myPHLIP

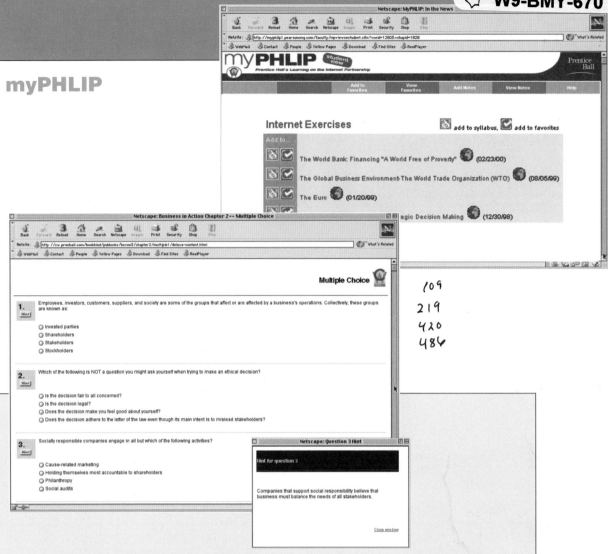

109
219
420
484

Prentice Hall's Learning on the Internet Partnership/Companion Web Site (PHLIP) is the most advanced text-specific site available on the Web! Developed *by professors for professors and their students*, the new myPHLIP provides professors with a customized course Web site, including new communication tools, one-click navigation of chapter content, and great PHLIP resources, such as current events and Internet exercises. It also features an interactive and exciting online *Student Study Guide*.

myPHLIP also supports students with:

● Free online tutorial assistance

● Free online study guide with practice tests—students get immediate feedback

● Free online study skills

● And more!

MANAGEMENT

Seventh Edition

Stephen P. Robbins
San Diego State University

Mary Coulter
Southwest Missouri State University

Prentice
Hall

Upper Saddle River, New Jersey 07458

Library of Congress Cataloging-in-Publication Data
Robbins, Stephen P.,
  Management/ Stephen P. Robbins, Mary Coulter.— 7th ed.
  p. cm.
  Includes bibliographical references and index.
  ISBN 0-13-031965-1
  1. Management. I. Coulter, Mary K. II. Title.
  HD31 .R5647 2001   2001021527
  658—dc21

Executive Editor: David Shafer
Editor-in-Chief: Jeff Shelstad
Managing Editor (Editorial): Jennifer Glennon
Assistant Editor: Michele Foresta
Editorial Assistant: Kim Marsden
Media Project Manager: Michele Faranda
Marketing Manager: Shannon Moore
Marketing Assistant: Katie Mulligan
Managing Editor (Production): Judy Leale
Production Assistant: Dianne Falcone
Permissions Coordinator: Suzanne Grappi
Associate Director, Manufacturing: Vincent Scelta
Production Manager: Arnold Vila
Manufacturing Buyer: Diane Peirano
Design Manager: Pat Smythe
Art Director: Cheryl Asherman
Interior Design: Amanda Kavanaugh
Cover Design: Laura Ospanik
Illustrator (Interior): Electragraphics
Associate Director, Multimedia Production: Karen Goldsmith
Manager, Print Production: Christy Mahon
Composition: UG / GGS Information Services, Inc.
Full-Service Project Management: Terri O'Prey, UG / GGS Information Services, Inc.
Printer/Binder: R. R. Donnelley

Credits and acknowledgments borrowed from other sources and reproduced, with permission, in this textbook appear on appropriate page within text. Photo credits appear on pages 641–42.

10 9 8 7 6 5 4 3 2
ISBN 0-13-031965-1

Stephen P. Robbins received his Ph.D. from the University of Arizona. He previously worked for the Shell Oil Company and Reynolds Metals Company. Since completing his graduate studies, Dr. Robbins has taught at the University of Nebraska at Omaha, Concordia University in Montreal, the University of Baltimore, Southern Illinois University at Edwardsville, and San Diego State University. Dr. Robbins' research interests have focused on conflict, power, and politics in organizations, as well as the development of effective interpersonal skills. His articles on these and other topics have appeared in such journals as *Business Horizons,* the *California Management Review, Business and Economic Perspectives, International Management, Management Review, Canadian Personnel and Industrial Relations,* and the *Journal of Management Education.*

In recent years, Dr. Robbins has been spending most of his professional time writing textbooks. In addition to *Management, Seventh Edition,* these include *Organizational Behavior, Ninth Edition* (Prentice Hall, 2001); *Fundamentals of Management, Third Edition,* with David DeCenzo (Prentice Hall, 2001); *Supervision Today!, Third Edition,* with David DeCenzo (Prentice Hall, 2001); *Business Today* (Harcourt, 2001); *Human Resource Management, Sixth Edition,* with David DeCenzo (Wiley, 1999); *Managing Today!, Second Edition* (Prentice Hall, 2000); *Essentials of Organizational Behavior, Sixth Edition* (Prentice Hall, 2000); *Training in Interpersonal Skills, Second Edition,* with Philip Hunsaker (Prentice Hall, 1996); and *Organization Theory, Third Edition* (Prentice Hall, 1990). These books are used at more than a thousand U.S. colleges and universities, as well as hundreds of schools throughout Canada, Latin America, Australia, New Zealand, Asia, Scandinavia, and Europe.

In Dr. Robbins' "other life," he participates in masters' track competition. Since turning 50 in 1993, he has set numerous indoor and outdoor world sprint records. He's also won gold medals in World Veteran Games in 100m, 200m, and 400m. In 1995, Robbins was named the year's outstanding age-40-and-over male track and field athlete by the Masters Track and Field Committee of USA Track & Field, the national governing body for athletes in the United States.

Mary Coulter received her Ph.D. in Management from the University of Arkansas in Fayetteville. Before completing her graduate work, she held different jobs including high school teacher, legal assistant, and government program planner. She has taught at Drury University, the University of Arkansas, Trinity University, and since 1983, at Southwest Missouri State University. Dr. Coulter's research interests have focused on competitive strategies for not-for-profit arts organizations and the use of new media in the educational process. Her research on these and other topics has appeared in such journals as *Journal of Business Strategies, Journal of Business Research, Journal of Nonprofit and Public Sector Marketing, International Journal of Business Disciplines,* and *Case Research Journal.* In addition to *Management,* Dr. Coulter has published two other books with Prentice Hall, *Strategic Management in Action, Second Edition,* and *Entrepreneurship in Action.* When she's not busy teaching or writing, she enjoys puttering around in her flower gardens, playing the piano, reading all different types of books, and enjoying many different activities with husband Ron and daughters Sarah and Katie.

BRIEF CONTENTS

CONTENTS

There's no doubt that the world has changed, is changing, and continues to change. The dynamic nature of today's organizations means both rewards *and* challenges for those individuals who will be managing those organizations. Management is a dynamic discipline and a textbook on the subject must constantly undergo significant changes to prepare you to manage under these conditions. Therefore, we've carefully revised this seventh edition of *Management* to provide you with the best possible understanding of what it means to be a manager. We've retained the basic four-functions approach, content, and features that have proven successful in previous editions. And, importantly, we've added new topics and features that better reflect the field of management and capture its excitement in the twenty-first century.

RETAINED FROM THE PREVIOUS EDITION

Adopters continually praise this book for its strong applications orientation. This is not just a book describing management theories. In addition to including explanatory examples (which most other textbooks now do), we go out and talk with real managers. Then we bring their experiences to our readers. No other textbook has so successfully blended management theory with management practice. And based on feedback that we get from faculty and students, we remain confident that this new edition continues to make management concepts meaningful and to excite readers about the possibilities for careers in management. We'd like to describe some of the features we have retained in this edition.

- *Manager's Dilemma* and *Managers Respond.* We have continued this unique feature in this edition. Each chapter opens with a dilemma that a real-life manager is facing. Some of these managers include Shigeki Tomoyama of Gazoo.com, Catherine Deslauriers of the city of Vancouver, Val Ackerman of the WNBA, and Glen Kelman of Plumtree Software. Each dilemma ends with the statement "What would you do?" providing an opportunity for student participation and active learning. Then, each chapter closes with a section titled "Managers Respond" where two real, practicing managers provide a short discussion of what they'd do if they were faced with the dilemma, drawing on the management concepts and tools presented in the chapter. These managers also come from a broad and varied spectrum of types of organizations, levels in organizations, and sizes of organizations. Their responses help students link management concepts to management practice.

- *Managers Speak Out.* In several chapters, you'll find this theme box in which we interview real managers and ask them a broad range of questions. Some of these managers include Jose Carlos de Guia, of a Philippines company called Microphase, Ian Weatherhead of the London Chamber of Commerce, Dan Shapiro of Microsoft, and Suzanne Cohen of the Neurofibramatosis Foundation. The information in these interviews provides a diverse perspective of managers and managerial philosophies and illustrates the real challenges that these managers are facing. Again, we believe that bringing in real managers makes the text more practical and shows the relevance of this book's content to a manager's daily job.

- *Testing, Testing . . . 1,2,3.* We introduced this innovation in the previous edition as a way for students to review their comprehension of chapter material at the time they finished reading it. In multiple places throughout each chapter, you'll find a box that lists three questions addressing specific factual information in the section you just read. Answers to these questions can be found in the accompanying Instructor's

Manual and also on the R.O.L.L.S. Web site, which can be reached through www.prenhall.com/robbins.

- *Skills Modules.* Management students need to learn how *to do* management tasks as well as to learn *about* management. Today, the "how's" of being a manager have become just as important as the "what's." To reflect the importance being placed on skills, we retained our Skills Modules. The 22 key skills found in the Skills Modules encompass the four management functions (planning, organizing, leading, and controlling).

- *Video Cases.* Because entrepreneurship and small business management are important aspects of management, we have retained several of the SB2000 videos. In addition, there are new custom part-ending videos that illustrate the integrative nature of management. These videos were filmed at monster.com, Clif Bar, Arnold Worldwide, Spiewak, and i2Go.

- *Emphasis on Workforce Diversity, Ethics Dilemmas,* and *Managing Your Career.* These topics are important to today's management students. We have chosen to continue these topics by highlighting them in boxed features throughout various chapters.

- *Writing Style.* This revision continues both authors' commitment to present management concepts in a lively and conversational style. We carefully blend theories and examples. Our goal is to present chapter material in an interesting and relevant manner without oversimplifying the discussion. Of course, writing style is a subjective interpretation; only you can judge whether we've successfully achieved our goal.

NEW TO THIS EDITION

We want our readers to know that we listened to what you were telling us! A couple of the major changes that we've made in *Management,* 7e, bring back the "tried and true." However, there are also several new content topics and features that have been included in this revision. New topics include e-business, workplace spirituality, stakeholder relationship management, virtual teams, team building, workplace violence, high performance organizations, value chain management, and work-life balance. The research base also has been updated to provide you with the most current thinking in management. In addition, we've added some new features that we think reflect the changing world of management. Here's a short description of the changes we've made.

- *Managing in an E-Business World.* One major change that managers must deal with in today's organizations is managing in an e-business world. Because of its importance and relevance to many different managerial topics, we chose to present this material in a boxed feature in several chapters. In these discussions, we look at important issues that managers face as they attempt to effectively manage in an e-business world. For example, some of the topics we address include the following: Planning: How Will it Work in E-Businesses?, Leadership in a Digital World, Nurturing Innovation in E-business Organizations, and Motivational Issues in E-Business Organizations.

- *Managing Entrepreneurial Ventures.* Entrepreneurship is playing an increasingly important role in economies around the world, and an increasing number of students are choosing careers as entrepreneurs. Effective management is just as important in entrepreneurial ventures as it is in large, corporate organizations. We think entrepreneurship is such an important topic that we address issues associated with managing entrepreneurial ventures in five separate sections including The Context of Entrepreneurship, Start-Up and Planning Issues, Organizing Issues, Leading Issues, and Controlling Issues. These separate sections on entrepreneurship can be easily located by the tinted pages after Parts 2, 3, 4, 5, and 6.

- *PRISM (PRactical Interactive Skills Modules) Web site.* In addition to the Skills Modules found in the book, we've developed an interactive skills Web site that provides you with different "virtual" management situations in an organization called MediaPlex. You will be role-playing different managers at Mediaplex who are faced with decisions that require action. The interactive decision-tree design of the management situations provides you with an opportunity to make different decisions and to learn why certain decisions are better than others. The skills included on PRISM are linked closely to appropriate chapters and reinforce important management concepts, theories, and skills. The link to PRISM is found on the main R.O.L.L.S. (Robbins OnLine Learning System) Web site.

- *Internet and Team Exercises.* The pervasiveness of the Internet and teamwork in organizations led us to design two new exercises at the end of every chapter. The first, called *Log On,* is an Internet-based assignment that explores and exploits the many helpful resources available on the Internet. Also, because many of you work on team class projects throughout your college career and are likely to work on teams throughout your work career, we've included a team-based exercise called *Working Together* that explores and builds on concepts or theories presented in the chapter.

- *Completely Revised Operations Management Chapter.* The operations management chapter has been totally rewritten around the concept of value chain management. As organizations look for ways to effectively and efficiently "produce" their product or service, they're applying the concepts of value chain management. We believe that the completely revised chapter better reflects the realities of managing operations in today's environment.

- *Major Changes to Planning Chapter.* Planning is one of the four important functions that managers perform. The chapter on planning has been rewritten to reflect more accurately what's involved with "doing" planning.

- *New Chapter on Managerial Communication and Information Technology.* Based on feedback from adopters, we brought back the conceptual material on communication from the fifth edition and updated it to reflect what managers need to know about communication and information technology.

- *Early Motivation and Leadership Theories Moved Back to Respective Chapters.* Similarly, based on comments from adopters, we moved the discussions of early motivation and leadership theories back to their respective chapters. Although we thought our approach to the historical development of managerial thought presented in the last edition of the book made sense, faculty told us they preferred the more conventional approach. We listened!

IN-TEXT LEARNING AIDS

A good textbook should teach as well as present ideas. Toward that end, we've tried to make this book an effective learning tool. We'd like to point out some specific pedagogical features that we designed to help readers better assimilate the material presented.

- *Chapter Learning Objectives.* Before you start a trip, it's valuable to know where you're headed. That way, you can minimize possible problems or detours. The same holds true in reading a textbook. To make your learning more efficient, each chapter opens with a list of learning objectives that describe what you should be able to do after studying the chapter. These objectives are designed to focus your attention on the major issues within each chapter.

- *Chapter Summaries.* Just as objectives clarify where you're going, chapter summaries remind you of where you've been. Each chapter concludes with a concise summary organized around the opening learning objectives.

- *Key Terms.* Every chapter highlights a number of key terms that you'll need to know. These terms are highlighted in bold print when they first appear and are defined at that time in the adjoining margin.

- *Testing, Testing . . . 1,2,3 Boxes.* Key factual material is highlighted by way of ongoing questions included in boxes throughout the chapters.

- *Thinking Critically About Ethics.* Being able to think critically about issues is important for managers. In the body of every chapter, you'll find a "Thinking Critically About Ethics" box. This learning aid provides material that stresses the ethical values in managerial decisions.

- *Thinking About Management Issues Questions.* Every chapter has five questions that are designed to get you to think about management issues. These questions require you to demonstrate that you not only know the key facts in the chapter but also can apply those facts in dealing with more complex issues.

- *Case Application and Questions.* Each chapter includes a case application and questions for analysis. A case is simply a description of a real-life managerial situation. By reading and analyzing the case and answering the questions at the end of the case, you can see if you understand and can apply the management concepts discussed in the chapter.

SUPPLEMENTS

The seventh edition supplements package has been revised and expanded to include increased media integration, technology, and test questions for your classroom needs.

- *Instructor's Manual: The Multi-Media Guide.* In addition to extensive chapter outlines, teaching notes to various boxed elements, answers to "Testing, Testing . . . 1, 2, 3" questions, and notes to all video cases, the *Instructor's Manual* contains integrated media teaching tips in a design unique to the seventh edition!

- *New: Two Test Item Files.* Test Item File 1, revised from the last edition, contains multiple choice, true/false, scenario, and essay questions. Together, the questions cover the content of each chapter in a variety of ways providing flexibility in testing the students' knowledge of the text.

  Test Item File 2, the new, alternative Test Bank, contains new multiple-choice, fill-in-the-blank, and scenario questions. It also features questions covering the Skills Modules. This Test Bank can be used either alone or in conjunction with Test Item File 1.

- *Instructor's Resource CD-ROM.* Contains the electronic IM, 2 Win/PH Test Managers, and PowerPoint Electronic Transparencies. The seventh edition's PowerPoints have been improved to contain up to 30 slides per chapter and feature extensive chapter content, newly-created art, and actual line art from the text.

- *2 Win/PH Test Managers.* Containing all of the questions in the printed Test Item Files, Test Manager is a comprehensive suite of tools for testing and assessment. Test Manager allows educators to create and distribute tests for their courses easily, either by printing and distributing through traditional methods or by on-line delivery via a Local Area Network (LAN) server.

- *Overhead Color Transparencies.* Designed to aid the educator and enhance classroom lectures, approximately 100 of the most critical PowerPoint electronic transparencies are chosen for inclusion in this package as full-color acetates and are provided on high quality mylar.

- *Study Guide.* Contains chapter objectives, detailed chapter outlines, and review questions for each chapter. Also contains teaching notes to various boxed features.

- *New 2-Video Package.* Video one features new part-ending *On Location!* segments. Created specifically for *Management, Seventh Edition,* this video library contains real-world footage from some of today's most intriguing companies such as Monster.com and Spiewak. Topics include international expansion, teams, and technology in human resources. Video 2 features chapter-ending *Small Business 2000* segments, offered to reinforce the conceptual material. These videos are offered as a package only.

- *Mastering Management from the Mastering Business Series. The multimedia tool that means business.* Mastering Business is a technologically innovative CD-ROM that uses video and interactive exercises to actively engage students in learning core business concepts across core business disciplines. For more information, pricing, or to request a Mastering Business Demo CD-ROM, please contact your local sales representative.

- *Self-Assessment Library Version 2.0.* Updated with new exercises and now available on CD-ROM, in print, and online.

- *The R.O.L.L.S (Robbins OnLine Learning System) Internet site.* Features myPHLIP, PRISM (Student Skills Exercises), Self-Assessment Library version 2.0, answers to "Testing, Testing . . . 1, 2, 3," and "Frequently Asked Questions" answered by the authors themselves. Parts of this site are pin code-protected. www.prenhall.com/robbins.

- Description of myPHLIP. The new myPHLIP provides professors with a customized course Web site including new communication tools, one-click navigation of chapter content, and great PHLIP resources such as current events and Internet exercises. It also features an interactive and exciting online Student Study Guide.

- *PRISM (PRactical Interactive Skills Modules) Web site.* As mentioned earlier, PRISM presents different "virtual" management situations in an organization called *MediaPlex.* The interactive decision-tree design of the management situations gives students the chance to try different management approaches and to learn why certain approaches are better than others.

- *Online Courses.* Online courses are available in both premium and standard versions, exclusively through Prentice Hall.

  WebCT. This robust Course Management System includes page tracking, progress tracking, class and student management, gradebook, communication, calendar, reporting tools, and more. www.prenhall.com/webct.

  Blackboard. Prentice Hall now makes its class-tested online course content available in Blackboard's easy-to-use interface. www.prenhall.com/blackboard.

  CourseCompass. www.prenhall.com/coursecompass.

ACKNOWLEDGMENTS

Every author relies on the comments of reviewers and ours were particularly helpful. We want to thank the following people for their comments and suggestions: Dr. Isaiah O. Ugboro, North Carolina AT&T State University; Emilia S. Westney, Texas Tech University;

Sheila Pechinski, University of Maine; Dr. Tracey Huneycutt Sigler, Western Washington University; Thomas G. Thompson, University of Maryland, University College; Gary M. Lande, M.D., Montana State University; Dr. Charles V. Goodman, Texas A&M University; Bobbie Williams, Georgia Southern University; Joseph Atallah, Devry Institute of Technology; and Dr. Roger R. Stanton, California State University.

Regardless of how good the manuscript is that we turn in, it's only a few computer disks until our friends at Prentice Hall swing into action. Then PH's crack team of editors, production experts, technology whizzes, designers, marketing specialists, and sales representatives turn those couple of million digital characters into a bound textbook and see that it gets into faculty and students' hands. Our thanks on making this book "go" include David Shafer, Shannon Moore, Michael Campbell, Jennifer Glennon, Michele Foresta, Michele Faranda, Judy Leale, Cheryl Asherman, Kim Marsden, Katie Mulligan, Elisa Adams, Melinda Alexander, and Natalie Anderson.

A special thank-you goes to Laura Ospanik Robbins (Steve's wife) who designed the wonderful cover that graces *Management, 7/e.* Another special thank-you goes to Amanda Quebbeman (who graduated from Southwest Missouri State University in December 2000 and is now working for Eli Lilly as a pharmaceutical representative). She played a significant role in developing the PRISM Web site and also coordinated the responses coming from the various managers. We also appreciate and thank all of those managers who so graciously gave of their time to either be part of the "Managers Speak Out" feature or the "Managers Respond" feature. Without these people, our belief in showing managers as "people, people, people" would be hard to implement.

Finally, Steve would like to acknowledge the support of his wife, Laura. Her insights and understanding make the job of textbook writing a lot more enjoyable. And her creative contributions make all his books better. Mary would like to acknowledge and thank her extremely understanding and tolerant husband, Ron, and their beautiful and talented daughters, Sarah and Katie.

Learning Objectives

After reading and studying this chapter, you should be able to:

1. Explain what a manager is and how the role of a manager has changed.

2. Define *management*.

3. Distinguish between efficiency and effectiveness.

4. Describe the basic management functions and the management process.

5. Identify the roles performed by managers.

6. Describe the skills managers need.

7. Explain what managers do using the systems perspective.

8. Identify what managers do using the contingency perspective.

9. Describe what an organization is and how the concept of an organization has changed.

10. Explain the value of studying management.

A MANAGER'S DILEMMA

You might be surprised to find the passionate emphasis placed on people management at a CPA firm.[1] Yet, at Lipschultz, Levin & Gray (www.thethinkers.com), self-described "head bean counter," Steven P. Siegel, recognizes that his people make the organization. He describes his primary responsibility as assuring that LLG's clients have the best professionals working for them. And the best way to do this, Siegel feels, is by developing the creativity, talent, and diversity of its staff so that new knowledge can be acquired and shared without getting hung up on formal organizational relationships or having employees shut away in corner offices.

Siegel has implemented several significant changes at LLG. Because he's convinced that people do their best intellectual work in nontraditional settings, every telltale sign of what most people consider boring, dull CPA work has been eliminated. None of the firm's employees or partners has an office or desk to call his or her own. Instead, everyone is part of a nomadic group that wheels stuff (files, phones, laptops) to a new spot every day. Everywhere you look in the company's office, you see versatility, comfort, and eccentricity. For instance, a miniature golf course is located in the middle of everything. The motivation behind this open office design is to create opportunities for professionals to gather—on purpose or by accident—without walls, cubicles, or offices to get in the way.

CHAPTER ONE

Introduction to Management and Organizations

1

Visitors to LLG realize that the firm is different as soon as they walk in the door. A giant wall-mounted abacus (remember the image of bean counters) decorates the interior. And visitors are greeted by a "Welcome Wall" with a big-screen television that flashes a continuous slide show of one-liners about business, life, and innovation.

Keeping professionals excited about work that can be routine and standardized is a major challenge for Siegel. Now put yourself in Siegel's shoes. What managerial skills would you use to maintain an environment that encourages innovation and professionalism in his CPA firm?

WHAT WOULD YOU DO?

Steven Siegel is an excellent example of what today's successful managers are like and the skills they must have in dealing with the problems and challenges of managing in the twenty-first century. These managers may not be what you might expect! They can be found from under age 18 to over 80. They run large corporations as well as entrepreneurial start-ups. They're found in government departments, hospitals, small businesses, not-for-profit agencies, museums, schools, and even such nontraditional organizations as political campaigns and consumer cooperatives. Managers can also be found doing managerial work in every country on the globe. In addition, some managers are at the top level of their organizations whereas others are near the bottom, and today they are just as likely to be women as they are men. However, although women are well represented in the lower and middle levels of management, the number in top executive positions remains low. Data collected by Catalyst, a nonprofit research group (www.catalystwomen.org), found that only 11.9 percent of corporate officers at the 500 largest U.S. companies are women. That figure drops to 5.1 percent if you look at only the elite top-level managerial jobs of chairman, president, chief executive officer, chief operating officer, and executive vice president. A number of organizations including Southwest Airlines, Avon, Hewlett-Packard, Kraft Foods, Xerox, and Golden West Financial have taken significant steps to attract and promote women executives.[2] But no matter where managers are found or what gender they are, the fact is that managers have exciting jobs!

This book is about the fun, exciting, and challenging work that Steven Siegel and millions of other managers like him do. It recognizes the reality facing today's managers—that management is changing. In workplaces of all types—factories, offices, restaurants, retail stores, and the like—new technologies and new ways of organizing work are radically altering old approaches. This new world has changed how work is done and the relationship between workers and managers. In this chapter, we introduce you to managers and management by looking at who managers are, what management is, what managers do, and what an organization is. Finally, we'll wrap up the chapter by discussing why it's important to study management.

Anne Robinson is the new owner and executive director of Caswell-Massey USA, the 250-year-old toiletries firm. She fell in love with the company when she joined it several years ago and is now leading a needed revitalization effort. Thanks to her efforts to cut costs, improve distribution, refocus the company's image as an upscale marketer, and introduce a flood of new packages and new products, the company has returned to profitability.

⟩ WHO ARE MANAGERS?

It used to be fairly simple to define who managers were: They were the organizational members who told others what to do and how to do it. It was easy to differentiate *managers* from *nonmanagerial employees*; the latter term described those organizational members who worked directly on a job or task and had no one reporting to them. But it isn't quite that simple anymore! The changing nature of organizations and work has, in many organizations, blurred the clear lines of distinction between managers and nonmanagerial employees. Many traditional jobs now include managerial activities, especially on teams. For instance, team members often develop plans, make decisions, and monitor their own performance. And as these nonmanagerial employees assume responsibilities that traditionally were part of management, definitions we've used in the past no longer describe every type of managerial situation.

How *do* we define who managers are? A **manager** is someone who works with and through other people by coordinating their work activities in order to accomplish organizational goals. That may mean coordinating the work of a departmental group, or it might mean supervising a single person. It could involve coordinating the work activities of a team composed of people from several different departments or even people outside the organization such as temporary employees or employees who work for the organization's suppliers. Keep in mind, also, that managers may have other work duties not related to coordinating and integrating the work of others. For example, an insurance claims supervisor may also process claims in addition to coordinating the work activities of other claims clerks.

Is there some way to classify managers in organizations? There is, particularly for traditionally structured organizations—that is, those organizations in which the number of employees is greater at the bottom than at the top. (These types of organizations are often pictured as being shaped like a pyramid.) As shown in Exhibit 1.1, we typically describe managers as first-line, middle, or top in this type of organization. Identifying exactly who the managers are in these organizations isn't difficult, although you should be aware that managers may have a variety of titles. **First-line managers** are the lowest level of management and manage the work of non-managerial individuals who are involved with the production or creation of the organization's products. They're often called *supervisors* but may also be called line managers, office managers, or even foremen. **Middle managers** include all levels of management between the first-line level and the top level of the organization. These managers manage the work of first-line managers and may have titles such as department head, project leader, plant manager, or division manager. At or near the top of the organization are the **top managers**, who are responsible for making organization-wide decisions and establishing the plans and goals that affect the entire organization. These individuals typically have titles such as executive vice president, president, managing director, chief operating officer, chief executive officer, or chairman of the board. In the chapter-opening case, Steven Siegel is a top-level manager. He holds the title of managing member and is involved in creating and implementing broad and comprehensive changes that affect the entire organization.

manager

Someone who works with and through other people by coordinating their work activities in order to accomplish organizational goals.

first-line managers

Managers at the lowest level of the organization who manage the work of nonmanagerial employees who are involved with the production or creation of the organization's products.

middle managers

Managers between the first-line level and the top level of the organization who manage the work of first-line managers.

top managers

Managers at or near the top level of the organization who are responsible for making organization-wide decisions and establishing the goals and plans that affect the entire organization.

Exhibit	1.1
Organizational Levels	

Top Managers

Middle Managers

First-Line Managers

Nonmanagerial Employees

Throughout this book, we'll be discussing organizations and managers from this more traditional pyramidal perspective, although not all organizations may reflect this arrangement. But even organizations that are more flexibly and loosely configured need individuals to fulfill the role of manager—that is, someone who works with and through other people by coordinating their work to accomplish organizational goals.

1. **How are managers different from nonmanagerial employees?**

2. **Explain why it isn't always easy to determine exactly who the managers are in an organization.**

3. **Contrast the three different levels of management.**

❭ WHAT IS MANAGEMENT?

management

The process of coordinating work activities so that they are completed efficiently and effectively with and through other people.

Simply speaking, management is what managers do. However, this simple statement doesn't tell us much. We define **management** as the process of coordinating work activities so that they are completed efficiently and effectively with and through other people. Let's look at some specific parts of this definition.

The *process* represents the ongoing functions or primary activities engaged in by managers. These functions are typically labeled planning, organizing, leading, and controlling. We'll elaborate on these functions and the management process when we discuss what managers do.

We already know that the second part of the definition—coordinating the work of others—is what distinguishes a managerial position from a nonmanagerial one. In addition, management involves the efficient and effective completion of organizational work activities, or at least that's what managers aspire to do.

efficiency

Getting the most output from the least amount of inputs; referred to as "doing things right."

Efficiency refers to getting the most output from the least amount of inputs. Because managers deal with scarce inputs—including resources such as people, money, and equipment—they are concerned with the efficient use of those resources. For instance, at the Beiersdorf Inc. factory in Cincinnati, where employees make body braces and supports, canes, walkers, crutches, and other

? THINKING CRITICALLY ABOUT ETHICS

How far should a manager go to achieve efficiency or effectiveness? Suppose that you're the catering manager at a local country club and you're asked by the club manager to lie about information you have on your work group's efficiency. Suppose that by lying you'll save an employee's job. Is that okay? Is lying always wrong, or might it be acceptable under certain circumstances? What, if any, would those circumstances be? What about simply distorting information that you have? Is that always wrong, or might it be acceptable under certain circumstances? When does "distorting" become "lying"?

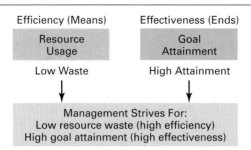

medical assistance products, efficient manufacturing techniques were implemented by cutting inventory levels, decreasing the amount of time to manufacture products, and lowering product reject rates. These efficient work practices paid off as the company was named one of *Industry Week's* best plants.[3] From this perspective, efficiency is often referred to as "doing things right"— that is, not wasting resources. However, it's not enough just to be efficient. Management is also concerned with being effective, completing activities so that organizational goals are attained. **Effectiveness** is often described as "doing the right things"—that is, those work activities that will help the organization reach its goals. For instance, at the Beiersdorf factory, goals included open communication between managers and employees and cutting costs. Through various work programs, these goals were pursued *and* achieved. Whereas efficiency is concerned with the means of getting things done, effectiveness is concerned with the ends, or attainment of organizational goals (see Exhibit 1.2). Management is concerned, then, not only with getting activities completed and meeting organizational goals (effectiveness) but also with doing so as efficiently as possible. In successful organizations, high efficiency and high effectiveness typically go hand in hand. Poor management is most often due to both inefficiency and ineffectiveness or to effectiveness achieved through inefficiency. ◄─────────────────

effectiveness

Completing activities so that organizational goals are attained; referred to as "doing the right things."

Testing...Testing...1,2,3

4. **How is management a process?**

5. **Define efficiency and effectiveness.**

6. **Explain why efficiency and effectiveness are important to management.**

> ❯ | WHAT DO MANAGERS DO?

Describing what managers do isn't an easy or simple task! Just as no two organizations are alike, no two managers' jobs are alike. But management writers and researchers have, after many years of study, developed some specific categorization schemes to describe what managers do. What are these categorization schemes? We're going to look at what managers do in terms of functions and process, roles, skills, managing systems, and situational analysis.

MANAGEMENT FUNCTIONS AND PROCESS

In the early part of the twentieth century, a French industrialist by the name of Henri Fayol proposed that all managers perform five management functions: planning, organizing, commanding, coordinating, and controlling.[4] In the mid-1950s, a management textbook first used the functions of planning, organizing, staffing, directing, and controlling as a framework. Most management textbooks (and this one is no exception) still continue to be organized around the management functions, although they have been condensed down to four basic and very important functions: planning, organizing, leading, and controlling (see Exhibit 1.3). Let's briefly define what each of these management functions encompasses.

If you have no particular destination in mind, then you can take any road. However, if you have someplace in particular you want to go, then you've got to plan the best way to get there. Because organizations exist to achieve some particular purpose, someone must clearly define that purpose and the means for its achievement. Management is that someone. The **planning** function involves the process of defining goals, establishing strategies for achieving those goals, and developing plans to integrate and coordinate activities.

Managers are also responsible for arranging work to accomplish the organization's goals. We call this function **organizing**. It involves the process of determining what tasks are to be done, who is to do them, how the tasks are to be grouped, who reports to whom, and where decisions are to be made.

Every organization includes people, and management's job is to work with and through people to accomplish organizational goals. This is the **leading** function. When managers motivate subordinates, influence individuals or teams as they work, select the most effective communication channel, or deal in any way with employee behavior issues, they are leading.

The final management function managers perform is **controlling**. After the goals are set and the plans are formulated (planning), the structural arrangements determined (organizing), and the people hired, trained, and motivated (leading), there has to be some evaluation of whether things are going as planned. To ensure that work is going as it should, managers must monitor and evaluate performance. Actual performance must be compared with the previously set goals. If there are any significant deviations, it's management's job to get work performance back on track. This process of monitoring, comparing, and correcting is what we mean by the controlling function.

The reality of managing isn't quite as simplistic as these descriptions of the management functions might lead you to believe. There are no simple, cut-and-dried beginning or ending points as managers plan, organize, lead, and control. As managers do their jobs, they often find themselves doing some planning, some organizing, some leading, and some controlling, and maybe not even in that sequential order. It's probably more realistic to describe the functions managers perform from the perspective of a process. The **management process** is

planning

Management function that involves the process of defining goals, establishing strategies for achieving those goals, and developing plans to integrate and coordinate activities.

organizing

Management function that involves the process of determining what tasks are to be done, who is to do them, how the tasks are to be grouped, who reports to whom, and where decisions are to be made.

leading

Management function that involves motivating subordinates, influencing individuals or teams as they work, selecting the most effective communication channels, or dealing in any way with employee behavior issues.

controlling

Management function that involves monitoring actual performance, comparing actual to standard, and taking action, if necessary.

management process

The set of ongoing decisions and work activities in which managers engage as they plan, organize, lead, and control.

Exhibit	1.3

Management Functions

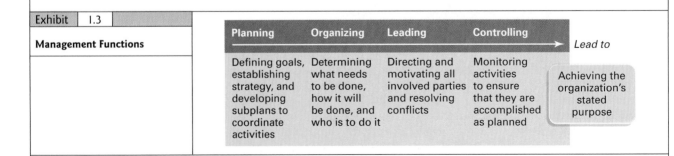

Planning	Organizing	Leading	Controlling	
				Lead to
Defining goals, establishing strategy, and developing subplans to coordinate activities	Determining what needs to be done, how it will be done, and who is to do it	Directing and motivating all involved parties and resolving conflicts	Monitoring activities to ensure that they are accomplished as planned	Achieving the organization's stated purpose

the set of ongoing decisions and work activities in which managers engage as they plan, organize, lead, and control. What this means is that as managers manage, their work activities are usually done in a continuous manner—that is, in a process.

The continued popularity of the functional and process approaches to describe what managers do is a tribute to their clarity and simplicity—managers plan, organize, lead, and control. But are these descriptions accurate?[5] Let's look at another perspective.

MANAGEMENT ROLES

Henry Mintzberg, a prominent management researcher, says that what managers do can best be described by looking at the roles they play at work.[6] From his study of actual managers at work, Mintzberg developed a categorization scheme for defining what managers do. He concluded that managers perform 10 different but highly interrelated roles. The term **management roles** refers to specific categories of managerial behavior. (Think of the different roles you play and the different behaviors you're expected to exhibit and play in these roles as a student, a sibling, an employee, a volunteer, and so forth.) As shown in Exhibit 1.4, Mintzberg's 10 managerial roles can be grouped as those primarily concerned with interpersonal relationships, the transfer of information, and decision making.

The **interpersonal roles** are roles that involve people (subordinates and persons outside the organization) and other duties that are ceremonial and symbolic in nature. The three interpersonal roles include being a figurehead, leader, and liaison. The **informational roles** involve receiving, collecting, and disseminating information. The three informational roles include a monitor, disseminator, and spokesperson. Finally, the **decisional roles** revolve around making choices. The four decisional roles include entrepreneur, disturbance handler, resource allocator, and negotiator.

A number of follow-up studies have tested the validity of Mintzberg's role categories among different types of organizations and at different levels within given organizations.[7] The evidence generally supports the idea that managers—regardless of the type of organization or level in the organization—perform similar roles. However, the emphasis that managers give to the various roles seems to change with their organizational level.[8] Specifically, the roles of disseminator, figurehead, negotiator, liaison, and spokesperson are more important at the higher levels of the organization; whereas the leader role (as Mintzberg defined it) is more important for lower-level managers than it is for either middle- or top-level managers.

So which approach to describing what managers do is correct—functions or roles? Each has merit. However, the functional approach still represents the more useful way of

management roles

Specific categories of managerial behavior.

interpersonal roles

Managerial roles that involve people and other duties that are ceremonial and symbolic in nature.

informational roles

Managerial roles that involve receiving, collecting, and disseminating information.

decisional roles

Managerial roles that revolve around making choices.

In addition to the challenge of tackling the planning, organizing, leading, and controlling tasks of an operation as unusual as a children's zoo, John Chapo, the executive director of the Folsom Children's Zoo in Lincoln, Nebraska, has also had to find a way to help troubled employees stay on the job and even make full recoveries. His research into employee assistance programs has paid off, helping one employee survive a debilitating personal crisis and return to work within six months.

Exhibit 1.4	Role	Description	Examples of Identifiable Activities
Mintzberg's Managerial Roles			
	Interpersonal		
	Figurehead	Symbolic head; obliged to perform a number of routine duties of a legal or social nature	Greeting visitors; signing legal documents
	Leader	Responsible for the motivation of subordinates; responsible for staffing, training, and associated duties	Performing virtually all activities that involve subordinates
	Liaison	Maintains self-developed network of outside contacts and informers who provide favors and information	Acknowledging mail; doing external board work; performing other activities that involve outsiders
	Informational		
	Monitor	Seeks and receives wide variety of internal and external information to develop thorough understanding of organization and environment	Reading periodicals and reports; maintaining personal contacts
	Disseminator	Transmits information received from outsiders or from subordinates to members of the organization	Holding informational meetings; making phone calls to relay information
	Spokesperson	Transmits information to outsiders on organization's plans, policies, actions, results, etc.	Holding board meetings; giving information to the media
	Decisional		
	Entrepreneur	Searches organization and its environment for opportunities and initiates "improvement projects" to bring about changes	Organizing strategy and review sessions to develop new programs
	Disturbance handler	Responsible for corrective action when organization faces important, unexpected disturbances	Organizing strategy and review sessions that involve disturbances and crises
	Resource allocator	Responsible for the allocation of organizational resources of all kinds—making or approving all significant organizational decisions	Scheduling; requesting authorization; performing any activity that involves budgeting and the programming of subordinates' work
	Negotiator	Responsible for representing the organization at major negotiations	Participating in union contract negotiations

Source: H. Mintzberg, *The Nature of Managerial Work* (New York: Harper & Row, 1973), pp. 93–94. Copyright © 1973 by Henry Mintzberg. Reprinted by permission of Harper & Row, Publishers, Inc.

conceptualizing the manager's job. "The classical functions provide clear and discrete methods of classifying the thousands of activities that managers carry out and the techniques they use in terms of the functions they perform for the achievement of goals."[9] Many of Mintzberg's roles align smoothly with one or more of the functions. For instance, resource allocation is part of planning, as is the entrepreneurial role, and all three of the interpersonal roles are part of the leading function. Although most of the other roles fit into one or more of the four functions, not all of them do. The difference can be explained by the fact that all managers do some work that isn't purely managerial.[10] Our decision to use the management functions to describe what managers do doesn't mean that Mintzberg's role categories are invalid as he clearly offered new insights into managers' work. ◀

MANAGEMENT SKILLS

As you can see from the preceding discussion, a manager's job is varied and complex. Managers need certain skills to perform the duties and activities associated with being a manager. What types of skills does a manager need? Research by Robert L. Katz found that managers need three essential skills or competencies.[11] **Technical skills** include knowledge of and proficiency in a certain specialized field, such as engineering, computers, accounting, or manufacturing. These skills are more important at lower levels of management since these managers are dealing directly with employees doing the organization's work. **Human skills** involve the ability to work well with other people both individually and in a group. Because managers deal directly with people, this skill is crucial! Managers with good human skills are able to get the best out of their people. They know how to communicate, motivate, lead, and inspire enthusiasm and trust. These skills are equally important at all levels of management. Finally, **conceptual skills** are the skills managers must have to think and to conceptualize about abstract and complex situations. Using these skills, managers must be able to see the organization as a whole, understand the relationships among various subunits, and visualize how the organization fits into its broader environment. These skills are most important at the top management levels. Exhibit 1.5 shows the relationship of these skills and the levels of management.

How relevant are management skills to today's managers? In today's demanding and dynamic workplace, employees who are invaluable to an organization must be willing to constantly upgrade their skills and take on extra work outside their own specific job area. There's no doubt that skills will continue to be an important way of describing what a manager does. In fact, understanding and developing management skills are so important that we've incorporated a condensed skills feature in the text. At the end of the textbook and on our Web site (www.prenhall.com/robbins), you'll find material on skill building, including our Web-based interactive skills exercises. The skills we've chosen to feature in these skill-building modules reflect a broad cross section of managerial activities that we and most experts believe are important elements of the four management functions. A matrix showing the relationship between these skills and the

Testing...Testing...1,2,3

7. **Briefly describe the four functions all managers perform.**

8. **What is the management process, and how does it reflect what managers do?**

9. **Describe Mintzberg's 10 management roles and how they are used to explain what managers do.**

technical skills

Knowledge of and proficiency in a specialized field.

human skills

The ability to work well with other people individually and in a group.

conceptual skills

The ability to think and to conceptualize about abstract and complex situations.

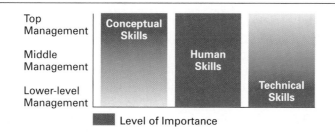

Top Management — Conceptual Skills
Middle Management — Human Skills
Lower-level Management — Technical Skills

Level of Importance

Exhibit 1.5

Skills Needed at Different Management Levels

Martha E. Barkman, Project Manager, Residential Real Estate Development, Harbor Properties, Inc., Seattle, Washington

Describe your job.

As a project manager for a real estate development company, my primary responsibility is the oversight of the conceptualization, finance, design, and ultimate construction of a building. Coordination of many different firms and managing a constant flow of information is the primary role I play rather than being the source of the decisions. I spend the majority of my days anticipating what the designers and contractors need, securing a timely answer, monitoring their progress, and reporting the results back to the owner or our in-house staff. Keeping the budget and schedules on target is also part of this process.

Why are managers important to organizations?

Managers are important in facilitating the flow of information to the people who need it. The tools and resources a company might provide aren't useful if they are not made available to improve the effectiveness of their employees. Managers are most effective when they can delegate the work to others, provided that they can monitor the progress. Managers are needed to anticipate and find solutions to the issues that impede their work team from reaching optimal effectiveness and job satisfaction.

What skills are needed for a manager to be effective today?

A manager must be able to communicate effectively in both traditional (paper) and new (electronic) methods. The high-tech world has brought true advantages in the ability to reach more people very rapidly. However, today's manager must be equally prepared to respond rapidly. An effective manager must also keep an eye on employee satisfaction, retain key employees, and prioritize the workload.

management functions is shown in Exhibit 1.6. Note that many of the skills are important to more than one function. As you study the management functions in more depth in later chapters of the book, you'll have the opportunity to practice some of the key skills that are part of doing what a manager does. Although no skill-building module can make you an instant expert in a certain area, these exercises can provide you an introductory understanding and appreciation of some of the skills you'll need to master in order to be an effective manager.

Testing...Testing...1,2,3

10. **Describe the three skills Katz felt were essential to managers.**

11. **How does the importance of these three skills change depending on management level?**

12. **Are skills important to today's managers? Explain.**

system

A set of interrelated and interdependent parts arranged in a manner that produces a unified whole.

closed systems

Systems that are not influenced by or do not interact with their environment.

open systems

Systems that dynamically interact with their environment.

MANAGING SYSTEMS

Another way to look at the manager's job is from the perspective of managing systems. A **system** is a set of interrelated and interdependent parts arranged in a manner that produces a unified whole. It's a concept taken from the physical sciences and applied to organizations. The two basic types of systems are closed and open. **Closed systems** are not influenced by and do not interact with their environment. In contrast, **open systems** dynamically interact with their environment. Today, when we call organizations systems, we mean open systems, that is, an organization that constantly interacts with its environment. Exhibit 1.7 shows a diagram of an organization from an open systems perspective. As you can see, an organization takes in inputs (resources) from the environment and transforms or processes these

Skill	Function			
	Planning	**Organizing**	**Leading**	**Controlling**
Acquiring power		√	√	
Active listening			√	√
Assessing cross-cultural differences		√	√	
Budgeting	√			√
Choosing an effective leadership style			√	
Coaching			√	
Creating effective teams		√	√	
Delegating (empowerment)		√	√	
Designing motivating jobs		√	√	
Developing trust			√	
Disciplining			√	√
Interviewing		√	√	
Managing resistance to change		√	√	√
Managing time	√			√
Mentoring			√	
Negotiating			√	
Providing feedback			√	√
Reading an organization's culture		√	√	
Running productive meetings	√	√	√	√
Scanning the environment	√			√
Setting goals	√			√
Solving problems creatively	√			

Exhibit 1.6

Management Skills and Management Functions Matrix

resources into outputs that are distributed into the environment. The organization is "open" to its environment and continually interacts with that environment.

How does the systems perspective add to our understanding of what managers do? Systems researchers envisioned an organization as being made up of "interdependent factors, including individuals, groups, attitudes, motives, formal structure, interactions, goals, status, and authority."[12] Using this approach, then, the

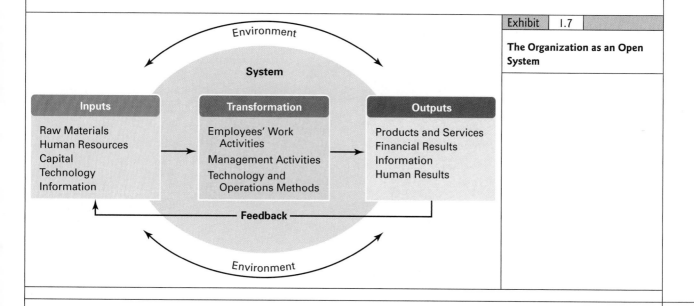

Exhibit 1.7

The Organization as an Open System

job of a manager is to coordinate the work activities of the various parts of the organization and ensure that all the interdependent parts of the organization are working together so that the organization's goals can be achieved.

In addition, the systems view of a manager's job implies that decisions and actions taken in one organizational area will affect others and vice versa (this is the interdependency characteristic of systems). For instance, no matter how efficient an organization's production department might be, if the marketing department does not anticipate changes in consumer tastes and work with the product development department in creating products consumers want, the organization's overall performance will suffer.

Finally, an important part of a manager's job is recognizing and understanding the impact of the various external factors. The open systems approach recognizes that organizations are not self-contained. They rely on their environment for essential inputs and as sources to absorb their outputs. No organization can survive for long if it ignores government regulations, supplier relations, or the varied external constituencies upon which it depends. (We'll cover these external environmental forces in Chapter 3 as we discuss how managers must understand the environment and the constraints it imposes.)

Just how relevant is the systems approach for describing what a manager does? It appears to be quite relevant, particularly since a manager's job entails working with and through other people by coordinating various work activities so that the system (the organization) meets its goals. Think, for example, of a day-shift manager at a local Wendy's restaurant who every day must coordinate the work of individuals taking and filling customer orders at the front counter and the drive-through windows, direct the delivery and unloading of food supplies, and address

Most organizations can be viewed as systems, and one as large as United Airlines is a fairly complex system indeed. United Airlines is made up of individual workers; groups of workers such as pilots, mechanics, and flight attendants; and structures such as work rules, flight schedules, and pricing strategies. It is an open system that interacts with customers, suppliers, government agencies, union leaders, and investors to achieve its goal of providing air transportation at a profit.

any customer concerns that come up. The manager "manages" all the parts of this "system" so that the restaurant's daily sales goals are met. Although the systems perspective doesn't provide specific descriptions of what managers do, it does provide a more general and broader picture than other perspectives do. Moreover, viewing the manager's job as linking the organization to its environment makes the organization appear more sensitive and responsive to its key constituencies such as customers, suppliers, government agencies, the community, and so forth.

MANAGING IN DIFFERENT AND CHANGING SITUATIONS

Management is not (and cannot be) based on simplistic principles. Different and changing situations require managers to use different approaches and techniques. Managing an entrepreneurial start-up requires different actions and decisions than managing a departmental work team in a large corporate setting. The **contingency perspective** (sometimes called the situational approach) of management underscores and emphasizes the fact that because organizations are different, they face different circumstances (contingencies) and, thus, may require different ways of managing. Therefore, when we describe what managers do from this perspective, we're recognizing that managers must "read" and attempt to interpret the situational contingencies facing them before deciding the best way to work with and through others as they coordinate work activities.

contingency perspective

An approach that says that organizations are different, face different situations (contingencies), and require different ways of managing.

A contingency approach to describing what managers do is intuitively logical because organizations and even units within the same organization are diverse—in size, objectives, work being done, and the like. It would be surprising to find universally applicable management principles that would work in *all* situations. But, of course, it's one thing to say that the way to manage "depends on the situation" and another to say what it depends upon. Management researchers have been working to identify these "what" variables. Exhibit 1.8 describes four popular contingency variables. The list is by no means comprehensive—more than 100 different "what" variables have been identified—but it represents those most widely used and gives you an idea of what we mean by the term *contingency variable*. As you can see from this short list, the contingency variables can have a significant

---

Organization Size. The number of people in an organization is a major influence on what managers do. As size increases, so do the problems of coordination. For instance, the type of organization structure appropriate for an organization of 50,000 employees is likely to be inefficient for an organization of 50 employees.

Routineness of Task Technology. To achieve its purpose, an organization uses technology; that is, it engages in the process of transforming inputs into outputs. Routine technologies require organizational structures, leadership styles, and control systems that differ from those required by customized or nonroutine technologies.

Environmental Uncertainty. The degree of uncertainty caused by political, technological, sociocultural, and economic changes influences the management process. What works best in a stable and predictable environment may be totally inappropriate in a rapidly changing and unpredictable environment.

Individual Differences. Individuals differ in terms of their desire for growth, autonomy, tolerance of ambiguity, and expectations. These and other individual differences are particularly important when managers select motivation techniques, leadership styles, and job designs.

Exhibit	1.8
Popular Contingency Variables	

Testing...Testing... 1,2,3

13. Describe an organi-
    zation using the sys-
    tems perspective.

14. Explain how the sys-
    tems perspective is
    used to describe
    what managers do.

15. What is the contin-
    gency perspective,
    and how is it used to
    describe what man-
    agers do?

impact on what managers do. The primary value of the contingency approach to describing what managers do is that it stresses that there are no simplistic or universal rules for managers to follow in doing their jobs. Instead, a manager's job involves managing different and changing situations, and managers' actions should be appropriate for the situations in which they find themselves.

SUMMARY OF MULTIPLE PERSPECTIVES ON THE MANAGER'S JOB

As we've shown throughout this section, a manager's job can be described from various perspectives: functions, roles, essential skills, systems, and contingencies. Each approach provides a different perspective on the manager's job. Although we'll use the functions approach as our framework for our study of management, we're not just forgetting the other perspectives! You'll see aspects of each as we discuss various management topics in the rest of the book.

❯ WHAT IS AN ORGANIZATION?

organization

A deliberate arrangement of people to accomplish some specific purpose.

Managers work in organizations. If there were no organizations, there would be no need for managers. What is an organization? An **organization** is a deliberate arrangement of people to accomplish some specific purpose. Your college or university is an organization; so are fraternities and sororities, government departments, churches, Amazon.com, your neighborhood video store, the United Way, the Colorado Rockies baseball team, and the Mayo Clinic. These are all organizations because they all share three common characteristics as shown in Exhibit 1.9.

First, each organization has a distinct purpose. This purpose is typically expressed in terms of a goal or a set of goals that the organization hopes to accomplish. Second, each organization is composed of people. One person working alone is not an organization, and it takes people to perform the work that's necessary for the organization to achieve its goals. Third, all organizations develop some deliberate structure so that their members can do their work. That structure may be open and flexible, with no clear and precise delineations of job duties or strict adherence to any explicit job arrangements—in other words, it may be a simple network of loose relationships. Or the structure may be more traditional with clearly defined rules, regulations, and job descriptions, and some members may be identified as "bosses" who have authority over other members. But no matter what type of structural arrangement an organization uses, it does require some deliberate structure so members' work relationships are clarified. In sum-

Exhibit	1.9	
Characteristics of Organizations		

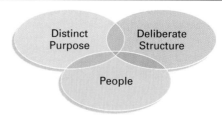

mary, the term *organization* refers to an entity that has a distinct purpose, includes people or members, and has some type of deliberate structure.

Although these three characteristics are important to our definition of *what* an organization is, the concept of an organization is changing. It's no longer appropriate to assume that all organizations are going to be structured like Procter & Gamble, Exxon-Mobil, or General Motors, with clearly identifiable divisions, departments, and work units. In fact, one of GM's subsidiaries, Saturn Corporation, may be more characteristic of what contemporary organizations look like, with its flexible work arrangements,

The 2000 U.S. women's national soccer team is an organization. How? It has a distinct purpose, includes people, and has a deliberate structure.

employee work teams, open communication systems, and supplier alliances. Just how is the concept of an organization changing? Exhibit 1.10 lists some differences between traditional organizations and new organizations. As these comparisons show, today's organizations are becoming more open, flexible, and responsive to changes.[13]

Why are organizations changing? Because the world around them has changed and is continuing to change. Societal, economic, global, and technological changes have created an environment in which successful organizations (those that consistently attain their goals) must embrace new ways of getting work done. Examples of how the world is changing include the increased dependence on e-business models and approaches, continuing spread of information technology and its impact on workplaces, increasing globalization, and changing employee expectations. Even though the concept of organizations may be changing, managers and management continue to be important to organizations.

Testing...Testing...1,2,3

16. **What are the three characteristics of organizations?**

17. **How are organizations changing?**

18. **Why are organizations changing?**

Traditional Organization	New Organization
• Stable	• Dynamic
• Inflexible	• Flexible
• Job-focused	• Skills-focused
• Work is defined by job positions	• Work is defined in terms of tasks to be done
• Individual-oriented	• Team-oriented
• Permanent jobs	• Temporary jobs
• Command-oriented	• Involvement-oriented
• Managers always make decisions	• Employees participate in decision making
• Rule-oriented	• Customer-oriented
• Relatively homogeneous workforce	• Diverse workforce
• Workdays defined as 9 to 5	• Workdays have no time boundaries
• Hierarchical relationships	• Lateral and networked relationships
• Work at organizational facility during specific hours	• Work anywhere, anytime

Exhibit | 1.10

The Changing Organization

> ## WHY STUDY MANAGEMENT?

You may be wondering why you need to study management. If you're an accounting major, a marketing major, or any major other than management, you may not understand how studying management is going to help you in your career. We can explain the value of studying management by looking at the universality of management, the reality of work, and the rewards and challenges of being a manager.

THE UNIVERSALITY OF MANAGEMENT

Just how universal is the need for management in organizations? We can say with absolute certainty that management is needed in all types and sizes of organizations, at all organizational levels, in all organizational work areas, and in all organizations, no matter in what country they're located. This is known as the **universality of management**. (See Exhibit 1.11.) Managers in all these settings will plan, organize, lead, and control. However, this is not to say that management is done the same way in all these scenarios. The differences in what a supervisor in a software applications testing facility at Cisco Systems does versus what the president of Cisco does are a matter of degree and emphasis, not of function. Because both are managers, both will plan, organize, lead, and control.

Since management is universally needed in all organizations, we have a vested interest in improving the way organizations are managed. Why? We interact with organizations every single day of our lives. Does it frustrate you when you have to spend three hours in a department of motor vehicles office to get your driver's license renewed? Are you irritated when none of the salespeople in a department store seem interested in helping you? Do you get annoyed when you call an airline three times and its sales representatives quote you three different prices for the same trip? These are all examples of problems created by poor management. Organizations that are well managed—and we'll share many examples of these throughout the text—develop a loyal customer base, grow, and prosper. Those that are poorly managed find themselves with a declining customer base and reduced revenues. By studying

universality of management

The reality that management is needed in all types and sizes of organizations, at all organizational levels, in all organizational areas, and in organizations in all countries around the globe.

Exhibit	1.11

Universal Need for Management

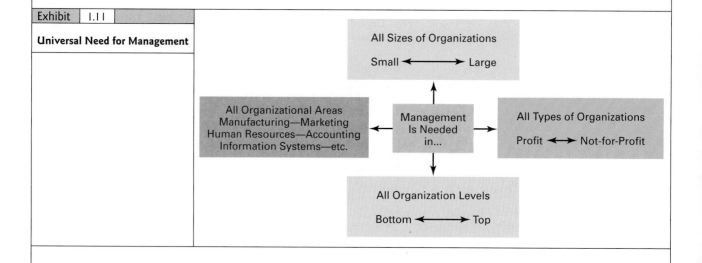

MANAGING YOUR CAREER | Career Opportunities in Management

Are management jobs disappearing? You might think so based on news coverage about organizational restructurings. The truth is there are abundant opportunities for management jobs and the future looks bright![14]

The U.S. Bureau of Labor Statistics estimates a 10 to 20 percent growth in all executive, administrative, and managerial jobs through the year 2008. These jobs, however, may not be in the organizations or fields that you'd expect. The demand for managers in traditional, Fortune 500 organizations and particularly in the area of

traditional manufacturing is not going to be as hot as the demand for managers in small and medium-sized organizations in the services field, particularly information and health care services. Keep in mind that a good place to land a management position can be a smaller-sized organization. So, what's the bottom line for you? Learn all you can about management, build your management skills, keep your options open, be willing to move into new areas, and soon a managerial position can be yours!

---

management, you'll be able to recognize poor management and work to correct it. In addition, you'll be able to recognize good management and encourage it, whether it's in an organization with which you're simply interacting or whether it's in an organization in which you're employed.

THE REALITY OF WORK

Another reason for studying management is the reality that for most of you, once you graduate from college and begin your career, you will either manage or be managed. For those who plan on management careers, an understanding of the management process forms the foundation upon which to build your management skills. For those of you who don't see yourself in a management position, you are still likely to have to deal with managers. Assuming that you will have to work for a living and recognizing that you are very likely to work in an organization, you'll probably have some managerial responsibilities even

if you're not a manager. Our experience tells us that you can gain a great deal of insight into the way your boss behaves and the internal workings of organizations by studying management. Our point is that you don't have to aspire to be a manager to gain something valuable from a course in management.

REWARDS AND CHALLENGES OF BEING A MANAGER

We can't leave our discussion of the value of studying management without looking at the rewards and challenges of being a manager. (See Exhibit 1.12.) What *does* it mean to be a manager?

Being a manager in today's dynamic workplace presents many challenges. Being a manager *is* hard work. It can be a tough and often thankless job. You may have to

Whirlpool plans to remain the leader in the major home appliance market. One way it hopes to do so is through an unusual training program during which a group of new hires live together in a large house for two months, getting familiar with the company's refrigerators, dishwashers, and dryers by using them over and over. Whirlpool's managers are a critical part of this intensive training. Here, training manager Kurt Gersonde introduces the dishwasher to the trainees.

Exhibit	1.12	**Rewards**	**Challenges**
Rewards and Challenges of Being a Manager		• Create a work environment in which organizational members can work to the best of their ability • Have opportunities to think creatively and use imagination • Help others find meaning and fulfillment in work • Support, coach, and nurture others • Work with a variety of people • Receive recognition and status in organization and community • Play a role in influencing organizational outcomes • Receive appropriate compensation in form of salaries, bonuses, and stock options • Good managers are needed by organizations	• Do hard work • Have to deal with a variety of personalities • Often have to make do with limited resources • Motivate workers in chaotic and uncertain situations • Successfully blend knowledge, skills, ambitions, and experiences of a diverse work group • Success depends on others' work performance

deal with a variety of personalities and often have to make do with limited resources. It can be a challenge to motivate workers in the face of uncertainty and chaos. And managers may find it difficult to effectively blend the knowledge, skills, ambitions, and experiences of a diverse group of employees. Finally, as a manager, your success typically depends on others' work performance.

Despite these seemingly difficult challenges, being a manager *can be* very rewarding. The most important work of any organization anywhere is creating a work environment in which organizational members can do their work to the best of their ability and help the organization achieve its goals. And managers get to do that! In addition, as a manager, you often have the opportunity to think creatively and use your imagination. You help others find meaning and fulfillment in their work. You get to support, coach, and nurture others and help them make good decisions. Also, as a manager, you'll get to meet and work with a variety of people—both inside and outside the organization. Other rewards of being a manager may include receiving recognition and status in the organization and in the community, playing a role in influencing organizational outcomes, and receiving appropriate compensation in the form of salaries, bonuses, and stock options. Finally, organizations need good managers. Nothing great ever happens alone! It's through the combined efforts of motivated and passionate people working together that organizations accomplish their goals. As a manager, you can get satisfaction from knowing that your efforts, skills, and abilities are needed.

Testing...Testing...1,2,3

19. **What does the concept of universality of management mean?**

20. **Why is an understanding of management important even if you don't plan to be a manager?**

21. **Describe the challenges and rewards of being a manager.**

Managers Respond to "A Manager's Dilemma"

Shannon McMurtrey

President, McMurtrey/Whitaker & Associates, Inc., Springfield, Missouri

I see the task of managing people and their careers as bordering on "sacred ground." I agree with Siegel in his recognition of his responsibility to his customers to ensure that they have the best professionals working for them. I would extend his view to encompass the responsibility that he has to his employees.

I view a major part of my responsibility as a manager as helping my employees fulfill their capacities as humans. I do not see them as "cogs in the professional services wheel" that turn solely on the whims of our clients. I find that our employees produce outstanding results for our clients whey they feel that they can serve in an environment that allows them to grow and excel.

With that said, I would agree with Siegel's approach in creating a fun, stimulating work environment. I would suggest that he add opportunities for professional development, training, and continuing education; allow significant personal time that can be used for employees' families or their own growth; and spend time with each employee to get to know him or her personally and professionally.

James G. Amalfitano, Esq.

Vice President of National Accounts, ILX Systems, New York, New York

In a CPA firm, professionalism is important. Clients trust that the individuals working on their account are competent and skilled. Even though the setting may have changed, the goal of producing the best intellectual work and acquiring and retaining business shouldn't have changed. The managerial skills that Siegel should use to maintain an environment of innovation and professionalism include emphasizing the importance of building and maintaining client trust, letting employees know the expectations, and reviewing employees on their merit.

To build client trust, Siegel should review the reasons why clients trusted their business to the organization all along. Then Siegel should emphasize to employees why it's important to continue to do those things. To let employees know the expectations, Siegel should make them aware of the guidelines for working in such a nontraditional setting. Although the eccentric workplace will be stimulating for professional creativity, there will be times when employees need to focus on serious business situations that call for more traditional approaches. Finally, employees need to know that they are productive and that they are recognized as contributors. Therefore, evaluations should be customized to the new organizational style.

Chapter Summary

This summary is organized by the chapter-opening objectives found on p. 2.

1. A manager is someone who works with and through other people by coordinating their work activities in order to accomplish organizational goals. The changing nature of organizations and work has altered the role of managers. The clear lines of distinction between managers and nonmanagerial employees have been blurred.

2. Management is the process of coordinating work activities so they're completed efficiently and effectively with and through other people.

3. Efficiency refers to getting the most output from the least amount of inputs. Effectiveness is concerned with completing activities so that organizational goals are attained. Efficiency is concerned with the means of getting things done and effectiveness is concerned with the ends.

4. Planning involves defining an organization's goals and establishing strategies and plans to achieve those goals. Organizing includes designing a structure to carry out the plans. Leading involves motivating subordinates, influencing individuals or teams, communicating effectively, and dealing with employee behavior issues. Finally, controlling includes monitoring, comparing, and correcting the organization's performance. The process of management refers to the idea that management consists of a set of ongoing decisions and actions in which managers engage as they plan, organize, lead, and control.

5. Henry Mintzberg concluded that managers perform 10 different roles or behaviors. He classified them into three sets. One set is concerned with interpersonal relationships (figurehead, leader, liaison). The second set is related to the transfer of information (monitor, disseminator, spokesperson). The third set deals with decision making (entrepreneur, disturbance handler, resource allocator, negotiator).

6. Robert Katz identified three skills managers need: technical, human, and conceptual. He showed that the relative importance of these skills varied according to the management level within the organization.

7. The systems perspective can be used to describe what a manager does because organizations are open systems with interrelated and interdependent parts. Within this "system," managers coordinate the various work activities so that the organization can meet its goals.

8. The contingency perspective (sometimes called the situational approach) is a reflection of the fact that organizations are different and face different circumstances (contingencies); thus, they may require different ways of managing.

9. An organization is a deliberate arrangement of people to accomplish some specific purpose. Organizations are becoming more open, flexible, and responsive to changes.

10. It's important to study management because it is universal, the reality of work is that you will either manage or be managed, and there are rewards and challenges in being a manager.

Thinking About Management Issues

1. Is your course instructor a manager? Discuss in terms of managerial functions, managerial roles, skills, the systems perspective, and the contingency perspective.

2. "The manager's most basic responsibility is to focus people toward performance of work activities to achieve desired outcomes." What's your interpretation of this statement? Do you agree with this statement? Why or why not?

3. Why do you think skills of job candidates have become so important to employers? What are the implications for (a) managers in general and (b) you personally?

4. Is there one best "style" of management? Why or why not?

5. Does management matter to organizations? Why or why not? Support your answer.

Is there some way for managers to find out about changes in how management is practiced in organizations and what trends are affecting the way managers manage? One source that provides this type of information is the American Management Association (AMA) Web site. The AMA, a practitioner-oriented membership-based organization, offers a wide range of management development programs for managers and organizations around the globe. Log on to AMA's Web site (www.amanet.org) and find the section entitled AMA

Research. Choose two current reports. Read through these and make a bulleted list of the key information. Then write a description of how this information might affect the way a manager plans, organizes, leads, and controls.

Once you've completed this portion of the assignment, search for another Web site that discusses trends in management. Write a description of that site and what you found there. Be sure to provide the URL (Web site address).

myPHLIP Companion Web Site

myPHLIP (**www.prenhall.com/myphlip**) is a fully customizable homepage that ties students and faculty to text-specific resources.
- **For students**, myPHLIP provides an online study guide tied chapter-by-chapter to the text—current events and Internet exercises, lecture notes, downloadable software, the Career Center, the Writing Center, Ask the Tutor, and more.
- **For faculty**, myPHLIP provides a syllabus tool that allows you to manage content, communicate with students, and upload personal resources.

Working Together: Team-Based Exercise

By this time in your life, all of you have had to work with individuals in managerial positions (or maybe *you* were the manager), either through work experiences or through other organizational experiences (social, hobby/interest, religious, and so forth). What do you think makes some managers better than others? Are there certain characteristics that distinguish good managers? Form small groups of three to four class members. Discuss your experiences with managers—good and bad. Draw up a list of the characteristics of those individuals you felt were good managers. For each item, indicate under which management function you think it falls. As a group, be prepared to share your list with the class and to explain your choice of management function.

Case Application

Sweet Music

For well over a century and a half, the C. F. Martin Guitar Company (established in 1833) of Nazareth, Pennsylvania, has been producing acoustic instruments considered to be among the finest in the world (www.cfmartin.com). Like a Steinway grand piano, a Rolls Royce automobile, a Buffet clarinet, or a Baccarat crystal vase, a Martin guitar—which can cost more than $10,000—is among the best that money can buy. This family business has managed to defy the odds and survive through six generations. Current CEO Christian Frederick Martin IV—better known as Chris—continues to be committed to the guitar maker's

craft. He even travels to Martin dealerships around the world to hold instructional clinics. Few companies have had the staying power of Martin Guitar. Why? What are the keys to the company's success? A primary one has to be the managerial guidance and skills of a talented leader who has kept organizational members focused on important issues such as quality.

From the very beginning, quality has played an important role in everything that C. F. Martin Guitar Company does. Even through dramatic changes in product design, distribution systems, and manufacturing methods, the company has remained committed to making quality products. The company's steadfast adherence to high standards of musical excellence and providing a product to meet the needs of a demanding customer base permeates everything that happens in the organization, top to bottom and in all work areas. Part of that quality approach encompasses a long-standing ecological policy. Since the company depends on natural wood products to manufacture its guitars, it has embraced the judicious and responsible use of traditional natural materials and encouraged the introduction of sustainable-yield alternative wood species. Based on thorough customer research, Martin introduced guitars that utilized structurally sound woods with natural cosmetic defects that were once considered unacceptable. In addition, Martin follows the directives of CITES, the Convention on International Trade in Endangered Species of Wild Fauna and Flora (www. cites.org).

C. F. Martin Guitar Company is an interesting blend of old and new. Although the equipment and tools may have changed over the years, employees remain true to the principle of high standards of musical excellence. Building a guitar to meet these standards requires considerable attention and patience. Family member Frank Henry Martin explained to potential customers in the preface to a 1904 catalog, "How to build a guitar to give this tone is not a secret. It takes care and patience. Care in selecting the materials, laying out the proportions, and attending to the details which add to the player's comfort. Patience in giving the necessary time to finish every part. A good guitar cannot be built for the price of a poor one, but who regrets the extra cost for a good guitar?" Almost one hundred years later, this statement is still an accurate expression of the company's philosophy. Although the company is firmly rooted in its past, Chris is not reluctant to take the company in new directions. For instance, in the late 1990s, he made the bold decision to start selling guitars in the under-$800 market segment. This segment accounts for 65 percent of the acoustic guitar industry's sales. The company's DXM model was introduced in 1998. Although it doesn't look, smell, or feel like the company's pricier models, customers claim it has a better sound than most other instruments in that price range. Chris justified his decision by saying that "If Martin just worships its past without trying anything new, there won't be a Martin left to worship."

The company is doing well under Chris's management. Revenues have continued to increase and in 2000 were close to $60 million. The manufacturing facility in Nazareth was expanded and new guitar models continue to be introduced. Employees describe his management style as friendly and personal, yet firm and direct. Although C. F. Martin Guitar Company continues to spread its wings in new directions, it hasn't lost sight of the commitment to making the absolute finest products it can. And under Chris's management, it won't.

Chris Martin, CEO of C.F. Martin Guitar Company.

QUESTIONS

1. Which management skill—conceptual, human, or technical—do you think would be most important to Chris Martin? Explain your choice.

2. Check out the CITES Web site. What information could a manager find there? How might an organization's commitment to social responsibility affect the way managers perform the managerial functions?

3. What management roles would Chris be playing as he (a) visits Martin dealerships around the world, (b) assesses the feasibility of new guitar models, and (c) keeps employees focused on the company's long-standing principles? Explain your choices.

4. Chris made the statement that "If Martin just worships its past without trying anything new, there won't be a Martin left to worship." What are the implications for managers throughout the company as they plan, organize, lead, and control?

5. Chris's management style was described by employees as friendly and personal, yet firm and direct. What do you think this means as far as the way he plans, organizes, leads, and controls? Do you think this style would work in other organizations or does this style work only because it's a family business and Chris is the sixth generation of the family to run the business? Explain.

Sources: Information on company from Web site (www. cfmartin.com), June 27, 2000; and S. Fitch, "Stringing Them Along," *Forbes*, July 26, 1999, pp. 90–91.)

Caring Management

SMALL BUSINESS 2000

Although caring may not be a word many people would normally associate with management, Cheryl Womack of Kansas City, Missouri, has built a $45 million company by caring about her customers *and* her employees. She started her business—VCW Inc., which she laughingly says stands for Very Cute Women—in 1981 in the basement of her home with one telephone and call-waiting. What does VCW Inc. do? The company oversees the National Association of Independent Truckers. VCW offers cost-effective insurance coverage, retirement benefit plans, low-interest credit cards, and other benefits to thousands of independent truck drivers who belong to this association. In addition, many large motor carriers who hire independent drivers also are her customers.

Womack's customers are a unique breed, indeed! Independent truck drivers "move the world" as they haul across the country the products we use every day. Independent truck drivers also are businesspeople and must run their businesses efficiently and effectively or they won't survive in this intensely competitive industry. How does VCW show that it cares about its customers—these independent truckers? It provides an answer to a problem that many of them face: where to find cost-effective insurance coverage that other insurance companies refuse to carry. Womack subscribes to the belief that if you can help solve a customer's problem, you'll be successful. She and her employees *have* been successful at solving their customers' problems and caring about them by providing outstanding customer service. But Womack's caring management doesn't stop with her customers. It extends to her employees, as well.

Her most telling statement about her management philosophy is that "everything I do here is designed to cultivate and grow employees." From the beautifully designed offices to the formal dinners and travel experiences she provides, Womack sees her role as a mentor for employees, not as a boss. She wants her employees to not only do their jobs but also to recreate, redesign, and expand them. Employees can earn $1,000 for proposing suggestions that help them do the job better. VCW Inc. also has a profit-sharing plan that gives employees a stake in the company's ability to make a profit. Womack also recognizes that employees need more than financial caring. To that end, she implemented on-site day care for employees' children, and employees enjoy inexpensive, delicious home-cooked meals at the office prepared by an employee who started at VCW in customer service but who had always dreamed of a job cooking for others. Cheryl strongly believes in the power of such benefits to show employees that she cares about them and wants them to be committed and productive at their jobs.

QUESTIONS

1. What characteristics of the "new organization" found in Exhibit 1.10 does Cheryl Womack's company, VCW Inc., exhibit? Explain your choices.

2. At which of the four management functions does Cheryl Womack seem to be particularly strong? Which of the management skills? Provide examples supporting your choices.

3. What can you learn about being a manager from Cheryl Womack? Be specific.

4. What do you think it means to be a mentor, not a boss?

Source: Based on *Small Business* 2000, *Show 110.*

After reading and studying this chapter, you should be able to:

1. Discuss management's relationship to other academic fields of study.

2. Explain the value of studying management history.

3. Identify some major pre-twentieth-century contributions to management.

4. Summarize the contributions of the scientific management advocates.

5. Describe the contributions of the general administrative theorists.

6. Summarize the quantitative approach to management.

7. Describe the contributions of the early organizational behavior advocates.

8. Explain the importance of the Hawthorne Studies to management.

9. Describe the following trends that are affecting management practices: globalization, workforce diversity, entrepreneurship, e-business applications, need for innovation and flexibility, quality management, learning organizations and knowledge management, and workplace spirituality.

A MANAGER'S DILEMMA

Toyota Motor Corporation is renowned worldwide for its many outstanding business accomplishments.[1] Many experts have tried to decipher the keys to Toyota's successes. Assessments of the company demonstrate over and over again that Toyota's successes can be attributed to finely tuned and coordinated work activities. For instance, manufacturing work processes, activities, and production flows are rigidly scripted yet exceedingly flexible and adaptable. How can a rigid system also be flexible? As Toyota has discovered over five decades of being in business, it's those very rigid manufacturing specifications that nourish and preserve employees' work flexibility and creativity. However, the creativity and innovation behind Toyota's manufacturing system pales in comparison to the project Shigeki Tomoyama and a fellow engineer pioneered—a project so momentous that it had the potential to transform Toyota into one of the New Economy's most daring players.

In a small office in Toyota city, Tomoyama and Akio Toyoda (the son of Honorary Chairman Shoichiro Toyoda) put together a simple computer network that allowed car dealers to display online photos of used Toyotas. Through their innovative approach, the number of consumers looking at the used cars increased. Test marketing showed that the use of the computer reduced the average stay of a used car on dealers' lots from 90 days to 10 days.

Management Yesterday and Today

2

From this simple beginning, their Web site, now called Gazoo.com, has become one of Japan's most popular online portals. The company's Gazoo.com division has more than 50 vendors and 500,000 members. Over 2,000 new members sign up every day. The Web site is so popular that over 13,000 convenience stores want Gazoo.com terminals placed in their stores. Through these Gazoo kiosks, customers place orders and pick up their deliveries later at the store.

Put yourself in Tomoyama's position. How can he make sure that Gazoo.com maintains its innovation and flexibility—two important organizational characteristics needed for success in this new e-business venture?

WHAT WOULD YOU DO?

Toyota's push into Web-based operations isn't all that unusual today. Many other organizations, large and small, have made similar commitments to understanding the challenges and rewards of doing business on the Web. The practice of management has always reflected the times and social conditions, so now we are seeing organizations responding to technology breakthroughs and developing Web-based operations. These new business models reflect today's reality: Information can be shared and exchanged instantaneously anywhere on the planet. Although Tomoyama must build an organizational division that is flexible and innovative, he recognizes that it's not always easy to implement new ideas. In fact, the history of management practice is filled with examples of evolutions and revolutions in implementing new ideas about how organizations should be managed.

The purpose of this chapter is to demonstrate that a knowledge of management history can help you understand today's management theory and practice. We'll introduce you to the origins of many contemporary management concepts and show how they have evolved to reflect the changing needs of organizations and society as a whole. We'll also introduce important trends and issues that managers currently face in order to link the past with the future and to demonstrate that the field of management is still evolving.

> ## MANAGEMENT'S CONNECTION TO OTHER FIELDS OF STUDY

Why do college faculty make you take courses in psychology or political science if you're a business major? College courses frequently appear to be independent bodies of knowledge. Too often, little of what is taught in one course is linked to other courses. As a result, many students don't believe that they need to remember what they've previously learned. This has been especially true in most business curriculums. There is typically a lack of connectedness between core business courses and between other business courses and liberal arts courses. Accounting classes, for instance, make little reference to marketing; and marketing classes typically make little reference to courses in economics or political science. College curriculums resemble a group of silos with each silo representing a separate and distinct discipline. However, a number of management educators have begun to recognize the need to build bridges between these silos by integrating courses across the college curriculum. Management courses have a rich heritage from humanities and social science courses. Let's briefly look at some of these courses that have directly affected management theories and practices.

Anthropology is the study of societies, which helps us learn about humans and their activities. Anthropologists' work on cultures and environments, for instance, has helped managers better understand differences in fundamental values, attitudes, and behavior between people in different countries and within different organizations.

Economics is concerned with the allocation and distribution of scarce resources. It provides us with an understanding of the changing economy as well as the role of competition and free markets in a global context. For instance, why are most athletic shoes made in Asia? Why does Mexico now have more automobile plants than Detroit? Economists provide the answers to these questions when they discuss comparative advantage. Similarly, an understanding of free trade and protectionist policies is absolutely essential to any manager operating in the global marketplace.

Philosophy courses examine the nature of things, particularly values and ethics. Ethical concerns go directly to the existence of organizations and what constitutes appropriate behavior within them. For instance, the liberty ethic (John Locke) proposed that freedom, equality, justice, and private property were legal rights; the Protestant ethic (John Calvin) encouraged individuals to be frugal, work hard, and attain success; and the market ethic (Adam Smith) argued that the market and competition, not government, should be the sole regulators of economic activity. These ethics have shaped today's organizations by providing a basis for legitimate authority, linking rewards to performance, and justifying the existence of business and the corporate form of organization.

Political science studies the behavior of individuals and groups within a political environment. Specific topics of concern to political scientists include structuring of conflict, allocating power in an economic system, and manipulating power for individual self-interest. Managers are affected by a nation's form of government—whether it allows citizens to hold property, by citizens' ability to engage in and enforce contracts, and by the appeal mechanisms available to redress grievances. A nation's position on property, contracts, and justice, in turn, shapes the type, form, and policies of its organizations.

We can't leave the topic of management's connection to other disciplines without recognizing the important role that *psychology* and *sociology* have played in its development. Psychology is the science that seeks to measure, explain, and sometimes change the behavior of humans and other animals. Sociology is the study of people in relation to their fellow human beings. Both disciplines have contributed greatly to our understanding of people and their behavior at work, both as individuals and in groups. Most of what we know about motivation, leadership, communication, group processes, teamwork, and other behavioral issues in organizations is based on concepts and theories from the fields of psychology and sociology.

Several academic disciplines including economics, psychology, sociology, and others have contributed to the development of management theories and practices.

> ## HISTORICAL BACKGROUND OF MANAGEMENT

Organized endeavors directed by people responsible for planning, organizing, leading, and controlling activities have existed for thousands of years. The Egyptian pyramids and the Great Wall of China, for instance, are tangible evidence that projects of tremendous scope, employing tens of thousands of people, were undertaken well before modern times. The pyramids are a particularly interesting example. The construction of a single pyramid occupied more than 100,000 workers for 20 years.[2] Who told each worker what to do? Who ensured that there would be enough stones at the site to keep workers busy? The answer to such questions is *managers*. Regardless of what managers were called at the time, someone had to plan what was to be done, organize people and materials to do it,

The largest of the pyramids contained more than 2 million blocks, each weighing several tons. Someone had to design the structure, find a stone quarry, and arrange for the stones to be cut and moved—possibly over land and by water—to the construction site. Then someone had to organize the people and materials, lead and direct the workers, and impose controls to ensure that everything was completed as planned.

lead and direct the workers, and impose some controls to ensure that everything was done as planned.

Another example of early management can be seen during the 1400s in the city of Venice, Italy, a major economic and trade center. The Venetians developed an early form of business enterprise and engaged in many activities common to today's organizations. For instance, at the arsenal of Venice, warships were floated along the canals and at each stop materials and riggings were added to the ship. Doesn't that sound a lot like a car "floating" along an automobile assembly line and components being added to it? In addition to this assembly line, the Venetians also had a warehouse and inventory system to monitor its contents, personnel (human resource management) functions required to manage the labor force, and an accounting system to keep track of revenues and costs.[3]

These examples from the past demonstrate that organizations have been around for thousands of years and that management has been practiced for an equivalent period. However, two pre-twentieth-century events played particularly significant roles in promoting the study of management.

First, in 1776, Adam Smith published a classical economics doctrine, *The Wealth of Nations*, in which he argued the economic advantages that organizations and society would gain from the **division of labor**, the breakdown of jobs into narrow and repetitive tasks. Using the pin manufacturing industry as an example, Smith claimed that 10 individuals, each doing a specialized task, could produce about 48,000 pins a day among them. However, if each person worked separately and had to perform each task, it would be quite an accomplishment to produce even 10 pins a day! Smith concluded that division of labor increased productivity by increasing each worker's skill and dexterity, by saving time lost in changing tasks, and by creating labor-saving inventions and machinery. The continued popularity of job specialization—for example, specific tasks performed by members of a hospital surgery team, specific meal preparation tasks done by workers in restaurant kitchens, or specific positions played by players on a football team—is undoubtedly due to the economic advantages cited by Adam Smith.

The second, and possibly most important, pre-twentieth-century influence on management was the **Industrial Revolution**. Starting in the eighteenth century in Great Britain, the revolution had crossed the Atlantic to America by the end of the Civil War. The major contribution of the Industrial Revolution was the substitution of machine power for human power, which, in turn, made it more economical to manufacture goods in factories rather than at home. These large, efficient factories using power-driven equipment required managerial skills. Why? Managers were needed to forecast demand, ensure that enough material was on hand to make products, assign tasks to people, direct daily activities, coordinate

division of labor

The breakdown of jobs into narrow and repetitive tasks.

Industrial Revolution

The advent of machine power, mass production, and efficient transportation.

the various tasks, ensure that the machines were kept in good working condition and work standards were maintained, find markets for the finished products, and so forth. Planning, organizing, leading, and controlling became necessary, and the development of large corporations would require formal management practices. The need for a formal theory to guide managers in running these organizations had arrived. However, it wasn't until the early 1900s that the first major step toward developing such a theory was taken.

The development of management theories has been characterized by differing beliefs about what managers do and how they should do it. In the next sections we present the contributions of four approaches. Scientific management looked at management from the perspective of improving the productivity and efficiency of manual workers. General administrative theorists were concerned with the overall organization and how to make it more effective. Then a group of theorists focused on developing and applying quantitative models to management practices. Finally, a group of researchers emphasized human behavior in organizations, or the "people" side of management.

Keep in mind that each is concerned with the same "animal"; the differences reflect the backgrounds and interests of the writer. A relevant analogy is the classic story of the blind men and the elephant, in which each man declares the elephant to be like the part he is feeling: The first man touching the side declares that the elephant is like a wall; the second touches the trunk and says the elephant is like a snake; the third feels one of the elephant's tusks and believes the elephant to be like a spear; the fourth grabs a leg and says an elephant is like a tree; and the fifth touches the elephant's tail and concludes that the animal is like a rope. Each is encountering the same elephant, but what each observes depends on where he stands. Similarly, each of the four management perspectives is correct and contributes to our overall understanding of management. However, each is also a limited view of a larger animal. (See Exhibit 2.1.) We'll begin our journey into management's past by looking at the contributions of scientific management. ◄—

Testing…Testing…1,2,3

1. **What are some early evidences of management practice?**

2. **Explain why division of labor and the Industrial Revolution are important to the study of management.**

3. **What are the four major approaches to the study of management?**

| Exhibit | 2.1 | **Development of Major Management Theories** |

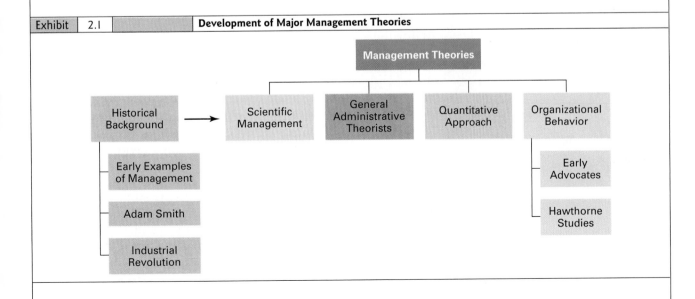

> **SCIENTIFIC MANAGEMENT**

If you had to pinpoint the year modern management theory was born, 1911 might be a logical choice. That was the year Frederick Winslow Taylor's *Principles of Scientific Management* was published. Its contents became widely accepted by managers around the world. The book described the theory of **scientific management**: the use of scientific methods to define the "one best way" for a job to be done.

scientific management

The use of the scientific method to determine the "one best way" for a job to be done.

IMPORTANT CONTRIBUTIONS

Important contributions to scientific management theory were made by Frederick W. Taylor and Frank and Lillian Gilbreth. Let's look at what they did.

Frederick W. Taylor   Taylor did most of his work at the Midvale and Bethlehem Steel Companies in Pennsylvania. As a mechanical engineer with a Quaker and Puritan background, he was continually appalled by workers' inefficiencies. Employees used vastly different techniques to do the same job. They were inclined to "take it easy" on the job, and Taylor believed that worker output was only about one-third of what was possible. Virtually no work standards existed. Workers were placed in jobs with little or no concern for matching their abilities and aptitudes with the tasks they were required to do. Managers and workers were in continual conflict. He set out to correct the situation by applying the scientific method to shop floor jobs. He spent more than two decades passionately pursuing the "one best way" for each job to be done.

Taylor's experiences at Midvale led him to define clear guidelines for improving production efficiency. He argued that these four principles of management (see Exhibit 2.2) would result in prosperity for both workers and managers.[4] How did these scientific principles really work? Let's look at an example.

Probably the best known example of Taylor's scientific management was the pig iron experiment. Workers loaded "pigs" of iron (each weighing 92 pounds) onto rail cars. Their daily average output was 12.5 tons. However, Taylor believed that by scientifically analyzing the job to determine the "one best way" to load pig iron, output could be increased to 47 or 48 tons per day. After scientifically trying different combinations of procedures, techniques, and tools, Taylor succeeded in getting that level of productivity. How? He put the right person on the job with the correct tools and equipment, had the worker follow his instructions exactly, and motivated the worker with an economic incentive of a significantly higher daily wage. Using similar approaches to other jobs, Taylor was able to define the "one best way" for doing each job. Overall, Taylor achieved consistent productivity improvements in the range of 200 percent or more. Through his groundbreaking studies of manual work using scientific principles, Taylor became known as the "father" of scientific management. His ideas spread in the United States and also in France, Germany, Russia, and Japan, and inspired others to study and develop methods of scientific management. His most prominent followers were Frank and Lillian Gilbreth.

Frederick W. Taylor (1856–1915) was the father of scientific management. Working at Midvale Steel Company, Taylor witnessed work inefficiencies. He sought to create a mental revolution among both workers and managers by defining clear guidelines for improving production efficiency.

Exhibit   2.2

**Taylor's Four Principles
of Management**

1. Develop a science for each element of an individual's work, which will replace the old rule-of-thumb method.
2. Scientifically select and then train, teach, and develop the worker. (Previously, workers chose their own work and trained themselves as best they could.)
3. Heartily cooperate with the workers so as to ensure that all work is done in accordance with the principles of the science that has been developed.
4. Divide work and responsibility almost equally between management and workers. Management takes over all work for which it is better fitted than the workers. (Previously, almost all the work and the greater part of the responsibility were thrown on the workers.)

Frank and Lillian Gilbreth A construction contractor by trade, Frank Gilbreth gave up his contracting career in 1912 to study scientific management after hearing Taylor speak at a professional meeting. Frank and his wife Lillian, a psychologist, studied work to eliminate wasteful hand-and-body motions. The Gilbreths also experimented with the design and use of the proper tools and equipment for optimizing work performance.[5]

Frank is probably best known for his experiments in bricklaying. By carefully analyzing the bricklayer's job, he reduced the number of motions in laying exterior brick from 18 to about 5, and on laying interior brick the motions were reduced from 18 to 2. Using Gilbreth's techniques, the bricklayer could be more productive and less fatigued at the end of the day.

therbligs

A classification scheme for labeling 17 basic hand motions.

The Gilbreths were among the first researchers to use motion pictures to study hand-and-body motions. They invented a device called a microchronometer that recorded a worker's motions and the amount of time spent doing each motion. Wasted motions missed by the naked eye could be identified and eliminated. The Gilbreths also devised a classification scheme to label 17 basic hand motions (such as search, grasp, hold), which they called **therbligs** (*Gilbreth* spelled backward with the *th* transposed). This scheme allowed the Gilbreths a more precise way of analyzing a worker's exact hand movements.

HOW DO TODAY'S MANAGERS USE SCIENTIFIC MANAGEMENT?

The guidelines that Taylor and others devised for improving production efficiency are still used in organizations today.[6] When managers analyze the basic work tasks that must be performed, use time-and-motion study to eliminate wasted motions, hire the best qualified workers for a job, and design incentive systems based on output, they're using the

Frank and Lillian Gilbreth, parents of 12 children, ran their household using scientific management principles and techniques. Two of their children wrote a book, *Cheaper by the Dozen*, that described life with the two masters of efficiency.

principles of scientific management. But current management practice isn't restricted to the scientific management approach. In fact, we can see theories and ideas from the next major approach we'll discuss—the general administrative approach—being used as well.

Testing...Testing...1,2,3

4. **What relevance does scientific management have to current management practices?**

5. **Describe Taylor's contributions to scientific management.**

6. **Explain Frank and Lillian Gilbreth's contributions to scientific management.**

〉 GENERAL ADMINISTRATIVE THEORISTS

general administrative theorists

Writers who developed general theories of what managers do and what constitutes good management practice.

Another group of writers looked at the subject of management but focused on the entire organization. We call them the **general administrative theorists**. They developed more general theories of what managers do and what constituted good management practice. Let's look at some important contributions to this perspective.

IMPORTANT CONTRIBUTIONS

The two most prominent theorists behind the general administrative approach were Henri Fayol and Max Weber.

Henri Fayol We mentioned Fayol in Chapter 1 because he described management as a universal set of functions that included planning, organizing, commanding, coordinating, and controlling. Because his ideas were important, let's look closer at what he had to say.[7]

Fayol wrote during the same time period as Taylor. While Taylor was concerned with management at the lowest organizational level and used the scientific method, Fayol's attention was directed at the activities of *all* managers. He wrote from personal experience as a practitioner since he was the managing director of a large French coal-mining firm.

principles of management

Fundamental rules of management that could be taught in schools and applied in all organizational situations.

Fayol described the practice of management as something distinct from accounting, finance, production, distribution, and other typical business functions. He argued that management was an activity common to all human endeavors in business, government, and even in the home. He then proceeded to state 14 **principles of management**—fundamental rules of management that could be taught in schools and applied in all organizational situations. These principles are shown in Exhibit 2.3.

bureaucracy

A form of organization characterized by division of labor, a clearly defined hierarchy, detailed rules and regulations, and impersonal relationships.

Max Weber Weber (pronounced VAY-ber) was a German sociologist who studied organizational activity. Writing in the early 1900s, he developed a theory of authority structures and relations.[8] Weber described an ideal type of organization he called a **bureaucracy**—a form of organization characterized by division of

1. *Division of work*. Specialization increases output by making employees more efficient.
2. *Authority*. Managers must be able to give orders. Authority gives them this right. Along with authority, however, goes responsibility.
3. *Discipline*. Employees must obey and respect the rules that govern the organization.
4. *Unity of command*. Every employee should receive orders from only one superior.
5. *Unity of direction*. The organization should have a single plan of action to guide managers and workers.
6. *Subordination of individual interests to the general interest*. The interests of any one employee or group of employees should not take precedence over the interests of the organization as a whole.
7. *Remuneration*. Workers must be paid a fair wage for their services.
8. *Centralization*. This term refers to the degree to which subordinates are involved in decision making.
9. *Scalar chain*. The line of authority from top management to the lowest ranks is the scalar chain.
10. *Order*. People and materials should be in the right place at the right time.
11. *Equity*. Managers should be kind and fair to their subordinates.
12. *Stability of tenure of personnel*. Management should provide orderly personnel planning and ensure that replacements are available to fill vacancies.
13. *Initiative*. Employees who are allowed to originate and carry out plans will exert high levels of effort.
14. *Esprit de corps*. Promoting team spirit will build harmony and unity within the organization.

Exhibit	2.3

Fayol's 14 Principles of Management

labor, a clearly defined hierarchy, detailed rules and regulations, and impersonal relationships. Weber recognized that this "ideal bureaucracy" didn't exist in reality. Instead he intended it as a basis for theorizing about work and how work could be done in large groups. His theory became the model structural design for many of today's large organizations. The features of Weber's ideal bureaucratic structure are outlined in Exhibit 2.4.

Exhibit	2.4	**Weber's Ideal Bureaucracy**

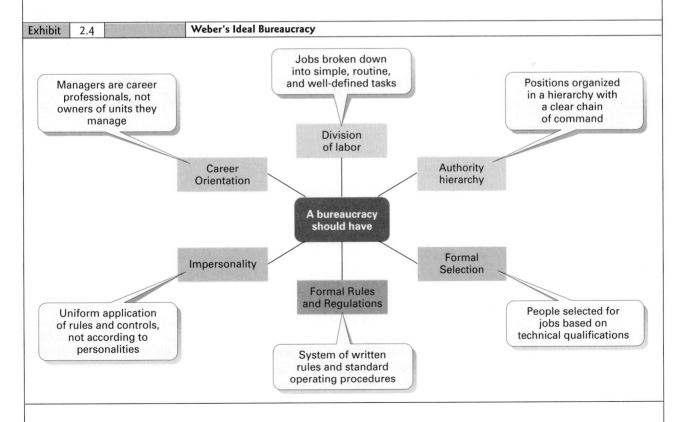

Bureaucracy, as described by Weber, is a lot like scientific management in its ideology. Both emphasize rationality, predictability, impersonality, technical competence, and authoritarianism. Although Weber's writings were less operational than Taylor's, the fact that his "ideal type" still describes many contemporary organizations attests to the importance of his work.

HOW DO TODAY'S MANAGERS USE GENERAL ADMINISTRATIVE THEORIES?

Some of our current management ideas and practices can be directly traced to the contributions of the general administrative theorists. For instance, the functional view of the manager's job can be attributed to Fayol. And even though the contingency perspective of a manager's job (which we introduced in Chapter 1) proposed that universalistic management principles for all types of organizations are not feasible, Fayol's 14 principles do serve as a frame of reference from which many current management concepts and theories of planning, organizing, leading, and controlling have evolved.

Weber's bureaucracy was an attempt to formulate an ideal prototype for designing organizations. Although many characteristics of Weber's bureaucracy are still evident in large organizations, his model isn't as popular today as it was throughout most of the twentieth century. Many contemporary managers feel that bureaucracy's emphasis on strict division of labor, adherence to formal rules and regulations, and impersonal application of rules and controls takes away the individual employee's creativity and the organization's ability to respond quickly to an increasingly dynamic environment. However, even in highly flexible organizations of talented professionals—such as General Electric or Cisco Systems—some bureaucratic mechanisms are necessary to ensure that resources are used efficiently and effectively.

❯ QUANTITATIVE APPROACH TO MANAGEMENT

quantitative approach

The use of quantitative techniques to improve decision making.

The **quantitative approach** involves the use of quantitative techniques to improve decision making. This approach has also been labeled *operations research* or *management science*.

IMPORTANT CONTRIBUTIONS

The quantitative approach evolved out of the development of mathematical and statistical solutions to military problems during World War II. After the war was over, many of the techniques that had been used for military problems were applied to the business sector. One group of military officers, nicknamed the Whiz Kids, joined Ford Motor Company in the mid-1940s and immediately began using statistical methods and quantitative models to improve decision making. Two of these individuals whose names you might recognize are Robert McNamara (who went on to become president of Ford, U.S. Secretary of Defense, and head of the World Bank) and Charles "Tex" Thornton (who founded Litton Industries).

What exactly does the quantitative approach do? This approach to management involves applications of statistics, optimization models, information models, and computer simulations to management activities. Linear programming, for instance, is a technique that managers use to improve resource allocation decisions. Work scheduling can be more efficient as a result of critical-path scheduling analysis. Decisions on determining a company's optimum inventory levels have been significantly influenced by the economic order quantity model. Each of these is an example of quantitative techniques being applied to improve managerial decision making.

HOW DO TODAY'S MANAGERS USE THE QUANTITATIVE APPROACH?

The quantitative approach has contributed directly to management decision making in the areas of planning and control. For instance, when managers make budgeting, scheduling, quality control, and similar decisions, they typically rely on quantitative techniques. The availability of sophisticated computer software programs to aid in developing models, equations, and formulas has made the use of quantitative techniques somewhat less intimidating for managers, although they must still be able to interpret the results. We cover some of the more important quantitative techniques in Chapters 9 and 20.

The quantitative approach, although important in its own way, has not influenced management practice as much as the next one we're going to discuss—organizational behavior—for a number of reasons. These include the fact that many managers are unfamiliar with and intimidated by quantitative tools, behavioral problems are more widespread and visible, and it is easier for most students and managers to relate to real, day-to-day people problems than to the more abstract activity of constructing quantitative models.

Quantitative tools such as the economic order quantity model can help managers avoid the kind of buildup of inventory that plagued Williams-Sonoma Inc. at the end of 1999. Overstocked in anticipation of generating more Internet business than actually materialized on its new Web site during the holiday season, the company ended up announcing a drop in fourth-quarter profits that sent its stock price into a temporary slide.

---

7. **Describe Fayol's principles of management and how they compare to Taylor's.**

8. **What did Weber contribute to the general administrative theories of management?**

9. **Explain how the quantitative approach evolved and how it has contributed to the field of management.**

Testing...Testing...1,2,3

> ## TOWARD UNDERSTANDING ORGANIZATIONAL BEHAVIOR

As we know, managers get things done by working with people. This explains why some writers and researchers have chosen to look at management by focusing on the organization's human resources. The field of study concerned with the actions (behavior) of people at work is called **organizational behavior (OB)**. Much of what currently makes up the field of human resources management and contemporary views on motivation, leadership, trust, teamwork, and conflict management have come out of organizational behavior research.

organizational behavior (OB)

The field of study concerned with the actions (behavior) of people at work.

EARLY ADVOCATES

Although there were a number of people in the late 1800s and early 1900s who recognized the importance of the human factor to an organization's success, four individuals stand out as early advocates of the OB approach. They are Robert Owen, Hugo Munsterberg, Mary Parker Follett, and Chester Barnard. The contributions of these individuals were varied and distinct, yet they all had in common a belief that people were the most important asset of the organization and should be managed accordingly. Their ideas provided the foundation for such management practices as employee selection procedures, employee motivation programs, employee work teams, and organization–external environment management techniques. Exhibit 2.5 summarizes the most important ideas of these early advocates.

THE HAWTHORNE STUDIES

Hawthorne Studies

A series of studies during the 1920s and 1930s that provided new insights in individual and group behavior.

Without question, the most important contribution to the developing OB field came out of the **Hawthorne Studies**, a series of studies conducted at the Western Electric Company Works in Cicero, Illinois. These studies, started in 1924 and continued through the early 1930s, were initially designed by Western Electric industrial engineers as a scientific management experiment. They wanted to examine the effect of various illumination levels on worker productivity.

| Exhibit | 2.5 | | **Early Advocates of OB** |

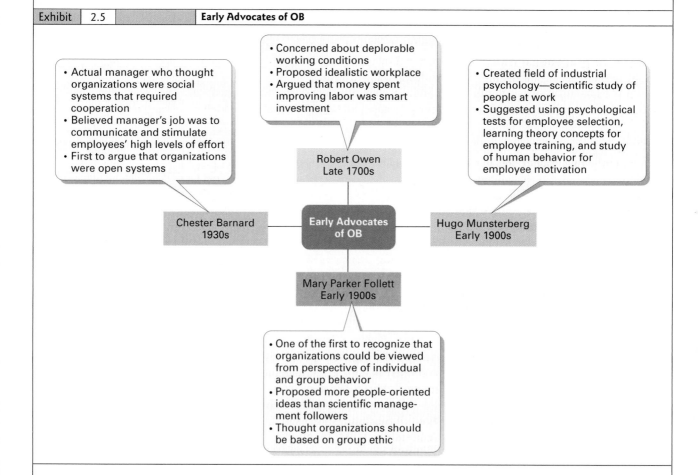

Gordon R. Wadge, Associate Director, OSA Archdiocese of New Orleans, New Orleans, Louisiana

Describe your job.

As associate director for a large nonprofit social service agency, I have diverse responsibilities ranging from fund-raising to program development and personnel oversight. In an agency with 350 employees, 1,500 volunteers, an annual budget of $9 million, and services in 40 civil parishes (counties), management demands are significant. Fund-raising and public relations responsibilities require approximately 65 percent of my time. Building community collaboratives and new program development absorb about 20 percent of my time with the remaining 15 percent devoted to personnel supervision and oversight.

What types of skills do you think tomorrow's managers will need?

To paraphrase the words of James Carville, "It's relationships, stupid!" There is no substitute for relationship skills. With stiff competition for hiring and retaining quality staff, the ability of a manager to build work teams, communicate with all levels of staff, and affirm individual staff members is fundamental to success in any organization. This reality is amplified in the nonprofit world where salaries and benefits are often less competitive than in for-profit companies. Along with relationship skills, the future will demand that managers be able to juggle multiple projects and master the effective use of technology.

What types of management issues have you had to deal with in your organization?

Building community collaboratives has been a challenging issue in our community. Increasingly in the world of nonprofits and social services, funders at all levels demand collaboration. Setting up effective management structures for community partnerships presents a unique set of challenges and at times seems to require the diplomacy of a Middle East negotiator. Trying to get multiple agencies to agree on a set project mission, goals, and then to be accountable is truly an art form.

Control and experimental groups were set up with the experimental group being exposed to various lighting intensities, and the control group working under a constant intensity. If you were one of the industrial engineers in charge of this experiment, what would you have expected to happen? That individual output in the experimental group would be directly related to the intensity of the light? Seems perfectly logical, doesn't it? However, they found that as the level of light was increased in the experimental group, output for both groups increased. Then, much to the surprise of the engineers, as the light level was decreased in the experimental group, productivity continued to increase in both groups. In fact, a productivity decrease was observed in the experimental group *only* when the level of light was reduced to that of a moonlit night. What would explain these unexpected results? The engineers couldn't explain what they had witnessed but concluded that illumination intensity was not directly related to group productivity, and that something else must have contributed to the results. However, they weren't able to pinpoint what that "something else" was.

In 1927, the Western Electric engineers asked Harvard professor Elton Mayo and his associates to join the study as consultants. Thus began a relationship that would last through 1932 and encompass numerous experiments in the redesign of jobs, changes in workday and workweek length, introduction of rest periods, and individual versus group wage plans.[9] For example, one experiment was designed to evaluate the effect of a group piecework incentive pay system on group productivity. The results indicated that the incentive plan had less effect on a worker's output than did group pressure, acceptance, and the accompanying security. The researchers concluded that social norms or group standards were the key determinants of individual work behavior.

Scholars generally agree that the Hawthorne Studies had a dramatic impact on the direction of management beliefs about the role of human behavior in organizations. Mayo concluded that behavior and sentiments are closely related, that group influences significantly affect individual behavior, that group standards establish individual worker output, and that money is less a factor in determining output than are group standards, group sentiments, and security. These conclusions led to a new emphasis on the human behavior factor in the functioning of organizations and the attainment of their goals.

However, the conclusions from the Hawthorne Studies weren't without criticism. Critics attacked the research procedures, analyses of findings, and the conclusions.[10] From a historical standpoint, however, it's of little importance whether the studies were academically sound or their conclusions justified. What *is* important is that they stimulated an interest in human behavior in organizations. The Hawthorne Studies played a significant role in changing the dominant view at the time that employees were no different from any other machines that the organization used.

Testing... Testing... 1,2,3

10. **What is organizational behavior?**

11. **What were some of the contributions of the early advocates of OB?**

12. **Describe the Hawthorne Studies and their contribution to management practice.**

HOW DO TODAY'S MANAGERS USE THE BEHAVIORAL APPROACH?

The behavioral approach has largely shaped today's contemporary organizations. From the way that managers design motivating jobs to the way that they work with employee teams to the way that they open up communication channels, we can see elements of the behavioral approach. The behavioral approach also influences decision making, organization structure design, and the types of control tools and techniques used. Much of what the early OB advocates proposed and the conclusions from the Hawthorne Studies provided the foundation for our current theories of motivation, leadership, group behavior and development, and numerous other behavioral topics. We'll address these topics fully in later chapters.

> **CURRENT TRENDS AND ISSUES**

Where are we today? What current management concepts and practices are shaping "tomorrow's history"? In this section, we'll attempt to answer those questions by introducing several trends and issues that we believe are changing the way managers do their jobs: globalization, workforce diversity, entrepreneurship, managing in an e-business world, need for innovation and flexibility, quality management, learning organizations and knowledge management, and workplace spirituality. Throughout the text we focus more closely on many of these themes in various boxes, examples, and exercises included in each chapter.

GLOBALIZATION

Management is no longer constrained by national borders. BMW, a German firm, builds cars in South Carolina. McDonald's, a U.S. firm, sells hamburgers in China. Toyota, a Japanese firm, makes cars in Kentucky. Australia's leading real estate company, Lend Lease Corporation, built the Bluewater shopping complex in Kent, England, and has contracts with Coca-Cola to build all the soft-drink maker's bottling plants in Southeast Asia. Swiss company ABB Ltd. has constructed power generating plants in Malaysia, South Korea, China, and Indonesia. The world has definitely become a global village!

Managers in organizations of all sizes and types around the world are faced with the opportunities and challenges of operating in a global market.[11] Globalization is such a significant topic that we devote one chapter to it (Chapter 4) and integrate discussion of its impact on the various management functions throughout the text. In fact, you'll see that several of our chapter-opening manager dilemmas, end-of-chapter cases, and chapter examples feature global managers and organizations.

WORKFORCE DIVERSITY

One of the major challenges facing managers in the twenty-first century will be coordinating work efforts of diverse organizational members in accomplishing organizational goals. Today's organizations are characterized by **workforce diversity**—a workforce that's more heterogeneous in terms of gender, race, ethnicity, age, and other characteristics that reflect differences. How diverse is the workforce? A report on work and workers in the twenty-first century, called *Workforce 2020*, stated that the U.S. labor force would continue its ethnic diversification, although at a fairly slow pace.[12] Throughout the early years of the twenty-first century, minorities will account for slightly more than one-half of net new entrants to the U.S. workforce. The fastest growth will be Asian and Hispanic workers. However, this report also stated that a more significant demographic force affecting workforce diversity during the next decade will be the aging of the population. This trend will significantly affect the U.S. workforce in three ways. First, these aging individuals may choose to continue full-time work, work part-time, or retire completely. Think of the implications for an organization when longtime employees with their vast wealth of knowledge, experience, and skills choose to retire, or imagine workers who refuse to retire and block opportunities for younger and higher-potential employees. Second, these aging individuals typically begin to receive public entitlements (mainly Social Security and Medicare). Having sufficient tax rates to sustain these programs has serious implications for organizations and younger workers since there will be more individuals demanding entitlements and a smaller base of workers contributing dollars to the program budgets. Finally, the aging population will become a powerful consumer force driving demand for certain types of products and services. Organizations in industries of potentially high market demand (such as entertainment, travel, and other leisure-time pursuits; specialized health care; financial planning, home repair, and other professional services; etc.) will require larger workforces to meet that demand whereas organizations in industries in which market demand faces potential declines (such as singles bars, ski resorts, etc.) may have to make adjustments in their workforces through layoffs and downsizing.

workforce diversity

A workforce that's more heterogeneous in terms of gender, race, ethnicity, age, and other characteristics that reflect differences.

Mary Furlong (bottom left) heads the company that operates ThirdAge.com, a Web portal designed for computer users 40 and up. The site gets more than 1 million visitors a month and has signed up about 10,000 people for courses in online technology. One-fourth of the company's workforce, some of whose members are shown here, are both technically savvy and over 50.

Workforce diversity is an issue facing managers of organizations in Japan, Australia, Germany, Italy, and other countries. For instance, as the level of immigration increases in Italy, the number of women entering the workforce rises in Japan, and the population ages in Germany, managers are finding they need to effectively manage diversity.

Does the fact that workforce diversity is a current issue facing managers mean that organizations weren't diverse before? No. They were, but diverse individuals made up a small percentage of the workforce, and organizations, for the most part, ignored the issue. Prior to the early 1980s, people took a "melting pot" approach to differences in organizations. We assumed that people who were "different" would somehow automatically want to assimilate. But we now recognize that employees don't set aside their cultural values and lifestyle preferences when they come to work. The challenge for managers, therefore, is to make their organizations more accommodating to diverse groups of people by addressing different lifestyles, family needs, and work styles. The melting pot assumption has been replaced by the recognition and celebration of differences.[13] Smart managers recognize that diversity can be an asset because it brings a broad range of viewpoints and problem-solving skills to a company. An organization that uses *all* of its human resources will enjoy a powerful competitive advantage. Many companies such as Levi Strauss, Advantica, Dole Food, Avis Rent A Car, SBC Communications, Avon Products, and Xerox have strong diversity management programs.[14] We'll highlight many diversity-related issues and how companies are responding to those issues throughout this text in our "Managing Workforce Diversity" boxes.

ENTREPRENEURSHIP

Practically everywhere you turn these days you'll read or hear about entrepreneurs. If you pick up a current newspaper or general news magazine or log on to one of the Internet's news sites, chances are you'll find at least one story (and probably many more) about an entrepreneur or an entrepreneurial business. Entrepreneurship is a popular topic! But what exactly *is* it?

entrepreneurship

The process whereby an individual or a group of individuals uses organized efforts and means to pursue opportunities to create value and grow by fulfilling wants and needs through innovation and uniqueness, no matter what resources are currently controlled.

Entrepreneurship is the process whereby an individual or a group of individuals uses organized efforts and means to pursue opportunities to create value and grow by fulfilling wants and needs through innovation and uniqueness, no matter what resources are currently controlled. It involves the discovery of opportunities and the resources to exploit them. Three important themes stick out in this definition of entrepreneurship. First is the pursuit of opportunities. Entrepreneurship is about pursuing environmental trends and changes that no one else has seen or paid attention to. For example, Jeff Bezos, founder of Amazon.com, was a successful programmer at an investment firm on Wall Street in the mid-1990s. However, statistics on the explosive growth in the use of the Internet and World Wide Web (at that time, it was growing about 2,300 percent a month) kept nagging at him. He decided to quit his job and pursue what he felt were going to be enormous retailing opportunities on the Internet. And the rest, as they say, is history. Today, Amazon sells books, music, home improvement products, cameras, cars, furniture, jewelry, and numerous other items from its popular Web site.

The second important theme in entrepreneurship is innovation. Entrepreneurship involves changing, revolutionizing, transforming, and introducing new approaches—that is, new products or services or new ways of doing business.

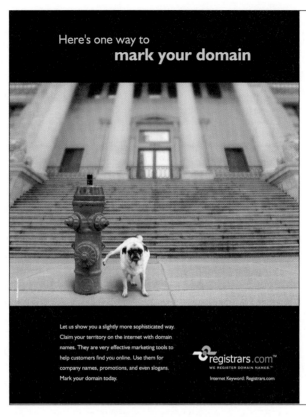

Here's one way to
mark your domain

Let us show you a slightly more sophisticated way. Claim your territory on the internet with domain names. They are very effective marketing tools to help customers find you online. Use them for company names, promotions, and even slogans. Mark your domain today.

registrars.com™
WE REGISTER DOMAIN NAMES.™

Internet Keyword: Registrars.com

The spirit of innovation that motivates an entrepreneur to start a new venture often permeates every aspect of the young firm, from its products or services to its corporate culture and even its advertising.

Dineh Mohajer is a prime example of this facet of entrepreneurship. As a fashion-conscious young woman, she hated the brilliant and bright nail polishes that were for sale in stores. The bright colors clashed with her trendy pastel-colored clothing. She wanted pastel nail colors that would match what she was wearing. When she couldn't find the nail polish colors she was looking for, Mohajer decided to mix her own. When her friends raved over her homemade colors, she decided to take samples of her nail polish to exclusive stores in Los Angeles. They were an instant hit! Today, her company, Hard Candy, sells a whole line of cosmetics in trendy and fashionable stores across the United States—all the result of Mohajer's innovative ideas.

The final important theme in entrepreneurship is growth. Entrepreneurs pursue growth. They are not content to stay small or to stay the same in size. Entrepreneurs want their businesses to grow and work very hard to pursue growth as they continually look for trends and continue to innovate new products and new approaches.

Entrepreneurship will continue to be important to societies around the world.[15] For-profit and even not-for-profit organizations will need to be entrepreneurial—that is, pursuing opportunities, innovations, and growth—if they want to be successful. We think that an understanding of entrepreneurship is so important that at the end of each major section in this book we've included a special entrepreneurship module that looks at the topics presented in that section from the perspective of entrepreneurship. ◄

Testing...Testing...1,2,3

13. **How is globalization affecting the way managers do their jobs?**

14. **What is workforce diversity, and what implications does it have for managers?**

15. **Discuss the three important themes in the definition of entrepreneurship.**

MANAGING IN AN E-BUSINESS WORLD

What a difference three years makes! The last time we revised this book, the Internet and World Wide Web were still a novelty to most managers and organizations. E-mail as a form of communication was gaining in popularity, and occasionally you saw Web addresses in company advertisements. Those days are long gone! Now, everywhere you look, organizations (small to large, all types, global and domestic, and in all industries) are becoming e-businesses. Today's managers must manage in an e-business world! In fact, as a student, your learning may increasingly be taking place in an electronic environment. What do we know about this e-business world?

E-business (electronic business) is a comprehensive term describing the way an organization does its work by using electronic (Internet-based) linkages with its key constituencies (employees, managers, customers, suppliers, and partners) in order to efficiently and effectively achieve its goals. It's more than e-commerce, although e-business can include e-commerce. **E-commerce (electronic commerce)** is any form of business exchange or transaction in which the parties interact electronically.[16] Firms such as Dell (computers), Varsitybooks (textbooks), and PC Flowers and Gifts (flowers and other gifts) are engaged in e-commerce because they sell products over the Internet. Exhibit 2.6 explains the main forms of e-commerce transactions. Although e-commerce applications will continue to grow in volume, they are only one part of an e-business.

Not every organization is or needs to be a total e-business. Exhibit 2.7 illustrates three categories of e-business involvement.[17] The first type is what we're going to call an e-business *enhanced* organization, a traditional organization that sets up e-business capabilities, usually e-commerce, while maintaining its traditional structure. Many *Fortune 500* type organizations are evolving into e-businesses using this approach. They use the Internet to *enhance* (not to replace) their traditional ways of doing business. For instance, Sears, a traditional bricks-and-mortar retailer with thousands of physical stores worldwide started an Internet division whose goal is to make Sears "the definitive online source for the home."[18] Although Sears Internet division, Sears.com, represents a radical departure for an organization founded in 1886 as a catalog-sales company, it's intended to expand, not replace, the company's main source of revenue. Many other traditional organizations—for

---

e-business (electronic business)

A comprehensive term describing the way an organization does its work by using electronic (Internet-based) linkages with its key constituencies in order to efficiently and effectively achieve its goals.

e-commerce (electronic commerce)

Any form of business exchange or transaction in which the parties interact electronically.

Exhibit	2.6

Types of E-Commerce Transactions

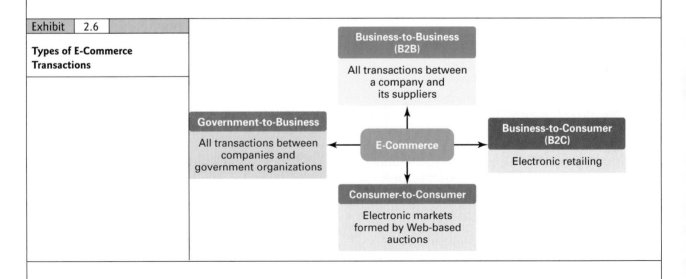

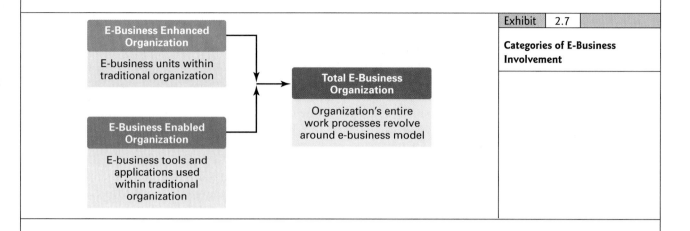

Exhibit | 2.7

Categories of E-Business Involvement

instance, Merrill Lynch, Office Depot, Starbucks, Tupperware, and Whirlpool—have become e-business enhanced organizations.

Another category of e-business involvement is an e-business *enabled* organization. In this type of e-business, an organization uses the Internet to perform its traditional business functions better but not to sell anything. In other words, the Internet *enables* organizational members to do their work more efficiently and effectively. There are numerous organizations using electronic linkages to communicate with employees, customers, or suppliers and to support them with information. For instance, Levi Strauss & Co. uses its Web site to interact with customers, providing them the latest information about the company and its products, but they can't buy Levis there. It also uses an **intranet**, an internal organizational communication system that uses Internet technology and is accessible only by organizational employees, to communicate with its global workforce. Other organizations are using enterprise-wide software solutions that link together all organizational areas and levels. For example, employees at Silicon Graphics can access over 800 specialized internal Web sites containing more than 144,000 pages of technical information and can access all corporate databases. Information that used to take days to get can now be obtained in a matter of a few minutes simply by linking, pointing, and clicking. These organizations have found that being an e-business enabled organization makes them more competitive.

The last category of e-business involvement is when an organization becomes a total e-business. Many organizations—such as Amazon.com, Yahoo, E*Trade, and eBay—started as total e-business organizations. Their whole existence is made possible by and revolves around the Internet. Other organizations, such as Charles Schwab & Company, have evolved into e-business organizations that seamlessly integrate traditional and e-business functions. When an organization becomes a total e-business, there's a complete transformation in the way it does its work. For instance, at Schwab when managers made the decision to merge its traditional and e-business operations, it had to reprice its core products, retrain all of its employees, and renovate all of its systems.[19] Was it worth it? Analysts describe Schwab as the best positioned of all retail brokerages in an e-business world.

Managing in an e-world, whether as an e-business enhanced, e-business enabled, or total e-business organization requires new insights and perspectives. To help you acquire these, we've included "Managing in an E-Business World" boxes in a number of chapters.

intranet

An internal organizational communication system that uses Internet technology and is accessible only by organizational employees.

16. **How is e-commerce different from e-business, and what are the main forms of e-commerce transactions?**

17. **Describe the three categories of e-business involvement.**

18. **Why should managers be concerned about innovation and flexibility?**

total quality management (TQM)

A philosophy of management that is driven by customer needs and expectations and focuses on continual improvement in work processes.

NEED FOR INNOVATION AND FLEXIBILITY

Innovation has been called the most precious capability that any organization in today's economy must have and nurture. Without a constant flow of new ideas—not only for new products and services, but also for new ways of doing things—an organization is doomed to obsolescence or even worse, failure.[20] In a survey about what makes an organization valuable, innovation showed up at the top of the list.[21] Which companies were cited as the most innovative in this study? Intel, Procter & Gamble, and AOL came out on top. There is absolutely no doubt that innovation is crucial. How do managers encourage innovative thinking among all organizational members? That's an important question and one that all managers at all levels must resolve. We'll cover the topic of managing innovation in Chapter 13.

Another demand facing today's organizations and managers is the need for flexibility. In a context in which customers' needs may change overnight, in which new competitors come and go at breathtaking speed, and in which employees and their skills are shifted as needed from project to project, you can see how flexibility might be valuable. As we discuss organizational strategy, organizational design, and job design (Chapters 8, 10, and 16), we'll examine the role of flexibility.

QUALITY MANAGEMENT

A quality revolution swept through both the business and public sectors during the 1980s and 1990s.[22] The generic term used to describe this revolution was **total quality management**, or **TQM** for short. It was inspired by a small group of quality experts, the most famous being W. Edwards Deming and Joseph M. Juran. The ideas and techniques espoused by these two men in the 1950s had few supporters in the United States but were enthusiastically embraced by Japanese organizations. As Japanese manufacturers began beating out U.S. competitors in quality comparisons, Western managers soon began taking a more serious look at TQM. Deming's and Juran's ideas became the basis for today's organizational quality management programs.

TQM is a philosophy of management driven by continual improvement and responding to customer needs and expectations. (See Exhibit 2.8.) The term *customer* in TQM has expanded beyond the original definition of the purchaser out-

---

Exhibit 2.8	
What Is TQM?	

1. Intense focus on the *customer*. The customer includes not only outsiders who buy the organization's products or services but also internal customers (such as shipping or accounts payable personnel) who interact with and serve others in the organization.
2. Concern for *continual improvement*. TQM is a commitment to never being satisfied. "Very good" is not good enough. Quality can always be improved.
3. *Process-focused*. TQM focuses on work processes as the quality of goods and services is continually improved.
4. Improvement in the *quality of everything* the organization does. TQM uses a very broad definition of quality. It relates not only to the final product but also to how the organization handles deliveries, how rapidly it responds to complaints, how politely the phones are answered, and the like.
5. *Accurate measurement*. TQM uses statistical techniques to measure every critical variable in the organization's operations. These are compared against standards or benchmarks to identify problems, trace them to their roots, and eliminate their causes.
6. *Empowerment of employees*. TQM involves the people on the line in the improvement process. Teams are widely used in TQM programs as empowerment vehicles for finding and solving problems.

side the organization to include anyone who interacts with the organization's product or services internally or externally. It encompasses employees and suppliers as well as the people who purchase the organization's goods or services. The objective is to create an organization committed to continuous improvement in work processes.

TQM is a departure from earlier management theories that were based on the belief that low costs were the only road to increased productivity. For example, the U.S. car industry is often used as a classic example of what can go wrong when managers focus solely on trying to keep costs down. In the late 1970s, GM, Ford, and Chrysler built products that many consumers rejected. Your second author remembers vividly purchasing a new Pontiac Grand Prix in 1978, driving it off the lot, pulling up to a gas pump, filling the gas tank and watching gas pour out on the ground because of a hole in the car's gas tank! When the costs of rejects, repairing shoddy work, product recalls, and expensive controls to identify quality problems were considered, U.S. manufacturers actually were *less* productive than many foreign competitors. The Japanese demonstrated that it *was* possible for the highest-quality manufacturers to be among the lowest-cost producers. American manufacturers in the car and other industries soon realized the importance of TQM and implemented many of its basic components.

Quality management is important, and we'll discuss it throughout this book. For example, we'll show how it can contribute to a competitive advantage in Chapter 8, is used for benchmarking competition in Chapter 9, and plays a role in value chain management in Chapter 19.

"Being the best in manufacturing means eliminating waste and knocking out unnecessary costs," says Ko Nishimura, CEO of Solectron Corp., the world's largest and fastest-growing contract manufacturer. "You have to find that gray zone between too much and not enough. If you go too far, you're gaudy and wasteful. If you don't go far enough, you're shoddy and inelegant."

LEARNING ORGANIZATIONS AND KNOWLEDGE MANAGEMENT

Today's managers confront an environment in which change takes place at an unprecedented rate. Constant innovations in information and computer technologies combined with the globalization of markets have created a chaotic world. As a result, many of the past management guidelines and principles—created for a world that was more stable and predictable—no longer apply. Successful organizations of the twenty-first century must be able to learn and respond quickly. These organizations will be led by managers who can effectively challenge conventional wisdom, manage the organization's knowledge base, and make needed changes. In other words, these organizations will need to be learning organizations. A **learning organization** is one that has developed the capacity to continuously learn, adapt, and change. Exhibit 2.9 clarifies how a learning organization is different from a traditional organization.

Part of a manager's responsibility in fostering an environment conducive to learning is to create learning capabilities throughout the organization—from lowest level to highest level and in all areas. How can managers do this? An important step is understanding the value of knowledge as an important resource, just like cash, raw materials, or office equipment. To illustrate the value of knowledge, think about how you register for college classes. Do you talk to others who have had a certain professor? Do you listen to their experiences with this individual and make your decision based on what they have to say (their knowledge about the situation)? If you do, you're tapping into the value

learning organization

An organization that has developed the capacity to continuously learn, adapt, and change.

Exhibit 2.9		Traditional Organization	Learning Organization
Learning Organization versus Traditional Organization	Attitude toward change	If it's working, don't change it.	If you aren't changing, it won't be working for long.
	Attitude toward new ideas	If it wasn't invented here, reject it.	If it was invented or reinvented here, reject it.
	Who's responsible for innovation?	Traditional areas such as R & D	Everyone in organization
	Main fear	Making mistakes	Not learning; not adapting
	Competitive advantage	Products and service	Ability to learn, knowledge and expertise
	Manager's job	Control others	Enable others

knowledge management

Cultivating a learning culture in which organizational members systematically gather knowledge and share it with others in the organization to achieve better performance.

of knowledge. But in an organization, just recognizing the value of accumulated knowledge or wisdom isn't enough. Managers must deliberately manage that base of knowledge. **Knowledge management** involves cultivating a learning culture in which organizational members systematically gather knowledge and share it with others in the organization so as to achieve better performance.[23] For instance, accountants and consultants at Ernst & Young, one of the Big Five professional services firms, document best practices they have developed, unusual problems they have dealt with, and other work information. This "knowledge" is then shared with all employees through computer-based applications and through COIN (community of interest) teams that meet regularly throughout the company. Many other organizations—General Electric, Toyota, Hewlett-Packard, Buckman Laboratories—have recognized the importance of knowledge management to being a learning organization.

Organizations that are continually learning are faced with changing and improving the way work is done. Managers play an important role in planning, organizing, and leading change efforts, and managers themselves are having to change their styles. They're transforming themselves from bosses to team leaders. Instead of telling people what to do and how to do it, managers are finding that they are more effective when they listen, motivate, coach, and nurture.

? THINKING CRITICALLY ABOUT ETHICS

Information is power—those who have information have power. Because information gives people power, it's human nature to want to keep that information and not share it. Knowledge hoarding is a business habit that's hard to break. In fact, it's an attitude that still characterizes many business organizations. In a learning organization, however, we're asking people to share information.

Getting people to share information may turn out to be one of the key challenges facing managers. Is it ethical to ask people to share information that they've worked hard to learn? What if performance evaluations are based on how well individuals do their jobs, and how well they do their jobs depends on the special knowledge that they have? Is it ethical to ask them to share that information? What ethical implications are inherent in creating an organizational environment that promotes learning and knowledge sharing?

WORKPLACE SPIRITUALITY

At first, the words *workplace* and *spirituality* might seem incongruous. After all, how can an organizational system that's based on rationality, logic, and "rules" of management (think of Weber, Fayol, Barnard, and other management theorists we've introduced in this chapter) ever be consistent with spirituality? Yet, we're seeing a growing interest in spirituality at work by employees at all levels and in all areas of organizations.[24] Companies such as Taco Bell, Pizza Hut, and subsidiaries of Wal-Mart have hired chaplains from all religious backgrounds to counsel employees on life issues and challenges. The chairman of Aetna International (the insurance company) has shared with employees the benefits of meditation and talked with them about using spirituality in their careers. This search for spirituality in the workplace is impacting organizations and the job of managers.

What is **workplace spirituality**? It's *not* about organized religious practices. Rather, it's "a recognition of an inner life that nourishes and is nourished by meaningful work that takes place in the context of community."[25] Employees are looking for meaning, purpose, and a sense of connectedness or community from their work and their workplace. Why? Where is this trend coming from?

In part, what we see happening is just a reflection of broader trends in society. People are searching for a deeper understanding of who they are and why they're here on Earth. They want more from their lives than just a steady job and a paycheck. They want to feel that there is some meaning in their lives and that they're part of something greater than just themselves. Since those feelings of meaning, connectedness, and fulfillment aren't coming from family or community structures anymore as people are more mobile and working longer hours, they're looking to the workplace—where they spend a significant portion of their waking hours—to provide these. Another contributing factor to the increase in workplace spirituality appears to be the change and uncertainty so descriptive of the environment facing today's organizations. Uncertainty makes people anxious. Practicing spirituality—in whatever ways they're comfortable with—provides employees with a sense of calm, belonging, connection, fulfillment, and meaning.

What are the implications for managers? Is workplace spirituality just another management fad? These are difficult questions to answer. However, research studies looking at the connection between workplace spirituality and productivity have shown some interesting results, which might tend to make you believe that issues of workplace spirituality won't be fleeting. One study showed that when companies implemented programs that used spiritual techniques for their employees, productivity improved and turnover was significantly reduced. Another study found that employees who worked for organizations they considered to be spiritual were less fearful, less likely to compromise their values, and more able to commit to their jobs.[26]

As a current issue affecting managers, workplace spirituality is likely to be manifested in how managers treat employees and how employees' contributions are respected and valued. It may be seen in the degree of trust that exists in all organizational dealings (both internal and external) and how organizational partners are treated. It can also be seen in how ethical and responsible managers are as they make decisions and take actions. ◄──

More employees and managers feel free to be open about their spirituality these days. Jeffrey Swartz, CEO of Timberland, says he often consults his rabbi about some of the tougher business decisions he must make. "He gives me perspective on how to make choices," says Swartz.

workplace spirituality

A recognition of an inner life that nourishes and is nourished by meaningful work that takes place in the context of community.

Testing...Testing...1,2,3

19. **What is TQM, and how is it affecting managers' jobs?**

20. **How does knowledge management fit into the concept of a learning organization?**

21. **What is workplace spirituality, and how is it an issue that managers must deal with?**

Managers Respond to "A Manager's Dilemma"

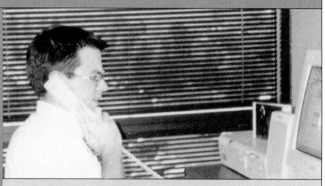

Marilyn Farrar-Wagner

Hospital Manager, Ridgewood Veterinary Hospital, Ridgewood, New Jersey

Adam Ferguson

Data Resource Coordinator, Cox Health Systems, Springfield, Missouri

To maintain innovation in any company, a manager must identify the client's needs, follow trends, and successfully predict what those needs will be in the future. I would suggest using a simple questionnaire (two or three questions) that clients be required to complete to place an order online. The responses could help accurately target clients' current and future needs. We did this when expanding our veterinary business. We asked clients what they would like to see. By investing in what we know our customers want, we've succeeded in surpassing their expectations.

It's also important for Tomoyama to be flexible in what the Web site offers. However, he also needs to maintain credibility while being flexible. With numerous online companies offering countless products and services, success will be achieved faster with reputation and quality. Toyota's credibility doesn't lie in dishwashers, for example. If Toyota wishes to diversify and maintain the quality expected, some research and development must be used to determine what other types of online services users might want.

With any e-application, it's of the utmost importance to be able to first maintain what you already have. As a site's traffic increases, there is the necessity to keep new information posted—not to mention the hardware and software requirements for larger volume. You don't want your site to lose speed or have people not be able to even get on your site due to traffic. If you have established yourself as a leader in a particular area, the loss of quality is much more visible than an increase in it.

The second thing I would do is surround myself with many intelligent and young people. I believe I remember hearing Gene Kranz (former flight director of NASA in the 1960s and 1970s) say that the average age of Mission Control employees for the Apollo 13 mission was around 25. I believe that smart application of young innovation is what dictates who goes and who stays in the e-world.

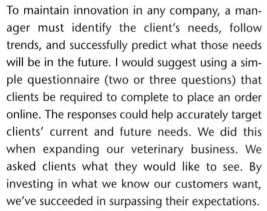

Chapter Summary

This summary is organized by the chapter-opening objectives found on p. 26.

1. Management is connected to other fields of study including anthropology (helps managers understand differences in fundamental values, attitudes, and behavior between people), economics (helps managers understand comparative advantage, free trade, and protectionist policy in a global marketplace), philosophy (helps managers understand why organizations exist and what constitutes appropriate behavior in organizations), political science (helps managers understand conflict, power, and government influence), psychology (helps managers understand behavior of humans), and sociology (helps managers understand people in relation to others).

2. Studying management history helps you to understand theory and practice as they are today. It also helps you to see how current management concepts have evolved over time. Current management concepts are the result of continual development, testing, modification, retesting, and so on.

3. Some important pre-twentieth-century contributions to management include the building of the Egyptian pyramids, management practices in Venice, Adam Smith's writings on division of labor, and the Industrial Revolution.

4. Scientific management made dramatic increases in productivity possible. The application of scientific principles moved management from being "seat of the pants" to a serious, scientific discipline. Frederick W. Taylor proposed four principles of management. Frank and Lillian Gilbreth were best known for their study of work arrangements to eliminate wasteful hand-and-body motions and their design of proper tools and equipment for optimizing work performance.

5. Henri Fayol was the first to define management as a universal set of functions. He argued that management is an activity common to all human undertakings, and he identified 14 principles of management that could be taught. Max Weber defined the bureaucracy as the ideal form of organization.

6. The quantitative approach to management advocated the use of statistical models, equations, formulas, and simulations for management decision making in planning and controlling.

7. Robert Owen proposed an idealistic workplace and argued that money spent on improving labor was a smart investment. Hugo Munsterberg created the field of industrial psychology. He suggested using psychological tests for employee selection, learning theory concepts for employee training, and the study of human behavior for employee motivation. Mary Parker Follett was one of the first to recognize that organizations could be viewed from the perspective of individual and group behavior. She proposed more people-oriented ideas and thought that organizations should be based on a group ethic. Finally, Chester Barnard thought that organizations were social systems that required cooperation. He believed the manager's job was to communicate and stimulate employees to high levels of effort.

8. The Hawthorne Studies led to a new emphasis on the human factor in the functioning of organizations and provided new insights into group norms and behavior.

9. Globalization affects all sizes and types of organizations. Workforce diversity requires managers to recognize and acknowledge employee differences. Entrepreneurship is important to societies around the world and all types and sizes of organizations will need to be entrepreneurial to be successful. Managers need to recognize the realities of an e-world, whether as an e-business enhanced, e-business enabled, or total e-business organization. Successful organizations will need to be innovative and flexible, and managers will need to encourage innovation and flexibility. Managers who emphasize quality management processes are committed to continuous improvement of work activities. Managers will need to foster the development of learning organizations and cultivate a knowledge management culture. Finally, managers will have to recognize the impact that workplace spirituality is having on management practices.

Thinking About Management Issues

1. What kind of workplace would Henri Fayol create? How about Mary Parker Follett? How about Frederick W. Taylor?

2. Can a mathematical (quantitative) technique help a manager solve a "people" problem such as how to motivate employees or how to distribute work equitably? Explain.

3. In an e-business world, is globalization an issue? Explain.

4. "Entrepreneurship is only for small, start-up businesses." Do you agree or disagree with this statement? Explain.

5. Would you feel more comfortable in a learning organization or in a traditional organization? Explain your choice.

Log On: Internet-Based Exercise

It's 10:49 P.M. and you're just sitting down at your computer to finish tomorrow's assignment for your management course, which is "Using the Internet, find five interesting facts about each of the following individuals and events that were instrumental in the development of management theories—Frederick W. Taylor, the Gilbreths, and the Hawthorne studies. Type up your facts about these early contributors to management in a bulleted list and be sure to note the URLs of the Web sites that you used."

After about 45 minutes of uninterrupted Web surfing, you finish up your assignment. Or so you think! Upon closer inspection of the assignment that your professor e-mailed you after class, you notice that it also includes the following: "Find and briefly describe three Web sites for each of the following current management issues: workforce diversity, innovation, learning organizations or knowledge management, and workplace spirituality. Be sure to note the URLs of the Web sites that you find." You jump back on the Web and finish this part of the assignment.

myPHLIP Companion Web Site

myPHLIP **(www.prenhall.com/myphlip)** *is a fully customizable homepage that ties students and faculty to text-specific resources.*
- *For students*, myPHLIP *provides an online study guide tied chapter-by-chapter to the text—current events and Internet exercises, lecture notes, downloadable software, the Career Center, the Writing Center, Ask the Tutor, and more.*
- *For faculty*, myPHLIP *provides a syllabus tool that allows you to manage content, communicate with students, and upload personal resources.*

Working Together: Team-Based Exercise

Building a base of knowledge that others in an organization can tap into and use to help do their jobs better is a bottom-line goal of knowledge management. Form groups of three to four class members. Your task is to do some preliminary work on creating a knowledge base for your college. Think about what organizational members could learn from each other in this organization. What common tasks might they perform that they could learn from each other about how best to do those tasks? What unique tasks do they perform that others might learn something from? After discussing these issues, come up with an outline of major areas of important knowledge for this organization. (Here are a couple of hints that might help you get started—using technology in classrooms, keeping in touch with former students and alumni.) As a group, be prepared to share your outline with the class and to explain your choices.

Case Application

Image Is Everything

Snapshots. You probably have photo albums filled with them. They capture historical moments and provide visual links to the past—to that brief moment in time when the photo was snapped. Photographs play an important role in telling stories, whether that story is personal or whether it's part of a report for your boss or used to help explain and illustrate a news story that you're reading. With a database of over 70 million photographs and an estimated 30,000 hours of film, Seattle-based Getty Images, Inc. (www.gettyimages.com), a stock photo company, has one

foot firmly planted in the past and another firmly planted in the future. Mark Getty, cofounder and executive chairman of Getty Images, is carefully transforming his company by embracing the new rules of Web-based business and culture. It's not been an easy transition.

When you read a book (such as this one) or a magazine, where do the photos and other visual images come from? Unless they're custom-shot photos, they're probably from stock photo businesses—companies that purchase photos from numerous professional photographers around the world, organize those photos into categories, and sell the photos to customers (creative and design

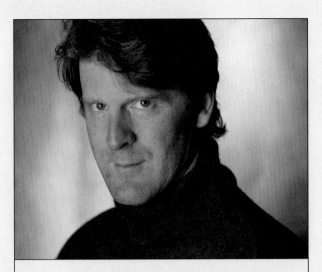

Mark Getty, cofounder and executive chairman of Getty Images.

professionals, other businesses, and consumers). In the "old" economy, it often took days, even weeks for customers to get a photo. They'd have to look through pages and pages of expensively produced color catalogs, trying to find that perfect image for the project on which they were working. If they couldn't find it, they might have to pay a research assistant at an image company to search through many thousands of photos to help find just what they were looking for. After numerous phone calls and selecting that perfect image, a package would show up at the customer's door with the chosen image. It would be on a square of film that would have to be digitized and eventually returned to the stock agency. And if you were working late at night or rushing to meet a project deadline, you were out of luck! Mark Getty perceived that there were opportunities in making this whole inefficient and cumbersome process better through the power of the Internet. He's transforming the old ways and in the process creating a company poised to profit in an e-business world.

Getty Image's integrated Web site can be accessed anytime, anywhere by customers. Using a key-word search, customers can receive a series of relevant images. Customers can immediately take a rough image for free and see what it looks like in a page layout. Buying a final image is very simple—enter a credit card number and download the image. But getting the process to this point hasn't been as simple!

Getty Images is a blend of acquired businesses, most of which were competitors. It began with two big acquisitions: London-based Tony Stone Images and Seattle-based PhotoDisc. These two companies couldn't have been more different. Tony Stone, a traditional stock photo company, was known for its superior artistic quality. PhotoDisc was a start-up that pioneered the delivery of images on

CDs at discount stores and other types of retailers. Old meets new! As difficult and often unpleasant as the merger between the two companies was, eventually company executives realized that they had the opportunity to create something new, unique, and potentially valuable by combining the best of both companies. The process of integrating new businesses has become easier as Getty Images has grown through other acquisitions.

One of the company's innovative approaches is an idea bank committee, a group of 10 people that meets once a month. Their job is to direct ideas from the company's more than 2,600 employees to the person best equipped to decide whether the idea is feasible and how to do it. The group has no formal leader, and it processes between 40 and 80 ideas per month. Some ideas are small; others have had enormous impact on the company. For instance, based on multiple requests, the group lobbied to allow customers to create customized packages of CDs by choosing their own mix of images. This customization option now accounts for over 40 percent of sales revenue. Then there's the backroom operation of Getty Images where two shifts of technicians digitally scan an average of 750 photos every 12 hours. These teams work to add value to the basic photos. For instance, they tag the photo with digital information that customers can use to control their computer settings to get more accurate color. Or the team might create special options in some photo files by, for instance, changing the background.

Through extensive training, radical restructuring, and investments in technology, Getty Images is positioned as a leader and innovator in the visual content market. However, success today doesn't guarantee success tomorrow, especially in a Web-based economy. Mark and other managers at Getty know that they'll have to stay focused on providing customers with the ultimate in imagery. Yes, to them, image is everything!

QUESTIONS

1. Being a Web-based business, would principles of scientific management ever be useful to Getty Images? Explain. Would the quantitative approach be useful? Explain.

2. Does Getty Images fit the description of a learning organization? Why or why not?

3. What type of e-business would you call Getty Images? Explain your choice.

4. What characteristics and management practices does this company exhibit that might be important for successful organizations in the twenty-first century?

Sources: Information from company Web site (www.gettyimages.com) and Hoover's Online (www.hoovers.com), July 17, 2000; C. Dahle, "Image Isn't Everything," *Fast Company*, June 2000, pp. 346–357.

Learning Objectives

After reading and studying this chapter, you should be able to:

1. Differentiate the symbolic from the omnipotent view of management.

2. Define organizational culture.

3. Identify the seven dimensions that make up an organization's culture.

4. Explain how cultures can be strong or weak.

5. Describe the various ways that employees learn culture.

6. Explain how culture constrains managers.

7. Describe the various components in an organization's specific and general environments.

8. Contrast certain and uncertain environments.

9. Identify the various stakeholders with whom managers may have to deal.

10. Clarify how managers manage relationships with external stakeholders.

A MANAGER'S DILEMMA

One of the most beautiful cities in North America has to be Vancouver, British Columbia. The city is surrounded by jagged mountain peaks, sandy beaches, and sparkling English Bay. Vancouver's multiethnic population of over 543,000 people resides in 23 distinct communities. Catherine Deslauriers, the city of Vancouver's staff and organizational development coordinator, is focused on training the city's managers to be more accountable for the quality of city services and ultimately to increase citizen satisfaction.[1] Deslauriers's job is made more challenging by the fact that the city's "product" is always on public display.

Deslauriers accepted this job in January 2000. Part of her job duties involves designing and delivering training programs for city employees. Prior to her arrival, the city's various training programs had consisted of ongoing classes in a number of areas including leadership and change management. Even though individual training sessions received positive participant feedback, they had not been well planned and integrated across all business units. As Deslauriers soon discovered, each business unit in the city had its own culture. She explained, "How fire and rescue workers think and operate is quite different from those in engineering and public works." However, employee training is only part of what Deslauriers does.

CHAPTER THREE

Organizational Culture and Environment: The Constraints

3

One of her other major job responsibilities as outlined by Vancouver's City Council includes improving public involvement in city decisions and actions. Although it may sound like the residents of Vancouver aren't actively involved in city issues, that's not the case. Over a period of three years in the 1990s, more than 20,000 residents participated in developing a vision for the city's future. Vancouver's citizens care about the quality of services provided by the city. How can Deslauriers use what she knows about stakeholder relationship management to help her effectively and efficiently fulfill this mandate by City Council to improve public involvement? Put yourself in her position.

WHAT WOULD YOU DO?

atherine Deslauriers recognizes the roles that both internal organizational culture and external environment play in making her organization—the city of Vancouver—successful. She also recognizes the challenges facing the organization in trying to manage both its internal culture and external environment. But how much actual impact does a manager such as Deslauriers have on an organization's success or failure? In the following section, we explore this important question.

> ## THE MANAGER: OMNIPOTENT OR SYMBOLIC?

omnipotent view of management

The view that managers are directly responsible for an organization's success or failure.

symbolic view of management

The view that managers have only a limited effect on substantive organizational outcomes because of the large number of factors outside their control.

The dominant view in management theory and society in general is that managers are directly responsible for an organization's success or failure. We'll call this perspective the **omnipotent view of management**. In contrast, some observers have argued that much of an organization's success or failure is due to forces outside management's control. In other words, external forces, not management, determine outcomes. This perspective has been labeled the **symbolic view of management**. Let's look more closely at each of these perspectives so we can try to clarify just how much credit or blame managers should receive for their organization's performance.

THE OMNIPOTENT VIEW

In Chapter 1, we discussed the importance of managers and management to organizations. This view reflects a dominant assumption in management theory: The quality of an organization's managers determines the quality of the organization itself. It's assumed that differences in an organization's effectiveness or efficiency are due to the decisions and actions of its managers. Good managers anticipate change, exploit opportunities, correct poor performance, and lead their organizations toward their objectives, which even may be changed if necessary. When profits are up, management takes the credit and rewards itself with bonuses, stock options, and the like. When profits are down, the board of directors often replaces top management in the belief that "new blood" will bring improved results. For instance, it only took nine months for the board of directors at Lands' End, the catalog retailer, to replace its top manager when its operating income declined and holiday sales fell far short of expectations.

The view of managers as omnipotent is consistent with the stereotypical picture of the take-charge business executive who can overcome any obstacle in carrying out the organization's objectives. This omnipotent view, of course, isn't limited to business organizations. We can also use it to help explain the high turnover among college and professional sports coaches, who can be considered the "managers" of their teams. Coaches who lose more games than they win are seen as ineffective. They are fired and replaced by new coaches who, it is hoped, will correct the inadequate performance.

In the omnipotent view, when organizations perform poorly, someone has to be held accountable regardless of the reasons why, and in our society, that "someone" is the manager. Of course, when things go well, we need someone to praise. So managers also get the credit—even if they had little to do with achieving positive outcomes.

THE SYMBOLIC VIEW

Winn-Dixie Stores operates 1,188 grocery stores across a 14-state southern region. When the company decided to close 10 percent of its stores and cut 11,000 jobs in April 2000, competitors such as Kroger found its business volume and revenues increasing. Was the increase in sales for Kroger the result of managers' decisions and actions, or was it beyond the control of the organizations' managers? The symbolic view would suggest that the positive performance wasn't due to anything that the managers did but instead was due to forces beyond their control.

The symbolic view says that a manager's ability to affect outcomes is influenced and constrained by external factors.[2] In this view, it's unreasonable to expect managers to significantly affect an organization's performance. Instead, an organization's results are influenced by factors outside the control of management. These factors include the economy, market (customer) changes, governmental policies, competitors' actions, conditions in the particular industry, control over proprietary technology, and decisions made by previous managers.

According to the symbolic view, managers have a limited effect on organizational outcomes.[3] A manager's roles are seen as creating meaning out of randomness, confusion, and ambiguity or trying to innovate and adapt. Managers symbolize control and influence by developing plans, making decisions, and engaging in other managerial activities. They do so for the benefit of stockholders, customers, employees, and the public. However, according to this view, the actual part that managers play in organizational success or failure is minimal.

ABC's managers were quite surprised at the sensational, almost overnight, success of the network television program "Who Wants to Be a Millionaire?" But how much impact did those managers really have on the show's success? Was the popularity of the show due to anything the managers did or was it just a reflection of the fickle tastes of television audiences? The symbolic view would say that this outcome was due to forces beyond managers' control.

REALITY SUGGESTS A SYNTHESIS

In reality, managers are neither helpless nor all-powerful. Internal constraints that restrict a manager's decision options exist within every organization. These internal constraints arise from the organization's culture. In addition, external constraints come from the organization's environment.

Exhibit 3.1 shows managers as operating within the constraints imposed by the organization's culture and environment. Yet, despite these constraints, managers are not powerless. They can still influence an organization's performance. In the remainder of this chapter, we'll discuss organizational culture and environment as constraints. However, as we'll see in other chapters, these constraints don't mean that a manager's hands are tied. As Catherine Deslauriers in our chapter-opening dilemma recognizes, managers may be able to change and influence their culture and environment and, thus, expand their area of discretion as they plan, organize, lead, and control.

| Organizational Environment | → | Managerial Discretion | ← | Organizational Culture |

Exhibit	3.1

Parameters of Managerial Discretion

Testing...Testing...1,2,3

1. **Why does the omnipotent view of management dominate management theory?**

2. **Explain the symbolic view of management.**

3. **Which view—omnipotent or symbolic—is more appropriate in reality? Explain.**

> ### THE ORGANIZATION'S CULTURE

We know that every person has a unique personality. An individual's personality is a set of relatively permanent and stable traits. Our personality influences the way we act and interact with others. When we describe someone as warm, open, relaxed, or conservative, we're describing personality traits. An organization, too, has a personality, which we call its *culture*.

WHAT IS ORGANIZATIONAL CULTURE?

organizational culture

A system of shared meaning within an organization that determines, in large degree, how employees act.

What is **organizational culture**? It's a system of shared meaning and beliefs held by organizational members that determines, in large degree, how they act. It represents a common perception held by the organization's members. Just as tribal cultures have rules and taboos that dictate how members will act toward each other and outsiders, organizations have cultures that govern how its members should behave. In every organization, there are systems or patterns of values, symbols, rituals, myths, and practices that have evolved over time.[4] These shared values determine to a large degree what employees see and how they respond to their world.[5] When confronted with problems or work issues, the organizational culture—the "way we do things around here"—influences what employees can do and how they conceptualize, define, analyze, and resolve issues.

Our definition of culture implies several things. First, culture is a perception. Individuals perceive the organizational culture on the basis of what they see, hear, or experience within the organization. Second, even though individuals may have different backgrounds or work at different organizational levels, they tend to describe the organization's culture in similar terms. That is the *shared* aspect of culture. Finally, *organizational culture* is a descriptive term. It's concerned with how members perceive the organization, not with whether they like it. It describes rather than evaluates.

Research suggests that there are seven dimensions that capture the essence of an organization's culture.[6] These dimensions are described in Exhibit 3.2. As you can see, each of these characteristics exists on a continuum from low to high. Appraising an organization on these seven dimensions gives a composite picture of the organization's culture. In many organizations, one

In the dizzyingly fast world of the Internet, an organization's culture can make or break it. At E*Trade, an online brokerage, employee teamwork is critical. To learn about and to stress the importance of teamwork, E*Trade managers took a cooking class together where they had to depend on each other to prepare a gourmet meal.

Exhibit	3.2		**Dimensions of Organizational Culture**

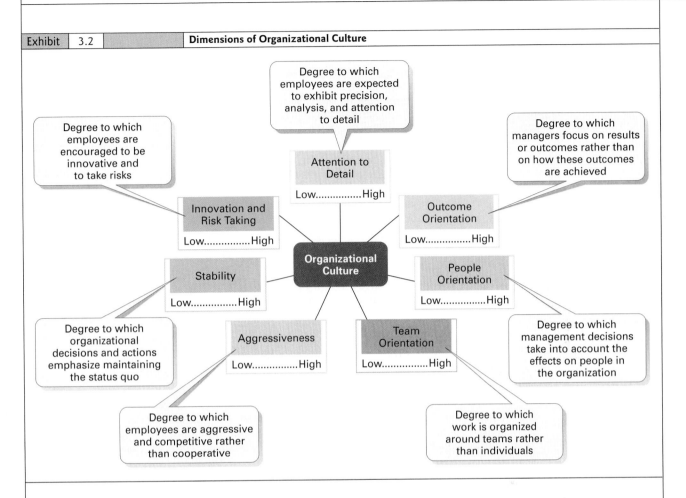

of these cultural dimensions often rises above the others and essentially shapes the organization's personality and the way organizational members do their work. For instance, at Sony Corporation the focus is on product innovation. The company "lives and breathes" new-product development (outcome orientation), and employees' work decisions, behaviors, and actions support that goal. In contrast, Southwest Airlines has made its employees a central part of its culture (people orientation). Exhibit 3.3 demonstrates how these dimensions can be mixed to create significantly different organizations.

STRONG VERSUS WEAK CULTURES

Although all organizations have cultures, not all cultures have an equal impact on employees' behaviors and actions. **Strong cultures**—cultures in which the key values are deeply held and widely shared—have a greater influence on employees than do weak cultures. The more that employees accept the organization's key values and the greater their commitment to those values, the stronger the culture is.

Whether an organization's culture is strong, weak, or somewhere in between depends on factors such as the size of the organization, how long it has been around, how much turnover there has been among employees, and the intensity with which the culture was originated. Some organizations do not make clear

strong cultures

Organizations in which the key values are intensely held and widely shared.

Exhibit 3.3	Organization A
Contrasting Organizational Cultures	This organization is a manufacturing firm. Managers are expected to fully document all decisions, and "good managers" are those who can provide detailed data to support their recommendations. Creative decisions that incur significant change or risk are not encouraged. Because managers of failed projects are openly criticized and penalized, managers try not to implement ideas that deviate much from the status quo. One lower-level manager quoted an often-used phrase in the company: "If it ain't broke, don't fix it."

Employees are required to follow extensive rules and regulations in this firm. Managers supervise employees closely to ensure that there are no deviations. Management is concerned with high productivity, regardless of the impact on employee morale or turnover.

Work activities are designed around individuals. There are distinct departments and lines of authority, and employees are expected to minimize formal contact with other employees outside their functional area or line of command. Performance evaluations and rewards emphasize individual effort, although seniority tends to be the primary factor in the determination of pay raises and promotions.

Organization B

This organization is also a manufacturing firm. Here, however, management encourages and rewards risk taking and change. Decisions based on intuition are valued as much as those that are well rationalized. Management prides itself on its history of experimenting with new technologies and its success in regularly introducing innovative products. Managers or employees who have a good idea are encouraged to "run with it," and failures are treated as "learning experiences." The company prides itself on being market driven and rapidly responsive to the changing needs of its customers.

There are few rules and regulations for employees to follow, and supervision is loose because management believes that its employees are hardworking and trustworthy. Management is concerned with high productivity but believes that this comes through treating its people right. The company is proud of its reputation as being a good place to work.

Job activities are designed around work teams, and team members are encouraged to interact with people across functions and authority levels. Employees talk positively about the competition between teams. Individuals and teams have goals, and bonuses are based on achievement of outcomes. Employees are given considerable autonomy in choosing the means by which the goals are attained. |

what is important and what is not; this lack of clarity is a characteristic of weak cultures. In such organizations, culture is unlikely to greatly influence managers. Most organizations, however, have moderate to strong cultures. There is relatively high agreement on what's important, what defines "good" employee behavior, what it takes to get ahead, and so forth. In fact, one study of organizational culture found that employees in organizations with strong cultures were more committed to their organization than were employees in organizations with weak cultures. The organizations with strong cultures also used their recruitment efforts and socialization practices to build employee commitment.[7] And an increasing

---

? THINKING CRITICALLY ABOUT ETHICS

How strong an organization's culture is will have an influence on how ethical managers will be. If the culture is strong and supports high ethical standards, it should have a powerful, positive influence on a manager's behavior. However, in a weak organizational culture, the norms and standards of work groups and departments will more strongly influence ethical behavior.

What do you think a culture that encourages high ethical standards will look like? Do you think it's possible for a manager with high ethical standards to live by those values in an organizational culture that tolerates, or even encourages, unethical practices? How could managers deal with such situations?

body of evidence suggests that strong cultures are associated with high organizational performance.[8] What are the implications for the way managers manage? As an organization's culture becomes stronger, it has an increasing impact on what managers do.[9] ←

THE SOURCE OF CULTURE

An organization's current customs, traditions, and general way of doing things are largely due to what it has done before and the degree of success it has had with those endeavors. The original source of an organization's culture usually reflects the vision or mission of the organization's founders. Because the founders had the original idea, they also may have biases on how to carry out the idea. Their focus might be on aggressiveness or it might be on treating employees as family. The founders establish the early culture by projecting an image of what the organization should be. They're not constrained by previous customs or approaches. And the small size of most new organizations helps the founders instill their vision in all organizational members.

Let's look at an example of how an individual can have an enormous influence on shaping his or her organization's culture. Yvon Chouinard, the founder of the outdoor gear company Patagonia, Inc. (www.patagonia.com), was an avid "extreme adventurer." He approached the business in a laid-back, casual manner. For instance, he hired employees not on the basis of any specific business skills but because he had climbed, fished, or surfed with them. Employees were friends, and work was treated as something fun to do. In a speech Chouinard gave a few years ago, he is said to have uttered the timeless line, "Let my people go surfing!"

Testing...Testing...1,2,3

4. **What is organizational culture?**

5. **Describe the seven dimensions of organizational culture.**

6. **Will strong or weak cultures have the greater impact on managers? Why?**

" M A N A G E R S S P E A K O U T "

Trenham Ian Weatherhead, Head of Defense & Security, London Chamber of Commerce, London, England

Describe your job.

I'm the manager of corporate events and head of the defense and security division of the London Chamber of Commerce. As manager of corporate events, I am responsible for 35 of the London Chamber's events for small businesses and for presidential lunches and dinners with ministers and heads of state. As head of the Chamber's defense and security division, I am responsible for assisting companies in their world-wide defense and security exports and investments.

What types of skills do you think tomorrow's managers will need?

Good communication skills, both with the understanding and use of the computer, but just as important, excellent interpersonal skills and being a good "team player."

How do your employees "learn" your organization's culture?

We have an excellent Human Resource division constantly training staff along their career path. Many staff members learn from one another. Also, we have regular staff meetings to update everyone on future development of the Chamber.

What are the most serious external (those outside your organization) issues facing your organization?

The lack of continuity of staff within companies with whom we work. If staff move on, it makes a good relationship between companies difficult to adjust. Another serious issue that I see is the security of the Internet and company computer networks.

Although the company (now called Lost Arrow) has more than 1,000 employees and revenues of over $182 million (2000), its culture still reflects Chouinard's values and philosophy. To keep employees happy, it offers child care and yoga classes at work and donates 1 percent of its sales to green causes. And if the surf is good, employees are free to go enjoy it!

HOW EMPLOYEES LEARN CULTURE

Culture is transmitted to employees in a number of ways. The most significant are stories, rituals, symbols, and language.

Stories Organizational "stories" typically contain a narrative of significant events or people including such things as the organization's founders, rule breaking, reactions to past mistakes, and so forth.[10] For instance, managers at Nike feel that stories told about the company's past help shape the future. Whenever possible, corporate "storytellers" (senior executives) explain the company's heritage and tell stories that celebrate people getting things done. These stories provide prime examples that people can learn from.[11] To help employees learn the culture, organizational stories anchor the present in the past, provide explanations and legitimacy for current practices, and exemplify what is important to the organization.[12]

Rituals Corporate rituals are repetitive sequences of activities that express and reinforce the values of the organization, what goals are most important, and which people are important and which ones are expendable.[13] One of the best-known corporate rituals is Mary Kay Cosmetics' annual meeting for its sales representatives.[14] Looking like a cross between a circus and a Miss America pageant, the awards ceremony takes place in a large auditorium, on a stage in front of a large, cheering audience, with all the participants dressed in glamorous evening clothes. Salespeople are rewarded for their success in achieving sales goals with an array of flashy gifts including gold and diamond pins, furs, and pink Cadillacs. This "show" acts as a motivator by publicly acknowledging outstanding sales performance. In addition, the ritual aspect reinforces founder Mary Kay's determination and optimism, which enabled her to overcome personal hardships, found her own company, and achieve material success. It conveys to her salespeople that reaching their sales goals is important and that, through hard work and encouragement, they too can achieve success. Your second author had the experience of being on a flight out of Dallas one year with a planeload of Mary Kay sales representatives headed home from the annual awards meeting. Their contagious enthusiasm and excitement made it obvious that this annual "ritual" played a significant role in establishing desired levels of motivation and behavioral expectations, which, after all, is what an organization's culture should do.

Material Symbols When you walk into different businesses, do you get a "feel" for the place—formal, casual, fun, serious, and so forth? These feelings you get demonstrate the power of material symbols in creating an organization's personality. The layout of an organization's facilities, how employees dress, the types of automobiles top executives are provided, and the availability of corporate aircraft are examples of material symbols. Others include the size of offices, the elegance of furnishings, executive "perks" (extra "goodies" provided to managers such as health club memberships, use of company-owned resort facilities, and so forth), the existence of employee lounges or on-site dining facilities, and reserved parking spaces for certain employees. These material symbols convey to employees who is important, the degree of equality desired by top management, and the kinds of behavior (for example, risk taking, conservative, authoritarian, participative, individualistic, and so forth) that are expected and appropriate.

Language Many organizations and units within organizations use language as a way to identify members of a culture. By learning this language, members attest to their acceptance of the culture and their willingness to help to preserve it. For instance, Microsoft, the software company, has its own unique vocabulary: *work judo* (the art of deflecting a work assignment to someone else without making it appear that you're avoiding it; *eating your own dog food* (a strategy of using your own software programs or products in the early stages as a way of testing them even if the process is disagreeable); *flat food* (goodies from the vending machine that can be slipped under the door to a colleague who's working feverishly on deadline); *facemail* (actually talking to someone face-to-face; considered by Microsoft employees a technologically backward means of communicating); *death march* (the countdown to shipping a new product); and so on.[15]

Over time, organizations often develop unique terms to describe equipment, key personnel, suppliers, customers, or products that are related to their business. New employees are frequently overwhelmed with acronyms and jargon that, after a short period of time, become a natural part of their language. Once learned, this language acts as a common denominator that unites members of a given culture.

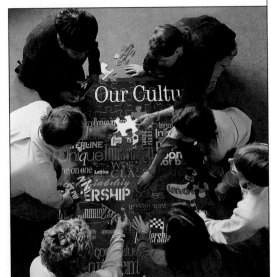

Important values at W.L. Gore & Associates—the company makes medical, electronic, and industrial products, and Gore-Tex fabrics—include innovation, equality, fairness, and teamwork. There are no managers or employees at W.L. Gore. Instead, there are sponsors and associates. Material symbols are minimal at the company. Instead, the company's workspaces are designed to promote its values.

HOW CULTURE AFFECTS MANAGERS

Because it constrains what they can and cannot do, an organization's culture is particularly relevant to managers. These constraints are rarely explicit. They're not written down. It's unlikely that they'll even be spoken. But they're there, and all managers quickly learn what to do and not to do in their organization. For instance, you won't find the following values written down anywhere, but each comes from a real organization.

Look busy even if you're not.

If you take risks and fail around here, you'll pay dearly for it.

Before you make a decision, run it by your boss so that he or she is never surprised.

We make our product only as good as the competition forces us to.

What made us successful in the past will make us successful in the future.

If you want to get to the top here, you have to be a team player.

The link between values such as these and managerial behavior is fairly straightforward. If an organization's culture supports the belief that profits can be increased by cost cutting and that the company's best interests are served by

Take a close look at this ad for Hewitt International. Obviously, a symphony without people can't make music. What organizational cultural value does this illustrate? There's no doubt that they're making the point that people are important! Think about how a manager's actions and behavior would be influenced by this cultural value.

achieving slow but steady increases in quarterly earnings, managers throughout the organization are unlikely to pursue programs that are innovative, risky, long term, or expansionary. For organizations that value and encourage workforce diversity, the organizational culture and, thus, managers' decisions and actions should be supportive of diversity efforts. (See the "Managing Workforce Diversity" box for more information on creating an inclusive workplace.) In an organization whose culture conveys a basic distrust of employees, managers are more likely to use an authoritarian leadership style than a democratic one. Why? The culture establishes for managers what is appropriate behavior. For instance, at St. Luke's advertising agency in London, a culture shaped by the value placed on freedom of expression, a lack of coercion and fear, and a determination to make work fun

◢◲◖ MANAGING WORKFORCE DIVERSITY	**Creating an Inclusive Workplace Culture**

We know from our discussion in Chapter 2 that managing a diverse workforce is a key challenge facing today's managers. As the composition of the workforce changes, managers must take a long hard look at their organizational culture to see if the shared meaning and beliefs that were appropriate for a more homogeneous workforce will support diverse views. How can managers create a workplace culture that advocates and encourages diversity?[17]

Diversity efforts by organizations are no longer driven simply by federal mandate. Instead, organizations have recognized that inclusive workplaces are good for business. Among other things, diversity contributes to creative solutions to problems and enhances employee morale. Creating a workplace culture that supports and encourages the inclusion of all diverse individuals and views is a major organizational effort. Managers throughout the organization must value diversity and show that they do by their decisions and actions. An organization that truly wants to promote inclusiveness must shape its culture to allow diversity to flourish. One way to do this is for managers to assimilate diverse perspectives while performing the managerial functions. For example, at the Marriott Marquis Hotel in

New York's Times Square, managers are taught in required diversity training classes that the best way to cope with diversity-related conflict is to focus narrowly on performance and never to define problems in terms of gender, culture, or race. And at Prudential, the annual planning process includes key diversity performance goals that are measured and tied to managers' compensation.

Beyond the day-to-day managerial activities, organizations should consider developing ways to reinforce employee behaviors that exemplify inclusiveness. Some suggestions include encouraging individuals to value and defend diverse views, creating traditions and ceremonies that celebrate diversity, rewarding appropriate "heroes" and "heroines" who accept and promote inclusiveness, and communicating formally and informally about employees who champion diversity issues.

Developing an organizational culture that supports diversity and inclusiveness may be challenging but offers high potential benefits. Organizations that allow diversity to prosper and thrive see cultural or environmental changes not as constraints but as opportunities to bring out the best in all of their members.

influences the way employees work and the way that managers plan, organize, lead, and control. The organization's culture is also reinforced by the office environment, which is open, versatile, and creative.[16]

An organization's culture, especially a strong one, constrains a manager's decision-making options in all management functions. As shown in Exhibit 3.4, the major areas of a manager's job are influenced by the culture in which he or she operates.

Planning
The degree of risk that plans should contain
Whether plans should be developed by individuals or teams
The degree of environmental scanning in which management will engage

Organizing
How much autonomy should be designed into employees' jobs
Whether tasks should be done by individuals or in teams
The degree to which department managers interact with each other

Leading
The degree to which managers are concerned with increasing employee job satisfaction
What leadership styles are appropriate
Whether all disagreements—even constructive ones—should be eliminated

Controlling
Whether to impose external controls or to allow employees to control their own actions
What criteria should be emphasized in employee performance evaluations
What repercussions will occur from exceeding one's budget

Exhibit | 3.4

Managerial Decisions Affected by Culture

7. **What is the source of an organization's culture?**

8. **Describe how stories, rituals, material symbols, and language shape an organization's culture.**

9. **How does culture affect what a manager does?**

〉 THE ENVIRONMENT

Our discussion in Chapter 1 of an organization as an open system explained that an organization interacts with its environment as it takes in inputs and distributes outputs. Anyone who questions the impact of the external environment on managing should consider the following:

> The Cadillac Division of General Motors has watched its faithful buyers grow silver-haired. Its average new-car buyer is now over 60 years old. To counteract this demographic trend, the company's managers are looking at ways to attract a new generation of buyers.

> The year 2000 brought a harsh dose of reality to the booming stock market as the dramatic fall in the Nasdaq stock index affected the ability of companies, especially Internet companies, to raise additional capital. Some companies even canceled their initial public offerings (IPOs) of stock because of the dramatic decline in the stock market.

As these two examples show, there are forces in the environment that play a major role in shaping managers' actions. In this section, we'll identify some of the critical environmental forces that affect management and show how they constrain managerial discretion.

DEFINING THE EXTERNAL ENVIRONMENT

external environment

Outside institutions or forces that potentially affect an organization's performance.

The term **external environment** refers to forces and institutions outside the organization that potentially can affect the organization's performance. The external environment is made up of two components, the specific environment and the general environment, as shown in Exhibit 3.5.

specific environment

The part of the environment that is directly relevant to the achievement of an organization's goals.

The Specific Environment The **specific environment** includes those constituencies that have a direct and immediate impact on managers' decisions and actions and are directly relevant to the achievement of the organization's goals. Each organization's specific environment is unique and changes with conditions. For instance, Timex and Rolex both make watches, but their specific environments differ because they operate in distinctly different market niches. What constituencies make up the specific environment? The main ones are customers, suppliers, competitors, and pressure groups.

Customers. Organizations exist to meet the needs of customers. It's the customer or client who absorbs the organization's output. This is true even for governmental organizations. (Think back to our chapter opener.) They exist to provide services, and we're reminded, especially at election time, that we indicate by our votes how satisfied we are as customers.

Exhibit | 3.5

The External Environment

Customers obviously represent potential uncertainty to an organization. Their tastes can change; they can become dissatisfied with the organization's product or service. Of course, some organizations face considerably more uncertainty as a result of their customers than do others. For example, what do you think of when you think of Club Med? Club Med's image was traditionally one of carefree singles having fun in the sun at exotic locales. Club Med found, however, that as their target customers married and had children, these same individuals were looking for family-oriented vacation resorts where they could bring the kids. Although Club Med responded to the changing demands of its customers by offering different types of vacation experiences, including family-oriented ones, the company found it hard to change its original image.

Suppliers. When you think of an organization's suppliers, you typically think in terms of organizations that provide materials and equipment. For Walt Disney World resorts in Florida, these include organizations that sell soft-drink syrups, computers, food, flowers and other nursery stock, concrete, and paper products. But the term *suppliers* also includes providers of financial and labor inputs. Stockholders, banks, insurance companies, pension funds, and other similar organizations are needed to ensure a continuous supply of money. Labor unions, colleges and universities, occupational associations, trade schools, and local labor markets are sources of employees. When the sources of employees dry up, it can constrain managers' decisions and actions. For example, a lack of qualified nurses, a problem

What's your image of a Harley rider? Do you picture leather, chains, and a rough appearance? Managers at Harley Davidson face uncertainty as they constantly try to balance its "outlaw" image that so many traditional Harley riders proudly brandish and its desire to attract new riders including professionals and women.

MANAGING IN AN E-BUSINESS WORLD Managing the External Environment

Managers had a lot to deal with when their work world *wasn't* so interconnected. Now, when suppliers or customers are just a keystroke away and interactions with external stakeholders can take place 24 hours a day, 7 days a week (24-7, in e-business language), it's even more complicated![18] One critical external environment issue facing managers in an e-business world is the evolving nature of relationships with customers, suppliers, and competitors—we know each of these as important parts of the specific environment of an organization.

There used to be clear-cut distinctions among an organization's customers, suppliers, and competitors. Each group had its own characteristics, goals, and requirements for the economic relationships that existed. Suppliers provided the inputs necessary to produce the products and services that were being sold to customers; customers bought the output (products and services) of an organization; and competitors battled for those same customers to purchase *their* products and services. It's not quite that simple anymore! In an e-business world, the economic relationships between an organization and its customers, suppliers, and competitors have become more interconnected.

Remember that an organization exists to meet the needs of customers—in other words, an organization *needs* customers. In an e-business world, customers play a more active role in the economic exchanges taking place. What are some ways that they're more involved? Organizations get instantaneous feedback from customers about their satisfying or not-so-satisfying experiences and, in many instances, may tell others about it via chat rooms or other online communication forums. Organizations have partnered with customers and even turned customers into salespersons. Take the case of Hotmail, now the world's largest Web-based e-mail provider. (Maybe *you* have a Hotmail account.) Started in 1995, the company has grown a subscriber base (now more than 34 million) more quickly than any other new company, yet has spent less than $500,000 on marketing, advertising, and promotion. How did it accomplish this? By making each new user a company salesperson. Every time a Hotmail user sends an e-mail, the outbound message conveys an advertisement about Hotmail and an implied endorsement by the sender. Other successful e-business organizations have partnered with customers for various reasons: highly customizable products (Dell Computers, General Motors, and various investment and brokerage Web sites), streamlined fulfillment systems (FedEx and UPS delivery services), customized pricing (Priceline.com, online auctions), and online product sales (Amazon.com, PC Flowers and Gifts, and so forth).

Relationships with suppliers have been turned upside down as well. To succeed in an e-business environment, there must be a seamless integration between an organization and its suppliers. Why? Because speed is essential in this Internet economy. Although having the right materials at the right time and in the right place to produce products or services has always been a goal of organizations, e-business is speeding up this process. To make it work, e-business organizations must have close and interdependent relationships with suppliers. For example, to meet its goal of making a custom car within five days of receiving an order from a customer, Toyota Motor Corporation has established electronic linkages with suppliers to ensure that it has the right materials at the right time and in the right place. Other companies, large and small, are establishing Internet-based transactions with suppliers and eliminating the old-fashioned time-consuming approach—sales representatives from various suppliers call on the customer and make presentations to the purchasing manager, the purchasing manager decides on a supplier and completes the purchase requisition, the purchase requisition is approved and the purchase order is submitted to the supplier, the purchase order is received by the supplier, the supplier completes the order and ships it to the customer, and so forth. The e-business world has made this process much more efficient and effective. In fact, many analysts believe that these business-to-business (B2B) transactions (between purchasing organizations and suppliers) are likely to become the most important applications of e-business models.

Finally, in an e-business world, organizations are partnering with competitors. Yes, it may sound strange—cooperating with the "enemy"—but organizations are discovering that meeting customers' needs in a fast-changing world may require collaborating with competitors in areas such as product innovation and purchasing supplies. In a dynamic and complex environment, which perfectly describes the e-business world, partnering with competitors may be the only way to reduce supply costs and to foster innovation. For instance, Nortel Networks, IBM, Matsushita Electric Industrial, and five other companies announced the creation of an Internet market called e2open.com in which computer makers and suppliers can buy and sell electronic products and services. And in the hotel industry, competitors Marriott and Hyatt have partnered in an online marketplace for room reservations.

Yes, it *is* a different external environment in which managers find themselves! However, managers can successfully navigate these treacherous waters by effectively managing all of these external relationships—with customers, suppliers, and competitors. In an e-business world, it's absolutely critical!

plaguing the health care industry, is making it difficult for health care providers to fulfill demand and achieve objectives.

Managers seek to ensure a steady flow of needed inputs at the lowest price available. Because these inputs represent uncertainties—that is, their unavailability or delay can significantly reduce the organization's effectiveness—managers typically go to great efforts to ensure a steady, reliable flow. The application of e-business principles and methods is changing the way that organizations deal with suppliers. (The "Managing in an E-Business World" box looks at this issue as well as how e-business is affecting other external constituencies.)

Competitors. All organizations have one or more competitors. Although the U.S. Postal Service has a monopoly on mail service, it competes with FedEx, UPS, and other forms of communication such as the telephone, e-mail, and fax. Nike competes against Reebok, Adidas, and Fila among others. Coca-Cola competes against Pepsi and other soft-drink companies. Not-for-profit organizations such as the Metropolitan Museum of Art and Girl Scouts USA also compete for dollars, volunteers, and customers.

Managers cannot afford to ignore the competition. When they do, they pay dearly. For instance, until the 1980s, the three major broadcast networks—ABC, CBS, and NBC—virtually controlled what you watched on television. Now, with digital cable, DVD players and VCRs, and even the World Wide Web, customers have a much broader choice of what to watch. As technological capabilities continue to expand, the number of viewing options will provide even more competition for the broadcast networks. The Internet is also having an impact on whom an organization's competitors are because it has virtually eliminated the geographic boundaries. Through the power of Internet marketing, a small maple syrup maker in Vermont can compete with the likes of Pillsbury, Quaker Oats, and Smuckers.

These examples illustrate that competitors—in terms of pricing, new products developed, services offered, and the like—represent an environmental force that managers must monitor and to which they must be prepared to respond.

Pressure Groups. Managers must recognize the special-interest groups that attempt to influence the actions of organizations. For instance, PETA's (People for the Ethical Treatment of Animals) pressure on McDonald's Corporation over its handling of animals during the slaughter process led McDonald's to stop buying beef from one of its suppliers until it met McDonald's standards for processing cattle. And it would be an unusual week if we didn't read that environmental or human rights activists were picketing, boycotting, or threatening some organization in order to get managers to change some decision or action.

As social and political attitudes change, so too does the power of pressure

Special-interest groups can and do impact organizations. For instance, these individuals protesting actions by the World Bank Monetary Fund were making their voices heard and hoping to influence decisions.

groups. For example, through their persistent efforts, groups such as MADD (Mothers Against Drunk Driving) and SADD (Students Against Destructive Decisions) have not only managed to make changes in the alcoholic beverage and restaurant and bar industries but have also raised public awareness about the problem of drunk drivers.

general environment

Broad external conditions that may affect the organization.

The General Environment The **general environment** includes the broad economic, political/legal, sociocultural, demographic, technological, and global conditions that *may* affect the organization. Changes in any of these areas usually do not have as large an impact as the specific environment has, but managers must consider these areas as they plan, organize, lead, and control.

Economic Conditions. Interest rates, inflation, changes in disposable income, stock market fluctuations, and the stage of the general business cycle are some of the economic factors in the general environment that can affect management practices in an organization. For example, many specialty retailers such as Ikea, The Limited, and Williams-Sonoma are acutely aware of the impact the level of consumer disposable income has on their sales. When consumers' incomes fall or when their confidence about job security declines, they will postpone purchasing anything that isn't a necessity. Even charitable organizations such as the United Way or the Muscular Dystrophy Association feel the impact of economic factors. During economic downturns, not only does the demand for their services increase but their contributions typically decrease.

Political/Legal Conditions. Federal, state, and local governments influence what organizations can and cannot do. Some federal legislation has significant implications. For example, the Americans with Disabilities Act of 1990 (ADA) was designed to make jobs and facilities more accessible to people with disabilities. Exhibit 3.6 lists other significant legislation affecting business firms.

Organizations spend a great deal of time and money to meet governmental regulations, but the effects of these regulations go beyond time and money.[19] They also reduce managerial discretion by limiting the choices available to managers. Consider the decision to dismiss an employee.[20] Historically, employees were free to quit an organization at any time and employers had the right to fire an employee at any time with or without cause. Laws and court decisions, however, have put increasing limits on what employers may do. Employers are increasingly expected to deal with employees by following the principles of good faith and fair dealing. Employees who feel that they've been wrongfully discharged can take their case to court. Juries are increasingly deciding what is or is not "fair." This trend has made it more difficult for managers to fire poor performers or to dismiss employees for off-duty conduct.

Other aspects of the political/legal sector are political conditions and the general stability of a country in which an organization operates and the attitudes that elected governmental officials hold toward business. In the United States, for example, organizations have generally operated in a stable political environment. However, management is a global activity. Managers should attempt to forecast major political changes in countries in which they operate because these political conditions can influence decisions and actions.

Exhibit   3.6

Selected U.S. Legislation Affecting Business

Legislation	Purpose
Occupational Safety and Health Act of 1970	Requires employer to provide a working environment free from hazards to health
Consumer Product Safety Act of 1972	Sets standards on selected products; requires warning labels, and orders product recalls
Equal Employment Opportunity Act of 1972	Forbids discrimination in all areas of employer-employee relations
Employee Retirement Income Security Act of 1974	Enacted by Congress to protect an employee's right to his or her pension
Tax Reform Act of 1986	Provided for a major restructuring of the U.S. federal income tax rate system
Worker Adjustment and Retraining Notification Act of 1988	Requires employers with 100 or more employees to provide 60 days' notice before a facility closing or mass layoff
Americans with Disabilities Act of 1990	Prohibits employers from discriminating against individuals with physical or mental disabilities or the chronically ill; also requires organizations to reasonably accommodate these individuals
Civil Rights Act of 1991	Reaffirms and tightens prohibition of discrimination; permits individuals to sue for punitive damages in cases of intentional discrimination
Women's Business Development Act of 1991	Assists the development of small business concerns owned and controlled by women through a training program and a loan program that eases access to credit through the Small Business Administration (SBA) loan program
Family and Medical Leave Act of 1993	Grants 12 weeks of unpaid leave each year to employees for the birth or adoption of a child or the care of a spouse, child, or parent with a serious health condition; covers organizations with 50 or more employees
North American Free Trade Agreement of 1993	Created a free-trade zone between the United States, Canada, and Mexico
Child Safety Protection Act of 1994	Provides for labeling requirements on certain toys that contain parts or packaging that could harm children and requires manufacturers of such toys to report any serious accidents or deaths of children to the Consumer Product Safety Commission
General Agreement on Tariffs and Trade (GATT) of 1994	Provides for the lowering of tariffs globally by roughly 40%, extending intellectual property protection worldwide, and tightening rules on investment and trade in services
U.S. Economic Espionage Act of 1996	Makes theft or misappropriation of trade secrets a federal crime
Electronic Signatures in Global and National Commerce Act of 2000	Gives online contracts (those signed by computer) the same legal force as equivalent paper contracts

Sociocultural Conditions.   Managers must adapt their practices to the changing expectations of the society in which they operate. As societal values, customs, and tastes change, managers must also change. For instance, as workers have begun seeking more balance to their lives, organizations have had to adjust by offering family leave policies, more flexible work hours and arrangements, and even on-site child care facilities. Other sociocultural changes in the United States that have been identified include the increasing fear of crime and violence; more acceptance of gambling and gaming activities; more emphasis on religion and spiritual activities; pursuit of healthy lifestyles; and acceptance of technology in our lives.

As society continues to value the importance of healthy lifestyles, organizations are encouraging their employees to exercise and work out. In fact, many organizations offer on-site wellness centers and gyms.

Each of these trends may pose a potential constraint to managers' decisions and actions. If an organization does business in other countries, managers need to be familiar with those countries' values and cultures and manage in ways that recognize and embrace those specific sociocultural aspects.

Demographic Conditions. The demographic conditions encompass trends in the physical characteristics of a population such as gender, age, level of education, geographic location, income, family composition, and so forth—the type of information that the U.S. Census Bureau collects.

One particular population group that you may have heard a lot about is the "baby boomers." This group typically includes individuals who were born from 1946 to 1964. The reason you hear so much about the baby boomers is that there are so many of them. Through every life stage they've entered (going to elementary school, teenage years, climbing the career ladder, and now the middle-age years), they've had an enormous impact because of their sheer numbers. Other age cohorts besides boomers that have been identified include the Depression group (born 1912–1921); the World War II group (born 1922–1927); the Postwar group (born 1928–1945); the Generation X or "zoomers" group (born 1965–1977); and Generation Y or baby boomlet generation (born 1978–1994). This last group is predicted to be as large as, if not larger than, its boomer parents. And the latter-born of this age group have been described as the Digital or Net generation because of their immersion into and acceptance of computers and all things digital.[21] The members of this generation are thinking, learning, creating, shopping, and playing in fundamentally different ways that are likely to greatly impact organizations and managers.

Technological. In terms of the general environment, the most rapid changes during the past quarter-century have occurred in technology. We live in a time of continuous technological change. For instance, the human genetic code has been cracked. Just think of the implications of such an incredible breakthrough! Information gadgets are getting smaller and more powerful. We have automated offices, electronic meetings, robotic manufacturing, lasers, integrated circuits, faster and more powerful microprocessors, synthetic fuels, and entirely new models of doing business in an electronic age. Companies that capitalize on technology such as General Electric and Nokia prosper. In addition, many successful retailers such as Wal-Mart and The Limited use sophisticated inventory information systems to keep on top of current sales trends. Other organizations such as Prime Trucking Inc. with its on-board truck computers, American Airlines with its Sabre Reservation System, and Amazon.com use information as a competitive advantage and have adopted technologically advanced e-business systems to stay ahead of their competitors. Similarly, hospitals, universities, airports, police departments, and even military organizations that adapt to major technological advances have a competitive edge over those that do not. The whole area of technology is radically changing the fundamental ways that organizations are structured and the way that managers manage. We consider it so important that we've addressed technological issues and their impact on managers throughout several chapters.

Global. As we discussed in Chapter 2, globalization is one of the major factors affecting managers and organizations. Managers of both large and small organizations are challenged by an increasing number of global competitors and consumer markets as part of the external environment. We'll cover this component of the external environment in detail in the next chapter. ◄

HOW THE ENVIRONMENT AFFECTS MANAGERS

Knowing *what* the various components of the environment are is important to managers. However, understanding *how* the environment affects managers is equally as important. The environment affects managers through the degree of environmental uncertainty that is present and through the various stakeholder relationships that exist between the organization and its external constituencies.

Assessing Environmental Uncertainty Not all environments are the same. They differ by what we call their degree of **environmental uncertainty**, which is determined by two dimensions: degree of change and degree of complexity in an organization's environment. Environmental uncertainty can be described as shown in the matrix in Exhibit 3.7. Let's take a closer look at the two dimensions that comprise environmental uncertainty.

The first of these dimensions is the degree of change. If the components in an organization's environment change frequently, we call it a *dynamic* environment. If change is minimal, we call it a *stable* one. A stable environment might be one in which there are no new competitors, no new technological breakthroughs by current competitors, little activity by pressure groups to influence the organization, and so forth. For instance, Zippo Manufacturing (www.zippo.com), best known for its Zippo lighters, faces a relatively stable environment. There are few competitors and little technological change. Probably the main environmental concern for the company is the declining trend in tobacco smokers, although the company's lighters have other uses and global markets remain attractive because tobacco use around the world is still strong.

Testing...Testing...1,2,3

10. **Define an organization's environment.**

11. **Describe the four factors in an organization's specific environment.**

12. **Describe the six factors in an organization's general environment.**

environmental uncertainty

The degree of change and complexity in an organization's environment.

Degree of Change		Exhibit	3.7
Stable	**Dynamic**	**Environmental Uncertainty Matrix**	

	Degree of Complexity — Simple	Degree of Complexity — Simple
	Cell 1 Stable and predictable environment Few components in environment Components are somewhat similar and remain basically the same Minimal need for sophisticated knowledge of components	**Cell 2** Dynamic and unpredictable environment Few components in environment Components are somewhat similar but are in continual process of change Minimal need for sophisticated knowledge of components
	Cell 3 Stable and predictable environment Many components in environment Components are not similar to one another and remain basically the same High need for sophisticated knowledge of components	**Cell 4** Dynamic and unpredictable environment Many components in environment Components are not similar to one another and are in continual process of change High need for sophisticated knowledge of components

An environment that's highly uncertain and unpredictable. That's the reality that managers at high-tech firms face. To cope with this uncertainty, managers pay close attention to what's happening in their external environment.

In contrast, the Big Five of the music industry (Sony, Warner, BMG, EMI, and Universal) face a highly uncertain and unpredictable environment. Digital formats such as MP3 and music-swapping Internet services such as Napster Inc. are turning the recorded music industry upside down. Although the music companies have long earned revenues by selling physical commodities such as LP records, cassettes, CDs, and the like, the digital future represents chaos and uncertainty. This environment can definitely be described as dynamic.

What about rapid change that's predictable? Is that considered a dynamic environment? Bricks-and-mortar retail department stores provide a good example. They typically make one quarter to one third of their sales in December. The drop-off from December to January is significant. However, because the change is predictable, we don't consider the environment to be dynamic. When we talk about degree of change, we mean change that is unpredictable. If change can be accurately anticipated, it's not an uncertainty that managers must confront.

environmental complexity

The number of components in an organization's environment and the extent of an organization's knowledge about its environmental components.

The other dimension of uncertainty describes the degree of **environmental complexity**. The degree of complexity refers to the number of components in an organization's environment and the extent of the knowledge that the organization has about those components. For example, Hasbro Toy Company, the second largest toy manufacturer (behind Mattel) has simplified its environment by acquiring many of its competitors such as Tiger Electronics, Wizards of the Coast, Kenner Toys, Parker Brothers, and Tonka Toys. The fewer competitors, customers, suppliers, government agencies, and so forth that an organization must deal with, the less complexity and, therefore, the less uncertainty there is in its environment.

Complexity is also measured in terms of the knowledge an organization needs to have about its environment. For instance, managers at the online brokerage E*Trade must know a great deal about their Internet service provider's operations if they want to ensure that their Web site is available, reliable, and secure for their stock-trading customers. On the other hand, managers of grocery stores have a minimal need for sophisticated knowledge about their suppliers.

How does the concept of environmental uncertainty influence managers? Looking again at Exhibit 3.7, each of the four cells represents different combinations of degree of complexity and degree of change. Cell 1 (an environment that is stable and simple) represents the lowest level of environmental uncertainty. Cell 4 (an environment that is dynamic and complex) is the highest. Not surprisingly, managers' influence on organizational outcomes is greatest in cell 1 and least in cell 4.

Because uncertainty is a threat to an organization's effectiveness, managers try to minimize it. Given a choice, managers would prefer to operate in environments such as those in cell 1. However, managers rarely have full control over that choice. In addition, most industries today are facing more dynamic change, making their environments more uncertain.

STAKEHOLDER RELATIONSHIP MANAGEMENT

What has made VH1 *the* TV channel for music-loving baby boomers? One reason is that VH1 President John Sykes knows the importance of building relationships with the organization's various external stakeholders: viewers, music celebrities, advertisers, affiliate TV stations, public service groups, and others. The nature of external stakeholder relationships is another way in which the environment influences managers. The more obvious and secure these relationships become, the more influence managers will have over organizational outcomes. In this section, we want to look at how we define these external stakeholder relationships, explain why managing external stakeholder relationships is important, and examine various ways of managing these relationships.

Who Are Stakeholders? **Stakeholders** are any constituencies in the organization's external environment that are affected by the organization's decisions and actions. These groups have a stake in or are significantly influenced by what the organization does. In turn, these groups can influence the organization. For example, think of the groups that might be affected by the decisions and actions of Starbucks—coffee bean suppliers, employees, specialty coffee competitors, local communities, and so forth. Some of these stakeholders also may impact decisions and actions of Starbucks' managers. The idea that organizations have stakeholders is now widely accepted by both management academics and practicing managers.[22]

With what types of stakeholders might an organization have to deal? Exhibit 3.8 identifies some of the most common. Note that these stakeholders include internal and external groups. Why? Because both can affect what an organization does and how it operates. However, we're primarily interested in the external groups and their impact on managers' discretion in planning, organizing, leading,

stakeholders

Any constituency in the environment that is affected by an organization's decisions and policies and that can influence the organization.

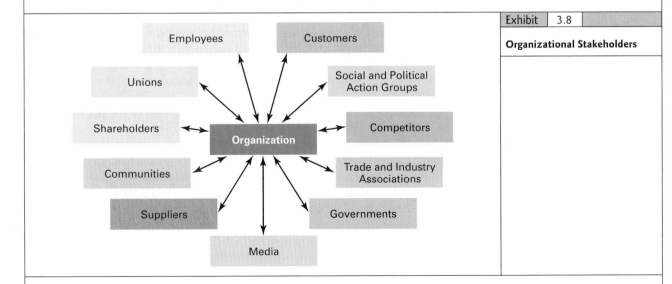

Exhibit	3.8

Organizational Stakeholders

As the world's largest retailer, it might seem that managers at Wal-Mart wouldn't have to consider its stakeholders as they make decisions. However, that's not the case at all! What stakeholders do you think would be important to Wal-Mart? Which of those stakeholders might managers find critical?

and controlling. This doesn't mean that the internal stakeholders aren't important, but we explain managing these relationships, primarily with organizational members (employees), throughout the rest of the book.

Why Is Stakeholder Relationship Management Important? Why should managers even care about managing stakeholder relationships?[23] One reason is that it can lead to other organizational outcomes such as improved predictability of environmental changes, more successful innovations, greater degrees of trust among stakeholders, and greater organizational flexibility to reduce the impact of change. But does it affect organizational performance? The answer is yes! Management researchers who have looked at this issue are finding that managers of high-performing companies tend to consider the interests of all major stakeholder groups as they make decisions.[24]

Another reason given for managing external stakeholder relationships is that it's the "right" thing to do. What does this mean? It means that an organization depends on these external groups as sources of inputs (resources) and as outlets for outputs (goods and services), and managers should consider their interests as they make decisions and take actions. We'll address this issue in more detail in Chapter 5 as we look at the concepts of managerial ethics and corporate social responsibility.

How Can These Relationships Be Managed? There are four steps in managing external stakeholder relationships. The first step is identifying who the organization's stakeholders are. Which of the various external groups might be impacted by decisions that managers make and which external groups might influence those decisions? Those external groups that are likely to be influenced by and to influence organizational decisions are the organization's stakeholders. The second step is for managers to determine what particular interests or concerns these stakeholders might have—product quality, financial issues, safety of working conditions, environmental protection, and so forth. Next managers must decide how critical each stakeholder is to the organization's decisions and actions. In other words, how critical is it to consider this stakeholder's concerns as managers plan, organize, lead, and control? The very idea of a stakeholder—a group that has a "stake" in what the organization does—means that it is important. But some stakeholders are more critical to the organization's decisions and actions than others. For instance, a critical stakeholder of a publicly supported state university would be the state legislature because it controls how much budget money the university gets each year. On the other hand, the university's computer hardware and software suppliers are important but not critical. Once managers have determined these things, the final step is determining what specific approach they should use to manage the external stakeholder relationships. This decision depends on how critical the external stakeholder is to the organization and how uncertain the environment is.[25] The more critical the stakeholder and the more uncertain the environment, the more that managers need to rely on establishing explicit stakeholder partnerships. Exhibit 3.9 illustrates the various approaches to managing stakeholder relationships.

Exhibit   3.9

**Managing Stakeholder
Relationships**

	Stakeholder Importance	
	Critically Important	Important but Not Critical
High Uncertainty	Stakeholder Partnerships	Boundary Spanning
Low Uncertainty	Stakeholder Management	Scanning and Monitoring the Environment

(Environmental Uncertainty)

When external stakeholders are important but not critical and environmental uncertainty is low, managers usually rely on simply scanning and monitoring the environment for trends and forces that may be changing. In this situation, it's not necessary for managers to take specific actions to manage stakeholders. They just need to stay informed about what's happening with them, what concerns they might have, and whether these concerns are changing. (We'll discuss environmental scanning techniques in Chapter 9.)

When the stakeholder is important but not critical and environmental uncertainty is high, managers need to be more proactive in their efforts to manage the stakeholder relationships. They can do this by using **boundary spanning**, which involves interacting in more specific ways with various external stakeholders to gather and disseminate important information. In boundary spanning, organizational members move freely between the organization and external stakeholders. The boundaries of the organization become more flexible and permeable. Boundary spanners are often said to have their feet in multiple settings—that is, they span the organizational boundaries. For instance, individuals who interact day in and day out with external stakeholders as they do their jobs—such as a salesperson for Pfizer who interacts with doctors and health care professionals, a public relations manager who talks with newspaper and television reporters, a buyer at Target who works with clothing suppliers in Asia, an equipment installation specialist for GE Medical Systems who collaborates with a competitor in installing an expensive imaging machine for a hospital, and so forth—would establish closer and more explicit relationships with the various stakeholders. It's a step beyond just simply scanning and monitoring the environment because boundary spanners actively interact with stakeholders as they gather and disseminate information.

When the stakeholder is critical and environmental uncertainty is low, managers can use more direct stakeholder management efforts such as conducting customer marketing research, encouraging competition among suppliers, establishing governmental relations departments or lobbying efforts, initiating public relations connections with public pressure groups, and so forth. For instance, when Nike wanted to address the issue of the working conditions in its overseas factories, it worked with several stakeholders including customers, suppliers, government agencies, and public pressure groups to manage the situation.

boundary spanning

Interacting in specific ways with various external stakeholders to gather and disseminate important information.

stakeholder partnerships

Proactive arrangements between an organization and a stakeholder to pursue common goals.

Finally, when the stakeholder is critical and environmental uncertainty is high, managers should use **stakeholder partnerships**, which are proactive arrangements between an organization and a stakeholder to pursue common goals. These types of partnering activities allow organizations to build bridges—organization–supplier, organization–customer, organization–local communities, organization–competitor, and so forth—to their stakeholders. For instance, Compaq and IBM initiated a partnership to structure their data storage capabilities to work together. Together they're spending over $1 billion to achieve compatibility in their data storage devices. Stakeholder partnerships involve significant levels of commitment among the partners to be more interdependent rather than independent. This whole notion of stakeholder partnerships is the premise behind value chain management, which we'll discuss in detail in Chapter 19.

As we have seen, organizations are not self-contained or self-sufficient. They interact with and are influenced by their environment. Organizations depend on their environment as a source of inputs and as a recipient of their outputs. Many of the environmental forces—both specific and general—are dynamic and create considerable uncertainty for managers. The greater the environmental uncertainty an organization faces, the more the environment limits managers' options. However, through various approaches, managers are learning how to better manage those external relationships to minimize the constraints.

Testing...Testing...1,2,3

13. **What are the two components of environmental uncertainty?**

14. **Who are stakeholders, and why should managers be concerned about managing the relationship with them?**

15. **Describe the four different ways for managers to manage stakeholder relationships.**

Managers Respond to "A Manager's Dilemma"

Ricardo Mendiola

Senior Community Liaison, Houston Department of Health and Human Services, Houston, Texas

The key elements to successful stakeholder relationships between the community and the city are: cooperative objectives established by both; structured communication; focus on ways to enhance the relationship; strategies to effectively deliver services; regularly scheduled meetings; ongoing evaluation of services; and consideration of funding.

The long term success and vision of a city depends so much on its ability to establish and enhance a solid relationship between its community (stakeholders) and the city. By analyzing both the community and the city objectives, you can establish the City's approach and delivery of services.

I think it is essential that the city recognize the importance and value of the community and include them in the service delivery process. This makes the community feel that its stake in the service delivery process is recognized and valued.

Lynee Pauk

Laboratory Supervisor and Medical Technologist, St. John's Regional Health Center, Springfield, Missouri

In any situation, it is important to first recognize the goal of what is to be done. The goal in this situation is to improve public involvement in Vancouver's city issues.

Second, it's important to identify problem(s) which hinder the goal from being met. In this case, Deslauriers has identified the isolation of the business units as a problem.

To resolve this, it would be helpful to establish stakeholder relationships between the business units and the community to encourage involvement. How could she accomplish this? She would need to identify the relevant stakeholders and pinpoint their concerns and interests. Once she had done this, Deslauriers would need to prioritize these concerns and then determine an effective approach to use in managing the stakeholder relationships which would depend on how critical the stakeholder is and how uncertain the environment is.

Chapter Summary

This summary is organized by the chapter-opening objectives found on p. 54.

1. The omnipotent view is dominant in management theory and in society. It argues that managers are directly responsible for the success or failure of an organization. In contrast, the symbolic view argues that management has only a limited effect on organizational outcomes because of the large number of external forces beyond managers' control; however, managers symbolize control and influence.

2. Organizational culture is a system of shared meaning and beliefs held by organizational members that determines, in large degree, how they act.

3. An organization's culture is composed of seven dimensions: innovation and risk taking, attention to detail, outcome orientation, people orientation, team orientation, aggressiveness, and stability.

4. A strong culture is one in which the key values are intensely held and widely shared. Strong cultures have a greater influence on employees than do weak cultures. In many organizations, particularly those with strong cultures, one of the seven cultural dimensions often rises above the others and shapes the organization's personality and the way organizational members do their work.

5. The various ways that employees learn an organization's culture include stories, rituals, material symbols, and language. Organizational stories typically contain a narrative of significant events or people that portray the unique culture. Rituals are repetitive sequences of activities that express and reinforce the key values, important goals, and important people. Material symbols include the layout of the facilities, dress codes, elegance of office furnish-

ings, and other observable (tangible) items. Language refers to special and unique terms, jargon, and acronyms that are related to an organization's business.

6. Culture constrains managers because it acts as an automatic filter that biases managers' perceptions, thoughts, feelings, and actions. Strong cultures particularly constrain managers' decision-making options by conveying which alternatives are acceptable and which are not.

7. The components of the specific environment include customers, suppliers, competitors, and pressure groups. The components of the general environment include broad economic, political/legal, sociocultural, demographic, technological, and global conditions.

8. Environmental uncertainty is determined by the degree of change and the degree of complexity in the environment. Stable and simple environments are relatively certain. The more dynamic and complex the environment, the greater the uncertainty.

9. Managers may have to deal with both internal and external stakeholders. Internal stakeholders include employees and unions. External stakeholders include customers, suppliers, local communities, shareholders and investors, competitors, creditors, social and political action groups, trade or industry associations, and governments.

10. Depending on how critical the stakeholder is to the organization and on the level of environmental uncertainty, managers can scan and monitor the external environment, or they can use boundary spanning, stakeholder management, or stakeholder partnering.

Thinking About Management Issues

1. Refer to Exhibit 3.3. How would a first-line manager's job differ in these two organizations?

2. Describe an effective culture for (a) a relatively stable environment and (b) a dynamic environment.

3. Classrooms have cultures. Describe your classroom culture using the seven dimensions of organizational culture. Does the culture constrain your instructor? How?

4. "Businesses are built on relationships." What do you think this statement means? What are the implications for managing the external environment?

5. What would be the drawbacks to managing stakeholder relationships through approaches such as boundary spanning, stakeholder management, and stakeholder partnering?

Managers at Abercrombie & Fitch, the casual clothing retailer, recognize that their company's financial success hinges on sales to teens and young adults (13-year-olds to 24-year-olds). You've been hired as a consultant to tell them all about the demographics of this group. After searching the Web for information, type up a bulleted list with your findings. The more information you provide Abercrombie's managers, the more impressed they will be—and you know what that means for your perfor-mance evaluation! Be sure to note the URLs of the Web sites you use.

In addition, Abercrombie's managers want a report on the Web sites of their main competitors. They're particularly interested in uncovering the corporate values being promoted by these competitors. Search the Web and write a short paragraph describing this information for Abercrombie's managers. Be sure to provide them with the URLs for each of the competitors' Web sites.

myPHLIP Companion Web Site

myPHLIP **(www.prenhall.com/myphlip)** *is a fully customizable homepage that ties students and faculty to text-specific resources.*
- **For students**, *myPHLIP provides an online study guide tied chapter-by-chapter to the text—current events and Internet exercises, lecture notes, downloadable software, the Career Center, the Writing Center, Ask the Tutor, and more.*
- **For faculty**, *myPHLIP provides a syllabus tool that allows you to manage content, communicate with students, and upload personal resources.*

Working Together: Team-Based Exercise

Although all organizations face environmental constraints, the forces in their specific and general environments differ. Get into a small group with three to four other class members and choose two organizations in different industries. Identify and describe the specific and general external factors for each organization. How are your descriptions different? How are they similar? Now, using the same two organizations, see if you can identify the important stakeholders for these organizations. Also indicate whether these stakeholders are critical for the organization and why they are or are not. As a group, be prepared to share your information with the class and to explain your choices.

Case Application

The Roman Empire Meets the Web

The main goal of the Roman Empire, undoubtedly one of the great institutions in history, was to spread civilization. Talk about a grandiose mission! For Michael Saylor, CEO of MicroStrategy (www.microstrategy.com), the goal pursued by the Romans sets a perfect example for his company. He believes that small missions produce small companies. To get people to look at work as more than a place to spend 40 hours a week, you must have a mission that employees will pursue with passion and intensity and that they will follow to the ends of the earth. So what *is* MicroStrategy's mission? Four words sum it up: Make Intelligence Accessible Everywhere. MicroStrategy wants everyone in the world to have the right information at the right time in order to gain insight, security, and to make better decisions. Says Saylor, "We live in an ignorant world. Our mission is to purge that ignorance." So what *does* MicroStrategy do?

MicroStrategy is a software company headquartered in Vienna, Virginia. Its products let companies sift through their databases for sales trends, customer behavior, and other hidden data patterns useful for decision makers. As one of the largest vendors of decision-support software, its client list includes more than 900 companies. For instance, McDonald's uses the company's decision-support software to evaluate which hamburger promotion attracts the most middle-class males during lunch hour. And until MicroStrategy came along, Victoria's Secret stocked every store with the same lingerie. Now it knows through data mining that, for whatever reason, New Yorkers prefer lavender underwear and Chicago women have larger bra sizes. Using MicroStrategy's software, companies also can distribute information over the Internet and through e-mail, wireless phones, and personal digital assistants. In addition, MicroStrategy offers consulting, training, and support services. Founded in 1989 by Saylor, a new graduate from MIT, the company at first only offered customized decision-support system consulting services. Then in 1993 it introduced its first packaged software product. By 2000, the company had grown significantly to over 1,600 employees in over 40 offices worldwide with revenues of $224 million. But this is just part of what MicroStrategy really *is*!

Like any information technology company, MicroStrategy is only as good as the human capital it attracts and keeps. It does this through an organizational culture that's a curious mix of military and fraternity experiences—experiences that shaped CEO and founder Saylor. The atmosphere at work is collegial. Bright kids work side by side and learn intense amounts of information. They question authority and are empowered to pursue their work in whatever passionate way they desire. Most of the company's employees are hired from top-tier schools. The top criterion for recruits is intelligence. However, they also need a combination of passion, curiosity, and perfectionism. Top jobs in the organization are earned on merit, not on seniority. For instance, the two top managers for one of the company's newest projects that has the potential to transform the whole area of personal intelligence devices are ages 28 and 24. Then there's also the mandatory six-week boot camp for new hires—a grueling introduction to MicroStrategy's business model and technology. Another unique feature of the company's approach to business are the company outings. Every year in January for a week, virtually the entire company goes on a cruise in the Caribbean. Although it is a lot of fun, it's an opportunity for employees to review the previous 12 months and recharge for the coming year. In many ways, this week reflects the company's "work hard, play hard" attitude. Saylor's perspective on the cruise is that it's not a reward but an entitlement. That entitlement cost the company $3.5 million in 1999. The payoff in employee morale is immeasurable, however. The company has also implemented a "Friends and Family Weekend" in April of every year. Employees receive $750 to fly in family or friends and give them a close-up glimpse of what it's like working at MicroStrategy. Beyond all the fun and the parties, a strong sense of

These MicroStrategy employees are taking a fun break from the annual conference that the company holds for customers, partners, and employees.

community permeates MicroStrategy. The employee handbook, available on the company's intranet, has detailed profiles of every employee.

The company's culture can be summed up as "Never be satisfied, never stop improving, never go through the motions." MicroStrategy never loses sight of wanting to be the best. And as for the Roman Empire, today it would probably look to MicroStrategy for inspiration!

QUESTIONS

1. Using Exhibit 3.2, describe MicroStrategy's organizational culture.

2. Describe how you think new hires at MicroStrategy "learn" the culture.

3. How might MicroStrategy's culture constrain the behavior of a newly hired executive?

4. What role has founder Michael Saylor played in MicroStrategy's culture? How might the beliefs of a strong founder become a liability to an organization?

Source: Information from company Web site (www.microstrategy.com), July 5, 2000; C. Salter, "MicroStrategy, Inc.," *Fast Company*, April 2000, pp. 190–202; E. Thomas, "Caesar and Edison and . . . Saylor?," *Newsweek*, January 1, 2000, pp. 48–49; and D. Roth, "The Value of Vision," *Fortune*, May 24, 1999, pp. 285–88.

Video Case Application

The Bean Queue

SMALL BUSINESS 2000

There's the Bean Queen. There are Bean Counters. And there are Human Beans. All can be found at Buckeye Beans and Herbs in Spokane, Washington. Jill Smith is the Bean Queen. She's a self-proclaimed hippie artist turned entrepreneur who started her company in 1983 with an investment of $1,000. From that small, inauspicious beginning, Buckeye Beans reached sales revenue approaching $8 million and employed 50 people (human beans). Buckeye Beans has been innovative in expanding its product line, which started out with one product, Buckeye Bean Soup, and now includes a line of all-natural soups, chili, bread mixes, and pasta. Buckeye Beans also pioneered special-occasion-shaped pasta, that is, pasta shaped like Christmas trees, hearts, bunnies, dolphins, leaves, grapes, baseballs, and even golf balls. But what strikes you most about Buckeye Beans isn't its unique products—it's the unusual organizational culture that melds this company together.

That unusual organizational culture is reflected in the company's simple mission statement: Make people smile. Smith's belief is that cooking should be fun and that the experience of cooking can be a fun escape, not drudgery. That's why the first ingredient listed on all Buckeye's product packages is a cup of good wine for the cook. Buckeye's strategy that its products go beyond just a simple bag of beans and instead serve as entertainment is also seen in the company's HEHE principle: humor, education, health, and environment. That's what Jill Smith, husband Doug, and other Buckeye employees believe in and value.

Shared values are very important to Smith and her employees. Not only are many of Buckeye's employees family and long-time friends, but they all share similar values. As Smith built Buckeye Beans, she felt it was important that her employees have the same value systems. And although she admits that her approach wouldn't work for every organization, she does think it's important for managers to identify their basic values and what they're trying to accomplish. Smith suggests asking what kinds of values are important and what kind of organization is desired. For Buckeye Beans, the approach has been to create a "different" type of company—a new model—in which the business is run and employee and customer relationships operate on the basis of trust, confidence, loyalty, and working hard together to get something done. As Smith so earnestly stresses, it's easier to work hard when you have a philosophy like that.

QUESTIONS

1. Using Exhibit 3.2 as a guide, how would you describe Buckeye Beans' organizational culture?

2. How does Buckeye Beans use stories, rituals, material symbols, and language to transmit its culture to employees? Give specific examples.

3. If Buckeye Beans and Herbs continues to grow in size, what challenges will it face in maintaining its organizational culture? What advice would you give Jill Smith about maintaining the culture?

4. In 1999, Buckeye Beans and Herbs was closed due to bankruptcy. The company was liquidated at auction on July 20, 1999. Yet, as the video showed, Buckeye seemed to have its act together. What lesson can be learned from this?

Source: Based on *Small Business 2000, Show 203*.

Mastering Management

In Episode 7 of the Mastering Management *series, you'll learn about the cultural challenges facing growing firms. CanGo's shift to a more formal organizational structure leads some employees to complain that the company has lost its distinctive edge. Liz and the management team must find ways to blend the new structure with the best of CanGo's old spirit.*

Learning Objectives

After reading and studying this chapter, you should be able to:

1. Explain the importance of viewing management from a global perspective.

2. Identify the three different attitudes toward global business.

3. Describe the different regional trading alliances.

4. Explain why so many countries have become part of regional trading alliances.

5. Contrast multinational, transnational, and borderless organizations.

6. Describe the typical stages by which organizations go global.

7. Explain the four dimensions of country culture.

8. Describe U.S. culture according to the four dimensions of country culture.

9. Identify the adjustment challenges faced by a manager on global assignment.

A MANAGER'S DILEMMA

It's the world's third-largest cement producer and has excelled in global markets by continually working to improve the service it provides its customers, wherever they are. Cemex (www.cemex.com), based in Monterrey, Mexico, follows certain principles that it believes make "the Cemex difference."[1] These principles include enhancing customer service, customer-focused technology, operating efficiency, management development, ecological efficiency, empowering people, market leadership, strategic thinking, a passion for learning, *and* a global perspective. Cemex believes that to succeed in a competitive global environment, managers need multicultural perspectives. It has implemented several initiatives including educational programs that foster effective communication and unity among Cemex's worldwide offices, an expatriate program in which executives of different nationalities are assigned key positions in facilities in foreign countries, and other activities that give managers the opportunity to broaden their global expertise. Company managers such as Raymundo Gonzalez, an international trading division manager, are discovering how important it is to understand managing in a global environment.

Although he's based out of Monterrey, Mexico, Gonzalez will be working frequently in Cemex's Asian operations, primarily in Indonesia. Cemex has a 25 percent stake in Indonesian cement maker, Semen Gresik. This manufacturing operation is the largest for Cemex outside Mexico. Before

Managing in a Global Environment

4

formally joining with Gresik, Cemex had done a great deal of cement trading in Asia. There's no doubt that the Asian business is important to Cemex's future plans.

There are some similarities between Mexico and Indonesia. Both are developing nations where companies must establish a favorable working climate and where they sometimes have to work with limited technology. But the differences seem far greater. For instance, the cultural character-istics of the two countries are dramatically different. Religious preferences (Catholicism versus Muslim), musical tastes, and cuisine are a few of the differences Cemex managers will have to face. Put yourself in Gonzalez's position. How can he make the adjustment easier for other Cemex managers—Mexican and Indonesian—who will be working with him?

WHAT WOULD YOU DO?

The Cemex example demonstrates that the challenges of managing in the global environment don't go away even for a large global corporation. The global marketplace is a whole new ball game for managers. With the entire world as a market and national borders becoming increasingly irrelevant, the potential for organizations to grow expands dramatically. For example, a study of 1,250 highly diverse U.S. manufacturing firms found that companies that operated in multiple countries had twice the sales growth and significantly higher profitability than strictly domestic firms.[2]

However, as the opening dilemma also implies, the opening of global borders can work both ways! There are considerable challenges in managing a global business as well. Managers must deal with economic, political, and cultural differences. And new competitors can suddenly appear at any time from any place on the globe. Managers who don't closely monitor changes in their global environment or who don't take the specific characteristics of their location into consideration as they plan, organize, lead, and control are likely to find limited global success. In this chapter, we're going to discuss the issues managers have to face in managing in a global environment.

> ## WHO OWNS WHAT?

One way to grasp the nature of the global environment is to consider the country of ownership origin for some familiar products and companies. You might be surprised to find that many products you thought were made by U.S. companies aren't! Take the following quiz[3] and then check your answers at the end of the chapter on p. 109.

1. Ben and Jerry's Ice Cream is owned by a company based in:
   a. Mexico   b. Saudi Arabia   c. United Kingdom   d. United States

2. The Bic Pen Company is:
   a. Japanese   b. British   c. American (United States)   d. French

3. PowerBar nutrition energy bars are products of a company based in:
   a. Brazil   b. Switzerland   c. United States   d. Germany

4. RCA television sets are produced by a company based in:
   a. France   b. United States   c. Malaysia   d. Taiwan

5. Skippy peanut butter is a product of a company based in:
   a. United States   b. Canada   c. Venezuela   d. United Kingdom

6. The owners of Godiva chocolate are:
   a. American (United States)   b. Swiss   c. French   d. Swedish

7. The company that produces Vaseline is based in:
   a. France   b. United Kingdom   c. United States   d. Germany

8. The parent company of Braun electric shavers is located in:
   a. Switzerland   b. Germany   c. United States   d. Japan

9. Greyhound Bus Lines is owned by a company located in:
   a. Mexico   b. United States   c. Canada   d. France

10. Burger King's Whopper is a trademark product of a company located in:
   a. United Kingdom   b. United States   c. Mexico   d. Norway

Company	Non-U.S. Revenues as % of Total
Manpower	77.0%
ExxonMobil	71.8
Colgate-Palmolive	71.6
Texas Instruments	67.8
Avon	65.8
McDonald's	61.6
Coca-Cola	61.2
Gillette	60.1

Exhibit 4.1

Selected Companies with Significant Revenues from Non-U.S. Operations

Source: B. Zajac, "Global Giants," *Forbes*, July 24, 2000, pp. 335–38.

How well did you score? Were you aware of how many products that we use every day that are actually made by companies *not* based in the United States?

To further emphasize our point about the international aspects of business today, take a look at Exhibit 4.1. This is a partial list of U.S. companies that derive more than half of their revenues from foreign operations. As you can see, these companies represent a broad cross section of products, markets, and industries.

❯ WHAT'S YOUR GLOBAL PERSPECTIVE?

It's not unusual for Germans, Italians, or Indonesians to speak three or four languages. Most Japanese schoolchildren begin studying English in the early elementary grades. On the other hand, most U.S. children study only English in school. Americans tend to think of English as the only international business language and don't see a need to study other languages.

Monolingualism is just one of the signs that a nation suffers from **parochialism**. That is, it views the world solely through its own eyes and perspectives.[4] People with a parochial attitude do not recognize that other people have different ways of living and working. Parochialism is a significant obstacle for many managers working in a global business world. If managers fall into the trap of ignoring foreign values and customs and rigidly apply an attitude of "ours is better than theirs" to foreign cultures, they will find it difficult to compete with other managers and organizations around the world that *are* seeking to understand foreign customs and market differences. But this type of selfish, parochialistic attitude isn't the only approach that managers might take toward managing in a global environment. Managers might have one of three attitudes toward international business: ethnocentric (home country-oriented), polycentric (host country-oriented), or geocentric (world-oriented).[5] Exhibit 4.2 summarizes the key points about each of these global attitudes. Let's look at each more closely.

An **ethnocentric attitude** is the parochialistic belief that the best work approaches and practices are those of the home country (the country in which

parochialism

A narrow view of the world; an inability to recognize differences between people.

ethnocentric attitude

The parochialistic belief that the best work approaches and practices are those of the home country.

Among the nearly 3,000 different languages used around the world today, Spanish is the second most important for global business (English is the first).

the company's headquarters are located). Managers with an ethnocentric attitude believe that people in foreign countries do not have the needed skills, expertise, knowledge, or experience to make the best business decisions as people in the home country do. They wouldn't trust foreign employees with key decisions or technology.

The **polycentric attitude** is the view that the managers in the host country (the foreign country in which the organization is doing business) know the best

polycentric attitude

The view that the managers in the host country know the best work approaches and practices for running their business.

Exhibit 4.2		Ethnocentric	Polycentric	Geocentric
Key Information about Three Global Attitudes	**Orientation**	**Home Country**	**Host Country**	**World**
	Advantages	• Simpler structure • More tightly controlled	• Extensive knowledge of foreign market and workplace • More support from host government • Committed local managers with high morale	• Forces understanding of global issues • Balanced local and global objectives • Best people and work approaches used regardless of origin
	Drawbacks	• More ineffective management • Inflexibility • Social and political backlash	• Duplication of work • Reduced efficiency • Difficult to maintain global objectives because of intense focus on local traditions	• Difficult to achieve • Managers must have both local and global knowledge

work approaches and practices for running their business. Managers with a polycentric attitude view every foreign operation as different and hard to understand. Thus, these managers are likely to leave their foreign facilities alone and let foreign employees figure out how best to do things.

The last type of global attitude that managers might have is the **geocentric attitude**, which is a world-oriented view that focuses on using the best approaches and people from around the globe. Managers with this type of attitude believe that it's important to have a global view both at the organization's headquarters in the home country *and* in the various foreign work facilities. Major issues and decisions are viewed globally by looking for the best approaches and people regardless of origin.

Successful global management requires enhanced sensitivity to differences in national customs and practices. Management practices that work in Chicago might not be appropriate in Bangkok or Berlin. Read the examples in Exhibit 4.3 of the cultural blunders that can happen when managers ignore foreign values and customs and rigidly apply their own. Later in this chapter and throughout the rest of the book, you'll see how a geocentric attitude toward managing requires eliminating parochial attitudes and carefully developing an understanding of cultural differences between countries.

geocentric attitude

A world-oriented view that focuses on using the best approaches and people from around the globe.

- You're in Shanghai on business. Walking down the street one day, you pass a Chinese colleague. He asks you, "Have you eaten yet?" You answer, "No, not yet." He rushes off, looking embarrassed and uncomfortable. The phrase, "Have you eaten yet?" is a common greeting—just like "Hi, how are you?" in the United States. It's the Chinese way of saying "Is your belly full today?" or "Is life treating you well?"
- A U.S. manager transferred to Saudi Arabia successfully obtained a signature on a million dollar contract from a Saudi manufacturer. The manufacturer's representative had arrived at the meeting several hours late, but the U.S. executive considered this tardiness unimportant. The American was certainly surprised and frustrated to learn later that the Saudi had no intention of abiding by the contract. He had signed it only to be polite after showing up late for the appointment.
- A U.S. executive visiting Germany for the first time was invited to the home of his largest customer. He decided to be a good guest and brought the hostess a bouquet of a dozen red roses. He later learned that in Germany it is bad luck to present an even number of flowers and that red roses are symbolic of a strong romantic interest.
- A U.S. executive based in Peru was viewed by Peruvian managers as cold and unworthy of trust because, in face-to-face discussions, he kept backing away. He didn't understand that in Peru and other Latin countries, the custom is to stand quite close to the person with whom you are speaking.
- The "thumbs up" gesture is considered offensive in Middle East, rude in Australia, and a sign of "OK" in France.
- It's rude to cross your arms while facing someone in Turkey.

Exhibit	4.3

Examples of Cross-Cultural Blunders

Source: See D.A. Ricks, M.Y.C. Fu, and J.S. Arpas, *International Business Blunders* (Columbus, OH: Grid, 1974); A. Bennett, "American Culture Is Often a Puzzle for Foreign Managers in the U.S." *Wall Street Journal*, February 12, 1986, p. 29; C.F. Valentine, "Blunders Abroad," *Nation's Business*, March 1989, p. 54; R.E. Axtell (ed.), *Do's and Taboos around the World*, 3rd ed. (New York: John Wiley & Sons, 1993); B. Pachter, "When in Japan, Don't Cross Your Legs," *Business Ethics*, March–April 1996, p. 50; and V. Frazee, "Keeping Up on Chinese Culture," *Global Workforce*, October 1996, pp. 16–17.

1. **How does a global economy create both opportunities and challenges for managers?**

2. **What is parochialism, and how does it create problems for managers?**

3. **Contrast the three different attitudes toward global business.**

❯ UNDERSTANDING THE GLOBAL ENVIRONMENT

As we mentioned in Chapter 2, management is no longer constrained by national borders. Managers in all sizes and types of organizations are faced with the opportunities and challenges of managing in a global environment. What is the global environment like? Two important features of the global environment that managers must understand are regional trading alliances and the different types of global organizations.

REGIONAL TRADING ALLIANCES

Just a few years ago, international competition was best described in terms of country against country—the United States versus Japan, France versus Germany, Mexico versus Canada. Now, global competition has been reshaped by the creation of regional trading and cooperation agreements including the European Union (EU), North American Free Trade Agreement (NAFTA) , and the Association of Southeast Asian Nations (ASEAN).

European Union (EU)

A union of 15 European nations created as a unified economic and trade entity.

The European Union The signing of the Maastricht Treaty (named for the Dutch town where the treaty was signed) in February 1992 created the formation of the **European Union (EU)**. This treaty united 12 countries—Belgium, Denmark, France, Greece, Ireland, Italy, Luxembourg, the Netherlands, Portugal, Spain, the United Kingdom, and Germany—as a unified economic and trade entity. Three other countries—Austria, Finland, and Sweden—joined the group in 1995. (See Exhibit 4.4.) Six countries (Poland, Hungary, the Czech Republic, Cyprus, Slovenia, and Estonia) are in membership negotiations to join the EU but won't be admitted before 2003.[6] Seven other countries (Turkey, Romania, Slovakia, Bulgaria, Latvia, Lithuania, and Malta) are considering starting membership negotiations. The current EU membership covers a population base of over 374 million people. Adding the seven countries in membership negotiations brings the total population base covered by the EU to over 437 million—a significant source of economic power.

Before the creation of the EU, each of these nations had border controls, taxes, and subsidies; nationalistic policies; and protected industries. Now, as a single market, there are no national barriers to travel, employment, investment, and trade. The EU took an enormous step toward full unification in 1999 when 11 of the 15 countries became part of the EMU—the economic and monetary union, the formal name for the system in which participating countries share the same

Exhibit	4.4	**European Union Countries**

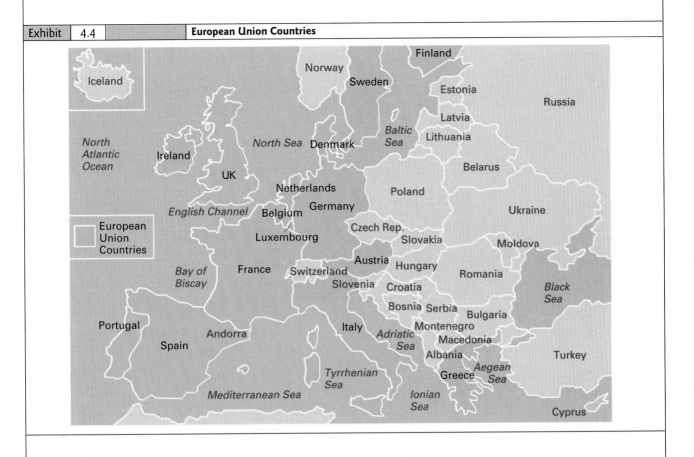

currency, the euro.[7] After 2002, the mark, the lira, and other currencies of participating countries will no longer be used. (The four countries currently not in the EMU are Greece, Sweden, United Kingdom, and Denmark.)

The primary motivation for the joining of these European nations was to allow them to reassert their economic position against the strength of the United States and Japan. Working in separate countries with barriers against one another, European industries couldn't develop the efficiency of American and Japanese businesses. As the EU continues to evolve, it continues to assert its economic power in one of the world's richest markets. European businesses will continue to play an important role in the global economy. For instance, Unilever PLC of the United Kingdom is a powerful force in consumer products (look back at the "Who Owns What" quiz), DaimlerChrysler AG of Germany is a solid competitor in automobiles, and Nokia of Finland is a dominant player in wireless technology.

North American Free Trade Agreement (NAFTA) When agreements in key issues covered by the **North American Free Trade Agreement (NAFTA)** were reached by the Mexican, Canadian, and U.S. governments on August 12, 1992, a vast economic bloc was created. Since 1994, when NAFTA went into effect, and 1998 (the most recent year for complete statistics), U.S. trade with Canada increased 56 percent to $329.9 billion (almost $1 billion per day), and U.S. trade with Mexico increased 113 percent to $173.4 billion.[8] Eliminating the barriers to

North American Free Trade Agreement (NAFTA)

An agreement among the Mexican, Canadian, and U.S. governments in which barriers to free trade have been eliminated.

Consumers such as these Mexican shoppers as well as their counterparts in Canada and the United States have benefited from trade increases among the three countries that resulted from the implementation of NAFTA in 1994, which created a huge economic trading bloc.

free trade (tariffs, import licensing requirements, customs user fees) has resulted in a strengthening of the economic power of all three countries.

Other Latin American nations are moving to become part of free-trade blocs. Colombia, Mexico, and Venezuela led the way when, in 1994, all three governments signed an economic pact eliminating import duties and tariffs. Now 36 countries in the Caribbean region, South America, and Central America are negotiating a Free Trade Area of the Americas (FTAA) trade agreement.[9] Already in existence is another free-trade bloc known as the Southern Cone Common Market, or Mercosur.[10] (See Exhibit 4.5.) As new trading blocs are created in this part of the globe, we're likely to see changes in how organizations are managed, particularly those with significant business interests in these regions.

Exhibit	4.5

Mercosur Members

Mercosur Members
Argentina
Brazil
Bolivia
Chile
Paraguay
Uruguay

Source: Based on C. Sims, "Chile Will Enter a Big South American Free-Trade Bloc," *New York Times*, June 26, 1996, p. C2.

Association of Southeast Asian Nations (ASEAN) The **ASEAN** is a trading alliance of 10 Southeast Asian nations. (See Exhibit 4.6.) During the years ahead, Asia, and particularly the Southeast Asian region, promises to be one of the fastest-growing economic regions of the world. It will be an increasingly important regional economic and political alliance whose impact eventually could rival that of both NAFTA and the EU.

Other regions around the world continue to look at the creation of regional trading alliances. For instance, nine African nations (Djibouti, Egypt, Kenya, Madagascar, Malawi, Mauritius, Sudan, Zambia, and Zimbabwe) have combined into a free trade area that encompasses 170 million people. In addition, these nine countries are members of the 21-nation Common Market for Eastern and Southern Africa (COMESA). These countries have pledged to permit the free flow of skilled labor by 2004, to allow the free movement of citizens by 2014, and to establish a common currency by 2025.[11]

DIFFERENT TYPES OF GLOBAL ORGANIZATIONS

Companies doing business globally aren't anything new. Siemens, Remington, and Singer, for instance, were selling their products in many countries in the late 1800s. Ford Motor Company set up its first overseas sales branch in France in 1908. By the 1920s, other companies, including Fiat, Unilever, and Royal Dutch/Shell, had gone multinational. But it wasn't until the mid-1960s that **multinational corporations (MNCs)** became commonplace. These organizations—which maintain significant operations in multiple countries but are managed from a base in the home country—inaugurated the rapid growth in international trade. With its focus on control from the home country, the MNC is characteristic of the ethnocentric attitude. Some examples of companies that can be considered MNCs include Sony, Deutsche Bank AG, ExxonMobil, and Merrill

Association of Southeast Asian Nations (ASEAN)

A trading alliance of 10 Southeast Asian nations.

multinational corporation (MNC)

A company that maintains significant operations in multiple countries but manages them from a base in the home country.

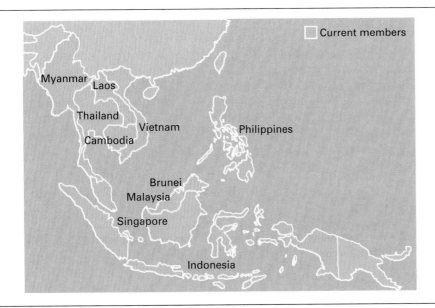

Exhibit	4.6

ASEAN Members

Source: Based on J. McClenahen and T. Clark, "ASEAN at Work," *IW*, May 19, 1997, p. 42.

Wal-Mart learned through experience how to operate as a transnational organization. Although the influence of American culture and the English language are increasing around the world, Wal-Mart needed to tailor both its products and its marketing strategies in order to compete successfully in Argentina. After racking up losses initially, Wal-Mart's Argentine operation has begun to show a profit only after changing everything from the colors of the makeup and the cuts of meat it sells to the width of the aisles and the ceramic tile in its seafood display cases.

transnational corporation (TNC)

A company that maintains significant operations in more than one country but decentralizes management to the local country.

borderless organization

A global type of organization in which artificial geographical barriers are eliminated.

Lynch. Although these companies have considerable global holdings, management decisions with company-wide implications are made from headquarters in the home country.

Another type of global organization is called the **transnational corporation (TNC)**—a company that maintains significant operations in more than one country but decentralizes management to the local country. This type of organization doesn't attempt to replicate its domestic successes by managing foreign operations from its home country. Instead, nationals typically are hired to run operations in each country, and marketing strategies for each country are tailored to that country's unique characteristics. This type of global organization reflects the polycentric attitude. For example, Switzerland-based Nestlé, the world's largest food company, can be described as a transnational. With operations in almost every country on the globe, its managers match the company's products to its consumers. In parts of Europe, Nestlé sells products that are not available in the United States or Latin America. Another example of a transnational is Frito-Lay, a division of PepsiCo, which markets a Dorito chip in the British market that differs in both taste and texture from the U.S. and Canadian version. Many consumer companies manage their global businesses as TNCs because they must adapt their products and services to meet the needs of the local markets.

Because of the increasingly global environment, many large, well-known companies are moving to more effectively globalize their management structure by eliminating structural divisions that impose artificial geographical barriers. This type of global organization is called a **borderless organization**. The borderless organization approaches global business from a geocentric attitude. For example, IBM dropped its organizational structure based on country and reorganized into 14 industry groups. Bristol-Myers Squibb changed its consumer business to become more aggressive in international sales and created a management position responsible for worldwide consumer medicines such as Bufferin and Excedrin. And Spain's Telefonica eliminated the geographic divisions between its headquarters in Madrid and its widespread phone companies. The company will be organized, instead, along business lines such as Internet services, cellular phones, and media operations. Borderless management is an attempt by organizations to increase efficiency and effectiveness in a competitive global marketplace.[12]

Testing...Testing...1,2,3

4. **Describe the three major regional trading alliances including what they are and why they were formed.**

5. **Contrast MNCs, TNCs, and borderless organizations.**

6. **Which global attitude does each of the global organization types represent?**

〉 HOW ORGANIZATIONS GO GLOBAL

How does an organization do business globally? Most proceed through three stages as shown in Exhibit 4.7. Each successive stage requires more investment globally and, thus, entails more risk.

In Stage I, managers make the first push toward going international merely by **exporting** the organization's products to other countries—that is, by making products at home and selling them overseas. In addition, an organization might choose initially to go global by **importing** products, that is, selling products at home that are made overseas. Both exporting and importing are nominal steps toward being a global business involving minimal investment and minimal risk. Most organizations start doing business globally this way. Many of these organizations, especially small businesses, continue with exporting and importing as their approaches to global involvement. For instance, Haribhai's Spice Emporium, a small business in Durban, South Africa, exports spices and rice to customers all over Africa, Europe, and the United States. However, some organizations have built multimillion dollar businesses by importing or exporting. For instance, that's what specialty retailer Pier 1 has done. It imports exotic products for sale in its stores around the world.

In Stage II, managers make more of an investment by committing to sell products in foreign countries or to have them made in foreign factories, but there is still no physical presence of company employees outside the company's home country. Instead, what is typically done on the sales side is sending domestic employees on regular business trips to meet foreign customers or hiring foreign agents or brokers to represent the organization's product line. On the manufacturing side, managers will contract with a foreign firm to produce the organization's products.

Stage III represents the most serious commitment by managers to pursue global markets. As shown in Exhibit 4.7, managers can do this in different ways. **Licensing** and **franchising** are similar approaches since both involve an organization's giving another organization the right to use its brand name, technology,

exporting

An approach to going global that involves making products at home and selling them overseas.

importing

An approach to going global that involves selling products at home that are made overseas.

licensing

An approach to going global by manufacturing organizations that involves giving other organizations the right to use your brand name, technology, or product specifications.

franchising

An approach to going global by service organizations that involves giving other organizations the right to use your brand name, technology, or product specifications.

Exhibit	4.7

How Organizations Go Global

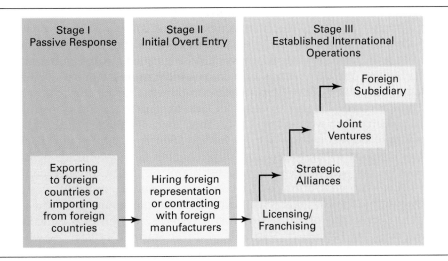

“ M A N A G E R S   S P E A K   O U T ”

Jose Carlos C. DeGuia, General Manager, MicroPhase Enterprise Company, Makati City, Philippines

Describe your job.

I am currently the general manager of MicroPhase Enterprise Company. As a general manager, I set the company direction, objectives, and strategies. I also oversee the day-to-day company operations to ensure our competitiveness in the market.

In what ways do global issues affect your organization?

Due to instability of the U.S. dollar exchange rate, our annual forecast and targets are becoming vague. Prices increase almost every week. Margins are dropping and becoming unacceptable. Also, losses due to the sinking peso are inevitable.

What skills are needed for a manager to be effective today?

An effective manager today must have a vision, should take on challenges, and be flexible enough to act on changes at the speed of a speedboat whether decisions are traditional or alternative.

What global issue do you see as the most challenging for your organization?

The instability of the U.S. dollar exchange rate is a challenge. Also, bringing information technology to a third world market (Philippines) is a challenging issue for our organization.

---

strategic alliances

An approach to going global that involves partnerships between an organization and a foreign company in which both share resources and knowledge in developing new products or building production facilities.

joint venture

An approach to going global that is a specific type of strategic alliance in which the partners agree to form a separate, independent organization for some business purpose.

foreign subsidiary

An approach to going global that involves a direct investment in a foreign country by setting up a separate and independent production facility or office.

or product specifications in return for a lump-sum payment or a fee usually based on sales. The only difference is that licensing is primarily used by manufacturing organizations and franchising is used by service organizations. For example, Thai consumers can enjoy Bob's Big Boy hamburgers, Filipinos can dine on Shakey's Pizza, and Malaysians can consume Schlotzky's deli sandwiches—all because of franchises in these countries. And Anheuser-Busch chose to license the right to brew and market Budweiser beer to other brewers, such as Labatt in Canada, Modelo in Mexico, and Kirin in Japan. **Strategic alliances** are partnerships between an organization and a foreign company in which both share resources and knowledge in developing new products or building production facilities. The partners also share the risks and rewards of this alliance. For example, IBM of the United States, Toshiba of Japan, and Siemens of Germany formed a partnership to develop new generations of computer chips. A specific type of strategic alliance in which the partners agree to form a separate, independent organization for some business purpose is called a **joint venture**. For example, Hewlett-Packard has had numerous joint ventures with various suppliers around the globe to develop different components for its computer equipment. These partnerships provide a fast and less expensive way for companies to compete globally than would doing it on their own. Finally, in Stage III, managers can make a direct investment in a foreign country by setting up a **foreign subsidiary**, a separate and independent production facility or office. This subsidiary can be managed as an MNC (domestic control), a TNC (foreign control), or as a borderless organization (global control). As you can probably guess, this arrangement involves the greatest commitment of resources and poses the greatest amount of risk. For instance, Motorola invested $2 billion in a semiconductor-manufacturing facility in Scotland in an attempt to bolster its wireless telecommunications business.

> ## MANAGING IN A GLOBAL ENVIRONMENT

Assume for a moment that you're an American manager going to work for a branch of a global organization in a foreign country. You know that your environment will differ from the one at home, but how? What should you be looking for?

Any manager who finds himself or herself in a foreign country faces new challenges. In this section, we'll look at some challenges and offer guidelines for responding. Although our discussion is presented through the eyes of a U.S. manager, our analytical framework could be used by any manager regardless of national origin who has to manage in a foreign environment.

THE LEGAL-POLITICAL ENVIRONMENT

Managers in the United States are accustomed to stable legal and political systems. Changes are slow, and legal and political procedures are well established. Elections are held at regular intervals. Even changes in political parties after an election do not produce any radical or quick transformations. The stability of laws governing the actions of individuals and institutions allows for accurate predictions. The same can't be said for all nations. Managers in a global organization must stay informed of the specific laws in countries where they do business.

Also, some countries have a history of unstable governments. Some South American and African countries have had six governments in as many years. With new government have come new rules. The goal of one government may be to nationalize the country's key industries whereas the goal of the next may be to encourage free enterprise. Managers of businesses in these countries face dramatically greater uncertainty as a result of political instability. Political interference is also a fact of life in many Asian countries. For instance, many large businesses have postponed doing business in China because the Chinese government still has too much control over what these organizations do and how they do it. As Chinese consumers gain more power, that governmental attitude is likely to change.

The legal-political environment doesn't have to be unstable or revolutionary to be a concern to managers. Just the fact that a country's laws and political system differ from that of the United States is important. Managers must recognize these differences if they hope to understand the constraints under which they operate and the opportunities that exist.

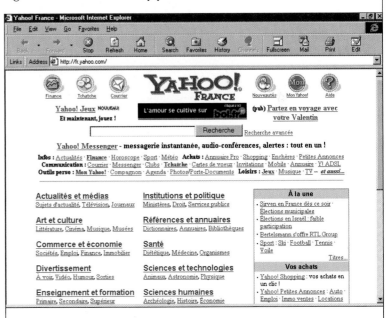

The clash of the Internet's global, borderless nature and local laws was played out in a French courtroom as Yahoo! defended itself against two antiracism groups that sued to prevent Nazi memorabilia and other content deemed racist from being seen in France on Yahoo's Web auction site. It is illegal in France to sell any type of Nazi objects. The company added warnings to some Web pages with sensitive material, alerting French surfers that they risked breaking French law by viewing them.

? THINKING CRITICALLY ABOUT ETHICS

Foreign countries often have lax product-labeling laws. As a product manager for a U.S. drug company, you're responsible for the profitability of a new drug whose side effects can be serious, although not fatal. Adding this information to the label or even putting an informational insert into the package will add significantly to the product's cost, threatening profitability margins. What will you do? Why? What factors will influence your decision?

THE ECONOMIC ENVIRONMENT

The global manager has economic concerns that the manager who operates in a single country doesn't have. Three of the most obvious are fluctuating currency exchange rates, inflation rates, and diverse tax policies.

A global firm's profits can vary dramatically depending on the strength of its home currency and the currencies of the countries in which it operates. Any devaluation of a nation's currency significantly affects the level of a company's profits. The strength of a foreign nation's currency can also affect managers' decisions.

Economic inflation rates can vary widely in different regions of the world. For example, in late 1999, the annual inflation rate in Turkey had decreased to 100 percent. Between September 1999 and April 2000, the exchange rate for Turkish lira went from 462,000 per U.S. dollar to 611,000! Even larger and more industrialized countries such as Brazil and Russia have suffered from high inflation rates. For instance, it has sometimes reached 2,700 percent in Brazil. The inflation rate influences prices paid for raw materials, labor, and other supplies. In addition, it affects the price that a company can charge for its goods and services.

Finally, diverse tax policies are a major worry for a global manager. Some host countries are more restrictive than the organization's home country. Others are far more lenient. About the only certainty is that tax rules differ from country to country. Managers need exact information on the various tax rules in countries in which they operate to minimize their business's overall tax obligation. But tax rules aren't the only economic information managers want to monitor. They also want to stay on top of the other economic factors we described—currency exchange rates and inflation rates.

THE CULTURAL ENVIRONMENT

The final global area of concern to managers is the cultural differences between nations. As we know from Chapter 3, organizations have different cultures. Countries have cultures too, as anthropologists have long been telling us. Like organizational culture, **national culture** is the values and attitudes shared by individuals from a specific country that shape their behavior and their beliefs about what is important.[13]

Which is more important to a manager—national culture or organizational culture? For example, is an IBM facility in Germany more likely to reflect German culture or IBM's corporate culture? Research indicates that national culture has a greater effect on employees than does their organization's culture.[14] German employees at an IBM facility in Munich will be influenced more by German culture than by IBM's culture. This means that as influential as organizational culture may be on managerial practice, national culture is even more influential.

Testing...Testing...1,2,3

7. **Describe the first two stages of global involvement.**

8. **Contrast the various approaches to Stage III of global involvement.**

9. **What are the legal-political and economic factors that managers need to be aware of in managing globally?**

national culture

The values and attitudes shared by individuals from a specific country that shape their behavior and beliefs about what is important.

Legal, political, and economic differences among countries are fairly obvious. The Japanese manager who works in the United States or his or her American counterpart in Japan can get information about a country's laws or tax policies without too much difficulty. Getting information about a country's cultural differences isn't quite that easy! The primary reason is that it's hard for natives to explain their country's unique cultural characteristics to someone else. If you're an American raised in the United Sates, how would you characterize U.S. culture? In other words, what are Americans like? Think about it for a moment and then see how many of the points in Exhibit 4.8 you identified.

National culture plays a large role in employee behavior. For example, the definition of sexual harassment to which U.S. firms must adhere is a relatively new concept in France, where male and female employees, like these colleagues enjoying a lunch break, typically greet one another every morning with a peck on both cheeks. A woman can bring harassment charges in France but only against an offending superior (not an equal or subordinate), and she must prove her career has been harmed by her refusal of sexual advances.

The most valuable framework to help managers better understand differences between national cultures was developed by Geert Hofstede. His research showed that national culture had a major impact on employees' work-related values and attitudes. In fact, it explained more of the differences than did age, sex, profession, or organizational position. More important, Hofstede identified four dimensions of national culture: (1) individualism versus collectivism, (2) power distance, (3) uncertainty avoidance, and (4) quantity versus quality of life.[15] We don't have the space to review Hofstede's entire results for the 40 countries studied, although we provide 12 examples in Exhibit 4.9.

	Exhibit	4.8
Americans are very *informal*. They tend to treat people alike even when there are great differences in age or social standing.	**What Are Americans Like?**	

Americans are very *informal*. They tend to treat people alike even when there are great differences in age or social standing.

Americans are *direct*. They don't talk around things. To some foreigners, this may appear as abrupt or even rude behavior.

Americans are *competitive*. Some foreigners may find Americans assertive or overbearing.

Americans are *achievers*. They like to keep score, whether at work or at play. They emphasize accomplishments.

Americans are *independent* and *individualistic*. They place a high value on freedom and believe that individuals can shape and control their own destiny.

Americans are *questioners*. They ask a lot of questions, even of someone they have just met. Many of these questions may seem pointless ("How ya' doin'?") or personal ("What kind of work do you do?").

Americans *dislike silence*. They would rather talk about the weather than deal with silence in a conversation.

Americans *value punctuality*. They keep appointment calendars and live according to schedules and clocks.

Americans *value cleanliness*. They often seem obsessed with bathing, eliminating body odors, and wearing clean clothes.

Source: Based on M. Ernest (ed.), *Predeparture Orientation Handbook: For Foreign Students and Scholars Planning to Study in the United States* (Washington, DC: U.S. Information Agency, Bureau of Cultural Affairs, 1984), pp. 103–05; A. Bennett, "American Culture Is Often a Puzzle for Foreign Managers in the U.S.," *Wall Street Journal*, February 12, 1986, p. 29; "Don't Think Our Way's the Only Way," *The Pryor Report*, February 1988, p. 9; and B.J. Wattenberg, "The Attitudes behind American Exceptionalism," *U.S. News & World Report*, August 7, 1989, p. 25.

Exhibit 4.9

Examples of Hofstede's Cultural Dimensions

Country	Individualism/ Collectivism	Power Distance	Uncertainty Avoidance	Quantity of Life[a]
Australia	Individual	Small	Moderate	Strong
Canada	Individual	Moderate	Low	Moderate
England	Individual	Small	Moderate	Strong
France	Individual	Large	High	Weak
Greece	Collective	Large	High	Moderate
Italy	Individual	Moderate	High	Strong
Japan	Collective	Moderate	High	Strong
Mexico	Collective	Large	High	Strong
Singapore	Collective	Large	Low	Moderate
Sweden	Individual	Small	Low	Weak
United States	Individual	Small	Low	Strong
Venezuela	Collective	Large	High	Strong

Source: Based on G. Hofstede, "Motivation, Leadership, and Organization: Do American Theories Apply Abroad?" *Organizational Dynamics*, Summer 1980, pp. 42–63.
[a]A weak quantity score is equivalent to high quality of life.

individualism

A cultural dimension that describes when people are supposed to look after their own interests and those of their immediate family.

collectivism

A cultural dimension that describes when people expect others in their group to look after them and to protect them when they are in trouble.

power distance

A cultural measure of the extent to which a society accepts the unequal distribution of power in institutions and organizations.

uncertainty avoidance

A cultural measure of the degree to which people tolerate risk and unconventional behavior.

Individualism versus Collectivism **Individualism** refers to a loosely knit social framework in which people are supposed to look after their own interests and those of their immediate family. They can do so because of the large amount of freedom that an individualistic society allows its citizens. The opposite is **collectivism**, which is characterized by a tight social framework in which people expect others in groups of which they are a part (such as a family or an organization) to look after them and to protect them when they are in trouble. In exchange, they feel they owe absolute loyalty to the group.

Hofstede found that the degree of individualism in a country was closely related to that country's wealth. Wealthier countries such as the United States, Great Britain, and the Netherlands are very individualistic. Poorer countries such as Colombia and Pakistan are very collectivistic.

Power Distance People naturally vary in terms of physical and intellectual abilities. This variation, in turn, creates differences in wealth and power. How does a society deal with those inequalities? Hofstede used the term **power distance** as a measure of the extent to which a society accepts the fact that power in institutions and organizations is distributed unequally. A large power distance society accepts wide differences in power in organizations. Employees show a great deal of respect for those in authority. Titles, rank, and status carry a lot of weight. When negotiating in large power distance countries, companies find that it helps to send representatives with titles at least as impressive as those with whom they are bargaining. In contrast, a low power distance society plays down inequalities as much as possible. Superiors still have authority, but employees are not afraid of or in awe of the boss.

Uncertainty Avoidance **Uncertainty avoidance** is a cultural measure of the degree to which people tolerate risk and unconventional behavior. We live in a world of uncertainty. The future is largely unknown and always will be.

Societies respond to this uncertainty in different ways. Some socialize their members into accepting it. People in such societies are relatively comfortable with risks. They're also relatively tolerant of behavior and opinions that differ from their own because they don't feel threatened by them. Hofstede describes such societies as having low uncertainty avoidance.

A society that's high in uncertainty avoidance is characterized by a high level of anxiety among its people, which manifests itself in nervousness, high stress, and aggressiveness. Because people in these cultures feel threatened by uncertainty and ambiguity, political and social mechanisms are created to provide security and to reduce risk. Organizations in these cultures are likely to have formal rules and little tolerance for unusual ideas and behaviors.

Although it is an economically rich country, Japan scores high on collectivism. This trait helps explain the popularity and success of teams at Japanese automotive factories.

Quantity versus Quality of Life The fourth cultural dimension, like individualism and collectivism, is a dichotomy. Some cultures emphasize the **quantity of life** and value things such as assertiveness and the acquisition of money and material goods. Other cultures that emphasize **quality of life** value relationships and show sensitivity and concern for the welfare of others.

quantity of life

A national culture attribute describing the extent to which societal values are characterized by assertiveness and materialism.

quality of life

A national culture attribute that reflects the emphasis placed upon relationships and concern for others.

A Guide for U.S. Managers We used the United States as a point of reference, so we'll conclude this section by reviewing how the United States ranked on Hofstede's four dimensions and considering how a U.S. manager working in another country might be able to use Hofstede's research findings. Comparing 40 countries on these four dimensions, Hofstede found U.S. culture to be highest among all countries on individualism, below average on power distance, well below average on uncertainty avoidance, and well above average on quantity of life. These conclusions are consistent with how the world views the United States. That is, the United States is seen as stressing the individualistic ethic, having a representative government with democratic ideals, being relatively free from threats of uncertainty, and having a capitalistic economy that values and rewards aggressiveness and materialism. In which countries are U.S. managers likely to fit best? Which are likely to create the biggest adjustment problems? All we have to do is identify those countries that are most and least like the United States on the four dimensions. For instance, the United States is strongly individualistic but low on power distance. This same pattern was exhibited by Great Britain, Australia, Canada, the Netherlands, and New Zealand. Those least similar to the United States on those dimensions were Venezuela, Colombia, Pakistan, Singapore, and the Philippines. The United States scored low on uncertainty avoidance and high on quantity of life. This same pattern was shown by Ireland, Great Britain, the Philippines, Canada, New Zealand, Australia, India, and South Africa. Those least similar to the United States on these dimensions were Chile and Portugal. These results empirically support what many of us suspected—that the U.S. manager

culture shock

The feelings of confusion, disorientation, and emotional upheaval caused by being immersed in a new culture.

transferred to London, Toronto, Melbourne, or a similar Anglo city would have to make the fewest adjustments. In addition, the results further identify the countries in which **culture shock** (the feelings of confusion, disorientation, and emotional upheaval caused by being immersed in a new culture) is likely to be greatest and the need to modify one's managerial style to be the most critical.

Testing...Testing...1,2,3

10. **Contrast national culture and organizational culture.**

11. **Describe Hofstede's four dimensions of national culture.**

12. **How can an understanding of Hofstede's four dimensions help managers be more effective in managing in a global environment?**

> **IS A GLOBAL ASSIGNMENT FOR YOU?**

How do organizations decide who will be sent on global assignments? Typically the decision is based on employee selection criteria that are influenced by the company's experience and commitment to global operations. Exhibit 4.10 lists several specific criteria that have been used by global organizations from Australia, the United States, Great Britain, Canada, France, New Zealand, and Asia in global employee selection decisions. Obviously, technical skills are important for success in global assignments, but other skills such as language fluency, flexibility, and family adaptability are needed as well. You can see by the list that both technical and human factors are usually considered. Organizations that don't consider both are likely to experience a failure rate in sending employees on global assignment.[16]

Exhibit 4.10 — **Criteria for Making Global Employee Selection Decisions Ranked in Order of Importance**	Australian Managers N = 47	Expatriate Managers[a] N = 52	Asian Managers N = 15
1. Ability to adapt	1	1	2
2. Technical competence	2	3	1
3. Spouse and family adaptability	3	2	4
4. Human relations skills	4	4	3
5. Desire to serve overseas	5	5	5
6. Previous overseas experience	6	7	7
7. Understanding of host country culture	7	6	6
8. Academic qualifications	8	8	8
9. Knowledge of language of country	9	9	9
10. Understanding of home country culture	10	10	10

Source: R.J. Stone, "Expatriate Selection and Failure," *Human Resource Planning* 14, No. 1 (1991), p. 10. Used with permission.
[a]American, British, Canadian, French, New Zealand, or Australian managers working for a multinational corporation outside their home countries.
1 = most important
10 = least important

Once an employee has been selected as a good candidate for a global managerial position, there are several individual and organizational factors that determine whether he or she can effectively adjust to a global assignment. (See Exhibit 4.11.)

As the figure shows, there are two major types of adjustments individuals make when they go to another country: preassignment adjustment and in-country adjustment. The preassignment adjustment period is affected by a number of factors. For one thing, it's important that an individual has accurate expectations of the realities of the job and of the country before taking a global assignment. A person's expectations are affected by the level of predeparture training and previous experience with the assigned country or similar cultures. Predeparture training including cross-cultural seminars or workshops that provide information about the culture and work life can help make the transition easier. Also, the adjustment will be easier for a person who has had previous experience with the culture of the assigned country (or one like it) than it will be for a person who has not.

There also are certain things that an organization can do to make the preassignment adjustment easier. For instance, the organization should have appropriate selection criteria and processes in place for choosing individuals for global assignments. By carefully selecting individuals for global assignments, an organization can alleviate many of the transition problems.

Once a person has been relocated, there's a period of in-country adjustment that also involves individual and organizational factors. Individual factors include the person's abilities to (1) remain upbeat, positive, and productive even

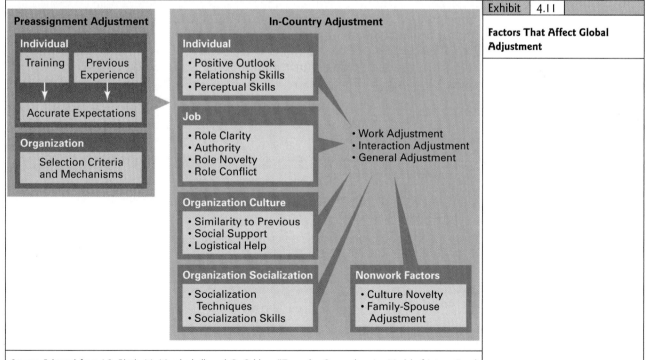

Exhibit 4.11

Factors That Affect Global Adjustment

Source: Adapted from J.S. Black, M. Mendenhall, and G. Oddou, "Toward a Comprehensive Model of International Adjustment: An Integration of Multiple Theoretical Perspectives," *Academy of Management Review*, April 1991, p. 303.

in new situations that may be stressful, (2) interact effectively with host country co-workers, and (3) accurately perceive and adapt to the country's cultural values and norms.

Organizational factors easing the transition include the job that the person will be doing, the organization's culture, and the level of organizational socialization. The important job factors for successful adjustment to a new country are related to the clarity of job expectations, the authority the individual has to make decisions, familiarity with the work activities, and the amount of role conflict that exists. If these job factors are not properly considered, a person faces a long period of adjustment or maybe never adjusting.

Organizational culture factors that should be considered for successful transition include how similar the organizational culture is to what the individual has experienced, the social support provided by the current organizational culture, and the amount of help provided by the organization to make the adjustment easier. Again, if these factors aren't properly addressed, a transferred person may not adjust as quickly or effectively to being a productive employee.

organizational socialization

The process that employees go through to adapt to an organization's culture.

Another factor that determines the success of an individual's adjustment to a global assignment is his or her skills of **organizational socialization**, the process that employees go through to adapt to an organization's culture. The cultural transition will be easier if socialization processes are in place and the individual can quickly learn "the way things are done around here."

Finally, it's important to note that nonwork considerations also influence how effectively an individual adjusts to a global assignment. These include how an individual personally adjusts to the unfamiliar culture and how the individual's family and spouse adjust. The family-spouse adjustment can be a major source of problems. The realities of living in a different culture, where simple tasks such as shopping for groceries, driving a car, or going to a movie can be logistical challenges, create stresses for individuals and their families. Culture shock is a real and normal reaction. If transferred individuals can make it through that initial period of adjustment, studies have shown that most people effectively and comfortably adjust to a new culture after about four to six months.[17]

Testing...Testing...1,2,3

13. **What selection criteria might companies use in determining which individuals to send on global assignments?**

14. **What types of preassignment adjustments does an individual going on a global assignment have to make?**

15. **What types of in-country adjustment does an individual going on a global assignment have to make?**

Managers Respond to "A Manager's Dilemma"

Photo not available.

Douglas Heatherly

Global Operations Planning Director, DuPont, Wilmington, Delaware

The first thing a manager should do is to work on his or her own perspective. Meet with colleagues who have worked in Asia (and specifically Indonesia) to gain their perspectives of work and social customs. Visit Indonesia and take some time to learn something of its country and people. Attend cross-cultural workshops to explore the similarities and differences of the cultures. Most importantly, focus on a common understanding of business goals so that everyone can find a winning position.

Find things you like in the other culture so you can focus on this instead of on the things that are different. Find ways each culture celebrates success and do this in your joint meeting. Learn some of each other's language so that you can acknowledge each other, order from a menu, or make a phone call through an operator. Above all else, it's important to remember you are not trying to convert the Asians to Mexico's culture, nor are you adopting the Asian culture, but rather you are seeking a working relationship and a way your company can earn a profit from the venture.

Kenneth Toh Eng Kian

Senior Manager, Program Promotions/Creative Services, Singapore Cable Vision, Singapore

It's of foremost importance for someone in Gonzalez's position to keep an open mind. His main goals should be to gain acceptance among his colleagues as well as to set the stage for conveying key business goals.

In order to gain acceptance by others, he must first be cognizant of his personal prejudices and learn to put them aside when dealing with individuals of other cultures. Rather than focusing on the differences, he is better off highlighting the similarities in both cultures—their love of music, dance, and spicy food, for example—and their shared professional goals. In addition, by keeping an open mind in this exchange, he will be able to gain invaluable cross-cultural insights, helping him better understand the subtleties inherent to the decision-making process in international trading.

Differences in opinion are certain to arise. However, if he has been able to successfully build a foundation of shared interests and goals by downplaying the differences, he is more likely to be able to rally people around him to achieve the tasks at hand.

Chapter Summary

This summary is organized by the chapter-opening objectives found on p. 84.

1. Competitors and markets are no longer defined by national borders. New competitors can suddenly appear from anywhere in the world. New markets are opening up in countries around the world. Managers must think globally if their organizations are going to succeed over the long term.

2. The three different global attitudes are ethnocentric, polycentric, and geocentric. An ethnocentric attitude is the parochialistic belief that the best work approaches and practices are those of the home country. A polycentric attitude is the view that the managers in the host country know the best work practices and approaches for running their business. The geocentric attitude is a world-oriented view that focuses on using the best approaches and people from anywhere around the globe.

3. The European Union (EU) is a 15-nation trading alliance whose purpose is to have common customs duties, unified industrial and commercial policies, and a common monetary currency. NAFTA (North American Free Trade Agreement) is a trading alliance between the United States, Mexico, and Canada. ASEAN (Association of Southeast Asian Nations) is a 10-nation trading alliance in one of the fastest-growing economic regions in the world.

4. Regional trading alliances create more powerful economic entities. Many countries have joined these alliances in order to compete more effectively. For instance, countries joined the EU to compete more aggressively against such economically powerful countries as the United States and Japan.

5. Multinational corporations (MNCs) have significant operations in two or more countries but are managed from the home country. Transnationals (TNCs) also have significant operations in multiple countries but decentralize management to the local (host) countries. Borderless organizations are a global type of organization that has eliminated artificial geographical barriers.

6. Organizations typically go global in three stages. Stage I is exporting to or importing from foreign countries. Stage II involves hiring foreign representatives to sell the organization's products or contracting with foreign manufacturers to make the organization's products. Stage III is the most serious commitment to global business and involves licensing, franchising, strategic alliances, joint ventures, or foreign subsidiaries.

7. The four primary dimensions of national culture are individualism versus collectivism, power distance, uncertainty avoidance, and quantity versus quality of life. Individualism refers to a loosely knit social framework in which people are supposed to look after their own interests and those of their immediate family. A collectivistic society is characterized by a tight social framework in which people expect others in groups of which they are a part to look after them and to protect them in times of trouble. Power distance is a measure of the extent to which a society accepts the fact that power in institutions and organizations is distributed unequally. Uncertainty avoidance is a measure of the degree to which people tolerate risk and unconventional behavior. Finally, cultures that emphasize quantity of life value things such as assertiveness and the acquisition of money and material goods. Those that emphasize quality of life value relationships and show sensitivity and concern for the welfare of others.

8. U.S. culture is characterized as being high on individualism, small power distance, low uncertainty avoidance, and strong quantity of life.

9. A manager on global assignment faces two periods of adjustment: the time before going to a foreign country and the time while in the new country. Both individual and organizational factors influence how successfully a manager adjusts to global assignments.

Thinking About Management Issues

1. What are the managerial implications of a borderless organization?

2. Can the Hofstede framework presented in this chapter be used to guide managers in a Thai hospital or a government agency in Venezuela? Explain.

3. Compare the advantages and drawbacks of the various approaches to going global.

4. What challenges might confront a Mexican manager transferred to the United States to manage a manufacturing plant in Tucson, Arizona? Will these be the same for a U.S. manager transferred to Guadalajara? Explain.

5. In what ways do you think global factors have changed the way organizations select and train managers? What impact might the Internet have on this? Explain.

You're the manager of new market development for Ralston Purina pet foods. Because of perceived market opportunities, your company's top managers are considering whether to make a major push into Mexico, Finland, and the Philippines. One of the major issues on which they want information is the status of regional trading alliances affecting these countries. Using the Internet, research whether these countries are part of regional trading alliances. If they do belong to such an alliance, compile a separate one-page report on each alliance for your managers.

The executive team would also like specific economic, political-legal, and cultural information on each country that they're considering. Again, using the Internet, compile a separate one-page report on each country covering this information.

myPHLIP Companion Web Site

myPHLIP **(www.prenhall.com/myphlip)** *is a fully customizable homepage that ties students and faculty to text-specific resources.*
- *For students*, myPHLIP *provides an online study guide tied chapter-by-chapter to the text—current events and Internet exercises, lecture notes, downloadable software, the Career Center, the Writing Center, Ask the Tutor, and more.*
- *For faculty*, myPHLIP *provides a syllabus tool that allows you to manage content, communicate with students, and upload personal resources.*

Working Together: A Team-Based Exercise

Moving to a foreign country isn't easy, no matter how many times you've done it or how receptive you are to new experiences. Successful global organizations are able to identify the best candidates for global assignments, and one of the ways they do this is through individual assessments prior to assigning people to overseas facilities. Form groups of three to five individuals. Each of you represents a different department at Cemex (the company described in the chapter-opening "Manager's Dilemma"). Your newly formed team, the Global Assignment Task Force, has been given the responsibility for developing a global aptitude assessment form for Cemex. Because Cemex is expanding its global operations significantly, it wants to make sure that it's sending the best possible candidates to the various global locations. Your team's assignment is to come up with a rough draft of a global aptitude assessment form for individual employees. Think about what questions you would want to ask candidates for global relocation. Your team's initial rough draft should cover only personal (not organizational) criteria and should be at least one-half page but no longer than one page. Be prepared to present your rough draft to Cemex's top management team—your classmates and professor.

Case Application

On the Rebound—Shooting for Success

Using an exceptionally well-executed game plan, the National Basketball Association (NBA) emerged as the first truly global sports league. The transformation of a once faltering domestic sport into a global commercial success reflected a keen understanding of managing in a global environment. Professional basketball sparked the interest of fans and players around the globe in the mid-1990s, and the NBA cashed in on the game's universal appeal. At one time, if you had asked someone in China what the most popular basketball team was, the answer would have been the "Red Oxen" from Chicago (the Bulls).

The league wanted to be a global entertainment leader and had the resources and capabilities to make it happen. However, that all changed during the 1998–99 season. A brutal contract negotiation with players forced the cancellation of more than one-third of the league's games. The lockout frustrated and angered fans. David Stern, NBA commissioner (the top manager), found the league's many global business initiatives grinding to a halt. Then there was the issue of the NBA's most celebrated and revered icon, Michael Jordan. His retirement

NBA Commissioner David Stern.

The NBA's Web site is a constantly changing cornucopia of everything basketball. The NBA is pushing its games and merchandise to fans around the world via their computers. In conjunction with the Internet site, the NBA signed a deal with USA Networks to sell league merchandise on its Home Shopping Network. However, some experts questioned whether fashion trends had moved away from sports apparel altogether and whether global consumers would want NBA merchandise since there are no "local" teams to support. Without the benefit of a globally appealing star such as Michael Jordan, the sales of team apparel and other merchandise are in question.

Another management action that Stern took was the creation and debut of NBA.com TV in November 1999. Created at a cost of $10 million, NBA.com TV is the first television network ever created by a U.S. sports league. As an extension of the league's Web site, NBA.com TV is a big step forward in the NBA's evolution as a global multimedia producer. However, the NBA had to walk a fine line between offering game broadcasts without competing with game telecasts of NBA licensees NBC Networks and Turner Sports Network. Although an immediate impact on the NBA's financial position is unlikely, the long-term potential is great. With this new venture, the league hopes to be positioned for growth of sports programming.

in 1999 took away one of the league's key draws, both as a player and as a celebrity. From its winning streak, the NBA was suddenly struggling. However, Stern wasn't throwing in the towel.

To address the challenges facing the NBA, Commissioner Stern looked at what the league had to offer. What it had was consumer familiarity with basketball both domestically and globally, some talented young players (even if they weren't well known yet), and a recognized image and track record. If those things could be exploited, the NBA might be able to get back in the game.

One of the actions that Stern took was to expand its network of offices globally. Why? The league hoped to reignite the NBA's popularity with global consumers by being visible. However, Stern wasn't ready to commit to franchising teams outside the United States. He explained, "The model is the rock concert. Sell lots of records. Tour occasionally." Latin America seems to be Stern's target for future growth. What is the league doing there? It's opening offices in Brazil and Argentina and conducting publicity blitzes in Mexico for newly signed superstar Eduardo Najera.

Another thing that Stern did was enhance the league's Internet presence through its Web site (www.nba.com).

QUESTIONS

1. What global attitude do you think the NBA and its member teams exhibit? Explain why this attitude has or hasn't contributed to the NBA's global success.

2. What legal-political, economic, and cultural differences might be significant to an NBA team recruiting a player from a foreign country? How would you deal with these differences?

3. Suppose you were hired as a talent scout for one of the NBA's teams and assigned to Shanghai, China. What would you do to make a successful adjustment both personally and professionally?

4. How has the NBA exhibited effective and efficient managing in the global environment?

Sources: "Spin Master Stern," *Latin Trade*, July 2000, p. 32; Information from NBA's Web page (www.nba.com), March 31, 2000; J. Tagliabue, "Hoop Dreams, Fiscal Realities," *New York Times*, March 4, 2000, pp. B1+; D. Roth, "The NBA's Next Shot," *Fortune*, February 21, 2000, pp. 207–16; A. Bianco, "Now It's NBA All-the-Time TV," *Business Week*, November 15, 1999, pp. 241–42; and D. McGraw and M. Tharp, "Going Out on Top," *U.S. News and World Report*, January 25, 1999, p. 55.

Video Case Application

Shopping the World

SMALL BUSINESS 2000

From his home in Tampa, Florida, Jimmy Fand shops the world . . . literally. As the owner of The Tile Connection, North America's largest ceramic tile importer, Fand scours the world for different and unique tile. He got into this business because he found such poor selections and high prices when he was shopping for ceramic tile for a home he was building for his family in Tampa. Growing up in Colombia, where tile is a common fixture in homes and offices, he knew there had to be better choices than he was finding. He decided to go into business himself and search out and import tile from foreign tile manufacturers. His global searches have led him to high-quality tile manufacturers in Spain, Portugal, Colombia, Brazil, Argentina, Japan, Turkey, and other places all around the world.

Fand's background is quite interesting, as well. He came to New York City at the age of 19 and found the city to be a truly exciting place that fulfilled his every expectation of a large cosmopolitan city. And, despite the fact that he was a high school dropout, Fand went on to complete three university degrees. It's likely that his success and confidence in being a global businessperson came from his willingness to absorb new experiences.

Fand is truly comfortable dealing with suppliers from other countries. He speaks numerous languages including Spanish, English, Italian, and Portuguese. He thinks that everyone should look at the global marketplace because of the numerous business opportunities it offers, but he also recognizes that many people are afraid to do business outside the United States. His advice for those who are fearful of taking the plunge into the global marketplace includes: (1) Be cautious about who you deal with. Know your business contacts. (2) Go to trade shows, domestically and internationally. Get to know others within your industry. (3) Do your homework. Know your products and know the pricing. Fand goes on to say that after you've done your research, don't be afraid to weed out unacceptable business partners. After all, your business image and reputation are at stake. You wouldn't want to jeopardize those by accepting shoddy products or services.

QUESTIONS

1. Would you describe Jimmy Fand as parochialistic? Why or why not?

2. Suppose that you were looking to locate ceramic tile manufacturers in an Asian country from whom you could possibly import tile. What information would you want about the country before doing business there?

3. What do you think about Fand's advice for doing business globally? Would you add anything to his list? Be specific.

Source: Based on *Small Business 2000, Show 405*.

Answers To "Who Owns What" Quiz

1. c. United Kingdom

   Ben & Jerry's Ice Cream was purchased by Unilever, PLC in April 2000.

2. d. French

   Bic Pen Company is a part of Société BIC S.A.

3. b. Switzerland

   PowerBar was purchased by Swiss giant Nestlé in 2000.

4. a. France

   RCA television sets are produced by Thomson Multimedia SA, a French company.

5. d. United Kingdom

   Skippy peanut butter is a product of BestFoods, which Unilever PLC purchased in 2000.

6. a. American (United States)

   Godiva Chocolates are a business division of Campbell Soup Company.

7. b. United Kingdom

   Vaseline is a product of Unilever PLC.

8. c. United States

   Braun electric shavers are a part of the Gillette Company.

9. c. Canada

   Greyhound Bus Lines is a division of Canadian company, Laidlaw Industries.

10. a. United Kingdom

    Burger King is a division of Diageo PLC.

After reading and studying this chapter, you should be able to:

1. Explain the classical and socioeconomic views of social responsibility.

2. List the arguments for and against business's being socially responsible.

3. Differentiate between social obligation, social responsiveness, and social responsibility.

4. Explain the relationship between corporate social responsibility and economic performance.

5. Describe values-based management and how it's related to organizational culture.

6. Explain what the "greening" of management is and how organizations are "going green."

7. Differentiate between the four views of ethics.

8. Identify the factors that affect ethical behavior.

9. Discuss various ways organizations can improve the ethical behavior of their employees.

A MANAGER'S DILEMMA

With a name like Digital Mafia Entertainment (www.digitalmafia.com), you might question a company's commitment to social responsibility. Yet, the name of Darien Dash's company, DME (Digital Mafia Entertainment) Interactive Holdings, Inc., in no way reflects his strong commitment to social responsibility.[1]

Dash started DME in 1994 when he realized that large cable companies weren't committed to bringing digital services to urban communities. In his job as vice president of sales for Digital Music Xpress, which provided CD-quality music through a regular cable box, Dash was repeatedly rejected by upper-level managers when he suggested bringing the service to inner cities. So he left the company and formed DME. His mission is to expand the hardware and software infrastructure of minority communities. Today DME is a total Internet services company based in Englewood Cliffs, New Jersey. Its employees provide network design, e-commerce, Web site maintenance, and advertising for a variety of clients including HBO Home Video, the New York Knicks, Lugz, and MSBET. As the company has evolved into a well-rounded information technology company, Dash's vision has remained the same: "expanding the hardware and software infrastructure within minority communities." Doing that, however, hasn't been easy.

Social Responsibility and Managerial Ethics

5

Although wiring inner cities is an admirable social goal and one to which Dash is steadfastly committed, it's not been the quickest way to generate revenues. Like many new businesses, DME initially didn't have sufficient cash flow to pay employees and to develop important business relationships. To pay the bills, Dash began consulting with other companies on how best to leverage multimedia and Internet technology. Soon the Web development side of the business was bringing in much-needed cash flow. Now that Dash has resolved this particular managerial worry, he would like to build a values-based organization. Put yourself in his position. What would you do to develop values that all DME employees could share?

WHAT WOULD YOU DO?

Helping your organization develop shared values that can act as guides for managerial action is just one example of the types of ethical and social responsibility issues with which managers may have to cope as they plan, organize, lead, and control. As managers go about their business, social factors can and do influence their actions. In this chapter, we'll introduce you to the often complicated issues involved with social responsibility and managerial ethics. The discussion of these topics is placed at this point in the text to link them to the preceding and following subjects. That is, we'll discover that both social responsibility and ethics are responses to a changing environment and are influenced by organizational culture (Chapter 3). Also, both social responsibility and ethics are important considerations when making decisions (Chapter 6).

> ## WHAT IS SOCIAL RESPONSIBILITY?

Empowered by Internet technology from digital formats such as MP3 and music-swapping Internet services such as Napster, music lovers all over the world obtain and share their favorite recordings for minimal costs. Large global corporations look to lower their costs and be more competitive by locating in countries where human rights are not a high priority and justify it by saying that they're bringing in jobs and helping strengthen the local economies. Automobile manufacturers build enormous, gas-guzzling sport utility vehicles that have the potential to seriously injure people in smaller, more fuel-efficient vehicles because customers want them and are willing to pay the high prices for them. Are these companies being socially responsible? What factors influenced managers' decisions in these situations? Managers now regularly face decisions that have a dimension of social responsibility: Employee relations, philanthropy, pricing, resource conservation, product quality and safety, and doing business in countries that violate human rights are some of the more obvious. How do managers make such decisions? Let's begin by looking at two different perspectives on what it means to be socially responsible.

TWO OPPOSING VIEWS OF SOCIAL RESPONSIBILITY

Few terms have been defined in as many different ways as *social responsibility*. For instance, it's been called "profit making only," "going beyond profit making," "voluntary activities," "concern for the broader social system," and "social responsiveness."[2] A great deal of attention has been focused on the extremes. On one side, there's the classical—or purely economic—view that management's only social responsibility is to maximize profits. On the other side stands the socioeconomic position, which holds that management's responsibility goes well beyond making profits to include protecting and improving society's welfare.

classical view

The view that management's only social responsibility is to maximize profits.

The Classical View The **classical view** holds that management's only social responsibility is to maximize profits. The most outspoken advocate of this approach is economist and Nobel laureate Milton Friedman.[3] He argues that managers' primary responsibility is to operate the business in the best interests of the stockholders (the true owners of a corporation). What are those interests? Friedman contends that stockholders have a single concern: financial return. He also argues that anytime managers decide on their own to spend their organization's resources for the "social good," they are adding to the costs of doing business. These costs have to be passed on to consumers either through higher prices or absorbed by stockholders through a smaller profit returned as dividends. Do note that Friedman is not saying that organizations should *not* be socially responsible; he thinks they should. But the extent of that responsibility is to maximize organizational profits for stockholders.

The Socioeconomic View The **socioeconomic view** is the view that management's social responsibility goes beyond making profits to include protecting and improving society's welfare. This position is based on the belief that society's expectations of business have changed. Corporations are *not* independent entities responsible only to stockholders. They also have a responsibility to the larger society that endorses their creation through various laws and regulations and supports them by purchasing their products and services.

The socioeconomic view that sees social responsibility as including protecting and benefiting society has led the drug manufacturer Merck, for instance, to become a long-term supporter of the Mectizan Donation Program to treat river blindness in Africa. Merck, in fact, is continually one of the top U.S. corporate philanthropists.

In addition, proponents of the socioeconomic view believe that business organizations are not just merely economic institutions. Society accepts and even encourages businesses to become involved in social, political, and legal issues. For instance, proponents of the socioeconomic view would say that Avon Products Inc. was being socially responsible when it initiated its Breast Cancer Awareness Crusade to provide women, particularly those who had limited access to medical care and treatment, with breast cancer education and early detection screening services.[4] And they would say that the educational programs implemented by Brazilian cosmetics manufacturer Natura Cosméticos SA in public primary schools in São Paulo to improve children's literacy and decision-making skills were socially responsible.[5] Why? Through these programs, the managers were protecting and improving society's welfare. More and more organizations around the world are taking their social responsibilities seriously. In fact, a survey of business owners reported that 68 percent would continue socially responsible practices even if they found that the activities were cutting into profits.[6]

socioeconomic view

The view that management's social responsibility goes beyond making profits to include protecting and improving society's welfare.

ARGUMENTS FOR AND AGAINST SOCIAL RESPONSIBILITY

Another way to understand the role that social responsibility plays in influencing how managers make decisions as they plan, organize, lead, and control is by looking at the arguments for and against social responsibility. What are the specific arguments for and against business's assuming social responsibilities? Exhibit 5.1 outlines the major points that have been presented.[7]

How much and what type of social responsibility businesses should pursue continues to be a topic of interest and heated debate. Now is probably a good time to pinpoint exactly what we mean by the term *social responsibility*.

Exhibit 5.1	For	Against
Arguments For and Against Social Responsibility	*Public expectations* Public opinion now supports businesses pursuing economic and social goals *Long-run profits* Socially responsible companies tend to have more secure long-run profits *Ethical obligation* Businesses should be socially responsible because responsible actions are the right thing to do *Public image* Businesses can create a favorable public image by pursuing social goals *Better environment* Business involvement can help solve difficult social problems *Discouragement of further governmental regulation* By becoming socially responsible, businesses can expect less government regulation *Balance of responsibility and power* Businesses have a lot of power and an equally large amount of responsibility is needed to balance against that power *Stockholder interests* Social responsibility will improve a business's stock price in the long run *Possession of resources* Businesses have the resources to support public and charitable projects that need assistance *Superiority of prevention over cures* Businesses should address social problems before they become serious and costly to correct	*Violation of profit maximization* Business is being socially responsible only when it pursues its economic interests *Dilution of purpose* Pursuing social goals dilutes business's primary purpose—economic productivity *Costs* Many socially responsible actions do not cover their costs and someone must pay those costs *Too much power* Businesses have a lot of power already and if they pursue social goals they will have even more *Lack of skills* Business leaders lack the necessary skills to address social issues *Lack of accountability* There are no direct lines of accountability for social actions

FROM OBLIGATIONS TO RESPONSIVENESS

social responsibility

A business firm's obligation, beyond that required by law and economics, to pursue long-term goals that are good for society.

We define **social responsibility** as a business firm's obligation, beyond that required by law and economics, to pursue long-term goals that are good for society.[8] Note that this definition assumes that an organization obeys laws and pursues economic interests. We take as a given that all business firms—those that are considered socially responsible and those that aren't—will obey all relevant laws that society enacts. Also note that this definition views business as a moral agent. In its effort to do good for society, it must differentiate between right and wrong.

We can understand social responsibility better if we compare it to two similar concepts: social obligation and social responsiveness.[9] As Exhibit 5.2 illustrates, **social obligation** is the obligation of a business to meet its economic and legal responsibilities. The organization does the minimum required by law. Following an approach of social obligation, a firm pursues social goals only to the extent that they contribute to its economic goals. This approach is based on the classical view of social responsibility; that is, the business feels its only social duty is to its

social obligation

The obligation of a business to meet its economic and legal responsibilities.

Exhibit 5.2

Levels of Social Involvement

stockholders. In contrast to social obligation, however, both social responsibility and social responsiveness go beyond merely meeting basic economic and legal standards.

Social responsibility adds an ethical imperative to do those things that make society better and not to do those that could make it worse. A socially responsible organization goes beyond what it must do by law or chooses to do only because it makes economic sense to do what it can to help improve society because that's the right, or ethical, thing to do. As Exhibit 5.3 describes, social responsibility requires business to determine what is right or wrong and to make ethical decisions and engage in ethical business activities. A socially responsible organization does what is right because it feels it has a responsibility to act that way. On the other hand, **social responsiveness** refers to the capacity of a firm to adapt to changing societal conditions. The idea of social responsiveness stresses that managers make practical decisions about the societal actions in which they engage.[10] A socially responsive organization acts the way it does because of its desire to satisfy some popular social need. Social responsiveness is guided by social norms. The value of social norms is that they can provide managers with a meaningful guide for decision making. The following example might help make the distinction between responsibility and responsiveness clearer:

> Suppose, for example, that a company makes multiple products and it states its intention to be socially responsible by producing reasonably safe products. Similarly, the same firm is responsive every time it produces an unsafe product: it withdraws the product from the market as soon as the product is found to be unsafe. After say, ten product recalls because of safety concerns, will the firm be recognized as socially responsible? Will the firm be recognized as socially responsive? The likely answers to these questions are "No" to the first, but "Yes" to the second.[11]

social responsiveness

The capacity of a firm to adapt to changing social conditions.

	Social Responsibility	Social Responsiveness
Major consideration	Ethical	Pragmatic
Focus	Ends	Means
Emphasis	Obligation	Responses
Decision framework	Long term	Medium and short term

Exhibit 5.3

Social Responsibility versus Social Responsiveness

Source: Adapted from S.L. Wartick and P.L. Cochran, "The Evolution of the Corporate Social Performance Model," *Academy of Management Review*, October 1985, p. 766.

The preceding organization's decision to continue producing unsafe products, even though it espoused a responsibility to produce reasonably safe products, would make it appear socially irresponsible in the eyes of the public; that is, it wasn't doing the right, or ethical, thing. However, the organization's quick action in withdrawing unsafe products from the market would make it socially responsive because it was responding to what the public demanded it do.

In the United States, a company that meets pollution control standards established by the federal government or does not discriminate against employees over the age of 40 in promotion decisions is meeting its social obligation and nothing more because there are laws mandating these actions. However, when it provides on-site child care facilities for employees, packages products in 100 percent recycled paper, or announces that it will not purchase, process, or sell any tuna caught in association with dolphins, it is being socially responsive. Why? Working parents, environmentalists, and consumers have demanded such actions.

Advocates of social responsiveness believe that the concept replaces philosophical talk with practical action. They see it as a more tangible and achievable objective than social responsibility.[12] Rather than assessing what's good for society in the long term, managers in a socially responsive organization identify the prevailing social norms and then change their social involvement to respond to changing societal conditions. For instance, environmental stewardship seems to be an important social norm at present and many companies are looking at ways to be environmentally responsible. Alcoa of Australia developed a novel way to recycle the used linings of aluminum smelting pots and Denso generates its own electricity and steam at many of its Japanese manufacturing facilities. Other organizations are addressing other popular social issues. For example, large media companies—such as Prentice Hall, McGraw-Hill, the *New York Times*, and the *Washington Post*—are involved in efforts to increase literacy. And other companies such as Reebok International Ltd., Liz Claiborne Inc., and Mattel Inc. have taken steps to address human rights issues in their overseas factories. These are examples of socially responsive actions for today.

Testing...Testing...1,2,3

1. **Contrast the classical and socioeconomic views of social responsibility.**

2. **What are the arguments for and against businesses being socially responsible?**

3. **Differentiate between social obligation, social responsiveness, and social responsibility.**

> ## SOCIAL RESPONSIBILITY AND ECONOMIC PERFORMANCE

In this section, we want to answer the question: How do socially responsible activities affect a company's economic performance? A number of research studies have looked at this question.[13] What have they found?

The majority showed a positive relationship between social involvement and economic performance. For instance, one study found that firms' corporate social performance was positively associated with both *prior* and *future* financial performance.[14] But we should be cautious about making any compelling assumptions from these findings because of methodological questions associated with trying to measure "social responsibility" and "economic performance."[15] Most of these studies determined a company's social performance by analyzing the content of annual reports, citations of social actions in news articles on the company, or public perception "reputation" indexes. Such criteria certainly have drawbacks as reliable measures of social responsibility. Although measures of economic performance (such as net income, return on equity, or per share stock prices) are more objective, they are generally used to indicate only short-term economic performance. It may well be that the impact of social responsibility on a firm's profits—positive or negative—takes a number of years to manifest itself. If there is a time lag, studies that use short-term financial measures are not likely to show valid results. There is also the issue of causation. If, for example, the evidence showed that social involvement and economic performance were positively related, this wouldn't necessarily mean that social involvement *caused* higher economic performance. It very well could be the opposite. That is, it might mean that high profits afforded companies the luxury of being socially involved.[16] These methodological "cautions" shouldn't be taken lightly. In fact, one study found that if the flawed empirical analyses in these studies were "corrected," social responsibility had a neutral impact on a company's financial performance.[17]

The financial services firm Charles Schwab, headquartered in San Francisco, has been cited as among the 100 best corporate citizens of the United States. With its reputation for excellent service to employees and a positive corporate culture, the firm is able to boast that employees come to Schwab "for something more than just the bottom line." At the same time, the firm fulfills its responsibility to its shareholders and customers with solid financial performance.

Another way to look at the issue of social responsibility and economic performance is by evaluating socially conscious mutual stock funds. Typically, these funds use some type of **social screening**, that is, apply social criteria to investment decisions. For instance, these funds usually will not invest in companies that are involved in liquor, gambling, tobacco, nuclear power, weapons, price fixing, or fraud. These mutual funds provide a way for individual investors to support socially responsible companies. Many of these funds (equity, bond, and money market) have outperformed the market average over the last five years.[18] However, because many of these funds invest in technology companies (these types of companies tend to meet the social screens employed), they've certainly been vulnerable to the ups and downs in the stock market.

social screening

Applying social criteria (screens) to investment decisions.

What conclusion can we draw from all of this? The most meaningful conclusion we can make is that there is little evidence to say that a company's socially responsible actions significantly hurt its long-term economic performance. Given political and societal pressures on business to be socially responsible, this means that managers should take social goals into consideration as they plan, organize, lead, and control.

⟩ VALUES-BASED MANAGEMENT

Values-based management is an approach to managing in which managers establish, promote, and practice an organization's shared values. An organization's values reflect what it stands for and what it believes in. As we discussed in Chapter 3, the shared organizational values form the organization's culture and

values-based management

An approach to managing in which managers establish, promote, and practice an organization's shared values.

influence the way the organization operates and how employees behave.[19] For instance, Patagonia, a maker of outdoor sports clothing and gear, passionately pursues environmental preservation. Its strong environmental commitment influences employees' work actions and decisions in areas from product design to marketing to shipping. In addition, Patagonia gives 10 percent of its profits to support environmental causes and actively seeks to educate its customers and suppliers about environmental issues. The company lives and practices its values. For any company that believes in and practices values-based management, the shared corporate values serve many purposes.

PURPOSES OF SHARED VALUES

The values that organizational members share serve at least four main purposes. (See Exhibit 5.4.) The first purpose of shared values is that they act as guideposts for managerial decisions and actions.[20] For instance, at Tom's of Maine, a maker of all-natural personal care products, the Statement of Beliefs guides managers as they plan, organize, lead, and control organizational activities. One of the company's eight beliefs states that "We believe that different people bring different gifts and perspectives to the team and that a strong team is founded on a variety of gifts."[21] This statement expresses to managers the value of diversity—diversity of opinions, diversity of abilities—and serves as a guide for managing teams of people. Another of the company's beliefs states that "We believe in products that are safe, effective, and made of natural ingredients." Again, think about how this statement would influence and guide company managers as they do their jobs.

Another purpose of shared values is the impact they have on shaping employee behavior and communicating what the organization expects of its members. For example, employees at Herman Miller, which manufactures office, residential, and health care furniture, practice company values as they design, manufacture, and ship furniture around the world. What are those company values? A commitment to innovation and uncompromising quality, participative management, and environmental stewardship.[22]

Shared corporate values also influence marketing efforts. For example, we previously mentioned Avon Products Inc.'s commitment to educating women about breast cancer. Its support for this program came about after the company asked women what their number one health concern was and breast cancer was the answer. How does Avon's commitment to women's health influence its marketing efforts? The company's global sales force of more than half a million individuals educates women about the disease by bringing brochures on their sales visits. The director of the Breast Cancer Awareness Crusade says, "All of the interaction that happens with an Avon rep on something as important as breast cancer should

| Exhibit | 5.4 | | **Purposes of Shared Values** |

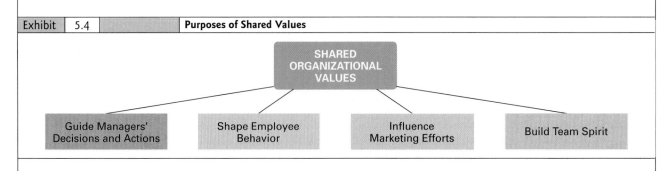

In an effort to be (or at least appear to be) socially responsible, many organizations donate dollars to philanthropic and charitable causes. In addition, many organizations ask their employees to make individual donations to these causes. Suppose you're the manager of a work team, and you know that several of your employees can't afford to pledge money right now because of various personal and financial problems. You've also been told by your supervisor that the CEO has been known to check the list of individual contributors to see who is and is not "supporting these very important causes." What would you do? What ethical guidelines might you suggest for individual and organizational contributions to philanthropic and charitable causes?

improve customer relations and make for easier sales." Avon has found a way to link its business to an important social concern and to improve its marketing efforts all at the same time.

Finally, shared values are a way to build team spirit in organizations.[23] When employees embrace the stated corporate values, they develop a deeper personal commitment to their work and feel obligated to take responsibility for their actions. Because the shared values influence the way work is done, employees become more enthusiastic about working together as a team to support values they believe in. At companies such as Tom's of Maine, Avon, Herman Miller, and numerous others, employees know what is expected of them on the job. They use the shared corporate values to shape the way they work. But how do organizations develop a set of shared values?

DEVELOPING SHARED VALUES

As any company that uses values-based management will tell you, it's not easy to establish the shared corporate values. At Tom's of Maine, the process involved everyone in the company. All the employees, working in groups of four to six, took a hard look at defining "who are we" and "what are we about." But the commitment by Tom's employees to developing shared corporate values didn't stop there. They realized that they were to actually *use* the values they helped define and develop. They realized that those shared values really mattered. They began to understand that they were part of a unique corporate culture in which values shaped the business strategy.[24]

A survey of Fortune 1000 companies found that 95 percent of the respondents were convinced they would have to adopt more socially responsible business practices in coming years to preserve their competitive edge.[25] Getting employees to buy into a set of core values that emphasize a commitment to doing good requires strong corporate leadership. Managers are responsible for shaping the organization so that its values, norms, and ideals appeal strongly to employees. Some specific suggestions for developing a good corporate values statement are listed in Exhibit 5.5.

Companies that live and practice values-based management have accepted a broad perspective regarding their commitment to being socially responsible and socially responsive. One value in particular that many managers are beginning to recognize as important has to do with the environmental responsibility of the organization and of individuals. This "greening" of management is what we're going to look at next. ◄——

Testing...Testing...1,2,3

4. **What have research studies found about the relationship between an organization's social involvement and its economic performance?**

5. **How is values-based management related to the concepts of social responsibility and social responsiveness?**

6. **What purposes do shared values serve, and how should shared values be developed?**

Exhibit	5.5
Suggestions for Creating a Good Corporate Values Statement	

1. Involve everyone in the company.
2. Allow customizing of the values by individual departments or units.
3. Expect and accept employee resistance.
4. Keep the statement short.
5. Avoid trivial statements.
6. Leave out religious references.
7. Challenge it.
8. Live it.

Source: Based on A. Farnham, "State Your Values: Hold the Hot Air," *Fortune*, April 19, 1993, pp. 117–24.

> **THE "GREENING" OF MANAGEMENT**

Until the late 1960s, few people (and organizations) paid attention to the environmental consequences of their decisions and actions.[26] Although there were some groups—mainly the Sierra Club and other smaller environmental activist groups—that were concerned with conserving the land and its natural resources, about the only popular reference to saving the environment you would have seen at that time was the ubiquitous printed request "Please Do Not Litter." A number of highly visible ecological problems and environmental disasters (Exxon *Valdez* oil spill, mercury poisoning in Japan, and Three Mile Island and Chernobyl nuclear power plant accidents) brought about a new spirit of environmentalism among individuals, groups, and organizations. Increasingly, managers began to confront questions about an organization's impact on the natural environment. This recognition of the close link between an organization's decisions and activities and its impact on the natural environment is referred to as the **greening of management**. Let's look at some issues managers may have to address as they "go green."

greening of management

The recognition of the close link between an organization's decisions and activities and its impact on the natural environment.

GLOBAL ENVIRONMENTAL PROBLEMS

One "green" issue managers must deal with as they become more involved in preserving the natural environment is recognizing the key global environmental problems and how these problems are changing. The list of global environmental problems is long. Some of the more serious ones include natural resource depletion, global warming, pollution (air, water, and soil), industrial accidents, and toxic wastes. How did these problems occur? Much of the blame can be placed on industrial activities in developed (economically affluent) countries over the last half century.[27] Various reports have shown that affluent societies account for more than 75 percent of the world's energy and resource consumption and create most of the industrial, toxic, and consumer waste.[28] An equally disturbing picture is that as the world population continues to grow and as emerging countries become more market oriented and affluent, global environmental problems can be expected to worsen.[29] However, many organizations around the world, large and small, have embraced their responsibility to respect and protect the natural environment. What role *can* organizations play in addressing global environmental problems? In other words, how can they "go green?"

HOW ORGANIZATIONS GO GREEN

There are many things that managers and organizations can do to protect and preserve the natural environment.[30] Some organizations do no more than what is required by law (that is, they fulfill their social obligation); others have made radical changes in the way they do their business. Products and production processes have become cleaner. For instance, the 3M Corporation has been a leader in waste-reduction efforts with its 3 Ps Program (Pollution Prevention Pays). Hangers Cleaners uses a pollution-free process to clean clothes. Whirlpool won an appliance industry competition and a $30 million prize for developing a CFC-free high-efficiency refrigerator. (CFCs, short for chlorofluorocarbons, have been linked to the degradation of the ozone layer surrounding the earth.) And DuPont, Xerox, and IBM have focused their environmental programs on preventing pollution, not just on cleaning it up. There are numerous other examples of environmentally friendly actions taken by global organizations. Although these examples are interesting, they really don't tell us much about how organizations go green. One approach to organizational roles in environmental responsibility uses the terms *shades of green* to describe different approaches that organizations may take.[31] What are these shades of green?

Exhibit 5.6 illustrates four approaches organizations can take with respect to environmental issues. The first approach simply is doing what is required legally: the *legal approach*. Under this approach, organizations exhibit little environmental sensitivity. They obey laws, rules, and regulations willingly and without legal challenge, and they may even try to use the law to their own advantage, but

Many companies are trying to do more to protect the natural environment. This ad from Phillips Petroleum Company introduces a new process the firm is developing to remove more than 90 percent of sulfur, an ingredient of gasoline and a contributor to air pollution, from its products.

Exhibit   5.6

Approaches to Being Green

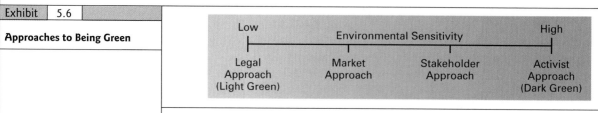

Source: Based on R.E. Freeman, J. Pierce, and R. Dodd, *Shades of Green: Business Ethics and the Environment* (New York: Oxford University Press, 1995).

that's the extent of their being green. For example, many durable product manufacturers and oil refiners have taken the legal approach and comply with the relevant environmental laws and regulations, but they go no further. This approach is a good illustration of social obligation: These organizations simply are following their legal obligations of pollution prevention and environmental protection. As an organization becomes more aware of and sensitive to environmental issues, it may adopt the *market approach*. In this approach, organizations respond to the environmental preferences of their customers. Whatever customers demand in terms of environmentally friendly products will be what the organization provides. For example, the DuPont company developed a new type of herbicide that has helped farmers around the world reduce their annual use of chemicals by more than 45 million pounds. By developing this product, DuPont was responding to the demands of its customers (farmers) who wanted to minimize the use of chemicals on their crops. Under the next approach, the *stakeholder approach*, the organization chooses to respond to multiple demands made by stakeholders. We know from an earlier chapter that stakeholders are any constituencies in the organization's external environment that are affected by the organization's decisions and actions. Under the stakeholder approach, the green organization will work to meet the environmental demands of groups such as employees, suppliers, or the community. For example, Compaq Computer Corporation developed corporate programs to minimize harmful emissions, to recycle, and to reduce both waste and energy consumption in response to demands by its various stakeholders. Both the market approach and the stakeholder approach are good illustrations of social responsiveness. Finally, if an organization pursues an *activist* (also called a dark green) *approach*, it looks for ways to respect and preserve the earth and its natural resources. For example, Ecover, a Belgian company that produces cleaning products from natural soaps and renewable raw materials, operates a near-zero-emissions factory. This green factory is an environmentally sound engineering marvel. The activist approach exhibits the highest degree of environmental sensitivity and is a good illustration of social responsibility.

SUMMING UP SOCIAL RESPONSIBILITY

The key issues in social responsibility are easier to understand if we think in terms of the people to whom managers are responsible. Classicists would say that stockholders or owners are an organization's only legitimate concern. Progressives would respond that managers are responsible to any group affected by the organization's decisions and actions: that is, the stakeholders.[32]

Lesser	**Social Responsibility**		Greater
Stage 1 Owners and Management	**Stage 2** Employees	**Stage 3** Constituents in the Specific Environment	**Stage 4** Broader Society

Exhibit	5.7
To Whom Is Management Responsible?	

Exhibit 5.7 illustrates a four-stage model of the progression of an organization's social responsibility.[33] What you do as a manager in terms of pursuing social goals depends on the person or persons to whom you believe you're responsible—that is, the stakeholders. A Stage 1 manager will promote stockholders' interests by seeking to minimize costs and maximize profits. Although all laws and regulations will be followed, Stage 1 managers do not feel obligated to satisfy other societal needs. This is consistent with Friedman's classical view of social responsibility. At Stage 2, managers will accept their responsibility to employees and focus on human resource concerns. Because they'll want to recruit, keep, and motivate good employees, Stage 2 managers will improve working conditions, expand employee rights, increase job security, and the like.

At Stage 3, managers expand their responsibilities to other stakeholders in the specific environment—that is, customers and suppliers. Social responsibility goals of Stage 3 managers include fair prices, high-quality products and services, safe products, good supplier relations, and similar actions. Their philosophy is that they can meet their responsibilities to stockholders only by meeting the needs of their other constituents.

Finally, Stage 4 characterizes the extreme socioeconomic definition of social responsibility. At this stage, managers feel a responsibility to society as a whole. Their business is seen as a public entity, and they feel a responsibility for advancing the public good. The acceptance of such responsibility means that managers actively promote social justice, preserve the environment, and support social and cultural activities. They take these stances even if such actions negatively affect profits. For instance, Tom Chappell of Tom's of Maine, described earlier, would be described as a Stage 4 manager.

Each stage implies an increasing level of managerial discretion. As managers move to the right along the continuum shown in Exhibit 5.7, they have to make more judgment calls. For example, when is a product dangerous to society? Is Philip Morris Company doing "right" for society when it sells Kraft cheese but "wrong" when it sells cigarettes? Or is producing a product with high fat and sodium content also wrong? Is a public utility company that operates nuclear power plants behaving irresponsibly toward society? Is it wrong for a company to market bioengineered produce even though the produce is more disease resistant? These are the types of social responsibility judgment calls managers must make.

There is no simple right-wrong dichotomy to help managers make socially responsible decisions. Clearly, managers

William C. Ford, Jr., chairman of Ford Motor, fits the profile of a Stage 4 manager in his involvement in environmental causes. Mr. Ford even acknowledged in May 2000 that sport utility vehicles, the firm's most profitable products, might in fact be as unsafe and environmentally damaging as their critics say, and he pledged to make improvements in their fuel efficiency and safety, increasing miles per gallon, for instance, by 25 percent over the next 5 years. In the company's "corporate citizenship report" to its shareholders, Mr. Ford also said, "Not so long ago, cars and trucks were things to aspire to. But . . . now the whole notion of social liability has crept in."

Testing...Testing...1,2,3

7. **What is the greening of management, and why is it important?**

8. **Describe how organizations can go green.**

9. **Explain the role that stakeholders play in the four stages of social responsibility.**

ethics

Rules and principles that define right and wrong conduct.

utilitarian view of ethics

A view of ethics that says that ethical decisions are made solely on the basis of their outcomes or consequences.

rights view of ethics

A view of ethics that is concerned with respecting and protecting individual liberties and privileges.

have a basic responsibility to obey the laws in the communities and countries in which they operate and to make a profit. Failure to achieve either of these goals threatens the organization's survival. Beyond that, however, managers need to identify the people to whom they believe they're responsible. By focusing on stakeholders and their expectations of the organization, managers can reduce the likelihood that they will ignore their responsibilities to critical issues and make more responsible choices.

› MANAGERIAL ETHICS

Is it ethical for a salesperson to offer a bribe to a purchasing agent as an inducement to buy? Would it make any difference if the bribe came out of the salesperson's commission? Is it ethical for someone to use a company car for private use? How about using company e-mail for personal correspondence?

The term **ethics** refers to rules and principles that define right and wrong conduct.[34] In this section, we examine the ethical dimension of managerial decisions. Many decisions that managers make require them to consider who may be affected—in terms of the result as well as the process.[35] To better understand the complicated issues involved in managerial ethics, we'll look at four different views of ethics, look at the factors that influence a manager's ethics, and offer some suggestions for what organizations can do to improve the ethical behavior of employees.

FOUR VIEWS OF ETHICS

The four perspectives on business ethics include utilitarian view, rights view, theory of justice view, and integrative social contracts theory.[36] The **utilitarian view of ethics** says that ethical decisions are made solely on the basis of their outcomes or consequences. Utilitarian theory uses a quantitative method for making ethical decisions by looking at how to provide the greatest good for the greatest number. Following the utilitarian view, a manager might conclude that laying off 20 percent of a plant's workforce is justified because it will increase the plant's profitability, improve job security for the remaining 80 percent, and be in the best interests of stockholders. Utilitarianism encourages efficiency and productivity and is consistent with the goal of profit maximization. However, it can result in biased allocations of resources, especially when some of those affected by the decision lack representation or a voice in the decision. Utilitarianism can also result in the rights of some stakeholders being ignored.

Another ethical perspective is the **rights view of ethics**, which is concerned with respecting and protecting individual liberties and privileges such as the rights to privacy, freedom of conscience, free speech, life and safety, and due process. This would include, for example, protecting the free speech rights of employees who report legal violations by their employers. The positive side of the rights perspective is that it protects individuals' basic rights, but it has a negative side for organizations. It can present obstacles to high productivity and efficiency by creating a work climate that is more concerned with protecting individuals' rights than with getting the job done.

The next view is the **theory of justice view of ethics**. Under this approach, managers are to impose and enforce rules fairly and impartially and do so by following all legal rules and regulations. A manager would be using the theory of justice perspective by deciding to provide the same rate of pay to individuals who are similar in their levels of skills, performance, or responsibility and not basing that decision on arbitrary differences such as gender, personality, race, or personal favorites. Using standards of justice also has pluses and minuses. It protects the interests of those stakeholders who may be underrepresented or lack power, but it can encourage a sense of entitlement that might make employees reduce risk taking, innovation, and productivity.

The final ethics perspective, the **integrative social contracts theory**, proposes that ethical decisions should be based on empirical (what is) and normative (what should be) factors. This view of ethics is based on the integration of two "contracts": the general social contract that allows businesses to operate and defines the acceptable ground rules, and a more specific contract among members of a community that addresses acceptable ways of behaving. For instance, in deciding what wage to pay workers in a new factory in Ciudad Juarez, Mexico, managers following the integrative social contracts theory would base the decision on existing wage levels in the community. This view of business ethics differs from the other three in that it suggests that managers need to look at existing ethical norms in industries and companies in order to determine what constitutes right and wrong decisions and actions.

Which approach to ethics do most businesspeople follow? It probably isn't a surprise that most businesspeople follow the utilitarian approach.[37] Why? It's consistent with such business goals as efficiency, productivity, and profits. However, that perspective needs to change because of the changing world facing managers. Trends toward individual rights, social justice, and community standards mean that managers need ethical standards based on nonutilitarian criteria. This is an obvious challenge for managers because making decisions on such criteria involves far more ambiguities than using utilitarian criteria such as efficiency and profits. The result, of course, is that managers increasingly find themselves struggling with ethical dilemmas.

In an effort to overcome past problems, many firms are turning to the rights view of ethics and allowing independent factory audits of their overseas locations to be performed by human rights groups. Reebok International Ltd. is among the firms that released their audit reports to the public. The firm seems committed to protecting the human rights of its workers and may succeed in leading other firms to follow its example. "We have raised the ante with external monitoring," says Reebok CEO Paul B. Fireman.

theory of justice view of ethics

A view of ethics in which managers impose and enforce rules fairly and impartially and do so by following all legal rules and regulations.

integrative social contracts theory

A view of ethics that proposes that ethical decisions should be based on empirical (what is) and normative (what should be) factors.

FACTORS THAT AFFECT MANAGERIAL ETHICS

Whether a manager acts ethically or unethically is the result of complex interactions between the manager's stage of moral development and several moderating variables including individual characteristics, the organization's structural design, the organization's culture, and the intensity of the ethical issue. (See Exhibit 5.8.)

Exhibit 5.8

Factors That Affect Ethical and Unethical Behavior

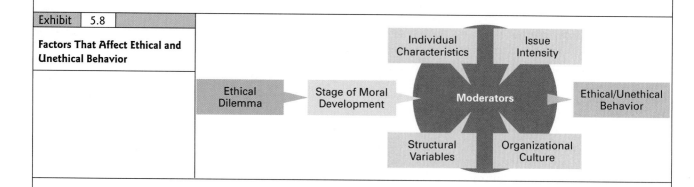

People who lack a strong moral sense are much less likely to do the wrong things if they're constrained by rules, policies, job descriptions, or strong cultural norms that disapprove of such behaviors. Conversely, intensely moral individuals can be corrupted by an organizational structure and culture that permits or encourages unethical practices. Moreover, managers are more likely to make ethical decisions when high moral intensity is involved. Let's look more closely at the various factors that influence whether managers behave ethically or unethically.

Stage of Moral Development Research confirms the existence of three levels of moral development, each composed of two stages.[38] At each successive stage, an individual's moral judgment becomes less and less dependent on outside influences. The three levels and six stages are described in Exhibit 5.9.

The first level is labeled *preconventional*. At this level, a person's choice between right or wrong is based on personal consequences involved, such as physical punishment, reward, or exchange of favors. Ethical reasoning at the *conventional* level indicates that moral values reside in maintaining expected standards and living up to the expectations of others. At the *principled* level, individuals make a clear effort to define moral principles apart from the authority of the groups to which they belong or society in general.

Exhibit 5.9

Stages of Moral Development

Level	Description of Stage
Principled	6. Following self-chosen ethical principles even if they violate the law
	5. Valuing rights of others and upholding absolute values and rights regardless of the majority's opinion
Conventional	4. Maintaining conventional order by fulfilling obligations to which you have agreed
	3. Living up to what is expected by people close to you
Preconventional	2. Following rules only when doing so is in your immediate interest
	1. Sticking to rules to avoid physical punishment

Source: Based on L. Kohlberg, "Moral Stages and Moralization: The Cognitive-Development Approach," in T. Lickona (ed.), *Moral Development and Behavior: Theory, Research, and Social Issues* (New York: Holt, Rinehart & Winston, 1976), pp. 34–35.

We can draw some conclusions from research on the levels and stages of moral development.[39] First, people proceed through the six stages sequentially. They move up the moral ladder, stage by stage. Second, there is no guarantee of continued moral development. An individual's moral development can stop at any stage. Third, the majority of adults are at Stage 4. They are limited to obeying the rules and will be inclined to behave ethically. For instance, a manager at Stage 3 is likely to make decisions that will receive peer approval; a manager at Stage 4 will try to be a "good corporate citizen" by making decisions that respect the organization's rules and procedures; and a Stage 5 manager is likely to challenge organizational practices that he or she believes to be wrong. Efforts by colleges to raise students' ethical awareness and standards are focused on helping them move to the principled level—the highest level of moral development.

From their first days as ice cream entrepreneurs, Ben Cohen and Jerry Greenfield (*left to right*), the founders of Ben & Jerry's Homemade, emphasized social responsibility as a key component of the firm's corporate mission. As Greenfield says, "Working on combining social issues with profit opportunities is the field in which we labor." Even though the firm has been sold (to the European conglomerate Unilever), the two hope to retain its strong commitment to ethical business practices, such as its generous donations to various charities, through the establishment of an independent board on which Cohen and Greenfield will serve.

Individual Characteristics Every person joins an organization with a relatively entrenched set of **values**. Our values—developed in our early years from parents, teachers, friends, and others—represent basic convictions about what is right and wrong. Thus, managers in the same organization often possess very different personal values.[40] Although *values* and *stage of moral development* may seem similar, they are not the same. Values are broad and cover a wide range of issues; the stage of moral development specifically is a measure of independence from outside influences.

Two personality variables also have been found to influence an individual's actions according to his or her beliefs about what is right or wrong: ego strength and locus of control. **Ego strength** is a personality measure of the strength of a person's convictions. People who score high on ego strength are likely to resist impulses to act unethically and instead follow their convictions. That is, individuals high in ego strength are more likely to do what they think is right. We would expect managers with high ego strength to be more consistent in their moral judgments and moral actions than those with low ego strength.

Locus of control is a personality attribute that measures the degree to which people believe they control their own fate. People with an *internal* locus of control believe that they control their own destinies; those with an *external* locus believe that what happens to them is due to luck or chance. How does this influence a person's decision to act ethically or unethically? Externals are less likely to take personal responsibility for the consequences of their behavior and are more likely to rely on external forces. Internals, on the other hand, are more likely to take responsibility for consequences and rely on their own internal standards of right and wrong to guide their behavior.[41] Managers with an internal locus of control are likely to be more consistent in their moral judgments and moral actions than will those with an external locus of control.

Structural Variables An organization's structural design helps shape whether managers behave ethically. Some structures provide strong guidance, whereas others only create ambiguity and uncertainty for managers. Structural designs

values

Basic convictions about what is right and wrong.

ego strength

A personality measure of the strength of a person's convictions.

locus of control

A personality attribute that measures the degree to which people believe they control their own fate.

Testing...Testing...1,2,3

10. **What is ethics, and why is it important for managers to be aware of ethics?**

11. **Contrast the four views of business ethics. Which is the most popular among businesspeople and why?**

12. **How might the stages of moral development, individual characteristics, and structural variables affect a manager's decision to behave ethically or unethically?**

that minimize ambiguity and uncertainty and continuously remind managers of what is ethical are more likely to encourage ethical behavior.

Formal rules and regulations reduce ambiguity. Job descriptions and written codes of ethics are examples of formal guides that can promote consistent behavior. Research continues to show, though, that the behavior of superiors is the strongest single influence on an individual's own choice to act ethically or unethically.[42] People check to see what those in authority are doing and use that as a benchmark for acceptable practices and expectations. Some organizational performance appraisal systems focus exclusively on outcomes. Others evaluate means as well as ends. When managers are evaluated only on outcomes, they may be pressured to do "whatever is necessary" to look good on the outcome variables and not be concerned with how they got those results. Closely associated with the appraisal system is the way rewards are allocated. The more reward or punishment depends on specific goal outcomes, the more pressure there is on managers to do whatever they must to reach those goals and perhaps compromise their ethical standards. Structures also differ in the amount of time, competition, cost, and similar pressures placed on employees. The greater the pressure, the more likely it is that managers will compromise their ethical standards.

Organization's Culture   The content and strength of an organization's culture also influence ethical behavior.[43] An organizational culture most likely to encourage high ethical standards is one that is high in risk tolerance, control, and conflict tolerance. Managers in such a culture are encouraged to be aggressive and innovative, are aware that unethical practices will be discovered, and feel free to openly challenge expectations they consider to be unrealistic or personally undesirable.

A strong culture will exert more influence on managers than a weak one. If the culture is strong and supports high ethical standards, it should have a very powerful and positive influence on managers' decision to act ethically or unethically. The Boeing Company, for example, has a strong culture that has long stressed ethical corporate dealings with customers, employees, the community, and stockholders. To reinforce the importance of ethics, the company developed a series of serious and thought-provoking posters (see page 129) designed to get employees to recognize that their individual decisions and actions are important in the way the organization is viewed. In a weak organizational culture, however, managers are more likely to rely on work group and departmental norms as a behavioral guide.

Issue Intensity   A student who would never consider breaking into an instructor's office to steal an accounting exam doesn't think twice about asking a friend who took the same accounting course from the same instructor last semester what questions were on the exam. Similarly, a manager might think nothing about taking home a few office supplies yet be highly concerned about the possible embezzlement of company funds.

These examples illustrate the final factor that affects a manager's ethical behavior: the intensity of the ethical issue itself.[44] As Exhibit 5.10 shows, six characteristics have been identified as relevant in determining issue intensity: greatness of harm, consensus of wrong, probability of harm, immediacy of consequences, proximity to victim(s), and concentration of effect.[45] These six factors determine how important an ethical issue is to an individual. According to these guidelines, the larger the number of people harmed, the more agreement that the action is wrong,

The Boeing Company's imaginative poster series reinforces the core values of integrity and ethical behavior for its employees.

the greater the likelihood that the action will cause harm, the more immediately that the consequences of the action will be felt, the closer the person feels to the victim(s), and the more concentrated the effect of the action on the victim(s), the greater the issue intensity. When an ethical issue is important—that is, the more intense it is—the more we should expect managers to behave ethically.

Exhibit	5.10	**Determinants of Issue Intensity**

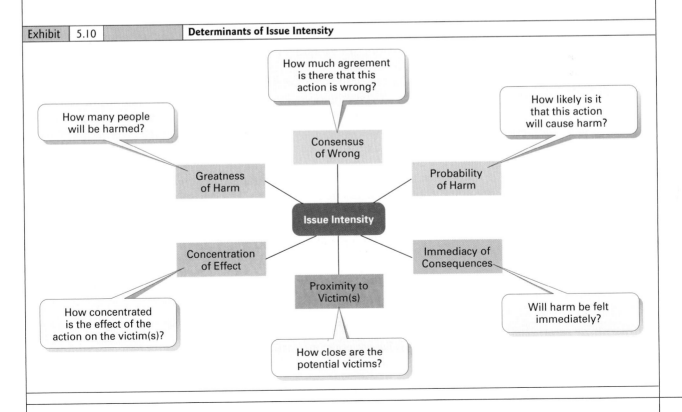

It is often said that ethical behavior in an organization begins at the top. Malcolm Walker heads a British retail food and appliance chain called Iceland that has made him a multimillionaire. "I wear a suit. I run a company. I'm interested in profit," he says. "But I'm a member of Greenpeace because no sane person can argue with what they stand for. They want to stop whaling, nuclear pollution and factories dumping poisons in rivers. What's wrong with any of that?" Iceland's refrigerator products are free of chemicals that harm Earth's protective ozone layer.

ETHICS IN AN INTERNATIONAL CONTEXT

Are ethical standards universal? Hardly! Social and cultural differences between countries are important environmental factors that determine ethical and unethical behavior. For example, the manager of a Mexican firm bribes several high-ranking government officials in Mexico City to secure a profitable government contract. Such a practice would be seen as unethical, if not illegal, in the United States. But it is a standard business practice in Mexico.

Should Coca-Cola employees in Saudi Arabia adhere to U.S. ethical standards, or should they follow local standards of acceptable behavior? If Airbus (a European company) pays a $10 million "broker's fee" to an intermediary to get a major contract with a Middle Eastern airline, should the Boeing Company be restricted from doing the same because such practices are considered improper in the United States?

In the case of payments to influence foreign officials or politicians, there is a law to guide U.S. managers. The Foreign Corrupt Practices Act makes it illegal for U.S. firms to knowingly corrupt a foreign official. However, even this law doesn't always reduce ethical dilemmas to black and white. In some Latin American countries, for example, government bureaucrats are paid ridiculously low salaries because custom dictates that they receive small payments from those they serve. Payoffs to these bureaucrats "grease the machinery" of government and ensure that things get done. The Foreign Corrupt Practices Act does not expressly prohibit small payoffs to foreign government employees whose duties are primarily administrative or clerical *when* such payoffs are an accepted part of doing business in that country.

Although it is important for individual managers working in foreign cultures to recognize the various social, cultural, and political and legal influences on what is appropriate and acceptable behavior, global organizations must also clarify their ethical guidelines so that employees know what is expected of them while working in a foreign location. This adds another dimension to making ethical judgments.

At the World Economic Forum in January 1999, the United Nations Secretary-General challenged world business leaders to "embrace and enact" the Global Compact, a document outlining nine principles for doing business globally in the areas of human rights, labor, and environment.[46] These nine principles are listed in Exhibit 5.11. Global businesses have been asked to incorporate these guidelines into their business activities. Companies making this commitment are doing so because they believe that the world business community plays a significant role in improving economic and social conditions.

Testing...Testing...1,2,3

13. **How does an organization's culture influence ethical behavior?**

14. **What determines the degree of intensity of an ethical issue?**

15. **What factors influence ethics internationally?**

Exhibit	5.11

Human Rights

Principle 1:	Support and respect the protection of international human rights within their sphere of influence
Principle 2:	Make sure business corporations are not complicit in human rights abuses

Labor Standards

Principle 3:	Freedom of association and the effective recognition of the right to collective bargaining
Principle 4:	The elimination of all forms of forced and compulsory labor
Principle 5:	The effective abolition of child labor
Principle 6:	The elimination of discrimination in respect of employment and occupation

Environment

Principle 7:	Support a precautionary approach to environmental challenges
Principle 8:	Undertake initiatives to promote greater environmental responsibility
Principle 9:	Encourage the development and diffusion of environmentally friendly technologies

Source: The Global Compact Web site (www.unglobalcompact.org), August 14, 2000.

TOWARD IMPROVING ETHICAL BEHAVIOR

Managers can do a number of things if they're serious about reducing unethical behaviors in their organization. They can seek to hire individuals with high ethical standards, establish codes of ethics and decision rules, lead by example, delineate job goals and performance appraisal mechanisms, provide ethics training, conduct social audits, and provide support to individuals facing ethical dilemmas. Taken individually, these actions will probably not have much impact. But when all or most of them are implemented as part of a comprehensive ethics program, they have the potential to significantly improve an organization's ethical climate. The key term here, however, is *potential*. There are no guarantees that a well-designed ethics program will lead to the desired outcome. For instance, retailing giant Sears has a long history of encouraging ethical business practices and, in fact, has a corporate Office of Ethics and Business Practices. However, the company's ethics programs didn't stop managers from illegally trying to collect payments from bankrupt charge account holders or from routinely deceiving automotive service center customers into thinking they needed unnecessary repairs.[47]

Employee Selection Given that individuals are at different stages of moral development and possess different personal value systems and personalities, an organization's employee selection process—interviews, tests, background checks, and so forth—should be used to eliminate ethically questionable applicants. The selection process should be viewed as an opportunity to learn about an individual's level of moral development, personal values, ego strength, and locus of control.[48] But this isn't an easy task! Even under the best of circumstances, individuals with questionable standards of right and wrong will be hired. However, this shouldn't pose a problem if other types of ethics controls are in place.

Codes of Ethics and Decision Rules Ambiguity about what is and is not ethical can be a problem for employees. A **code of ethics**, a formal statement of an organization's primary values and the ethical rules it expects its employees to follow, is a

code of ethics

A formal statement of an organization's primary values and the ethical rules it expects its employees to follow.

popular choice for reducing that ambiguity. For instance, nearly 95 percent of Fortune 500 companies now have codes of conduct. And codes of ethics are becoming more popular globally. A survey of business organizations in 22 countries found that 78 percent have formally stated ethics standards and codes of ethics.[49]

What should a code of ethics look like? It has been suggested that codes should be specific enough to show employees the spirit in which they are supposed to do things yet loose enough to allow for freedom of judgment.[50] A survey of various codes of ethics found that their content tended to fall into three categories: (1) Be a dependable organizational citizen; (2) do not do anything unlawful or improper that will harm the organization; and (3) be good to customers.[51] Exhibit 5.12 lists the variables included in each of these clusters.

But how well do codes of ethics work? The reality is that they're not always effective in encouraging ethical behavior in organizations. A survey of employees in U.S. businesses with ethics codes found that 75 percent of those surveyed had observed ethical or legal violations in the previous 12 months including such things as deceptive sales practices, unsafe working conditions, sexual harassment, conflicts of interest, and environmental violations.[52] Does this mean that codes of ethics shouldn't be developed? No. But there are some suggestions that managers can follow. First, ethical codes shouldn't be developed and applied in isolation. Information about ethical expectations and reminders about the organization's commitment to ethics

---

Exhibit	5.12

Clusters of Variables Found in 83 Corporate Codes of Business Ethics

Cluster 1. Be a Dependable Organizational Citizen
1. Comply with safety, health, and security regulations.
2. Demonstrate courtesy, respect, honesty, and fairness.
3. Illegal drugs and alcohol at work are prohibited.
4. Manage personal finances well.
5. Exhibit good attendance and punctuality.
6. Follow directives of supervisors.
7. Do not use abusive language.
8. Dress in business attire.
9. Firearms at work are prohibited.

Cluster 2. Do Not Do Anything Unlawful or Improper That Will Harm the Organization
1. Conduct business in compliance with all laws.
2. Payments for unlawful purposes are prohibited.
3. Bribes are prohibited.
4. Avoid outside activities that impair duties.
5. Maintain confidentiality of records.
6. Comply with all antitrust and trade regulations.
7. Comply with all accounting rules and controls.
8. Do not use company property for personal benefit.
9. Employees are personally accountable for company funds.
10. Do not propagate false or misleading information.
11. Make decisions without regard for personal gain.

Cluster 3. Be Good to Customers
1. Convey true claims in product advertisements.
2. Perform assigned duties to the best of your ability.
3. Provide products and services of the highest quality.

Source: F.R. David, "An Empirical Study of Codes of Business Ethics: A Strategic Perspective," paper presented at the 48th Annual Academy of Management Conference, Anaheim, CA, August 1988.

Exhibit 5.13

12 Questions for Examining the Ethics of a Business Decision

1. Have you defined the problem accurately?

2. How would you define the problem if you stood on the other side of the fence?

3. How did this situation occur in the first place?

4. To whom and to what do you give your loyalty as a person and as a member of the corporation?

5. What is your intention in making this decision?

6. How does this intention compare with the probable results?

7. Whom could your decision or action injure?

8. Can you discuss the problem with the affected parties before you make the decision?

9. Are you confident that your position will be as valid over a long period of time as it seems now?

10. Could you disclose without qualm your decision or action to your boss, your chief executive officer, the board of directors, your family, society as a whole?

11. What is the symbolic potential of your action if understood? If misunderstood?

12. Under what conditions would you allow exceptions to your stand?

Source: Reprinted by permission of *Harvard Business Review.* An exhibit from "Ethics without the Sermon" by L.L. Nash, November–December 1981, p. 81. Copyright © 1981 by the President and Fellows of Harvard College; all rights reserved.

should be continually relayed to employees. Second, all levels of management should support and continually reaffirm the importance of the code of ethics and consistently discipline those who break the code. When managers consider the code of ethics to be important, regularly affirm its content, and publicly reprimand rule breakers, ethics codes can supply a strong foundation for an effective corporate ethics program.[53] Finally, an organization's code of ethics might be designed around the 12 questions listed in Exhibit 5.13 that can be used as decision rules in guiding managers as they handle ethical dilemmas in decision making.[54]

Top Management's Leadership Doing business ethically requires a commitment from top managers. Why? Because it's the top managers who set the cultural tone. They are role models in terms of both words and actions, though what they *do* is far more important than what they *say*. If top managers, for example, use company resources for their personal use, inflate their expense accounts, or give favored treatment to friends, they imply that such behavior is acceptable for all employees.

Top managers also set the cultural tone by their reward and punishment practices. The choice of whom and what are rewarded with pay increases and promotions sends a strong signal to employees. The promotion of a manager for achieving impressive results in an ethically questionable manner indicates to others that those questionable ways are acceptable. When wrongdoing is uncovered, managers who want to emphasize their commitment to doing business ethically must punish the offender and publicize the fact by making the outcome visible to everyone in the organization. This practice sends a message that doing wrong has a price and it's not in employees' best interests to act unethically!

16. Describe how the employee selection process might be used to encourage ethical behavior.

17. What are codes of ethics, and how can their effectiveness be improved?

18. What role does top management's leadership play in encouraging ethical behavior?

Testing...Testing...1,2,3

Fannie Mae's mission is to provide affordable housing and home ownership for low-, moderate-, and middle-income Americans. The company encourages employee involvement in community service by helping employees find meaningful volunteer opportunities, granting 10 hours of paid leave per month for volunteer work, supporting those employees who participate in volunteer activities, and recognizing employees for their accomplishments as volunteers.

Job Goals and Performance Appraisal Employees should have realistic and tangible goals. Explicit goals can create ethical problems if they make unrealistic demands on employees. Under the stress of unrealistic goals, otherwise ethical employees may have the attitude that "anything goes." When goals are clear and realistic, they reduce ambiguity for employees and motivate rather than punish.

Whether an individual achieves his or her job goals is usually a key issue in performance appraisal. Keep in mind, though, that when performance appraisals focus only on economic goals, ends will begin to justify means. If an organization wants its employees to uphold high ethical standards, it must include this dimension in its performance appraisal process. For example, a manager's annual review might include a point-by-point evaluation of how his or her decisions measured up against the company's code of ethics and on how well goals were met.

Ethics Training More and more organizations are setting up seminars, workshops, and similar ethics training programs to encourage ethical behavior. Ethics researchers estimate that over 40 percent of U.S. companies provide some form of ethics training.[55] But these training programs aren't without controversy. The primary debate is whether you can actually teach ethics. Critics, for instance, stress that the effort is pointless because people establish their individual value systems when they're very young. Proponents, however, note that several studies have found that values can be learned after early childhood. In addition, they cite evidence that shows that teaching ethical problem solving can make an actual difference in ethical behaviors;[56] that training has increased individuals' level of moral development;[57] and that, if it does nothing else, ethics training increases awareness of ethical issues in business.[58]

How do you teach ethics? Let's look at how it's done at the Boeing Company.[59] Its training program, called "Questions of Integrity: The Ethics Challenge," consists of 54 different ethics situations and four possible ways of dealing with each. In work group discussions, supervisors discuss each situation and then ask their employees to choose the best outcome by holding up cards marked A, B, C, or D. For instance, one of the situations asks employees, "When walking through the halls, you constantly hear one of your male co-workers call any female employee 'babe.' What do you do?" Possible answers include "A. Speak to your co-worker in a nonconfrontational manner about the sexist comment. B. Tell his manager that the employee should be fired for sexual harassment. C. Nothing. Calling a woman 'babe' is a form of endearment. D. Tell your supervisor that you feel this is demeaning in the workplace." The "correct" answers are A and D. Other examples of the realistic ethical scenarios used in the training include selling Amway products at work, wearing a prochoice t-shirt, and staying at a supplier's beach house. The Boeing Company's ethics training program was designed to bring ethics to life for employees and make it more relevant to their everyday workplace behaviors.

Ethics training sessions can provide a number of benefits.[60] They reinforce the organization's standards of conduct. They're a reminder that top managers want employees to consider ethical issues in making decisions. They clarify what practices are and are not acceptable. Finally, when employees discuss common concerns among themselves, they are reassured that they're not alone in facing ethical dilemmas. This reassurance can strengthen their confidence when they have to take unpopular but ethically correct stances.

Independent Social Audits An important element of unethical behavior is fear of being caught. Independent social audits, which evaluate decisions and management practices in terms of the organization's code of ethics, increase the likelihood of detection. These audits can be routine evaluations, performed on a regular basis just as financial audits are, or they can occur randomly with no prior announcement. An effective ethical program should probably have both. To maintain integrity, auditors should be responsible to the company's board of directors and present their findings directly to the board. This practice gives the auditors clout and lessens the opportunity for retaliation from those being audited.

Formal Protective Mechanisms Our last recommendation is for organizations to provide formal mechanisms to protect employees who face ethical dilemmas so that they can do what's right without fear of reprimand. An organization might designate ethical counselors. When employees face an ethics dilemma, they could go to these advisers for guidance. The ethical counselor's role would be a sounding board—a channel to let employees openly verbalize their ethical problem, the problem's cause, and their own options. After the options are clear, the adviser might take on the role of advocate who champions the ethically "right" alternatives. Other organizations have appointed ethics officers who design, direct, and modify the organization's ethics programs as needed. In addition, the organization might create a special appeals process that employees could use without personal or career risk to themselves to raise ethical issues or blow the whistle on violators.[61]

> | A FINAL THOUGHT

It seems that news headlines abound with stories of unethically questionable practices at large and well-known companies: Pepsico acknowledges its role in putting Coca-Cola under inquiry by the European Commission because it believed Coke was abusing its dominant position in the European market; Warner Music Group is criticized for distributing violent rap lyrics; Prudential Insurance Company is accused of sales fraud and forgery; Columbia/HCA is investigated for inflating the severity of patient illnesses to receive larger Medicare and Medicaid payments; and Bausch and Lomb is accused of using deceptive accounting principles and practices in order to meet strict numbers-oriented performance goals. What's going on? Has ethics taken a back seat in business?

A survey of employees shows that workplace pressures are leading more and more of them to consider acting unethically or illegally on the job.[62] The results indicated that 56 percent of those surveyed felt pressure to act unethically or illegally on the job, with 48 percent saying they have actually committed such activities. What types of unethical business activities were reported? Here is a sampling that respondents admitted to: cut corners on quality control (16 percent); covered up incidents (14 percent); abused or lied about sick days (11 percent); lied to or deceived customers (9 percent); put inappropriate pressure on others (7 percent); falsified numbers or reports (6 percent); lied to or deceived superiors on serious matters (5 percent); withheld important information (5 percent); misused or stole company property (4 percent); took credit for someone's work or idea (4 percent); and engaged in copyright or software infringement (3 percent).

As we well know, unethical behaviors are prevalent across our society. Cheating, for instance, is a common occurrence in education. A range of studies shows that anywhere from 75 percent to 98 percent of students admit to having cheated in high school.[63] And a survey of college students by *U.S. News and World Report* showed some ethically alarming results: 90 percent believe cheaters never pay the price; 90 percent say when they see someone cheating, they don't turn the person in; 84 percent believe they need to cheat to get ahead in the world today; and 63 percent say it's fair for parents to help with their kids' homework.[64] It's not surprising that organizations have difficulty upholding high ethical standards when their future employees—these students—so readily accept unethical behavior.

What are the implications for managers, current and future? Doing the right thing—that is, managing ethically—isn't always easy. However, because society's expectations of its institutions are regularly changing, managers must continually monitor those expectations. What is ethically acceptable today may be a poor guide for the future.

Testing...Testing...1,2,3

19. **How can job goals and performance appraisal be used to encourage ethical behavior?**

20. **Describe how independent social audits and formal protective mechanisms can encourage ethical behavior.**

21. **What are the implications for managers of the surveys showing the status of ethical behavior in the workplace?**

Managers Respond to "A Manager's Dilemma"

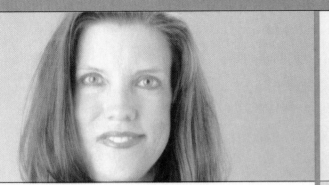

Lois Boyle

Owner, Chief Creative Officer, J. Schmid & Associates, Inc., Shawnee Mission, Kansas

As a marketer, I see this as an incredible market differentiation opportunity. The Internet industry has spawned thousands of "me-too" companies with few organizations owning a clear, defined niche. Creating a values-based organization would enable DME to define a mission statement that includes key points of differentiation.

Dash should educate and empower DME's employees by creating a meaningful mission statement and communicating it to all employees. To become part of the everyday business culture, the mission statement must be emphasized at all points of decision making. Visual reminders and managerial encouragement should be used to reiterate these values. Employees should ask themselves "will this decision promote our values as stated in the mission statement?"

In addition, the mission statement should be printed on every internal and external communication. This creates market awareness and ultimately market strength.

Finally, when a milestone has been reached that supports the values expressed in the mission statement, an internal celebration should take place. Recognizing efforts that support the mission statement will help reinforce the values within the minds and actions of employees.

Amanda Quebbeman

Pharmaceutical Sales Representative, Eli Lilly and Company, St. Louis, Missouri

There are several things I would recommend Dash do to develop values for his company. First, get all employees to participate in the process. This would ensure that they will "buy into" what organizational values are ultimately agreed upon. This won't be easy, but I think it's critical. Next, I think Dash should form small groups to take a close look at defining these values. The fact that the company was founded upon a desire to empower minority communities is a great place to start. Once these employee teams have carefully considered the important values, it's time for a company-wide meeting to discuss them. This may not be easy or pleasant, but is critical to getting employee commitment. Then, a written statement of core company values can be developed. It is important for Dash and his employees to understand that these values won't ever be changed. As organizational circumstances change, the values statement should reflect these changes.

Finally, I want to emphasize how important Dash's leadership is to this whole process. Without his continued support of the company's values, employees aren't likely to use them to guide their decisions and actions.

Chapter Summary

This summary is organized by the chapter-opening objectives found on p. 110.

1. According to the classical view, business's only social responsibility is to maximize financial returns for stockholders. The opposing socioeconomic view holds that business has a responsibility to the larger society.

2. The arguments for business's being socially responsible include public expectations, long-run profits, ethical obligation, public image, a better environment, fewer governmental regulations, balancing of responsibility and power, stockholder interests, possession of resources, and the superiority of prevention over cures. The arguments against hold that social responsibility violates the profit-maximization objective, dilutes the organization's purpose, costs too much, gives business too much power, requires skills that business does not have, lacks accountability, and lacks wide public support.

3. Social obligation is when an organization has met its economic and legal responsibilities and no more. Social responsiveness refers to the capacity of a firm to respond to social pressures and is guided by social norms. Social responsibility refers to business's pursuit of long-term goals that are good for society and requires a business to determine what is right or wrong by seeking out fundamental truths.

4. Although many studies have shown a positive relationship between social involvement and social performance, we need to be cautious about drawing conclusions because of methodological concerns. The most meaningful conclusion we can make is that there is little evidence to say that a company's socially responsible actions significantly hurt its long-term economic performance.

5. Values-based management refers to an approach to managing in which managers establish, promote, and practice the organization's shared values. The shared values comprise the organization's culture and influence the way the organization operates and employees behave.

6. The greening of management is the recognition of the close link between an organization's decisions and actions and its impact on the natural environment. Organizations might go green using any of four approaches: legal, market, stakeholder, and activist.

7. The utilitarian view makes decisions on the basis of their outcomes or consequences. The rights view seeks to respect and protect basic rights of individuals. The theory of justice view seeks to impose and enforce rules fairly and impartially. The integrative social contracts view recognizes the implicit contracts between organizations and the ethical standards of the community within which they operate.

8. Whether a manager acts ethically or unethically is the result of complex interactions between the manager's stage of moral development, his or her individual characteristics, the organization's structural design, the organization's culture, and the intensity of the ethical issue.

9. A comprehensive ethical program would include hiring individuals with high ethical standards, establishing codes of ethics and decision rules, leading by example, delineating job goals and performance appraisal mechanisms, providing ethics training, conducting social audits, and providing support to individuals facing ethical dilemmas.

Thinking About Management Issues

1. What does social responsibility mean to you personally? Do *you* think business organizations should be socially responsible? Explain.

2. Do you think values-based management is just a "do-gooder" ploy? Explain your answer.

3. Internet programs that allow individuals to share files are popular among college students. These programs work by allowing nonorganizational users to access any local network in which desired files are located. Because these types of file-sharing programs tend to clog bandwidth, local users' ability to access and use a local network is reduced. What ethical and social responsibilities does a university have in this situation? To whom does it have a responsibility? What guidelines might you suggest for university decision makers?

4. A whistle-blower is someone who reports his or her employer's unethical practices to outsiders. What are some problems that could be associated with employee whistle-blowing for (a) the whistle-blower and (b) the organization?

5. Describe the characteristics and behaviors of someone you consider to be an ethical person. How could the types of decisions and actions in which this person engages be encouraged in a workplace?

An increasing number of organizations are making a commitment to understanding the impact of their decisions and actions on the natural environment. Using the Web, find two examples of companies that fit the profile of each of the four approaches to going green. For each example, describe what specific activities the company is doing. Be sure to give the Web site addresses for the examples you find.

myPHLIP Companion Web Site

myPHLIP *(www.prenhall.com/myphlip) is a fully customizable homepage that ties students and faculty to text-specific resources.*
- ***For students**, myPHLIP provides an online study guide tied chapter-by-chapter to the text—current events and Internet exercises, lecture notes, downloadable software, the Career Center, the Writing Center, Ask the Tutor, and more.*
- ***For faculty**, myPHLIP provides a syllabus tool that allows you to manage content, communicate with students, and upload personal resources.*

Working Together: Team-Based Exercise

You have obviously faced many ethical dilemmas already in your life—at school, in social settings, and even at work. Form groups of three to five individuals. Appoint a spokesperson to present your group's findings to the class. Each member of the group is to think of some unethical behaviors he or she has observed in organizations. The incidents could be something experienced as an employee, customer, client, or an action observed informally.

Once everyone has identified some examples of ethically questionable behaviors, the group should identify three important criteria that could be used to determine whether a particular action is ethical. Think carefully about these criteria. They should differentiate between ethical and unethical behavior. Write your choices down. Use these criteria to assess the examples of unethical behavior described by group members.

When asked by your instructor, the spokesperson should be ready to describe several of the incidents of unethical behavior witnessed by group members, your criteria for differentiating between ethical and unethical behavior, and how you used this criteria for assessing these incidents.

Case Application

Blowout

Tires shredding as the rubber peels away from the rim. A driver struggling to maintain control of a vehicle going down the highway at 65+ miles an hour. It's a horrible nightmare situation that no driver ever expects to have to face. However, that nightmare was a reality for dozens of unfortunate drivers. A federal investigation into at least 88 deaths and more than 300 incidents involving tires that shredded on the highway led to a late summer 2000 recall of 6.5 million Bridgestone/Firestone tires. These tires were found mainly on Ford Explorers (the company's extremely popular sport utility vehicle) and other Ford light trucks. This tire recall, the second largest in history, raised significant social responsibility and ethical issues for both companies. Decisions by managers at both companies came under fire.

Indications that something could be wrong with the Firestone tires may have appeared as early as the beginning of the 1990s. In August 2000, a Firestone spokeswoman said her company is aware of being sued 51 times. A spokeswoman for Ford said that no judgments have been awarded against Ford. In fact, the only case tried before a jury in Arizona in 1997 resulted in a judgment for Ford and Firestone. But the pattern in these cases was virtually the same—the tread of a rear tire separated causing the vehicle to swerve out of control and usually flip over. Martin Inglis, vice president in charge of Ford North America, said that Ford had tested the Firestone tires at its desert proving grounds in Arizona but had never witnessed such a failure. Yet, early in 1999, Ford began receiving troubling reports from overseas markets. In some Persian Gulf and Latin American countries, Ford received complaints of the suspect Firestone tires failing suddenly at high temperatures and under heavy loads. In response to customer complaints, Ford replaced Firestone tires on more than 46,000 of its Explorer sport utility vehicles in Saudi Arabia, Venezuela, Thailand, and Malaysia. Mr. Inglis stated that, "The incidents overseas seemed incidental," and that Ford didn't understand what the issues were in the United States. However, other Ford officials said they had been looking at reports of tire tread separation on Ford Explorers for some time. At the time of the recall one official stated, "It didn't just happen in the last 10 days."

After the problems surfaced in Venezuela, Ford examined 243 tires with more than 50,000 miles of use from customers in the United States who had brought their vehicles in for service. Engineers at Ford's research facilities in Arizona examined the tires with X-ray imaging and cut the tires apart. They found no evidence of tread separation. Ford also brought in tire experts from Firestone to do their own tests and they, too, found nothing. One Ford executive admitted that their primary problem was not discerning initially that anything was wrong. "Taken across the aggregate number of vehicles out there, the incident reports involved a very minuscule number," he said.

However, as Ford wrapped up its tire tests in early May 2000, the National Highway Traffic Safety Administration (NHTSA) began its initial engineering analysis involving the tires, much to the surprise of Ford's officials. Ford decided to begin an intensive in-house investigation, which was still going on at the time of the tire recall. In July 2000, the NHTSA disclosed that it was investigating consumer complaints and deaths involved with the sudden failure of the Firestone tires. As the NHTSA probe attracted wider publicity, Ford's senior managers got involved to try and calm customers' fears about safety. One of their actions involved contacting Goodyear (another supplier of the same-sized tires to Ford in the mid-1990s) and studying its warranty information. Ford was able to confirm that Goodyear's tires had not experienced the same type of problem.

Then, by July 2000, Ford's investigators were growing increasingly concerned about the speed of Firestone's analysis of its warranty information. Firestone didn't have the same level of expertise at this analysis as did Goodyear. The two companies agreed that a joint analysis would be appropriate. Working from a "war room" at Ford headquarters in Dearborn, Michigan, a team of top executives; people from the legal, purchasing, and communications departments; safety experts; and people from Ford's truck group tried to find a common denominator in the tire incident reports. Others began contacting tire makers worldwide to see if there would be enough tires available to accommodate a recall. The public impression was that the two companies were working closely together. However, the reality was that there was a lot of tension between the two. For instance, they disagreed on recommended tire inflation levels. By early August as the war team continued to work, the data being studied "were suggesting some trends we found alarming" said one Ford official. It became clear to the Ford and Firestone investigators that the problem tires appeared to have come from Firestone's Decatur, Illinois, plant during specific periods of production. Also, it became obvious that the bulk of the tread separation incidents had occurred in warm weather states—Arizona, California, Florida, and Texas—a finding consistent with the information from overseas markets. Ford and Firestone officials met with NHTSA officials and the decision was made to go ahead with the recall, although Firestone said in its statement that the incidence of tire-shredding accidents was small compared to the millions of tires produced.

Firestone's response to the recall was immediately lambasted by frustrated and frightened customers. Because it didn't have enough tires in stock to replace all those being recalled, Firestone decided to use a phased recall process to take place over a year, meaning that many customers would have to wait months for replacements. The recall began in southern states because heat was believed to be a contributing factor. However, customers in phases 2 and 3 of the recall (primarily midwestern and northern states) showed up at dealers (Firestone and Ford) demanding that their tires be replaced immediately. Experts on crisis management criticized Firestone's handling of the recall. One said, "After they announced the recall, they were not prepared to deal with it." Others questioned whether the tire manufacturer was too slow in issuing its recall. "The fact that the company is just step-ping up to the bat tells me they've never really had the consumer as the principal focus of their thinking," said a professor at Harvard Business School.

Faced with growing criticism, Ford Motor Company took the step of telling its almost 3,000 dealers not to wait for the phased recall. The automaker authorized its dealers to replace suspect tires immediately with models from Goodyear, General, Michelin, and Uniroyal. A Ford spokesman said, "The main thing is to get the recalled tires replaced as quickly as possible." In addition, Ford pointed a finger at Firestone's plant in Decatur, Illinois. Ford's vice president of communications said, "The data and the analysis of the data is that there's a problem with Decatur and that other plants are world-class." During the time of the production of the suspect tires, workers at the plant were on strike and it was operating with replacement workers and managers. Bridgestone/Firestone countered that the strike, which ended in 1995, had nothing to do with the problems.

QUESTIONS

1. Identify the main stakeholders involved in this situa-tion. What concerns might each stakeholder have? Are any of the stakeholders' concerns in conflict with each other? Explain. What are the implications for the two main parties—Ford and Bridgestone/Firestone?

2. Using Exhibit 5.10, analyze the intensity of the ethical dilemma facing managers at Ford and at Firestone.

How might the other factors that affect ethical and unethical behavior be involved? (See Exhibit 5.8.)

3. Was Ford (a) meeting its social obligation, (b) being socially responsive, or (c) being socially responsible? Explain your choice. How about Firestone?

4. Do some research on crisis management. What should each company have done differently?

Sources: The Associated Press, "Firestone Recall Criticized," *Springfield News Leader*, August 15, 2000, p. 6A; The Associated Press, "Ford Links Many Recalled Tires to Strike," *Springfield News Leader*, August 14, 2000, p. 1A; T. Aeppel and N. Shirouzu, "Bridgestone/Firestone Handling of Recall Results in Consumer Confusion, Chaos," *Wall Street Journal*, August 11, 2000, pp. A3+; R.E. Silverman and K.J. Dunham, "Bridgestone/Firestone's Handling of Recall Gets Mixed Reviews," *Wall Street Journal*, August 11, 2000, p. A6; R.L. Simison and others, "How the Tire Problem Turned into a Crisis for Firestone and Ford," *Wall Street Journal*, August 10, 2000, pp. A1+; T. Aeppel, "Firestone Will Replace 6.5 Million Tires," *Wall Street Journal*, August 10, 2000, pp. A3+; R.B. Schmitt, "Lawyer Famed as Tire Defects Expert Enters Spotlight with Firestone Recall," *Wall Street Journal*, August 10, 2000, p. A12; N. Shirouzu and K. Lundegaard, "Firestone Plans Sweeping Recall of Tires," *Wall Street Journal*, August 9, 2000, pp. A3+; R.B. Schmitt and K. Lundegaard, "Lawyers Are Gearing Up for More Tire Lawsuits," *Wall Street Journal*, August 9, 2000, p. A10; and T. Aeppel, "Tire Dilemma Puts Focus on Process of Manufacturing," *Wall Street Journal*, August 9, 2000, p. A10.

Video Case Application

When You Care Enough to Send the Very Best

SMALL BUSINESS 2000

Although "caring enough to send the very best" may be the marketing slogan for the world's largest manufacturer of greeting cards, caring and compassion also are fitting descriptions of Judi Jacobsen's Madison Park Greeting Card Company of Seattle (www.madpark.com). The slogan, however, would have to be changed to "caring enough to *do* the very best." Jacobsen's compassion is directed at the com-munity where her business is located and at the people she employs.

At the age of 30, Jacobsen decided to pursue her desire to paint. People who saw and bought her paintings told her that they would make good greeting cards. Taking that advice to heart, Jacobsen started Madison

Park Greeting Card Company. Today she sells her greet-ing cards in more than 6,000 specialty shops around the United States. At the time of this case, Madison Park employed 25 people and had reached the $3 million sales mark. The admirable part of this story isn't just the fact that Jacobsen was able to pursue *her* dream but that she also had a strong commitment to helping others. Her community involvement started with her decision to locate her business in a rundown section of the city and to help revitalize the area. In addition, she has a strong and specific concern for her employees.

Jacobsen's management philosophy is that one of the best things you can do for your people is to give them meaningful work. To put this philosophy into practice, she hired Cambodian refugees who couldn't speak English but who could pack cards into boxes. She hired hearing-impaired employees and displaced mothers for other jobs at Madison Park. Jacobsen strongly believes that people count more than the bottom line and that, although she understands that businesses must do well to be able to help others, having a balance between profits and people is important. She says, "If I had to choose people or profits, I'd put people first."

QUESTIONS

1. What types of values do you think Judi Jacobsen's Madison Park Greeting Card Company embraces?

2. Would you call Judi Jacobsen socially responsive or socially responsible? Explain your choice.

3. Using Exhibit 5.7, in which stage of social responsibility would you place Madison Park? Explain your choice.

4. Give your opinion of Judi's statement, "If I had to choose people or profits, I'd put people first." What would this type of philosophy imply as far as management decisions and actions?

Source: Based on *Small Business 2000, Show 104.*

Mastering Management

In Episode 8 of the Mastering Management *series, Andrew faces a difficult dilemma. One of his staff members confides that she is thinking of leaving CanGo. Soon after, Andrew has to decide whether to give this person access to potentially important information about the company. Andrew's dilemma serves as an opportunity to wrestle with the complexity of business ethics.*

MANAGING ENTREPRENEURIAL VENTURES

The Context of Entrepreneurship

Donna Dubinsky is an entrepreneur. First she cofounded Palm, the hand-held computing giant. Then she left and cofounded its highly successful rival, Handspring. By her mid-40s, she had created two companies with a total market value of more than $37 billion.

In this module on entrepreneurship, we're going to look at the activities that entrepreneurs like Donna Dubinsky engage in. We'll start by describing what entrepreneurship is and why it's important. Then, we'll discuss the entrepreneurial process, what entrepreneurs do, and the social responsibility and ethical issues affecting entrepreneurs.

What Is Entrepreneurship?

As we discussed in Chapter 2, entrepreneurship is the process where individuals or a group of individuals risk time and money in pursuit of opportunities to create value and grow through innovation regardless of the resources they currently control. The three important themes in this definition are (1) the pursuit of opportunities, (2) innovation, and (3) growth. Entrepreneurs are pursuing opportunities to grow a business by changing, revolutionizing, transforming, or introducing new products or services. For example, PixStream Inc. of Waterloo, Ontario, Canada, innovated a "better mousetrap" to take advantage of opportunities in the competitive battle between phone companies and cable television companies to deliver video services.[1] PixStream's networking equipment, used by phone companies to broadcast up to 96 different channels simultaneously, revolutionized conventional wisdom about what it takes to deliver video services. Its video server is about the size of a large microwave oven instead of 27 racks of equipment housed in a large room. Through its innovative products, PixStream successfully solved its customers' problems.

Many people think that entrepreneurial ventures and small businesses are one and the same, but they're not. There are some key differences between the two. Entrepreneurs create **entrepreneurial ventures**—organizations that are pursuing opportunities, are characterized by innovative practices, and have growth and profitability as their main goals. A **small business**, on the other hand, is one that is independently owned, operated, and financed; has fewer than 100 employees; doesn't necessarily engage in any new or innovative practices, and has relatively little impact on its industry.[2] A small business isn't necessarily entrepreneurial because it's small. To be entrepreneurial means being innovative and seeking out new opportunities. Even though entrepreneurial ventures may start small, they pursue growth.

Some new small firms may grow, but many remain small businesses, by choice or by default.

Why Is Entrepreneurship Important?

Entrepreneurship is, and continues to be, important to every industry sector in the United States and in most advanced countries.[3] Its importance in the United States can be shown in three areas: innovation, number of new start-ups, and job creation.

Innovation Innovating is a process of changing, experimenting, transforming, revolutionizing, and is a key aspect of entrepreneurial activity. The "creative destruction" process that characterizes innovation leads to technological changes and employment growth. Entrepreneurial firms act as "agents of change" by providing an essential source of new and unique ideas that might otherwise go untapped.[4] Statistics back this up. New small organizations generate 24 times more innovations per research and development dollar spent than do Fortune 500 organizations, and they account for over 95 percent of new and "radical" product developments.[5]

Number of New Start-Ups Because all businesses—whether they fit the definition of entrepreneurial or not—were new start-ups at one point in time, the most convenient measure we have of the role that entrepreneurship plays in the number of new start-ups is to look at the number of new firms over a period of time. Data collected by the U.S. Small Business Administration shows that the number of new start-ups rose between 1995 and 2000. If we assume that some of these new businesses engage in innovative practices and pursue profitability and growth, then entrepreneurship has contributed to the overall creation of new firms.

Job Creation We know that job creation is important to the overall long-term economic health of communities, regions, and nations. The latest figures show that virtually *all* new net jobs were generated by firms with fewer than 500 employees. Very small businesses (those with fewer than 20 employees) accounted for a whopping 77.2 percent of this growth![6] New organizations have been creating jobs at a fast pace even as many of the world's largest and well-known global corporations continued to downsize. These numbers reflect the importance of entrepreneurial firms as job creators.

But what about entrepreneurial activity outside the United States? What kind of impact has it had? An annual assessment of global entrepreneurship called the Global Entrepreneurship Monitor (GEM) studies the impact of entrepreneurial activity on economic growth in various countries. (You can download the year 2000 report at [www.entreworld.org/GEM2000]) The GEM 2000 report covered 21 countries that were divided into three levels of entrepreneurship. (See Exhibit P2.1.)

What did the researchers find? Among the major industrialized G-7 countries (group of seven countries including Canada, France, Germany, Italy, Japan, the United Kingdom, and the United States) in particular, there was a very strong relationship between the level of entrepreneurial activity and annual economic growth. "The GEM report provides conclusive evidence that promoting entrepreneurship and enhancing the entrepreneurial dynamics of a country should be an integral element of any government's commitment to boosting economic well being."[7] From a global perspective, therefore, we also can conclude that entrepreneurship plays an important role in a country's economic growth.

Testing...Testing...1,2,3

1. **Differentiate between entrepreneurial ventures and small businesses.**

2. **Why is entrepreneurship important in the United States?**

3. **Is the pursuit of entrepreneurship important only in the United States? Explain.**

The Entrepreneurial Process

What's involved in the entrepreneurial process? There are four key steps that entrepreneurs must address as they start and manage their entrepreneurial ventures. The first of these is *exploring the entrepreneurial context*. The context includes the realities of the new economy, society's laws and regulations that compose the legal environment, and the realities of the changing world of work. It's important to look at each of these aspects of the entrepreneurial context because they determine the "rules" of the game and what decisions and actions are likely to meet with success. Also, it's through exploring the context that entrepreneurs confront that next critically important step in the entrepreneurial process—*identifying opportunities and possible competitive advantages*. We know from our definition of entrepreneurship that the pursuit of opportunities is an important aspect. Once entrepreneurs have explored the entrepreneurial context and identified opportunities and possible competitive advantages, they must look at the issues involved with actually bringing their entrepreneurial venture to life. Therefore, the next step in the entrepreneurial process is *starting the venture*. Included in this phase are researching the feasibility of the venture, planning the venture, organizing the venture, and launching the venture. Finally, once the entrepreneurial venture is up and running, the last step in the entrepreneurial process is *managing the venture*, which an entrepreneur does by managing processes, managing people, and managing growth. We'll

Exhibit P2.1			
Level of Entrepreneurial Activity	**Top Level**	**Middle Level**	**Lowest Level**
	Australia	Argentina	France
	Canada	Belgium	Japan
	Korea	Brazil	
	Norway	Denmark	
	United States	Finland	
		Germany	
		India	
		Israel	
		Ireland	
		Italy	
		Singapore	
		Spain	
		Sweden	
		United Kingdom	

Source: Based on "Economic Growth Linked to Levels of Business Start-Ups," *GEM2000* Report, found online at [www.babson.edu/press/gemGrowth2000.html], December 22, 2000.

explore each of these important steps in the entrepreneurial process in the entrepreneurship modules at the end of Parts 3, 4, 5, and 6.

What Do Entrepreneurs Do?

Describing what entrepreneurs do isn't an easy or simple task! No two entrepreneurs' work activities are exactly alike. In a general sense, entrepreneurs are creating something new, something different. They're searching for change, responding to it, and exploiting it.[8]

Initially, an entrepreneur is engaged in assessing the potential for the entrepreneurial venture and then dealing with start-up issues. In exploring the entrepreneurial context, entrepreneurs are gathering information, identifying potential opportunities, and pinpointing possible competitive advantage(s). Then, armed with this information, the entrepreneur begins researching the venture's feasibility—uncovering business ideas, looking at competitors, and exploring financing options. After looking at the potential of the proposed venture and assessing the likelihood of pursuing it successfully, the entrepreneur proceeds to planning the venture. This includes such activities as developing a viable organizational mission, exploring organizational culture issues, and creating a well-thought-out business plan. Once these planning issues have been resolved, the entrepreneur must look at organizing the venture which involves choosing a legal form of business organization, addressing other legal issues such as patent or copyright searches, and coming up with an appropriate organizational design for structuring how work is going to be done. After these start-up activities have been completed, the entrepreneur is ready to actually launch the venture. This involves setting goals and strategies, and establishing the technology-operations methods, marketing plans, information systems, financial-accounting systems, and cash flow management systems.

Once the entrepreneurial venture is up and running, the entrepreneur's attention switches to managing it. What's involved with actually managing the entrepreneurial venture? An important activity is managing the various processes that are part of every business: making decisions, establishing action plans, analyzing external and internal environments, measuring and evaluating performance, and making needed changes. Also, the entrepreneur must perform activities associated with managing people including selecting and hiring, appraising and training, motivating, managing conflict, delegating tasks, and being an effective leader. Finally, the entrepreneur must manage the venture's growth which includes such activities as developing and designing growth strategies, dealing with crises, exploring various avenues for financing growth, placing a value

on the venture, and perhaps even eventually exiting the venture.

Social Responsibility and Ethics Issues Facing Entrepreneurs

As they launch and manage their ventures, entrepreneurs are faced with the often difficult issues of social responsibility and ethics. Just how important are these issues to entrepreneurs? An overwhelming majority of respondents (95 percent) in a study of small companies believed that developing a positive reputation and relationship in communities where they do business was important for achieving business goals.[9] However, despite the importance these individuals placed on corporate citizenship, more than half lacked formal programs for connecting with their communities. In fact, some 70 percent of the respondents admitted that they failed to consider community goals in their business plans. Yet, there are some entrepreneurs who take their social responsibilities seriously. For example, Josie Ippolito, president of La Canasta Mexican Food Products, Inc., in Phoenix, manages a factory that turns out 1 million tortillas daily and is located in the middle of an inner-city neighborhood.[10] The company is committed to the economic well-being of its neighborhood and employs about 100 workers from the local area. La Canasta is growing and rather than abandoning the neighborhood, Josie added an expansion to her current facility that will double capacity. She says, "Where are these people going to get jobs?"

Other entrepreneurs have pursued opportunities with products and services that protect the global environment. For example, Univenture Inc. of Columbus, Ohio, makes recyclable sleeves and packaging for disc media. Its products are better for the environment as compared to the traditional jewel boxes most compact discs are packaged in. Ross Youngs, president and CEO says "Our products won't break. If someone throws it away, it's because they don't want it. Hopefully they will end up in the recycle bin because our products are recyclable."[11]

Ethical considerations also play a role in decisions and actions of entrepreneurs. Entrepreneurs do need to be aware of the ethical consequences of what they do. The example they set, particularly if there are other employees, can be profoundly significant in influencing behavior. For example, Charlie Wilson, founder of Houston-based SeaRail International Inc., made ethics a consideration in putting together guidelines for his sales representatives. He said, "Ethics is what's spearheading our growth. It creates an element of trust, familiarity, and predictability in the business . . . You don't get a good reputation doing things that way [unethically]. And, if you do [act unethically], eventually customers won't want to do business with you."[12]

The importance that entrepreneurs place on ethics can be seen in the results of a study of approximately 300 entrepreneurs and corporate managers. It showed that entrepreneurs generally have stricter ethical standards than do managers and are also better able to live by their beliefs, probably because they have more control over their decisions and actions. Only half of the entrepreneur respondents said that they would sacrifice personal ethics to achieve business goals as compared to 71 percent of the corporate managers.[13]

Testing...Testing...1,2,3

4. **Describe the four key steps in the entrepreneurial process.**

5. **What do entrepreneurs do?**

6. **Why are social responsibility and ethical considerations important to entrepreneurs?**

INTEGRATED VIDEO CASE **PART 2**

Managing in a Global Environment

On Location

This video takes us to the offices of Arnold Worldwide, the marketing/public relations agency; Spiewak, Inc., the New York-based outdoor clothing retail company; and Monster.com, the online recruiting and job assistance firm.

Each of these U.S. firms also manages a growing overseas operation. In this segment, you'll hear executives from all three describe the challenges and opportunities they have faced in their expanding international businesses. For Arnold, growth overseas led the company to change its name to Arnold Worldwide, signifying its willingness to venture abroad where many of its clients were already working successfully.

Although it has been exporting its products since the end of World War II, Spiewak truly ventured abroad only when foreign customers began to seek out its fashion clothing and uniform lines. After doing business with a Japanese buyer for several years, the company approached him with an offer to sell Spiewak's line to other Japanese customers. The firm now sells to many countries in Asia and Europe. Spiewak's managers already knew the market existed; the question was how to reach it.

Monster.com believes its service—job counseling and placement—is nearly universal. What differs when the firm moves abroad is the language and culture—but the company's managers know that the technology supporting its growing list of Web sites is easily transferable to new markets. Its sites in Spain, France, New Zealand, India, Germany, and other countries—which you can visit from its U.S. homepage—all are built on the same model and offer similar features.

Stepping into the international arena has brought new challenges for all three firms. Spiewak has found that it must adapt to the local culture in such everyday matters as getting paid. Its Japanese customers proved most adept at dealing with currency translation and the intricacies of international transactions. In France, customers were less interested in adapting to the many nuances of global transactions and expected Spiewak to operate as if it were a French manufacturer. Think about why the firm decided to make its dealings in France as transparent to

French wholesalers as possible. Spiewak faced yet a different kind of challenge in Italy. Do you think its international operations share any logistical challenges with the foreign branches of Monster.com or Arnold?

Arnold has approached international growth by acquiring small marketing firms overseas and, on occasion, staffing them with the best people from its U.S. headquarters to ensure that the business grows as expected. You might notice in the film segment that having a high-ranking person from the U.S. office on board creates other benefits for Arnold as well. How do you think Monster.com might ensure that its corporate mission and culture travel well overseas?

Consider the cultural challenges faced by Arnold Worldwide and Monster.com in particular. When companies expand to the international marketplace, they often find that working conditions and employee expectations in regard to salary, benefits, and promotion are very different from what they are at home.

DISCUSSION QUESTIONS

1. Arnold Worldwide strives to transfer its business philosophy intact to each new international office it opens, yet Monster.com deliberately operates under a different philosophy abroad, striving to be the number-one firm in its market, than it does in the United States, where it already is the top firm. How do you think its philosophy affects the day-to-day operations of Monster.com's international offices?

2. What do you think of Arnold Worldwide's growth strategy of making international acquisitions? What are some of the advantages and disadvantages of such a strategy in general?

3. Spiewak adapts its business practices to the environment in which it operates, using a distributor in Italy, for instance, because it ensures that collections run smoothly. Does a company lose anything by following an adaptive strategy?

4. What impact do you think the Internet has had on the international operations of each of these firms? Do you think their experiences are representative of other service, product, and Web-based firms?

Learning Objectives

After reading and studying this chapter, you should be able to:

1. Outline the steps in the decision-making process.

2. Explain why decision making is so pervasive in organizations.

3. Describe the rational decision maker.

4. Contrast the perfectly rational and boundedly rational approaches to decision making.

5. Explain the role that intuition plays in the decision-making process.

6. Identify the two types of decision problems and the two types of decisions that are used to solve them.

7. Differentiate the decision conditions of certainty, risk, and uncertainty.

8. Describe the different decision-making styles.

A MANAGER'S DILEMMA

Its bicycles are loved by customers and respected by competitors. Cannondale Corporation (www.cannondale.com) based in Bethel, Connecticut, is a leading maker of mountain, road racing, multisport, recreational, and specialty bicycles.[1] Not content to stay on a gentle, smooth, and predictable path, Cannondale's managers decided to go in a new direction by introducing a new line of off-road motorcycles in the spring of 2000. Mario Galasso, vice president of product development at the company who also races bikes in his off-hours, helped design the new dirt bike.

It's hoped that the company's new motorcycle will help double sales and give a boost to the stock price that's been languishing around $5 1/2 a share, down from a high of $28 in 1998. However, to accomplish these lofty goals, the company will have to steal market share from some serious competition: Yamaha, Suzuki, Kawasaki, and Honda. Yet, there's some good news as well. Recreational off-road biking is extremely popular now. This boom is being fed by televised motocross competitions. Galasso says, "The whole thing is kind of going crazy." He hopes that the new bike his group has designed will attract wide consumer interest.

The path to the introduction of Cannondale's new motorcycle was about as unpredictable and bumpy as some of the trails that the company's customers love to traverse. Bringing a new product out is a

Decision-Making: The Essence of the Manager's Job

6

difficult proposition for any company, and Cannondale's product development expertise, although extremely proficient in high-end bicycles, was put to the test. The whole process took a couple of years longer than expected. Galasso relished the challenge, however. He explained, "The point of riding and racing is trying to make your bike lighter, faster, trying to get an edge over a guy. You don't get into this if you don't think you can do it better."

Now that the new bike is out, how could Galasso evaluate the effectiveness of the decision? What decision criteria might he use?

WHAT WOULD YOU DO?

Like managers everywhere, Mario Galasso needs to make good decisions at Cannondale Corporation. Making good decisions is something that every manager strives to do since the overall quality of managerial decisions has a major influence on organizational success or failure. In this chapter, we examine the concept of decision making and how managers make decisions.

> ### THE DECISION-MAKING PROCESS

decision

A choice from two or more alternatives.

Individuals at all levels and in all areas of organizations make **decisions**. That is, they make choices from two or more alternatives. For instance, top-level managers make decisions about their organization's goals, where to locate manufacturing facilities, what new markets to move into, and what products or services to offer. Middle and lower-level managers make decisions about setting weekly or monthly production schedules, handling problems that arise, allocating pay raises, and selecting or disciplining employees. But making decisions isn't something that just managers do. All organizational members make decisions that affect their jobs and the organization they work for. How do they make those decisions?

Although decision making is typically described as "choosing among alternatives," that view is too simplistic. Why? Because decision making is a comprehensive process, not just a simple act of choosing among alternatives. Even for something as straightforward as deciding where to go for lunch, you do more than just choose burgers or pizza. Granted, you may not spend a lot of time contemplating the lunch decision, but you still engage in the steps in the decision-making process. What *does* the decision-making process involve?

decision-making process

A set of eight steps including identifying a problem, selecting an alternative, and evaluating the decision's effectiveness.

Exhibit 6.1 illustrates the **decision-making process**, a set of eight steps that begins with identifying a problem and decision criteria and allocating weights to those criteria; moves to developing, analyzing, and selecting an alternative that can resolve the problem; implements the alternative; and concludes with evaluating the decision's effectiveness. This process is as relevant to your personal decision about what movie to see on a Friday night as it is to a corporate action such as Cannondale's decision to start manufacturing and marketing motorcycles. The process also can be used to describe both individual and group decisions. Let's take a closer look at the process in order to understand what each step involves.

STEP 1: IDENTIFYING A PROBLEM

problem

A discrepancy between an existing and a desired state of affairs.

The decision-making process begins with the existence of a **problem** or, more specifically, a discrepancy between an existing and a desired state of affairs.[2] Let's develop an example that illustrates this point and that we can use throughout our discussion of the decision-making process. To keep it simple, let's make the example something most of us can relate to: the decision to buy a new laptop computer. Take the case of Joan, a sales manager whose sales representatives need new laptops because their old ones aren't fast enough and don't have sufficient memory to handle the volume of work. Again, for simplicity's sake, assume that it's not economical to simply add memory to the old ones and that it's corporate policy that managers purchase new computers rather than lease them. Now we have a problem. There's a disparity between the sales representatives' current computers and their need to have larger, faster computers. Joan has a decision to make.

Exhibit   6.1

The Decision-Making Process

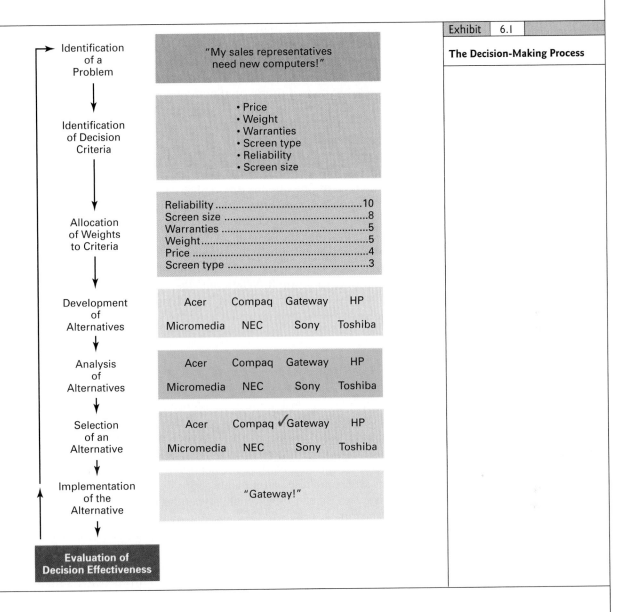

Unfortunately, this example doesn't tell us much about how managers identify problems. In the real world, most problems don't come with neon signs flashing "problem." The sales representatives' complaints about inadequate computing ability to do their jobs effectively might be a clear signal to Joan that she needs to get them new computers, but few problems are that obvious. Is a 5 percent drop in sales a problem? Or are declining sales merely a symptom of other problems, such as unsatisfactory products or poor advertising? Also, keep in mind that what one manager considers a problem might not be considered a problem by another manager. Problem identification is subjective. Furthermore, the manager who mistakenly resolves the wrong problem perfectly is likely to perform just as poorly as the manager who doesn't identify the right problem and does nothing. Problem identification isn't simple or insignificant.[3] Before something can be characterized as a problem, managers have to be aware of the problem, be under pressure to take action, and have the resources needed to take action.[4]

How do managers become aware of a problem? They obviously have to compare their current state of affairs against where they want to be. If they're not where they want to be or if things aren't going as they should, then a problem (or discrepancy) exists. In our computer buying example, the problem is that the current computers aren't sufficient for the sales representatives to do their jobs efficiently and effectively.

A discrepancy without pressure to take action becomes a problem that can be postponed. To initiate the decision process, then, the problem must be such that it exerts some type of pressure on the manager to act. Pressure might come from organizational policies, deadlines, financial crises, competitor actions (think of our chapter-opening manager's dilemma), complaints from customers or subordinates, expectations from the boss, or an upcoming performance evaluation.

Finally, managers aren't likely to characterize something as a problem if they perceive that they don't have the authority, budget, information, or other resources necessary to act on it. When managers become aware of a problem and are under pressure to act but feel they have inadequate resources, they usually describe the situation as one in which unrealistic expectations are being placed on them.

STEP 2: IDENTIFYING DECISION CRITERIA

decision criteria

Criteria that define what's relevant in a decision.

Once a manager has identified a problem that needs attention, the **decision criteria** important to resolving the problem must be identified. That is, managers must determine what's relevant in making a decision. In our computer buying example, Joan has to assess what factors are relevant to her decision. These might include criteria such as price, product model and manufacturer, standard features, optional equipment, service warranties, repair record, and service support after purchase. After careful consideration, Joan decides that price, weight, warranties, screen type, reliability, and screen size are the relevant criteria in her decision.

Whether they are explicitly stated or not, every decision maker has criteria that guide his or her decisions. Note that, in this step in the decision-making process, what *isn't* identified is as important as what *is*. If Joan doesn't consider a service warranty a decision criterion, then it will not influence her final choice of computers.

Testing...Testing...1,2,3

1. **What is a decision, and who makes decisions in organizations?**

2. **In the first step of the decision-making process, how do managers know when there is a problem?**

3. **What are decision criteria, and why are they important to decision makers?**

STEP 3: ALLOCATING WEIGHTS TO THE CRITERIA

The criteria identified in Step 2 aren't all equally important, so the decision maker must weight the items in order to give them the correct priority in the decision. How do you weight criteria? A simple approach is to give the most important criterion a weight of 10 and then assign weights to the rest against that standard. Thus, a criterion with a weight of 10 would be twice as important as one given a 5. Of course, you could use 100 or 1,000 or any number you select as the highest weight. The idea is to use your personal preferences to prioritize the criteria you identified in Step 2 by assigning a weight to each.

Exhibit 6.2 lists the criteria and weights that Joan developed for her computer replacement decision. As you can see, reliability is the most important criterion in her decision, with such factors as price and screen type having low weights.

Criterion	Weight		Exhibit 6.2
			Criteria and Weights for Computer Replacement Decision
Reliability	10[a]		
Screen size	8		
Warranty period	5		
Weight	5		
Price	4		
Screen type	3		

[a]In this example, the highest rating for a criterion is 10 points.

STEP 4: DEVELOPING ALTERNATIVES

The fourth step requires the decision maker to list the viable alternatives that could resolve the problem. No attempt is made in this step to evaluate the alternatives, only to list them. Our sales manager, Joan, identified eight laptop models as viable choices including Acer TravelMate 734TL, Compaq Presario 1800XL186, Gateway Solo 2550LS, Hewlett-Packard Omnibook 900, Micromedia Computers Millennium 3000, NEC Direct Versa Note VX 14.1, Sony Vaio PCG-X18, and Toshiba Satellite Pro 4280.

STEP 5: ANALYZING ALTERNATIVES

Once the alternatives have been identified, the decision maker must critically analyze each one. Each alternative is evaluated by appraising it against the criteria established in Steps 2 and 3. From this comparison, the strengths and weaknesses of each alternative become evident. Exhibit 6.3 shows the assessed values that Joan gave each of her eight alternatives after she had talked to some computer experts and read the latest information from computer magazines.

Keep in mind that the ratings (on a 1 to 10 scale) given the eight computer models shown in Exhibit 6.3 are based on the personal assessment made by Joan. Some assessments can be done pretty objectively. For instance, the purchase price represents the best price she can get from local retailers, and performance data and weight were reported in computer magazines. However, the assessment of reliability is often a personal judgment. The point is that most decisions by managers involve judgments—the criteria chosen in Step 2, the weights given to the criteria in Step 3, and the evaluation of alternatives in Step 5. This explains why two computer buyers with the same amount of money may look at two totally different sets of alternatives or even rate the same alternatives differently.

When making decisions, as in our computer purchase for example, managers must identify the criteria—model, brand, price, warranty period—that are important.

Model	Reliability	Screen Size	Warranty	Weight	Price	Screen Type
Acer TravelMate 734TL	8	3	5	10	3	5
Compaq Presario 1800 XL186	8	5	10	5	6	5
Gateway Solo 2550 LS	10	8	5	10	3	10
Hewlett-Packard Omnibook 900	8	5	5	10	3	10
Micromedia Computers Millennium 3000	6	8	5	10	6	10
NEC Direct Versa Note VX 14.1	10	8	5	5	3	10
Sony Vaio PCG-X18	2	10	5	10	10	10
Toshiba Satellite Pro 4280	4	10	5	10	10	5

Exhibit 6.3 represents only an assessment of the eight alternatives against the decision criteria. It doesn't reflect the weighting done in Step 3. If one choice had scored 10 on every criterion, you wouldn't need to consider the weights. Similarly, if the weights were all equal, you could evaluate each alternative merely by summing up the appropriate lines in Exhibit 6.3. For instance, the Acer TravelMate 734TL would have a score of 34, and the Sony Vaio PCG-X18 would have a score of 47. However, if you multiply each alternative assessment (Exhibit 6.3) by its weight (Exhibit 6.1), you get Exhibit 6.4. The sum of these scores represents an evaluation of each alternative against both the established criteria and weights. Notice that the weighting of the criteria significantly changes the ranking of alternatives in our example.

STEP 6: SELECTING AN ALTERNATIVE

The sixth step is the important act of choosing the best alternative from among those considered. We have determined all the pertinent criteria in the decision, weighted them, and identified and analyzed viable alternatives. Now we merely have to choose the alternative that generated the highest score in Step 5. In our computer purchase example (Exhibit 6.4), Joan would choose the Gateway Solo 2550 LS computer since it scored highest (281 points) on the basis of the criteria identified, the weights given to the criteria, and Joan's assessment of each computer's ranking on the criteria. It's the "best" alternative and the one she should choose.

Model	Reliability	Screen Size	Warranty	Weight	Price	Screen Type	Total
Acer TravelMate 734TL	80	24	25	50	12	15	206
Compaq Presario 1800 XL186	80	40	50	25	24	15	234
Gateway Solo 2550 LS	100	64	25	50	12	30	281
Hewlett-Packard Omnibook 900	80	40	25	50	12	30	237
Micromedia Computers Millennium 3000	60	64	25	50	24	30	253
NEC Direct Versa Note VX 14.1	100	64	25	25	12	30	256
Sony Vaio PCG-X18	20	80	25	50	40	30	245
Toshiba Satellite Pro 4280	40	80	25	50	40	15	250

STEP 7: IMPLEMENTING THE ALTERNATIVE

Although the choice process is completed in the previous step, the decision may still fail if it isn't implemented properly. Therefore, Step 7 is concerned with putting the decision into action.

Implementation involves conveying the decision to those affected by it and getting their commitment to it. As we'll discuss in Chapter 15, groups or teams can help a manager with commitment. If the people who must carry out a decision participate in the process, they're more likely to enthusiastically support the outcome than if they are just told what to do. For instance, in our decision example, if the sales representatives had participated in the purchase decision, they'd probably enthusiastically support the computer model chosen and any new training necessary. (Parts Three through Five of this book detail how decisions are implemented by effective planning, organizing, and leading.)

implementation

Conveying a decision to those affected and getting their commitment to it.

STEP 8: EVALUATING DECISION EFFECTIVENESS

The last step in the decision-making process involves appraising the outcome of the decision to see if the problem has been resolved. Did the alternative chosen in Step 6 and implemented in Step 7 accomplish the desired result? How to evaluate results is detailed in Part Six of this book, where we look at the control function.

What would happen if, as a result of this evaluation, the problem still existed? The manager would then need to carefully assess what went wrong. Was the problem incorrectly defined? Were errors made in the evaluation of the various alternatives? Was the right alternative selected but poorly implemented? Answers to questions such as these might send the manager back to one of the earlier steps. It might even require starting the whole decision process over.

〉 THE PERVASIVENESS OF DECISION MAKING

Everyone in an organization makes decisions, but decision making is particularly important in a manager's job. As Exhibit 6.5 shows, decision making is part of all four managerial functions. That is why managers—when they plan, organize, lead, and control—are frequently called *decision makers*. In fact, we can say that *decision making* is synonymous with *managing*.[5]

Exhibit	6.5
Decisions in the Management Functions	

Planning
What are the organization's long-term objectives?
What strategies will best achieve those objectives?
What should the organization's short-term objectives be?
How difficult should individual goals be?

Organizing
How many employees should I have report directly to me?
How much centralization should there be in the organization?
How should jobs be designed?
When should the organization implement a different structure?

Leading
How do I handle employees who appear to be low in motivation?
What is the most effective leadership style in a given situation?
How will a specific change affect worker productivity?
When is the right time to stimulate conflict?

Controlling
What activities in the organization need to be controlled?
How should those activities be controlled?
When is a performance deviation significant?
What type of management information system should the organization have?

Testing...Testing...1,2,3

4. **Why is the allocation of weights to criteria important in making decisions?**

5. **How do managers develop, analyze, select, and implement alternatives and then assess whether the decision was effective?**

6. **Why are managers typically described as decision makers?**

The fact that almost everything a manager does involves making decisions doesn't mean that decisions are always long, complex, or clearly evident to an outside observer. Much of a manager's decision making is routine. Every day of the year you make a decision about the problem of when to eat dinner. It's no big deal. You've made the decision thousands of times before. It's a pretty simple decision and can usually be handled quickly. It's the type of decision you almost forget *is* a decision. Managers make dozens of these routine decisions every day. Keep in mind that even though a decision seems easy to make or has been faced by a manager a number of times before, it still is a decision.

〉 THE MANAGER AS DECISION MAKER

Although we've described the steps in the decision-making process, we still don't know much about the manager as a decision maker and how decisions are actually made in organizations. How can we best describe the decision-making situation and the person who makes the decisions? We look at those issues in this section. We'll start by looking at three perspectives on how decisions are made.

MAKING DECISIONS: RATIONALITY, BOUNDED RATIONALITY, AND INTUITION

rational decision making

Describes choices that are consistent and value maximizing within specified constraints.

Managerial decision making is assumed to be **rational**. By that we mean that managers make consistent, value-maximizing choices within specified constraints.[6] What are the underlying assumptions of rationality, and how valid are those assumptions?

Assumptions of Rationality A decision maker who was perfectly rational would be fully objective and logical. He or she would carefully define a problem and would have a clear and specific goal. Moreover, making decisions using rationality would consistently lead toward selecting the alternative that maximizes the likelihood of achieving that goal. Exhibit 6.6 summarizes the assumptions of rationality.

The assumptions of rationality apply to any decision. Because we're concerned with managerial decision making, however, we need to add one further assumption. Rational managerial decision making assumes that decisions are made in the best *economic* interests of the organization. That is, the decision maker is assumed to be maximizing the organization's interests, not his or her own interests.

How realistic are these assumptions about rationality? Managerial decision making can follow rational assumptions if the following conditions are met:

Exhibit 6.6

Assumptions of Rationality

Lead to

- The problem is clear and unambiguous.
- A single, well-defined goal is to be achieved.
- All alternatives and consequences are known.
- Preferences are clear.
- Preferences are constant and stable.
- No time or cost constraints exist.
- Final choice will maximize payoff.

Rational Decision Making

The manager is faced with a simple problem in which the goals are clear and the alternatives limited, in which the time pressures are minimal and the cost of seeking out and evaluating alternatives is low, for which the organizational culture supports innovation and risk taking, and in which the outcomes are relatively concrete and measurable.[7] But most decisions that managers face in the real world don't meet all those tests.[8] So how are most decisions in organizations usually made? The concept of bounded rationality can help answer that question.

Bounded Rationality Despite the limits to perfect rationality, managers are expected to follow a rational process when making decisions.[9] Managers know that "good" decision makers are supposed to do certain things: identify problems, consider alternatives, gather information, and act decisively but prudently. Managers, thus, are expected to exhibit the correct decision-making behaviors. By doing so, managers signal to their superiors, peers, and subordinates that they are competent and that their decisions are the result of intelligent and rational deliberation. However, certain aspects of the decision-making process are not realistic with respect to how managers make decisions. Instead, managers tend to operate under assumptions of **bounded rationality**; that is, they behave rationally within the parameters of a simplified decision-making process that is limited (or bounded) by an individual's ability to process information.[10] Because they can't possibly analyze all information on all alternatives, managers **satisfice** rather than maximize. That is, they accept solutions that are "good enough." They are being rational within the limits (bounds) of their information processing ability. Let's look at an example. Suppose that you're a finance major and upon graduation you want a job, preferably as a personal financial planner, with a minimum salary of $32,000 and within a hundred miles of your hometown. You accept a job offer as a business credit analyst—not exactly a personal financial planner but still in the finance field—at a bank 50 miles from home at a starting salary of $33,000. A more comprehensive job search would have revealed a job in personal financial planning at a trust company only 25 miles from your hometown and starting at a salary of $35,000. Because the first job offer was satisfactory (or "good enough"), you behaved in a boundedly rational manner by accepting it, although according to the assumptions of perfect rationality, you didn't maximize your decision by searching all possible alternatives and choosing the best.

Since most decisions that managers make don't fit the assumptions of perfect rationality, they instead make those decisions using a boundedly rational approach. That is, they make decisions based on alternatives that are satisfactory. However, keep in mind that their decision making also may be strongly influenced by the organization's culture, internal politics, power considerations, and by a phenomenon called **escalation of commitment**, which is an increased commitment to a previous decision despite evidence that it may have been wrong.[11] For example, studies of the events leading up to the *Challenger* space shuttle disaster point to an escalation of commitment by decision makers to launch the shuttle on that fateful day even though the decision was questioned by certain individuals. Why would decision makers want to escalate commitment to a bad decision? Because they don't want to admit that their initial decision may have been flawed. Rather than search for new alternatives, they simply increase their commitment to the original solution.

bounded rationality

Behavior that is rational within the parameters of a simplified decision-making process, which is limited (or bounded) by an individual's ability to process information.

satisficing

Acceptance of solutions that are "good enough."

escalation of commitment

An increased commitment to a previous decision despite evidence that it may have been wrong.

Exhibit	6.7		**What Is Intuition?**

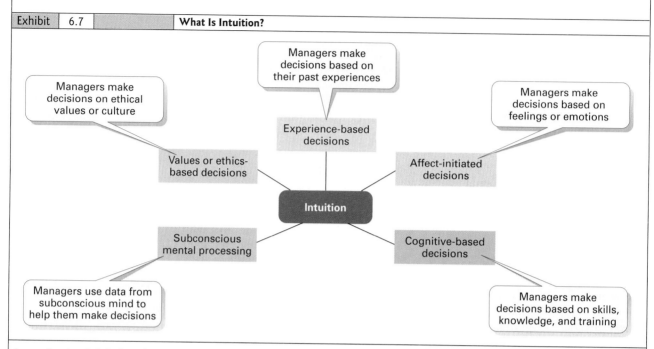

Source: Based on L.A. Burke and M.K. Miller, "Taking the Mystery Out of Intuitive Decision Making," *Academy of Management Executive,* October 1999, pp. 91–99.

intuitive decision making

A subconscious process of making decisions on the basis of experience and accumulated judgment.

Role of Intuition What role does intuition play in managerial decision making? Managers regularly use their intuition and it may actually help improve their decision making.[12] What is **intuitive decision making**? It's a subconscious process of making decisions on the basis of experience and accumulated judgment. Researchers studying managers' use of intuitive decision making identified five different aspects of intuition, which are described in Exhibit 6.7.

Making a decision on intuition or "gut feeling" doesn't necessarily happen independently of rational analysis; rather, the two complement each other. A manager who has had experience with a particular, or even similar, type of problem or situation often can act quickly with what appears to be limited information. Such a manager doesn't rely on a systematic and thorough analysis of the problem or identification and evaluation of alternatives but instead uses his or her experience and judgment to make a decision.

How common is intuitive decision making? One survey of managers and other organizational employees revealed that almost one-third of them emphasized "gut feeling" over cognitive problem solving and decision making.[13]

Testing...Testing...1,2,3

7. **Describe decision making from the rationality and bounded rationality views.**

8. **What is escalation of commitment and how does it influence decision making?**

9. **Describe the role of intuition in decision making.**

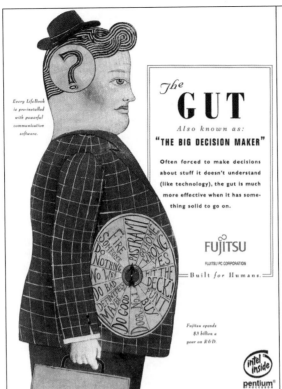

This humorous ad for the Fujitsu PC Corporation acknowledges the power of intuitive decision making.

TYPES OF PROBLEMS AND DECISIONS

Managers will be faced with different types of problems and decisions as they do their jobs. Depending on the nature of the problem, the manager can use different types of decisions.

Well-Structured Problems and Programmed Decisions Some problems are straightforward. The goal of the decision maker is clear, the problem is familiar, and information about the problem is easily defined and complete. Examples of these types of problems might include a customer's wanting to return a purchase to a retail store, a supplier's being late with an important delivery, a news team's responding to an unexpected and fast-breaking event, or a college's handling of a student wanting to drop a class. Such situations are called **well-structured problems** since they are straightforward, familiar, and easily defined problems. For instance, a server in a restaurant spills a drink on a customer's coat. The manager has an upset customer and he or she needs to do something. Because drinks are frequently spilled, there's probably some standardized routine for handling the problem. For example, the manager offers to have the coat cleaned at the restaurant's expense. In handling this problem situation, the manager uses a **programmed decision**.

Decisions are programmed to the extent that they are repetitive and routine and to the extent that a definite approach has been worked out for handling them. Because the problem is well structured, the manager doesn't have to go to the trouble and expense of going through an involved decision process.

well-structured problems

Straightforward, familiar, and easily defined problems.

programmed decision

A repetitive decision that can be handled by a routine approach.

Programmed decision making is relatively simple and tends to rely heavily on previous solutions. The "develop-the-alternatives" stage in the decision-making process either doesn't exist or is given little attention. Why? Because once the structured problem is defined, its solution is usually self-evident or at least reduced to very few alternatives that are familiar and that have proved successful in the past. In many cases, programmed decision making becomes decision making by precedent. The spilled drink on the customer's coat doesn't require the restaurant manager to identify and weight decision criteria or to develop a long list of possible solutions. Rather, the manager falls back on a systematic procedure, rule, or policy.

A **procedure** is a series of interrelated sequential steps that a manager can use for responding to a structured problem. The only real difficulty is in identifying the problem. Once the problem is clear, so is the procedure. For instance, a purchasing manager receives a request from the sales department for 15 Palm Pilots for use by the company's customer service representatives. The purchasing manager knows that there is a definite procedure for handling this decision. The decision-making process in this case is merely executing a simple series of sequential steps.

A **rule** is an explicit statement that tells a manager what he or she can or cannot do. Rules are frequently used by managers when they confront a well-structured problem because they are simple to follow and ensure consistency. For example, rules about lateness and absenteeism permit supervisors to make disciplinary decisions rapidly and with a relatively high degree of fairness.

A third guide for making programmed decisions is a **policy**. It provides guidelines to channel a manager's thinking in a specific direction. In contrast to a rule, a policy establishes parameters for the decision maker rather than specifically stating what should or should not be done. Policies typically contain an ambiguous term that leaves interpretation up to the decision maker. For instance, each of the following is a policy statement:

The customer always comes first and should always be *satisfied*.

We promote from within, *whenever possible*.

Employee wages shall be *competitive* within community standards.

Notice that *satisfied, whenever possible,* and *competitive* are terms that require interpretation. The policy to pay competitive wages does not tell a company's human resources manager the exact amount he or she should pay, but it does give direction to the decision he or she makes.

Poorly Structured Problems and Nonprogrammed Decisions As you can well imagine, not all problems that managers face are well structured and solvable by a programmed decision. Many organizational situations involve **poorly structured problems**, which are problems that are new or unusual and for which information is ambiguous or incomplete. For example, the selection of an architect to design a new corporate manufacturing facility in Bangkok is an example of a poorly structured problem. So too is the problem of whether to invest in a new unproven technology or whether to shut down a money-losing division. When problems are poorly structured, managers must rely on nonprogrammed decision making in order to develop unique solutions. **Nonprogrammed decisions** are unique and nonrecurring. When a manager confronts a poorly structured problem, or one that is unique, there is no cut-and-dried solution. It requires a custom-made response through nonprogrammed decision making.

---

procedure

A series of interrelated sequential steps that can be used to respond to a well-structured problem.

rule

An explicit statement that tells managers what they can or cannot do.

policy

A guideline that establishes parameters for making decisions.

poorly structured problems

Problems that are new or unusual and for which information is ambiguous or incomplete.

nonprogrammed decisions

A unique decision that requires a custom-made solution.

Integration Exhibit 6.8 describes the relationship among the types of problems, the types of decisions, and organizational level. Because lower-level managers confront familiar and repetitive problems (well structured), they mostly rely on programmed decisions such as procedures, rules, and organizational policies. The problems confronting managers usually become more poorly structured as they move up the organizational hierarchy. Why? Because lower-level managers handle the routine decisions themselves and turn over to upper-level managers the decisions they find unusual or difficult. Similarly, higher-level managers turn over routine decisions to their subordinates so they can deal with more difficult issues.

Keep in mind, however, that few managerial decisions in the real world are either fully programmed or nonprogrammed. These are extremes, and most decisions fall somewhere in between. Few programmed decisions are designed to eliminate individual judgment completely. At the other extreme, even a unique situation requiring a nonprogrammed decision can be helped by programmed routines. It's best to think of decisions as *mainly* programmed or *mainly* nonprogrammed rather than as completely one or the other.

A final thought on this topic is that organizational efficiency is facilitated by the use of programmed decision making, which may explain its wide popularity. Whenever possible, management decisions are likely to be programmed. Obviously, using programmed decisions isn't too realistic at the top level of the organization because most of the problems that top managers confront are nonrecurring. But there are strong economic incentives for top managers to create standard operating procedures (SOPs), rules, and policies to guide other managers as they make decisions.

Programmed decisions minimize the need for managers to exercise discretion. This is important because discretion can cost money. The more nonprogrammed decision making a manager is required to do, the greater the judgment needed. Because sound judgment isn't all that common, it costs more to acquire the services of managers who possess it. Some organizations try to economize by hiring less skilled or experienced managers but then don't develop programmed decision guides for them to follow. This, too, can be costly! Take, for example, a small women's clothing store chain whose owner, because he chooses to pay low

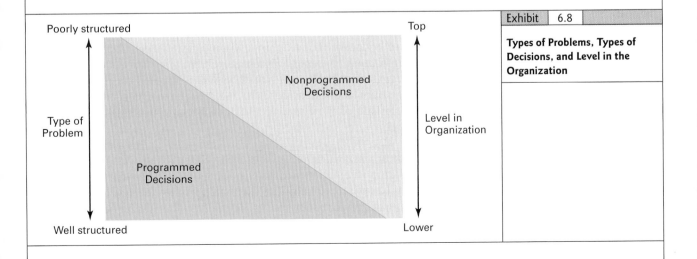

Exhibit | 6.8

Types of Problems, Types of Decisions, and Level in the Organization

salaries, hires store managers with little experience and limited ability to make good judgments. This practice, by itself, might not be a problem. The trouble is that the owner doesn't provide either training or explicit rules and procedures to guide his store managers' decisions. Each handles problems a little bit differently. The result is continuous complaints by customers about things such as promotional discounts, processing credit sales, and the handling of returns.

One of the more challenging tasks facing managers as they make decisions—programmed or nonprogrammed—is analyzing decision alternatives (Step 5 in the decision-making process). In the next section, we'll look at analyzing alternatives under different conditions.

Testing... Testing...1,2,3

10. **Describe well-structured problems and programmed decisions.**

11. **Differentiate between procedures, policies, and rules.**

12. **Describe poorly structured problems and nonprogrammed decisions.**

DECISION-MAKING CONDITIONS

There are three conditions that managers may face as they make decisions: certainty, risk, and uncertainty. What are the characteristics of each of these decision-making conditions?

certainty

A situation in which a manager can make accurate decisions because all outcomes are known.

Certainty The ideal situation for making decisions is one of **certainty**, that is, a situation in which a manager can make accurate decisions because the outcome of every alternative is known. For example, when North Dakota's state treasurer is deciding in which bank to deposit excess state funds, he knows exactly how much interest is being offered by each bank and will be earned on the funds. He is certain about the outcomes of each alternative. As you might expect, this condition isn't characteristic of most managerial decision situations. It's more idealistic than realistic.

risk

Those conditions in which the decision maker is able to estimate the likelihood of certain outcomes.

Risk A far more common situation is one of **risk**, those conditions in which the decision maker is able to estimate the likelihood of certain alternatives or outcomes. The ability to assign probabilities to outcomes may be the result of personal experiences or secondary information. Under the conditions of risk, managers have historical data that allow them to assign probabilities to different alternatives. Let's work through an example.

▲ **MANAGING YOUR CAREER** | **Taking Risks**

"IYAD-WYAD-YAG-WYAG: If you always do what you've always done, you'll always get what you've always got! So if your life is ever going to improve, you'll have to take chances."[14]

How will you approach your various career moves in the time you spend working over the course of your lifetime? Will you want to do what you've always done? Or will you want to take chances, and how comfortable will you be taking chances? Taking career risks doesn't have to be a gamble. Responsible risk taking can make outcomes more predictable. Here are some suggestions for being a responsible, effective risk taker in career decisions. It's important to thoroughly evaluate the risk. Before committing to a career risk, consider what you could lose or who might be hurt. How important are those things or those people to you? Explore whether you can reach your goal in another way, thus making the risk unnecessary. Find out everything you can about what taking this career risk involves—the timing; the people involved; the changes it will entail; and the potential gains and losses, both in the short run and the long run. Examine closely your feelings about taking this risk: Are you afraid? Are you ready to act now? Will you know if you have risked more than you can afford to lose?

As with any decision involving risk, the more information you have available, the better able you are to assess the risk. Then, armed with this information, you can make a more informed decision. And even though you won't be able to eliminate all the negatives associated with taking the risk, you can, at least, know about them.

Suppose that you manage a ski resort in the Colorado Rockies. You're thinking about adding another lift to your current facility. Obviously, your decision will be significantly influenced by the additional revenue that the new lift would generate, and additional revenue will depend on snowfall. The decision is made somewhat clearer because you have reasonably reliable past weather data on snowfall levels in your area. The data show that during the past 10 years, you had three years of heavy snowfall, five years of normal snowfall, and two years of light snow. Can you use this information to help you make your decision about adding the new lift? If you have good information on the amount of revenues generated during each level of snow, the answer is yes.

You can calculate expected value, the conditional return from each possible outcome, by multiplying expected revenues by snowfall probabilities. The result is the average revenue you can expect over time if the given probabilities hold. As Exhibit 6.9 shows, the expected revenue from adding a new ski lift is $687,500. Of course, whether that justifies a decision to build or not depends on the costs involved in generating that revenue—such as the cost of building the lift, the additional annual operational expenses for another lift, the interest rate for borrowing money, and so forth.

Event	Expected Revenues	× Probability	= Expected Value of Each Alternative
Heavy snowfall	$850,000	0.3	$255,000
Normal snowfall	725,000	0.5	362,500
Light snowfall	350,000	0.2	70,000
			$687,500

Exhibit 6.9

Expected Value for Revenues from the Addition of One Ski Lift

Uncertainty What happens if you have a decision to make when you're not certain about the outcomes and can't even make reasonable probability estimates? We call such a condition uncertainty. Managers do face decision-making situations of uncertainty. Under conditions of uncertainty, the choice of alternative is influenced by the limited amount of information available to the decision maker.

Another factor that influences choices under conditions of uncertainty is the psychological orientation of the decision maker. The optimistic manager will follow a *maximax* choice (maximizing the maximum possible payoff), the pessimist will follow a *maximin* choice (maximizing the minimum possible payoff), and the manager who desires to minimize his maximum "regret" will opt for a *minimax* choice. Let's look at these different choice approaches using an example.

Consider the case of a marketing manager at Visa International. She has determined four possible strategies (S_1, S_2, S_3, and S_4) for promoting the Visa card throughout the southeastern United States. The marketing manager also knows that major competitor MasterCard has three competitive actions (CA_1, CA_2, CA_3) it's using to promote its card in the same region. In this case, we'll assume that the Visa executive has no previous knowledge that would allow her to place probabilities on the success of any of the four strategies. With these facts, the Visa manager formulates the matrix shown in Exhibit 6.10 to show the various Visa strategies and the resulting profit to Visa depending on the competitive action used by MasterCard.

In this example, if our Visa manager is an optimist, she'll choose S_4 because that could produce the largest possible gain: $28 million. Note that this choice maximizes the maximum possible gain (maximax choice).

If our manager is a pessimist, she'll assume that only the worst can occur. The worst outcome for each strategy is as follows: S_1 = $11 million; S_2 = $9 million; S_3 = $15 million; S_4 = $14 million. These are the most pessimistic outcomes from each strategy. Following the *maximin* choice, she would maximize the minimum payoff; in other words, she'd select S_3 ($15 million is the largest of the minimum payoffs).

When Sona Wang began trying to line up institutional investors for the first venture fund to target women entrepreneurs, very few women had landed more than $1 million in venture capital before. So Wang was not surprised that the decision to come on board the fund was seen as risky. "We knew it was risky," she says. Now her Chicago-based firm, Inroads Capital, is the largest fund of its kind, managing $50 million in venture capital.

uncertainty

A situation in which a decision maker has neither certainty nor reasonable probability estimates available.

Exhibit	6.10
Payoff Matrix	

(in millions of dollars)

Visa Marketing Strategy	MasterCard's Response		
	CA_1	CA_2	CA_3
S_1	13	14	11
S_2	9	15	18
S_3	24	21	15
S_4	18	14	28

(in millions of dollars)				Exhibit 6.11
Visa Marketing Strategy	MasterCard's Response			Regret Matrix
	CA_1	CA_2	CA_3	
S_1	11	7	17	
S_2	15	6	10	
S_3	0	0	13	
S_4	6	7	0	

In the third approach, managers recognize that once a decision is made, it will not necessarily result in the most profitable payoff. There may be a regret of profits forgone (given up)—*regret* referring to the amount of money that could have been made had a different strategy been used. Managers calculate regret by subtracting all possible payoffs in each category from the maximum possible payoff for each given event, in this case for each competitive action. For our Visa manager, the highest payoff, given that MasterCard engages in CA_1, CA_2, or CA_3, is $24 million, $21 million, or $28 million, respectively (the highest number in each column). Subtracting the payoffs in Exhibit 6.10 from those figures produces the results shown in Exhibit 6.11.

The maximum regrets are S_1 = $17 million; S_2 = $15 million; S_3 = $13 million; and S_4 = $7 million. The *minimax* choice minimizes the maximum regret, so our Visa manager would choose S_4. By making this choice, she'll never have a regret of profits forgone of more than $7 million. This result contrasts, for example, with a regret of $15 million had she chosen S_2 and MasterCard had taken CA_1.

Although managers will try to quantify a decision when possible by using payoff and regret matrices, uncertainty often forces them to rely more on intuition, creativity, hunches, and "gut feeling." Regardless of the decision situation, each manager has his or her own style of making decisions.

DECISION-MAKING STYLES

Suppose that you were a new manager at Cannondale Corporation or at the local YMCA. How would you approach decision making? One perspective on decision-making styles proposes that people differ along two dimensions in the way they approach decision making.[15] The first is an individual's *way of thinking*. Some of us tend to be rational and logical in the way we think or process information. A rational type looks at information in order and makes sure that it's logical and consistent before making a decision. Others of us tend to be creative and intuitive. Intuitive types don't have to process information in a certain order but are comfortable looking at it as a whole.

Shirley DeLibero, a hands-on manager who favors empowerment of her employees, has faced her share of tough decisions. When she took over New Jersey Transit in 1990 it was a system plagued by unpopular fare hikes, late trains, and delayed maintenance. With a combination of directive-style and behavioral-style decisions, DeLibero has increased ridership, decreased customer complaints, improved maintenance, and brought several long-delayed improvement projects to fruition. Creative financing decisions prevented fare hikes for several years.

The other dimension describes an individual's *tolerance for ambiguity*. Again, some of us have a low tolerance for ambiguity. These types must have consistency and order in the way they structure information so that ambiguity is minimized. On the other hand, some of us can tolerate high levels of ambiguity and are able to process many thoughts at the same time. When we diagram these two dimensions, four decision-making styles are evident: directive, analytic, conceptual, and behavioral (see Exhibit 6.12). Let's look more closely at each style.

- *Directive style.* People using the **directive style** have low tolerance for ambiguity and are rational in their way of thinking. They're efficient and logical. Directive types make fast decisions and focus on the short run. Their efficiency and speed in making decisions often result in their making decisions with minimal information and assessing few alternatives.

- *Analytic style.* Decision makers with an **analytic style** have much greater tolerance for ambiguity than do directive types. They want more information before making a decision and consider more alternatives than a directive-style decision maker does. Analytic decision makers are best characterized as careful decision makers with the ability to adapt or cope with unique situations.

- *Conceptual style.* Individuals with a **conceptual style** tend to be very broad in their outlook and will look at many alternatives. They focus on the long run and are very good at finding creative solutions to problems.

- *Behavioral style.* Decision makers with a **behavioral style** work well with others. They're concerned about the achievements of subordinates and are receptive to suggestions from others. They often use meetings to communicate, although they try to avoid conflict. Acceptance by others is important to this decision-making style.

directive style

A decision-making style characterized by low tolerance for ambiguity and a rational way of thinking.

analytic style

A decision-making style characterized by a high tolerance for ambiguity and a rational way of thinking.

conceptual style

A decision-making style characterized by a high tolerance for ambiguity and an intuitive way of thinking.

behavioral style

A decision-making style characterized by a low tolerance for ambiguity and an intuitive way of thinking.

Exhibit	6.12

Decision-Making Styles

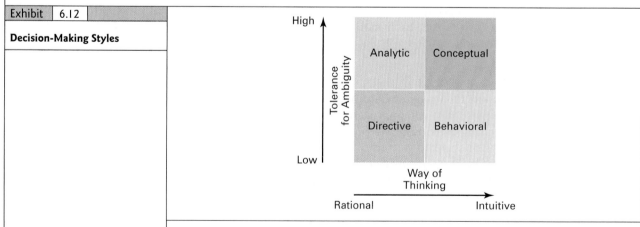

Source: S.P. Robbins and D.A. De Cenzo, *Supervision Today,* 2nd ed. (Upper Saddle River, NJ: Prentice Hall, 1998), p. 166.

MANAGING WORKFORCE DIVERSITY   The Value of Diversity in Decision Making

Have you decided what your major is going to be? How did you decide? Do you feel your decision is a good one? Is there anything you could have done differently to make sure that your decision was the best one?[16]

Making good decisions is tough! Managers, as we know, are continuously making decisions—for instance, developing new products, establishing weekly or monthly goals, implementing an advertising campaign, reassigning an employee to a different work group, resolving a customer's complaint, or purchasing new laptops for sales representatives. One important suggestion for making better decisions is to tap into the diversity of the work group. Drawing upon diverse employees can prove valuable to a manager's decision making. Why? Diverse employees can provide fresh perspectives on issues. They can offer differing interpretations on how a problem is defined and may be more open to trying new ideas. Diverse employees usually are more creative in generating alternatives and more flexible in resolving issues. And getting input from diverse sources increases the likelihood that creative and unique solutions will be generated.

Even though diversity in decision making can be valuable, there are drawbacks. The lack of a common perspective usually means that more time is spent discussing issues. Communication may be a problem particularly if language barriers are present. In addition, seeking out diverse opinions can make the decision-making process more complex, confusing, and ambiguous. And with multiple perspectives on the decision, it may be difficult to reach a single agreement or to agree on specific actions. Although these drawbacks are valid concerns, the value of diversity in decision making outweighs the potential disadvantages.

Now, about that decision on a major. Did you ask others for their opinions? Did you seek out advice from professors, family members, friends, or co-workers? Getting diverse perspectives on an important decision such as this could have helped you make the best decision! Managers also should consider the value to be gained from diversity in decision making.

Although these four decision-making styles are distinct, most managers have characteristics of more than one style. It's probably more realistic to think of a manager's dominant style and his or her alternate styles. Although some managers will rely almost exclusively on their dominant style, others are more flexible and can shift their style depending on the situation.

Managers should also recognize that their employees may use different decision-making styles. Some employees may take their time carefully weighing alternatives and considering riskier options (analytic style) whereas other employees may be more concerned about getting suggestions from others before making decisions (behavioral style). This doesn't make one approach better than the other. It just means that their decision-making styles are different. The Managing Workforce Diversity box addresses some of the issues associated with valuing diversity in decision making.

SUMMING UP MANAGERIAL DECISION MAKING

How can we best sum up managerial decision making? Exhibit 6.13 provides a concise overview. Because it's in their best interests, managers *want* to make good decisions—that is, choose the "best" alternative, implement it, and determine whether or not it takes care of the situation that called for a decision in the first place. Their decision-making process is affected by four factors including the decision-making approach being followed, the decision-making conditions, the

Exhibit	6.13		Overview of Managerial Decision Making

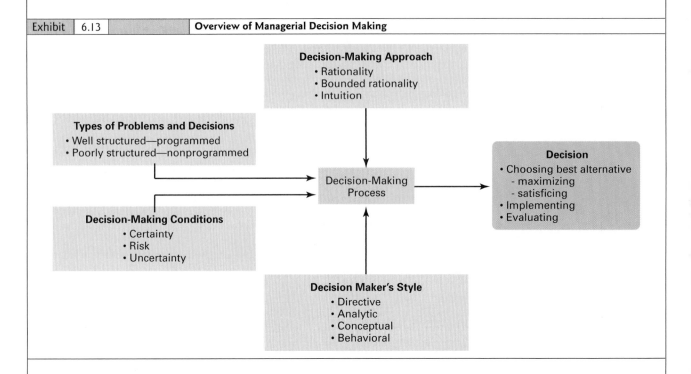

type of problem being dealt with, and the decision-maker's own style of decision making. Each of these factors plays a role in determining how a manager makes a decision. So whether that decision involves addressing an employee's habitual tardiness, resolving a problem with product quality, or determining whether to enter a new market (as in our chapter-opening case), remember that it has been shaped by a number of factors.

Testing...Testing...1,2,3

13. **Contrast the characteristics of decision making under the conditions of certainty, risk, and uncertainty.**

14. **Contrast the four decision-making styles.**

15. **What factors influence management decision making?**

Managers Respond to "A Manager's Dilemma"

Stacey Renee Unger

Media Specialist, Edward Jones, St. Louis, Missouri

Lynee Pauk

Medical Technologist/Lab Evening Supervisor, St. John's Regional Health Center, Springfield, Missouri

Mario Galasso wants to know if adding a new off-road motorcycle product line was a good business decision. I would start by evaluating the:

- Product's cost to develop and possible return
- Resources that the new product is taking away from currently profitable products
- Brand awareness in motorcycles
- Market share within the industry
- Inventory numbers
- Integration of the new product with other existing products

Then I would establish specific decision effectiveness criteria by developing a five-year marketing plan for the new motorcycle that would include revenue goals, market share goals, inventory goals, and brand awareness levels. Finally, I would develop an integrated marketing/advertising plan for all the new products in a targeted market.

If goals aren't reached after five years, I would consider selling the product line to competitors, discontinuing the product, or updating the motorcycle with consumer input. Although introducing a new product isn't easy, an established plan will help Mario decide if the motorcycle was a good business decision.

There are a couple of important decision criteria Galasso might use to evaluate the effectiveness of the decision to produce the new bike. First, Galasso should look to see what goals were established when the bike decision was being considered. Those goals should be part of the criteria to evaluate the decision's effectiveness.

Then Galasso could get firsthand feedback by sponsoring racers. Put them on the bike to see if they like how it handles. Galasso not only could get feedback on the bike from individuals who have ridden some of their top competitors' bikes, but it would also get Cannondale's name out into the biking circuit.

Next, Galasso could also get feedback from the numbers—how is the motorcycle industry doing as a whole? Has Cannondale's market share increased? If so, is it due to the introduction of the new bike? How is customer response to the product?

Chapter Summary

This summary is organized by the chapter-opening objectives found on p. 148.

1. Decision making is an eight-step process: (1) formulating problems, (2) identifying decision criteria, (3) allocating weights to the criteria, (4) developing alternatives, (5) analyzing alternatives, (6) selecting an alternative, (7) implementing the alternative, and (8) evaluating decision effectiveness.

2. Everyone in organizations makes decisions. Decision making is particularly important in every aspect of a manager's job, that is, in planning, organizing, leading, and controlling.

3. The rational decision maker is assumed to have a clear problem, have no goal conflict, know all options, have a clear preference ordering, keep all preferences constant, have no time or cost constraints, and select a final choice that maximizes his or her payoff.

4. The perfectly rational approach to decision making assumes that the following conditions are met: The manager is faced with a simple problem in which the goals are clear and the alternatives limited, in which the time pressures are minimal and the cost of seeking out and evaluating alternatives is low, for which the organizational culture supports innovation and risk taking, and in which the outcomes are relatively concrete and measurable. Under these conditions, the decision maker can choose the alternative with the maximum payoff. On the other hand, the boundedly rational approach to decision making says that managers behave rationally within the parameters of a simplified decision-making process that is limited (or bounded) by an individual's ability to process information. Because they can't possibly analyze all information on all alternatives, managers satisfice rather than maximize.

5. Managers regularly use their intuition in making decisions. Intuitive decision making is a subconscious process of making decisions on the basis of experience and accumulated judgment.

6. Managers face well and poorly structured problems. Well-structured problems are straightforward, familiar, easily defined, and are solved using programmed decisions. Poorly structured problems are new or unusual, involve ambiguous or incomplete information, and are solved using nonprogrammed decisions.

7. The ideal situation for making decisions occurs when the manager can make accurate decisions because he or she knows the outcome from every alternative. Such certainty, however, is rare. A far more realistic situation is one of risk, in which the decision maker can estimate the likelihood of certain alternatives or outcomes. If neither certainty nor reasonable probability estimates are available, uncertainty exists, and the decision maker's choice will be influenced by intuition.

8. Decision-making style can be described by a person's way of thinking (rational or intuitive) and tolerance for ambiguity (low or high). The various combinations of these characteristics give us the directive style (low tolerance for ambiguity and rational way of thinking), analytic style (high tolerance for ambiguity and rational way of thinking), conceptual (high tolerance for ambiguity and intuitive way of thinking), and behavioral (low tolerance for ambiguity and intuitive way of thinking).

Thinking About Management Issues

1. Why is decision making often described as the essence of a manager's job?

2. How might an organization's culture influence the way managers make decisions?

3. All of us bring biases to the decisions we make. What types of biases might a manager have? What would be the drawbacks of having biases? Could there be any advantages to having biases? Explain. What are the implications for managerial decision making?

4. Would you call yourself a systematic or intuitive thinker? What are the decision-making implications of these labels? What are the implications for choosing an employer?

5. "As managers use computers and software tools more often, they'll be able to make more rational decisions." Do you agree or disagree with this statement? Why?

Log On: Internet-Based Exercise

Developing alternatives for making decisions often requires individuals to be creative. Using the Internet, find five sites that offer ideas on how to improve creativity. Then write two to three paragraphs explaining what role

creativity should play in decision making and what you learned from your search about how you can be a more creative decision maker.

myPHLIP Companion Web Site

myPHLIP **(www.prenhall.com/myphlip)** *is a fully customizable homepage that ties students and faculty to text-specific resources.*
- **For students**, *myPHLIP provides an online study guide tied chapter-by-chapter to the text—current events and Internet exercises, lecture notes, downloadable software, the Career Center, the Writing Center, Ask the Tutor, and more.*
- **For faculty**, *myPHLIP provides a syllabus tool that allows you to manage content, communicate with students, and upload personal resources.*

Working Together: Team-Based Exercise

Being effective in decision making is something that managers obviously desire. What is involved with being a good decision maker? Form groups of three to four students. Discuss your experiences making decisions—for example, buying a car or some other major purchase, choosing classes and professors, making summer or spring break plans, and so forth. Each of you should share times when you felt you made good decisions. Analyze

what happened during that decision-making process that contributed to it being a good decision. Then consider some decisions that you felt were bad. What happened to make them bad? What common characteristics, if any, did you identify among the good decisions? The bad decisions? Come up with a bulleted list of practical suggestions for making good decisions. As a group, be prepared to share your list with the class.

Case Application

Framing a Good Decision

The frames aren't just around the artwork anymore at the Museum of Modern Art (MoMA) in New York City. As the museum began a major remodeling and expansion construction project, the wisdom of that decision was raising questions.

MoMA (www.moma.org), a not-for-profit educational institution, is supported by admission and membership fees, sales of publications and services, and of course, contributions from wealthy donors. It was founded in 1929 by three private citizens who were determined to make modern and contemporary art available to the public. MoMA was the first museum to devote its art program and collection entirely to the modern movement. And the quality and diversity of the museum's current collection offers visitors a unique and unparalleled overview of modern and contemporary art.

Early in the 1990s, museum director Glenn Lowry and museum trustees decided that MoMA should not be "a shrine to the twentieth century but rather a vital, forward-looking institution committed to the art of the present as well as to the great achievements of the modern tradition." With this guiding philosophy, the decision was made to expand the museum's facilities and radically alter its exhibit space. Their rationale was that the museum needed more and better-designed space to accommodate its various existing functions as well as new and different space to meet the challenges of the future and to better articulate its programs devoted to education about and celebration of modern art.

To accomplish these lofty goals, MoMA's decision makers directed that the planned expansion and renovation result in a building that would showcase the best of modern art in the most compelling way possible, respect the work of a diverse professional staff, and make judi-

The Museum of Modern Art (MOMA), New York City.

cious use of the institution's resources, both in the long run and in day-to-day operations. They wanted a building that would be both an example of great architecture and a great museum as well. With the completion of the new space in late 2004 or early 2005, they hoped to attract a million more visitors, or 2.5 million total, annually. Fulfilling this dream wouldn't be easy.

Since the decision to expand was made in the early 1990s, costs of everything from real estate to construction have skyrocketed. (Costs for the entire project are estimated at $650 million.) Since MoMA's endowment is relatively small (a mere $387 million as compared to the Metropolitan Museum of Art's endowment of more than $1 billion), managers have had to look for alternatives. One decision they made was to pursue a for-profit joint business venture—a Web site selling everything from coffee cups to furniture—with the Tate Gallery in London. Some people felt that the move demeaned the integrity of the museum and created controversy among staffers, an allegation that MoMA officials, of course, denied. And then there's MoMA's relationship with its "trustees"—individuals who donate large sums of money and are "rewarded" with a seat on the prestigious museum board. To fund the expansion, museum officials have sought contributions from current and potential trustees, a common practice for not-for-profit organizations during a major fund-raising campaign. Despite the concerns, MoMA does have a solid financial

history and had a budget surplus for five years in the last years of the 1990s. However, wealthy donors will be paying off their pledges for years and if the museum needs additional cash for any reason, it's not going to have many places to turn.

The construction project itself has turned out to be more complicated than originally planned. When the project was first proposed, its cost was a modest $200 million for about 30 percent more space, and the museum itself was expected to remain open throughout the entire process (estimated to be about 18 months). However, initial blueprints were quickly shoved aside for more aggressive plans. The architectural design by influential Japanese architect Yoshio Taniguchi increases the museum space by 50 percent and is slated to take 48 months to complete. Rather than staying open throughout the process, managers decided to temporarily transfer a major portion of the museum's operations to a former Swingline stapler factory in Queens. Being in a section of the city not considered as glamorous as its midtown location, attendance (and revenues) could suffer, and after completion, there's no guarantee that the new facility will attract the hoped-for additional visitors.

Concerns about the viability of the proposed project led MoMA's managers to cut some costs—$50 million from the architects' budget and by using lesser-quality construction materials. However, Director Lowry says that MoMA is not taking on too much with this expansion. His goal unapologetically remains, "To be the No. 1 modern museum in the world."

QUESTIONS

1. What types of problems and decisions do you see MoMA managers dealing with in this story? Explain your choices.

2. Explain how each of the following might have been used in the decisions that had to be made in pursuing the museum expansion: (a) perfectly rational decision making, (b) boundedly rational decision making, (c) intuition.

3. Would you characterize the conditions surrounding MoMA's expansion decision as conditions of certainty, risk, or uncertainty? Explain your choice.

4. Is escalation of commitment evident in this situation? Explain. What can you learn about decision making from this situation?

Sources: Information from MoMA's Web site (www.moma.org), August 28, 2000; and D. Costello, "Museum of Modern Art's Ambitious Expansion Plan Faces Trouble," *Wall Street Journal*, June 7, 2000, pp. B1+.

Video Case Application

Grace Under Fire

SMALL BUSINESS 2000

You probably wouldn't know quite what to expect from a business named Pyro Media, but you'd figure it was going to be something pretty unusual. Grace Tsujikawa Boyd's business, Pyro Media, has pursued a pretty unusual direction, but the decision to do something different wasn't made randomly or without thought.

Boyd's Pyro Media started as a manufacturer of huge ceramic glazed pots such as the ones you might see holding trees or plants in the lobbies of large hotels. Using her degree in art, Boyd herself initially made the high-quality glazed pots, which sold for about $1,500 each. As her business grew to the point at which it had backorders of 8 to 12 weeks, Boyd decided it was time to move to a bigger facility and to invest in equipment and employees. She says, "We were in business making money and assumed that business was going to grow at the same rate it had been." Grace soon found, however, that Pyro Media's revenues didn't keep increasing by 30 percent as they had been but instead were dropping off. Upon investigating the situation, she found that big corporations had begun importing and distributing terra cotta planters, essentially stealing away her business.

Boyd knew that she had to do something. She had invested in equipment, a 56,000-square-foot facility, and employees who knew ceramics. She called in some consultants to see what other markets her business might pursue. Their study, which took about six months, recom-

mended that Pyro Media look into high-tech ceramic applications: In other words, take the same technology that Boyd had developed and used in making ceramic pots and apply it to a new area. On the basis of that information, Boyd hired a ceramics engineer and went after the ceramics "castables" market. The company's decision to move into this new market proved to be successful.

Recognizing that business was falling off and analyzing the reason behind the loss of revenue were instrumental in Pyro Media's continued success. Boyd says that being able to recognize a problem is critical, especially for small businesses. Why? Because small businesses have no money or time to waste. If problems are ignored and not analyzed, the business might face quick failure.

QUESTIONS

1. A decision to move into a new market as Boyd's Pyro Media did is a major decision. How could Boyd have used the decision-making process to help her make this decision?

2. Would you call declining revenues a problem or a symptom of a problem? Why?

3. Using Exhibit 6.12, identify the type of decision-making style you think Boyd uses. Explain your choice.

4. Do you agree with Boyd's assertion that being able to recognize a problem is critical, especially for small businesses? Why or why not?

Source: Based on *Small Business 2000, Show 108.*

Mastering Management

Through Episode 9 of the Mastering Management *series, you can learn about the processes that are involved in decision making as Andrew must choose between staying with CanGo and pursuing an alternative career.*

After reading and studying this chapter, you should be able to:

1. Define planning.

2. Explain why managers plan.

3. Describe what role goals play in planning.

4. Distinguish among the different types of plans.

5. Tell how goals are established.

6. Describe the characteristics of well-designed goals.

7. Identify three contingency factors in planning.

8. Explain the approaches to developing plans.

9. Discuss the criticisms of planning.

10. Describe what it takes to effectively plan in a dynamic environment.

A MANAGER'S DILEMMA

gazoontite.com. Its name may be light-hearted, but its CEO, Soon-Chart Yu, is serious about capturing a significant portion of a $30 billion market for allergy and asthma sufferers.[1] Yu honed his managerial skills as a brand manager for the Formula 409 cleaning product line at Clorox. During his four-year tenure at Clorox, he won company-wide recognition for best advertising, best promotion, and best new product. However, he always had a desire to build his own business. Yu really didn't know what business he wanted to pursue until he started putting together data on something he knew about personally: allergies and asthma. Like half of all U.S. households, Yu and his family had suffered for years. After researching the allergy/asthma market and learning about the intricacies of retailing through a part-time job at a Crate & Barrel store, he took the plunge.

In May 1999, gazoontite.com opened as the "definitive one-stop shop for breathing happier and healthier." Offering over 1,000 high-quality products such as hypoallergenic toys, bed sheets, air cleaners, and other items for people with breathing problems, gazoontite.com sells its products online, in retail outlets, and through catalogs distributed in doctors' offices. Yu says that his goal is to make purchasing products as convenient as possible to everyone who needs them.

Getting his business up and running took significant amounts of planning. Yu had to convince investors to "cough up" an initial $4 million

Foundations of Planning

7

and to invest an additional $30 million a few months into the business. However, because he had prepared well-thought-out objectives and plans and showed investors that he was serious about making his business successful, getting them to provide funds wasn't at all difficult.

Launching a business and then managing its continued successful growth require different managerial actions. Yu had effectively planned for the launch of his business; now he needs to plan to keep it going. Describe the different types of plans that Yu might need.

WHAT WOULD YOU DO?

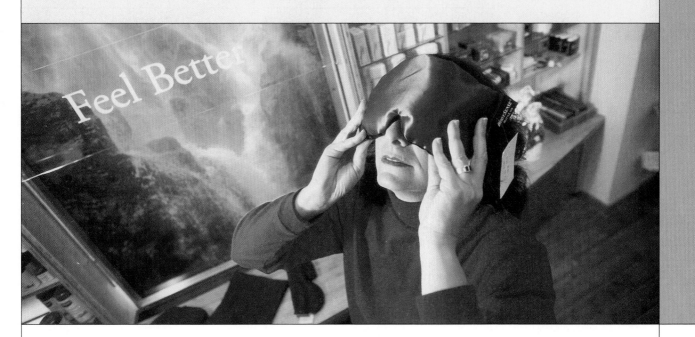

Feel Better

In this chapter we present the basics of planning. In the following pages, you'll learn what planning is, why managers plan, how they plan, and about some contemporary issues in planning.

› WHAT IS PLANNING?

planning

A process that involves defining the organization's goals, establishing an overall strategy for achieving those goals, and developing a comprehensive set of plans to integrate and coordinate organizational work.

As we stated in Chapter 1, **planning** involves defining the organization's goals, establishing an overall strategy for achieving those goals, and developing a comprehensive set of plans to integrate and coordinate organizational work. It's concerned with both ends (what's to be done) and means (how it's to be done).

Planning can either be formal or informal. All managers engage in some planning, but their planning might be informal. In informal planning, nothing is written down, and there is little or no sharing of goals with others in the organization. This type of planning often is done in many small businesses where the owner-manager has a vision of where he or she wants the business to go and how to get there. Informal planning is general and lacks continuity. Although it's more common in smaller organizations, informal planning exists in some large organizations as well. And some small businesses have very sophisticated planning processes and formal plans.

When we use the term *planning* in this book, we mean *formal* planning. In formal planning, specific goals covering a period of years are defined. These goals are written down and shared with organizational members. Finally, specific action programs exist for the achievement of these goals; that is, managers clearly define the path they want to take to get the organization and the various work units from where they are to where they want them to be.

› WHY DO MANAGERS PLAN?

Setting goals, establishing strategies to achieve those goals, and developing a set of plans to integrate and coordinate activities seem pretty complicated. Given that fact, why should managers want to plan? What impact does planning have on performance?

PURPOSES OF PLANNING

We can identify at least four reasons for planning. Planning gives direction, reduces the impact of change, minimizes waste and redundancy, and sets the standards used in controlling. Let's look at each of these purposes.

Planning establishes coordinated effort. It gives direction to managers and nonmanagers alike. When employees know where the organization or work unit is going and what they must contribute to reach goals, they can coordinate their activities, cooperate with each other, and do what it takes to accomplish those goals. Without planning, departments and individuals might be working at cross purposes, preventing the organization from moving efficiently toward its goals.

Planning also reduces uncertainty by forcing managers to look ahead, anticipate change, consider the impact of change, and develop appropriate responses. It also clarifies the consequences of actions managers might take in response to change. Even though planning can't eliminate change, managers plan in order to anticipate changes and develop the most effective response to them.

In addition, planning reduces overlapping and wasteful activities. When work activities are coordinated around established plans, wasted time and resources and redundancy can be minimized. Furthermore, when means and ends are made clear through planning, inefficiencies become obvious and can be corrected or eliminated.

Finally, planning establishes goals or standards that are used in controlling. If we're unsure of what we're trying to accomplish, how can we determine whether we have actually achieved it? In planning, we develop the goals and the plans. Then, through controlling, we compare actual performance against the goals, identify any significant deviations, and take any necessary corrective action. Without planning, there would be no way to control.

PLANNING AND PERFORMANCE

Is planning worthwhile? Do managers and organizations that plan outperform those that don't? Intuitively, you would expect the answer to be a resounding yes. Although studies of performance in organizations that plan are generally positive, we can't say that organizations that formally plan *always* outperform those that don't plan.

Numerous studies have been done to test the relationship between planning and performance.[2] On the basis of these studies, we can draw the following conclusions. First, generally speaking, formal planning is associated with higher profits, higher return on assets, and other positive financial results. Second, the quality of the planning process and the appropriate implementation of the plans probably contribute more to high performance than does the extent of planning. Next, in those studies in which formal planning didn't lead to higher performance, the external environment often was the culprit. Governmental regulations, powerful labor unions, and other critical environmental forces constrain managers' options and reduce the impact of planning on an organization's performance. Finally, the planning/performance relationship is influenced by the planning time frame. Organizations need at least four years of systematic formal planning before performance is impacted. ◄————

Testing...Testing...1,2,3

1. **Define planning.**

2. **What purposes does planning serve?**

3. **What is the relationship between planning and organizational performance?**

❯ HOW DO MANAGERS PLAN?

Planning is often called the primary management function because it establishes the basis for all the other functions that managers perform. Without planning, managers wouldn't know what to organize, lead, or control. In fact, without plans, there wouldn't *be* anything to organize, lead, or control! So how *do* managers plan? That's what we want to look at in this section. Planning involves two important elements: goals and plans.

Goals, or desired outcomes, drive the creation of most plans. Although the Summer Olympics of 2008 are years away, Beijing wants to be the host of the games. To improve its chances, the city is encouraging citizens to learn some English, setting a goal of teaching half of all Beijingers 100 English phrases in preparation. Here drivers and conductors in the city's public transportation system receive basic English lessons.

THE ROLE OF GOALS AND PLANS IN PLANNING

Goals are desired outcomes for individuals, groups, and entire organizations.[3] *Goals* are *objectives*, and we use the two terms interchangeably. They provide the direction for all management decisions and form the criterion against which actual work accomplishments can be measured. That's why they're often called the foundation of planning. If you don't know what that desired target or outcome is, how could you establish plans for reaching it? **Plans** are documents that outline how goals are going to be met and that typically describe resource allocations, schedules, and other necessary actions to accomplish the goals. As managers plan, they're developing both goals and plans.

Types of Goals At first glance, it might appear that organizations have a single objective: for business firms, to make a profit; for not-for-profit organizations, to meet the needs of some constituent group(s). In reality, all organizations have multiple objectives. Businesses also want to increase market share and keep employees enthused about the organization. A church provides a place for religious practices but also assists economically disadvantaged individuals in its community and acts as a social gathering place for church members. No one single measure can evaluate whether an organization is successful. Emphasis on one goal, such as profit, ignores other goals that must also be reached if long-term success is to be achieved. Also, as we discussed in Chapter 5, using a single objective such as profit can result in unethical practices because managers will ignore other important parts of their jobs in order to look good on that one measure.

Exhibit 7.1 provides a sampling of both financial and strategic goals from some well-known U.S. corporations. Financial goals are related to the financial performance of the organization; strategic goals are related to other areas of an organization's performance. Except for a few of the financial ones, these goals could apply to a not-for-profit organization as well. Notice, too, that although survival isn't specifically mentioned as a goal, it's of utmost importance to all organizations. Some of the goals listed in Exhibit 7.1 contribute directly to profits, but obviously, an organization must survive if other goals are to be achieved.

Another way to describe goals is in terms of whether they're real or stated. Exhibit 7.1 is a list of **stated goals**—official statements of what an organization says, and what it wants its various stakeholders to believe, its goals are. However, stated goals—which can be found in an organization's charter, annual report, public relations announcements, or in public statements made by managers— are often conflicting and excessively influenced by what society believes organizations should do.

goals

Desired outcomes for individuals, groups, or entire organizations.

plans

Documents that outline how goals are going to be met including resource allocations, schedules, and other necessary actions to accomplish the goals.

stated goals

Official statements of what an organization says, and what it wants its various stakeholders to believe, its goals are.

Financial Objectives	Strategic Objectives	Exhibit 7-1
		Stated Objectives From Large U.S. Companies

Financial Objectives

- Faster revenue growth
- Faster earnings growth
- Higher dividends
- Wider profit margins
- Higher returns on invested capital
- Stronger bond and credit ratings
- Bigger cash flows
- A rising stock price
- Recognition as a "blue chip" company
- A more diversified revenue base
- Stable earnings during recessionary periods

Strategic Objectives

- A bigger market share
- A higher, more secure industry rank
- Higher product quality
- Lower costs relative to key competitors
- Broader or more attractive product line
- A stronger reputation with customers
- Superior customer service
- Recognition as a leader in technology and/or product innovation
- Increased ability to compete in international markets
- Expanded growth opportunities

Source: A.A. Thompson Jr. and A.J. Strickland III, *Strategic Management* (New York: McGraw-Hill/Irwin, 2001), p. 43.

The conflict in stated goals exists because organizations respond to a variety of stakeholders. These stakeholders frequently evaluate the organization by different criteria. For example, when Ford Motor Company chairman, Bill Ford Jr., announced his company's goal to make its vehicles more fuel efficient and more environmentally friendly as a way to best serve its shareholders, environmentalists and Ford executives viewed it differently.[4] The company reached out to environmental groups by initiating discussions on fuel economy issues. It also released a corporate citizenship report that acknowledged "very real conflicts" between Ford's stated commitment to the environment and its continued marketing of gas-guzzling SUVs. Environmentalists, although encouraged by the company's concern, were wary of its ultimate intent. Ford executives, well aware of the need to produce vehicles that the public demanded and that added dollars to the bottom line, had long been battered by environmentalists' criticisms, thus making them reluctant to cooperate in any collaborative discussions. Was the goal of being more environmentally friendly true and the goal of doing the best for its shareholders false? No. Both were true, but they did conflict.

Have you ever read an organization's objectives as stated in its company literature? For instance, Lands End Inc. says, "We are dedicated to providing outstanding customer service." At SBC Communications, goals include "growing our customer base by expanding into new markets; providing service over state-of-the-art networks; selling more services to each of our customers; and executing our strategy better than any other company." And Colgate-Palmolive identifies its goals as "strong global growth, building marketing leadership, increasing profitability, and living the company's values."[5] These types of statements are, at best, vague and are more likely to represent management's public relations skills than serve as meaningful guides to what the organization is actually trying to accomplish. It shouldn't be surprising then to find that an organization's stated goals are often quite irrelevant to what actually goes on.[6] The content of such goals is substantially determined by what various stakeholders want to hear. If you want to know an organization's **real goals**—those goals that an organization actually pursues—closely observe what organizational members are doing. Actions define priorities.

real goals

Goals that an organization actually pursues, as defined by the actions of its members.

Laurie McCartney runs an online firm called eStyle, which is geared to busy women and has expanded to Babystyle and Kidstyle as well. McCartney sees eStyle's international expansion as a long-term goal. Her short-term goal is to focus on the United States. "We see a huge demand for our product, and we also see lots of potential partnerships," says McCartney of potential roll-outs in Europe and Asia. "That said, the market here is fairly large and significant. We really want to continue to focus on the U.S. market."

For example, universities that proclaim the goal of limiting class size, facilitating close student-faculty relations, and actively involving students in the learning process and that then put students into lecture classes of 300 or more are pretty common! An awareness that real and stated objectives differ is important, if for no other reason than to understand what might otherwise seem to be management inconsistencies.

Types of Plans The most popular ways to describe organizational plans are by their breadth (strategic versus operational), time frame (short term versus long term), specificity (directional versus specific), and frequency of use (single-use versus standing). These planning classifications aren't independent. As Exhibit 7.2 illustrates, strategic plans are long term, directional, and single use. Operational plans are short term, specific, and standing. Let's describe each of these types of plans.

Strategic plans are plans that apply to the entire organization, establish the organization's overall goals, and seek to position the organization in terms of its environment. Plans that specify the details of how the overall goals are to be achieved are called **operational plans**. How do the two types of plans differ? Strategic plans tend to cover a longer time frame. They also cover a broader view of the organization. Strategic plans also include the formulation of goals whereas operational plans define ways to achieve the goals. Also, operational plans tend to cover short time periods—monthly, weekly, and day-to-day.

The difference in years between short-term and long-term plans has shortened considerably. It used to be that long term meant anything over seven years. Try to imagine what you'd like to be doing in seven years and you can begin to appreciate how difficult it can be for managers to establish plans that far in the future. As organizational environments have become more uncertain, the definition of *long term* has changed. We're going to define **long-term plans** as those with a time frame beyond three years.[7] We'll define **short-term plans** as those covering one year or less. The intermediate term is any time period in between. Although these time classifications are fairly common, an organization can designate any time frame it wants to use for planning purposes.

strategic plans

Plans that apply to the entire organization, establish the organization's overall goals, and seek to position the organization in terms of its environment.

operational plans

Plans that specify the details of how the overall goals are to be achieved.

long-term plans

Plans with a time frame beyond three years.

short-term plans

Plans covering one year or less.

Exhibit 7.2				
Types of Plans	**Breadth**	**Time Frame**	**Specificity**	**Frequency of Use**
	Strategic	Long term	Directional	Single use
	Operational	Short term	Specific	Standing

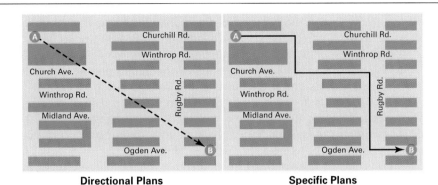

Exhibit   7.3

Specific Versus Directional Plans

Directional Plans   Specific Plans

Intuitively, it would seem that specific plans would be preferable to directional, or loosely guided, plans. **Specific plans** are clearly defined and leave no room for interpretation. They have specifically stated objectives. There's no ambiguity and no problem with misunderstandings. For example, a manager who seeks to increase his or her unit's work output by 8 percent over a given 12-month period might establish specific procedures, budget allocations, and schedules of activities to reach that goal. The drawbacks of specific plans are that they require clarity and a sense of predictability that often do not exist.

When uncertainty is high and management must be flexible in order to respond to unexpected changes, directional plans are preferable. **Directional plans** are flexible plans that set out general guidelines. (Exhibit 7.3 illustrates the difference between specific and directional planning.) They provide focus but do not lock managers into specific goals or courses of action. Instead of detailing a specific plan to cut costs by 4 percent and increase revenues by 6 percent in the next six months, managers might formulate a directional plan for improving profits by 5 to 10 percent over the next six months. The flexibility inherent in directional plans must be weighed against the loss of clarity provided by specific plans.

Some plans that managers develop are ongoing while others are used only once. A **single-use plan** is a one-time plan specifically designed to meet the needs of a unique situation. For instance, when Charles Schwab and Company introduced its online discount stock brokerage service, top-level executives used a single-use plan to guide the creation and implementation of the new service. In contrast, **standing plans** are ongoing plans that provide guidance for activities performed repeatedly. Standing plans include policies, rules, and procedures that we defined in Chapter 6. An example of a standing plan would be the sexual harassment policy developed by the University of Arizona. It provides guidance to university administrators, faculty, and staff as they perform their job duties. ◄

ESTABLISHING GOALS

Taylor has just been elected president of her business school's honorary fraternity. She wants the organization to be more actively involved in the business school than it has been in the past. Marcel graduated from the university with a degree in marketing and computers three years ago and went to work for a regional consulting services firm. He recently was promoted to manager of the eight-person e-commerce

specific plans

Plans that are clearly defined and that leave no room for interpretation.

directional plans

Plans that are flexible and that set out general guidelines.

single-use plan

A one-time plan specifically designed to meet the needs of a unique situation.

standing plans

Ongoing plans that provide guidance for activities performed repeatedly.

Testing...Testing...1,2,3

4. **Differentiate between goals and plans.**

5. **What are the different types of goals?**

6. **Describe each of the different types of plans.**

development team and hopes to strengthen the team's financial contributions to the firm. What should Taylor and Marcel do now? The first thing they should do is establish some goals. How? That's what we're going to look at in this section.

Approaches to Establishing Goals As we stated earlier, goals provide the direction for all management decisions and actions and form the criterion against which actual accomplishments are measured. Everything organizational members do should be oriented toward helping their work units and the organization achieve its goals. These goals can be established through a process of traditional goal setting or management by objectives.

The central theme in **traditional goal setting** is that goals are set at the top and then broken down into subgoals for each level of the organization. For example, the president of a manufacturing business tells the production vice president what he expects manufacturing costs to be for the coming year and tells the marketing vice president what level he expects sales to reach for the year. Then, at some later point, performance is evaluated to determine whether the assigned goals have been achieved. This traditional perspective assumes that top managers know what's best because they see the "big picture." Thus, the goals that are established and passed down to each succeeding level of the organization serve to direct and guide, and in some ways, constrain, individual employees' work behaviors. Employees' work efforts at the various levels and in the various work areas are geared to meet the goals that have been assigned in their areas of responsibility.

One of the problems with this traditional approach is that if top managers define the organization's goals in broad terms—achieving "sufficient" profits or increasing "market leadership"—these ambiguous goals have to be made more specific as they flow down through the organization. At each level, managers define the goals, applying their own interpretations and biases as they make them more specific. However, what often results is that goals lose clarity and unity as they make their way down from the top of the organization to lower levels. Exhibit 7.4 illustrates what can happen in this situation.

However, when the hierarchy of organizational goals *is* clearly defined, it forms an integrated network of goals, or a **means-ends chain**. This means that higher-level goals, or ends, are linked to lower-level goals, which serve as the means for their accomplishment. In other words, the achievement of goals at a low level

---

traditional goal setting

An approach to setting goals in which goals are set at the top level of the organization and then broken down into subgoals for each level of the organization.

means-ends chain

An integrated network of goals in which the accomplishment of goals at one level serves as the means for achieving the goals, or ends, at the next level.

Exhibit	7.4

Traditional Objective Setting

1. The organization's overall objectives and strategies are formulated.	**Exhibit** 7.5
2. Major objectives are allocated among divisional and departmental units.	
3. Unit managers collaboratively set specific objectives for their units with their managers.	**Steps in a Typical MBO Program**
4. Specific objectives are collaboratively set with all department members.	
5. Action plans, defining how objectives are to be achieved, are specified and agreed upon by managers and employees.	
6. The action plans are implemented.	
7. Progress toward objectives is periodically reviewed, and feedback is provided.	
8. Successful achievement of objectives is reinforced by performance-based rewards.	

becomes the means to reach the goals at the next level (ends). And the accomplishment of goals at that level becomes the means to achieve the goals at the next level (ends). And so forth and so on, up through the different levels of the organization. This is how the traditional goal-setting approach is supposed to work.

Instead of traditional goal setting, many organizations use **management by objectives (MBO)**. In this management system specific performance goals are jointly determined by employees and their managers, progress toward accomplishing these goals is periodically reviewed, and rewards are allocated on the basis of this progress. Rather than using goals only as controls, MBO uses them to motivate employees as well.

Management by objectives consists of four elements: goal specificity, participative decision making, an explicit time period, and performance feedback.[8] Its appeal lies in its focus on the accomplishment of participatively set objectives as the reason for and motivation behind individuals' work efforts. Exhibit 7.5 lists the steps in a typical MBO program.

Do MBO programs work? Studies of actual MBO programs confirm that MBO increases employee performance and organizational productivity. A review of 70 programs, for example, found organizational productivity gains in 68 of them.[9] This same review also identified top-management commitment and involvement as important conditions for MBO to succeed.

One problem of MBO programs is that they can be useless in times of dynamic environmental change. An MBO program needs some stability for employees to work toward accomplishing the set goals. If new goals must be set every few weeks, there's no time for employees to work on accomplishing the goals and measuring that accomplishment. Another problem of MBO programs is that an

management by objectives (MBO)

A management system in which specific performance goals are jointly determined by employees and their managers, progress toward accomplishing those goals is periodically reviewed, and rewards are allocated on the basis of this progress.

? THINKING CRITICALLY ABOUT ETHICS

"I'm telling you. After my talk with my manager today about my work goals for the next quarter, I think our company's MBO program actually stands for 'manipulating' by objectives, not management by objectives," Carlos complained to his friend Sabrina. He went on, "She came in and outlined what she thought I should be working on and then asked me what I thought of it. I guess that's her way of getting me to participate in the goal setting."

Is it unethical for a manager to enter a participative goal-setting session with a pre-established set of goals that he or she wants the employee to accept? Why or why not? Is it unethical for a manager to use his or her formal position to impose specific goals on an employee? Why or why not?

One characteristic of well-designed goals is that they are outcome-based. Entrepreneurs Mike and Maureen Birdsall, co-owners of Birdsall Designs, Inc., a Web design firm in San Francisco, pay for their employees' home Internet connections so that work can be fit around family needs. Working traditional business hours is less important to the firm than the goal of getting the job done.

overemphasis by an employee on accomplishing his or her goals without regard to others in the work unit can be counterproductive. A manager must work closely with all members of the work unit to assure that employees aren't working at cross purposes. Finally, if MBO is viewed simply as an annual exercise in filling out paperwork, employees won't be motivated to accomplish the goals.

Characteristics of Well-Designed Goals Goals are not all created equal! Some goals are better than others. How do you tell the difference? What makes a "well-designed" goal?[10] Exhibit 7.6 outlines the characteristics of well-designed goals.

A well-designed goal should be *written in terms of outcomes* rather than actions. The desired end result is the most important element of any goal and, therefore, the goal should be written to reflect this. Next, a goal should be *measurable and quantifiable*. It's much easier to determine if a goal has been met if it's measurable. For instance, suppose one of your goals is to "produce a high-quality product." What exactly do you mean by high quality? Because there are numerous ways to define quality, the goal should state specifically how you will measure whether or not the product is high quality. This means that even in areas in which it may be difficult to quantify your intent, you should try to find some specific way to measure whether that goal is accomplished. Otherwise, why have the goal if you can't measure whether it's been met? In line with specifying a quantifiable measure of accomplishment, a well-designed goal should also be *clear as to a time frame*. Although open-ended goals may seem preferable because of their supposed flexibility, in fact, goals without a time frame make an organization less flexible. This happens because you're never sure when the goal has been met or when you should call it quits because the goal will never be met regardless of how long you work at it. A well-designed goal will specify a time frame for accomplishment. Next, a well-designed goal should be *challenging but attainable*. Goals that are too easy to accomplish are not motivating and neither are goals that are not attainable even with exceptional effort. Next, well-designed goals should be *written down*. Although actually writing down goals may seem too time consuming, the process of writing the goals forces people to think them through. In addition, the written goals become visible and tangible evidence of the importance of working toward something. Finally, well-designed goals are *communicated to all organizational members* who need to know the goals. Why? Making people aware of the goals ensures that they're all "on the same page" and working in ways to ensure the accomplishment of the organizational goals.

Exhibit	7.6		
Characteristics of Well-Designed Goals		• Written in terms of outcomes rather than actions • Measurable and quantifiable • Clear as to a time frame	• Challenging yet attainable • Written down • Communicated to all necessary organizational members

Gerrit Grunert, Managing Director, Rheintor Vermoegensverwaltung GmbH, Neuss, Germany

Describe your job.

My job is managing a commercial real estate portfolio in prime locations in Germany's major cities. As a managing director, my job is to generate and maximize annual revenues, under consideration of an optimal increase in value for the whole portfolio over a long time period. The job requires not only managing the portfolio and the staff of the company but also coordinating external people such as architects, consultants, lawyers, and others.

What types of skills do you think tomorrow's managers will need?

Apart from overall flexibility, high motivation, and knowledge, it is vital to have an affinity for computers and e-business. Since business is becoming more and more global, fluency in other languages and experiences in foreign countries will be important. Managers must be able to pursue a lifelong learning approach.

How do you use planning in your job?

Apart from annual planning of revenues and costs, a long-term planning process for a minimum of 10 years has to be done. This strategic planning includes assumptions about the current, intermediate, and long-term status of the property within the real estate life cycle of the national market. The main goal is to assure that new investments will be made when the market is weak and that properties will be sold with a maximum profit when the market is as close to the peak of the life cycle as possible.

How important are goals to what you do?

The whole operational work that has to be carried out by the managing director depends on meeting the target yield goal. Every lease contract, refurbishment, and investment/sale of a property have to be carried out so that the main target is not jeopardized. Goals determine every transaction that has to be carried out.

Steps in Goal Setting What steps should managers follow to set goals? The goal-setting process consists of five steps.

1. Review the organization's **mission**, which is the purpose of an organization. These broad statements of what the organization's purpose is and what it hopes to accomplish provide an overall guide to what organizational members think is important. (We'll look more closely at organizational mission in Chapter 8.) It's important to review these statements before writing goals because the goals should reflect what the mission statement says.

2. Evaluate available resources. You don't want to set goals that are impossible to achieve given your available resources. Even though goals should be challenging, they should be realistic. After all, if the resources you have to work with won't allow you to achieve a goal no matter how hard you try or how much effort is exerted, that goal shouldn't be set. That would be like the person with a $50,000 annual income and no other financial resources setting a goal of building a $1 million house in two years. No matter how hard he or she works at it, it's not going to happen.

3. Determine the goals individually or with input from others. These goals reflect desired outcomes and should be congruent with the organizational mission and goals in other organizational areas. These goals should be measurable, specific, and include a time frame for accomplishment.

mission

The purpose of an organization.

Testing...Testing...1,2,3

7. **Distinguish between traditional goal setting and management by objectives.**

8. **What characteristics do well-designed goals have?**

9. **How should managers set goals?**

4. Write down the goals and communicate them to all who need to know. We've already explained the benefit of writing down and communicating goals.

5. Review results to see whether goals are being met. Change, as needed.

Once the goals have been established, written down, and communicated, a manager is ready to develop plans for pursuing the goals.

DEVELOPING PLANS

The process of developing plans is influenced by three contingency factors and by the planning approach followed.

Contingency Factors in Planning Look back at our chapter-opening Manager's Dilemma. How will Soon-Chart Yu know what types of plans to develop for gazoontite.com? Will strategic or operational plans be needed? How about specific or directional plans? In some situations, long-term plans make sense; in others they do not. What are these situations? Three contingency factors affect planning: level in the organization, degree of environmental uncertainty, and length of future commitments.[11]

Exhibit 7.7 shows the general relationship between a manager's level in the organization and the type of planning done. For the most part, operational planning dominates managers' planning efforts at lower levels. At higher organizational levels, the planning becomes more strategy oriented.

The second contingency factor that affects planning is environmental uncertainty. When environmental uncertainty is high, plans should be specific but flexible. Managers must be prepared to rework and amend plans as they're implemented. At times, managers may even have to abandon their plans.[12] For example, at Continental Airlines, CEO Gordon M. Bethune and other executives established a specific goal of focusing on what customers wanted most—on-time flights—to help the company become more competitive in the highly uncertain airline industry. Because of the high level of uncertainty, the management team identified a "destination but not a flight plan," and was willing to change plans as necessary to achieve that goal of on-time service. Also, it's important for managers to continue formal planning efforts through periods of environmental uncertainty because studies have shown that it takes at least four years of such efforts before any positive impact on organizational performance is seen.[13]

Exhibit	7.7	
Planning in the Hierarchy of Organizations		

Strategic Planning

Top Executives

Middle-Level Managers

First-Level Managers

Operational Planning

The last contingency factor affecting planning is also related to the time frame of the plans. The more that current plans affect future commitments, the longer the time frame is for which managers should plan. This **commitment concept** means that plans should extend far enough to meet those commitments made when the plans were developed. Planning for too long or for too short a time period is inefficient and ineffective. To see how important the commitment concept is to planning, just look at the shores of Lake Erie in Cleveland, where several distinct geometric forms are combined into an impressive building—the Rock and Roll Hall of Fame. In the early 1980s, a group of music industry professionals founded the Rock and Roll Hall of Fame to honor music greats, but the hall had no physical facility. The hall's board decided in 1986 to build an actual hall and museum. Initial plans were developed, but building cost estimates proved to be too low and the project was delayed. The original groundbreaking, scheduled for 1990, didn't take place until 1993. By that time, it wasn't feasible to back out of the project, even with the delays and higher costs. Instead, construction proceeded and the hall and museum opened in September 1995. How does this example illustrate the commitment concept? The decision made back in the early 1980s became a commitment for future actions and expenditures. Once the board decided to build a facility, it had to plan for the increased costs and the construction delays. The future impact of the decision to build was that it committed the board to live with the decision and all its consequences, good and bad.

Approaches to Planning Federal, state, and local government officials work together on a plan to boost populations of wild salmon in the northwestern United States. Managers in the Global Fleet Graphics division (which makes premium, durable graphic-marking systems for buildings, signs, vehicles, and heavy equipment) of the 3M Company are developing plans detailing innovative solutions for satisfying increasingly demanding customers and battling more aggressive competitors. Emilio Azcárraga Jean, chairman and president of Grupo Televisa, the Mexican broadcasting company, gets input from many different people before setting company goals and then turns over the planning for achieving the goals to various executives. In each of these situations, planning is done a little differently. *How* an organization plans can best be understood by looking at *who* does the planning.

In the traditional approach, planning was done entirely by top-level managers who were often assisted by a **formal planning department**, a group of planning specialists whose sole responsibility was helping to write the various organizational plans. Under this approach, plans developed by top-level managers flowed down through other organizational levels, much like the traditional approach to goal setting. As they flowed down through the organization, plans were tailored to the particular needs of each level. Although this approach helped make managerial planning thorough, systematic, and coordinated, all too often the focus was on developing "the plan," a thick binder (or binders) full of meaningless information, that was stuck away on a shelf and never used by anyone for guiding or coordinating work efforts. In fact, in a survey of managers about formal top-down organizational planning processes, over 75 percent said that their

Strategic planning takes place at the higher levels of an organization. A plan to put a computer, printer, and Internet access in the home of every one of the company's 346,000 employees is the idea of Ford's chief executive Jacques E. Nasser. Ford is spending between $50 and $150 million to carry out Nasser's plan to make the company a customer-focused powerhouse.

commitment concept

Plans should extend far enough to meet those commitments made when the plans were developed.

formal planning department

A group of planning specialists whose sole responsibility is helping to write various organizational plans.

company's planning approach was unsatisfactory.[14] A common complaint was that "plans are documents that you prepare for the corporate planning staff and later forget." Although this traditional top-down approach to planning is still used by many organizations, it can be effective only if managers understand the importance of creating a workable, usable document that organizational members actually draw on for direction and guidance, not a document that looks impressive but is never used.

Another approach to planning is to involve more organizational members in the process. In this approach, plans aren't handed down from one level to the next but instead are developed by organizational members at the various levels and in the various work units to meet their specific needs. For instance, at Dell Computer Corporation's server manufacturing facility in Austin, Texas, employees from production, supply management, and channel management meet weekly to make plans based on current product demand and supply. In addition, work teams set their own daily schedules and track their progress against those schedules. If a team falls behind, team members develop "recovery" plans to try to get back on schedule.[15] When organizational members are more actively involved in planning, they see that the plans are more than just something written down on paper. They can actually see that the plans are used in directing and coordinating work.

⟩ CONTEMPORARY ISSUES IN PLANNING

We conclude this chapter by addressing two contemporary issues in planning. Specifically, we're going to look at criticisms of planning, and then at how managers can plan effectively in dynamic environments.

CRITICISMS OF PLANNING

Formalized organizational planning became popular in the 1960s and, for the most part, it still is today. It makes sense for an organization to establish some direction. But critics have challenged some of the basic assumptions underlying planning. What are the primary arguments directed at formal planning?

1. *Planning may create rigidity.*[16] Formal planning efforts can lock an organization into specific goals to be achieved within specific timetables. When these goals were set, the assumption may have been that the environment wouldn't change during the time period the goals covered. If that assumption is faulty, managers who follow a plan may face trouble. Rather than remaining flexible—and possibly throwing out the plan—managers who continue to do the things required to achieve the original goals may not be able to cope with the changed environment. Forcing a course of action when the environment is fluid can be a recipe for disaster.

2. *Plans can't be developed for a dynamic environment.*[17] Most organizations today face dynamic environments. If a basic assumption of making plans—that the environment won't change—is faulty, then how can you make plans at all? Today's business environment is often chaotic, at best. By definition, that means random and unpredictable. Managing under those conditions requires flexibility, and that may mean not being tied to formal plans.

3. *Formal plans can't replace intuition and creativity.*[18] Successful organizations are typically the result of someone's innovative vision. But visions have a tendency to become formalized as they evolve. Formal planning efforts typically involve a thorough investigation of the organization's capabilities and opportunities and a mechanical analysis that reduces the vision to some type of programmed routine. That approach can spell disaster for an organization. For example, the rapid growth of Apple Computer in the late 1970s and throughout the 1980s was attributed, in part, to the innovative and creative approaches of one of its co-founders, Steven Jobs. As the company grew, Jobs felt there was a need for more formalized management—something he was uncomfortable doing. He hired a CEO who ultimately ousted Jobs from his own company.

Managers can't see the future, but they can and do plan in an often-unpredictable environment. Tools like software can help to make forecasting easier. At the Mexican steel maker IMSA, for instance, operations-planning manager Francisco Leal bought software programs that anticipate demand and centralize order data in order to improve the planning process.

With Jobs's departure came increased organizational formality, including detailed planning—the same things that Jobs despised so much because he felt that they hampered creativity. By the mid-1990s, Apple, once an industry leader, was struggling for survival. The situation became so bad that Jobs was brought back as CEO to get Apple back on track, which he eventually did by refocusing on innovation.

4. *Planning focuses managers' attention on today's competition not on tomorrow's survival.*[19] Formal planning has a tendency to focus on how to best capitalize on existing business opportunities within an industry. It often doesn't allow managers to consider creating or reinventing an industry. Consequently, formal plans may result in costly blunders and high catch-up costs when other competitors take the lead. On the other hand, companies such as Intel, ABB (Asea Brown Boveri), and Sony have found success from forging into uncharted waters, spawning new industries as they go.[20]

5. *Formal planning reinforces success, which may lead to failure.*[21] Success breeds success. That's an "American tradition." If it's not broken, don't fix it, right? Well, maybe not! Success may, in fact, breed failure in an uncertain environment. It's hard to change or discard previously successful plans—to leave the comfort of what works for the anxiety of the unknown. Successful plans, however, may provide a false sense of security, generating more confidence in the formal plans than is warranted. Many managers will not face the unknown until they're forced to do so by environmental changes. By then, it may be too late!

How valid are these criticisms? Should managers forget about planning? No, managers shouldn't forget about planning! Although the criticisms have merit when directed at rigid, inflexible planning, today's managers can be effective planners if they understand planning in dynamic uncertain environments.

EFFECTIVE PLANNING IN DYNAMIC ENVIRONMENTS

A wireless technology called Bluetooth that links together information devices such as mobile phones, laptops, and handheld organizers is threatening to revolutionize all kinds of industries. Honeywell is using the Internet to help fashion a customized prototype of products from fan blades to golf club heads. Mexican cement maker Cemex is using Internet-based truck dispatch systems to speed deliveries to customers. Consumers continue to increase how much they spend on eating out instead of cooking at home. The Euro is now the official currency of a majority of countries in the European Union.

How can managers effectively plan when the external environment is continually changing? We already discussed uncertain environments as one of the main contingency factors that affect the types of plans managers develop. Because dynamic environments are more the norm than the exception for today's managers, let's revisit how to plan in an uncertain environment.

In an uncertain environment, managers want to develop plans that are specific but flexible. Although this may seem contradictory, it's not. To be useful, plans need some specificity, but the plans should not be cast in stone. Managers must recognize that planning is an ongoing process. The plans serve as a road map even though the destination may be changing constantly due to dynamic market conditions. They should be willing to change directions if environmental conditions warrant. This flexibility is particularly important as plans are implemented. Managers must stay alert to environmental changes that could impact the effective implementation of plans and make changes as needed. Keep in mind, also, that it's important to continue formal planning efforts, even when the environment is highly uncertain, in order to see any effect on organizational performance. It's the persistence in planning efforts that contributes to significant performance improvement. Why? It seems that, as with most activities, managers "learn to plan" and the quality of their planning improves when they continue to do it.[23]

Testing...Testing...1,2,3

10. **How do contingency factors affect planning?**

11. **What are the major arguments against formal planning?**

12. **How can managers effectively plan in a dynamic environment?**

🌐 MANAGING IN AN E-BUSINESS WORLD

How Will Planning Work in E-Businesses?

Just how fast is Internet fast?[22] Start-up business Accompany Inc. (www.accompany.com), a San Francisco-based online buying club, went from an idea being tossed around by friends to a full-fledged company (including business plan, start-up money, and launch) in three months. Goodhome.com (www.goodhome.com), an online home-furnishings retailer, went from idea to business plan to venture capital funding to start-up in just 10 weeks. E-business failures are just as fast. After only six months in business, the hip clothing Web site boo.com shut down its Web site and liquidated the company. Other e-businesses have suffered the same quick demise. In a hyperspeed evolving and changing environment, how can managers in e-businesses ever hope to plan effectively?

The impact of Internet time on planning is revolutionary. It forces managers to abandon any plans that end in -year (such as three-year, one-year, and so forth). In Internet time, many e-businesses are writing and rewriting plans every quarter or even every week. The organizational hierarchy is flattened as the responsibility for establishing goals and developing plans is shoved to the lowest organizational levels since there's no time for goals and plans to flow down from the top. Budgeting decisions are speeded up as organizations have to be ready to allocate resources to critical areas at a moment's notice. However, probably the biggest change for planning in e-businesses is that customers are calling the shots. Customers tell the companies what they want and companies have to respond or lose out. In effect, the customers are establishing the goals and the direction of e-businesses. One expert described the situation as the difference between a bus and a taxi. Driving a bus is similar to the traditional approach to managerial planning—it follows a set route. Planning in e-businesses has to be more like driving a taxi that goes where customers tell it to go. Both will get you to the destination, but the taxi is more likely to get you there sooner, especially during the chaos of rush hour.

Managers Respond to "A Manager's Dilemma"

Gyl Wadge Kovalik

Project Director, Texas Department of Health, Austin, Texas

Carrie Lundy

Area Service Manager, CHEP USA, Gladstone, Missouri

Since Gazoontite.com has been in business for a while, it's likely that Yu has hired some key management personnel and other employees to work in his organization. The first step in planning for the company's future would be to develop a strategic, long-term plan with key management staff to map out the general direction of the company over the next three or more years. The strategic plan would be directional and allow flexibility for line-level managers to adjust to and plan for external environmental realities.

The next step in planning would be involving all employees in a management by objectives exercise to establish specific performance goals for the short term and long term related to the strategic and financial goals in the strategic plan.

Yu might want to consider hiring planning consultants to assist with the first planning cycle because his past managerial experience with an established company might not translate well into the volatile world of an Internet start-up.

In planning for the ongoing operation of his business, Yu would need to do some different types of planning that would cover different areas of his business. First, he would need formal plans for both long-range and immediate staffing needs. This is particularly important in light of the difficulties that Internet companies often face because of the scarcity of people with the talents needed to take the company to the next level.

Next, Yu would need plans for compiling, evaluating, and reacting to ever-changing customer needs. The volatility of the Internet world makes some type of planning in this area necessary. Yu would also need plans for staying aware of the competition, both online and traditional. It's important to have some systematic approach to identifying and evaluating competitors.

Finally, he would need plans for negotiating with vendors and suppliers. Since gazoontite.com is essentially a retailer of others' products, Yu would need to plan for the relationships he desires with his vendors and suppliers, especially as the business continues to grow.

Chapter Summary

This summary is organized by the chapter-opening objectives found on p. 174.

1. Planning involves defining the organization's goals, establishing an overall strategy for achieving those goals, and developing a comprehensive set of plans to integrate and coordinate organizational work. It's concerned with both the ends (what's to be done) and the means (how it's to be done).

2. Managers plan for four reasons: planning gives direction by establishing coordinated efforts, planning reduces the impact of change, planning minimizes wasted time and resources and redundancy, and planning sets the standards used in controlling.

3. Goals—desired outcomes for individuals, groups, or an entire organization—are often called the foundation of planning because they provide the direction for all management decisions and form the criterion against which actual work accomplishments are measured.

4. Strategic plans cover an extensive time period, cover broad issues, and include the formulation of objectives. Operational plans cover shorter time periods, focus on specifics, and assume that objectives are already known. Long-term plans are those with a time frame beyond three years. Short-term plans are those covering one year or less. Specific plans are clearly defined and leave no room for interpretation. Directional plans are flexible plans that set out general guidelines. A single-use plan is a one-time plan specifically designed to meet the needs of a unique situation. Standing plans are ongoing plans that provide guidance for activities performed repeatedly.

5. Goals can be established by traditional goal setting or by management by objectives. Traditional goal setting is an approach in which goals are set at the top organizational level and then broken down into subgoals for each level of the organization. Management by objectives is a management system in which specific performance goals are jointly determined by employees and their managers, progress toward accomplishing these goals is periodically reviewed, and rewards are allocated on the basis of this progress.

6. Well-designed goals have the following characteristics: written in terms of outcomes rather than actions; measurable and quantifiable; clear as to a time frame; challenging but attainable; written down; and communicated to all organizational members who need to know the goals.

7. Three contingency factors that affect planning include the level in the organization, the degree of environmental uncertainty, and the length of future commitments.

8. The traditional approach to developing plans was that it was done by top-level managers who were often assisted by a formal planning department. The plans developed by top managers flowed down through other organizational levels and were tailored to the particular needs of each level. Another approach to planning is to involve more organizational members in the process. Instead of plans being handed down from one level to the next, they are developed by organizational members at the different levels and in the various work units to meet their specific needs.

9. The major criticisms of formal planning are: (a) It may create rigidity in organizational decisions and actions; (b) plans can't be developed for a dynamic environment; (c) formal plans can't replace intuition and creativity; (d) planning focuses managers' attention on today's competition, not on tomorrow's survival; and (e) formal planning reinforces success and thereby ultimately may lead to failure.

10. Effective planning in a dynamic environment means developing plans that are specific but flexible; being willing to change directions if environmental conditions warrant; staying alert to environmental changes that could impact the effective implementation of plans and making changes as needed; and continuing formal planning efforts even when the environment is highly uncertain.

Thinking About Management Issues

1. Will planning become more or less important to managers in the future? Why?

2. If planning is so crucial, why do some managers choose not to do it? What would you tell these managers?

3. Explain how planning involves making decisions today that will have an impact later.

4. How might planning in a not-for-profit organization such as the American Cancer Society differ from planning in a for-profit organization such as Coca-Cola?

5. What types of planning do you do in your personal life? Describe these plans in terms of being (a) strategic or operational, (b) short or long term, and (c) specific or directional.

Log On: Internet-Based Exercise

Find five organizations that have goals listed on their Web sites. These could be for-profit or not-for-profit organizations. Write down these goals (be sure to include the organization's Web site address) and evaluate them according to the characteristics of well-designed goals. Rewrite the goals that don't meet the characteristics so that they do meet them. Explain what changes you have made.

myPHLIP Companion Web Site

myPHLIP **(www.prenhall.com/myphlip)** *is a fully customizable homepage that ties students and faculty to text-specific resources.*
- **For students**, *myPHLIP provides an online study guide tied chapter-by-chapter to the text—current events and Internet exercises, lecture notes, downloadable software, the Career Center, the Writing Center, Ask the Tutor, and more.*
- **For faculty**, *myPHLIP provides a syllabus tool that allows you to manage content, communicate with students, and upload personal resources.*

Working Together: Team-Based Exercise

People Power[2], a corporate training company that markets its human resource programs to organizations around the globe, has had several requests to design a training program to teach an organization's employees how to use the Internet for researching information. This training program will then be marketed to potential corporate customers. Your team is spearheading this important project. The first thing your team has to do is identify three or four goals for each of the three stages of the project: (1) researching corporate customer needs, (2) researching the Internet for specific information sources and techniques that could be used in the training module, and (3) designing and writing specific training modules.

Form small groups of three or four individuals. Complete your assigned work as described. Be sure that your goals are well designed. Be prepared to share your goals with the rest of the class.

Case Application

Building for the Future

"Every project we take on starts with a question: How can we do what's never been done before?" That's the guiding philosophy of Australia's Lend Lease Corporation (www. lendlease.com). And it's done some pretty spectacular things: built the foundations for the Sydney Opera House, constructed the Newington Olympic Village for the 2000 Summer Olympics, and created the soundstages for *The Matrix* and *Mission Impossible* 2. But building isn't the company's only business. It's also a market leader in terms of being a global integrated real estate business with expertise in real estate investment funds management, project management and construction, and property development.

One of Lend Lease's successful real estate projects.

Lend Lease is one of Australia's business success stories and is seen as one of the most exciting companies to work for in Australia. How does Lend Lease manage to be consistently successful *and* persistently different? Effective managerial planning plays an important role. One of its recent projects, the Bluewater shopping complex in Kent, England, illustrates how planning is approached at Lend Lease.

In the mid-1990s, two Lend Lease executives—chairman Stuart Hornery and director of special projects Malcolm Latham—were standing at the edge of an abandoned limestone quarry about 20 miles outside of London, surveying the barren landscape. Instead of seeing what most people would—one of Europe's industrial wastelands—they envisioned a dramatic and unique civic space that would be a community gathering place in addition to being a popular retail shopping center. They made the decision to purchase the site from Blue Circle Industries, a British cement company that had been trying to develop it for more than eight years. Upon signing the deal, Lend Lease got a preapproved development plan that was in place for the site. Company executives chose to abandon everything in this plan but the project's name: Bluewater. That's when the company's own planning efforts got serious.

Less than three weeks after that initial visit to the site, a team of Lend Lease employees including Hornery and Latham and six of the company's best retail, property, and project management experts met with Eric Kuhne, a well-respected and influential U.S. architect, in rented office space in London. The team's goal was to give life to the vision that Hornery and Latham believed was possible at the Bluewater site. What they developed was an innovative, break-the-mold plan, simply titled, "The Bluewater

Factors." The team's plan outlined a shopping complex featuring a glowing white roofscape; 1.6 million square feet of retail space (one of the largest shopping complexes in Europe); a 13,000-car parking garage; and over 50 acres of parks, seven lakes, and more than 1 million trees and shrubs. The project's scale would prove to be an enormous undertaking. However, the company's effective planning would once again prove up to the task.

Lend Lease uses project-control groups (PCG) to blend creativity and accountability. Each major project gets a PCG, which plays a role similar to a corporate board of directors. Members of a PCG don't work on the project day to day but are accountable for it. Project managers are challenged to assemble a PCG with the best possible diverse mix of skills, intuition, and experiences of people from both inside *and* outside the company. These PCGs can include as few as three people or as many as fifteen. They meet every six or seven weeks during the project's duration. And these meetings are serious. There's a precise agenda, a set of minutes, a financial review, and several other reports on the key aspects of the project. But these meetings aren't just about making sure that deadlines and budgets are being met. They're also an opportunity to engage in active questioning and exploration of ideas for better implementation. They're a cross between dreams and discipline. One project manager said, "We know that we have to make a case for why we are doing something in the first place. That means we're not afraid to stop things. We're brutal about pulling the plug and moving on, even when we've already spent a lot of time and money on a project."

The PCG for the Bluewater project included Hornery (Lend Lease's chairman), Latham (Lend Lease's director of special projects), Kuhne (the architect), the CEO of Lend Lease's European business, and the investment director of Prudential (one of Lend Lease's biggest investors). It also included a revolving group of architects; engineers; manufacturers; community advocates; local planning authorities; experts on construction, retail, and finance; *and* customers. Every five to six weeks, the PCG met to discuss budgets, agendas, and proposals for innovations. Did this commitment to effective planning work?

The time from initial idea to final leasing stage was just 1,628 days (a little under 4½ years). The project came in two weeks ahead of schedule, on budget, and fully leased with more than 320 retailers from around the world. The Bluewater complex is a sprawling triangle with three two-story malls. Each mall's shopping streets connect with the surrounding landscape and each mall features a "leisure village" that integrates its shopping area with nearby recreational space. The complex features health clubs, restaurants, and a cinema complex. There are even "welcome" halls decorated like luxury hotels and staffed by full-time concierges. Since the grand opening in March 2000, an average of more than 75,000 people have visited Bluewater each day.

QUESTIONS

1. What role do you think goals play in planning done at Lend Lease? Explain.

2. How does Lend Lease illustrate effective planning in a dynamic environment?

3. What approach to developing plans does Lend Lease appear to follow? Explain.

4. Would Lend Lease's approach work in other organizations? Why or why not?

Sources: Information on company from Hoover's Online (www.hoovers.com), September 19, 2000; from company's Web site (www.lendlease.com), August 15, 2000; and P. LaBarre, "A Company Without Limits," *Fast Company*, September 1999, pp. 160–186.

Learning Objectives

After reading and studying this chapter, you should be able to:

1. Explain the importance of strategic management.

2. Describe the steps in the strategic management process.

3. Explain SWOT analysis.

4. Differentiate corporate-, business-, and functional-level strategies.

5. Differentiate the various grand strategies.

6. Explain what competitive advantage is and why it's important to organizations.

7. Describe the five competitive forces.

8. Identify the various competitive strategies.

A MANAGER'S DILEMMA

The ball is in Val Ackerman's court. As president of the WNBA (Women's National Basketball Association), Ackerman is facing some tough strategic issues.[1]

The WNBA, formed in 1997, is wholly owned by the NBA, the professional basketball association that has spotlighted superstars such as Michael Jordan, Magic Johnson, Shaquille O'Neal, and Kobe Bryant. The WNBA's 16 teams are located in the same cities as NBA teams and most play in the same arenas. With the nurturing and financial support of its parent, the WNBA is the best hope for women's team play in professional sports. It has national television exposure and outstanding facilities to showcase players' talents. And it has captured the hearts of fans in the communities with WNBA teams. Ackerman states, "We are pioneers. We are succeeding where many others have failed."

Although the league seems to have several things going for it, there are plenty of problems. Ticket sales and television viewer levels have been flat. Players complain about low pay, and some have left for European and Australian leagues where player salaries can top six figures. In the WNBA, rookies start at $26,000 per year plus benefits, and salaries cap out at $80,000. Some top draft picks earn as little as $56,000 while a few select players can earn six-figure incomes with sponsor contracts and bonuses. However, the women who have achieved these lofty levels are

8

Strategic Management

few and far between. The league is caught between needing to recruit talent with fan drawing power and to keep operating costs low enough to maintain reasonable ticket prices.

The WNBA's core target market is women and children. They comprise around 75 percent of ticket buyers and 50 percent of the television audience. Many male sports fans have been unimpressed with the women's quality of play. And with the continuing limited ability to attract top-notch talent, the level of play isn't likely to improve. Put yourself in Ackerman's position. How could she use a SWOT (strengths, weaknesses, opportunities, threats) analysis to strategically manage the WNBA's future?

WHAT WOULD YOU DO?

The importance of having a good strategy can be seen by what Val Ackerman is attempting to do with the WNBA. By designing strategies to help the WNBA attract fans and players, Ackerman is trying to build the league into a prosperous, thriving organization. An underlying theme in this chapter is that good strategies result in high organizational performance.

› THE IMPORTANCE OF STRATEGIC MANAGEMENT

Effective managers around the world recognize the role that strategic management plays in their organization's performance. Through well-designed strategies, Swedish company Electrolux has "conquered" Europe and is looking at the United States. Hindustan Lever Ltd., an Indian company that makes soaps, detergents, and food preparations, has achieved a three-year total return to stockholders of 120 percent as a result of developing and implementing effective strategies. And Millennium Pharmaceuticals of Cambridge, Massachusetts, is poised to exploit its scientific knowledge and capabilities in gene-based medicine and jump into the ranks of the world's top pharmaceutical companies. These companies illustrate the value of strategic management. In this section, we want to look at what strategic management is and why it's considered important to managers.

WHAT IS STRATEGIC MANAGEMENT?

To begin to understand the basics of strategy and strategic management you need look no further than at what's happened in the discount retail industry. The industry's two largest competitors—Wal-Mart and Kmart—have battled for market dominance since 1962, the year both companies were founded. The two chains have other striking similarities as well: store atmosphere, names, markets served, and organizational purpose. Yet, Wal-Mart's performance (financial and otherwise) has surpassed that of Kmart. Why? Organizations vary in how well they perform because of differences in their strategies and differences in competitive abilities.[2] Wal-Mart is good at strategic management, whereas Kmart struggles to find the right combination.

strategic management

That set of managerial decisions and actions that determines the long-run performance of an organization.

Strategic management is that set of managerial decisions and actions that determines the long-run performance of an organization.[3] It entails all of the basic management functions; that is, the organization's strategies must be planned, organized, put into effect, and controlled. We'll discuss in detail the process of how strategic management takes place in an organization at a later point in the chapter.

PURPOSES OF STRATEGIC MANAGEMENT

Why is strategic management considered so important? Because it's involved in many of the decisions that managers make. Most of the significant current business events reported in the various business publications involve strategic management. For instance, in a recent week, there were reports of Chase Manhattan Bank's bid to purchase J.P. Morgan & Co., of questions being raised about Ford's response to the failures of Firestone tires on its Ford Explorers, and of the impact of rising fuel prices on Italian airline Alitalia. All are examples of managers making strategic decisions. Also, a survey of business owners found that 69 percent had strategic plans, and among those owners, 89 percent responded that they found their plans to be effective.[4] They stated, for example, that strategic planning gave them specific goals and provided their staff with a unified vision. Although some management analysts claim that strategic planning is "dead," others emphasize its importance.[5] In addition, studies of the effectiveness of strategic planning and management have found that, as with planning in general, companies with formal strategic management systems had higher financial returns than did companies with no such system.[6]

Today, strategic management has moved beyond for-profit business organizations to include governmental agencies, hospitals, and other not-for-profit organizations. For instance, when the U.S. Postal Service found itself in intense competitive battles with overnight package delivery companies, electronic mail services, and private mailing facilities, the U.S. Postmaster General (the Postal Service's CEO) used strategic management to help pinpoint important issues and to design appropriate strategic responses including the popular self-adhesive stamps and an electronic postmark used to certify e-mail messages. Although strategic management in not-for-profits has not been as well researched as that in for-profit organizations, we know that it's important for these organizations as well.

❯ THE STRATEGIC MANAGEMENT PROCESS

The **strategic management process**, as illustrated in Exhibit 8.1, is an eight-step process that encompasses strategic planning, implementation, and evaluation. Although the first six steps describe the planning that must take place, implementation and evaluation are just as important. Even the best strategies can fail if management doesn't implement or evaluate them properly. Let's examine in detail the eight steps in the strategic management process.

strategic management process

An eight-step process that encompasses strategic planning, implementation, and evaluation.

STEP 1: IDENTIFYING THE ORGANIZATION'S CURRENT MISSION, OBJECTIVES, AND STRATEGIES

Every organization needs a mission—a statement of the purpose of an organization. The mission answers the question: What is our reason for being in business? Defining the organization's mission forces managers to carefully identify the

Exhibit 8.1 **The Strategic Management Process**

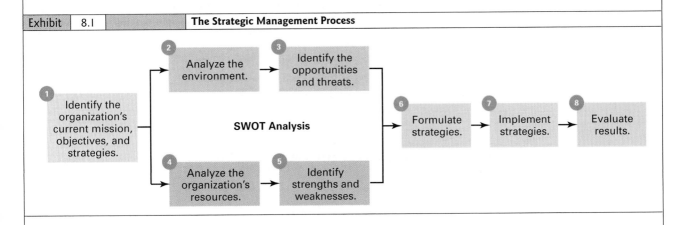

scope of its products or services. For instance, the mission of Prime Trucking Inc., a trucking company headquartered in Missouri, is "to prosper while providing excellent service to our customers." The mission statement for the U.S. Federal Bureau of Prisons reads, "The Federal Bureau of Prisons protects society by confining offenders in the controlled environments of prisons and community-based facilities that are safe, humane, and appropriately secure, and which provide work and other self-improvement opportunities to assist offenders in becoming law-abiding citizens." The mission statement of The Body Shop International PLC says that it "dedicates its business to the pursuit of social and environmental change." These statements provide clues to what these organizations see as their reason for being in business. Exhibit 8.2 provides a description of the typical components of mission statements.

Determining the purpose or reason for one's business is as important for not-for-profit organizations as it is for business firms. A college, for instance, must decide if it's training students for the professions, training students for particular

Exhibit	8.2

Components of a Mission Statement

Customers: **Who are the organization's customers?**
We believe our first responsibility is to the doctors, nurses, and patients, to mothers and all others who use our products and services. (Johnson & Johnson)

Products or services: **What are the organization's major products or services?**
AMAX's main products are molybdenum, coal, iron ore, copper, lead, zinc, petroleum and natural gas, potash, phosphates, nickel, tungsten, silver, gold, and magnesium. (AMAX)

Markets: **Where does the organization compete geographically?**
Our emphasis is on North American markets, although global opportunities will be explored. (Blockway)

Technology: **How technologically current is the organization?**
The common technology in these areas is discrete particle coatings. (Nashua)

Concern for survival, growth, and profitability: **Is the organization committed to growth and financial stability?**
In this respect, the company will conduct its operations prudently, and will provide the profits and growth which will assure Hoover's ultimate success. (Hoover's Universal)

Philosophy: **What are the organization's basic beliefs, values, aspirations, and ethical priorities?**
It's all part of the Mary Kay philosophy—a philosophy based on the golden rule. A spirit of sharing and caring where people give cheerfully of their time, knowledge, and experience. (Mary Kay Cosmetics)

Self-concept: **What is the organization's major competitive advantage and core competencies?**
Crown Zellerbach is committed to leapfrogging competition within 1,000 days by unleashing the constructive and creative abilities and energies of each of its employees. (Crown Zellerbach)

Concern for public image: **How responsive is the organization to societal and environmental concerns?**
To share the world's obligation for the protection of the environment. (Dow Chemical)

Concern for employees: **Does the organization consider employees a valuable asset?**
Bama seeks people who want to learn and contribute in a team environment. We provide a safe work environment, operate as an equal opportunity employer, focus on employee development and retention, develop mutual respect and trust for each other and support promotion from within. We value the voice of each employee. (The Bama Companies)

Source: Based on F. David, *Strategic Management*, 8e (Upper Saddle River, NJ: Prentice Hall, 2001), pp. 65–66.

jobs, or educating students through a well-rounded liberal arts education. Is it seeking students from the top 5 percent of high school graduates, students with low academic grades but high aptitude test scores, or students in the vast middle ground? Does it seek to attract older, working students or recent high school graduates? Answers to questions such as these clarify the organization's current purpose. For instance, many colleges have made significant investments in distance-learning and Internet-based courses and are tapping into markets that they previously could not serve.

It's also important for managers to identify the goals currently in place and the strategies currently being pursued. As we explained in Chapter 7, goals are the foundation of planning. A company's goals provide the measurable performance targets that employees strive to reach. Knowing the company's current goals gives managers a basis for deciding whether those goals need to be changed. For the same reasons, it's important for managers to identify the organization's current strategies. ◄

Testing...Testing...1,2,3

1. Define strategic management and explain how it entails the four management functions.

2. Why is strategic management important?

3. What happens in the first step in the strategic management process?

STEP 2: ANALYZING THE ENVIRONMENT

In Chapter 3, we described the external environment as an important constraint on a manager's actions. Analyzing that environment is a critical step in the strategy process. Why? Because an organization's environment, to a large degree, defines management's options. A successful strategy will be one that aligns well with the environment.[7] Managers in every organization need to analyze the environment. They need to know, for instance, what the competition is doing, what pending legislation might affect the organization, and what the labor supply is like in locations where it operates. In analyzing the external environment, managers should examine both the specific and general environments to see what trends and changes are occurring. For instance, managers in the sporting goods industry are finding that the industry is going through a metamorphosis.[8] Long dominated by the large traditional sporting goods companies such as Nike and Rawlings, the industry is being changed by dozens of smaller companies whose products are aimed at extreme sports enthusiasts—sports participants who value risk taking and pushing themselves to the limits. Many of these smaller companies credit their success to the X Games, the ESPN competition that features everything from skateboarding to sky surfing to street luge. Managers at both the traditional sporting goods companies and at the smaller companies want to stay on top of changes taking place in the external environment so they can take appropriate action. Step 2 of the strategic management process is complete when managers have an accurate grasp of what is taking place in the external environment and are aware of important trends that might affect the organization.

STEP 3: IDENTIFYING OPPORTUNITIES AND THREATS

After analyzing the environment, managers need to assess what they have learned in terms of opportunities that the organization can exploit and threats it faces. **Opportunities** are positive trends in external environmental factors; **threats** are negative trends.

Keep in mind that the same environment can present opportunities to one organization and pose threats to another in the same industry because of their different management of resources and capabilities. For example, Southwest Airlines

opportunities

Positive trends in external environmental factors.

threats

Negative trends in external environmental factors.

Shoestore owner Richard Polk is testing the possibilities of delivering text ads for his stores directly to cell phone users in his Boulder, Colorado marketplace. He identified the opportunity to take part in a trial run by a wireless-advertising firm after realizing that "you can't plan the weather two weeks out and buy a newspaper ad." But with the precision targeting of the wireless Web, "we can market directly to the customer relative to the conditions at the moment."

and Continental Airlines have prospered in a turbulent industry, whereas other airlines such as TWA and United have faltered.

STEP 4: ANALYZING THE ORGANIZATION'S RESOURCES AND CAPABILITIES

Now we move from looking outside the organization to looking inside. For example, what skills and abilities do the organization's employees have; what resources does the organization have; has it been successful at innovating products; what is the organization's financial position; how do customers perceive the organization and the quality of its products or services? This step forces managers to recognize that every organization, no matter how large or successful, is constrained in some ways by the resources and capabilities it has available.

The internal analysis provides important information about an organization's specific resources and capabilities. If any of these organizational capabilities or resources are exceptional or unique, they're called the organization's **core**

core competencies

An organization's major value-creating skills, capabilities, and resources that determine its competitive weapons.

competencies. The core competencies are the organization's major value-creating skills, capabilities, and resources that determine the organization's competitive weapons.[9] For instance, Ram Mukunda, CEO of Startec Global Communications, has built a company that's regarded as one of the world's leading international communications companies. Startec has succeeded by serving the needs of many ethnic communities throughout the United States and around the world. The company's core competency is communicating with customers in their native languages and then tailoring high-value programs and products to meet their changing needs. Because of its capabilities in these areas, Startec's customer base has grown nearly 4,000 percent since the mid-1990s.[10]

strengths

Any activities the organization does well or any unique resources that it has.

weaknesses

Activities the organization does not do well or resources it needs but does not possess.

STEP 5: IDENTIFYING STRENGTHS AND WEAKNESSES

The analysis in Step 4 should lead to a clear assessment of the organization's internal resources (such as financial capital, technical expertise, skilled workforce, experienced managers, and so forth). It should also point out the organization's capabilities in performing the different functional activities (such as marketing, production and manufacturing, research and development, financial and accounting, information systems, human resources management, and so forth). Any activities the organization does well or any unique resources that it has are called **strengths**. **Weaknesses** are activities the organization does not do well or resources it needs but does not possess. Look back at our chapter-opening dilemma. What might Val Ackerman look at in determining her organization's strengths and weaknesses?

An understanding of the organization's culture and its strengths and drawbacks is a crucial part of Step 5 that's often overlooked.[11] Managers should be aware that strong and weak cultures have different effects on strategy and that the content of a culture has a major effect on strategies pursued.

As we discussed in Chapter 3, an organization's culture is its personality. It reflects the shared values, beliefs, and valued behaviors that embody the "way things are done around here." In a strong culture, almost all employees will have a clear understanding of what the organization is about. This clarity should make it easy for managers to convey to new employees the organization's core competencies and strengths. At a department store chain such as Nordstrom, which has a very strong culture of customer service and satisfaction, managers are able to instill cultural values in new employees in a much shorter time than could a competitor with a weak culture. The negative side of a strong culture, of course, is that it's more difficult to change. A strong culture may act as a significant barrier to accepting any changes in the organization's strategies. Successful organizations with strong cultures may become prisoners of their own successes.

As we know, cultures also differ in the degree to which they encourage taking risks, exploiting innovations, and rewarding performance. These cultural factors influence managers' preferences for certain strategies. In a risk-aversive culture, for example, managers are likely to favor strategies that are defensive, that minimize financial exposure, and that react to changes in the environment rather than try to anticipate those changes. Conversely, where innovation is highly valued, managers are likely to favor new technology and product development.

Lands' End has succeeded in translating its core competency, the outstanding (and uniquely folksy) customer service provided by its phone reps, to the new frontier of Internet shopping. The company more than doubled its online sales in 1999 and, according to Senior Vice President for E-Commerce Bill Bass, it will continue to build on that competency with new Web site features like personalization.

Organizational culture also can promote or hinder an organization's strategic actions. One study showed that firms with "strategically appropriate cultures" outperformed other corporations with less appropriate cultures.[12] What is a strategically appropriate culture? It's one that supports the firm's chosen strategy. For instance, at Hewlett-Packard, a high-tech company with over $48 billion in annual revenues, growth is the chosen strategy, and employees' product innovation efforts are enthusiastically encouraged and supported within the corporate culture. In fact, HP's culture, renowned for its openness, employee freedom and

Many company Web sites have an "About Us" link that provides information about the company and its products or services—past, present, and future. This information is available for anyone to read, even competitors. In an intensely competitive industry where it's difficult for a company to survive, much less be successful, would it be wrong for managers to include misleading or even false information? Why or why not? Suppose that the industry wasn't intensely competitive? Would you feel differently? Explain.

When General Mills discovered it was wasting money by sending cereal shipments out in half-empty trucks, it needed to address that weakness quickly. The company soon came up with an Internet-based system that allows it to "carpool" its freight onto trucks shared by a dozen different companies. Says Kevin J. Schoen, General Mills' Director of Strategic Alliances, "The only way now to boost productivity is to go outside our walls—collaborate with other companies."

SWOT analysis

An analysis of the organization's strengths, weaknesses, opportunities, and threats.

autonomy, has played a key role in the company's successful implementation of its global growth strategies.

The merging of Steps 3 and 5 results in an assessment of the organization's internal resources and capabilities and external environmental opportunities. (See Exhibit 8.3.) This is frequently called **SWOT analysis** because it's an analysis of the organization's *strengths*, *weaknesses*, *opportunities*, and *threats*. Based on the SWOT analysis, managers can identify a strategic niche that the organization might exploit.

In light of the SWOT analysis, managers also reevaluate the organization's current mission and goals. Are they realistic? Do they need modification? Are we where we want to be right now? If changes are needed in the overall direction, this is where they are likely to originate. If no changes are necessary, managers are ready to begin the actual formulation of strategies.

STEP 6: FORMULATING STRATEGIES

Strategies need to be established for the corporate, business, and functional levels of the organization, and we'll describe each of these types of strategies shortly. The formulation of strategies follows the decision-making process we discussed in Chapter 6. Managers need to develop and evaluate strategic alternatives and then select strategies that support and complement each other and that allow the organization to best capitalize on its strengths and environmental opportunities. Step 6 is complete when managers have developed a set of strategies that will give the organization a relative advantage over its rivals. Successful managers will choose strategies that give their organization the most favorable competitive edge, and then they will try to sustain that advantage.

STEP 7: IMPLEMENTING STRATEGIES

After strategies are formulated, they must be implemented. A strategy is only as good as its implementation. No matter how effectively an organization has planned its strategies, it can't succeed if the strategies aren't implemented properly. The rest of the chapters in this book address a number of issues related to strategy implementation. For instance, in Chapter 10, we discuss the strategy-structure relationship. In Chapter 12, we show that if new strategies are to suc-

Exhibit	8.3

Identifying the Organization's Opportunities

Organization's Resources/Abilities   **Organization's Opportunities**   Opportunities in the Environment

---

⚐ MANAGING YOUR CAREER | Doing a Personal SWOT Analysis

A SWOT analysis can be a useful tool for examining your own skills, abilities, career preferences, and career opportunities. Doing a personal SWOT analysis involves taking a hard look at what your individual strengths and weaknesses are and then assessing the opportunities and threats of various career paths that might interest you.[13]

Step 1: Assessing personal strengths and weaknesses. All of us have special skills, talents, and abilities. Each of us enjoys doing certain activities and not others. For example, some people hate sitting at a desk all day; others panic at the thought of having to interact with strangers. List the activities you enjoy and the things you are good at. Also, identify some things you don't enjoy and you're not so good at. It's important to recognize your weaknesses so that you can either try to correct them or stay away from careers in which those things would be important. List your important individual strengths and weaknesses and highlight those you think are particularly significant.

Step 2: Identifying career opportunities and threats. We know from this chapter and Chapter 3 that different industries face different external opportunities and threats. It's important to identify these external factors for the simple reason that your initial job offers and future career advancement can be significantly influenced by the opportunities and threats. A company that's in an industry in which there are significant nega-

tive trends will offer few job openings or career advancement opportunities. On the other hand, job prospects will be bright in industries that have significant positive external trends. List two or three industries you have an interest in and critically evaluate the opportunities and threats facing those industries.

Step 3: Outlining five-year career goals. Taking your SWOT assessments, list four or five career goals that you would like to accomplish within five years of graduation. These goals might include things such as the type of job you'd like to have, how many people you might be managing, or the type of salary you'd like to be making. Keep in mind that ideally you should try to match your individual strengths with industry opportunities.

Step 4: Outlining a five-year career action plan. Now it's time to get specific! Write a specific career action plan for accomplishing each of the career goals you identified in the previous step. State exactly what you will do, and by when, in order to meet each goal. If you think you will need special assistance, state what it is and how you will get it. For example, your SWOT analysis may indicate that in order to achieve your desired career goal, you need to take more courses in management. Your career action plan should indicate when you will take those courses. Your specific career action plan will provide you with guidance for making decisions, just as an organization's plans provide direction to managers.

---

ceed, they often require hiring new people with different skills, transferring some current employees to new positions, or laying off some employees. Also, since more and more organizations are using teams, the ability to build and manage effective teams is an important part of implementing strategy. We cover teams in Chapter 15. Finally, top management leadership is a necessary ingredient in a successful strategy. So, too, is a motivated group of middle- and lower-level managers to carry out the organization's specific strategies. Chapters 16 and 17 discuss ways to motivate people and offer suggestions for improving leadership effectiveness.

STEP 8: EVALUATING RESULTS

The final step in the strategic management process is evaluating results. How effective have our strategies been? What adjustments, if any, are necessary? Anne Mulcahy, the president and chief operating officer of Xerox Corporation, has made strategic adjustments to improve her company's competitiveness in the information services industry. She developed these strategic actions after assessing the results of previous strategies and determining that changes were needed. We discuss this step in our coverage of the control process in Chapter 18. ◀

Testing...Testing...1,2,3

4. **What information do managers gather when they're analyzing the environment and the organization's resources and capabilities?**

5. **How is a SWOT analysis useful?**

6. **Why are implementation and evaluation important steps in the strategic management process?**

> ## TYPES OF ORGANIZATIONAL STRATEGIES

Organizational strategies include strategies at the corporate level, business level, and functional level. (See Exhibit 8.4.) Managers at the top level of the organization typically are responsible for corporate-level strategies. Managers at the middle level typically are responsible for business-level strategies. And managers at the lower levels of the organization typically are responsible for the functional-level strategies. Let's look at each of these types of strategies.

CORPORATE-LEVEL STRATEGY

corporate-level strategy

An organizational strategy that seeks to determine what businesses a company should be in or wants to be in.

A **corporate-level strategy** seeks to determine what businesses a company should be in or wants to be in. Corporate-level strategy determines the direction that the organization is going and the roles that each business unit in the organization will play in pursuing that direction. For instance, PepsiCo's corporate-level strategy integrates the strategies of its various business units—Soft Drinks (Pepsi, Mountain Dew, Slice), Snacks (Frito-Lay and Rold Gold pretzels), Other Beverages (Tropicana Juices, Aquafina bottled water, All Sport sports drinks, Dole Juices, and Lipton tea), and Quaker Oats—so the company can grow. PepsiCo once owned a restaurant division that included Taco Bell, Pizza Hut, and KFC, but, because of intense competitive pressures in the fast-food industry and the restaurant division's inability to contribute to corporate growth, PepsiCo changed its corporate-level strategy to concentrate on its soda and snack food divisions. It spun off that division as a separate and independent business entity called Tricon Global Restaurants, Inc. The most popular approach for describing an organization's corporate-level strategies is the grand strategies framework, which we'll look at first. We'll conclude our discussion of corporate-level strategies with a description of a strategy tool to help managers evaluate the various businesses the company is in.

Charles C. Conaway, the CEO of Kmart Corp., is working to turn the retailing icon around. He plans to revamp the company by investing in new technology to improve inventory and stocking processes, introducing 24-hour customer-service centers, instituting an employee reward system to encourage superior service and generate ideas to cut waste, focusing on private-label brands, and clarifying the image and mission of the nationwide chain. Although it will likely be at least a year before anyone knows whether his plans succeed, Conaway will be measuring results throughout the process. The first step is a customer-feedback loop that encourages customers to call an 800 number on the back of their receipt and rate their shopping experience via an automated voice-response system.

Kellogg Company, Wal-Mart, and Westinghouse are profitable companies, but they seem to be going in different directions. Until recently, Kellogg's management was content to maintain the status quo and remain in the breakfast food industry. Wal-Mart, on the other hand, is rapidly expanding its operations and developing new business and retailing concepts. It's also pursuing global opportunities. Meanwhile, sluggish sales and an uncertain outlook in heavy industrial products and services such as turbine generators and electric and nuclear power generation have prompted Westinghouse Electric Corporation to scale back and sell some of its businesses. These different directions can be explained in terms of grand, or all-encompassing, strategies.[14] Exhibit 8.5 shows each of the grand strategies in relation to the SWOT analysis.

Exhibit | 8.4 | **Levels of Organizational Strategy**

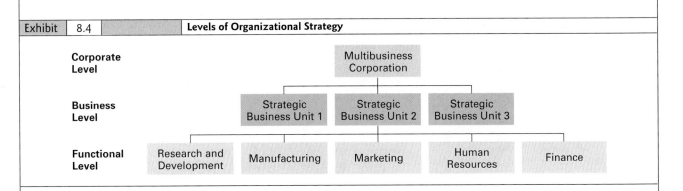

Grand Strategy—Stability A **stability strategy** is a corporate-level strategy characterized by an absence of significant change. Examples of this strategy include continuing to serve the same clients by offering the same product or service, maintaining market share, and sustaining the organization's return-on-investment results.

When should managers pursue stability? When they view the organization's performance as satisfactory and the environment appears to be stable and unchanging; that is, the organization is content to continue what it has been doing and sees no reason to change.

It's not easy to identify organizations pursuing a stability strategy, if for no other reason than few top managers are willing to admit they are doing it. Growth tends to have universal appeal, and retrenchment is often accepted as a necessary evil. But managers who actively pursue stability might be considered complacent or even smug. You should be aware, however, that many *small* business owners and managers may follow a stability strategy indefinitely. Why? These individuals may feel that their business is successful enough just as it is and that it adequately meets their personal goals.

stability strategy

A corporate-level strategy characterized by an absence of significant change.

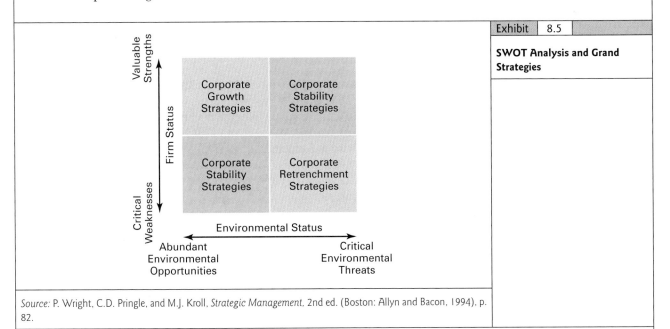

Exhibit | 8.5

SWOT Analysis and Grand Strategies

Source: P. Wright, C.D. Pringle, and M.J. Kroll, *Strategic Management,* 2nd ed. (Boston: Allyn and Bacon, 1994), p. 82.

Whirlpool Corp. is employing a growth strategy in all its international markets, particularly Asia and Latin America. Among the components of its strategy are building brand awareness and loyalty, and reducing costs by designing products on a "global platform" that relies on the fact that 60 to 70 percent of the materials and technology behind its products are the same around the world. In Brazil, where this young couple is shopping for a washer, Whirlpool holds about 45 percent of the appliance market.

growth strategy

A corporate-level strategy that seeks to increase the level of the organization's operations.

We mentioned Kellogg Company as an example of a company that had followed a stability strategy. However, due to fierce competition in global cereal markets in which it was beginning to lose its unique niche and leadership position, Kellogg's management finally began to branch out by acquiring Worthington Foods (meats and meat alternatives) and Keebler Foods (cookies and snacks). Although the Kellogg Company can no longer be considered as pursuing a stability strategy, when an organization's managers *are* content to stick with what they are doing and are reluctant to move into other areas, that would be an example of the stability strategy.

Grand Strategy—Growth The **growth strategy** is a corporate-level strategy that seeks to increase the level of the organization's operations. This includes increasing such popular quantitative measures as sales revenues, number of employees, and market share. Growth can be achieved through direct expansion, vertical integration, horizontal integration, or diversification.

Growth through direct expansion (also called concentration) is achieved by internally increasing a firm's sales, production capacity, or workforce. No other firms are acquired or merged with; instead the company chooses to grow by itself through its own business operations. For instance, McDonald's has pursued a growth strategy by way of direct expansion. The company has grown by awarding franchises to people who are willing to be trained in the "McDonald's way" and by opening company-owned outlets. In addition, it's pursued other restaurant formats, such as Chipotle's Mexican Grill and Aroma Café, but again has chosen to do that on its own.

A company might also choose to grow by vertical integration, which is an attempt to gain control of inputs (backward vertical integration), outputs (forward vertical integration), or both. In backward vertical integration, the organization attempts to gain control of its inputs by becoming its own supplier. For instance, United Airlines has created its own in-flight food services business. In forward vertical integration, the organization gains control of its outputs (products or services) by becoming its own distributor. For example, Gateway Computer's retail stores are an example of an organization controlling its distribution.

In horizontal integration, a company grows by combining with other organizations in the same industry—that is, combining operations with competitors. For instance, H.J. Heinz, Inc., the food-processing company, combined operations with an organic baby food company, Earth's Best, to help its own Heinz baby foods division become more competitive. Because combining with competitors might decrease the amount of competition in an industry, the U.S. Federal Trade Commission assesses the impact of such proposed growth actions and must approve any proposed horizontal integration strategy. Other countries have similar restrictions. For instance, managers at America Online Inc. and Time Warner Inc. had to make concessions before the European Commission, the "watchdog" for the European Union, would allow their merger to stand.

Finally, an organization can grow through diversification, either related or unrelated. **Related diversification** is when a company grows by merging with or acquiring firms in different but related industries. For example, American Standard Cos., based in Piscataway, New Jersey, is in a variety of businesses including bathroom fixtures, air-conditioning and heating units, plumbing parts, and pneumatic brakes for trucks. The company's "strategic fit" is its exploitation of efficiency-oriented manufacturing techniques developed in its bathroom fixtures business and transferred to its other businesses. **Unrelated diversification** is when a company grows by merging with or acquiring firms in different and unrelated industries. For instance, Lancaster Colony Corporation makes salad dressing, car mats, and scented candles. These industries are different *and* unrelated.

Grand Strategy—Retrenchment A **retrenchment strategy** is a corporate-level strategy designed to address organizational weaknesses that are leading to performance declines. There's no shortage of companies that have pursued a retrenchment strategy. A partial list includes some of the biggest corporate names: Procter & Gamble, AT&T, Kodak, Reebok, IBM, Toyota Motor Corporation, Mitsubishi, Daimler Chrysler, and Union Carbide. When an organization is facing performance problems, a retrenchment strategy helps it stabilize operations, revitalize organizational resources and capabilities, and prepare to compete once again.

Corporate Portfolio Analysis When an organization's corporate strategy involves a number of businesses, managers can manage this collection, or portfolio, of businesses using a corporate portfolio matrix.[15] The first portfolio matrix—the **BCG matrix**—developed by the Boston Consulting Group, introduced the idea that an organization's businesses could be evaluated and plotted using a 2 × 2 matrix (see Exhibit 8.6) to identify which ones offered high potential and which were a drain on organizational resources.[16] The horizontal axis represents market share, which was evaluated as either low or high; and the vertical axis indicates anticipated market growth, which also was evaluated as either low or high. Based on its evaluation, the business was placed in one of four categories:

- *Cash cows* (low growth, high market share). Businesses in this category generate large amounts of cash, but their prospects for future growth are limited.
- *Stars* (high growth, high market share). These businesses are in a fast-growing market and hold a dominant share of that market. Their contribution to cash flow depends on their need for resources.
- *Question marks* (high growth, low market share). These businesses are in an attractive industry but hold a small market share percentage.

Under the leadership of CEO M. Bruce Nelson, Office Depot is pursuing a retrenchment strategy that has put a lid on new-store openings and also may include closing some of the chain's retail locations. "We're looking at every single store," says Nelson. The strategy is designed to help the firm recoup financial losses and reverse the defection of key customers.

related diversification

When a company grows by merging with or acquiring firms in different but related industries.

unrelated diversification

When a company grows by merging with or acquiring firms in different and unrelated industries.

retrenchment strategy

A corporate-level strategy designed to address organizational weaknesses that are leading to performance declines.

BCG matrix

A strategy tool that guides resource allocation decisions on the basis of market share and growth rate of SBUs.

Exhibit	8.6

The BCG Matrix

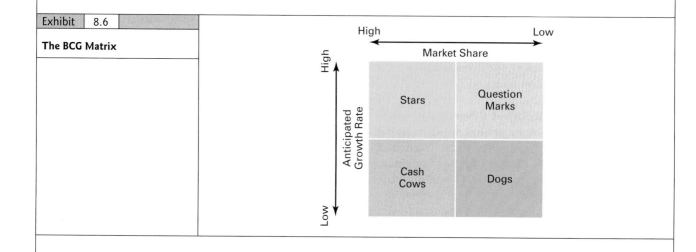

- *Dogs* (low growth, low market share). Businesses in this category do not produce or consume much cash. They have a low market share in a low-growth industry.

What are the strategic implications of the BCG matrix? Managers should "milk" cash cows for as much as they can, limit any new investment in them, and use the large amounts of cash generated to invest in stars and question marks with strong potential to improve market share. Heavy investment in stars will help take advantage of the market's growth and help maintain high market share. The stars, of course, will eventually develop into cash cows as their markets mature and sales growth slows. The hardest decision for managers is related to the question marks. After close and careful analysis, some will be sold off and others turned into stars. The dogs should be sold off or liquidated as they have low market share in markets with low growth potential.

A corporate portfolio matrix, such as the BCG matrix, can be a useful strategic management tool. It provides a framework for understanding diverse businesses and helps managers establish priorities for making resource allocation decisions.

Testing...Testing...1,2,3

7. **Differentiate between a stability strategy and a retrenchment strategy.**

8. **Describe the different ways an organization can pursue a growth strategy.**

9. **What does the BCG matrix show?**

BUSINESS-LEVEL STRATEGY

business-level strategy

An organizational strategy that seeks to determine how an organization should compete in each of its businesses.

Now we move to the business level. A **business-level strategy** seeks to determine how an organization should compete in each of its businesses. For a small organization in only one line of business or the large organization that has not diversified into different products or markets, the business-level strategy typically overlaps with the organization's corporate strategy. For organizations in multiple businesses, however, each division will have its own strategy that defines the products or services it will offer, the customers it wants to reach, and the like. For example, the French company LVMH-Moët Hennessy Louis Vuitton has different business-level strategies for its businesses including Christian Dior couture, Louis Vuitton leather goods, Guerlain perfume, Fred Joailler jewels, Hennessy champagne and cognac, and other luxury products. Each division has developed its own unique approach for competing. When an organization is in several different businesses, these single businesses that are independent and that formulate their own strategies are often called **strategic business units**.

The Role of Competitive Advantage Developing an effective business-level competitive strategy requires an understanding of competitive advantage, a key concept in strategic management.[17] **Competitive advantage** is what sets an organization apart, that is, its distinct edge. That distinct edge comes from the organization's core competencies, which, as we know from earlier in the chapter, might be in the form of organizational capabilities—the organization does something that others cannot do or does it better than others can do it. For example, Dell has developed a competitive advantage from its ability to create a direct-selling channel that's highly responsive to customers. And Southwest Airlines has a competitive advantage because of its skills at giving passengers what they want—quick, convenient, and fun service. Or those core competencies that lead to competitive advantage also can come from organizational assets or resources—the organization has something that its competitors do not have. For instance, Wal-Mart's state-of-the-art information system allows it to monitor and control inventories and supplier relations more efficiently than its competitors, which Wal-Mart has turned into a price advantage. And Harley-Davidson, Nike, and Coca-Cola all have well-known global trademarks that they use to get premium prices for their products.

If implemented properly, quality can be a way for an organization to create a sustainable competitive advantage.[18] That's why many organizations apply quality management concepts to their operations in an attempt to set themselves apart from competitors.

As we first discussed in Chapter 2, quality management focuses on quality and continuous improvement. To the degree that an organization can satisfy a customer's need for quality, it can differentiate itself from competitors and attract a loyal customer base. Moreover, constant improvement in the quality and reliability of an organization's products or services may result in a competitive advantage that can't be taken away.[19] Product innovations offer little opportunity for sustained competitive advantage, particularly in today's dynamic environment, because they are usually copied by competitors as soon as they hit the market. But incremental improvement—an essential element of quality management—is something that might be developed into a competitive advantage. Let's look at how two very different companies use quality management to gain competitive advantage.

strategic business units

Single businesses of an organization in several different businesses that are independent and that formulate their own strategies.

competitive advantage

What sets an organization apart; its distinct edge.

In 1998 Alex Nesbitt founded a company called Shipper.com to enable e-commerce firms to make next-day deliveries to their customers. When he realized the market for same-day delivery was even bigger, Nesbitt refocused the company on a new competitive advantage and renamed it Sameday.com. Not all e-commerce firms offer the same marketing edge; a firm called WhyRunOut.com offers convenience by picking up your film, dry cleaning, and rented videos, among other things.

MANAGING IN AN E-BUSINESS WORLD   E-Business Strategies

When the external environment is characterized by rapid, chaotic change, like it is in an e-business world, what are the strategy implications for e-business organizations?[20] After all, managers in these organizations do need to formulate and implement strategies that will serve as blueprints to successful performance, just as managers in non-e-business organizations do. Let's look at some of the major implications of increasingly dynamic and uncertain environments for e-business strategies.

Environmental analysis will become an important part of everyone's job. E-businesses can't afford to have only certain people or groups monitor changes and trends in the external environment. Because technology, competitors, and customers can change rapidly, everyone in an e-business must stay alert to changing patterns and relationships. For instance, at Priceline.com, the Web site where visitors name their price for airline tickets, hotel reservations, phone service, and other items, customer demand is monitored very carefully by employees who manage the Web site. If customers start asking for services not currently offered or complain about certain aspects of current services, employees do something about it. They don't wait for someone else to analyze the trends.

Strategy will become increasingly short term in orientation. In an environmental context where customers can appear—and disappear—with a keystroke, where technology can become obsolete in the blink of an eye, and where competitors from anywhere in the world can emerge practically overnight, the time frame of strategies must, by necessity, be short. In an e-world, it's no longer the survival of the fittest but the survival of the fastest. In addition, managers must be prepared to abandon a strategy if conditions warrant, no matter how many resources have been committed. This short-term orientation tends to be most difficult for traditional companies making the shift to e-businesses. Why? Because traditional organizations are used to predictable and regular planning cycles and procedures. In an e-business world, strategic management is an ongoing, real-time activity.

Barriers to entry are practically nonexistent. In an e-business world, there are few barriers keeping competitors from entering an industry. For example, if you were starting a traditional nursery business, you'd have to build or lease a building, find a wholesaler and set up purchasing arrangements, arrange the plants and flowers when they arrive, hire sales clerks, distribute marketing fliers, and take care of all sorts of other details—enough details that a person might think twice about starting the business. In an e-business world, starting a nursery business can be as simple as registering a Web site (domain) name, hiring a Web site designer, and making arrangements with a wholesaler to ship the plants direct to customers when you get online orders. You don't have to invest in physical resources other than a computer. Everything else can be done through online interactions with customers and suppliers.

A sustainable competitive advantage will be harder to achieve. As you know, organizations need a competitive advantage to be successful. Yet, in an e-business world, a competitive advantage will not be easy to sustain unless the organization has a core competency that is hard to imitate. Because an organization's culture and its human resources are difficult for competitors to imitate, they increasingly will become important sources of competitive advantage. New products and new technologies are easier for competitors to duplicate so managers in e-business organizations instead need to focus on the intangible resources and capabilities. In the best e-businesses, the culture is robust and provides a healthy environment for motivated employees. For example, at Sun Microsystems, corporate values and vision are continually communicated to employees through its internal communication network. Also, CEO Scott McNealy regularly communicates corporate values through communication sources such as Sun Talk Radio, an internal corporate broadcast system.

Even given the unique challenges of the e-business world, strategic management *is* important. Managers need to ensure that all employees are monitoring key external trends and changes so the organization can quickly exploit opportunities and steer away from threats. In addition, managers need to strengthen the organization's culture and human resources because it's difficult for competitors to imitate that unique mix.

At Granite Rock Company of Watsonville, California, the quality management program is an important strategic tool. What types of strategic quality innovations does the company use? It found through numerous customer surveys that on-time delivery was its customers' highest priority. Granite Rock set about establishing standards for achieving on-time performance. It studied Domino's Pizza outlets, which guarantee fast, accurate delivery. From that study, Granite Rock instituted a program in which customers simply drive up in their trucks, insert a card, and tell the machine how much of which material is needed—a process similar to using a bank ATM. The truck is loaded automatically, and a bill is sent to the customer later. The company's Granite Xpress is open 24 hours a day, seven days a week to meet customer needs.

LM Ericsson, a Swedish company, is a world leader in designing and supplying mobile telephone networks for communications companies in Europe and around the world.[21] Its products are known for their high quality and innovativeness, a fact of which Ericsson is proud. In fact, the company is poised to exploit the next major trend in communications, the mobile Internet, as Ericsson is the sole supplier of these networks for several different commercial operators around the globe.

We can find numerous other examples of organizations worldwide that are using quality management as a competitive weapon. From the U.S.-based Motorola Corporation to South Korea's Daewoo Corporation, organizations are recognizing the value of quality management as a competitive advantage.

Given the fact that every organization has resources and capabilities, what makes some organizations more successful than others? Why do some professional baseball teams consistently win championships or draw large crowds? Why do some organizations have consistent and continuous growth in revenues and profits? Why do some colleges, universities, or departments experience continually increasing enrollments? Why do some companies consistently appear at the top of lists ranking the "best," or the "most admired," or the "most profitable"? Although every organization has resources and work systems to do whatever it's in business to do, not every one is able to effectively exploit its resources or capabilities and to develop the core competencies that can provide it with a competitive advantage. And it's not enough for an organization simply to create a competitive advantage; it must be able to sustain it. That is, a sustainable competitive advantage enables the organization to keep its edge despite competitors' actions or evolutionary changes in the industry.

Testing...Testing...1,2,3

10. **What does an organization's business-level strategy seek to determine?**

11. **Why is competitive advantage an important concept?**

12. **How can quality management be a competitive advantage?**

Competitive Strategies Many important ideas in strategic management have come from the work of Michael Porter.[22] His competitive strategies framework identifies three generic strategies from which managers can choose. Success depends on selecting the right strategy—one that fits the competitive strengths (resources and capabilities) of the organization and the industry it's in. Porter's major contribution has been to carefully explain how managers can create and sustain a competitive advantage that will give a company above-average profitability. An important element in doing this is an industry analysis.

Porter proposes that some industries are inherently more profitable (and, therefore, more attractive to enter and remain in) than others. For example, the pharmaceutical industry is one with historically high profit margins, and the airline industry has notoriously low ones. But a company can still make a lot of money in a "dull" industry and lose money in a "glamorous" industry. The key is to exploit a competitive advantage.

In any industry, five competitive forces dictate the rules of competition. Together, these five forces (see Exhibit 8.7) determine industry attractiveness and profitability. Managers assess an industry's attractiveness using the following five factors.

1. *Threat of new entrants.* Factors such as economies of scale, brand loyalty, and capital requirements determine how easy or hard it is for new competitors to enter an industry.

2. *Threat of substitutes.* Factors such as switching costs and buyer loyalty determine the degree to which customers are likely to buy a substitute product.

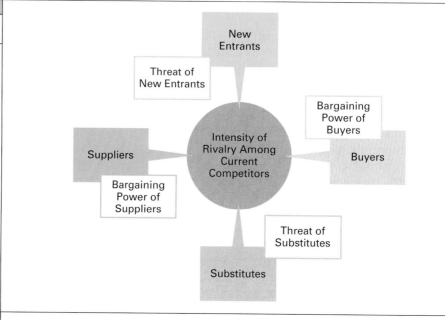

Source: Based on M.E. Porter, *Competitive Strategy: Techniques for Analyzing Industries and Competitors* (New York: The Free Press, 1980).

3. *Bargaining power of buyers.* Factors such as number of customers in the market, customer information, and the availability of substitutes determine the amount of influence that buyers have in an industry.

4. *Bargaining power of suppliers.* Factors such as the degree of supplier concentration and availability of substitute inputs determine the amount of power that suppliers have over firms in the industry.

5. *Existing rivalry.* Factors such as industry growth rate, increasing or falling demand, and product differences determine how intense the competitive rivalry will be among existing firms in the industry.

Once managers have assessed the five forces and determined what threats and opportunities exist, they're ready to select an appropriate competitive strategy. According to Porter, no firm can be successful by trying to be all things to all people. He proposes that managers select a strategy that will give the organization a competitive advantage. Porter goes on to say that a competitive advantage comes from either having lower costs than all other industry competitors or by being significantly different from competitors. On that basis, managers can choose one of

European management companies like the Schiphol Group are far ahead of the United States and most of Asia when it comes to finding new ways to generate extra profits from airports. One of the ways in which Schiphol Airport in Amsterdam has differentiated itself is by adding a plush casino, a shiatsu massage facility, and Indonesian dining.

three strategies: cost leadership, differentiation, or focus. Which one managers select depends on the organization's strengths and core competencies and its competitors' weaknesses. (See Exhibit 8.8.)

When an organization sets out to be the lowest-cost producer in its industry, it's following a **cost leadership strategy**. A low-cost leader aggressively searches out efficiencies in production, marketing, and other areas of operation. Overhead is kept to a minimum, and the firm does everything it can to cut costs. You won't find expensive art or interior decor at offices of low-cost leaders. For example, at Wal-Mart's headquarters in Bentonville, Arkansas, office furnishings are sparse and drab but functional. Although low-cost leaders don't place a lot of emphasis on "frills," the product or service being sold must be perceived as comparable in quality to that offered by rivals or at least be acceptable to buyers. Examples of companies that have used the low-cost leader strategy include Wal-Mart, Hyundai, and Southwest Airlines.

The company that seeks to offer unique products that are widely valued by customers is following a **differentiation strategy**. Sources of differentiation might be exceptionally high quality, extraordinary service, innovative design, technological capability, or an unusually positive brand image. The key to this competitive strategy is that whatever product or service attribute is chosen for differentiating must set the firm apart from its competitors and be significant enough to justify a price premium that exceeds the cost of differentiating.

Practically any successful consumer product or service can be identified as an example of the differentiation strategy: Nordstrom's (customer service); Sony (reputation for quality and innovative design); Coach handbags (design and brand image); and Kimberly-Clark's Huggies Pull-Ups (product design).

cost leadership strategy

A business-level strategy in which the organization is the lowest-cost producer in its industry.

differentiation strategy

A business-level strategy in which a company offers unique products that are widely valued by customers.

Generic Strategy	Commonly Required Skills and Resources	Common Organizational Requirements	Exhibit 8.8
			Requirements for Successfully Pursuing Porter's Competitive Strategies
Overall cost leadership	Sustained capital investment and access to capital Process engineering skills Intense supervision of labor Products designed for ease in manufacture Low-cost distribution system	Tight cost control Frequent, detailed control reports Structured organization and responsibilities Incentives based on meeting strict quantitative targets	
Differentiation	Strong marketing abilities Product engineering Creative flair Strong capability in basic research Corporate reputation for quality or technological leadership Long tradition in the industry or unique combination of skills drawn from other businesses Strong cooperation from channels	Strong coordination among functions in R&D, product development, and marketing Subjective measurement and incentives instead of quantitative measures Amenities to attract highly skilled labor, scientists, or creative people	
Focus	Combination of the foregoing policies directed at the particular strategic target	Combination of the foregoing policies directed at the particular strategic target	

Source: Reprinted from M.E. Porter, *Competitive Strategy: Techniques for Analyzing Industries and Competitors* (New York: Free Press, 1980), pp. 40–41.

focus strategy

A business-level strategy in which a company pursues a cost or differentiation advantage in a narrow industry segment.

The first two of Porter's competitive strategies seek a competitive advantage in the broad marketplace. However, the **focus strategy** aims at a cost advantage (cost focus) or a differentiation advantage (differentiation focus) in a narrow segment. That is, managers select a market segment or group of segments in an industry and don't attempt to serve the broad market. The goal of a focus strategy is to exploit a narrow segment of a market. These segments can be based on product variety, type of end buyer, distribution channel, or geographical location of buyers. For example, at Cia. Chilena de Fosforos, a large Chilean wood products manufacturer, Vice Chairman Gustavo Romero devised a focus strategy to sell chopsticks in Japan. Competitors and even some other company managers thought he was crazy. However, by focusing on this narrow segment, Romero's strategy managed to create more demand for his company's chopsticks than it had mature trees with which to make the products. Whether a focus strategy is feasible depends on the size of the segment and whether the organization can support the additional cost of focusing. Research suggests that the focus strategy may be the most effective choice for small businesses because they typically do not have the economies of scale or internal resources to successfully pursue one of the other two strategies.[23]

stuck in the middle

A situation in which an organization hasn't been able to develop either a low cost or a differentiation competitive advantage.

What happens if an organization is unable to develop a cost or differentiation advantage? Porter uses the term **stuck in the middle** to describe those organizations, which find it very difficult to achieve long-term success. Porter goes on to note that successful organizations frequently get into trouble by reaching beyond their competitive advantage and ending up stuck in the middle.

However, studies have shown that a dual emphasis on low costs and differentiation *can* result in high performance.[24] To successfully pursue both competitive advantages, though, an organization must be strongly committed to quality products or services, and consumers of those products or services must value quality. By providing high-quality products or services, an organization differentiates itself from its rivals. Consumers who value high quality will purchase more of the organization's products, and the increased demand will lead to economies of scale and lower per unit costs. For example, companies such as Anheuser-Busch, Federal Express, Intel, and Coca-Cola differentiate their products while at the same time maintain low-cost operations.

functional-level strategy

An organizational strategy that seeks to determine how to support the business-level strategy.

FUNCTIONAL-LEVEL STRATEGY

A **functional-level strategy** seeks to determine how to support the business-level strategy. For organizations that have traditional functional departments such as manufacturing, marketing, human resources, research and development, and finance, these strategies need to support the business-level strategy. For example, when R. R. Donnelley & Sons Company, a Chicago-based printer, made a business-level strategy decision to invest significant dollars in high-tech digital printing methods, its marketing department had to develop new sales plans and promotional pieces, the production department had to incorporate the digital equipment in the printing plants, and the human resources department had to update its employee selection and training programs. We don't cover specific functional strategies in this book as they are the content of other business courses you take.

No matter what corporate strategy, competitive advantage or competitive strategy, or functional strategies an organization chooses to pursue, keep in mind that all are part of the strategic management process that plays a crucial role in organizational success. Without the strategic management process to guide and direct their strategic planning decisions and actions, managers would have little chance of designing effective and efficient strategies.

Testing...Testing...1,2,3

13. **What does the five forces model show?**

14. **Describe three possible competitive strategies.**

15. **What do the organization's functional strategies seek to determine?**

Managers Respond to "A Manager's Dilemma"

Donald Weeks

**Vice President, Finance & Operations,
Zerus Hardware, Springfield, Missouri**

The SWOT analysis is a useful tool that allows you to look at the big picture—a quick list of what you do well and what you don't. When I put together a SWOT analysis, the first place I look when developing a strategy is the weaknesses. If you can discover what makes you weak, then you can develop a plan to turn it into a strength or at least to neutralize it as a weakness.

From the information in a SWOT analysis, Ackerman should first utilize the strong nurturing support of the NBA to do more cross-promotions for the WNBA. Players and management of the NBA team should assist and promote their women counterparts. Second, she should raise salaries in order to raise the level of play and retain players. This is very important for the long-term success of the league. The funding for these salary increases would come from the NBA in the short term. In the long term, the expanded fan base and greater advertising revenues could offset the cost.

Ted Schaefer

**Partner, PriceWaterhouseCoopers,
Denver, Colorado**

Ackerman has a great opportunity to drive the WNBA to a much higher level. A SWOT analysis will help her assess the organization and develop strategies that are sorely needed to survive.

The key to moving this organization forward is having top talent to draw in the fans. The players are the product and marquee names will draw in women *and* men. Although upgrading the talent will cost money, it is a necessity to drive revenue. The United States has top talent and the WNBA needs to have a goal of retaining all top U.S. talent. Although financing will be needed, I believe the league needs to be aggressive or it risks going out of business like the other U.S. women's basketball league. High quality needs to be the core strategy.

Once the decision is made to obtain top talent, Ackerman needs to leverage that talent. The NBA is a quality organization and the fans expect a certain level of play. The WNBA needs to meet the quality standards of the NBA if it expects to move ahead.

Chapter Summary

This summary is organized by the chapter-opening objectives found on p. 196.

1. In a dynamic and uncertain environment, strategic management is important because it can provide managers with a systematic and comprehensive means for analyzing the environment, assessing their organization's strengths and weaknesses, and identifying opportunities for which they could develop and exploit a competitive advantage.

2. The strategic management process includes eight steps: (1) identifying the organization's current mission, goals, and strategies; (2) analyzing the environment; (3) identifying the opportunities and threats in the environment; (4) analyzing the organization's resources and capabilities; (5) identifying the organization's strengths and weaknesses; (6) formulating strategies; (7) implementing strategies; and (8) evaluating results.

3. SWOT analysis refers to analyzing the organization's internal strengths and weaknesses as well as the external opportunities and threats in order to identify a niche that the organization can exploit.

4. Corporate-level strategy seeks to determine what businesses a company should be in or wants to be in. Business-level strategy seeks to determine how an organization should compete in each of its businesses. Functional-level strategy seeks to determine how to support the business-level strategy.

5. The corporate grand strategies are stability, growth, and retrenchment. A firm that's pursuing a stability strategy is not making any significant changes. A growth strategy means that a firm is increasing the level of its operations. When a firm is following a retrenchment strategy, it's addressing organizational weaknesses that are leading to performance declines.

6. Competitive advantage is what sets an organization apart; its competitive edge. It's important because an organization needs to be able to effectively exploit its resources and capabilities and to develop the core competencies to keep its edge despite competitors' actions or evolutionary changes in the industry.

7. The five competitive forces include the threat of new entrants, threat of substitutes, bargaining power of buyers, bargaining power of suppliers, and existing rivalry. The threat of new entrants is determined by barriers to entry, which include factors such as economies of scale, brand loyalty, and capital requirements. The threat of substitutes includes factors such as switching costs and buyer loyalty. The bargaining power of buyers includes factors such as number of customers in the market, customer information, and the availability of substitutes. The bargaining power of suppliers includes factors such as degree of supplier concentration and availability of substitute inputs. Existing rivalry includes factors such as industry growth rate, increasing or falling demand, and product differences.

8. The various competitive strategies include cost leadership, differentiation, and focus. A cost leadership strategy is the strategy an organization follows when it wants to be the lowest-cost producer in its industry. The differentiation strategy is the strategy a firm follows when it wants to be unique in its industry along dimensions widely valued by customers. The focus strategy is the strategy a company follows when it pursues a cost or a differentiation advantage in a narrow industry segment.

Thinking About Management Issues

1. Perform a SWOT analysis on a local business you think you know well. What, if any, competitive advantage does this organization have?

2. How might the process of strategy formulation, implementation, and evaluation differ for (a) large businesses, (b) small businesses, (c) not-for-profit organizations, and (d) global businesses?

3. "The concept of competitive advantage is as important for not-for-profit organizations as it is for for-profit organizations." Do you agree or disagree with this statement? Explain, using examples to make your case.

4. Should ethical considerations be included in analyses of an organization's internal and external environments? Why or why not?

5. How could the Internet be helpful to managers as they follow the steps in the strategic management process?

Log On: Internet-Based Exercise

An organization's mission statement should be an important expression of its purpose, philosophy, values, and strategic intent. Using the Internet, find and write down five examples of organizational mission statements; at least two of these should be not-for-profit organizations.

Now, using the mission statements as your guide, describe what types of corporate-level and business-level strategies each organization might pursue to fulfill that mission statement. Explain your rationale for choosing each strategy.

Working Together: Team-Based Exercise

Examples of organizational strategies are found everywhere in business and general news periodicals. You should be able to recognize the different types of strategies from these news stories.

Form groups of three or four individuals. Using materials that your instructor provides you, find examples of

five different organizational strategies. Determine whether the examples are at the corporate level, business level, or functional level and explain why your group made that choice. Be prepared to share your examples with the class.

myPHLIP Companion Web Site

myPHLIP **(www.prenhall.com/myphlip)** *is a fully customizable homepage that ties students and faculty to text-specific resources.*
- **For students**, myPHLIP *provides an online study guide tied chapter-by-chapter to the text—current events and Internet exercises, lecture notes, downloadable software, the Career Center, the Writing Center, Ask the Tutor, and more.*
- **For faculty**, myPHLIP *provides a syllabus tool that allows you to manage content, communicate with students, and upload personal resources.*

Case Application

Turbulent Flight Plan

Eighty-two percent. That's the market share held by Air Canada, the sole remaining major Canadian airline, after its takeover of money-losing Canadian Airlines in the spring of 2000. And the Canadian airline industry now is going through some major upheavals. Consumers facing an airline market that's more reliant on a single carrier than any other major Western nation—even Germany's Lufthansa only has 60 percent of the market—are complaining about the almost total monopoly. They are critical of flights being overbooked, extremely long lines at check-in, telephone call centers with half-hour-plus waits on hold, and prices that cost the passenger less to fly to Europe than to the next province. In response, the Canadian government encouraged discount airlines and stood behind their attempts to make it in the market. The House of Commons passed legislation in May 2000 that defined "abuse of dominant position" and empowered the Competition Bureau (equivalent to the U.S. Federal

Trade Commission) to punish companies engaging in price gouging. This legislative move was prompted by Air Canada's competitive attack on WestJet Airlines for moving into markets in eastern Canada. WestJet Airlines is one discount airline struggling for a smooth flight in this increasingly turbulent environment.

Of the six scheduled discount airlines started in Canada in the last 20 years, only WestJet, based in Calgary, Alberta, is still flying. It serves 13 western Canadian cities and has 5 percent of the Canadian market. But Stephen C. Smith, president of WestJet, has made a strategic decision to take the company national.

WestJet, started in 1996, mimics the Southwest Airlines strategic model. Southwest Airlines, a U.S. airline, has enjoyed phenomenal success with a strategic formula of low fares and short-haul routes. WestJet's fares are an average of 40 percent lower than Air Canada's. It offers one class of seating, has no meals on board or executive lounges in airports, and concentrates on flights of 400 miles or less. Passengers don't have tickets, only confir-

sure in the airline industry) were up 54 percent for the first four months of 2000. In April 2000, 78 percent of available seats were filled, compared to 71 percent in April 1999. WestJet also consistently makes a profit. A spokesperson for a Canadian consumer group said, "WestJet is tightly run and well managed . . . There are not many [passenger] complaints." However, some experts say that Smith's strategic decision to compete nationally is a gamble that will either make or break WestJet. "It's a risk, and this isn't an industry that tolerates a lot of mistakes." To accommodate its national expansion, WestJet ordered 20 new Boeing 737 jets to be delivered over eight years and plans to lease 10 more. Also, WestJet's competitor, Air Canada, started its own discount carrier in summer 2000, serving WestJet's stronghold, western Canada. Although industry analysts say that unionized Air Canada will have a hard time matching nonunionized WestJet's cost structure, some feel that WestJet may be overextending itself and expanding faster than demand for its services.

mation numbers. And to cut costs, WestJet encourages ticket sales through the Internet, which now accounts for about 11 percent of its tickets sold. Whenever possible, it lands at smaller airports that charge low user fees. One deviation from Southwest's strategy is that WestJet does assign passengers—or guests—to specific seats.

As many of these strategies illustrate, Smith has made a commitment to keeping operating costs low. In addition, like Southwest, WestJet flies one class of jet, the Boeing 737, which minimizes pilot training, maintenance costs, and gate turnaround time. To keep its employees (over 1,100 of them) nonunionized and, thus, giving the company more control over wages and salaries, WestJet uses several incentives. A major one is that all workers who have been with the company at least three months participate in a profit-sharing plan—$4 million was shared among eligible employees in 1999. In addition, 70 percent of the employees participate in a stock purchase plan, in which WestJet matches employee contributions up to 20 percent of their salary.

Smith's no-frills model appears to be working. During its four years of operation, WestJet's growth has been steady. Revenue passenger miles (a key operating mea-

QUESTIONS

1. What competitive advantage(s) do you think WestJet has? What competitive advantages do you think Air Canada has? Explain your choices.

2. What competitive strategy does WestJet appear to be following? Explain your choice.

3. How could Stephen Smith have used SWOT analysis in developing his strategy to go national? Do an abbreviated SWOT analysis using information from the case.

4. What do you think of WestJet's strategic decision to compete nationally? What suggestions might you make to Stephen Smith?

Sources: J. Brooke, "Taking Off? And for a Lot Less," *New York Times*, June 3, 2000, pp. B1+; and J. Baglole, "Canada's WestJet Battles Giant," *Wall Street Journal*, April 24, 2000, p. A26.

Video Case Application

Not Just Toying Around

SMALL BUSINESS 2000

The toy industry, like all others, has its good points and its bad points. One person who's trying to take advantage of the good points—that is, what he sees as the many growth opportunities in the toy industry—is Charlie Woo of Los Angeles.

Woo and his family came to the United States from Hong Kong in the late 1970s. To support the family, his mother and father initially started a restaurant but found that ven-

ture to be too time consuming. They looked to start another business and settled on the toy industry. By using their contacts in Hong Kong and by bringing their four sons into the business, the Woo family opened ABC Toys. The company's initial goal was to manufacture and distribute toys to small wholesalers who couldn't get products from the large toy makers because they weren't big enough customers; that is, they didn't buy in enough volume. ABC Toys had identified a specific niche and wasn't even attempting to compete with the likes of Mattel, Hasbro, or the other large toy manufacturers. Charlie, who was just about to complete his

Ph.D. in physics from UCLA, found himself making a major career switch—from physics to toys.

ABC Toys purchased several run-down warehouses on a blighted corner of downtown Los Angeles. Charlie's vision was to encourage other small toy manufacturers and distributors to rent from them and together create a "toy town." He recalls that in the beginning, ABC Toys was located there by itself. But Charlie reasoned that this strategy was good because it would enable customers to come to one location, shop comparatively, and, he hoped, end up buying more products than they would if they had to travel to separate stores. As more and more small toy companies joined ABC Toys in Toy Town, word soon spread and customers began coming from all over. Now there are more than 500 wholesale toy dealers within a few blocks of each other in Toy Town.

In 1989, Charlie and one of his brothers spun off a separate business, Megatoys, out of ABC Toys. This spin-out company employs 30 people and has hit $16 million in sales. And Charlie isn't finished yet! He believes that there is still good potential for growth in his business. Why? The changing global trade environment is opening up many potentially profitable areas. After all, in this business, if you want to be successful, you can't just toy around!

QUESTIONS

1. Charlie wants to continue Megatoys' growth. How might he use strategic management concepts to help him achieve his goals?

2. Would SWOT analysis be useful to Charlie in managing Megatoys? Why or why not? Explain your choice.

3. Charlie has asked you to make a presentation to his employees about competitive advantage. Draw up a list of the main ideas you'd want to tell them.

Source: Based on *Small Business* 2000, *Show* 107.

Learning Objectives

After reading and studying this chapter, you should be able to:

1. Describe three techniques for assessing the environment.

2. Describe four techniques for allocating resources.

3. Tell why budgets are popular planning tools.

4. Differentiate Gantt and load charts.

5. Identify the steps in developing a PERT network.

6. State the factors that determine the breakeven point.

7. Describe the requirements for using linear programming.

8. Explain the concept of project management.

9. Tell how managers might use scenarios in planning.

A MANAGER'S DILEMMA

"The best-managed company in China." What else needs to be said about a manager who earns this distinction for his company? Lots! Wang Guoduan, founder of Kelon Electrical Holdings Company has proven that you don't have to be a dot-com to take on the world.[1]

Guoduan's business is China's largest and most successful refrigerator maker. The company sold almost $677 million of refrigerators, air conditioners, and other appliances in 2000 and captured nearly a quarter of the domestic Chinese market. Kelon also sells its minibar-style refrigerators at Wal-Mart in the United States and is pushing into other global locations including Europe and Southeast Asia. The company has repeatedly won awards as the best-run and most investor-friendly company in China, beating out companies such as China Telecom and computer manufacturer Giant.

Guoduan himself has an interesting background. In the early 1980s, he was managing a dilapidated, state-owned rice cooker factory in Rongqi, located in the Guangdong province. With demand for its rice cookers stagnant, Guoduan and some friends looked for a replacement product to manufacture. When they saw their first modern refrigerator, they immediately recognized the opportunity. This was at a time when the Chinese government was becoming less restrictive, and Guoduan believed that new governmental policies eventually would lead to

Planning Tools and Techniques

9

increased consumer incomes. And with increased incomes, consumers would be looking for ways to make their everyday lives easier and more convenient. Well-designed, modern refrigerators would seem to be a highly desired consumer product. Having pinpointed the product, the Kelon team took apart a Japanese-made refrigerator to find out what made it work. Then after going through all the governmental channels of approval, the company started manufacturing refrigerators. By 1991, Kelon had become the country's number one refrigerator maker.

Now, however, Kelon's future is uncertain. A saturated market, sluggish economy, and increased competition are some of the challenges facing Guoduan. Put yourself in his position. What planning tools might prove useful to Guoduan?

WHAT WOULD YOU DO?

In this chapter we'll discuss some basic planning tools and techniques that managers such as Wang Guoduan or managers at any businesses—large or small—could use. We'll begin by looking at some techniques for assessing the environment. Then we'll review techniques for allocating resources. Finally, we'll discuss some contemporary planning techniques including project management and scenarios.

> ## TECHNIQUES FOR ASSESSING THE ENVIRONMENT

In our description of the strategic management process in Chapter 8, we discussed the importance of assessing the organization's environment. In this section, we review three techniques that have been developed to help managers with this task: environmental scanning, forecasting, and benchmarking.

ENVIRONMENTAL SCANNING

How can managers become aware of potentially important environmental changes such as a new law in eastern Germany permitting shopping for "tourist items" on Sunday? Toy retailer Toys R Us deciding to partner with Amazon.com in response to other competitors' strategic alliances with major Internet portals? The trend toward early retirement in the United States, France, Germany, and Japan? Managers in both small and large organizations use **environmental scanning**, which is the screening of large amounts of information to anticipate and interpret changes in the environment. Extensive environmental scanning is likely to reveal issues and concerns that could affect an organization's current or planned activities. Research has shown that companies with advanced environmental scanning systems increased their profits and revenue growth.[2] Organizations that don't keep on top of environmental changes are likely to face the opposite situation. For instance, Tupperware, the company that created airtight, easy-to-use, plastic food storage containers, enjoyed unprecedented success during the 1960s and 1970s selling its products at home-hostessed parties where housewives played games, socialized, and saw product demonstrations. However, as U.S. society changed—more women working full-time outside the home, an increasing divorce rate, and young adults waiting longer to marry—the popularity of Tupperware parties began to decline because no one had time to go to them. The company's North American market share fell from 60 percent to 40 percent while Rubbermaid, a competitor that marketed its plastic food storage containers in retail outlets, increased its market share from 5 percent to 40 percent. By the early 1990s, most American women had no desire to go to a Tupperware party or knew how to find Tupperware products. Yet, Tupperware's president, obviously clueless about the changed environment, predicted that before the end of the 1990s, the party concept would be popular once again.[3] This example shows how a once successful company can suffer by failing to recognize how the environment has changed.

One of the fastest-growing areas of environmental scanning is **competitor intelligence**.[4] It's a process by which organizations gather information about their competitors and get answers to questions such as: Who are they? What are

environmental scanning

The screening of large amounts of information to anticipate and interpret changes in the environment.

competitor intelligence

Environmental scanning activity that seeks to identify who competitors are, what they are doing, and how their actions will affect the organization.

they doing? How will what they're doing affect us? Let's look at an example of how one organization used competitor intelligence in its planning. Dun & Bradstreet (D&B), a leading provider of business credit, marketing, and purchasing information to companies that need this information, has an active business intelligence division. The manager of this division received a call from an assistant vice president for sales in one of the company's geographic territories. This person had been on a sales call with a major customer and the customer happened to mention in passing that another company had visited and made a major presentation about its services. What was interesting was that, although D&B has plenty of competitors, this particular company wasn't one of them. The business intelligence division manager jumped into action and gathered together a team that sifted through dozens of sources (research services, Internet, personal contacts, and other external sources) and quickly became convinced that there was something to this—that this company was "aiming its guns right at us." Managers at D&B jumped into action to develop plans to counteract this competitive attack.[5]

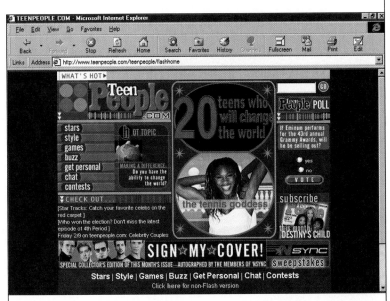

In order to hit just the right note in marketing to the notoriously fickle teen market, *People* magazine launched what has become an enormously successful offshoot, *Teen People* magazine. Its interactive Web site [www.teenpeople.com] is full of targeted features like news about teen idols, style and fashion tips, games, gossip, chat rooms, advice, horoscopes, and questionnaires for reader input in the magazine. Another way to gather the kind of market information that makes the print magazine successful is to tap research firms that specialize in environmental scanning, like Teenage Research Unlimited.

Competitor intelligence experts suggest that 80 percent of what managers need to know about competitors can be found out from their own employees, suppliers, and customers.[6] Competitor intelligence doesn't necessarily have to involve organizational spying. Advertisements, promotional materials, press

? THINKING CRITICALLY ABOUT ETHICS

Here are some techniques that have been suggested for gathering competitor information: (1) Get copies of lawsuits and civil suits that may have been filed against competitors. These court proceedings are public records and can expose surprising details. (2) Call the Better Business Bureau and ask if competitors have had complaints filed against them because of fraudulent product claims or questionable business practices. (3) Pretend to be a journalist and call competitors to ask them questions. (4) Get copies of your competitors' in-house newsletters and read them. (5) Buy a single share of competitors' stock so you get the annual report and other information the company sends out. (6) Send someone from your organization to apply for a job at a competitor and have that person ask specific questions. (7) Dig through a competitor's trash.

Which, if any, of these are unethical? Defend your choices. What ethical guidelines would you suggest for competitor intelligence activities?

In the hotly contested overnight shipping market, competitor intelligence has sometimes given the advantage to FedEx, and sometimes to UPS. FedEx was the first company to let customers track their packages via a computerized private information network. That left UPS flat-footed for a time, but when customers balked at having to invest in FedEx's proprietary software, UPS came up with a way to send delivery notices directly to its customers' accounting systems.

Testing...Testing...1,2,3

1. **What is environmental scanning?**

2. **Describe competitor intelligence.**

3. **When would global scanning be an important planning tool?**

forecasts

Predictions of outcomes.

releases, reports filed with governmental agencies, annual reports, want ads, newspaper reports, and industry studies are examples of readily accessible sources of information. Attending trade shows and debriefing the salesforce can be other good sources of competitor information. Many firms even regularly buy competitors' products and have their own engineers study them (through a process called *reverse engineering*) to learn about new technical innovations. In addition, the Internet has opened up vast sources of competitor intelligence as many corporate Web pages include new product information and other press releases.

The questions and concerns that often arise about competitor intelligence pertain to the ways in which competitor information is gathered. Competitor intelligence becomes illegal corporate spying when it involves the theft of proprietary materials or trade secrets by any means. Often there's a fine line between what's considered *legal and ethical* and what's considered *legal but unethical*. And, although the top manager at one competitive intelligence firm contends that 99.9 percent of intelligence gathering is legitimate, there's no question that some people or companies will go to any lengths to get information about competitors.[7]

One type of environmental scanning that is particularly important is global scanning. The value of global scanning to managers, of course, is largely dependent on the extent of the organization's global activities. For a company that has significant global interests, global scanning can be quite valuable. Because world markets are complex and dynamic, managers have expanded the scope of their scanning efforts to gain vital information on global forces that might affect their organizations.[8] Some organizations, such as American Can Company and Mitsubishi Trading Company, have elaborate information networks and computerized systems to monitor global changes.[9]

The sources that managers use for scanning the domestic environment are too limited for global scanning. Managers need to globalize their perspectives and information sources. For instance, they can subscribe to information clipping services that review newspapers and business periodicals throughout the world and provide summaries of desired information. Also, there are numerous electronic services that provide topic searches and even provide automatic and continual updates in global areas of special interest to managers.

FORECASTING

The second technique managers can use to assess the environment is forecasting. Forecasting is an important part of organizational planning and managers need forecasts that will allow them to predict future events effectively and in a timely manner. Environmental scanning creates the foundation for **forecasts**, which are predictions of outcomes. Virtually any component in the organization's general and specific environments can be forecasted. Let's look at how managers forecast and how effective forecasts are.

Forecasting Techniques Forecasting techniques fall into two categories: quantitative and qualitative. **Quantitative forecasting** applies a set of mathematical rules to a series of past data to predict outcomes. These techniques are preferred when managers have sufficient hard data that can be used. **Qualitative forecasting**, in contrast, uses the judgment and opinions of knowledgeable individuals to predict outcomes. Qualitative techniques typically are used when precise data are limited or hard to obtain. Exhibit 9.1 describes some popular forecasting techniques.

Today, many organizations collaborate on forecasts by using Internet-based software known as CFAR, which stands for collaborative forecasting and replenishment.[10] CFAR offers a standardized way for retailers and manufacturers to use the Internet to exchange data. Each organization relies on its own data about past sales trends, promotion plans, and other factors to calculate a demand forecast for a particular product. If their respective forecasts differ by a certain amount (say, 10 percent), the retailer and manufacturer use the Internet to exchange more data and written comments until they arrive at a more accurate forecast. This mutual collaborative forecasting helps both organizations do a better job of planning.

Forecasting Effectiveness The goal of forecasting is to provide managers with information that will facilitate decision making. Despite forecasting's importance to planning, managers have had mixed success in forecasting trends and events.[11]

quantitative forecasting

Forecasting that applies a set of mathematical rules to a series of past data to predict outcomes.

qualitative forecasting

Forecasting that uses the judgment and opinions of knowledgeable individuals to predict outcomes.

Exhibit 9.1

Forecasting Techniques

Technique	Description	Application
Quantitative		
Time series analysis	Fits a trend line to a mathematical equation and projects into the future by means of this equation	Predicting next quarter's sales on the basis of four years of previous sales data
Regression models	Predicts one variable on the basis of known or assumed other variables	Seeking factors that will predict a certain level of sales (for example, price, advertising expenditures)
Econometric models	Uses a set of regression equations to simulate segments of the economy	Predicting change in car sales as a result of changes in tax laws
Economic indicators	Uses one or more economic indicators to predict a future state of the economy	Using change in GNP to predict discretionary income
Substitution effect	Uses a mathematical formula to predict how, when, and under what circumstances a new product or technology will replace an existing one	Predicting the effect of DVD players on the sale of VHS players
Qualitative		
Jury of opinion	Combines and averages the opinions of experts	Polling the company's human resource managers to predict next year's college recruitment needs
Salesforce composition	Combines estimates from field sales personnel of customers' expected purchases	Predicting next year's sales of industrial lasers
Customer evaluation	Combines estimates from established purchases	Surveying major car dealers by a car manufacturer to determine types and quantities of products desired

Forecasting techniques are most accurate when the environment is not rapidly changing. The more dynamic the environment, the more likely managers are to forecast ineffectively. Also, forecasting is relatively ineffective in predicting non-seasonal events such as recessions, unusual occurrences, discontinued operations, and the actions or reactions of competitors.

Although forecasting has a mixed record, there are ways to improve its effectiveness.[12] First, use simple forecasting methods. They tend to do as well as or often better than complex methods that tend to mistakenly confuse random data for meaningful information. For instance, at St. Louis–based Emerson Electric, CEO Chuck Knight found that forecasts developed as part of the company's planning process were indicating that the competition wasn't just domestic anymore but global. He didn't use any complex mathematical techniques to come to this conclusion but instead relied on the information already collected as part of his company's planning process. Next, compare every forecast with "no change." A no-change forecast is accurate approximately half the time. Third, don't rely on a single forecasting method. Make forecasts with several models and average them, especially when making long-range forecasts. Fourth, don't assume that you can accurately identify turning points in a trend. What is typically perceived as a significant turning point often turns out to be simply a random event. Fifth, shorten the length of forecasts to improve their accuracy because accuracy decreases as the time period you're trying to predict increases. And, finally, remember that forecasting *is* a managerial skill and as such can be practiced and improved. The availability of easy-to-use forecasting software has made the task somewhat less mathematically challenging, although the "number crunching" is only a small part of the activity. Interpreting the forecast and incorporating that information into planning decisions is the challenge facing managers.

BENCHMARKING

Suppose that you are a talented pianist or track sprinter. To make yourself better, you want to learn from the best so you watch outstanding musicians or athletes for motions and techniques they use as they perform. That's what is involved in the final technique for assessing the environment we're going to discuss— **benchmarking**. This is the search for the best practices among competitors or noncompetitors that lead to their superior performance.[13] The basic idea behind benchmarking is that managers can improve quality by analyzing and then copying the methods of the leaders in various fields. Even small companies have found that benchmarking can bring big benefits. For instance, Manco, Inc., a small producer of duct tape based in Cleveland, benchmarks itself against some big names—Wal-Mart, Rubbermaid, and PepsiCo. Why? To help it compete better against rival 3M Corporation.[14]

The history behind benchmarking is quite interesting. In the 1970s, Japanese firms were aggressively copying the successes of others and applying what they learned in visits to companies around the world to improve their own products and processes. Xerox Corporation, a U.S. company, couldn't figure out how Japanese copier manufacturers were able to sell midsized copiers in the United States for considerably less than Xerox's costs. Xerox's director of manufacturing traveled with a team to Japan to make a detailed study of their competitors' costs and processes. What the team found was shocking. Their Japanese rivals were light-years ahead of Xerox in efficiency. So Xerox began

benchmarking

The search for the best practices among competitors or noncompetitors that lead to their superior performance.

David Raphael, Managing Director, Raphael Executive and Marketing Services, Balgowlah, Australia

Describe your job.

Our business is corporate education. As managing director, I manage the success of the business. This involves analyzing the market, finding new prospects, and even conducting workshops on "Consultative Selling," "Successful Account Management," "Quality Customer Service," and so forth.

What types of skills do you think tomorrow's managers will need?

Successful CEOs and board-level managers must be able to analyze their market and predict the changes. They must then set realistic, measurable goals for their people

to achieve, provide systems and processes to maximize productivity, understand the latest business tools and use them, develop their company's differentiation basis, and have the same skills as middle managers.

Middle managers must understand the business goals, provide leadership to their people so that they achieve the goals set, and provide feedback to board-level managers about successes and challenges in the market.

How do you monitor and assess the external changes that might affect how you do your job?

I listen proactively to my customers and ask them what is happening in their businesses. I read and analyze papers, television news, and information from the Internet. I use business models to predict changes in things such as interest rates, economic recessions/booms, and so forth. Finally, I monitor, watch, and adapt our business plans to government policy changes that affect our business.

benchmarking those efficiencies and turning around its performance. Today, companies such as AT&T, DuPont, Ford, and Kodak use benchmarking as a standard tool in their quest for performance improvement. In fact, some companies have chosen some pretty unusual benchmarking partners! Southwest Airlines, for example, studied Indy 500 pit crews, who can change a race tire in under 15 seconds, to see how they could make their gate turnaround even faster. IBM studied Las Vegas casinos looking for ways to discourage employee theft. And Giordano Holdings Ltd., a Hong Kong–based manufacturer and retailer of mass-market casual wear, borrowed its "good quality, good value" concept from Marks & Spencer, used The Limited to benchmark its point-of-sales computerized information system, and modeled its simplified product offerings on McDonald's menu approach.

What does the benchmarking process involve? As shown in Exhibit 9.2, it typically follows four steps:

1. A benchmarking planning team is formed. The team's initial task is to identify what is to be benchmarked, identify comparative organizations, and determine data collection methods.
2. The team collects data internally on its own work methods and externally from other organizations.
3. The data are analyzed to identify performance gaps and the cause of differences.
4. An action plan that will result in meeting or exceeding the standards of others is prepared and implemented.

How does a manager or benchmarking team get data on other organizations?[15] First, you need to decide against whom you're going to benchmark.

Exhibit | 9.2

Steps in Benchmarking

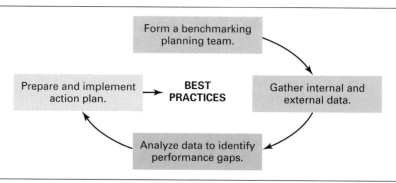

Source: Based on Y.K. Shetty, "Aiming High: Competitive Benchmarking for Superior Performance," *Long Range Planning,* February 1993, p. 42.

Testing...Testing...1,2,3

4. **How effective is fore-casting as a planning technique?**

5. **What does the benchmarking process involve?**

6. **How can managers get data on other organizations?**

Use your network of contacts among customers, suppliers, and employees for organizations they think are best at the process you're trying to improve. Trade associations and industry experts often know what organizations have revolutionary practices. And watch for organizations that may have won local, regional, or national quality awards as potential benchmarking partners. Also, use the Internet. Rivals' Web sites can be rich sources of information. Many company Web sites describe new products or services being developed and often have financial information that can be analyzed. Experts also suggest that managers not overlook the possibility of developing partnerships with other organizations, even rivals, to share benchmarking data. Obviously, this will work only if you have something that others want. But if, for example, you're looking to improve your customer satisfaction process and you already have a great order system in place, you may be able to swap data with another organization that has complementary needs.

How can managers ensure that their benchmarking efforts are effective? Exhibit 9.3 lists some suggestions for improving the process.

Exhibit | 9.3

Suggestions for Improving Benchmarking Efforts

1. Link benchmarking efforts to strategic objectives.
2. Have the right-sized team—between six and eight people is most effective.
3. Involve those individuals who will be directly affected by benchmarking efforts.
4. Focus on specific, targeted issues rather than broad, general ones.
5. Set realistic timetables.
6. Choose benchmarking targets carefully.
7. Observe proper protocol when gathering benchmarking information by dealing with the appropriate individuals.
8. Don't collect excessive, unnecessary data.
9. Look at the processes behind the numbers, not just at the numbers themselves.
10. Identify benchmarking targets and then be sure to take action.

Source: Based on J.H. Sheridan, "Where Benchmarkers Go Wrong," *Industry Week,* March 15, 1993, pp. 28–34.

⟩ TECHNIQUES FOR ALLOCATING RESOURCES

As we know from Chapter 7, once an organization's goals (or ends) have been established, an important aspect of planning is the focus on the "means"—that is, determining how those goals are going to be accomplished. Before managers can organize and lead in order to implement the goals, they must have resources. **Resources** are the assets of the organization and include financial (debt, equity, retained earnings, and other financial holdings); physical (equipment, buildings, raw materials, or other tangible assets); human (experiences, skills, knowledge, and competencies of people); intangible (brand names, patents, reputation, trademarks, copyrights, registered designs, and databases); and structural/cultural (history, culture, work systems, working relationships, level of trust, policies, and structure). How are these resources allocated effectively and efficiently so that organizational goals are met? That's what we want to look at in this section. Although managers can choose from a number of techniques for allocating resources (many of which are covered in courses on accounting, finance, human resources, and operations management), we'll discuss four techniques here: budgeting, scheduling, breakeven analysis, and linear programming.

resources

The assets of the organization including financial, physical, human, intangible, and structural/cultural.

BUDGETING

Most of us have had some experience, as limited as it might be, with budgets. We probably learned about them at a very early age when we discovered that unless we allocated our "revenues" carefully, our weekly allowance was spent on "expenses" before the week was half over.

A **budget** is a numerical plan for allocating resources to specific activities. Managers typically prepare budgets for revenues, expenses, and large capital expenditures such as equipment. It's not unusual, though, for budgets to be used for improving time, space, and use of material resources. These types of budgets substitute non-dollar numbers for dollar amounts. Such items as person-hours, capacity utilization, or units of production can be budgeted for daily, weekly, or monthly activities. Exhibit 9.4 describes the different types of budgets that managers might use.

Why are budgets so popular? Probably because they're applicable to a wide variety of organizations and work activities within organizations. We live in a world in which almost everything is expressed in monetary units. Dollars, pesos, euros, yen, and the like are used as common measuring units. It seems only logical, then, that monetary budgets would be a useful tool for allocating resources and guiding work in such diverse departments as manufacturing and marketing research or at various levels in an organization. Budgets are one planning technique that most managers, regardless of organizational level, help formulate. It's an important managerial activity because it forces financial discipline and structure throughout the organization. However, many managers don't like preparing budgets because they feel the process is time consuming, inflexible, inefficient, and ineffective.[16] How can the budgeting process be

budget

A numerical plan for allocating resources to specific activities.

Dr. Rita Colwell, a microbiologist who is the first woman to head the National Science Foundation, controls the Federal agency's $3.6 billion budget. That task means deciding how to spend the money on various new and ongoing projects in basic nonmedical research in the areas of science and engineering.

Source: Based on R.S. Russell and B.W. Taylor III, *Production and Operations Management* (Upper Saddle River, NJ: Prentice Hall, 1995), p. 287.

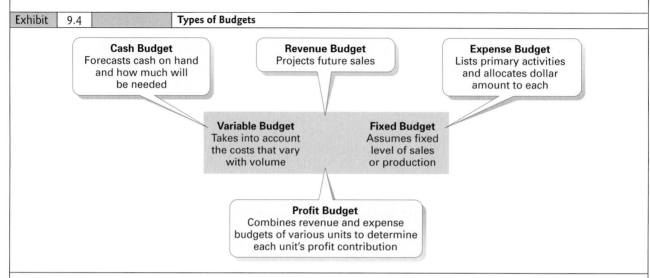

Exhibit	9.4		**Types of Budgets**

improved? Exhibit 9.5 provides some suggestions. Organizations such as Texas Instruments, Ikea, Volvo, and Svenska Handelsbanken (the most consistently profitable bank in Europe) incorporated several of these suggestions as they revamped their budgeting processes. (See the Budgeting Skills Module on pp. 585–86 for an explanation of the mechanics of the budgeting process.)

SCHEDULING

If you observed a group of supervisors or department managers for a few days, you would see them regularly allocating resources by detailing what activities have to be done, the order in which they are to be completed, who is to do each, and when they are to be completed. These managers are doing what we call **scheduling**. In this section, we'll review some useful scheduling devices including Gantt charts, load charts, and PERT network analysis.

Gantt Charts The **Gantt chart** was developed during the early 1900s by Henry Gantt, an associate of the scientific management expert Frederick Taylor. The idea behind a Gantt chart is simple. It's essentially a bar graph with time on the horizontal axis and the activities to be scheduled on the vertical axis. The bars show output, both planned and actual, over a period of time. The Gantt chart visually shows when tasks are supposed to be done and compares that with the actual progress on each. It's a simple but important device that lets managers detail eas-

scheduling

Detailing what activities have to be done, the order in which they are to be completed, who is to do each, and when they are to be completed.

Gantt chart

A scheduling chart developed by Henry Gantt that shows actual and planned output over a period of time.

Exhibit	9.5	
Suggestions for Improving Budgeting		• Be flexible.
		• Goals should drive budgets—budgets should not determine goals.
		• Coordinate budgeting throughout the organization.
		• Use budgeting/planning software when appropriate.
		• Remember that budgets are tools.
		• Remember that profits result from smart management, not because you budgeted for them.

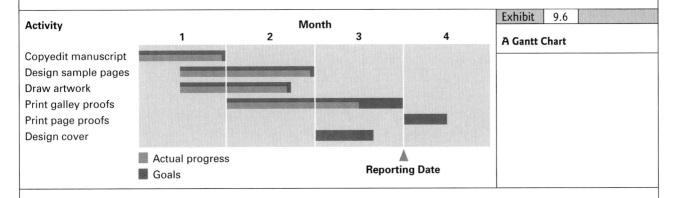

Exhibit 9.6

A Gantt Chart

ily what has yet to be done to complete a job or project and to assess whether an activity is ahead of, behind, or on schedule.

Exhibit 9.6 depicts a simplified Gantt chart for book production developed by a manager in a publishing company. Time is expressed in months across the top of the chart. The major work activities are listed down the left side. Planning involves deciding what activities need to be done to get the book finished, the order in which those activities need to be completed, and the time that should be allocated to each activity. Where a box sits within a time frame reflects its planned sequence. The shading represents actual progress. The chart also serves as a control tool because the manager can see deviations from the plan. In this example, both the design of the cover and the printing of galley proofs are running behind schedule. Cover design is about three weeks behind, and galley proof printing is about two weeks behind schedule. Given this information, the manager might need to take some action to either make up for the lost weeks or to ensure that no further delays will occur. At this point, the manager can expect that the book will be published at least two weeks later than planned if no action is taken.

Load Charts A **load chart** is a modified Gantt chart. Instead of listing activities on the vertical axis, load charts list either entire departments or specific resources. This arrangement allows managers to plan and control capacity utilization. In other words, load charts schedule capacity by work areas.

For example, Exhibit 9.7 shows a load chart for six production editors at the same publishing company. Each editor supervises the production and design of

load chart

A modified Gantt chart that schedules capacity by entire departments or specific resources.

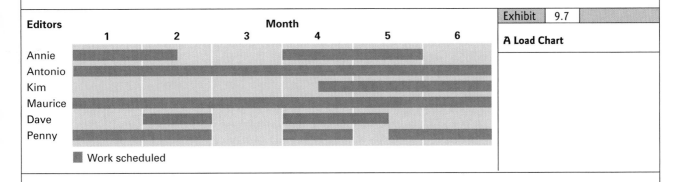

Exhibit 9.7

A Load Chart

Testing...Testing...1,2,3

7. **What types of resources do managers allocate?**

8. **Why are budgets popular resource allocation tools?**

9. **Contrast a Gantt chart with a load chart.**

PERT network

A flowchartlike diagram showing the sequence of activities needed to complete a project and the time or costs associated with each.

---

events

End points that represent the completion of major activities in a PERT network.

---

activities

The time or resources needed to progress from one event to another in a PERT network.

---

slack time

The amount of time an individual activity can be delayed without delaying the whole project.

---

critical path

The longest sequence of events and activities in a PERT network.

---

several books. By reviewing a load chart, the executive editor, who supervises the six production editors, can see who is free to take on a new book. If everyone is fully scheduled, the executive editor might decide not to accept any new projects, to accept new projects and delay others, to make the editors work overtime, or to employ more production editors. In Exhibit 9.7, only Antonio and Maurice are completely scheduled for the next six months. The other editors have some unassigned time and they might be able to accept new projects or be available to help other editors who get behind.

PERT Network Analysis   Gantt and load charts are useful as long as the activities being scheduled are few in number and independent of each other. But what if a manager had to plan a large project such as a departmental reorganization, the implementation of a cost-reduction program, or the development of a new product that required coordinating inputs from marketing, manufacturing, and product design people? Such projects require coordinating hundreds and even thousands of activities, some of which must be done simultaneously and some of which can't begin until preceding activities have been completed. If you're constructing a building, you obviously can't start putting up the walls until the foundation is laid. How, then, can managers schedule such a complex project? The Program Evaluation and Review Technique (PERT) is highly appropriate for such projects.

A **PERT network** is a flowchartlike diagram that depicts the sequence of activities needed to complete a project and the time or costs associated with each activity. With a PERT network, a manager must think through what has to be done, determine which events depend on one another, and identify potential trouble spots. PERT also makes it easy to compare the effects alternative actions might have on scheduling and costs. Thus, PERT allows managers to monitor a project's progress, identify possible bottlenecks, and shift resources as necessary to keep the project on schedule.

To understand how to construct a PERT network, you need to know four terms. **Events** are end points that represent the completion of major activities. **Activities** represent the time or resources required to progress from one event to another. **Slack time** is the amount of time an individual activity can be delayed without delaying the whole project. The **critical path** is the longest or most time-consuming sequence of events and activities in a PERT network. Any delay in completing events on this path would delay completion of the entire project. In other words, activities on the critical path have zero slack time.

Developing a PERT network requires that a manager identify all key activities needed to complete a project, rank them in order of occurrence, and estimate each activity's completion time. Exhibit 9.8 explains the steps in this process.

Most PERT projects are complicated and include numerous activities. Such complicated computations can be done with specialized PERT software. However, let's work through a simple example. Assume that you're the superintendent at a construction company and have been assigned to oversee the construction of an office building. Because time really is money in your business, you must determine how long it will take to get the building completed. You've determined the specific activities and events. Exhibit 9.9 outlines the major events in the construction project and your estimate of the expected time to complete each. Exhibit 9.10 on page 236 shows the PERT network based on the

I. *Identify every significant activity that must be achieved for a project to be completed.* The accomplishment of each activity results in a set of events or outcomes.

2. *Determine the order in which these events must be completed.*

3. *Diagram the flow of activities from start to finish, identifying each activity and its relationship to all other activities.* Use circles to indicate events and arrows to represent activities. This results in a flowchart diagram called a PERT network.

4. *Compute a time estimate for completing each activity.* This is done with a weighted average that uses an *optimistic* time estimate (t_o) of how long the activity would take under ideal conditions, a *most likely* estimate (t_m) of the time the activity normally should take, and a *pessimistic* estimate (t_p) that represents the time that an activity should take under the worst possible conditions. The formula for calculating the expected time (t_e) is then

$$t_e = \frac{t_o + 4t_m + t_p}{6}$$

5. *Using the network diagram that contains time estimates for each activity, determine a schedule for the start and finish dates of each activity and for the entire project.* Any delays that occur along the critical path require the most attention because they can delay the whole project.

Exhibit 9.8

Steps in Developing a PERT Network

data in Exhibit 9.9. You've also calculated the length of time that each path of activities will take:

A-B-C-D-I-J-K (44 weeks)

A-B-C-D-G-H-J-K (50 weeks)

A-B-C-E-G-H-J-K (47 weeks)

A-B-C-F-G-H-J-K (47 weeks)

Your PERT network shows that if everything goes as planned, the total project completion time will be 50 weeks. This is calculated by tracing the project's critical path (the longest sequence of activities): A-B-C-D-G-H-J-K and adding up the times. You know that any delay in completing the events on this path would delay the completion of the entire project (in other words, there is no slack time). Taking six weeks instead of four to put in the floor covering and paneling (Event I) would have no effect on the final completion date. Why? Because that event isn't on the critical path. However, taking seven weeks instead of six to dig the subterranean garage (Event B) would likely delay the total project. A manager

Event	Description	Expected Time (in weeks)	Preceding Event
A	Approve design and get permits.	10	None
B	Dig subterranean garage.	6	A
C	Erect frame and siding.	14	B
D	Construct floor.	6	C
E	Install windows.	3	C
F	Put on roof.	3	C
G	Install internal wiring.	5	D,E,F
H	Install elevator.	5	G
I	Put in floor covering and paneling.	4	D
J	Put in doors and interior decorative trim.	3	I, H
K	Turn over to building management group.	I	J

Exhibit 9.9

A PERT Network for Constructing an Office Building

Exhibit 9.10

A PERT Network for Constructing an Office Building

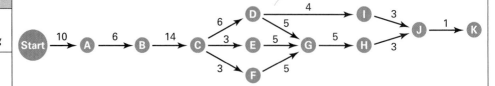

who needed to get back on schedule or to cut the 50-week completion time would want to concentrate on those activities along the critical path that could be completed faster. How might the manager do this? He or she could look to see if any of the other activities *not* on the critical path had slack time in which resources could be transferred to activities that *were* on the critical path.

BREAKEVEN ANALYSIS

breakeven analysis

A technique for identifying the point at which total revenue is just sufficient to cover total costs.

Managers at Glory Foods (www.gloryfoods.com) want to know how many units of their new frozen food products must be sold in order to break even—that is, the point at which total revenue is just sufficient to cover total costs. **Breakeven analysis** is a widely used resource allocation technique to help managers determine breakeven point.[17]

Breakeven analysis is a simple calculation, yet it's valuable to managers because it points out the relationship between revenues, costs, and profits. To compute breakeven point *(BE)*, a manager needs to know the unit price of the product being sold *(P)*, the variable cost per unit *(VC)*, and total fixed costs *(TFC)*. An organization breaks even when its total revenue is just enough to equal its total costs. But total cost has two parts: fixed and variable. *Fixed costs* are expenses that do not change regardless of volume. Examples include insurance premiums, rent, and property taxes. *Variable costs* change in proportion to output and include raw materials, labor costs, and energy costs.

The breakeven point can be computed graphically or by using the following formula:

$$BE = \frac{TFC}{P-VC}$$

Exhibit 9.11

Breakeven Analysis

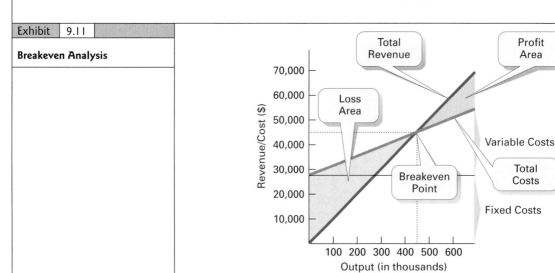

This formula tells us that (1) total revenue will equal total costs when we sell enough units at a price that covers all variable unit costs and (2) the difference between price and variable costs, when multiplied by the number of units sold, equals the fixed costs. Let's work through an example.

Assume that Miguel's Photocopying Service charges $0.10 per photocopy. If fixed costs are $27,000 a year and variable costs are $0.04 per copy, Miguel can compute his breakeven point as follows: $27,000 ÷ ($0.10 – $0.04) = 450,000 copies, or when annual revenues are $45,000 (450,000 copies × $0.10). This same relationship is shown graphically in Exhibit 9.11.

As a planning tool, breakeven analysis could help Miguel set his sales goal. For example, he could determine the profit he wants and then calculate what sales level is needed

Some e-businesses are thriving, and others are having trouble reaching their breakeven point. Overcrowded markets, thin profit margins, and high costs are having adverse effects on the profitability of firms such as Blue Nile, Gear, and Peapod.

to reach that profit. Breakeven analysis could also tell Miguel how much volume has to increase to break even if he's currently operating at a loss or how much volume he can afford to lose and still break even.

LINEAR PROGRAMMING

Kamie Bousman manages a manufacturing plant that produces two kinds of cinnamon-scented home fragrance products: wax candles and a woodchip-based potpourri sold in bags. Business is good and she can sell all of the products she can produce. This is her problem: Given that the bags of potpourri and the wax candles are produced in the same manufacturing departments, how many of each product should she produce to maximize profits? Kamie can use **linear programming** to solve her resource allocation problem.

Although linear programming can be used here, it can't be applied to all resource allocation problems because it requires that there be limited resources, that the goal be outcome optimization, that there be alternative ways of combining resources to produce a number of output mixes, and that there be a linear relationship between variables (a change in one variable must be accompanied by an exactly proportional change in the other).[18] For Kamie's business, that last condition would be met if it took exactly twice the amount of raw materials and hours of labor to produce two of a given home fragrance product as it took to produce one.

What kinds of problems can be solved with linear programming? Some applications include selecting transportation routes that minimize shipping costs, allocating a limited advertising budget among various product brands, making the optimal assignment of people among projects, and determining how much of each product to make with a limited number of resources. Let's return to Kamie's problem and see how linear programming could help her solve it. Fortunately, her problem is relatively simple, so we can solve it rather quickly. For complex linear programming problems, there are computer software programs designed specifically to help develop optimizing solutions.

First, we need to establish some facts about Kamie's business. Kamie has computed the profit margins on her home fragrance products at $10 for a bag of pot-

linear programming

A mathematical technique that solves resource allocation problems.

	Number of Hours Required (per unit)		
Department	**Potpourri Bags**	**Scented Candles**	**Monthly Production Capacity (in hours)**
Manufacturing	2	4	1,200
Assembly	2	2	900
Profit per unit	$10	$18	

Exhibit 9.12

Production Data for Cinnamon-Scented Products

pourri and $18 for a scented candle. These numbers establish the basis for Kamie to be able to express her *objective function* as maximum profit = $10P + $18S, where P is the number of bags of potpourri produced and S is the number of scented candles produced. The objective function is simply a mathematical equation that can predict the outcome of all proposed alternatives. In addition, Kamie knows how much time each fragrance product must spend in each department and the monthly production capacity (1,200 hours in manufacturing and 900 hours in assembly) for the two departments. (See Exhibit 9.12.) The production capacity numbers act as *constraints* on her overall capacity. Now Kamie can establish her constraint equations:

$$2P + 4S \leq 1,200$$
$$2P + 2S \leq 900$$

Of course, Kamie can also state that $P \geq 0$ and $S \geq 0$, because neither fragrance product can be produced in a volume less than zero.

Kamie has graphed her solution in Exhibit 9.13. The shaded area represents the options that don't exceed the capacity of either department. What does this mean? Well, let's look first at the manufacturing constraint line BE. We know that total manufacturing capacity is 1,200 hours, so if Kamie decides to produce all potpourri bags, the maximum she can produce is 600 (1,200 hours ÷ 2 hours required to produce a bag of potpourri). If she decides to produce all scented can-

Exhibit 9.13

Graphical Solution to Linear Programming Problem

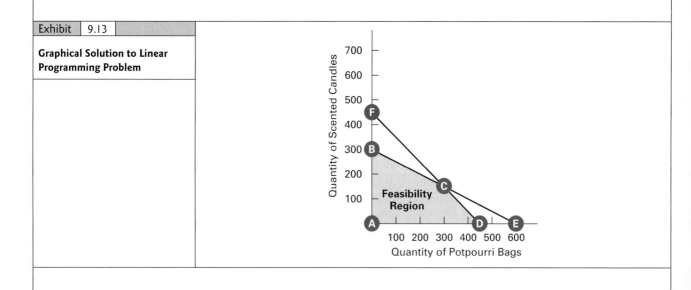

dles, the maximum she can produce is 300 (1,200 hours ÷ 4 hours required to produce a scented candle). The other constraint Kamie faces is that of assembly, shown by line DF. If Kamie decides to produce all potpourri bags, the maximum she can assemble is 450 (900 hours production capacity ÷ 2 hours required to assemble). Likewise, if Kamie decides to produce all scented candles, the maximum she can assemble is also 450 because the scented candles also take 2 hours to assemble. The constraints imposed by these capacity limits establish Kamie's *feasibility region*. Her optimal resource allocation will be defined at one of the corners within this feasibility region. Point C provides the maximum profits within the constraints stated. How do we know? At point A, profits would be 0 (no production of either potpourri bags or scented candles). At point B, profits would be $5,400 (300 scented candles × $18 profit and 0 potpourri bags produced = $5,400). At point D, profits would be $4,500 (450 potpourri bags produced × $10 profit and 0 scented candles produced = $4,500). At point C, however, profits would be $5,700 (150 scented candles produced × $18 profit and 300 potpourri bags produced × $10 profit = $5,700). ◄

Testing...Testing...1,2,3

10. How would a manager construct and use a PERT network for planning?

11. What is the value of breakeven analysis as a planning tool?

12. For what types of planning situations is linear programming appropriate?

〉 CONTEMPORARY PLANNING TECHNIQUES

Today's managers face the challenges of planning in an environment that's both dynamic and complex. Two planning techniques that are appropriate for this type of environment are project management and scenario planning. Both techniques emphasize *flexibility*, something that's important to making planning more effective and efficient in this type of organizational environment.

PROJECT MANAGEMENT

Different types of organizations, ranging from manufacturers such as DaimlerChrysler and Boeing to software design firms such as Purple Moon and Microsoft, do their work using projects. A **project** is a one-time-only set of activities that has a definite beginning and ending point in time.[19] Projects vary in size and scope—from a NASA space shuttle launch to a sorority's holiday party. **Project management** is the task of getting a project's activities done on time, within budget, and according to specifications.[20]

More and more organizations are using project management because the approach fits well with the need for flexibility and rapid response to perceived market opportunities. When organizations undertake projects that are unique, have specific deadlines, contain complex interrelated tasks requiring specialized skills, and are temporary in nature, these projects often do not fit nicely and neatly into the standardized planning procedures that guide an organization's other routine and ongoing work activities. Instead, managers use project management techniques to effectively and efficiently accomplish the project's goals. What does the project management process involve?

project

A one-time-only set of activities that has a definite beginning and ending point in time.

project management

The task of getting a project's activities done on time, within budget, and according to specifications.

Project Management Process In the typical project, the work is done by a project team whose members are assigned from their respective work areas to the project and who report to a project manager. The project manager coordinates the project's activities with other departments. When the project team accomplishes its

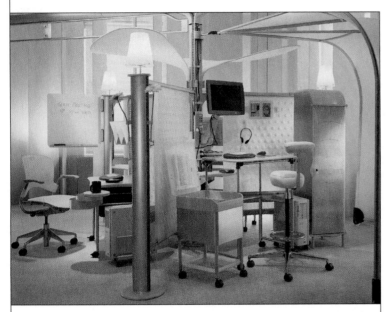

When Herman Miller Inc., one of the world's leading office-furniture manufacturers, wanted to come up with a completely new approach to designing office environments, it turned to the project approach. Led by respected industrial designer Ayse Birsel, the project team in its early stages would meet in a different city every few months to visit companies, study their workplaces, and develop a shared idea of what eventually became the Resolve office system (shown here).

goals, it disbands and members move on to other projects or back to their permanent work area.

The essential features of the project planning process are shown in Exhibit 9.14. The process begins by clearly defining the project's goals. This step is necessary because the manager and the team members need to know what's expected. All activities in the project and the resources needed to do them must then be identified. What materials and labor are needed to complete the project? This step may be time consuming and complex, particularly if the project is unique and there is no history or experience with similar projects. Once the activities have been identified, the sequence of completion needs to be determined. What activities must be completed before others can begin? Which can be done simultaneously? This step typically is done using flowchart-type diagrams such as a Gantt chart, a load chart, or a PERT network. Next, the project activities need to be scheduled. Time estimates for each activity are done and these estimates are used to develop an overall project schedule and completion date. Then the project schedule is compared to the goals, and any necessary adjustments are made. If the project completion time is too long, the manager might assign more resources to critical activities so they can be completed faster.

Today, the project management process can take place online as a number of Internet-based project collaboration software packages are available. For instance, one package, OnProject.com (www.onproject.com), described as an Internet workspace, allows users to share and manage information associated with projects. Even suppliers and customers can be part of the process.[21]

The Role of the Project Manager The temporary nature of projects makes managing them different from, say, overseeing a production line and preparing a weekly tally of costs on an ongoing basis. The one-shot nature of the work makes a project manager the organizational equivalent of a hired gunman. There's a job to be done. It has to be defined—in detail. And the project manager is responsible for how it's done.

Exhibit	9.14	Project Planning Process

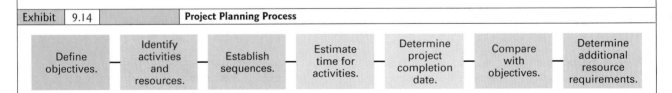

Define objectives.	Identify activities and resources.	Establish sequences.	Estimate time for activities.	Determine project completion date.	Compare with objectives.	Determine additional resource requirements.

Source: Based on R.S. Russell and B.W. Taylor III, *Production and Operations Management* (Upper Saddle River, NJ: Prentice Hall, 1995), p. 287.

Even with the availability of sophisticated computerized and online scheduling programs and other project management tools, the role of project manager is challenging because he or she is managing people who are still linked to their permanent work areas. The only real influence project managers have is their communication skills and their power of persuasion. To make matters worse, team members seldom work on just one project. They're usually assigned to two or three at any given time. So project managers end up competing with each other to focus a worker's attention on his or her particular project.

SCENARIO PLANNING

We already know how important it is that today's managers monitor and assess the external environment for trends and changes. As they assess the environment, issues and concerns that could affect their organization's current or planned operations are likely to be revealed. All of these won't be equally important, so it's usually necessary to focus on a limited set that are most important and to develop scenarios based on each.

A **scenario** is a consistent view of what the future is likely to be. Developing scenarios also can be described as contingency planning; that is, if this is what

scenario

A consistent view of what the future is likely to be.

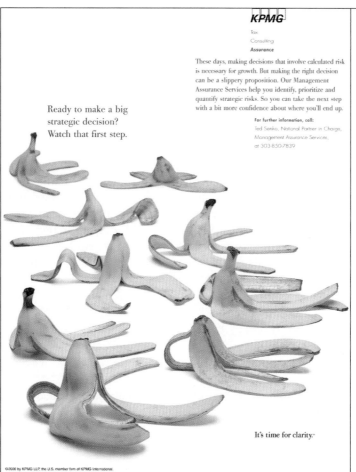

As this ad for the accounting and consulting firm KPMG LLP makes clear, risk and uncertainty are a fact of business life. While no one can foresee every potential "slip," a strategic risk assessment offers senior management insight into some of the more important uncertainties in their business environment.

Exhibit 9.15	• Identify potential unexpected events.
Preparing for Unexpected Events	• Determine if any of these events would have early indicators.
	• Set up an information-gathering system to identify early indicators.
	• Have appropriate responses (plans) in place if these unexpected events occur.

Source: S. Caudron, "Frontview Mirror," *Business Finance*, December 1999, pp. 24–30.

happens, then these are the actions we need to take. If, for instance, environmental scanning reveals increasing interest by the U.S. Congress for raising the national minimum wage, managers at Shoney's Restaurants could create multiple scenarios to assess the possible consequences of such an action. What would be the implications for its labor costs if the minimum wage were raised to $8.00 an hour? How about $9.00 an hour? What effect would these changes have on the chain's bottom line? How might competitors respond? Different assumptions lead to different outcomes. The intent of scenario planning is not to try to predict the future but to reduce uncertainty by playing out potential situations under different specified conditions.[22] Shoney's could, for example, develop a set of scenarios ranging from optimistic to pessimistic in terms of the minimum wage issue. It would then be prepared to implement new strategies to get and keep a competitive advantage. An expert in scenario planning said, "Just the process of doing scenarios causes executives to rethink and clarify the essence of the business environment in ways they almost certainly have never done before."[23]

Although scenario planning is useful in anticipating events that *can be* anticipated, it's difficult to forecast random events—the major surprises and aberrations that can't be foreseen. For instance, an earthquake in Taiwan in 1999 that destroyed a large portion of the country's chip-manufacturing facilities was a wild card for global computer makers. Other random events that surfaced in the last decade would be the rapid spread of AIDS and the sudden popularity of the Internet. And there certainly will be random events that materialize in the twenty-first century. As difficult as it may be for managers to anticipate and deal with these random events, they're not totally vulnerable to the consequences. Exhibit 9.15 lists some suggestions for preparing for unexpected events.

Planning tools and techniques can help managers prepare confidently for the future. But they should remember that all of the techniques we've described in this chapter are simply tools. They will never replace the manager's skills and capabilities in using the information gained to develop effective and efficient plans.

Testing...Testing...1,2,3

13. **Why is project management a popular planning technique?**

14. **List the essential steps in the project planning process.**

15. **How would scenario planning be useful in today's environment?**

Managers Respond to "A Manager's Dilemma"

Richard F. Unger

President, Unger, Sletten, and Associates, St. Louis, Missouri

Cindy Brewer

Corporate Trainer, Sears, Inc., Chicago, Illinois

Mr. Guoduan has a lot of challenges facing him! However, there must be other new-product opportunities available to get the company back in a growth position.

He should try identifying successful new-product entries in other countries that may apply to the Chinese market and that Kelon could manufacture—maybe something such as the George Foreman grill. Once a list of potential new products is identified, it would be easy to conduct some market research to evaluate consumer demand.

If consumer demand turns out to be attractive, he should look at doing break-even analysis to determine if it will be feasible to produce the new products. If so, he might want to use linear programming to help him determine the mix of products that will allow him to maximize resource allocation.

Mr. Guoduan has proven himself to be an effective manager, and he should be able to adapt to the changing environment. To help him do this, he should do some type of environmental scanning that will pinpoint emerging trends, not only in China but in other global markets also. Part of this planning analysis should be some type of competitor intelligence. Who are these competitors that are coming into the market? What do they offer that Kelon doesn't? What are their strengths and weaknesses? With this information, Guoduan should be able to pinpoint future growth possibilities for his company.

Once he has identified potential product or market opportunities, Guoduan might find financial planning tools such as budgets and break-even analysis useful. After all, if the proposed products won't make money, then the decision needs to be reconsidered.

Chapter Summary

This summary is organized by the chapter-opening objectives found on p. 222.

1. Three techniques for assessing the environment include environmental scanning, forecasting, and benchmarking. Environmental scanning is the screening of large amounts of information to anticipate and interpret changes in the environment. Forecasting is predicting outcomes. Quantitative forecasting applies a set of mathematical rules to a series of past data to predict outcomes. Qualitative forecasting uses the judgment and opinions of knowledgeable individuals to predict outcomes. Benchmarking is the search for the best practices among competitors or noncompetitors that lead to their superior performance.

2. There are four important techniques for allocating resources: budgeting, scheduling, breakeven analysis, and linear programming. Budgeting involves developing budgets, numerical plans for allocating resources to specific activities. Scheduling involves detailing what activities need to be done, the order in which they are to be completed, who is to do each, and when they are to be completed. Breakeven analysis is a resource allocation technique for identifying the point at which total revenue is just sufficient to cover total costs. Linear programming is a mathematical technique that solves resource allocation problems.

3. Budgets are popular planning tools because money is a universal common denominator that can be used in all types of organizations and by managers at all levels.

4. Gantt and load charts are both scheduling tools. Both are bar graphs. However, Gantt charts monitor planned and actual activities over time. Load charts focus on capacity utilization by monitoring whole departments or specific resources.

5. The five steps in developing a PERT network are (1) identifying every significant activity that must be achieved for a project to be completed; (2) determining the order in which those activities must be completed; (3) diagramming the flow of activities in a project from start to finish; (4) estimating the time needed to complete each activity; and (5) using the network diagram to determine a schedule for the start and finish dates of each activity and for the entire project.

6. A product's breakeven point is determined by the unit price of the product, its variable cost per unit, and its total fixed cost.

7. For linear programming to be applicable, a resource allocation problem must have limited resources, an objective function to maximize, alternative ways of combining resources, and a linear relationship between variables.

8. Project management involves getting a project's activities done on time, within budget, and according to specifications. A project is a one-time-only set of activities that has a definite beginning and ending point in time.

9. A scenario is a consistent view of what the future is likely to be. The intent of scenario planning is to come up with multiple scenarios that lead to different outcomes. Although scenario planning can't predict the future, it can reduce uncertainty by playing out potential situations under different specified conditions.

Thinking About Management Issues

1. It's a waste of time and other resources to develop a set of sophisticated scenarios for situations that may never occur. Do you agree or disagree? Support your position.

2. Do intuition and creativity have any relevance in quantitative planning tools and techniques? Explain.

3. The *Wall Street Journal* and other business periodicals often carry reports of companies that have not met their sales or profit forecasts. What are some reasons a company might not meet its forecast? What suggestions could you make for improving the effectiveness of forecasting?

4. In what ways is managing a project different from managing a department or other structured work area? In what ways are they the same?

5. "People can use statistics to prove whatever it is they want to prove." What do you think? What are the implications for managers and how they plan?

You've been hired as a summer intern in the business intelligence division of McDonald's Corporation. Your manager has asked you to compile information on four of the company's most important competitors. Specifically, she'd like you to find out (1) any new products these competitors may be introducing; (2) annual sales and profits for the last five years; and (3) other strategic changes the competitors may be planning.

Determine what four competitors you're going to research. Using the Internet, find the desired information. Compile the information, by competitor, using a bulleted list format. You'd like to impress your manager with your hard work and motivated effort so she'll give you a good reference at the end of your internship. Therefore, any additional information you can find on competitors is likely to score points with her.

myPHLIP *(www.prenhall.com/myphlip)* is a fully customizable homepage that ties students and faculty to text-specific resources.
- *For students*, myPHLIP provides an online study guide tied chapter-by-chapter to the text—current events and Internet exercises, lecture notes, downloadable software, the Career Center, the Writing Center, Ask the Tutor, and more.
- *For faculty*, myPHLIP provides a syllabus tool that allows you to manage content, communicate with students, and upload personal resources.

Benchmarking can be an important tool and source of information for managers. It also can be useful to students. Form small groups of three to four students. In your small group, discuss study habits that each of you has found to be effective from your years of being in school. As a group, come up with a bulleted list of at least eight suggestions in the time period allotted by your instructor. When the instructor calls time, each group should combine with one other group and share ideas, again in the time allotted by

your instructor. In this larger group, be sure to ask questions about suggestions that each small group had. Each small group should make sure that it understands the suggestions of the other small group it's working with. When the instructor calls time, each small group will then present and explain the study habit suggestions of the other small group it was working with. After all groups have presented, the class will come up with what it feels are the "best" study habits of all the ideas presented.

MTV's World

Even though it was founded over two decades ago (in 1980), MTV Networks is still a global trendsetter in the youth market. Like it or not, we live in an MTV world. From a dance floor in Hull, England, to Moscow's Red Square where 200,000 Russian teens gathered for an MTV concert, to the Philippines where it's the number-two cable channel, MTV definitely is in control. And for global product marketers—such as Nike, Gap, Ericsson, Levi Strauss, and Procter & Gamble—hoping to capture the teen and young adult market, MTV is the premiere platform for showcasing their products.

MTV Networks, a division of Viacom Inc., owns and operates the cable networks MTV, VH1, and Nickelodeon. Since Viacom's merger with television network CBS, MTV includes CMT (Country Music Television) and TNN (The Nashville Network). In addition, its other cable properties include Nick at Nite and TV Land. Under the leadership of CEO Tom Freston, the company generated $1 billion in profit in 1999, up 25 percent from 1998, but only $50 million of that came from global operations.

As the prime purveyor of the rock video as entertainment, MTV has cultivated and nurtured the evolution of rock videos from plain and simple staging of music stars singing their hit songs to today's stylistic and futuristic

Pictured left to right are chairman of MTV Networks board of directors Tom Freston and producer of MTV Russia Boris Zosimov.

mini-events showcasing music stars, stage sets, computer graphics, props, and dancers. Young people around the world—Viacom estimates that every second of every day almost 2 million people, 1.2 million of those outside the United States—tune in to watch MTV on-air celebrities do their thing. Punjabi hip-hop sheiks spin rap in India, Chinese veejays promote the likes of Ricky Martin, and Italian hosts combine cooking with a music countdown.

How does Freston keep MTV tuned in to the elusive and faddish whims of its target audience? Through intense quantitative research. Freston says that consumer research is the key. MTV does hundreds of different types of research from videotaping teens to going to clubs to surveying viewing habits. The challenge for MTV is that these young people grow up and move on, and just as it gets accustomed to serving one group and their particular attitudes, a whole new generation comes into the pipeline. However, MTV's success comes from more than just knowing what tools and techniques to use. Freston says it also comes from having employees around the world who are enthusiastically interested in what they do and who have good instincts and a good sense of cultural

shifts. The company's culture nurtures this environment, even in its global divisions. For instance, management of MTV India, based in Bombay, is now 100 percent local. However, when the division was getting off the ground, managers from the home office in New York trained the locals in the company culture and operational activities. Freston says that managers at MTV India are expected to "be inside the Indian's head." Today the Indian channel produces 21 shows hosted by local veejays who speak Hinglish, a hip blend of Hindi and English. And, like MTV affiliates around the world, they promote social causes such as AIDS awareness, the environment, and voter registration. Managers at MTV's other global divisions also are expected to know their markets and run their businesses accordingly. In fact, Freston believes that locally produced programs are the key to turning MTV's 22 global channels into high-profit businesses. Although MTV faces tough competition from foreign rivals that mimic its look and style and foreign governmental regulations that often threaten its plans, it seems to have a formula that captivates young audiences around the world.

QUESTIONS

1. Given the unusual nature of MTV's business, what planning tools and techniques might be most useful? Explain your choices.

2. Suppose that some organization wanted to use MTV Networks as a benchmark. What types of things might it learn from MTV?

3. Does the fact that MTV Networks is such a global company complicate its planning? Explain. What might be the implications for MTV's managers around the world as they choose specific planning tools and techniques?

Sources: Information on company from Hoovers Online (www.hoovers.com), September 30, 2000; Gannett News Service, "Bubble Gum Pop," *Springfield News-Leader*, September 28, 2000; S. Beatty and C. Hymowitz, "How MTV Stays Tuned In to Teens," *New York Times*, March 21, 2000, pp. B1+; and B. Pulley and A. Tanzer, "Sumner's Gemstone," *Forbes*, February 21, 2000, pp. 106–11.

Mastering Management

In Episode 10 of the Mastering Management *series, you can see the connection between planning theory and practical application. Using a number of planning tools, CanGo must come up with a detailed plan for implementing their online gaming initiative.*

As we discussed in the last entrepreneurship module, the first thing that entrepreneurs must do is to identify opportunities and possible competitive advantages. Once they've done this, they're ready to start the venture by researching its feasibility and then planning for its launch. These start-up and planning issues are what we're going to look at in this second entrepreneurship module.

Identifying Environmental Opportunities and Competitive Advantage

In 1994, when Jeff Bezos first saw that Internet usage was increasing by 2,300 percent a month, he knew that something dramatic was happening. "I hadn't seen growth that fast outside of a petri dish," he said. Bezos was determined to be a part of it. He quit his successful career as a stock market researcher and hedge fund manager on Wall Street and pursued his vision for online retailing, now the Amazon.com Web site.[1] What would you have done if you had seen that type of number somewhere? Ignored it? Wrote it off as a fluke? The skyrocketing Internet usage that Bezos observed is a prime example of identifying environmental opportunities. Remember from Chapter 8 that opportunities are positive trends in external environmental factors. These trends provide unique and distinct possibilities for innovating and creating value. Entrepreneurs need to be able to pinpoint these pockets of opportunities that a changing context provides. After all, "organizations do not see opportunities, individuals do."[2] Peter Drucker, a well-known management author identified seven potential sources of opportunity that entrepreneurs might look for in the external context.[3] These include the unexpected, the incongruous, the process need, industry and market structures, demographics, changes in perception, and new knowledge. Let's take a closer look at each.

1. *The unexpected.* When situations and events are unanticipated, opportunities can be found. The event might be an unexpected success (positive news) or an unexpected failure (bad news). Either way, there can be opportunities for entrepreneurs to pursue. For instance, the well-publicized 2000 U.S. presidential vote count and recounts acquainted people with the term "chad" and all its variations (hanging, pregnant, dimpled, and so forth). Savvy entrepreneurs began fashioning jewelry, t-shirts, and other products using the chad image. And publicity surrounding the accidental skiing deaths of two well-known individuals (Sonny Bono and Michael Kennedy) proved to be a bonanza for ski helmet manufacturers as novice and seasoned skiers alike began to wear protective head-

gear. These events were unexpected and proved to be opportunities for entrepreneurs.

2. *The incongruous.* When something is incongruous, there are inconsistencies and incompatibilities in the way it appears. Things "ought to be" a certain way, but aren't. When conventional wisdom about the way things should be no longer holds true, for whatever reason, there are opportunities to capture. Entrepreneurs who are willing to "think outside the box"—that is, to think beyond the traditional and conventional approaches—may find pockets of potential profitability. Sigi Rabinowicz, CEO of Tefron, an Israeli firm, recognized incongruities in the way that women's lingerie was made. He knew that a better way was possible. His company has spent over a decade adapting a circular hosiery knitting machine to make women's underwear that is nearly seamless.[4] Another example of how the incongruous can be a potential source of entrepreneurial opportunity is Fred Smith, founder of FedEx, who recognized in the early 1970s the inefficiencies in the delivery of packages and documents. His approach was: Why not? Who says that overnight delivery is impossible? Smith's recognition of the incongruous led to the creation of Fed Ex, now a multi-billion dollar corporation.

3. *The process need.* What happens when technology doesn't immediately come up with the "big discovery" that's going to fundamentally change the very nature of some product or service? What happens is that there can be pockets of entrepreneurial opportunity in the various stages of the process as researchers and technicians continue to work for the monumental breakthrough. Because the full leap hasn't been possible, opportunities abound in the tiny steps. Take the medical products industry, for example. Although researchers haven't yet discovered a cure for cancer, there have been many successful entrepreneurial biotechnology ventures created as knowledge about a possible cure continues to grow. The "big breakthrough" hasn't happened, but there have been numerous entrepreneurial opportunities throughout the process of discovery.

4. *Industry and market structures.* When changes in technology change the structure of an industry and market, existing firms can become obsolete if they're not attuned to the changes or are unwilling to change. Even changes in social values and consumer tastes can shift the structures of industries and markets. These markets and industries become open tar-

gets for nimble and smart entrepreneurs. The whole Internet experience provides several good examples of existing industries and markets being challenged by upstart entrepreneurial ventures. For instance, eBay has prospered as an online middleman between buyers and sellers. And it's not just Beanie Babies or used books being bought and sold by individuals. Even businesses are getting in on the auction action. For example, computer giant Sun Microsystems lists up to 150 items per day on eBay, including its e4500 servers that sell for around $15,000. And the Disney Company uses the site to auction off authentic studio props from its movies. Meg Whitman, eBay's CEO says that the company's job is connecting people, not selling them things. And connect them, they do! The online auction firm had 22.5 million registered users in early 2001.[5]

5. *Demographics.* The characteristics of the world population are changing. These changes influence industries and markets by altering the types and quantities of products and services desired and customers' buying power. Although many of these changes are fairly predictable if you stay alert to demographic trends, others aren't as obvious. Either way, there can be significant entrepreneurial opportunities in anticipating and meeting the changing needs of the population. For example, Thay Thida is one of the three partners in Khmer Internet Development Services (KIDS) in Phnom Penh, Cambodia. She and her co-founders saw the opportunities in bringing Internet service to Cambodians and have profited from their entrepreneurial venture.[6]

6. *Changes in perception.* Perception is one's view of reality. When changes in perception take place, the facts do not vary, but their meaning does. Changes in perception get at the heart of people's psychographic profiles—what they value, what they believe in, and what they care about. Changes in these attitudes and values create potential market opportunities for alert entrepreneurs. For example, think about your perception of healthy foods. As our perception of whether or not certain food groups are good for us has changed, there have been product and service opportunities for entrepreneurs to recognize and capture. For example, John Mackey started Whole Foods Market in Austin, Texas, as a place for customers to purchase food and other items free of pesticides, preservatives, sweeteners, and animal cruelty. Now, as the nation's number-one natural foods supermarket chain, Mackey's entrepreneurial venture consists of about 110 stores in more than 20 states.[7]

7. *New knowledge.* New knowledge is a significant source of entrepreneurial opportunity. Although not all knowledge-based innovations are significant, new knowledge ranks pretty high on the list of sources of entrepreneurial opportunity! It does take more than just having new knowledge, though. Entrepreneurs must be able to do something with that knowledge and to protect important proprietary information from competitors. For example, French scientists are using new knowledge about textiles to develop a wide array of innovative products that keep wearers healthy and smelling good. Neyret, the Parisian lingerie maker, innovated lingerie products woven with tiny perfume microcapsules that stay in the fabric through about 10 washings. Another French company, Francital, developed a fabric that is treated with chemicals to absorb perspiration and odors.[8]

Being alert to entrepreneurial opportunities is only part of an entrepreneur's initial efforts. He or she must also understand competitive advantage. As we discussed in Chapter 8, when an organization has a competitive advantage, it has something that other competitors don't, does something better than do other organizations, or does something that others can't. Competitive advantage is a necessary ingredient for an entrepreneurial venture's long-term success and survival. Getting and keeping a competitive advantage is tough to do and getting tougher. However, it is something that entrepreneurs must consider as they begin researching the venture's feasibility.

Testing...Testing...1,2,3

1. **How are opportunities important to entrepreneurial ventures?**

2. **Describe each of the seven sources of potential opportunity.**

3. **Why is it important for entrepreneurs to understand competitive advantage?**

Researching the Venture's Feasibility— Generating and Evaluating Ideas

It's important for entrepreneurs to research the venture's feasibility by generating and evaluating business ideas. Entrepreneurial ventures thrive on ideas. Generating ideas is an innovative, creative process. It's also one that will take time, not only in the beginning stages of the entrepreneurial venture, but throughout the life of the business. Where do ideas come from?

Generating Ideas. Studies of entrepreneurs have shown that the sources of their ideas are unique and varied. One survey found that "working in the same industry" was the major source (60 percent of respondents) of ideas for an entrepreneurial venture.[9] Other sources included personal interests or hobbies, looking at familiar and unfamiliar products and services, and opportunities in external environmental sectors (technological, sociocultural, demographics, economic, or legal-political).

What should entrepreneurs look for as they explore these idea sources? They should look for limitations of what's currently available, new and different approaches, advances and breakthroughs, unfilled niches, or trends and changes. For example, John C. Diebel, founder of Meade Instruments Corporation, the Irvine, California telescope maker, came up with the idea of putting computerized attachments on the company's inexpensive consumer models so that amateur astronomers could enter on a keypad the coordinates of planets or stars they wanted to see. The telescope would then automatically locate and focus on the desired planetary bodies. It took the company's engineers two years to figure out how to do it, but Meade now controls more than half the $230 million market for sales to these amateur astronomers.[10]

Evaluating Ideas. Evaluating entrepreneurial ideas revolves around personal and marketplace considerations. Each of these assessments will provide an entrepreneur with key information about the idea's potential. Exhibit P3.1 describes some questions that entrepreneurs might ask as they evaluate potential ideas.

A more structured evaluation approach that an entrepreneur might want to use is a **feasibility study**—an analysis of the various aspects of a proposed entrepreneurial venture designed to determine its feasibility. Not only is a well-prepared feasibility study an effective evaluation tool to determine whether an entrepreneurial idea is a potentially successful one, it can serve as a basis for the all-important business plan.

A feasibility study should give descriptions of the most important elements of the entrepreneurial venture and the entrepreneur's analysis of the viability of these elements. Exhibit P3.2 provides an outline of a possible approach to a feasibility study. Yes, it covers a lot of territory and it takes a significant amount of time, energy, and effort to prepare it. However, an entrepreneur's potential future success is worth that investment.

Researching the Venture's Feasibility— Researching Competitors

Part of researching the venture's feasibility is looking at the competitors. As we discussed in Chapter 9, researching the competition through competitor intelligence can be a powerful tool.

What would entrepreneurs like to know about their potential competitors? Here are some possible questions: What types of products or services are competitors offering? What are the major characteristics of these products or services? What are their products' strengths and weaknesses? How do they handle marketing, pricing, and distributing? What do they attempt to do differently from

Personal Considerations	Marketplace Considerations	Exhibit P3.1
		Evaluating Potential Ideas
Do you have the capabilities to do what you've selected?	Who are the potential customers for your idea: who, where, how many?	
Are you ready to be an entrepreneur?	What similar or unique product features does your proposed idea have compared to what's currently on the market?	
Are you prepared emotionally to deal with the stresses and challenges of being an entrepreneur?	How and where will potential customers purchase your product?	
Are you prepared to deal with rejection and failure?	Have you considered pricing issues and whether the price you'll be able to charge will allow your venture to survive and prosper?	
Are you ready to work hard?	Have you considered how you will need to promote and advertise your proposed entrepreneurial venture?	
Do you have a realistic picture of the venture's potential?		
Have you educated yourself about financing issues?		
Are you willing and prepared to do continual financial and other types of analyses?		

Exhibit   P3.2

Feasibility Study

A. Introduction, historical background, description of product or service:
   1. Brief description of proposed entrepreneurial venture
   2. Brief history of the industry
   3. Information about the economy and important trends
   4. Current status of the product or service
   5. How you intend to produce the product or service
   6. Complete list of goods or services to be provided
   7. Strengths and weaknesses of the business
   8. Ease of entry into the industry, including competitor analysis

B. Accounting considerations:
   1. Proforma balance sheet
   2. Proforma profit and loss statement
   3. Projected cash flow analysis

C. Management considerations:
   1. Personal expertise—strengths and weaknesses
   2. Proposed organizational design
   3. Potential staffing requirements
   4. Inventory management methods
   5. Production and operations management issues
   6. Equipment needs

D. Marketing considerations:
   1. Detailed product description
   2. Identify target market (who, where, how many)
   3. Describe place product will be distributed (location, traffic, size, channels, etc.)
   4. Price determination (competition, price lists, etc.)
   5. Promotion plans (role of personal selling, advertising, sales promotion, etc.)

E. Financial considerations:
   1. Start-up costs
   2. Working capital requirements
   3. Equity requirements
   4. Loans—amounts, types, conditions
   5. Breakeven analysis
   6. Collateral
   7. Credit references
   8. Equipment and building financing—costs and methods

F. Legal considerations:
   1. Proposed business structure (type; conditions, terms, liability, and responsibility; insurance needs; buyout and succession issues)
   2. Contracts, licenses, and other legal documents

G. Tax considerations: (sales/property/employee; federal, state, and local)

H. Appendix: charts/graphs, diagrams, layouts, résumés, etc.

other competitors? Do they appear to be successful at it? Why or why not? What are they good at? What competitive advantage(s) do they appear to have? What are they not so good at? What competitive disadvantage(s) do they appear to have? How large and profitable are these competitors?

For instance, Ezra Dabah, CEO of Children's Place, carefully examined the competition as he took his chain of children's clothing stores nationwide. Although he faces stiff competition from the likes of GapKids, J.C. Penney, and Gymboree, he feels that his company's approach to manufacturing and marketing will give it a competitive edge.[11]

Once an entrepreneur has this information, he or she should assess how the proposed entrepreneurial venture is going to "fit" into this competitive arena? Will the entrepreneurial venture be able to compete successfully? This type of competitor analysis becomes an important part of the feasibility study and the business plan. If, after all this analysis, the situation looks promising, the final part of researching the venture's feasibility is to look at the various financing options. This isn't the final determination of how much funding the venture will need or where this funding will come from, but is simply gathering information about various financing alternatives.

Testing...Testing...1,2,3

4. **What should entrepreneurs look for as they generate ideas?**

5. **What is a feasibility study, and why is it important to entrepreneurs?**

6. **Why should entrepreneurs research competitors?**

Researching the Venture's Feasibility— Researching Financing

Chances are that funds will be needed to start the entrepreneurial venture. A significant number of financing options are available to entrepreneurs. Exhibit P3.3 lists the various options.

Planning the Venture—Developing a Business Plan

Planning is important to entrepreneurial ventures, also. Once the venture's feasibility has been thoroughly researched, the entrepreneur then must look at planning the venture. The most important thing that an entrepreneur does in planning the venture is developing a **business plan**—a written document that summarizes a business opportunity and defines and articulates how the identified opportunity is to be seized and exploited.

For many would-be entrepreneurs, developing and writing a business plan seems like a daunting task, indeed. However, a good business plan is valuable. It pulls together all the elements of the entrepreneur's vision into a single coherent document. The business plan requires careful planning and creative thinking, but if done well, can be a convincing document that serves many functions. It serves as a blueprint and road map for operating the business. And the business plan is a "living" document that guides organizational decisions and actions throughout the life of the business, not just in the start-up stage.

If an entrepreneur has completed a feasibility study, much of the information included in it becomes the basis for the business plan. A good business plan should cover six major areas. These are the executive summary, analysis of opportunity, analysis of the context, description of the business, financial data and projections, and supporting documentation. What's included in each of these sections?

Executive Summary. The executive summary summarizes the key points that the entrepreneur wants to make about the proposed entrepreneurial venture. These might include a brief mission statement; primary goals; brief history of entrepreneurial venture maybe in the form of a time line; key people involved in the venture; nature of the business; concise product or service descriptions; brief explanations of market niche, competitors, and competitive advantage; proposed strategies; and selected key financial information.

Analysis of Opportunity. In this section of the business plan, an entrepreneur presents the details of the perceived opportunity. Essentially, this means (1) sizing up the market by describing the demographics of the target market; (2) describing and evaluating industry trends; and (3) identifying and evaluating competitors.

Analysis of the Context. Whereas the opportunity analysis focuses on the opportunity in a specific industry and market, the context analysis takes a much broader perspective. Here, the entrepreneur decribes the broad external changes and trends taking place in the economic, political-legal, technological, and global environments.

- Entrepreneur's personal resources (personal savings, home equity, personal loans, credit cards, etc.)
- Financial institutions (banks, savings and loan institutions, government-guaranteed loan, credit unions, etc.)
- **Venture capitalists**—external equity financing provided by professionally-managed pools of investor money
- **Angel investors**—a private investor who offers financial backing to an entrepreneurial venture in return for equity in the venture
- **Initial public offering (IPO)**—the first public registration and sale of a company's stock
- National, state, and local governmental business development programs
- Unusual sources (television shows, judged competitions, etc.)

Exhibit	P3.3
Possible Financing Options	

Description of the Business. In this section, an entrepreneur describes how the entrepreneurial venture is going to be organized, launched, and managed. It includes a thorough description of the mission statement; a description of the desired organizational culture; marketing plans including overall marketing strategy, pricing, sales tactics, service-warranty policies, and advertising and promotion tactics; product development plans such as an explanation of development status, tasks, difficulties and risks, and anticipated costs; operational plans including a description of proposed geographic location, facilities and needed improvements, equipment, and work flow; human resource plans including a description of key management persons, composition of board of directors including their background experience and skills, current and future staffing needs, compensation and benefits, and training needs; and an overall schedule and timetable of events.

Financial Data and Projections. Every effective business plan contains financial data and projections. Although these calculations and interpretation may be difficult, they are absolutely critical. No business plan is complete without financial information. Financial plans should cover at least three years and contain projected income statements, pro forma cash flow analysis (monthly for the first year and quarterly for the next two), pro forma balance sheets, breakeven analysis, and cost-controls. If major equipment or other capital purchases are expected, the items, costs, and available collateral should be listed. All financial projections and analyses should include explanatory notes, especially where the data seem contradictory or questionable.

Supporting Documentation. This *is* an important component of an effective business plan. The entrepreneur should back up descriptions with charts, graphs, tables, photographs, or other visual tools. In addition, it might be important to include information (personal and work related) about the key participants in the entrepreneurial venture.

Just as the idea for an entrepreneurial venture takes time to germinate, so does the writing of a good business plan. It's important for the entrepreneur to put serious thought and consideration into the plan. It's not an easy thing to do. However, the resulting document should be valuable to the entrepreneur in current and future planning efforts.

Testing...Testing...1,2,3

7. **List possible financial options for entrepreneurs.**

8. **What is a business plan?**

9. **Describe the six major sections of a business plan.**

On Location

Strategic Management

This video introduces the strategic issues at three of the featured firms: Arnold Worldwide, the marketing/public relations agency; Clif Bar, the health-food company; and Spiewak, Inc., the New York-based outdoor clothing retail company.

Among the strategies you'll hear discussed are ideas for managing growth in various ways, for marketing products and services produced by the three firms, and for maintaining a competitive advantage. Each of the three executives in the segment will also talk about his firm's vulnerabilities and how the company is positioned to overcome them. You might want to make particular note of the differences among the approaches these firms take in shaping their strategies, given that one is a service firm (Arnold). Also, of the two manufacturers, one produces a very small line of perishable items (Clif Bar) and the other one, which is also considerably older, makes a wide variety of outdoor clothing (Spiewak).

Spiewak has recently changed its corporate strategy to focus on two completely different markets, the industrial/uniform market and the fashion retail market. Michael Spiewak, president of the company, describes the creation of separate marketing, sales, and logistics areas for the new fashion label, which carries its own brand name. Consider whether the company is likely to have separate business-level and functional-level strategies for its two separate businesses. You might also notice that Fran Kelley, president and chief operating officer of Arnold Worldwide, talks about strategies for controlling growth in terms of levels also. At Arnold, some strategies are the same throughout the company, while others are tailored for each department so the firm can be more responsive to its individual clients. What level of strategy do you think Kelley is describing?

Note the competitive edge, or core competency, described by each executive. Spiewak depends on its relatively small size to keep it more nimble than its larger competitors, who can't move as quickly in response to fashion trends. Clif Bar focuses on a small range of prod-

ucts and lavishes attention on quality, innovation, taste, and unique packaging. Notice that its marketing plan is also highly focused. Arnold Worldwide has developed a proprietary "brand essence" approach to its marketing campaigns, but perhaps even more important are its people, whom the firm considers "our most important asset."

Finally, each manager describes a set of vulnerabilities the firm must face. These are identified by a constant process of analyzing the external environment to identify opportunities and threats and to identify strengths and weaknesses. Decide whether you think each company's vulnerable spots are likely to change in the near or long-term future, or not at all.

DISCUSSION QUESTIONS

1. Gary Erickson, chief executive officer and owner of Clif Bar, says in the segment that part of the company's mission is to maintain the integrity of a product that was originally developed in a kitchen, not in a lab: "If we don't come out with a good-tasting, healthy product, we're off the market." How do you think this mission can be translated into corporate, business, and functional-level strategies?

2. How is Arnold Worldwide using the Internet as part of its competitive advantage? Do you think the Internet could or should also be part of the competitive advantage of Spiewak and/or Clif Bar? If so, why and how?

3. Fran Kelley of Arnold Worldwide says the best managers are "paranoid," and Michael Spiewak says "we run scared." What do you think that means in the context of strategic management? Do you think it is a good model for managers to follow?

4. Part of Clif Bar's growth strategy is *not* to try to be all things to all people. What advantages and disadvantages can you think of in applying this focus strategy at a small firm? A large firm?

5. How do you think each of the three firms evaluates the results of its strategic management decisions? Consider the differences between them in your answer.

Learning Objectives

After reading and studying this chapter, you should be able to:

1. Define organizational structure and organizational design.

2. Explain why structure and design are important to an organization.

3. Describe the six key elements of organizational structure.

4. Differentiate mechanistic and organic organizational designs.

5. Identify the four contingency factors that influence organizational design.

6. Describe a simple structure, a functional structure, and a divisional structure.

7. Explain team-based structures and why organizations are using them.

8. Describe matrix structures, project structures, autonomous internal units, and boundaryless organizations.

9. Explain the concept of a learning organization and how it influences organizational design.

A MANAGER'S DILEMMA

Nokia, headquartered in Finland, is the world's leading maker of mobile phones and has a well-known brand. CEO Jorma Ollila isn't content with the company's current success and wants to position Nokia for the future.[1]

The company has evolved dramatically since its founding in 1865 as a wood-pulp mill. Over the years, it moved into a number of diverse industries ranging from paper to chemicals and rubber. But during the 1990s, the company took a radically new direction as it shifted into the burgeoning field of telecommunications. Today, Nokia is a global company whose primary growth areas are in wireless and wired telecommunications. It has more than 56,000 employees worldwide, and one in every three employees works in some form of product research. Its commitment to innovation is reflected in the fact that throughout the 1990s, Nokia again and again introduced better products than any of its competitors. It was also able to get its products to retailers and cellular phone companies in the right quantity and at the right time. How? Ollila says there's something about the way Nokia works that makes it more pragmatic, more focused, and more flexible than other companies. This is how he described it, "It's the way the organization creates a meeting of minds among people. How do you send a very strong signal that this is a meritocracy, and this is a place where you are allowed to have a bit of

Organizational Structure and Design

10

fun, to think unlike the norm, where you are allowed to make a mistake?"

Ollila has structured Nokia to be very nonhierarchical. Often, it's unclear who's in charge, although employees love the freedom once they get used to it. This kind of hands-off management encourages creativity, entrepreneurship, and personal responsibility. To balance this flexibility, rigorous financial targets keep employees focused on the organization's work. Ollila believes that Nokia could be even better if it became a learning organization. Put yourself in Ollila's position. What could he do to make his company a learning organization?

WHAT WOULD YOU DO?

lthough Jorma Ollila's desire to make his organization more of a learning organization might not be right for others, it does illustrate how important it is for managers to design an organizational structure that helps accomplish organizational goals and objectives. In this chapter, we'll present information about designing appropriate organizational structures. We'll look at the various elements of organizational structure and what contingency factors influence the design. We'll look at some traditional and contemporary organizational designs. And, finally, we'll describe a learning organization and what executives like Jorma Ollila can do to turn their organization into one.

> ## DEFINING ORGANIZATIONAL STRUCTURE

No other topic in management has undergone as much change in the past few years as that of organizing and organizational structure. Traditional approaches to organizing work are being questioned and reevaluated as managers search out structural designs that will best support and facilitate employees' doing the organization's work—ones that can achieve efficiency but also have the flexibility that's necessary for success in today's dynamic environment. Recall from Chapter 1 that **organizing** is defined as the process of creating an organization's structure. That process is important and serves many purposes. (See Exhibit 10.1.) The challenge for managers is to design an organizational structure that allows employees to effectively and efficiently do their work.

Just what is an organization's structure? An **organizational structure** is the formal framework by which job tasks are divided, grouped, and coordinated. When managers develop or change an organization's structure, they are engaged in **organizational design**, a process that involves decisions about six key elements: work specialization, departmentalization, chain of command, span of control, centralization and decentralization, and formalization.[2]

WORK SPECIALIZATION

Remember our discussion of Adam Smith in Chapter 2, who first identified division of labor in the late eighteenth century and concluded that it contributed to increased employee productivity. Early in the twentieth century, Henry Ford used this concept in an assembly line where every Ford worker was assigned a specific, repetitive task. By breaking jobs into small standardized tasks, which could be performed over and over again, Ford was able to produce cars at the rate of one every 10 seconds, while using relatively low-skilled workers.

Today we use the term **work specialization** to describe the degree to which tasks in an organization are divided into separate jobs. The essence of work spe-

---

organizing

The process of creating an organization's structure.

organizational structure

The formal framework by which jobs tasks are divided, grouped, and coordinated.

organizational design

Developing or changing an organization's structure.

work specialization

The degree to which tasks in an organization are divided into separate jobs; also known as division of labor.

Exhibit 10.1	
Some Purposes of Organizing	Divides work to be done into specific jobs and departments
	Assigns tasks and responsibilities associated with individual jobs
	Coordinates diverse organizational tasks
	Clusters jobs into units
	Establishes relationships among individuals, groups, and departments
	Establishes formal lines of authority
	Allocates and deploys organizational resources

cialization is that an entire job is not done by one individual but instead is broken down into steps, and each step is completed by a different person. Individual employees specialize in doing part of an activity rather than the entire activity.

During the first half of the twentieth century, managers viewed work specialization as an unending source of increased productivity. And for a time it was! Because it wasn't widely used, when work specialization *was* implemented, employee productivity rose. By the 1960s, however, it had become evident that a good thing could be carried too far. The point had been reached in some jobs where human diseconomies from work specialization—boredom, fatigue, stress, poor quality, increased absenteeism, and higher turnover—more than offset the economic advantages. In such instances, worker productivity could be increased by enlarging, not narrowing, the scope of job activities. In addition, managers found that employees who were given a variety of work to do, allowed to do the activities necessary to complete a whole job, and put into teams with interchangeable skills often achieved significantly higher output with increased employee satisfaction.

Most managers today see work specialization as an important organizing mechanism but not as a source of ever-increasing productivity. They recognize the economies it provides in certain types of jobs, but they also recognize the problems it creates when it's carried to extremes. McDonald's, for example, uses high work specialization to efficiently make and sell its fast-food products, and most employees in health care organizations are specialized. However, other organizations, such as Saturn Corporation, Hallmark, and Ford Australia, have successfully broadened the scope of jobs and reduced work specialization.

The prestige of the Mayo Clinic, renowned for its expertise in every branch of medicine, is largely due to the specialization of its 2,000 physicians and 35,000 allied health staff members in biology and molecular biology, dermatology, diagnostic radiology, medical genetics, oncology, surgery, and urology, to name a few.

DEPARTMENTALIZATION

Does your college have an office of student services? A financial aid department? Once jobs have been divided up through work specialization, they have to be grouped back together so that common tasks can be coordinated. The basis by which jobs are grouped together is called **departmentalization**. Every organization will have its own specific way of classifying and grouping work activities. Exhibit 10.2 shows the five common forms of departmentalization.

Functional departmentalization groups jobs by functions performed. This approach can be used in all types of organizations, although the functions change

departmentalization

The basis by which jobs are grouped together.

functional departmentalization

Groups jobs by functions performed.

| Exhibit | 10.2 | **The Five Common Forms of Departmentalization** |

Functional Departmentalization

```
                    Plant Manager

Manager,      Manager,      Manager,         Manager,          Manager,
Engineering   Accounting    Manufacturing    Human Resources   Purchasing
```

+ Efficiencies from putting together similar specialties and
  people with common skills, knowledge, and orientations
+ Coordination within functional area
+ In-depth specialization
− Poor communication across functional areas
− Limited view of organizational goals

Geographical Departmentalization

```
                    Vice President
                      for Sales

Sales Director,   Sales Director,    Sales Director,      Sales Director,
Western Region    Southern Region    Midwestern Region    Eastern Region
```

+ More effective and efficient handling of specific regional
  issues that arise
+ Serve needs of unique geographic markets better
− Duplication of functions
− Can feel isolated from other organizational areas

Product Departmentalization

Source: Bombardier Annual Report

```
                         Bombardier, Ltd.

        Mass Transit          Recreational and         Rail Products
          Sector            Utility Vehicles Sector        Sector

   Mass Transit    Bombardier–Rotax                  Rail and Diesel
    Division          (Vienna)                       Products Division

Recreational Products   Logistic Equipment    Industrial Equipment   Bombardier–Rotax
      Division              Division                Division           (Gunskirchen)
```

+ Allows specialization in particular products and services
+ Managers can become experts in their industry
+ Closer to customers
− Duplication of functions
− Limited view of organizational goals

Process Departmentalization

```
                         Plant
                      Superintendent

Sawing        Planing          Assembling    Lacquering       Finishing      Inspection
Department    and Milling      Department    and Sanding      Department     and Shipping
Manager       Department       Manager       Department       Manager        Department
              Manager                        Manager                         Manager
```

+ More efficient flow of work activities
− Can only be used with certain types of products

| Exhibit | 10.2 | The Five Common Forms of Departmentalization (*continued*) |

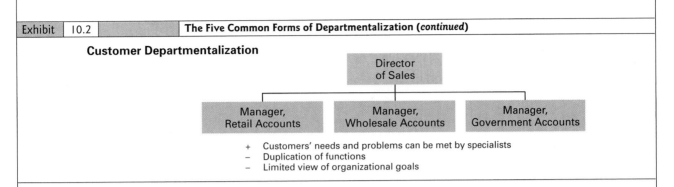

Customer Departmentalization

+ Customers' needs and problems can be met by specialists
− Duplication of functions
− Limited view of organizational goals

to reflect the organization's objectives and work activities. **Product departmentalization** groups jobs by product line. In this approach, each major product area is placed under the authority of a manager who's a specialist in, and is responsible for, everything having to do with that product line. **Geographical departmentalization** groups jobs on the basis of territory or geography such as southern, midwestern, or northwestern regions for an organization operating only in the United States; or for a global company, maybe U.S., European, Canadian, and Asian-Pacific regions. **Process departmentalization** groups jobs on the basis of product or customer flow. In this approach, work activities follow a natural processing flow of products or even of customers. Finally, **customer departmentalization** groups jobs on the basis of common customers who have common needs or problems that can best be met by having specialists for each.

Large organizations often combine most or all of these forms of departmentalization. For example, a major Japanese electronics firm organizes each of its divisions along functional lines, its manufacturing units around processes, its sales units around seven geographic regions, and its sales regions into four customer groupings.

Two trends are currently popular regarding departmentalization. First, customer departmentalization is increasingly being used as an approach to better monitor customers' needs and to be better able to respond to changes in those needs. For example, L. L. Bean organized around a half-dozen customer groups on the basis of what customers generally purchased. This arrangement allowed the company to better understand its customers and to respond faster to their needs. Second, managers are using **cross-functional teams**, groups of individuals who are experts in various specialties and who work together.[3] For instance, at Thermos Corporation (known worldwide for its beverage containers and lunch boxes) flexible interdisciplinary teams replaced the old tradition-bound functionally departmentalized structure. One of these teams—the Lifestyle Team—developed a new electric grill that has been extremely popular with consumers. This team of individuals from engineering, marketing, and manufacturing was involved in every aspect of bringing this winning product to market—from defining the target market, to defining the product, to working with manufacturing on a feasible design. We'll discuss the use of cross-functional teams more fully in Chapter 15. ◄

CHAIN OF COMMAND

For many years, the chain-of-command concept was a cornerstone of organizational design. As you'll see, it has far less importance today. But contemporary managers still need to consider its implications when deciding how best to structure their organizations.

---

product departmentalization

Groups jobs by product line.

geographical departmentalization

Groups jobs on the basis of territory or geography.

process departmentalization

Groups jobs on the basis of product or customer flow.

customer departmentalization

Groups jobs on the basis of common customers.

cross-functional teams

Groups of individuals who are experts in various specialties who work together.

Testing...Testing...1,2,3

1. **Why is organizing important?**

2. **What are the advantages and drawbacks of work specialization?**

3. **Describe the ways that managers can departmentalize work activities.**

With over 1,000 employees in facilities around the world, from the Caribbean to China to its Copiague (NY) headquarters, TII Industries, Inc., is an example of a firm organized by geography. To keep in touch with 70-plus key managers of the firm, Chief Operating Officer George S. Katsarakes begins every morning with a conference call with a time limit of 21 minutes.

chain of command

The continuous line of authority that extends from upper organizational levels to the lowest levels and clarifies who reports to whom.

authority

The rights inherent in a managerial position to tell people what to do and to expect them to do it.

responsibility

The obligation to perform any assigned duties.

unity of command

The management principle that each person should report to only one manager.

span of control

The number of employees a manager can efficiently and effectively manage.

The **chain of command** is the continuous line of authority that extends from upper organizational levels to the lowest levels and clarifies who reports to whom. It helps employees answer questions such as "Who do I go to if I have a problem?" or "To whom am I responsible?"

You can't discuss the chain of command without discussing three other concepts: authority, responsibility, and unity of command. **Authority** refers to the rights inherent in a managerial position to tell people what to do and to expect them to do it.[4] To facilitate decision making and coordination, an organization's managers are part of the chain of command and are granted a certain degree of authority to meet their responsibilities. As managers coordinate and integrate the work of employees, those employees assume an obligation to perform any assigned duties. This obligation or expectation to perform is known as **responsibility**. Finally, the **unity of command** principle (one of Fayol's 14 principles of management) helps preserve the concept of a continuous line of authority. It states that a person should report to only one manager. Without unity of command, conflicting demands and priorities from multiple bosses can create problems.

Early management theorists (Fayol, Weber, Taylor, and others) were enamored with the concepts of chain of command, authority, responsibility, and unity of command. However, times change and so do the basic tenets of organizational design. These concepts are considerably less relevant today because of information technology and employee empowerment. Employees throughout the organization can access information that used to be available only to top managers in a matter of a few seconds. Also, using computers, employees communicate with anyone else anywhere in the organization without going through formal channels—that is, the chain of command. Moreover, as employees are empowered to make decisions that previously were reserved for management, as more organizations use self-managed and cross-functional teams, and as new organizational designs with multiple bosses continue to be implemented, the traditional concepts of authority, responsibility, and chain of command are becoming less relevant.

SPAN OF CONTROL

How many employees can a manager efficiently and effectively manage? This question of **span of control** is important because, to a large degree, it determines the number of levels and managers an organization has. All things being equal, the wider or larger the span, the more efficient the organization. An example can show why.

Assume that we have two organizations, both of which have approximately 4,100 employees. As Exhibit 10.3 shows, if one organization has a uniform span of four and the other a span of eight, the wider span will have two fewer levels and approximately 800 fewer managers. If the average manager made $42,000 a year, the organization with the wider span would save over $33 million a year in management salaries alone! Obviously, wider spans are more efficient in terms of cost. However, at some point, wider spans reduce effectiveness. That is,

Exhibit | 10.3

Contrasting Spans of Control

Members at Each Level

(Highest) Assuming Span of 4 | Assuming Span of 8

Organizational Level

Level	Span of 4	Span of 8
1	1	1
2	4	8
3	16	64
4	64	512
5	256	4,096
6	1,024	
7	4,096	

(Lowest)

Span of 4:
Employees: = 4,096
Managers (level 1–6) = 1,365

Span of 8:
Employees: = 4,096
Managers (level 1–4) = 585

when the span becomes too large, employee performance suffers because managers no longer have the time to provide the necessary leadership and support.

The contemporary view of span of control recognizes that many factors influence the appropriate number of employees that a manager can efficiently *and* effectively manage. These factors encompass the skills and abilities of the manager and the employees and characteristics of the work being done. For instance, the more training and experience employees have, the less direct supervision they'll need. Therefore, managers with well-trained and experienced employees can function quite well with a wider span. Other contingency variables that will determine the appropriate span include similarity of employee tasks, the complexity of those tasks, the physical proximity of subordinates, the degree to which standardized procedures are in place, the sophistication of the organization's information system, the strength of the organization's culture, and the preferred style of the manager.[5]

The trend in recent years has been toward larger spans of control. Wide spans of control are consistent with managers' efforts to reduce costs, speed up decision making, increase flexibility, get closer to customers, and empower employees. However, to ensure that performance doesn't suffer because of these wider spans, organizations are investing heavily in employee training. Managers recognize that they can handle a wider span when employees know their jobs inside and out or can turn to co-workers if they have questions.

CENTRALIZATION AND DECENTRALIZATION

In some organizations, top managers make all the decisions and lower-level managers and employees simply carry out their directives. At the other extreme are organizations in which decision making is pushed down to the managers who are closest to the action. The former organizations are highly centralized, and the latter are decentralized.

Although he maintains a close personal involvement in every aspect of his successful men's clothing business, Karl Kani of Karl Kani Infinity, based in Los Angeles, also sees the need to delegate some control. "It's very hard to be an expert at designing, marketing, manufacturing, and distribution . . . The smartest thing to do was to enlist experts so that I could attend to the thing I do best"—designing the clothes that carry his name.

centralization

The degree to which decision making is concentrated at a single point in the organization.

decentralization

The degree to which lower-level employees provide input or actually make decisions.

Centralization describes the degree to which decision making is concentrated at a single point in the organization. If top managers make the organization's key decisions with little or no input from below, then the organization is centralized. In contrast, the more that lower-level employees provide input or actually make decisions, the more **decentralization** there is. Keep in mind that the concept of centralization-decentralization is a relative, not an absolute, one. What we mean is that an organization is never completely centralized or decentralized. Few organizations could function effectively if all decisions were made by only a select group of top managers; nor could they function if all decisions were delegated to employees at the lowest levels.

Consistent with efforts to make organizations more flexible and responsive, there's been a distinct trend toward decentralizing decision making. In large companies, especially, lower-level managers are "closer to the action" and typically have more detailed knowledge about problems and how best to solve them than do top managers. For instance, when Interstate Bakeries Corporation purchased the Hostess and Wonder Bread brands from Ralston Purina Company, it immediately revived the lagging sales of familiar brands such as Twinkies, Ding Dongs, and HoHos—something that Ralston had not been able to do. How did Interstate accomplish what Ralston could not? Ralston was highly centralized and nearly all decisions were made by top managers. In contrast, Interstate pushed decision making down to individual plant and brand managers. They could react to local conditions in making decisions.[6] Another example of this trend toward decentralization can be seen at Honeywell of Australia and New Zealand, which moved from a hierarchical management structure to one that is much flatter and team based. Before the change, nearly all decisions were made at headquarters, but authority was pushed down to individual plant and brand managers. The results have been increased revenues and a more intimate knowledge and understanding of the company's major customers.[7] Likewise, at the Bank of Montreal, all 1,164 branches were organized into 236 "communities"—that is, a group of branches within a limited geographical area. Each community is led by a community area manager, who typically works within a 20-minute drive of the other branches. This area manager can respond faster and more intelligently to problems in his or her community than could some senior executive in Montreal.[8]

Exhibit 10.4	More Centralization	More Decentralization
Factors That Influence the Amount of Centralization and Decentralization	• Environment is stable. • Lower-level managers are not as capable or experienced at making decisions as upper-level managers. • Lower-level managers do not want to have a say in decisions. • Decisions are significant. • Organization is facing a crisis or the risk of company failure. • Company is large. • Effective implementation of company strategies depends on managers retaining say over what happens.	• Environment is complex, uncertain. • Lower-level managers are capable and experienced at making decisions. • Lower-level managers want a voice in decisions. • Decisions are relatively minor. • Corporate culture is open to allowing managers to have a say in what happens. • Company is geographically dispersed. • Effective implementation of company strategies depends on managers having involvement and flexibility to make decisions.

What determines whether an organization will move toward more centralization or decentralization? Exhibit 10.4 lists some of the factors that have been identified as influencing the amount of centralization or decentralization an organization has.[9]

FORMALIZATION

Formalization refers to the degree to which jobs within the organization are standardized and the extent to which employee behavior is guided by rules and procedures. If a job is highly formalized, then the person doing that job has a minimum amount of discretion over what is to be done, when it's to be done, and how he or she could do it. Employees can be expected to handle the same input in exactly the same way, resulting in consistent and uniform output. In organizations with high formalization, there are explicit job descriptions, numerous organizational rules, and clearly defined procedures covering work processes. Where formalization is low, job behaviors are relatively unstructured and employees have a great deal of freedom in how they do their work. Because an individual's discretion on the job is inversely related to the amount of behavior in that job that is preprogrammed by the organization, the greater the standardization, the less input the employee has into how work is done. Standardization not only eliminates the possibility that employees will engage in alternative behaviors, it even removes the need for employees to consider alternatives.

The degree of formalization can vary widely between organizations and even within organizations. For instance, at a newspaper publisher, news reporters often have a great deal of discretion in their jobs. They may pick their news topic, find their own stories, research them the way they want, and write them up, usually within minimal guidelines. On the other hand, the compositors and typesetters who lay out the newspaper pages don't have that type of freedom. They have constraints—both time and space—that standardize how they do their work. ◄

formalization

The degree to which jobs within the organization are standardized and the extent to which employee behavior is guided by rules and procedures.

Testing...Testing...1,2,3

4. **How are the chain-of-command and span of control concepts used in organizing?**

5. **Describe the factors that influence greater centralization and those factors that influence greater decentralization.**

6. **What role does formalization play in an organization's structure?**

> ## ORGANIZATIONAL DESIGN DECISIONS

Organizations are not all structured in exactly the same way. A company with 30 employees isn't going to look like one with 30,000 employees. But even organizations of comparable size don't necessarily have similar structures. What works for one organization may not work for another. How do managers decide what organizational design to use? That decision depends upon certain contingency factors. In this section, we'll look at two generic models of organizational design and then at the contingency factors that favor each.

MECHANISTIC AND ORGANIC ORGANIZATIONS

Exhibit 10.5 describes two organizational forms.[10] The **mechanistic organization** is a rigid and tightly controlled structure. It's characterized by high specialization, rigid departmentalization, narrow spans of control, high formalization, a limited information network (mostly downward communication), and little participation in decision making by lower-level employees.

mechanistic organization

An organizational design that's rigid and tightly controlled.

Exhibit	10.5

Mechanistic versus Organic Organization

Mechanistic	**Organic**
• High Specialization	• Cross-Functional Teams
• Rigid Departmentalization	• Cross-Hierarchical Teams
• Clear Chain of Command	• Free Flow of Information
• Narrow Spans of Control	• Wide Spans of Control
• Centralization	• Decentralization
• High Formalization	• Low Formalization

Mechanistic types of organizational structures tend to be efficiency machines, well oiled by rules, regulations, standardized tasks, and similar controls. This organizational design tries to minimize the impact of differing personalities, judgments, and ambiguity because these human traits are seen as inefficient and inconsistent. Although no pure form of a mechanistic organization exists in reality, almost all large corporations and governmental agencies have at least some of these mechanistic characteristics.

organic organization

An organizational design that's highly adaptive and flexible.

In direct contrast to the mechanistic form of organization is the **organic organization**, which is as highly adaptive and flexible a structure as the mechanistic organization is rigid and stable. Rather than having standardized jobs and regulations, the organic organization is flexible, which allows it to change rapidly as needs require. Organic organizations have division of labor, but the jobs people do are not standardized. Employees are highly trained and empowered to handle diverse job activities and problems, and these organizations frequently use employee teams. Employees in organic-type organizations require minimal formal rules and little direct supervision. Their high levels of skills and training and the support provided by other team members make formalization and tight managerial controls unnecessary.

When is a mechanistic structure preferable and when is an organic one more appropriate? Let's look at the key contingency factors that influence the decision.

The organic, flexible organizational structure of ad agency TBWA Worldwide allows most of its employees to work as informally as they want, whether they are meeting in the company dining room or working at home in their pajamas.

CONTINGENCY FACTORS

Top managers of most organizations typically put a great deal of thought into designing an appropriate structure. What that appropriate structure is depends on four contingency variables: the organization's strategy, size, technology, and degree of environmental uncertainty.

Strategy and Structure An organization's structure should facilitate the achievement of goals. Because goals are influenced by the organization's strategies, it's only logical that strategy and structure should be closely linked. More specifically, structure should follow strategy. If managers significantly change the organization's strategy, they will need to modify the structure to accommodate and support the change.

Daniel J. Shapiro, Lead Program Manager, Microsoft, Redmond, Washington

Describe your job.

I'm a program manager at Microsoft. My job is cyclical and my primary responsibilities vary depending on the stage my product is in. In the early stages of the product, I work closely with marketing, our larger customers, samples of individual customers, and our corporate partners to develop a vision of the key problems we will solve and innovations we will introduce. Next, I design a product plan, working closely with the development team to make sure it can be implemented and the testing team to make sure it is measurable. Finally, I oversee the long, difficult path from concept to completed code: prioritizing features, cutting functionality if deadlines loom, directing attention to the most pressing problems, and ensuring that all the details are in place. My role is part product planner, part diplomat, part engineer, and part cattle rancher.

What types of skills do you think tomorrow's managers will need?

The business world is becoming more complex and the domain of the specialist is shrinking. Managers must focus on growing their skills outside their comfort zone. The best thing managers can do is to find the area of their business that they find the most distasteful and spend some time learning about it. Not only will it enrich their decision-making skills, but it also will foster a closer relationship with that work group.

How has technology changed the structure of your organization?

The concept of the "open door" has been around for ages. It's a noble aspiration but rarely works in practice. The greatest gift of technology is the "open in-box." Every employee at my company knows the e-mail addresses of our top managers. Each employee also knows that any and all concerns brought to those executives' attention will be addressed. I have seen new employees directly out of college engage the CEO directly in an e-mail exchange about our corporate strategy.

Alfred Chandler initially researched the strategy-structure relationship.[11] He studied several large U.S. companies over a period of 50 years and concluded that changes in corporate strategy led to changes in an organization's structure. He found that these organizations usually began with a single product or product line that required only a simple or loose form of organization. However, as these organizations grew, their strategies became more ambitious and elaborate and the structure changed to support the chosen strategy.

Most current strategy frameworks tend to focus on three dimensions: (1) innovation, which reflects the organization's pursuit of meaningful and unique innovations; (2) cost minimization, which reflects the organization's pursuit of tightly controlled costs; and (3) imitation, which reflects an organization's seeking to minimize risk and maximize profit opportunities by copying the market leaders. What structural design works best with each?[12] Innovators need the flexibility and free-flowing information of the organic structure, whereas cost minimizers seek the efficiency, stability, and tight controls of the mechanistic structure. Imitators use structural characteristics of both—the mechanistic structure to maintain tight controls and low costs and the organic structure to pursue new and innovative directions.

Size and Structure There's considerable evidence that an organization's size significantly affects its structure.[13] For instance, large organizations—those with 2,000 or more employees—tend to have more specialization, departmentalization, centralization, and rules and regulations than do small organizations. However, the relationship isn't linear. Rather, size affects structure at a decreasing

Testing...Testing...1,2,3

7. Describe the differences between mechanistic and organic organizations.

8. Summarize the strategy-structure relationship.

9. How does the size of an organization influence its structure?

unit production

The production of items in units or small batches.

mass production

The production of items in large batches.

process production

The production of items in continuous processes.

rate; that is, size has less impact as an organization grows. Why? Essentially, once an organization has around 2,000 employees, it's already fairly mechanistic. Adding an additional 500 employees to a firm with 2,000 employees won't have much of an impact. On the other hand, adding 500 employees to an organization that has only 300 members is likely to result in a shift toward a more mechanistic structure.

Technology and Structure Every organization has at least one form of technology to convert its inputs into outputs. For instance, workers at Maytag Corporation build its washers, dryers, and other home appliances on a standardized assembly line. Employees at Kinkos Copies produce custom jobs for individual customers. And employees at Bayer AG work on a continuous-flow production line for manufacturing its pharmaceuticals. Each of these organizations represents a different type of technology.

The initial interest in technology as a determinant of structure can be traced to the work of a British scholar, Joan Woodward.[14] She studied several small manufacturing firms in southern England to determine the extent to which structural design elements were related to organizational success. Woodward was unable to find any consistent pattern until she segmented the firms into three categories based on the size of their production runs. The three categories, representing three distinct technologies, had increasing levels of complexity and sophistication. The first category, **unit production**, described the production of items in units or small batches. The second category, **mass production**, described large-batch manufacturing. Finally, the third and most technically complex group, **process production**, included continuous-process production. A summary of her findings is shown in Exhibit 10.6.

Since Woodward's initial work, numerous studies have been done on the technology-structure relationship. These studies generally demonstrate that organizations adapt their structures to their technology.[15] The processes or methods that transform an organization's inputs into outputs differ by their degree of routineness. In general, the more routine the technology, the more standardized and mechanistic the structure can be. Organizations with more nonroutine technology are more likely to have organic structures.[16]

Environmental Uncertainty and Structure In Chapter 3 we introduced the organization's environment and the amount of uncertainty in that environment as constraints on managerial discretion. Why should an organization's structure be affected by its environment? Because of environmental uncertainty! Some organizations face relatively stable and simple environments; others face dynamic and com-

Exhibit 10.6		Unit Production	Mass Production	Process Production
Woodward's Findings on Technology, Structure, and Effectiveness	Structural characteristics	Low vertical differentiation	Moderate vertical differentiation	High vertical differentiation
		Low horizontal differentiation	High horizontal differentiation	Low horizontal differentiation
		Low formalization	High formalization	Low formalization
	Most effective structure	Organic	Mechanistic	Organic

plex environments. Because uncertainty threatens an organization's effectiveness, managers will try to minimize it. One way to reduce environmental uncertainty is through adjustments in the organization's structure.[17] The greater the uncertainty, the greater the need for the flexibility offered by an organic design. On the other hand, in stable, simple environments, mechanistic designs tend to be most effective.

The evidence on the environment-structure relationship helps to explain why so many managers are restructuring their organizations to be lean, fast, and flexible. Global competition, accelerated product innovation by competitors, and increased demands from customers for high quality and faster deliveries are examples of dynamic environmental forces. Mechanistic organizations are not equipped to respond to rapid environmental change and environmental uncertainty. As a result, we're seeing organizations being designed to be more organic. ◄───

> ## COMMON ORGANIZATIONAL DESIGNS

What organizational designs do Ford, Toshiba, Procter & Gamble, and eBay have? In making organizational design decisions, managers have some common structural designs from which to choose. We'll first look at some traditional organizational designs and then at some more contemporary designs.

TRADITIONAL ORGANIZATIONAL DESIGNS

In designing a structure to support the efficient and effective accomplishment of organizational goals, managers may choose to follow more traditional organizational designs. These designs—the simple structure, functional structure, and divisional structure—tend to be more mechanistic. Exhibit 10.7 summarizes the strengths and weaknesses of each of these designs.

Simple Structure Most organizations start as entrepreneurial ventures with a simple structure consisting of owners and employees. A **simple structure** is an organizational design with low departmentalization, wide spans of control, authority centralized in a single person, and little formalization.[18] This structure is most com-

simple structure

An organizational design with low departmentalization, wide spans of control, centralized authority, and little formalization.

Simple Structure
Strengths: Fast; flexible; inexpensive to maintain; clear accountability
Weaknesses: Not appropriate as organization grows; reliance on one person is risky

Functional Structure
Strengths: Cost-saving advantages from specialization (economies of scale, minimal duplication of people and equipment) and employees are grouped with others who have similar tasks
Weaknesses: Pursuit of functional goals can cause managers to lose sight of what's best for overall organization; functional specialists become insulated and have little understanding of what other units are doing

Divisional Structure
Strengths: Focuses on results—division managers are responsible for what happens to their products and services
Weaknesses: Duplication of activities and resources increases costs and reduces efficiency

Exhibit | 10.7

Strengths and Weaknesses of Common Traditional Organizational Designs

Each unit of the media conglomerate Viacom International, Inc. is managed in a separate division of the company. Viacom's divisional structure enables it to oversee Nickelodeon, MTV, Showtime, CBS-TV, Blockbuster, Paramount, and Simon & Schuster.

monly used by small businesses in which the owner and manager are one and the same.

Many organizations, do not, by choice or by design, remain simple structures. As an organization grows, it generally reaches a point where it has to add employees to help cope with the additional duties and requirements of operating at that level. As the number of employees rises, the structure tends to become more specialized and formalized. Rules and regulations are introduced, work becomes specialized, departments are created, levels of management are added, and the organization becomes increasingly bureaucratic. (You can review Weber's concept of bureaucracy in Chapter 2.) At this point, a manager might choose to organize around a functional structure or a divisional structure.

functional structure

An organizational design that groups similar or related occupational specialties together.

Functional Structure A **functional structure** is an organizational design that groups similar or related occupational specialties together. It's the functional approach to departmentalization applied to the entire organization. For instance, Revlon, Inc. is organized around the functions of operations, finance, human resources, and product research and development.

divisional structure

An organizational structure made up of separate, semiautonomous units or divisions.

Divisional Structure The **divisional structure** is an organizational structure made up of separate units or divisions.[19] In this design, each unit or division has relatively limited autonomy, with a division manager responsible for performance and who has strategic and operational authority over his or her unit. In divisional structures, however, the parent corporation typically acts as an external overseer to coordinate and control the various divisions, and it often provides support services such as financial and legal. Take Wal-Mart Stores, Inc., for example. Its divisions include Wal-Mart Realty, International, Specialty Stores, Sam's Clubs, and Supercenters. The Limited Inc. is another example of an organization with a divisional structure. Its divisions include Apparel (The Limited, Express, Lerner New York, Lane Bryant, Structure, Limited Too, and Mast Industries), Intimate Brands Inc. (Victoria's Secret Stores, Victoria's Secret Catalogue, Bath & Body Works, White Barn Candle Company, and Gryphon Development LP), Other Retail (Henri Bendel and Galyan's Trading Company), and Center Functions (Limited Distribution Services, Limited Store Planning, Limited Real Estate, Limited Design Services, Limited Brand and Creative Services, and Limited Technology Services).

Testing...Testing...1,2,3

13. **When would the simple structure be the preferred organizational design?**

14. **Contrast functional and divisional structures.**

15. **What are the strengths and weaknesses of the traditional organizational designs?**

CONTEMPORARY ORGANIZATIONAL DESIGNS

As our chapter-opening Manager's Dilemma illustrated, managers in contemporary organizations are finding that these traditional hierarchical designs often aren't appropriate for the increasingly dynamic and complex environments they face. In response to marketplace demands for being lean, flexible, and innovative, managers are finding creative ways to structure and organize work and to make their organizations more responsive to the needs of customers, employees, and other organizational constituents.[20] Now, we want to introduce you to some of the more contemporary concepts in organizational design.

Team-Based Structures In a **team-based structure**, the entire organization is made up of work groups or teams that perform the organization's work.[21] Needless to say, in a team-based structure, employee empowerment is crucial because there is no line of managerial authority from top to bottom. Rather, employee teams are free to design work in the way they think is best. However, the teams are also held responsible for all work activity and performance results in their respective areas. Let's look at some examples of organizations that are organized around teams.

Whole Foods Market, Inc., the largest natural-foods grocer in the United States, is structured entirely around teams.[22] Every one of Whole Foods' stores is an autonomous profit center composed of an average of 10 self-managed teams, each with a designated team leader. The team leaders in each store are a team; store leaders in each region are a team; and the company's six regional presidents are a team. At Sun Life Assurance of Canada's U.S. office in Wellesley, Massachusetts, customer representatives have been reorganized into eight-person teams trained to expedite all customer requests. Now, when customers call in, they're not switched from one specialist to another but to one of the teams that takes care of every aspect of the customer's request.

In large organizations, the team structure complements what is typically a functional or divisional structure. This allows the organization to have the efficiency of a bureaucracy while providing the flexibility that teams provide. To improve productivity at the operating level, for instance, companies such as Saturn, Motorola, and Xerox extensively use self-managed teams. And at Boeing, Baxter International, and Hewlett-Packard, cross-functional teams are used to design new products or coordinate major projects.

Matrix and Project Structures Other popular contemporary designs are the matrix and project structures. The **matrix structure** is an organizational structure that assigns specialists from different functional departments to work on one or more projects

team-based structure

An organizational structure in which the entire organization is made up of work groups or teams.

matrix structure

An organizational structure that assigns specialists from different functional departments to work on one or more projects.

General Electric has made hundreds of deals and mergers in the last few years. When the company decided to build an internal database for sharing best practices from those experiences, it turned to a handful of employee teams whose members interviewed fellow GE workers and collected their tips and anecdotes. The teams came from human resources, finance, and more than a dozen other corporate functions. Here, Don Borwhat, human resources senior vice president of GE Fanuc Automation, talks with team members.

being led by project managers. Exhibit 10.8 shows an example of the matrix structure used in an aerospace firm. Along the top are the familiar organizational functions. The specific projects the firm is currently working on are listed along the left-hand side. Each project is managed by an individual who staffs his or her project with people from each of the functional departments. The addition of this vertical dimension to the traditional horizontal functional departments, in effect, "weaves together" elements of functional and product departmentalization—hence, the term *matrix*. One other unique aspect you need to know about the matrix design is that it creates a *dual chain of command*. It explicitly violates the classical organizing principle of unity of command. How does the matrix work in reality?

Employees in a matrix organization have two managers: their functional department manager and their product or project manager, who share authority. The project managers have authority over the functional members who are part of their project team in areas relative to the project's goals. However, decisions such as promotions, salary recommendations, and annual reviews remain the functional manager's responsibility. To work effectively, project and functional managers have to communicate regularly, coordinate work demands on employees, and resolve conflicts together.

Although the matrix structure works well—and continues to be an effective structural design choice for many organizations—some organizations are using a more "advanced" type of **project structure**, in which employees continuously work on projects. Unlike the matrix structure, a project structure has no formal departments to which employees return at the completion of a project. Instead, employees take their specific skills, abilities, and experiences to other work projects. In addition, all work activities in project structures are performed by teams of employees who become part of a project team because they have the appropriate work skills and abilities. For instance, at Oticon Holding A/S, a Danish hearing-aid manufacturer, there are no organizational departments or employee job titles. All work activities are project based, and these project teams form, disband, and form again as the work requires. Employees "join" project teams because they bring needed skills and abilities to that project. Once the project is completed, however, they move on to the next one.[23]

project structure

An organizational structure in which employees continuously work on projects.

Exhibit | **10.8** | **A Matrix Organization in an Aerospace Firm**

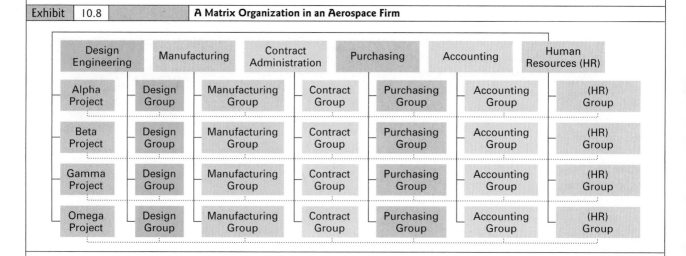

Project structures tend to be very fluid and flexible organizational designs. There's no departmentalization or rigid organizational hierarchy to slow down decision making or taking actions. In this type of structure, managers serve as facilitators, mentors, and coaches. They "serve" the project teams by eliminating or minimizing organizational obstacles and by ensuring that the teams have the resources they need to effectively and efficiently complete their work.

Autonomous Internal Units Some large organizations with numerous business units or divisions have adopted a design that's nothing more than a collection of **autonomous internal units**—that is, independent decentralized business units, each with its own products, clients, competitors, and profit goals. Although this may sound similar to the divisional structure we described earlier, the key difference is that these business units are *autonomous*. There is no centralized control or resource allocation as you'd find in the divisional structure. An example of an organization using this structure is ABB (Asea Brown Boveri), a global organization with annual revenues exceeding $24 billion. It makes equipment for power transmission and distribution; automation systems; petroleum technologies and equipment; and electrical and mechanical products. ABB is actually about 1,000 companies operating in more than 140 countries around the globe. The whole operation is managed by just eight top executives at headquarters in Zurich, Switzerland. The autonomous internal unit structure allows ABB remarkable flexibility to acquire new businesses, respond to competitors, and exploit market opportunities.[24]

autonomous internal units

Separate decentralized business units, each with its own products, clients, competitors, and profit goals.

---

16. **Describe a team-based structure.**

17. **Compare and contrast a matrix structure and a project structure.**

18. **When might an organization design its structure around autonomous internal units?**

Testing...Testing...1,2,3

The Boundaryless Organization Another approach to contemporary organizational design is the idea of the **boundaryless organization**, an organization whose design is not defined by, or limited to, the horizontal, vertical, or external boundaries imposed by a predefined structure.[25] The term was coined by Jack Welch, former chairman of General Electric, who wanted to eliminate vertical and horizontal boundaries within GE and break down external barriers between the company and its customers and suppliers. This idea may sound odd, yet many of today's most successful organizations are finding that they can most effectively operate in today's environment by remaining flexible and *un*structured: that the ideal structure for them is *not* having a rigid, predefined structure. Instead, the boundaryless organization seeks to eliminate the chain of command, to have appropriate spans of control, and to replace departments with empowered teams.[26]

What do we mean by "boundaries"? Think of the horizontal boundaries imposed by work specialization and departmentalization, the vertical boundaries that separate employees into organizational levels and hierarchies, and the external boundaries that separate the organization from its customers, suppliers, and other stakeholders. By removing *vertical* boundaries through such structural approaches as cross-hierarchical teams and participative decision making, the hierarchy is flat-

boundaryless organization

An organization whose design is not defined by, or limited to, the horizontal, vertical, or external boundaries imposed by a predefined structure.

When DaimlerChrysler began production of its M-Class sport utility vehicles in its Tuscaloosa, Alabama plant in 1997, it took a big step toward being a boundaryless organization. The former CEO of Mercedes-Benz U.S. International, Andreas Renschler, proposed letting employees in the firm's Alabama plant operate "in a kind of empowerment zone" where management will "set the frame, set the goals, and let people work." The organizational design approach seems to be working as a major expansion for the plant was announced in late summer 2000.

tened. Managers can remove *horizontal* boundaries by using cross-functional teams and organizing work activities around work processes instead of around functional departments. And *external* boundaries can be minimized or eliminated by using strategic alliances with suppliers, or value chain management customer-organization linkages, concepts described in Chapter 19.

The Learning Organization We first introduced the concept of a learning organization in Chapter 2 as we looked at some of the current issues facing managers. The concept of a learning organization doesn't involve a specific organizational design per se but instead describes an organizational mind-set or philosophy that has significant design implications. What is a **learning organization**? It's an organization that has developed the capacity to continuously adapt and change because all members take an active role in identifying and resolving work-related issues.[28] In a learning organization, employees are practicing knowledge management by continually acquiring and sharing new knowledge and are willing to apply that knowledge in making decisions or performing their work. Some organizational design theorists even go so far as to say that an organization's ability to do this—that is, to learn and to apply that learning as they perform the organization's work—may be the only sustainable source of competitive advantage.[29]

What would a learning organization look like? As you can see in Exhibit 10.9, the important characteristics of a learning organization revolve around

learning organization

An organization that has developed the capacity to continuously adapt and change because all members take an active role in identifying and resolving work-related issues.

Exhibit   10.9

Characteristics of a Learning Organization

Organizational Design
- Boundaryless
- Teams
- Empowerment

Organizational Culture
- Strong Mutual Relationships
- Sense of Community
- Caring
- Trust

THE LEARNING ORGANIZATION

Information Sharing
- Open
- Timely
- Accurate

Leadership
- Shared Vision
- Collaboration

Source: Based on P.M. Senge, *The Fifth Discipline: The Art and Practice of Learning Organizations* (New York: Doubleday, 1990); and R.M. Hodgetts, F. Luthans, and S.M. Lee, "New Paradigm Organizations: From Total Quality to Learning to World Class," *Organizational Dynamics*, Winter 1994, pp. 4–19.

MANAGING IN AN E-BUSINESS WORLD Structuring the E-Business Organization

The digital age is revamping our notions of how organizations should be structured for maximum efficiency and effectiveness in accomplishing organizational goals.[27] Traditional organizing concepts of dividing up work activities and then recombining these activities according to some prescribed arrangement just doesn't work in an e-business world. Why? Because the structure of an e-business organization encompasses more than just work arrangements and relationships among employees. Other organizational relationships also are essential to e-businesses—relationships with customers, vendors, suppliers, and others anywhere around the world who interact with the organization at any time. Let's look at an example of an e-business—Amazon.com—to illustrate what we mean. What organizational relationships does it have? There are several including (1) the authors and readers who write online book commentaries for its Web site and participate in online chats; (2) the publishers who provide content for the site; (3) the employees at Ingram Distribution, FedEx, and UPS who fulfill customers' book orders; (4) the staff at book-review publications who provide reviews for the site; and, of course, (5) Amazon's employees who do the behind-the-scenes work of managing a Web-based business. What kind of organizational design takes into account these diverse organizational relationships? And what are the implications for managers who are structuring e-business organizations?

In a broad sense, e-businesses tend to take on organic properties. To achieve the flexibility, openness, and speed necessary for success in this digital world, these organizations need high vertical, horizontal, and lateral communication; cross-hierarchical and cross-functional teams; extensive employee empowerment; and low formalization. And yes, an e-business organization fits our description of a boundaryless organization because that, in essence, is what an e-business is. It's an organization without boundaries where information and work activities flow freely among the various organizational participants. Any effective and efficient e-business structural design needs to recognize, accommodate, and nurture these boundaryless organizational relationships.

organizational design, information sharing, leadership, and culture. Let's take a closer look at each.

What types of organizational design elements would be necessary for learning to take place? In a learning organization, it's critical for members to share information and collaborate on work activities throughout the entire organization—across different functional specialties and even at different organizational levels. This can be done by minimizing or eliminating the existing structural and physical boundaries. In this type of boundaryless environment, employees are free to work together and collaborate in doing the organization's work the best way they can and to learn from each other. Because of this need to collaborate, teams also tend to be an important feature of a learning organization's structural design. Employees work in teams on whatever activities need to be done, and these employee teams are empowered to make decisions about doing their work or resolving issues. With empowered employees and teams, there's little need for "bosses" to direct and control. Instead, managers serve as facilitators, supporters, and advocates for employee teams.

Learning can't take place without information. For a learning organization to "learn," information must be shared among members; that is, organizational employees must engage in knowledge management. This means sharing information openly, in a timely manner, and as accurately as possible. Because there are few structural and physical barriers in a learning organization, the environment is conducive to open communication and extensive information sharing.

Away from a keyboard since his high school typing class, Louie Pokrywka is now learning to use elaborate computer schematics in his job at Kimberly-Clark's paper products mill in Connecticut. Computer technology has transformed his work and the way other Kimberly-Clark employees learn.

Leadership plays an important role as an organization moves to become a learning organization. What should leaders in a learning organization do? One of their most important functions is facilitating the creation of a shared vision for the organization's future and then keeping organizational members working toward that vision. In addition, leaders should support and encourage the collaborative environment that's critical to learning. Without strong and committed leadership throughout the organization, it would be extremely difficult to be a learning organization.

Finally, the organizational culture is an important aspect of being a learning organization. A learning organization's culture is one in which everyone agrees on a shared vision and everyone recognizes the inherent interrelationships among the organization's processes, activities, functions, and external environment. There is a strong sense of community, caring for each other, and trust. In a learning organization, employees feel free to openly communicate, share, experiment, and learn without fear of criticism or punishment.

No matter what structural design managers choose for their organizations, the design should help employees do their work in the best—most efficient and effective—way they can. The structure needs to help, not hinder, organizational members as they carry out the organization's work. After all, the structure is simply a means to an end.

Testing...Testing...1,2,3

19. **What is a boundaryless organization?**

20. **Describe the types of organizational boundaries that are minimized or eliminated in boundaryless organizations.**

21. **Describe the characteristics of a learning organization.**

Managers Respond to "A Manager's Dilemma"

Susan Colegrove

Project Manager, Industrial Participation Programs, Military Aircraft and Missile Systems Division, The Boeing Company, St. Louis, Missouri

Joe Jakubielski

I/T Analyst, Hallmark Cards, Inc., Kansas City, Missouri

Most companies would have to agree that their product or service line isn't the same today as it was when they were first established. Nokia is not unusual in that respect. However, in order to stay competitive in this fast-changing environment, Nokia must provide its customers with a better product and delivery plan. The company has been able to do this quite well.

Ollila's idea of reorganizing his company into a learning organization should not be difficult. Some workplace cultures could not make this change immediately. However, Nokia has a less rigid structure already in place. The company encourages innovation, communication, and teamwork. These three factors can only be beneficial in supporting his idea. In addition, he can support this change by communicating the new philosophy and desired outcomes, encouraging open communication and participation, and by providing proper leadership.

Creating a learning organization requires the sharing of knowledge among employees. By creating a work atmosphere in which employees are encouraged and rewarded for sharing their expertise, Ollila could improve upon Nokia's past successes. It sounds as if the organizational structure is already in place for this to happen. Employees are given the freedom to do their jobs the best way they know how. Under such an approach, group goals and rewards should take precedence over individual ones.

In addition, another suggestion would be to place higher emphasis on training. The company could make it mandatory for employees to attend a greater number of training classes per year. Displaying a commitment to learning such as this would show employees the intentions that Ollila has to turn Nokia into a learning organization.

Chapter Summary

This summary is organized by the chapter-opening objectives found on p. 254.

1. An organizational structure is the organization's formal framework by which job tasks are divided, grouped, and coordinated. When managers develop or change an organization's structure, they are engaged in organizational design.

2. Structure and design are important to an organization because they clarify expectations of what is to be done; divide work to avoid duplication, wasted effort, conflict, and misuse of resources; provide for logical flow of work activities; establish communication channels; provide coordinating mechanisms; focus work efforts on accomplishing objectives; and enhance planning and controlling.

3. Work specialization describes the degree to which tasks in the organization are divided into separate jobs. Departmentalization describes the way in which jobs are grouped in order to accomplish organizational goals. The chain of command is a continuous line of authority that extends from the upper levels of the organization down to the lowest levels and clarifies who reports to whom. Span of control refers to how many subordinates a manager can effectively and efficiently supervise. Centralization describes the degree to which decision making is concentrated at a single point in the organization. Decentralization describes when lower-level employees provide input and actually make decisions. Formalization refers to the degree to which jobs within the organization are standardized and the extent to which employee behavior is guided by rules and procedures.

4. Mechanistic organizations are rigid and tightly controlled structures. They are characterized by high specialization, extensive departmentalization, narrow spans of control, high formalization, a limited information network (mostly downward), and little participation in decision making by lower-level employees. On the other hand, organic organizations are highly adaptive and flexible. There is division of labor, but jobs are not highly standardized. Formalization and tight managerial controls are unnecessary because employees are highly trained.

5. The four contingency factors that influence an organization's design are strategy, size, technology, and environment.

6. A simple structure is an organizational design with low departmentalization, wide spans of control, authority centralized in a single person, and little formalization. A functional structure is an organizational design that groups similar or related occupational specialties together. A divisional structure is an organizational structure made up of separate units or divisions.

7. In a team-based structure, the entire organization is made up of work groups or teams that perform the organization's work. Organizations are using teams because it breaks down departmental barriers and decentralizes decision making to the level of the work team.

8. A matrix structure is an organizational design that assigns specialists from different functional departments to work on one or more projects being led by a project manager. A project structure is an organizational design in which employees continuously work on projects. Autonomous internal units are independent decentralized business units, each with its own products, clients, competitors, and profit goals. A boundaryless organization is an organizational design in which the structure is not defined by, or limited to, the boundaries imposed by traditional structures.

9. A learning organization is an organization that has developed the capacity to continuously adapt and change because all members take an active role in making decisions or performing their work. It influences organizational design because an organization's ability to learn is enhanced (or hindered) by its structural and physical boundaries and the amount of collaborative work efforts.

Thinking About Management Issues

1. Can an organization's structure be changed quickly? Why or why not?

2. Would you rather work in a mechanistic or an organic organization? Why?

3. What types of skills would a manager need to effectively work in a project structure? In a boundaryless organization? In a learning organization?

4. The boundaryless organization has the potential to create a major shift in our living and working patterns. Do you agree or disagree? Explain.

5. With the availability of advanced information technology that allows an organization's work to be done anywhere at any time, is organizing still an important managerial function? Why or why not?

Log On: Internet-Based Exercise

If an **organizational chart** (a visual drawing of an organization's structure) isn't available, an organization's choice of structural design often can be determined by reading descriptions of what it does. Find seven companies on the Web. Describe in a short paragraph what organizational structural design each is using and how you came to that conclusion.

myPHLIP Companion Web Site

myPHLIP **(www.prenhall.com/myphlip)** is a fully customizable homepage that ties students and faculty to text-specific resources.

- **For students**, myPHLIP provides an online study guide tied chapter-by-chapter to the text—current events and Internet exercises, lecture notes, downloadable software, the Career Center, the Writing Center, Ask the Tutor, and more.
- **For faculty**, myPHLIP provides a syllabus tool that allows you to manage content, communicate with students, and upload personal resources.

Working Together: Team-Based Exercise

In relatively decentralized organizations, managers must delegate (assign or turn over) authority to another person to carry out specific duties. Read through the Skills Module (see pp. 590–91) on Delegating. Form groups of three or four students. Your instructor will assign groups to either "effective delegating" or "ineffective delegating." Come up with a role-playing situation that illustrates your group's assignment (effective or ineffective delegating) that you will present in class. Be prepared to explain how your situation was an example of effective or ineffective delegating.

Case Application

In the Know

Buckman Laboratories (www.buckman.com), headquartered in Memphis, Tennessee, manufactures more than 1,000 specialty chemicals. The company employs over 1,300 people in 90 countries and its annual revenues exceed $300 million. Although this small, privately-held company depends on its research laboratories for the products that bring in its revenues, the whole company itself is a learning laboratory.

What is it about Buckman Labs that attracts executives from AT&T, 3M, Champion International, US West, and other *Fortune* 500 companies, who trek to Memphis to see and learn? They're coming to see how the company stays so fast, global, and interactive. Bob Buckman, Buckman Lab's CEO from 1978 to April 2000, recognized the power of knowledge and information long before others did. Buckman and his associates began treating knowledge as the company's most important corporate asset back in 1984. They believed that being (and remaining) competitive in a knowledge-intensive global environment required three things: (1) closing the gap between the organization and the customer; (2) staying in touch with each other; and (3) bringing *all* of the company's brainpower together to solve problems for each customer. Beginning in the early 1980s, Buckman was concerned with staying connected, sharing knowledge, and functioning anytime, anywhere, no matter what.

Buckman Labs has organized its associates and their work around its knowledge network, K'Netix®. This global electronic communications network resulted from Buckman's desire to close the gap between his associates and his customers—instantly. He started thinking about how important information and knowledge were—not just to him but to *all* of Buckman Labs' associates. What he needed and what his associates needed was a steady

Bob Buckman, CEO of Buckman Laboratories.

stream of the latest information about products, markets, and customers. And this information needed to be easily accessible and easily shared. As an ardent reader of business and management literature, Buckman remembered a comment from the well-known and well-respected CEO Jan Carlzon (Scandinavian Airlines' former CEO) that stuck in his mind, "An individual without information cannot take responsibility; an individual who is given information cannot help but take responsibility."

Buckman realized that the way to maximize each individual associate's power was to connect each associate to the world. He wrote down the characteristics of his ideal knowledge transfer system. Here's what he wrote: (1) It would be possible for people to talk to each other directly one on one, to minimize distortion. (2) It would give everyone access to the company's knowledge bases. (3) It would allow each individual in the company to enter knowledge into the system. (4) It would be available 24 hours a day, seven days a week. (5) It would be easy to use. (6) It would communicate in whatever language was best for the user. (7) It would be updated automatically, capturing questions and answers for a future knowledge base. But the technology of the system was not the most important barrier to knowledge sharing. Such a system would require a total cultural transformation—literally turning the organization upside down by getting associates to be deeply involved with knowledge sharing and collaboration. And that's what Bob Buckman set out to do. It wasn't easy however, to transform the company from an old top-down, bureaucratic, command-and-control organization into an organization in which every associate had complete

access to all information and one in which no one would be controlling associates by telling them what to do all the time.

Getting the physical hardware and software in place to support such a system was the easy part of the battle. Getting associates to use the knowledge base *and* contribute to it required a corporate culture change. After all, a knowledge-based company is successful only if knowledge is shared among all its organizational members, because knowledge has value only when it moves across the organization. What was particularly difficult about this type of cultural transformation was that employees in traditional organizations had always been rewarded on their ability to hoard knowledge and, thus, gain recognition and power. This is how the situation at Buckman Labs was described: "There were people whose file cabinets were locked and filled with everything they knew, and that was the source of their power." But that philosophy had to change if the knowledge system was going to work. Not long after K'Netix® went online, Buckman made his expectations clear: "Those of you who have something intelligent to say now have a forum in which to say it. Those of you who will not or cannot contribute also become obvious. If you are not willing to contribute or participate, then you should understand that the many opportunities offered to you in the past will no longer be available." What ultimately emerged at Buckman Labs has been a mixture of visible incentives and invisible pressure to use K'Netix® the Buckman Knowledge Network.

Because Buckman Labs competes in a variety of markets, often against competitors three to five times its size, its commitment to knowledge takes on a new urgency. Salespeople need the right answer for each customer and they need it fast. K'Netix® has made getting answers simple and rapid. But the company's commitment to speed, associate interactivity and knowledge sharing, and its embrace of globalization would not be possible without a recognition of the learning which is taking place.

QUESTIONS

1. On the basis of the case information, describe what decisions you think Buckman Labs has made regarding the six key elements of organizational design. Be as specific as possible.

2. Would you describe Buckman Labs as more of a mechanistic or an organic organization? Explain.

3. According to Exhibit 10.9, is Buckman Labs a learning organization? Explain.

4. Go to Buckman's Web site. Answer the following:
   - Find the statement of mission. What is it?
   - Locate the company's code of ethics. Summarize some of the company's basic principles.

- Find the Knowledge Nurture page. What is the Buckman Room? What is the Starter Kit? What is the Library?
- Find the page that describes K'Netix®. What does it say about the Buckman Knowledge Network?

5. What could other organizations learn from Buckman Labs' approach?

Sources: Company's Web site (www.buckman.com), February 24, 2000; S. Thurm, "What Do You Know?" *Wall Street Journal*, June 21, 1999, pp. R10+; B.P. Sunoo, "How HR Supports Knowledge Sharing," *Workforce*, March 1999, pp. 30–32; G. Rifkin, "Buckman Labs Is Nothing But Net," *Fast Company* Web page (www.fastcompany.com), April 17, 1997; and A. Bruzzese, "Sharing Knowledge Breaks Hierarchy," *Springfield News Leader*, October 17, 1997, p. 7A.

Mastering Management

In Episode 6 of the Mastering Management *series, you'll learn about the relationship between work design, job satisfaction, and productivity. Some of CanGo's employees feel under-motivated, under-appreciated, and out of the loop. Warren and Liz must work together to solve the problem.*

After reading and studying this chapter, you should be able to:

1. Define communication.

2. Explain the interpersonal communication process.

3. Describe the factors on which the different communication methods can be evaluated and on what the choice of communication method depends.

4. Tell how nonverbal communication affects managers.

5. Explain the barriers to effective interpersonal communication and how to overcome them.

6. Contrast the different organizational communication flows and networks.

7. Describe two developments in information technology that have had a significant impact on managerial communication.

8. Discuss how information technology affects organizations.

A MANAGER'S DILEMMA

Semifreddi's is an artisan-bread bakery (bakers of specialty bread and bread shaped in unusual and artistic ways) in Emeryville, California. CEO Tom Frainier has built a company whose annual revenues are over $7 million.[1] He describes himself as an "accessible, available, communicative guy." However, language barriers are proving to be a challenge for Tom and his workers, most of who come from Mexico, Laos, China, Peru, Cambodia, Yemen, and Vietnam. Even though his workers have limited English language skills, Tom feels that he is communicating sufficiently well with his diverse workforce because no major problems have arisen—at least yet.

Consider the recent problem when customers began making comments about the lack of parking on one side of the bakery. As Tom did anytime there were issues to be discussed, he called an employee meeting. He asked workers not to park in the spaces reserved for customers. Some employees misunderstood and thought that he was telling them not to drive to work. Tom said later that his mistake was talking slowly and loudly and assuming that his employees would understand him. However, the miscommunication over the parking issue was minor in comparison to another of Tom's communication challenges.

Tom is a staunch supporter of open book management, a management approach that entails regularly "opening up the financial statements" to employees and sharing this information with them in order to make them

Managerial Communication and Information Technology

11

feel more a part of the business. He recently gathered together employees from different work shifts for a meeting and rattled off a bunch of numbers. Then Tom asked everybody if they understood the information, and all heads nodded in agreement. Tom said later, "I didn't realize that they were just being polite." His desire to involve employees by letting them see the financial results of their actions wasn't having the intended effect.

Put yourself in Tom's position. What could he do to improve the effectiveness of his communications?

WHAT WOULD YOU DO?

om Frainier of Semifreddi's recognizes the importance of effectively communicating with his employees. Communication between managers and employees provides the information necessary to get work done effectively and efficiently in organizations. As such, there's no doubt that communication is fundamentally linked to managerial performance.[2] In this chapter, we'll present basic concepts in managerial communication. We'll explain the interpersonal communication process, methods of communicating, barriers to effective communication, and ways to overcome those barriers. We'll also look at organizational communication issues including communication flow and communication networks. Finally, because managerial communication is so greatly influenced by information technology, we'll look at contemporary issues and challenges associated with electronic communications and other forms of information technology.

> ## UNDERSTANDING MANAGERIAL COMMUNICATION

The importance of effective communication for managers can't be overemphasized for one specific reason: Everything a manager does involves communicating. Not *some* things, but everything! A manager can't make a decision without information. That information has to be communicated. Once a decision is made, communication must again take place. Otherwise, no one would know that a decision was made. The best idea, the most creative suggestion, the best plan, or the most effective job redesign can't take shape without communication. Managers need effective communication skills. We aren't suggesting, however, that good communication skills alone make a successful manager. We can say, though, that ineffective communication skills can lead to a continuous stream of problems for a manager.

WHAT IS COMMUNICATION?

communication

The transfer and understanding of meaning.

Communication is the transfer and understanding of meaning. The first thing to note about this definition is the emphasis on the *transfer* of meaning. This means that if no information or ideas have been conveyed, communication hasn't taken place. The speaker who isn't heard or the writer who isn't read hasn't communicated. More importantly, however, communication involves the *understanding* of meaning. For communication to be successful, the meaning must be imparted and understood. A letter written in Portuguese addressed to a person who doesn't read Portuguese can't be considered communication until it's translated into a language the person does read and understand. Perfect communication, if such a thing existed, would be when a transmitted thought or idea was perceived by the receiver exactly as it was envisioned by the sender.

Another point to keep in mind is that *good* communication is often erroneously defined by the communicator as *agreement* with the message instead of clearly understanding the message.[3] If someone disagrees with us, many of us assume that the person just didn't fully understand our position. In other words, many of us define good communication as having someone accept our views. But I can clearly understand what you mean and just *not* agree with what you say. In fact, many times when a conflict has gone on a long time, people will say it's because the parties aren't communicating effectively. That assumption reflects the tendency to think that effective communication equals agreement.

The final point we want to make about managerial communication is that it encompasses both **interpersonal communication**—communication between two or more people—and **organizational communication**—all the patterns, networks, and systems of communication within an organization. We're going to explore a manager's interpersonal communication first.

> ## THE PROCESS OF INTERPERSONAL COMMUNICATION

Before communication can take place, a purpose, expressed as a **message** to be conveyed, must exist. It passes between a source (the sender) and a receiver. The message is converted to symbolic form (called **encoding**) and passed by way of some medium (**channel**) to the receiver, who retranslates the sender's message (called **decoding**). The result is the transfer of meaning from one person to another.[4] Exhibit 11.1 illustrates the seven elements of the **communication process**: the communication source, the message, encoding, the channel, decoding, the receiver, and feedback. In addition, note that the entire process is susceptible to **noise**—disturbances that interfere with the transmission, receipt, or feedback of a message. Typical examples of noise include illegible print, phone static, inattention by the receiver, or background sounds of machinery or co-workers. Remember that anything that interferes with understanding can be noise, and noise can create distortion at any point in the communication process. Let's look at how distortions can happen with the sender, the message, the channel, the receiver, and the feedback loop.

A *sender* initiates a message by *encoding* a thought. Four conditions influence the effectiveness of that encoded message: the skills, attitudes, and knowledge of the sender, and the sociocultural system. How? We'll use ourselves, as your textbook authors, as an example. If we don't have the requisite skills, our message won't reach you, the reader, in the form desired. Our success in communicating to you depends on our writing skills. In addition, any preexisting ideas (attitudes) that we may have about numerous topics will affect how we communicate. For instance, our attitudes about managerial ethics, labor unions, or the importance of managers to organizations influence our writing. Next, the amount of knowledge we have about a subject affects the message(s) we are transferring. We can't communicate what we don't know; and if our knowledge is too extensive, it's pos-

Glossary (margin)

interpersonal communication

Communication between two or more people.

organizational communication

All the patterns, networks, and systems of communication within an organization.

message

A purpose to be conveyed.

encoding

Converting a message into symbols.

channel

The medium a message travels along.

decoding

Retranslating a sender's message.

communication process

The seven elements involved in transferring meaning from one person to another.

noise

Any disturbances that interfere with the transmission, receipt, or feedback of a message.

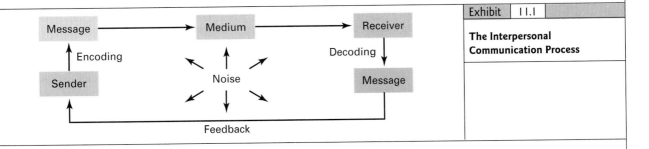

Exhibit	11.1

The Interpersonal Communication Process

sible that our writing won't be understood by the readers. Finally, the socio-cultural system in which we live influences us as communication senders. Our beliefs and values (all part of culture) act to influence what and how we communicate. Think back to our chapter-opening Manager's Dilemma and how Tom Frainier wants to be an effective communicator. As he encodes his ideas into messages when communicating with employees, he'll need to reflect on his skill, attitudes, knowledge, and the sociocultural system (of both the United States and his employees' countries of origin) in order to reduce any possible noise.

The *message* itself can distort the communication process, regardless of the kinds of supporting tools or technologies used to convey it. A message is the actual physical product encoded by the source. It can be the written document, the oral speech, and even the gestures and facial expressions we use. The message is affected by the symbols used to transfer meaning (words, pictures, numbers, etc.), the content of the message itself, and the decisions that the sender makes in selecting and arranging both the symbols and the content. Noise can distort the communication process in any of these areas.

The *channel* chosen to communicate the message also has the potential to be affected by noise. Whether it's a face-to-face conversation, an e-mail message, or a company-wide memorandum, distortions can and do occur. Managers need to recognize that certain channels are more appropriate for certain messages. Obviously, if the office is on fire, a memo to convey that fact is inappropriate! And if something is important, such as an employee's performance appraisal, a manager might want to use multiple channels—perhaps an oral review followed by a written letter summarizing the points. This decreases the potential for distortion.

The *receiver* is the individual to whom the message is directed. Before the message can be received, however, the symbols in it must be translated into a form that the receiver can understand. This is the *decoding* of the message. Just as the sender was limited by his or her skills, attitudes, knowledge, and sociocultural system, so is the receiver. And just as the sender must be skillful in writing or speaking, the receiver must be skillful in reading or listening. A person's knowledge influences his or her ability to receive. Moreover, the receiver's attitudes and sociocultural background can distort the message.

The final link in the communication process is a *feedback loop*. Feedback returns the message to the sender and provides a check on whether understanding has been achieved. Because feedback can be transmitted along the same types of channels as the original message, it faces the same potential for distortion.

Testing...Testing...1,2,3

1. **What are the two important parts of the definition of communication?**

2. **What types of communication does managerial communication encompass?**

3. **Describe the seven elements of the communication process.**

METHODS OF COMMUNICATING INTERPERSONALLY

You need to communicate to your employees the organization's new policy on sexual harassment; you want to compliment one of your workers on the extra hours she's put in to help your work group complete a customer's order; you must tell one of your employees about changes to her job; or you would like to get employees' feedback on your proposed budget for next year. In each of these instances, how would you communicate this information? Managers have a wide variety of communication methods from which to choose. These include face-to-face, telephone, group meetings, formal presentations, memos, traditional mail, fax machines, employee publications, bulletin boards, other company publications, audio- and videotapes, hot lines, electronic mail, computer conferencing, voice mail, teleconferences, and videoconferences. All of these communication channels include oral or written symbols, or both. How do you know which to use? Managers can use 12 questions to help them evaluate the various communication methods.[5]

1. Feedback—how quickly can the receiver respond to the message?

2. Complexity capacity—can the method effectively process complex messages?

3. Breadth potential—how many different messages can be transmitted using this method?

4. Confidentiality—can communicators be reasonably sure their messages are received only by those intended?

5. Encoding ease—can sender easily and quickly use this channel?

6. Decoding ease—can receiver easily and quickly decode messages?

7. Time-space constraint—do senders and receivers need to communicate at the same time and in the same space?

Face-to-face communication works especially well in situations where the message tends to be complex. At this office of the brokerage firm Charles Schwab, in New York City's Chinatown, an employee helps a customer understand some of the company's many online services.

8. Cost—how much does it cost to use this method?

9. Interpersonal warmth—how well does this method convey interpersonal warmth?

10. Formality—does this method have the needed amount of formality?

11. Scanability—does this method allow the message to be easily browsed or scanned for relevant information?

12. Time of consumption—does the sender or receiver exercise the greater control over when to deal with the message?

Exhibit 11.2 provides a comparison of the various communication methods on these 12 criteria. Which method a manager ultimately chooses should reflect the needs of the sender, the attributes of the message, the attributes of the channel, and the needs of the receiver. For instance, if you need to communicate to an employee the changes being made in her job, face-to-face communication would be a better choice than a memo since you want to be able to address immediately any questions and concerns that she might have.

We can't leave the topic of interpersonal communication methods without looking at the role of **nonverbal communication**—that is, communication transmitted without words. Some of the most meaningful communications are neither spoken nor written. A loud siren or a red light at an intersection tells you something without words. When a college instructor is teaching a class, she doesn't need words to tell her that her students are bored when their eyes are glassed over or they begin to read the school newspaper. Similarly, when students start putting their papers, notebooks, and book away, the message is clear: Class time is about over. The size of a person's office or the clothes he or she wears also conveys messages to others. These are all forms of nonverbal communication. The best-known types of nonverbal communication are body language and verbal intonation.

nonverbal communication

Communication transmitted without words.

Exhibit 11.2 — Comparison of Communication Methods

Channel	Feedback Potential	Complexity Capacity	Breadth Potential	Confidentiality	Encoding Ease	Decoding Ease	Time-Space Constraint	Cost	Personal Warmth	Formality	Scanability	Consumption Time
Face-to-face	1	1	1	1	1	1	1	2	1	4	4	S/R
Telephone	1	4	2	2	1	1	3	3	2	4	4	S/R
Group meetings	2	2	2	4	2	2	1	1	2	3	4	S/R
Formal presentations	4	2	2	4	3	2	1	1	3	3	5	Sender
Memos	4	4	2	3	4	3	5	3	5	2	1	Receiver
Postal mail	5	3	3	2	4	3	5	3	4	1	1	Receiver
Fax	3	4	2	4	3	3	5	3	3	3	1	Receiver
Publications	5	4	2	5	5	3	5	2	4	1	1	Receiver
Bulletin boards	4	5	1	5	3	2	2	4	5	3	1	Receiver
Audio/videotapes	4	4	3	5	4	2	3	2	3	3	5	Receiver
Hot lines	2	5	2	2	3	1	4	2	3	3	4	Receiver
E-mail	3	4	1	2	3	2	4	2	4	3	4	Receiver
Computer conference	1	2	2	4	3	2	3	2	3	3	4	S/R
Voice mail	2	4	2	1	2	1	5	3	2	4	4	Receiver
Tele-conference	2	3	2	5	2	2	2	2	3	3	5	S/R
Video-conference	3	3	2	4	2	2	2	1	2	3	5	S/R

Note: Ratings are on a 1–5 scale where 1 = high and 5 = low. Consumption time refers to who controls the reception of communication. S/R means the sender and receiver share control.
Source: P.G. Clampitt, *Communicating for Managerial Effectiveness* (Newbury Park, CA: Sage Publications, 1991). p. 136.

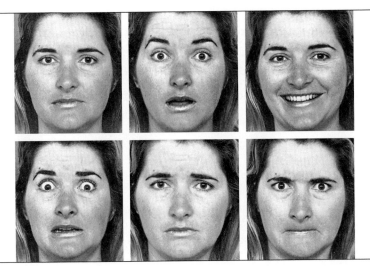

Source: S.E. Taylor, L.A. Peplan, and D.O. Sears, *Social Psychology*, 9th ed. (Upper Saddle River, NJ: Prentice Hall, 1997), p. 98; photographs by Paul Ekman, Ph.D. Used with permission.

Exhibit 11.3

Facial Expressions Convey Emotions

Each picture portrays a different emotion. Try to identify them before looking at the answers. (Top, left to right: neutral, surprise, happiness. Bottom: fear, sadness, anger.)

Body language refers to gestures, facial expressions, and other body movements that convey meaning. A person frowning "says" something different from one who's smiling. Hand motions, facial expressions, and other gestures can communicate emotions or temperaments such as aggression, fear, shyness, arrogance, joy, and anger. (See Exhibit 11.3.)

body language

Gestures, facial expressions, and other movements of the body that convey meaning.

Verbal intonation refers to the emphasis someone gives to words or phrases that conveys meaning. To illustrate how intonations can change the meaning of a message, consider the student who asks the instructor a question. The instructor replies, "What do you mean by that?" The student's reaction will vary, depending on the tone of the instructor's response. A soft, smooth vocal tone conveys interest and creates a different meaning from one that is abrasive and puts a strong emphasis on saying the last word. Most of us would view the first intonation as coming from someone sincerely interested in clarifying the student's concern, whereas the second suggests that the person is defensive or aggressive.

verbal intonation

An emphasis given to words or phrases that conveys meaning.

The fact that every oral communication also has a nonverbal message can't be overemphasized. Why? Because the nonverbal component usually carries the greatest impact. "It's not *what* you said, but *how* you said it." People respond to *how* something is said as well as *what* is said. Managers should remember this as they communicate.

Nonverbal communication can include all sorts of gestures and body motions that convey meaning to others who know how to read them, such as these futures traders on the Chicago stock exchange, who use signs and signals to place trades. Such language can be both very precise and very powerful.

4. **Explain the criteria managers can use to evaluate the various communication methods.**

5. **How do the various communication methods compare on these criteria?**

6. **Why is nonverbal communication an important part of interpersonal communication?**

BARRIERS TO EFFECTIVE INTERPERSONAL COMMUNICATION

In our discussion of the interpersonal communication process, we noted the continual potential for distortion. What causes distortion? In addition to the general distortions identified in the communication process, managers face other barriers to effective communication.

filtering

The deliberate manipulation of information to make it appear more favorable to the receiver.

Filtering **Filtering** is the deliberate manipulation of information to make it appear more favorable to the receiver. For example, when a person tells his or her manager what the manager wants to hear, that individual is filtering information. Does this happen much in organizations? Yes, it does! As information is communicated up through organizational levels, it's condensed and synthesized by senders so those on top don't become overloaded with information. Those doing the condensing filter communications through their personal interests and perceptions of what is important.

The extent of filtering tends to be a function of the number of vertical levels in the organization and the organizational culture. The more vertical levels there are in an organization, the more opportunities there are for filtering. As organizations become less dependent on strict hierarchical arrangements and instead use more collaborative, cooperative work arrangements, information filtering may become less of a problem. In addition, the ever-increasing use of e-mail to communicate in organizations reduces filtering because communication is more direct as intermediaries are bypassed. Finally, the organizational culture encourages or discourages filtering by the type of behavior it rewards. The more that organizational rewards emphasize style and appearance, the more that managers will be motivated to filter communications in their favor.

selective perception

When people selectively interpret what they see or hear on the basis of their interests, background, experience, and attitudes.

Selective Perception **Selective perception** is when people selectively interpret what they see or hear on the basis of their interests, background, experience, and attitudes. The receiver in the communication process selectively sees and hears communications depending on his or her needs, motivations, experience, background, and other personal characteristics. The receiver also projects his or her interests and expectations into communications as they are decoded. An employment interviewer who expects female job applicants to put family before career is likely to *see* that in female candidates, regardless of whether the applicants actually feel that way.

Emotions How a receiver feels when a message is received influences how he or she interprets it. You'll often interpret the same message differently, depending on whether you're happy or distressed. Extreme emotions are most likely to hinder

MANAGING WORKFORCE DIVERSITY   Communication Styles of Men and Women

"You don't understand what I'm saying, and you never listen!" "You're making a big deal out of nothing." Have you said or heard these statements or ones like them to friends of the opposite sex? Most of us probably have! Research shows us that men and women tend to have different communication styles.[6] Let's look more closely at these differing styles and the problems that can arise and try to suggest ways to minimize the barriers.

Deborah Tannen has studied the ways that men and women communicate and reports some interesting differences. The essence of her research is that men use talk to emphasize status, whereas women use it to create connection. She states that communication between the sexes can be a continual balancing act of juggling our conflicting needs for intimacy, which suggests closeness and commonality, and independence, which emphasizes separateness and differences. It's no wonder, then, that communication problems arise! Women speak and hear a language of connection and intimacy. Men hear and speak a language of status and independence. For many men, conversations are merely a way to preserve independence and maintain status in a hierarchical social order. Yet for many women, conversations are negotiations for closeness and seeking out support and confirmation. Let's look at a few examples of what Tannen has described.

Men frequently complain that women talk on and on about their problems. Women, however, criticize men for not listening. What's happening is that when a man hears a women talking about a problem, he frequently asserts his desire for independence and control by offering solu-

tions. Many women, in contrast, view conversing about a problem as a way to promote closeness. The woman talks about a problem to gain support and connection, not to get the male's advice.

Here's another example: Men are often more direct than women in conversation. A man might say, "I think you're wrong on that point." A woman might say, "Have you looked at the marketing department's research report on that issue?" The implication in the woman's comment is that the report will point out the error. Men frequently misread women's indirectness as "covert" or "sneaky," but women aren't as concerned as men with the status and one-upmanship that directness often creates.

Finally, men often criticize women for seeming to apologize all the time. Men tend to see the phrase "I'm sorry" as a sign of weakness because they interpret the phrase to mean the woman is accepting blame, when he may know she's not to blame. The woman also knows she's not at fault. Yet she's typically using "I'm sorry" to express regret: "I know you must feel badly about this and I do, too."

Because effective communication between the sexes is important in *all* organizations, how can we manage these differences in communication styles? To keep gender differences from becoming persistent barriers to effective communication requires acceptance, understanding, and a commitment to communicate adaptively with each other. Both men and women need to acknowledge that there are differences in communication styles, that one style isn't better than the other, and that it takes real effort to "talk" with each other successfully.

effective communication. In such instances, we often disregard our rational and objective thinking processes and substitute emotional judgments. It's best to avoid reacting to a message when you're upset because you're not likely to be thinking clearly.

Information Overload A marketing manager goes on a week-long sales trip to Spain where he doesn't have access to his e-mail and is faced with 600 messages on his return. It's not possible to fully read and respond to each and every one of those messages without facing **information overload**—when the information we have to work with exceeds our processing capacity. Today's typical executive frequently complains of information overload. The demands of keeping up with e-mail, phone calls, faxes, meetings, and professional reading create an onslaught of data that is nearly impossible to process and assimilate. What happens when individuals have more information than they can sort and use? They tend to select out, ignore, pass over, or forget information. Or they may put off further processing until the overload situation is over. Regardless, the result is lost information and less effective communication.

information overload

The information we have to work with exceeds our processing capacity.

Differences in language can create obvious communication barriers, and managers must sometimes be creative about preventing and solving communication problems in today's increasingly diverse workplace. Few safety manuals or other documents in the construction industry are available in any language other than English at present, for example, although the Building and Construction Trades Council of Greater New York includes an English-as-a-second-language component in its apprenticeship programs. Here Walter Suarez, left, helps translate English into Spanish for coworker Nelson Diaz at a construction site in New York.

jargon

Specialized terminology or technical language that members of a group use to communicate among themselves.

Defensiveness When people feel that they're being threatened, they tend to react in ways that reduce their ability to achieve mutual understanding. That is, they become defensive—engaging in behaviors such as verbally attacking others, making sarcastic remarks, being overly judgmental, and questioning others' motives.[7] When individuals interpret another's message as threatening, they often respond in ways that hinder effective communication.

Language Words mean different things to different people. Age, education, and cultural background are three of the more obvious variables that influence the language a person uses and the definitions he or she gives to words. Author/journalist William F. Buckley and rap artist Dr. Dre both speak English, but the language each uses is vastly different.

In an organization employees typically come from diverse backgrounds (think back to our chapter-opening Manager's Dilemma) and have different patterns of speech. Even employees who work for the same organization but in different departments often have different **jargon**—specialized terminology or technical language that members of a group use to communicate among themselves.

Keep in mind that while we may speak the same language, our use of that language is far from uniform. Senders tend to assume that the words and phrases they use mean the same to the receiver as they do to them. This, of course, is incorrect and creates communication barriers. Knowing how each of us modifies the language would help minimize those barriers.

National Culture As the chapter-opening Manager's Dilemma pointed out, communication differences can also arise from the different languages that individuals use to communicate and the national culture of which they are a part. Interpersonal communication isn't conducted the same way around the world. For example, let's compare countries that place a high value on individualism (such as the United States) with countries where the emphasis is on collectivism (such as Japan).[8]

In the United States, communication patterns tend to be oriented to the individual and clearly spelled out. U.S. managers rely heavily on memoranda, announcements, position papers, and other formal forms of communication to state their positions on issues. U.S. supervisors may hoard information in an attempt to make themselves look good and as a way of persuading their employees to accept decisions and plans. And for their own protection, lower-level employees also often engage in this practice.

In collectivist countries, such as Japan, there's more interaction for its own sake and a more informal manner of interpersonal contact. The Japanese manager, in contrast to the U.S. manager, engages in extensive verbal consultation with sub-ordinates over an issue first and draws up a formal document later to outline the agreement that was made. The Japanese value decisions by consensus, and open communication is an inherent part of the work setting. Also, face-to-face communication is encouraged.

Cultural differences can affect the way a manager chooses to communicate. And these differences undoubtedly can be a barrier to effective communication if not recognized and taken into consideration.

OVERCOMING THE BARRIERS TO EFFECTIVE INTERPERSONAL COMMUNICATION

Given these barriers to communication, what can managers do to overcome them? The following suggestions should help you make your interpersonal communication more effective.

Use Feedback Many communication problems can be directly attributed to mis-understandings and inaccuracies. These problems are less likely to occur if the manager uses the feedback loop in the communication process. This feedback can be verbal or nonverbal.

If a manager asks a receiver, "Did you understand what I said?" the response represents feedback. Good feedback should include more than yes-and-no answers. The manager can ask a set of questions about a message to determine whether or not the message was received and understood as intended. Better yet, the manager can ask the receiver to restate the message in his or her own words. If the manager hears what was intended, understanding and accuracy should improve. Feedback includes subtler methods than directly asking questions or having the receiver summarize the message. General comments can give a man-ager a sense of the receiver's reaction to a message.

Of course, feedback doesn't have to be conveyed in words. Actions *can* speak louder than words. A sales manager sends an e-mail to his or her staff describing a new monthly sales report that all sales representatives will need to complete. If some of them don't turn in the new report, the sales manager has received feed-back. This feedback suggests that the sales manager needs to clarify further the initial communication. Similarly, when you're talking to others, you watch their eyes and look for other nonverbal clues to tell you whether they're getting your message or not.

Simplify Language Because language can be a barrier, managers should choose words and structure their messages in ways that will make those messages clear and understandable to the receiver. The manager needs to simplify his or her lan-guage and consider the audience to whom the message is directed so that the lan-guage can be tailored to the receivers. Remember, effective communication is achieved when a message is both received and *understood*. Understanding is improved by simplifying the language used in relation to the audience intended. This means, for example, that a hospital administrator should always try to com-municate in clear, easily understood terms and that the language used in messages to the surgical staff should be purposefully different from that used with office employees. Jargon can facilitate understanding when it's used within a group of those who know what it means, but it can cause many problems when used outside that group.

Listen Actively   When someone talks, we hear. But too often we don't listen. Listening is an active search for meaning, whereas hearing is passive. In listening, two people are engaged in thinking: the sender *and* the receiver.

Many of us are poor listeners. Why? Because it's difficult and it's usually more satisfying to be on the offensive. Listening, in fact, is often more tiring than talking. It demands intellectual effort. Unlike hearing, **active listening**, which is listening for full meaning without making premature judgments or interpretations, demands total concentration. The average person normally speaks at a rate of about 125 to 200 words per minute. However, the average listener can comprehend up to 400 words per minute.[9] The difference obviously leaves lots of idle time for the brain and opportunities for the mind to wander.

Active listening is enhanced by developing empathy with the sender—that is, by placing yourself in the sender's position. Because senders differ in attitudes, interests, needs, and expectations, empathy makes it easier to understand the actual content of a message. An empathetic listener reserves judgment on the message's content and carefully listens to what is being said. The goal is to improve your ability to receive the full meaning of a communication without having it distorted by premature judgments or interpretations. Other specific behaviors that active listeners demonstrate are listed in Exhibit 11.4.

Constrain Emotions   It would be naive to assume that managers always communicate in a rational manner. We know that emotions can severely cloud and distort the transference of meaning. A manager who is emotionally upset over an issue is more likely to misconstrue incoming messages and fail to communicate his or her outgoing messages clearly and accurately. What can the manager do? The simplest answer is to refrain from communicating until he or she has regained composure.

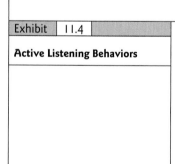

active listening

Listening for full meaning without making premature judgments or interpretations.

Exhibit	11.4

Active Listening Behaviors

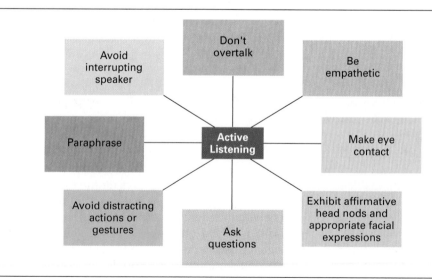

Source: Based on P.L. Hunsaker, *Training in Management Skills* (Upper Saddle River, NJ: Prentice Hall, 2001).

Watch Nonverbal Cues If actions speak louder than words, then it's important to watch your actions to make sure they align with and reinforce the words that go along with them. The effective communicator watches his or her nonverbal cues to ensure that they convey the desired message. ◄

Testing...Testing...1,2,3

7. **Describe the various barriers to effective interpersonal communication.**

8. **Explain how managers can overcome the barriers to effective interpersonal communication.**

9. **How can managers actively listen?**

› ORGANIZATIONAL COMMUNICATION

An understanding of managerial communication isn't possible without looking at the fundamentals of organizational communication. In this section, we look at several important aspects of organizational communication including formal versus informal communication, the flow patterns of communication, and formal and informal communication networks.

FORMAL VERSUS INFORMAL COMMUNICATION

Communication within an organization is often described as formal or informal. **Formal communication** refers to communication that follows the official chain of command or is part of the communication required to do one's job. For example, when a manager asks an employee to complete a task, he or she is communicating formally. So is the employee who brings a problem to the attention of his or her manager. Any communication that takes place within prescribed organizational work arrangements would be classified as formal.

Informal communication is organizational communication that is not defined by the organization's structural hierarchy. When employees talk with each other in the lunch room, as they pass in hallways, or as they're working out at the company exercise facility, that's informal communication. Employees form friendships and communicate with each other. The informal communication system fulfills two purposes in organizations: (1) It permits employees to satisfy their need for social interaction, and (2) it can improve an organization's performance by creating alternative, and frequently faster and more efficient, channels of communication.

formal communication

Communication that takes place within prescribed organizational work arrangements.

informal communication

Communication that is not defined by the organization's structural hierarchy.

DIRECTION OF COMMUNICATION FLOW

Organizational communication can flow downward, upward, laterally, or diagonally. Let's look at each.

Downward Any communication that flows downward from a manager to employees is **downward communication**. Downward communication is used to inform, direct, coordinate, and evaluate employees. When managers assign goals to their employees, they're using downward communication. Managers are also using downward communication by providing employees with job descriptions, informing them of organizational policies and procedures, pointing out problems that need attention, or evaluating their performance. Downward communication can take place through any of the communication methods we described earlier.

downward communication

Communication that flows downward from a manager to employees.

Upward Communication Managers rely on their employees for information. Reports are given to managers to inform them of progress toward goals and any current problems. **Upward communication** is communication that flows

upward communication

Communication that flows upward from employees to managers.

Communication flows in many directions in every organization. The Dean of the Darden School of Business at the University of Virginia, Edward A. Snyder, enjoys chatting with students every morning over coffee, a ritual that has endeared him to many and that typifies a kind of lateral communication. Says Snyder of these meetings, "You've got to treat students as colleagues, as part of a community, and as partners in the institution."

lateral communication

Communication that takes place among any employees on the same organizational level.

diagonal communication

Communication that cuts across work areas and organizational levels.

communication networks

The variety of patterns of vertical and horizontal flows of organizational communication.

upward from employees to managers. It keeps managers aware of how employees feel about their jobs, their co-workers, and the organization in general. Managers also rely on upward communication for ideas on how things can be improved. Some examples of upward communication include performance reports prepared by employees, suggestion boxes, employee attitude surveys, grievance procedures, manager-employee discussions, and informal group sessions in which employees have the opportunity to identify and discuss problems with their manager or even representatives of top-level management.

The extent of upward communication depends on the organizational culture. If managers have created a climate of trust and respect and use participative decision making or empowerment, there will be considerable upward communication as employees provide input to decisions. However, in a highly mechanistic and authoritarian environment, upward communication still takes place but will be limited both in style and content.

Lateral Communication Communication that takes place among any employees on the same organizational level is called **lateral communication**. In today's often chaotic and rapidly changing environment, horizontal communications are frequently needed to save time and facilitate coordination. Cross-functional teams, for instance, rely heavily on this form of communication interaction. However, it can create conflicts if employees don't keep their managers informed about decisions they've made or actions they've taken.

Diagonal Communication **Diagonal communication** is communication that cuts across both work areas *and* organizational levels. When a credit analyst in the credit department communicates directly with a regional marketing manager—note the different department and different organizational level—about a customer problem, that's diagonal communication. In the interest of efficiency and speed, diagonal communication can be beneficial. And the increased use of e-mail facilitates diagonal communication. In many organizations, any employee can communicate by e-mail with any other employee, regardless of organizational work area or level. However, just as with lateral communication, diagonal communication has the potential to create problems if employees don't keep their managers informed.

ORGANIZATIONAL COMMUNICATION NETWORKS

The vertical and horizontal flows of organizational communication can be combined into a variety of patterns called **communication networks**. Exhibit 11.5 illustrates three common communication networks.

Types of Communication Networks In the *chain* network, communication flows according to the formal chain of command, both downward and upward. The *wheel* network represents communication flowing between a clearly identifiable and strong leader and others in a work group or team. The leader serves as the hub

Exhibit   11.5

Three Common Organizational Communication Networks and How They Rate on Effectiveness Criteria

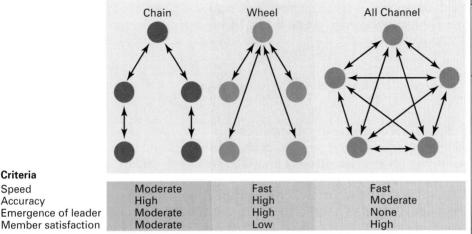

Criteria	Chain	Wheel	All Channel
Speed	Moderate	Fast	Fast
Accuracy	High	High	Moderate
Emergence of leader	Moderate	High	None
Member satisfaction	Moderate	Low	High

through whom all communication passes. Finally, in the *all-channel* network, communication flows freely among all members of a work team.

As a manager, which network should you use? The answer depends on your goal. Exhibit 11.5 also summarizes the effectiveness of the various networks according to four criteria: speed, accuracy, the probability that a leader will emerge, and the importance of member satisfaction. One observation is immediately apparent: No single network is best for all situations. If you are concerned with high member satisfaction, the all-channel network is best; if having a strong and identifiable leader is important, the wheel facilitates this; and if accuracy is most important, the chain and wheel networks work best.

The Grapevine We can't leave our discussion of communication networks without discussing the **grapevine**—the informal organizational communication network. The grapevine is active in almost every organization. Is it an important source of information? You bet! One survey reported that 75 percent of employees hear about matters first through rumors on the grapevine.[10]

What are the implications for managers? Certainly, the grapevine is an important part of any group or organization communication network and well worth understanding.[11] It identifies for managers those bewildering issues that employees consider important and anxiety producing. It acts as both a filter and a feedback mechanism, picking up on the issues employees consider relevant. More importantly, from a managerial point of view, it *is* possible to analyze what is happening on the grapevine—what information is being passed, how information seems to flow along the grapevine, and which individuals seem to be key conduits of information on the grapevine. By being aware of the grapevine's flow and patterns, managers can stay on top of issues that concern employees and, in turn, can use the grapevine to disseminate important information. Since the grapevine can't be eliminated, managers should "manage" it as an important information network.

Rumors that flow along the grapevine also can never be eliminated entirely. What managers can do, however, is minimize the negative consequences of

grapevine

The informal organizational communication network.

Testing...Testing... 1,2,3

10. **Distinguish between formal and informal organizational communication.**

11. **Describe the four ways that organizational communication can flow.**

12. **Compare the different types of communication networks.**

rumors by limiting their range and impact. How? By communicating openly, fully, and honestly with employees, particularly in situations in which employees may not like proposed or actual managerial decisions or actions.

⟩ UNDERSTANDING INFORMATION TECHNOLOGY

Technology is changing the way we live and work. Take the following four examples: Japanese employees and managers, housewives, and teens use wireless interactive Web phones to send e-mail, surf the Web, swap photos, and play computer games. At Postnet, the Swedish postal service's Internet subsidiary, employees work at tables with electrical and data-connection cables to plug in their laptop computers. Postnet's CEO spends her days walking around the office carrying her mobile phone, which is connected to the postal system's main switchboard. Over 75 percent of IBM's 316,000 employees regularly use instant messaging software for communicating and for workplace collaboration. At Chevron's worldwide headquarters in San Francisco, employees often meet to share information and to exchange ideas in "visualization centers" where data and graphics can be displayed on enormous screens.[12]

The world of managerial communication is not what it used to be! Managers are challenged to keep their organizations functioning smoothly while continually improving work operations *and* staying competitive even though both the organization and the environment are changing rapidly. Although changing technology has been a significant source of the environmental uncertainty facing organizations, these same technological advances have enabled managers to coordinate the work efforts of employees in ways that can lead to increased efficiency and effectiveness. Information technology now touches every aspect of almost every company's business. The implications for managerial communication are profound.

HOW TECHNOLOGY AFFECTS MANAGERIAL COMMUNICATION

Technology, and more specifically information technology, has radically changed the way organizational members communicate. For example, it has significantly improved a manager's ability to monitor individual or team performance, it has allowed employees to have more complete information to make faster decisions, and it has provided employees more opportunities to collaborate and share information. In addition, information technology has made it possible for people in organizations to be fully accessible, any time, regardless of where they are. Employees don't have to be at their desk with their computer turned on in order to communicate with others in the organization. Two developments in information technology seem to be having the most significant impact on current managerial communication: networked computer systems and wireless capabilities.

Networked Computer Systems In a networked computer system, an organization links its computers together through compatible hardware and software, creating an organizational network. Organizational members can then communicate with each other and tap into information whether they're down the hall, across town, or halfway across the world. Although we won't get into the mechanics of how a network system works, we will address some of its communication applications including e-mail, instant messaging, voice mail, fax, electronic data interchange, teleconferencing and videoconferencing, intranets and extranets, and the talking Internet.

E-mail is the instantaneous transmission of written messages on computers that are linked together. Messages wait at the receiver's computer and are read at the receiver's convenience. E-mail is fast and cheap and can be used to send the same message to numerous people at the same time. It's a quick and convenient way for organizational members to share information and communicate.

Some organizational members who find e-mail slow and cumbersome are using **instant messaging (IM)**. This is interactive real-time communication that takes place among computer users who are logged onto the computer network at the same time. IM first became popular among teens and preteens who wanted to communicate with their friends online.

The speed and convenience of e-mail has changed business communication forever. Along with the enormous growth of intranets (internal electronic communications webs) and other forms of electronic communication, the market for e-mail monitoring systems has doubled in the last year and continues to surge. Hundreds of companies like Canada's Ritvik now routinely store and review employees' incoming and outgoing e-mail messages and Web site visits, in an effort to reserve the organization's resources for company use. Here Andrew Quinn, Ritvik's systems manager, monitors co-workers' correspondence.

Now, it's moving to the workplace. With IM, there's no waiting around for a colleague to read e-mail. Whatever information needs to be communicated can be done so instantaneously. However, there are a couple of drawbacks to instant messaging. It requires groups of users to be logged on to the organization's computer network at the same time. This leaves the network open to security breaches. Also, IM software is currently incompatible with important business applications software.[13] However, as new versions of IM software are created, these drawbacks are likely to be addressed.

e-mail

The instantaneous transmission of written messages on computers that are linked together.

instant messaging (IM)

Interactive real-time communication that takes place among computer users logged on the computer network at the same time.

❓ THINKING CRITICALLY ABOUT ETHICS

Pogo.com reported that in one recent month, over 1 million people visited its game site from work and the *average* workplace player spent more than 2 hours and 34 minutes per visit glued to a Pogo.com game. Funny stories, jokes, and pictures make their way from one employee's e-mail inbox to another's, to another's, and so forth. An elf bowling game sent by e-mail was a favorite diversion last holiday season.

Although these may seem like fun and harmless activities, it's estimated that such Internet distractions cost businesses $54 billion annually. While there's a high dollar cost associated with using the Internet at work for other than business reasons, is there a psychological benefit to be gained by letting employees do something to relieve the stress of pressure-packed jobs? What are the ethical issues associated with widely available Internet access at work for both employees and for organizations?[14]

voice mail

A communication system that digitizes a spoken message, transmits it over a network, and stores the message on disk for the receiver to retrieve later.

fax

Communication through machines that allow the transmission of documents containing both text and graphics over ordinary telephone lines.

electronic data interchange (EDI)

A way for organizations to exchange standard business transaction documents using direct computer-to-computer networks.

teleconferencing

Communication system that allows a group of people to confer simultaneously using telephone or e-mail group communications software.

videoconferencing

A simultaneous communication conference in which participants can see each other.

intranet

An organizational communication network that uses Internet technology and is accessible only by organizational employees.

extranet

An organizational communication network that uses Internet technology and allows authorized users inside the organization to communicate with certain outsiders.

A **voice-mail** system digitizes a spoken message, transmits it over the network, and stores the message on disk for the receiver to retrieve later.[15] This capability allows information to be transmitted even though a receiver may not be physically present to take the information. Receivers can choose to save the message for future use, delete it, or route it to other parties.

Fax machines allow the transmission of documents containing both text and graphics over ordinary telephone lines. A sending fax machine scans and digitizes the document. A receiving fax machine reads the scanned information and reproduces it in hard copy form. Information that is best viewed in printed form can be easily and quickly shared by organizational members.

Electronic data interchange (EDI) is a way for organizations to exchange standard business transaction documents, such as invoices or purchase orders, using direct computer-to-computer networks. Organizations often use EDI with vendors, suppliers, and customers because it saves time and money. How? Information on transactions is transmitted from one organization's computer system to another through a telecommunications network. The printing and handling of paper documents at one organization are eliminated as is the inputting of data at the other organization.

Meetings—one-on-one, team, divisional, or organization-wide—have always been one way to share information. The limitations of technology used to dictate that meetings take place among people in the same physical location, but that's no longer the case! **Teleconferencing** allows a group of people to confer simultaneously using telephone or e-mail group communications software. If meeting participants can see each other over video screens, the simultaneous conference is called **videoconferencing**. Work groups, large and small, which might be in different locations, can use these communication network tools to collaborate and share information.

Networked computer systems have allowed the development of organizational intranets and extranets. An **intranet** is an organizational communication network that uses Internet technology and is accessible only by organizational employees. Many organizations are using intranets as ways for employees to share information and collaborate on documents and projects from different locations. For example, through the intranet at Buckman Laboratories International, a manufacturer of specialty chemicals based in Memphis, Tennessee, employees find information about products, markets, and customers that's easily accessible and easily shared. They contribute information to and pull information from this knowledge network known as K'Netix®. An **extranet** is an organizational communication network that uses Internet technology and allows authorized users inside the organization to communicate with certain outsiders such as customers or vendors. For instance, Harley-Davidson has developed an extranet that allows faster and more convenient communications with dealers.

Finally, we're all aware of the tremendous impact that the Internet has had and continues to have on organizations. Now, instead of being a communication medium just for text, colorful graphics, and the occasional music and video clip, the Internet is being used for voice communication. Popular Web sites such as Yahoo! and Exite@Home let users chat verbally with each other. America Online has introduced a Web browser that lets users click on a button to talk to others. Many companies are moving to Internet-based voice communication. For instance, in the New Jersey offices of Merrill Lynch & Co., 6,500 Internet phones have been installed for employees to use in conference calls or for instant messaging communication. On Compaq Computer Corporation's Web site, visitors can click on an icon and speak live to a company representative.[16]

Wireless Capabilities While the communication possibilities for a manager in a networked world are exciting, the real potential is yet to come! Networked computer systems require organizations (and organizational employees) to be connected by wires. Wireless communication depends on signals sent through air or space without any physical connection using things such as microwave signals, satellites, radio waves and radio antennas, or infrared light rays. Wireless smart phones, notebook computers, and other pocket communication devices have spawned a whole new way for managers to "keep in touch." In Japan and Europe, over 9 million users have wireless technology that allows them to send and receive information from anywhere.[17] Employees don't have to be at their desks with their computers plugged in and turned on in order to communicate with others in the organization. As technology continues to improve in this area, we'll see more and more organizational members using wireless communication as a way to collaborate and share information.

HOW INFORMATION TECHNOLOGY AFFECTS ORGANIZATIONS

Employees—working in teams or as individuals—need information to make decisions and do their work. After describing the communications capabilities managers have at their disposal, it's clear that technology *can* significantly affect the way that organizational members communicate, share information, and do their work.

Communications and the exchange of information among organizational members are no longer constrained by geography or time. Collaborative work efforts among widely dispersed individuals and teams, sharing of information, and integration of decisions and work throughout an entire organization have the potential to increase organizational efficiency and effectiveness. And while the economic benefits of information technology are obvious, managers must not forget to address the psychological drawbacks.[18] For instance, what is the psychological cost of an employee being constantly accessible? Will there be increased pressure for employees to "check in" even during their off-hours? How important is it for employees to separate their work lives and their personal lives? While there are no easy answers to these questions, they are issues that managers will have to face.

Just one example of the way in which the Internet has dramatically changed the gathering, sharing, and storing of information is the handiwork of Boeing's Barbara Claitman, director of e-business for the firm's commercial aviation division. In May 2000, Boeing began offering airlines an information-packed interactive Web site called myboeingfleet.com, which contains the same information Boeing's customers used to receive in the form of mountains of paper. Now, along with technical manuals, parts lists, and other maintenance documents, airlines can find links to news sources and chat rooms for discussing maintenance issues. In addition to making it possible to save millions of dollars a year in printing and mailing costs, the Web site's two-way flow of communication might enable Boeing to track changes its customers make to its planes after they leave the factory. That could result in greater safety in the air.

13. **Describe the various communication applications made possible by networked computer systems.**
14. **What impact is wireless communication technology having on managerial communication?**
15. **How is information technology affecting organizations?**

Testing...Testing...1,2,3

Managers Respond to "A Manager's Dilemma"

Michael J. Stabile, Ph.D.

Principal, Nagel Middle School, Cincinnati, Ohio

Jeff Sneed

Customer Service Manager, LaserWorks, Inc., Springfield, Missouri

Sometimes the "antidote can become the poison." Tom's leadership style, as effective and successful as it has been in the past, may not be practical for the type of employees he currently has. Open management style is not the issue—it is the communication process and perception of his employees. I would suggest he try the following:

- He needs to talk the language(s) of his employees through memorandums and other written directives. By communicating in his employees' native languages, he shows that he is interested in them.

- He needs to understand the culture(s) of his workers and what they value and what motivates them. Again, this type of personal interest in employees can be beneficial for Tom when he needs to communicate changes to them.

- He needs to find individuals with leadership potential from the diverse work group who could communicate and translate company goals and plans. By involving capable employees, Tom can improve the total communication in the work situation.

If I were Tom, I would definitely make some changes in order to communicate with my employees. Without question, their efficiency will be greatly reduced if they didn't understand the message I was trying to relay.

What I would do first is pick out the employees that I felt spoke the best English and try to communicate with them individually. By getting the employees in a more one-on-one situation, I think they would be more comfortable and more likely to actually understand and not just say they do. These individuals could then act as team leaders and explain the information to other employees who speak the same language, making sure that they comprehend it.

Another possibility would be to use a language translator—there are many Web sites with this capability. Tom could type a memo stating what he was trying to communicate and the Web site would translate the memo into the necessary languages.

Chapter Summary

This summary is organized by the chapter-opening objectives found on p. 280.

1. Communication is the transfer and understanding of meaning. Managerial communication encompasses both interpersonal communication—communication between two or more people—and organizational communication—all the patterns, networks, and systems of communication within an organization.

2. The communication process starts with a purpose, expressed as a message. This message is converted to symbolic form (called encoding) and passed by way of some medium (channel) to the receiver who retranslates the sender's message (called decoding). The entire process is susceptible to noise—disturbances that interfere with the transmission, receipt, or feedback of a message.

3. Communication methods can be compared on the basis of feedback potential, complexity capacity, breadth potential, confidentiality, encoding ease, decoding ease, time-space constraint, cost, personal warmth, formality, scanability, and consumption time. Which communication method (face-to-face, telephone, group meetings, formal presentations, memos, postal mail, fax, publications, bulletin boards, audio/videotapes, hot lines, e-mail, computer conference, voice mail, teleconference, or videoconference) a manager ultimately chooses, depends on the needs of the sender, the attributes of the message, the attributes of the channel, and the needs of the receiver.

4. Nonverbal communication is communication transmitted without words and is reflected by body language and verbal intonation. It affects managers because every oral communication has a nonverbal message as well. That nonverbal message usually carries the greatest impact.

5. The barriers to effective interpersonal communication include filtering (deliberately manipulating information to make it appear more favorable), selective perception (selectively interpreting what we see or hear based on our interests, background, experience, and attitudes), emotions, information overload (information received exceeds our processing capacity), defensiveness, language, and national culture. Overcoming the barriers involves using feedback, simplifying language, listening actively, constraining emotions, and watching nonverbal cues.

6. Organizational communication can flow in four ways. Downward communication is any communication that flows downward from manager to employees. Upward communication is communication that flows upward from employees to manager. Lateral communication is communication that takes place among employees on the same organizational level. Diagonal communication is communication that cuts across both work areas and organizational levels. There are three common organizational communication networks: the chain, the wheel, and the all-channel networks. In addition, managers must recognize the grapevine—the informal organizational communication network.

7. Two developments in information technology that have impacted managerial communication include networked computer systems and wireless capabilities. Some of the communication applications of networked computer systems include e-mail, instant messaging, voice mail, fax machines, electronic data interchange, teleconferencing and videoconferencing, intranets and extranets, and Internet voice communications. Wireless communications mean that organizational members don't have to be plugged into the computer network to send and receive information.

8. Information technology affects organizations through the way that organizational members communicate, share information, and do their work. Communication and the exchange of information among organizational members are no longer constrained by geography or time.

Thinking About Management Issues

1. Why isn't effective communication synonymous with *agreement*?

2. Which do you think is more important for the manager: speaking accurately or listening actively? Why?

3. "Ineffective communication is the fault of the sender." Do you agree or disagree with this statement? Discuss.

4. How might managers use the grapevine for their benefit?

5. Is information technology helping managers be more effective and efficient? Explain your answer.

Log On: Internet-Based Exercise

There's no doubt that managers *and* organizations need to communicate effectively. Look for the best example of poor organizational communication you can find on a company's Web site. Now, look for the best example of good organizational communication you can find on a company's Web site. How are the two different? What makes the one example "poor" communication, and what makes the other example "good" communication?

Now, find five companies whose primary business is helping organizational employees improve their interpersonal communication skills. What common characteristics, if any, did you find in the programs these companies offer?

myPHLIP Companion Web Site

myPHLIP **(www.prenhall.com/myphlip)** *is a fully customizable homepage that ties students and faculty to text-specific resources.*
- *For students*, *myPHLIP provides an online study guide tied chapter-by-chapter to the text—current events and Internet exercises, lecture notes, downloadable software, the Career Center, the Writing Center, Ask the Tutor, and more.*
- *For faculty*, *myPHLIP provides a syllabus tool that allows you to manage content, communicate with students, and upload personal resources.*

Working Together: Team-Based Exercise

Form groups of five or six individuals. Each group should choose one person to remain in the room while the other members of each group leave the room. Your instructor will give you instructions on what happens next.

After the exercise is over, each group should discuss where communication errors (both in sending and receiving information) occurred. You should also discuss what you learned about managerial communication from this exercise. Be prepared to share your important ideas with the class.

Case Application

Miscommunications Lead to Tragedies

When managers or employees miscommunicate information, it may create organizational or work problems, but most of the time there are no serious or tragic consequences associated with the miscommunication. But in the airline industry, miscommunications can be deadly as all too many recent examples illustrate. Consider the following events.

Alaska Airlines Flight 261 plunged into the waters off the coast of California in February 2000 killing all 88 people onboard. Probes into the crash focused on certain written maintenance records that were inadequately filled out. Crash investigators focused on the possibility that the results of a 1997 service test on the plane's jackscrew, a part of the horizontal stabilizer that helps keep a plane level, had been altered to allow the plane to return to service quickly.

In September 1997, a Garuda Airlines jetliner crashed into a jungle, just 20 miles south of the Medan Airport on the island of Sumatra. All 234 people aboard were killed. The cause of this disaster was the pilot and the air traffic controller confusing the words "left" and "right" as the plane approached the airport under extremely poor visibility conditions.

On December 20, 1995, American Airlines Flight 965 was approaching the Cali, Colombia, airport. The pilot expected to hear either the words "cleared as filed" (meaning he was to follow the flight plan filed before leaving Miami) or "cleared direct" (meaning fly straight from where you are to Cali, a slightly different route from the filed flight plan). The controller intended to clear the flight "as filed" but said "cleared to Cali." The pilot interpreted that as a direct clearance. When he checked back, the controller said "affirmative." On the final approach to the airport, the plane crashed into a mountain, killing 160 people.

Clear communication is critical in air traffic control work.

In 1993, Chinese pilots flying a U.S.-built MD-80 tried to land in heavy fog at Urumqi, in northwest China. They were puzzled by an audio alarm from the jet's ground proximity warning system, which alerts pilots that they're approaching the ground too quickly. Just before impact, the cockpit recorder recorded one crew member saying to the other in Chinese: "What does 'pull up' mean?" The plane hit power lines and crashed, killing 12 people.

In 1990, pilots on a Colombian airline Avianca flight told controllers as they neared New York Kennedy Airport that their Boeing 707 was "running low on fuel" after several holding patterns caused by bad weather. Controllers hear those words all the time so they took no special action. While the pilots knew there was a serious problem, they failed to use a key phrase—"fuel emergency"—that would have compelled controllers to direct the Avianca flight ahead of all others and clear it to land as soon as possible. In addition, the vocal tone of the pilots didn't convey the severity or urgency of the fuel problem to the air traffic controllers. The controllers at Kennedy never understood the true crisis facing the pilots. The jet ran out of fuel and crashed 16 miles from the airport, killing 73 people.

Finally, history's deadliest aviation disaster occurred in 1977 at Tenerife in the Canary Islands. On a particularly foggy evening, the captain of a KLM flight thought the air traffic controller had cleared him to take off. But the controller intended only to give departure instructions. Although the language spoken between the Dutch KLM captain and the Spanish controller was English, the heavy accents and improper terminology created confusion. The KLM Boeing 747 hit a Pan Am 747 at full throttle on the runway—a disaster caused by miscommunication that killed a total of 583 people.

All these examples illustrate how miscommunication can have tragic consequences. Although the circumstances of most managerial communication aren't as dramatic as these, the fact remains that good communication is essential to any group's or organization's effectiveness.

QUESTIONS

1. What barriers to communication do you see in these examples? How might these barriers have been overcome?

2. Would nonverbal communication play a role in the miscommunications between pilots and air traffic controllers? Explain.

3. How could active listening have prevented these crashes? Be specific.

4. As our chapter-opening Manager's Dilemma demonstrated and as this case illustrates, language can be a definite communication barrier. What are the implications for managers who manage diverse work groups in which employees may not speak the native language as fluently?

Sources: Information from ABC News.com Web site (www.abcnews.go.com), September 13, 2000; S. Carey, "Alaska Air Aims to Restore Credibility After Plane Crash," *Wall Street Journal*, April 28, 2000, p. B4; A. Kotarumalos, "Pilot Confused Before Deadly Jetliner Crash," *Seattle Post-Intelligencer*, September 30, 1997, p. A2; P. Garrison, "Can Culture Cause a Crash?," *Conde Nast Traveler*, July 1997, pp. 24–28; J. Ritter, "Poor Fluency in English Means Mixed Signals," *USA Today*, January 18, 1996, p. 1A; and E. Weiner, "Right Word Is Crucial in Air Control," *New York Times*, January 29, 1990, p. B5.

Mastering Management

In Episode 12 of the Mastering Management *series, you'll see the importance of effective communication to successful management. The management team at CanGo learns that they must be much clearer in their communication, particularly with new employees.*

Learning Objectives

After reading and studying this chapter, you should be able to:

1. Explain the strategic importance of human resource management.

2. Describe the human resource management process.

3. Differentiate between job descriptions and job specifications.

4. Contrast recruitment and decruitment options.

5. Describe the selection devices that work best with various kinds of jobs.

6. Identify the various training categories.

7. Explain the various approaches to performance appraisal.

8. Describe what an organization's compensation system should include.

9. Discuss the current issues affecting human resource management.

A MANAGER'S DILEMMA

As a new breed of entrepreneur in Europe, Eric Perbos-Brinck (standing in background in photo) gave up a promising management career at the large French retailer, Promodes, to start an Internet company called Bravonestor.com (www.bravonestor.com).[1] Like any new entrepreneur, Perbos-Brinck has struggled to get his business up and running.

One challenge Perbos-Brinck faced was the traditional inward-looking French culture. Although France is a member of the European Union (EU) and supports free trade among EU members, it remains a very nationalistic and proud country. A growing class of rebels, including Perbos-Brinck, has an outlook that embraces the globe, not just France or Europe. These new thinkers are independent, favor individual enterprise, question authority, and are using the realities of the new economy to shake up the way French business traditionally has been conducted. One tradition, though, has been hard to change, and it's creating quite a problem for Perbos-Brinck's business.

That tradition is the European mentality about immigration. Historically, Europeans have been passionately opposed to immigrants. However, the strong European economy, with declining unemployment levels and business leaders pushing to catch up with the United States in high technology, has created a situation where this parochialistic attitude may no longer be realistic.

CHAPTER TWELVE

Human Resource Management

12

When Perbos-Brinck launched his business in November 1999, the only employees were himself and another person. Six months later, that number had grown to 10 with five more individuals hired in early summer 2000. To fill the jobs with employees who have the necessary skills for working in an e-business, Perbos-Brinck has had to cast a wide net. One of his programmers is Moroccan. His search engine designer is Senegalese. Perbos-Brinck found these two, who were studying in France as part of an exchange program, after an intense employee search. As Perbos-Brinck continues to bring highly skilled people from various countries on board, he needs an effective employee orientation program to help them assimilate into his company as well as the French culture. Put yourself in his position. What should this orientation program include?

WHAT WOULD YOU DO?

The challenge facing Eric Perbos-Brinck of orienting his diverse employees to his company and to the French culture reflects only a small aspect of the human resource management (HRM) challenges facing today's managers. If an organization doesn't take its HRM responsibilities seriously, work performance and goal accomplishment may suffer. The quality of an organization is, to a large degree, merely the summation of the quality of people it hires and keeps. Getting and keeping competent employees are critical to the success of every organization, whether the organization is just starting or has been in business for years. Therefore, part of every manager's job in the organizing function is human resource management.

❯ WHY HUMAN RESOURCE MANAGEMENT IS IMPORTANT

high-performance work practices

Work practices that lead to both high individual and high organizational performance.

John Yokoyama, owner of Pike Place Fish Market in Seattle, knows first-hand the value of treating his employees like partners in his business. Having created an environment in which he could "give employees and customers the best experience they've ever had," Yokoyama enjoys intense employee loyalty. One recent January, when business was slow, he suggested shortening workers' hours to cut costs. Instead, Pike Place employees came back with a telemarketing plan they had created themselves and set a record high for January sales.

"Our people are our most important asset." Many organizations are using this phrase, or something close to it, to acknowledge the important role that employees play in organizational success. These organizations also recognize that *all* managers must engage in some human resource management activities—even in large organizations that have a specialized HRM department. These managers interview job candidates, orient new employees, and evaluate their employees' work performance.

Can HRM be an important strategic tool? *Can* it help establish an organization's sustainable competitive advantage? The answers to these questions seem to be yes. Various studies have concluded that an organization's human resources can be a significant source of competitive advantage.[2]

Achieving competitive success through people requires a fundamental change in how managers think about their employees and how they view the work relationship. It involves working with and through people and seeing them as partners, not just as costs to be minimized or avoided. That's what organizations such as Southwest Airlines, Cisco Systems, and Timberland are doing. In addition to their potential importance as part of organizational strategy and contribution to competitive advantage, an organization's HRM practices have been found to have a significant impact on organizational performance.

Studies that have looked at the link between HRM policies and practices and organizational performance have found that certain policies and practices have a positive impact on performance.[3] What type of positive impact? One study reported that significantly improving an organization's HRM practices could increase its market value by as much as 30 percent.[4] The term used to describe these practices that lead to such results is **high-performance work practices**. High-performance work practices can lead to both high individual and high organizational performance. Exhibit 12.1 lists examples of high-performance work practices. The common thread in these practices seems to be a commitment to improving the knowledge, skills, and abilities of an organization's

• Self-directed work teams	• Implementation of employee suggestions	**Exhibit 12.1**
• Job rotation	• Contingent pay based on performance	
• High levels of skills training	• Coaching and mentoring	**Examples of High-Performance Work Practices**
• Problem-solving groups	• Significant amounts of information sharing	
• Total quality management procedures and processes	• Use of employee attitude surveys	
• Encouragement of innovative and creative behavior	• Cross-functional integration	
• Extensive employee involvement and training	• Comprehensive employee recruitment and selection procedures	

Source: Based on M. Huselid, "The Impact of Human Resource Management Practices on Turnover, Productivity, and Corporate Financial Performance," *Academy of Management Journal*, June 1995, p. 635; and B. Becker and B. Gerhart, "The Impact of Human Resource Management on Organizational Performance: Progress and Prospects," *Academy of Management Journal*, August 1996, p. 785.

employees, increasing their motivation, reducing loafing on the job, and enhancing the retention of quality employees while encouraging nonperformers to leave.

Whether an organization chooses to implement high-performance work practices or not, there are certain HRM activities that must be completed in order to ensure that the organization has qualified people to perform the work that needs to be done. These activities constitute the human resource management process.

❭ THE HUMAN RESOURCE MANAGEMENT PROCESS

Exhibit 12.2 introduces the key components of an organization's **human resource management process**, which consists of eight activities necessary for staffing the organization and sustaining high employee performance. The first three activities

human resource management process

Activities necessary for staffing the organization and sustaining high employee performance.

Exhibit 12.2   **The Human Resource Management Process**

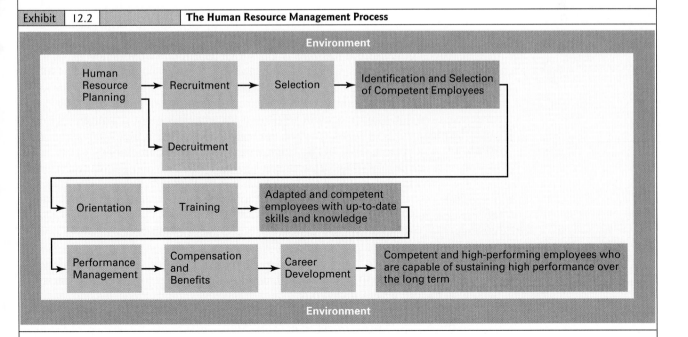

U.S. unions are broadening their goals and looking abroad. The American Union of Needle Trades Industrial & Textile Employees recently lobbied successfully for an agreement in which the United States will import more textiles from Cambodia and the Cambodian government will let foreign monitors inspect the country's factories, such as this one, to ensure that working conditions are being improved.

labor union

An organization that represents workers and seeks to protect their interests through collective bargaining.

affirmative action

Programs that enhance the organizational status of members of protected groups.

ensure that competent employees are identified and selected; the next two activities involve providing employees with up-to-date knowledge and skills; and the final three activities entail making sure that the organization retains competent and high-performing employees who are capable of sustaining high performance.

Notice in Exhibit 12.2 that the entire HRM process is influenced by the external environment. We elaborated on the constraints that the environment puts on managers in Chapter 3, but let's briefly review those environmental factors that most directly influence the HRM process—employee labor unions and governmental laws and regulations.

A **labor union** is an organization that represents workers and seeks to protect their interests through collective bargaining. In unionized organizations, many HRM decisions are regulated by the terms of collective agreements. These agreements usually define such things as recruitment sources; criteria for hiring, promotions, and layoffs; training eligibility; and disciplinary practices. Although only about 13.9 percent of the workforce in the United States is unionized, that percentage is higher in other countries. In Japan and Germany, respectively, 24.1 percent and 32.1 percent of the labor force belong to a union. And in Mexico an estimated 25 percent of workers belong to a union.[5] Although labor unions can significantly affect an organization's HRM practices, no environmental constraint can match the influence of governmental laws and regulations, especially in North America.

The federal government has greatly expanded its influence over HRM by enacting a number of laws and regulations (see Exhibit 12.3 for examples). As a result, today's employers must ensure that equal employment opportunities exist for job applicants and current employees. Decisions regarding who will be hired, for instance, or which employees will be chosen for a management training program must be made without regard to race, sex, religion, age, color, national origin, or disability. Exceptions can occur only when special circumstances exist. For instance, a community fire department can deny employment to a firefighter applicant who is confined to a wheelchair, but if that same individual is applying for a desk job, such as a fire department dispatcher, the disability cannot be used as a reason to deny employment. The issues involved, however, are rarely that clear-cut. For example, employment laws protect most employees whose religious beliefs require a specific style of dress—robes, long shirts, long hair, and the like. However, if the specific style of dress may be hazardous or unsafe in the work setting (e.g., when operating machinery), a company could refuse to hire a person who won't adopt a safer dress code.[6]

Trying to balance the "shoulds and should-nots" of these laws often falls within the realm of **affirmative action**. Many organizations have affirmative

Year	Law or Regulation	Description
1963	Equal Pay Act	Prohibits pay differences based on sex for equal work
1964	Civil Rights Act, Title VII (amended in 1972)	Prohibits discrimination based on race, color, religion, national origin, or sex
1967	Age Discrimination in Employment Act	Prohibits age discrimination against employees between 40 and 65 years of age
1973	Vocational Rehabilitation Act	Prohibits discrimination on the basis of physical or mental disabilities
1974	Privacy Act	Gives employees the legal right to examine personnel files and letters of reference concerning them
1978	Mandatory Retirement Act	Prohibits the forced retirement of most employees before the age of 70; upper limit on age was removed in 1986
1986	Immigration Reform and Control Act	Prohibits unlawful employment of aliens and unfair immigration-related employment practices
1988	Polygraph Protection Act	Limits an employer's ability to use lie detectors
1988	Worker Adjustment and Retraining Notification Act	Requires employers with 100 or more employees to provide 60 days' notice before a facility closing or mass layoff
1990	Americans with Disabilities Act	Prohibits employers from discriminating against individuals with physical or mental disabilities or the chronically ill; also requires organizations to reasonably accommodate these individuals
1991	Civil Rights Act of 1991	Reaffirms and tightens prohibition of discrimination; permits individuals to sue for punitive damages in cases of intentional discrimination
1993	Family and Medical Leave Act of 1993	Permits employees in organizations with 50 or more workers to take up to 12 weeks of unpaid leave each year for family or medical reasons

Exhibit 12.3

Major U.S. Federal Laws and Regulations Related to HRM

action programs to ensure that decisions and practices enhance the employment, upgrading, and retention of members from protected groups such as minorities and females. That is, the organization not only refrains from discrimination but actively seeks to enhance the status of members from protected groups.

Managers are not completely free to choose whom they hire, promote, or fire. Although these laws and regulations have significantly helped to reduce employment discrimination and unfair employment practices, they have, at the same time, reduced managers' discretion over human resource decisions. ◄──────

Testing...Testing...1,2,3

1. **What strategic importance does HRM have for organizations?**

2. **List the eight steps in the HRM process.**

3. **How does the external environment affect the HRM process?**

> ## HUMAN RESOURCE PLANNING

Human resource planning is the process by which managers ensure that they have the right number and kinds of people in the right places, and at the right times, who are capable of effectively and efficiently performing assigned tasks. HR planning can be condensed into two steps: (1) assessing current human resources and (2) assessing future human resource needs and developing a program to meet those future needs.

human resource planning

The process by which managers ensure that they have the right number and kinds of people in the right places, and at the right times, who are capable of effectively and efficiently performing assigned tasks.

CURRENT ASSESSMENT

Managers begin HR planning by reviewing the organization's current human resource status, usually through a *human resource inventory*. This information is derived from forms filled out by employees, which includes items such as name, education, training, prior employment, languages spoken, special capabilities, and specialized skills. The availability of sophisticated databases makes keeping and getting this information quite easy.

Another part of the current assessment is the **job analysis**, which is an assessment that defines jobs and the behaviors necessary to perform them. For instance, what are the duties of a purchasing specialist, level 3, who works for Boise Cascade? What minimal knowledge, skills, and abilities are necessary to be able to adequately perform this job? How do these requirements compare with those for a level 2 purchasing specialist, or for a purchasing manager? Information for a job analysis can be gathered through the following methods: directly observing or filming individuals on the job, interviewing employees individually or in a group, having employees complete a structured questionnaire, having job "experts" (usually managers) identify a job's specific characteristics, and having employees record their daily activities in a diary or notebook.

With information from the job analysis, managers develop or revise job descriptions and job specifications. A **job description** is a written statement of what a jobholder does, how it is done, and why it is done. It typically describes job content, environment, and conditions of employment. A **job specification** states the minimum qualifications that a person must possess to perform a given job successfully. It identifies the knowledge, skills, and attitudes needed to do the job effectively. Both the job description and specification are important documents when managers begin recruiting and selecting.

job analysis

An assessment that defines jobs and the behaviors necessary to perform them.

job description

A written statement of what a jobholder does, how it is done, and why it is done.

job specification

A statement of the minimum qualifications that a person must possess to perform a given job successfully.

Conditions of employment, such as the number of hours worked per week, are an important part of most job descriptions. The French government recently passed a law requiring companies in France to reduce the workweek to 35 hours. The move was protested by some who fear it will reduce productivity instead of accomplishing its intended purpose, helping to lower France's unemployment rate.

MEETING FUTURE HUMAN RESOURCE NEEDS

Future human resource needs are determined by the organization's goals and strategies. Demand for employees is a result of demand for the organization's products or services. On the basis of its estimate of total revenue, managers can attempt to establish the number and mix of employees needed to reach that revenue. In some cases, however, that situation may be reversed. When particular skills are necessary but in short supply, the availability of appropriate human resources determines revenues.

After they have assessed both current capabilities and future needs, managers are able to estimate HR shortages—both in number and in type—and to highlight areas in which the organization will be understaffed or overstaffed. With this information, managers are ready to proceed to the next step in the HRM process.

› RECRUITMENT AND DECRUITMENT

Once managers know their current human resource status and their future needs, they can begin to do something about any inconsistencies. If one or more vacancies exist, they can use the information gathered through job analysis to guide them in **recruitment**—that is, the process of locating, identifying, and attracting capable applicants.[7] On the other hand, if HR planning shows a surplus of employees, management may want to reduce the organization's workforce through **decruitment**.[8]

RECRUITMENT

Potential job candidates can be found by using several sources, including the Internet. Exhibit 12.4 explains these sources. The source that's used is influenced by three factors: (1) the local labor market—it's generally easier to recruit in large labor markets; (2) the type or level of position—the more specialized the position, the more that recruitments efforts might have to be regional or national searches; and (3) the size of the organization—in general, the larger the organization, the easier it is to recruit.

Do certain recruiting sources produce superior candidates? The answer is generally "yes." The majority of studies have found that employee referrals generally produce the best candidates.[9] The explanation is intuitively logical. First, applicants referred by current employees are prescreened by these employees. Because the recommenders know both the job and the person being recommended, they tend to

recruitment

The process of locating, identifying, and attracting capable applicants.

decruitment

Techniques for reducing the labor supply within an organization.

Source	Advantages	Disadvantages
Internal search	Low cost; builds employee morale; candidates are familiar with organization	Limited supply; may not increase proportion of employees from protected groups
Advertisements	Wide distribution; can be targeted to specific groups	Generates many unqualified candidates
Employee referrals	Knowledge about the organization provided by current employee; can generate strong candidates because a good referral reflects on the recommender	May not increase the diversity and mix of employees
Public employment agencies	Free or nominal cost	Candidates tend to be unskilled or minimally trained
Private employment agencies	Wide contacts; careful screening; short-term guarantees often given	High cost
School placement	Large, centralized body of candidates	Limited to entry-level positions
Temporary help services	Fills temporary needs	Expensive; may have limited understanding of organization's overall goals and activities
Employee leasing and independent contractors	Fills temporary needs, but usually for more specific, longer-term projects	Little commitment to organization other than current project
Web-based advertising	Reaches large numbers of people; can get immediate feedback	Generates many unqualified candidates

Exhibit 12.4

Major Sources of Potential Job Candidates

Exhibit 12.5	Option	Description
Decruitment Options	Firing	Permanent involuntary termination
	Layoffs	Temporary involuntary termination; may last only a few days or extend to years
	Attrition	Not filling openings created by voluntary resignations or normal retirements
	Transfers	Moving employees either laterally or downward; usually does not reduce costs but can reduce intraorganizational supply-demand imbalances
	Reduced workweeks	Having employees work fewer hours per week, share jobs, or perform their jobs on a part-time basis
	Early retirements	Providing incentives to older and more senior employees for retiring before their normal retirement date
	Job sharing	Having employees share one full-time position

refer applicants who are well qualified. Also, because current employees often feel that their reputation is at stake with a referral, they tend to refer others only when they are reasonably confident that the referral will not make them look bad.

DECRUITMENT

The other approach to controlling labor supply is the process of decruitment. In the last decade, many large U.S. corporations, government agencies, and small businesses have reduced the size of their workforce or restructured their skill base.[10] Downsizing is a way to meet the demands of a dynamic environment. For instance, through mergers designed to make themselves more competitive globally, companies such as DaimlerChrysler and ExxonMobil have cut thousands of jobs.

Decruitment is not a pleasant task for any manager. The decruitment options are shown in Exhibit 12.5. Obviously people can be fired, but other choices may be more beneficial to the organization. Keep in mind that, regardless of the method used to reduce the number of employees in the organization, there is no easy way to do it, even though it may be absolutely necessary.

Testing...Testing...1,2,3

4. **Why is a job analysis important for the job description and job specification?**

5. **What are possible recruitment sources?**

6. **What is decruitment?**

> **SELECTION**

Once the recruiting effort has developed a pool of candidates, the next step in the HRM process is to determine who is best qualified for the job. This step is called the **selection process**, the process of screening job applicants to ensure that the most appropriate candidates are hired.

selection process

The process of screening job applicants to ensure that the most appropriate candidates are hired.

WHAT IS SELECTION?

Selection is an exercise in prediction. It seeks to predict which applicants will be successful if hired. Successful in this case means performing well on the criteria the organization uses to evaluate employees. In filling a sales position, for example, the selection process should be able to predict which applicants will generate a high volume of sales; for a position as a network administrator, it should predict which applicants will be able to effectively install, debug, and manage the organization's computer network.

Exhibit 12.6

Selection Decision Outcomes

	Selection Decision	
	Accept	**Reject**
Successful	Correct decision	Reject error
Unsuccessful	Accept error	Correct decision

Later Job Performance

Consider, for a moment, that any selection decision can result in four possible outcomes. As shown in Exhibit 12.6, two of these outcomes would be correct, and two would indicate errors.

A decision is correct when the applicant was predicted to be successful and proved to be successful on the job, or when the applicant was predicted to be unsuccessful and would perform accordingly if hired. In the first case, we have successfully accepted; in the second case, we have successfully rejected.

Problems arise when errors are made in rejecting candidates who would have performed successfully on the job (reject errors) or accepting those who ultimately perform poorly (accept errors). These problems can be significant. Given today's HR laws and regulations, reject errors can cost more than the additional screening needed to find acceptable candidates. They can expose the organization to charges of discrimination, especially if applicants from protected groups are disproportionately rejected. The costs of accept errors include the cost of training the employee, the profits lost because of the employee's incompetence, the cost of severance, and the subsequent costs of further recruiting and selection screening. The major thrust of any selection activity should be to reduce the probability of making reject errors or accept errors while increasing the probability of making correct decisions. Managers do this by using selection procedures that are both valid and reliable.

VALIDITY AND RELIABILITY

Any selection device that a manager uses should demonstrate **validity**. That is, there must be a proven relationship between the selection device and some relevant criterion. For example, the law prohibits managers from using a test score as a selection device unless there is clear evidence that, once on the job, individuals with high scores on this test outperform individuals with low test scores. The burden is on managers to support that any selection device they use to differentiate applicants is related to job performance.

In addition to being valid, a selection device must also demonstrate **reliability**, which indicates whether the device measures the same thing consistently. For example, if a test is reliable, any single individual's score should remain fairly consistent over time, assuming that the characteristics the test is measuring are also stable. No selection device can be effective if it is low in reliability. Using such a device would be like weighing yourself every day on an erratic scale. If the scale is unreli-

validity

The proven relationship that exists between a selection device and some relevant job criterion.

reliability

The ability of a selection device to measure the same thing consistently.

able—randomly fluctuating, say 10 to 15 pounds every time you step on it—the results will not mean much. To be effective predictors, selection devices must possess an acceptable level of consistency.

TYPES OF SELECTION DEVICES

Managers can use a number of selection devices to reduce accept and reject errors. The best-known devices include an analysis of the applicant's completed application form, written and performance-simulation tests, interviews, background investigations, and in some cases, a physical examination. Let's briefly review each of these devices. Exhibit 12.7 lists the strengths and weaknesses of each.[11]

Exhibit	12.7

Selection Devices

The Application Form
Strengths:
- Relevant biographical data and facts that can be verified have been shown to be valid performance measures for some jobs.
- When items on the form have been weighted to reflect job relatedness, this device has proved to be a valid predictor for diverse groups.

Weaknesses:
- Usually only a couple of items on the form prove to be valid predictors of job performance and then only for a specific job.
- Weighted-item applications are difficult and expensive to create and maintain.

Written Tests
Strengths:
- Tests of intellectual ability, spatial and mechanical ability, perceptual accuracy, and motor ability are moderately valid predictors for many semiskilled and unskilled lower-level jobs in industrial organizations.
- Intelligence tests are reasonably good predictors for supervisory positions.

Weaknesses:
- Intelligence and other tested characteristics can be somewhat removed from actual job performance, thus reducing their validity.

Performance-Simulation Tests
Strengths:
- Based on job analysis data and easily meet the requirement of job relatedness.
- Have proven to be valid predictors of job performance.

Weaknesses:
- Expensive to create and administer.

The Interview
Strengths:
- Must be structured and well organized to be effective predictors.
- Interviewers must use common questioning to be effective predictors.

Weaknesses:
- Interviewers must be aware of legality of certain questions.
- Subject to potential biases, especially if interviews are not well structured and standardized.

Background Investigations
Strengths:
- Verifications of background data are valuable sources of information.

Weaknesses:
- Reference checks are essentially worthless as a selection tool.

Physical Examination
Strengths:
- Has some validity for jobs with certain physical requirements.
- Done primarily for insurance purposes.

Weaknesses:
- Must be sure that physical requirements are job related and do not discriminate.

? THINKING CRITICALLY ABOUT ETHICS

Prospective employees commonly provide a résumé, summarizing background, education, work experiences, and accomplishments. Should it be 100 percent truthful? Is it wrong to embellish a résumé? For instance, Eva P. made $2,700 a month when she left her previous job. On her résumé, she stated that she was making $2,900. Jason E. left a job for which his job title was "credit clerk." When looking for a new position, he described his previous title as "credit analyst" because he thought it sounded more impressive. Are these "creative enhancements" wrong? What problems could such misinformation create for managers? What deviations from the truth, if any, might be acceptable when writing a résumé?

The Application Form Almost all organizations require job candidates to fill out an application. It may be only a form on which the person gives his or her name, address, and telephone number. Or it might be a comprehensive personal history profile, detailing the person's activities, skills, and accomplishments.

Written Tests Typical types of written tests include tests of intelligence, aptitude, ability, and interest. Such tests have been used for years, although their popularity tends to run in cycles. Today, personality, behavioral, and aptitude assessment tests are popular among businesses. Managers need to be careful regarding their use, however, since legal challenges against the use of such tests have been successful when they're not job related or when they elicit information concerning sex, race, age, or other areas protected by equal employment opportunity laws.[12]

Managers are aware that poor hiring decisions are costly and that properly designed tests can reduce the likelihood of making poor decisions. In addition, the cost of developing and validating a set of written tests for a specific job has decreased significantly.

Performance-Simulation Tests What better way is there to find out whether an applicant for a technical writing position at Matsushita can write technical manuals than by having him or her do it? Performance-simulation tests are made up of actual job behaviors. The best-known performance-simulation tests are work sampling and assessment centers.

Work sampling involves presenting applicants with a miniature model of a job and having them perform a task or set of tasks central to it. Applicants demonstrate that they have the necessary skills and abilities by actually doing the tasks. This type of test is appropriate for routine jobs.

Assessment centers are places in which job candidates undergo performance-simulation tests that evaluate managerial potential. In assessment centers, executives, supervisors, or trained psychologists evaluate candidates for managerial positions as they go through extensive exercises that simulate real problems they would confront on the job.[13] Activities might include interviews, in-basket problem-solving exercises, group discussions, and business decision games.

The Interview The interview, like the application form, is an almost universal selection device.[14] Not many of us have ever gotten a job without one or more interviews. However, the value of the interview as a selection device has been

work sampling

A selection device in which job applicants are presented with a miniature replica of a job and are asked to perform tasks that are central to it.

assessment centers

Places in which job candidates undergo performance-simulation tests that evaluate managerial potential.

Exhibit 12.8	1. Structure a *fixed set of questions* for all applicants.
Suggestions for Interviewing	2. Have *detailed information about the job* for which applicants are interviewing.
	3. *Minimize any prior knowledge* of applicants' background, experience, interests, test scores, or other characteristics.
	4. *Ask behavioral questions* that require applicants to give detailed accounts of actual job behaviors.
	5. Use a *standardized evaluation form.*
	6. *Take notes* during the interview.
	7. *Avoid short interviews* that encourage premature decision making.
	Source: Based on D.A. DeCenzo and S.P. Robbins, *Human Resource Management*, 6th ed. (New York: Wiley, 1999, pp. 205–06.)

widely debated.[15] Managers can make interviews more valid and reliable by following the suggestions listed in Exhibit 12.8.

Another important factor in interviewing job candidates is the legality of certain interview questions. Employment law attorneys caution managers to be extremely cautious in the types of questions they ask candidates. Exhibit 12.9 lists some examples of typical interview questions that managers *shouldn't* ask because they could expose the organization to lawsuits by job applicants.

Background Investigations Background investigations are of two types: verifications of application data and reference checks. The first type has proved to be a valuable source of selection information while the latter is essentially worthless as a selection tool because applicants' references tend to be almost universally positive. After all, a person isn't going to ask someone to write a reference if that person is likely to write a negative one.

Physical Examination This device would be useful only for a small number of jobs that have certain physical requirements. Instead, the physical examination is mostly used for insurance purposes because organizations want to be sure that new hires will not submit insurance claims for injuries or illnesses they had before being hired.

WHAT WORKS BEST AND WHEN?

Many selection devices are of limited value to managers in making selection decisions. Exhibit 12.10 summarizes the validity of these devices for particular types of jobs. Managers should use those devices that effectively predict for a given job.

Exhibit 12.9	• What is your date of birth?
Examples of Interview Questions Managers Shouldn't Ask	• Have you ever filed a workers' compensation claim?
	• What is your place of birth?
	• Do you own a home?
	• What is your native language?
	• Do you have children? Plan to have children? Have child care?
	• Do you have a physical or mental disability that would prevent you from doing this job?
	• What religion do you practice?
	Source: Based on J.S. Pauliot, "Topics to Avoid with Applicants," *Nation's Business*, July 1992, pp. 57–58; and L.M. Litvan, "Thorny Issues in Hiring," *Nation's Business*, April 1996, pp. 34–36.

Selection Device	Senior Management	Middle and Lower Management	Complex Nonmanagerial	Routine Work
		Position		
Application form	2	2	2	2
Written tests	1	1	2	3
Work samples	—	—	4	4
Assessment center	5	5	—	—
Interviews	4	3	2	2
Verification of application data	3	3	3	3
Reference checks	1	1	1	1
Physical exam	1	1	1	2

Note: Validity is measured on a scale from 5 (highest) to 1 (lowest). A dash means "not applicable."

Exhibit 12.10

Quality of Selection Devices as Predictors

realistic job preview (RJP)

A preview of a job that provides both positive and negative information about the job and the company.

In addition, managers who treat the recruiting and hiring of employees as if the applicants must be sold on the job and exposed only to an organization's positive characteristics are likely to have a workforce that is dissatisfied and prone to high turnover.[16]

During the hiring process, every job applicant develops a set of expectations about the company and about the job for which he or she is interviewing. When the information an applicant receives is excessively inflated, a number of things happen that have potentially negative effects on the company. First, mismatched applicants are less likely to withdraw from the selection process. Second, because inflated information builds unrealistic expectations, new employees are likely to become quickly dissatisfied and to leave the organization. Third, new hires are prone to becoming disillusioned and less committed to the organization when they face the unexpected harsh realities of the job. In many cases, these individuals may feel that they were misled during the hiring process and may become problem employees.

To increase job satisfaction among employees and reduce turnover, you should consider providing a **realistic job preview (RJP)**. An RJP includes both positive and negative information about the job and the company. For instance, in addition to the positive comments typically expressed during an interview, the job applicant might be told that there are limited opportunities to talk to co-workers during work hours, that promotional advancement is slim, or that work hours fluctuate so erratically that employees may be required to work during what are usually off-hours (nights and weekends). Research indicates that applicants who have been given a realistic job preview hold lower and more realistic job expectations for the jobs they will be performing and are better able to cope with the frustrating elements of the job than are applicants who have been given only inflated information. The result is fewer unexpected resignations by new employees.

Realistic job previews include both good and potentially bad news about the company and the position it seeks to fill. At A. C. Nielsen, such a preview would include the information that employees have a say in the bonuses managers earn. Chief financial officer Robert Chrenc and senior vice president Althea DeBrule find that this participation has increased employee satisfaction by 50 percent.

Testing...Testing...1,2,3

7. What is the major intent of any selection activity?

8. Describe the advantages and disadvantages of the various selection devices.

9. Why is a realistic job preview important?

〉 ORIENTATION

Did you participate in some type of organized "introduction to college life" when you started school? If you did, you may have been told about your school's rules and regulations, the procedures for activities such as applying for financial aid or cashing a check or registering for classes, and you were probably introduced to some of the college administrators. A person starting a new job needs the same type of introduction to his or her job and the organization. This introduction is called **orientation**.

orientation

Introduction of a new employee to his or her job and the organization.

There are two types of orientation. *Work unit orientation* familiarizes the employee with the goals of the work unit, clarifies how his or her job contributes to the unit's goals, and includes an introduction to his or her new co-workers. *Organization orientation* informs the new employee about the organization's objectives, history, philosophy, procedures, and rules. This should include relevant human resource policies and benefits such as work hours, pay procedures, overtime requirements, and fringe benefits. In addition, a tour of the organization's work facilities is often part of the organization orientation.

" MANAGERS SPEAK OUT "

Suzanne J. Cohen, Deputy Director, National Neurofibromatosis Foundation, New York, NY (on right in photo)

Describe your job.

I'm the deputy director of the National Neurofibromatosis Foundation, a national nonprofit organization. My role is to manage our day-to-day operations, which include human resources, patient programs, fundraising, financing, and marketing and public relations.

What types of skills do you think tomorrow's managers will need?

No matter what field, managers can no longer work in isolation. All of tomorrow's managers will need an ability to think beyond their immediate jobs and integrate all aspects of a company's business into their work. Now and in the future, solid communication skills—writing, creativity, and strategic thinking—are essential for success.

What are the important issues facing human resource managers?

Competition is one of the most important issues facing human resource managers. In an expanding economy, it becomes harder to recruit and retain employees as salaries increase and benefits packages are "sweetened." This translates to a human resource professional who must be more flexible and innovative in his or her work.

How does your organization encourage employees to manage their careers?

Our organization has a strong tradition of promoting from within. We recognize the skills, experiences, and strengths employees bring and find ways to help them grow within our organization. We look most closely at employees' abilities to contribute their ideas and creativity to improving the organization's business practices.

Many organizations, particularly large ones, have formal orientation programs, which might include a tour of the work facilities, a film describing the history of the organization, and a short discussion with a representative from the human resources department who describes the organization's benefit programs. Other organizations use a more informal orientation program in which, for instance, the manager assigns the new employee to a senior member of the work group who introduces the new employee to immediate co-workers and shows him or her the locations of the copy room, coffee machine, rest rooms, cafeteria, and the like.

Managers have an obligation to make the integration of the new employee into the organization as smooth and as free of anxiety as possible. They need to openly discuss employee beliefs regarding mutual obligations of the organization and the employee.[17] It is in the best interests of the organization and the new employee to get the person up and running in the job as soon as possible. Successful orientation, whether formal or informal, results in an outsider-insider transition that makes the new member feel comfortable and fairly well adjusted, lowers the likelihood of poor work performance, and reduces the probability of a surprise resignation by the new employee only a week or two into the job.

❯ EMPLOYEE TRAINING

Using fun techniques such as safety fairs, games of safety Jeopardy, and forklift rodeos, employees at Motorola's Network Solutions Sector learn about safety on the job.[18] Employee safety training is only one of many types of training that organizations provide employees. As job demands change, employee skills have to be altered and updated. It's been estimated that U.S. business firms spend $54 billion on formal courses and training programs to build workers' skills.[19] Managers, of course, are responsible for deciding what type of training employees need, when they need it, and what form that training should take.

SKILL CATEGORIES

Employee skills can be grouped into three categories: technical, interpersonal, and problem solving. Most employee training activities seek to modify an employee's skills in one or more of these areas.

Most training is directed at upgrading and improving an employee's *technical* skills, including basic skills—the ability to read, write, and do math computations—as well as job-specific competencies.[20] The majority of jobs today have become more complex than they were a decade or two ago. Computerized factories and offices, digital equipment, and other types of sophisticated technology require that employees have math, reading, and computer skills. How, for example, can employees master statistical process control or the careful measurement and self-inspection needed for tool changes in flexible manufacturing systems if they can't perform basic math calculations or read detailed operating manuals? Or how can clerical employees do their jobs effectively without the ability to understand word processing, database management, or e-mail programs?

Almost every employee belongs to a work group or unit. To some degree, work performance depends on an employee's ability to interact effectively with his or her co-workers and manager. Some employees have excellent *interpersonal* skills while other

In an effort to weather the decline of its textile industries, the Dominican Republic is hoping to attract high-tech ventures for which it can supply skilled employees. To train workers like those shown here, critical for a nation in which formal schooling averages five years and the illiteracy rate is over 15 percent, the government has created the Technological Institute of the Americas to provide training that will range from short skills courses to master's degrees in computer programming and engineering.

employees require training to improve theirs. This type of training often includes learning how to be a better listener, how to communicate ideas more clearly, and how to reduce conflict. For instance, employees at Big Y Foods in Springfield, Massachusetts, learned to develop cooperation, teamwork, and trust through an experience-based inter-personal skills training program.

Many employees have to solve problems on their job, particularly in nonroutine jobs. When the *problem-solving* skills of employees are deficient, managers might want to improve them through training. This would include participating in activities to sharpen logic, reasoning, and skills at defining problems; assessing causation; being creative in developing alternatives; analyzing alternatives; and selecting solutions. For example, managers at fabric supplier F. Schumacher receive training in problem solving and conflict resolution.

TRAINING METHODS

Most training takes place on the job because this approach is simple to implement and is usually inexpensive. However, on-the-job training can disrupt the workplace and result in an increase in errors while learning takes place. Also, some skill training is too complex to learn on the job. In such cases, it should take place outside the work setting. Exhibit 12.11 summarizes the more popular training methods, both on-the-job and off-the-job types.

Exhibit 12.11	
Employee Training Methods	**Sample On-the-Job Training Methods**

Job rotation	Lateral transfers allowing employees to work at different jobs. Provides good exposure to a variety of tasks.
Understudy assignments	Working with a seasoned veteran, coach, or mentor. Provides support and encouragement from an experienced worker. In the trades industry, this may also be an apprenticeship.

Sample Off-the-Job Training Methods

Classroom lectures	Lectures designed to convey specific technical, interpersonal, or problem-solving skills.
Films and videos	Using media to explicitly demonstrate technical skills that are not easily presented by other training methods.
Simulation exercises	Learning a job by actually performing the work (or its simulation). May include case analyses, experiential exercises, role playing, and group interaction.
Vestibule training	Learning tasks on the same equipment that one actually will use on the job but in a simulated work environment.

❭ EMPLOYEE PERFORMANCE MANAGEMENT

Managers need to know whether their employees are performing their jobs efficiently and effectively or whether there is need for improvement. Evaluating employee performance is part of a **performance management system,** which is a process of establishing performance standards and appraising employee performance in order to arrive at objective human resource decisions as well as to provide documentation to support those decisions. The performance appraisal is a critical part of a performance management system. Let's look at some different methods of doing performance appraisal.

PERFORMANCE APPRAISAL METHODS

Managers can choose from seven performance appraisal methods. The advantages and disadvantages of each of these methods are shown in Exhibit 12.12.

Written Essays The **written essay** is a performance appraisal technique in which an evaluator writes out a description of an employee's strengths and weaknesses, past performance, and potential. The evaluator would also make suggestions for improvement.

Critical Incidents The use of **critical incidents** focuses the evaluator's attention on those critical or key behaviors that separate effective from ineffective job performance. The appraiser writes down anecdotes that describe what the employee did that was especially effective or ineffective. The key here is that only specific behaviors, not vaguely defined personality traits, are cited.

Graphic Rating Scales One of the oldest and most popular performance appraisal methods is **graphic rating scales**. This method lists a set of performance factors such as quantity and quality of work, job knowledge, cooperation, loyalty, attendance, honesty, and initiative. The evaluator then goes down the list and

performance management system

A process of establishing performance standards and evaluating performance in order to arrive at objective human resource decisions as well as to provide documentation to support those decisions.

written essay

A performance appraisal technique in which an evaluator writes out a description of an employee's strengths and weaknesses, past performance, and potential.

critical incidents

A performance appraisal technique in which the evaluator focuses on the critical behaviors that separate effective from ineffective job performance.

graphic rating scales

A performance appraisal technique in which an employee is rated on a set of performance factors.

Method	Advantage	Disadvantage
Written essay	Simple to use	More a measure of evaluator's writing ability than of employee's actual performance
Critical incidents	Rich examples; behaviorally based	Time-consuming; lack quantification
Graphic rating scales	Provide quantitative data; less time-consuming than others	Do not provide depth of job behavior assessed
BARS	Focus on specific and measurable job behaviors	Time-consuming; difficult to develop
Multiperson comparisons	Compares employees with one another	Unwieldy with large number of employees
MBO	Focuses on end goals; results oriented	Time-consuming
360 degree appraisal	Thorough	Time-consuming

Exhibit 12.12

Advantages and Disadvantages of Performance Appraisal Methods

rates the employee on each factor using an incremental scale. The scales typically specify five points; for instance, a factor such as job knowledge might be rated from 1 ("poorly informed about work duties") to 5 ("has complete mastery of all phases of the job").

Behaviorally Anchored Rating Scales One increasingly popular performance appraisal approach is **behaviorally anchored rating scales (BARS)**. These scales combine major elements from the critical incident and graphic rating scale approaches. The appraiser rates an employee according to items along a numerical scale, but the items are examples of actual behavior on a job rather than general descriptions or traits.

behaviorally anchored rating scales (BARS)

A performance appraisal technique that appraises an employee on examples of actual job behavior.

Multiperson Comparisons **Multiperson comparisons** compare one individual's performance with that of one or more others. It's a relative, not an absolute, measuring device. The three most popular approaches to multiperson comparisons include group order ranking, individual ranking, and paired comparison. The **group order ranking** requires the evaluator to place employees into a particular classification such as "top one-fifth" or "second one-fifth." The **individual ranking** approach requires the evaluator merely to list the employees in order from highest to lowest. In the **paired comparison** approach, each employee is compared with every other employee in the comparison group and rated as either the superior or weaker member of the pair. After all paired comparisons are made, each employee is assigned a summary ranking based on the number of superior scores he or she received.

multiperson comparisons

Performance appraisal techniques that compare one individual's performance with that of one or more other individuals.

group order ranking

A multiperson comparison that requires the evaluator to place employees into a particular classification.

individual ranking

A multiperson comparison that requires the evaluator to list employees in order from lowest to highest.

Objectives We previously introduced management by objectives (MBO) as we discussed planning in Chapter 7. MBO is also a mechanism for appraising performance. In fact, it's the preferred method for assessing managers and professional employees.[21] With MBO, employees are evaluated by how well they accomplish a specific set of goals that has been determined to be critical in the successful completion of their jobs.

paired comparison

A multiperson comparison in which each employee is compared with every other employee in the comparison group and rated as either the superior or weaker member of the pair.

360 Degree Feedback **360 degree feedback** is a performance appraisal method that utilizes feedback from supervisors, employees, and co-workers. In other words, this type of review utilizes information from the full circle of people with whom the manager interacts. Companies such as Alcoa, Pitney Bowes, AT&T, DuPont, Levi Strauss, and UPS are using this innovative approach. Users of this approach caution that, although it's effective for career coaching and helping a manager recognize his or her strengths and weaknesses, it's not appropriate for determining pay, promotions, or terminations.

360 degree feedback

A performance appraisal method that utilizes feedback from supervisors, employees, and co-workers.

Testing...Testing...1,2,3

10. **What is the goal of orientation?**

11. **Identify three skill categories for which organizations do employee training.**

12. **How can managers evaluate their employees' performance?**

⟩ COMPENSATION AND BENEFITS

Would you work 40 hours a week (or more) for an organization for no pay and no benefits? Although we might consider doing so for some "social cause" organization, most of us expect to receive some compensation from our employer. Developing an effective and appropriate compensation system is an important part of the HRM process.[22] An effective and appropriate compensation system can help attract and retain competent and talented individuals who can help the organization accomplish its mission and goals. In addition, an organization's compensation system has been shown to have an impact on its strategic performance.[23]

Managers must develop a compensation system that reflects the changing nature of work and the workplace in order to keep people motivated. Organizational compensation can include many different types of rewards and benefits such as base wages and salaries, wage and salary add-ons, incentive payments, and other benefits and services.

How do managers determine who receives $9 an hour and who receives $350,000 a year? Several factors influence the differences in compensation and benefit packages for different employees. Exhibit 12.13 summarizes these factors, which are both job based and business or industry based. Many organizations today, however, are using an alternative approach to determining compensation called skill-based pay.

Because employees' levels of skills tend to affect work efficiency and effectiveness, many organizations have implemented **skill-based pay** systems, which reward employees for the job skills and competencies they can demonstrate. In a skill-based pay system, an employee's job title doesn't define his or her pay category; skills do.[24] For example, the highest pay a machine operator at Polaroid Corporation can earn is $14 an hour. However, because the company has a skill-based pay plan, machine operators can earn up to a 10 percent premium if they broaden their skills and perform tasks such as material accounting, equipment maintenance, and quality inspection.[25] Skill-based pay systems seem to mesh nicely with the changing nature of jobs and today's work environment. As one expert noted, "Slowly, but surely, we're becoming a skill-based society where your market value is tied to what you can do and what your skill set is. In this new world where skills and knowledge are what really count, it doesn't make sense to treat people as jobholders. It makes sense to treat them as people with specific skills and to pay them for these skills."[26]

Although many factors influence the design of an organization's compensation system, flexibility is becoming a key consideration. The traditional approach to paying people reflected a time of job stability when an employee's pay was largely determined by seniority and job level. Given the dynamic environments that many organizations face in which the employee skills that are absolutely critical to organizational success can change in a matter of months, the trend is to make pay systems more flexi-

skill-based pay

A pay system that rewards employees for the job skills they can demonstrate.

At Baptist Hospital in Pensacola, Florida, president Quinton Studer improved admissions and patient satisfaction dramatically in just two years, in large part by coming up with new ways to measure employee performance. Studer discovered that what employees wanted most was prompt feedback. So 90-day work plans are now developed for employees at all levels, and every 90 days four standards are measured against the plans: customer service, efficiency, expense management, and employee turnover.

Exhibit | 12.13 | **Factors That Influence Compensation and Benefits**

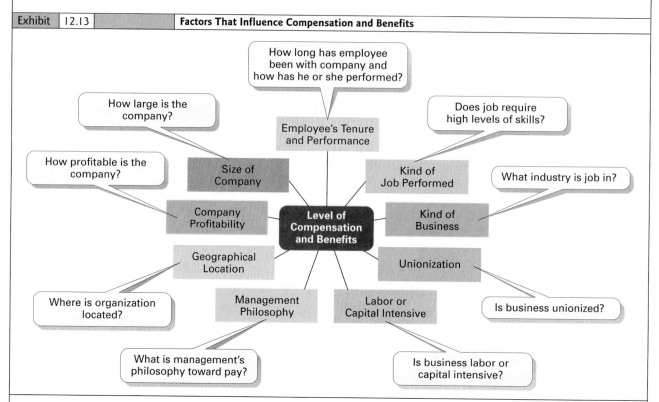

Sources: Based on R.I. Henderson, *Compensation Management,* 6th ed. (Upper Saddle River, NJ: Prentice Hall, 1994), pp. 3–24; and A. Murray, "Mom, Apple Pie, and Small Business," *Wall Street Journal,* August 15, 1994, p. A1.

ble and to reduce the number of pay levels. However, whatever approach managers take, they must establish a fair, equitable, and motivating compensation system that allows the organization to recruit and keep a productive workforce.

› CAREER DEVELOPMENT

The term *career* has several meanings. In popular usage, it can mean advancement ("she is on a management career track"), a profession ("he has chosen a career in accounting"), or a lifelong sequence of jobs ("his career has included 12 jobs in six organizations"). For our purposes, we define a **career** as the sequence of positions held by a person during his or her lifetime.[27] Using this definition, it's apparent that we all have, or will have, a career. Moreover, the concept is as relevant to unskilled laborers as it is to software designers or physicians. But career development isn't what it used to be![28]

career

A sequence of positions held by a person during his or her lifetime.

THE WAY IT WAS
Although career development has been an important topic in management courses for years, we've witnessed some dramatic changes in the concept. Career development programs were typically designed by organizations to help

employees advance their work lives within a specific organization. The focus of such programs was to provide the information, assessment, and training needed to help employees realize their career goals. Career development was also a way for organizations to attract and retain highly talented people. Those purposes have all but disappeared in today's workplace. Widespread organizational changes have led to uncertainty and chaos concerning the concept of a traditional organizational career. Downsizing, restructuring, and other organizational adjustments have brought us to one significant conclusion about career development: The individual—not the organization—is responsible for his or her own career! You, therefore, must be prepared to do what is necessary to advance your career. You must take responsibility for designing, guiding, and developing your own career. Your career will be managed by you, not by the organization.[29] Both organizations and individuals are adjusting to the notion that organizational members have to look out for themselves and become more self-reliant.

Although it has its drawbacks, the chance of getting an assignment abroad can be one of the attractions of a growing number of career paths today. John McNamara (shown here with Agate), national director of international assignments for Deloitte & Touche, enjoyed aspects of his 11-year stint in Saudi Arabia, although cultural differences imposed many restrictions on him and his wife Agate and their two sons.

YOU AND YOUR CAREER TODAY

The idea of increased personal responsibility for one's career has been described as a *boundaryless career* in which individuals rather than organizations define career progression, organizational loyalty, important skills, and marketplace value.[30] The challenge for individuals is that there are no norms and few rules to guide them in these new circumstances. Instead, individuals assume primary responsibility for career planning, career goal setting, and education and training.[31]

One of the first career decisions you have to make is career choice. The optimum career choice is one that offers the best match between what you want out of life and your interests, abilities, and market opportunities. Good career choice outcomes should result in a series of positions that give you an opportunity to be a good performer, make you want to maintain your commitment to your career, lead to highly satisfying work, and give you the proper balance between work and personal life. A good career match, then, is one in which you are able to develop a positive self-concept, to do work that you think is important, and to lead the kind of life you desire.[32] Exhibit 12.14 provides the results of a survey of college graduates regarding what is important to them in their first jobs. How would you have ranked these items?

Once you have identified a career choice, it's time to initiate the job search. We aren't going to get into the specifics of job hunting, writing a résumé, or interviewing successfully, although those career actions are important. Let's fast for-

Exhibit 12.14	(ranked in order of importance)	
Top 10 Important Job Factors for College Graduates	**1.** Enjoying what they do	**6.** Recognition for good performance
	2. Opportunity to use skills and abilities	**7.** Friendly co-workers
	3. Opportunity for personal development	**8.** Job location
	4. Feeling what they do matters	**9.** Lots of money
	5. Benefits	**10.** Working on teams.

Source: Based on V. Frazee, "What's Important to College Grads in Their First Jobs?" *Personnel Journal*, July 1996, p. 21.

Testing...Testing...1,2,3

13. Why is it important for an organization to have an effective compensation system?

14. What factors influence the pay employees receive?

15. How has the concept of career development changed?

ward through all that and assume that your job search was successful. It's time to go to work! How do you survive and excel in your career? Exhibit 12.15 lists some suggestions for a successful management career.[33] By taking an active role in managing your career, your work life can be more exciting, enjoyable, and satisfying.

> **CURRENT ISSUES IN HUMAN RESOURCE MANAGEMENT**

We'll conclude this chapter by looking at some contemporary HRM issues facing today's managers. These include managing workforce diversity, sexual harassment, and work-life balance.

MANAGING WORKFORCE DIVERSITY

We've discussed the changing makeup of the workforce in several places throughout the book. Let's look at how workforce diversity affects such basic HRM concerns as recruitment, selection, and orientation and training.

Exhibit 12.15	
Some Suggestions for a Successful Management Career	Develop a Network
	Continue Upgrading Your Skills
	Consider Lateral Career Moves
	Stay Mobile
	Support Your Boss
	Find a Mentor
	Don't Stay Too Long in Your First Job
	Stay Visible
	Gain Control of Organizational Resources
	Learn the Power Structure
	Present the Right Image
	Do Good Work
	Select Your First Job Judiciously

Recruitment To improve workforce diversity, managers need to widen their recruiting net. For example, the popular practice of relying on employee referrals as a source of job applicants tends to produce candidates who are similar to present employees. However, some organizations, such as Exabyte of Boulder, Colorado, have been able to recruit and hire diverse individuals by relying on their current employees. The company's successful experience with a hearing-impaired employee led to hiring other nonhearing employees through employee referrals. But not every organization has the employee resources needed to achieve workforce diversity through employee referrals. So managers may have to look for job applicants in places where they might not have looked before. To increase diversity, managers are turning to nontraditional recruitment sources such as women's job networks, over-50 clubs, urban job banks, training centers for the physically challenged, ethnic newspapers, and gay rights organizations. This type of outreach should enable the organization to broaden its pool of diverse applicants.

Selection Once a diverse set of applicants exists, efforts must be made to ensure that the selection process does not discriminate. Moreover, applicants need to be made comfortable with the organization's culture and be made aware of management's desire to accommodate their needs. For instance, although only a small percentage of women apply for Microsoft's technical jobs, the company makes every effort to hire a high percentage of the female applicants and strives to make sure that these women have a successful experience once they are on the job.[34]

Orientation and Training The outside-insider transition is often more challenging for women and minorities than for white males. Many organizations provide special workshops to raise diversity awareness issues. For example, at a Kraft manufacturing facility in Missouri, managers developed an ambitious diversity program reflecting the increased value the organization had placed on incorporating diverse perspectives. One thing they did was to reward "diversity champions," individual employees who supported and promoted the benefits of diversity. They also added diversity goals to employee evaluations, encouraged nontraditional promotions, sponsored six ethnic meal days annually, and trained over half of the plant's employees in diversity issues.[35]

SEXUAL HARASSMENT
Sexual harassment is a serious issue in both public and private sector organizations. More than 16,000 complaints are filed with the Equal Employment Opportunity Commission (EEOC) each year.[36] Data indicate that almost all *Fortune* 500 companies in the United States have had complaints lodged by employees, and about a third of them have been sued.[37] Not only were the settlements in these cases very costly for the companies in terms of litigation, it is estimated that sexual harassment costs a "typical *Fortune* 500 company $6.7

A tight labor market has brought a new kind of diversity to Denver Bookbinding Co., where CEO Gail Laindley has hired paroled prisoners and political refugees to fill jobs that would otherwise go begging. The rate of work errors has risen and productivity is down, due to less skilled employees and the personal and social problems they bring with them. To cope, Laindley has lengthened the workday and makes regular accommodations for employees with special needs like meetings with their parole officers.

million per year in absenteeism, low productivity, and turnover."[38] Sexual harassment, however, isn't just a problem in the United States. It's a global issue. For instance, sexual harassment charges have been filed against employers in such countries as Japan, Australia, the Netherlands, Belgium, New Zealand, Sweden, Ireland, and Mexico.[39] Even though discussions of sexual harassment cases often focus on the large awards granted by a court, there are other concerns for employers. Sexual harassment creates an unpleasant work environment and undermines workers' ability to perform their job.

sexual harassment

Any unwanted activity of a sexual nature that affects an individual's employment.

Sexual harassment is defined as any unwanted activity of a sexual nature that affects an individual's employment. It can occur between members of the opposite sex or of the same sex. Although such activity is generally covered under employment discrimination laws, in recent years this problem has gained more recognition. By most accounts, prior to the mid-1980s this problem was generally viewed as isolated incidents, with the individual at fault being solely responsible (if at all) for his or her actions.[40] Yet, charges of sexual harassment continue to appear in today's headlines on a regular basis.

Much of the problem associated with sexual harassment is determining exactly what constitutes this illegal behavior. The EEOC cites three situations in which sexual harassment can occur. These are instances in which verbal or physical conduct toward an individual (1) creates an intimidating, offensive, or hostile environment; (2) unreasonably interferes with an individual's work; or (3) adversely affects an employee's employment opportunities. For many organizations, it's the offensive or hostile environment issue that is problematic. Managers must be aware of what constitutes such an environment. The key is being attuned to what makes fellow employees uncomfortable—and if we don't know, we should ask![41]

If sexual harassment carries with it potential costs to the organization, what can a company do to protect itself?[42] The courts want to know two things: Did the organization know about, or should it have known about, the alleged behavior? And what did management do to stop it? With the number and dollar amounts of the awards against organizations increasing, there is a greater need for management to educate all employees on sexual harassment matters and have mechanisms available to monitor employees.

WORK-LIFE BALANCE

What kinds of work-life balance issues can arise that might affect an employee's job performance? Here are some examples:

● Is it OK for workers to bring their babies to work because of an emergency crisis with normal child care arrangements?

● Should a manager praise an employee for flying to Singapore on business the day after his wife gives birth? Should a manager discipline an employee who refuses to go for the same reason?

● A manager has an assignment that requires a lot of travel. In deciding whom to give it to, should the manager consider which workers have young children?

● Is it OK for workers to cover their work areas with pictures of their newborn babies or drawings scrawled by their young children?

Organizations are beginning to recognize that employees can't (and don't) leave their families and personal lives behind when they walk into work. An organization hires a person who has feelings, a personal life outside the office, personal problems, and family commitments. Although managers can't be sympathetic with every detail of an employee's family life, we *are* seeing organizations more attuned to the fact that employees have sick children, elderly parents who need special care, and other family issues that may require special arrangements. To accommodate employees' needs for work-life balance, many companies are offering **family-friendly benefits** that include a wide range of work and family programs to help employees. These might include such benefits as flextime, child care, part-time employment, relocation programs, summer camps for employees' children, parental leave, and adoption benefits.[43] Companies such as CompUSA, Excalibur Hotel, Barnes & Noble, and Summit Systems currently offer such benefits.[44] At the heart of such programs are increasing child and elder care benefits. In addition, another work-life concern arises with the large number of **dual-career couples**— couples in which both partners have professional, managerial, or administrative occupations. An organization's HRM policies should reflect the special needs this situation creates.

As we've seen, getting and keeping quality employees is critical because the quality of an organization's human resources directly influences how well the organization performs. Therefore, managers at all organizational levels must take their HRM responsibilities seriously.

family-friendly benefits

Benefits that accommodate employees' needs for work-life balance.

dual-career couples

Couples in which both partners have a professional, managerial, or administrative occupation.

16. **Why is managing workforce diversity an important HRM issue?**

17. **What is sexual harassment, and what role do managers play in minimizing occurrences of sexual harassment?**

18. **How can organizations make their HRM programs and practices more accommodating to employees' needs for work-life balance?**

Testing...Testing...1,2,3

Managers Respond to "A Manager's Dilemma"

Marvin Fisher

Regional Recruiting Manager, Toys "R" Us, Joliet, Illinois

It's important to spend a few hours orienting a new hire to the company's history and culture. This process lessens the anxiety and stress of starting a new job. Another important process is personally introducing foreign new hires to the current staff. These introductions should be administered in a fun and informative way to help foster open communication.

Orienting someone to a new culture should be an ongoing process. It would also be beneficial to move some company events outside of the office. Have meetings at a neutral site to increase everyone's exposure to the French culture. Arrange for lunch or dinner at different restaurants. Plan for corporate outings to different events. This process helps the foreign employees become familiar with the culture in a comfortable environment and builds rapport within the team.

Finally, establish a mentor program with the new hires. Not only can a mentor help the new person learn the French culture, but the mentor can also learn about the culture and uniqueness of the new hires.

Stacy Renee Unger

Media Specialist, Edward Jones, St. Louis, Missouri

There are several challenges to this situation. First, there are the rapid changes taking place in the online world. Second, Perbos-Brinck also must deal with bringing in new hires who may be highly skilled but who are unfamiliar with the company and with the French culture.

I would suggest that all new employees should have a French mentor in the company for the first six months. This mentor could provide some security in terms of being there to answer questions, to give advice, and to just be a sounding board.

Also, Perbos-Brinck might want to have these new hires take training classes at a French university. For example, at Edward Jones, all of our London headquarters associates from the United States go to a two-month training class at the London Business School. This class lets them experience business cultural barriers and gives individuals who are new to a culture opportunities to see what challenges they might face and how to deal with them.

Chapter Summary

This summary is organized around the chapter-opening objectives found on p. 304.

1. Human resource management is strategically important because various studies have concluded that an organization's human resources can be a significant source of competitive advantage. Also, other studies have shown that certain HRM policies and practices, called high-performance work practices, can lead to both high individual and high organizational performance.

2. The human resource management process seeks to staff the organization and sustain high employee performance through human resource planning, recruitment or decruitment, selection, orientation, training, performance management, compensation and benefits, and career development.

3. A job description is a written statement of what a jobholder does, how it is done, and why it is done. A job specification states the minimum acceptable qualifications that a jobholder must possess to perform a given job successfully.

4. Recruitment seeks to develop a pool of potential job candidates. Typical sources include an internal search, advertisements, employee referrals, public and private employment agencies, Web-based advertising, school placement centers, and temporary help services. Decruitment reduces the labor supply within an organization through options such as firing, layoffs, attrition, transfers, reduced workweeks, and early retirements.

5. Selection devices must match the job in question. Work sampling works best with low-level jobs. Assessment centers work best for managerial positions. The validity of the interview as a selection device increases for progressively higher levels of management.

6. Most employee training seeks to modify skills in one or more of three areas: technical, interpersonal, or problem solving. Technical skills include basic skills such as the ability to read, write, or do math as well as job-specific competencies. Interpersonal skills include the ability to interact effectively with co-workers and managers. Problem-solving skills include logic, reasoning and skills at defining problems; assessing causation; being creative in developing alternatives; and selecting solutions.

7. There are seven major performance appraisal approaches. In the written essay, an evaluator writes out a description of the employee's strengths and weaknesses, past performance, and potential. In the critical incidents, the evaluator writes down examples of what the employee did that was effective or ineffective. The graphic rating scales approach lists a set of performance factors on which the evaluator rates the employee by using an incremental scale. In the behaviorally anchored rating scales, the appraiser uses a numerical scale to rate an employee according to descriptions of actual behavior on a job. The multiperson comparisons approach compares one individual's performance with that of one or more others. Also, an evaluator can appraise a person's accomplishment of a specific set of goals. Finally, 360 degree feedback is an approach that utilizes feedback from supervisors, employees, and co-workers.

8. An organization's compensation system should reflect the changing nature of work and the workplace and typically includes base wages and salaries, wage and salary add-ons, incentive payments, and other benefits and services.

9. Current HRM issues facing managers include managing workforce diversity, sexual harassment, and work-life balance. HRM practices can facilitate workforce diversity by widening the recruitment effort, eliminating any discriminatory selection practices, communicating to applicants the willingness to accommodate their needs and providing employee diversity training and education programs. Sexual harassment is a concern for management because it intimidates employees, interferes with job performance, and exposes the organization to liability. Finally, organizations are beginning to recognize that employees have families and personal lives and many are offering family-friendly benefits to accommodate these realities.

Thinking About Management Issues

1. Are there limits on how far a prospective employer should delve into an applicant's personal life by means of interviews or tests? Explain.

2. Should an employer have the right to choose employees without governmental interference? Support your answer.

3. Studies show that women's salaries still lag behind men's and, even with equal opportunity laws and regulations, women are paid about 79 percent of what men are paid. How would you design a compensation system that would address this issue?

4. What drawbacks, if any, do you see in implementing flexible benefits? (Consider this question from the perspectives of both the organization and the employee.)

5. What are the benefits and drawbacks of realistic job previews? (Consider this question from the perspectives of both the organization and the employee.)

Log On: Internet-Based Exercise

The United States Equal Employment Opportunity Commission (EEOC) handles all aspects of ensuring that employees (current and potential) have equal access and opportunity in employment. How does an individual file an EEOC charge? Research the procedure an employee must follow in filing an EEOC charge. Write down the main steps.

Also, the EEOC keeps summary statistics on sexual harassment cases. Research the following: How many sexual harassment cases have been filed during the last three years for which data are available? How many cases were settled? What monetary benefits have been awarded? What guidelines are suggested for dealing with sexual harassment? Put this information into a bulleted list format.

myPHLIP Companion Web Site

myPHLIP **(www.prenhall.com/myphlip)** *is a fully customizable homepage that ties students and faculty to text-specific resources.*
- **For students**, myPHLIP *provides an online study guide tied chapter-by-chapter to the text—current events and Internet exercises, lecture notes, downloadable software, the Career Center, the Writing Center, Ask the Tutor, and more.*
- **For faculty**, myPHLIP *provides a syllabus tool that allows you to manage content, communicate with students, and upload personal resources.*

Working Together: Team-Based Exercise

You work as director of human resources for a gift registry Web site based in St. Paul, Minnesota. Your company currently has 30 employees, but due to the popularity of your Web site, the company is growing rapidly. To handle customer demand, at least 30 additional employees are going to be needed in the next three months. In filling those positions, the company's CEO is committed to increasing employee diversity because she feels that diverse employees will add unique perspectives on the types of gift services provided by the company. She's asked you to head up a team to propose some specific practices for recruiting diverse individuals.

Form teams of three or four class members. Identify specific steps that your company can take to recruit diverse individuals. Be creative and be specific. Write down your proposed steps and be prepared to share your ideas with the class.

Case Application

Accounting for People

In an industry where 12- to 14-hour workdays, six and even seven days a week, are the norm, not the exception, Ernst & Young International (E&Y) is rewriting the rules for its people. As the fourth largest of the Big Five accounting firms, E&Y offers accounting services from over 675 offices in more than 130 countries. Its tax practice, one of the world's largest, helps international clients deal with the myriad tax laws of various countries. The company is privately held, and revenues for 2000 were estimated at $9.5 billion, a decrease of approximately 23 percent over 1999's revenues.

Becoming more employee friendly hasn't been an easy transition for the company. The accounting services industry is intensely competitive and employees have long been expected to "serve the client at any cost." Yet, as chairman Phil Laskawy had discovered, that cost had a price tag. Part of that price tag was losing new hires—23 percent of the women and 18 percent of the men each year—and spending hundreds of thousands of dollars to fill each vacant position. In addition, a study of E&Y's senior management by Catalyst, the New York City–based organization that studies issues affecting women in business, showed that about 60 percent of the women and 57 percent of the men were dissatisfied with working long hours. Laskawy knew something had to change. He also knew it wouldn't be easy. How can you bring work-life balance to a profession that traditionally has demanded brutally long hours? How can work be flexible when a client has a tight deadline and is paying big bucks to see the organization working—around the clock if necessary—to meet it? How can you make it okay to talk about personal needs with partners and clients? All of these were important issues that ultimately would have to be addressed if the organization was going to make any progress toward becoming more employee oriented.

Laskawy's first step was to create an Office for Retention, headed up by Deborah Holmes, who had been working as a work-life consultant in her job as research director of Catalyst. To get people's attention and to make it clear how important this whole issue was, he asked her to present the findings of the Catalyst study of E&Y to the firm's partners at one of its triannual meetings. Then the two went on a six-week road trip to meet the senior partners at the firm's top offices. At these meetings, Laskawy emphasized to the partners that Holmes reported directly to him. He wanted to make sure they knew that what she was going to be doing was vitally important to the company's future. Even after four years, Laskawy's support hasn't wavered. He often mentions the Office of Retention in his company-wide voice-mail messages to employees. And just what types of people programs has E&Y implemented?

Holmes's initial push was developing and launching four pilot programs. Three of these programs were aimed directly at E&Y's women professionals and addressed issues of internal networking, mentoring, and external networking. All three have proved reasonably effective. The fourth program was, by far, the most ambitious as it covered all of E&Y's employees. The goal of that program was to balance employees' work-life equation. From the start, Holmes made it clear that this program wasn't just

E&Y chairman Phil Laskawy.

about establishing flextime or job-sharing initiatives but about incorporating the reality of people's lives into the company's business strategy. An ambitious goal, needless to say!

From her prior consulting experiences with other traditional organizations, Holmes recognized that to make this program successful, her office had to create highly visible prototypes involving as many employees as possible. Two offices—San Jose and Palo Alto—appeared to be ideal candidates. The San Jose office was one of the company's most lucrative offices, yet it was losing a great number of people to high-tech companies in Silicon Valley. The managing partner for these offices, Roger Dunbar, added a great deal of credibility as he was known as both an innovative leader and a big moneymaker.

Dunbar immediately recognized the value of this life-balance initiative. He assembled a steering committee of 16 top partners and senior managers. They spent a day with Holmes trying to pinpoint the causes underlying the employee retention problem. Some partners felt that opening a day care center or starting concierge services would fix the problem. But Holmes said the problem was deeper than that and these benefits alone weren't the answer. By the end of that meeting, the steering committee had identified substantive issues that needed to be addressed. Eight teams, made up of rank-and-file managers, were appointed to study each issue and to come up with viable solutions.

After working for four months, the teams proposed some simple actions—such as making every day casual dress day, encouraging people not to check their e-mail and voice mail on the weekend, and supporting telecommuting options. Others got right to the heart of the issue of how people worked, communicated, and related to clients. The biggest change had to do with *how* people managed their work, not *where* they got it done. Like most professional services firms, E&Y staffers willingly accepted projects because billable hours reflected their value to the firm. The result was unduly large workloads and rapid job burnout. The teams recommended a change in this philosophy. Now two committees—one for senior partners and managers, the other for junior staff—review time sheets to make sure that no one was overburdened with projects. A senior audit manager in the San Jose office said, "There are a lot of type-A personalities here who will work themselves to frustration and then quit. We wanted to get to them before that happened." During 1999, the committees reduced the workloads of 48 people. The company has taken other steps to create a flexible workplace where people can feel good about their professional career, where they have the time to pursue their passions, and where people have "jobs for life."

QUESTIONS

1. What do you think Ernst & Young's philosophy might be regarding the role of strategic human resource management? Explain.

2. On the basis of information included in the case, create a recruitment advertisement for a junior tax accountant that E&Y might use.

3. What do you think of the company's life-balance initiatives? Do you agree with the company's philosophy? Or does a person who pursues a profession, such as accounting, just have to face the reality of what being a professional entails?

4. What could other companies learn from E&Y's experiences?

5. Check out Ernst & Young's Web site (www.ey.com). Describe what information you find there about the company's life-balance initiative.

Sources: Information from Hoover's Online (www.hoovers.com), April 2, 2001; information from company's Web site (www.ey.com), October 16, 2000; and P. Kruger, "Jobs for Life," *Fast Company*, May 2000, pp. 236–52.

Video Case Application

The Fine Art of Managing People

SMALL BUSINESS 2000

Every business has three basic components, or the three Ps: the *product*, or service being provided; the *process*, or the way the product or service is delivered; and the *people*. Of those three components, the most crucial is the people. Successful business owners are likely to say that the single most important factor in their business's success is the people. Although there's some science behind managing people, there's a lot of art as well. Let's take a look at what some successful businesspeople have to say about the fine art of managing people.

Jeff Gordon, owner of an ad agency in Washington, DC, says that recruitment is the single most important task of any business leader. He recruits full time, and he may have to sift through 150 to 300 people to get that one outstanding person. However, in his business, he has to put that kind of effort into recruiting to find the "gems" who are so critical to his company's success.

Jill and Doug Smith approached people management somewhat differently than what experts advise. They developed their business, Buckeye Beans and Herbs of Spokane, Washington, using friends and family. And as Jill says, this approach can be either a tremendous negative or a tremendous positive. It's been the latter for their business because they all share similar values. In fact, she describes her business as a values-added people company.

When Dale Crownover, owner of Texas Nameplate of Dallas, implemented a quality improvement program, he found that his employees wanted more communication opportunities. At the company's monthly meetings, all employees (not just managers) get involved. Crownover says it's really all about sharing and communicating; letting employees know the goals, the plans, why they're doing what they're doing, and how they're doing. Very simply, he's found that employees want to be part of something.

Finally, Greg Thurman of Harford Communication in Priest River, Idaho, says he doesn't tell people what to do but asks them what they think they should do to solve a problem. His goal was to create an environment in which people didn't feel stifled. As Thurman says, "I don't know every job as well as the people doing the job." Therefore, instead of telling them how to do their jobs, he encourages employees to look for answers and then together they "polish" a solution.

Q U E S T I O N S

1. What "people" advice did each of the four business owners profiled give?

2. What's your opinion of the advice these business owners gave?

3. How could the advice that each of these business owners described help in the design of an organization's HRM programs and actions? Be specific.

Source: Based on *Small Business 2000, Show 413*.

Mastering Management

In Episode 11 of the Mastering Management *series, you'll observe Warren's performance appraisal evaluation with Nick. While Nick is an underachieving employee, the appraisal process turns out not to be effective in identifying his strengths and weaknesses. You'll evaluate the performance appraisal process and the methods that CanGo uses to evaluate employees.*

After reading and studying this chapter, you should be able to:

1. Contrast the calm waters and white-water rapids metaphors of change.

2. Describe what managers can change in organizations.

3. Explain why people are likely to resist change.

4. List techniques for reducing resistance to change.

5. Describe the situational factors that facilitate cultural change.

6. Explain how process reengineering is related to change.

7. Describe techniques for reducing employee stress.

8. Differentiate between creativity and innovation.

9. Explain how organizations can stimulate and nurture innovation.

A MANAGER'S DILEMMA

In a geographic region where currency crises, political upheavals, and natural disasters are an unavoidable fact of life, Panamerican Beverages Inc. (Panamco, www.panamco.com) has learned how to not only survive but thrive in a chaotic and unpredictable environment. Panamco is Latin America's largest Coca-Cola bottler and distributor and a vital part of Coke's global operations. Its sales account for about 6 percent of the worldwide unit case volume of Coca-Cola's soft-drink sales. Or put another way, just Panamco's sales are equivalent to one bottle in every case of Coca-Cola's global soft-drink sales.[1] In Latin America, Panamco sells a lot of Coke!

Francisco Sánchez-Loaeza, Panamco's chairman and CEO, is well aware of his company's strategic importance both to Coca-Cola and to numerous Latin American economies. He proclaims that his most important managerial responsibility is keeping the company's employees focused on successful performance in a sea of change. Sánchez-Loaeza says that adaptability is his company's core survival skill and the secret to its ever-expanding business. "Our organization is designed to shift gears rapidly. At all levels, we allow for immediate changes in direction." Other organizational factors he identifies as important to the company's success include its democratic and decentralized management philosophy,

Managing Change and Innovation

logistical expertise, innovative merchandising strategies, and excellent financial stewardship.

Sánchez-Loaeza has always encouraged managers at Panamco to focus on flexibility, good communication, and quick reaction. Local managers are given a lot of autonomy to make decisions and respond independently to market forces in their territories. They have the authority to implement their own programs and initiatives. Although Panamco's managers appreciate and support the need for continual adaptation to marketplace demands, regular nonmanagerial employees often don't understand why so much change is necessary. Put yourself in Sánchez-Loaeza's position. How would you educate your employees about the importance and necessity of change?

WHAT WOULD YOU DO?

The managerial challenges facing Sánchez-Loaeza in educating his employees about the importance and necessity of change are certainly not unique. Big companies, small businesses, universities and colleges, state and city governments, and even the military are being forced to significantly change the way they do things. Although change has always been a part of the manager's job, it has become even more important in recent years. We'll describe why change is important and how managers can manage change in this chapter. We'll also discuss ways in which managers can nurture innovation and increase their organization's adaptability.

〉 | WHAT IS CHANGE?

organizational change

Any alterations in people, structure, or technology.

If it weren't for **organizational change**—that is, any alterations in people, structure, or technology—the manager's job would be relatively easy. Planning would be simple because tomorrow would be no different from today. The issue of effective organizational design would also be solved because the environment would be free from uncertainty and there would be no need to adapt. Similarly, decision making would be dramatically streamlined because the outcome of each alternative could be predicted with almost certain accuracy. It would, indeed, simplify the manager's job if, for example, competitors did not introduce new products or services, if customers didn't demand new and improved products, if governmental regulations were never modified, or if employees' needs never changed. But that's not the way it is. Change is an organizational reality. Managing change is an integral part of every manager's job. In this chapter, we address the key issues related to managing change.

〉 | FORCES FOR CHANGE

In Chapter 3, we pointed out that there are both external and internal forces that constrain managers. These same forces also bring about the need for change. Let's briefly look at the factors that can create the need for change.

EXTERNAL FORCES

The external forces that create the need for change come from various sources. In recent years, the *marketplace* has affected firms such as Dell Computer as competition from Gateway, Apple, and Toshiba intensified in the battle for consumers' computer purchases. These companies must constantly adapt to changing consumer desires as they develop new PCs and improve marketing strategies. *Governmental laws and regulations* are a frequent impetus for change. For example, the passage of the Americans with Disabilities Act required thousands of organizations (for-profit and not-for-profit firms) to reconfigure restrooms, add ramps, widen doorways, and take other actions to improve accommodations for persons with disabilities. And the new law that gives electronic signatures the same legal weight as pen-and-ink signatures is bringing changes in many organizational areas.

Technology also creates the need for change. For example, technological improvements in expensive diagnostic equipment have created significant economies of scale for hospitals and medical centers. Assembly-line technology in other industries is changing dramatically as organizations replace human labor with robots. Even in the greeting card industry, electronic mail and the Internet have dramatically changed the way that people send greeting cards. The fluctuation in *labor markets* also forces managers to change. For instance, the demand for Web page designers and Web site managers made it necessary for organizations that need those kinds of employees to change their human resource management activities to attract and retain skilled employees in the areas of greatest need.

Economic changes, of course, affect almost all organizations. For instance, global recessionary pressures force organizations to become more cost-efficient. But even in a strong economy, uncertainties about interest rates, federal budget deficits, and currency exchange rates create conditions that may force organizations to change.

These immigrant garment workers became an internal force for change in Israel when, in response to the owner's attempts to fire them, they locked themselves inside their factory for a month. They and their 50 or so coworkers now own the factory and constitute the first textile cooperative in Israel.

INTERNAL FORCES

In addition to the external forces we just described, internal forces also can stimulate the need for change. These internal forces tend to originate primarily from the internal operations of the organization or from the impact of external changes.

A redefinition or modification of an organization's *strategy* often introduces a host of changes. For instance, when Gordon Bethune took over as CEO of bankrupt Continental Airlines, he turned it into a well-run and profitable company with extremely committed employees by orchestrating a series of well-planned and dramatic strategic changes.[2] In addition, an organization's *workforce* is rarely static. Its composition changes in terms of age, education, ethnic background, sex, and so forth. In a stable organization with a large pool of seasoned executives, for instance, there might be a need to restructure jobs in order to retain younger managers at lower ranks. The compensation and benefits system might also need to be adapted to reflect the needs of an older workforce. The introduction of new *equipment* represents another internal force for change. Employees may have their jobs redesigned, need to undergo training on how to operate the new equipment, or be required to establish new interaction patterns within their work group. *Employee attitudes* such as increased job dissatisfaction may lead to increased absenteeism, more voluntary resignations, and even labor strikes. Such events will, in turn, often lead to changes in management policies and practices.

THE MANAGER AS CHANGE AGENT

Changes within an organization need a catalyst. People who act as catalysts and assume the responsibility for managing the change process are called **change agents**.

Any manager can be a change agent. As we discuss the information on change, we assume that it's initiated and coordinated by a manager within the organization. However, the change agent could be a nonmanager—for example, a change specialist from the human resources department or even an outside consultant

change agents

People who act as catalysts and assume the responsibility for managing the change process.

Testing...Testing...1,2,3

1. **Why is handling change an integral part of every manager's job?**

2. **What external and internal forces create the need for organizations to change?**

3. **Who are change agents, and what role do they play in the change process?**

whose expertise is in change implementation. For major systemwide changes, an organization will often hire outside consultants to provide advice and assistance. Because they're from the outside, they can offer an objective perspective that insiders may lack. However, outside consultants are usually at a disadvantage because they have an extremely limited understanding of the organization's history, culture, operating procedures, and people. Outside consultants are also prone to initiate more drastic change than insiders would (which can be either a benefit or a disadvantage) because they don't have to live with the repercussions after the change is implemented. In contrast, internal managers who act as change agents may be more thoughtful, and possibly overcautious, because they must live with the consequences of their decisions.

> TWO VIEWS OF THE CHANGE PROCESS

We can use two very different metaphors to describe the change process.[3] One metaphor envisions the organization as a large ship crossing a calm sea. The ship's captain and crew know exactly where they're going because they've made the trip many times before. Change comes in the form of an occasional storm, a brief distraction in an otherwise calm and predictable trip. In the other metaphor, the organization is seen as a small raft navigating a raging river with uninterrupted white-water rapids. Aboard the raft are half a dozen people who have never worked together before, who are totally unfamiliar with the river, who are unsure of their eventual destination, and who, as if things weren't bad enough, are traveling at night. In the white-water rapids metaphor, change is a natural state, and managing change is a continual process. These two metaphors present very different approaches to understanding and responding to change. Let's take a closer look at each one.

THE CALM WATERS METAPHOR

Up until the late 1980s, the calm waters metaphor was fairly descriptive of the situation that managers faced. It's best illustrated by Kurt Lewin's three-step description of the change process.[4] (See Exhibit 13.1.)

According to Lewin, successful change can be planned and requires *unfreezing* the status quo, *changing* to a new state, and *refreezing* to make the change permanent. The status quo can be considered an equilibrium state. To move from this equilibrium, unfreezing is necessary. Unfreezing can be thought of as preparing

Exhibit	13.1

The Change Process

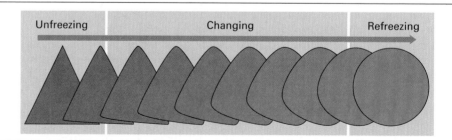

for the needed change. It can be achieved by increasing the *driving forces*, which are forces that drive change and direct behavior away from the status quo, by decreasing the *restraining forces*, which are forces that resist change and push behavior toward the status quo, or by combining the two approaches.

Once unfreezing has been accomplished, the change itself can be implemented. However, merely introducing change doesn't ensure that the change will take hold. The new situation needs to be *refrozen* so that it can be sustained over time. Unless this last step is done, there's a strong chance that the change will be short-lived as employees revert back to the old equilibrium state—that is, the old ways of doing things. The objective of refreezing, then, is to stabilize the new situation by reinforcing the new behaviors.

Note how Lewin's three-step process treats change simply as a break in the organization's equilibrium state. The status quo has been disturbed and change is necessary to establish a new equilibrium state. This calm waters view no longer appropriately describes the kind of environment that managers in today's organizations face.

White-water rapids make an apt metaphor for the pace of change at Yahoo! Inc. Heather Killen, senior vice president of international operations, faces a daily stream of unique decisions brought about by the dizzying pace of technological advances and the clash of cultures made possible by the Internet. In one case in France, Killen defended the rights of U.S. Yahoo! members to auction such controversial items as Nazi memorabilia, the sale of which is illegal in France. The ability of sellers outside the country to offer such items was not even possible before the widespread use of the Internet for commerce.

WHITE-WATER RAPIDS METAPHOR

The white-water rapids metaphor is consistent with our discussion of uncertain and dynamic environments in Chapter 3. It's also consistent with the dynamics of a world that's increasingly dominated by information, ideas, and knowledge.

To get a feeling of what managing change might be like when you have to continually maneuver in uninterrupted rapids, consider attending a college that had the following rules: Courses vary in length. Unfortunately, when you sign up, you don't know how long a course will run. It might go for two weeks or 30 weeks. Furthermore, the instructor can end a course at any time with no prior warning. If that isn't bad enough, the length of the class changes each time it meets: Sometimes the class lasts 20 minutes; other times it runs for three hours. And the time of the next class meeting is set by the instructor during this class. There's one more thing. All exams are unannounced, so you have to be ready for a test at any time. To succeed in this college environment, you would have to be incredibly flexible and able to respond quickly to changing conditions. Students who were overly structured, "slow" to respond, or uncomfortable with change would not survive.

Growing numbers of managers are coming to accept that their job is much like what a student would face in such a college. The stability and predictability of the calm waters metaphor do not exist. Disruptions in the status quo are not occasional and temporary, and they are not followed by a return to calm waters. Many managers never get out of the rapids. They face constant change, bordering on chaos. These managers must play a game that they've never played before, and the game is governed by rules that are created as the game progresses.[5]

Is the white-water rapids metaphor an exaggeration? No! Although you'd expect this type of chaotic and dynamic environment in high-tech industries, even organizations in non-high-tech industries are faced with constant change. Take the case of Converse Inc., an athletic shoe manufacturer based in Massachusetts.[6] In the intensely competitive athletic shoe business, a company has to be prepared for any possibility. Kids (a major target market) are no longer content with new sneaker styles every season. They want new and unique styles more often. Large megaretailers who sell the shoes are demanding more from manufacturers such as holding more inventory, replenishing supplies faster, and helping to find ways to sell more shoes. And competition is hot! Industry leaders Adidas, Reebok, and Nike keep the pressure on. Managers at Converse knew that if they wanted to remain in business and be successful, they had to change. They decided on a series of changes: reviving the once-popular Chuck Taylor line of canvas basketball shoes, signing new spokespersons, making shoes for mountain biking and skateboarding, and implementing a company-wide quality management program. These types of significant organizational changes were essential for Converse to survive the white-water rapids environment in which it operates.

PUTTING THE TWO VIEWS IN PERSPECTIVE

Does *every* manager face a world of constant and chaotic change? No, but the number who don't is dwindling rapidly. Managers in such businesses as wireless telecommunications, computer software, and women's high-fashion clothing have long confronted a world of white-water rapids. These managers used to envy their counterparts in industries such as banking, publishing, oil exploration, and air transportation where the environment was historically more stable and predictable. However, those days of stability and predictability are long gone!

Today, an organization that treats change as the occasional disturbance in an otherwise calm and stable world is running a great risk. Too much is changing too fast for any organization or its managers to be complacent. It's no longer business as usual. And managers must be ready to efficiently and effectively manage the changes facing their organization or their work area. How? That's what we'll discuss next.

> | **MANAGING CHANGE**

Managers at Hallmark, the world's largest greeting card company, recognized that buyers of greeting cards were changing even though the reasons they sent cards were still the same. What organizational changes might these managers have to make to accommodate customers' changing needs? As change agents, managers should be motivated to initiate change because they are committed to improving their organization's performance. Initiating change involves identifying what organizational areas might need to be changed and putting the change process in motion. For instance, those managers at Hallmark made some important changes including developing its Web site to market all kinds of Hallmark products and offering alternative cards for serious subjects including job loss and drug rehabilitation and a whole line of pet greeting cards. But that's not all there is to managing change. Managers must manage employee resistance to change. Here we look at the types of change that managers can make and at how managers can deal with resistance to change.

TYPES OF CHANGE

What *can* a manager change? The manager's options for change essentially fall into three categories: structure, technology, and people. (See Exhibit 13.2.) Changing *structure* includes any alteration in authority relations, coordination mechanisms, degree of centralization, job redesign, or similar structural variables. Changing *technology* encompasses modifications in the way work is performed or the methods and equipment that are used. Changing *people* refers to changes in employee attitudes, expectations, perceptions, and behavior.

Changing Structure We discussed structural issues in Chapter 10. Managers' organizing responsibilities include such activities as choosing the organization's formal design, allocating authority, and determining the degree of formalization. Once those structural decisions have been made, however, they aren't final. Changing conditions or changing strategies bring about the need to make changes in structure. As a result, the manager, in his or her role as change agent, might need to modify the structure.

What options does the manager have for changing structure? Essentially the manager has the same options we introduced in our discussion of structure and design. A few examples should make them clearer. Recall from Chapter 10 that an organization's structure is defined in terms of work specialization, departmentalization, chain of command, span of control, centralization and decentralization, and formalization. Managers can alter one or more of these *structural components*. For instance, departmental responsibilities could be combined, organizational levels eliminated, or spans of control widened to make the organization flatter and less bureaucratic. Or more rules and procedures could be implemented to increase standardization. An increase in decentralization can be used to make decision making faster. Even organizational downsizing efforts involve changes in structure.

Another option would be to make major changes in the actual *structural design*. For instance, the merger between Southwestern Bell Corporation and Pacific Telesis Group (now called SBC Communications Inc.) involved structural design changes in which a number of employees' duties were expanded. Or structural design changes might include a shift from a functional to a product structure or

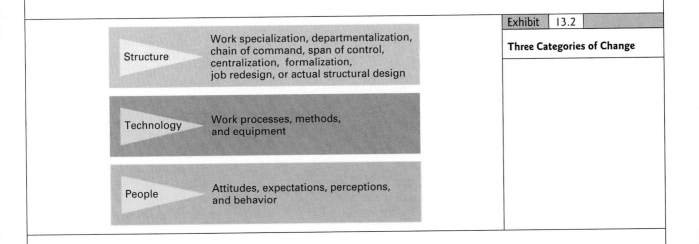

Exhibit	13.2
Three Categories of Change	

Structure — Work specialization, departmentalization, chain of command, span of control, centralization, formalization, job redesign, or actual structural design

Technology — Work processes, methods, and equipment

People — Attitudes, expectations, perceptions, and behavior

Structural design can bring about major change. In its recent restructuring, office furniture manufacturer Herman Miller Inc. created an entirely new division to run its Holland, MI plant. The division is called SQA, which stands for "simple, quick, affordable" and characterizes its approach to operations, which is notable for linking all sales and purchasing functions via the Internet. CEO Michael Volkema believes "no one is going to lead in this industry without leading in technology." Having proved its worth, the SQA division was folded back into the company to serve as a blueprint for improving efficiency companywide.

the creation of a project structure design. Polaroid Corporation, for example, has replaced its traditional functional structure with a new design that arranges work around cross-functional teams.

Changing Technology Managers can also change the technology used to convert inputs into outputs. Most early studies in management—such as the work of Taylor and the Gilbreths—dealt with efforts aimed at technological change. If you recall, scientific management sought to implement changes that would increase production efficiency based on time-and-motion studies. Today, major technological changes usually involve the introduction of new equipment, tools, or work methods; automation; or computerization.

Competitive factors or new innovations within an industry often require managers to introduce *new equipment, tools,* or *work methods*. For example, coal mining companies in New South Wales have updated work methods, installed more efficient coal-handling equipment, and made changes in work practices to be more productive. Even the U.S. Army applied sophisticated technology to its operations, including such advancements as three-dimensional shootout training devices and e-mail capability among troops on the battlefield.[7]

Automation is a technological change that replaces certain tasks done by people with machines. It began during the Industrial Revolution and continues today as one of a manager's options for structural change. Automation has been introduced (and sometimes resisted) in organizations such as the U.S. Postal Service where automatic mail sorters are used, or in automobile assembly lines, where robots are programmed to do jobs that blue-collar workers used to perform.

Probably the most visible technological changes in recent years, though, have come through managers' efforts to expand *computerization*. Most organizations now have sophisticated information systems. For instance, grocery stores and other retailers use scanners linked to computers that provide instant inventory information. Also, it's very uncommon for an office not to be computerized. At BP Amoco, employees had to learn how to deal with the personal visibility and accountability brought about by the implementation of an enterprise-wide information system. The integrative nature of this system meant that what any employee did on his or her computer automatically affected other computer systems on the internal network.[8] Or take, for example, Bennetton Group SpA, which uses computers to link together its manufacturing plants outside Treviso, Italy, with the company's various sales outlets and a highly automated warehouse that employs only 19 people to handle 30,000 boxes a day.[9]

organizational development (OD)

Techniques or programs to change people and the nature and quality of interpersonal work relationships.

Changing People For well over 30 years now, academic researchers and actual managers have been interested in helping individuals and groups within organizations work together more effectively. The term **organizational development (OD)**, though occasionally referring to all types of change, essentially

| Exhibit | 13.3 | **Organizational Development Techniques** |

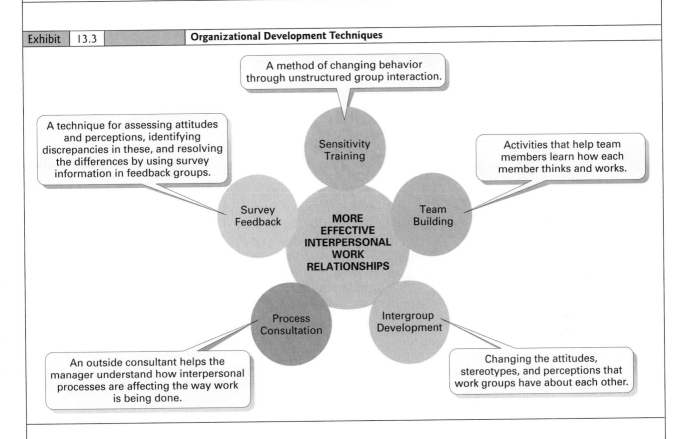

focuses on techniques or programs to change people and the nature and quality of interpersonal work relationships.[10] The most popular OD techniques are described in Exhibit 13.3. The common thread in these techniques is that each seeks to bring about changes in or among the organization's people. For example, George Fisher, former CEO of Eastman Kodak, applied various forms of organizational development to boost employee morale. While past Kodak CEOs tended to be autocratic and inaccessible, Fisher rebuilt the company through respect for people, trust and support, openness, the sharing of power, and participation.

DEALING WITH RESISTANCE TO CHANGE

Change can be a threat to people in an organization. Organizations can build up inertia that motivates people to resist changing their status quo, even though change might be beneficial. Why do people resist change and what can be done to minimize their resistance?

Why People Resist Change It's often said that most people hate any change that doesn't jingle in their pockets. This resistance to change is well documented.[11] Why *do* people resist change? An individual is likely to resist change for three reasons: uncertainty, concern over personal loss, and the belief that the change is not in the organization's best interest.[12]

Good communication would have helped lower resistance to change at France's Alcatel, says Patrick Liot, who heads the high-tech firm's Silicon Valley division. One of Alcatel's acquisitions, a Southern California firm called Xylan, was marred by the departure of scores of valuable Xylan employees who hadn't been fully informed of the benefits Alcatel expected from the merger. "We learned a lesson from that one," says Liot.

Change replaces the known with ambiguity and uncertainty. Regardless of how much you may dislike attending college, at least you know what to do. You know what's expected of you. When you leave college for the world of full-time employment, regardless of how eager you are to get out of college, you'll trade the known for the unknown. Employees in organizations are faced with similar uncertainty. For example, when quality control methods based on sophisticated statistical models are introduced into manufacturing plants, many quality control inspectors have to learn the new methods. Some inspectors may fear that they will be unable to do so and may, therefore, develop a negative attitude toward the change or behave poorly if required to use new methods.

The second cause of resistance is the fear of losing something already possessed. Change threatens the investment you've already made in the status quo. The more that people have invested in the current system, the more they resist change. Why? They fear the loss of status, money, authority, friendships, personal convenience, or other benefits that they value. This helps explain why older workers tend to resist change more than younger workers. Older employees have generally invested more in the current system and, thus, have more to lose by changing.

A final cause of resistance is a person's belief that the change is incompatible with the goals and interests of the organization. An employee who believes that a new job procedure proposed by a change agent will reduce product quality or productivity can be expected to resist the change. If the employee expresses his or her resistance positively (perhaps by directly and clearly expressing it to the change agent, along with substantiation), this type of resistance can be beneficial to the organization.

Techniques for Reducing Resistance When managers see resistance to change as dysfunctional, what actions can they take? There are six actions they can use to deal with resistance to change.[13] These six actions described in Exhibit 13.4 include education and communication, participation, facilitation and support, negotiation, manipulation and cooptation, and coercion. Depending on the type and source of the resistance, managers might choose to use any of these actions.

Testing...Testing...1,2,3

4. **What types of change can managers make in organizations?**

5. **Why do people resist change?**

6. **Describe the techniques for reducing resistance to change.**

Exhibit | 13.4

Managerial Actions to Reduce Resistance to Change

Education and Communication
- Communicate with employees to help them see the logic of change.
- Educate employees through one-on-one discussions, memos, group meetings, or reports.
- Appropriate if source of resistance is either poor communication or misinformation.
- Must be mutual trust and credibility between managers and employees.

Participation
- Allows those who oppose a change to participate in the decision.
- Assumes that they have expertise to make meaningful contributions.
- Involvement can reduce resistance, obtain commitment to seeing change succeed, and increase quality of change decision.

Facilitation and Support
- Provide supportive efforts such as employee counseling or therapy, new skills training, or short paid leave of absence.
- Can be time consuming and expensive.

Negotiation
- Exchange something of value to reduce resistance.
- May be necessary when resistance comes from a powerful source.
- Potentially high costs and likelihood of having to negotiate with other resisters.

Manipulation and Cooptation
- Manipulation is covert attempts to influence such as twisting or distorting facts, withholding damaging information, or creating false rumors.
- Cooptation is a form of manipulation and participation.
- Inexpensive and easy ways to gain support of resisters.
- Can fail miserably if targets feel they've been tricked.

Coercion
- Using direct threats or force.
- Inexpensive and easy way to get support.
- May be illegal. Even legal coercion can be perceived as bullying.

MANAGING YOUR CAREER | Reinvent Yourself

Face it. The only constant thing about change is that it is constant. These days you don't have the luxury of dealing with change only once in a while. No, the workplace seems to change almost continuously. How can you reinvent yourself to deal with the demands of a constantly changing workplace?[14]

Being prepared isn't a credo just for the Boy Scouts; it should be your motto for dealing with a workplace that is constantly changing. Being prepared means taking the initiative and being responsible for your own personal career development. Rather than depending on your organization to provide you with career development and training opportunities, do it yourself. Take advantage of continuing education or graduate courses at local colleges. Sign up for workshops and seminars that can help you enhance your skills. Upgrading your skills to keep them current is one of the most important things you can do to reinvent yourself.

It's also important for you to be a positive force when faced with workplace changes. We don't mean that you should routinely accept any change that's being implemented. If you think that a proposed change isn't appropriate or won't be effective, speak up. Voice your concerns in a constructive manner. Being constructive may mean suggesting an alternative. However, if you feel that the change is beneficial, support it wholeheartedly and enthusiastically.

The changes that organizations make in response to a dynamic environment can be overwhelming and stressful. However, you can take advantage of these changes by reinventing yourself.

> ❭ | CONTEMPORARY ISSUES IN MANAGING CHANGE

Today's change issues—changing organizational cultures, continuous quality improvement versus process reengineering, and handling employee stress—are critical concerns for managers. What can managers do to change an organization's culture when that culture no longer supports the organization's mission? How do managers effectively implement continuous incremental change or how do they implement radical change? And what can managers do to handle the stress created by today's dynamic environment? We'll look at each of these issues in this section and discuss the actions managers should consider in dealing with them.

CHANGING ORGANIZATIONAL CULTURE

The fact that an organization's culture is made up of relatively stable and permanent characteristics (see Chapter 3) tends to make that culture very resistant to change.[15] A culture takes a long time to form and, once established, it tends to become entrenched. Strong cultures are particularly resistant to change because employees have become so committed to them. For instance, Durk I. Jager, former CEO of Procter & Gamble, worked hard to make over the company's deep-rooted culture hoping that the changes would help the company respond better to the changing demands of its markets. He wasn't successful and was replaced by A.G. Lafley in June 2000.[16] If, over time, a certain culture becomes inappropriate to an organization and a handicap to management, there might be little a manager can do to change it, especially in the short run. Even under the most favorable conditions, cultural changes have to be viewed in years, not weeks or even months.

Understanding the Situational Factors What are the favorable conditions that might facilitate cultural change? The evidence suggests that cultural change is most likely to take place when most or all of the following conditions exist:

● *A dramatic crisis occurs.* This can be the shock that weakens the status quo and makes people start thinking about the relevance of the current culture. Examples are a surprising financial setback, the loss of a major customer, or a dramatic technological innovation by a competitor.

● *Leadership changes hands.* New top leadership, who can provide an alternative set of key values, may be perceived as more capable of responding to the crisis than the former leaders were. Top leadership includes the organization's chief executive and also might include all senior managers.

● *The organization is young and small.* The younger the organization, the less entrenched its culture. Similarly, it is easier for managers to communicate new values in a small organization than in a large one.

● *The culture is weak.* The more widely held the values and the higher the agreement among members on those values, the more difficult it will be to change. Conversely, weak cultures are more receptive to change than are strong ones.[17]

These situational factors help to explain why a company such as Procter & Gamble faced challenges in reshaping its culture. For the most part, employees liked the old ways of doing things and didn't see the company's problems as critical.

• Conduct a cultural analysis to identify cultural elements needing change. • Make it clear to employees that the organization's survival is legitimately threatened if change is not forthcoming. • Appoint new leadership with a new vision. • Initiate a reorganization. • Introduce new stories and rituals to convey the new vision. • Change the selection and socialization processes and the evaluation and reward systems to support the new values.	**Exhibit 13.5** **The Road to Cultural Change**

How Can Cultural Change Be Accomplished? Now we ask the question: If conditions are right, how do managers go about changing culture? The challenge is to show the ineffectiveness of the current culture, implement the new "ways of doing things," and reinforce those new values. No single action is likely to have the impact necessary to change something that's so ingrained and highly valued. Thus, there needs to be a comprehensive and coordinated strategy for managing cultural change, as shown in Exhibit 13.5.

As you can see, these suggestions focus on specific actions that managers can take to change the ineffective culture. Following these suggestions, however, is no guarantee that a manager's change efforts will succeed. Organizational members don't quickly let go of values that they understand and that have worked well for them in the past. Managers must, therefore, be patient. Change, if it comes, will be slow. And managers must stay constantly alert to protect against any return to old, familiar practices and traditions.

CONTINUOUS QUALITY IMPROVEMENT PROGRAMS VERSUS PROCESS REENGINEERING

We know that quality management is important to managers since having quality products and services is essential to organizational success in today's global economy. Achieving desired levels of quality involves making changes in the way people work. Managers can make those changes either by using continuous quality improvement programs or by using a more radical process reengineering approach. Exhibit 13.6 summarizes the key differences between the two approaches.

MANAGING WORKFORCE DIVERSITY — The Paradox of Diversity

When organizations bring diverse individuals in and socialize them into the culture, a paradox is created.[18] Managers want these new employees to accept the organization's core cultural values. Otherwise, the employees may have a difficult time fitting in or being accepted. At the same time, managers want to openly acknowledge, embrace, and support the diverse perspectives and ideas that these employees bring to the workplace.

Strong organizational cultures put considerable pressure on employees to conform and the range of acceptable values and behaviors is limited. Therein lies the paradox. Organizations hire diverse individuals because of their unique strengths, yet their diverse behaviors and strengths are likely to diminish in strong cultures as people attempt to fit in.

A manager's challenge in this paradox of diversity is to balance two conflicting goals: to encourage employees to accept the organization's dominant values and to encourage employees to accept differences. When changes are made in the organization's culture, managers need to remember the importance of keeping diversity alive.

Exhibit 13.6	Continuous Quality Improvement	Reengineering
Continuous Quality Improvement Versus Reengineering	• Continuous, incremental change • Fixing and improving • Mostly "as is" • Works from bottom up in organization	• Radical change • Redesigning—starting over • Mostly "what can be" • Initiated by top management

Continuous Quality Improvement Programs Many quality management programs rely on continuous, small, and incremental changes. These programs are compatible with the calm waters metaphor because they recognize that organizations must continuously find ways to navigate the problems that arise as they strive to improve. In these types of quality programs, the change efforts are focused on fixing and improving current work activities. They're about continually improving activities that are basically OK. As continuous quality improvement is focused on individuals continually looking for ways to improve the way they work, participative decision making from the bottom levels up is important in both planning and implementing this type of program.

Process Reengineering In today's white-water rapids world, however, where long-term marketplace success increasingly belongs to the flexible and adaptive organization, there's a need for a different approach to change. Turbulent times require revolutionary, not orderly, change. And process reengineering is about dramatic and radical shifts in the way the organization performs its work—that is, its work processes.[19] It focuses on quantum changes by throwing out the old ways of doing things and starting over in redesigning the way work is done.

Reengineered manufacturing processes at Honda rely on robots that can be programmed quickly and cheaply. The high speed and low cost of Honda's model changeovers set new standards for the auto industry. Says one industry analyst, "Honda is already a leader in flexibility, and now they're going to get more flexible? That has to be scary to the competition."

It involves defining customer needs and then designing work processes to best meet those needs. For instance, Eaton Corporation reengineered its new-product-development process to help the company reach aggressive growth goals. The managers' and workers' redesign of the product innovation process led to a doubling of revenues and profits during a five-year period. At Sweden's ICA Handlarnas, reengineering work processes resulted in linking all the company's more than 3,300 retail stores to a single mainframe database so that inventory information was instantly available to managers. Because of the extensive nature of process reengineering, it's initiated by top management. However, because the process itself requires significant hands-on input from managers and workers, participative decision making is an important element.

7. **What situational factors might facilitate cultural change in an organization?**

8. **How can cultural change be implemented?**

9. **Contrast continuous quality improvement programs and process reengineering.**

HANDLING EMPLOYEE STRESS

For many employees, change creates stress. A dynamic and uncertain environment characterized by mergers, restructurings, process reengineering efforts, forced retirements, and downsizing has created a large number of employees who are overworked and stressed out.[20] In this section, we review what stress is, what causes it, how to identify it, and what managers can do to reduce it.

What Is Stress? **Stress** is a dynamic condition a person faces when confronted with an opportunity, constraint, or demand related to what he or she desires and for which the outcome is perceived to be both uncertain and important.[21] This is a complicated definition, so let's look at its components more closely.

Stress, in and of itself, is not necessarily bad. Although stress is often discussed in a negative context, it also has a positive value, particularly when it offers a potential gain. Functional stress allows an athlete, stage performer, or employee to perform at his or her highest level in crucial situations.

However, stress is more often associated with constraints and demands. A constraint prevents you from doing what you desire; demands refer to the loss of something desired. When you take a test at school or have your annual performance review at work, you feel stress because you confront opportunity, constraints, and demands. A good performance review may lead to a promotion, greater responsibilities, and a higher salary. But a poor review may keep you from getting the promotion. An extremely poor review might lead to your being fired.

Just because the conditions are right for stress to surface doesn't always mean it will. Two conditions are necessary for *potential* stress to become *actual* stress.[22] There must be uncertainty over the outcome, and the outcome must be important. Regardless of the conditions, a stressful condition exists only when there is doubt or uncertainty regarding whether the opportunity will be seized, whether the constraint will be removed, or whether the loss will be avoided. That is, stress is highest for individuals who are uncertain whether they will win or lose and lowest for individuals who think that winning or losing is a certainty. The importance of the outcome is also a critical factor. If winning or losing is unimportant, there is no stress. An employee who feels that keeping a job or earning a promotion is unimportant will experience no stress before a performance review.

Causes of Stress As shown in Exhibit 13.7, the causes of stress can be found in issues related to the organization or in personal factors that evolve out of the employee's private life. Clearly, change of any kind has the potential to cause stress. It can present opportunities, constraints, or demands. Moreover, changes are frequently created in a climate of uncertainty and around issues that are important to employees. It's not surprising, then, that change is a major stressor.

stress

A dynamic condition a person faces when confronted with an opportunity, constraint, or demand related to what he or she desires and for which the outcome is perceived to be both uncertain and important.

Exhibit 13.7

Causes of Stress

Personal Factors → STRESS ← Job-Related Factors

Signs of Stress What signs indicate that an employee's stress level might be too high? Stress shows itself in a number of ways. For instance, an employee who is experiencing high stress may become depressed, accident prone, or argumentative; may have difficulty making routine decisions; may be easily distracted, and so on. As Exhibit 13.8 shows, stress symptoms can be grouped under three general categories: physiological, psychological, and behavioral. Of these, the physiological symptoms are least relevant to managers. Of greater importance are the psychological and behavioral symptoms since these directly affect an employee's work.

Reducing Stress As we mentioned earlier, not all stress is dysfunctional. Since stress can never be totally eliminated from a person's life, either off the job or on, managers are concerned with reducing the kind of stress that leads to dysfunctional behavior. This can occur through controlling certain organizational factors to reduce organizational stress, and to a more limited extent, offering help for personal stress.

Things that managers can do in terms of organizational factors begin with employee selection. Managers need to make sure that an employee's abilities match the job requirements. When employees are in over their heads, their

Exhibit 13.8

Symptoms of Stress

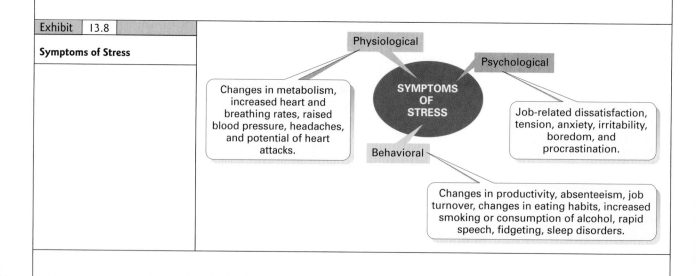

Physiological — Changes in metabolism, increased heart and breathing rates, raised blood pressure, headaches, and potential of heart attacks.

SYMPTOMS OF STRESS

Psychological — Job-related dissatisfaction, tension, anxiety, irritability, boredom, and procrastination.

Behavioral — Changes in productivity, absenteeism, job turnover, changes in eating habits, increased smoking or consumption of alcohol, rapid speech, fidgeting, sleep disorders.

? THINKING CRITICALLY ABOUT ETHICS

Although numerous organizations provide stress reduction programs, many employees choose not to participate. Why? Many employees are reluctant to ask for help, especially if a major source of that stress is job insecurity. After all, there's still a stigma associated with stress. Employees don't want to be perceived as being unable to handle the demands of their job. Although they may need stress management now more than ever, few employees want to admit that they're stressed. What can be done about this paradox? Do organizations even *have* an ethical responsibility to help employees deal with stress?

stress levels typically will be high. A realistic job preview during the selection process can also minimize stress by reducing ambiguity over job expectations. Improved organizational communications will keep ambiguity-induced stress to a minimum. Similarly, a performance planning program such as MBO will clarify job responsibilities, provide clear performance goals, and reduce ambiguity through feedback. Job redesign is also a way to reduce stress. If stress can be traced to boredom or to work overload, jobs should be redesigned to increase challenge or to reduce the workload. Redesigns that increase opportunities for employees to participate in decisions and to gain social support have also been found to lessen stress.[23]

Stress from an employee's personal life raises two problems. First, it's difficult for the manager to control directly. Second, there are ethical considerations. Specifically, does the manager have the right to intrude—even in the most subtle ways—in an employee's personal life? If a manager believes it's ethical and the employee is receptive, there are a few approaches the manager can consider. Employee *counseling* can provide stress relief. Employees often want to talk to someone about their problems, and the organization—through its managers, in-house human resource counselors, or free or low-cost outside professional help—can meet that need. Companies such as Citicorp, AT&T, and Johnson & Johnson provide extensive counseling services for their employees. A *time management program* can help employees whose personal lives suffer from a lack of planning that, in turn, creates stress. Such a program may help employees sort out their priorities.[24] For instance, Honeywell provides such a service. Still another approach is organizationally sponsored *wellness programs*. Mutual of Omaha, for example, has a Wellness Center in its Omaha offices. Other companies such as Coors Brewing

Does insufficient sleep cause stress? Or does a good nap relieve stress? Managers at Deloitte Consulting in Pittsburgh are taking no chances either way. Here senior consultant Philippe Truche takes a short refresher in the company's nap room. Many firms offer more active ways to relieve stress including game rooms, sports facilities, and classes in meditation, exercise, and yoga.

Testing...Testing...1,2,3

10. **Is stress all bad? Explain.**

11. **What signs might indicate to a manager that an employee's stress level is too high?**

12. **Describe what managers can do to reduce employee stress levels.**

Company in Golden, Colorado, the Quaker Oats Company in Chicago, and HBO in New York have set up on-site exercise centers for employees.[25] And at Philadelphia-based Cigna Corporation, employees are encouraged to take up to 15 minutes for a stress break when and where they need it. The company's philosophy is that "a few minutes of stretching or deep breathing can enhance personal health as well as attitudes, work performance, and overall teamwork."[26]

⟩ STIMULATING INNOVATION

"Winning in business today demands innovation."[27] Such is the stark reality facing today's managers. In the dynamic, chaotic world of e-business and global competition, organizations must create new products and services and adopt state-of-the-art technology if they are to compete successfully. Coors, for instance, has long been known for its technical innovations; it was the first beer company to use aluminum cans for packaging its products and was also the first to produce cold-filtered beer. However, the company isn't resting on its past successes. It continues to innovate products and processes.

What companies come to mind when you think of successful innovators? Maybe Sony Corporation, with its Walkman, PlayStation, Aibo robot pets, and Vaio PCs. Maybe 3M Corporation with its Post-it notes, Scotch-Guard protective coatings, and cellophane tape. Maybe Intel Corporation with its continual advancements in chip designs and new product introductions. What's the secret to the success of these innovator champions? What, if anything, can other managers do to make their organizations more innovative? In the following pages, we'll try to answer those questions as we discuss the factors behind innovation.

CREATIVITY VERSUS INNOVATION

creativity

The ability to combine ideas in a unique way or to make unusual associations between ideas.

Creativity refers to the ability to combine ideas in a unique way or to make unusual associations between ideas.[28] An organization that stimulates creativity develops unique ways to work or novel solutions to problems. **Innovation** is the process of taking a creative idea and turning it into a useful product, service, or work method. Thus, the innovative organization is characterized by its ability to channel creativity into useful outcomes. When managers talk about changing an organization to make it more creative, they usually mean they want to stimulate and nurture innovation. Sony, 3M, and Intel are aptly described as innovative because they take novel ideas and turn them into profitable products and work methods.

innovation

The process of taking a creative idea and turning it into a useful product, service, or work method.

STIMULATING AND NURTURING INNOVATION

By using the systems model we introduced in Chapter 1, we can better understand how organizations become more innovative.[29] (See Exhibit 13.9.) We see from the model that to get our desired output (creative products and work methods), we have to look at the inputs and the transformation of those inputs. Inputs include creative people and groups within the organization. But

MANAGING IN AN E-BUSINESS WORLD | Nurturing Innovation in an E-Business

Although innovation is important for all organizations, it's absolutely critical for e-businesses. As John Chambers, CEO of Cisco Systems, states so clearly, "The first company to capitalize on an innovation reaps the greatest rewards and most improved operating margins. When competitors start to use the same technologies, your competitive advantage or differentiation gets commoditized. Then it's time to move on to the next new thing."[30] The statement "innovate or lose" takes on added urgency in an e-business world.

The e-business world is definitely a white-water rapids environment. Change is continual, unpredictable, and sudden. In this type of environment, how can managers nurture the innovations that are so vital to success? As we discuss in the chapter, is the support provided through structural, cultural, and human resource variables also important to creating a climate of innovation in e-businesses? The answer would have to be a resounding "yes"! Let's take a closer look.

The structural characteristics of e-businesses are almost always organic in nature, which is exactly what innovation needs to take root and thrive. There is a high level of flexibility and openness. Employees can easily collaborate with others both inside the organization *and* outside. Also, easy access to information facilitates knowledge sharing among employees throughout the organization, which is critical for stimulating and nurturing innovative efforts. For instance, the loose structure at Tivoli Systems, a fast-moving software division of IBM, allows employees to share ideas and critique each other's efforts openly. Tivolians (as they like to call themselves) are comfortable with taking stands, speaking their minds, and challenging authority.

The cultures of e-business organizations are critical to the nurturing of innovation. From encouraging experimentation, risk, and conflict to accepting ambiguity, the cultures of e-businesses must value the pursuit of imagination, experimentation, and agility. And that culture begins with a compelling vision. Innovative e-businesses must have a clear and inspiring vision that serves as the motivation for people to come up with big ideas. Then the values embodied in the organization's culture need to support the pursuit of those ideas. Take General Electric, for instance, where former CEO Jack Welch fashioned a vision of GE as a nimble Web-savvy competitor even in its traditional, old-fashioned industries. Welch's vision established a cultural environment of innovation in which GE's employees continually share best practices and transfer knowledge among units.

Finally, human resource variables are important to innovation in e-businesses. Because of the hyperdynamic and competitive forces of the e-business world, everyone must play the role of idea champion. It's unrealistic in the fast-changing world of e-business to think that only a few people could be champions of change. It's imperative for success and survival that everyone in an e-business be actively engaged in searching for innovative products or services and innovative ways of doing work. It's fast paced and it's frenetic. The brutal realities of working in this type of setting will drive out those individuals who can't deal with hyperchange. But on a more positive note, those individuals who thrive in this type of environment tend to be those who are willing to try the new, the untested, the innovative. And that's exactly the type of people e-businesses need.

just having creative people isn't enough. It takes the right environment for the innovation process to take hold and prosper, just as a flower requires the proper soil, nutrients, water, and light to grow. What does this "right" environment look like? We've identified three sets of variables that have been found to stimulate innovation: the organization's structure, culture, and human resource practices. (See Exhibit 13.10.)

Inputs	Transformation	Outputs
Creative individuals, groups, organizations	Creative process Creative situation	Creative product(s), work methods

Exhibit 13.9

Systems View of Innovation

Source: Adapted from R.W. Woodman, J.E. Sawyer, and R.W. Griffin, "Toward a Theory of Organizational Creativity," *Academy of Management Review*, April 1993, p. 309.

<table>
<tr><td>

Exhibit 13.10

Innovation Variables

</td><td>

Structural Variables

- Organic Structures
- Abundant Resources
- High Interunit Communication

Cultural Variables

- Acceptance of Ambiguity
- Tolerance of the Impractical
- Low External Controls
- Tolerance of Risk
- Tolerance of Conflict
- Focus on Ends
- Open-System Focus

Human Resource Variables

- High Commitment to Training and Development
- High Job Security
- Creative People

STIMULATE INNOVATION

</td></tr>
</table>

Structural Variables Research into the effect of structural variables on innovation shows three things.[31] First, organic structures positively influence innovation. Because this type of organization is low in formalization, centralization, and work specialization, organic structures facilitate the flexibility, adaptability, and cross-fertilization necessary in innovation. Second, the easy availability of plentiful resources provides a key building block for innovation. With an abundance of resources, managers can afford to purchase innovations, can afford the cost of instituting innovations, and can absorb failures. Finally, frequent interunit communication helps break down barriers to innovation.[32] Cross-functional teams, task forces, and other such organizational designs facilitate interaction across departmental lines and are widely used in innovative organizations. 3M, for instance, is highly decentralized and takes on many of the characteristics of small, organic organizations. The company also has the "deep pockets" needed to support its policy of allowing scientists and engineers to use up to 15 percent of their time on projects of their own choosing.[33]

Cultural Variables Innovative organizations tend to have similar cultures.[34] They encourage experimentation, reward both successes and failures, and celebrate mistakes. An innovative culture is likely to have the following characteristics.

- *Acceptance of ambiguity.* Too much emphasis on objectivity and specificity constrains creativity.
- *Tolerance of the impractical.* Individuals who offer impractical, even foolish, answers to what-if questions are not stifled. What at first seems impractical might lead to innovative solutions.

- *Low external controls.* Rules, regulations, policies, and similar organizational controls are kept to a minimum.

- *Tolerance of risk.* Employees are encouraged to experiment without fear of consequences should they fail. Mistakes are treated as learning opportunities.

- *Tolerance of conflict.* Diversity of opinions is encouraged. Harmony and agreement between individuals or units are *not* assumed to be evidence of high performance.

- *Focus on ends rather than means.* Goals are made clear, and individuals are encouraged to consider alternative routes toward meeting the goals. Focusing on ends suggests that there might be several right answers to any given problem.

- *Open-system focus.* Managers closely monitor the environment and respond to changes as they occur.

Human Resource Variables Within the human resource category, we find that innovative organizations actively promote the training and development of their members so that their knowledge remains current, offer their employees high job security to reduce the fear of getting fired for making mistakes, and encourage individuals to become "champions" of change. **Idea champions** actively and enthusiastically support new ideas, build support, overcome resistance, and ensure that innovations are implemented. Research finds that these idea champions have common personality characteristics: extremely high self-confidence, persistence, energy, and a tendency toward risk taking. Champions also display characteristics associated with dynamic leadership. They inspire and energize others with their vision of the potential of an innovation and through their strong personal conviction in their mission. They're also good at gaining the commitment of others to support their mission. In addition, champions have jobs that provide considerable decision-making discretion. This autonomy helps them introduce and implement innovations in organizations.[35] For instance, the tiny, self-powered, self-guided rover vehicle named *Sojourner* that explored the surface of Mars never would have been built had it not been for an idea champion by the name of Donna L. Shirley. As the head of Mars exploration at NASA's Jet Propulsion Laboratory in Pasadena, California, Shirley had been working since the early 1980s on the idea of putting roving vehicles on Mars. Despite ongoing funding and management support problems, she continued to champion the idea until it was approved in the early 1990s. The successful Mars Pathfinder mission with *Sojourner's* roving over Mars's surface attests to the power of an idea champion.[36]

Steve Taylor's creativity led him to see that there was more to marketing lettuce than just bringing it to market. The innovation developed by his firm, Fresh Express of Salinas, California, became a $1.4 billion industry: the salad in a bag.

idea champion

Individuals who actively and enthusiastically support new ideas, build support, overcome resistance, and ensure that innovations are implemented.

13. **Differentiate between creativity and innovation.**

14. **How can the systems model be used to help organizations become more innovative?**

15. **Describe the specific structural, cultural, and human resource variables associated with innovation.**

Testing...Testing...1,2,3

Managers Respond to "A Manager's Dilemma"

Rick Allen Gladden

Manager, IT, FedEx Services, Collierville, Tennessee

Adam Ferguson

Data Resource Coordinator, Cox Health Systems, Springfield, Missouri

Helping those who work for and with me to remember that it's through change that we all succeed is a management function of highest priority. In Francisco's situation, I would attempt to head off all doubt and skepticism by sharing what truths are self-evident about the changes to my managers and I expect them to do the same with their staff. I find shared knowledge of the decisions and its process helps the staff to feel part of the decision, to take ownership, and to embrace the change. Management must take the initiative by sharing their vision and reinforcing how these changes fit the overall team mission as it relates to the staff. Changes that require training and development need to be scoped, budgeted, and planned for before the announcement of the changes. Lastly, I would follow up with my management team to make sure the changes were being implemented smoothly and efficiently.

As a computer professional in the ever-changing world of health care, I'm constantly confronted with changes—in the technical arena and in interoffice work flow. The manipulation of data provides a steady stream of small to system-wide changes.

When confronting the obstacle of changing the way people do things, or the form in which they are used to getting information, I try to focus as much attention as I can on the "why" instead of the "what." I have found it beneficial to look at changes from the viewpoint of *why* the change is needed. When I pass that angle on to my co-workers, while projecting a positive and enthusiastic attitude, the transition becomes much smoother. I also believe that people appreciate this type of explanation and excitement; they feel that they are "in the loop" of what's going on. With the "why" firmly in place and understood, it's been my experience that the "what" naturally follows with little or no resistance.

Chapter Summary

This summary is organized around the chapter-opening objectives found on p. 336.

1. The calm waters metaphor views change as a break in the organization's equilibrium state. Organizations are seen as stable and predictable, disturbed by an occasional crisis. The white-water rapids metaphor views change as continual and unpredictable. Managers must deal with ongoing and almost chaotic change.

2. Managers can change the organization's *structure* by altering structural components such as work specialization, departmentalization, chain of command, span of control, centralization and decentralization, formalization, or the organization's actual structural design; change the organization's *technology* by altering work processes, methods, and equipment; or change the organization's *people* by altering attitudes, expectations, perceptions, or behaviors.

3. Change is often resisted because of the uncertainty and ambiguity it creates, the concern for personal loss, and the belief that it might not be in the organization's best interest.

4. Six tactics reduce resistance to change: education and communication, participation, facilitation and support, negotiation, manipulation and cooptation, and coercion.

5. Dramatic crises and changes in top leadership facilitate cultural change by providing major shocks to employees and the status quo. Having a small or young organization and a weak culture facilitates cultural change by providing a more impressionable base with which to work.

6. Process reengineering is related to change since it involves radically redesigning an organization's work processes. These activities involve changes in structure, technology, and human resources.

7. Techniques for reducing employee stress include carefully matching applicants with jobs in the selection process, having clear performance objectives, redesigning jobs to increase challenges and reduce the workload, counseling employees, providing time management programs, and sponsoring wellness programs.

8. Creativity refers to the ability to combine ideas in a unique way or to make unusual associations between ideas. Innovation is the process of taking a creative idea and turning it into a useful product, service, or work method.

9. Organizations can stimulate and nurture innovation by having structures that are flexible, having easy access to resources, and having fluid communication. Innovation is also nurtured in a culture that is relaxed, is supportive of new ideas, encourages monitoring of the environment, and has creative people who are well trained, current in their fields, and secure in their jobs.

Thinking About Management Issues

1. Can a low-level employee be a change agent? Explain your answer.

2. Innovation requires allowing people to make mistakes. However, being wrong too many times can be damaging to one's career. Do you agree? Why or why not? What are the implications for nurturing innovation?

3. How are opportunities, constraints, and demands related to stress? Give an example of each.

4. Planned change is often thought to be the best approach to take in organizations. Can unplanned change ever be effective? Explain.

5. Organizations typically have limits to how much change they can absorb. As a manager, what signs would you look for that might suggest that your organization has exceeded its capacity to change?

Log On: Internet-Based Exercise

Change is a given for most organizations. What types of changes do they make? Find five examples of organizations that have made significant changes in the past year. Discuss the change by describing the type of change and what managers did to manage the change. Has the change impacted organizational performance? How?

Because organizational changes may involve major issues, managers often decide to hire outside organizational change consultants to assist in the change effort. Find five companies whose primary business is helping organizations manage change. What common characteristics, if any, did you find in the programs these companies offer?

Working Together: Team-Based Exercise

Stress is something that all of us face, and college students, particularly, may have extremely stressful lives. How do you recognize when you're under a lot of stress? What do you do to deal with that stress? Form teams of three or four students. Each person in the group should describe how he or she knows when he or she is under a lot of stress. What symptoms does each person show? Make a list of these symptoms and categorize them. Then each person should also describe things that he or she has found to be particularly effective in dealing with stress. Make a list of these stress-handling techniques. Out of that list, identify your top three stress reducers and be prepared to share these with the class.

Case Application

Reading Between the Lines

Reader's Digest. You may not admit to reading it, but you've undoubtedly seen the undersized magazine at your grandparents' house or in the waiting room at your doctor's office. It's the world's number-one general-interest magazine, translated into 19 languages for over 100 million readers worldwide. The Reader's Digest Association, Inc. publishes *Reader's Digest* in addition to books, music, videos, TV movies, and special-interest magazines. The company's products are marketed through well-targeted direct mailings and an extensive consumer database that's considered one of the world's best. Even with some significant operational and marketing strengths, the company has struggled through difficult times. In the mid-1990s, revenues and profits in key businesses were falling. Even the venerable flagship publication, *Reader's Digest,* had declining circulation and readership. Thomas O. Ryder, CEO, had some serious changes to make. However, getting a company with a long history and traditions to change wasn't an easy assignment.

The Reader's Digest Association was founded in 1922 by Lila and DeWitt Wallace. They published their first issue with articles of "enduring value and interest" out of their apartment in Greenwich Village. That purpose is still pursued today but in a broad range of media formats. The company is committed to informing, enriching, entertaining, and inspiring people of all ages and cultures.

Over the years, the company established itself as a solid publisher, growing by moving into different areas both geographically and in terms of products. However, along with the growth in size, Reader's Digest Association, like many traditional organizations, developed a slow-moving, entrenched bureaucracy with a culture described as "like molasses." Reader's Digest employees grew accustomed to a genteel way of doing business and enjoyed a work lifestyle that was paternalistic and cultured. For instance, a $100 million art collection graced company headquarters in Pleasantville, New York (its home since 1939). Founder DeWitt Wallace was known to give rides on the corporate jet to employees who had never flown before. And at 4:30 P.M. sharp, bells rang to signal the workday's end. It was a company clinging to the trappings of a bygone era.

As the company's performance continued to deteriorate, strategic and management changes were attempted. The company's board of directors hired (and fired) four CEOs in as many years. These individuals tried and failed to reshape the company. Then Thomas O. Ryder was hired in 1998. Talk about someone shaking up the place! Ryder was the shot in the arm the company needed, although his medicine was difficult to swallow for many of the company's longtime employees.

Coming from American Express Company, Ryder had a much more relaxed management style than the typical Reader's Digest executive. He was open, accessible, and

Reader's Digest Global Headquarters in Pleasantville, New York.

sociable. However, he knew that the company had to make some serious changes and that these changes weren't going to be easy. A $350 million cost-cutting program led to 1,000 people being laid off, the sale of the corporate jet, and the elimination of senior executive perks such as country club memberships. Then there was the sale of the company's art collection. Many longtime employees were upset by the sale, but Ryder believed that the art collection was an amenity that the company could no longer afford if it was going to be a nimble, Web-savvy publisher and direct marketer. Then Ryder tackled the company's way of working. Upon discovering it took almost a year to develop mailing campaigns, he hired outside firms to do some of the work. Some employees

resisted tinkering with decades of standard procedure. Ryder says the cost-cutting strategies were signals that "everyone would have to change the way they worked." To further instill a sense of moving forward, Ryder entered into several strategic alliances to expand the company's strong brand, including life insurance and credit cards.

Even though the changes seem to have made a difference in the company's financial performance, some long-time employees say that Ryder's attempts to create a sense of energy and drive are no different from other previous failed efforts. They don't think the enthusiasm shown at top levels has filtered down to the lower levels. As Ryder's predecessor said, "When you have a company as successful as the Digest was, the processes become embedded, and trying to change them is hard." Ryder counters by saying that his changes are different because he respects the Reader's Digest brand and the talents of its workforce, which he says had simply "lost its way."

QUESTIONS

1. Explain what external and internal forces created the need for Reader's Digest Association to change. Would you describe this change situation as calm waters or white-water rapids? Why?

2. What conditions for facilitating cultural change existed in this company?

3. What problems did Ryder encounter in trying to change the company's culture? Why did employees seem to be resisting change?

4. What could this situation teach you about changing organizational cultures?

Sources: Information from company's Web site (www.readers digest.com), October 23, 2000; information from Hoover's Online (www.hoovers.com), October 23, 2000; and M. Rose, "Mr. Ryder Rewrites the Musty Old Books at Reader's Digest," *Wall Street Journal*, April 18, 2000, pp. A1+.

Mastering Management

In Episode 3 of the Mastering Management *series, you'll learn about some of the difficulties associated with organizational change. With the possibility of an IPO looming, Liz feels that CanGo must adopt a more formal organizational structure. Her suggestion prompts a heated discussion among the members of the management team about the relationship between CanGo's culture and its future performance.*

Michael Hannon, president of Graphic Laminating Inc. in Solon, Ohio, redesigned his organization's structure by transforming it into an employee-empowered company. He wanted to drive authority down through the organization so that employees were responsible for their own efforts. One way he did this was by creating employee teams to handle specific projects. Employees with less experience were teamed with veteran employees. He says, "I want to build a good team and give people the ability to succeed. Sometimes that means giving them the ability to make mistakes, and I have to keep that in perspective. The more we allow people to become better at what they do, the better they will become—and the better we all will do."[1]

Once the start-up and planning issues for the entrepreneurial venture have been addressed, the entrepreneur is ready to begin organizing the entrepreneurial venture. What organizing issues will an entrepreneur have to deal with? There are five issues including the legal forms of organization, organizational design and structure, human resource management, stimulating and making changes, and the continuing importance of innovation.

Legal Forms of Organization

The first organizing decision that an entrepreneur must make is a critical one. It's the form of legal ownership for the venture. The two primary factors that affect this decision are taxes and legal liability. An entrepreneur wants to minimize the impact of both of these factors. The right choice can protect the entrepreneur from legal liability as well as save tax dollars, in both the short run and the long run.

What alternatives are available? There are three basic ways to organize an entrepreneurial venture: sole proprietorship, partnership, and corporation. However, when you include the variations of these basic organizational alternatives, you end up with six possible choices, each with its own tax consequences, liability issues, and pros and cons. These six choices are sole proprietorship, general partnership, limited liability partnership (LLP), C corporation, S corporation, and limited liability company (LLC). Let's briefly look at each one with their advantages and drawbacks. (Exhibit P4.1 summarizes the basic information about each organizational alternative.)

Sole Proprietorship. A **sole proprietorship** is a form of legal organization in which the owner maintains sole and complete control over the business and is personally liable for business debts. There are no legal requirements for establishing a sole proprietorship other than obtaining necessary local business licenses and permits. In a sole proprietorship, income and losses "pass through" to the owner and are taxed at the owner's personal income tax rate. The biggest drawback, however, is the unlimited personal liability for any and all debts of the business.

General Partnership. A **general partnership** is a form of legal organization in which two or more business owners share the management and risk of the business. Even though a partnership is possible without a written agreement, the potential and inevitable problems that arise in any partnership make a written partnership agreement drafted by legal counsel a highly recommended thing to do.

Can partnerships work? Can best friends in personal life be best friends at work? Gail Tessler and Norma Menkin, long-time best friends, are partners and co-presidents of Gainor Staffing, a staffing firm located in New York City. Each woman brings a particular strength to the business. And even though they have had their disagreements, both women know that they have a rarity in partnerships—an arrangement that has worked successfully for them.[2]

Limited Liability Partnership (LLP). The **limited liability partnership (LLP)** is a form of legal organization in which there are general partner(s) and limited liability partner(s). The general partners actually operate and manage the business. They are the ones who have unlimited liability. There must be at least one general partner in an LLP. However, there can be any number of limited partners. These partners are usually passive investors, although they can make management suggestions to the general partners. They also have the right to inspect the business and make copies of business records. The limited partners are entitled to a share of the business's profits as agreed to in the partnership agreement, and their risk is limited to the amount of their investment in the LLP.

C Corporation. Of the three basic types of ownership, the corporation (also known as a C corporation) is the most complex to form and operate. A **corporation** is a legal business entity that is separate from its owners and managers. Many entrepreneurial ventures are organized as a **closely held corporation**, which, very simply, is a corporation owned by a limited number of people who do not trade the stock publicly. Whereas the sole proprietorship and partnership forms of organization do not exist separately from the entrepreneur, the corporation does. The corporation functions as a distinct legal entity and, as such, can make contracts, engage in business activities, own property, sue and be sued, and of course, pay taxes. A corporation must operate in accordance with its charter and the laws of the state in which it operates.

| Exhibit | P4.1 | | **Legal Forms of Business Organization** | | | |

Structure	Ownership Requirements	Tax Treatment	Liability	Advantages	Drawbacks
Sole proprietorship	One owner	Income and losses "pass through" to owner and are taxed at personal rate	Unlimited personal liability	*Low start-up costs* Freedom from most regulations *Owner has direct control* All profits go to owner *Easy to exit business*	Unlimited personal liability *Personal finances at risk* Miss out on many business tax deductions *Total responsibility* May be more difficult to raise financing
General partnership	Two or more owners	Income and losses "pass through" to partners and are taxed at personal rate; *flexibility in profit-loss allocations to partners*	Unlimited personal liability	*Ease of formation* Pooled talent *Pooled resources* Somewhat easier access to financing *Some tax benefits*	Unlimited personal liability *Divided authority and decisions* Potential for conflict *Continuity of transfer of ownership*
Limited liability partnership (LLP)	Two or more owners	Income and losses "pass through" to partners and are taxed at personal rate; *flexibility in profit-loss allocations to partners*	Limited, although one partner must retain unlimited liability	*Good way to acquire capital from limited partners*	Cost and complexity of forming can be high *Limited partners cannot participate in management of business without losing liability protection*
C corporation	Unlimited number of shareholders; *no limits on types of stock or voting arrangements*	Dividend income is taxed at corporate and personal shareholder levels; *losses and deductions are corporate*	Limited	*Limited liability* Transferable ownership *Continuous existence* Easier access to resources	Expensive to set up *Closely regulated* Double taxation *Extensive record keeping* Charter restrictions
S corporation	Up to 75 shareholders; *no limits on types of stock or voting arrangements*	Income and losses "pass through" to partners and are taxed at personal rate; *flexibility in profit-loss allocation to partners*	Limited	*Easy to set up* Enjoy limited liability protection and tax benefits of partnership *Can have a tax-exempt entity as a shareholder*	Must meet certain requirements *May limit future financing options*
Limited liability company (LLC)	Unlimited number of "members"; *flexible membership arrangements for voting rights and income*	Income and losses "pass through" to partners and are taxed at personal rate; *flexibility in profit-loss allocations to partners*	Limited	*Greater flexibility* Not constrained by regulations on C and S corporations *Taxed as partnership, not as corporation*	Cost of switching from one form to this can be high *Need legal and financial advice in forming operating agreement*

S Corporation. The **S corporation** (also called a subchapter S corporation) is a specialized type of corporation that has the regular characteristics of a corporation but is unique in that the owners are taxed as a partnership as long as certain criteria are met. The S corporation has been the classic organizing approach for getting the limited liability of a corporate structure without incurring corporate tax. However, this form of legal organization must meet strict criteria. If any of these criteria are violated, a venture's S status is automatically terminated.

Limited Liability Company (LLC). The **limited liability company (LLC)** is a relatively new form of business organization that's a hybrid between a partnership and a corporation. The LLC offers the liability protection of a corporation, the tax benefits of a partnership, and fewer restrictions than on an S corporation. However, the main drawback of this approach is that it's quite complex and expensive to set up. Legal and financial advice is an absolute necessity in forming the LLC's **operating agreement**, which is the document that outlines the provisions governing the way the LLC will conduct business.

Summary of Legal Forms of Organization. The organizing decision regarding the legal form of organization is an important one because it can have significant tax and liability consequences. Although the legal form of organization can be changed, it's not an easy thing to do. An entrepreneur needs to think carefully about what's important, especially in the areas of flexibility, taxes, and amount of personal liability in choosing the best form of organization.

Organizational Design and Structure

The choice of an appropriate organizational structure is also an important decision when organizing the entrepreneurial venture. At some point, successful entrepreneurs find that they can't do everything alone. More people are needed. The entrepreneur must then decide on the most appropriate structural arrangement for effectively and efficiently carrying out the organization's activities. Without some suitable type of organizational structure, the entrepreneurial venture may soon find itself in a chaotic situation.

In many small firms, the organizational structure tends to evolve with very little conscious and deliberate planning by the entrepreneur. For the most part, the structure may be very simple—one person who does whatever is needed. As the entrepreneurial venture grows and the entrepreneur finds it increasingly difficult to go it alone, employees are brought on board to perform certain functions or duties that the entrepreneur can't handle. These individuals tend to keep doing those same functions as the company grows. Then, as the entrepreneurial venture continues to grow, each of these functional areas may require managers and employees.

With the evolution to a more deliberate structure, the entrepreneur faces a whole new set of challenges. All of a sudden, he or she must share decision making and operating responsibilities. This is typically one of the most difficult things for an entrepreneur to do—letting go and allowing someone else to make decisions. After all, he or she reasons, how can anyone know this business as well as I do? Also, what might have been a fairly informal, loose, and flexible atmosphere that worked well when the organization was small may no longer be effective. Many entrepreneurs are greatly concerned about keeping that "small company" atmosphere alive even as the venture grows and evolves into a more structured arrangement. But having a structured organization doesn't necessarily mean giving up flexibility, adaptability, and freedom. In fact, the structural design may be as fluid as the entrepreneur feels comfortable with and yet still have the rigidity it needs to operate efficiently.

Organizational design decisions in entrepreneurial ventures revolve around the six key elements of organizational structure that we discussed in Chapter 10: work specialization, departmentalization, chain of command, span of control, amount of centralization-decentralization, and amount of formalization. Decisions about these six elements will determine whether an entrepreneur designs a more mechanistic or a more organic organizational structure (concepts we also discussed in Chapter 10). When would each be preferable? A mechanistic structure would be preferable when cost efficiencies are critical to the venture's competitive advantage; where more control over employees' work activities is important; if the venture produces standardized products in a routine fashion; and when the external environment is relatively stable and certain. An organic structure would be most appropriate when innovation is critical to the organization's competitive advantage; for smaller organizations where rigid approaches to dividing and coordinating work aren't necessary; if the organization produces customized products in a flexible setting; and where the external environment is dynamic, complex, and uncertain.

Testing...Testing...1,2,3

1. **Contrast the six different forms of legal organization.**

2. **What organizational design issues do entrepreneurs face as the venture grows?**

3. **When would a more mechanistic structure be preferable? An organic structure?**

Human Resource Management Issues in Entrepreneurial Ventures

As an entrepreneurial venture grows, additional employees will need to be hired to perform the increased workload. As employees are brought on-board, the entrepreneur faces certain human resource management issues. Two HRM issues of particular importance to entrepreneurs are employee recruitment and employee retention.

Employee Recruitment. An entrepreneur wants to ensure that the venture has the people it needs to do the work that's required. And recruiting new employees is one of the biggest challenges that entrepreneurs face. In fact, the ability of small firms to successfully recruit appropriate employees is consistently rated as one of the most important factors influencing organizational success.[3]

Entrepreneurs, particularly, are looking for high potential people who can perform multiple roles during various stages of venture growth. They look for individuals who "buy into" the venture's entrepreneurial culture—individuals who have a passion for the business.[4] Unlike their corporate counterparts who often focus on filling a job by matching a person to the job requirements, entrepreneurs look to fill in critical skills gaps. They're looking for people who are exceptionally capable and self-motivated, flexible, multiskilled, and who can help grow the entrepreneurial venture. While corporate managers tend to focus on using traditional HRM practices and techniques, entrepreneurs are more concerned with matching characteristics of the person to the values and culture of the organization; that is, they focus on matching the person to the organization.[5]

Employee Retention. Getting competent and qualified people into the venture is just the first step in effectively managing the human resources. An entrepreneur wants to keep the people he or she has hired and trained. Sabrina Horn, president of The Horn Group, based in San Francisco, understands the importance of having good people on board and keeping them. Her public relations firm employs around 45 employees who create PR for technology firms. In this rough-and-tumble, intensely competitive industry, Sabrina knows that the loss of talented employees could harm client services. To combat this, she offers employees a wide array of desirable benefits such as raises of six percent or more each year, profit sharing, trust funds for employees' children, paid sabbaticals, personal development funds, and so forth. But, more importantly, Sabrina recognizes that employees have a life outside the office and treats them accordingly. This type of HRM approach has kept her employees loyal and productive.[6]

A unique and important employee retention issue entrepreneurs must deal with is compensation. Whereas traditional organizations are more likely to view compensation from the perspective of monetary rewards (base pay, benefits, and incentives), smaller entrepreneurial firms are more likely to view compensation from a total rewards perspective. For these firms, compensation encompasses psychological rewards, learning opportunities, and recognition, in addition to monetary rewards (base pay and incentives).[7]

Stimulating and Making Changes

We know from an earlier module that the context facing entrepreneurs is one of dynamic change. Both external and internal forces (see Chapter 13) may bring about the need for making changes in the entrepreneurial venture. Entrepreneurs need to be alert to problems and opportunities that may create the need to change. In fact, of the many hats an entrepreneur wears, that of change agent may be one of the most important.[8] If changes are needed in the entrepreneurial venture, often it is the entrepreneur who first recognizes the need for change and acts as the catalyst, coach and cheerleader, and chief change consultant. Change isn't easy in any organization, but it can be particularly challenging for entrepreneurial ventures. Even if a person is comfortable with taking risks, as entrepreneurs usually are, change can be hard. That's why it's important for an entrepreneur to recognize the critical roles he or she plays in stimulating and implementing change. For instance, Terry Elrich, publisher and editor-in-chief of *Hemmings Motor News* [www.hemmings.com] knows how important it is to act as a catalyst for change. He has built the magazine to its role as "the bible of the car-collector hobby market" by being a savvy businessperson *and* a savvy change-agent. He hasn't been afraid to take risks and make changes in his entrepreneurial venture.[9]

During any type of organizational change, an entrepreneur also may have to act as chief coach and cheerleader. Since organizational change of any type can be disruptive and scary, the entrepreneur must assume the role of explaining the change and encouraging change efforts by supporting, explaining, getting employees excited about the change, building employees up, and motivating employees to put forth their best efforts. In other words, doing those things that coaches and cheerleaders do for a team.

Finally, the entrepreneur may have to guide the actual change process as changes in strategy, technology, products, structure, or people are being implemented. In this role, the entrepreneur answers questions, makes suggestions, gets needed resources, facilitates conflict, and does whatever else is necessary to get the change(s) implemented.

The Continuing Importance of Innovation

In today's dynamic chaotic world of global competition, organizations must continually innovate new products and services if they want to compete successfully. We know that innovation is a key characteristic of entrepreneurial ventures. In fact, you can say that innovation is what makes the entrepreneurial venture "entrepreneurial."

What must an entrepreneur do to encourage innovation in the venture? Having an innovation-supportive culture is crucial. What does such a culture look like?[10] It's one in which employees perceive that supervisory support and organizational reward systems are consistent with a commitment to innovation. It's also important in this type of culture that employees not perceive that their workload pressures are excessive or unreasonable. And research has shown that firms with cultures supportive of innovation tend to be smaller, have fewer formalized human resource practices, and less abundant resources.[11]

Although having an innovation-supportive culture is important, employees also need to be able to do something with those innovations. For instance, employees at Monarch Marking Systems Inc. in Miamisburg, Ohio, know how to turn ideas into action. To improve the productivity levels in one particular area, an employee team pondered several potential remedies, tested theories, and ultimately implemented five solutions. The team's innovative solutions reduced the amount of time to change over the production line from 60 minutes to four minutes. And, even better, the innovative solutions made the employees' jobs easier.[12]

Testing...Testing...1,2,3

4. **What unique HRM issues must entrepreneurs deal with?**

5. **Why is the role of change agent an important one for entrepreneurs?**

6. **Describe what an innovation-supportive culture for an entrepreneurial venture looks like.**

HUMAN RESOURCES AND TECHNOLOGY

On Location

In this video segment we hear from executives at three of the featured firms—i2Go, producers of digital media products; Clif Bar, the health-food company; and Monster.com, the online recruiting and job assistance firm.

In all three firms, and in many others like them in manufacturing and service industries of all kinds, technology has become a highly valued asset, embedded in strategy and decision making at every level. It has transformed nearly all these organizations' business processes, and in this segment you can see its impact on the human resources function in particular.

Perhaps the most dramatic change that technology has brought to human resources is the ability of the Internet to speed and facilitate the job search and placement process for both employee and employer. This ability to match people with jobs is in fact at the heart of Monster.com's own business, but it is also one that many firms now take advantage of in their hiring. Monster.com itself hired its chief technology officer through an online posting. Only a year ago, Clif Bar had a full-time recruiter on staff; now the firm does virtually all its recruiting online in about half the time. With sales doubling every year, the company constantly seeks new hires to help maintain its growth.

Other technology applications in human resources include Intranets that keep employees in close contact with management and with each other even if they are separated by thousands of miles. At Monster.com, employees at 29 locations in 14 different countries can watch the company's president and the CEO discuss sales and strategies via monthly streaming videos broadcast on the firm's Intranet. Benefits administration, employment record-keeping tasks, and forecasts of future employment needs are also made simpler and more accurate with online systems at all three firms.

You will probably notice that all three managers firmly believe people to be their companies' best or strongest asset, and they stress that human resources management remains a very people-oriented process. Try to note some of the reasons that these managers offer for finding some limitations on the use of technology in HR, despite the tremendous improvements in efficiency, accuracy, and speed that it offers. Decide what human resource functions you think are best handled face to face. Are there circumstances under which you think your decision would change?

DISCUSSION QUESTIONS

1. How do you think the widespread use of online recruiting affects the employment process from the prospective employee's point of view? Will you handle your next job search differently knowing that it is likely to be conducted, at least initially, online? What do you think you would do differently, and why?

2. Do you think there could be any drawbacks to using computer technology to assist in sorting and pre-qualifying job candidates, as described by Jim Saccone of i2Go? If so, what are they? How can human resource managers avoid them?

3. If you were a human resources manager planning an online system to enable employees to choose their own benefits packages and maintain their benefits files, what kind of information would you want the system to provide to employees? What kind of safeguards do you think would be required?

4. Clif Bar's human resources efforts are focused as much on retention as on recruiting. Do you think this balance is appropriate for a firm? Why or why not? How can technology help in employee retention?

5. In what sense do you think it is true that the human resources function has evolved to the status of being a "partner" on the senior management team at a firm like Monster.com?

Learning Objectives

After reading and studying this chapter, you should be able to:

1. Define the focus and goals of organizational behavior.

2. Describe the three components of an attitude.

3. Identify the role that consistency plays in attitudes.

4. Explain the relationship between satisfaction and productivity.

5. Tell how managers can use the Myers-Briggs personality type framework and the big-five model of personality.

6. Define emotional intelligence.

7. Describe attribution theory and its use in explaining individual behavior.

8. Identify the types of shortcuts managers use in judging others.

9. Explain how managers can shape employee behavior.

A MANAGER'S DILEMMA

How would you feel if you were a new employee, your boss asked you to do something, and you had to admit that you didn't know how to do it? Most of us would feel inadequate and incompetent. Now imagine how strange and uncomfortable it would be if, after experiencing such an incident, you went home with the boss because you two are roommates and have been friends since fourth grade. This, in fact, is a situation faced by John Kim (on right in photo), an employee at Plumtree Software (www.plumtree.com) and his boss, Glen Kelman (left front in photo), co-founder and vice president of product management and marketing. A third roommate, Conan Reidy (background in photo), also works at Plumtree.[1] The three roommates are finding that mixing work and friendships can be tricky!

At home, the roommates are equals. They share a single bathroom and housework. However, at work, equality is out the door! For instance, a problem with office assignments erupted when Plumtree moved into new headquarters. As part of the four-person management team, Kelman has a corner office with windows. Reidy, who works in a cubicle, was annoyed at Kelman for not standing up for him when offices were assigned. However, Reidy didn't complain because he didn't want to get an office only because of his closeness with Kelman. Another problem brewing is that the roommates compete to outlast one another working

Foundations of Behavior

14

late. Reidy's boss worries that he's going to burn out. Other awkward situations arise whenever the company's performance is being discussed. Often Kelman wants to complain about work but has to stop himself. When the company's president calls, Kelman goes into his bedroom and shuts the door. And, if the company decides to sell stock to the public, Kelman's financial wealth could increase dramatically, creating some interesting emotional issues for the roommates. Although it might seem easy to say "move," it's too expensive and these guys are his good friends. Put yourself in Kelman's position. How could he use information about emotions and attitudes to handle this situation?

WHAT WOULD YOU DO?

Y ou're probably already well aware of the fact that people differ in their attitudes and behavior. For instance, you interact daily with people who have different types of personalities. And haven't you seen family members or friends behave in ways that prompted you to wonder: Why did they do that? As the chapter-opening case illustrates, effective managers need to understand behavior. This chapter introduces several psychological factors that influence employee behavior and then considers the implications of each for management practice.

❭ WHY LOOK AT INDIVIDUAL BEHAVIOR?

The material in this and the next three chapters draws heavily on the field of study that is known as *organizational behavior (OB)*. Although it's concerned with the subject of **behavior**—that is, the actions of people—**organizational behavior** is concerned more specifically with the actions of people at work.

One of the challenges in understanding organizational behavior is that it addresses issues that aren't obvious. Like an iceberg, OB has a small visible dimension and a much larger hidden portion. (See Exhibit 14.1.) What we see when we look at organizations is their visible aspects: strategies, goals, policies and procedures, structure, technology, formal authority relationships, and chain of command. But under the surface are other elements that managers need to understand—elements that also influence how employees work. As we'll show, OB provides managers with considerable insights into these important, but hidden, aspects of the organization.

FOCUS OF ORGANIZATIONAL BEHAVIOR

Organizational behavior focuses primarily on two major areas. First, OB looks at *individual behavior*. Based predominantly on contributions from psychologists, this area includes such topics as attitudes, personality, perception, learning, and motivation. Second, OB is concerned with *group behavior*, which includes norms,

behavior

The actions of people.

organizational behavior

The actions of people at work.

Exhibit 14.1

The Organization as an Iceberg

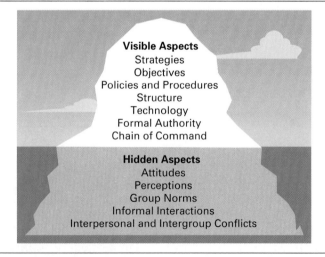

Visible Aspects
Strategies
Objectives
Policies and Procedures
Structure
Technology
Formal Authority
Chain of Command

Hidden Aspects
Attitudes
Perceptions
Group Norms
Informal Interactions
Interpersonal and Intergroup Conflicts

roles, team building, leadership, and conflict. Our knowledge about groups comes basically from the work of sociologists and social psychologists. Unfortunately, the behavior of a group of employees can't be understood by merely summing up the actions of the individuals in the group because individuals in a group setting behave differently from individuals acting alone. You see this characteristic at its extreme, for instance, when a street gang harasses innocent people. The gang members, acting individually, might never engage in such behavior. Therefore, because employees in an organization are both individuals and members of groups, we need to study them at two levels. In this chapter, we'll provide the foundation for understanding individual behavior. Then, in the next chapter, we'll introduce the basic concepts related to understanding group behavior.

GOALS OF ORGANIZATIONAL BEHAVIOR

The goals of OB are to *explain, predict,* and *influence* behavior. Why do managers need to be able to do these? Simply, in order to manage their employees' behavior. We know that a manager's success depends on getting things done through people. To do this, the manager needs to be able to explain why employees engage in some behaviors rather than others, predict how employees will respond to various actions the manager might take, and influence how employees behave.

Willis T. White is president of West Coast Valet Service, a California commercial laundry and dry cleaner. When it comes to employees' emotions, he says, "Give them a high priority, because they affect productivity." White's attitude reflects the same focus as the field of organizational behavior—the psychological aspects of human behavior at work.

What employee behaviors are we specifically concerned about explaining, predicting, and influencing? We'll emphasize employee productivity, absenteeism, and turnover. We'll also look at job satisfaction. Although job satisfaction is an attitude rather than a behavior, it is an outcome that concerns many managers. In the following pages, we'll address how an understanding of employee attitudes, personality, perception, and learning can help us predict, explain, and influence employee productivity, absenteeism and turnover rates, and job satisfaction.

---

1. **Define organizational behavior.**

2. **Why is the concept of the organization as an iceberg important to understanding organizational behavior?**

3. **What are the goals of organizational behavior?**

Testing...Testing...1,2,3

> | **ATTITUDES**

Attitudes are evaluative statements—either favorable or unfavorable—concerning objects, people, or events. They reflect how an individual feels about something. When a person says, "I like my job," he or she is expressing an attitude about work.

To better understand the concept of attitudes, we should look at an attitude as being made up of three components: cognition, affect, and behavior.[2] The **cognitive component** of an attitude is made up of the beliefs, opinions, knowledge,

attitudes

Evaluative statements, either favorable or unfavorable, concerning objects, people, or events.

cognitive component

The part of an attitude that's made up of the beliefs, opinions, knowledge, or information held by a person.

affective component

The part of an attitude that's the emotional or feeling part.

behavioral component

The part of an attitude that refers to an intention to behave in a certain way toward someone or something.

job satisfaction

An employee's general attitude toward his or her job.

job involvement

The degree to which an employee identifies with his or her job, actively participates in it, and considers his or her job performance to be important to self-worth.

organizational commitment

An employee's orientation toward the organization in terms of his or her loyalty to, identification with, and involvement in the organization.

organizational citizenship behavior (OCB)

Discretionary behavior that is not part of an employee's formal job requirements but that nevertheless promotes the effective functioning of the organization.

or information held by a person. The belief that "discrimination is wrong" illustrates a cognition. The **affective component** of an attitude is the emotional or feeling part of an attitude. Using our example, this component would be reflected by the statement, "I don't like Jon because he discriminates against minorities." Finally, affect can lead to behavioral outcomes. The **behavioral component** of an attitude refers to an intention to behave in a certain way toward someone or something. To continue our example, I might choose to avoid Jon because of my feelings about him. Looking at attitudes as being made up of three components—cognition, affect, and behavior—helps show the complexity of attitudes. But for the sake of clarity, keep in mind that the term *attitude* usually refers only to the affective component.

Naturally, managers aren't interested in every attitude an employee might hold. They're especially interested in job-related attitudes. The three most popular of these are job satisfaction, job involvement, and organizational commitment.[3] **Job satisfaction** is an employee's general attitude toward his or her job. A person with a high level of job satisfaction holds positive attitudes toward the job, while a person who is dissatisfied with the job holds negative attitudes. When people speak of employee attitudes, they usually are referring to job satisfaction. **Job involvement** is the degree to which an employee identifies with his or her job, actively participates in it, and considers his or her job performance to be important to his or her self-worth. **Organizational commitment** represents an employee's orientation toward the organization in terms of his or her loyalty to, identification with, and involvement in the organization.

Another job-related concept that managers may find important in understanding employee attitudes is that of **organizational citizenship behavior (OCB),** which is discretionary behavior that is not part of an employee's formal job requirements but that nevertheless promotes the effective functioning of the organization.[4] Examples of good OCB include helping others on one's work team, volunteering for extended job activities, avoiding unnecessary conflicts, and making constructive statements about one's work group and the organization. In today's workplace, where teamwork and cooperation are increasingly relied on to get things done, organizations are likely to prefer having employees who exhibit organizational citizenship behavior.

In recent years, all of these—job satisfaction, job involvement, organizational commitment, and organizational citizenship behavior—have been popular topics for organizational researchers.[5]

Testing...Testing...1,2,3

4. **What are the three components of an attitude?**

5. **Describe the three job-related attitudes.**

6. **What is organizational citizenship behavior?**

ATTITUDES AND CONSISTENCY

Did you ever notice that people change what they say so it doesn't contradict what they do? Perhaps a friend of yours has repeatedly argued that she thinks joining a sorority is an important part of college life, but then she goes through

rush and doesn't get accepted. All of a sudden, she's saying that she thinks sororities are dumb and sorority life isn't all that it's cracked up to be.

Research has generally concluded that people seek consistency among their
attitudes *and* between their attitudes and behavior.[6] This means that individuals
try to reconcile differing attitudes and align their attitudes and behavior so they
appear rational and consistent. When there is an inconsistency, individuals will
take steps to make it consistent either by altering the attitudes or the behavior or
by developing a rationalization for the inconsistency.

For example, a campus recruiter for R&S Company, who visits college cam-
puses, identifies qualified job candidates, and sells them on the advantages of
R&S as a good place to work, would experience conflict if he personally believed
that R&S had poor working conditions and few opportunities for promotion.
This recruiter could, over time, find his attitudes toward R&S becoming more
positive. He may, in effect, convince himself by continually articulating the
merits of working for the company. Another alternative is that the recruiter
could become openly negative about R&S and the opportunities within the
company for prospective applicants. The original enthusiasm that the recruiter
might have shown would dwindle, probably to be replaced by outright cynicism
toward the company. Finally, the recruiter might acknowledge that R&S is an
undesirable place to work but, as a professional recruiter, realize that his obligation is to present the positive aspects of working for the company. He might further rationalize that no workplace is perfect and that his job is not to present
both sides of the issue but to present a favorable picture of the company.

COGNITIVE DISSONANCE THEORY

Can we assume from this consistency principle that an individual's behavior can
always be predicted if we know his or her attitude on a subject? The answer,
unfortunately, is more complex than merely "yes" or "no." The reason is cognitive dissonance theory.

Cognitive dissonance theory sought to explain the relationship between attitudes and behavior.[7] **Cognitive dissonance** is any incompatibility or inconsistency between attitudes or between behavior and attitudes. The theory argued
that any form of inconsistency is uncomfortable and that individuals will try to
reduce the dissonance and, thus, the discomfort. In other words, individuals seek
stability with a minimum of dissonance.

cognitive dissonance

Any incompatibility or
inconsistency between attitudes
or between behavior and
attitudes.

Of course, no one can completely avoid dissonance. You know that cheating
on your tax return is wrong, but you "fudge" the numbers a bit every year and
hope that you won't be audited. Or you tell your children to brush their teeth
after every meal, but you don't do it yourself. In each of these instances, there's an
inconsistency between attitude and behavior. How do people cope with cognitive
dissonance? The theory proposed that the desire to reduce dissonance is determined by the *importance* of the factors creating the dissonance, the degree of *influence* the individual believes he or she has over those factors, and the *rewards* that
may be involved in dissonance.

If the factors creating the dissonance are relatively unimportant, the pressure
to correct the inconsistency will be low. For instance, say that a corporate manager—Mrs. Sanchez—believes strongly that no company should treat assembly-
line employees unfairly or inhumanely. Unfortunately, Mrs. Sanchez because of
job requirements is placed in the position of having to make decisions that would

trade off her company's profitability against her attitudes on compassionate treatment of employees. She knows that running an efficient manufacturing facility is in her company's best interest. What will she do? Clearly, Mrs. Sanchez will be experiencing a high degree of cognitive dissonance. Because of the importance of the issue to Mrs. Sanchez, we can't expect her to ignore the inconsistency, but there are several paths that she can follow to deal with her discomfort. She can change her behavior by using her authority to order that employees be treated fairly and humanely. Or she can reduce dissonance by concluding that the dissonant behavior isn't so important after all ("I've got to have a job, and in my role as a corporate decision maker, I often have to place the good of my company above that of society"). A third alternative would be for Mrs. Sanchez to change her attitude ("There's nothing wrong with the way our employees are treated. After all, they do have a job"). Still another choice would be for her to identify compatible factors that outweigh the dissonant ones ("The benefits to society from our giving people jobs more than offset the cost to society of not always treating employees compassionately").

The degree of influence that individuals believe they have over the factors also will affect their reaction to the dissonance. If they perceive the dissonance to be an uncontrollable result—something about which they have no choice—they are not likely to be receptive to attitude change or to feel a need for it. If, for example, the dissonance-producing behavior was required as a result of a manager's order, the pressure to reduce dissonance would be less than if the behavior had been performed voluntarily. Although dissonance would exist, it could be rationalized and justified by the need to follow the manager's orders—that is, the individual has no choice and control.

Finally, rewards also influence the degree to which individuals are motivated to reduce dissonance. Coupling high dissonance with high rewards tends to reduce the discomfort inherent in the dissonance, by motivating the individual to believe that there is consistency.

These moderating factors suggest that just because individuals experience dissonance, they will not necessarily move toward consistency—that is, attempting to reduce the dissonance. If the issues contributing to the dissonance are of minimal importance, if an individual perceives that the dissonance is externally imposed and is substantially uncontrollable by him or her, or if rewards are significant enough to offset the dissonance, the individual will not be pressured to reduce the dissonance.

ATTITUDE SURVEYS

attitude surveys

Surveys that elicit responses from employees through questions about how they feel about their jobs, work groups, supervisors, or the organization.

Many organizations regularly survey their employees about their attitudes. Exhibit 14.2 shows what an attitude survey might look like. Typically, **attitude surveys** present employees with a set of statements or questions eliciting how they feel about their jobs, work groups, supervisors, or the organization. Ideally, the items will be designed to obtain the specific information that managers desire. An attitude score is achieved by summing up responses to individual questionnaire items. These scores can then be averaged for job groups, departments, divisions, or the organization as a whole. For instance, Trident Precision Manufacturing of Webster, New York, administers a twice-yearly employee satisfaction survey to gauge their employees' overall satisfaction with the company and its practices.[8]

Exhibit 14.2

Sample Attitude Survey

Please answer each of the following statements using the following rating scale:

5 = Strongly agree
4 = Agree
3 = Undecided
2 = Disagree
1 = Strongly disagree

Statement	Rating
1. This company is a pretty good place to work.	_____
2. I can get ahead in this company if I make the effort.	_____
3. This company's wage rates are competitive with those of other companies.	_____
4. Employee promotion decisions are handled fairly.	_____
5. I understand the various fringe benefits the company offers.	_____
6. My job makes the best use of my abilities.	_____
7. My workload is challenging but not burdensome.	_____
8. I have trust and confidence in my boss.	_____
9. I feel free to tell my boss what I think.	_____
10. I know what my boss expects of me.	_____

Source: Based on T. Lammers, "The Essential Employee Survey," *Inc.*, December 1992, pp. 159–61.

THE SATISFACTION-PRODUCTIVITY CONTROVERSY

For a good part of the twentieth century, it was widely believed that happy workers were productive workers. As a result of the Hawthorne Studies (discussed in Chapter 2), managers generalized that if their employees were satisfied with their jobs, that satisfaction would translate to working hard. Many of the paternalistic actions by managers—things such as forming company bowling teams and credit unions, having company picnics, and training supervisors to be sensitive to the concerns of employees—were supposed to make workers happy. But belief in the happy worker idea was based more on wishful thinking than on hard evidence.

A careful review of research indicates that if satisfaction does have a positive effect on productivity, it's quite small.[9] However, looking at contingency variables has improved the relationship.[10] For example, the relationship is strongest when the employee's behavior isn't constrained or controlled by outside factors. An employee's productivity on machine-paced jobs, for instance, is going to be more heavily influenced by the speed of the machine than by his or her level of satisfaction. Another important contingency variable seems to be job level. The satisfaction-performance correlations are strongest for higher-level employees. Thus, we might expect the relationship to be more relevant for individuals in professional, supervisory, and managerial positions than for regular employees.

Unfortunately, most studies on the relationship between satisfaction and productivity used research designs that could not prove cause and effect. Studies that controlled for a causal relation indicated that a more valid conclusion was that productivity led to satisfaction rather than the other way around.[11] If you do a good job, you intrinsically feel good about it. In addition, assuming that the organization rewards productivity, your higher productivity should increase verbal recognition, your pay level, and promotion opportunities. These rewards, in turn, increase your level of satisfaction with the job.

Does productivity lead to job satisfaction, or is it the other way around? In either case, employees at the Richmond, VA firm Xperts Inc., an information technology consulting firm, have been productive enough to make their firm a fast-growing contender with almost no employee turnover in its highly competitive field. Each was recently given a stipend of up to $1,500 to individually decorate his or her own workspace with paint, furniture, materials, and even the advice of interior decorators if needed. Here Kendall Tyler, director of sales, enjoys her office.

IMPLICATIONS FOR MANAGERS

What are the implications for managers of what we know about attitudes? One implication concerns managing cognitive dissonance. We know that employees will try to reduce dissonance. If employees are required to do things that appear inconsistent to them or that are at odds with their attitudes, managers should remember that pressure to reduce the dissonance is minimized when employees perceive that the dissonance is externally imposed and uncontrollable. The pressure is also decreased if rewards are significant enough to offset the dissonance. So the manager might point to external forces such as competitors, customers, or other factors when explaining the need to perform some work activity about which workers may have some dissonance. Or the manager can provide rewards that workers desire in order to decrease their attempts to eliminate the dissonance.

Another implication for managers is that there is relatively strong evidence that committed and satisfied employees have low rates of turnover and absenteeism.[12] Given that managers want to keep resignations and absences down—particularly among their most productive employees—they will want to do those things that will generate positive job attitudes. Measuring employee satisfaction through attitude surveys can alert managers to any significant changes. In addition, research has shown that job satisfaction influences organizational citizenship behavior, primarily through perceptions of fairness. What does this mean? If employees don't feel that their supervisors or the organization's procedures or pay policies are fair, their job satisfaction is likely to suffer significantly. However, when employees perceive organizational processes and outcomes to be fair, trust is developed. And when employees trust their employer, they're more willing to voluntarily engage in behaviors that go beyond the formal job requirements.[13]

Finally, the findings about the satisfaction-productivity relationships have important implications for managers. They suggest that the goal of making employees happy on the assumption that their being happy will lead to high productivity is probably misdirected. Managers who follow this strategy could end up with a very content, but very unproductive, group of employees. Managers would get better results by directing their attention primarily to what will help employees become more productive. Then successful job performance should lead to feelings of accomplishment, increased pay, promotions, and other rewards—all desirable outcomes—that then lead to job satisfaction.

Testing...Testing...1,2,3

7. **Explain how individuals reconcile inconsistencies between attitudes and behaviors.**

8. **What are attitude surveys, and how might they help managers?**

9. **Describe the relationship between job satisfaction and productivity.**

❯ PERSONALITY

Some people are quiet and passive; others are loud and aggressive. When we describe people using terms such as *quiet, passive, loud, aggressive, ambitious, extroverted, loyal, tense,* or *sociable,* we're categorizing them in terms of personality traits. An individual's **personality** is the unique combination of the psychological traits we use to describe that person.

personality

The unique combination of psychological traits that describes a person.

PERSONALITY TRAITS

How would you describe your personality? There are dozens of personality traits you could use; for instance, aggressive, shy, ambitious, loyal, and lazy. Over the years, researchers have attempted to focus specifically on which traits would lead to identifying one's personality. Two of the most widely recognized efforts include the Myers-Briggs Type Indicator and the five-factor model of personality.

Myers-Briggs Type Indicator Personality assessment tests are commonly used to reveal an individual's personality traits. One of the most popular personality tests is the Myers-Briggs Type Indicator (MBTI). It consists of more than a hundred questions that ask people how they usually act or feel in different situations.[14] The way you respond to these questions puts you at one end or another of four dimensions:

1. *Social interaction*: Extrovert or Introvert (E or I)   An extrovert is someone who is outgoing, dominant, and often aggressive and who wants to change the world. Extroverts need a work environment that is varied and action oriented, that lets them be with others, and that gives them a variety of experiences. An individual who's shy and withdrawn and focuses on understanding the world is described as an introvert. Introverts prefer a work environment that is quiet and concentrated, that lets them be alone, and that gives them a chance to explore in depth a limited set of experiences.

2. *Preference for gathering data*: Sensing or Intuitive (S or N)   Sensing types dislike new problems unless there are standard ways to solve them; they like an established routine, have a high need for closure, show patience with routine details, and tend to be good at precise work. On the other hand, intuitive types are individuals who like solving new problems, dislike doing the same thing over and over again, jump to conclusions, are impatient with routine details, and dislike taking time for precision.

3. *Preference for decision making:* Feeling or Thinking (F or T)   Individuals who are feeling types are aware of other people and their feelings, like harmony, need occasional praise, dislike telling people unpleasant things, tend to be sympathetic, and relate well to most people. Thinking types are unemotional and uninterested in people's feelings, like analysis and putting things into logical order, are able to reprimand people and fire them when necessary, may seem hard-hearted, and tend to relate well only to other thinking types.

4. *Style of making decisions:* Perceptive or Judgmental (P or J)   Perceptive types are curious, spontaneous, flexible, adaptable, and tolerant. They focus on starting a task, postpone decisions, and want to find out all about the task

before starting it. Judgmental types are decisive, good planners, purposeful, and exacting. They focus on completing a task, make decisions quickly, and want only the information necessary to get a task done.

Combining these preferences provides descriptions of 16 personality types. Exhibit 14.3 summarizes a few of them.

How could the MBTI help managers? Proponents of the assessment believe that it's important to know these personality types because they influence the way people interact and solve problems. For instance, if your boss is an intuitive type and you're a sensing type, you'll gather information in different ways. An intuitive type prefers gut reactions, whereas a sensor prefers facts. To work well with your boss, you would have to present more than just facts about a situation and bring out how you feel about it. The MBTI has been used to help managers select employees who are well matched to certain types of jobs. All in all, the MBTI can be a useful tool for understanding personality and predicting people's behavior.

The Big-Five Model of Personality Although the MBTI is very popular, it suffers from one major criticism. It lacks evidence to support its validity. That same criticism can't be applied to the five-factor model of personality, more often called the **big-five model**.[15] The big-five personality traits are:

big-five model

Five-factor model of personality that includes extraversion, agreeableness, conscientiousness, emotional stability, and openness to experience.

1. *Extraversion*: The degree to which someone is sociable, talkative, and assertive.

2. *Agreeableness*: The degree to which someone is good-natured, cooperative, and trusting.

3. *Conscientiousness*: The degree to which someone is responsible, dependable, persistent, and achievement oriented.

4. *Emotional stability*: The degree to which someone is calm, enthusiastic, and secure (positive) or tense, nervous, depressed, and insecure (negative).

5. *Openness to experience*: The degree to which someone is imaginative, artistically sensitive, and intellectual.

Exhibit 14.3	Type	Description
Examples of MBTI Personality Types	INFJ (introvert, intuitive, feeling, judgmental)	Quietly forceful, conscientious, and concerned for others. Such people succeed by perseverance, originality, and the desire to do whatever is needed or wanted. They are often highly respected for their uncompromising principles.
	ESTP (extrovert, sensing, thinking, perceptive)	Blunt and sometimes insensitive. Such people are matter-of-fact and do not worry or hurry. They enjoy whatever comes along. They work best with real things that can be assembled or disassembled.
	ISFP (introvert, sensing, feeling, perceptive)	Sensitive, kind, modest, shy, and quietly friendly. Such people strongly dislike disagreements and will avoid them. They are loyal followers and quite often are relaxed about getting things done.
	ENTJ (extrovert, intuitive, thinking, judgmental)	Warm, friendly, candid, and decisive; also usually skilled in anything that requires reasoning and intelligent talk, but may sometimes overestimate what they are capable of doing.

Source: Based on I. Briggs-Myers, *Introduction to Type* (Palo Alto, CA: Consulting Psychologists Press, 1980), pp. 7–8.

The big five provide more than just a personality framework. Research has shown that important relationships exist between these personality dimensions and job performance. For example, one study examined five categories of occupations: *professionals* (such as engineers, architects, attorneys), *police, managers, salespeople*, and *semiskilled and skilled employees*.[16] Job performance was defined in terms of employee performance ratings, training competence, and personnel data such as salary level. The results of the study showed that conscientiousness predicted job performance for all five occupational groups. Predictions for the other personality dimensions depended on the situation and on the occupational group. For example, extraversion predicted performance in managerial and sales positions—occupations in which high social interaction is necessary. Openness to experience was found to be important in predicting training competency. Ironically, emotional security wasn't positively related to job performance. Although one might expect calm and secure workers to perform better than nervous ones, that wasn't the case. Perhaps that result is a function of the likelihood that emotionally stable workers often keep their jobs while emotionally unstable workers often do not. Given that all the people who participated in the study were employed, the variance on that dimension was small and insignificant.

The big-five model of personality posits five major personality traits, one of which—agreeableness—is exemplified by David Lein, Mary Morse's boss at Autodesk, a computer-aided design company in San Rafael, California. Like other bosses Morse has had at the firm, Lein has been supportive and understanding, asking her about her career plans and ensuring that she has both the time and the opportunity to train for advancement. While being accommodating comes easily to Lein, many managers are realizing that it can play a major role in retaining prized employees.

EMOTIONAL INTELLIGENCE

Research into the area of emotional intelligence has offered some new insights into personality.[17] **Emotional intelligence (EI)** is an assortment of noncognitive skills, capabilities, and competencies that influence a person's ability to succeed in coping with environmental demands and pressures. It's composed of five dimensions:

Self-awareness: The ability to be aware of what you're feeling.
Self-management: The ability to manage one's own emotions and impulses.
Self-motivation: The ability to persist in the face of setbacks and failures.
Empathy: The ability to sense how others are feeling.
Social skills: The ability to handle the emotions of others.

EI has been shown to be positively related to job performance at all levels. For instance, one study looked at the characteristics of Bell Lab engineers who were rated as stars by their peers. The researchers concluded that stars were better at relating to others. That is, it was EI, not academic intelligence, that characterized high performers. A second study of Air Force recruiters generated similar findings.

emotional intelligence (EI)

An assortment of noncognitive skills, capabilities, and competencies that influence a person's ability to succeed in coping with environmental demands and pressures.

Top-performing recruiters exhibited high levels of EI. What can we conclude from these results? EI appears to be especially relevant to success in jobs that demand a high degree of social interaction.

PREDICTING BEHAVIOR FROM PERSONALITY TRAITS

Five personality traits have proved to be the most powerful in explaining individual behavior in organizations. They are *locus of control, Machiavellianism, self-esteem, self-monitoring*, and *risk propensity*.

Locus of Control Some people believe that they control their own fate. Others see themselves as pawns, believing that what happens to them in their lives is due to luck or chance. The **locus of control** in the first case is *internal*; these people believe that they control their own destiny. The locus of control in the second case is *external*; these people believe that their lives are controlled by outside forces.[18] Research evidence indicates that employees who rate high on externality are less satisfied with their jobs, more alienated from the work setting, and less involved in their jobs than are those who rate high on internality.[19] A manager might also expect externals to blame a poor performance evaluation on their boss's prejudice, their co-workers, or other events outside their control; internals would explain the same evaluation in terms of their own actions.

Machiavellianism The second characteristic is called **Machiavellianism** (Mach) named after Niccolo Machiavelli, who wrote in the sixteenth century on how to gain and manipulate power. An individual who is high in Machiavellianism is pragmatic, maintains emotional distance, and believes that ends can justify means.[20] "If it works, use it" is consistent with a high Mach perspective. Do high Machs make good employees? That depends on the type of job and whether you consider ethical factors in evaluating performance. In jobs that require bargaining skills (such as a purchasing manager) or that have substantial rewards for winning (such as a salesperson working on commission), high Machs are productive. In jobs in which ends do not justify the means or that lack absolute measures of performance, it's difficult to predict the performance of high Machs.

Self-Esteem People differ in the degree to which they like or dislike themselves. This trait is called **self-esteem**.[21] The research on self-esteem (SE) offers some interesting insights into organizational behavior. For example, self-esteem is directly related to expectations for success. High SEs believe that they possess the ability they need in order to succeed at work. Individuals with high self-esteem will take more risks in job selection and are more likely to choose unconventional jobs than are people with low self-esteem.

The most common finding on self-esteem is that low SEs are more susceptible to external influence than are high SEs. Low SEs are dependent on receiving positive evaluations from others. As a result, they're more likely to seek approval from others and are more prone to conform to the beliefs and behaviors of those they respect than are high SEs. In managerial positions, low SEs will tend to be concerned with pleasing others and, therefore, will be less likely to take unpopular stands than are high SEs.

Not surprisingly, self-esteem has also been found to be related to job satisfaction. A number of studies confirm that high SEs are more satisfied with their jobs than are low SEs.

---

locus of control

The degree to which people believe they are masters of their own fate.

Machiavellianism

A measure of the degree to which people are pragmatic, maintain emotional distance, and believe that ends justify means.

---

self-esteem

An individual's degree of like or dislike for himself or herself.

Self-Monitoring Another personality trait that has received increasing attention is called **self-monitoring**.[22] It refers to an individual's ability to adjust his or her behavior to external, situational factors. Individuals high in self-monitoring show considerable adaptability in adjusting their behavior. They're highly sensitive to external cues and can behave differently in different situations. High self-monitors are capable of presenting striking contradictions between their public persona and their private selves. Low self-monitors cannot adjust their behavior. They tend to display their true dispositions and attitudes in every situation, and there's high behavioral consistency between who they are and what they do.

Research on self-monitoring is fairly new; thus, predictions are hard to make. However, preliminary evidence suggests that high self-monitors pay closer attention to the behavior of others and are more flexible than are low self-monitors.[23] We might also hypothesize that high self-monitors will be successful in managerial positions that require them to play multiple, and even contradictory, roles. The high self-monitor is capable of putting on different "faces" for different audiences.

self-monitoring

A personality trait that measures an individual's ability to adjust his or her behavior to external situational factors.

Risk Taking People differ in their willingness to take chances. Differences in the propensity to assume or to avoid risk have been shown to affect how long it takes managers to make a decision and how much information they require before making their choice. For instance, in one study, a group of managers worked on simulated exercises that required them to make hiring decisions. High risk-taking managers took less time to make decisions and used less information in making their choices than did low risk-taking managers. Interestingly, the decision accuracy was the same for the two groups. To maximize organizational effectiveness, managers should try to align employee risk-taking propensity with specific job demands.[24] For instance, high risk-taking propensity may lead to effective performance for a commodities trader in a brokerage firm because this type of job demands rapid decision making. On the other hand, high risk-taking propensity might prove a major obstacle to accountants auditing financial statements.

Willingness to take risks differs widely among individuals. When Hiroshi Mikitani, 34, created a new online shopping mall a few years ago in Japan, only 5 million of his fellow Japanese used the Internet, and then mostly for sending e-mail. The odds that his company, Rakuten, Inc. would be a success, were against him. But today Rakuten [www.rakuten.co.jp] houses 2,000 retailers, ranging from big department stores to fresh fish sellers and *sake* brewers, and it is profitable and growing fast thanks to a recent IPO. "I want to make Rakuten the most exciting place to buy, sell, or trade products and services," says Mikitani.

PERSONALITY TYPES IN DIFFERENT CULTURES

We know that there are certainly no common personality types for a given country. You can, for instance, find high risk takers and low risk takers in almost any culture. Yet a country's culture can influence *dominant* personality characteristics of its people. We can see this effect of national culture by looking at one of the personality traits we just discussed: locus of control.

National cultures differ in terms of the degree to which people believe they control their environment. For instance, North Americans believe that they can dominate their environment; other societies, such as those in Middle Eastern countries, believe that life is essentially predetermined. Notice how closely this distinction parallels the concept of internal and external locus of control. On the basis of this particularly cultural characteristic, we should expect a larger proportion of internals in the U.S. and Canadian workforces than in the workforces of Saudi Arabia and Iran.

As we have seen throughout this section, personality traits influence employees' behavior. For global managers, understanding how personality traits differ takes on added significance when looking at it from the perspective of national culture.

IMPLICATIONS FOR MANAGERS

The major value in understanding personality differences probably lies in employee selection. Managers are likely to have higher-performing and more satisfied employees if consideration is given to matching personalities with jobs. The best-documented personality–job fit theory has been developed by psychologist John Holland.[25] His theory states that an employee's satisfaction with his or her job, as well as his or her likelihood of leaving that job, depends on the degree to which the individual's personality matches the occupational environment. Holland identified six basic personality types. Exhibit 14.4 describes each of the six types, their personality characteristics, and sample occupations.

Holland's theory proposes that satisfaction is highest and turnover lowest when personality and occupation are compatible. Social individuals should be in "people" type jobs, and so forth. A realistic person in a realistic job will be more satisfied than a realistic person in an investigative job. The key points of this theory are that (1) there do appear to be intrinsic differences in personality among

Exhibit 14.4			
Holland's Typology of Personality and Sample Occupations	**Type**	**Personality Characteristics**	**Sample Occupations**
	Realistic. Prefers physical activities that require skill, strength, and coordination	Shy, genuine, persistent, stable, conforming, practical	Mechanic, drill press operator, assembly-line worker, farmer
	Investigative. Prefers activities involving thinking, organizing, and understanding	Analytical, original, curious, independent	Biologist, economist, mathematician, news reporter
	Social. Prefers activities that involve helping and developing others	Sociable, friendly, cooperative, understanding	Social worker, teacher, counselor, clinical psychologist
	Conventional. Prefers rule-regulated, orderly, and unambiguous activities	Conforming, efficient, practical, unimaginative, inflexible	Accountant, corporate manager, bank teller, file clerk
	Enterprising. Prefers verbal activities in which there are opportunities to influence others and attain power	Self-confident, ambitious, energetic, domineering	Lawyer, real estate agent, public relations specialist, small business manager
	Artistic. Prefers ambiguous and unsystematic activities that allow creative expression	Imaginative, disorderly, idealistic, emotional, impractical	Painter, musician, writer, interior decorator

Source: Based on J.L. Holland, *Making Vocational Choices: A Theory of Vocational Personalities and Work Environments,* 2d ed. (Upper Saddle River, NJ: Prentice Hall, 1985).

individuals; (2) there are different types of jobs; and (3) people in job environments compatible with their personality types should be more satisfied and less likely to resign voluntarily than should people in incongruent jobs.

In addition, there are other benefits to a manager's understanding of personality. By recognizing that people approach problem solving, decision making, and job interactions differently, a manager can better understand why, for instance, an employee is uncomfortable with making quick decisions or why another employee insists on gathering as much information as possible before addressing a problem. Or, for instance, managers can expect that individuals with an external locus of control may be less satisfied with their jobs than internals and also that they may be less willing to accept responsibility for their actions.

Finally, being a successful manager and accomplishing goals means working well together with others both inside and outside the organization. In order to work effectively together, you need to understand each other. This understanding comes, at least in part, from recognizing the ways in which people differ from each other—that is, from an appreciation of personality traits. ◄───────

Testing...Testing...1,2,3

10. **Contrast the MBTI and the big-five models in terms of understanding personality.**

11. **What are the five dimensions of emotional intelligence?**

12. **Describe the five personality traits that have proved to be the most powerful in explaining individual behavior in organizations.**

> PERCEPTION

Perception is a process by which individuals give meaning to their environment by organizing and interpreting their sensory impressions. Research on perception consistently demonstrates that individuals may look at the same thing yet perceive it differently. One manager, for instance, can interpret the fact that her assistant regularly takes several days to make important decisions as evidence that the assistant is slow, disorganized, and afraid to make decisions. Another manager with the same assistant might interpret the same tendency as evidence that the assistant is thoughtful, thorough, and deliberate. The first manager would probably evaluate her assistant negatively; the second manager would probably evaluate the person positively. The point is that none of us sees reality. We interpret what we see and call it reality. And, of course, as the example shows, we behave according to our perceptions.

perception

The process of organizing and interpreting sensory impressions in order to give meaning to the environment.

FACTORS THAT INFLUENCE PERCEPTION

How do we explain the fact that people can perceive the same thing differently? A number of factors act to shape and sometimes distort perception. These factors can reside in the *perceiver*; in the object, or *target*, being perceived; or in the context of the *situation* in which the perception occurs.

The Perceiver When an individual looks at a target and attempts to interpret what he or she sees, the individual's personal characteristics will heavily influence the interpretation. These personal characteristics include attitudes, personality, motives, interests, experiences, and expectations.

The Target The characteristics of the target being observed can also affect what's perceived. Loud people are more likely than quiet people to be noticed in a group. So, too, are extremely attractive or unattractive individuals. Because targets aren't looked at in isolation, the relationship of a target to its background also influ-

Exhibit | 14.5 | **Perception Challenges: What Do You See?**

Old woman or young woman?   Two faces or an urn?   A knight on a horse?

ences perception, as does our tendency to group close things and similar things together. You can experience these tendencies by looking at the visual perception examples shown in Exhibit 14.5. Notice how what you see changes as you look differently at each one.

The Situation The context in which we see objects or events is also important. The time at which an object or event is seen can influence attention, as can location, light, heat, color, and any number of other situational factors.

ATTRIBUTION THEORY

Much of the research on perception is directed at inanimate objects. Managers, though, are more concerned with people. Our discussion of perception, therefore, should focus on how we perceive people.

Our perceptions of people differ from our perceptions of inanimate objects because we make inferences about the behaviors of people that we don't make about objects. Objects don't have beliefs, motives, or intentions; people do. The result is that when we observe an individual's behavior, we try to develop explanations of why they behave in certain ways. Our perception and judgment of a person's actions, therefore, will be significantly influenced by the assumptions we make about the person.

attribution theory

A theory used to explain how we judge people differently depending on the meaning we attribute to a given behavior.

Attribution theory was developed to explain how we judge people differently depending on the meaning we attribute to a given behavior.[26] Basically, the theory suggests that when we observe an individual's behavior, we attempt to determine whether it was internally or externally caused. Internally caused behaviors are those that are believed to be under the personal control of the individual. Externally caused behavior results from outside factors; that is, the person is forced into the behavior by the situation. That determination, however, depends on three factors: distinctiveness, consensus, and consistency.

Distinctiveness refers to whether an individual displays a behavior in many situations or whether it's particular to one situation. Is the employee who arrived late today the same person that some employees are complaining is a "goof-off?"

What we want to know is whether this behavior is unusual. If it's unusual, the observer is likely to attribute the behavior to external forces, something beyond the control of the person. However, if the behavior isn't unusual, it will probably be judged as internal.

If everyone who's faced with a similar situation responds in the same way, we can say the behavior shows *consensus*. A tardy employee's behavior would meet this criterion if all employees who took the same route to work were also late. From an attribution perspective, if consensus is high, you're likely to give an external attribution to the employee's tardiness; that is, some outside factor—maybe road construction or a traffic accident—caused the behavior. However, if other employees who come the same way to work made it on time, you would conclude that the cause of the late behavior was internal.

To break down some of the stereotypes about themselves that can hamper male executives, London-based management trainer James Traeger runs a men-only seminar to help men understand the value of emotion in workplace relationships. One participant says, "The program is about breaking down the stereotype of an aggressive, controlling, and competitive man who always wants to be right, take charge, solve problems, and also has to have the last word. It's about learning to listen and work in harmony."

Finally, an observer looks for *consistency* in a person's actions. Does the person engage in the behaviors regularly and consistently? Does the person respond the same way over time? Coming in 10 minutes late for work isn't perceived in the same way if, for one employee, it represents an unusual case (she hasn't been late in months), while for another employee, it's part of a routine pattern (she's late two or three times every week). The more consistent the behavior, the more the observer is inclined to attribute it to internal causes.

Exhibit 14.6 summarizes the key elements of attribution theory. It would tell us, for instance, that if an employee—let's call him Mr. Liu—generally per-

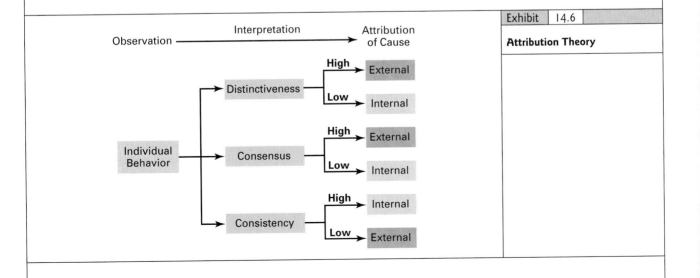

Exhibit 14.6 **Attribution Theory**

forms at or about the same level on other related tasks as he does on his current task (low distinctiveness), if other employees frequently perform differently (better or worse) than Mr. Liu does on that current task (low consensus), and if Mr. Liu's performance on this current task is consistent over time (high consistency), his manager or anyone else who is judging Mr. Liu's work is likely to hold him primarily responsible for his task performance (internal attribution).

One of the most interesting findings drawn from attribution theory is that there are errors or biases that distort attributions. For instance, there's substantial evidence to support the fact that when we make judgments about the behavior of other people, we have a tendency to *underestimate* the influence of external factors and to *overestimate* the influence of internal or personal factors.[27] This tendency is called the **fundamental attribution error** and can explain why a sales manager may be prone to attribute the poor performance of her sales representative to laziness rather than to the innovative product line introduced by a competitor. There's also a tendency for individuals to attribute their own successes to internal factors such as ability or effort while putting the blame for personal failure on external factors such as luck. This tendency is called the **self-serving bias** and suggests that feedback provided to employees in performance reviews will be predictably distorted by them depending on whether it's positive or negative.

SHORTCUTS FREQUENTLY USED IN JUDGING OTHERS

We use a number of shortcuts when we judge others. Perceiving and interpreting what others do is a lot of work. As a result, individuals develop techniques for making the task more manageable. These techniques are frequently valuable; they let us make accurate perceptions rapidly and provide valid data for making predictions. However, they aren't perfect. They can and do get us into trouble. An understanding of these shortcuts can be helpful for recognizing when they can result in significant distortions.

Individuals cannot assimilate all they observe, so they engage in **selectivity**. They take in bits and pieces of the vast amounts of stimuli bombarding their senses. These bits and pieces aren't chosen randomly; they are selectively chosen depending on the interests, background, experience, and attitudes of the observer. Selective perception allows us to "speed read" others but not without the risk of being inaccurate.

It's easy to judge others if we assume that they're similar to us. In **assumed similarity**, or the "like me" effect, the observer's perception of others is influenced more by the observer's own characteristics than by those of the person observed. For example, if you want challenges and responsibility in your job, you'll assume that others want the same. People who assume that others are like them can, of course, be right, but most of the time they're wrong.

When we judge someone on the basis of our perception of a group he or she is part of, we're using the shortcut called **stereotyping**. For instance, "married people are more stable employees than single persons" and "union people expect something for nothing" are examples of stereotyping. To the degree that a stereotype is based on fact, it may produce accurate judgments. However, many stereotypes have no foundation in fact. In such cases, stereotyping distorts judgment.[28]

fundamental attribution error

The tendency to underestimate the influence of external factors and overestimate the influence of internal factors when making judgments about the behavior of others.

self-serving bias

The tendency for individuals to attribute their own successes to internal factors while putting the blame for failures on external factors.

selectivity

The process by which people assimilate certain bits and pieces of what they observe, depending on their interests, background, and attitudes.

assumed similarity

The belief that others are like oneself.

stereotyping

Judging a person on the basis of one's perception of a group to which he or she belongs.

When we form a general impression about a person on the basis of a single characteristic, such as intelligence, sociability, or appearance, we're being influenced by the **halo effect**. This effect frequently occurs when students evaluate their classroom instructor. Students may isolate a single trait such as enthusiasm and allow their entire evaluation to be slanted by the perception of this one trait. An instructor may be quiet, assured, knowledgeable, and highly qualified, but if his classroom teaching style lacks enthusiasm, he might be rated lower on a number of other characteristics.

halo effect

A general impression of an individual based on a single characteristic.

IMPLICATIONS FOR MANAGERS

Managers need to recognize that their employees react to perceptions, not to reality. So whether a manager's appraisal of an employee is actually objective and unbiased or whether the organization's wage levels are among the highest in the community is less relevant than what employees perceive them to be. If individuals perceive appraisals to be biased or wage levels as low, they'll behave as if those conditions actually exist. Employees organize and interpret what they see, so there is always the potential for perceptual distortion.

The message to managers should be clear: Pay close attention to how employees perceive both their jobs and management actions. Remember, the valuable employee who quits because of an inaccurate perception is just as great a loss to an organization as the valuable employee who quits for a valid reason. ◀

Testing...Testing...1,2,3

13. **How can an understanding of perception help managers better understand individual behavior?**

14. **What role does attribution theory play in perception?**

15. **Name four shortcuts used in judging others. What effect does each have on perception?**

❯ LEARNING

The last individual behavior concept we're going to introduce is learning. It is included for the obvious reason that almost all complex behavior is learned. If we want to explain, predict, and influence behavior, we need to understand how people learn.

What is learning? Psychologists' definition of learning is considerably broader than the average person's view that "it's what we do in school." In actuality, each of us is constantly learning. Learning occurs all the time as we continuously learn from our experiences. A workable definition of **learning** is, therefore, any relatively permanent change in behavior that occurs as a result of experience. How do people learn, then? We're going to look at two learning theories relevant to understanding how and why individual behavior occurs: operant conditioning and social learning. Then we'll discuss how managers can use learning principles to shape employees' behaviors.

learning

Any relatively permanent change in behavior that occurs as a result of experience.

OPERANT CONDITIONING

Operant conditioning argues that behavior is a function of its consequences. People learn to behave to get something they want or to avoid something they don't want. Operant behavior describes voluntary or learned behavior in contrast to reflexive or unlearned behavior. The tendency to repeat learned behavior is influenced by the reinforcement or lack of reinforcement that happens as a result of the behavior. Reinforcement, therefore, strengthens a behavior and increases the likelihood that it will be repeated.

operant conditioning

A type of learning in which desired voluntary behavior leads to a reward or prevents a punishment.

As a senior consultant at the Hay Group in Chicago, Brad Hill teaches hourly employees such as meatpackers and health-care workers how to create their own gain-sharing programs to benefit both their companies and themselves. In these tough rank-and-file jobs it is often difficult for employees to accept new ideas, and sometimes even to believe that change can work for their benefit. To convince his clients that they can still learn new things about their jobs and about themselves, Hill starts every new assignment by teaching a crew of volunteers from each department in the client firm how to juggle, an art he taught himself at the age of 35.

Building on earlier work in the field, B. F. Skinner's research widely expanded our knowledge of operant conditioning.[29] Even his most outspoken critics admit that his operant concepts work.

Behavior is assumed to be determined from without—that is, *learned*—rather than from within—reflexive or unlearned. Skinner argued that creating pleasing and desirable consequences to follow some specific behavior would increase the frequency of that behavior. People will most likely engage in desired behaviors if they are positively reinforced for doing so, and rewards are most effective if they immediately follow the desired response. In addition, behavior that isn't rewarded or is punished is less likely to be repeated.

You see examples of operant conditioning everywhere. Any situation in which it's either explicitly stated or implicitly suggested that reinforcements (rewards) are contingent on some action on your part is an example of operant conditioning. Your instructor says that if you want a high grade in this course, you must perform well on tests by giving correct answers. A salesperson working on commission knows that earning a sizable income is contingent upon generating high sales in his or her territory. Of course, the linkage between behavior and reinforcement can also work to teach the individual to behave in ways that work against the best interests of the organization. Assume that your boss tells you that if you'll work overtime during the next three-week busy season, you'll be compensated for it at the next performance appraisal. Then, when performance appraisal time comes, you are given no positive reinforcements (such as being praised for pitching in and helping out when needed). What will you do the next time your boss asks you to work overtime? You'll probably refuse. Your behavior can be explained by operant conditioning: If a behavior isn't positively reinforced, the probability that the behavior will be repeated declines.

SOCIAL LEARNING

Individuals also can learn by observing what happens to other people and just by being told about something as well as by direct experiences. So, for example, much of what we have learned comes from watching others (models)—parents, teachers, peers, television and movie actors, managers, and so forth. This view that we can learn both through observation and direct experience is called **social learning theory**.

social learning theory

A theory of learning that says people can learn through observation and direct experience.

The influence of others is central to the social learning viewpoint. The amount of influence that these models will have on an individual is determined by four processes:

1. *Attentional processes.* People learn from a model only when they recognize and pay attention to its critical features. We tend to be most influenced by models who are attractive, repeatedly available, thought to be important, or are seen as similar to us.

2. *Retention processes.* A model's influence will depend on how well the individual remembers the model's action, even after the model is no longer readily available.

3. *Motor reproduction processes*. After a person has seen a new behavior by observing the model, the watching must become doing. This process then demonstrates that the individual can actually do the modeled activities.

4. *Reinforcement processes*. Individuals will be motivated to exhibit the modeled behavior if positive incentives or rewards are provided. Behaviors that are reinforced will be given more attention, learned better, and performed more often.

SHAPING: A MANAGERIAL TOOL

Because learning takes place on the job as well as prior to it, managers are concerned with how they can teach employees to behave in ways that most benefit the organization. Thus, managers will often attempt to "mold" individuals by guiding their learning in graduated steps. This process is called **shaping behavior**.

Consider the situation in which an employee's behavior is significantly different from that sought by his or her manager. If the manager reinforced the individual only when he or she showed desirable responses, there might be very little reinforcement taking place. In such a case, shaping offers a logical approach toward achieving the desired behavior.

shaping behavior

The process of systematically reinforcing each successive step that moves an individual closer to the desired behavior.

| ▲ MANAGING YOUR CAREER | **Learning to Get Along with Difficult People** |

We've all been around people who are, to put it nicely, difficult to get along with. These people might be chronic complainers, they might be meddlers who think they know everything about everyone else's job and don't hesitate to tell you so, or they might exhibit any number of other unpleasant interpersonal characteristics. They can make your job as a manager extremely hard and your workday very stressful if you don't know how to deal with them. Being around difficult people tends to bring out the worst in all of us. What can you do? How do you learn to get along with these difficult people?[30]

Getting along with difficult people takes patience, planning, and preparation. What you need is an approach that helps you diffuse a lot of the negative aspects of dealing with these individuals. For instance, it helps to write down a detailed description of the person's behavior. Describe what this person does that bothers you. Then try to understand that behavior. Put yourself in that person's shoes and attempt to see things from his or her perspective. Doing these things initially might help you better understand, predict, and influence behavior.

Unfortunately, trying to understand the person usually isn't enough for getting along. You'll also need some specific strategies for coping with different types of difficult personalities. Here are some of the most common types of

difficult people you'll meet and some strategies for dealing with them.

The Hostile, Aggressive Types. With this type, you need to stand up for yourself; give them time to run down; don't worry about being polite, just jump in if you need to; get their attention carefully; get them to sit down; speak from your own point of view; avoid a head-on fight; and be ready to be friendly.

The Complainers. With the complainers you need to listen attentively; acknowledge their concerns; be prepared to interrupt their litany of complaints; don't agree, but do acknowledge what they're saying; state facts without comment or apology; and switch them to problem solving.

The Silent or Nonresponsive Types. With this type, you need to ask open-ended questions; use the friendly, silent stare; don't fill the silent pauses for them in conversations; comment on what's happening; and help break the tension by making them feel more at ease.

The Know-It-All Experts. The keys to dealing with this type are be on top of things; listen and acknowledge their comments; question firmly, but don't confront; avoid being a counterexpert; and work with them to channel their energy in positive directions.

? THINKING CRITICALLY ABOUT ETHICS

Is shaping behavior a form of manipulative control? Animal trainers use rewards to get dogs, porpoises, and whales to perform extraordinary stunts. Behavioral psychologists put rats through thousands of experiments by manipulating their food supply. Trainers and researchers shape the behavior of animals by controlling consequences. Such learning techniques may be appropriate for animals performing in zoos, circuses, or laboratories, but are they appropriate for managing the behavior of people at work?

Suppose an employee does something the organization judges to be wrong but that was motivated by a manager's control of rewards. Say, for instance, an employee inflates the numbers on a sales report because bonuses are based on sales volume. Is that employee any less responsible for his or her actions than if such rewards had not been involved? Explain your position.

We shape behavior by systematically reinforcing each successive step that moves the individual closer to the desired behavior. If an employee who has chronically been a half-hour late for work comes in only 20 minutes late, we can reinforce the improvement. Reinforcement would increase as an employee gets closer to the desired behavior.

There are four ways to shape behavior: positive reinforcement, negative reinforcement, punishment, or extinction. When a behavior is followed by something pleasant, such as when a manager praises an employee for a job well done, it's called *positive reinforcement*. Positive reinforcement will increase the likelihood of the desired behavior being repeated. Rewarding a response with the elimination or withdrawal of something unpleasant is called *negative reinforcement*. A manager who says "I won't dock your pay if you start getting to work on time" is using negative reinforcement. The desired behavior (getting to work on time) is being encouraged by the withdrawal of something unpleasant (the employee's pay being docked). On the other hand, *punishment* penalizes undesirable behavior and will eliminate it. Suspending an employee for two days without pay for habitually coming to work late is an example of punishment. Finally, eliminating any reinforcement that's maintaining a behavior is called *extinction*. When a behavior isn't reinforced, gradually it disappears. In meetings, managers who wish to discourage employees from continually asking irrelevant or distracting questions can eliminate this behavior by ignoring those employees when they raise their hands to speak. Soon this behavior will disappear.

Both positive and negative reinforcement results in learning. They strengthen a desired behavior and increase the probability that the desired behavior will be repeated. Both punishment and extinction also result in learning; however, they weaken an undesired behavior and tend to decrease its frequency.

IMPLICATIONS FOR MANAGERS

Employees are going to learn on the job. The only issue is whether managers are going to manage their learning through the rewards they allocate and the examples they set or allow it to occur haphazardly. If marginal employees are rewarded with pay raises and promotions, they will have little reason to change their behavior. In fact, productive employees, seeing that marginal performance gets rewarded, might change their behavior. If managers want behavior A but reward behavior B, they shouldn't be surprised to find employees learning to engage in behavior B. Similarly, managers should expect that employees will look to them as models. Managers who are consistently late to work, or take two hours for lunch, or help themselves to company office supplies for personal use should expect employees to read the message they are sending and model their behavior accordingly.

Testing...Testing...1,2,3

16. **How could operant conditioning help a manager understand, predict, and influence behavior?**

17. **What is social learning theory, and what are its implications for managing people at work?**

18. **How can managers "shape" employees' behavior?**

Managers Respond to "A Manager's Dilemma"

Karen Armstrong

Vice President, Human Resources, extendedcare.com, Northbrook, Illinois

Lee Lesser

Principal, Behavioral Momentum Associates, LLC, Parsippany, New Jersey

The personal and work challenges these three individuals are facing are becoming more common in this world of overnight start-up dot-com companies. Although one peer getting promoted above another often happens, their situation is exacerbated because they live together.

It's important for all three to do an assessment of how they are feeling, what is causing them to feel that way, and what they can do to improve the situation. After their individual assessments, I would have all three sit down and discuss their perceptions and concerns as a team and establish ground rules for how they want to interact together—both on and off the job. Because of Kelman's leadership role, it would be helpful for him to recognize how important it is for him to listen to Kim and Reidy without judging or trying to defend himself.

Sometimes simply acknowledging that there is a problem and getting it out in the open is a powerful first step forward. If all parties can approach the situation in a positive and mature manner, a workable solution can often be found.

Kelman appears to be a high self-monitor personality. He is capable of portraying striking differences between his public (work) and private (at-home) personas. Kim and Reidy seem to have low self-esteem. Kim could not ask for help when he didn't know how to do something and Reidy chose not to complain about not getting the office he wanted. These significant differences in their personality traits represent the sources of their emotional and attitudinal issues.

Kelman should use his ability as a high self-monitor to pay close attention to the behavior of others and to be more flexible. To handle the situation, Kelman should modify his behavior to be more like his two roommates. In addition, he should try to understand the low self-esteem behaviors of his roommates. By Kelman demonstrating more consistency between who he is and what he does, displaying his true disposition and attitude in more situations, the emotional friction and issues between he and his lifelong friends will be reduced.

Chapter Summary

This summary is organized by the chapter-opening objectives found on p. 368.

1. The field of organizational behavior is concerned with the actions of people at work in organizations. By focusing on individual- and group-level concepts, OB seeks to explain, predict, and influence behavior. Because they get things done through other people, managers will be more effective if they have an understanding of behavior.

2. The three components of an attitude are cognitive, affective, and behavioral. The cognitive component consists of the beliefs, opinions, knowledge, or information held by a person. The affective component is the emotional or feeling part of an attitude. Finally, the behavioral component is an intention to behave in a certain way toward someone or something.

3. People seek consistency between their attitudes and their behavior. They seek to reconcile different attitudes and to align their attitudes and behavior so they appear rational and consistent. They also seek consistency to reduce the level of cognitive dissonance or discomfort they feel when their attitudes and behaviors aren't aligned.

4. The correlation between satisfaction and productivity tends to be low. Research evidence suggests that productivity leads to satisfaction rather than, as was popularly believed, the other way around.

5. The Myers-Briggs Type Indicator (MBTI) is a personality assessment test that asks people how they usually act or feel in different situations. A person fits into one of 16 personality types according to the way he or she responds to the questions. The MBTI can help

managers understand, predict, and influence behavior. The big-five model of personality proposes that there are five important personality factors: extraversion, agreeableness, conscientiousness, emotional stability, and openness to experience. Research has shown that important relationships exist between these personality dimensions and job performance.

6. Emotional intelligence (EI) is defined as an assortment of noncognitive skills, capabilities, and competencies that influence a person's ability to succeed in coping with environmental demands and pressures. The five dimensions of EI include self-awareness, self-management, self-motivation, empathy, and social skills.

7. Attribution theory can help explain how we judge people differently depending on what meaning we attribute to a given behavior. When we observe an individual's behavior, we attempt to determine whether it was internally or externally caused. That determination is based on three factors: distinctiveness, consensus, and consistency.

8. There are four shortcuts managers use in judging others. Selectivity is the process by which people assimilate selected bits and pieces of what they observe, depending on their interests, background, and attitudes. Assumed similarity is the belief that others are like oneself. Stereotyping is judging a person on the basis of a group to which he or she belongs. The halo effect is a general impression of an individual based on a single characteristic.

9. Managers can shape employee behavior by systematically reinforcing each successive step that moves the employee closer to the desired behavior.

Thinking About Management Issues

1. How, if at all, does the importance of knowledge of OB differ based on a manager's level in the organization? Be specific.

2. "A growing number of companies are now convinced that people's ability to understand and to manage their emotions improves their performance, their collaboration with peers, and their interaction with customers." What are the implications of this statement for managers?

3. What behavioral predictions might you make if you knew that an employee had (a) an external locus of control, (b) a low Mach score, (c) low self-esteem, or (d) high self-monitoring tendencies?

4. "Managers should never use discipline with a problem employee." Do you agree or disagree? Discuss.

5. In the winter of 2000–01, unemployment was at a 30-year low. Managers realized that they had to do more than pay employees competitive salaries and give them attractive benefits if they wanted to keep them. They also had to be nice. A Gallup poll showed that most workers rated having a caring boss even higher than they valued money or fringe benefits. How should managers interpret this information? What are the implications?

Log On: Internet-Based Exercise

Do workers in different countries have differing levels of job satisfaction? Find the best and latest data that describe the level of job satisfaction in (a) the United States, (b) Canada, (c) Japan, and (d) Australia. What conclusions can you draw from these data?

myPHLIP Companion Web Site

myPHLIP **(www.prenhall.com/myphlip)** *is a fully customizable homepage that ties students and faculty to text-specific resources.*
- **For students**, myPHLIP *provides an online study guide tied chapter-by-chapter to the text—current events and Internet exercises, lecture notes, downloadable software, the Career Center, the Writing Center, Ask the Tutor, and more.*
- **For faculty**, myPHLIP *provides a syllabus tool that allows you to manage content, communicate with students, and upload personal resources.*

Working Together: Team-Based Exercise

When we use shortcuts to judge others, are the consequences always negative? Form teams of three to four students. Your instructor will assign each class team either to "yes, the consequences are always negative" or to "no, the consequences aren't always negative." After these assignments are made, your group should discuss this question. Come up with evidence and examples to support your group's argument. Be prepared to debate your group's position in class.

Case Application

Risky Business

What kind of employees do you think it's going to take for an organization to prosper in the dynamic and chaotic world of the Internet and e-businesses? Joe Liemandt, president and CEO of Trilogy Software, based in Austin, Texas, is convinced that employees need, among other things, a willingness to take risks. He's focused on recruiting and keeping the kind of employees that can help Trilogy prosper in such an environment.

Trilogy, founded in 1989 by five Stanford University students, is an industry leader in e-business solutions. The company's software suite helps e-businesses around the world handle procurement, customer service, relationship management, and data integration. Its e-business solutions are used in a wide range of industries including automotive, computers, telecommunications, retail, and financial services. Clients include many notable corporate icons such as IBM, Ericsson, and General Electric. Liemandt has fashioned a strategy for Trilogy that encompasses maintaining the high energy of a start-up with the experience of an established company. An important part of that strategy is continually recruiting "Only the Best"—the brightest, most dynamic employees from the best universities, business schools, and industries. By hiring great people and giving them significant responsibilities from day one, Trilogy ensures that it has the resources to respond to competitive challenges, to keep the entrepreneurial spirit alive, and to achieve its goals of being a high-energy, high-impact company.

New recruits are wooed to Austin with dinners, cultural and recreational outings, and competitive salaries. Once there, the recruits go through "boot camp"—an intensive training program conducted at Trilogy University. And it's not an easy time!

In classes led by Liemandt and other Trilogy veterans during the first week, the new Trilogians learn about programming languages, product plans, and marketing. Classes start at 8 A.M. and in the first month, at least, last until midnight. During the second week, the new hires are divided into small teams and given three weeks to complete projects ranging from making an existing Trilogy product run faster to creating new products from

Joe Liemandt, president and CEO of Trilogy Software.

scratch. Their performance on these projects will affect where the new hires are eventually placed and also affect whether they're rewarded with a trip to Las Vegas at the end of boot camp. The stakes are high. Recruits are told that effort won't be enough. In a presentation given by Liemandt about the team projects, the recruits are shown a slide that says ominously, "No Reward for Trying." He flatly states, "If you set a hard goal and don't make it, you don't win points." It's a harsh, but necessary, reality that the new recruits need to face. However, if the new recruits make it through training, life at Trilogy can be very rewarding and satisfying.

The company's atmosphere combines work and play. Trilogy empowers employees with the responsibilities and resources to reach their highest goals. The organizational

culture encourages maximizing employee passion, energy, and commitment. And the company rewards its employees for their performance. Company benefits are intended to keep employees motivated and excited. For instance, it offers fully stocked kitchens, company trips, discounted memberships at local gyms, the use of company ski boats on two Austin lakes, comprehensive medical and dental insurance, life insurance, and an on-site concierge service to take care of personal errands.

QUESTIONS

1. How does Liemandt's managerial approach to training new recruits reflect an understanding of individual behavior? What would you tell Liemandt about individual behavior?

2. What type of personality characteristics would best fit into Trilogy's culture?

3. Design an employee attitude survey that Trilogy's managers might use. If you want, check out information on the company's Web site (www.trilogy.com).

4. How might perception and learning affect employee behavior at Trilogy? What would be the implications for managers?

Sources: Information from company's Web site (www.trilogy.com) and Hoover's Online (www.hoovers.com), October 29, 2000; E. Ramstad, "High Rollers," *Wall Street Journal*, September 21, 1998, pp. A1+; and N.M. Tichy, "No Ordinary Boot Camp," *Harvard Business Review*, April 2001, pp. 63–70.

Mastering Management

In Episode 4 of the Mastering Management *series, you'll learn more about attribution theory as Warren must decide whom to promote to a managerial position. In so doing, he is forced to reflect on his understanding of his subordinates' capabilities.*

Learning Objectives

After reading and studying this chapter, you should be able to:

1. Differentiate between formal and informal groups.

2. Describe the five stages of group development.

3. Identify how roles and norms influence an employee's behavior.

4. Describe the key components in the group behavior model.

5. Identify the advantages and disadvantages of group decision making.

6. Explain the increased popularity of teams in organizations.

7. Describe the four most common types of teams used in organizations.

8. List the characteristics of effective teams.

9. Identify how managers can build trust.

A MANAGER'S DILEMMA

"We're revolutionizing the world of international advertising." A pretty bold goal for a small ad agency with just 25 people in its offices in Amsterdam.[1] Yet, for Karen Drakenberg, the Swedish chief executive of StrawberryFrog (www.strawberryfrog.com), the goal is not only ambitious but, she feels, also achievable. "StrawberryFrog is dead set on not becoming or being just a local player."

The team at StrawberryFrog depends on a network of about 50 people around the globe who can pitch in when they're needed on various projects. With no cumbersome administrative bureaucracy to slow it down, the agency has landed some large ad campaigns—one for Pharmacia Corporation, another for Tektronics printers, and one to promote elle.com (the online interactive version of *Elle* magazine). Other potential clients, though, have gone elsewhere for their global ad campaigns because they felt that bigger global agencies had the advantage in putting together sophisticated and integrated ad campaigns. The team at StrawberryFrog, however, feels that good global campaigns are found in big ideas, not in big bureaucracies.

The key to StrawberryFrog's approach is its new model of virtual work. By relying on a web of freelancers around the globe, the agency enjoys a network of talent without all the unnecessary overhead and complexity of work arrangements. The inspiration for this approach came from the

Understanding Groups and Teams

15

film and construction industries. If you look at the film industry, people are essentially "free agents" who move from project to project applying their skills—directing, talent search, costuming, makeup, acting, set design—as needed. And the construction industry has mastered the art of managing multiskilled teams all working together on one shared vision. Those are the hallmarks of what Drakenberg is trying to do. However, managing such a loose configuration of talent creates some challenges in itself. Put yourself in Drakenberg's position. How can she effectively manage the virtual teams that work to develop successful ad campaigns for clients?

WHAT WOULD YOU DO?

Virtual teams are one of the realities—and challenges—of managing in today's dynamic global environment. Thousands of organizations have made the move to restructure work around teams rather than individuals. Why? What do these teams look like? How can managers build effective teams? These are some of the types of questions we'll be answering in this chapter. First, however, let's begin by developing our understanding of group behavior.

> ### ⟩ UNDERSTANDING GROUP BEHAVIOR

The behavior of a group is not merely the sum total of the behaviors of all the individuals in the group. Why? Because individuals act differently in groups than they do when they are alone. Therefore, if we want to understand organizational behavior more fully, we need to study groups.

WHAT IS A GROUP?

group

Two or more interacting and interdependent individuals who come together to achieve particular goals.

A **group** is defined as two or more interacting and interdependent individuals who come together to achieve particular goals. Groups can either be formal or informal. *Formal groups* are work groups established by the organization that have designated work assignments and specific tasks. In formal groups, appropriate behaviors are established by and directed toward organizational goals. Exhibit 15.1 provides some examples of different types of formal groups in today's organizations.

In contrast, *informal groups* are social. These groups occur naturally in the workplace in response to the need for social contact. Informal groups tend to form around friendships and common interests.

STAGES OF GROUP DEVELOPMENT

Group development is a dynamic process. Most groups are in a continual state of change. Even though groups probably never reach complete stability, there's a general pattern that describes how most groups evolve. Research shows that groups pass through a standard sequence of five stages.[2] As shown in Exhibit 15.2, these five stages are *forming, storming, norming, performing,* and *adjourning.*

Exhibit	15.1
Examples of Formal Groups	

Command groups. These are the basic, traditional work groups determined by formal authority relationships and depicted on the organizational chart. They typically include a manager and those employees who report directly to him or her.

Cross-functional teams. These bring together the knowledge and skills of individuals from various work areas in order to come up with solutions to operational problems. Cross-functional teams also include groups whose members have been trained to do each other's jobs.

Self-managed teams. These are essentially independent groups that, in addition to doing their operating jobs, take on traditional management responsibilities such as hiring, planning and scheduling, and performance evaluations.

Task forces. These are temporary groups created to accomplish a specific task. Once the task is complete, the group is disbanded.

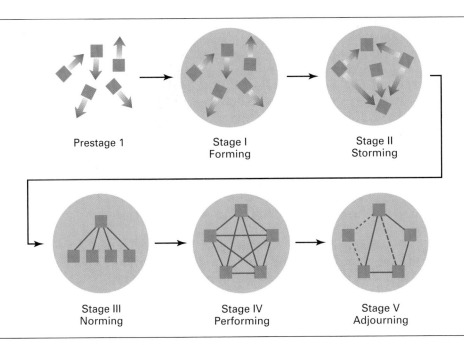

Exhibit 15.2

Stages of Group Development

Prestage 1

Stage I
Forming

Stage II
Storming

Stage III
Norming

Stage IV
Performing

Stage V
Adjourning

The first stage, **forming**, has two aspects. First, people join the group either because of a work assignment, in the case of a formal group, or for some other benefit desired (such as status, self-esteem, affiliation, power, or security), in the case of an informal group.

Once the group's membership is in place, the second part of the forming stage begins: the task of defining the group's purpose, structure, and leadership. This phase is characterized by a great deal of uncertainty. Members are "testing the waters" to determine what types of behavior are acceptable. This stage is complete when members begin to think of themselves as part of a group.

The **storming** stage is one of intragroup conflict. Members accept the existence of the group but resist the control that the group imposes on individuality. Furthermore, there is conflict over who will control the group. When this stage is complete, there will be a relatively clear hierarchy of leadership within the group and agreement on the group's direction.

The third stage is one in which close relationships develop and the group demonstrates cohesiveness. There's now a strong sense of group identity and camaraderie. This **norming** stage is complete when the group structure solidifies and the group has assimilated a common set of expectations of what defines correct member behavior.

The fourth stage is **performing**. The group structure at this point is fully functional and accepted. Group energy has moved from getting to know and understand each other to performing the task at hand.

Performing is the last stage in the development of permanent work groups. Temporary groups—such as committees, task forces, and similar groups—that have a limited task to perform have a fifth stage, **adjourning**. In this stage, the group prepares to disband. High levels of task performance are no longer the group's top priority. Instead, attention is directed at wrapping up activities. Responses of group members vary at this stage. Some are upbeat, basking in the

forming

The first stage of group development in which people join the group and then define the group's purpose, structure, and leadership.

storming

The second stage of group development, which is characterized by intragroup conflict.

norming

The third stage of group development, which is characterized by close relationships and cohesiveness.

performing

The fourth stage of group development when the group is fully functional.

adjourning

The final stage of group development for temporary groups during which group members are concerned with wrapping up activities rather than task performance.

group's accomplishments. Others may be saddened by the loss of camaraderie and friendships gained during the work group's life.

Most of you have probably experienced each of these stages in working on a class group project. Group members are selected and then meet for the first time. There's a "feeling out" period to assess what the group is going to do and how it's going to do it. This is usually rapidly followed by a battle for control: Who's going to be in charge? Once this issue is resolved and a "hierarchy" agreed on, the group identifies specific aspects of the task, who's going to do them, and dates by which the assigned work needs to be completed. General expectations are established and agreed upon for each member. These decisions form the foundation for what you hope will be a coordinated group effort culminating in a project well done. Once the group project is complete and turned in, the group breaks up. Of course, some groups don't get much beyond the first or second stage; these groups typically turn in disappointing work and get lower grades.

Should you assume from the preceding discussion that a group becomes more effective as it progresses through the first four stages? Some researchers argue that effectiveness of work groups increases at advanced stages, but it's not that simple.[3] That assumption may be generally true, but what makes a group effective is a complex issue. Under some conditions, high levels of conflict are conducive to high levels of group performance. We might expect to find situations in which groups in Stage II outperform those in Stage III or IV. Similarly, groups don't always proceed clearly from one stage to the next. Sometimes, in fact, several stages may be going on simultaneously, as when groups are storming and performing at the same time. Groups even occasionally regress to previous stages. Therefore, one shouldn't always assume that all groups precisely follow this developmental process or that Stage IV is always the most preferable. It's better to think of this model as a general framework. It reminds you that groups are dynamic entities and can help you better understand the problems and issues that are most likely to surface during a group's life. Even virtual groups, like those described in our chapter-opening Manager's Dilemma, go through the various stages of group development as they perform their tasks.

BASIC GROUP CONCEPTS

In this section we introduce several concepts to help you begin to understand group behavior. These include *roles, norms, conformity, status systems, group size, group cohesiveness*, and *conflict management*.

Roles We introduced the concept of roles in Chapter 1 when we discussed what managers do. (Remember Mintzberg's managerial roles.) Of course, managers are not the only individuals in an organization who play various roles. The concept of roles applies to all employees in organizations and to their life outside the organization as well.

A **role** refers to a set of expected behavior patterns attributed to someone who occupies a given position in a social unit. In a group, individuals are expected to perform certain roles because of their position in the group. These roles tend to be oriented toward either task accomplishment or maintaining group member satisfaction.[4] Think about groups that you've been in and the roles that you played. Were you continually trying to keep the group focused on getting its work done? If so, you were filling a task accomplishment role. Or were you more concerned

---

Testing...Testing... 1,2,3

1. **Contrast formal and informal groups.**

2. **What are some types of formal groups in organizations?**

3. **Describe the five stages of group development.**

---

role

A set of behavior patterns expected of someone occupying a given position in a social unit.

that group members had the opportunity to offer ideas and that they were satisfied with the experience? If so, you were performing a group member satisfaction role. Both roles are important to the ability of a group to function effectively and efficiently.

A general problem that arises in understanding role behavior is that individuals play multiple roles, adjusting their roles to the group to which they belong at the time. They read their job descriptions, get suggestions from their manager, and watch what their co-workers do. When that individual is confronted by different role expectations, he or she experiences *role conflict*. Employees often face role conflicts. A credit manager expects her credit analysts to process a minimum of 30 applications a week but the work group pressures members to restrict output to 20 so that everyone has work to do and no one gets laid off. A young college instructor's colleagues want him to give very few high grades in order to maintain the department's reputation for having tough standards, but students want him to give out high grades to enhance their grade point averages. To the degree that the instructor wants to satisfy the expectations of both his colleagues and his students, he faces role conflict.

Norms and Conformity All groups have established **norms**, or acceptable standards or expectations that are shared by the group's members. Norms dictate factors such as work output levels, absenteeism, promptness, and the amount of socializing allowed on the job.

Norms, for example, dictate the "arrival ritual" among office assistants at Coleman Trust and Realty. The workday begins at 8 A.M. Most employees typically arrive a few minutes before and put their coat, purse, lunch bag, and other personal items on their chair or desk so everyone knows they're "at work." They then go down to the company cafeteria to get coffee and chat. Employees who violate this norm by starting work sharply at 8 o'clock are teased and pressured to encourage behavior that conforms to the group's standard.

Although each group will have its own unique set of norms, there are common types of norms in most organizations. These focus on effort and performance, dress, and loyalty. Probably the most widespread norms are related to levels of effort and performance. Work groups typically provide their members with explicit cues on how hard to work, what level of output to have, when to look busy, when it's acceptable to goof off, and the like. These norms are very powerful in influencing an individual employee's performance. They're so powerful that performance predictions that are based solely on an employee's ability and level of personal motivation often prove to be wrong. And dress norms frequently dictate the kind of clothing that should be worn to work. Of course, what's acceptable dress in one organization may be very different from what is acceptable in another. Finally, loyalty norms will influence whether individuals work late, work on weekends, or move to locations they might not prefer to live.

Because individuals want to be accepted by groups to which they belong, they're susceptible to conformity pressures. The impact that group pressures for conformity can have on an individual member's judgment and attitudes was demonstrated in research by Solomon Asch.[5] In his conformity experiments, groups of seven or eight people were asked to compare two cards held up by the

In the intensely creative world of Industrial Light and Magic (ILM), which has produced many Academy Award-winning special effects for films like *Forrest Gump* and *Jurassic Park*, group norms allow for a lot of flexibility. Visual-effects supervisor Eric Brevig, shown here with digital painter Bridget Goodman, must approve scenes as they are developed by ILM's teams of artists and animators. In meetings he follows this strict but unwritten rule: *Never tell people how to do their jobs. Instead, present them with a challenge, and then let them choose the best way to attack it.* "That way," says Brevig, "they feel like part of the team—and they usually come up with a better idea than mine."

norms

Acceptable standards or expectations shared by a group's members.

Exhibit 15.3

**Examples of Cards
Used in the Asch Study**

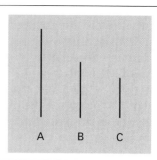

experimenter. One card had three lines of different lengths and the other had one line that was equal in length to one of the three lines on the other card (see Exhibit 15.3). The object was for each group member to announce aloud which of the three lines matched the single line. Asch wanted to know what would happen if members began to give incorrect answers. Would the pressures to conform cause individuals to align with the others? The experiment was "fixed" so that all but one of the members (the unsuspecting subject) had been told ahead of time to start giving obviously incorrect answers after one or two rounds of these matching exercises. Over many experiments and trials, the unsuspecting subject conformed over a third of the time; that is, the person gave answers he or she knew were wrong but that were consistent with the replies of other group members.

What can we conclude from this study? The results suggest that there are group norms that push us toward conformity. We desire to be one of the group and to avoid being visibly different. We can generalize further to say that when an individual's opinion of objective data differs significantly from that of others in the group, he or she feels extensive pressure to align his or her opinion to conform with the opinions of others.

Status Systems **Status** is a prestige grading, position, or rank within a group. As far back as researchers have been able to trace groups, they have found status hierarchies. Status systems are an important factor in understanding behavior. Status is a significant motivator and has behavioral consequences when individuals see a disparity between what they perceive their status to be and what others perceive it to be.

status

A prestige grading, position, or rank within a group.

Status in a group may be informally conferred by characteristics such as education, age, skill, or experience. Anything can have status value if others in the group evaluate it that way. Of course, just because status is informal doesn't mean that it's unimportant or that it is hard to determine who has it or who does not. Members of groups have no problem placing people into status categories, and they usually agree about who has high, middle, or low status.

Status is also formally conferred, and it's important for employees to believe that the organization's formal status system is congruent—that is, there's equity between the perceived ranking of an individual and the status symbols he or she is given by the organization. For instance, status incongruence would occur when a supervisor earns less than his or her subordinates, a desirable office is occupied by a person in a low-ranking position, or paid country club memberships are provided to division managers but not to vice presidents. Employees expect the "things" an individual has and receives to be congruent with his or her status.

? THINKING CRITICALLY ABOUT ETHICS

You've been hired as a summer intern in the auditing section of an accounting firm in Dallas. After working there about a month, you conclude that the attitude in the office is "anything goes." Employees know that supervisors won't discipline them for ignoring company rules. For example, employees have to turn in expense reports, but the process is a joke; nobody submits receipts to verify reimbursement, and nothing is ever said. In fact, when you tried to turn in your receipts with your expense report, you were told, "Nobody else turns in receipts and you don't really need to, either." You know that no expense check has ever been denied because of failure to turn in a receipt, even though the employee handbook says that receipts are required. Also, your co-workers use company phones for personal long-distance calls even though that is prohibited by the employee handbook. And one permanent employee told you to "help yourself" to any paper, pens, or pencils you might need here or at home.

What are the norms of this group? Suppose that you were the supervisor in this area. How would you go about changing the norms?

Testing...Testing...1,2,3

4. **What is the influence of roles on group behavior?**

5. **How can group norms both help and hurt an organization?**

6. **How might status issues influence group behavior?**

When they're not, employees are likely to question the authority of their managers. Also, the motivational potential of promotions declines, and the general pattern of order and consistency in the organization is disturbed. ◄───────

Group Size Does the size of a group affect the group's overall behavior? The answer is a definite yes, but the effect depends on the outcomes on which you're focusing.[6] The evidence indicates, for instance, that small groups are faster at completing tasks than are larger ones. However, if the group is engaged in problem solving, large groups consistently get better results than smaller ones. Translating these findings into specific numbers is a bit more difficult, but we can offer some guidelines. Large groups—those with a dozen or more members—are good for getting diverse input. Thus, if the goal of the group is to find facts, a larger group should be more effective. On the other hand, smaller groups are better at doing something productive with those facts. Groups of approximately seven members tend to be more effective for taking action.

One of the more disturbing findings related to group size is that, as groups get incrementally larger, the contribution of individual members often tends to decrease.[7] The best explanation for this reduction of effort is a phenomenon known as the **free rider tendency**. The dispersion of responsibility within a group encourages individuals to slack off. When the results of the group can't be attributed to any one person, the relationship between an individual's input and the group's output is clouded. In such situations, individuals may be tempted to become "free riders" and coast on the group's efforts. In other words, efficiency will decline when individuals think that their contributions can't be measured. The obvious conclusion from this finding is that when managers use work teams they should also have a way to identify individual efforts.

free rider tendency

A group phenomenon in which individual members reduce their individual efforts and contributions as the group increases in size.

Group Cohesiveness Intuitively, it makes sense that groups in which there's a lot of internal disagreement and lack of cooperation are less effective in completing their tasks than are groups in which members generally agree, cooperate, and like each other. Research in this area has focused on **group cohesiveness**, or the degree to which members are attracted to a group and share the group's goals.

group cohesiveness

The degree to which group members are attracted to one another and share the group's goals.

Group cohesiveness, or the degree to which team members share the group's goals, may seem like an intangible quality to most of us. But it was very real to this group from ad agency Leo Burnett Co. After the agency split its departments into more flexible teams in an effort to recoup some lost business, securing the Heinz account was one of its biggest goals. The team in this photo won the account for Burnett, based on three factors: It successfully targeted the teen market, its ads were better developed, and Heinz believed the Burnett team was "more cohesive" than its competitor's.

Research has generally shown that highly cohesive groups are more effective than are less cohesive ones.[8] The relationship between cohesiveness and effectiveness, however, is more complex. A key moderating variable is the degree to which the group's attitude aligns with its goals or with the goals of the organization.[9] The more cohesive a group is, the more its members will follow its goals. If the goals are desirable (for instance, high output, quality work, cooperation with individuals outside the group), a cohesive group is more productive than a less cohesive group. But if cohesiveness is high and attitudes are unfavorable, productivity decreases. If cohesiveness is low and goals are supported, productivity increases but not as much as when both cohesiveness and support are high. When cohesiveness is low and goals are not supported, cohesiveness has no significant effect on productivity. These conclusions are illustrated in Exhibit 15.4.

Conflict Management As a group performs its assigned tasks, disagreements or conflicts inevitably will arise. When we use the term **conflict**, we're referring to *perceived* incompatible differences resulting in some form of interference or opposition. Whether the differences are real or not is irrelevant. If people in a group perceive that differences exist, then there is conflict. In addition, our definition includes the extremes—from subtle, indirect, and highly controlled forms of interferences to overt acts such as strikes, riots, or wars.

Over the years, three different views have evolved regarding conflict.[10] One view argues that conflict must be avoided, that it indicates a problem within the group. We call this the **traditional view of conflict**. A second view, the

conflict

Perceived incompatible differences that result in interference or opposition.

traditional view of conflict

The view that all conflict is bad and must be avoided.

Exhibit	15.4

The Relationship Between Cohesiveness and Productivity

		Cohesiveness	
		High	Low
Alignment of Group and Organizational Goals	High	Strong Increase in Productivity	Moderate Increase in Productivity
	Low	Decrease in Productivity	No Significant Effect on Productivity

human relations view of conflict, argues that conflict is a natural and inevitable outcome in any group and need not be negative but, rather, has potential to be a positive force in contributing to a group's performance. The third and most recent perspective proposes that not only can conflict be a positive force in a group but also that some conflict is *absolutely necessary* for a group to perform effectively. This third approach is called the **interactionist view of conflict**.

The interactionist view is not suggesting that all conflicts are good. Some conflicts are seen as supporting the goals of the work group and improving its performance; these are **functional conflicts** of a constructive nature. Other conflicts are destructive and prevent a group from achieving its goals. These are **dysfunctional conflicts**. Exhibit 15.5 on page 406 illustrates the challenge facing managers.

What differentiates functional from dysfunctional conflict? The evidence indicates that you need to look at the *type* of conflict.[11] Three types have been identified: task, relationship, and process.

Task conflict relates to the content and goals of the work. **Relationship conflict** focuses on interpersonal relationships. **Process conflict** refers to how the work gets done. Studies demonstrate that relationship conflicts are almost always dysfunctional. Why? It appears that the friction and interpersonal hostilities inherent in relationship conflicts increase personality clashes and decrease mutual understanding, thereby hindering the completion of organizational tasks. On the other hand, low levels of process conflict and low to moderate levels of task conflict are functional. For process conflict to be productive, it must be kept to a mimimum. Intense arguments about who should do what become dysfunctional when they create uncertainty about task roles, increase the time to complete tasks, and lead to members working at cross-purposes. A low to moderate level of task conflict consistently demonstrates a positive effect on group performance because it stimulates discussions of ideas that help groups to perform better. Because we have yet to devise a sophisticated measuring instrument for assessing whether a given task, relationship, or process conflict level is optimal, too high, or too low, the manager must make intelligent judgments.

When the conflict level is too high, what techniques can managers use to reduce it? They can select from five conflict-resolution options: avoiding, accommodating, forcing, compromising, and collaborating.[12] (See Exhibit 15.6 on page 406 for a description of each of these techniques.) Keep in mind that no one option is ideal for every situation. Which approach to use depends on the manager's desire to be more or less cooperative and more or less assertive. ◄───────

GROUP DECISION MAKING

Many organizational decisions are made by groups. It's a rare organization that doesn't at some time use committees, task forces, review panels, study teams, or similar groups to make decisions. In addition, studies show that managers may spend up to 70 percent of their time in group meetings.[13] Undoubtedly, a large portion of that time is spent formulating problems, developing solutions, and determining how to implement the solutions. It's possible, in fact, for groups to be assigned any of the eight steps in the decision-making process. (Refer to Chapter 6 for a review of the steps in the decision-making process.) In this section, we'll look at the advantages and disadvantages of group decision making, discuss when groups would be preferred, and review some techniques for improving group decision making.

---

human relations view of conflict

The view that conflict is a natural and inevitable outcome in any group.

interactionist view of conflict

The view that some conflict is necessary for a group to perform effectively.

functional conflicts

Conflicts that support a group's goals and improve its performance.

dysfunctional conflicts

Conflicts that prevent a group from achieving its goals.

task conflict

Conflicts over content and goals of the work.

relationship conflict

Conflict based on interpersonal relationships.

process conflict

Conflict over how work gets done.

Testing...Testing...1,2,3

7. **What is the most effective size for a group?**

8. **Describe the relationship between group cohesiveness and productivity.**

9. **How does conflict management influence group behavior?**

Exhibit | 15.5

Conflict and Group Performance

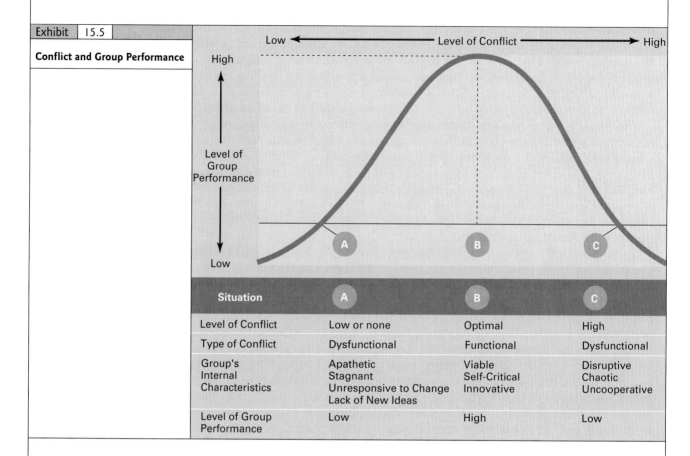

Situation	A	B	C
Level of Conflict	Low or none	Optimal	High
Type of Conflict	Dysfunctional	Functional	Dysfunctional
Group's Internal Characteristics	Apathetic Stagnant Unresponsive to Change Lack of New Ideas	Viable Self-Critical Innovative	Disruptive Chaotic Uncooperative
Level of Group Performance	Low	High	Low

Exhibit | 15.6

Conflict-Resolution Techniques

Source: Adapted from K.W. Thomas, "Conflict and Negotiation Processes in Organizations," in M.D. Dunnette and L.M. Hough (eds.), *Handbook of Industrial and Organizational Psychology*, vol. 3, 2d ed. (Palo Alto, CA: Consulting Psychologists Press, 1992), p. 668. With permission.

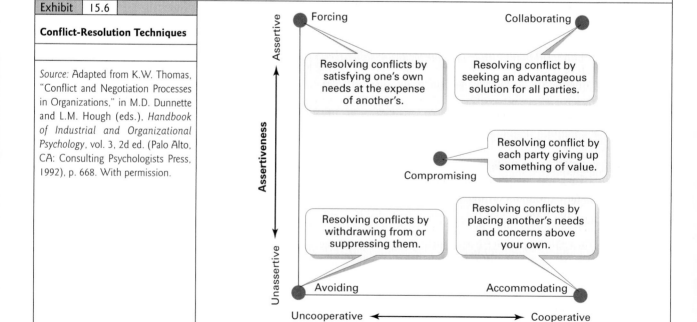

Advantages and Disadvantages What advantages do group decisions have over individual decisions?

1. *Provide more complete information.* There is truth to the saying that two heads are better than one. A group brings a diversity of experience and perspectives to the decision process that an individual cannot.

2. *Generate more alternatives.* Because groups have a greater amount and diversity of information, they can identify more alternatives than an individual. This advantage is particularly evident when group members represent different areas of expertise. For instance, a team made up of individuals from engineering, accounting, production, marketing, and human resources will generate alternatives that reflect their diverse perspectives.

3. *Increase acceptance of a solution.* Many decisions fail after the final choice has been made because people do not accept the solution. Group members are reluctant to fight or undermine a decision they have helped develop.

4. *Increase legitimacy.* The group decision-making process is consistent with democratic ideals, and decisions made by groups may be perceived as more legitimate than decisions made unilaterally by one person.

If groups are so good at making decisions, how did the phrase, "A camel is a horse put together by a committee" become so popular? The answer, of course, is that group decisions also have disadvantages.

1. *Time consuming.* Putting a group together takes time as does any decision making within the group. The result is that groups almost always take more time to reach a solution than it would take an individual.

2. *Minority domination.* Members of a group are never perfectly equal. They may differ in organizational rank, experience, knowledge about the problem, influence with other members, verbal skills, assertiveness, and so forth. This inequality creates the opportunity for one or more members to dominate others. A dominant and vocal minority frequently can have an excessive influence on the final decision.

3. *Pressures to conform.* As we know from our earlier discussion, there are pressures to conform in groups. This can lead to a phenomenon known as **groupthink**, which is a type of conformity in which group members withhold different or unpopular views in order to give the appearance of agreement. Groupthink undermines critical thinking in the group and eventually harms the quality of the final decision.[14]

4. *Ambiguous responsibility.* Group members share responsibility, but who is actually responsible for the final outcome? In an individual decision, it's clear who is responsible. In a group decision, the responsibility of any single member is diluted.

groupthink

A type of conformity in which group members withhold deviant, minority, or unpopular views in order to appear in agreement.

Effectiveness and Efficiency of Group Decision Making Determining whether groups are effective at making decisions depends on the criteria you use to assess effectiveness.[15] Exhibit 15.7 summarizes when groups or individuals are most effective.

Keep in mind, however, that the effectiveness of group decision making is also influenced by the size of the group. The larger the group, the greater the opportunity for diverse representation. On the other hand, a larger group requires more coordination and more time for members to contribute their ideas. So groups probably should not be too large. Evidence indicates, in fact, that groups of five,

Exhibit 15.7	Criteria of Effectiveness	Groups	Individuals
Group versus Individual Decision Making	Accuracy	√	
	Speed		√
	Creativity	√	
	Degree of acceptance	√	
	Efficiency		√

and to a lesser extent, seven, are the most effective.[16] Having an odd number in the group helps avoid decision deadlocks. Also, these groups are large enough for members to shift roles and withdraw from unfavorable positions but still small enough for quieter members to participate actively in discussions.

Techniques for Improving Group Decision Making We know that groups can be effective decision makers. However, when members of a group meet and interact, they create the potential for groupthink. They can censor themselves and pressure other group members into agreement. How can managers make group decisions more creative? Exhibit 15.8 describes three possible techniques.

UNDERSTANDING WORK GROUP BEHAVIOR

Why are some groups more successful than others? The answer to that is complex, but it includes variables such as the abilities of the group's members, the size of the group, the level of conflict, and the internal pressures on members to conform to the group's norms. Exhibit 15.9 presents the major components that determine group performance and satisfaction.[17] It can help you sort out the key variables and their interrelationships.

External Conditions Imposed on the Group To begin understanding the behavior of a formal work group, we need to view it as a subsystem of a larger system.[18] As a subset of a larger organizational system, the work group is influenced by exter-

Exhibit 15.8	
Techniques for Making More Creative Group Decisions	

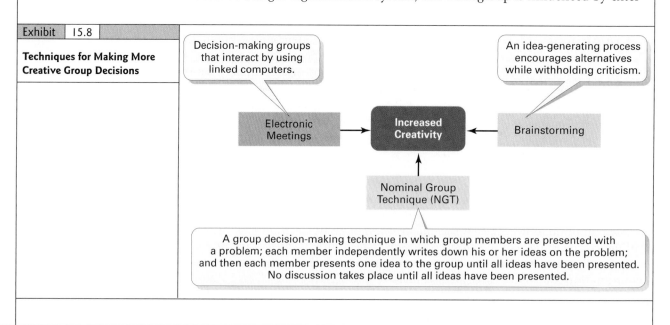

Decision-making groups that interact by using linked computers.

An idea-generating process encourages alternatives while withholding criticism.

Electronic Meetings → Increased Creativity ← Brainstorming

↑ Nominal Group Technique (NGT)

A group decision-making technique in which group members are presented with a problem; each member independently writes down his or her ideas on the problem; and then each member presents one idea to the group until all ideas have been presented. No discussion takes place until all ideas have been presented.

Tasks can be generalized as being either simple or complex. Simple tasks are routine and standardized. Complex tasks are ones that tend to be novel or non-routine. We would hypothesize that the more complex the task, the more the group will benefit from discussion among group members about alternative work methods. If the task is simple, group members don't need to discuss such alternatives. They can rely on standard operating procedures. Similarly, if there's a high degree of interdependence among the tasks that group members must perform, they'll need to interact more. Effective communication and controlled conflict should, therefore, be most relevant to group performance when tasks are complex and interdependent. ◄——

Testing...Testing...1,2,3

10. What are the advantages and disadvantages of group decision making?

11. When would groups be the best choice for making decisions?

12. Why are some groups more successful than others? (Hint: Use the group behavior model.)

> ## TURNING GROUPS INTO EFFECTIVE TEAMS

Work teams are popular in organizations. A recent study by the Center for the Study of Work Teams found that 80 percent of organizations with over 100 employees reported that half their employees were on at least one team.[23] And the popularity of teams is likely to continue. Why? Exhibit 15.10 summarizes some reasons. In this section, we'll discuss what a work team is, the different types of teams that organizations might use, and how to develop and manage work teams.

WHAT IS A TEAM?

Most of you are already familiar with teams especially if, for no other reason, than you've watched organized sports activity. Although a sports team has many of the same characteristics as a work team, work teams *are* different and have their own unique traits. Just what are **work teams**? They are formal groups made up of interdependent individuals who are responsible for the attainment of a goal.[24]

TYPES OF TEAMS

Although there are many ways to categorize teams, one convenient way is to look at teams in terms of four characteristics: purpose, duration, membership, and structure.[25] (See Exhibit 15.11.) Let's explain these characteristics in more detail.

work teams

Formal groups made up of interdependent individuals who are responsible for the attainment of a goal.

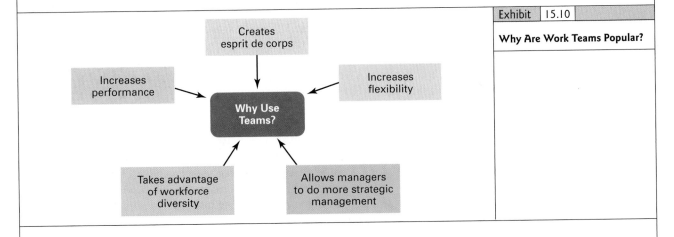

Exhibit	15.10

Why Are Work Teams Popular?

Exhibit | 15.11 |

Categories of Teams

Purpose
- Product Development
- Problem Solving
- Reengineering
- Any Other Organizational Purposes Desired

Structure
- Supervised
- Self-Managed

Membership
- Functional
- Cross-Functional

Duration
- Permanent
- Temporary

Teams can vary in their purpose or goal. A team might be involved in product development, problem solving, as part of a process reengineering effort, or in any other number of work-related activities. For instance, at Motorola's facility in Austin, teams are used in work process optimization projects. And Toyo Australia uses multiskilled teams in manufacturing the colored inks used in magazine production and other print-related products.[26]

A team is either permanent or temporary. Departmental teams and others that are part of the organization's formal structure are types of permanent teams. Temporary teams include task forces, project teams, problem-solving teams, and any other type of short-term team formed to develop, analyze, or study a work-related issue.

Team membership can either be functional or cross-functional. A departmental team is functional because its members come from a specific functional area. However, as we already discussed in Chapter 10, many organizations are using cross-functional teams as a way to foster innovation, cooperation, and commitment.

Finally, teams can be either supervised or self-managed. A supervised team will be under the direction of a manager who is responsible for guiding the team in setting goals, performing the work activities, and evaluating performance. On the other hand, a self-managed team assumes the responsibilities of managing itself.

The four most common types of teams you're likely to find in organizations today are functional teams, self-managed teams, virtual teams, and cross-functional teams.[27]

Functional teams are composed of a manager and his or her employees from a particular functional area. Within this functional area, issues such as authority, decision making, leadership, and interactions are relatively simple and clear. Functional teams are often involved in efforts to improve work activities or to solve specific problems within their particular functional area. For example, at GTE Directories in Dallas/Fort Worth, publication teams work on actually producing the telephone directories and customer service teams work on resolving customer complaints.[28]

Another type of team commonly being used in organizations is the **self-managed team**, a formal group of employees who operate without a manager and are responsible for a complete work process or segment. The self-managed team is responsible for getting the work done *and* for managing themselves. This usually includes planning and scheduling work, assigning tasks to members, collective control over the pace of work, making operating decisions, and taking action on prob-

functional team

A type of work team composed of a manager and his or her subordinates from a particular functional area.

self-managed team

A type of work team that operates without a manager and is responsible for a complete work process or segment.

lems. For instance, teams at Corning have no shift supervisors and work closely with other manufacturing divisions to solve production-line problems and coordinate deadlines and deliveries. The teams have the authority to make and implement decisions, finish projects, and address problems.[29] Other organizations such as Xerox, General Motors, Coors Brewing, PepsiCo, Hewlett-Packard, and Federal Express use self-managed teams in deciding how best to do the work. How effective are self-managed teams? Most organizations that use them find them to be successful and plan to expand their use in the coming years.[30]

The third type of team we want to discuss is the **virtual team**. Virtual teams are teams that use computer technology to link physically dispersed members in order to achieve a common goal. The advertising project teams at StrawberryFrog, described in the chapter-opening Manager's Dilemma, are examples of virtual teams. In a virtual team, members collaborate using communication links such as wide area networks, videoconferencing, fax, e-mail, or even Web sites where the team can hold online conferences.[31] Virtual teams can do all the things that other teams can—share information, make decisions, and complete tasks; however, they miss the normal give-and-take of face-to-face discussions. Because of this omission, virtual teams tend to be more task oriented, especially if the team members have never personally met.

The last type of team we want to discuss is the **cross-functional team**, which we introduced in Chapter 10 and defined as a hybrid grouping of individuals who are experts in various specialties and who work together on various tasks. Many organizations are using cross-functional teams. For example, at Hallmark Cards in Kansas City, editors, writers, artists, and production specialists join with employees from manufacturing, graphic arts, sales, and distribution to work on everything from developing new-product ideas to improving customer deliveries.[32] And at Hewlett-Packard's North American distribution facility in Bridgewater, New Jersey, a cross-functional team was formed to redesign inefficient work processes.[33]

Teams serve many different purposes in organizations. This specially selected "Speed Team" was created at IBM for the single, focused purpose of shortening the time it took the company's information technology group—100,000 people worldwide—to complete the development of Internet applications. Jane Harper (far left) decided with co-leader Ray Blair (far right) that "we will have failed if the Speed Team is still together three years from now," and so it has been designed to last for about six months and then disband.

virtual team

A type of work team that uses computer technology to link physically dispersed members in order to achieve a common goal.

cross-functional team

A type of work team that's a hybrid grouping of individuals who are experts in various specialties and who work together on various tasks.

> ### DEVELOPING AND MANAGING EFFECTIVE TEAMS

Teams are not automatic productivity enhancers. They can also be disappointments to management. We need to look more closely at how managers can develop and manage effective teams.

CHARACTERISTICS OF EFFECTIVE TEAMS

Research on teams provides insights into the characteristics associated with effective teams.[34] Let's look more closely at these characteristics as listed in Exhibit 15.12.

Testing...Testing...1,2,3

13. **Compare groups and teams.**

14. **Why have teams become so popular in organizations?**

15. **Describe functional, self-managed, virtual, and cross-functional teams.**

Exhibit | 15.12

Characteristics of Effective Teams

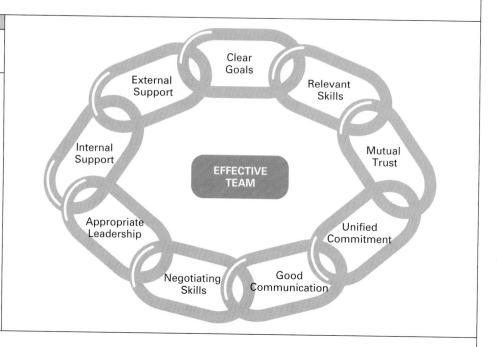

Clear Goals High-performance teams have both a clear understanding of the goals to be achieved and a belief that the goals embody important results. Moreover, the importance of these goals encourages individuals to redirect personal concerns to achieving team goals. In effective teams, members are committed to the team's goals, know what they're expected to accomplish, and understand how they will work together to achieve these goals.

Relevant Skills Effective teams are composed of competent individuals. They have the necessary technical and interpersonal skills to achieved the desired goals while working well together. This last point is important and often overlooked. Not everyone who is technically competent has the skills to work well as a team member. High-performing teams have members who possess both technical and interpersonal skills.

Mutual Trust Effective teams are characterized by high mutual trust among members. That is, members believe in the ability, character, and integrity of each other. But as you probably know from personal relationships, trust is fragile. It takes a long time to build and it can be easily destroyed. Maintaining trust requires careful attention by managers.

Work teams have gone international, and the best of them can boast spectacular results. Maxus Energy, the U.S. subsidiary of Argentine corporation YPF, formed a team with fellow subsidiary Maxus-Southeast Sumatra. Its members, from the United States, Holland, Great Britain, and Indonesia, had little in common but their problem: to prevent an anticipated 15 percent drop in oil production from a new field. They succeeded by pooling their expertise and even added oil reserves to their stockpiles in the process.

	Exhibit	15.13

1. *Communicate.* Keep team members and subordinates informed by explaining decisions and policies and providing accurate feedback. Be candid about your own problems and limitations.
2. *Be supportive.* Be available and approachable. Encourage and support team members' ideas.
3. *Be respectful.* Delegate real authority to team members and listen to their ideas.
4. *Be fair.* Give credit where it's due, be objective and impartial in performance evaluations, and be generous with your praise.
5. *Be predictable.* Be consistent in your daily affairs. Make good on your explicit and implied promises.
6. *Demonstrate competence.* Develop the admiration and respect of team members by demonstrating technical and professional ability and good business sense.

Six Suggestions for Helping Managers Build Trust

Source: Adapted from F. Bartolome, "Nobody Trusts the Boss Completely—Now What?" *Harvard Business Review*, March–April 1989, pp. 135–42.

The climate of trust within a group tends to be strongly influenced by the organization's culture and the actions of management. Organizations that value openness, honesty, and collaborative processes and that encourage employee involvement and autonomy are more likely to create trusting cultures. Exhibit 15.13 lists six recommended actions that can help managers build and maintain trust.

Unified Commitment Members of an effective team exhibit intense loyalty and dedication to the team. They're willing to do whatever it takes to help their team succeed. We call this loyalty and dedication *unified commitment.*

Studies of successful teams have found that members identify with their teams.[35] Members redefine themselves to include membership in the team as an important aspect of the self. Unified commitment, then, is characterized by dedication to the team's goals and a willingness to expend extraordinary amounts of energy to achieve them.

Good Communication Not surprisingly, effective teams are characterized by good communication. Members convey messages between each other in ways that are readily and clearly understood. This includes nonverbal as well as spoken messages. Good communication is also characterized by a healthy dose of feedback from team members and managers. Feedback helps to guide team members and to correct misunderstandings. Like a couple who has been together for many years, members on high-performing teams are able to quickly and efficiently share ideas and feelings.

Negotiating Skills When jobs are designed around individuals, their job descriptions, the organization's rules and procedures, and other types of formalized documentation clarify employee roles. Effective teams, on the other hand, tend to be flexible and are continually making adjustments in who does what. This flexibility requires team members to possess negotiating skills. Problems and relationships are regularly changing in teams and members need to be able to confront and reconcile differences.

Achieving greatness is the goal of the Boston restaurant called Radius, and teamwork is the means its owners have chosen to get there. "This restaurant is about creating something bigger than any of us could accomplish alone," says co-owner and chef Michael Schlow (right). Christopher Myers (left) is co-owner and wine director, and Esti Benson is the general manager. Myers and Benson run daily meetings of the entire staff to discuss the evening's reservations, menu, and ingredients and to build the spirit of teamwork that is making the restaurant a rising star.

Appropriate Leadership Effective leaders can motivate a team to follow them through the most difficult situations. How? They help clarify goals. They demonstrate that change is possible by overcoming inertia. And they increase the self-confidence of team members, helping members to more fully realize their potential. It's important to note that the best leaders aren't necessarily directive or controlling. Increasingly, effective team leaders act in the roles of coach and facilitator. They help guide and support the team but don't control it. This condition obviously applies to self-managed teams but also increasingly applies to cross-functional, virtual, and functional teams in which the members themselves are empowered. For some traditional managers, changing their role from "boss" to facilitator is a difficult transition. Although most managers relish sharing authority or understand its advantages, some hard-nosed dictatorial managers aren't well suited to the team concept and must be transferred or replaced.

Internal and External Support The final condition necessary for an effective team is a supportive climate. Internally, the team should have a sound infrastructure. This includes proper training, a clear and reasonable measurement system that team members can use to evaluate their overall performance, an incentive program that recognizes and rewards team activities, and a supportive human resource system.[36] The right infrastructure should support members and reinforce behaviors that lead to high levels of performance. Externally, managers should provide the team with the resources needed to get the job done.

MANAGING TEAMS

What's involved in managing a team? We can look at the task of managing a team using the four management functions: planning, organizing, leading, and controlling.[37]

Planning Goal determination is an important part of the planning process. As we pointed out previously, effective teams have clear goals. It's important that team members understand and accept the team's goals.[38] Whether the goals are provided for the team or whether the team develops its own goals, every team member needs to know what the goals are. An easy way to check team members' understanding of the goals is to have each person write down the goals and then look at their statements. If there are any misconceptions about the team's goals, the manager needs to clear them up.

According to H. David Aycock, the former chairman, CEO, and president of steel-products manufacturer Nucor Corp. in Charlotte, North Carolina, the successful teamwork on which the firm is built relies on seven key ingredients: a clear mission, positive thinking, unselfish effort, mutual respect, trust, small size, and strong management. Says Aycock, the team leader or manager "must always be on the lookout for distractions, tangents, and unproductive or ancillary issues. If the leader spots the project going astray, it's his or her responsibility to get it back on track—*fast*."

Organizing Organizing tasks in managing a team include clarifying authority and structural issues. A key question is "How much authority do we have?" A self-managed team has been empowered to make certain decisions and perform specific work activities. A team's authority will be influenced by the organization's culture and its support of employee involvement and autonomy. Structural issues also need to be resolved within the team itself. Has a leader been appointed, or will the team designate one? What tasks need to be done in order to accomplish the team's goals? How should the work be done efficiently and effectively? Who's going to be assigned to the various tasks, and how will these assignments be made?

- Ask appropriate questions to bring out ideas and stimulate discussion.
- Listen closely and intently to members' ideas and concerns.
- Manage group discussions to encourage shy team members to participate.
- Establish an informal and nonthreatening climate so members feel free to candidly speak their thoughts.
- Use the consensus method to reach decisions on key team issues.
- Involve team members in setting goals.
- Implement meeting guidelines to minimize wasted time in group meetings.
- Encourage respect for each other so each member knows that his or her contributions are valued.
- Identify and deal with dysfunctional behaviors immediately.
- Celebrate the achievement of milestones and other team accomplishments.
- Use recognition, task assignments, and other techniques to motivate team members.

Exhibit	15.14

Types of Interpersonal Skills Used in Managing Teams

Source: Based on G.M. Parker, *Cross-Functional Teams* (San Francisco: Jossey-Bass, 1994), pp. 57–58.

Leading Important issues in leading that a team must address include, among others, what role the leader will play, how disagreements will be handled, and what communication processes will be used. Dealing with the human dynamics of the team is often the most difficult part of managing a team. Exhibit 15.14 lists some people skills that are important in leading a team.

Controlling Two important controlling issues are: How will the team's performance be evaluated, and what type of reward system will be used? As organizations use teams more and more, their performance management systems will have to change. How?

Performance criteria need to be modified to incorporate teamwork behaviors in employee evaluations.[39] Not only should individual performance be evaluated, but also factors that indicate how well the individual works in the team context should be considered. For instance, at Ideo, an industrial design firm, performance appraisals include comments from team peers as well as from managers.[40]

Changes in the appraisal process to incorporate team efforts are only half the story. Managers also need to look at how teams are rewarded for their efforts and performance levels. A popular approach to group incentives is **gainsharing**, an incentive program that shares the gains of the efforts of employees with those employees. In gainsharing, rewards are directly related to performance. If the team succeeds, team members are rewarded. Team-based organizations also may use one-time bonuses, team incentive systems, employee-based recognition programs, and informal team recognition. For example, Hallmark Cards added an annual bonus based on achievement of team goals to its basic individual incentive system. Trigon Blue Cross/Blue Shield changed its system to reward both individual goals and teamlike behaviors.[41] No matter what approach is used, the team itself should be the primary force in deciding what types of rewards and recognition are important.[42]

gainsharing

A group incentive program that shares the gains of the efforts of group members with those group members.

16. **What characteristics do effective teams exhibit?**

17. **What types of planning, organizing, and leading issues must be addressed when managing a team?**

18. **How should performance evaluations and reward systems be handled in teams?**

Testing...Testing...1,2,3

Managers Respond to "A Manager's Dilemma"

Jeff Wasson

CEO, Travelnow.com, Springfield, Missouri

Peter H. Nalen

Vice President, Management Supervisor, The Sawtooth Group, Woodbridge, New Jersey

Karen will not be able to manage these virtual teams without establishing some boundaries or guidelines. I would recommend that she develop a template model that is process based. She should empower account managers from her local staff. This would allow her to manage multiple projects through her account managers. Her account managers would be responsible for managing the processes that utilize the talent pool from around the globe.

With the assistance of her account managers, Karen should define the services offered by StrawberryFrog. This management team also needs to develop procedures and realistic time-lines for each ad campaign. Account managers would monitor the budget for each project as well as define terms of accountability expected from the independent employees.

Finally, it would be necessary to communicate these guidelines to all participants in the talent pool before formally adding them to the resource list. This method will ensure that expectations are delivered without adding unnecessary overhead or work complexity.

The number-one objective for Drakenberg will be to ensure clear, concise direction from her clients in order to deliver specific assignments to her virtual team. Because the team is geographically dispersed, they will not have the luxury of continual personal interaction that helps define individual roles within a project or clarify potentially misinterpreted objectives.

She will need to assign a clear and strong team leader who will have the responsibility of defining and assigning each piece of the campaign project. For each campaign, the team leader will need to effectively communicate to each team member his or her role in the overall project, as well as the specific campaign objectives, goals, assigned tasks, responsibilities, and dates.

Once having made the initial assignments, the team leader will also proactively manage a feedback loop to and from each member to ensure the project moves forward on time and on goal.

Chapter Summary

This summary is organized by the chapter-opening objectives found on p. 396.

1. Formal groups are work groups established by the organization that have designated work assignments and specific tasks. Informal groups are social groups that occur naturally in the workplace in response to the need for social contact.

2. The five stages of group development are forming, storming, norming, performing, and adjourning. Forming is the stage in which people join the group and define the group's purpose, structure, and leadership. Storming is a stage of intragroup conflict over control issues. During the norming stage, close relationships develop and the group demonstrates cohesiveness. Performing is the stage at which the group is doing the task at hand. Finally, adjourning is the stage when temporary groups with limited tasks to perform prepare for disbanding.

3. A role refers to a set of behavior patterns expected of someone occupying a given position in a social unit. At any given time, employees adjust their role behaviors (task accomplishment or maintaining group member satisfaction) to the group of which they are a part. Norms are standards shared by group members. They informally convey to employees which behaviors are acceptable and which are unacceptable.

4. There are five variables in the group behavior model that explain the group's performance and satisfaction. First, a group is influenced by the larger organization of which it is a part. Second, a group's potential level of performance depends to a large extent on the resources that its members individually bring to the group. Third, there is a group structure that shapes the behavior of members. Fourth, there are internal processes within the group that aid or hinder interaction and the ability of the group to perform.

Finally, the impact of group processes on the group's performance and member satisfaction depends on the task that the group is doing.

5. The advantages of group decision making are more complete information, more alternatives, increased acceptance of a solution, and greater legitimacy. The disadvantages include the amount of time it takes, the likelihood of being dominated by a minority, the pressure to conform, and the blurring of responsibility.

6. Teams have become increasingly popular in organizations because they build esprit de corps, free up management to do more strategic thinking, permit more flexible decision making, utilize workforce diversity, and usually increase performance.

7. The four most common types of teams used in organizations are functional teams, self-managed teams, virtual teams, and cross-functional teams. Functional teams are made up of a manager and his or her employees from a particular functional area. A self-managed team is a formal group of employees that operates without a manager and is responsible for a complete work process or segment. Virtual teams are teams that use computer technology to link physically dispersed members in order to achieve a common goal. A cross-functional team is a hybrid grouping of individuals who are experts in various specialties and who work together on various tasks.

8. Effective work teams are characterized by clear goals, members with relevant skills, mutual trust among members, unified commitment, good communication, adequate negotiating skills, appropriate leadership, and external and internal support.

9. Managers can build trust by communicating openly; supporting team members' ideas; being respectful, fair, and predictable; and demonstrating competence.

Thinking About Management Issues

1. Think of a group to which you belong (or have belonged). Trace its development through the stages of group development shown in Exhibit 15.2. How closely did its development parallel the group development model? How might the group development model have been used to improve the group's effectiveness?

2. How do you think scientific management theorists would react to the increased reliance on teams in organizations? How would the behavioral science theorists react?

3. How do you explain the popularity of work teams in the United States when its culture places such high value on individualism and individual effort?

4. Why might a manager want to stimulate conflict in a group or team? How could conflict be stimulated?

5. Do you think that everyone should be expected to be a team player, given the trends we're seeing in the use of teams? Discuss.

Log On: Internet-Based Exercise

1. Work teams are popular in U.S. organizations. Does this popularity extend to organizations in other countries? Research the use of work teams in organizations in Mexico, Australia, Sweden, and Japan. In what countries are work teams used the most? What types of work teams seem to be popular in these countries?

2. Identify three organizations that specialize in team building, team facilitation, or team development. What types of programs do these organizations offer? How are they similar? How are they different? Which of the programs do you think would be most effective? Why?

myPHLIP Companion Web Site

myPHLIP (**www.prenhall.com/myphlip**) is a fully customizable homepage that ties students and faculty to text-specific resources.
- **For students**, myPHLIP provides an online study guide tied chapter-by-chapter to the text—current events and Internet exercises, lecture notes, downloadable software, the Career Center, the Writing Center, Ask the Tutor, and more.
- **For faculty**, myPHLIP provides a syllabus tool that allows you to manage content, communicate with students, and upload personal resources.

Working Together: Team-Based Exercise

What happens when groups are presented with a task that must be completed within a certain time frame? Does the group exhibit characteristics of the stages of group development? Can the group behavior model (Exhibit 15.9) explain what happens in the group? Your instructor will divide the class into groups and give you instructions about what to do next.

Case Application

Team Adventures at Evart Glass

One exercise involves team members' randomly throwing and catching various objects (such as tennis balls, hackey sacs, or koosh balls) and attempting to juggle the objects simultaneously. Another involves passing a bicycle inner tube around a circle of people who are holding hands without either breaking the circle or letting the tube touch the ground. You might think we're describing activities at a summer camp for 10-year-olds, but these are exercises being used to show one company's work teams what it means to be a team player.

Evart Glass Plant, an automobile glass manufacturer, is a division of DaimlerChrysler and the primary supplier of windows for the Chrysler Jeep Grand Cherokee. Based on the results of an employee survey, each division was challenged to improve its organizational culture and climate. Evart Glass's culture committee decided to focus on improving interactions between employees on work teams and between work teams. As many U.S. organizations have done, the Evart Glass Plant had moved to a team-based structure. The plant manager stated, "As we move toward a team-focused approach in our operation, team effort is what counts." However, getting employees to function effectively and efficiently as team members and getting teams to perform at high levels doesn't just happen. That's why the decision was made to send the company's employees (almost 300 of them) through a team-building and team-training program.

The team-training experiences were made more challenging by combining the employees into cross-functional teams, which were not their normal work groups. For instance, one team consisting of a forklift driver, a receptionist, a maintenance person, and a shift supervisor had to share ideas about how to move each member of the team from one side of an "electric" fence to the other without touching the fence. The team lesson to be learned from that exercise was that support and trust are vital parts of teamwork because sometimes team members have to be willing to open up and ask for help in order to do their jobs successfully. After a full day of completing different types of team adventures, team members gathered together to discuss their experiences and to compare them with workplace challenges they faced. The company's human resource manager said that this experience allowed everyone to "get to know the people in different work areas and to feel more comfortable about going to each other to talk and solve a work-related problem and share information."

Employees weren't initially thrilled about the idea of team-building exercises. Some workers, primarily union members, resisted the mandatory team training. To ease the uncertainty over what the training was about, the company provided information to workers well in advance of the actual training. In addition, the team-building program was based on a "challenge by choice" philosophy, meaning that workers were not required to participate in activities that made them uncomfortable, but they would be expected to take an active support role

and cheer on their team members as they completed the activity. In the end, a follow-up survey of reactions to the training was positive; many employees stated that they would like to do it again with their own work groups. In addition, employees from all organizational levels commented that they noticed changes in attitude; for instance, people now went out of their way to help others and were making more of an effort to include everyone's opinions in discussions. One person from the finance department summed up the whole experience by stating, "I saw the whole concept of teamwork being played out, showing you have to work together rather than just taking it all on yourself."

QUESTIONS

1. "You can't train people to be team players." Build arguments to support this statement. Then come up with arguments against it.

2. Describe the advantages and disadvantages of using cross-functional team training rather than using the actual work teams of which employees are part.

3. How might the team-building exercises such as the ones briefly described contribute to making a team more effective?

4. It's your chance to be creative! Think of a team-building exercise that would help a team achieve one of the characteristics of an effective team. (See Exhibit 15.12.) Describe the characteristic you chose and then describe the exercise you'd use to help a team develop or enhance that characteristic.

Source: H. Campbell, "Adventures in Teamland," *Personnel Journal*, May 1996, pp. 56–62.

Mastering Management

In Episode 5 of the Mastering Management *series, Maria heads a team charged with the task of putting together a promotional presentation for CanGo. The problems she faces in getting the team to act in an organized and effective manner give you a chance to explore key issues in team formation and performance.*

After reading and studying this chapter, you should be able to:

1. Define the motivation process.

2. Describe three early motivation theories.

3. Explain how goals motivate people.

4. Differentiate reinforcement theory from goal-setting theory.

5. Identify ways to design motivating jobs.

6. Describe the motivational implications of equity theory.

7. Explain the key relationships in expectancy theory.

8. Describe current motivation issues facing managers.

9. Identify management practices that are likely to lead to more motivated employees.

A MANAGER'S DILEMMA

Angel Lorenzo is a shift supervisor at Grupo M, the largest private employer in the Dominican Republic.[1] Its 13,000 employees make clothes for Abercrombie & Fitch, Hugo Boss, and Tommy Hilfiger in 26 factories. Lorenzo began working at Grupo M as a sewing machine operator and was promoted to a job as a quality control inspector. Now, Lorenzo manages 14 teams of machine operators, making sure that their work flow is smooth and that jobs are done on time. He says that his job is to let his employees know that they are the most important people in the factory. If they don't do their jobs well, the business loses customers.

Grupo M defies the stereotypical image of garment manufacturers found in many Third World countries. The company is not a sweatshop nor does it employ child labor. Its factories are clean, brightly lit, and nice places to work. The company's founder, Fernando Capellan, envisioned an exemplary business that would be an innovator in the garment industry. And Grupo M has earned a reputation as a remarkably progressive employer whose labor practices strengthen it. For instance, in 1999, it earned a corporate conscience award (from the U.S.-based Council on Economic Priorities) for "empowering employees." Capellan says, "We have proven that you don't have to run a factory like a sweatshop in order to be profitable and to grow. In fact, we believe that we have been able to innovate, to expand, and to do what we have done because of the way

16

Motivating Employees

that we treat our people. Everything that we give to our workers gets returned to us in terms of efficiency, quality, loyalty, and innovation. It's just smart business."

Although the company's philosophy is admirable, managers such as Lorenzo are challenged to keep employees motivated. After all, even though Grupo M factories are clean and modern, employees still are required to do fast-paced, mind-numbing work. Put yourself in Lorenzo's position. How could you motivate your workers to do their jobs well?

WHAT WOULD YOU DO?

Motivating and rewarding employees is one of the most important and one of the most challenging activities that managers perform. Successful managers, such as Angel Lorenzo, in our chapter-opening Manager's Dilemma, understand that what motivates them personally may have little or no effect on others. Just because *you're* motivated by being part of a cohesive work team, don't assume everyone is. Or just because you're motivated by challenging work doesn't mean that everyone is. Effective managers who want their employees to put forth maximum effort recognize that they need to know how and why employees are motivated and to tailor their motivational practices to satisfy the needs and wants of those employees.

〉 WHAT IS MOTIVATION?

motivation

The willingness to exert high levels of effort to reach organizational goals, conditioned by the effort's ability to satisfy some individual need.

need

An internal state that makes certain outcomes appear attractive.

One way to motivate employees to high levels of performance is to satisfy their need to contribute to organizational goals in a creative and freewheeling environment. That's the kind of atmosphere that's provided every day at Play, a small and highly creative marketing agency in Richmond, VA. Here chief operating officer Lynn Spitzer gets creative with some of the company's highly motivated staff.

To understand what motivation is, let's begin by pointing out what motivation is not. Why? Because many people incorrectly view motivation as a personal trait— that is, a trait that some people have and others don't. Although in reality a manager might describe a certain employee as unmotivated, our knowledge of motivation tells us that we can't label people that way. What we *do* know is that motivation is the result of the interaction between the person and the situation. Certainly, individuals differ in motivational drive, but overall motivation varies from situation to situation. As we analyze the concept of motivation, keep in mind that the level of motivation varies both between individuals and within individuals at different times.

Motivation is the willingness to exert high levels of effort to reach organizational goals, conditioned by the effort's ability to satisfy some individual need. Although, in general, motivation refers to effort exerted toward any goal, we're referring to organizational goals because our focus is on work-related behavior. Three key elements can be seen in this definition: effort, organizational goals, and needs.

The *effort* element is a measure of intensity or drive. A motivated person tries hard. But high levels of effort are unlikely to lead to favorable job performance unless the effort is channeled in a direction that benefits the organization.[2] Therefore, we must consider the quality of the effort as well as its intensity. Effort that is directed toward, and consistent with, organizational goals is the kind of effort that we should be seeking. Finally, we will treat motivation as a need-satisfying process, as shown in Exhibit 16.1.

A **need** refers to some internal state that makes certain outcomes appear attractive. An unsatisfied need creates tension that stimulates drives within an individual. These drives lead to a search behavior to find particular goals that, if attained, will satisfy the need and reduce the tension.

We can say that motivated employees are in a state of tension. To relieve this tension, they exert effort. The greater the tension, the higher the effort level. If this effort leads to need satisfaction, it reduces tension. Because we're interested in work behavior, this tension-reduction effort must also be directed toward organizational goals. Therefore, inherent in our definition of motivation is the requirement

Exhibit | 16.1

The Motivation Process

that the individual's needs be compatible with the organization's goals. When the two don't match, individuals may exert high levels of effort that run counter to the interests of the organization. Incidentally, this isn't all that unusual. Some employees regularly spend a lot of time talking with friends at work to satisfy their social need. There's a high level of effort but little being done in the way of work.

Motivating high levels of employee performance is an important organizational consideration. Both academic researchers and practicing managers have been trying to understand and explain employee motivation for years. In this chapter, we're going to first look at the early motivation theories and then at the contemporary theories. We'll finish by looking at some current issues in motivation and then providing some practical suggestions managers can use in motivating employees.

> EARLY THEORIES OF MOTIVATION

We're going to be looking at three early theories of motivation that, although now somewhat questionable in terms of validity, are probably still the best-known explanations for employee motivation. These three theories are *Maslow's hierarchy of needs, McGregor's Theories X and Y*, and *Herzberg's motivation-hygiene theory*. Although more valid explanations of motivation have been developed, you should know these early theories for at least two reasons: (1) They represent the foundation from which contemporary motivation theories were developed, and (2) practicing managers continue to regularly use these theories and their terminology in explaining employee motivation.

MASLOW'S HIERARCHY OF NEEDS THEORY

The best-known theory of motivation is probably Abraham Maslow's **hierarchy of needs theory**.[3] Maslow was a humanistic psychologist who proposed that within every person is a hierarchy of five needs:

1. **Physiological needs:** food, drink, shelter, sexual satisfaction, and other physical requirements.
2. **Safety needs:** security and protection from physical and emotional harm, as well as assurance that physical needs will continue to be met.
3. **Social needs:** affection, belongingness, acceptance, and friendship.
4. **Esteem needs:** internal esteem factors such as self-respect, autonomy, and achievement and external esteem factors such as status, recognition, and attention.
5. **Self-actualization needs:** growth, achieving one's potential, and self-fulfillment; the drive to become what one is capable of becoming.

hierarchy of needs theory

Maslow's theory that there is a hierarchy of five human needs: physiological, safety, social, esteem, and self-actualization.

physiological needs

A person's needs for food, drink, shelter, sexual satisfaction, and other physical needs.

safety needs

A person's needs for security and protection from physical and emotional harm.

social needs

A person's needs for affection, belongingness, acceptance, and friendship.

esteem needs

A person's needs for internal factors such as self-respect, autonomy, and achievement, and external factors such as status, recognition, and attention.

self-actualization needs

A person's need to become what he or she is capable of becoming.

Exhibit	16.2

Maslow's Hierarchy of Needs

Theory X

The assumption that employees dislike work, are lazy, avoid responsibility, and must be coerced to perform.

Theory Y

The assumption that employees are creative, enjoy work, seek responsibility, and can exercise self-direction.

Physiological and safety needs brought the grandparents of these workers from Italy to Argentina over 50 years ago in search of job opportunities and a better way of life. Now poor economic conditions in Argentina are inspiring many children of Italian immigrants, like these in line outside the Italian consulate in Buenos Aires, to seek passports to return to Italy.

In terms of motivation, Maslow argued that each level in the hierarchy must be substantially satisfied before the next is activated and that once a need is substantially satisfied it no longer motivates behavior. In other words, as each need is substantially satisfied, the next need becomes dominant. In terms of Exhibit 16.2, the individual moves up the needs hierarchy. From the standpoint of motivation, Maslow's theory proposed that, although no need is ever fully satisfied, a substantially satisfied need will no longer motivate an individual. If you want to motivate someone, according to Maslow, you need to understand what level that person is on in the hierarchy and focus on satisfying needs at or above that level. Managers who accepted Maslow's hierarchy attempted to change their organizations and management practices so that employees' needs could be satisfied.

In addition, Maslow separated the five needs into higher and lower levels. Physiological and safety needs were described as *lower-order needs*; social, esteem, and self-actualization were described as *higher-order needs*. The difference between the two levels was made on the premise that higher-order needs are satisfied internally while lower-order needs are predominantly satisfied externally. In fact, the natural conclusion from Maslow's classification is that, in times of economic prosperity, almost all permanently employed workers have their lower-order needs substantially met.

Maslow's need theory received wide recognition, especially among practicing managers during the 1960s and 1970s. This recognition can be attributed to the theory's intuitive logic and ease of understanding. Unfortunately, however, research hasn't generally validated the theory. Maslow provided no empirical support for his theory, and several studies that sought to validate it could not.[4]

MCGREGOR'S THEORY X AND THEORY Y

Douglas McGregor is best known for his formulation of two sets of assumptions about human nature: Theory X and Theory Y.[5] Very simply, **Theory X** presents an essentially negative view of people. It assumes that workers have little ambition, dislike work, want to avoid responsibility, and need to be closely controlled to work effectively. **Theory Y** offers a positive view. It assumes that workers can exercise self-direction, accept and actually seek out responsibility, and consider work to be a natural activity. McGregor believed that Theory Y assumptions better captured the true nature of workers and should guide management practice.

What did McGregor's analysis imply about motivation? The answer is best expressed in the framework presented by Maslow. Theory X assumed that lower-order needs dominated individuals, and Theory Y assumed that higher-order needs dominated. McGregor himself held to the belief that the assumptions of Theory Y were more valid than those of Theory X. Therefore, he proposed that participation in decision making, responsible and challenging jobs, and good group relations would maximize employee motivation.

Unfortunately, there is no evidence to confirm that either set of assumptions is valid or that accepting Theory Y assumptions and altering your actions accordingly will make employees more motivated. For instance, when Bob McCurry was vice president of Toyota's U.S. marketing operations, he essentially followed Theory X. He drove his employees hard and used a "crack-the-whip" style, yet he was extremely successful at increasing Toyota's market share in a highly competitive environment.

HERZBERG'S MOTIVATION-HYGIENE THEORY

Frederick Herzberg's **motivation-hygiene theory** proposes that intrinsic factors are related to job satisfaction and motivation, whereas extrinsic factors are associated with job dissatisfaction.[6] Believing that an individual's relation to his or her work is a basic one and that his or her attitude toward work determines success or failure, Herzberg investigated the question "What do people want from their jobs?" He asked people for detailed descriptions of situations in which they felt exceptionally good or bad about their jobs. These findings are shown in Exhibit 16.3.

Herzberg concluded from his analysis of the findings that the replies people gave when they felt good about their jobs were significantly different from the replies they gave when they felt badly. Certain characteristics were consistently related to job satisfaction (factors on the left side of the exhibit) and others to job dissatisfaction (factors on the right side). Those factors associated with job satisfaction were intrinsic and included things such as achievement, recognition, and responsibility. When people felt good about their work, they tended to attribute these characteristics to themselves. On the other hand, when they were dissatis-

motivation-hygiene theory

The motivation theory that intrinsic factors are related to job satisfaction and motivation, whereas extrinsic factors are associated with job dissatisfaction.

Motivators	Hygiene Factors
• Achievement	• Supervision
• Recognition	• Company Policy
• Work Itself	• Relationship with
• Responsibility	Supervisor
• Advancement	• Working Conditions
• Growth	• Salary
	• Relationship with Peers
	• Personal Life
	• Relationship with
	Subordinates
	• Status
	• Security
Extremely Satisfied	Neutral Extremely Dissatisfied

Exhibit | 16.3

Herzberg's Motivation-Hygiene Theory

Exhibit	16.4

Contrasting Views of Satisfaction-Dissatisfaction

Traditional View

Satisfied	Dissatisfied

Herzberg's View

Motivators		Hygiene Factors	
Satisfaction	No Satisfaction	No Dissatisfaction	Dissatisfaction

fied, they tended to cite extrinsic factors such as company policy and administration, supervision, interpersonal relationships, and working conditions.

In addition, Herzberg believed that the data suggested that the opposite of satisfaction was not dissatisfaction, as traditionally had been believed. Removing dissatisfying characteristics from a job would not necessarily make that job more satisfying (or motivating). As shown in Exhibit 16.4, Herzberg proposed that his findings indicated the existence of a dual continuum: The opposite of "satisfaction" is "no satisfaction," and the opposite of "dissatisfaction" is "no dissatisfaction."

According to Herzberg, the factors that led to job satisfaction were separate and distinct from those that led to job dissatisfaction. Therefore, managers who sought to eliminate factors that created job dissatisfaction could bring about workplace harmony but not necessarily motivation. Because they don't motivate employees, the extrinsic factors that create job dissatisfaction were called **hygiene factors**. When these factors are adequate, people will not be dissatisfied, but they will not be satisfied (or motivated) either. To motivate people on their jobs, Herzberg suggested emphasizing **motivators**, the intrinsic factors that increase job satisfaction.

Herzberg's theory enjoyed wide popularity from the mid-1960s to the early 1980s, but criticisms were raised about his procedures and methodology. Although today we say the theory was too simplistic, it has had a strong influence on how we currently design jobs.

hygiene factors

Factors that eliminate job dissatisfaction but don't motivate.

motivators

Factors that increase job satisfaction and motivation.

Testing...Testing...1,2,3

1. **What is motivation, and how is Maslow's hierarchy of needs theory a theory of motivation?**

2. **What are McGregor's Theory X and Theory Y assumptions?**

3. **Describe Herzberg's motivation-hygiene theory.**

> ⟩ | **CONTEMPORARY THEORIES OF MOTIVATION**

The theories and approaches we're going to look at in this section represent current state-of-the-art explanations of employee motivation. Although these may not be as well known as some of the early theories of motivation, they do tend to have substantive research support.[7] What are these contemporary motivation approaches? We're going to look at six: three-needs theory, goal-setting theory, reinforcement theory, designing motivating jobs, equity theory, and expectancy theory.

THREE-NEEDS THEORY

David McClelland and others have proposed the **three-needs theory**, which says there are three needs that are major motives in work.[8] These three needs include the **need for achievement (nAch)**, which is the drive to excel, to achieve in relation to a set of standards, and to strive to succeed; the **need for power (nPow)**, which is the need to make others behave in a way that they would not have behaved otherwise; and the **need for affiliation (nAff)**, which is the desire for friendly and close interpersonal relationships. Of these three needs, the need for achievement has been researched most extensively. What has this research showed us?

People with a high need for achievement are striving for personal achievement rather than for the trappings and rewards of success. They have a desire to do something better or more efficiently than it's been done before.[9] They prefer jobs that offer personal responsibility for finding solutions to problems, in which they can receive rapid and unambiguous feedback on their performance in order to tell whether they're improving, and in which they can set moderately challenging goals. High achievers aren't gamblers; they dislike succeeding by chance. They are motivated by and prefer the challenge of working at a problem and accepting the personal responsibility for success or failure. An important point is that high achievers avoid what they perceive to be very easy or very difficult tasks. Also, a high need to achieve doesn't necessarily lead to being a good manager, especially in large organizations. A high nAch salesperson at Merck does not necessarily make a good sales manager and good managers in large organizations such as AT&T, Wal-Mart, or Microsoft do not necessarily have a high need to achieve. The reason high achievers don't necessarily make good managers is probably because high achievers focus on their *own* accomplishments while good managers emphasize helping *others* accomplish their goals.[10] However, we do know that employees can be trained to stimulate their achievement need.[11]

The other two needs in the three-needs theory haven't been researched as extensively as the need for achievement. However, we do know that the needs for affiliation and power are closely related to managerial success.[12] The best managers tend to be high in the need for power and low in the need for affiliation.

How do you find out your levels of each of these three needs? All three motives typically are measured using a projective test (known as the Thematic Apperception Test or TAT) in which respondents react to a set of pictures. Each picture is shown to a subject who then writes a story based on the picture. (See Exhibit 16.5 for some examples of these pictures.) Trained interpreters then determine an individual's levels of nAch, nPow, and nAff from the stories written.

GOAL-SETTING THEORY

Before a big assignment or major class project presentation, has a teacher ever said to you "Just do your best"? What does that vague statement, "do your best," mean? Would your performance on a class project have been higher if that teacher

three-needs theory

The motivation theory that says three needs—achievement, power, and affiliation—are major motives in work.

need for achievement (nAch)

The drive to excel, to achieve in relation to a set of standards, and to strive to succeed.

need for power (nPow)

The need to make others behave in a way that they would not have behaved otherwise.

need for affiliation (nAff)

The desire for friendly and close interpersonal relationships.

The need for achievement is usually accompanied by a sense of commitment and even passion about the goal. Tom Iseghohi, director of global car pricing for Ford Motor Co., describes the need for achievement this way: "Talented people don't want an easy slam dunk. They're passionate about winning, and they want the people around them to share that passion."

Exhibit	16.5	Examples of Pictures Used for Assessing Levels of nAch, nAff, and nPow

goal-setting theory

The proposition that specific goals increase performance and that difficult goals, when accepted, result in higher performance than do easy goals.

had said that you needed to score a 93 percent to keep your A in the class? Would you have done better in high school English if your parents had said, "You should strive for 85 percent or higher on all your work in English class" rather than telling you to do your best? Research on goal-setting theory addresses these issues, and the findings, as you'll see, are impressive in terms of the effect that goal specificity, challenge, and feedback have on performance.[13]

There is substantial support for the proposition that specific goals increase performance and that difficult goals, when accepted, result in higher performance than do easy goals. This proposition is known as **goal-setting theory**.

Intention to work toward a goal is a major source of job motivation. Studies on goal setting have demonstrated the superiority of specific and challenging goals as motivating forces.[14] Specific, hard goals produce a higher level of output than does the generalized goal of "do your best." The specificity of the goal itself acts as an internal stimulus. For instance, when a FedEx delivery truck driver commits to making 10 weekly round-trip hauls between Toronto and Buffalo, New York, this intention gives him a specific goal to try to attain. We can say that, all things being equal, the delivery person with a specific goal will outperform someone else operating with no goals or the generalized goal of "do your best."

You may have noticed what appears to be a contradiction between the research findings on achievement motivation and goal setting. Is it a contradiction that achievement motivation is stimulated by moderately challenging goals, whereas goal-setting theory says that motivation is maximized by difficult goals? No, and our explanation is twofold.[15] First, goal-setting theory deals with people in general. The conclusions on achievement motivation are based on people who have a high nAch. Given that no more than 10 to 20 percent of North Americans are naturally high achievers and that proportion is undoubtedly lower in underdeveloped countries, difficult goals are still recommended for the majority of employees. Second, the conclusions of goal-setting theory apply to those who accept and are committed to the goals. Difficult goals will lead to higher performance only if they are accepted.

Will employees try harder if they have the opportunity to participate in the setting of goals? Although we can't say that having employees participate in the goal-setting process is *always* desirable, participation is probably preferable to assigning goals when you expect resistance to accepting difficult challenges.[16] In some cases, participatively set goals elicited superior performance; in other cases, individuals performed best when their manager assigned goals. But a major advantage

Specific goals can help motivate workers, even though researchers are uncertain whether motivation is stronger when employees set their own goals or accept goals set by their managers. Workers like these at Amazon.com will have easily quantifiable goals, such as number of orders packed, against which their work effort can be measured. What information do you think they would need from their managers if they set their own goals?

of participation may be in increasing acceptance of the goal itself as a desirable one toward which to work.

Finally, people will do better when they get feedback on how well they're progressing toward their goals because feedback helps identify discrepancies between what they have done and what they want to do; that is, feedback acts to guide behavior. But all feedback isn't equally effective. Self-generated feedback—where the employee is able to monitor his or her own progress—has been shown to be a more powerful motivator than externally generated feedback.[17]

Are there any contingencies in goal-setting theory, or can we just assume that difficult and specific goals always lead to higher performance? In addition to feedback, three other factors have been found to influence the goals-performance relationship. These are goal commitment, adequate self-efficacy, and national culture. Goal-setting theory presupposes that an individual is committed to the goal—that is, an individual is determined not to lower or abandon the goal. Commitment is most likely to occur when goals are made public, when the individual has an internal locus of control, and when the goals are self-set rather than assigned.[18] **Self-efficacy** refers to an individual's belief that he or she is capable of performing a task.[19] The higher your self-efficacy, the more confidence you have in your ability to succeed in a task. So, in difficult situations, we find that people with low self-efficacy are likely to reduce their effort or give up altogether, whereas those with high self-efficacy will try harder to master the challenge.[20] In addition, individuals with high self-efficacy seem to respond to negative feedback with increased effort and motivation, whereas those with low self-efficacy are likely to reduce their effort when given negative feedback.[21] Finally, goal-setting theory is culture bound. It is well adapted to countries such as the United States and Canada because its main ideas align reasonably well with North American cultures. It assumes that subordinates will be reasonably independent (not too high a score on

self-efficacy

An individual's belief that he or she is capable of performing a task.

Exhibit | 16.6 | | **Goal-Setting Theory**

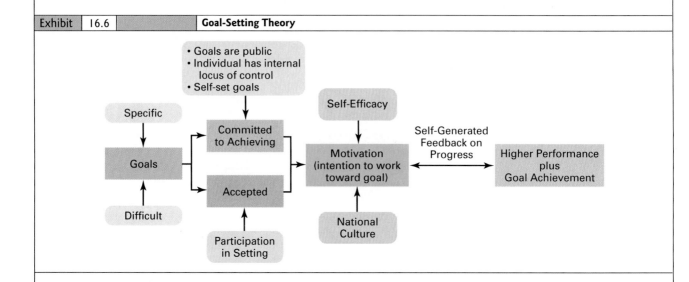

power distance), that managers and employees will seek challenging goals (low in uncertainty avoidance), and that performance is considered important by both managers and subordinates (high in quantity of life). So don't expect goal setting to necessarily lead to higher employee performance in countries such as Portugal or Chile, where the country's cultural characteristics aren't like this.

Exhibit 16.6 summarizes the relationships among goals, motivation, and performance. Our overall conclusion from goal-setting theory is that intentions—as articulated in terms of hard and specific goals—are a powerful motivating force. Under the proper conditions, they can lead to higher performance. However, there is no evidence that such goals are associated with increased job satisfaction.[22]

REINFORCEMENT THEORY

In contrast to goal-setting theory, **reinforcement theory** says that behavior is a function of its consequences. Goal-setting theory proposes that an individual's purpose directs his or her behavior. Reinforcement theory argues that behavior is externally caused. What controls behavior are **reinforcers**, consequences that, when given immediately following a behavior, increase the probability that the behavior will be repeated.

The key to reinforcement theory is that it ignores factors such as goals, expectations, and needs. Instead, it focuses solely on what happens to a person when he or she takes some action. This idea helps explain why publishers such as Pearson Education provide incentive clauses in their authors' contracts. If every time an author submits a completed chapter the company sends an advance check against future royalties, the person is motivated to keep writing and submitting chapters.

In Chapter 14 we showed how reinforcers shape behavior and help people to learn. But the concept of reinforcement is also widely believed to explain motivation. According to B. F. Skinner, reinforcement theory can be explained as follows: People will most likely engage in desired behaviors if they are rewarded for doing so; these rewards are most effective if they immediately follow a desired behavior, and behavior that isn't rewarded, or is punished, is less likely to be repeated.[23]

reinforcement theory

The theory that behavior is a function of its consequences.

reinforcers

Any consequence immediately following a response that increases the probability that the behavior will be repeated.

Since you're reading this textbook, you're likely enrolled in a class that's helping you earn credit toward a college degree. You're also likely taking the courses you need to earn a college degree because you hope to get a good job (or a better job, if you're already working) upon graduating. With all this effort you're putting forth, have you ever stopped to think about what you really want from your job?[24] A high salary? Work that challenges you? Autonomy and flexibility? Perhaps the results of a recent survey of workers will give you some insights into what you might want from your job. The top reasons that employees stay with their jobs are as follows:

Reason	Percentage of Respondents
Good co-workers	71 percent
Pleasant work environment	68 percent
Easy commute	68 percent
Challenging work	65 percent
Flexible work hours	54 percent

Do any of these characteristics describe what you want from your job? Whether they do or don't, you should spend some time reflecting on what you want your job to provide you. Then, when it's time to do that all-important job search, look for situations that will provide you what you're looking for.

Following reinforcement theory, managers can influence employees' behavior by reinforcing actions they deem desirable. However, because the emphasis is on positive reinforcement, not punishment, managers should ignore, not punish, unfavorable behavior. Even though punishment eliminates undesired behavior faster than nonreinforcement does, its effect is often only temporary and may later have unpleasant side effects including dysfunctional behavior such as workplace conflicts, absenteeism, and turnover.

Research has shown that reinforcement is undoubtedly an important influence on work behavior. But reinforcement isn't the only explanation for differences in employee motivation.[25] Goals also affect motivation, as do levels of achievement needs, job design, inequities in rewards, and expectations.

Reinforcement theory says that we behave in response to what we see as the consequences of our behavior. Carolyn Jones, president of C.J. Enterprises in Chattanooga, TN, understands that well. "When people are having personal problems or they're working on a project, don't just throw them to the wolves and not show them your appreciation," she says. "You don't have to baby them, just show them that you care about what's going on with them. Be a little bit lenient. Bend when you need to bend."

Testing...Testing...1,2,3

4. **What are the three needs McClelland proposed are present in work situations?**

5. **Describe how goal-setting theory explains employee motivation.**

6. **What does reinforcement theory tell us about employee motivation?**

DESIGNING MOTIVATING JOBS

Because managers are primarily interested in how to motivate individuals on the job, we need to look at ways to design motivating jobs. If you look closely at what an organization is and how it works, you'll find that it's composed of thousands of tasks. These tasks, in

job design

The way tasks are combined to form complete jobs.

turn, are aggregated into jobs.[26] We use the term **job design** to refer to the way tasks are combined to form complete jobs. The jobs that people perform in an organization should not evolve by chance. Managers should design jobs deliberately and thoughtfully to reflect the demands of the changing environment as well as the organization's technology, skills and abilities, and preferences of its employees.[27] When jobs are designed with those things in mind, employees are motivated to reach their full productive capabilities. What are some ways that managers can design motivating jobs?

Job Enlargement As we saw earlier in Chapters 2 and 10, job design historically has concentrated on making jobs smaller and more specialized. Yet, when jobs are narrow in focus and highly specialized, motivating employees is a real challenge. Thus, many organizations have looked at other job design options. One of the earliest efforts at overcoming the drawbacks of job specialization involved the horizontal expansion of a job through increasing **job scope**—the number of different tasks required in a job and the frequency with which these tasks are repeated. For instance, a dental hygienist's job could be enlarged so that in addition to dental cleaning, he or she is pulling patients' files, refiling them when finished, and cleaning and storing instruments. This type of job design option is called **job enlargement**.

job scope

The number of different tasks required in a job and the frequency with which those tasks are repeated.

Efforts at job enlargement that focused solely on increasing the number of tasks done have had less than exciting results. As one employee who experienced such a job redesign said, "Before I had one lousy job. Now, thanks to job enlargement, I have three lousy jobs!" However, one study that looked at how *knowledge* enlargement activities (expanding the scope of knowledge used in a job) affected workers found benefits such as more satisfaction, enhanced customer service, and fewer errors.[28] Even so, most job enlargement efforts provided few challenges and little meaning to workers' activities, although they addressed the lack of variety in overspecialized jobs.

job enlargement

The horizontal expansion of a job by increasing job scope.

Job Enrichment Another approach to designing motivating jobs is through the vertical expansion of a job by adding planning and evaluating responsibilities—**job enrichment**. Job enrichment increases **job depth**, which is the degree of control employees have over their work. In other words, employees are empowered to assume some of the tasks typically done by their managers. Thus, the tasks in an enriched job should allow workers to do a complete activity with increased freedom, independence, and responsibility. These tasks should also provide feedback so that individuals can assess and correct their own performance. For instance, in an enriched job, our dental hygienist, in addition to dental cleaning, could schedule appointments and follow up with clients. Although job enrichment can improve the quality of work, employee motivation, and satisfaction, the research evidence on the use of job enrichment programs has been inconclusive.[29]

job enrichment

The vertical expansion of a job by adding planning and evaluating responsibilities.

job depth

The degree of control employees have over their work.

Job Characteristics Model Even though many organizations have implemented job enlargement and job enrichment programs and experienced mixed results, neither of these job design approaches provided a conceptual framework for analyzing jobs or for guiding managers in designing motivating jobs. The **job characteristics model (JCM)** offers such a framework.[30] It identifies five primary job characteristics, their interrelationships, and their impact on employee productivity, motivation, and satisfaction.

job characteristics model (JCM)

A framework for analyzing and designing jobs that identifies five primary job characteristics, their interrelationships, and their impact on outcomes.

According to the JCM, any job can be described in terms of five core dimensions, defined as follows:

- **Skill variety**, the degree to which a job requires a variety of activities so that an employee can use a number of different skills and talents
- **Task identity**, the degree to which a job requires completion of a whole and identifiable piece of work
- **Task significance**, the degree to which a job has a substantial impact on the lives or work of other people
- **Autonomy**, the degree to which a job provides substantial freedom, independence, and discretion to the individual in scheduling the work and determining the procedures to be used in carrying it out
- **Feedback**, the degree to which carrying out work activities required by a job results in the individual's obtaining direct and clear information about the effectiveness of his or her performance

Exhibit 16.7 presents the model. Notice how the first three dimensions—skill variety, task identity, and task significance—combine to create meaningful work. What we mean is that if these three characteristics exist in a job, we can predict that the person will view his or her job as being important, valuable, and worthwhile. Notice, too, that jobs that possess autonomy give the job incumbent a feeling of personal responsibility for the results and that, if a job provides feedback, the employee will know how effectively he or she is performing.

From a motivational standpoint, the JCM suggests that internal rewards are obtained when an employee *learns* (knowledge of results through feedback) that he or she *personally* (experienced responsibility through autonomy of work) has performed well on a task that he or she *cares about* (experienced meaningfulness through skill variety, task identity, and/or task significance).[31] The more these three conditions characterize a job, the greater the employee's motivation, performance, and satisfaction and the lower his or her absenteeism and likelihood of resigning. As the model shows, the links between the job dimensions and the outcomes are moderated by the strength of the individual's growth need (the person's

skill variety

The degree to which a job requires a variety of activities so that an employee can use a number of different skills and talents.

task identity

The degree to which a job requires completion of a whole and identifiable piece of work.

task significance

The degree to which a job has a substantial impact on the lives or work of other people.

autonomy

The degree to which a job provides substantial freedom, independence, and discretion to the individual in scheduling work and determining the procedures to be used in carrying it out.

feedback

The degree to which carrying out work activities required by a job results in the individual's obtaining direct and clear information about his or her performance effectiveness.

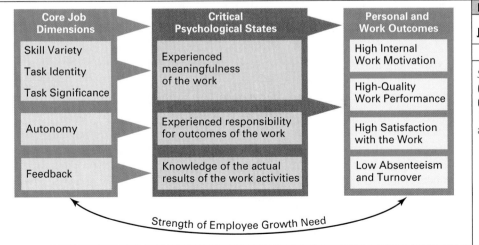

Exhibit	16.7

Job Characteristics Model

Source: J.R. Hackman and J.L. Suttle (eds.), *Improving Life at Work* (Glenview, IL: Scott, Foresman, 1977). With permission of the authors.

Open and immediate feedback is a key feature of good job design. Telephone order takers, like these employees of GiftCertificates.com, can check the accuracy of their work as they go along by confirming with customers such information as the dollar amount of the sale and the customer's address, credit card number, and other billing information. Jonas Lee, founder of the online marketing firm, is shown at left training an employee.

desire for self-esteem and self-actualization). This means that individuals with a high growth need are more likely to experience the critical psychological states and respond positively when their jobs include the core dimensions than are individuals with a low growth need. This may explain the mixed results with job enrichment: Individuals with low growth need don't tend to achieve high performance or satisfaction by having their jobs enriched.

The JCM provides specific guidance to managers for job design. (See Exhibit 16.8.) The following suggestions, which are based on the JCM, specify the types of changes in jobs that are most likely to lead to improvement in each of the five core job dimensions. You'll notice that two of these suggestions from the JCM incorporate the earlier job design concepts we discussed (job enlargement and job enrichment), although the other suggestions also involve more than vertically and horizontally expanding jobs.

1. *Combine tasks.* Managers should put existing fragmented tasks back together to form a new, larger module of work (job enlargement) to increase skill variety and task identity.

2. *Create natural work units.* Managers should design tasks that form an identifiable and meaningful whole to increase employee "ownership" of the work and encourage employees to view their work as meaningful and important rather than as irrelevant and boring.

3. *Establish client relationships.* The client is the external or internal user of the product or service on which the employee works. Whenever possible, managers should establish direct relationships between workers and their clients to increase skill variety, autonomy, and feedback. For instance, at San Francisco's Park Lane Hotels International, guests nominate their favorite staff for awards including Sony televisions and free nights at the hotel.[32]

4. *Expand jobs vertically.* Vertical expansion (job enrichment) gives employees responsibilities and controls that were formerly reserved for managers. It partially closes the gap between the "doing" and the "controlling" aspects of the job and increases employee autonomy.

5. *Open feedback channels.* Feedback lets employees know not only how well they are performing their jobs but also whether their job performance is improving, deteriorating, or remaining constant. Ideally, employees should receive performance feedback directly as they do their jobs rather than from managers on an occasional basis. For example, frequent fliers at Continental Airlines bestow Pride in Performance certificates to employees who have been helpful. Employees can then redeem the coupons for valuable merchandise.[33]

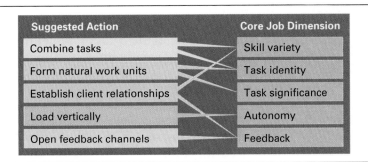

Exhibit 16.8

Guidelines for Job Redesign

Source: J.R. Hackman and J.L. Suttle (eds.), *Improving Life at Work* (Glenview, IL: Scott, Foresman, 1977). With permission of the authors.

EQUITY THEORY

Do you ever wonder what kind of grade the person sitting next to you in class makes on a test or on a major class project? Most of us do! Being human, we tend to compare ourselves with others. If someone offered you $60,000 a year on your first job after graduating from college, you'd probably jump at the offer and report to work enthusiastic, ready to tackle whatever needed to be done, and certainly satisfied with your pay. How would you react, though, if you found out a month into the job that a co-worker—another recent graduate, your age, with comparable grades from a comparable school, and with comparable work experience—was getting $65,000 a year? You'd probably be upset! Even though in absolute terms $60,000 is a lot of money for a new graduate to make (and you know it!), that suddenly isn't the issue. You see the issue now as relative rewards and what you believe is *fair*—what is *equitable*. The term *equity* is related to the concept of fairness and equal treatment compared with others who behave in similar ways. There's considerable evidence that employees compare their job inputs and outcomes relative to others and that inequities influence the degree of effort that employees exert.[34]

Equity theory, developed by J. Stacey Adams, proposes that employees perceive what they get from a job situation (outcomes) in relation to what they put into it (inputs) and then compare their inputs-outcomes ratio with the inputs-outcomes ratios of relevant others (Exhibit 16.9). If an employee perceives her ratio to be equal to those of relevant others, a state of equity exists. In other words, she perceives that her situation is fair—that justice prevails. However, if the ratio is unequal, inequity exists and she views herself as underrewarded or overrewarded. When inequities occur, employees attempt to do something about

equity theory

The theory that an employee compares his or her job's inputs-outcomes ratio with that of relevant others and then corrects any inequity.

Exhibit 16.9

Equity Theory

Perceived Ratio Comparison[a]	Employee's Assessment
$\dfrac{\text{Outcomes A}}{\text{Inputs A}} < \dfrac{\text{Outcomes B}}{\text{Inputs B}}$	Inequity (underrewarded)
$\dfrac{\text{Outcomes A}}{\text{Inputs A}} = \dfrac{\text{Outcomes B}}{\text{Inputs B}}$	Equity
$\dfrac{\text{Outcomes A}}{\text{Inputs A}} > \dfrac{\text{Outcomes B}}{\text{Inputs B}}$	Inequity (overrewarded)

[a]Person A is the employee, and person B is a relevant other or referent.

it. What will employees do when they perceive an inequity? Let's look more closely at their probable behavioral responses.

Equity theory proposes that employees might (1) distort either their own or others' inputs or outcomes, (2) behave in some way to induce others to change their inputs or outcomes, (3) behave in some way to change their own inputs or outcomes, (4) choose a different comparison person, or (5) quit their job. These types of employee reactions have generally proved to be correct.[35] A review of the research consistently confirms the equity thesis: Employee motivation is influenced significantly by relative rewards as well as by absolute rewards. Whenever employees perceive inequity, they'll act to correct the situation.[36] The result might be lower or higher productivity, improved or reduced quality of output, increased absenteeism, or voluntary resignation.

The other aspect we need to examine in equity theory is who these "others" are against whom people compare themselves. The **referent** is an important variable in equity theory.[37] Three referent categories have been defined: other, system, and self. The "other" category includes other individuals with similar jobs in the same organization but also includes friends, neighbors, or professional associates. On the basis of what they hear at work or read about in newspapers or trade journals, employees compare their pay with that of others. The "system" category includes organizational pay policies and procedures and the administration of the system. Whatever precedents have been established by the organization regarding pay allocation are major elements of this category. The "self" category refers to inputs-outcomes ratios that are unique to the individual. It reflects past personal experiences and contacts and is influenced by criteria such as past jobs or family commitments. The choice of a particular set of referents is related to the information available about the referents as well as to their perceived relevance.

However applicable it might be to understanding employee motivation, we shouldn't conclude that equity theory is flawless. The theory leaves some issues unclear.[38] For instance, how do employees define inputs and outcomes? How do they combine and weigh their inputs and outcomes to arrive at totals? When and how do the factors change over time? And how do people choose referents? Despite these problems, equity theory does have an impressive amount of research support and offers us some important insights into employee motivation.

EXPECTANCY THEORY

The most comprehensive and widely accepted explanation of employee motivation to date is Victor Vroom's **expectancy theory**.[39] Although the theory has its critics,[40] most research evidence supports it.[41]

Expectancy theory states that an individual tends to act in a certain way based on the expectation that the act will be followed by a given outcome and on the attractiveness of that outcome to the individual. It includes three variables or relationships (see Exhibit 16.10):

1. *Expectancy* or *effort-performance linkage* is the probability perceived by the individual that exerting a given amount of effort will lead to a certain level of performance.

2. *Instrumentality* or *performance-reward linkage* is the degree to which the individual believes that performing at a particular level is instrumental in attaining the desired outcome.

---

referents

The persons, systems, or selves against which individuals compare themselves to assess equity.

Testing...Testing...1,2,3

7. **Define job enlargement and job enrichment.**

8. **Describe the job characteristics model as a way to design motivating jobs.**

9. **What are the motivation implications of equity theory?**

expectancy theory

The theory that an individual tends to act in a certain way based on the expectation that the act will be followed by a given outcome and on the attractiveness of that outcome to the individual.

3. *Valence* or *attractiveness of reward* is the importance that the individual places on the potential outcome or reward that can be achieved on the job. Valence considers both the goals and needs of the individual.

This explanation of motivation might sound complex, but it really isn't that difficult to visualize. It can be summed up in the questions: How hard do I have to work to achieve a certain level of performance, and can I actually achieve that level? What reward will performing at that level get me? How attractive is the reward to me, and does it help me achieve my goals? Whether you are motivated to put forth effort (that is, to work) at any given time depends on your particular goals and your perception of whether a certain level of performance is necessary to attain those goals. Let's look at the theory's features and go through an example of how it works.

First, what perceived outcomes does the job offer the employee? Outcomes (rewards) may be positive—things such as pay, security, companionship, trust, fringe benefits, a chance to use talents or skills, or congenial relationships. Or the employee may view the outcomes as negative—fatigue, boredom, frustration, anxiety, harsh supervision, or threat of dismissal. Keep in mind that reality isn't relevant here. The critical issue is what the individual *perceives* the outcomes to be, regardless of whether the perceptions are accurate.

As chief information officer of Service Advantage International, a customer service research firm in Detroit that he helped to found, 20-year-old Matthew G. Newell didn't have time for a full course load at Eastern Michigan University, so he cut back his class schedule drastically. For Matthew, the link between his work at the firm and the satisfaction he derives from contributing to its growth—and his $35,000 a year salary—is strong enough to outweigh his desire to finish college in the traditional four years.

Second, how attractive are the outcomes or rewards to employees? Are they valued positively, negatively, or neutrally? This obviously is a personal and internal issue that depends on the individual's needs, attitudes, and personality. A person who finds a particular reward attractive—that is, values it positively—would rather get it than not get it. Others may find it negative and, therefore, prefer not getting it. Still others may be neutral about the outcome.

Third, what kind of behavior must the employee exhibit in order to achieve these rewards? The rewards aren't likely to have any effect on an individual employee's performance unless he or she knows, clearly and unambiguously, what must be done to achieve them. For example, what is "doing well" in terms of performance appraisal? What criteria will be used to judge the employee's performance?

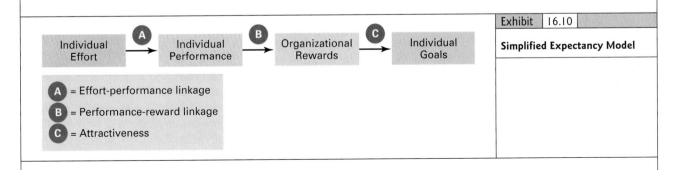

Individual Effort → (A) → Individual Performance → (B) → Organizational Rewards → (C) → Individual Goals

(A) = Effort-performance linkage
(B) = Performance-reward linkage
(C) = Attractiveness

Exhibit | 16.10

Simplified Expectancy Model

Finally, how does the employee view his or her chances of doing what is asked? After an employee has considered his or her own skills and ability to control those variables that lead to success, what's the likelihood that he or she can successfully perform at the necessary level?[42]

Let's work through an example of how expectancy theory works by looking at your level of motivation for a particular course. Most students prefer that their instructor tell them what the course expectations are. They want to know what assignments and exams will be like, when they're going to be due or given, and how much weight each carries in determining the final grade. They also like to think that the amount of effort exerted in attending classes, taking notes, completing assignments, and studying outside class will be reasonably related to the grade they'll make.

Five weeks into a class that you're really enjoying, you get a test back. You studied hard for the test and put in a number of hours reading the chapters and going over your notes. When you've studied this hard in the past, you've consistently made As and Bs on tests. You work this hard to make top grades, which you believe are important for getting a good job after graduation or even for going on to graduate school. When you get this test back, you're shocked. You scored a 46. The class median was 72, and 10 percent of the class got an A. The minimum passing score was 50. You're angry. You're frustrated. What happens now?

Several interesting things might happen to your behavior. You're probably no longer interested in attending this class regularly. Your amount of studying is likely to decrease considerably. And when you do attend class, you might daydream a lot and take fewer class notes. "Lacking in motivation" would probably be an apt description at this point. Why did your motivation level change? Let's explain it by using expectancy theory.

Using Exhibit 16.10 to understand this situation, we can say the following: You studied and prepared for the course (put forth effort) in order to correctly answer the test questions (performance). Correct answers produce a high grade (reward), which, in turn, are important for getting a good job with security, prestige, and other benefits (individual goal).

The attractiveness of the outcome (a good grade) is high. But what about the performance-reward linkage? Do you feel that your grade truly reflected your knowledge of the material? In other words, did the test fairly measure what you knew? If the answer is yes, then this linkage is strong. If the answer is no, then at least part of the reason for your reduced motivation is your belief that the test wasn't a fair measure of your performance.

Another possible demotivating force may be the effort-performance relationship. If, after you took the test, you believed that you couldn't have passed it even with the amount of studying you had done, then your motivation to study would drop. Because a low value had been placed on all the hard work and study efforts that you thought would lead to answering test questions correctly, your motivational level and effort would decrease.

Let's summarize some of the key points about expectancy theory. The key to expectancy theory is understanding an individual's goal and the linkage between effort and performance, between performance and rewards, and finally, between rewards and individual goal satisfaction. It emphasizes payoffs, or rewards. As a result, we have to believe that the rewards an organization is offering align with what the individual wants. Expectancy theory recognizes that there is no universal principle for explaining what motivates individuals and, thus, stresses that managers must understand why employees view certain outcomes as attractive or unattractive. After all, we want to reward individuals with those things they value positively. Also, expectancy theory emphasizes expected behaviors. Do employees know what is expected of them and how they'll be evaluated? Finally, the theory is concerned with perceptions. Reality is irrelevant. An individual's own perceptions of performance, reward, and goal satisfaction outcomes, not the outcomes themselves, will determine his or her motivation (level of effort).

INTEGRATING CONTEMPORARY THEORIES OF MOTIVATION

We have presented six contemporary motivation theories. You might be tempted to view them independently, but doing so would be a mistake. Many of the ideas underlying the theories are complementary, and you'll better understand how to motivate people if you see how the theories fit together.[43] Exhibit 16.11 presents a model that integrates much of what we know about motivation. Its basic foundation is the expectancy model shown in Exhibit 16.10. Let's work through this model, starting on the left.

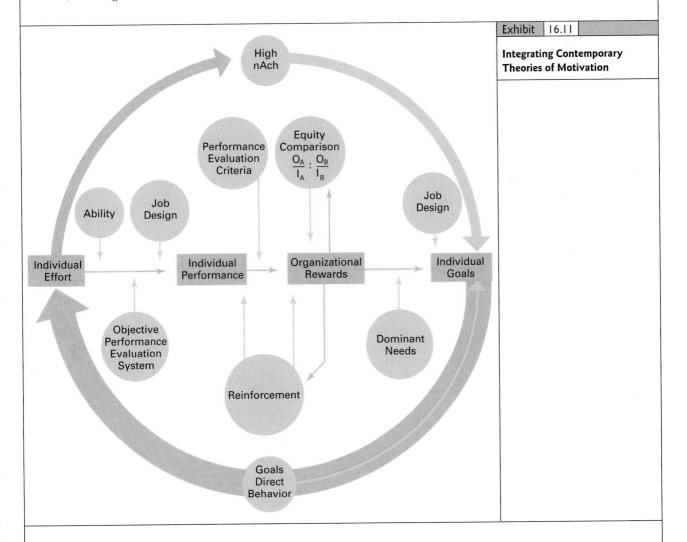

Exhibit | 16.11

Integrating Contemporary Theories of Motivation

The individual effort box has an arrow leading into it. This arrow flows from the individual's goals. Consistent with goal-setting theory, this goals-effort link is meant to illustrate that goals direct behavior. Expectancy theory predicts that an employee will exert a high level of effort if he or she perceives that there is a strong relationship between effort and performance, performance and rewards, and rewards and satisfaction of personal goals. Each of these relationships is, in turn, influenced by certain factors. You can see from the model that the level of individual performance is determined not only by the level of individual effort but also by the individual's ability to perform and by whether the organization has a fair and objective performance evaluation system. The performance-reward relationship will be strong if the individual perceives that it is performance (rather than seniority, personal favorites, or some other criterion) that is rewarded. The final link in expectancy theory is the rewards-goal relationship. Need theories come into play at this point. Motivation would be high to the degree that the rewards an individual received for his or her high performance satisfied the dominant needs consistent with his or her individual goals.

A closer look at the model also shows that it considers the achievement need, reinforcement, equity, and JCM theories. The high achiever isn't motivated by the organization's assessment of his or her performance or organizational rewards, hence, the jump from effort to individual goals for those with a high nAch. Remember that high achievers are internally driven as long as the jobs they're doing provide them with personal responsibility, feedback, and moderate risks. They're not concerned with the effort-performance, performance-reward, or rewards-goals linkage.

Reinforcement theory is seen in the model by recognizing that the organization's rewards reinforce the individual's performance. If managers have designed a reward system that is seen by employees as "paying off" for good performance, the rewards will reinforce and encourage continued good performance. Rewards also play a key part in equity theory. Individuals will compare the rewards (outcomes) they have received from the inputs or efforts they made with the inputs-outcomes ratio of relevant others. If inequities exist, the effort expended may be influenced.

Finally, we can see the JCM in this integrative model. Task characteristics (job design) influence job motivation at two places. First, jobs that are designed around the five core job dimensions are likely to lead to higher actual job performance because the individual's motivation will be stimulated by the job itself—that is, they will increase the linkage between effort and performance. Second, jobs that are designed around the five core job dimensions also increase an employee's control over key elements in his or her work. Therefore, jobs that offer autonomy, feedback, and similar task characteristics help to satisfy the individual goals of employees who desire greater control over their work.

Testing...Testing...1,2,3

10. **Describe the three key linkages in expectancy theory.**

11. **What role does perception play in expectancy theory?**

12. **How might the contemporary motivation theories be integrated to explain employee motivation?**

⟩ CURRENT ISSUES IN MOTIVATION

So far, we've covered a lot of the theoretical bases of employee motivation. Understanding and predicting employee motivation continues to be one of the most popular areas in management research. However, even current studies of employee motivation are influenced by several significant workplace issues— issues such as motivating a diverse workforce, pay-for-performance programs, open-book management, and motivating the "new workforce." Let's take a closer look at each of these issues.

MOTIVATING A DIVERSE WORKFORCE

To maximize motivation among today's diverse workforce, managers need to think in terms of *flexibility*. For instance, studies tell us that men place more importance on having autonomy in their jobs than do women. In contrast, the opportunity to learn, convenient and flexible work hours, and good interpersonal relations are more important to women.[44] Managers need to recognize that what motivates a single mother with two dependent children who is working full time to support her family may be very different from the needs of a single part-time employee or an older employee who is working only to supplement his or her retirement income. Employees have different personal needs and goals that they are hoping to satisfy through their job. A diverse array of rewards is needed to motivate employees with such varied needs.

Flexible Working Schedules Many of the so-called family-friendly benefits (see Chapter 12) that organizations have implemented are a response to the varied needs of a diverse workforce. In addition, many organizations have developed flexible working schedules that recognize different needs. What are some of these types of flexible working schedules?

A **compressed workweek** is a workweek in which employees work longer hours per day but fewer days per week. The most common form is four 10-hour days (a 4-40 program). However, organizations could design whatever schedules they wanted to fit employees' needs. For example, employees at ChevronTexaco's headquarters work nine hours every Monday through Thursday, eight hours on a Friday, and zero hours the next Friday. This compressed workweek provides employees with time off for running errands, pursuing hobbies, or taking care of family problems.[45]

Another alternative is **flexible work hours** (also popularly known as **flextime**), which is a scheduling system in which employees are required to work a specific number of hours a week but are free to vary those hours within certain limits. In a flextime schedule, there are certain common core hours when all employees are required to be on the job, but starting, ending, and lunch-hour times are flexible. Flextime is one of the most desired benefits employees want from their employers.[46] And employers have responded, according to a survey indicating that 57 percent of employers were offering flextime in 1999.[47]

Another job scheduling option that can be effective in motivating a diverse workforce is **job sharing**—the practice of having two or more people split a full-time job. This type of job schedule might be attractive, for example, to individuals with school-age children or retirees, who want to work but do not want the demands and hassles of a full-time position.

compressed workweek

A workweek in which employees work longer hours per day but fewer days per week.

flexible work hours (flextime)

A scheduling system in which employees are required to work a certain number of hours per week but are free, within limits, to vary the hours of work.

job sharing

The practice of having two or more people split a full-time job.

MANAGING WORKFORCE DIVERSITY

Developing Employee Potential: The Bottom Line of Diversity

One of a manager's more important goals is helping employees develop their potential.[48] This is particularly important in managing talented diverse employees who can bring new perspectives and ideas to the business but who may find that the workplace environment is not as conducive as it could be to accepting and embracing these different perspectives. For instance, managers at Lucent Technologies' distinguished Bell Labs have worked hard to develop an environment in which the ideas of diverse employees are encouraged openly. What can managers do to ensure that their diverse employees have the opportunity to develop their potential? One thing they can do is make sure that there are diverse role models in leadership positions so that others see that there are opportunities to grow and advance. Giving motivated, talented, hardworking, and enthusiastic diverse employees opportunities to excel in decision-making roles can be a powerful motivator to other diverse employees to work hard to develop their own potential. A mentoring program in which diverse employees are given the opportu-

nity to work closely with organizational leaders can be a powerful tool. At Silicon Graphics, for instance, new employees become part of a mentoring group called "Horizons." Through this mentoring group, diverse employees have the opportunity to observe and learn from key company decision makers.

Another way for managers to develop the potential of their diverse employees is to offer developmental work assignments that provide a variety of learning experiences in different organizational areas. DaimlerChrysler, for example, started its Corporate University, which offers a comprehensive series of learning opportunities for all employees. The company's director of diversity and work/family says that employees who are provided the opportunity to learn new processes and new technology are more likely to excel at their work and to stay with the company. These types of developmental opportunities are particularly important for diverse employees because it empowers them with tools that are critical to professional development.

---

telecommuting

A job approach in which employees work at home and are linked to the workplace by computer and modem.

Another alternative made possible by information technology is **telecommuting**. Here, employees work at home and are linked to the workplace by computer and modem. Many jobs can be done at home, and this approach might be close to the ideal job for some people because there is no commuting, the hours are flexible, there is freedom to dress as you please, and there are little or no interruptions from colleagues. However, keep in mind that not all employees embrace the idea of telecommuting. Some workers relish the informal interactions at work that satisfy their social needs as well as being a source of new ideas.

Cultural Differences in Motivation Managing a diverse workforce also means that managers need to be flexible by being aware of cultural differences and show flexibility in responding to those differences. The motivation theories we've just studied were developed largely by U.S. researchers and were validated with U.S. workers. These theories may need to be modified for different cultures.[49]

Take, for instance, Maslow's needs hierarchy. The hierarchy aligns well with American culture. But in countries where uncertainty avoidance characteristics are strong—such as in Japan, Greece, and Mexico—security needs would be on top of the needs hierarchy. In countries with high scores on quality of life, such as Denmark, Sweden, Norway, the Netherlands, and Finland, social needs would be on top.[50]

Although equity theory has a strong following in the United States, evidence suggests that in collectivist cultures—especially in the former socialist countries of Central and Eastern Europe—employees expect rewards to reflect their individual needs as well as their performance.[51] Moreover, consistent with a legacy of communism and centrally planned economies, employees exhibited an entitlement attitude—that is, they expected outcomes to be *greater* than their inputs.[52]

Don't assume, however, that there aren't *any* cross-cultural consistencies. For instance, the desire for interesting work seems important to almost all workers, regardless of their national culture. As a case in point, in a study of employees in Belgium, Britain, Israel, and the United States, "interesting work" ranked number one among 11 work goals. And this factor was ranked either second or third in Japan, the Netherlands, and Germany.[53] And in a study comparing job-preference outcomes among graduate students in the United States, Canada, Australia, and Singapore, growth, achievement, and responsibility were rated as the top three and had identical rankings.[54] Both of these studies suggest that there is some universality to the importance of intrinsic factors.

PAY-FOR-PERFORMANCE PROGRAMS

Why do most people work? Although there may be many reasons why people work, most of us do so because it pays us an amount of money that allows us to satisfy our needs and wants. Because monetary compensation is an important type of reward, how can managers use pay to motivate high levels of employee performance? The relation between pay and motivation explains the intent and logic behind pay-for-performance programs.

Pay-for-performance programs are compensation plans that pay employees on the basis of some performance measure.[55] Piece-rate pay plans, wage incentive plans, profit sharing, and lump-sum bonuses are examples. What differentiates these forms of pay from more traditional compensation plans is that instead of paying a person for time on the job, pay is adjusted to reflect some performance measure. These performance measures might include such things as individual productivity, team or work group productivity, departmental productivity, or the overall organization's profit performance. For instance, employee teams at ExxonMobil Corporation are eligible for team-performance-based incentives of as much as 30 percent of base pay. And employees at Comfort Shoe Specialists, a retail store located in a shopping center outside St. Louis, each get a weekly $50 bonus if sales for the week exceed those of the previous week.[56]

Pay-for-performance compensation is probably most compatible with expectancy theory. Specifically, individuals should perceive a strong relationship between their performance and the rewards they receive for motivation to be maximized. If rewards are allocated only on nonperformance factors—such as seniority, job title, or across-the-board pay raises—then employees are likely to reduce their efforts. From a motivation perspective, making some or all of an employee's pay conditional on some performance measure focuses his or her attention and effort toward that measure and then reinforces the continuation of the effort with a reward. If the employee, team, or organization's performance declines, so does the reward. Thus, there's an incentive to keep efforts and motivation strong.

Pay-for-performance programs are gaining in popularity. In the late 1990s, 72 percent of large U.S. companies had some form of pay-for-performance plan for

One of the first challenges faced by Carly Fiorina when she was first named as CEO of Hewlett-Packard, was to improve the functioning of the computer giant's U.S. sales force. "We have had compensation systems that failed to drive superior performance," Fiorina announced early in her tenure. One of her solutions was to institute a pay-for-performance system.

pay-for-performance programs

Compensation plans that pay employees on the basis of some performance measure.

❓ THINKING CRITICALLY ABOUT ETHICS

You have been hired as a telephone sales representative at World Adventures Travel in Dover, Delaware. In this job, you help customers who have called to book vacations by finding what works best for them and their needs as you check airline flights, times, and fares and also help with rental car and hotel reservations.

Most car rental firms and hotels run contests for the sales representative who books the most cars or most hotel rooms. The contest winners receive very attractive rewards! For instance, if you book just 50 clients for one rental car company, your name is put in a drawing for $1,000. If you book 100 clients, the drawing is for $2,500. And if you book 200 clients, you receive an all-expenses-paid, one-week Caribbean vacation. So the incentives are attractive enough to encourage you to "steer" customers toward one of those companies even though it might not be the best or cheapest for them. Your manager doesn't discourage participation in this program.

Do you see anything wrong with this situation? Explain. What ethical issues do you see for (1) the employee, (2) the organization, and (3) the customer? How could an organization design performance incentive programs that encourage high levels of performance without compromising ethics?

Testing...Testing...1,2,3

13. **What are some options for motivating a diverse workforce?**

14. **Why do managers need to be aware of cultural differences when designing motivational approaches?**

15. **How is performance-based compensation compatible with expectancy theory?**

---

open-book management

A motivational approach in which an organization's financial statements (the "books") are shared with all employees.

---

nonexecutives.[57] These types of pay plans are also becoming more popular in other countries such as Canada and Japan. About 35 percent of Canadian companies and 21.8 percent of Japanese companies now have company-wide pay-for-performance plans.[58]

Do pay-for-performance programs work? Studies seem to indicate that, yes, they do. For instance, one study found that companies that used pay-for-performance programs performed better financially than those that did not.[59] Another study showed that pay-for-performance programs with outcome-based incentives had a positive impact on sales, customer satisfaction, and profits.[60]

OPEN-BOOK MANAGEMENT

Many organizations of various sizes are involving their employees in workplace decisions by opening up the financial statements (the "books"). They share that information so that employees will be motivated to make better decisions about their work and better able to understand the implications of what they do, how they do it, and the ultimate impact on the bottom line. This approach is called **open-book management**.[61] According to a study by Ernst & Young LLP, workers who are treated as business partners are more likely to be productive and motivated to contribute to their company's profitability.[62]

The goal of open-book management is to get employees to think like an owner by seeing the impact their decisions and actions have on financial results. But most employees don't have the knowledge or background to understand the financials, so they have to be taught how to read and understand the organization's financial statements. And once employees have this knowledge, managers need to share the numbers regularly with them.

Some organizations take open-book management a step further. For instance, at Springfield Remanufacturing Company in Springfield, Missouri, employees not only get financial information but also receive bonuses and incentive pay based on profit improvements.[63] Through this type of sharing arrangement, employees begin to see the link between their efforts, level of performance, and operational results. Most firms that have introduced open-book management say that it has significantly helped the business. For instance, Allstate's Business Insurance Group used open-book management to boost return on equity from 2.9 percent to 16.5 percent in just three years. The unit's president said, "It got employees involved and committed, and it gave them some ownership. They understood they had an impact on the bottom line."[64]

MOTIVATING THE "NEW WORKFORCE"

Special groups present unique motivational challenges. In this section we look at some of the unique problems faced in trying to motivate professional employees, contingent workers, and low-skilled, minimum-wage employees.

Motivating Professionals In contrast to a generation ago, the typical employee today is more likely to be a highly trained professional with a college degree than a blue-collar factory worker. These professionals receive a great deal of intrinsic satisfaction from their work. They tend to be well paid. What special concerns should managers be aware of when trying to motivate a team of engineers at Intel, software designers at SAS Institute, or a group of consultants at Accenture?

Professionals are typically different from nonprofessionals.[65] They have a strong and long-term commitment to their field of expertise. Their loyalty is more often to their profession than to their employer. To keep current in their field, they need to regularly update their knowledge, and because of their commitment to their profession they rarely define their workweek as 8 A.M. to 5 P.M. five days a week.

What motivates professionals? Money and promotions typically are low on their priority list. Why? They tend to be well paid and they enjoy what they do. In contrast, job challenge tends to be ranked high. They like to tackle problems and find solutions. Their chief reward in their job is the work itself. Professionals also value support. They want others to think that what they are working on is important. That may be true for all employees, but professionals tend to be focused on their work as their central life interest, whereas nonprofessionals typically have other interests outside of work that can compensate for needs not met on the job.

The preceding description implies a few guidelines to keep in mind when motivating professionals. Provide them with ongoing, challenging projects. Give them autonomy to follow their interests, and allow them to structure their work in ways they find productive. Reward them with educational opportunities—additional training, workshops, attending conferences—that allow them to keep current in their field. Also reward them with recognition, and ask questions and use other actions that demonstrate to them that you're sincerely interested in what they're doing and value it.

The needs and motivation of contingent workers vary. For Barbara Judd, a contingent worker at Microsoft for two years, the perks and benefits she was denied were demotivating, as were the different-colored ID badge she was issued and the special designation attached to her name on company e-mails. Judd would have been willing to accept a full-time staff position with the company, but the offer never came and her assignment with the company came to an abrupt end. Microsoft was later the target of legal action, still pending, stemming from its treatment of the contingent workers who sometimes make up as much as 25 percent of its workforce.

Motivating Contingent Workers The elimination of jobs through downsizing and other organizational restructurings has increased the number of openings for part-time, contract, and other types of

MANAGING IN AN E-BUSINESS WORLD   **Motivational Issues in E-Business Organizations**

Are there unique challenges to motivating employees in e-businesses?[66] The answer appears to be "yes." One of these challenges is that employees in e-businesses are more susceptible to distractions that can negatively affect their work effort and reduce their productivity. In addition, technical and professional employees in e-businesses often have skills that make them very marketable, and many realize their employers' dependence on these skills. As a result, employees in e-businesses often have different compensation expectations than do their peers in more traditional organizations.

Although employees have always been susceptible to distractions at work (interruptions by colleagues, personal phone calls, etc.), access to computers and the Internet has significantly broadened these potential distractions. If the work itself isn't interesting or creates excessive stress, employees are likely to be motivated to do something else such as surfing the Net, playing online games, sending personal e-mails, trading stocks, shopping online, and maybe even searching for other jobs. What can managers do? The solution includes making jobs more interesting, providing formal breaks to alleviate monotony, and establishing clear guidelines for computer and Internet use. In fact, many employers are installing Web-monitoring software, although there is evidence that such efforts can negatively affect trust and have an adverse impact on employee morale.

It's difficult for e-businesses to find and keep talented technical and professional employees. Many have implemented an extensive list of desirable incentives and benefits rarely seen by nonmanagerial employees in typical organizations—such as signing bonuses, stock options, cars, free health-club memberships, full-time on-site concierges, and cell phone subsidies. For instance, at

Etensity, a Virginia-based Web consulting and services firm, employees can get up to $400 a month to pay for a new car through the company's Hot Wheels program; and another program called Raise the Roof, gives employees $10,000 toward the purchase of a new home. These types of incentives may benefit their recipients, but there are drawbacks. One is the effect these rewards have on others who don't get them. Another is the increasing problem created by stock options. Although these look very good while a business is growing and the stock market values them favorably, stock options can become demotivating when stock market conditions take a dive. The shakeout among dot-com stocks during 2000 and 2001 illustrates that the use of stock options as motivators is a two-way street. As long as the market was rising, employees were willing to give up a large salary in exchange for stock options. However, when stock prices dropped, many of these stock options became worthless. For individuals who joined and stayed with an e-business for the opportunity to get rich through stock options, a declining market can be a powerful demotivator. Another problem is that the potential for perceived inequities is very high among employees in e-businesses. There are often glaring discrepancies between the rewards provided to technical talent and those provided to other employees. This creates the potential for demotivating those who feel they're being treated inequitably. Also, many e-business employees, being quite aware of their marketability, have little loyalty to their organization and are always chasing the next wealth-creating opportunity.

Managing the types of compensation and benefits to reward employees in e-businesses is tricky! What can managers do? Maybe the key is looking at other ways to motivate than using compensation and benefits.

temporary workers. Contingent workers don't have the security or stability that permanent employees have, and they don't identify with the organization or display the commitment that other employees do. Temporary workers also typically get little or no benefits such as health care or pensions.[67]

There's no simple solution for motivating contingent employees. For that small set of temps who prefer the freedom of their temporary status—for instance, some students, working mothers, retirees—the lack of stability may not be an issue. In addition, temporariness might be preferred by highly compensated physicians, engineers, accountants, or financial planners who don't want the demands of a full-time job. But these are the exceptions. For the most part, temporary employees are not temporary by choice.

What will motivate involuntarily temporary employees? An obvious answer is the opportunity to become a permanent employee. In cases in which permanent employees are selected from a pool of temps, the temps will often work hard in hopes of becoming permanent. A less obvious answer is the opportunity for training. The ability of a temporary employee to find a new job is largely dependent on his or her skills. If the employee sees that the job he or she is doing can help develop marketable skills, then motivation is increased. From an equity standpoint, you should also consider the repercussions of mixing permanent and temporary workers when pay differentials are significant. When temps work alongside permanent employees who earn more, and get benefits, too, for doing the same job, the performance of temps is likely to suffer. Separating such employees or perhaps converting all employees to a variable-pay or skill-based pay plan might help minimize the problems.

Motivating Low-Skilled, Minimum-Wage Employees Suppose that in your first managerial position after graduating, you're responsible for managing a work group composed of low-skilled, minimum-wage employees. Offering more pay to these employees for high levels of performance is out of the question: Your company just can't afford it. In addition, these employees have limited education and skills. What are your motivational options at this point? One of the toughest motivational challenges a manager faces is how to achieve and keep high-performance levels among these types of workers.[68]

One trap we often fall into is thinking that people are motivated only by money. Although money is important as a motivator, it's not the only reward that people seek and that managers can use. In motivating minimum-wage employees, managers should look at other types of rewards that help motivate employee performance. What are some other rewards managers might use? One that many companies use is employee recognition programs such as employee of the month, quarterly employee performance awards ceremonies, or other celebrations of employees' accomplishments. For instance, at many fast-food restaurants or retail stores, you'll often see plaques hanging in prominent places featuring the names of "Employee of the Month." These types of programs serve the purpose of highlighting employees whose work performance has been of the type and level the organization wants to encourage in all its employees. Many managers also recognize the power of praise. However, you need to be sure that these "pats on the back" are sincere and given for the right reasons.

What else can managers do to motivate high levels of performance from minimum-wage employees? Again, we can look to job design and expectancy theories for some answers. In service industries such as travel and hospitality, retail sales, child care, and maintenance in which pay for frontline employees generally does not exceed the minimum-wage level, successful companies are empowering these frontline employees with more authority to address customers' problems. If we use the JCM to examine this change, we can see that this type of job redesign provides enhanced motivation because employees now experience increased skill variety, task identity, task significance, autonomy, and feedback. For instance, almost every job at Marriott International has been redesigned to place more workers in contact with more guests more of the time.[69] These employees are now able to take care of customer complaints and requests that formerly were referred to a manager or another department. In addition, employees have at least part of their pay tied to customer satisfaction, so there's a clear link between level of performance and reward (instrumentality linkage from expectancy theory). So, even though motivating minimum-wage workers may be a challenge, we can still use what we know about employee motivation to help us find some answers.

> ### FROM THEORY TO PRACTICE: SUGGESTIONS FOR MOTIVATING EMPLOYEES

In this chapter, we've covered a lot of information about motivation. If you're a manager concerned with motivating your employees, what specific recommendations can you draw from the theories and issues presented in this chapter? Although there's no simple, all-encompassing set of guidelines, the following suggestions draw on the essence of what we know about motivating employees.

Recognize individual differences. Almost every contemporary motivation theory recognizes that employees aren't identical. They have different needs, attitudes, personality, and other important individual variables.

Match people to jobs. There's a great deal of evidence showing the motivational benefits of carefully matching people to jobs. For example, high achievers should have jobs that allow them to participate in setting moderately challenging goals and that involve autonomy and feedback. Also keep in mind that not everybody is motivated by jobs that are high in autonomy, variety, and responsibility.

Use goals. The literature on goal-setting theory suggests that managers should ensure that employees have hard, specific goals and feedback on how well they're doing in achieving those goals. Should the goals be assigned by the manager or should employees participate in setting them? The answer depends on your perception of goal acceptance and the organization's culture. If you expect resistance to goals, participation should increase acceptance. If participation is inconsistent with the culture, use assigned goals.

Ensure that goals are perceived as attainable. Regardless of whether goals are actually attainable, employees who see goals as unattainable will reduce their effort because they'll be thinking "why bother." Managers must be sure, therefore, that employees feel confident that increased efforts *can* lead to achieving performance goals.

Individualize rewards. Because employees have different needs, what acts as a reinforcer for one may not for another. Managers should use their knowledge of employee differences to individualize the rewards they control, such as pay, promotions, recognition, desirable work assignments, autonomy, and participation.

Link rewards to performance. Managers need to make rewards contingent on performance. Rewarding factors other than performance will only reinforce those other factors. Important rewards such as pay increases and promotions should be given for the attainment of specific goals. Managers should also look for ways to increase the visibility of rewards, making them potentially more motivating.

Check the system for equity. Employees should perceive that rewards or outcomes are equal to the inputs. On a simple level, experience, ability, effort, and other obvious inputs should explain differences in pay, responsibility, and other obvious outcomes. And remember that one person's equity is another's inequity, so an ideal reward system should probably weigh inputs differently in arriving at the proper rewards for each job.

Don't ignore money. It's easy to get so caught up in setting goals, creating interesting jobs, and providing opportunities for participation that you forget that money is a major reason why most people work. Thus, the allocation of performance-based wage increases, piecework bonuses, and other pay incentives is important in determining employee motivation. A review of 80 studies evaluating motivational methods and their impact on employee productivity supports this point.[70] Goal setting alone produced, on average, a 16 percent increase in productivity; job redesign efforts to enrich jobs yielded 8 to 16 percent increases; employee participation in decision making produced a median increase of less than 1 percent; and monetary incentives led to an average increase of 30 percent. We're not saying that managers should focus solely on money as a motivational tool. Rather, we're simply stating the obvious—that is, if money is removed as an incentive, people aren't going to show up for work. The same can't be said for removing goals, enriched work, or participation.

16. **Describe open-book management and its use in motivation.**

17. **What are some special challenges in motivating (a) professionals, (b) contingent workers, and (c) low-skilled, minimum-wage workers?**

Testing...Testing...1,2,3

18. **List some practical suggestions for motivating employees.**

Managers Respond to "A Manager's Dilemma"

Cindy Brewer

Corporate Trainer, Sears, Inc., Chicago, Illinois

The company that Lorenzo works for has made significant strides in helping motivate employees. However, he is still concerned that there is more that he can be doing to motivate his workers.

He should try reinforcement theory in which desired work behavior—good work quality and quantity—is immediately followed by a positive response. By reinforcing desired behavior, Lorenzo can ensure that these behaviors will be repeated.

Finally, I would suggest that Lorenzo try employee recognition programs as a form of motivation—perhaps an employee of the week award, quarterly employee performance awards, or other ways to celebrate employees' accomplishments. What these types of programs do is highlight employees whose performance has been of the type and level the organization wants to encourage.

Stacey Ficken

Branch Manager–Loan Officer, Guardian Savings, St. Louis, Missouri

Here are some suggestions that Angel Lorenzo might try in motivating his workers to do their jobs well:

- Allow employees to have a part in deciding the production quotas that will need to be met for their department.
- Communicate to employees how their job or department affects the company as a whole and let them know where the company wants to be in the future.
- Set up a reward and recognition system for accuracy and high production for both individuals and the group as a whole.
- Provide timely feedback about work performance regardless of whether it is positive or negative.
- Thank employees and let them know that they are a necessary and important part of the organization.

Chapter Summary

This summary is organized by the chapter-opening objectives found on p. 422.

1. Motivation is the willingness to exert high levels of effort toward organizational goals, conditioned by the effort's ability to satisfy some individual need. The motivation process begins with an unsatisfied need, which creates tension, and drives an individual to search for goals that, if attained, will satisfy the need and reduce the tension.

2. Early motivation theories included Maslow's hierarchy of needs theory, McGregor's Theory X and Theory Y, and Herzberg's motivation-hygiene theory. Maslow's hierarchy of needs theory states that there are five needs people attempt to satisfy in a steplike progression: physiological, safety, social, esteem, and self-actualization. Theory X is basically a negative view of human nature and how people approach work, whereas Theory Y is basically positive. Herzberg's motivation-hygiene theory proposed that not all job factors can motivate employees. The hygiene factors simply serve to reduce employee dissatisfaction, whereas it is the motivation factors that produce job satisfaction.

3. Intention to work toward a goal is a major source of job motivation. Goals motivate employees by providing specific and challenging benchmarks to guide and stimulate performance. Specific hard goals produce a higher level of output than does the generalized goal of "do your best."

4. Reinforcement theory says that behavior is a function of its consequences. It emphasizes the pattern in which rewards are administered and states that only positive, not negative, reinforcement be used, and then only to reward desired behavior. Goal-setting theory proposes that an individual's internal purpose (intention to work toward a goal) guides his or her behavior.

5. Organizations have attempted to design motivating jobs by using job enlargement, job enrichment, and the job characteristics model (JCM). Job enlargement is the horizontal expansion of a job that increases job scope, the number of different tasks required in a job, and the frequency with which those tasks are repeated. Job enrichment is the vertical expansion of a job that increases job depth, which is the degree of control employees have over their work. The JCM proposes that jobs have five core dimensions—skill variety, task identity, task significance, autonomy, and feedback—that can be combined to create more motivating jobs.

6. In equity theory, individuals compare their job's inputs-outcomes ratio with those of relevant others. If they perceive that they are being underrewarded, their work motivation declines. Or they may even resign. When individuals perceive that they are being overrewarded, they often are motivated to work harder in order to justify their pay.

7. Expectancy theory states that an individual tends to act in a certain way based on the expectation that the act will be followed by a given outcome and on the attractiveness of that outcome to the individual. The key relationships are effort-performance linkage (expectancy), performance-reward linkage (instrumentality), and attractiveness of the reward (valence).

8. The current motivation issues facing managers include motivating a diverse workforce, designing appropriate pay-for-performance programs, using open-book management, and motivating the new workforce (professionals, contingent workers, and low-skilled, minimum-wage workers).

9. Management practices that are likely to lead to more motivated employees include recognizing individual differences, matching people to jobs, using goals, ensuring that employees perceive goals as attainable, individualizing rewards, linking rewards to performance, checking the reward system for equity, and realizing that money is an important incentive.

Thinking About Management Issues

1. Most of us have to work for a living, and a job is a central part of our lives. So why do managers have to worry so much about employee motivation issues?

2. Describe a task you have done recently for which you exerted a high level of effort. Explain your behavior using any three of the motivation approaches described in this chapter.

3. If you had to develop an incentive system for a small company that makes flour and corn tortillas with mostly unskilled labor, which elements from which motivation approaches or theories would you use? Why? Would your choice be the same if it were a software design firm with mostly skilled labor?

4. Could managers use any of the motivation theories or approaches to encourage and support workforce diversity efforts? Explain.

5. Many job design experts who have studied the changing nature of work say that people do their best work when they're motivated by a sense of purpose rather than by the pursuit of money. Do you agree? Explain your position.

Log On: Internet-Based Exercise

How popular are flexible work schedules? Research this question by finding out how many businesses are actually using any of the types of flexible work schedules. Then find examples of three companies that are using flexible work schedules for their employees. Describe what these organizations are doing. Be sure to note what type of flexible work schedule each organization is using. If the organizations provided any performance data on these schedules, what did they find?

myPHLIP Companion Web Site

myPHLIP (**www.prenhall.com/myphlip**) *is a fully customizable homepage that ties students and faculty to text-specific resources.*
- **For students**, myPHLIP *provides an online study guide tied chapter-by-chapter to the text—current events and Internet exercises, lecture notes, downloadable software, the Career Center, the Writing Center, Ask the Tutor, and more.*
- **For faculty**, myPHLIP *provides a syllabus tool that allows you to manage content, communicate with students, and upload personal resources.*

Working Together: Team-Based Exercise

List five criteria (e.g., pay, recognition, challenging work, friendships, status, the opportunity to do new things, the opportunity to travel, etc.) that would be most important to you in a job. Rank them by order of importance.

Break into small groups (three or four other class members) and compare your responses. What patterns, if any, did you find?

Case Application

Is This Any Way to Motivate Employees?

Click Commerce's offices are similar to other dot-com businesses—casual attire, white boards everywhere for employees to write or sketch on, and an entertainment room with three pinball machines and six Daytona 500 simulators. The company (www.clickinteractive.com) is a leading provider of business-to-business software that manufacturing companies use to manage relationships with business partners and customers. It also offers software for managing accounting, inventory, marketing, and ordering. The Chicago-based company was originally founded in 1996 as Click Interactive, Inc., but changed its name to Click Commerce in December 1999 to better reflect its focus on the business-to-business e-commerce market. CEO Michael Ferro (photo left), one of the "Top 40 Entrepreneurs Under 40," has led the company through the difficulties of an Internet start-up to a successful initial public offering of stock in June 2000. However, his approach to

Michael Ferro and Jim Heising of Click Interactive, Inc.

times. For programmers who are used to wearing the more typical jeans and T-shirt, wearing suits and ties is somewhat humiliating. In addition, most programmers, who enjoy their insulated lifestyle, don't relish giving up the cloistered existence of working full-time on their computer and instead of writing software they have to call on customers. This isn't easy for people who are used to interacting with a computer and who have chosen this profession to a large degree because of the job's independence and isolation.

Although there is a stigma attached to being temporarily assigned to sales, some of the programmers do acknowledge the value of the assignment. Jim Heising (photo right), for example, admits he gained some valuable insights into customers while forced to make sales calls. Now the company's chief technology officer, Heising says that although sometimes customers' requests are far-fetched, other times they come up with great ideas that can actually be implemented.

QUESTIONS

1. Explain the advantages and disadvantages of Ferro's motivational approach using Maslow's hierarchy of needs theory, reinforcement theory, and expectancy theory.

2. If you were a Click programmer, what would you think about being assigned to the penalty box?

3. Log on to Click Commerce's Web site (www.click interactive.com) and find the information on Careers. Click on two of the job titles listed there and assess these jobs according to the job characteristics model.

4. At a time when most managers are encouraged to be nice to their employees, would you suggest to Ferro that he change his motivational approach? Explain your answer.

Sources: Company information from Click Commerce's Web site (www.clickinteractive.com), November 10, 2000, and Hoover's Online (www.hoovers.com), November 10, 2000; and E. Brown, "Spare the Rod . . . ," *Forbes*, May 18, 1998, pp. 76–78.

motivation can be described as a bit unusual because it involves taking employees out of their normal work environment and requiring them to do something completely different as a form of "punishment."

Ferro believes that an occasional kick in the pants is good for employee motivation. He has created what he calls "the penalty box" for his programmers who are burned out or who act overly cocky. In actuality, this is a temporary assignment—from a few weeks to a few months—in the company's sales department. While those chosen may see such a stint as a penalty, Ferro focuses on the positive—it gives isolated programmers new experiences and broadens their responsibilities.

The "punishment" part of the box is that all salespeople, including programmers on temporary assignment, are required to wear professional business attire at all

---

Mastering Management

In Episodes 1 and 6 of the Mastering Management *series, you'll see how managers must deal with issues of motivation. In Episode 1, the management team must motivate the employees to take on a set of new and challenging tasks. In Episode 6, Warren and Liz must use the concepts of work design, job satisfaction, and productivity to address employee motivational problems.*

After reading and studying this chapter, you should be able to:

1. Explain the difference between managers and leaders.

2. Describe the trait and behavioral theories of leadership.

3. Explain the Fiedler contingency model.

4. Contrast the Hersey-Blanchard and leader participation models of leadership.

5. Summarize the path-goal model.

6. Contrast transactional and transformational leaders.

7. Describe the main characteristics of charismatic, visionary, and team leaders.

8. Explain the various sources of power a leader might possess.

9. Describe how leaders can create a culture of trust.

10. Explain gender and cultural differences in leadership.

A MANAGER'S DILEMMA

Bob Ross Buick (www.bobrossauto.com) has cornered the automotive market in Dayton, Ohio, literally and figuratively.[1] Located at a major highway intersection in Dayton, it has been the number-one Buick dealer in Ohio for five consecutive years. Following the unexpected and untimely death of founder Bob Ross Sr., his wife, Norma (seated in car), took over as president and CEO, and son Robert Jr. and daughter Jenell became co–vice presidents. Norma said, "It never occurred to us to sell or combine the business or walk away from it all." In fact, one day after Bob's death, Norma and her children came together as a united front to prove to employees, customers, and auto representatives that they could continue what Bob Sr. had built.

What Bob Ross Sr. had built was a business with a legacy of excellence and prosperity. He started as a car salesman in 1962 and distinguished himself by qualifying for 10 years straight for the Buick Sales Master Club. His accomplishments led to him being selected to participate in the very first class of the prestigious General Motors Minority Dealer Academy, and Bob was the first graduate of the program to be awarded a GM dealership. For almost 20 years, he built his business into one of the premiere automobile facilities in the Dayton area.

It wasn't just Bob's business acumen that contributed to his company's excellence and success. Daughter Jenell said, "Dad always fos-

CHAPTER SEVENTEEN

Leadership

17

tered the philosophy that we're only as good as our employees." He treated his employees well, and employee satisfaction was high. Many of the employees had been with the company for years.

Norma Ross has big shoes to fill. She has the leadership challenge of following someone who was loved and respected by his employees. Jenell explained, "When any leader dies, this is the biggest time when people leave ship." Put yourself in Norma Ross's position. How can she create a culture of trust with the business's employees so that they remain loyal and committed to the organization?

WHAT WOULD YOU DO?

Norma Ross is facing a big leadership challenge! It's important that she be able to create this culture of trust and be seen as an effective leader. Why is leadership so important? Because it's the leaders in organizations who make things happen. If leadership is so important, it's only natural to ask: What differentiates leaders from nonleaders? What's the most appropriate style of leadership? And what can you do if you want to be seen as a leader? In this chapter, we'll try to answer these and other questions about leaders.

〉 MANAGERS VERSUS LEADERS

Let's begin by clarifying the distinction between managers and leaders. Authors and practitioners often equate the two, although they're not necessarily the same. Managers are appointed to their position. Their ability to influence is based on the formal authority inherent in that position. In contrast, leaders may either be appointed or emerge from within a work group. Leaders are able to influence others to perform beyond the actions dictated by formal authority.

Should all managers be leaders? Conversely, should all leaders be managers? Because no one yet has been able to demonstrate either through research or logical argument that leadership ability is a handicap to a manager, we believe that all managers should *ideally* be leaders. However, not all leaders necessarily have the capabilities or skills of effective managers and, thus, not all leaders should be managers. The fact that an individual can influence others does not mean that he or she can also plan, organize, and control. Given (even if only ideally) that all managers should be leaders, we'll study leadership from a managerial perspective. Therefore, our definition of a **leader** is someone who can influence others and who has managerial authority. What is **leadership** then? It's the process of influencing a group toward the achievement of goals.

Leadership, like motivation, is an organizational behavior topic that has been heavily researched and most of that research has been aimed at answering the question: What is an effective leader? We can clearly see an evolution in our understanding of the leadership process in the various theories proposed to explain it. We'll begin our study of leadership by looking at some early leadership theories.

leader

Someone who can influence others and who has managerial authority.

leadership

The process of influencing a group toward the achievement of goals.

〉 EARLY LEADERSHIP THEORIES

Leadership has always been an issue of high interest from the early days of people gathering together in groups to accomplish goals. However, it wasn't until the early part of the twentieth century that researchers began to study leadership. These early leadership theories focused on the leader (trait theories) and how the leader interacted with his or her group members (behavioral theories). Let's take a closer look at what each of these approaches has contributed to our understanding of leadership.

TRAIT THEORIES

Leadership research in the 1920s and 1930s focused basically on leader traits—characteristics that might be used to differentiate leaders from nonleaders. The intent was to isolate one or more traits that leaders possessed but that nonleaders did not. Some of the traits studied included physical stature, appearance, social class, emotional stability, fluency of speech, and sociability. Despite the best efforts of researchers, it proved to be impossible to identify a set of traits that would *always* differentiate a leader (the person) from a nonleader. However, later attempts to identify traits consistently *associated* with leadership were more successful. Six traits associated with effective leadership included drive, the desire to lead, honesty and integrity, self-confidence, intelligence, and job-relevant knowledge.[2] These traits are briefly described in Exhibit 17.1.

Researchers agreed that traits alone were not sufficient for explaining effective leadership. Explanations based solely on traits ignored the interactions of leaders and their group members as well as situational factors. Possessing the appropriate traits only made it more likely that an individual would be an effective leader. Therefore, leadership research from the late 1940s to the mid-1960s concentrated on the preferred behavioral styles that leaders demonstrated. Researchers wondered whether there was something unique in what effective leaders *did*—in other words, in their *behavior*.

BEHAVIORAL THEORIES

Researchers hoped that the **behavioral theories** approach would not only provide more definitive answers about the nature of leadership but, if successful, would also have practical implications quite different from those of the trait approach. If trait research had been successful, it would have provided a basis for *selecting* the "right" people to assume formal leadership positions in organizations. In contrast, if behavioral studies turned up critical behavioral determinants of leadership, people could be *trained* to be leaders. There are four main leader behavior studies we need to look at. Exhibit 17.2 provides a summary of the major leader behavior dimensions and the conclusions of each of these studies.

behavioral theories

Leadership theories that identified behaviors that differentiated effective leaders from ineffective leaders.

Exhibit	17.1

Six Traits Associated with Leadership

1. *Drive*. Leaders exhibit a high effort level. They have a relatively high desire for achievement, they are ambitious, they have a lot of energy, they are tirelessly persistent in their activities, and they show initiative.
2. *Desire to lead*. Leaders have a strong desire to influence and lead others. They demonstrate the willingness to take responsibility.
3. *Honesty and integrity*. Leaders build trusting relationships between themselves and followers by being truthful or nondeceitful and by showing high consistency between word and deed.
4. *Self-confidence*. Followers look to leaders for an absence of self-doubt. Leaders, therefore, need to show self-confidence in order to convince followers of their rightness of goals and decisions.
5. *Intelligence*. Leaders need to be intelligent enough to gather, synthesize, and interpret large amounts of information, and they need to be able to create visions, solve problems, and make correct decisions.
6. *Job-relevant knowledge*. Effective leaders have a high degree of knowledge about the company, industry, and technical matters. In-depth knowledge allows leaders to make well-informed decisions and to understand the implications of those decisions.

Source: S.A. Kirkpatrick and E.A. Locke, "Leadership: Do Traits Really Matter?" *Academy of Management Executive*, May 1991, pp. 48–60.

Exhibit 17.2		**Behavioral Dimension**	**Conclusion**
Behavioral Theories of Leadership	University of Iowa	*Democratic style*: involving subordinates, delegating authority, and encouraging participation *Autocratic style*: dictating work methods, centralizing decision making, and limiting participation *Laissez-faire style*: giving group freedom to make decisions and complete work	Democratic style of leadership was most effective, although later studies showed mixed results.
	Ohio State	*Consideration*: being considerate of followers' ideas and feelings *Initiating structure*: structuring work and work relationships to meet job goals	High-high leader (high in consideration and high in initiating structure) achieved high subordinate performance and satisfaction, but not in all situations.
	University of Michigan	*Employee oriented*: emphasized interpersonal relationships and taking care of employees' needs *Production oriented*: emphasized technical or task aspects of job	Employee-oriented leaders were associated with high group productivity and higher job satisfaction.
	Managerial Grid	*Concern for people*: measured leader's concern for subordinates on a scale of 1 to 9 (low to high) *Concern for production*: measured leader's concern for getting job done on a scale of 1 to 9 (low to high)	Leaders performed best with a 9,9 style (high concern for production and high concern for people).

autocratic style

A leader who tended to centralize authority, dictate work methods, make unilateral decisions, and limit employee participation.

democratic style

A leader who tended to involve employees in decision making, delegate authority, encourage participation in deciding work methods and goals, and use feedback as an opportunity for coaching employees.

laissez-faire style

A leader who generally gave the group complete freedom to make decisions and complete the work in whatever way it saw fit.

University of Iowa Studies The University of Iowa studies (conducted by Kurt Lewin and his associates) explored three leadership styles.[3] The **autocratic style** described a leader who typically tended to centralize authority, dictate work methods, make unilateral decisions, and limit employee participation. The **democratic style** described a leader who tended to involve employees in decision making, delegate authority, encourage participation in deciding work methods and goals, and use feedback as an opportunity for coaching employees. Finally, the **laissez-faire style** leader generally gave the group complete freedom to make decisions and complete the work in whatever way it saw fit. Lewin and his associates researched which style was the most effective. Their results seemed to indicate that the democratic style contributed to both good quantity and quality of work. Had the answer to the question of the most effective leadership style been found? Unfortunately, it wasn't that simple. Later studies of the autocratic and democratic styles showed mixed results. For instance, the democratic style sometimes produced higher performance levels than the autocratic style, but at other times, it produced lower or equal performance levels. More consistent results were found, however, when a measure of subordinate satisfaction was used. Group members' satisfaction levels were generally higher under a democratic leader than under an autocratic one.[4]

Now leaders had a dilemma! Should they focus on achieving higher performance or on achieving higher member satisfaction? This recognition of the dual nature of a leader's behavior—that is, focusing on the work to be done (the task) and on the people within the group (the members)—was also a key characteristic of the other important early behavioral studies.

The Ohio State Studies The Ohio State studies identified two important dimensions of leader behavior.[5] Beginning with a list of more than 1,000 behavioral dimensions, the researchers eventually narrowed it down to just two that accounted for most of the leadership behavior described by group members. The first one they called **initiating structure**, which referred to the extent to which a leader was likely to define and structure his or her role and the roles of group members in the search for goal attainment. It included behavior that involved attempts to organize work, work relationships, and goals. The second one was called **consideration**, which was defined as the extent to which a leader had job relationships characterized by mutual trust and respect for group members' ideas and feelings. A leader who was high in consideration helped group members with personal problems, was friendly and approachable, and treated all group members as equals. He or she showed concern for (was considerate of) his or her followers' comfort, well-being, status, and satisfaction.

Were these behavioral dimensions adequate descriptions of leader behavior? Research found that a leader who was high in both initiating structure and consideration (a **high-high leader**) achieved high group task performance and satisfaction more frequently than one who rated low on either dimension or both. However, the high-high style didn't always yield positive results. Enough exceptions were found to indicate that perhaps situational factors needed to be integrated into leadership theory.

University of Michigan Studies Leadership studies conducted at the University of Michigan's Survey Research Center at about the same time as those being done at Ohio State had a similar research objective: identify behavioral characteristics of leaders that were related to performance effectiveness. The Michigan group also came up with two dimensions of leadership behavior, which they labeled employee oriented and production oriented.[6] Leaders who were *employee oriented* were described as emphasizing interpersonal relationships; they took a personal interest in the needs of their followers and accepted individual differences among group members. The *production-oriented* leaders, in contrast, tended to emphasize the technical or task aspects of the job, were concerned mainly with accomplishing their group's tasks, and regarded group members as a means to that end. The conclusions of the Michigan researchers strongly favored leaders who were employee oriented. Employee-oriented leaders were associated with high group productivity and higher job satisfaction. Production-oriented leaders were associated with low group productivity and lower job satisfaction.

The Managerial Grid The behavioral dimensions from these early leadership studies provided the basis for the development of a two-dimensional grid for appraising leadership styles. This **managerial grid** used the behavioral dimensions "concern for people" and "concern for production" and evaluated a leader's use of these behaviors, ranking them on a scale from 1 (low) to 9 (high).[7] Although the grid (shown in Exhibit 17.3) had 81 potential categories into which a leader's behavioral style might fall, emphasis was placed on five: impoverished management (1,1), task management (9,1), middle-of-the-road management (5,5), coun-

initiating structure

The extent to which a leader was likely to define and structure his or her role and the roles of group members in the search for goal attainment.

consideration

The extent to which a leader had job relationships characterized by mutual trust and respect for group members' ideas and feelings.

high-high leader

A leader high in both initiating structure and consideration behaviors.

managerial grid

A two-dimensional grid of two leadership behaviors—concern for people and concern for production—which resulted in five different leadership styles.

| Exhibit | 17.3 | | **The Managerial Grid** |

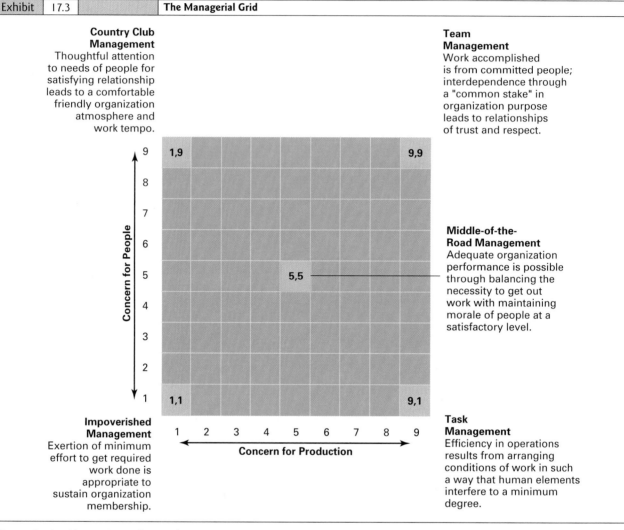

Country Club Management
Thoughtful attention to needs of people for satisfying relationship leads to a comfortable friendly organization atmosphere and work tempo.

Team Management
Work accomplished is from committed people; interdependence through a "common stake" in organization purpose leads to relationships of trust and respect.

Middle-of-the-Road Management
Adequate organization performance is possible through balancing the necessity to get out work with maintaining morale of people at a satisfactory level.

Impoverished Management
Exertion of minimum effort to get required work done is appropriate to sustain organization membership.

Task Management
Efficiency in operations results from arranging conditions of work in such a way that human elements interfere to a minimum degree.

Concern for People

Concern for Production

1,9   9,9
5,5
1,1   9,1

Source: Reprinted by permission of *Harvard Business Review*. An exhibit from "Breakthrough in Organization Development" by Robert R. Blake, Jane S. Mouton, Louis B. Barnes, and Larry E. Greiner, November–December 1964, p. 136. Copyright © 1964 by the President and Fellows of Harvard College; all rights reserved.

try club management (1,9), and team management (9,9). Of these five styles, the researchers concluded that managers performed best when using a 9,9 style. Unfortunately, the grid offered no answers to the question of what made a manager an effective leader; it only provided a framework for conceptualizing leadership style. In fact, there's been little substantive evidence to support the conclusion that a 9,9 style is most effective in all situations.[8]

It became increasingly clear that predicting leadership success involved something more complex than isolating a few leader traits or preferable behaviors. The failure to attain consistent results led to a new focus on situational influences. The relationship between leadership style and effectiveness suggested that under condition *a*, leadership style *x* would be appropriate, whereas style *y* would be more suitable for condition *b*, and style *z* for condition *c*. But what were these situational conditions? It was one thing to say that leadership effectiveness depended on the situation and another to be able to isolate those situational conditions or contingencies.

1. Explain how someone can be a manager but not a leader, a leader but not a manager, and both a manager and a leader.

2. What are leadership traits, and what has leadership research shown about traits?

3. Contrast the findings of (a) the University of Iowa studies; (b) the Ohio State studies; (c) the University of Michigan studies; and (d) the managerial grid.

〉 CONTINGENCY THEORIES OF LEADERSHIP

In this section we examine four contingency theories—the Fiedler, Hersey-Blanchard, leader participation, and path-goal models. Each looks at defining leadership style and the situation and attempts to answer the *if-then* contingencies (i.e., *if* this is my situation, *then* this is the best leadership style for me to use).

THE FIEDLER MODEL

The first comprehensive contingency model for leadership was developed by Fred Fiedler.[9] The **Fiedler contingency model** proposed that effective group performance depended on the proper match between the leader's style of interacting with his or her followers and the degree to which the situation allowed the leader to control and influence. The model was based on the premise that a certain leadership style would be most effective in different types of situations. The key was to define those leadership styles and the different types of situations and then to identify the appropriate combinations of style and situation. In order to understand Fiedler's model, let's look at the first of these variables—leadership style.

Fiedler proposed that a key factor in leadership success was an individual's basic leadership style. He further suggested that a person's style was one of two types: task oriented or relationship oriented. To measure a leader's style, Fiedler developed the **least-preferred co-worker (LPC) questionnaire**. This questionnaire contained 16 pairs of contrasting adjectives—for example, pleasant-unpleasant, cold-warm, boring-interesting, and friendly-unfriendly. Respondents were asked to think of all the co-workers they had ever had and to describe that one person they *least enjoyed* working with by rating him or her on a scale of 1 to 8 (the 8 always described the positive adjective out of the pair and the 1 always described the negative adjective out of the pair) for each of the 16 sets of adjectives. Fiedler believed that you could determine a person's basic leadership style on the basis of the responses to the LPC questionnaire. What were his descriptions of these styles?

Fiedler believed that if the leader described the least preferred co-worker in relatively positive terms (in other words, a "high" LPC score), then the respondent was primarily interested in good personal relations with co-workers. That is, if you

Fiedler contingency model

A leadership theory that proposed that effective group performance depended on the proper match between a leader's style of interacting with his or her followers and the degree to which the situation allowed the leader to control and influence.

least-preferred co-worker (LPC) questionnaire

A questionnaire that measured whether a leader was task or relationship oriented.

Gordon Binder, former CEO of the highly successful biotech firm Amgen, Inc., provides an example of a leadership style suited to a particular situation (the model on which contingency theories of leadership are based). In mid-1989, Amgen's first product was ready to ship, but management feared a competitor would trigger an injunction against the new drug. To get the drug out within 24 hours of FDA approval, Binder joined 20 staff members and packed boxes all night, beating the industry standard of one month between approval and delivery. (And the injunction never came.)

leader-member relations

One of Fiedler's situational contingencies that described the degree of confidence, trust, and respect employees had for their leader.

task structure

One of Fiedler's situational contingencies that described the degree to which job assignments were formalized and procedurized.

position power

One of Fiedler's situational contingencies that described the degree of influence a leader had over power-based activities such as hiring, firing, discipline, promotions, and salary increases.

described the person that you least liked to work with in favorable terms, your style would be described as *relationship oriented*. In contrast, if you saw the least preferred co-worker in relatively unfavorable terms (a low LPC score), you were primarily interested in productivity and getting the job done; thus, your style would be labeled as *task oriented*. Fiedler did acknowledge that there was a small group of people who fell in between these two extremes and who did not have a cut-and-dried personality sketch. One other point we need to make is that Fiedler assumed that a person's leadership style was always the same (fixed) regardless of the situation. In other words, if you were a relationship-oriented leader, you'd always be one, and the same if you were task oriented.

After an individual's basic leadership style had been assessed through the LPC, it was necessary to evaluate the situation in order to match the leader with the situation. Fiedler's research uncovered three contingency dimensions that defined the key situational factors for determining leader effectiveness. These were:

- **Leader-member relations**: the degree of confidence, trust, and respect employees had for their leader; rated as either good or poor

- **Task structure**: the degree to which job assignments were formalized and procedurized; rated as either high or low

- **Position power**: the degree of influence a leader had over power-based activities such as hiring, firing, discipline, promotions, and salary increases; rated as either strong or weak

Each leadership situation was evaluated in terms of these three contingency variables. Mixing these variables produced eight possible situations in which a leader could find himself or herself (see the bottom of the chart in Exhibit 17.4). Situations I, II, and III were classified as very favorable for the leader. Situations IV, V, and VI were moderately favorable for the leader. And situations VII and VIII were described as very unfavorable for the leader.

In order to define the specific contingencies for leadership effectiveness, Fiedler studied 1,200 groups in which he compared relationship-oriented versus task-oriented leadership styles in each of the eight situational categories. He concluded that task-oriented leaders tended to perform better in situations that were very favorable to them and in situations that were very unfavorable. (See top of Exhibit 17.4 in which performance is shown on the vertical axis and situation favorableness is shown on the horizontal axis.) On the other hand, relationship-oriented leaders seemed to perform better in moderately favorable situations.

Remember that Fiedler treated an individual's leadership style as fixed. Therefore, there were only two ways to improve leader effectiveness. First, you could bring in a new leader whose style better fit the situation. For instance, if the group situation was rated as highly unfavorable but was led by a relationship-oriented leader, the group's performance could be improved by replacing that person with a task-oriented leader. The second alternative was to change the situation to fit the leader. This could be done by restructuring tasks or increasing or decreasing the power that the leader had over factors such as salary increases, promotions, and disciplinary actions.

Exhibit 17.4   **Findings of the Fiedler Model**

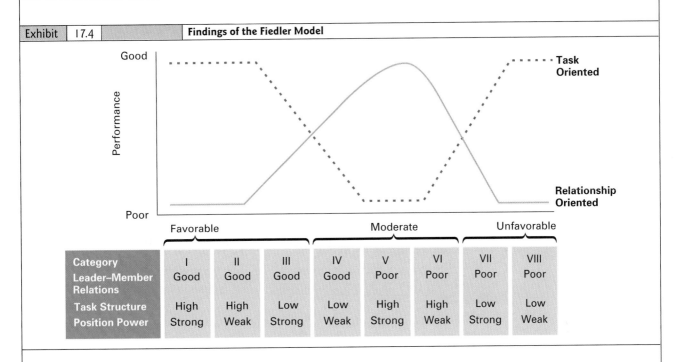

Category	I	II	III	IV	V	VI	VII	VIII
Leader–Member Relations	Good	Good	Good	Good	Poor	Poor	Poor	Poor
Task Structure	High	High	Low	Low	High	High	Low	Low
Position Power	Strong	Weak	Strong	Weak	Strong	Weak	Strong	Weak

Reviews of the major studies undertaken to test the overall validity of Fiedler's model have shown considerable evidence to support the model.[10] However, it wasn't without shortcomings. For instance, additional variables were probably needed to fill in some gaps in the model. Moreover, there were problems with the LPC, and the practicality of it needed to be addressed. In addition, it's probably unrealistic to assume that a person can't change his or her leadership style to fit the situation. Effective leaders can, and do, change their styles to meet the needs of a particular situation. Finally, the contingency variables were complex and difficult for practitioners to assess. It was often difficult in practice to determine how good the leader-member relations were, how structured the task was, and how much position power the leader had.[11] Despite its shortcomings, the Fiedler model provided evidence that effective leadership style needed to reflect situational factors.

HERSEY AND BLANCHARD'S SITUATIONAL LEADERSHIP THEORY

Paul Hersey and Ken Blanchard have developed a leadership theory that has gained a strong following among management development specialists.[12] This model called **situational leadership theory (SLT)** is a contingency theory that focuses on followers' readiness. Hersey and Blanchard argue that successful leadership is achieved by selecting the right leadership style, which is contingent on the level of the followers' readiness. Before we proceed, there are two points we need to clarify: why a leadership theory focuses on the followers, and what is meant by the term *readiness.*

The emphasis on the followers in leadership effectiveness reflects the reality that it *is* the followers who accept or reject the leader. Regardless of what the

situational leadership theory (SLT)

A leadership contingency theory that focuses on followers' readiness.

leader does, effectiveness depends on the actions of his or her followers. This is an important dimension that has been overlooked or underemphasized in most leadership theories. And **readiness**, as defined by Hersey and Blanchard, refers to the extent to which people have the ability and willingness to accomplish a specific task.

SLT uses the same two leadership dimensions that Fiedler identified: task and relationship behaviors. However, Hersey and Blanchard go a step further by considering each as either high or low and then combining them into four specific leadership styles (see Exhibit 17.5) described as follows:

- *Telling* (high task–low relationship): The leader defines roles and tells people what, how, when, and where to do various tasks.
- *Selling* (high task–high relationship): The leader provides both directive and supportive behavior.
- *Participating* (low task–high relationship): The leader and follower share in decision making; the main role of the leader is facilitating and communicating.
- *Delegating* (low task–low relationship): The leader provides little direction or support.

The final component in the model is the four stages of follower readiness:

- *R1*: People are both unable and unwilling to take responsibility for doing something. They're neither competent nor confident.
- *R2*: People are unable but willing to do the necessary job tasks. They're motivated but currently lack the appropriate skills.
- *R3*: People are able but unwilling to do what the leader wants.
- *R4*: People are both able and willing to do what is asked of them.

readiness

The extent to which people have the ability and willingness to accomplish a specific task.

Exhibit	17.5

Hersey and Blanchard's Situational Leadership Model

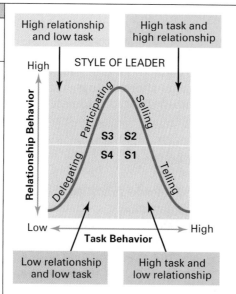

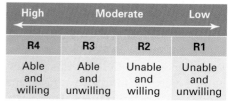

High	Moderate		Low
R4	R3	R2	R1
Able and willing	Able and unwilling	Unable and willing	Unable and unwilling

Follower Readiness

SLT essentially views the leader-follower relationship as analogous to that of a parent and a child. Just as a parent needs to relinquish control as a child becomes more mature and responsible, so, too, should leaders. As followers reach high levels of readiness, the leader responds not only by continuing to decrease control over their activities but also by continuing to decrease relationship behavior. The SLT says if followers are *unable* and *unwilling* to do a task, the leader needs to give clear and specific directions (telling); if followers are *unable* and *willing*, the leader needs to display high task orientation to compensate for the followers' lack of ability and high relationship orientation to get followers to "buy into" the leader's desires (selling); if followers are *able* and *unwilling*, the leader needs to use a supportive and participative style (participating); and if employees are both *able* and *willing*, the leader doesn't need to do much (delegating).

SLT has an intuitive appeal. It acknowledges the importance of followers and builds on the logic that leaders can compensate for ability and motivational limitations in their followers. Yet research efforts to test and support the theory generally have been disappointing.[13] Why? Possible explanations include internal ambiguities and inconsistencies in the model itself as well as problems with research methodology in tests of the theory. So in spite of its intuitive appeal and wide popularity among practicing managers, at least at this point in time, any enthusiastic endorsement should be done with caution. ◄

Testing...Testing...1,2,3

4. **What are the situational factors in Fiedler's contingency model?**

5. **According to Fiedler's model, when are (a) task-oriented leaders more effective, and (b) relationship-oriented leaders more effective?**

6. **How does follower readiness affect the choice of leadership style in situational leadership theory?**

LEADER PARTICIPATION MODEL

Another early contingency model, developed by Victor Vroom and Phillip Yetton, was the **leader participation model**, which related leadership behavior and participation in decision making.[14] Developed in the early 1970s, the model argued that leader behavior must adjust to reflect the task structure— whether it was routine, nonroutine, or anywhere in between. Vroom and Yetton's model is what we call a *normative* one; it provides a sequential set of rules (norms) that the leader should follow in determining the form and amount of participation in decision making, as determined by the different types of situations.

The leader participation model has changed as studies continue to provide additional insights and understanding of effective leadership style.[15] A current model reflects *how* and *with whom* decisions are made and uses variations of the same five leadership styles identified in the original model (see a description of these styles in Exhibit 17.6). It also expands upon the decision-making contingencies leaders look at in determining what leadership style would be most effective.[16] These contingencies—decision significance, importance of commitment, leader expertise, likelihood of

leader participation model

A leadership contingency model that related leadership behavior and participation in decision making.

The amount of decision making a leader allows is the basis of the leader participation model. At American Standard, the maker of plumbing supplies, employees are allowed considerable input in decision making, especially when it concerns their own careers. High-ranking executives act as "coaches" who guide their employees along career paths with increasing levels of pay and responsibility. Here Perry Gilbert (left) and his coach Earl Berg, discuss Perry's career at American Standard's Trane Industries in Trenton, New Jersey.

Exhibit 17.6		
Leadership Styles in the Vroom Leader Participation Model	*Decide:*	Leader makes the decision alone and either announces or sells it to group.
	Consult Individually:	Leader presents the problem to group members individually, gets their suggestions, and then makes the decision.
	Consult Group:	Leader presents the probelm to group members in a meeting, gets their suggestions, and then makes the decision.
	Facilitate:	Leader presents the problem to the group in a meeting and, acting as facilitator, defines the problem and the boundaries within which a decision must be made.
	Delegate:	Leader permits the group to make the decision within prescribed limits.

Source: Based on: V. Vroom, "Leadership and the Decision-Making Process," *Organizational Dynamics*, vol. 28, no. 4, (2000), p. 84.

commitment, group support, group expertise, and team competence—are either present in the situation (H for high) or absent (L for low). Exhibit 17.7 shows a current leader participation model—the Time-Driven Model, which is short-term in its orientation and concerned with making effective decisions with minimum cost. To use the model, a leader works through it from left to right determining whether each contingency factor is high or low. After assessing all these contingencies in the particular situation, the most effective leadership style is identified on the far right-hand side of the model. Another model—the Development-Driven Model—is structured the same way but emphasizes making effective decisions with maximum employee development outcomes and places no value on time.

PATH-GOAL MODEL

Currently, one of the most respected approaches to understanding leadership is **path-goal theory**, which states that it's the leader's job to assist his or her followers in attaining their goals and to provide the direction or support needed to ensure that their goals are compatible with the overall objectives of the group or organization. Developed by Robert House, path-goal theory is a contingency model of leadership that takes key elements from the expectancy theory of motivation.[17] The term *path-goal* is derived from the belief that effective leaders clarify the path to help their followers get from where they are to the achievement of their work goals and make the journey along the path easier by reducing roadblocks and pitfalls.

According to path-goal theory, a leader's behavior is *acceptable* to group members to the degree that they view it as an immediate source of satisfaction or as a means of future satisfaction. A leader's behavior is *motivational* to the extent that it (1) makes the satisfaction of subordinates' needs contingent on effective performance and (2) provides the coaching, guidance, support, and rewards that are necessary for effective performance. To test these statements, House identified four leadership behaviors:

path-goal theory

A leadership theory that says it's the leader's job to assist his or her followers in attaining their goals and to provide the direction or support needed to ensure that their goals are compatible with the overall objectives of the group or organization.

- *Directive leader*: lets subordinates know what's expected of them, schedules work to be done, and gives specific guidance on how to accomplish tasks
- *Supportive leader*: is friendly and shows concern for the needs of followers
- *Participative leader*: consults with group members and uses their suggestions before making a decision
- *Achievement-oriented leader*: sets challenging goals and expects followers to perform at their highest level

Exhibit 17.7

Time-Driven Model

Problem Statement	Decision Significance	Importance of Commitment	Leader Expertise	Likelihood of Commitment	Group Support	Group Expertise	Team Competence	
	H	H	H	H	–	–	–	Decide
				L	H	H	H	Delegate
							L	Consult (Group)
						L	–	Consult (Group)
					L	–		Consult (Group)
			L	H	H	H	H	Facilitate
							L	Consult (Individually)
						L	–	Consult (Individually)
					L	–		Consult (Individually)
				L	H	H	H	Facilitate
							L	Consult (Group)
						L	–	Consult (Group)
					L	–		Consult (Group)
		L	H	–	–	–	–	Decide
			L	–	H	H	H	Facilitate
							L	Consult (Individually)
						L	–	Consult (Individually)
					L	–		Consult (Individually)
	L	H	–	H	–	–	–	Decide
				L	–	–	H	Delegate
							L	Facilitate
		L	–	–	–	–	–	Decide

Source: Adapted from V. Vroom, "Leadership and the Decision-Making Process," *Organizational Dynamics*, vol. 28, no. 4, (2000), p. 87.

In contrast to Fiedler's view that a leader couldn't change his or her behavior, House assumes that leaders are flexible. In other words, path-goal theory assumes that the same leader can display any or all of these leadership styles depending on the situation.

As Exhibit 17.8 illustrates, path-goal theory proposes two classes of situational or contingency variables that moderate the leadership behavior–outcome relationship: those in the *environment* that are outside the control of the follower (factors including task structure, formal authority system, and the work group) and those that are part of the personal characteristics of the *follower* (including locus of control, experience, and perceived ability). Environmental factors determine the type of leader behavior required if subordinate outcomes are to be maximized;

Exhibit   17.8

Path-Goal Theory

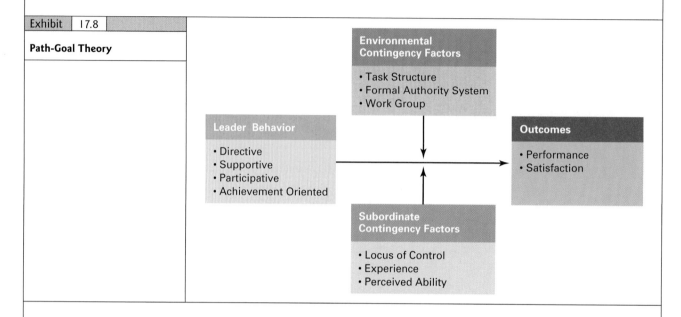

personal characteristics of the follower determine how the environment and leader behavior are interpreted. The theory proposes that leader behavior will be ineffective when it's redundant with sources of environmental structure or incongruent with follower characteristics. For example, some hypotheses from path-goal theory are:

- Directive leadership leads to greater satisfaction when tasks are ambiguous or stressful than when they are highly structured and well laid out.
- Supportive leadership results in high employee performance and satisfaction when subordinates are performing structured tasks.
- Directive leadership is likely to be perceived as redundant among subordinates with high perceived ability or with considerable experience.
- The clearer and more bureaucratic the formal authority relationships, the more leaders should exhibit supportive behavior and deemphasize directive behavior.
- Directive leadership will lead to higher employee satisfaction when there is substantive conflict within a work group.
- Subordinates with an internal locus of control will be more satisfied with a participative style.
- Subordinates with an external locus of control will be more satisfied with a directive style.
- Achievement-oriented leadership will increase subordinates' expectancies that effort will lead to high performance when tasks are ambiguously structured.

Research to validate hypotheses such as these is generally encouraging. Although not every study has found positive support, the majority of the evidence supports the logic underlying path-goal theory.[18] That is, employee performance and satisfaction are likely to be positively influenced when the leader compensates for shortcomings in either the employee or the work setting. However, if the leader spends time explaining tasks when those tasks are already clear or when the employee has the ability and experience to handle them without interference, the employee is likely to see such directive behavior as redundant or even insulting. ◄

> ### 〉 CUTTING-EDGE APPROACHES TO LEADERSHIP

7. **Describe the leader participation model.**

8. **Explain the meaning of *path* and *goal* to the path-goal theory.**

9. **How does path-goal theory explain leadership?**

What are the latest views of leadership in organizations? In this section, we want to look at three contemporary approaches to leadership including transformational-transactional leadership, charismatic-visionary leadership, and team leadership.

TRANSFORMATIONAL-TRANSACTIONAL LEADERSHIP

Most of the leadership theories presented so far in this chapter have described **transactional leaders**, that is, leaders who guide or motivate their followers in the direction of established goals by clarifying role and task requirements. But there's another type of leader who inspires followers to transcend their own self-interests for the good of the organization and is capable of having a profound and extraordinary effect on his or her followers. These are **transformational leaders**, and examples include Leslie Wexner of The Limited retail chain, Jack Welch, former chairman of General Electric, and Richard Branson of The Virgin Group. They pay attention to the concerns and developmental needs of individual followers; they change followers' awareness of issues by helping those followers look at old problems in new ways; and they are able to excite, arouse, and inspire followers to put out extra effort to achieve group goals.

transactional leaders

Leaders who guide or motivate their followers in the direction of established goals by clarifying role and task requirements.

transformational leaders

Leaders who provide individualized consideration, intellectual stimulation, and possess charisma.

Transactional and transformational leadership shouldn't be viewed as opposing approaches to getting things done.[19] Transformational leadership is built on top of transactional leadership. Transformational leadership produces levels of employee effort and performance that go beyond what would occur with a transactional approach alone. Moreover, transformational leadership is more than charisma since the transformational leader attempts to instill in followers the ability to question not only established views but those views held by the leader.[20]

The evidence supporting the superiority of transformational leadership over the transactional variety is overwhelmingly impressive. For instance, a number of studies of U.S., Canadian, and German military officers found, at every level, that transformational leaders were evaluated as being more effective than their transactional counterparts.[21] And managers at FedEx who were rated by their followers as exhibiting more transformational leadership were eval-

CEO Jack Welch, Jr. (left) has long been considered a transformational leader, turning General Electric into what many management experts regard as the model U.S. corporation. His ability to lead the firm with a clear vision and finely-tuned strategy, and to inspire its individual employees with a continuous stream of personal (even hand-written) communications, is legendary. In November 2000, Jeffrey R. Immet (right) was named to succeed the departing Welch in a gradual transition expected to last about a year.

uated by their immediate supervisors as higher performers and more promotable.[22] In summary, the overall evidence indicates that transformational leadership is more strongly correlated with lower turnover rates, higher productivity, and higher employee satisfaction.[23]

CHARISMATIC-VISIONARY LEADERSHIP

Wacko and *genius*, two seemingly contradictory terms, have been used to describe Pat Farrah, the chief merchandising officer for Home Depot, Inc.[24] In the intensely competitive building supply and home improvement industry, Farrah's enthusiastic leadership has helped reenergize the company's spirit and performance. Farrah is what we call a **charismatic leader**—that is, an enthusiastic, self-confident leader whose personality and actions influence people to behave in certain ways.

Several authors have attempted to identify personal characteristics of the charismatic leader.[25] The most comprehensive analysis identified five such characteristics—charismatic leaders have a vision, are able to articulate that vision, are willing to take risks to achieve that vision, are sensitive to both environmental constraints and follower needs, and exhibit behaviors that are out of the ordinary—that differentiate charismatic leaders from noncharismatic ones.[26]

What can we say about the charismatic leader's effect on his or her followers? There's an increasing body of evidence that shows impressive correlations between charismatic leadership and high performance and satisfaction among followers.[27]

If charisma is desirable, can people learn to be charismatic leaders? Or are charismatic leaders born with their qualities? Although a small number of experts still think that charisma can't be learned, most believe that individuals can be trained to exhibit charismatic behaviors.[28] For example, researchers have succeeded in teaching undergraduates to "be" charismatic. How? They were taught to articulate a broad goal, communicate high performance expectations, exhibit confidence in the ability of subordinates to meet those expectations, and empathize with the needs of their subordinates; they learned to project a powerful, confident, and dynamic presence; and they practiced using a captivating and engaging voice tone. To further capture the dynamics and energy of charisma, the researchers trained the student leaders to use charismatic nonverbal behaviors including leaning toward the follower when communicating, maintaining direct eye contact, and having a relaxed posture and animated facial expressions. These students learned how to project charisma. Moreover, their group members had higher task performance, higher task adjustment, and better adjustment to the leader and to the group than did group members who worked in groups led by noncharismatic leaders.

One last thing we need to say about charismatic leadership is that it may not always be needed to achieve high levels of employee performance. It may be most appropriate when the follower's task has an ideological purpose or when the environment involves a high degree of stress and uncertainty.[29] This may explain why and when charismatic leaders surface, it's more likely to be in politics, religion, or wartime, or when a business firm is starting up or facing a survival crisis. For example, Franklin D. Roosevelt used his charisma in fashioning a vision to lead the country out of the Great Depression; Martin Luther King Jr. was unyielding in his desire to bring about social equality through nonviolent means; and Steve Jobs achieved unwavering loyalty and commitment from Apple Computer's technical staff in the early 1980s by articulating a vision of personal computers that would dramatically change the way people lived.

---

charismatic leader

An enthusiastic, self-confident leader whose personality and actions influence people to behave in certain ways.

Although the term *vision* is often linked with charismatic leadership, **vision-ary leadership** goes beyond charisma since it's the ability to create and articulate a realistic, credible, and attractive vision of the future that improves on the present situation.[30] This vision, if properly selected and implemented, is so energizing that it "in effect jump-starts the future by calling forth the skills, talents, and resources to make it happen."[31]

A vision should offer clear and compelling imagery that taps into people's emotions and inspires enthusiasm and energy to pursue the organization's goals. It should be able to generate possibilities that are inspirational and unique and that offer a new way of doing things and will lead to organizational distinction. A vision is likely to fail if it does not offer a view of the future that is clearly better for the organization and its members. Desirable visions fit the times and circumstances and reflect the uniqueness of the organization. People in the organization must also believe that the vision is attainable. It should be perceived as challenging yet doable. Visions that are clearly articulated and have powerful imagery are easily grasped and accepted. For instance, Michael Dell (Dell Computer) has created a vision of a business that sells and delivers a finished PC directly to a customer in less than eight days. Jeff Bezos's vision for Amazon.com was to be the Internet's largest retailer. Mary Kay Ash's vision of women as entrepreneurs, selling products that improved their self-image, gave impetus to her cosmetics company, Mary Kay Cosmetics.

What skills do visionary leaders exhibit? Once the vision is identified, these leaders appear to have three qualities that are related to effectiveness in their visionary roles.[32] First is the *ability to explain the vision to others*. The visionary leader needs to make the vision clear in terms of required goals and actions through clear oral and written communication. The second skill needed is the *ability to express the vision not just verbally but through behavior*. This skill requires behaving in ways that continually convey and reinforce the vision. For example, Herb Kelleher of Southwest Airlines lived and breathed his commitment to customer service. He was legendary within the company for his boundless energy and for jumping in, when needed, to help check in passengers, load baggage, fill in for flight attendants, or do anything else to make the customers' experiences more pleasant and memorable. The third skill visionary leaders need is the *ability to extend or apply the vision to different leadership contexts*. For instance, the vision has to be as meaningful to the people in accounting as to those in production, to employees in Cleveland as to those in Sydney.

TEAM LEADERSHIP

Leadership is increasingly taking place within a team context. As more organizations use work teams, the role of the leader in guiding team members becomes increasingly important. The role of team leader *is* different from the traditional leadership role, as J. D. Bryant, a supervisor at Texas Instruments' Forest Lane plant in Dallas, discovered.[33] One day he was contentedly overseeing a staff of 15 circuit board assemblers. The next day he was told that the company was going to use employee teams and he was to become a "facilitator." He said, "I'm supposed to teach the teams everything I know and then let them make their own decisions." But, confused about his new role, he admitted, "There was no clear plan on what I was supposed to do." What *is* involved in being a team leader?

Many leaders are not equipped to handle the change to employee teams. As one consultant noted, "Even the most capable managers have trouble making the transition because all the command-and-control type things they were encouraged to do before are no longer appropriate. There's no reason to have any skill or sense of

visionary leadership

The ability to create and articulate a realistic, credible, and attractive vision of the future that improves upon the present situation.

Exhibit 17.9

Specific Team Leadership Roles

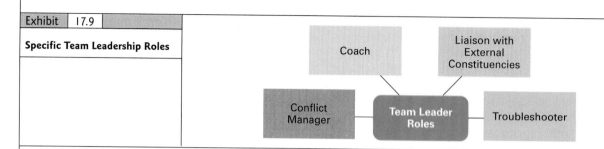

this."[34] This same consultant estimated that "probably 15 percent of managers are natural team leaders; another 15 percent could never lead a team because it runs counter to their personality. [That is, they're unable to moderate their dominating style for the good of the team.] Then there's that huge group in the middle: Team leadership doesn't come naturally to them, but they can learn it."[35]

The challenge for most managers is learning how to become an effective team leader. They have to learn skills such as having the patience to share information, being able to trust others and to give up authority, and understanding when to intervene. Effective team leaders have mastered the difficult balancing act of knowing when to leave their teams alone and when to get involved. New team leaders may try to retain too much control at a time when team members need more autonomy, or they may abandon their teams at times when the teams need support and help.[36]

One study of organizations that had reorganized themselves around employee teams found certain common responsibilities that all leaders had to assume. These included coaching, facilitating, handling disciplinary problems, reviewing team and individual performance, training, and communication.[37] You would probably agree that many of these responsibilities apply to managers' jobs in general. However, a more meaningful way to describe the team leader's job is to focus on two priorities: (1) managing the team's external boundary and (2) facilitating the team process.[38] These priorities can be broken down into four specific leadership roles. (See Exhibit 17.9.)

First, team leaders are *liaisons with external constituencies*. These may include upper management, other organizational work teams, customers, or suppliers. The leader represents the team to other constituencies, secures needed resources, clarifies others' expectations of the team, gathers information from the outside, and shares that information with team members.

Next, team leaders are *troubleshooters*. When the team has problems and asks for assistance, team leaders sit in on meetings and try to help resolve the problems. Troubleshooting rarely involves technical or operational issues because the team members typically know more about the tasks being done than does the team leader. The leader is most likely to contribute by asking penetrating questions, helping the team talk through problems, and getting needed resources to tackle problems.

Third, team leaders are *conflict managers*. When disagreements arise, they help process the conflict. They help identify issues such as the source of the conflict, who's involved, the issues, the resolution options available, and the advantages and disadvantages of each. By getting team members to address questions such as these, the leader minimizes the disruptive aspects of intrateam conflicts.

Finally, team leaders are *coaches*. They clarify expectations and roles, teach, offer support, cheerlead, and do whatever else is necessary to help team members keep their work performance levels high.

Testing...Testing...1,2,3

10. **Contrast transactional and transformational leaders.**

11. **Describe characteristics of *charismatic* and of *visionary* leaders.**

12. **What are the four specific leadership roles that team leaders play?**

> ## CONTEMPORARY ISSUES IN LEADERSHIP

As you can tell from the preceding discussion on the various leadership theories and approaches, the concept of "effective leadership" is continually being refined as researchers continue to study leadership in organizations and discover more about it. Let's take a closer look at some of the contemporary issues affecting leadership practice.

LEADERS AND POWER

Where do leaders get their power—that is, their capacity to influence work actions or decisions? Five sources of leader power have been identified: legitimate, coercive, reward, expert, and referent.[39]

MANAGING YOUR CAREER — The Ins and Outs of Office Politics

Office politics. You've probably heard the term before and probably have even experienced it if you've ever worked in an organization. Office politics is a fact of life in organizations.[40] Because organizations are made up of individuals and groups with different values, goals, and interests, the potential exists for conflict over resources. Departmental budgets, space allocations, project responsibilities, and salary adjustments are just a few of the examples of the types of resources over which organizational members will disagree about who gets how much. To gain control over these resources, people exert power. People want to carve out a niche from which to exert influence, to earn awards, and to advance their careers. When employees in organizations convert their power into action, we describe them as being engaged in office politics. Those with good political skills have the ability to use their various sources of power effectively to get what they need and want. Although you may not like the idea of engaging in office politics, it *is* important that you know how to be politically adept. You can use the following suggestions to improve *your* political effectiveness.

1. *Frame arguments in terms of organizational goals.* Effective politicking requires camouflaging your self-interests. People whose actions appear to blatantly further their own interests at the expense of the organization are almost universally denounced, are likely to *lose* influence, and may even be expelled from the organization.

2. *Develop the right image.* Know your organization's culture; understand what the organization wants and values from its employees. Because the assessment of your performance is not a fully objective process, you must pay attention to style as well as substance.

3. *Gain control of organizational resources.* The control of scarce and important organizational resources is a source of power. Knowledge and expertise are particularly effective resources to control.

4. *Make yourself appear indispensable.* If the organization's key decision makers believe that there is no ready substitute for what you bring to the organization, they are likely to go to great lengths to ensure that your desires are satisfied.

5. *Be visible.* Make your boss and those in power aware of your contributions. Routinely highlight your successes in reports, have satisfied customers express their satisfaction to your managers, be seen at company social functions, be active in your professional associations, develop powerful allies who speak positively about your accomplishments, and so forth.

6. *Develop powerful allies.* It helps to have powerful people on your side. Cultivate contacts with potentially influential people above you, at your own level, and at lower organizational levels. These allies can provide you with important information that might not otherwise be available.

7. *Avoid "tainted" members.* In every organization, there are individuals whose status is questionable. Their performance and loyalty are suspect. Keep your distance from such individuals so that your own effectiveness isn't compromised.

8. *Support your boss.* Your immediate future is in your boss's hands. Since he or she evaluates your performance, try to do whatever is necessary to have your boss on your side. Make every effort to help your boss look good and succeed, support your boss, and find out what criteria will be used to assess your effectiveness. Don't speak negatively of your boss to others and definitely don't undermine your boss.

legitimate power

The power a leader has as a result of his or her position in the organization.

coercive power

The power a leader has because of his or her ability to punish or control.

reward power

The power a leader has because of his or her ability to give positive benefits or rewards.

expert power

Influence that's based on expertise, special skills, or knowledge.

referent power

Power that arises because of a person's desirable resources or personal traits.

Legitimate power and authority are the same. Legitimate power represents the power a leader has as a result of his or her position in the organization. People in positions of authority are also likely to have reward and coercive power, but legitimate power is broader than the power to coerce and reward. Because of their legitimate power, when school principals, bank presidents, or army captains ask for something to be done, teachers, tellers, and lieutenants listen and usually comply.

Coercive power is the power that rests on the leader's ability to punish or control. Followers react to this power out of fear of the negative results that might occur if they do not comply. As a manager, you typically have some coercive power, such as being able to suspend or demote employees or to assign them work they find unpleasant or undesirable.

Reward power is the power to give positive benefits or rewards. These rewards can be anything that another person values. In an organizational context, that might include money, favorable performance appraisals, promotions, interesting work assignments, friendly colleagues, and preferred work shifts or sales territories.

Expert power is influence that's based on expertise, special skills, or knowledge. As jobs have become more specialized, managers have become increasingly dependent on staff "experts" to achieve the organization's goals. If an employee has skills, knowledge, or expertise critical to the operation of a work group, that person's expert power is enhanced. For instance, in many organizations, individuals who have good computer skills and are seen as "experts" when computer problems arise have the ability to influence because of their knowledge and skills—that is, they have expert power.

Finally, **referent power** is the power that arises because of a person's desirable resources or personal traits. If I admire and identify with you, you can exercise power over me because I want to please you. Referent power develops out of admiration of another and a desire to be like that person. You might consider the person you identify with as having what we discussed earlier, *charisma*. If you admire someone to the point of modeling your behavior and attitudes after him or her, that person has referent power over you.

Leadership, as you know, is about the process of influencing followers using various types of power. Most effective leaders rely on several different forms of power to affect the behavior and performance of their followers. For example, Commander Kathleen McGrath, the first woman to command a U.S. Navy warship at sea, employs different types of power in managing her crew and equipment. She gives orders to the crew (legitimate), praises them (reward), and disciplines those who commit infractions (coercive).[41]

Since less than 1 percent of the world's 360 million Internet users live in Africa, technical skills will become more and more highly prized among African employers as the rate of technology usage there begins to climb. Someone like Tany Accone, executive producer for M-Web Africa of Johannesburg, South Africa, has that kind of expert power. Her company builds online communities among Africans with web access.

CREATING A CULTURE OF TRUST

An important consideration for leaders is building credibility and trust. Followers want leaders who are credible and whom they can trust. But what do the terms *credibility* and *trust* mean?

The main component of credibility is honesty. Surveys have found that honesty is consistently singled out as the number-one characteristic of admired leaders. "Honesty is absolutely essential to leadership. If people are going to follow someone willingly, whether it be

? THINKING CRITICALLY ABOUT ETHICS

Your boss isn't satisfied with the way one of your colleagues is handling a project and she reassigns the project to you. She tells you to work with this person to find out what he has done already and to discuss any other necessary information that he might have. She wants your project report by the end of the month. This person is upset and angry over the reassignment and won't give you the information you need to even start, much less complete, the project. You won't be able to meet your deadline unless you get this information.

What type of power does your colleague appear to be using? What type of influence could you possibly use to gain his cooperation? If you were involved in this situation, what could you do to resolve it successfully yet ethically?

into battle or into the boardroom, they first want to assure themselves that the person is worthy of their trust." In addition to being honest, credible leaders have been found to be competent and inspiring.[42] They are personally able to communicate effectively their confidence and enthusiasm. Thus, followers judge a leader's **credibility** in terms of his or her honesty, competence, and ability to inspire.

Trust is closely entwined with the concept of credibility, and, in fact, the terms are often used interchangeably. **Trust** is defined as the belief in the integrity, character, and ability of a leader. Followers who trust a leader are willing to be vulnerable to the leader's actions because they are confident that their rights and interests will not be abused.[43] Research has identified five dimensions that make up the concept of trust:[44]

credibility

The degree to which followers perceive someone as honest, competent, and able to inspire.

trust

The belief in the integrity, character, and ability of a leader.

- *Integrity*: honesty and truthfulness
- *Competence*: technical and interpersonal knowledge and skills
- *Consistency*: reliability, predictability, and good judgment in handling situations
- *Loyalty*: willingness to protect a person, physically and emotionally
- *Openness*: willingness to share ideas and information freely

Consistent with the work on credibility, integrity and competence are the most critical characteristics that an individual looks for in determining another's trustworthiness. In fact, if you look back at our discussion of leadership traits, integrity and job-relevant knowledge were among the six traits found to be consistently associated with leadership. Although these qualities have always been important, workplace changes have reinforced their value in building trust.

The trend toward empowering individuals and creating self-managed work teams

Trust is a key component of any good relationship, particularly between manager and employees. Pamela Barefoot (center), president of Blue Crab Bay Co., a producer of specialty foods and gifts in Virginia, built trust with the two dozen employees of her growing company by relying on openness, integrity, and clear communications. As the firm prepares to move to larger quarters, Barefoot says of her staff, "They know how I feel about things, and when I leave here they can run this business just as well as I can, because they know the way I want it done."

has reduced or eliminated many of the traditional control mechanisms used to monitor employees. For instance, if a work team is free to schedule its own work, evaluate its own performance, and even make its own hiring decisions, trust becomes critical. Employees have to trust managers to treat them fairly, and managers have to trust employees to conscientiously fulfill their responsibilities. And the trend toward expanding nonauthority relationships within and between organizations widens the need for interpersonal trust. Leaders have to increasingly lead others who may not be in their work group—members of cross-functional teams, individuals who work for suppliers or customers, and perhaps even people who represent other organizations through strategic alliances. These situations do not allow leaders the luxury of falling back on their formal positions for influence. Many of these relationships, in fact, are fluid and fleeting. So the ability to quickly develop trust may be crucial to the success of the relationship. How crucial? One study of managers divided into high- and low-credibility groups based on scores on a credibility questionnaire found that employees who perceived their managers as having high credibility felt significantly more positive about and attached to their work and organizations than did those employees who perceived their managers as low in credibility.[45] In another study, individuals who reported that their manager was honest, competent, and inspiring were significantly more likely to feel a strong sense of teamwork and commitment to their organization than were those who reported their managers as not honest, competent, or inspiring.

Given the importance of trust to effective leadership, how should leaders seek to build trust? Here are some suggestions:[46]

- *Practice openness.* Mistrust comes as much from what people do not know as from what they do know. Openness leads to confidence and trust. Keep people informed, make the criteria on how decisions are made overtly clear, explain the rationale for your decisions, be candid about problems, and fully disclose relevant information.

- *Be fair.* Before making decisions or taking actions, consider how others will perceive them in terms of objectivity and fairness. Give credit where credit is due, be objective and impartial in performance appraisals, and pay attention to equity perceptions in reward distributions.

- *Speak your feelings.* Leaders who convey only hard facts come across as cold, distant, and uncaring. If you share your feelings, others will see you as real and human. They will know who you are, and their respect for you will increase.

- *Tell the truth.* If honesty is critical to credibility, you must be perceived as someone who tells the truth. People are generally more tolerant of learning something negative than of finding out that their leader lied to them.

- *Show consistency.* People want predictability. Mistrust comes from not knowing what to expect. Take the time to think about your values and beliefs. Then let them consistently guide your decisions and actions.

- *Fulfill your promises.* Trust requires that people believe you are dependable. Keep your word. Promises made must be promises kept.

- *Maintain confidences.* You trust people who are discreet and upon whom you can rely. If people make themselves vulnerable by telling you something in confidence, they need to feel assured that you won't discuss it with others or betray that confidence.

- *Demonstrate competence.* Develop the admiration and respect of others by demonstrating technical and professional ability. Pay particular attention to developing and practicing effective communication, negotiation, and other interpersonal skills.

LEADING THROUGH EMPOWERMENT

As we've described in different places throughout the text, managers are increasingly leading by empowering their employees. **Empowerment** involves increasing the decision-making discretion of workers. Millions of individual employees and employee teams are making the key operating decisions that directly affect their work. They're developing budgets, scheduling workloads, controlling inventories, solving quality problems, and engaging in similar activities that until very recently were viewed exclusively as part of the manager's job.[47] For instance, at Total Systems Services Inc. of Columbus, Georgia, employees are actively involved in work decisions, which at one point included the design of the company's new office complex. The importance of employees to the company is reflected in the brick river walk along the Chattahoochee River where each brick is engraved with an employee's name.[48]

Why are more and more companies empowering employees? One reason is the need for quick decisions by those people who are most knowledgeable about the issues—often those at lower organizational levels. If organizations are to successfully compete in a dynamic global economy, they have to be able to make decisions and implement changes quickly. Another reason is the reality that organizational downsizings during the last part of the twentieth century left many managers with larger spans of control. In order to cope with the increased work demands, managers had to empower their people. Although empowerment is not a universal panacea, when employees have the knowledge, skills, and experience to do their jobs competently and when they seek autonomy and possess an internal locus of control, empowerment can be beneficial.

empowerment

Increasing the decision-making discretion of workers.

Testing...Testing...1,2,3

13. **What are the various sources of power that a leader might use?**

14. **Why is a culture of trust so important in a workplace, and how can leaders build trust?**

15. **How is empowerment related to leadership?**

GENDER AND LEADERSHIP

There was a time when the question "Do males and females lead differently?" could be accurately characterized as a purely academic issue—interesting, but not very relevant. That time has certainly passed! Many women now hold management positions, and

Here's what Steve Miller, Group Managing Director of Royal Dutch/Shell, has to say about leadership and empowerment: "No leader can possibly have all the answers . . . The actual solutions about how best to meet the challenges of the moment have to be made by the people closest to the action . . . The leader has to find the way to empower these frontline people; to challenge them, to provide them with the resources they need, and then to hold them accountable. As they struggle with . . . this challenge, the leader becomes their coach, teacher, and facilitator. Change how you define leadership, and you change how you run a company."

As more and more women attain management and leadership positions, questions about possible gender differences in leadership styles will continue to emerge and be studied. Although Avon has long had a reputation for providing career opportunities for women and has several women on its board of directors, Andrea Jung is the first woman to be named CEO of the billion-dollar firm and was passed over once before becoming chief executive in November 1999. Acknowledged to have "a thorough knowledge of the company and the global beauty industry, as well as the passion to mobilize the organization," Jung joined a small group of female CEOs of *Fortune* 500 firms in the United States.

many more around the world will continue to join the management ranks. Misconceptions about the relationship between leadership and gender can adversely affect hiring, performance evaluation, promotion, and other human resource decisions for both men and women. So this topic needs to be addressed. First, however, a warning: This topic tends to be controversial.[49] If male and female styles differ, is one inferior? Moreover, if there is a difference, does labeling leadership styles by gender encourage stereotyping? These questions can't be easily dismissed and we'll address them shortly.

The Evidence A number of studies focusing on gender and leadership style have been conducted in recent years. Their general conclusion is that males and females *do* use different styles. Specifically, women tend to adopt a more democratic or participative style and a less autocratic or directive style than do men. Women are more likely to encourage participation, share power and information, and attempt to enhance followers' self-worth. They lead through inclusion and rely on their charisma, expertise, contacts, and interpersonal skills to influence others. Women tend to use transformational leadership, motivating others by transforming their self-interest into organizational goals. Men are more likely to use a directive, command-and-control style. They rely on the formal position authority for their influence. Men use transactional leadership, handing out rewards for good work and punishment for bad.[50]

There is an interesting qualifier to the preceding findings. The tendency for female leaders to be more democratic than males declines when women are in male-dominated jobs. Apparently, group norms and male stereotypes influence women and they tend to act more autocratically.[51]

Is Different Better? Although it's interesting to see how male and female leadership styles differ, a more important question is whether they differ in effectiveness. Although some researchers have shown that males and females tend to be equally effective as leaders,[52] an increasing number of comprehensive management studies have shown that women executives, when rated by their peers, employees, and bosses, score higher than their male counterparts on a wide variety of measures.[53] (See Exhibit 17.10 for a summary.) Why? One possible explanation is that in today's organizations, flexibility, teamwork and partnering, trust, and information sharing are rapidly replacing rigid structures, competitive individualism, control, and secrecy. The best managers listen, motivate, and provide support to their people. They inspire and influence rather than control. And women seem to do those things better than men. For example, the increased use of cross-functional teams means that effective managers must become skillful negotiators. Women's leadership style makes them better at negotiating. They don't focus on wins, losses, and competition as men do. Women treat negotiations in the context of a continuing relationship—trying hard to make the other party a winner in its own and others' eyes.[54]

Exhibit 17.10

**Where Female Managers Do Better:
A Scorecard**

None of the five studies set out to find gender differences. They stumbled on them while compiling and analyzing performance evaluations.

Skill (Each check mark denotes which group scored higher on the respective studies)	MEN	WOMEN
Motivating Others		✓ ✓ ✓ ✓ ✓
Fostering Communication		✓ ✓ ✓ ✓*
Producing High-Quality Work		✓ ✓ ✓ ✓ ✓
Strategic Planning	✓ ✓	✓ ✓*
Listening to Others		✓ ✓ ✓ ✓ ✓
Analyzing Issues	✓ ✓	✓ ✓*

*In one study, women's and men's scores in these categories were statistically even.
Data: Hagberg Consulting Group, Management Research Group, Lawrence A. Pfaff, Personnel Decisions International Inc., Advanced Teamware Inc.

Source: R. Sharpe, "As Leaders, Women Rule," *Business Week*, November 20, 2000, p. 75.

A Few Concluding Thoughts Although women rate highly on those leadership skills needed to succeed in today's dynamic global environment, we don't want to fall into the same trap as the early leadership researchers who tried to find the "one best leadership style" for all situations. We know that there is no one *best* style for all situations. Instead, which leadership style is effective will depend on the situation. So even if men and women differ in their leadership styles, we shouldn't assume that one is always preferable to the other. There are, for instance, organizations that have inexperienced and unmotivated workers performing ambiguous tasks in which directive leadership is likely to be most effective. In addition, we should recognize that some people are more flexible in adjusting their leadership behaviors to different situations than are others.[55] That said, it's probably best to think of gender as providing a behavioral *tendency* in leadership. Effective leaders may, for instance, tend toward being more participative but use an autocratic approach when the situation requires it.

LEADERSHIP STYLES AND DIFFERENT CULTURES

One general conclusion that surfaces from leadership research is that effective leaders do not use any single style. They adjust their style to the situation. Although not mentioned explicitly, national culture is certainly an important situational variable in determining which leadership style will be most effective. For instance, one study of Asian leadership styles revealed that Asian managers preferred leaders who were competent decision makers, effective communicators, and supportive of employees.[56]

National culture affects leadership style because it influences how followers will respond. Leaders can't (and shouldn't) just choose their styles freely. They are constrained by the cultural conditions their followers have come to expect. Consider the following: Korean leaders are expected to be paternalistic toward employees.[57] Arab leaders who show kindness or generosity without being asked to do so are seen by other Arabs as weak.[58] Japanese leaders are expected to be

MANAGING IN AN E-BUSINESS WORLD   **Leadership in a Digital World**

What does leadership mean in a digital world in which organizations are flexible and fluid and the pace of change is extremely rapid?[59] What's it like to lead in an e-business organization? Jomei Chang of Vitria Technology describes it as follows, "There's no place to hide. [The Internet] forces you to be on your toes every minute, every second." *Is* leadership in e-businesses really all that different from traditional organizations? Managers who've worked in both think it is. How? Three differences seem to be most evident: the speed at which decisions must be made, the importance of being flexible, and the need to create a vision of the future.

Making Decisions Fast. Managers in all organizations never have all the data they want when making decisions, but the problem is multiplied in e-businesses. The situation is changing rapidly and the competition is intense. For example, Meg Whitman, president and CEO of eBay, says, "We're growing at 40 percent to 50 percent per quarter. That pace absolutely changes the leadership challenge. Every three months we become a different company. In one year, we went from 30 employees to 140, and from 100,000 registered users to 2.2 million. At Hasbro [where she was previously an executive], we would set a yearlong strategy, and then we would simply execute against it. At eBay, we constantly revisit the strategy—and revise the tactics."

Leaders in e-businesses see themselves as sprinters and their contemporaries in traditional businesses as long-distance runners. They frequently use the term *Internet time*, which is a reference to a rapidly speeded-up working environment. "Every [e-business] leader today has to unlearn one lesson that was drilled into each of them: You gather data so that you can make considered decisions. You can't do that on Internet time."

Maintaining Flexibility. In addition to speed, leaders in e-businesses need to be highly flexible. They have to be able to roll with the ups and downs. They need to be able to redirect their group or organization when they find that something doesn't work. They have to encourage experimentation. This is what Mark Cuban, president and co-founder of Broadcast.com, had to say about the importance of being flexible. "When we started, we thought advertising would be the core of our business. We were wrong. We thought that the way to define our network was to distribute servers all over the country. We were wrong. We've had to recalibrate again and again—and we'll have to keep doing it in the future."

Focusing on the Vision. Although visionary leadership is important in every organization, in a hyperspeed environment, people require more from their leaders. The rules, policies, and regulations that characterize more traditional organizations provide direction and reduce uncertainty for employees. Such formalized guidelines typically don't exist in e-businesses and it becomes the responsibility of the leaders to provide direction through their vision. For instance, David Pottruck, co-CEO of Charles Schwab, gathered nearly 100 of the company's senior managers at the southern end of the Golden Gate Bridge. He handed each a jacket inscribed with the phrase "Crossing the Chasm" and led them across the bridge in a symbolic march to kick off his plan to turn Schwab into a full-fledged Internet brokerage. Getting people to buy into the vision may require even more radical actions. For instance, when Isao Okawa, chairman of Sega Enterprises, decided to remake his company into an e-business, his management team resisted—that is, until he defied Japan's consensus-charged, lifetime-employment culture by announcing that those who resisted the change would be fired, risking shame. Not so amazingly, resistance to the change vanished overnight.

---

humble and speak infrequently.[60] And Scandinavian and Dutch leaders who single out individuals with public praise are likely to embarrass those individuals rather than energize them.[61]

Remember that most leadership theories were developed in the United States, using U.S. subjects, so they have an American bias. They emphasize follower responsibilities rather than rights; assume self-gratification rather than commitment to duty or altruistic motivation; assume centrality of work and democratic value orientation; and stress rationality rather than spirituality, religion, or superstition.[62]

As a guide for adjusting your leadership style, you might consider the cultural value dimensions presented in Chapter 4. For example, an autocratic style is compatible with high power distance cultures, which we find in Arab, Far Eastern, and Latin countries. Power distance rankings should also be good indicators of employee willingness to accept participative leadership. Participation is likely to be most effective in low power distance cultures such as those in the United States, Norway, Finland, Denmark, and Sweden. Not incidentally, this may explain (1) why a number of leadership studies (such as the University of Michigan behavioral studies and the leader participation model) implicitly favor the use of a participative or people-oriented style, and (2) the recent enthusiasm in North American organizations for empowerment.

SOMETIMES LEADERSHIP IS IRRELEVANT!

The belief that some leadership style will always be effective regardless of the situation may not be true. Leadership may not always be important! Research indicates that, in some situations, any behaviors a leader exhibits are irrelevant. In other words, certain individual, job, and organizational variables can act as substitutes for leadership, negating the influence of the leader.[63]

For instance, follower characteristics such as experience, training, professional orientation, or need for independence can neutralize the effect of leadership. These characteristics can replace the employee's need for a leader's support or ability to create structure and reduce task ambiguity. Similarly, jobs that are inherently unambiguous and routine or that are intrinsically satisfying may place fewer demands on the leader. Finally, such organizational characteristics as explicit formalized goals, rigid rules and procedures, or cohesive work groups can substitute for formal leadership.

16. **Describe the relationship between gender and leadership style.**

17. **How does national culture affect the choice of effective leadership style?**

18. **Why might leadership not even be necessary in certain organizational situations?**

Testing...Testing...1,2,3

Managers Respond to "A Manager's Dilemma"

Jason Downing

Restaurant Manager, Chili's Grill & Bar, Springfield, Missouri

The change of power needs to be as translucent as possible. Norma should try not to make any major changes immediately because this could lead to feelings of employee insecurity. One of the first things she should do is to develop a mission statement covering important issues such as job security and future plans. Because Norma wants to ensure that the company's employees remain loyal and committed, she should get their input by asking for their ideas on increasing company growth and profitability.

It would also be helpful if the Rosses had an all-employee luncheon. They should start off by thanking their employees for their commitment to the success of the dealership. The Rosses should also focus on developing working relationships with their employees. They should try to learn about each one's family life and interests.

Finally, Norma should evaluate the company's financial situation and consider implementing a bonus or incentive program. In this way, she demonstrates her belief that the employees are (and have been) important to the company's success.

Peter G. Johnson

Director, Employment Services, Synovus Financial Corporation, Columbus, Georgia

The key to Norma Ross's success and continuing her husband's fine work will rest in her demonstrated leadership ability to effectively establish a level of trust with the employees. This will not happen overnight. She should strive for small successes and build on those.

Norma should gain a clear understanding of the strengths and needs of her people, attempt to leverage the unique talents each brings to the table, and model behaviors that will sustain an inclusive work environment. This includes showing a healthy respect for the history and accomplishments of the company and its people; making sure people are aligned on the company vision; being honest and delivering on any promises made; being visible; communicating effectively; being approachable; showing genuine interest in what people do; preaching and practicing employee empowerment; focusing on rewarding individuals and teams; and having fun!

In short, Norma should be patient, demonstrate good judgment, practice inclusive behaviors, be aware of and flexible to changing conditions, show confidence, and be fair and consistent in her decisions.

Chapter Summary

This summary is organized around the chapter-opening objectives found on p. 456.

1. Managers are appointed. Their ability to influence is based on the formal authority inherent in their positions. In contrast, leaders may either be appointed or emerge from within a group. Leaders can influence others to perform beyond the actions dictated by formal authority.

2. The trait theory of leadership focused on identifying those characteristics (traits) that might be used to differentiate leaders from nonleaders. It proved to be impossible to identify a set of traits that would *always* differentiate leaders from nonleaders. However, attempts to identify traits consistently associated with leadership were more successful. Behavioral leadership theories focused on the preferred behavioral styles that leaders demonstrated. The University of Iowa studies looked at the leadership styles of autocratic, democratic, and laissez-faire leaders. The Ohio State studies identified two leadership behavior dimensions: initiating structure and consideration. The University of Michigan studies also identified two dimensions of leadership behavior but called them employee oriented and production oriented. Blake and Mouton used two leader behaviors, concern for people and concern for production, in a two-dimensional managerial grid that conceptualized leadership style.

3. Fiedler's contingency model identifies two leadership styles (relationship oriented and task oriented) and three situational variables (leader-member relations, task structure, and position power). In situations that are highly favorable or highly unfavorable, task-oriented leaders tend to perform best. In moderately favorable situations, relationship-oriented leaders are preferred.

4. Hersey-Blanchard's situational leadership theory proposes that successful leadership is achieved by selecting the right leadership style, which is contingent on the level of the followers' readiness. On the other hand, the leader participation model related leadership behavior and follower participation in decision making by assessing task structure contingency variables through a decision-tree format.

5. The path-goal model proposes two classes of contingency variables: those in the environment and those that are part of the personal characteristics of the followers. Leaders select a specific type of behavior—directive, supportive, participative, or achievement oriented—that is congruent with the demands of the environment and the characteristics of the subordinates. According to this theory, it's the leader's job to assist his or her followers in attaining their goals and to provide the direction or support needed to ensure that their goals are compatible with the overall objectives of the group or organization.

6. Transactional leaders guide their followers in the direction of established goals by clarifying role and task requirements. Transformational leaders inspire followers to transcend their own self-interests for the good of the organization and are capable of having a profound and extraordinary effect on their followers.

7. Charismatic leaders have a vision, are able to articulate that vision, are willing to take risks to achieve that vision, are sensitive to both environmental constraints and follower needs, and exhibit behaviors that are out of the ordinary. Visionary leadership goes beyond charisma since visionary leaders have the ability to create and articulate a realistic, credible, and attractive vision of the future that improves upon the present situation. Visionary leaders have three qualities: the ability to explain the vision to others, the ability to express the vision not just verbally but through behavior, and the ability to extend or apply the vision to different leadership contexts. Team leaders have to fill four specific leadership roles: liaisons with external constituencies, troubleshooters, conflict managers, and coaches.

8. There are five sources of power a leader might possess: legitimate (power of position in the organization), coercive (power based on the ability to punish or control), reward (power to give positive benefits or rewards), expert (power based on expertise, special skills, or knowledge), and referent (power that arises because of a person's desirable resources or personal traits).

9. Leaders can create a culture of trust by practicing openness, being fair, sharing feelings, telling the truth, showing consistency, fulfilling promises, maintaining confidences, and demonstrating competence.

10. Research finds that men and women do use different styles. Women tend to adopt a more democratic and participative style. Men are more likely to use a directive, command-and-control style. National culture of followers will also affect the choice of effective leadership style. For instance, a manipulative or autocratic style would be best suited for cultures with high power distance. Along these same lines, participation is likely to be most effective in low power distance cultures.

Thinking About Management Issues

1. What types of power are available to you? Which ones do you use most? Why?

2. Do you think that most managers in real life use a contingency approach to increase their leadership effectiveness? Discuss.

3. If you were to ask people why a given individual is a leader, they tend to describe the person in terms such as *competent, consistent, self-assured, inspiring a shared vision,* and *enthusiastic.* How do these descriptions fit in with leadership concepts presented in the chapter?

4. What kinds of campus activities could a full-time college student do that might lead to the perception that he or she is a charismatic leader? In pursuing those activities, what might the student do to enhance this perception of being charismatic?

5. Do you think trust evolves out of an individual's personal characteristics or out of specific situations? Explain.

Log On: Internet-Based Exercise

Find five examples of highly visible corporate leaders, at least one of which is female. Describe the leadership styles of these individuals using one of the leadership theories discussed in the chapter. Give examples of how you think each person fits the leadership style that you've chosen.

myPHLIP Companion Web Site

myPHLIP (*www.prenhall.com/myphlip*) *is a fully customizable homepage that ties students and faculty to text-specific resources.*
- *For students, myPHLIP provides an online study guide tied chapter-by-chapter to the text—current events and Internet exercises, lecture notes, downloadable software, the Career Center, the Writing Center, Ask the Tutor, and more.*
- *For faculty, myPHLIP provides a syllabus tool that allows you to manage content, communicate with students, and upload personal resources.*

Working Together: Team-Based Exercise

You're the new manager of customer service operations at Preferred Bank Card, Inc., a credit card issuer with offices throughout California. Your predecessor, who was very popular with the customer service representatives and who is still with the company, concealed from your team how far behind they are on their goals this quarter. As a result, your team members are looking forward to a promised day off that they are not entitled to and will not be getting. It's your job to tell them the bad news. How will you do it?

Form small groups of no more than four people. Discuss this situation and how you would handle it. Then create a role-playing situation that illustrates your group's proposed approach. Be ready to do your role-play in front of the class. Also be prepared to provide the rest of the class with the specific steps that your group suggested be used in this situation.

Case Application

Toyota's Tough Boss

Hiroski Okuda isn't afraid to speak his mind or impose radical change in an organization. And because of these traits, he is memorable at Toyota Motor Corporation (www.global.toyota.com), where he is the chairman of the board. Prior to becoming chairman, Okuda served as Toyota's president—the first nonfamily member in over 30 years to head the company. He also is unusual among other Japanese executives because, in Japan, executives

Hiroski Okuda, chairman of the board, Toyota Motor Corporation.

are supposed to be unseen. Okuda justifies his outspoken and aggressive style as necessary to change a company that had become lethargic and overly bureaucratic.

Okuda moved ahead at Toyota by taking jobs that other employees didn't want. For example, in the early 1980s, the company was trying to build a manufacturing facility in Taiwan, but the Taiwanese government's demands for high local content, technology transfer, and guaranteed exports convinced many at Toyota that the project should be scrapped. Okuda thought differently. He successfully lobbied for the facility in the company, and it's now very profitable for Toyota. As Okuda noted, "Everyone wanted to give up. But I restarted the project and led it to success." His drive and ability to overcome obstacles were central to his rise in the company's hierarchy.

When Okuda ascended to the presidency of Toyota in early 1995, the company was losing market share in Japan to both Mitsubishi and Honda. Okuda attributed this problem to several factors. Toyota had been losing touch with Japanese customers for years. For example, when engineers redesigned the Corolla in 1991, they made it too big and too expensive for Japanese tastes. Then, four years later, in an attempt to lower costs significantly, they stripped out so many features in the car that the Corolla looked too cheap. Competitors, on the other hand, had also done a much better job at identifying the boom in recreational vehicles—especially the sport-utility market. Toyota's burdensome bureaucracy also bothered Okuda. A decision that took only five minutes to filter through at Suzuki Motor Corporation would take upwards of three weeks at Toyota.

In his first 18 months on the job, Okuda implemented some drastic changes. In a country where lifetime employment is consistent with the culture, he replaced nearly one-third of Toyota's highest-ranking executives. He revamped Toyota's long-standing promotion system based on seniority, adding performance as a factor. Some outstanding performers moved up several management levels at one time—something unheard of in the history of the company.

Okuda also worked with the company's vehicle designers to increase the speed at which a vehicle went from concept to market. What once took 27 months was shortened to 18. And now the company is making a custom car within five days of receiving an order.

Finally, Okuda is using the visibility of his job to address larger societal issues facing all Japanese businesses. For instance, he accused Japan's Finance Ministry of trying to destroy the auto industry by driving up the yen's value. And he has been an audible voice in the country, condemning the lax lending practices that forced Japanese banks to write off billions of dollars in bad loans that led, in part, to that country's economic crisis in the late 1990s and early 2000.

Unfortunately, some of Okuda's actions may have backfired. Speculation that he overstepped his boundary at times by his blunt demands for change and his refusal to bail out other members of the Toyota *keiretsu* may have offended the founding Toyoda family, leading to his removal as president of the company in June 1999. However, even though he was no longer president of the company, his strategic leadership helped him to be appointed to the chairman's job.

DISCUSSION QUESTIONS

1. How would you describe Hiroski Okuda's leadership style? Cite specific examples supporting your choice.

2. When a company is in crisis, do you believe that a radical change in leadership is required to turn the company around? Support your position.

3. Would you describe Okuda's leadership style as (a) charismatic, (b) visionary, and (c) culturally consistent with Japanese practices? Explain.

Sources: Information on company from Hoover's Online (www.hoovers.com), November 27, 2000, and from company's Web site (www.global.toyota.com), November 27, 2000; R. L. Simison, "Toyota Finds Way to Make a Custom Car in 5 Days," *Wall Street Journal*, August 6, 1999, p. A4; N. Shirouzu, "Toyota Is Tightening Control of Key Suppliers in Bid to Block Encroachment by Foreign Firms," *Wall Street Journal*, August 3, 1999, p. A18; N. Shirouzu, "Toyota Plans an Expansion of Capacity Due to Demand," *Wall Street Journal*, June 29, 1999, p. A8; B. McClennan, "New Toyota Chief Has U.S. Credentials," *Ward's Auto World*, June 1999,

p. 42; E. Thornton, "Mystery at the Top," *Business Week*, April 26, 1999, p. 52; N. Shirouzu, "Top-Level Reshuffle Expected at Toyota," *Wall Street Journal*, April 8, 1999, p. A20; E. Thornton, "This Isn't Your Simple Flat Tire," *Business Week*, February 1, 1999, p. 54; N. Shirouzu, "Toyota President Expected to Quit Post—Hiroski Okuda Is to Become Auto Maker's Chairman; Firm to Revamp," *Wall Street Journal*, January 11, 1999; and A. Taylor, III, "Toyota's Boss Stands Out in a Crowd," *Fortune*, November 25, 1996, pp. 116–22.

Video Case Application

Casting a Long Shadow

SMALL BUSINESS 2000

"All companies are shadows of their leader." This statement is made by Tom Velez of CTA, who has proven to be a huge shadow indeed. He has provided the strong leadership that guided his company as it grew from nothing to $150 million in sales revenues. What can Velez teach us about leadership?

The Velez family emigrated from Ecuador to the United States, and both of Tom's parents were uneducated. However, his father strongly believed in education and also believed in music. With these family values, it's not surprising that Velez attended the Julliard School of Music. However, he soon realized that, although he was a good violinist, he would never be great. He began to look at other career possibilities. At the time, there weren't many opportunities for Hispanics, but Velez knew that mathematics was easy for him. This self-knowledge guided him in his job search. He eventually ended up in a job at the National Aeronautics and Space Administration (NASA) and went on to get his Ph.D. in Mathematics from Georgetown University. Mathematics was a core skill that NASA needed in writing computer programs and understanding the physical phenomena coming from the data being gathered from space exploration, so Velez's skills seemed tailor made. However, in addition to his study of mathematics, Velez had studied philosophy. One of the philosophical ideas he took to heart was the idea of creative genius—that is, a person who makes things happen. Because of NASA's mission and reputation, he expected to find many creative geniuses there; instead,

he found that it was only a few people who made the biggest difference. From NASA, Velez went on to work at Martin Marietta, a large defense contractor.

Velez soon left Martin Marietta to form CTA with a partner. What does CTA do? It provides information systems and resource management capabilities to the U.S. government. How has Velez encouraged in his organization the type of creative genius he considers so important? His leadership approach has been based on the belief that people aren't always attracted to paychecks. Instead, they're attracted to challenge, to opportunities, and to culture. He advises finding a way to build a team incrementally and to be a leader. As a leader, admit you're not the best. Admit you need your team's help and then reward those creative geniuses who make it happen. How? Give them ownership in the business; give them freedom. And, he says, remember that creating the culture you want your business to have is a day-by-day, month-by-month, year-by-year process.

DISCUSSION QUESTIONS

1. What role do you think Velez's pursuit of creative genius plays in the way he leads CTA? Explain.

2. At NASA, what types of power do you think Velez might have had? Explain.

3. Do you agree with Velez's philosophy that people aren't always attracted to paychecks? Discuss.

4. What can you learn about leadership from Tom Velez?

Source: Based on *Small Business Today, Show 107.*

Mastering Management

In Episode 2 of the Mastering Management *series, you'll learn about a variety of approaches to leadership as Liz faces the challenge of leading two very different groups of followers. One is an experienced group of senior managers and the other is a group of young employees.*

MANAGING ENTREPRENEURIAL VENTURES

In Boise, Idaho, where industry giants like Micron Technology, Inc. and Hewlett-Packard compete for scarce talented employees, Pro-Team Inc. [www.pro-team.com], a manufacturer of specialty vacuum cleaners for industrial settings, has an impressive annual turnover rate below 5 percent. How has it achieved such success? CEO Larry R. Shideler recognizes the importance of leading and focusing the same level of excellence on the venture's human resources as it does on product excellence.[1]

Leading is an important function of entrepreneurs. As an entrepreneurial venture grows and people are brought on board, an entrepreneur takes on a new role—that of a leader. In this section on "Managing Entrepreneurial Ventures," we want to look at what's involved with the leading function. First, we're going to look at the unique personality characteristics of entrepreneurs. Then we're going to discuss the important role that entrepreneurs play in motivating employees through empowerment and leading the venture and employee teams.

Personality Characteristics of Entrepreneurs

Think of someone you know who is an entrepreneur. Maybe it's someone you know personally or maybe it's someone like Bill Gates of Microsoft, Dineh Mohajer of Hard Candy, or Larry Ellison of Sun Microsystems. How would you describe this person's personality? One of the most researched areas of entrepreneurship has been the search to determine what, if any, psychological characteristics entrepreneurs have in common, what types of per-

sonality traits entrepreneurs have that might distinguish them from nonentrepreneurs, and what traits entrepreneurs have that might predict who will be a successful entrepreneur.

Is there a classic "entrepreneurial personality?" Although trying to pinpoint specific personality characteristics that all entrepreneurs share has the same problem as the trait theories of leadership—that is, being able to identify specific personality traits that *all* entrepreneurs share—this hasn't stopped entrepreneurship researchers from listing common traits.[2] For instance, one list of personality characteristics included the following: high level of motivation, abundance of self-confidence, ability to be involved for the long term, high energy level, persistent problem solver, high degree of initiative, ability to set goals, and moderate risk-taker.[3] Another list of characteristics of "successful" entrepreneurs included high energy level, great persistence, resourcefulness, the desire and ability to be self-directed, and relatively high need for autonomy. Another recent development in defining entrepreneurial personality characteristics was the proposed use of a proactive personality scale to predict an individual's likelihood of pursuing entrepreneurial ventures. What is a **proactive personality**? Very simply, it describes those individuals who are more prone to take actions to influence their environment—that is, they're more proactive. Obviously, an entrepreneur is likely to exhibit proactivity as he or she searches for opportunities and acts to take advantage of those opportunities.[4] Various items on the proactive personality scale were found to be good indicators of a person's likelihood of becoming an entrepreneur, including gender, education,

---

	Exhibit P5.1
1. Aggressively pursues goals; pushes both self and others	**Type E's**
2. Seeks autonomy, independence, and freedom from boundaries; very individualistic	
3. Sends consistent messages; very focused and doesn't deviate from purpose	
4. Acts quickly, often without deliberating	
5. Keeps distance and maintains objectivity; expects others to be self-sufficient and tough-minded	
6. Pursues simple, practical solutions; able to cut through complexity and find the essential and important issues	
7. Is willing to take risks, comfortable with uncertainty	
8. Exhibits clear opinions and values; makes quick judgments; often finding fault and having high expectations	
9. Impatient regarding results and with others; "just do it" mentality	
10. Positive, upbeat, optimistic; communicates confidence	

Source: Based on J. Chun, "Type E Personality," *Entrepreneur*, January 1997, p. 10.

having an entrepreneurial parent, and possessing a proactive personality.

Another perspective on entrepreneurial personality has been suggested—that of Type E personalities. *Is* there a Type E (entrepreneurial) personality? One study suggests that entrepreneurs tend to share certain characteristics that set them apart from their corporate counterparts.[5] Exhibit P5.1 describes those characteristics.

Testing...Testing...1,2,3

1. **What does personality research attempt to show about entrepreneurs?**

2. **How does the concept of a proactive personality relate to entrepreneurs?**

3. **What characteristics does a Type E personality exhibit?**

Motivating Employees Through Empowerment

At Sapient Corporation (creators of Internet and software systems for e-commerce and for automating back-office tasks such as billing and inventory), cofounders Jerry Greenberg and J. Stuart Moore recognized that employee motivation was critically important to their company's ultimate success. They designed their organization so that individual employees are part of an industry-specific team that works on an entire project rather than on one small piece of it. Their rationale was that people often feel frustrated when they're doing a small part of a job and never get to see the whole job from start to finish. They figured people would be more productive if they got the opportunity to participate in all phases of a project. Their approach seems to be working as *Fortune* named Sapient one of the 100 Fastest Growing Companies in 2000.[6]

When you're motivated to do something, don't you find yourself energized and willing to work hard at doing whatever it is you're excited about? Wouldn't it be great if all of a venture's employees were energized, excited, and willing to work hard at their jobs? Having motivated employees is an important goal for any entrepreneur, and employee empowerment is an important motivational tool entrepreneurs can use.

Although it's not easy for entrepreneurs to do, employee empowerment—giving employees the power to make decisions and take actions on their own—is an important motivational approach. Why? Because successful entrepreneurial ventures must be quick and nimble, ready to pursue opportunities and go off in new directions. Empowered employees can provide that flexibility and speed. When employees are empowered, they often display stronger work motivation, better work quality, higher job satisfaction, and lower turnover. For example, the 5,600 employees at Butler International, Inc., a technology consulting services firm based in Montvale, New Jersey, work at client locations. Ed Kopko, president and CEO, recognized that employees had to be empowered to do their jobs if they were going to be successful. The company's commitment to and success with employee empowerment led to its being awarded the Arthur Andersen Global Best Practices Award for Motivating and Retaining Employees.[7] Another entrepreneurial venture that has found employee empowerment to be a strong motivational approach is Stryker Instruments in Kalamazoo, Michigan. Each of the company's 40 production units (consisting of about 40 employees each) has responsibility for its operating budget, cost reduction goals, customer-service levels, inventory management, training, production planning and forecasting, purchasing, human resource management, safety, and problem solving. In addition, unit members work closely with marketing, sales, and R&D during new product introductions and continuous improvement projects. Says one team supervisor, "Stryker lets me do what I do best and rewards me for that privilege."[8]

Empowerment is a philosophical concept that entrepreneurs have to "buy into." This doesn't come easily. In fact, it's hard for many entrepreneurs to do. Their life is tied up in the business. They've built it from the ground up. But continuing to grow the entrepreneurial venture is eventually going to require handing over more responsibilities to employees. How can entrepreneurs empower employees? For many entrepreneurs, it's a gradual process.

Entrepreneurs can begin by using participative decision making in which employees provide input into decisions. Although getting employees to participate in decisions isn't quite taking the full plunge into employee empowerment, it, at least, is a way to begin tapping into the collective array of employees' talents, skills, knowledge, and abilities.

Another way to empower employees is through delegation—the process of assigning certain decisions or specific job duties to employees. (See the Skills Module on "Delegating" in the back of the book to find out how to delegate effectively.) By delegating decisions and duties, the entrepreneur is turning over the responsibility for carrying them out.

When an entrepreneur is finally comfortable with the idea of employee empowerment, fully empowering employees means redesigning their jobs so they have discretion over the way they do their work. It's allowing employees to do their work effectively and efficiently by using their creativity, imagination, knowledge, and skills.

If an entrepreneur implements employee empowerment properly—that is, with complete and total commitment to the program and with appropriate employee training—results can be impressive for the entrepreneurial venture and for the empowered employees. The business can enjoy significant productivity gains, quality improvements, more satisfied customers, increased employee motivation, and improved morale. Employees can enjoy the opportunities to do a greater variety of work that is more interesting and challenging. In addition, employees are encouraged to take the initiative in identifying and solving problems and doing their work. For example, at Mine Safety Appliances in Murrysville, Pennsylvania, employees are empowered to change their work processes in order to meet the organization's challenging quality improvement goals. Getting to this point took an initial 40 hours of classroom instruction per employee in areas such as engineering drawing, statistical process control, quality certifications, and specific work instruction. However, the company's commitment to an empowered workforce has resulted in profitability increasing 91 percent over the last five years, 95 percent of the company's employees achieving multiskill certifications, and the company being named Home Depot's Supplier of the Year in 1999 in its first year of supplying the company.[9]

The Entrepreneur As Leader

The last topic we want to discuss in this module is the role of the entrepreneur as a leader. In this role, the entrepreneur has certain leadership responsibilities in leading the venture and in leading employee work teams.

Leading the venture. Today's successful entrepreneur must be like the leader of a jazz ensemble which is known for its improvisation, innovation, and creativity. Max DePree, former head of Herman Miller, Inc., a leading office furniture manufacturer known for its innovative leadership approaches said it best in his book, *Leadership Jazz*:

> Jazz band leaders must choose the music, find the right musicians, and perform—in public. But the effect of the performance depends on so many things—the environment, the volunteers playing the band, the need for everybody to perform as individuals and as a group, the absolute dependence of the leader on the members of the band,

the need for the followers to play well . . . The leader of the jazz band has the beautiful opportunity to draw the best out of the other musicians. We have much to learn from jazz band leaders, for jazz, like leadership, combines the unpredictability of the future with the gifts of individuals.[10]

The way an entrepreneur leads the venture should be much like the jazz leader—drawing the best out of other individuals even given the unpredictability of the situation. And one way that an entrepreneur does this is through the vision he or she creates for the organization. In fact, often the driving force through the early stages of the entrepreneurial venture is the visionary leadership of the entrepreneur. The entrepreneur's ability to articulate a coherent, inspiring, and attractive vision of the future is a key test of his or her leadership. But if an entrepreneur can do this, the results can be worthwhile. A study contrasting visionary and nonvisionary companies showed that visionary companies outperformed the nonvisionary ones by six times on standard financial criteria, and their stocks outperformed the general market by 15 times.[11]

Leading employee work teams. As we know from Chapter 15, many organizations, entrepreneurial and otherwise, are using employee work teams to perform organizational tasks, create new ideas, and resolve problems.

Employee work teams tend to be popular in entrepreneurial ventures. An *Industry Week* census of manufacturers showed that nearly 68 percent of survey respondents used teams to varying degrees.[12] The three most common ones the respondents said they used (similar to those we discussed in Chapter 15) included empowered teams (teams that have the authority to plan and implement process improvements), self-directed teams (teams that are nearly autonomous and responsible for many managerial activities), and cross-functional teams (teams that include a hybrid grouping of individuals who are experts in various specialties and who work together on various tasks).

These entrepreneurs also said that developing and using teams is necessary because technology and market demands are forcing them to make their products faster, cheaper, and better. And tapping into the collective wisdom of the venture's employees and empowering them to make decisions just may be one of the best ways to adapt to change. In addition, a team culture can improve the overall workplace environment and morale.

For team efforts to work, however, entrepreneurs must shift from the traditional command-and-control style to a coach-and-collaboration style (look back at the discussion on team leadership in Chapter 17). They must recognize that individual employees can understand the business and can innovate just as effectively as they can. For example, at Marque, Inc. of Goshen, Indiana, CEO Scott Jessup, recognized that he wasn't the smartest guy in the company as far as production problems, but he was smart enough to recognize that if his company wanted to expand its market share in manufacturing medical-emergency-squad vehicles, new levels of productivity needed to be reached. He decided to form a cross-functional team—bringing together people from production, quality assurance, and fabrication—that could spot production bottlenecks and other problems and then gave the team the authority to resolve the constraints.[13]

Testing...Testing...1,2,3

4. How can entrepreneurs empower employees?

5. Describe the analogy of an entrepreneur to the leader of a jazz ensemble.

6. How can entrepreneurs be effective at leading employee work teams?

TEAMWORK

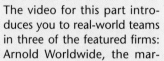

The video for this part introduces you to real-world teams in three of the featured firms: Arnold Worldwide, the marketing/public relations agency; Clif Bar, the health-food company; and i2Go, producers of digital media products.

Teams are an intrinsic part of the organizational structure and a critical source of creative synergy in each of these companies. You'll hear the firms' executives describe the various reasons teams are used in each organization, the way they are managed, and some of the benefits as well as the challenges of choosing teams for important organizational tasks. You may note in particular that teams are important both in small companies like Clif Bar where, because there are few employees, "everyone counts," and also in large companies like Arnold Worldwide, where many specific teams of all sizes exist but the organization itself is also viewed as one enormous team. Even the client company, such as Volkswagen, is considered part of the team at Arnold Worldwide.

One element the teams profiled in this segment have in common is their use of a creative incubator—a means by which new product ideas are generated, sifted, and developed, often by team members from several different functional areas of the firm. At Clif Bar, for instance, new product names are brainstormed in team sessions. At i2Go, quality-control experts who will eventually test new products and components are involved in the process as early as the development of new-product ideas. Since in each case the company is hoping its teams will come up with as many new ideas as possible so that the best ones can be selected, it's important for managers to be skillful in leading teams to arrive at good decisions efficiently and without unnecessary conflict. Listen for ways that all managers try to achieve this kind of team leadership.

Each executive in the segment offers his or her ideas about what makes for a high-performance team. You'll also hear about the value of good communication, strong leadership, and team autonomy. As you watch the segment, try to think about whether one of these factors is more important than the others. Decide whether you think there is any relationship among them, and how each contributes to successful teamwork.

DISCUSSION QUESTIONS

1. Fran Kelley of Arnold Worldwide says that one of the challenges of leading teams is setting standards that are high but achievable. Why do you think appropriate performance standards are valuable for teams? Is setting standards important for leading teams only, or for leading individuals also? Why?

2. Yana Kushner calls one of the advantages of the teamwork at Clif Bar the fact that "no one has to make a decision alone." Do you agree with her view that this is an advantage for a manager? Why or why not?

3. What are some of the challenges of relying on teams for creative decisions? List some mentioned in the video segment and some others of your own.

4. The video mentions some of the uses that teams at all three firms make of agendas, recaps, and status reports. Why do you think such written records are important for teams? Do you think it would be better for each person on the team to just keep his or her own records of meetings? Why or why not?

5. At Arnold Worldwide, management believes that nothing is as effective in good team management as face-to-face meetings among team members on a regular basis. Why do you think such meetings are important? What do you think management can do to foster success if getting people together is physically impossible, due to geographic or budget constraints?

Learning Objectives

After reading and studying this chapter, you should be able to:

1. Define control.

2. Describe the three approaches to control.

3. Explain why control is important.

4. Describe the control process.

5. Distinguish between the three types of control.

6. Describe the qualities of an effective control system.

7. Discuss the contingency factors that influence the design of an organization's control system.

8. Identify how controls need to be adjusted for cultural differences.

9. Explain how three contemporary issues—workplace privacy, employee theft, and workplace violence—affect control.

A MANAGER'S DILEMMA

Mohamed Saleem has a challenging control problem. As manager of electronic resource planning at Mohamed Mustafa & Shamsuddin Company (Mustafa's), a Singaporean retailer known for its low prices and vast array of products from around the world, he must figure out how to control customer fraud at the company's Web site.[1]

Controlling customer stealing isn't anything new for Mustafa's. To control pilfering opportunities at its two enormous department stores, Mustafa's makes customers leave their bags at the entrance; cashiers secure shopping bags with plastic grips so customers can't slip in unpaid items; and plainclothes security officers and security cameras monitor aisles crammed with silk saris, gold jewelry, electric fans, rice cookers, and similar merchandise. The two stores are located side by side in Singapore's Little India. Besides sheer variety, the stores also offer consistently lower prices than many of its rivals, especially on electronics goods. About 40 percent of Mustafa's customers are tourists. However efficient and effective the company's attempts are at controlling customer theft at its bricks-and-mortar stores, doing so in an electronic world isn't as easy!

In 1994, Mustafa's introduced a Web site storefront. The Web site offers about 5,000 (out of the 100,000) items stocked in the physical stores. It also boasts several innovative features including live foreign

Foundations of Control

18

exchange rates updated regularly. Orders are shipped to customers within hours. However, fraud problems started almost immediately. Although the company's software ensured that each transaction was encrypted to protect customers from theft of their financial information, customers weren't required to digitally verify their identities before making credit card payments online. And unfortunately, Mustafa's wasn't protected from fraudulent credit card transactions, a problem faced by all Internet retailers. When customers made credit card purchases using fraudulent means, Mustafa's was left holding the bill. Saleem has been directed to come up with a plan for addressing this problem for his company. Put yourself in his position. What steps might you take to control credit card fraud?

WHAT WOULD YOU DO?

Fraud and theft are just two common organizational control problems that managers can face. If an organization has inadequate controls, it may face sky-rocketing costs or it may find that it is not achieving its goals. Regardless of the thoroughness of the planning, a program or decision still may be poorly or improperly implemented without a satisfactory control system in place. To be effective, managers need to consider the benefits of a well-designed organizational control system.

〉 WHAT IS CONTROL?

control

The process of monitoring activities to ensure that they are being accomplished as planned and of correcting any significant deviations.

Control is the process of monitoring activities to ensure that they are being accomplished as planned and of correcting any significant deviations. All managers should be involved in the control function even if their units are performing as planned. Managers can't really know whether their units are performing properly until they've evaluated what activities have been done and have compared the actual performance with the desired standard.[2] An effective control system ensures that activities are completed in ways that lead to the attainment of the organization's goals. The criterion that determines the effectiveness of a control system is how well it facilitates goal achievement. The more it helps managers achieve their organization's goals, the better the control system.[3]

Ideally, every organization would like to efficiently and effectively reach its goals. Does this mean, however, that the control systems organizations use are identical? In other words, would SAS Institute, Inc., Matsushita, and BP Amoco have the same types of control systems? Probably not. Three different approaches to designing control systems have been identified: market, bureaucratic, and clan.[4] (See Exhibit 18.1.)

market control

An approach to control that emphasizes the use of external market mechanisms to establish the standards used in the control system.

Market control is an approach to control that emphasizes the use of external market mechanisms, such as price competition and relative market share, to establish the standards used in the control system. This approach is typically used by organizations in which the firm's products or services are clearly specified and distinct and in which there's considerable marketplace competition. Under such conditions, a company's divisions are often turned into profit centers and evaluated by the

Exhibit 18.1	Type of Control	Characteristics
Characteristics of Three Approaches to Control Systems	Market	Uses external market mechanisms, such as price competition and relative market share, to establish standards used in system. Typically used by organizations whose products or services are clearly specified and distinct and that face considerable marketplace competition.
	Bureaucratic	Emphasizes organizational authority. Relies on administrative and hierarchical mechanisms, such as rules, regulations, procedures, policies, standardization of activities, well-defined job descriptions, and budgets to ensure that employees exhibit appropriate behaviors and meet performance standards.
	Clan	Regulates employee behavior by the shared values, norms, traditions, rituals, beliefs, and other aspects of the organization's culture. Often used by organizations in which teams are common and technology is changing rapidly.

percentage of total corporate profits each contributes. For instance, at Matsushita, the various divisions (consumer products, industrial products, industrial equipment, and components) are evaluated according to the profits each generates. On the basis of these measures, corporate managers make decisions about future resource allocations, strategic changes, and other work activities that may need attention.

Another approach to a control system is **bureaucratic control**, which emphasizes organizational authority and relies on administrative rules, regulations, procedures, and policies. This type of control depends on standardization of activities, well-defined job descriptions, and other administrative mechanisms, such as budgets, to ensure that employees exhibit appropriate behaviors and meet performance standards. BP Amoco provides a good example of bureaucratic control. Although managers at BP Amoco's various divisions are allowed considerable autonomy and freedom to run their units as they see fit, they're expected to adhere closely to their budgets and stay within corporate guidelines.

Under **clan control**, employee behaviors are regulated by the shared values, norms, traditions, rituals, beliefs, and other aspects of the organization's culture. For instance, corporate rituals such as annual employee performance award dinners or holiday bonuses play a significant part in controlling behavior. Whereas bureaucratic control is based on strict hierarchical mechanisms, clan control depends on the individual and the group (or clan) to identify appropriate and expected behaviors and performance measures. Because clan controls arise from the shared values and norms of the group, this type of control system is often found in organizations in which teams are commonly used for work activities and in which technology changes often. For instance, at SAS Institute, individuals are well aware of the expectations regarding appropriate work behavior and performance standards. The organizational culture—through the shared values, norms, and stories about the company's founder, Jim Goodnight—conveys to individual employees "what's important around here" and "what's not important." Rather than relying on prescribed administrative controls, SAS employees are guided and controlled by the clan's culture.

Most organizations don't rely totally on just one of these approaches to designing an appropriate control system. Instead, organizations choose to emphasize either bureaucratic or clan control, in addition to using some market control measures. The key is designing an appropriate control system that helps the organization efficiently and effectively reach its goals.

Market control is one means of establishing standards in a control system. It relies on price competition and relative market share, two factors that will loom large in the race to dominate the Internet in Latin America in the next few years. Rance Hesketh is a Canadian executive who manages the Brazilian operations of OptiGlobe, a young Internet company that has just built a large new data center for 170 employees in São Paolo. "We are blowing through our numbers for next year already," says Hesketh.

bureaucratic control

An approach to control that emphasizes organizational authority and relies on administrative rules, regulations, procedures, and policies.

clan control

An approach to control in which employee behavior is regulated by the shared values, norms, traditions, rituals, beliefs, and other aspects of the organization's culture.

> ## WHY IS CONTROL IMPORTANT?

Why is control so important? Planning can be done, an organizational structure can be created to efficiently facilitate the achievement of goals, and employees can be motivated through effective leadership. Still, there's no assurance that activities are going as planned and that the goals managers are seeking are, in fact,

Exhibit 18.2

The Planning-Controlling Link

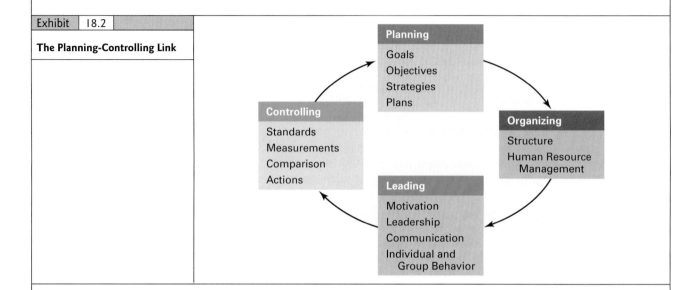

being attained. Control is important, therefore, because it's the final link in the management functions. It's the only way managers know whether organizational goals are being met and, if not, the reasons why. The specific value of the control function, however, lies in its relation to planning and delegating activities.

In Chapter 7, we described goals as the foundation of planning. Goals give specific direction to managers. However, just stating goals or having employees accept stated goals is no guarantee that the necessary actions to accomplish those goals have been taken. As the old saying goes, "The best-laid plans often go awry." The effective manager needs to follow up to ensure that what others are supposed to do is, in fact, being done and that goals are, in fact, being achieved. In reality, managing is an ongoing process, and controlling activities provide the critical link back to planning (Exhibit 18.2). If managers didn't control, they'd have no way of knowing whether their goals and plans were on target and what future actions to take.

Another reason controlling is important is managers delegate authority and empower employees. Many managers are reluctant to delegate or empower their employees because they fear that employees will do something wrong for which the manager would be held responsible. Thus, many managers are tempted to do things themselves and avoid delegating or empowering. This reluctance, however, can be reduced if managers develop an effective control system. Such a control system can provide information and feedback on employee performance. An effective control system is important, therefore, because managers need to delegate duties and empower employees to make decisions. But because managers are ultimately responsible for performance results, they also need a feedback mechanism, which the control system provides.

Testing...Testing...1,2,3

1. **What is the role of control in management?**

2. **Contrast market, bureaucratic, and clan control.**

3. **How are planning and controlling linked?**

⟩ | THE CONTROL PROCESS

The **control process** is a three-step process including measuring actual performance, comparing actual performance against a standard, and taking managerial action to correct deviations or inadequate standards. (See Exhibit 18.3.) Before we consider each step in detail, you should be aware that the control process assumes that performance standards already exist. These standards are the specific goals created during the planning process against which performance progress can be measured. If managers use a type of MBO system, then the designated objectives are the standards against which performance is measured and compared. However, even if MBO is not used, standards are the specific performance indicators that managers use. Our point is that these standards are developed in the planning process; planning must precede control.

MEASURING

To determine what actual performance is, a manager must acquire information about it. The first step in control, then, is measuring. Let's consider how we measure and what we measure.

How We Measure Four common sources of information frequently used by managers to measure actual performance are personal observation, statistical reports, oral reports, and written reports. Each has particular advantages and drawbacks; however, a combination of information sources increases both the number of input sources and the probability of getting reliable information.

To get firsthand, intimate knowledge of actual work activities, managers might use *personal observation*. This approach provides information that isn't filtered through others. It also permits intensive coverage because minor as well as major performance activities can be observed, and it provides opportunities for a manager to see what's actually going on. **Management by walking around (MBWA)** is a phrase used to describe when a manager is out in the work area, interacting directly with employees, and exchanging information about what's

---

control process

A three-step process including measuring actual performance, comparing actual performance against a standard, and taking managerial action to correct deviations or inadequate standards.

management by walking around (MBWA)

A term used to describe when a manager is out in the work area, interacting directly with employees, and exchanging information about what's going on.

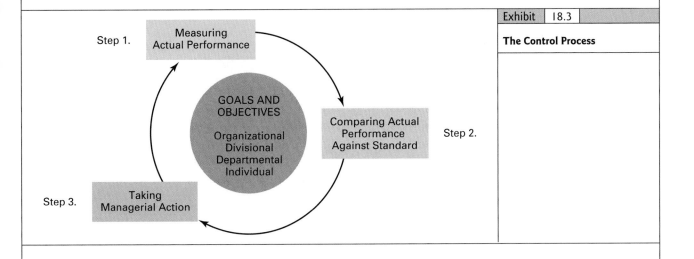

| Exhibit | 18.3 |

The Control Process

Step 1. Measuring Actual Performance

GOALS AND OBJECTIVES
Organizational
Divisional
Departmental
Individual

Comparing Actual Performance Against Standard — Step 2.

Step 3. Taking Managerial Action

going on. MBWA can pick up factual omissions, facial expressions, and tones of voice that may be missed by other sources. Unfortunately, in a time when quantitative information suggests objectivity, personal observation is often considered an inferior information source. And it does have some drawbacks. It's subject to personal biases; what one manager sees, another might not. Also, personal observation consumes a good deal of time. As companies continue to restructure and managers' spans of control continue to increase, this can be a significant drawback. Finally, this approach suffers from obtrusiveness. Employees might interpret a manager's overt observation as a sign of a lack of confidence in them or of mistrust.

The widespread use of computers has led managers to rely increasingly on *statistical reports* for measuring actual performance. This measuring device, however, isn't limited to computer outputs. It also includes graphs, bar charts, and numerical displays of any form that managers may use to assess performance. Although numerical data are easy to visualize and effective for showing relationships, they provide limited information about an activity. Statistics report on only a few areas that can be measured numerically and often ignore other important, often subjective, factors.

Information can also be acquired through *oral reports*—that is, through conferences, meetings, one-on-one conversations, or telephone calls. In organizations in which employees work in a virtual environment, this approach may be the best way to keep tabs on work performance. For instance, at the Ken Blanchard Companies in Escondido, California, managers are expected to hold one-on-one meetings with each of their employees at least once every two weeks.[5] The advantages and drawbacks of this approach to measuring performance are similar to those of personal observation. Although the information is filtered, it's fast, allows for feedback, and permits language expression and tone of voice, as well as words themselves, to convey meaning. Historically, one of the major drawbacks of oral reports was the problem of documenting information for later reference. However, information technology allows oral reports to be efficiently recorded and become as permanent as written records.

Actual performance may also be measured by *written reports*. Like statistical reports, these are slower yet more formal than first- or secondhand reports. This formality also often makes them more comprehensive and concise than oral reports. In addition, written reports are usually easy to file and retrieve.

Given the varied advantages and drawbacks of each of these four measurement approaches, comprehensive control efforts by managers should use all four.

What We Measure What we measure is probably more critical to the control process than how we measure. Why? The selection of the wrong criteria can result in serious dysfunctional consequences. Besides, what we measure determines, to a great extent, what people in the organization will attempt to excel at.[6]

Some control criteria are applicable to any management situation. For instance, because all managers, by definition, coordinate the work of others, criteria such as employee satisfaction or turnover and absenteeism rates can be measured. Most managers also have budgets set in dollar costs for their area of responsibility. Keeping costs within budget is, therefore, a fairly common control measure. However, any comprehensive control system needs to recognize the diversity of activities that managers do. For instance, a production manager at a paper tablet manufacturer might use measures such as the quantity of tablets produced per day, tablets produced per labor-hour, scrap tablet rate, or percentage of rejects returned by customers. On the other hand, the manager of an administrative unit in a governmental agency might use number of document pages typed per day, number of client requests processed per hour, or average time required to process paperwork. Marketing managers often use measures such as percentage of market held, average dollar per sale, number of customer visits per salesperson, or number of customer impressions per advertising medium.

As you might imagine, some activities are more difficult to measure in quantifiable terms. It's more difficult, for instance, for a manager to measure the performance of a research chemist or an elementary school counselor than of a person who sells life insurance. But most activities can be grouped into some objective segments that can be measured. The manager needs to determine what value a person, department, or division contributes to the organization and then convert the contribution into measurable standards.

Most jobs and activities can be expressed in tangible and measurable terms. When a performance indicator can't be stated in quantifiable terms, managers should look for and use subjective measures. Certainly, subjective measures have significant limitations. Still, they're better than having no standards at all and ignoring the control function. If an activity is important, the excuse that it's difficult to measure is unacceptable. Of course, any analysis or decisions based on subjective criteria should recognize the limitations of such information.

COMPARING

The comparing step determines the degree of variation between actual performance and the standard. Some variation in performance can be expected in all activities. It's critical, therefore, to determine the acceptable **range of variation**. (See Exhibit 18.4.) Deviations that exceed this range become significant and need the manager's attention. In the comparison stage, managers are particularly concerned with the size and direction of the variation. An example should make this concept clearer.

range of variation

The acceptable parameters of variance between actual performance and the standard.

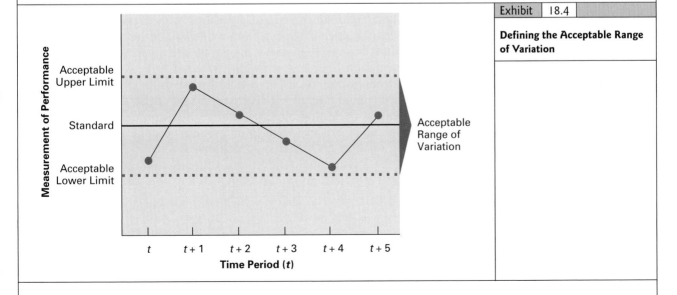

Exhibit | 18.4

Defining the Acceptable Range of Variation

Brand	Standard	(hundreds of cases) Actual	Over (Under)
Heineken	1,075	913	(162)
Molson	630	634	4
Irish Amber	800	912	112
Victoria Bitter	620	622	2
Labatt's	540	672	132
Corona	160	140	(20)
Amstel Light	225	220	(5)
Dos Equis	80	65	(15)
Tecate	170	286	116
Total cases	4,300	4,464	164

Chris Tanner is sales manager for Eastern States, a distributor of imported beers in several states on the U.S. East Coast. Chris prepares a report during the first week of each month that describes sales for the previous month, classified by brand name. Exhibit 18.5 displays both the sales goal (standard) and actual sales figures for the month of July.

Should Chris be concerned about July's sales performance? Sales were a bit higher than originally targeted, but does that mean there were no significant deviations? Even though overall performance was generally quite favorable, several brands might need to be examined more closely by Chris. However, the number of brands that deserve attention depends on what Chris believes to be *significant*. How much variation should Chris allow before corrective action is taken?

The deviation on several brands (Molson, Victoria Bitter, and Amstel Light) is very small and doesn't need special attention. On the other hand, are the shortages for Corona and Dos Equis brands significant? That's a judgment that Chris must make. Heineken sales were 15 percent below Chris's goal. This deviation is significant and needs attention. Chris should look for a cause. In this instance, Chris attributes the decrease to aggressive advertising and promotion programs by the big domestic producers, Anheuser-Busch and Miller. Because Heineken is his company's number-one selling import, it's most vulnerable to the promotion clout of the big domestic producers. If the decline in sales of Heineken is more than a temporary slump (that is, if it happens again next month), then Chris will need to cut back on inventory stock.

An error in understating sales can be as troublesome as an overstatement. For instance, is the surprising popularity of Tecate (up 68 percent) a one-month aberration, or is this brand becoming more popular with customers? If the brand is increasing in popularity, Chris will want to order more product to meet customer demand and not run short and risk losing customers. Again, Chris will have to interpret the information and make a decision. Our Eastern States' example illustrates that both overvariance and undervariance in any comparison of measures require managerial attention.

TAKING MANAGERIAL ACTION

The third and final step in the control process is taking managerial action. Managers can choose among three possible courses of action: They can do nothing; they can correct the actual performance; or they can revise the standards. Because "doing nothing" is fairly self-explanatory, let's look more closely at the other two.

Vic Cavallaro, Publisher, KidsBooks, Inc., New York, New York

Describe your job.

I'm the owner and hands-on publisher of a small, children's trade book company. My main responsibility is to direct and control all product development from concept to finished book, including editorial, design, and production—while keeping an eye on finances.

What types of skills do you think tomorrow's managers will need?

An increasingly scattered, freelance workforce will require more flexibility in adapting to quick-changing trends. The ability to disseminate information, communicate proce-

dures, evaluate results, *and* tie it all together will be a major challenge to tomorrow's manager.

Why are controls important to your organization?

Publishing for children requires a high degree of content sensitivity and control. It's a great responsibility to be dealing with developing minds. We have to be extra careful with grammar, accuracy of factual information, and subject matter. The primary task—as in all organizations—is to have a well-motivated, caring, and competent staff.

How do you implement controls in your organization?

Experts within each discipline scrutinize all nonfiction. We cross-edit a lot, so that different eyes and sensibilities review each manuscript. Conflicts are resolved by conferencing with senior editors. Hands-on, proactive involvement by senior management reduces the need for formal, stringent controls.

Correct Actual Performance If the source of the performance variation is unsatisfactory work, the manager will want to take corrective action. Examples of such corrective action might include changing strategy, structure, compensation practices, or training programs; redesigning jobs; or firing employees.

A manager who decides to correct actual performance has to make another decision: Should immediate or basic corrective action be taken? **Immediate corrective action** corrects problems at once to get performance back on track. **Basic corrective action** looks at how and why performance has deviated and then proceeds to correct the source of deviation. It's not unusual for managers to rationalize that they don't have the time to take basic corrective action and, therefore, must be content to perpetually "put out fires" with immediate corrective action. Effective managers, however, analyze deviations and, when the benefits justify it, take the time to pinpoint and correct the causes of variance.

To return to our Eastern States example, taking immediate corrective action on the negative variance for Heineken, Chris might contact the company's retailers and have them immediately drop the price on Heineken by 5 percent. However, taking basic corrective action would involve more in-depth analysis by Chris. After assessing how and why sales deviated, Chris might choose to increase instore promotional efforts, increase the advertising budget for this brand, or reduce future purchases from the breweries. The action Chris takes will depend on the assessment of each brand's potential profitability.

Revise the Standard It's possible that the variance was a result of an unrealistic standard; that is, the goal may have been too high or too low. In such cases, it's the standard that needs corrective attention, not the performance. In our example, Chris might need to raise the sales goal (standard) for Tecate to reflect its growing popularity.

immediate corrective action

Corrective action that corrects problems at once to get performance back on track.

basic corrective action

Corrective action that looks at how and why performance deviated and then proceeds to correct the source of deviation.

David Crosier, Staples' vice president for supply-chain management, was having a hard time getting enough stock of popular 3M products such as Scotch tape and Post-it notes because 3M's customer database was full of inaccurate information, causing errors and stockouts. Once 3M took corrective action, however, investing in new computer technology to build a reliable electronic base of solid sales information, it was able to set up an online ordering service that has reduced errors and improved efficiency and service. Crosier now has all the 3M office supplies he can sell.

The more troublesome problem is the revision of a performance standard downward. If an employee, work team, or work unit falls significantly short of reaching its goal, their natural response is to shift the blame for the variance to the goal. For instance, students who make a low grade on a test often attack the grade cutoff standards as too high. Rather than accept the fact that their performance was inadequate, students argue that the standards are unreasonable. Similarly, salespeople who fail to meet their monthly quota may attribute the failure to an unrealistic quota. It may be true that when standards are too high, it can result in a significant variation and may even contribute to demotivating those employees being measured against them. But keep in mind that if employees or managers don't meet the standard, the first thing they're likely to attack is the standard. If you believe that the standard is realistic, fair, and achievable, hold your ground. Explain your position, reaffirm to the employee, team, or unit that you expect future performance to improve, and then take the necessary corrective action to turn that expectation into reality.

SUMMARY OF MANAGERIAL DECISIONS

Exhibit 18.6 summarizes the manager's decisions in the control process. The standards evolve out of goals that are developed during the planning process. These goals

| Exhibit | 18.6 | **Managerial Decisions in the Control Process** |

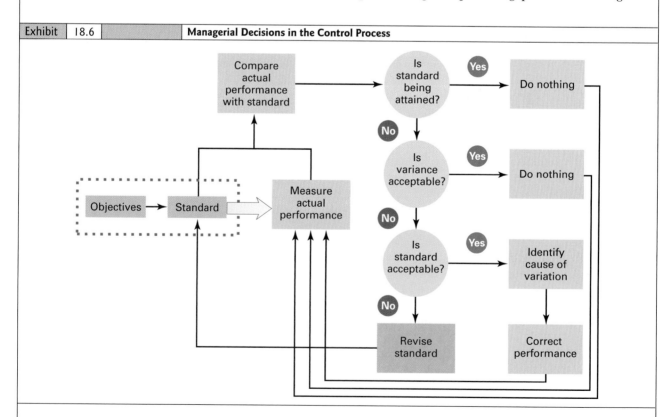

then provide the basis for the control process, which is essentially a continuous flow between measuring, comparing, and taking managerial action. Depending on the results of comparing, a manager's decisions about what course of action to take might be to do nothing, revise the standard, or correct the performance.

4. **What are the three steps in the control process?**

5. **Name four methods managers can use to acquire information about actual performance.**

6. **Contrast the managerial actions of correcting actual performance and revising standards.**

〉 TYPES OF CONTROL

Managers can implement controls *before* an activity begins, *during* the time the activity is going on, and *after* the activity has been completed. The first type is called *feedforward control*, the second is *concurrent control*, and the last is *feedback control*. (See Exhibit 18.7.)

FEEDFORWARD CONTROL

The most desirable type of control—**feedforward control**—prevents anticipated problems since it takes place in advance of the actual activity. It's future directed.[7] Let's look at some examples of feedforward control.

When McDonald's opened its first restaurant in Moscow, it sent company quality control experts to help Russian farmers learn techniques for growing high-quality potatoes and bakers to teach processes for baking high-quality breads. Why? Because McDonald's strongly emphasizes product quality no matter the geographical location. They want a cheeseburger in Moscow to taste like one in Omaha. Another example of feedforward control is the move by several prestigious U.S. accounting firms to dump potentially high-risk clients. The fear

feedforward control

A type of control that focuses on preventing anticipated problems since it takes place in advance of the actual work activity.

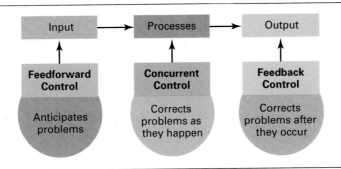

Exhibit	18.7

Types of Control

of costly litigation and damaged reputations led to decisions by high-level managers at the Big Five accounting firms to drop certain publicly traded companies as audit clients.[8] Still another example of feedforward control is the scheduled preventive maintenance programs on aircraft done by the major airlines. These are designed to detect and, it is hoped, to prevent structural damage that might lead to an accident.

The key to feedforward controls, therefore, is taking managerial action *before* a problem occurs. Feedforward controls are desirable because they allow managers to prevent problems rather than having to correct them later after the damage (such as poor-quality products, lost customers, lost revenue, and so forth) has already been done. Unfortunately, these controls require timely and accurate information that often is difficult to get. As a result, managers frequently end up using the other two types of controls.

CONCURRENT CONTROL

concurrent control

A type of control that takes place while a work activity is in progress.

feedback control

A type of control that takes place after a work activity is done.

Concurrent control, as its name implies, takes place while an activity is in progress. When control is enacted while the work is being performed, management can correct problems before they become too costly.

The best-known form of concurrent control is direct supervision. When a manager directly oversees the actions of employees, the manager can concurrently monitor their actions and correct problems as they occur. Although, obviously, there's some delay between the activity and the manager's corrective response, the delay is minimal. Problems can usually be addressed before much resource waste or damage has been done. Technical equipment (computers, computerized machine controls, and so forth) can be programmed to include concurrent controls. For instance, you may have experienced concurrent control when using a computer program such as word-processing software that alerts you to misspelled words or incorrect grammatical usage. In addition, many organizational quality programs rely on concurrent controls to inform workers if their work output is of sufficient quality to meet standards.

FEEDBACK CONTROL

The most popular type of control relies on feedback. The control takes place *after* the activity is done. For instance, the control report that Chris Tanner (from our earlier Eastern States' example) used for assessing beer sales is an example of **feedback control**.

The major drawback of this type of control is that by the time the manager has the information, the problems have already occurred and led to waste or damage. But for many activities, feed-

Concurrent controls are frequent in service businesses, such as the online pet supply company Petco.com, and vice president Tim Allen knows it. During the 1999 holiday season, a flood of orders overloaded one of the firm's distribution centers, and thousands of complaints resulted. The company responded with an apology to its customers and a budget of more than $10 million to develop new customer-service software that doubled the number of calls its service staff could handle.

back is the only viable type of control available. For instance, financial statements are an example of feedback controls. If, for example, the income statement shows that sales revenues are declining, the decline has already occurred. So at this point, the manager's only option is to try to determine why sales decreased and to correct the situation.

Feedback has two advantages over feedforward and concurrent control.[9] First, feedback provides managers with meaningful information on how effective their planning efforts were. Feedback that indicates little variance between standard and actual performance is evidence that the planning was generally on target. If the deviation is significant, a manager can use that information when formulating new plans to make them more effective. Second, feedback control can enhance employee motivation. People want information on how well they have performed. Feedback control provides that information.

Feedback is always useful, although it sometimes comes too late to prevent problems. When Chris Zane of Zane's Cycles agreed to work with General Mills on a bicycle-giveaway sweepstakes, he never anticipated that a grocery chain in Ohio would find a way to earn 28 Trek bicycles in the promotion and later sell the $260 bikes for $79 apiece. "It really screwed up the value of the product," Zane reports. Although he was able to ride out the crisis, Zane learned that there were certain elements of the market that he would not be able to control.

⟩ IMPLICATIONS FOR MANAGERS

A $165 million NASA Mars polar lander probe disappears without a trace. Marriott International implements its First Ten program, setting a standard for hassle-free guest check-in (based on the belief that guests ideally should be in their rooms within the first 10 minutes of their arrival). Better financial controls implemented by CEO Pamela D. A. Reeve improves the financial results of Lightbridge, a Massachusetts-based company that helps telecommunications carriers acquire new clients and retain them.[10] As these three examples illustrate, controlling plays an important role in results and *is* an important function of managing. Without controls, managers would have insufficient information to resolve problems, make decisions, or take appropriate actions. How can managers perform the control function efficiently and effectively? To answer this question, we're going to look at the qualities of an effective control system, the contingency factors that affect the design of control systems, and how controls need to be adjusted for national differences.

QUALITIES OF AN EFFECTIVE CONTROL SYSTEM
Effective control systems tend to have certain characteristics in common.[11] The importance of these qualities varies with the situation, but we can generalize that effective control systems have 10 characteristics. These characteristics are explained in Exhibit 18.8.

Exhibit | 18.8 | **Qualities of an Effective Control System**

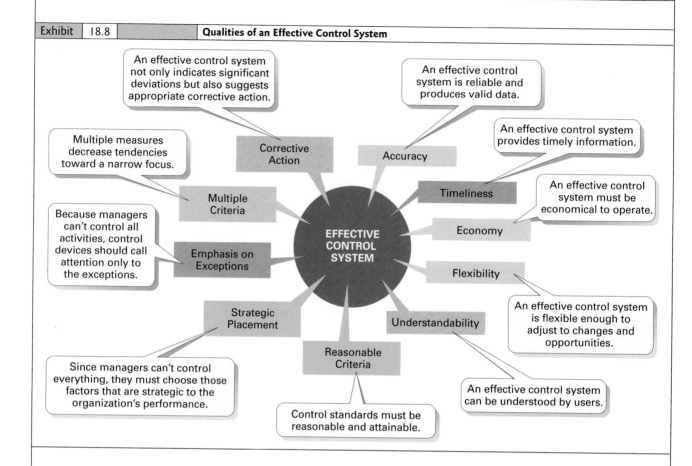

CONTINGENCY FACTORS IN CONTROL

Although our generalizations about effective control systems provide guidelines, their validity is influenced by situational factors. What types of contingency factors will affect the design of an organization's control system? These factors include the size of the organization, one's position and level in the organizational hierarchy, degree of decentralization, organizational culture, and importance of an activity. (See Exhibit 18.9.)

? **THINKING CRITICALLY ABOUT ETHICS**

Eric McKenzie owns and runs a political consulting business in Madison, Wisconsin. He has 14 employees. Last year, he devised a workplace policy that employees only have to tell their supervisor about their actions if they take home more than $3 of office supplies in a week. His philosophy is that office supplies are fairly inexpensive at wholesale prices, so the impact on the bottom line isn't that significant. Eric guesses that the average employee takes home about $25 a year in supplies, so he loses about $350 a year—about the same he figures he'd lose if his company had a more restrictive policy. The main difference, he believes, is that employees feel grateful about being trusted to use their common sense rather than feeling guilty.

What do you think about such a policy? Does it encourage other potentially unethical behavior? Would such a policy work in all types and sizes of organizations? Why or why not?

Exhibit | 18.9

Contingency Factors in the Design of Control Systems

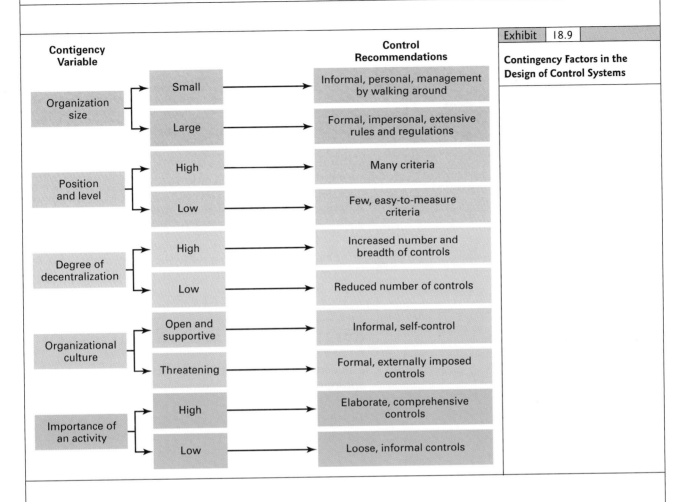

Contigency Variable		Control Recommendations
Organization size	Small	Informal, personal, management by walking around
	Large	Formal, impersonal, extensive rules and regulations
Position and level	High	Many criteria
	Low	Few, easy-to-measure criteria
Degree of decentralization	High	Increased number and breadth of controls
	Low	Reduced number of controls
Organizational culture	Open and supportive	Informal, self-control
	Threatening	Formal, externally imposed controls
Importance of an activity	High	Elaborate, comprehensive controls
	Low	Loose, informal controls

Control systems should vary according to the organization's size. A small organization relies more on informal and personal control approaches. Concurrent control through direct supervision is probably most cost-effective. However, as organizations increase in size, direct supervision is likely to be supplemented by an expanding formal control system of reports, regulations, and rules. Very large organizations will typically have highly formalized and impersonal feedforward and feedback controls.

The higher up one moves in the hierarchy, the greater the need for multiple sets of control criteria, tailored to the work unit's goals. This reflects the increased ambiguity in measuring performance as a person moves up the organizational hierarchy. Conversely, lower-level jobs have clearer definitions of performance, which allow for a narrower interpretation of job performance.

The greater the degree of decentralization, the more managers will need feedback on employees' decisions and performance results. Because managers who delegated the authority for making decisions and performing work are still ultimately responsible for the actions of those to whom it was delegated, they will want proper assurances that their employees' decisions and actions are both effective and efficient.

Control systems such as those that monitor the speed and accuracy of retail clerks are shaped by contingency factors like the size of the organization, one's position and level in the organization, the degree of centralization found in the firm, the importance of the activity, and the type of organizational culture. In the case of Wal-Mart's newest European acquisition, the British chain ASDA Group PLC, the size of the organization is very large, the clerk's position and level in the organization is low, centralization is relatively high, the activity is high in importance, and the culture is based on customer-friendly service, wide selection of items, and low prices.

The organizational culture may be one of trust, autonomy, and openness or one of fear, reprisal, and mistrust. In the former, we can expect to find informal self-control and, in the latter, externally imposed and formal control systems to ensure that performance is within standards. As we've discussed with leadership styles, motivation techniques, organizational structure decisions, conflict-management techniques, and the extent of participative decision making, the type and extent of controls should be consistent with the organization's culture.

Finally, the importance of an activity influences whether, and how, it will be controlled. If control is costly and the repercussions from error small, the control system isn't likely to be elaborate. However, if an error can be highly damaging to the organization, extensive controls are likely to be implemented—even if the cost is high.

ADJUSTING CONTROLS FOR CULTURAL DIFFERENCES

The concepts of control that we've been discussing are appropriate for an organization whose units are not geographically distant or culturally distinct. But what about global organizations? Would control systems be different, and what should managers know about adjusting controls for national differences?

Methods of controlling people and work can be quite different in other countries. The differences we see in organizational control systems of global organizations are primarily in the measurement and corrective action steps of the control process. In a global corporation, managers of foreign operations tend to be less controlled directly by the home office, if for no other reason than that distance keeps managers from being able to observe work directly. Because distance creates a tendency to formalize controls, the home office of a global company often relies on extensive formal reports for control. The global company also may use the power of information technology to control work activities. For instance, the Japanese retailer Ito-Yokado that owns the 7-Eleven convenience store chain uses automated cash registers not only to record sales and monitor inventory but also to schedule tasks for store managers and to track their use of the built-in analytical graphs and forecasts. If managers don't use them enough, they're told to increase their activities.[12]

Technology's impact on control also can be seen when comparing technologically advanced nations with less technologically advanced countries. In countries such as the United States, Japan, Canada, Great Britain, Germany, and Australia, managers of global companies use indirect control devices—particularly computer-related reports and analyses—in addition to standardized rules and direct supervision to ensure that work activities are going as planned. In less technologically advanced countries, managers tend to rely more on direct supervision and highly centralized decision making for control.

Also, constraints on what corrective actions managers can take may affect managers in foreign countries because laws in some countries do not allow managers the option of closing facilities, laying off employees, taking money out of the country, or bringing in a new management team from outside the country.

Finally, another challenge for global companies in collecting data is comparability. For instance, a company's manufacturing facility in Mexico might produce the same products as a facility in Scotland. However, the Mexican facility might be much more labor intensive than its Scottish counterpart (to take strategic advantage of lower labor costs in Mexico). If the top-level executives were to control costs by, for example, calculating labor costs per unit or output per worker, the figures would not be comparable. Managers in global companies must address these types of global control challenges.

Differences in national culture bring about differences in control mechanisms and the response that is expected if they fail. When Japan's Mitsubishi Motors became embroiled in public disgrace over the systematic cover-up of manufacturing defects that reached back over a period of 30 years, the company's president, Katsuhiko Kawasoe, bowed in apology to Japan's Transport Minister Hajime Morita and soon afterward resigned his position in the firm.

Testing...Testing...1,2,3

7. **Contrast the advantages and drawbacks of feedforward, concurrent, and feedback control.**

8. **What qualities will an effective control system have, and how will contingency factors affect the design of an organization's control system?**

9. **What types of control challenges do national differences present to managers?**

> ## CONTEMPORARY ISSUES IN CONTROL

There are issues that can arise as managers design efficient and effective control systems. Technological advances in computer hardware and software, for example, have made the process of controlling much easier, but these advances have brought with them difficult questions regarding what managers have the right to know about employees and how far they can go in controlling employee behavior. In this section, we're going to look at three contemporary issues in control: workplace privacy, employee theft, and workplace violence.

WORKPLACE PRIVACY

If you work, do you think you have a right to privacy at your workplace? What can your employer find out about you and your work? You might be surprised by the answers! Employers can (and do), among other things, read your e-mail

MANAGING IN AN E-BUSINESS WORLD — Controlling Issues in E-Business Organizations

What types of controlling issues do managers in e-businesses have to deal with?[13] The two most important ones are controlling distractions at work and controlling the potential for harassment, bias, discrimination, and other offensive behavior.

We discussed in Chapter 16 how employees in e-businesses are particularly susceptible to distractions at work, especially if their jobs aren't interesting or if they create excessive stress. Because computers are the lifeblood of any e-business, employees must have computers and access to online information. Thus, it's not possible to eliminate the distractions of Web surfing, playing online games, sending personal e-mail, shopping online, or engaging in any other type of online entertainment when employees are logged on in order to do their work. Another aspect of this particular control issue is that an e-business's employees may not even be on-site. Many e-business employees are virtual employees, located across town or maybe even halfway around the world. Their only contact with their manager and the company is via the computer. There's no opportunity for managing by walking around. The manager can't pop his or her head in the door at any time to see how things are going. Given these challenging realities, how can managers hope to control employee work performance in e-businesses?

It can help to think of control for potential work distractions in terms of feedforward, concurrent, and feedback mechanisms. In terms of feedforward control, the most productive e-business employees are likely to be those who can work effectively on their own and who can exercise self-control, so managers should try to hire those types of individuals. Establish work policies that are flexible yet that make it clear that work must be completed efficiently and effectively. As far as concurrent control, maintain open and continual communication—especially in a virtual environment where employees may not have physical contact with their managers for weeks or months at a time. And that communication shouldn't always take the form of e-mail, although that's the most obvious choice. Even the most reclusive e-business employee needs some verbal contact occasionally. It also may be necessary to occasionally monitor an employee's work using selected monitoring software. However, employees should be made aware that their work could be monitored. And recognize that employees may actually be more productive if they use some time while working to let off steam by surfing the Web or playing computer games. Finally, feedback controls should include having employees submit regular reports indicating the types and amount of work being accomplished.

The second major control issue that managers in e-businesses may have to contend with is the potential for harassment, bias, discrimination, and offensive sexual behavior from Internet and e-mail abuses. There is increasing evidence that many employees fail to use the same constraints in electronic communications that they use in traditional work settings. As one attorney noted, employees and managers "all know that they can't hang up a *Penthouse* calendar in the workplace. They all know they can't make a racist or sexist joke in the workplace." But those same people may think it's acceptable to send racial and sexist jokes via e-mail or to download pornography at work. After all, there's something about the ease of hitting that send or download button that seems to cause people to lose their sense of proper and legal behavior. How can e-business managers deal with this particular control issue?

All organizations, but especially e-businesses, need a policy that specifically defines inappropriate electronic communications. This policy also needs to reiterate management's right to monitor employee Internet and e-mail usage. If a harassment or discrimination allegation is made, electronic records can help establish what actually happened and can help managers react quickly. Finally, this policy should clearly specify disciplinary actions for any violations or transgressions.

(even those marked "personal or confidential"), tap your telephone, monitor your work by computer, store and review computer files, and monitor you in an employee bathroom or dressing room. And these actions aren't all that uncommon. Today, 45 percent of all companies and 17 percent of *Fortune* 1000 companies use monitoring software of some type. The use of other forms of surveillance, such as video cameras, brings that total up to 67 percent. Exhibit 18.10 summarizes the percentage of employers engaging in different forms of electronic monitoring.[14]

Track telephone calls (numbers and time spent)	39%	
Store and review employee e-mail messages	27%	
Store and review computer files	21%	
Log computer time and keystrokes entered	15%	
Record and review telephone conversations	11%	
Store and review voice-mail messages	6%	

Exhibit 18.10

Workplace Monitoring

Source: American Management Association in "Your Boss Is Watching," *PC Computing*, March 2000, p. 88.

Why do managers feel they must monitor what employees are doing? A big reason is that employees are hired to work, not to surf the Web checking stock prices, placing bets at online casinos, or shopping for presents for family or friends. Recreational on-the-job Web surfing has been said to cost a billion dollars in wasted computer resources and billions of dollars in lost work productivity annually.[15] That's a significant cost to businesses.

Another reason that managers monitor employee e-mail and computer usage is that they don't want to risk being sued for creating a hostile workplace environment because of offensive messages or an inappropriate image displayed on a co-worker's computer screen. Concern about racial or sexual harassment is one of the reasons why companies might want to monitor or keep backup copies of all e-mail. This electronic record can help establish what actually happened and can help managers react quickly.[16]

Finally, managers want to ensure that company secrets aren't being leaked.[17] Although protecting intellectual property is important for all businesses, it's especially important in high-tech industries. Managers need to be certain that employees are not, even inadvertently, passing information on to others who could use that information to harm the company.

The consequences of inappropriate workplace computer usage can be serious for employees and companies.[18] For instance, shortly before Christmas 1999, 23 workers at a *New York Times* administrative center in Norfolk, Virginia, were fired, and a number of other employees were reprimanded for violating the company's policy that prohibits using the corporate e-mail system to "create, forward, or display any offensive or disruptive messages, including photographs, graphics, and audio material." A number of Xerox employees were dis-

Personnel badges that function as sensors can be used to locate employees (for instance, doctors on call in a hospital) or as security devices to monitor employee arrival and departure and to safeguard restricted areas. Some employees and privacy advocates find such devices to be an invasion of privacy. Do you think they serve a good purpose? What are some of the privacy issues they raise?

missed for spending as much as eight hours a day browsing X-rated and e-shopping Web sites during work hours. Two executives at Salomon Smith Barney were fired after a routine check of corporate e-mail turned up pornographic material. And Lockheed Martin's e-mail system crashed for six hours after an employee sent 60,000 co-workers an e-mail (asking them to respond back using an attached e-receipt) about a national prayer day. Since Lockheed depended heavily on its internal e-mail communication system, this crash cost the company hundreds of thousands of dollars.

Even with all the workplace monitoring that managers can do, employees in the United States do have some protection through the federal Electronic Communications Privacy Act of 1986. The ECPA prohibits unauthorized interception of electronic communication. Although this law gives employees some privacy protection, it doesn't make workplace electronic monitoring illegal as employers are allowed to monitor communications for business reasons or when employees have been notified of the practice.[19] Although employees may think that it's unfair for a company to monitor their work electronically and to fire them for what they feel are minor distractions, the courts have ruled that, since the computer belongs to the company, managers have a right to view everything on it.[20]

Because of the potentially serious costs and given the fact that these days many jobs now entail work that involves using a computer, many companies are developing and enforcing workplace monitoring policies. The responsibility for doing this falls on managers. It's important to develop some type of viable workplace monitoring policy. What can managers do to maintain control but do so in a way that isn't demeaning to employees? They should develop an unambiguous computer usage policy and make sure that every employee knows about it. Tell employees up front that their computer use may be monitored at any time and provide clear and specific guidelines as to what constitutes acceptable use of company e-mail systems and the Web.

EMPLOYEE THEFT

Would it surprise you to find out that up to 85 percent of all organizational theft and fraud is committed by employees, not outsiders?[21] And, it's a costly problem—estimated to be around $200 billion each year for U.S. companies.[22] **Employee theft** is defined as any unauthorized taking of company property by employees for their personal use.[23] It can range from embezzlement to fraudulent filing of expense reports to removing equipment, parts, software, and office supplies from company premises. Although retail businesses have long faced particularly serious potential losses from employee theft, loose financial controls at start-ups and small companies and the ready availability of information technology have made employee stealing an escalating problem in all kinds and sizes of organizations. It's a control issue that managers need to educate themselves about and with which they must be prepared to deal.[24]

Why do employees steal? The answer depends on whom you ask.[25] Experts in various fields—industrial security, criminology, clinical psychology—all have different perspectives. The industrial security people propose that people steal because the opportunity presents itself through lax controls and favorable circumstances. Criminologists say that it's because people have financial-based

employee theft

Any unauthorized taking of company property by employees for their personal use.

Feedforward	Concurrent	Feedback	
			Exhibit 18.11
			Control Measures for Deterring or Reducing Employee Theft or Fraud
Careful prehiring screening.	Treat employees with respect and dignity.	Make sure employees know when theft or fraud has occurred—not naming names but letting people know this is not acceptable.	
Establish specific policies defining theft and fraud and discipline procedures.	Openly communicate the costs of stealing.	Use the services of professional investigators.	
Involve employees in writing policies.	Let employees know on a regular basis about their successes in preventing theft and fraud.	Redesign control measures.	
Educate and train employees about the policies.	Use video surveillance equipment if conditions warrant.	Evaluate your organization's culture and the relationships of managers and employees.	
Have professionals review your internal security controls.	Install "lock-out" options on computers, telephones, and e-mail.		
	Use corporate hot lines for reporting incidences.		
	Set a good example.		

Sources: Based on A.H. Bell and D.M. Smith, "Protecting the Company Against Theft and Fraud," *Workforce Online*, (www.workforce.com), December 3, 2000; J.D. Hansen, "To Catch a Thief," *Journal of Accountancy*, March 2000, pp. 43–46; and J. Greenberg, "The Cognitive Geometry of Employee Theft," in *Dysfunctional Behavior in Organizations: Nonviolent and Deviant Behavior* (Stamford, CT: JAI Press, 1998), pp. 147–93.

pressures (such as personal financial problems) or vice-based pressures (such as gambling debts). And the clinical psychologists suggest that people steal because they can rationalize whatever they're doing as being correct and appropriate behavior ("everyone does it," "they had it coming," "this company makes enough money and they'll never miss anything this small," "I deserve this for all that I put up with," and so forth).[26] Although each of these approaches provides compelling insights into employee theft and has been instrumental in program designs to deter it, unfortunately, employees continue to steal. So what can managers do? Let's look at some suggestions for managing employee theft.

We can use the concept of feedforward, concurrent, and feedback control to identify measures for deterring or reducing employee theft.[27] Exhibit 18.11 summarizes several possible managerial actions.

WORKPLACE VIOLENCE

The news headlines relate the sad details of an Atlanta stock day trader gunning down individuals at a brokerage office. The popular media coined the term *going postal* (because of incidences of postal employees gunning down their co-workers) to describe individuals who are pushed over the edge and become violent. Is workplace violence *really* an issue with which managers might have to deal?

Exhibit 18.12		
Workplace Violence	Witnessed yelling or other verbal abuse	42%
	Yelled at co-workers themselves	29%
	Cried over work-related issues	23%
	Seen someone purposely damage machines or furniture	14%
	Seen physical violence in the workplace	10%
	Struck a co-worker	2%

Source: Integra Realty Resources, October–November Survey of Adults 18 and Over, in "Desk Rage," *Business Week*, November 20, 2000, p. 12.

Although the number of workplace homicides is decreasing,[28] the U.S. Department of Justice estimates that workplace assaults of all types claim more than 1 million victims each year. Other experts put the figure at closer to 2 million. Exhibit 18.12 describes the results from a survey of workers and their experiences with office rage. Not only is workplace violence and office rage happening, it's a serious problem. The annual cost to U.S. businesses is estimated at between 20 and 35 billion dollars.[29]

What factors are believed to be contributing to workplace violence? Undoubtedly, employee stress caused by long hours, information overload, other daily interruptions, unrealistic deadlines, and uncaring managers play a role. Even office layout designs with small cubicles where employees work amidst the noise and commotion from those around them have been cited as contributing to the problem.[30] Other experts have described dangerously dysfunctional work environments characterized by the following as primary contributors to the problem[31]:

- Employee work driven by TNC (time, numbers, and crises).

- Rapid and unpredictable change in which instability and uncertainty plague employees.

- Destructive communication style in which managers communicate in an excessively aggressive, condescending, explosive, or passive-aggressive style; excessive workplace teasing or scapegoating.

- Authoritarian leadership with a rigid, militaristic mind-set of managers versus employees; employees aren't allowed to challenge ideas, participate in decision making, or engage in team-building efforts.

- Defensive attitude in which little or no performance feedback is given; only numbers count; and yelling, intimidation, and avoidance are the preferred ways of handling conflict.

- Double standards in terms of policies, procedures, and training opportunities for managers and employees.

- Unresolved grievances because there are no mechanisms or only adversarial ones in place for resolving them; dysfunctional individuals may be protected or ignored because of long-standing rules, union contract provisions, or reluctance to take care of problems.

- Emotionally troubled employees and no attempt by managers to get help for these people.

- Repetitive, boring work in which there's no chance of doing something else or of new people coming in.

- Faulty or unsafe equipment or deficient training that keeps employees from being able to work efficiently or effectively.

- Hazardous work environment in terms of temperature, air quality, repetitive motions, overcrowded spaces, noise levels, excessive overtime, and so forth. To minimize costs, no additional employees are hired when workload becomes excessive, leading to potentially dangerous work expectations and conditions.

- Culture of violence in which there's a history of individual violence or abuse; violent or explosive role models; or tolerance of on-the-job alcohol or drug abuse.

Reading through this list, you may feel that workplaces where you'll spend your professional life won't be anything like this. However, the competitive

Feedforward	Concurrent	Feedback	Exhibit 18.13
			Control Measures for Deterring or Reducing Workplace Violence
Management commitment to functional, not dysfunctional, work environments.	MBWA (managing by walking around) to identify potential problems; observe how employees treat and interact with each other.	Communicate openly about incidences and what's being done.	
Employee assistance programs (EAP) to help employees with serious behavioral problems.	Allow employees or work groups to "grieve" during periods of major organizational change.	Investigate incidences and take appropriate action.	
Organizational policy that any workplace rage, aggression, or violence will not be tolerated.	Be a good role model in how you treat others.	Review company policies and change, if necessary.	
Careful prehiring screening.	Use corporate hot lines or some mechanism for reporting and investigating incidences.		
Never ignore threats.	Use quick and decisive intervention.		
Train employees about how to avoid danger if situation arises.	Get expert professional assistance if violence erupts.		
Clearly communicate policies to employees.	Provide necessary equipment or procedures for dealing with violent situations (cell phones, alarm systems, code names or phrases, and so forth).		

Sources: Based on M. Gorkin, "Five Strategies and Structures for Reducing Workplace Violence," *Workforce Online* (www.workforce.com), December 3, 2000; "Investigating Workplace Violence: Where Do You Start?" *Workforce Online* (www.forceforce.com), December 3, 2000; "Ten Tips on Recognizing and Minimizing Violence," *Workforce Online* (www.workforce.com), December 3, 2000; and "Points to Cover in a Workplace Violence Policy," *Workforce Online* (www.workforce.com), December 3, 2000.

demands of succeeding in a 24-7 global economy put pressure on organizations and employees in many ways.

What can managers do to deter or reduce possible workplace violence? Once again, we can use the concept of feedforward, concurrent, and feedback control to identify actions that managers can take.[32] Exhibit 18.13 summarizes several suggestions.

Testing...Testing...1,2,3

10. **How do issues of workplace privacy affect managerial controls?**

11. **What can managers do to control employee theft?**

12. **Why is workplace violence an organizational control problem?**

Managers Respond to "A Manager's Dilemma"

Wayne Price

Director, Risk Management
O'Reilly Auto Parts, Springfield, Missouri

Diane L. Dudley

Partner, KPMG, LLP, Washington, DC

E-commerce has made many of the traditional approaches to security obsolete. However, to determine the true risk/reward potential, a risk assessment needs to be done and then a risk management strategy needs to be developed.

Saleem should assess risk by doing a thorough operational review of Web site sales projections, current percentage of fraudulent transactions, and what individual transaction limits currently exist. The risk management strategy should include one or more of the following: risk retention (profit potential outweighs costs), risk avoidance (Web-based sales potential doesn't justify risk exposure), risk transfer (insurance or noninsurance protection), and loss control (implementing various screening mechanisms such as digital verification, callback procedures, and so forth).

I think a key for Saleem is to access resources beyond Mustafa's. Credit card companies, Web site designers, and Internet consultants all see tremendous profit potential from Internet sales, but high costs from fraudulent transactions could deter such use. It's in these companies' best interests to help provide guidance and perhaps even a level of financial protection.

Internet fraud prevention requires several layers of security. Mustafa's Web site must provide a secure environment for customers and protect the company.

Mohamed should add some steps to validate each customer order in addition to obtaining the applicable credit card company authorization. Don't accept orders unless complete information (full address and phone number) is provided. Don't accept orders that come from free e-mail services. Mustafa's personnel should verify transactions with "bill to" addressed differently from the "ship to" addresses and orders that are larger than the typical amounts. For these, Mohamed should implement a policy to call customers and ask them to send a fax with their signature and a photocopy of their credit card.

Next, Mohamed should consider contracting with an Internet billing company to verify Mustafa's credit card sales transactions. These companies can screen credit card transactions and can identify questionable purchases. The cost of such a service is likely to be less than the resulting savings.

Finally, Mohamed should continually review the company's security procedures to ensure that its systems provide adequate prevention of fraud.

Chapter Summary

This summary is organized around the chapter-opening objectives found on p. 494.

1. Control is the process of monitoring activities to ensure that they're being accomplished as planned and of correcting any significant deviations.

2. The three approaches to control are market control, bureaucratic control, and clan control. Market control is an approach that emphasizes external market mechanisms, such as price competition and relative market share, to establish the standards used in the control system. Bureaucratic control emphasizes organizational authority and relies on administrative rules, regulations, procedures, and policies. Under clan control systems, employee behaviors are regulated by the shared values, norms, traditions, rituals, beliefs, and other aspects of the organizational culture.

3. Control is important because it monitors whether goals are being accomplished as planned and delegated authority is being abused.

4. In the control process, managers must first have performance standards, which come from the goals formed in the planning stage. Then managers must measure actual performance and compare that performance against the standards (goals). If a variance exists between actual and standard, managers must either adjust the performance, adjust the standards, or do nothing.

5. The three types of control are as follows: Feedforward control is future-directed and prevents problems. Concurrent control takes place while an activity is in progress. Feedback control takes place after the activity has been completed.

6. An effective control system is accurate, timely, economical, flexible, and understandable. It uses reasonable criteria, has strategic placement, emphasizes the exception, uses multiple criteria, and suggests corrective action.

7. The contingency factors that influence the design of an organization's control system include organizational size, level in hierarchy, degree of decentralization, organizational culture, and the activity's importance. As organizations grow in size, direct supervision is supplemented by more formal control measures. The higher one is in the organizational hierarchy, the more that multiple sets of control criteria are needed. The greater the degree of decentralization, the more performance feedback managers will need. In organizational cultures characterized by trust, autonomy, and openness, informal self-controls are likely; however, in cultures characterized by fear, reprisal, and mistrust, it's more likely that more external and formal control systems will be used. Finally, if an activity is important and errors can be highly damaging, extensive controls are likely to be implemented, no matter what the cost.

8. Controls need to be adjusted for national differences because methods of controlling people and work can be quite different in other countries. The differences are primarily in the measurement and corrective action steps of the control process.

9. Workplace privacy issues affect control since managers may feel they need to monitor what employees are doing because of wasted computer resources and lost work productivity, the risks of creating a hostile work environment because of offensive e-mail messages or inappropriate images displayed on workers' computer screens, and to ensure that company secrets aren't being leaked on purpose or inadvertently. Employee theft is an important control issue since it's a costly problem for U.S. businesses and there are ways to deter or reduce it. Finally, workplace violence affects control since it, too, is costly for U.S. businesses and can be deterred or reduced.

Thinking About Management Issues

1. What would an organization have to do to change its dominant control approach from bureaucratic to clan? From clan to bureaucratic?

2. In Chapter 13 we discussed the white-water rapids view of change. Do you think it's possible to establish and maintain effective standards and controls in this type of environment? Explain.

3. How could you use the concept of control in your own personal life? Be specific. (Think in terms of feedforward, concurrent, and feedback controls as well as controls for the different areas of your life.)

4. When do electronic surveillance devices such as computers, video cameras, and telephone monitoring step over the line from effective management controls to intrusions on employee rights?

5. "Every individual employee in the organization plays a role in controlling work activities." Do you agree, or do you think control is something for which only managers are responsible? Explain.

Log On: Internet-Based Exercise

Employee theft and fraud are common problems for organizations. Find three examples of organizations that have experienced employee theft and fraud. What type of theft or fraud took place? What steps did the organization take to deal with the problem immediately and in the future?

Find three companies that help organizations deal with employee theft and fraud. What suggestions do they give for managing these problems?

myPHLIP Companion Web Site

myPHLIP *(www.prenhall.com/myphlip) is a fully customizable homepage that ties students and faculty to text-specific resources.*

- ***For students**, myPHLIP provides an online study guide tied chapter-by-chapter to the text—current events and Internet exercises, lecture notes, downloadable software, the Career Center, the Writing Center, Ask the Tutor, and more.*
- ***For faculty**, myPHLIP provides a syllabus tool that allows you to manage content, communicate with students, and upload personal resources.*

Working Together: Team-Based Exercise

You're a professor in the School of Accountancy at Collins State College. Several of your colleagues have expressed an interest in developing some specific controls to minimize opportunities for students to cheat on homework assignments and exams. You and some other faculty members have volunteered to write a report outlining some suggestions that might be used.

Form teams of three or four and discuss this topic. Write a bulleted list of your suggestions from the perspective of controlling possible cheating (1) before it happens, (2) while in-class exams or assignments are being completed, and (3) after it has happened. Please keep the report brief (no more than two pages). Be prepared to present your suggestions before the rest of the class.

Case Application

Surf's Up

Digital dillydallying. Cyberloafing. As more and more organizations look to provide employees with the latest in technology and online access, the potential for workplace abuse of the newest tools, and the time that it takes away from doing a job, grows. More than any other recent technological advancement, the Internet and World Wide Web have created opportunities for on-the-job loafing. Over 90 percent of employees surveyed by an online career information specialist say they have surfed non-work-related Web sites at some point during the day. But that's not the only shocking statistic—37.1 percent of

these individuals say they continuously surf the Web at work; 58.8 percent say they have received sexually explicit or otherwise improper e-mail at work; 24 percent say they take preventive measures to keep their bosses from catching them surfing; and 54 percent of employers say they have caught employees surfing non-business-related Web sites at work.

From the cyberloafer's point of view, the Internet is a perfect substitute for work because an employee can appear busy while goofing off! After all, Web searches and e-mail can look like serious business. Although not every log-on to e-mail or visit to a Web site involves an employee's goofing off, many organizations are recogniz-

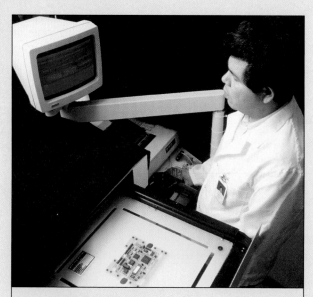

Western Digital employees, like countless other organizational employees, have at-work access to the Internet.

Canada, France, Germany, Hong Kong, Japan, Taiwan, United Kingdom, United Arab Emirates, and locations throughout the United States), Western Digital's managers knew that its communication system and customer service would benefit from employees' having access to the Internet. Western Digital's CEO, Matt Massengill continually emphasized and reinforced the importance of customer service. "Customers count on our commitment to excellence. Every product we design and manufacture, every customer contact, every internal task—everything we do—is measured by its contribution to customer satisfaction." Yet, these managers were also aware of the potential problems. Would the benefits of having employee Internet access outweigh the potential drawbacks? Managers thought they would. Western Digital's employees have at-work access to the Internet.

QUESTIONS

1. What other types of work benefits besides internal communication and customer service might be possible from Western Digital employees having access to the Internet and Web? Would these same types of benefits be applicable to other types of organizations? Explain.

2. What types of feedforward, concurrent, and feedback controls might Western Digital use in controlling the potential misuse of Internet access at work?

3. Develop a set of guidelines that Western Digital's managers could use to address the control issues of access to and use of the Internet and Web at work.

4. Given the fact that Western Digital operates in different global locations, would the company's Internet usage control system have to be different as well? Explain.

Sources: Company information from Hoover's Online (www.hoovers.com) and company's Web site (www.westerndigital.com), December 1, 2000; M.A. Verespej, "Everybody's Gone Surfing," *IW*, January 10, 2000, p. 11; and "Western Digital Corporation's Internet Access Policy," *Workforce Tools: Supplement to the January 1997 Issue of Workforce*, January 1997, pp. 1–3.

ing that they need to establish some controls for these new technologies.

At Western Digital Corporation, based in Irvine, California, managers weighed the pros and cons of providing Internet access to its 10,000 associates worldwide. Western Digital, founded in 1970, is a global provider of information storage products and services including a broad array of disk drives for personal and enterprise-wide computing. Its mission states: "Western Digital's mission is to satisfy our customers' requirements by providing world-class computing products and services. We will accomplish this mission through investments in people and technologies that generate sustained profitability." Employees carry out this vision doing their work using stated corporate values: integrity, leadership, customer satisfaction, individual responsibility, quality and continuous process improvement, and teamwork.

As a global company with employees in far-flung locations (including Malaysia, Singapore, Czech Republic,

---

Video Case Application

Keeping the Coffee Coming

SMALL BUSINESS 2000

At the Port of New Orleans, the largest coffee port in the United States, one company is handling an old-fashioned product in a new-fashioned way. Frederico Pacorini's SiloCaf, a fully computerized bulk coffee storage, handling, and processing facility, is a place where tradition meets technology.

SiloCaf was founded in 1933 as a forwarding company: in other words, a company that takes any product and moves it (forwards it) from one location to another location. Today, the company specializes in forwarding commodities, primarily coffee, and the way it handles coffee is about as high tech as it can get. Why has SiloCaf invested in technology for such a seemingly simple product? The main reason is that consumers want the same flavor from each and every can of coffee they buy. Coffee, however, is a natural product with impurities and defects, and coffee crops are never the same. Getting a consistent flavor is difficult without some way to control the coffee blend. SiloCaf is addressing this challenge by using computer and information systems technology.

Mossimo Toma is SiloCaf's systems and resources manager. He's responsible for overseeing the coffee-blending process. Coffee beans come into SiloCaf's warehouse from all over the world. Each week 10 million pounds of coffee are blended (about 4 million bags per year). The coffee never stays in SiloCaf's plant more than one week. Once it's been processed and blended, it's loaded into bags or in bulk and shipped to a coffee roasting company. At any one time, SiloCaf has from 35 million to 40 million pounds of coffee in its facility for processing. If you consider the price of a pound of coffee, SiloCaf has an extremely valuable resource in its possession. Actually, SiloCaf never owns the coffee; it's owned by the roasting company or the dealer who delivers the coffee to the roasting company.

All the mechanical parts in SiloCaf's New Orleans facility have been brought from Italy, which is where the company first developed its technology. Frederico Pacorini, the son of the founder and the manager of the New Orleans facility, says that technology in a business such as theirs is important because it allows them to make all the blends they need for their customers (coffee roasters), to optimize the way they do blends, and to control blends. SiloCaf's employees receive continual statistical reports for each one of the scales used to blend the coffee. The reports enable them to check the consistency of the scale's performance, which is important for achieving the product consistency that the end users (coffee drinkers) want.

You'd think that all this high-tech control would be expensive, but it's not. The nice thing about SiloCaf's solution to the blend consistency challenge is that the technology it's using is relatively simple. In fact, the company's initial investment was a mere 1 percent of all plant investment dollars spent.

QUESTIONS

1. What types of control do you see in this example? Be specific.
2. Given the nature of the product that SiloCaf processes, would feedforward controls be feasible? Why or why not? How about concurrent controls? Explain.
3. SiloCaf never owns the coffee it blends. Considering this fact, why would controls be important?
4. Do controls have to be expensive to be effective? Discuss.

Source: Based on *Small Business 2000, Show 109.*

Learning Objectives

After reading and studying this chapter, you should be able to:

1. Describe the role of the transformation process in operations management.

2. Explain why operations management is important to all types of organizations.

3. Define value chain management.

4. Discuss the goal of value chain management.

5. Explain the organizational and managerial requirements for value chain management.

6. Describe the benefits of and obstacles to value chain management.

7. Discuss technology's role in operations management.

8. Describe how quality affects operations management.

9. Explain ISO 9000 and Six Sigma.

A MANAGER'S DILEMMA

Titus Lokananta represents an interesting global phenomenon. He's an Indonesian Cantonese with a German passport working for a large Mexican company in the Czech Republic! As plant manager for Mexican food company Grupo Industrial Bimbo SA, his plant, located in Ostrava, Czech Republic, produces sweet, gooey gummy bears.[1]

Many Mexican multinationals are turning themselves into global powerhouses and fervently support globalization. Bimbo is a good example. In the late 1980s, a buyer for McDonald's stopped by the company's baked goods facilities in Mexico in search of a local supplier of buns. It only took a single bite for the buyer to reject Bimbo's product. That rejection inspired Bimbo's chairman to invest significant resources to bake a bun good enough for McDonald's. And it worked! Bimbo has progressed from being McDonald's preferred supplier to being its exclusive one. As McDonald's has moved into foreign markets, so has Bimbo. Today, Bimbo's global workforce of around 16,000 makes much of the sliced bread, snacks, and tortillas eaten by consumers in Latin America as well as candy and cakes in over 16 countries. It's hoping that the gummy bear factory in the Czech Republic can become a strong contributor to the company's global business.

In 1995, Bimbo realized that its candy-making technology was obsolete. To improve its candy making, it began to do contract work for Park

Operations and Value Chain Management

19

Lane Confectionery GmbH of Germany. After learning all it could from the Germans, Bimbo bought Park Lane from its bankrupt owners. The company selected Lokananta, one of its liaisons at Park Lane, to run the Czech candy factory.

Lokananta hired back most of the factory's former workforce and went to work boosting productivity. One of his first managerial actions was persuading assembly-line workers to take lunch breaks in shifts so production lines could run continuously. Now he's ready for the next challenge—boosting quality. Put yourself in Lokananta's position. What could he do to successfully implement a quality program in this plant?

WHAT WOULD YOU DO?

This chapter focuses on the importance of operations management to the organization. Operations management encompasses such topics as efficiency, productivity, value chain management, e-manufacturing, and quality. As our chapter-opening Manager's Dilemma points out, it's important for managers everywhere to have well-thought-out and well-designed operating systems, organizational control systems, and quality programs to survive in the increasingly competitive global environment. If managers such as Titus Lokananta have these systems, their organizations will be able to produce high-quality products and services at prices that meet or beat those of their competitors.

❯ WHAT IS OPERATIONS MANAGEMENT AND WHY IS IT IMPORTANT?

operations management

The design, operation, and control of the transformation process that converts resources into finished goods or services.

The term **operations management** refers to the design, operation, and control of the transformation process that converts such resources as labor and raw materials into goods and services that are sold to customers. Exhibit 19.1 portrays, in a very simplified fashion, the fact that every organization has an operations system that creates value by transforming inputs into outputs. The system takes in inputs—people, technology, capital, equipment, materials, and information—and transforms them through various processes, procedures, work activities, and so forth into finished goods and services. And just as every organization produces something, every unit in an organization also produces something. Marketing, finance, research and development, human resources, and accounting convert inputs into outputs such as sales, increased market share, high rates of return on capital, new and innovative products, motivated and committed employees, and accounting reports. As a manager, you'll need to be familiar with operations management concepts regardless of the area you manage in order to achieve your goals efficiently and effectively.

Why is operations management so important to organizations and managers? There are three reasons: It encompasses both services and manufacturing, it's important in effectively and efficiently managing productivity, and it plays a strategic role in an organization's competitive success.

SERVICES AND MANUFACTURING

manufacturing organizations

Organizations that produce physical goods.

Every organization produces something. Unfortunately, this fact is often overlooked except in obvious cases such as in the manufacturing of cars, cell phones, or candy gummy bears. After all, **manufacturing organizations** produce

Exhibit	19.1

The Operations System

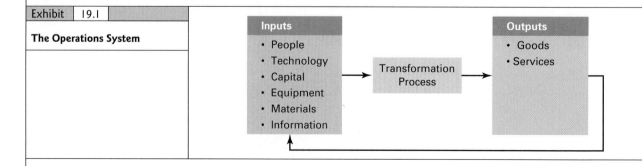

physical goods. It's easy to see the operations management (transformation) process at work in these types of organizations because raw materials are turned into recognizable physical products. But that transformation process isn't as readily evident in **service organizations** because they produce nonphysical outputs in the form of services. For instance, hospitals provide medical and health care services that help people manage their personal health, airlines provide transportation services that move people from one location to another, a cruise line provides a vacation and entertainment service, military forces provide defense capabilities, and the list goes on and on. All of these service organizations transform inputs into outputs, although the transformation process isn't as easily recognizable as that of manufacturing organizations. Take a university, for example. University administrators bring together inputs—professors, books, academic journals, audiovisual materials, computers, classrooms, and similar resources—to transform "unenlightened" students into educated and skilled individuals.

The reason we're making this point is that the U.S. economy has gone from being dominated by the creation and sale of manufactured goods to the creation and sale of services. In fact, most of the world's industrialized nations are predominantly service economies. In the United States, for instance, approximately 75 percent of all private sector jobs are now in service industries.[2] For a few other industrialized countries, services employment is as follows: United Kingdom—69 percent; Japan—65 percent; Chile—61 percent; Germany—68 percent; Canada—75 percent; Australia—73 percent; and Mexico—55 percent.[3]

Every organization produces something. Consumer's Medical Resource, for instance, is a service organization that provides the employees of Honeywell Inc. with up-to-date medical information they can use to make informed decisions about needed medical treatment. Consumer's Medical Resource transforms its resources, such as the expertise of researcher Lori Habersaat and Dr. Maureen Tierney, pictured here counseling a seriously ill patient via conference call, into outputs such as improved access to appropriate care.

MANAGING PRODUCTIVITY

Improving productivity has become a major goal in virtually every organization. By **productivity**, we mean the overall output of goods or services produced divided by the inputs needed to generate that output. For countries, high productivity can lead to economic growth and development. Employees can receive higher wages and company profits can increase without causing inflation. For individual organizations, increased productivity gives them a more competitive cost structure and the ability to offer more competitive prices.

Increasing productivity is a key to global competitiveness. For instance, a great deal of Japan's economic prosperity in the 1980s can be explained in terms of improved manufacturing productivity in businesses. As Japanese businesses become more competitive, U.S. businesses responded by making dramatic improvements to increase their efficiency. For example, at heavy equipment manufacturer Caterpillar, Inc., investments in productivity enhancements of both its workforce and technology resulted in higher customer satisfaction, an increasing market share, and 27 percent greater sales with 29 percent fewer employees.[4] DaimlerChrysler found that making simple changes such as having assembly-line workers take coffee breaks in shifts rather than all at once increased worker productivity by 10 to 12 percent in just two years.[5]

service organizations

Organizations that produce nonphysical outputs in the form of services.

productivity

The overall output of goods or services produced divided by the inputs needed to generate that output.

Increasing productivity has become a priority for many U.S. firms. Delphi Automotive Systems Corp., a company that is almost 100 years old, has changed more in the last 2 years than in most of its previous history. With 2,220 employees, including quality assembler Julia Nelson pictured here, the newly reconstructed plant makes customized catalytic converters for the auto industry. Says Peter Wood, manufacturing systems manager at the plant, "Delivery used to take 21 days. But now, if you order on Monday, we can deliver on that precise order by Friday."

Even today, organizations that hope to succeed globally are looking for ways to improve productivity. For example, McDonald's drastically reduced the amount of time it takes to cook its french fries—now only 65 seconds as compared to the 210 seconds it once took, saving time and other resources.[6] The Canadian Imperial Bank of Commerce based in Toronto automated its purchasing function, saving several million dollars annually.[7] And Skoda Auto a.s., the Czech car company owned by Germany's Volkswagen AG, improved its productivity through an intensive restructuring of its manufacturing process and now produces 500 cars per day, almost doubling the number it used to make.[8]

Productivity is a composite of people and operations variables. To improve productivity, managers must focus on both. W. Edwards Deming, a management consultant and quality expert, believed that managers, not workers, were the primary source of increased productivity. He outlined 14 points for improving management's productivity. (See Exhibit 19.2.) A close look at these suggestions reveals Deming's understanding of the interplay between people and operations. High productivity can't come solely from good "people management." The truly effective organization will maximize productivity by successfully integrating people into the overall operations system. For instance, field engineers for GE Medical Systems, a division of General Electric, used to haul around on service calls a trunkful of service and repair manuals weighing about 200 pounds to repair the company's massive imaging machines that were installed at hospitals and clinics around the world. If the technician didn't have the right manual on hand while working on the equipment, a trip to the car was necessary to get the right one. The engineers estimated that they wasted as much as 15 percent of their time during a service call going back and forth to their cars. The company solved the problem by equipping its field engineers (around 2,500 in the United States alone) with laptop computers that held all the information the technician might ever need. Although this investment in information technology cost millions of dollars, the field engineers' productivity rose by 9 percent.[9] The company recognized the important interplay between people and the operations system.

STRATEGIC ROLE OF OPERATIONS MANAGEMENT

The era of modern manufacturing originated over 95 years ago in the United States, primarily in Detroit's automobile factories. Then the success that U.S. manufacturers experienced during World War II led manufacturing executives to believe that troublesome production problems had been conquered and required little managerial attention. These executives focused on improving other functional areas such as finance and marketing. From the late 1940s through the mid-1970s, manufacturing activities in the United States were taken for granted, and to some extent, slighted. With an occasional exception (such as the aerospace industry), corporate managers gave manufacturing little attention.

Meanwhile, as U.S. executives neglected the production side of their businesses, managers in Japan, Germany, and other countries took the opportunity to

Exhibit 19.2

Deming's 14 Points for Improving Management's Productivity

1. Plan for the long-term future.
2. Never be complacent concerning the quality of your product.
3. Establish statistical control over your production processes and require your suppliers to do so as well.
4. Deal with the best and fewest number of suppliers.
5. Find out whether your problems are confined to particular parts of the production process or stem from the overall process itself.
6. Train workers for the job that you are asking them to perform.
7. Raise the quality of your line supervisors.
8. Drive out fear.
9. Encourage departments to work closely together rather than to concentrate on departmental or divisional distinctions.
10. Do not adopt strictly numerical goals.
11. Require your workers to do quality work.
12. Train your employees to understand statistical methods.
13. Train your employees in new skills as the need arises.
14. Make top managers responsible for implementing these principles.

Source: W.E. Deming, "Improvement of Quality and Productivity Through Action by Management," *National Productivity Review,* Winter 1981–1982, pp. 12–22. With permission. Copyright 1981 by Executive Enterprises, Inc., 22 West 21st St., New York, NY 10010-6904. All rights reserved.

develop modern, computer-based, and technologically advanced facilities that fully integrated manufacturing operations into strategic planning decisions. The competition's success realigned world manufacturing leadership. U.S. manufacturers soon discovered that foreign goods were being made not only less expensively but also with better quality. Finally, by the late 1970s, U.S. executives recognized that they were facing a true crisis and responded.[10] They invested heavily in improving manufacturing technology, increased the corporate authority and visibility of manufacturing executives, and began incorporating existing and future production requirements into the organization's overall strategic plan. Today, successful manufacturers recognize the crucial role that operations management plays as part of the overall organizational strategy to establish and maintain global leadership.

The strategic role that operations management plays in successful organizational performance can be seen clearly as more organizations move toward managing their operations from a value chain perspective, which we discuss next. ←

Testing...Testing...1,2,3

1. **What is operations management, and how is it used in both manufacturing and service organizations?**

2. **Explain why managing productivity is important in operations management.**

3. **What strategic role does operations management play?**

〉 VALUE CHAIN MANAGEMENT

It's 11 P.M., and you're listening to a voice mail from your parents saying they want to buy you a computer for your birthday this year. They want you to order it so you have it to help you in your studies this semester. You log on to Dell Computer's Web site and configure your dream machine that will serve even your most demanding computing needs for the remainder of your college years. You hit the order button and within three or four days, your dream computer is delivered to your front door, built to your exact specifications, ready to set up

The value chain for Nantucket Nectars begins with fresh fruit suppliers like Ocean Spray and links the company's bottling plants, headquarters, sales force, distributors, and retailers. With the help of sophisticated software the company can track sales records for various distributors by region and pass the information on to wholesalers to improve their ordering efficiency. Wholesalers in turn alert the local retailers they supply so customers can find plenty of fresh stock of the flavors they prefer.

and use immediately to type that management assignment due tomorrow. Or consider Deere and Company's Horicon Works, which makes lawn and garden tractors. Managers set a goal of seven-day replenishment of any tractor to any dealer in North America with a 90 percent first-time fill rate. Similarly, at Wainwright Industries in St. Peters, Missouri, employees produce stampings for a General Motors van-assembly plant that's located about six miles away. However, employees also operate a warehouse/just-in-time (JIT) sequencing facility dedicated to serving that GM customer. This warehouse handles some 1,500 parts made by 50 different suppliers, including Wainwright's products. Every seven minutes or so, a truck leaves the warehouse to make deliveries to the GM plant with the parts arranged in racks sequenced by color, size, and style as they will be needed on the van assembly line.[11]

As these examples show, closely integrated work activities among so many different players are possible. How? How can organizations deliver to customers in such a timely manner products to meet their unique needs? The answer lies in value chain management. The concepts of value chain management are transforming operations management strategies and turning organizations around the world into finely tuned models of efficiency and effectiveness strategically positioned to exploit competitive opportunities as they arise. In this section, we explore a number of different aspects of value chain management by defining what it is, describing its goals, outlining the requirements for successfully implementing it, explaining its benefits, and identifying the obstacles to its successful implementation.

WHAT IS VALUE CHAIN MANAGEMENT?

Every organization needs customers if it's going to survive and prosper. Even not-for-profit organizations must have "customers" who use its services or purchase its products. Customers want some type of value from the goods and services they purchase or use, and these end users determine what has value.[12] Organizations must provide that value to attract and keep customers. **Value** is the performance characteristics, features and attributes, and any other aspects of goods and services for which customers are willing to give up resources (usually money). For example, when you purchase Destiny Child's new CD at Best Buy, a new pair of Australian sheepskin Ugg boots online at the company's Web site, a Wendy's bacon cheeseburger at the drive-through location on campus, or a haircut from your local hair salon, you're exchanging (giving up) money in return for the value you need or desire from these products—providing music entertainment during your evening study time, keeping your feet warm *and* fashionable as winter cold sets in, alleviating the lunchtime hunger pangs quickly since your next class starts in 15 minutes, or looking professionally groomed for the job interview you've got next week. Or, using one of our earlier examples, even General Motors willingly exchanges money for the value of having on-time, as-needed delivery of presorted and prearranged parts to its van-assembly facility.

value

The performance characteristics, features and attributes, and any other aspects of goods and services for which customers are willing to give up resources.

How *is* value provided to customers? Through the transformation of raw materials and other resources into some product or service that end users need or desire where, when, and how they want it. However, that seemingly simple act of turning a variety of resources into something that customers value and are willing to pay for involves a vast array of interrelated work activities performed by different participants (suppliers, manufacturers, and even customers)—that is, it involves the value chain. The **value chain** is the entire series of organizational work activities that add value at each step beginning with the processing of raw materials and ending with finished product in the hands of end users.[13] In its entirety, the value chain can encompass the supplier's suppliers to the customer's customer.[14]

The concept of a value chain was popularized by Michael Porter in his 1985 book *Competitive Advantage: Creating and Sustaining Superior Performance.* He wanted managers to understand the sequence of organizational activities that created value for customers. Although he primarily focused on what was happening within a single organization, he did emphasize that managers must understand how their organization's value chain fit into the industry's overall creation of value.

Understanding and capturing the value created throughout the value chain isn't an easy task. But that's what value chain management is designed to help managers do. **Value chain management** is the process of managing the entire sequence of integrated activities and information about product flows along the entire value chain. In contrast to supply chain management, which is internally oriented and focuses on the efficient flow of incoming materials (resources) to the organization, value chain management is externally oriented and focuses on both incoming materials and outgoing products and services. And, although supply chain management is efficiency oriented (its goal is to reduce costs and make the organization more productive), value chain management is effectiveness oriented and aims to create the highest value for customers.[15]

GOAL OF VALUE CHAIN MANAGEMENT

Who has the power in the value chain? Is it the suppliers providing needed resources and materials? After all, they have the ability to dictate prices and quality. Is it the manufacturer that assembles those resources into a valuable product or service? Their contribution in creating a product or service is quite obvious. Is it the distributor that makes sure the product or service is available where and when the customer needs it? Actually, it's none of these! In value chain management, ultimately customers are the ones with power.[16] They're the ones who define what value is and how it's created and provided. Using value chain management, managers hope to find that unique combination in which customers are offered solutions that truly meet their unique needs incredibly fast and at a price that can't be matched by competitors. For example, in an effort to better anticipate customer demand and replenish customer stocks, Shell Chemical Company developed a supplier inventory management order network. The software used in this network allows managers to track shipment status, calculate safety stock levels, and prepare resupply schedules.

With this in mind then, the goal of value chain management is to create a value chain strategy that meets and exceeds customers' needs

value chain

The entire series of organizational work activities that add value at each step beginning with the processing of raw materials and ending with finished product in the hands of end users.

value chain management

The process of managing the entire sequence of integrated activities and information about product flows along the entire value chain.

The goal of value chain management at American Standard Cos., Inc., a venerable maker of plumbing supplies and other products, is to get a better idea what customers need and then to work backward through every link in the chain, from shipping to manufacturing to supply purchasing. "We were a very traditional, conservative company," says Hugh Hoffman, in charge of order fulfillment for chinaware products in the United States. "The business was changing. There was incredible pressure on prices, but also a need to innovate and to serve customers better. So we knew we had to change, and change fast." Since adopting its new approach to the value chain, the company has steadily improved its financial performance.

4. What is value, and what role does it play in value chain management?

5. Who has the power in the value chain? Explain.

6. Describe the goal of value chain management.

business model

A strategic design for how a company intends to profit from its broad array of strategies, processes, and activities.

and desires and allows for full and seamless integration among all members of the chain. A good value chain is one in which a sequence of participants work together as a team, each adding some component of value—such as faster assembly, more accurate information, better customer response and service, and so forth—to the overall process.[17] The better the collaboration among the various chain participants, the better the customer solutions. When value is created for customers and their needs and desires are satisfied, everyone along the chain benefits. For example, at Iomega Corporation, a manufacturer of personal computer storage devices such as Zip drives, managing the value chain started first with improved relationships with internal suppliers, then expanded out to external suppliers and customers. As the company's experience with value chain management intensified and improved, so did its connection with its customers, which ultimately pays off for all its value chain partners.[18]

REQUIREMENTS FOR VALUE CHAIN MANAGEMENT

Managing an organization from a value chain perspective isn't easy. Approaches to giving customers what they wanted that may have worked in the past are likely no longer efficient or effective. Yet, today's dynamic competitive environment facing global organizations demands new solutions. Understanding how and why value is determined by the marketplace has led some organizations to experiment with a new **business model**—that is, a strategic design for how a company intends to profit from its broad array of strategies, processes, and activities. For example, IKEA, the home furnishings manufacturer, transformed itself from a small Swedish mail-order furniture operation into the world's largest retailer of home furnishings by reinventing the value chain in the home furnishings industry. How? The company offers customers well-designed products at substantially lower prices in return for their willingness to take on certain key tasks traditionally done by manufacturers and retailers—assembling furniture and getting it home.[19] The company's definition of a new business model and willingness to abandon old methods and processes have worked well.

So what *does* successful value chain management require? Exhibit 19.3 summarizes the six main requirements: coordination and collaboration, technology investment, organizational processes, leadership, employees, and organizational culture and attitudes. Let's look more closely at each.

Exhibit	19.3

Six Requirements for Successful Value Chain Management

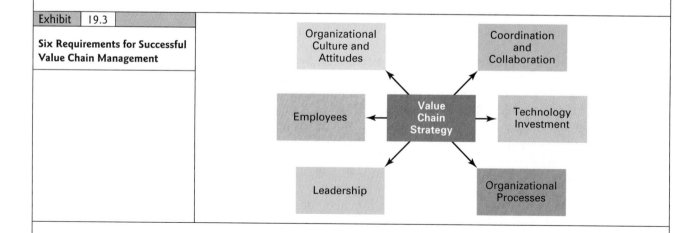

Coordination and Collaboration For the value chain to achieve its goal of meeting and exceeding customers' needs and desires, comprehensive and seamless integration among all members of the chain is absolutely necessary. Collaborative relationships must be developed. All partners in the value chain must identify things that they may not value but that customers do. And sharing information and being flexible as far as who in the value chain does what are important steps in building coordination and collaboration. This sharing of information and analysis requires more open communication among the various value chain partners. For example, Furon Company, a manufacturer of specialty polymer products, believes that better communication with customers and with suppliers has facilitated timely delivery of goods and services and opened up additional business opportunities.[20]

Technology Investment Successful value chain management isn't possible without a significant investment in information technology. The payoff from this investment, however, is that information technology can be used to restructure the value chain to better serve end users. For example, Rollerblade Inc. invested significant dollars in developing a Web site and uses it to educate customers about its products. Although the company has chosen not to sell its products over the Web for fear of antagonizing its dealer network, managers remain flexible about the issue and would reconsider if they felt that value could be better delivered to customers by doing so.[21]

Greencastle Metal Works has dramatically reconfigured the flow of material on the factory floor of its plant, reducing the square footage of its production area by about half and completely redesigning the work area. Instead of flowing back and forth several times in the same area, parts now flow in a U-shaped pattern. "Extra space means there's a place to lay a part down," says Stacy Alexander, process manager for the firm. "And if someone is laying it down, it's a waste—it's not adding value."

What types of technology are important? According to value chain management experts, the key tools include a supporting enterprise resource planning software (ERP) system that links all an organization's activities, sophisticated work planning and scheduling software, customer relationship management systems, business intelligence capabilities, and e-business connections with trading network partners. For instance, Dell Computer manages its supplier relationships almost exclusively online. The company has one Web site for customers and one for suppliers. The supplier Web site is the primary mode of communication between Dell and 33 of its largest suppliers.[22] The company's investment in this type of information technology allows it to meet customers' needs in a way that competitors haven't been able to match.

Organizational Processes Value chain management radically changes **organizational processes**—that is, the ways that organizational work is done.[23] When managers decide to manage operations using value chain management, old processes are no longer appropriate. Managers must critically evaluate all organizational processes from beginning to end by looking at core competencies—the organization's major skills, capabilities, and resources—to determine where value is being added. Non-value-adding activities should be eliminated. Questions such as "Where can internal knowledge be leveraged to improve the flow of material and information," "How can we better configure our product to satisfy both customers and suppliers," "How can the flow of material and information be improved," and

organizational processes

The ways that organizational work is done.

"How can we improve customer service" should be asked for each and every process. For example, when managers at Deere and Company implemented value chain management in its Worldwide Commercial and Consumer Equipment Division, a thorough process evaluation revealed that work activities needed to be better synchronized and interrelationships between multiple links in the value chain better managed. They changed numerous work processes division-wide in order to do this.[24]

Three important conclusions about how organizational processes must change can be made. First, better demand forecasting is necessary *and* possible because of closer ties with customers and suppliers. For example, in an effort to make sure that Listerine was on the store shelves when customers wanted it (known in the retail industry as product replenishment rates), Wal-Mart and Warner-Lambert's Consumer Group (now a division of Pfizer, Inc.) collaborated on improving product demand forecast information. Through their mutual efforts, the partners boosted Wal-Mart's sales of Listerine by $6.5 million, an excellent outcome for supplier and retailer. Customers also benefited (were provided value) because they were able to purchase the product when and where they wanted it.

Second, selected functions may need to be done collaboratively with other partners in the value chain. This collaboration may even extend to sharing employees. For instance, Furon Company places its own employees in customer sites and brings in employees of suppliers and customers to work on its premises. Furon's CEO J. Michael Hagan says this type of collaboration is essential if an organization wants to "go from being a mere component supplier to being a solutions provider."[25]

Finally, new metrics (measures) are needed for evaluating the performance of various activities along the value chain. Because the goal in value chain management is meeting and exceeding customers' needs and desires, managers need a better picture of how well this value is being created and delivered to customers. For example, when Nestlé USA implemented a value chain manage-

---

? THINKING CRITICALLY ABOUT ETHICS

What happens when one partner in the value chain wields its power like a bully? That seems to be an apt description of what some large retailers are doing in the e-commerce arena. Manufacturers are learning that the big retailers—the companies they've always depended on to sell most of their product—can be e-commerce bullies. Instead of the manufacturers using their Web sites to sell products and risk the wrath of their customers (that is, the retailers), most choose to refer potential online buyers to the "dealer nearest you." For example, Rubbermaid Home Products, a division of Newell Rubbermaid, Inc., up until mid-1999, sold a wide array of its products online. However, its Web site today has been stripped of its e-commerce capability. Why? Because of a letter sent by Home Depot to most of its suppliers recommending that they not sell their products to consumers over the Web.

Do you consider such "bully" behavior ethical? Why or why not? Would successful value chain management even be possible given the nature of the relationships here? Explain.

Source: D. Bartholomew, "E-Commerce Bullies," *Industry Week*, September 4, 2000, pp. 48–54.

ment approach, it redesigned its metrics system to focus on one consistent set of measurements—including, among other measures, accuracy of demand forecasts and production plans, on-time delivery, and customer service levels—that allowed them to more quickly identify problems and take actions to resolve them.[26]

Leadership The importance of leadership to value chain management is plain and simple—successful value chain management isn't possible without strong and committed leadership.[27] From top organizational levels to lower levels, managers must support, facilitate, and promote the implementation and ongoing practice of value chain management. J. Michael Hagan, CEO of Furon Company, describes his role as follows, "Value is a mindset that not only has to be driven from the top down, but also from the bottom up. Everyone has to be asking whether a given task adds value, and if it doesn't, why do it?"[28] Managers must make a serious commitment to identifying what value is, how that value can best be provided, and how successful those efforts have been. That type of organizational atmosphere or culture in which all efforts are focused on delivering superb customer value isn't possible without a serious commitment on the part of the organization's leaders.

Also, it's important that managers outline expectations for what's involved in the organization's pursuit of value chain management. Ideally, this should start with a vision or mission statement that expresses the organization's commitment to identifying, capturing, and providing the highest possible value to customers. For instance, when American Standard Companies of Piscataway, New Jersey, began its pursuit of value chain management, CEO Emmanueal A. Kampouris at dozens of meetings across the country explained the new competitive environment and why the company needed to create better working relationships with its value chain partners in order to better serve the needs of its customers.[29] Throughout the organization, then, managers should clarify expectations regarding each employee's role in the value chain. But clear expectations aren't just important for internal partners. Being clear about expectations also extends to external partners. For example, managers at American Standard Companies identified clear requirements for suppliers and was prepared to drop any that couldn't meet them. The company was so serious about its expectations that it did cut hundreds of suppliers from its plumbing, air-conditioning, and automotive businesses. The upside, though, was that those suppliers that met the expectations benefited from more business and American Standard had partners willing to work with it in delivering better value to customers.

Employees/Human Resources We know from our discussions of management theories and approaches throughout this textbook that employees are the organization's most important resource. Without employees, there would be no products produced or services delivered—in fact, there would be no organized efforts in the pursuit of common goals. So, not surprisingly, employees play an important role in value chain management. The three main human resource requirements for value chain management are flexible approaches to job design, an effective hiring process, and ongoing training.

Flexibility is the key description of job design in a value chain management organization. Traditional functional job roles—such as marketing, sales,

Many elements are important in making value chain management successful. Information technology plays a major role, but it is not the only ingredient. David Curry, director of external activities in the purchasing division of Honda of America, points out that "there is not one single element that will make [companies] totally successful. It takes a combination of things. And there are no cookbook answers. Each company is different. You have to pull together the ingredients that suit your tastes—your culture, your size, your particular processes, and so on. You have to create your own recipe for success."

accounts payable, customer service, and so forth—are inadequate in a value chain management environment. Instead, jobs need to be designed around work processes that link all functions involved in creating and providing value to customers. For example, at American Standard Companies, one employee carries the title of "process owner of chinaware order fulfillment." This employee is responsible for the delivery of all the company's chinaware, which involves overseeing every aspect from demand forecasting to collecting payment. This type of flexible job design supports the company's commitment to providing superb customer value.[30] In designing jobs for a value chain approach, the focus needs to be on how each activity performed by an employee can best contribute to the creation and delivery of customer value. That requires flexibility in what employees do and how they do it.

The fact that jobs in a value chain management organization must be flexible contributes to the second requirement concerning employees—that is, flexible jobs require employees who are flexible. In a value chain organization, employees may be assigned to work teams that tackle a given process and are often asked to do different things on different days depending on need. In such an environment in which customer value is best delivered through focusing on collaborative relationships that may change as customer needs change and in which there are no standardized processes or job descriptions, an employee's ability to be flexible is critical. Therefore, the organization's hiring process must be designed to identify those employees who have the ability to learn and adapt.

Finally, the need for flexibility also requires that there be a significant investment in continual and ongoing employee training. Whether the training involves learning how to use information technology software, how to improve the flow of materials throughout the chain, how to identify activities that add value, how to make better decisions faster, or how to improve any other number of potential work activities, managers must see to it that employees have the knowledge and tools they need to do their jobs efficiently and effectively. That means providing them with training opportunities. For example, at defense contractor Alenia Marconi Systems based in Portsmouth, England, ongoing training is part of the company's commitment to efficiently and effectively meeting the needs of customers. Employees continually receive technical training as well as training in strategic issues including the importance of emphasizing people and customers, not just sales and profits.[31]

Organizational Culture and Attitudes The last requirement for value chain management we need to discuss is the importance of having a supportive organizational culture and attitudes. From our extensive description of value chain management, you could probably guess the type of organizational culture and attitudes that are going to support its successful implementation. Those cultural attitudes include sharing, collaborating, openness, flexibility, mutual respect, and trust. And these attitudes encompass not only the internal partners in the value chain but extend to external partners as well. For instance, American Standard Companies has chosen to practice these attitudes the old-fashioned way—with lots of face time and telephone calls. One of the company's suppliers, St. Louis–based White Rodgers, described their relationship as follows: "Their goals are our goals, because both companies are focused on growth. The keys to the relationship are mutual respect and open communication at all levels. No one has to go through a liaison. If our engineers need to talk to theirs, we just go right to the source."[32] However, Dell Computer has taken a completely different approach as it works with its value chain partners almost exclusively through cyberspace.[33] Both approaches, however, reflect each company's commitment to developing long-lasting, mutually beneficial value chain relationships that best meet customers' needs.

7. Why is the concept of a business model important in value chain management?

8. What roles do coordination and collaboration, technology investment, and organizational processes play in value chain management?

9. How do leadership, employees, and organizational culture and attitudes contribute to value chain management?

BENEFITS OF VALUE CHAIN MANAGEMENT

Collaborating with external and internal partners in creating and managing a successful value chain strategy isn't easy! It takes significant investment in time, energy, and other resources, and a serious commitment by all chain partners. Given this, why would managers ever choose to implement value chain management in their organizations? There are several significant benefits that organizations receive from value chain management. Exhibit 19.4 highlights the results of a survey of manufacturers that had embarked on value chain management initiatives and the benefits they perceived.[34]

Exhibit 19.4

Value Chain Benefits

Value chain survey respondents indicated the following are a "major benefit" from sharing information with partners:

	% of companies in excellent or very good chains	% of companies in poor chains	% of all companies
Increased sales	41%	14%	26%
Cost savings	62%	22%	40%
Increased market share	32%	12%	20%
Inventory reductions	51%	18%	35%
Improved quality	60%	28%	39%
Accelerated delivery times	54%	27%	40%
Improved logistics management	43%	15%	27%
Improved customer service	66%	22%	44%

Source: G. Taninecz, "Forging the Chain," *Industry Week*, May 15, 2000, p. 44.

Improved customer service was the major benefit that companies (44 percent) reported. Managing from a value chain perspective gives organizations a better handle on customer needs at all points along the chain. As value chain partners collaborate and optimize their processes to better meet customers' needs, customer service *should* improve.

The next two most cited benefits from value chain management reported by companies were cost savings and accelerated delivery times (40 percent). As inefficiencies and non-value-added activities are driven out of the value chain, companies will achieve cost savings in different work activities and areas. In addition, as value chain partners collaborate by sharing information and linking important activities, delivery times can be accelerated.

The next most important benefit cited by survey respondents was improved quality (39 percent). As work processes are evaluated for value-added potential, quality should be one of the measures used.

Inventory reductions were the next most important benefit identified by survey respondents (35 percent). Inventory storage—both raw materials and finished products—can represent significant costs for organizations. Through close and careful collaboration among value chain partners, the flow of materials and information through the chain can be improved, leading to inventory reductions. For example, Deere and Company found that working with its suppliers to better control the suppliers' inventories had a positive impact on its own ability to respond to changes in product mix and volumes.[35]

As Exhibit 19.4 shows, three additional benefits are possible through value chain management. These include improved logistics management (27 percent), increased sales (26 percent), and increased market share (20 percent). Each of these benefits is important and desirable, as well.

OBSTACLES TO VALUE CHAIN MANAGEMENT

As desirable as these benefits may be, managers must deal with several obstacles in managing the value chain including organizational barriers, cultural attitudes, required capabilities, and people. (See Exhibit 19.5.)

Organizational Barriers Organizational barriers are among the most difficult obstacles managers handle. These barriers include refusal or reluctance to share information, reluctance to shake up the status quo, and security issues. Without shared information, close coordination and collaboration are impossible. And

Exhibit	19.5

Obstacles to Successful Value Chain Management

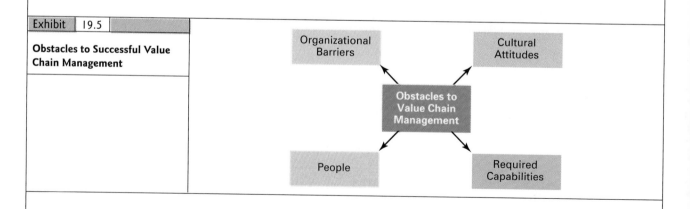

the reluctance or refusal of employees to shake up the status quo can impede efforts toward value chain management and prevent its successful implementation. Finally, because value chain management relies heavily on a substantial information technology infrastructure, system security and Internet security breaches are issues that need to be addressed. Many companies feel that if an organization such as the Pentagon can't keep its Web site secure, then they will never be able to.[36]

Cultural Attitudes Unsupportive cultural attitudes—especially trust and control—also can be obstacles to value chain management. The trust issue is a critical one, both lack of trust and too much trust. To be effective, partners in a value chain must trust each other. There must be a mutual respect for, and honesty about, each partner's activities all along the chain. When that trust doesn't exist, the partners will be reluctant to share information, capabilities, and processes. But too much trust also can be a problem. Just about any organization is vulnerable to theft of **intellectual property**—that is, proprietary company information that's critical to its efficient and effective functioning and competitiveness. A study by the American Society for Industrial Security found that those cultivating a trusting relationship with a company pose the most serious threat for intellectual property loss.[37] Although value chain partners need to trust each other, the potential for theft can be minimized by better understanding each other's operations and by being careful with proprietary intellectual property.

Another cultural attitude that can be an obstacle to successful value chain management is the belief that when an organization collaborates with external and internal partners, it no longer controls its own destiny. However, this just isn't the case. Even with the intense collaboration that must take place, organizations still control critical decisions including what customers value, how much value they desire, and what distribution channels are important.[38]

Required Capabilities We know from our earlier discussion of requirements for successful implementation of value chain management that there are a number of capabilities that value chain partners must have. Several of these, including extreme coordination and collaboration, the ability to configure products to satisfy customers and suppliers, and the ability to educate internal and external partners, aren't easy to develop or to do. But they're essential to capturing and exploiting the value chain. Many of the companies we've described throughout this section—American Standard Companies, Deere and Company, Furon Company, and so forth—endured critical and often difficult self-evaluations of their capabilities and processes in order to become more effective and efficient at managing their value chains.

People The final obstacles to successful value chain management can be an organization's members. Without their unwavering commitment and willingness to do whatever it takes, value chain management isn't going to be successful. If employees refuse or are reluctant to be flexible, it's going to be difficult to make the necessary changes to meet changing situational demands. After all, it's the employees who do the work. If they're not willing to be flexible in what work they do, and how and with whom they work, critical collaboration and cooperation throughout the value chain will be hard to achieve.

intellectual property

Proprietary company information that's critical to its efficient and effective functioning and competitiveness.

In addition, value chain management takes an incredible amount of time and energy by an organization's employees. Managers must motivate those high levels of effort from employees. It's not easy to do.

Finally, a major human resource problem faced by organizations pursuing value chain management is the lack of experienced managers who are able to lead value chain management initiatives. Because it's a relatively new approach to managing operations, there aren't a lot of managers who've done it successfully. However, this obstacle hasn't prevented progressive organizations from pursuing the benefits to be gained from value chain management.

Testing...Testing...1,2,3

10. **What types of benefits does value chain management provide?**

11. **Why are organizational barriers among the most difficult obstacle to value chain management for managers to handle?**

12. **How are cultural attitudes, required capabilities, and employees obstacles to value chain management?**

⟩ CURRENT ISSUES IN OPERATIONS MANAGEMENT

Capitalize on e-manufacturing technology! Successfully implement quality initiatives! Achieve ISO 9000 certification! These issues currently are at the top of managers' lists for improving operations management. Because managers consider them to be essential for making products and services competitive in global markets, we'll review each in this section.

TECHNOLOGY'S ROLE IN E-MANUFACTURING

As we know from our previous discussion of value chain management, today's competitive marketplace has put tremendous pressure on organizations to deliver products and services that customers value in a timely manner. And with all the hype about online purchasing and sales, it's easy to assume that operations management plays no role in e-businesses. However, smart companies are looking at ways to harness Web technology to improve operations management. For example, Schneider Automation Inc. (a North Andover, Massachusetts–based division of the French multinational, Schneider Electric SA) implemented its Transparent Factory initiative—a framework for linking plant-floor automation with enterprise-wide business network systems. With millions of device sensors and actuators on its factory floors running on stand-alone software but with no way to connect to the factory's system network, managers saw prime opportunities to capitalize on information technology solutions to manage its operations more effectively and efficiently.[39]

Although e-manufacturing is being driven by the recognition that the customer is king, managers still need to realize that the organization's production activities must be more responsive. For instance, operations managers need systems that can reveal available capacity, status of orders, and product quality while products are in the process of being manufactured, not just after the fact. To connect more closely with customers, operations across the enterprise, including manufacturing, must be synchronized. To avoid production and delivery bottlenecks, the manufacturing function must be a full partner in the entire e-business architecture.

What's making this type of extensive involvement and collaboration possible is technology. Technology is also allowing manufacturing plants to control costs particularly in the areas of predictive maintenance, remote diagnostics, and utility cost savings. For instance, let's look at how e-manufacturing technology is affecting the equipment maintenance function—an important operations management activity. New generations of Internet-compatible equipment contain embedded Web servers that can communicate proactively—that is, if a piece of equipment breaks or reaches certain preset parameters that it's about to break, it can ask for help. But technology can do more than sound an alarm or light up an indicator button. For instance, some devices have the ability to initiate e-mail or signal a pager at a supplier, the maintenance department, or contractor describing the specific problem and requesting parts and service. How much is such e-enabled maintenance control worth? It can be worth quite a lot if it prevents equipment breakdowns and subsequent production downtime.

Managers who understand the power of technology to contribute to more effective and efficient performance know that managing operations is more than the traditional view of manufacturing's role in producing the product. Instead, the emphasis is on working together with all the organization's business functions to find solutions to customers' business problems.

Customization of consumer products is one of the benefits of technology's increasing role in operations management. Levi's is able to make custom-fit jeans with a new scanning technology that feeds the customer's individual measurements into a central computer and produces animated displays via digital film. When it comes to choosing the fabric, however, the process falls back on the old-fashioned way—swatches.

QUALITY INITIATIVES

$2.1 billion. That's the amount that Toshiba Corporation paid to settle a lawsuit over defects in its laptop computers. (Your second author received a settlement of about $1,300 for the alleged problem with Toshiba laptops.) Palm, Inc., the leading manufacturer of personal digital assistants (PDAs), revealed that its first model with a color screen—first offered for sale in February 2000—had a tendency to crack. It offered customers free replacements for cracked units. Patriot Computer Corporation of Markham, Ontario, Canada, had to halt production when it discovered that a power-supply unit built in China was malfunctioning.[40] Alleged defects in certain Bridgestone/Firestone tires are believed to have led to serious sport-utility vehicle accidents. These are just a few of the quality problems still being experienced by businesses around the world.

Although quality management has been a part of many organizations' operations management strategies for several years, as the previous examples show, it *does* continue to be an important issue for managers. Many experts believe that organizations that do not produce high-quality products will be unable to compete successfully in the global marketplace. In fact, in an annual census of U.S. manufacturers conducted by *Industry Week*, a majority of corporate and plant-level executives stated that strategic initiatives that promoted quality and continuous improvement were critical to manufacturing excellence and their ultimate success.[41] One respondent, the vice president and general manager of Bettis

Candace Walton Manders, Microbiology Laboratory Supervisor, Children's Hospital, New Orleans, Louisiana

Describe your job.

I am a medical technologist and the microbiology supervisor of bacteriology, parasitology, virology, and mycology. I have set up all the labs at the hospital except virology. I review all results that go to the hospital units and outpatients for accuracy. I am in constant contact with the pathologist, who is the medical director of microbiology, about problems, unusual results, or unusual organisms. I am on the Infection Control Committee and report to it all significant isolates (bacteria, viruses, fungus, and parasites) from important sites. I prepare rotation schedules and time cards. I also work as a regular medical technologist and know how to do 99 percent of all the procedures in our four labs.

What types of managerial skills do you think tomorrow's managers wil need?

Flexibility is needed in a constantly changing health care field with cost constraints. Also needed are skills to cope with high employee turnover rates and increasing health care restrictions, and to train new employees quickly without compromising the quality of patient care. Computer and typing skills are important and managers must keep up-to-date on all aspects of their fields. Developing a support network with other professionals in the field is also helpful.

What types of management controls do you use?

I delegate appropriate tasks to competent employees I know will do the job within a set time frame. I stay open to suggestions from employees but let them come up with the solution. I work as a team member and give the appropriate person the correct job. Finally, I take a personal interest in each employee. I have an open door policy with my employees, my medical director, and the lab manager.

Why are management controls important?

When you have 20 to 25 different employees rotating through your department, you have to have management and quality controls in place. It's important that consistency in quality be maintained on all shifts through all types of employees—full-time, part-time, rotating generalists—24 hours a day, seven days a week.

Corporation in Waller, Texas (a manufacturer of pneumatic and hydraulic valve actuators), said, "I am a believer that you cannot afford not to focus on quality. You're just going to pay the price when something bad happens. A failure in the quality of our product could shut down a customer's plant. Continuous improvement is something we have to do to survive in the marketplace."[42] And look back at the chapter-opening Manager's Dilemma. Managers at Grupo Industrial Bimbo SA knew they would have to produce quality products in order to be a strong competitor in the intensely competitive global candy market.

What is quality? When you consider a product or service to have quality, what does that mean to you? Does it mean that the product doesn't break or quit working—that is, that it's reliable? Does it mean that the service is delivered in a way that you intended? Does it mean that the product does what it's supposed to do? Or does quality mean something else? Exhibit 19.6 provides a description of several quality dimensions. We're going to define **quality** as the ability of a product or service to reliably do what it's supposed to do and to satisfy customer expectations.

How is quality achieved? That's the issue managers must address. A good way to address quality initiatives is to think in terms of the management functions—planning, organizing, leading, and controlling—that need to take place.

quality

The ability of a product or service to reliably do what it's supposed to do and to satisfy customer expectations.

Exhibit | 19.6

Quality Dimensions of Goods and Services

Product Quality Dimensions

1. Performance—Operating characteristics
2. Features—Important special characteristics
3. Flexibility—Meeting operating specifications over some period of time
4. Durability—Amount of use before performance deteriorates
5. Conformance—Match with preestablished standards
6. Serviceability—Ease and speed of repair or normal service
7. Aesthetics—How a product looks and feels
8. Perceived quality—Subjective assessment of characteristics (product image)

Service Quality Dimensions

1. Timeliness—Performed in promised period of time
2. Courtesy—Performed cheerfully
3. Consistency—Giving all customers similar experiences each time
4. Convenience—Accessibility to customers
5. Completeness—Fully serviced, as required
6. Accuracy—Performed correctly each time

Source: Adapted from J.W. Dean, Jr., and J.R. Evans, *Total Quality: Management, Organization and Society* (St. Paul, MN: West Publishing Company, 1994); H.V. Roberts and B.F. Sergesketter, *Quality Is Personal* (New York: The Free Press, 1993); D. Garvin, *Managed Quality: The Strategic and Competitive Edge* (New York: The Free Press, 1988); and M.A. Hitt, R.D. Ireland, and R.E. Hoskisson, *Strategic Management*, 4th ed. (Cincinnati, OH: South-Western, 2001), p. 211.

Planning for Quality Managers must have quality improvement goals and strategies and plans formulated to achieve those goals. Goals can help focus everyone's attention toward some objective quality standard. For instance, at the Rockwell Collins avionics plant based in Decorah, Iowa (where Rockwell International's communications and navigation equipment is made), a quality goal being pursued by employees over the next four years is a 30 percent reduction in defects.[43] Although this goal is specific and challenging, managers and employees are partnering together to pursue well-designed strategies to achieve the goals and are confident they can do so.

Organizing and Leading for Quality Since quality improvement initiatives are carried out by organizational employees, it's important for managers to look at how they can best organize and lead them. For instance, at the Rockwell Collins avionics plant, every employee participates in process improvement workshops. A Rockwell executive says, "The spirit within that plant is high. They do seem to be excited about what they have accomplished. This is not something we are doing to them. This is something they are doing with us."[44]

Organizations with extensive and successful quality improvement programs tend to rely on two important people approaches: cross-functional work teams and self-directed or empowered work teams. Because achieving product quality is something in which all employees from upper levels to lower levels must participate, it's not surprising that quality-driven organizations rely on well-trained, flexible, and empowered employees. For example, at Compaq Computer Corporations Americas' Software Manufacturing and Distribution facility in Nashua, New Hampshire, employees have been trained in people skills as well as statistical analysis. Each employee is encouraged and empowered to find ways to

Quality remains a critical component of successful operations management. Controlling for quality can include product testing and inspection, such as is done at PAC International Ltd., outside Manchester, England. The company manufactures electronic access-control systems for the global market and has recently revamped all its operations. Here Rachel Gibson, an assembler for the firm, inspects a circuit board after soldering.

work smarter, not harder, and to stay focused on results that make a difference in total performance.[45] There's no doubt that, at this plant, empowered employees are making major differences.

Controlling for Quality Quality improvement initiatives aren't possible without having some way to monitor and evaluate their progress. Whether it involves standards for inventory control, defect rate, raw materials procurement, or any other operations management area, controlling for quality is important. For instance, at the Aeroquip-Inoac Company (AIC) plant in Livingston, Tennessee, a closely knit group of employees is dedicated to continuous improvement. They use employee suggestions, benchmarking visits, and other numerous quality initiatives and have built a reputation for delivering high-quality products. The company wasn't always this efficient or effective. Prior to 1992, the company's quality control was performed mainly by employees in the quality control department. However, when a new plant manager was hired, he wanted to see ownership of quality turned over to employees on the manufacturing floor. It wasn't an easy transformation as employees initially resisted any changes. However, the company's current quality assurance environment supports defect *prevention* rather than defect *detection*. Quality became the responsibility of *all* employees. Today, employees and managers work together to solve problems and provide customers with the quality products they value.[46]

These types of quality improvement success stories aren't just limited to U.S. companies. For example, at a Delphi Automotive Systems Corporation assembly plant in Matamoros, Mexico, employees have worked hard to improve quality and have made significant strides. For instance, the customer reject rate on shipped products is now 10 ppm (parts per million), down from 3,000 ppm just five years ago—an improvement of almost 300 percent.[47] Quality initiatives at several Australian companies including Alcoa of Australia, Wormald Security, and Carlton and United Breweries have led to significant quality improvements.[48] And at Valeo Klimasystemme GmbH of Bad Rodach, Germany, assembly teams build different climate-control systems for high-end German cars including the Mercedes E-Class, BMW 5 Series, and Opel Omega/Cadillac Catera. Quality initiatives by Valeo's employee teams have led to significant improvements in various quality standards.[49]

QUALITY GOALS

To publicly demonstrate their quality commitment, many organizations worldwide have pursued challenging quality goals—the two best-known being ISO 9000 and Six Sigma.

ISO 9000 **ISO 9000** is a series of international quality management standards established by the International Organization for Standardization (www.iso.ch) that set uniform guidelines for processes to ensure that products conform to cus-

ISO 9000

A series of international quality management standards that set uniform guidelines for processes to ensure that products conform to customer requirements.

			Exhibit	19.7
• Customer demands and expectations	• Production costs			
• Market advantage	• Quality		**Reasons for Pursuing ISO 9000 Certification**	
• Competitive pressures	• Corporate strategy			

Source: Based on "ISO 9000 Certified: To Be or Not to Be," *Modern Materials Handling,* November 1995, pp. 10–11.

tomer requirements. These standards cover everything from contract review to product design to product delivery. The ISO 9000 standards have become the internationally recognized standard for evaluating and comparing companies in the global marketplace. In fact, this type of certification is becoming a prerequisite for doing business globally. Gaining ISO 9000 certification provides proof that a quality operations system is in place. Exhibit 19.7 lists some reasons why companies pursue ISO 9000 registration.

The latest survey of ISO 9000 certificates showed that the number of registered sites worldwide exceeded nearly 272,000—an increase of almost 49,000.[50] New certifications of businesses in the United States and Italy led the increase. As a region, Europe continues to lead in the total number of ISO certificates with almost 61 percent of the total. However, other global regions continue to make strides in this area as businesses pursue quality initiatives.

Six Sigma Motorola popularized the use of stringent quality standards more than 30 years ago through a trademarked quality improvement program called Six Sigma.[51] Very simply, **Six Sigma** is a quality standard that establishes a goal of no more than 3.4 defects per million units or procedures. What does the name mean? *Sigma* is the Greek letter that statisticians use to define a standard deviation from a bell curve. The higher the sigma, the fewer the deviations from the norm—that is, the fewer the defects. At One Sigma, two-thirds of whatever is being measured falls within the curve. Two Sigma covers about 95 percent. At Six Sigma, you're about as close to being defect free as you can get.[52] It's an ambitious quality goal! Although it may be an extremely high standard to achieve, many quality-driven businesses are using it to judge their suppliers. For instance, Motorola, AlliedSignal, and GE have told suppliers that this is the quality standard they must use if they want their business. GE realized approximately $2 billion in savings through its Six Sigma program in 1999.[53] Other well-known companies pursuing Six Sigma include DuPont, Texas Instruments, Inc., Sony Corporation, Nokia Corporation, and Johnson & Johnson.[54] What impact can Six Sigma have? Let's look at an example.

When AlliedSignal merged with Honeywell, Inc., two companies with highly successful quality improvement programs were joined.[55] The new merged company's program called Six Sigma Plus is paying big dividends. Savings in 1999 amounted to $600 million and approximately $700 million in 2000. How are these types of results possible? The company's Six Sigma Plus program includes several steps: defining a problem, measuring how the process performs, analyzing causes of problems, improving the process to reduce defects and variations, and controlling the process to ensure continued, improved performance. For example, a Six Sigma Plus team consisting of employees from Honeywell, a customer (Phoenix-based PING Inc.), and a supplier (Remington Arms Company) was able

Six Sigma

A quality standard that establishes a goal of no more than 3.4 defects per million parts or procedures.

to produce a new type of golf club with Honeywell's PowderFlo metal-injection molding technology. Using Six Sigma Plus and e-business processes, the team was able to significantly reduce product development time (by 50 percent) and open up new markets for Honeywell and its customers (potentially $6 billion as new-product applications are developed in areas such as flatware, fan blades, and automobile turbine wheels).

Summary Although it's important for managers to recognize that many positive benefits can accrue from obtaining ISO 9000 certification or Six Sigma, the key benefit comes from the quality improvement journey itself. In other words, the goal of quality certification should be having work processes and an operations system in place that enable organizations to meet customers' needs and employees to perform their jobs in a consistently high-quality way.

Testing...Testing...1,2,3

13. **What role is e-manufacturing playing in operations management?**

14. **How should quality initiatives be pursued?**

15. **Describe two quality goals that organizations can pursue.**

Managers Respond to "A Manager's Dilemma"

Deborah Barnhart

Director, Network Medical Management Support, St. John's Health System, Springfield, Missouri

To successfully implement a quality program in his plant, Lokananta needs to create a corporate culture of quality. Here are the steps I think he needs to take to do this.

- Ensure that top management is committed to the program and has dedicated sufficient resources to the efforts.
- Establish a reward and recognition program for quality-related activities.
- Provide training for all employees on the quality process.
- Recognize that quality is every employee's job.
- Establish a communication program, internal and external, that supports the quality program.
- Establish minimum standards for each functional department. Each department should also identify and monitor key processes and create control charts, tracking indicators over time.
- Develop feedback systems to increase understanding of what is valued by your customers.
- When opportunities for improvement are identified, develop an action plan, implement it, check to see if the actions resulted in the desired improvements, and incorporate the change into the process or continue to improve.
- Celebrate successes and efforts made by employees to improve quality.

Cindy Brewer

Corporate Trainer, Sears, Inc., Chicago, Illinois

The parent company, Bimbo, knows that product quality is important. Although he has made the gummy bear plant more efficient, Lokananta must now work on product quality. There are several things he should do.

First, he should make sure that he has top management support for his quality management efforts. Then he's ready to take the quality management values to his employees. Employees should be educated as far as the need for quality. It's important that they "buy into" the need for managing quality. Employees should be provided quality management training. This may take some time.

Once employees have been educated and trained about managing quality, quality control programs should be implemented. It's important that employees be empowered to make necessary changes. Otherwise, if they see areas in which improvements can be made, the changes won't be made. Performance appraisal and reward and recognition systems should be designed around the company's culture of quality.

Finally, work quality needs to be stressed throughout the organization. Hold company-wide meetings to continually emphasize the importance of quality.

Chapter Summary

This summary is organized by the chapter-opening objectives found on p. 524.

1. The transformation process is the essence of operations management. Inputs (people, materials, etc.) are brought together and are transformed through the organization's work activities and processes into finished goods and services.

2. Operations management is important to all types of organizations for three reasons. First, the transformation process takes place in manufacturing and service organizations. Next, it's important in effectively and efficiently managing productivity. Finally, it plays a strategic role in an organization's competitive success.

3. Value chain management is the process of managing the entire sequence of integrated activities and information about product flows along the entire value chain.

4. The goal of value chain management is to create a value chain strategy that meets and exceeds customers' needs and desires and allows for full and seamless integration among all members of the value chain.

5. There are six main requirements for successful value chain management: coordination and collaboration among value chain partners including sharing information and being flexible about who does what; an investment in a technology infrastructure to support collaboration and sharing; appropriate organizational processes (the ways organizational work is done) including better demand forecasting, collaborative work, and better metrics for evaluating the performance of various activities along the value chain; strong and committed leadership; appropriate employee approaches including flexible job design, an effective hiring process, and ongoing training; and appropriate and supportive organizational culture and attitudes.

6. Benefits from value chain management include improved customer service, cost savings, accelerated delivery times, improved quality, inventory reductions, improved logistics management, increased sales, and increased market share. Obstacles to successful implementation of value chain management include organizational barriers, cultural attitudes, required capabilities, and people.

7. Companies use technology to manage operations more effectively and efficiently by monitoring such information as available capacity, status of orders, and product quality; by connecting with customers and suppliers; and by controlling costs.

8. Quality is an important issue for managers because it's important to global competitive success. Managers must plan, organize, lead, and control for quality.

9. ISO 9000 and Six Sigma are challenging quality goals that organizations might choose to pursue. ISO 9000 is a series of international quality management standards established by the International Organization for Standardization that set uniform guidelines for processes to ensure that products conform to customer requirements. Six Sigma is a quality standard that sets a goal of no more than 3.4 defects per million units or procedures.

Thinking About Management Issues

1. Do you think that manufacturing or service organizations have the greater need for operations management? Explain.

2. How might operations management apply to other managerial functions besides control?

3. How could you use value chain management concepts in your everyday life?

4. Which is more critical for success in organizations: continuous improvement or quality control? Support your position.

5. Choose a large organization that you're interested in studying. Research this company to find out what types of operations management strategies it is using. Focus on describing what it's doing that's unusual or effective or both.

Log On: Internet-Based Exercise

When a company pursues well-known quality goals such as ISO 9000 or Six Sigma, they promote that accomplishment and often use it as means of competitive differentiation. Find three examples of companies that have achieved ISO 9000 certification. Describe what unique quality initiatives these companies have implemented.

Are there any quality processes or activities that these organizations have in common?

Now do the same thing for Six Sigma. Find three examples of companies pursuing Six Sigma and describe what unique quality initiatives these companies have

implemented. Are there any quality processes or activities that these organizations have in common with each other? How about in common with the organizations that have achieved ISO 9000 certification?

Working Together: Team-Based Exercise

Break into groups of four to five students. Your team's task is to assess how you believe technology will change the way your college disseminates information to students a decade from now. Specifically, what do you believe the typical college's teaching technologies will look like in the year 2012? Here are some questions to consider:

1. Will there still be a need for a college campus spanning several hundred acres?
2. Do you believe every student will be required to have a laptop for classes?
3. Will there be computers in every classroom, coupled with high-tech media technologies?
4. Do you believe students will be required to physically come to campus for their classes?
5. What role will distance learning and telecommuting play in classroom activities?

You have 30 minutes to discuss these issues and develop your responses. Appoint someone on your team to present your team's findings to the class.

Case Application

Modern Manufacturing in the Twenty-first Century

As Europe's number-one car maker, Volkswagen AG produces 4.9 million cars, trucks, and vans every year. Its well-known models include the Jetta, Passat, and Beetle, as well as venerable luxury cars including Audi, Lamborghini, Rolls-Royce, and Bentley. In addition, it produces SEAT family cars in Spain and Skoda family cars in the Czech Republic. And, to boost its truck-making business and expand its market, VW purchased a 19 percent stake in Swedish commercial truck maker, Scania. But it's VW's futuristic South American facility that's grabbed attention. It's been described as a revolution in the auto industry. Why? The unusual manufacturing approach used there is likely to change the way cars will be built in the future all over the world.

Assembling vehicles has traditionally followed a conventional process. Many parts were put together on massive assembly lines where thousands of workers labored. The automobile components used typically came from suppliers that brought them to the assembly plant's loading dock. From there, the parts were moved either manually or in some automated fashion to the appropriate place on the assembly line. Finally, employees assembled what parts they could, and robotic manufacturing was used to do the rest.

However, that's not the way it is at VW's Resende truck plant outside Rio de Janeiro. Although employees build the company's new 1.5-ton truck called the Robust—the bulk of the 80,000 trucks produced there annually will be sold in the United States—none of them are Volkswagen employees.

At Resende, VW has essentially outsourced the entire assembly of its vehicles to its suppliers. This $250 million plant uses hundreds of suppliers that channel their materials through just seven final assemblers. Each of these assemblers is responsible for putting together one of the seven modules that comprises a finished truck. For example, German instrument maker VDO Kienzle starts with the steel shell of a truck cab. Up to 200 VDO employees install everything from seats to the instrument panels in the interior of the truck. Then they attach the finished cab to the chassis moving down the assembly line through various suppliers' spaces.

As a result of this approach, Volkswagen has saved money in a number of ways. It has fewer employees for which it is directly responsible. Suppliers pay their own employees as well as for their tools and fixtures. Suppliers are also responsible for incurring their own inventory costs—minimized, however, by a sophisticated just-in-time inventory system, in which parts arrive just one hour before they're needed on the assembly line. Finally, management seeks the advice and cooperation of suppliers in cutting costs and boosting productivity. And VW doesn't pay for or take delivery of the final truck product until all quality inspections have been completed and passed. The value of Volkswagen's approach is that it lets the company do what it believes it does best—designing and engineering vehicles, not assembling them, which others can do better, faster, and cheaper.

Given the success of VW's approach, other vehicle manufacturers are adopting similar approaches. For example, a strategic partnership between DaimlerChrysler, watchmaker SMH Swatch, and Mitsubishi Motors Corporation will use a modular approach to build the Smart—a small, four-seat car designed for urban transportation. DaimlerChrysler's Smart Unit and Mitsubishi are sharing the costs of developing the main components of the car. The car is being built in a new factory in western France, and the production run is divided into seven modules. Final assembly of each of the seven completed modules is done by the suppliers in the western France plant. And in the United States, DaimlerChrysler is using this approach with its suppliers of the Dodge Dakota pickup truck.

QUESTIONS

1. What advantages and drawbacks do you see to VW's approach at the Resende plant?

2. How would VW have to change the operations management system at Resende in order to implement value chain management?

3. Producing vehicles in modules appears to result in significant cost savings. Do you believe that quality would also be enhanced by such a process? Why or why not?

4. "Both Volkswagen and DaimlerChrysler are European-based and culturally influenced companies. These same processes would not work in an organization and culture of a vehicle manufacturer like General Motors." Do you agree or disagree with this statement? Defend your position.

5. Do you think VW's approach at the Resende plant is a model of how to set up a global operation? Why or why not?

Sources: Company information from Hoover's Online (www.hoovers.com), December 16, 2000; C.N. Tierney, "Daimler and VW: Changing Fortunes," *Business Week Online* (www.businessweek.com), November 20, 2000; R.S. Russell and B.W. Taylor, III, *Operations Management* (Upper Saddle River, NJ: Prentice Hall, 2000), p. 257; E.P. Lima, "VW's Revolutionary Idea," *Industry Week*, March 17, 1997, pp. 62–67; J.H. Sheridan, "Bonds of Trust," *Industry Week*, March 17, 1997, pp. 52–62; R. Collins, K. Bechler, and S. Pires, "Outsourcing in the Automotive Industry: From JIT to Modular Consortia," *European Management Journal*, p. 11; and D. Woodruff, I. Katz, and K. Naughton, "VW's Factory of the Future," *Business Week*, October 7, 1996, pp. 52–56.

Video Case Application

Wizards of Wheels

SMALL BUSINESS 2000

Bicycling is a booming industry. Enthusiasts point to its appeal as a great family sport that can be enjoyed at low cost and done in a variety of locations, particularly because bicycles are easily transported from one place to another— easily transported, that is, if the bicyclists have a reliable, safe, and easy-to-use bicycle rack on their vehicles. Some of the world's best bicycle racks are made by Sara and Chris Fortune's company, Graber Products (www.graber-products.com) of Madison, Wisconsin.

Chris says that consumers want products that are user friendly and so do dealers. Graber Products is striving to supply that product. He says that whenever Graber develops a new product, three very simple and very basic "musts" need to be met: (1) The bicycle racks must stay on the car; (2) the bikes must stay on the rack; and (3) the racks must not scratch or mar the owner's vehicle. These three "musts" guide product innovation and development at Graber.

Innovation is one of the top business issues that faces Graber Products. Through its product innovation process, Graber wants to go beyond what's already on the market. It doesn't want to merely copy what other industry competitors have already done because doing that would make it extremely difficult for the company to gain market recognition. And it isn't just Chris and Sara who recognize the importance of innovation to Graber's long-term success. *Everyone* at Graber talks about innovation. For instance, the company's talented toolmakers, who bend and mold the pieces of steel into the simple yet functional bicycle racks are constantly innovating. They have to, and they're given the freedom to do so by the company's cellular manufacturing system.

Cellular manufacturing is similar to assembly-line production, but assembly lines use some parts that are made elsewhere, whereas all parts used in cellular manufacturing are processed right in the plant. Employees can design and produce tools or processes that make them more efficient and help them achieve higher product quality levels. The cellular manufacturing system has led to two important results at Graber. First, it has improved the quality of parts because employees are now dealing with a much smaller production run. Second, it has improved efficiency by almost 25 percent.

QUESTIONS

1. What role do you think innovation plays in the operations management system at Graber? What role do you think innovation plays in value chain management?

2. Do you think there's a connection between innovativeness in *producing* a product and in *developing* a product? Explain.

3. How do you think the three product development "musts" that Chris Fortune describes might affect the innovation process at Graber Products?

4. Pretend that Sara and Chris Fortune have asked you to come to their plant in Madison, Wisconsin, to consult with them about value chain management. Make a list of the important points you'd want to tell them.

Source: Based on *Small Business 2000, Show 410.*

Learning Objectives

After reading and studying this chapter, you should be able to:

1. Define organizational performance.

2. Explain why measuring organizational performance is important.

3. Describe the different organizational performance measures.

4. Identify financial control tools used to monitor and measure organizational performance.

5. Explain how a management information system can be used as a tool for monitoring and measuring organizational performance.

6. Describe the balanced scorecard approach to monitoring and measuring organizational performance.

7. Tell how benchmarking of best practices can be used for monitoring and measuring organizational performance.

8. Discuss the manager's role in helping organizations achieve high levels of performance.

A MANAGER'S DILEMMA

In Seattle, on June 23, 2000, music lovers around the world rejoiced as the Experience Music Project (EMP), an interactive museum located at the foot of the city's famous Space Needle, opened.[1] EMP (www.emplive.com) is a tribute to American popular music, especially rock 'n' roll. Although Tom Chiado, project manager at EMP, may have one of the most fun and interesting jobs in the world, his job as manager isn't easy.

EMP is the brainchild of Microsoft co-founder, Paul Allen. Allen had amassed the world's largest collection of rock memorabilia including fragments of the electric guitar Jimi Hendrix smashed and burned at the 1967 Monterey International Pop Festival, feather boas worn by Janis Joplin, and turntables used by Grandmaster Flash. He needed a place to showcase it. About $100 million later, Allen's fascinating memorabilia had a home.

The building itself is a sight to see. Its wildly shaped exterior immediately attracts attention. But it's the interior that really grabs you. It's a technological fun house designed for experiencing music firsthand. Visitors can play live at the "on stage" exhibit and experience billowing smoke, lights sweeping the stage, and a filmed audience cheering wildly. Then there's the professional sound-mixing board where visitors can remix the Eurhythmics song "Sweet Dreams." There's even a crazy ride called Artist's Journey where visitors are strapped in for a ride that takes

Controlling for Organizational Performance

20

them from the middle of a filmed block party to a concert audience getting down with George Clinton's band.

Allen is determined to give visitors as much information as possible as they tour the museum. Therefore, upon arrival, visitors receive a hand-held multimedia device equipped with a small screen, headphones, and 4 MB computer hard drive that they can use to call up music and text on virtually every object on display. Despite all the high-tech touches, Chiado has some down-to-earth managing to do. One of his tasks is assessing EMP's performance. Put yourself in his position. How can he monitor how effective and efficient EMP is?

WHAT WOULD YOU DO?

Managers have many challenges when it comes to controlling for organizational performance. As the chapter-opening Manager's Dilemma points out, effectiveness and efficiency are just two of the measures that managers might use. In this chapter, we discuss several issues associated with controlling for organizational performance. We start by looking at what organizational performance is and why it's important to measure it. Then we look at different organizational performance measures and at some tools for monitoring and measuring organizational performance. We conclude the chapter by describing the manager's role in guiding organizations to high performance.

> ## ORGANIZATIONAL PERFORMANCE

Available seat-miles. Seat-miles flown. Revenue per passenger-miles. Passenger load factors. These are just a few of the important performance indicators that executives in the intensely competitive airline industry carefully measure and scrutinize. Then, of course, there's the Triple Crown—not the one awarded for winning three famous horse races—but the one awarded by the U.S. Department of Transportation's Air Travel Consumer Report for outstanding performance accomplishments in three areas: customer service, on-time performance, and baggage handling. One company, Southwest Airlines, has earned an unprecedented five consecutive Triple Crowns. Obviously, managers at Southwest Airlines recognized the importance of controlling for organizational performance. But managers in the airline industry aren't the only ones who want and need performance information. Managers in all types of businesses must manage organizational performance.

WHAT IS ORGANIZATIONAL PERFORMANCE?

performance

The end result of an activity.

When you hear the word *performance* what do you think of? A summer evening concert given by a local community orchestra? An Olympic athlete pushing all out for the finish line in a close race? A Southwest Airlines ramp agent in Tulsa, Oklahoma, loading passengers as quickly and efficiently as possible in order to meet the company's 20-minute gate turnaround goal? A Web site designer at Prentice Hall Publishers creating an online learning site that professors and students will find valuable? **Performance** is all of these. It's the end result of an activity.[2] And whether that activity is hours of intense practice before a concert or race or whether it's carrying out job responsibilities as efficiently and effectively as possible, performance is what results from that activity.

organizational performance

The accumulated end results of all the organization's work processes and activities.

Managers are concerned with **organizational performance**—the accumulated end results of all the organization's work processes and activities. It's a complex but important concept, and managers need to understand the factors that contribute to high organizational performance. After all, they don't want (or intend) to manage their way to mediocre performance. They *want* their organizations, work units, or work groups to achieve high levels of performance, no matter what mission, strategies, or goals are being pursued.

WHY IS MEASURING ORGANIZATIONAL PERFORMANCE IMPORTANT?

Managers measure and control organizational performance because it leads to better asset management, to an increased ability to provide customer value, and to improved measures of organizational knowledge. In addition, measures of organizational performance do have an impact on an organization's reputation. (See Exhibit 20.1.)

Better Asset Management The year was 1984, and the Chicago Bulls team was about as bad as it could be. This mediocre team had never won an NBA championship. Barely 6,000 people showed up at a game paying $15 a seat to watch the team play. However, that year the franchise owners and managers made a decision that would have a profound effect on the organization (and eventually on basketball history). They signed a young guard from the University of North Carolina by the name of Michael Jordan. By the end of the 1998 season, attendance had skyrocketed (24,000+ spectators per game willing to pay an average of $30 a ticket), the team had won six NBA championships in eight years, and the franchise itself benefited handsomely as its value soared (much like Michael Jordan himself) by 1,000 percent.[3] By all relevant performance measures, the Chicago Bulls basketball organization was successful.

The point of this story is that an organization's assets are only valuable if they're managed in a way that captures that value. The value created by Michael Jordan and other assets of the Bulls (coach Phil Jackson; other talented team players including Scottie Pippen and Dennis Rodman; experienced marketing, operations, and financial employees; and other resources including the arena and practice facilities, available capital, etc.) was possible only because they were managed extremely well as a portfolio of assets. That's what managers at high-performing companies do—they manage the organizational assets in ways that exploit their value. **Asset management** is the process of acquiring, manag-

Achieving world-class organizational performance requires getting everything right. Despite the enormous success of the brick-and-mortar retail giant Wal-Mart, the associated Web site (www.walmart.com) is still working its way to success. In 1999 the site was at a competitive disadvantage because it was unable to promise Christmas delivery of orders placed after December 14, and a newly expanded site that opened the following February was criticized for its cumbersome design, slow operation, and poor search engine. With many improvements now in store, CEO Jeanne Jackson thinks Walmart.com will win the race to the top. As she is known to say, "This is a marathon. It's not a sprint."

asset management

The process of acquiring, managing, renewing, and disposing of assets as needed, and of designing business models to exploit the value from these assets.

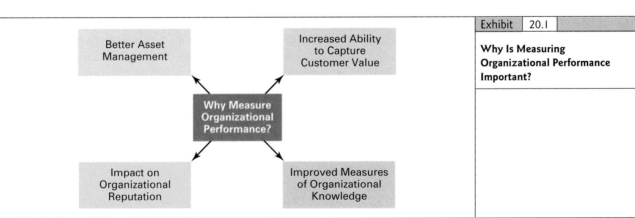

Exhibit	20.1

Why Is Measuring Organizational Performance Important?

You should consider the knowledge, experiences, and skills you'll gain from your job as personal career assets.[5] And you should manage these assets just as managers manage organizational assets—that is, manage them in ways that create value.

Creating value from managing your personal career asset portfolio may, some day, involve making a decision to leave your job. And you wouldn't be alone in such a decision. A poll conducted by CareerPath.com found that of the 1,400 workers surveyed, 40 percent said they planned to change jobs within a year. Although people will put a lot of thought into getting the next job, how many actually think about an exit strategy for the job they'll be leaving? Yet, the way you leave your current job says a lot about the way you value your work, your colleagues, your reputation, and your personal career assets.

Some actions you need to take in implementing an effective exit strategy include (1) deciding when to go public with your intention to leave, (2) anticipating how to answer the inevitable questions about your decision, (3) scheduling a workable transition plan, and (4) dealing with the emotions (joy, sorrow, guilt, panic, jealousy, and anger) associated with leaving and starting over. The goal in being prepared for each of these is protecting your hard-earned reputation and making sure people at the organization you're leaving feel good about your time there.

ing, renewing, and disposing of assets as needed, and of designing business models to take advantage of the value from these assets.[4] It's not just the top-level managers who are concerned with asset management. Managers at all organizational levels and in all work areas manage their available assets—people, information, equipment, and so forth—by making decisions that they hope will lead to high levels of performance. Because achieving high levels of organizational performance is important in both the short run and long run, managers look for ways to better manage their assets so that they look good on the key performance measures used by both internal *and* external evaluators.

Increased Ability to Provide Customer Value Providing value to customers is important for organizations. If customers aren't receiving something of value from their interactions with organizations, they'll look elsewhere. Managers should monitor how well they're providing customer value, and they can do that when they measure performance. For example, at IBM's Industry Solutions Laboratories in Hawthorne, New York, Stuttgart, Germany, and Yamato, Japan, customers interact with IBM researchers to come up with technological solutions that meet their unique and challenging needs.[6] For instance, Britain's Safeway Stores PLC and the Hawthorne Lab collaborated on a consumer application that gives top customers the ability to conveniently create and maintain personalized grocery shopping lists and preorder groceries using a portable handheld device. And the Hawthorne Lab completed a project for Southwest Airlines that automated the crew-pairing process—a company logistics nightmare in which 2,700 pilots, 4,500 flight attendants, and more than 2,400 daily departures had to be logistically coordinated. It was important for the lab's managers to be able to measure how well they solved customer problems and to gauge their ability to provide customer value.

Impact on Organizational Reputation You know that your personal reputation is important in what others think of you. It influences whether they will ask you for advice, listen to what you have to say, or trust you to complete assigned tasks. Organizations strive to have good reputations, as well. They want others—customers, suppliers, competitors, community, and so forth—to think highly of them. The advantages of a strong corporate reputation include greater consumer trust and the ability to command premium pricing.[7] In addition, there is a strong correlation between an organization's financial performance and its reputation. Which leads to the other? It's not always clear which comes first, but we do know it's difficult to have one without the other. In fact, a study of reputation and financial performance showed a strong correlation between good reputation and strong financial measures such as earnings growth and total return.[8]

Water has taken on new value as health-conscious consumers drink more of it and less soda, coffee, and tea. But just how much do consumers value water? Philip Hughes will soon find out. As proprietor of Ice Box Ltd., a major London supplier of pristine blocks of Greenland ice, Hughes is betting that water that froze in the pollution-free days of Cleopatra will succeed when marketed as a luxury product. "You get this sparkling effect as it releases oxygen," he says. Sales figures will soon provide Hughes with a gauge of that sparkle's value.

Improved Measures of Organizational Knowledge We know from our discussions in Chapters 2 and 10 that successful organizations of the twenty-first century must be able to learn and respond quickly—that is, they must be learning organizations. In learning organizations, organizational knowledge is recognized as a valuable asset, just like cash, equipment, or raw materials. What is **organizational knowledge**? It's knowledge that's created by means of collaborative information sharing and social interaction that lead to organizational members taking appropriate actions.[9] The key to valuable organizational knowledge is this connection between information and action. Organizational employees must share what they know and use that knowledge to make changes in work practices, processes, or products to achieve high levels of organizational performance.

Although intangible knowledge assets are increasingly overshadowing the value of tangible assets at many companies, it's not always easy to measure the value of organizational knowledge. In fact, the director of finance at defense contractor Lockheed Martin said, "We currently have no formal measure of knowledge assets, but these assets are our survival assets, and the most strategic for our long-term viability."[10] Successful managers do understand the importance of organizational knowledge to organizational performance even if it's much harder to manage knowledge assets than physical assets. And successful organizations have developed approaches to managing knowledge assets even though they have no formal measurement tools. For example, Genentech, Inc., the biotech firm, uses a metric of its own creation that looks at strategic research and development spending and the assets that are created from this spending.[11] It's not a perfect measure, but it works for them.

organizational knowledge

Knowledge that's created by collaborative information sharing and social interaction that lead to organizational members taking appropriate actions.

1. **What is performance? What is organizational performance?**

2. **Why is measuring organizational performance important?**

3. **How is organizational knowledge more than sharing information?**

Testing...Testing...1,2,3

MEASURES OF ORGANIZATIONAL PERFORMANCE

At Shandwick International, a public relations firm whose global clients come from such diverse industries as entertainment, financial communications, and health care, employees were "more afraid of talking about money than we are of talking about sex."[12] However, the company's chief learning officer decided to change that by creating a series of training programs to help employees understand how the company made money. Employees were shown the connection between what work they did and the company's performance. "If you know what makes figures move in the right direction, you can do your job differently and push them in that direction."[13]

Management author Peter Drucker would agree that an organization's employees need to see the connection between what they do and the outcomes. He said, "The focus of the organization must be on performance . . . The spirit of organization is high performance standards, for the group as well as for each individual."[14] But before employees can see this connection and work toward achieving high performance, managers need to specify the performance outcomes that will be measured. The most frequently used organizational performance measures include organizational productivity, organizational effectiveness, and industry rankings.

productivity

The overall output of goods or services produced divided by the inputs needed to generate that output.

Organizational Productivity We defined **productivity** in Chapter 19 as the overall output of goods or services produced divided by the inputs needed to generate that output. Organizations strive to be productive. They want the most goods and services produced using the least amount of inputs. Output is measured by the sales revenue an organization receives when those goods and services are sold (selling price × number sold). Input is measured by the costs of acquiring and transforming the organizational resources into the outputs.

It's management's job to increase this ratio. The easiest way to do this, of course, would be to raise the selling price of the outputs, but today's competitive environment makes this a risky choice that may, in fact, decrease the total output sold. The only other viable option, then, for increasing productivity is to decrease the input part of ratio—that is, the organization's expenses. Doing this means being more efficient in performing the organization's work activities. So, organizational productivity becomes a measure of how efficiently employees do their work.

Being efficient nowadays often means investing in technology. For example, when Ford Motor Company announced in February 2000 that it would provide each of its approximately 346,000 employees worldwide with a high-speed computer, a color printer, and unlimited Internet access for just $5 a month over three years, the company saw it not as an expense but as an investment in its employees' capabilities. The company's chief information officer said, "Even though the day-to-day tasks of many Ford employees don't currently involve the Internet, eventually everyone will be affected. We are increasing our company's capability by increasing the capability of our employees."[15] Ford was investing in its future productivity by making employees more efficient in their job-related use of the Internet.

organizational effectiveness

A measure of how appropriate organizational goals are and how well an organization is achieving those goals.

Organizational Effectiveness In Chapter 1, we defined managerial effectiveness as goal attainment. Can the same interpretation apply to organizational effectiveness? Yes, it can. **Organizational effectiveness** is a measure of how appropriate organizational goals are and how well an organization is achieving those goals. It's a common performance measure used by managers.

Other descriptions of organizational effectiveness have been suggested by management researchers.[16] For instance, the systems resource model of organizational effectiveness proposes that effectiveness is measured by the organization's ability

---

Diversity Success Stories

U.S. companies are making progress in their diversity programs. Although many still have a long way to go, some companies are doing their best to make employees of all races into full and active participants in their businesses.[17] Every year, *Fortune* identifies America's 50 Best Companies for Minorities. Each of the companies on this list has made an outstanding commitment to diversity at every organizational level and in every aspect—from new hires to suppliers, and even to the charitable causes supported. Who are some of these diversity champions and what are they doing? Let's look at a few examples.

Levi-Strauss is number two on the list. The company has a long history of funding projects that help bring together diverse groups of people. For instance, it founded Project Change, an organization devoted to combating racism in communities in which the company has manufacturing facilities. In addition, it was one of the first companies to integrate its factories in the southern United States. And it pioneered a program to buy supplies from minority-owned businesses.

Avis Rent A Car is number 8 on the list. It leads its industry in the share of total purchasing dollars spent with minority-owned companies. In addition, minorities make up 25 percent of the organization's managers and receive about 35 percent of job promotions.

Hyatt Corporation (thirteenth on the list) leads all companies in minority representation with 62.5 percent of the payroll. About 35 percent of Hyatt managers are from minority groups. Hyatt also started a program to introduce inner-city students to the culinary profession. It installed a $250,000 state-of-the-art industrial kitchen at Chicago's predominantly Hispanic Roberto Clemente High School. Several students discovered a passion for cooking and have gone on to culinary careers at Hyatt and other organizations.

Finally, Sempra Energy of San Diego is fourth on the list. Almost half of its workforce is made up of minorities. Sempra requires its human resources staff to evaluate all human resource management activities from job postings to employee benefit plans to ensure that minorities are treated equally. And supervisors must explain why minority candidates are rejected for promotions.

---

to exploit its environment in acquiring scarce and valued resources. The process model emphasizes the transformation processes of the organization and how well the organization converts inputs into desired outputs. Then, finally, the multiple constituencies model says that several different effectiveness measures should be used, reflecting the different criteria of the organization's constituencies. For example, customers, advocacy groups, suppliers, and security analysts each would have their own measures of how well the organization was performing. Although each of these different effectiveness models may have merit in measuring certain aspects of organizational effectiveness, the bottom line for managers continues to be how well the organization accomplishes its goals. That's what guides managerial decisions in designing strategies, work processes, and work activities, and in coordinating the work of employees.

Industry Rankings There's no shortage of different types of industry and company rankings. Exhibit 20.2 lists some of the more popular rankings that can be used to measure organizational performance. The rankings for each list are determined by specific performance measures. For instance, *Fortune's* Top Performing Companies of the *Fortune* 500 are determined by financial results including, for example, profits, return on revenue, and return on shareholder's equity; growth in profits for 1 year, 5 years, and 10 years; and revenues per employee, revenues per dollar of assets, and revenues per dollar of equity.[18] *Fortune's* 100 Best Companies to Work For are chosen by answers given by thousands of randomly selected employees on a questionnaire called the Great Place to Work Trust Index (www.greatplacetowork.com) and on materials filled out by thousands of

Exhibit	20.2

Popular Industry and Company Rankings

Fortune (www.fortune.com)
100 Best Companies to Work For
Fortune 1000
Fortune 1000 Top Performing Companies
Global 500
America's Most Admired Companies
World's Most Admired Companies
America's Best Wealth Creators
America's Best and Worst Boards of Directors
e50 Companies
America's 50 Best for Minorities

Business Week (www.businessweek.com)
Standard & Poor's 500
Global 1000

Forbes (www.forbes.com)
Forbes 500
Forbes International 500
500 Top Private Companies
200 Best Small Companies

Industry Week (www.industryweek.com)
100 Best Managed Companies
World's Best Plants
Technology and Innovation Awards of the Year
Census of Manufacturers
25 Fastest Growing Companies
Industry Week 1000

Customer Satisfaction Indexes
American Customer Satisfaction Index—
    University of Michigan Business School
(www.bus.umich.edu/research/nqrc/acsi.html)
Customer Satisfaction Measurement Association
(www.csmassociation.org)

Industry rankings have expanded in recent years to include more than just the largest or most profitable firms. Newer measures include firms that focus on work-life issues or family-friendly benefits and honor those organizations whose managers consistently set new standards in these areas. *Working Woman* magazine, for instance, publishes an annual list of the 100 Best Companies for Working Mothers. One entry for the year 2000 is the Stride-Rite Corporation. What put this 81-year-old maker of children's footwear on the list for the eighth time? It adopted several greatly improved work/life benefits, despite declining sales, including longer vacations, larger tuition reimbursements, and longer leaves for new fathers and adoptive parents.

company managers including a corporate culture audit created by the Great Place to Work Institute and a human resources questionnaire designed by Hewitt Associates, the largest compensation and benefits consultant in the United States.[19] *Industry Week's* Best Managed Plants are determined by organizational accomplishments and demonstrations of superior management skills in the areas of financial performance, innovation, leadership, globalization, alliances and partnerships, employee benefits and education, and community involvement.[20] The American Customer Satisfaction Index (ACSI), (www.bus.umich.edu/research/nqrc/acsi.html) measures customer satisfaction with the quality of goods and services available to household consumers in the United States and then links the results to financial returns.[21] Each of the other rankings listed in Exhibit 20.2 is compiled from specific performance measures chosen by the organization doing the ranking.

Testing...Testing...1,2,3

4. **How can managers increase organizational productivity?**

5. **What does organizational effectiveness measure?**

6. **Why might managers use industry rankings as performance measures?**

> ## TOOLS FOR MONITORING AND MEASURING ORGANIZATIONAL PERFORMANCE

Managers at Applebee's Neighborhood Grill & Bar restaurant chain play by their own rules. They're applying cutting-edge ideas to a traditional industry. Rather than carefully locating restaurants so that the sales of one don't eat into another's sales, Applebee's floods an area with stores in order to gain brand recognition and market dominance. For instance, in Kansas City, where its corporate headquarters are located, the company has 23 restaurants. In contrast, Chili's, its biggest competitor, only has four units. Applebee's philosophy: Faster is better. Get into a neighborhood before the competition. Keep things moving by giving customers a convenient experience.[22] What kinds of tools would Applebee's managers need for monitoring and measuring performance?

At Murata Manufacturing Company of Kyoto, Japan, managers know that performance will be measured against a challenging goal set by Yasutaka Morita, the company's chairman. That goal? Thirty percent of annual sales should come from new products. Since Murata manufactures components for information-age devices such as cellular phones, personal digital assistants, and so forth, measures of new-product innovation are key indicators.[23]

As these examples illustrate, managers need appropriate tools for monitoring and measuring organizational performance. Managers might use any of the following types of performance control tools: financial controls, information controls, balanced scorecard approach, or benchmarking best practices approach.

FINANCIAL CONTROLS

One of the primary purposes of every business firm is to earn a profit. In pursuit of this objective, managers need financial controls. Managers might, for instance, carefully analyze quarterly income statements for excessive expenses. They might also perform several financial ratio tests to ensure that sufficient cash is available to pay ongoing expenses, that debt levels haven't become too high, or that assets are being used productively. Or they might look at some newer financial control tools such as market value added (MVA) to see if the company's market value is greater than the capital invested in it.

Traditional Financial Control Measures Traditional financial measures managers might employ include ratio analysis and budget analysis. Exhibit 20.3 summarizes some of the most popular financial ratios used in organizations. Taken from the organization's main financial statements (the balance sheet and the income statement), they compare two significant figures and express them as a percentage or ratio. Because you've undoubtedly encountered these ratios in introductory accounting and finance courses, or you will in the near future, we aren't going to elaborate on how they're calculated.

Financial ratios are widely reported in the business press and carefully watched by investors. When Deutsche Telekom's CEO Ron Sommer announced that his firm would shift its goals following smaller than expected profits late in 2000, some investors expressed their disappointment in the company's performance by selling their shares, which caused share value to drop. Sommer's plans, which he announced to journalists in a conference call about the company's latest financial results, include backing out of the bidding war for a wireless network in Europe to avoid overpaying for access to countries where the company had no customer base.

Exhibit	20.3

Popular Financial Ratios

Objective	Ratio	Calculation	Meaning
Liquidity	Current ratio	$\dfrac{\text{Current assets}}{\text{Current liabilities}}$	Tests the organization's ability to meet short-term obligations
	Acid test	$\dfrac{\text{Current assets less inventories}}{\text{Current liabilities}}$	Tests liquidity more accurately when inventories turn over slowly or are difficult to sell
Leverage	Debt to assets	$\dfrac{\text{Total debt}}{\text{Total assets}}$	The higher the ratio, the more leveraged the organization
	Times interest earned	$\dfrac{\text{Profits before interest and taxes}}{\text{Total interest charges}}$	Measures how far profits can decline before the organization is unable to meet its interest expenses
Activity	Inventory turnover	$\dfrac{\text{Sales}}{\text{Inventory}}$	The higher the ratio, the more efficiently inventory assets are being used
	Total asset turnover	$\dfrac{\text{Sales}}{\text{Total assets}}$	The fewer assets used to achieve a given level of sales, the more efficiently management is using the organization's total assets
Profitability	Profit margin on sales	$\dfrac{\text{Net profit after taxes}}{\text{Total sales}}$	Identifies the profits that various products are generating
	Return on investment	$\dfrac{\text{Net profit after taxes}}{\text{Total assets}}$	Measures the efficiency of assets to generate profits

What do these ratios mean? The liquidity ratios measure an organization's ability to meet its current debt obligations. Leverage ratios examine the organization's use of debt to finance its assets and whether it's able to meet the interest payments on the debt. The activity ratios measure how efficiently the firm is using its assets. Finally, the profitability ratios measure how efficiently and effectively the firm is using its assets to generate profits. We mention these ratios only briefly here to remind you that managers use such ratios as internal control devices for monitoring how efficiently and profitably the organization uses its assets, debt, inventories, and the like.

We discussed budgets as a planning tool in Chapter 9. When a budget is formulated, it's a planning tool because it gives direction to work activities. It indicates what activities are important and how much resources should be allocated to each activity. As we noted, however, budgets are used for both planning and controlling.

Budgets also provide managers with quantitative standards against which to measure and compare resource consumption. By pointing out deviations between standard and actual consumption, they become control tools. If the deviations are judged to be significant enough to require action, the manager will want to examine what has happened and try to uncover the reasons behind the deviations. With this information, he or she can take whatever action is necessary. For example, if you use a personal budget for monitoring and controlling your monthly expenses, you might find one month that your miscellaneous expenses were higher than you had budgeted for. At that point, you might cut back spending in another area or work extra hours to try to get more income.

Other Financial Control Measures In addition to the traditional financial tools, managers are using measures such as economic value added (EVA) and market value added (MVA). The fundamental concept behind both of these financial tools is that companies are supposed to take in capital from investors and make it worth more. When managers do that, they've created wealth. When they take in capital and make it worth less, they've destroyed wealth.

Economic value added (EVA) is a tool for measuring corporate and divisional performance. It's calculated by taking after-tax operating profit minus the total annual cost of capital.[24] EVA is a measure of how much economic value is being created by what a company does with its assets, less any capital investments the company has made in its assets. As a performance control tool, EVA focuses managers' attention on earning a rate of return over and above the cost of capital. Companies such as Hewlett-Packard, Equifax, Boise Cascade Corporation, and even the U.S. Postal Service have integrated EVA measures into their organizations and improved their performance as a result.[25] When EVA is used as a performance measure, employees soon learn that they can improve their organization's or business unit's EVA by earning more profit without using more capital, by using less capital, or by investing capital in high-return projects.[26]

Market value added (MVA) adds a market dimension because it measures the stock market's estimate of the value of a firm's past and expected capital investment projects. If the company's market value (value of all outstanding stock plus the company's debt) is greater than all the capital invested in it (from shareholders, bondholders, and retained earnings), it has a positive MVA indicating that managers have created wealth. If the company's market value is less than all the capital invested in it, the MVA will be negative indicating that managers have destroyed wealth. Studies have shown that EVA is a predictor of MVA and that consecutive years of positive EVA generally lead to a high MVA.[27]

Both EVA and MVA can be powerful tools for managers as they monitor and measure organizational performance. In fact, they're becoming so popular that some people feel that they may replace some of the more traditional financial ratio measures such as return on investment.[28] ◄───────

INFORMATION CONTROLS

Information can be critical to monitoring and measuring an organization's performance. Managers need the right information at the right time and in the right amount. Inaccurate, incomplete, excessive, or delayed information will seriously impede performance. How can managers use information for control?

economic value added (EVA)

A financial tool for measuring corporate and divisional performance calculated by taking after-tax operating profit minus the total annual cost of capital.

market value added (MVA)

A financial tool that measures the stock market's estimate of the value of a firm's past and expected investment projects.

Testing...Testing...1,2,3

7. **How can financial ratios be used as tools for measuring organizational performance?**

8. **What performance measurement information do budgets provide?**

9. **Explain EVA and MVA.**

How do managers decide what to do when analysts tell them their industry's time has come and gone? Scott Little (left) and Peter Beaudrault, CFO and President of Hard Rock Café International, looked at information showing nearly a decade of declining growth and revenues for the theme dining industry and came to a different conclusion. They've just spent $50 million to refurbish Hard Rock's 105 worldwide locations, and $7 million to build a state-of-the-art network to handle digital streaming of live events via the Internet. Heeding customer input, they're also upgrading the menus and planning new locations with less emphasis on nostalgia. Their goal is nothing less than to create a new life for their 30-year-old brand.

management information system (MIS)

A system used to provide management with needed information on a regular basis.

data

Raw, unanalyzed facts.

information

Processed and analyzed data.

Management Information Systems Although there's no universally agreed-upon definition of a **management information system (MIS)**, we'll define it as a system used to provide management with needed information on a regular basis. In theory, this system can be manual or computer based, although all current discussions focus on computer-supported applications. The term *system* in MIS implies order, arrangement, and purpose. Furthermore, an MIS focuses specifically on providing managers with *information*, not merely *data*. These two points are important and require elaboration.

A library provides a good analogy. Although it can contain millions of volumes, a library doesn't do users much good if they can't find what they want quickly. That's why librarians spend a great deal of time cataloging a library's collections and ensuring that materials are returned to their proper locations. Organizations today are like well-stocked libraries. There's no lack of data. There is, however, an inability to process those data so that the right information is available to the right person when he or she needs it. Likewise, a library is almost useless if it has the book you need immediately but you can't find it or the library takes a week to retrieve it from storage. An MIS, on the other hand, has organized data in some meaningful way and can access the information in a reasonable amount of time. **Data** are raw, unanalyzed facts, such as numbers, names, or quantities. Raw unanalyzed facts are relatively useless to managers. When data are analyzed and processed, they become **information**. An MIS collects data and turns them into relevant information for managers to use.

How Are Information Systems Used in Controlling? Managers need information to monitor organizational performance and to control organizational activities. Without information, they would find it difficult to perform the activities we discussed in Chapter 18 as part of the controlling process. For instance, in measuring actual performance, managers need information about what is, in fact, happening within their area of responsibility. They need information about what the standards are in order to be able to compare actual performance with the standards; they need information to help them determine acceptable ranges of variation within these comparisons; and they rely on information to help them develop appropriate courses of action if there are significant deviations between actual and standard. As you can see, information is an important tool in monitoring and measuring organizational performance.

BALANCED SCORECARD APPROACH

The balanced scorecard approach to performance measurement was introduced as a way to evaluate organizational performance from more than just the financial perspective.[29] The **balanced scorecard** is a performance measurement tool that looks at four areas—financial, customer, internal processes, and people/innovation/growth assets—that contribute to a company's performance. According to this approach, managers should develop goals in each of the four areas and measures to determine if these goals are being met. For instance, a company might include cash flow, quarterly sales growth, and return on investment (ROI) as measures for success in the financial area. Or it might include percentage of sales coming from new products as a measure of customer goals.[30] The intent of the balanced scorecard is to emphasize that all of these areas are important to an organization's success and that there should be a balance among them.

Although a balanced scorecard makes sense, unfortunately, managers still tend to focus on areas that they believe drive their organization's success.[31] Their scorecards reflect their strategies. If those strategies center around the customer, for example, then the customer area is likely to get more attention than the other three areas. Yet, managers need to recognize that you really can't focus on one performance area without affecting the others. For instance, at IBM Global Services in Houston, managers developed a scorecard around an overriding strategy of customer satisfaction. However, the other areas (financial, internal processes, and people/innovation/growth) are intended to support that central strategy. The solutions manager for the balanced scorecard described the division's approach as follows, "The internal processes part of our business is directly related to responding to our customers in a timely manner, and the learning and innovation aspect is critical for us since what we're selling to our customers above all is our expertise. Of course, how successful we are with those things will affect our financial component."[32] And, in Canada, the Ontario Hospital Association developed a scorecard for 89 hospitals designed to evaluate four main areas: clinical utilization and outcomes, financial performance and financial condition of the hospital, patient satisfaction, and how the hospital was investing for the future. The scorecard was purposefully designed to recognize the synergies among each of these measures. After hospitals were evaluated on the scorecard measures, the results of the scorecard evaluations were made available to patients, giving them an objective basis for choosing a hospital.[33]

BENCHMARKING OF BEST PRACTICES

When the first 2001 Chrysler Sebring convertible rolled off the assembly line at DaimlerChrysler's assembly plant, the company was able to avoid $100 million in production costs because of manufacturing best practices shared by Mercedes-Benz, Chrysler's German owner.[34] We first introduced the concept of benchmarking in Chapter 9. Remember that **benchmarking** is the search for the best practices among competitors or noncompetitors that lead to their superior performance. At its most fundamental level, benchmarking means learning from

balanced scorecard

A performance measurement tool that looks at four areas—financial, customer, internal processes, and people/innovation/growth assets—that contribute to a company's performance.

benchmarking

The search for the best practices among competitors or noncompetitors that lead to their superior performance.

others.[35] As a tool for monitoring and measuring organizational performance, benchmarking can be used to help identify specific performance gaps and potential areas of improvement.[36] But managers shouldn't just look at external organizations for best practices. It's also important for managers to look for internal best practices that can be shared.

Did you ever work somewhere that had an employee suggestion box on a wall in an office or in the workplace? When an employee had an idea about a new way of doing something—such as reducing costs, improving delivery time, and so forth—it went into the suggestion box where it usually sat until someone decided to empty the box. Businesspeople frequently joked about the suggestion box and cartoons lambasted the futility of putting ideas in the employee suggestion box.

Unfortunately, this attitude about suggestion boxes still persists in many organizations, and it shouldn't. Research shows that best practices frequently already exist within an organization but usually go unidentified and unused.[37] That's a lot of valuable knowledge going to waste. In today's environment, organizations striving for high performance levels can't afford to ignore such potentially valuable information. Remember our discussion of knowledge management and the need to share performance-related information with others inside the organization. Some companies already have recognized the potential of internally benchmarking best practices as a tool for monitoring and measuring performance. For example, Toyota Motor Corporation developed a suggestion-screening system to prioritize best practices based on potential impact, benefits, and difficulty of implementation. Accenture and EDS, Inc. have hired knowledge managers who oversee and disseminate information about internal best practices. W. R. Grace & Company, a supplier of specialty chemical, construction, and container products, regularly updates profiles of its top salespeople as role models for others to learn from. And General Motors Corporation sends employees—from upper management to line employees—to different plants where they learn about internal and external best practices.[38]

Exhibit 20.4 provides a summary of what managers must do to implement an internal benchmarking best practices program.

Exhibit 20.4	
Steps to Successfully Implement an Internal Benchmarking Best Practices Program	**1.** *Connect best practices to strategies and goals.* The organization's strategies and goals should dictate what types of best practices might be most valuable to others in the organization. **2.** *Identify best practices throughout the organization.* Organizations must have a way to find out what practices have been successful in different work areas and units. **3.** *Develop best practices reward and recognition systems.* Individuals must be given an incentive to share their knowledge. The reward system should be built into the organization's culture. **4.** *Communicate best practices throughout the organization.* Once best practices have been identified, that information needs to be shared with others in the organization. **5.** *Create a best practices knowledge-sharing system.* There needs to be a formal mechanism for organizational members to continue sharing their ideas and best practices. **6.** *Nurture best practices on an ongoing basis.* Create an organizational culture that reinforces a "we can learn from everyone" attitude and emphasizes sharing information.
	Source: Based on T. Leahy, "Extracting Diamonds in the Rough," *Business Finance*, August 2000, pp. 33–37.

› A MANAGER'S ROLE IN HELPING ORGANIZATIONS ACHIEVE HIGH PERFORMANCE LEVELS

Only General Electric Company, Avon Products Inc., Cisco Systems, Inc., Cemex SA de CV, and 24 other companies have been named to *Industry Week's* 100 Best Managed Companies list for five straight years (1996–2000).[39] What distinguishes these high-performing companies from countless others worldwide? What do they do differently that leads to such accomplishments? Two judges who helped choose the companies for this prestigious list said, "All of the companies understand that the key to competitive advantage in this century will be the capacity of top leadership to create social architecture capable of penetrating intellectual capital. The best-managed companies are able to integrate and implement the new-economy virtues of speed and e-commerce with the old-economy virtues of generating profit, market share, and excellent customer service."[40]

Who guides these organizations in these directions? Who makes these decisions and choices? Note that these companies have the distinction of being best-*managed* companies. Obviously, managers have played an important role in their companies' achieving these high levels of performance. What role *do* managers play in achieving high performance? We made the point earlier that there are no managers who want to manage their way to mediocrity. Exhibit 20.5 identifies important responsibilities of managers in leading their employees and organizations to achieve at exemplary levels of performance.

One of the manager's first responsibilities in leading organizations to high performance levels is helping organizational members make the right choices during periods of organizational change.[41] We know that, for most organizations, change is a given in today's environment. Managers must provide direction by answering employees' questions about what the change entails, what it means for them, how their performance will now be evaluated, and what tools and support will be provided to them. These employee concerns are the same whether the change is organization-wide or simply within the work group. By providing direction and encouragement during periods of change, managers can influence employees to make choices about their work activities that will help them achieve high performance levels. And when employees are performing at high levels, the organization will be also.

Another responsibility of managers is to design a performance management system that identifies appropriate performance measures and addresses common performance measurement problems. It's an accepted fact in organizations that what gets measured is what gets done.[42] People will work on those things on which they're going to be evaluated. So managers have to make sure that they're measuring the right things. For instance, performance measures used at General Motors can tell you anything you want to know about the car's outcome—such as how much of every type of material that went into it, how

Proflowers.com is an online florist based in San Diego, with about $35 million in sales in 2000. When busy times hit, like Valentine's Day and Mother's Day, Penny Handscomb, vice president of human resources and training, resists hiring extra people who later have to be laid off. Instead, she trains every new hire, even computer programmers, in the skills of customer service. "When it comes to busy times," she says, "I put everybody on the phone." The result? Calls get answered, and everyone in the firm has a first-hand understanding of what makes customers happy. Such meticulous attention to customers, and such an innovative and effective way of catering to their needs, is what sets apart the best practices of successful firms.

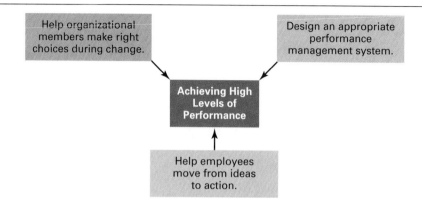

Exhibit　20.5

A Manager's Responsibilities in Helping Organizations Achieve High Levels of Performance

many defects it has, and how many labor-hours were expended in making it. In fact, the company has about 1,000 outcome measures. But what it lacks are work process performance measures. There are no measures to tell employees what they might be doing wrong and how they might improve their performance.[43]

So what *should* organizations measure? They should measure what's important to their customers, to the work processes they use to provide goods or services, and to the company itself.[44] It goes back to the importance of establishing appropriate goals during the planning function. If the chosen goals are important enough to be pursued, then they should be important enough to serve as performance measures.

Knowing what to measure is only half the battle. Managers must also address common problems that plague the performance measurement and reporting process. Exhibit 20.6 identifies the most common problems in performance measuring and reporting. Managers can resolve these problems by focusing on the key facts and figures that support organizational goals and reporting them in a way that's clear, specific, and timely.[45]

Finally, an important responsibility of managers in helping achieve high levels of performance is moving from ideas to action. Managers should encourage employees to develop great ideas and to think of these ideas as things that can actually be done.[46] In high-performing organizations, specific desired results are defined and employees map out the entire implementation process from conception to delivery. That's how companies such as Air Liquide in Paris has developed a great reputation

In 1970, it took an average of 24 units of energy to make $1 worth of industrial goods. Now it takes 16. One reason for the impressive reduction is that many manufacturers have been working to reduce their reliance on fuel, even during times when fuel prices were low. Two years ago, for instance, Blenko Glass of West Virginia worked with that state's Industries of the Future Development Office to come up with a more efficient laser cutter to separate finished glass pieces from the burner. Blenko expects this new tool to reduce the amount of energy used in the manufacturing process by half. Relevant measures like fuel consumption can help companies continually improve their performance.

MANAGING IN AN E-BUSINESS WORLD   E-Business Success Stories

In spite of the turmoil Internet-related stocks faced in the latter part of the year 2000, e-business is still alive and flourishing in many companies.[47] These e-businesses have been able to design successful strategies to capture and exploit customer value. In Chapter 2, we introduced three categories of e-business involvement: e-business-enhanced organizations, e-business-enabled organizations, and total e-business organizations. Let's look at some companies that have prospered in each category.

An e-business-enhanced organization has e-business units (usually e-commerce initiatives) within a traditional organization. Lands' End (www.landsend.com), the direct merchant of traditional, casual apparel for men, women, and children, sells more clothing online than any other company. How? By treating its Web site simply as the digital version of its catalog. Lands' End's vice president of e-commerce says, "This isn't rocket science. We're not suddenly selling clothes to people with purple hair. Because we've been a direct merchant for over 36 years, the customer service, the fulfillment operation—all of that was in place." Whereas Lands' End is an example of successful business-to-consumer e-commerce, another company, W. W. Grainger (www.grainger.com) has succeeded as an e-business-enhanced organization in the business-to-business category of e-commerce. Here was a company that the Internet was supposed to destroy. As a distributor of machine maintenance and repair supplies, e-commerce experts felt that either its suppliers would start selling directly online to customers or the 75-year-old company would be too slow and lazy to compete at Internet speed. However, Grainger has thrived on the Web. On its Web site, customers can search through over 220,000 products (vastly more than in its venerable catalog that lists only 70,000 products), do so in a fraction of the time, get up-to-the-minute pricing, and know immediately whether the products are in stock. The company's group president says, "The Internet is clearly the best vehicle for our customers."

E-business-enabled organizations use e-business tools and applications to perform traditional business functions better but not to sell anything. Pillsbury Company, the food giant, has developed Internet-based software that will analyze reams of data and change every aspect of Pillsbury from the way it develops new products to how it capitalizes on consumers' tastes to how it monitors production quality. The "digital dough-boy" is transforming itself from a staid Old Economy food company to a cutting-edge New Economy brand to beat. The company's future plans include providing Pillsbury employees a "library card" that gives them the freedom to roam online through stacks of consumer information to get the data they need. Another company using online capabilities to work more efficiently and effectively is Herman Miller, Inc., the second largest office furniture manufacturer in the United States. Its innovative SQA (simple, quick, affordable) division has linked all sales and purchasing operations via the Internet. The impact? SQA turns over its inventory 40 times (much better than the industry's average of 27 times), furniture selection and layout can be processed at a customer's office in two hours versus the weeks or months traditional furniture makers take, delivery is in three days to two weeks compared to six to eight weeks for other manufacturers, and order-entry errors have been reduced to almost zero from more than 20 percent.

A total e-business organization is one whose entire work processes are structured around the Internet. A stand-out company in this category is Yahoo! Japan. It was the top-performing company on *Business Week's* Info Tech 100 list for 2000. Like its U.S. affiliate, Yahoo! Japan has worked hard to make its name synonymous with the Internet. Its site is the most popular site in Japan—more than 85 percent of all Japanese Internet users visit each month. President and CEO Masahiro Inoue's strategy for the company is clear and direct: Borrow the best ideas from its American counterpart (which owns 34 percent of the company) and exploit the name for all it's worth. Then there's Yahoo!Finance, another part of the Web portal, Yahoo! Yahoo!Finance draws some 6.9 million monthly visitors—more than twice what its closest competitor MSN's Money Central does. Through various alliances with its partners, the Web site provides customers with online financial services tailored to their unique needs. Yahoo!Finance and its parent Yahoo! have created online tools that users want.

Exhibit 20.6
Common Performance Measuring and Reporting Problems

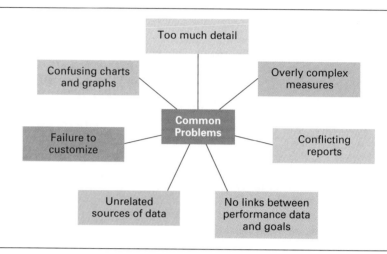

Source: Based on T. Leahy, "10 Cures for Performance Reporting Anxiety," *Business Finance*, December 1999, pp. 63–65.

for exemplary customer service, Baan NV in the Netherlands has implemented a successful product development process, and employees at General Electric have mastered problem-solving skills and techniques in its Six Sigma quality program.[48] Managers in these organizations have created an atmosphere in which employees turn ideas into action.

Testing...Testing...1,2,3

10. **How are information systems used in controlling?**

11. **Why is both external and internal benchmarking of best practices important?**

12. **What can managers do to help their organizations achieve high levels of performance?**

Managers Respond to "A Manager's Dilemma"

Catherine R. Holmes

Occupational Health Manager, Army & Air Force Exchange Service, Dallas, Texas

Tom's first task is to develop a written model of the desired EMP customer's experience. This must be the model against which he judges organizational effectiveness and efficiency. Once he has defined what he hopes customers experience during their visits, he can then determine if he is meeting that goal. Second, a diverse, knowledgeable, friendly, and helpful workforce is a necessity. Basic policies must be in place to ensure appropriate training and culture that exudes excitement and maximizes the visitor's overall experience. In addition, employees are in a unique position to assess organizational efficiency and can be a valuable source of information for improvements.

There are many ways to assess performance by obtaining visitor feedback or using focus groups. In addition, getting statistics on the number of visitors and developing a method for identifying repeat visitors will help Tom judge his organization's performance.

Adam Ferguson

Data Resource Coordinator, Cox Health Systems, Springfield, Missouri

One key to any successful business is the ability to quantify and accurately report work activity. With an elaborate technology system in place, Tom can collect data from visitors on an individual basis. Questions could be asked of visitors throughout the entire stay using their personal handheld device in a way so that the person wouldn't even be aware of the query *and* in a manner that wouldn't detract, or distract, from the experience. Tom could also program the devices to monitor what visitors are asking for. If a visitor isn't calling up any supplemental information, that might be a flag that he or she is not engaged with the experience.

What he chooses to track is the real question for Tom. Building a database and noting when changes to the museum experience have been made, he could have a very valuable tool for monitoring, improving, projecting, and knowing if EMP is having the desired impact on people.

Chapter Summary

This chapter is organized by the chapter-opening objectives found on p. 552.

1. Organizational performance is the accumulated end results of all the organization's work processes and activities.

2. Measuring organizational performance is important because it leads to better asset management, to an increased ability to provide customer value, and to improved measures of organizational knowledge. In addition, measures of organizational performance have an impact on an organization's reputation.

3. The most frequently used organizational performance measures include organizational productivity, organizational effectiveness, and industry rankings. Organizational productivity is the overall output of goods or services produced by an organization divided by the inputs needed to generate that output. Organizational effectiveness is a measure of how appropriate organizational goals are and how well an organization is achieving those goals. Industry rankings are lists created by various business publications and organizations that rate organizations on different performance measures.

4. Traditional financial control measures include ratio analysis and budget analysis. Managers can use ratio analysis as internal control devices for monitoring how efficiently and profitably an organization uses its assets, debt, inventories, and the like. Budgets provide managers with quantitative standards against which to measure and compare resource consumption. Other financial control measures include economic value added (EVA) and market value added (MVA). EVA is calculated by taking after-tax operating profit minus the total annual cost of capital. As a performance control tool, EVA focuses managers' atten-

tion on earning a rate of return over and above the cost of capital. MVA measures the stock market's estimate of the value of a firm's past and expected capital investment projects. The fundamental concept behind both EVA and MVA is that companies are supposed to take in capital from investors and make it worth more.

5. A management information system can provide managers with the information they need to monitor organizational performance and to control organizational activities. Without information, they would find it difficult to measure actual performance, compare actual performance against the performance standards, or develop appropriate courses of action if there are significant deviations between actual and standard.

6. The balanced scorecard is a performance measurement tool that looks at four areas—financial, customer, internal processes, and people/innovation/growth assets—that contribute to a company's performance. According to this approach, managers should develop goals in each of the four areas and measures to determine if these goals are being met.

7. Benchmarking of best practices can be used for monitoring and measuring organizational performance because it can identify specific performance gaps and potential areas of improvement.

8. In their role of helping organizations achieve high levels of performance, managers have certain responsibilities including helping organizational members make the right choices during periods of organizational change, designing a performance management system that identifies appropriate performance measures and addresses common performance measurement problems, and creating an atmosphere in which employees turn ideas into action.

Thinking About Management Issues

1. Could an organization be productive but not effective? Effective but not productive? Explain.

2. In what ways is information a unique resource for organizations? Give examples.

3. Would there be any situations in which an organization shouldn't be concerned with monitoring or measuring organizational performance? Explain.

4. Although measuring organizational performance is discussed as part of the managerial control function, does it have any relation to the other three management functions (planning, organizing, and leading)? Discuss.

5. Is there any connection between organizational knowledge and benchmarking of internal best practices? Explain.

Log On: Internet-Based Exercise

Several popular industry rankings were cited in this chapter. Choose one of the rankings and research the top five companies listed in that ranking. Make a bulleted list of the types of strategies, goals, and work activities, processes, and programs that each organization is using. Are there any common characteristics that these organizations share?

myPHLIP Companion Web Site

myPHLIP *(www.prenhall.com/myphlip) is a fully customizable homepage that ties students and faculty to text-specific resources.*
- *For students, myPHLIP provides an online study guide tied chapter-by-chapter to the text—current events and Internet exercises, lecture notes, downloadable software, the Career Center, the Writing Center, Ask the Tutor, and more.*
- *For faculty, myPHLIP provides a syllabus tool that allows you to manage content, communicate with students, and upload personal resources.*

Working Together: Team-Based Exercise

The balanced scorecard approach is designed for managers to get a well-rounded view of different important aspects of organizational performance, each being equally important. Might a balanced scorecard approach work for measuring student performance? Get into small groups of three or four class members. Create a balanced scorecard performance measurement tool that instructors might use for evaluating student performance in an introductory management course. Be prepared to share your scorecard with the rest of the class and defend your choice of performance measures.

Case Application

The Queen of Lifestyle

Martha Stewart. Most people have a definite opinion about America's most famous homemaker—they either love her or hate her. But no matter what you think about the public person you see cooking, decorating, or gardening, you have to admire the fact that she's building an impressive company, Martha Stewart Living Omnimedia, Inc. (MSO, www.marthastewart.com).

From the publication of her first book on entertaining in 1982 to today's multimedia empire, Stewart has capitalized on what she does best—helping people create a type of quality lifestyle in which the ultimate in cooking, decorating, entertaining, and other homemaking arts is emphasized and celebrated. And Martha's fans are many and loyal. Her various media properties are said to reach over 88 million people a month.

What exactly does MSO do? It's a leading creator of "how-to" content and related products for homemakers and other consumers. Company managers search for ways to leverage the "Martha Stewart" brand name across a broad range of media and retail outlets. As of October 2000, the company's merchandise included more than 3,700 distinct variations of products, including bed and bath products, baby items, interior paints, craft kits, outdoor furniture and garden tools, and a housewares line. The company aims to offer its customers quality, convenience, and choice across a wide range of outlets. Customers can purchase Martha Stewart merchandise at mass market retailers (Kmart), national department stores (Sears, Zellers, and P/Kaufmann), specialty paint stores and specialty craft and fabric stores, the Martha by Mail® catalog, the online Martha by Mail store, or through the shared Web site, BlueLight.com. Then there are MSO's various media properties including three magazines, the weekly television program, a daily cable television program, books, a weekly askMartha® newspaper column, the askMartha radio program, and the company's Web site.

Controlling for organizational performance given such a wide variety of activities is quite a challenge for company managers. Yet, everything they do is aimed at achieving the company's two main goals of (1) providing original "how-to" content and information to as many consumers as possible, and (2) turning consumers into "doers" by offering them the information and products they need for doing things the "Martha Stewart way."

Martha Stewart, CEO, Martha Stewart Living Omnimedia.

QUESTIONS

1. What types of information might the following managers at Martha Stewart Omnimedia need: (a) CEO Martha Stewart, (b) the manager in charge of obtaining new editorial content, and (c) the vice president of marketing?

2. Since all of MSO's products are aimed at exploiting the same "how-to" content and information, how might internal benchmarking be used among the various media and product divisions?

3. Does MSO seem to be doing a good job of asset management? Explain.

4. What types of performance measures might managers use to monitor how well the company is providing customer value? Be specific.

5. What might a balanced scorecard for MSO look like?

Sources: Company information from company Web site (www.marthastewart.com), December 19, 2000 and Hoover's Online (www.hoovers.com), December 19, 2000; and D. Brady, "Martha Inc.," *Business Week*, January 17, 2000, pp. 62–72.

MANAGING ENTREPRENEURIAL VENTURES

Entrepreneurs must look at controlling their venture's operations in order to survive and prosper in both the short run and long run. Those unique control issues that face entrepreneurs include managing growth, managing downturns, exiting the venture, and managing personal life choices and challenges.

Managing Growth

William Williams, cofounder of Glory Foods [www.gloryfoods.com], has taken an unusual approach to managing growth. His company, based in Columbus, Ohio, sells "down-home tasting" southern specialties that are quick and easy to prepare, an alternative to the traditional southern cooking that takes hours. Glory Foods has successfully cornered a market niche by following a conservative path to growth. Williams's decision to move slowly was based mostly on the fact that he didn't want to dilute the founders' equity positions down to minority levels in order to acquire the increased financing needed to grow. Although the slow growth approach may have taken more time, Williams and his partners felt it was worth it because they still have total control over what happens to the company.[1]

Growth is a natural and desirable outcome for entrepreneurial ventures. Growth is what distinguishes an entrepreneurial venture. In fact, it's part of our definition of entrepreneurship. Entrepreneurial ventures pursue growth.[2] However, growth doesn't have to be frantic and chaotic. Growing slowly can be just as successful, as William Williams discovered at Glory Foods.

Growing successfully doesn't occur just randomly or by luck. Successfully pursuing growth typically requires an entrepreneur to manage all the challenges associated with growing. This entails planning, organizing, and controlling for growth.

Planning for growth. Although it may seem we've reverted back to discussing planning issues instead of controlling issues, actually controlling is tied closely to planning as we know from our discussion in Chapter 18 (see Exhibit 18.2). And the best growth strategy is a well-planned one.[3] Ideally, the decision to grow doesn't come about spontaneously, but instead is part of the venture's overall business goals and plan. Rapid growth without planning can be disastrous. Entrepreneurs need to address growth strategies as part of their business planning but shouldn't be overly rigid in that planning. The plans should be flexible enough to exploit unexpected opportunities that arise. With plans in place, the successful entrepreneur must then organize for growth.

Organizing for growth. The key challenges for an entrepreneur in organizing for growth include finding capital, finding people, and strengthening the organizational culture.

Having enough capital is a major challenge facing growing entrepreneurial ventures. The money issue never seems to go away, does it? It does take capital to expand. The processes of finding capital to fund growth are much like going through the initial financing of the venture. However, at this time, hopefully, the venture has a successful track record to back up the request. If it doesn't, it may be extremely difficult to acquire the necessary capital. That's why we said earlier that the best growth strategy is a planned one. Part of that planning should be how growth will be financed. For example, The Boston Beer Company, which produces Samuel Adams beer, grew 30 percent to 60 percent a year for 12 years by focusing almost exclusively on increasing its top-selling product line. However, the company was so focused on increasing market share that it had few financial controls and an inadequate financial infrastructure. During periods of growth, cash flow difficulties would force company president and brewmaster Jim Koch, to tap into a pool of unused venture capital funding. However, when a chief financial officer joined the company in the late 1980s, he developed a financial structure that enabled the company to manage its growth more efficiently and effectively by setting up a plan for funding growth.[4]

Another important issue that a growing entrepreneurial venture needs to address is finding people. If the venture is growing quickly, this challenge may be intensified because of the time constraints. It's important to plan, as much as possible, the numbers and types of employees needed to support the increasing workload as the venture grows. Also, it may be necessary to provide additional training and support to employees to help them handle the increased pressures associated with a growing organization.

Finally, when a venture is growing, it's important to create a positive, growth-oriented culture that enhances the opportunities to achieve success, both organizationally and individually. This sometimes can be difficult to do, particularly when changes are happening rapidly. However, the values, attitudes, and beliefs that are established and reinforced during these times are critical to the entrepreneurial venture's continued and future success. Exhibit P6.1 lists some suggestions that entrepreneurs might use to ensure that their venture's culture is one that embraces and sup-

Exhibit P6.1	• Keep the lines of communication open—inform employees about major issues.
Suggestions for Achieving a Supportive Growth-Oriented Culture	• Establish trust by being honest, open, and forthright about the challenges and rewards of being a growing organization.
	• Be a good listener—find out what employees are thinking and facing.
	• Be willing to delegate duties.
	• Be flexible—be willing to change your plans if necessary.
	• Provide consistent and regular feedback by letting employees know the outcomes—good and bad.
	• Reinforce the contributions of each person by recognizing employees' efforts.
	• Continually train employees to enhance their capabilities and skills.
	• Maintain the focus on the venture's mission even as it grows.
	• Establish and reinforce a "we" spirit since a successful growing venture takes the coordinated efforts of all the employees.

ports a climate in which organizational growth is viewed as desirable and important. Keeping employees focused and committed to what the venture is doing is critical to the ultimate success of its growth strategies. If employees don't "buy into" the direction the entrepreneurial venture is headed, it's unlikely the growth strategies will be successful.

Controlling for growth. Another challenge that growing entrepreneurial ventures face is reinforcing already established organizational controls. Maintaining good financial records and financial controls over cash flow, inventory, customer data, sales orders, receivables, payables, and costs should be a priority of every entrepreneur—whether pursuing growth or not. However, it's particularly important to reinforce these controls when the entrepreneurial venture is expanding. It's all too easy to let things "get away" or to put off doing them when there's an unrelenting urgency to get things done. Rapid growth—or even slow growth—does not excuse the need to have effective controls in place. In fact, it's particularly important to have established procedures, protocols, and processes and to use them. Even though mistakes and inefficiencies can never be eliminated entirely, at least an entrepreneur should ensure that every effort is being made to achieve high levels of productivity and organizational effectiveness. For example, at Green Gear Cycling, CEO Alan Scholz recognized the importance of controlling for growth. How? By following a "Customers for Life" strategy. By continually monitoring customer relationships and orienting organizational work decisions around their possible impacts on customers, Green Gear's employees hope to keep customers for life. That's significant because they figured that if they could keep a customer for life, the value would range from $10,000 to $25,000 per lifetime customer.[5]

Testing...Testing...1,2,3

1. **Describe how entrepreneurs should plan for growth.**

2. **What are the key issues in organizing for growth?**

3. **Why is controlling for growth important?**

Managing Downturns

Although organizational growth is a desirable and important goal for entrepreneurial ventures, what happens when things turn sour—when the growth strategies don't result in the intended outcomes and, in fact, result in a decline in performance? There are challenges, as well, in managing the downturns.

Nobody likes to fail, especially entrepreneurs. However, when an entrepreneurial venture faces times of trouble, what can be done? How can downturns be managed successfully? The first step is recognizing that a crisis is brewing.

Recognizing crisis situations. An entrepreneur should be alert to the warning signs of a business in trouble. Some signals of potential performance decline include inadequate or negative cash flow, excess number of employees, unnecessary and cumbersome administrative procedures, fear of conflict and taking risks, tolerance of work incompetence, lack of a clear mission or goals, and ineffective or poor communication within the organization.[6]

Another perspective on recognizing performance declines revolves around what is known as the **"boiled frog" phenomenon**.[7] The "boiled frog" is a classic psychological response experiment. In one case, a live frog that's dropped into a boiling pan of water, reacts instantaneously and jumps out of the pan. But, in the second case, a live frog that's dropped into a pan of mild water that is gradually heated to the boiling point, fails to react and dies. A small firm may be particularly vulnerable to the boiled frog phenomenon because the entrepreneur may not recognize the "water heating up"—that is, the subtly declining situation. When changes in performance are gradual, a serious response may never be triggered or may be done too late to do anything about the situation. So what does the boiled frog phenomenon teach us? That entrepreneurs need to be alert to the signals that the venture's performance may be worsening. Don't wait until the water has reached the boiling point to react.

Dealing with downturns, declines, and crises. Although an entrepreneur hopes never to have to deal with organizational downturns, declines, or crises, there may come a time when he or she must do just that. After all, nobody likes to think about things going bad or taking a turn for the worse. But that's exactly what the entrepreneur should do—think about it *before* it happens (remember feedforward control from Chapter 18).[8] It's important to have an up-to-date plan for covering bad times. It's just like mapping out exit routes from your home in case of a fire. An entrepreneur wants to be prepared before an emergency hits. This plan should focus on providing specific details for controlling the most fundamental and critical aspects of running the venture—cash flow, accounts receivable, costs, and debt. Beyond having a plan for controlling the venture's critical inflows and outflows, other actions would involve identifying specific strategies for cutting costs and restructuring the venture.

Exiting the Venture

Getting out of an entrepreneurial venture might seem a strange thing for entrepreneurs to do. However, there may come a point when the entrepreneur decides it's time to move on. That decision may be based on the fact that the entrepreneur hopes to capitalize financially on the investment in the venture—called **harvesting**—or that the entrepreneur is facing serious organizational performance problems and wants to get out, or even on the entrepreneur's desire to focus on other pursuits (personal or business). The issues involved with exiting the venture include choosing a proper business valuation method and knowing what's involved in the process of selling a business.

Business valuation methods. Valuation techniques generally fall into three categories: (1) asset valuations, (2) earnings valuations, and (3) cash flow valuations.[9] Setting a value on a business can be a little tricky. In many cases, the entrepreneur has sacrificed much for the business and sees it as his or her "baby." Calculating the value of the baby based on objective standards such as cash flow or some multiple of net profits can sometimes be a shock. That's why it's important for an entrepreneur who wishes to exit the venture to get a comprehensive business valuation prepared by professionals.

Other important considerations in exiting the venture. Although the hardest part of preparing to exit a venture is valuing it, other factors also should be considered.[10] Exhibit P6.2 provides a listing of these issues. The process of exiting the entrepreneurial venture should be approached as carefully as the process of launching it. If the entrepreneur is selling the venture on a positive note, he or she wants to realize the value built up in the business. If the venture is being exited because of declining performance, the entrepreneur wants to maximize the potential return.

Managing Personal Life Choices and Challenges

Being an entrepreneur is extremely exciting and fulfilling, yet extremely demanding. There are long hours, difficult demands, and high stress. Yet, there are many rewards to being an entrepreneur, as well. In this section, we want to look at how entrepreneurs can make it work—that is, how can they be successful and effectively balance the demands of their work and personal lives?[11]

Entrepreneurs are a special group. They are focused and persistent, hardworking, and intelligent. Because

Exhibit	P6.2
Issues in Exiting the Entrepreneurial Venture	

Be prepared.

Decide who will sell the business.

Consider the tax implications.

Screen potential buyers.

Decide whether to tell employees before or after selling.

they put so much of themselves into launching and growing their entrepreneurial ventures, many may neglect their personal lives. Entrepreneurs often have to make sacrifices to pursue their entrepreneurial dreams. However, they can make it work. They can balance their work and personal lives. How?

One of the most important things an entrepreneur can do is to *become a good time manager*. Prioritize what needs to be done. Use a planner (daily, weekly, monthly) to help schedule priorities. Some entrepreneurs don't like taking the time to plan or prioritize or think it's a ridiculous waste of time. Yet, identifying the important duties and distinguishing them from those that aren't so important actually makes an entrepreneur more efficient and effective. In addition, part of being a good time manager is delegating to trusted employees those decisions and actions that the entrepreneur doesn't have to be involved in personally. Although it may be hard to let go of some of the things they've always done, entrepreneurs who delegate effectively will see their personal productivity levels rise. Another suggestion for finding that balance is to *seek professional advice* in those areas of business where it's needed. Although entrepreneurs may be reluctant to spend scarce cash, the time, energy, and potential problems saved in the long run are well worth the investment. Competent professional advisers can provide entrepreneurs with information to make more intelligent decisions. Also, it's important to *deal with conflicts* as they arise. This includes both workplace and family conflicts. If an entrepreneur doesn't deal with conflicts, negative feelings are likely to crop up and lead to communication breakdowns. When communication falls apart, vital information may get lost and people (employees *and* family members) may start assuming the worst. It can turn into a nightmare situation that feeds upon itself. So, the best

strategy is to deal with conflicts as they come up. Talk, discuss, argue (if you must), but an entrepreneur shouldn't avoid the conflict or pretend it doesn't exist. Another suggestion for achieving that balance between work and personal life is to *develop a network of trusted friends and peers*. Having a group of people to talk to is a good way for an entrepreneur to think through problems and issues. The support and encouragement offered by these groups of people can be an invaluable source of strength for an entrepreneur. Finally, *recognize when your stress levels are too high*. Entrepreneurs *are* achievers. They like to make things happen. They thrive on working hard. Yet, too much stress can lead to significant physical and emotional problems (as we discussed in Chapter 13). Entrepreneurs have to learn when stress is overwhelming them and to do something about it. After all, what's the point of growing and building a thriving entrepreneurial venture if you're not around to enjoy it?

Testing...Testing...1,2,3

4. **Describe the boiled frog phenomenon and why it's useful for entrepreneurs.**

5. **What issues does an entrepreneur need to consider when deciding to exit the entrepreneurial venture?**

6. **How can an entrepreneur balance the demands of his or her personal and work lives?**

OPERATIONS MANAGEMENT

On Location

This video takes us into the area of operations management at two companies— Spiewak, Inc., the New York-based outdoor clothing retail company and i2Go, producer of digital media products.

Although their products are very different, both of these firms consider themselves manufacturers. Spiewak's business is manufacturing sportswear and uniforms. At i2Go, according to vice president of operations Jim Saccone, "We manufacture technology." This focus on technology also gives the firm's operations managers the valuable tools they need for monitoring all its production processes for speed, efficiency, and innovation.

What does operations management as strategy mean for a high-tech firm that makes MP3 players, among other digital media products? In this case it often means uncovering new ways to collaborate effectively with member firms in i2Go's supply chain such as by bundling other manufacturers' products like memory chips with i2Go's products and using suppliers' brand names as part of the marketing strategy for those products.

i2Go also relies on operations management, assisted by technology, to improve customer service and product quality. The company tracks the number of product complaints or failure incidents experienced by a given customer, sorts the data by product, and feeds that information back into the product development process. Complaints or problems that occur repeatedly are easily pinpointed and guide the company's development group to faster solutions. In addition, customer histories provide service reps with a reliable way to speed future customer service responses.

Technology helps tie shipping, receiving, order processing, and billing into a seamless whole at both firms. Michael Spiewak, president of Spiewak, Inc., points out, however, that glitches can seem like the norm, even in well-run firms. When the supplier ships the wrong fabrics, for instance, an entire order can be manufactured incorrectly, and the correct items then reach the customer only by a company-wide effort that involves help from the original supplier and sometimes other fabric suppliers as well. Operations management helps minimize these problems and helps speed corrections that need to be made.

A company with many suppliers can experience logistical problems in getting the inputs it needs, in transforming them into finished goods, and in making promised deliveries on time. Michael Spiewak compares his company's products, which are seasonal, to perishable goods like bananas when he says, "If they sit on the dock for too long, they go bad." Think about whether this need for timeliness affects a company like i2Go, and if so, why. What factors might affect the perceived "freshness" of the products that each of these companies makes? What role does operations management play in preserving it?

DISCUSSION QUESTIONS

1. How do Spiewak, Inc., and i2Go gather customer input? Why does customer opinion matter to each of these firms? How does customer input contribute to operations management in general?

2. Can operations management ever make manufacturing processes foolproof? Why or why not? How can it contribute to success in an environment where occasional errors are unavoidable?

3. Michael Spiewak says, "The faster we do things, the better off we are." What does he mean? Why does speed matter to a product or service? How can operations management help a manufacturing firm achieve the speed it desires?

4. Consider a firm that manufactures a nonperishable, nonseasonal good like office furniture. List as many ways as you can think of in which operations management can contribute to the company's sales and marketing strategies.

5. Think of a service firm that you frequently patronize, such as a bank, a barber shop or salon, or a theater. How do you think the management of the firm defines productivity? How would you rate this firm's productivity, and what suggestions can you think of for improving it?

SKILL-BUILDING MODULES

In this section of the textbook, you will have the opportunity to learn about, practice, and reinforce specific management skills. We have included 22 skills that encompass the four functions of management: planning, organizing, leading, and controlling. (See the matrix that follows.)

For each of the skills, we provide the following: (1) A short introduction discusses some basic facts about the skill and defines it, if necessary. (2) A section called "Learning About" describes the suggested behaviors for doing that skill. These behaviors are presented in numbered lists in order to illustrate the specific actions associated with that skill. (3) A section entitled "Practice" presents a short scenario designed to provide you with an opportunity to practice the behaviors associated with the skill. Your professor may have you do different things with the practice scenarios. (4) A section entitled "Reinforcement" is designed to present additional activities that you could do to practice and reinforce the behaviors associated with the skill.

Management Skills and Management Functions Matrix

| | Functions | | | |
Skill	Planning	Organizing	Leading	Controlling
Acquiring power			X	X
Active listening			X	X
Assessing cross-cultural differences		X	X	
Budgeting	X			X
Choosing an effective leadership style			X	
Coaching			X	
Creating effective teams		X	X	
Delegating (empowerment)		X	X	
Designing motivating jobs		X	X	
Developing trust			X	
Disciplining			X	X
Interviewing		X	X	
Managing resistance to change		X	X	X
Managing time	X			X
Mentoring			X	
Negotiating			X	
Providing feedback			X	X
Reading an organization's culture		X	X	
Running productive meetings	X	X	X	X
Scanning the environment	X			X
Setting goals	X			X
Solving problems creatively	X			

ACQUIRING POWER

Power is a natural process in any group or organization, and to perform their jobs effectively, managers need to know how to acquire and use **power**—the capacity of a leader to influence work actions or decisions. We dis-cussed the concept of power in Chapter 17 and identified five different types of power for leaders including legitimate, coercive, reward, expert, and referent. Why is having power important? Because power makes you less dependent on others. When a manager has power, he or she is not as dependent on others for critical resources. And if the resources a manager controls are important, scarce, and nonsubstitutable, her power will increase because others will be more dependent on her for those resources.

Learning About Acquiring Power

You can be more effective at acquiring and using power if you use the following eight behaviors.

1. *Frame arguments in terms of organizational goals.* To be effective at acquiring power means camouflaging your self-interests. Discussions over who controls what resources should be framed in terms of the benefits that will accrue to the organization; do not point out how you personally will benefit.

2. *Develop the right image.* If you know your organization's culture, you already understand what the organization wants and values from its employees in terms of dress, associates to cultivate and those to avoid, whether to appear risk taking or risk aversive, the preferred leadership style, the importance placed on getting along well with others, and so forth. With this knowledge, you're equipped to project the appropriate image. Because the assessment of your performance isn't always a fully objective process, you need to pay attention to style as well as substance.

3. *Gain control of organizational resources.* Controlling organizational resources that are scarce *and* important is a source of power. Knowledge and expertise are particularly effective resources to control. They make you more valuable to the organization and, therefore, more likely to have job security, chances for advancement, and a receptive audience for your ideas.

4. *Make yourself appear indispensable.* Because we're dealing with appearances rather than objective facts, you can enhance your power by appearing to be indispensable. You don't really have *to be* indispensable as long as key people in the organization believe that you are.

5. *Be visible.* If you have a job that brings your accomplishments to the attention of others, that's great. However, if you don't have such a job, you'll want to find ways to let others in the organization know what you're doing by highlighting successes in routine reports, having satisfied customers relay their appreciation to senior executives, being seen at social functions, being active in your professional associations, and developing powerful allies who speak positively about your accomplishments. Of course, you'll want to be on the lookout for those projects that will increase your visibility.

6. *Develop powerful allies.* To get power, it helps to have powerful people on your side. Cultivate contacts with potentially influential people above you, at your own level, and at lower organizational levels. These allies often can provide you with information that's otherwise not readily available. In addition, having allies can provide you with a coalition of support if and when you need it.

7. *Avoid "tainted" members.* In almost every organization, there are fringe members whose status is questionable. Their performance and/or loyalty may be suspect. Keep your distance from such individuals.

8. *Support your boss.* Your immediate future is in the hands of your current boss. Because he or she evaluates your performance, you'll typically want to do whatever is necessary to have your boss on your side. You should make every effort to help your boss succeed, make him look good, support him if he is under siege, and spend the time to find out the criteria he will use to assess your effectiveness. Don't undermine your boss. And don't speak negatively of him to others.

Source: Based on H. Mintzberg, *Power In and Around Organizations* (Upper Saddle River, NJ: Prentice Hall, 1983), p. 24; and P.L. Hunsaker, *Training in Management Skills* (Upper Saddle River, NJ: Prentice Hall, 2001), pp. 339–364.

Practice: Acquiring Power

Read through the following scenario. Write down some notes about how you would handle the situation described. Be sure to refer to the eight behaviors described for acquiring power. Your professor will then tell you what to do next.

SCENARIO

You used to be the star marketing manager for Hilton Electronics Corporation. But for the past year, you've been outpaced again and again by Conor, a new manager in the design department, who has been accomplishing everything expected of her and more. Meanwhile your best efforts to do your job well have been sabotaged and undercut by Leonila—your and Conor's manager. For example, prior to last year's international consumer electronics show, Leonila moved $30,000 from your budget to Conor's. Despite your best efforts, your marketing team couldn't complete all the marketing materials normally developed to showcase all of your organization's new products at this important industry show. And Leonila has chipped away at your staff and budget ever since. Although you've been able to meet most of your goals with less staff and budget, Leonila has continued to slice away at the resources of your group. Just last week, she eliminated two positions in your team of eight marketing specialists to make room for a new designer and some extra equipment for Conor. Leonila is clearly taking away your resources while giving Conor whatever she wants and more. You think it's time to do something or soon you won't have any team or resources left.

Reinforcement: Acquiring Power

The following suggestions are activities you can do to practice and reinforce the behaviors associated with acquiring power.

1. Keep a one-week journal of your behavior describing incidents when you tried to influence others around you. Assess each incident by asking if you were successful at these attempts to influence others. Why or why not? What could you have done differently?

2. Review recent issues of a business periodical (such as *Business Week, Fortune, Forbes, Fast Company, Industry Week*, or the *Wall Street Journal*). Look for articles on reorganizations, promotions, or departures from management positions. Find at least two articles in which you believe power issues are involved. Relate the content of the articles to the concepts introduced in this skill module.

ACTIVE LISTENING

The ability to be an effective listener is often taken for granted. Hearing is often confused with listening, but hearing is merely recognizing sound vibrations. Listening is making sense of what we hear and requires paying attention, interpreting, and remembering. Effective listening is active rather than passive. Active listening is hard work and requires you to "get inside" the speaker's head in order to understand the communication from his or her point of view.

Learning About Active Listening

We can identify eight specific behaviors that effective active listeners demonstrate. You can be more effective at active listening if you use these behaviors.

1. *Make eye contact.* Making eye contact with the speaker focuses your attention, reduces the likelihood that you'll be distracted, and encourages the speaker.

2. *Exhibit affirmative nods and appropriate facial expressions.* The effective active listener shows interest in what's being said through nonverbal signals. Affirmative nods and appropriate facial expressions that signal interest in what's being said, when added to eye contact, convey to the speaker that you're really listening.

3. *Avoid distracting actions or gestures.* The other side of showing interest is avoiding actions that suggest your mind is elsewhere. When listening, don't look at your watch, shuffle papers, play with your pencil, or engage in similar distractions.

4. *Ask questions.* The serious active listener analyzes what he or she hears and asks questions. This behavior provides clarification, ensures understanding, and assures the speaker you're really listening.

5. *Paraphrase.* Restate *in your own words* what the speaker has said. The effective active listener uses phrases such as "What I hear you saying is . . . " or

"Do you mean . . .?". Paraphrasing is an excellent control device to check whether or not you're listening carefully and is also a control for accuracy of understanding.

6. *Avoid interrupting the speaker.* Let the speaker complete his or her thoughts before you try to respond. Don't try to second-guess where the speaker's thoughts are going. When the speaker is finished, you'll know it.

7. *Don't overtalk.* Most of us would rather speak our own ideas than listen to what others say. While talking might be more fun and silence might be uncomfortable, you can't talk and listen at the same time. The good active listener recognizes this fact and doesn't overtalk.

8. *Make smooth transitions between the roles of speaker and listener.* In most work situations, you're continually shifting back and forth between the roles of speaker and listener. The effective active listener makes transitions smoothly from speaker to listener and back to speaker.

Source: Based on C.R. Rogers and R.E. Farson, *Active Listening* (Chicago: Industrial Relations Center of the University of Chicago, 1976); and P.L. Hunsaker, *Training in Management Skills* (Upper Saddle River, NJ: Prentice Hall, 2001), pp. 61–62.

Practice: Active Listening

Read through the following scenario. Write down some notes about how you would handle the situation described. Be sure to refer to the eight behaviors described for active listening. Your professor will tell you what to do next.

SCENARIO

Ben Lummis has always been one of the most reliable technicians at the car stereo shop you manage. Even on days when the frantic pace stressed most other employees, Ben was calm and finished his work efficiently and effectively. You don't know much about his personal life except that he liked to read books about model railroading during his lunch break and he asked to listen to his favorite light jazz station on the shop radio for part of the day. Because his work has always been top-notch, you were happy to let him maintain his somewhat aloof attitude. But over the past month, you wish you knew Ben better. He's been averaging about an absence a week and he no longer spends his lunch break reading in the break room. When he returns from wherever it is he goes, he seems even more remote than when he left. You strongly suspect that something is wrong. Even his normally reliable work has changed. Several irate customers have returned with sound systems he installed improperly. At the time of these complaints, you reviewed each problem with him carefully and each time he promised to be more careful. In addition, you checked the company's work absence records and found that Ben has enough time saved up to take seven more sick days this year. But things don't seem to be improving. Just this week Ben took another suspicious sick day and another angry customer has demanded that his improperly installed system be fixed.

Reinforcement: Active Listening

The following suggestions are activities you can do to practice and reinforce the active listening behaviors.

1. In another lecture-format class, practice active listening for one day. Then ask yourself: Was this harder for me than a normal lecture? Did it affect my note taking? Did I ask more questions? Did it improve my understanding of the lecture's content?

2. For one week, practice active listening behaviors during phone conversations that you have with others. Keep a journal of whether listening actively was easy or difficult, what distractions there were, how you dealt with those distractions, and your assessment of whether or not active listening allowed you to get more out of the conversations.

ASSESSING CROSS-CULTURAL DIFFERENCES

Diverse is a realistic description of today's workforce, and workforce diversity is a major issue for managers in many organizations. The diversity that exists in today's workforce demands that managers become more sensitive to the differences that each cultural group brings to the workplace. How can managers develop this type of sensitivity? It starts with the ability to assess cross-cultural differences.

Learning About Assessing Cross-Cultural Differences

You can be more effective at assessing cross-cultural differences if you use the following six behaviors.

1. *Shift your philosophy from treating everyone alike to recognizing individual differences.* The first step for managers in assessing cross-cultural differences is often the hardest one: changing your belief that everyone is alike and must be treated alike. However, once you can get beyond this, you can begin to appreciate the challenges and rewards of diversity.

2. *Assume differences until similarity is proven.* Most of us have the tendency to assume that others are more similar to us than they really are. You're less likely to misunderstand, miscommunicate, or misperceive if you assume others are different rather than similar.

3. *When communicating, emphasize description rather than interpretation or evaluation.* Interpreting or evaluating what someone has said or done tends to be based more on the observer's culture and background than on the observed situation. Therefore, you should concentrate on describing until you've had sufficient time to observe and interpret situations from the differing perspectives of all cultures involved.

4. *Practice empathy.* Put yourself in the other person's shoes. What are his or her values, experiences, and frames of reference? What do you know about his or her education, upbringing, or background that can give you added insight? Try to see the other person as he or she really is.

5. *Respond to differences in ways that will encourage desired behaviors.* Value and defend diverse views. Accept that culturally diverse employees are going to have different values, beliefs, and ways of doing things, and as long as these differences do not detract from the organization's goals, they should be encouraged.

6. *Avoid any statements, decisions, or actions that could be interpreted as sexist, racist, or offensive to any diverse groups.* Although it's important for you to not treat everyone alike, you don't want to discriminate against diverse groups under the guise of being sensitive to differences.

Sources: Based on N.J. Adler, *International Dimensions of Organizational Behavior*, 3rd ed. (Cincinnati, OH: Southwestern, 1997); T. Cox, "The Multicultural Organization," *Academy of Management Executive*, May 1991, pp. 34–47; and W. Sonnenschein, *The Practical Executive and Workforce Diversity* (Lincolnwood, IL: NTC Business Books, 1997), pp. 39–40.

Practice: Assessing Cross-Cultural Differences

Read through the following scenario. Write down some notes about how you would handle the situation described. Be sure to refer to the six behaviors described for assessing cross-cultural differences. Your professor will then tell you what to do next.

SCENARIO

June Chavez is the manager of a large bank in downtown San Diego. She believes strongly in having her employees provide friendly and helpful service to the bank's customers, but she wonders how she's going to deal with the language conflicts going on in the bank. Over half of June's employees speak Spanish, which is a tremendous asset to the bank's many Spanish-speaking customers. However, at the last few weekly meetings that June holds with her supervisors, concerns over language continue to be raised. The supervisors have raised the issue that some employees who speak only English resent it when their colleagues converse in a language they can't understand. In fact, the supervisor of the bank's tellers said at the last meeting, "On the one hand, I have people who say this is America and people should speak English, and on the other, I've got people who say that there is freedom of speech here." The other supervisors all chimed in and agreed that they were having the same types of problems. June knows that if she doesn't take action soon, she's going to have a real problem on her hands.

Reinforcement: Assessing Cross-Cultural Differences

The following suggestions are activities you can do to practice and reinforce the behaviors associated with assessing cross-cultural differences.

1. Interview at least three people from a different country and get responses to the following questions: (a) What country do you come from? (b) What is your first language? What other languages do you speak? (c) Describe your country's culture in terms of the role of women in the workforce, the benefits provided to employees, how managers treat their employees, and general management practices. (d) What were the greatest difficulties you had in adopting to your new culture? (e) What advice would you give me if I were in a management position in your country? (If you don't know any individuals from another country, check for possible names with the office at your school that is responsible for international students.)

2. Review recent issues of a business periodical (such as *Business Week, Fortune, Forbes, Fast Company, Industry Week,* or the *Wall Street Journal*). Find two articles on global business and evaluate them by asking: What types of cross-cultural differences might arise in these situations? How might managers deal with those cross-cultural differences?

BUDGETING

Managers do not have unlimited resources to do their jobs. Most managers will have to deal with a **budget**, a numerical plan for allocating resources to specific activities. As planning tools, they indicate what activities are important and how many resources should be allocated to each activity. However, budgets aren't just used in planning. They're also used in controlling. As control tools, budgets provide managers with quantitative standards against which to measure and compare resource consumption. By pointing out deviations between standard and actual consumption, managers can use the budget for control purposes.

Learning About Budgeting

You can develop your skills at budgeting if you use the following seven suggestions.

1. *Determine which work activities are going to be pursued during the coming time period.* An organization's work activities are a result of the goals that have been established. Your control over which work activities your unit will be pursuing during a specific time period will depend on how much control you normally exercise over the work that must be done in order to meet those goals. In addition, the amount of control you have often depends on your managerial level in the organization.

2. *Decide which resources will be necessary to accomplish the desired work activities; that is, those that will ensure goals are met.* Although there are different types of budgets used for allocating resources, the most common ones involve monetary resources. However, you also may have to budget time, space, material resources, human resources, capacity utilization, or units of production.

3. *Gather cost information.* You'll need accurate cost estimates of needed resources. Previous budgets may be of some help, but you'll also want to talk with your manager, colleagues, and key employees, and use other contacts you have developed inside and outside your organization.

4. *Once you know which resources will be available to you, assign the resources as needed to accomplish the desired work activities.* In many organizations, managers are given a monthly, quarterly, or annual budget with which to work. The budget will detail which resources are available during the time period. As the manager, you have to assign the resources in an efficient and effective manner to ensure that your unit goals are met.

5. *It's wise to review the budget periodically.* Don't wait until the end of the time period to monitor whether you're over or under budget.

6. *Take action if you find that you're not within your budget.* Remember that a budget also serves as a control tool. If resources are being consumed more quickly than budgeted, you may need to determine why and take corrective action.

7. *Use past experience as a guide when developing your budget for the next time period.* Although every budgeted time period will be different, it is possible to use past experience to pinpoint trends and potential problems. This knowledge can help you prepare for any circumstances that may arise.

Source: Based on R.N. Anthony, J. Dearden, and N.M. Bedford, *Management Control Systems*, 5th ed. (Homewood, IL: Irwin, 1984), Chapters 5–7.

Practice: Budgeting

Read through the following scenario and complete the assigned questions. Be sure to refer to the seven behaviors described for budgeting. Your professor will tell you what to do next.

SCENARIO

You have recently been appointed as advertising manager for a new monthly health and lifestyle magazine, *Global Living for Life*, being developed by the Magazine Division of LifeTime Publications. You were previously an advertising manager on one of the company's established magazines. In this position, you will report to the new magazine's publisher, Molly Tymon.

Estimates of first-year subscription sales for *Global Living for Life* are 125,000 copies. Newsstand sales should add another 5,000 copies a month to that number, but your concern is with developing advertising revenue for the magazine. You and Molly have set a goal of selling advertising space totaling $6 million during the magazine's first year. You think you can do this with a staff of 10 people. Because this is a completely new publication, there is no previous budget for your advertising group. You've been asked by Molly to submit a preliminary budget for your group.

Write up a report (no longer than two pages in length) that describes in detail how you would go about fulfilling this request by Molly. For example, where would you get budget categories? Whom would you contact? Present your best ideas for creating this budget for your department.

Reinforcement: Budgeting

The following suggestions are activities you can do to practice and reinforce the budgeting skill behaviors.

1. Create a personal budget for the next month. Be sure to identify sources of income and planned expenditures. At the end of the month, answer the following questions: (a) Did your budget help you plan what you could and could not do this month? (b) Did unexpected situations arise that weren't included in the budget? How did you handle those? (c) How is a personal budget similar to and different from a budget for which a manager might be responsible?

2. Interview three managers from different organizations. Ask them about their budgeting responsibilities and the "lessons" they've learned about budgeting.

CHOOSING AN EFFECTIVE LEADERSHIP STYLE

Effective leaders are skillful at helping the groups they lead be successful as the group goes through various stages of development. There is no leadership style that is consistently effective. Situational factors, including follower characteristics, must be taken into consideration in the selection of an effective leadership style. The key situational factors that determine leadership effectiveness include stage of group development, task structure, position power, leader-member relations, the work group, employee characteristics, organizational culture, and national culture.

Learning About Choosing an Effective Leadership Style

You can choose an effective leadership style if you use the following six suggestions.

1. *Determine the stage in which your group or team is operating: forming, storming, norming, or performing.* Because each team stage involves specific and different issues and behaviors, it's important to know in

which stage your team is. Forming is the first stage of group development during which people join a group and then help define the group's purpose, structure, and leadership. Storming is the second stage characterized by intragroup conflict. Norming is the third stage characterized by close relationships and cohesiveness. Performing is the fourth stage when the group is fully functional.

2. *If your team is in the forming stage, there are certain leader behaviors you want to exhibit.* These include making certain that all team members are introduced to one another, answering member questions, working to establish a foundation of trust and openness, modeling the behaviors you expect from the team members, and clarifying the team's goals, procedures, and expectations.

3. *If your team is in the storming stage, there are certain leader behaviors you want to exhibit.* These behaviors include identifying sources of conflict and adopting a mediator role, encouraging a win-win philosophy, restating the team's vision and its core values and goals, encouraging open discussion, encouraging an analysis of team processes in order to identify ways to improve, enhancing team cohesion and commitment, and providing recognition to individual team members as well as the team.

4. *If your team is in the norming stage, there are certain leader behaviors you want to exhibit.* These include clarifying the team's goals and expectations, providing performance feedback to individual team members and the team, encouraging the team to articulate a vision for the future, and finding ways to publicly and openly communicate the team's vision.

5. *If your team is in the performing stage, there are certain leader behaviors you want to exhibit.* These behaviors include providing regular and ongoing performance feedback, fostering innovation and innovative behavior, encouraging the team to capitalize on its strengths, celebrating achievements (large and small), and providing the team whatever support it needs to continue doing its work.

6. *Monitor the group for changes in behavior and adjust your leadership style accordingly.* Because a group is not a static entity, it will go through up periods and down periods. You should adjust your leadership style to the needs of the situation. If the group appears to need more direction from you, provide it. If it appears to be functioning at a high level on its own, provide whatever support is necessary to keep it functioning at that level.

Source: Based on D.A. Whetten and K.S. Cameron, *Developing Management Skills*, 4th ed. (Upper Saddle River, NJ: Prentice Hall, 1998), chapter 9.

Practice: Choosing an Effective Leadership Style

Read through the following scenario. Write down some notes about how you would handle the situation described. Be sure to refer to the six suggestions given for choosing an effective leadership style. Your professor will then tell you what to do.

SCENARIO

You've been put in charge of a three-person team working on the implementation of a central accounting function for all training done by your *Fortune* 500 company. This project is new and your position is a new one. Two team members, Tony and Maria, used to be supervisors themselves but, due to an ongoing corporate reorganization, now find themselves reporting to you. You feel like the only way to get them to do anything is to stay on them all the time. The other team member, Corbett, typically has very good ideas but he's becoming quite reluctant to share them, particularly because Tony and Maria glare at him if he says anything. This situation is proving to be a real test of your leadership skills, but you've got a six-month deadline to complete this project, and one month is already over. You've got to figure out a way to lead this team to a successful completion of the project.

Reinforcement: Choosing an Effective Leadership Style

The following suggestions are activities you can do to practice and reinforce the behaviors in choosing an effective leadership style.

1. Think of a group or team to which you currently belong or of which you have been a part. What type of leadership style did the leader of this group appear to exhibit? Give some specific examples of the types of leadership behaviors he or she used. Evaluate the leadership style. Was it appropriate for the group? Why or why not? What would you have done differently? Why?

2. Observe a sports team (either college or professional) that you consider extremely successful and one that you would consider not successful. What leadership styles appear to be used in these team situations? Give some specific examples of the types of leadership behaviors you observe. How would you evaluate the leadership style? Was it appropriate for the team? Why or why not? To what degree do you think leadership style influenced the team's outcomes?

3. Interview three different managers about the leadership styles they use. Ask for specific examples of how they use their leadership style. Ask the managers how they chose the style they're using and how they know if they need to change their style.

COACHING

Effective managers are increasingly being described as *coaches* rather than as *bosses*. Just like coaches, they're expected to provide instruction, guidance, advice, and encouragement to help employees improve their job performance.

Learning About Coaching

There are three general skills that managers should exhibit if they are to help their employees generate performance breakthroughs. You can be more effective at coaching if you use those skills and practice the following specific behaviors associated with each.

1. *Analyze ways to improve an employee's performance and capabilities.* A coach looks for opportunities for an employee to expand his or her capabilities and improve performance. How? By using the following behaviors: Observe your employee's behavior on a daily basis. Ask questions of the employee: Why do you do a task this way? Can it be improved? What other approaches might be used? Show genuine interest in the employee as an individual, not merely as an employee. Respect his or her individuality. Listen to the employee.

2. *Create a supportive climate.* It's the coach's responsibility to reduce barriers to development and to facilitate a climate that encourages personal performance improvement. How? By using the following behaviors: Create a climate that contributes to a free and open exchange of ideas. Offer help and assistance. Give guidance and advice when asked. Encourage your employees. Be positive and upbeat. Don't use threats. Focus on mistakes as learning opportunities. Ask: What did we learn from this that can help us in the future? Reduce obstacles. Express to the employee that you value his or her contribution to the unit's goals. Take personal responsibility for the outcome, but don't rob employees of their full responsibility. Validate the employees' efforts when they succeed. Point to what was missing when they fail. Never blame the employees for poor results.

3. *Influence employees to change their behavior.* The ultimate test of coaching effectiveness is whether or not an employee's performance improves. The concern is with ongoing growth and development. How can you do this? By using the following behaviors: Encourage continual improvement. Recognize and reward small improvements and treat coaching as a way of helping employees to continually work toward improvement. Use a collaborative style by allowing employees to participate in identifying and choosing among improvement ideas. Break difficult tasks down into simpler ones. Model the qualities that you expect from your employees. If you want openness, dedication, commitment, and responsibility from your employees, you must demonstrate these qualities yourself.

Source: Based on C.D. Orth, H.E. Wilkinson, and R.C. Benfari, "The Managers' Role as Coach and Mentor," *Organizational Dynamics*, Spring 1987, p. 67.

Practice: Coaching

Read through the following scenario. Write down some notes about how you would handle the situation described. Be sure to refer to the three general coaching skills and the specific behaviors associated with each. Your professor will then tell you what to do next.

SCENARIO

Store manager Ian McCormick was thrilled with Barbara Kim's work. She was simply the best assistant department manager he had ever seen. Barbara made friends with everyone who came into the store and customers would often bring their items over to her and wait in line just for a chance to visit with her. When a department manager position opened up, Ian was glad to give Barbara the promotion. And Barbara was even happier! She told Ian, "I can't tell you how much this means to me. I'll do anything to make this work."

As a department manager, Barbara was just as friendly as ever—too friendly, in fact. She seemed incapable of saying "no" to her former co-workers. She let them off nearly every time they asked, throwing the work schedule into disarray and leaving checkout lines open. Customers who were once happy about Barbara were now complaining. Transaction error rates also increased. Ian brought this to Barbara's attention several times, and each time Barbara said she would talk to the clerks about being more careful. But mistakes continued. Ian knows that Barbara has potential but he's not sure what to do about this situation now. Something definitely needs to be done.

Reinforcement: Coaching

The following suggestions are activities you can do to practice and reinforce the coaching behaviors.

1. Talk to several instructors about ways that they deal with a student whose performance is not at the level it should be. What kinds of techniques do they use? Which, if any, of the coaching behaviors described do the instructors use?

2. Most of us are aware of coaches and what they do in an athletic team setting. Observe different coaches (on television or firsthand) and how they deal with individuals on their team. What types of behaviors do they exhibit? Based on what you see, what coaching advice could you use as a manager?

CREATING EFFECTIVE TEAMS

What differentiates a *team* from a group is that members are committed to a common purpose, have a set of specific performance goals, and hold themselves mutually accountable for the team's results. Teams can produce outputs that are greater than the sum of their individual contributions. The primary force that makes a work group an effective team—that is, a real high-performing team—is its emphasis on performance.

Learning About Creating Effective Teams

Managers and team leaders have a significant impact on a team's effectiveness. As a result, they need to be able to create effective teams. You can be more effective at creating effective teams if you use the following nine behaviors.

1. *Establish a common purpose.* An effective team needs a common purpose to which all members aspire. This purpose is a vision. It's broader than any specific goals. This common purpose provides direction, momentum, and commitment for team members.

2. *Assess team strengths and weaknesses.* Team members will have different strengths and weaknesses. Knowing these strengths and weaknesses can help the team leader build upon the strengths and compensate for the weaknesses.

3. *Develop specific individual goals.* Specific individual goals help lead team members to achieve higher performance. In addition, specific goals facilitate clear communication and help maintain the focus on getting results.

4. *Get agreement on a common approach for achieving goals.* Goals are the ends a team strives to attain. Defining and agreeing upon a common approach ensure that the team is unified on the *means* for achieving those ends.

5. *Encourage acceptance of responsibility for both individual and team performance.* Successful teams make members individually and jointly accountable for the team's purpose, goals, and approach. Members understand what they are individually responsible for and what they are jointly responsible for.

6. *Build mutual trust among members.* When there is *trust*, team members believe in the integrity, character, and ability of each other. When trust is lacking, members are unable to depend on each other. Teams that lack trust tend to be short-lived.

7. *Maintain an appropriate mix of team member skills and personalities.* Team members come to the team with different skills and personalities. To perform effectively, teams need three types of skills. First, teams need people with technical expertise. Next, they need people with problem-solving and decision-making skills to identify problems, generate alternatives, evaluate those alternatives, and make competent choices. Finally, teams need people with good interpersonal skills.

8. *Provide needed training and resources.* Team leaders need to make sure that their teams have both the training and the resources they need to accomplish their goals.

9. *Create opportunities for small achievements.* Building an effective team takes time. Team members have to learn to think and work as a team. New teams can't be expected to hit home runs every time they come to bat, especially at the beginning. Instead, team members should be encouraged to try for small achievements at the beginning.

Source: Based on P.L. Hunsaker, *Training in Management Skills* (Upper Saddle River, NJ: Prentice Hall 2001), Chapter 12.

Practice: Creating Effective Teams

Read through the following scenario. Write down some notes about how you would handle the situation described. Be sure to refer to the nine behaviors given for creating effective teams. Your professor will then tell you what to do next.

SCENARIO

You're the leader of a five-member project team that's been assigned the task of moving your engineering firm into the new booming area of high-speed rail construction. You and your team members have been researching the field, identifying specific business opportunities, negotiating alliances with equipment vendors, and evaluating high-speed rail experts and consultants from around the world. Throughout the process, Tonya, a highly qualified and respected engineer, has challenged everything you say during team meetings and in the workplace. For example, at a meeting two weeks ago, you presented the team with a list of 10 possible high-speed rail projects that had been identified by the team and started evaluating your organization's ability to compete for them. Tonya contradicted virtually all your comments, questioned your statistics, and was quite pessimistic about the possibility of contracts. After this latest display of displeasure, two other group members, Liam and Ahmed, came to you and complained that Tonya's actions were damaging the team's effectiveness. You originally put Tonya on the team for her unique expertise and insight. You'd like to find a way to reach her and get the team on the right track to its fullest potential.

Reinforcement: Creating Effective Teams

The following suggestions are activities you can do to practice and reinforce the skills in creating effective teams.

1. Interview three managers at different organizations. Ask them about their experiences in managing teams. What behaviors have they found that have been successful in creating an effective team? What about those behaviors that have not been successful in creating an effective team?
2. After completing a team project for one of your classes, assess the team's effectiveness by answering the following questions: Did everyone on the team know exactly why the team did what it did? Did team members have a significant amount of input into or influence on decisions that affected them? Did team members have open, honest, timely, and two-way communications? Did everyone on the team know and understand the team's priorities? Did the team members work together to resolve destructive conflicts? Was everyone on the team working toward accomplishing the same thing? Did team members understand the team's unwritten rules of how to behave within the group?

DELEGATING

Managers get things done through other people. Because there are limits to any manager's time and knowledge, effective managers need to understand how to delegate. **Delegation** is the assignment of authority to another person to carry out specific duties. It allows an employee to make decisions. Delegation should not be confused with participation. In participative decision making, there's a sharing of authority. In delegation, employees make decisions on their own.

Learning About Delegation

A number of actions differentiate the effective delegator from the ineffective delegator. There are five behaviors that effective delegators will use.

1. *Clarify the assignment.* Determine *what* is to be delegated and *to whom.* You need to identify the person who's most capable of doing the task and then determine whether or not he or she has the time and motivation to do the task. If you have a willing and able employee, it's your responsibility to provide clear information on what is being delegated, the results you expect, and any time or performance expectations you may have. Unless there's an overriding need to adhere to specific methods, you should delegate only the results expected. Get agreement on what is to be done and the results expected, but let the employee decide the best way to complete the task.
2. *Specify the employee's range of discretion.* Every situation of delegation comes with constraints. Although you're delegating to an employee the authority to perform some task or tasks, you're not delegating unlimited authority. You are delegating authority to act on certain issues within certain parameters. You need to specify what those parameters are so that employees know, without any doubt, the range of their discretion.
3. *Allow the employee to participate.* One of the best ways to decide how much authority will be necessary to accomplish a task is to allow the employee who will be held accountable for that task to participate in that decision. Be aware, however, that allowing employees to participate can present its own set of potential problems as a result of employees' self-interests and biases in evaluating their own abilities.
4. *Inform others that delegation has occurred.* Delegation shouldn't take place behind the scenes. Not only do the manager and employee need to know specifically what has been delegated and how much authority has been given, but so does anyone else who's likely to be affected by the employee's decisions and actions. This includes people inside and outside the organization. Essentially, you need to communi-

cate what has been delegated (the task and amount of authority) and to whom.

5. *Establish feedback controls*. To delegate without establishing feedback controls is inviting problems. The establishment of controls to monitor the employee's performance increases the likelihood that important problems will be identified and that the task will be completed on time and to the desired specifications. Ideally, these controls should be determined at the time of the initial assignment. Agree on a specific time for the completion of the task and then set progress dates when the employee will report back on how well he or she is doing and any major problems that may have arisen. These controls can be supplemented with periodic checks to ensure that authority guidelines aren't being abused, organizational policies are being followed, proper procedures are being met, and the like.

Source: Based on P.L. Hunsaker, *Training in Management Skills* (Upper Saddle River, NJ: Prentice Hall, 2001), pp. 135–36 and 430–32; R.T. Noel, "What You Say to Your Employees When You Delegate," *Supervisory Management*, December 1993, p. 13; and S. Caudron, "Delegate for Results," *Industry Week*, February 6, 1995, pp. 27–30.

Practice: Delegating

Read through the following scenario. Write down some notes about how you would handle the situation described. Be sure to refer to the five behaviors described for delegating. Your professor will then tell you what to do next.

SCENARIO

Ricky Lee is the manager of the contracts group of a large regional office supply distributor. His boss, Anne Zumwalt, has asked him to prepare by the end of the month the department's new procedures manual that will outline the steps followed in negotiating contracts with office products manufacturers who supply the organization's products. Because Ricky has another major project he's working on, he went to Anne and asked her if it would be possible to assign the rewriting of the procedures manual to Bill Harmon, one of his employees who's worked in the contracts group for about three years. Anne said she had no problems with Ricky reassigning the project as long as Bill knew the parameters and the expectations for the completion of the project. Ricky is preparing for his meeting in the morning with Bill regarding this assignment.

Reinforcement: Delegating

The following suggestions are activities you can do to practice and reinforce the behaviors in delegating.

1. Interview a manager regarding his or her delegation skills. What activities doesn't he or she delegate? Why?

2. Teach someone else how to delegate effectively. Be sure to identify to this person the behaviors needed in delegating effectively as well as explaining why these behaviors are important.

DESIGNING MOTIVATING JOBS

As a manager, it's likely you're going to have to design or redesign jobs at some point. How will you ensure that these jobs are motivating? What can you do regarding job design that will maximize your employees' motivation and performance? The job characteristics model, which defines five core job dimensions (skill variety, task identity, task significance, autonomy, and feedback) and their relationships to employee motivation, provides a basis for designing motivating jobs.

Learning About Designing Motivating Jobs

The following five suggestions, based on the job characteristics model, specify the types of changes in jobs that are most likely to lead to improving the motivating potential for employees.

1. *Combine tasks*. As a manager, you should put existing specialized and divided tasks back together to form a new, larger module of work. This step will increase skill variety and task identity.

2. *Create natural work units*. You should design work tasks that form an identifiable and meaningful whole. This step will increase "ownership" of the work and will encourage employees to view their work as meaningful and important rather than as irrelevant and boring.

3. *Establish client relationships*. The client is the user of the product or service that is the basis for an employee's work. Whenever possible, you should establish direct relationships between your workers and your clients. This step increases skill variety, autonomy, and feedback for the employees.

4. *Expand jobs vertically*. Vertical expansion of a job means giving employees responsibilities and controls that were formerly the manager's. It partially closes the gap between the "doing" and "controlling" aspects of the job. This step increases employee autonomy.

5. *Open feedback channels*. By increasing feedback, employees not only learn how well they are performing their jobs but also whether their performance is

improving, deteriorating, or remaining at a constant level. Ideally, this feedback should be received directly as the employee does the job rather than from his or her manager on an occasional basis.

Source: Based on J.R. Hackman, "Work Design," in J.R. Hackman and J.L. Suttle (eds.), *Improving Life at Work* (Santa Monica, CA: Goodyear, 1977), pp. 132–33.

Practice: Designing Motivating Jobs

Read through the following scenario. Write down some notes about how you would handle the situation described. Be sure to refer to the five suggestions described for designing motivating jobs. Your professor will tell you what to do next.

SCENARIO

You work for Sunrise Deliveries, a freight transportation company that makes local deliveries of products for your customers. In your position, you supervise Sunrise's six delivery drivers. Each morning your drivers drive their pre-loaded trucks to their destinations and wait for the products to be unloaded. There's a high turnover rate in the job. In fact, most of your drivers don't stay longer than six months. Not only is this employee turnover getting expensive, it's been hard to develop a quality customer service program when you've constantly got new faces. You've also heard complaints from the drivers that "all they do is drive." You know that you're going to have to do something to solve this problem.

Reinforcement: Designing Motivating Jobs

The following suggestions are activities you can do to practice and reinforce the behaviors associated with designing motivating jobs.

1. Think of the worst job you have ever had. Analyze the job according to the five dimensions identified in the job characteristics model. Redesign the job in order to make it more satisfying and motivating.

2. Interview two people in two different job positions on your campus. Ask them questions about their jobs using the job characteristics model as a guide. Using the information provided, list recommendations for making the jobs more motivating.

DEVELOPING TRUST

Trust plays an important role in the manager's relationships with his or her employees. Given the importance of trust, today's managers should actively seek to develop it within their work group.

Learning About Developing Trust

You can be more effective at developing trust among your employees if you use the following eight suggestions.

1. *Practice openness*. Mistrust comes as much from what people don't know as from what they do. Being open with employees leads to confidence and trust. Keep people informed. Make clear the criteria you use in making decisions. Explain the rationale for your decisions. Be forthright and candid about problems. Fully disclose all relevant information.

2. *Be fair*. Before making decisions or taking actions, consider how others will perceive them in terms of objectivity and fairness. Give credit where credit is due. Be objective and impartial in performance appraisals. Pay attention to equity perceptions in distributing rewards.

3. *Speak your feelings*. Managers who convey only hard facts come across as cold, distant, and unfeeling. When you share your feelings, others will see that you are real and human. They will know you for who you are and their respect for you is likely to increase.

4. *Tell the truth*. Being trustworthy means being credible. If honesty is critical to credibility, then you must be perceived as someone who tells the truth. Employees are more tolerant of hearing something "they don't want to hear" than of finding out that their manager lied to them.

5. *Be consistent*. People want predictability. Mistrust comes from not knowing what to expect. Take the time to think about your values and beliefs and let those values and beliefs consistently guide your decisions. When you know what's important to you, your actions will follow, and you will project a consistency that earns trust.

6. *Fulfill your promises*. Trust requires that people believe that you are dependable. You need to ensure that you keep your word. Promises made must be promises kept.

7. *Maintain confidences*. You trust those whom you believe to be discreet and those on whom you can rely. If people open up to you and make themselves vulnerable by telling you something in confidence, they need to feel assured you won't discuss it with others or betray that confidence. If people perceive you as someone who leaks personal confidences or someone who can't be depended on, you've lost their trust.

8. *Demonstrate competence*. Develop the admiration and respect of others by demonstrating technical and

professional ability. Pay particular attention to developing and displaying your communication, negotiation, and other interpersonal skills.

Source: Based on F. Bartolome, "Nobody Trusts the Boss Completely—Now What?" *Harvard Business Review*, March–April 1989, pp. 135–42; and J.K. Butler Jr., "Toward Understanding and Measuring Conditions of Trust: Evolution of a Condition of Trust Inventory," *Journal of Management*, September 1991, pp. 643–63.

Practice: Developing Trust

Read through the following scenario. Write down some notes about how you would handle the situation. Be sure to refer to the eight behaviors described for developing trust. Your professor will tell you what to do next.

SCENARIO

Donna Romines is the shipping department manager at Tastefully Tempting, a gourmet candy company based in Phoenix. Orders for the company's candy come from around the world. Your six-member team processes these orders. Needless to say, the two months before Christmas are quite hectic. Everybody counts the days until December 24 when the phones finally stop ringing off the wall, at least for a couple of days. You and all of your team members breathe a sigh of relief as the last box of candy is sent on its way out the door.

When the company was first founded five years ago, after the holiday rush, the owners would shut down Tastefully Tempting for two weeks after Christmas. However, as the business has grown and moved into Internet sales, that practice has become too costly. There's too much business to be able to afford that luxury. And the rush for Valentine's Day orders start pouring in the week after Christmas. Although the two-week postholiday company-wide shutdown has been phased out formally, some departments have found it difficult to get employees to gear up once again after the Christmas break. The employees who come to work after Christmas usually accomplish little. This year, though, things have got to change. You know that the cultural "tradition" won't be easy to overcome, but your shipping team needs to be ready to tackle the orders that have piled up. After all, Tastefully Tempting's customers want their orders filled promptly and correctly!

Reinforcement: Developing Trust

The following suggestions are activities you can do to practice and reinforce the behaviors associated with developing trust.

1. Keep a one-week log describing ways that your daily decisions and actions encouraged people to trust you or to not trust you. What things did you do that led to trust? What things did you do that may have led to distrust? How could you have changed your behavior so that the situations of distrust could have been situations of trust?

2. Review recent issues of a business periodical (such as *Business Week, Fortune, Forbes, Fast Company, Industry Week*, or the *Wall Street Journal*) for articles in which trust (or lack of trust) may have played a role. Find two articles and describe the situation. Explain how the person(s) involved might have used skills at developing trust to handle the situation.

DISCIPLINING

If an employee's performance regularly isn't up to par or if an employee consistently ignores the organization's standards and regulations, the manager may have to use discipline as a way to control behavior. What exactly is **discipline**? It's actions taken by a manager to enforce the organization's expectations, standards, and rules. The most common types of discipline problems managers have to deal with include attendance (absenteeism, tardiness, abuse of sick leave), on-the-job behaviors (failure to meet performance goals, disobedience, failure to use safety devices, alcohol or drug abuse), and dishonesty (theft, lying to managers).

Learning About Disciplining

You can be more effective at disciplining employees if you use the following eight behaviors.

1. *Respond immediately.* The more quickly a disciplinary action follows a behavior that requires disciplining, the more likely it is that the employee will associate the discipline with the behavior rather than with you as the disciplinarian. It's best to begin the disciplinary process as soon as possible after you notice a violation.

2. *Provide a warning.* You have an obligation to warn an employee before initiating disciplinary action. This means that the employee must be aware of and accept the organization's rules and standards of behavior and performance. Disciplinary action is more likely to be seen as fair when employees have received a warning that a given behavior will lead to discipline and when they know what that disciplinary action will be.

3. *State the problem specifically.* Give the date, time, place, individuals involved, and any extenuating circumstances surrounding the problem behavior. Be sure

to define the problem behavior in exact terms instead of just reciting company regulations. Explain why the behavior isn't acceptable by showing how it specifically affects the employee's job performance, the work unit's effectiveness, and the employee's colleagues.

4. *Allow the employee to explain his or her position.* Regardless of the facts you have, due process demands that an employee be given the opportunity to explain his or her position. From the employee's perspective, what happened? Why did it happen? What was his or her perception of the expectations, rules, regulations, and circumstances?

5. *Keep discussion impersonal.* Make sure that the discipline is directed at what the employee has done (or failed to do) and not at the employee personally.

6. *Be consistent.* Fair treatment of employees demands that disciplinary action be consistent. This doesn't mean, however, treating everyone exactly alike. Be sure to clearly justify disciplinary actions that might appear inconsistent to employees.

7. *Take progressive action.* Choose a disciplinary action that's appropriate to the problem behavior. Penalties should get progressively stronger if, or when, the problem is repeated. For example, you may start with an oral warning, then move progressively to a written warning, a suspension, and then, if the problem behavior warrants, dismissal. Keep in mind, however, that there may be some behaviors that warrant immediate dismissal and these should be made clear to employees.

8. *Obtain agreement on change.* Disciplining should include guidance and direction for correcting the problem behavior. Let the employee state what he or she plans to do in the future to ensure that the problem won't be repeated.

Source: Based on A. Belohlav, *The Art of Disciplining Your Employees* (Upper Saddle River, NJ: Prentice Hall, 1985); and R.H. Lussier, "A Discipline Model for Increasing Performance," *Supervisory Management*, August 1990, pp. 6–7.

Practice: Disciplining

Read through the following scenario. Write down some notes about how you would handle the disciplinary situation described. Be sure to refer to the eight behaviors sug-gested for effective disciplining. Your professor will then tell you what to do next.

SCENARIO

You're a team leader in the customer services department at Mountain View Microbrewery. Carla is the newest member of your 10-person team, having been there only six weeks. She came to Mountain View with good recommendations from her previous job as a customer support representative at a car dealership. However, not long after joining your team, she was late in issuing an important purchasing order. When you talked to her about it, she said it was "lost." But you discovered it in her in-box where it had been properly placed. Then, just last week, she failed to make an immediate return call to an unhappy customer who could easily have been satisfied at that point. Instead the customer worked himself into an unhappy rage and vented his unhappiness in a letter to the company's CEO. Now the latest incident with Carla came up just yesterday. As part of your company's continual quality improvement program, your team members prepare periodic reports on the service they provide to each customer and turn these reports over to an upper management team that evaluates them. Carla didn't meet the deadline for getting her report into this evaluation group and you received a call from one of the team members wanting to know where this report was. Because Carla is still on probation for another six weeks, it appears that the time has come for you to talk to her about her failure to meet expected work performance goals.

Reinforcement: Disciplining

The following suggestions are activities you can do to practice and reinforce the disciplining behaviors.

1. Talk with managers at three different organizations. Ask them what guidance they've received from their organizations in disciplining employees. Have them describe specific employee discipline problems they've faced and how they've handled them.

2. Interview three of your current or past instructors. Ask them about their approaches to discipline. How do they handle late papers, cheating, excessive absenteeism, or other disciplinary problems?

INTERVIEWING

The interview is used almost universally as part of the employee selection process. Not many of us have ever gotten a job without having gone through one or more interviews. Interviews can be valid and reliable selection tools, but they need to be structured and well organized.

Learning About Interviewing

You can be an effective interviewer if you use the following seven suggestions for interviewing job candidates.

1. *Review the job description and job specification.* Be sure that prior to the interview, you have reviewed pertinent information about the job. Why? Because this will

provide you with valuable information on which to assess the job candidate. Furthermore, knowing the relevant job requirements will help eliminate interview bias.

2. *Prepare a structured set of questions you want to ask all job applicants.* By having a set of prepared questions, you ensure that you'll get the information you want. Furthermore, by asking similar questions, you're able to better compare all candidates' answers against a common base.

3. *Before meeting a candidate, review his or her application form and résumé.* By doing this you'll be able to create a complete picture of the candidate in terms of what is represented on the résumé or application and what the job requires. You can also begin to identify areas to explore during the interview. That is, areas that are not clearly defined on the résumé or application but that are essential to the job can become a focal point in your discussion with the candidate.

4. *Open the interview by putting the applicant at ease and by providing a brief preview of the topics to be discussed.* Interviews are stressful for job candidates. Opening the discussion with small talk, such as the weather, can give the candidate time to adjust to the interview setting. By providing a preview of topics to come, you are giving the candidate an agenda. This helps the candidate begin framing what he or she will say in response to your questions.

5. *Ask your questions and listen carefully to the candidate's answers.* Select follow-up questions that flow naturally from the answers given. Focus on the candidate's responses as they relate to information you need to ensure that the person meets your job requirements. If you're still uncertain, use a follow-up question to further probe for information.

6. *Close the interview by telling the applicant what is going to happen next.* Applicants are anxious about the status of your hiring decision. Be up front with candidates regarding others who will be interviewed and the remaining steps in the hiring process. Let the person know your time frame for making a decision. In addition, tell the applicant how you will notify him or her about your decision.

7. *Write your evaluation of the applicant while the interview is still fresh in your mind.* Don't wait until the end of the day, after interviewing several people, to write your analysis of each person. Memory can (and often will) fail you! The sooner you write your impressions after an interview, the better chance you have of accurately noting what occurred in the interview and your perceptions of the candidate.

Source: Based on S.P. Robbins and D.A. DeCenzo, *Fundamentals of Management*, 3rd ed. (Upper Saddle River, NJ: Prentice Hall, 2001), p. 214.

Practice: Interviewing

Read through the following list. In preparing to do this exercise, be sure to refer to the seven suggestions for conducting effective interviews. Your professor will then tell you what to do next.

1. Break into groups of three.
2. Take up to 10 minutes to compose five challenging job interview questions that you think should be relevant in the hiring of new college graduates for a sales management training program at Kraft Foods. Each hiree will spend 18 to 24 months as a sales representative calling on retail grocery and restaurant accounts. After this training period, successful performers can be expected to be promoted to the position of district sales supervisor.
3. Exchange your five questions with another group.
4. Each group should allocate one of the following roles to their three members: interviewer, applicant, and observer. The person playing the applicant should rough out a brief résumé of his or her background and experience and then give it to the interviewer.
5. Role-play a job interview. The interview should include, but not be limited to, the five questions provided by the other group.
6. After the interview, the observer should evaluate the interviewer's behaviors in terms of the effective interview suggestions.

Reinforcement: Interviewing

The following suggestions are activities you can do to practice and reinforce the interviewing skill.

1. On your campus, there's probably a job and career placement service provided for graduating seniors. If possible, talk to two or three graduating seniors who have been interviewed by organizations through this campus service. Ask them to share what happened during their interviews. Then write a brief report describing what you found out and comparing the students' experiences with the suggestions for effective interviewing.
2. Interview a manager about the interview process he or she uses in hiring new employees. What types of information does the manager try to get during an interview? (Be sure that as you interview this manager that you're using the suggestions for good interviewing! Although you're not "hiring" this person, you are looking for information, which is exactly what managers are looking for during a job interview.)

MANAGING RESISTANCE TO CHANGE

Managers play an important role in organizational change—that is, they often serve as change agents. However, managers may find that change is resisted by employees. After all, change represents ambiguity and uncertainty, or it threatens the status quo. How can this resistance to change be effectively managed?

Learning About Managing Resistance to Change

You can be more effective at managing resistance to change if you use the following suggestions.

1. *Assess the climate for change.* One major factor why some changes succeed and others fail is the readiness for change. Assessing the climate for change involves asking several questions. The more affirmative answers you get, the more likely it is that change efforts will succeed.

   - Is the sponsor of the change high enough in the hierarchy to have power to effectively deal with resistance?

   - Is senior management supportive of the change and committed to it?

   - Is there a strong sense of urgency from senior managers about the need for change and is this feeling shared by others in the organization?

   - Do managers have a clear vision of how the future will look after the change?

   - Are there objective measures in place to evaluate the change effort and have reward systems been explicitly designed to reinforce them?

   - Is the specific change effort consistent with other changes going on in the organization?

   - Are managers willing to sacrifice their personal self-interests for the good of the organization as a whole?

   - Do managers pride themselves on closely monitoring changes and actions by competitors?

   - Are managers and employees rewarded for taking risks, being innovative, and looking for new and better solutions?

   - Is the organizational structure flexible?

   - Does communication flow both down *and* up in the organization?

   - Has the organization successfully implemented changes in the recent past?

   - Are employee satisfaction with and trust in management high?

   - Is there a high degree of interaction and cooperation between organizational work units?

   - Are decisions made quickly and do decisions take into account a wide variety of suggestions?

2. *Choose an appropriate approach for managing the resistance to change.* There are six tactics that have been suggested for dealing with resistance to change. Each is designed to be appropriate for different conditions of resistance. These include *education and communication* (used when resistance comes from lack of information or inaccurate information), *participation* (used when resistance stems from people not having all the information they need or when they have the power to resist), *facilitation and support* (used when those with power will lose out in a change), *manipulation and cooptation* (used when any other tactic will not work or is too expensive), and *coercion* (used when speed is essential and change agents possess considerable power). Which one of these approaches will be most effective depends on the source of the resistance to the change.

3. *During the time the change is being implemented and after the change is completed, communicate with employees regarding what support you may be able to provide.* Your employees need to know that you are there to support them during change efforts. Be prepared to offer the assistance that may be necessary to help your employees enact the change.

Source: Based on J.P. Kotter and L.A. Schlesinger, "Choosing Strategies for Change," Harvard Business Review, March–April 1979, pp. 106–14; and T.A. Stewart, "Rate Your Readiness to Change," Fortune, February 7, 1994, pp. 106–10.

Practice: Managing Resistance to Change

Read through the following scenario. Write down some notes about how you would handle the situation described. Be sure to refer to the three suggestions for managing resistance to change. Your professor will tell you what to do next.

SCENARIO

You're the nursing supervisor at a community hospital employing both emergency room and floor nurses. Each of these teams of nurses tends to work almost exclusively with others doing the same job. In your professional reading, you've come across the concept of cross-training nursing teams and giving them more varied responsibilities, which in turn has been shown to improve patient care while lowering costs. You call the two team leaders, Sue and

Scott, into your office to explain that you want the nursing teams to move to this approach. To your surprise, they're both opposed to the idea. Sue says she and the other emergency room nurses feel they're needed in the ER where they fill the most vital role in the hospital. They work special hours when needed, do whatever tasks are required, and often work in difficult and stressful circumstances. They think the floor nurses have relatively easy jobs for the pay they receive. Scott, leader of the floor nurse team, tells you that his group believes the ER nurses lack the special training and extra experience that the floor nurses bring to the hospital. The floor nurses claim they have the heaviest responsibilities and do the most exacting work. Because they have ongoing contact with patients and families, they believe they shouldn't be called away from vital floor duties to help the ER nurses complete their tasks.

Reinforcement: Managing Resistance to Change

The following suggestions are activities you can do to practice and reinforce the behaviors associated with effectively managing resistance to change.

1. Think about changes (major and minor) that you have dealt with over the last year. Perhaps these changes involved other people and perhaps they were personal. Did you resist the change? Did others resist the change? How did you overcome your resistance or the resistance of others to the change?

2. Interview managers at three different organizations about changes they have implemented. What was their experience in implementing the change? How did they manage resistance to the change?

MANAGING TIME

Time is a unique resource in that if it's wasted, it can never be replaced. Managers who use their time effectively know which activities they want to accomplish, the best order in which to do those activities, and when they want to complete those activities. **Time management** is a personal form of scheduling time effectively. The essence of time management is to use your time effectively.

Learning About Managing Time

You can be more effective at managing your time if you use the following five suggestions:

1. *Identify your goals.* What specific goals have you set for yourself or for your work unit? If you work in an organization that uses a form of MBO (management by objectives) or some other goal-setting method, these goals may already exist.

2. *Prioritize your goals.* Not all goals you have are equally important. Given limitations that exist on your time, you want to give the highest priority to the goals that are the most important.

3. *List the activities that must be done to accomplish your goals.* Planning really is the key here. You must identify the specific actions you need to take to achieve your goals. Record these activities on a sheet of paper, an index card, or even a computer-generated schedule. These activities become your "to-do" list. Your to-do list should cover, at a minimum, those things that need to be done over the next few days. The list should be reviewed throughout the day and updated when necessary. As items are completed, they should be crossed off the list.

4. *Prioritize your to-do list.* This step involves imposing a second set of priorities. Here you need to emphasize both importance and urgency. If the activity is not important, you should consider delegating it to someone else. If it's not urgent, usually it can wait. Completing this step will help you identify activities you *must* do, activities you *should* do, activities you'll do *when you can*, and activities that you can *get others to do for you*.

5. *Schedule your day.* After prioritizing your activities, develop a daily plan. Each morning (or the night before) identify what you want to accomplish during the day. Follow with those you should do, and so forth, but be realistic in your schedule. Depending on the nature of your activities, you may not be able to complete everything. Be realistic in what you can accomplish. The key is to concentrate on the "must-do's," making sure they do get done. Don't make the mistake of working on the "when you can" activities just because they may be easier to accomplish. You'll be spending time on activities that really won't add to your effectiveness.

Source: Based on R.A. Mackenzie, *The Time Trap* (New York: McGraw-Hill, 1975); R.A. Webber, *Time Is Money* (New York: The Free Press, 1980); M.E. Haynes, *Practical Time Management: How to Make the Most of Your Most Perishable Resource* (Tulsa, OK: Pennwell Books, 1985); and A. Deutschman, "The CEO's Secret of Managing Time," *Fortune*, June 1, 1992, pp. 135–46.

Practice: Managing Time

Have you ever thought about how you spend your time in a typical week? Do you know who or what "wastes" your time? For this exercise, you are to keep a time log for each day for the next week. Starting at midnight and in 15-minute increments, list what you do and who you interact with for 24 hours. To get the most accurate information, fill in each time period as it ends (except when you're asleep). Don't wait until later and attempt to complete it by memory. When you have tracked these data for a week, review the time log.

Answer the following questions. Can you identify times when you were most productive? How about those when you wasted time? Are there consistencies in the time wasters? That is, do they tend to occur at the same time, in the same place, or with the same individuals?

Finally, share your information with a partner in class. Look for similarities between your lists. Each of you should make two recommendations that would help the other person become a better time manager.

Reinforcement: Managing Time

The following suggestions are activities you can do to practice and reinforce the behaviors associated with managing your time.

1. Interview two of your professors regarding how they effectively manage their time. What similarities do you see in their responses? How do their responses fit in with the suggestions given for improving this skill?
2. Use your contacts to identify two individuals—one who has a long record of personal or career accomplishments; the other, a modest record. Interview each to learn how they manage their time. Now write a short paper analyzing to what degree their time management skills may have contributed to or hindered their record of accomplishments.

MENTORING

A **mentor** is someone in the organization, usually older, more experienced, and in a higher-level position, who sponsors or supports another employee (a protégé) who is in a lower-level position in the organization. A mentor can teach, guide, and encourage. Some organizations have formal mentoring programs, but even if your organization does not, mentoring is an important skill for you to develop.

Learning About Mentoring

You can be more effective at mentoring if you use the following six suggestions as you mentor another person.

1. *Communicate honestly and openly with your protégé.* If your protégé is going to learn from you and benefit from your experience and knowledge, you're going to have to be open and honest as you talk about what you've done. Bring up the failures as well as the successes. Remember that mentoring is a learning process and in order for learning to take place, you're going to have to be open and honest in "telling it like it is."
2. *Encourage honest and open communication from your protégé.* You need to know as the mentor what your protégé hopes to gain from this relationship. You should encourage the protégé to ask for information and to be specific about what he or she wants to gain.
3. *Treat the relationship with the protégé as a learning opportunity.* Don't pretend to have all the answers and all the knowledge, but do share what you've learned through your experiences. And in your conversations

and interactions with your protégé, you may be able to learn as much from that person as he or she does from you. So be open to listening to what your protégé is saying.

4. *Take the time to get to know your protégé.* As a mentor, you should be willing to take the time to get to know your protégé and his or her interests. If you're not willing to spend that extra time, you should probably not embark on a mentoring relationship.
5. *Remind your protégé that there is no substitute for effective work performance.* In any job, effective work performance is absolutely essential for success. It doesn't matter how much information you provide as a mentor if the protégé isn't willing to strive for effective work performance.
6. *Know when it's time to let go.* Successful mentors know when it's time to let the protégé begin standing on his or her own. If the mentoring relationship has been effective, the protégé will be comfortable and confident in handling new and increasing work responsibilities. And just because the mentoring relationship is over doesn't mean that you never have contact with your protégé. It just means that the relationship becomes one of equals, not one of teacher and student.

Source: Based on H. Rothman, "The Boss as Mentor," *Nation's Business*, April 1993, pp. 66–67; J.B. Cunningham and T. Eberle, "Characteristics of the Mentoring Experience: A Qualitative Study," *Personnel Review*, June 1993, pp. 54–66; S. Crandell, "The Joys of Mentoring," *Executive Female*, March–April 1994, pp. 38–42; and W. Heery, "Corporate Mentoring Can Break the Glass Ceiling," *HRFocus*, May 1994, pp. 17–18.

Practice: Mentoring

Read through the following scenario. Write down some notes about how you would handle the situation described. Be sure to refer to the six behaviors for mentoring. Your professor will then tell you what to do next.

SCENARIO

Lora Slovinsky has worked for your department in a software design firm longer than any of your other employees. You value her skills and commitment and you frequently ask for her judgment on difficult issues. Very often, her ideas have been better than yours and you've let her know through both praise and pay increases how much you appreciate her contributions. Recently, though, you've begun to question Lora's judgment. The fundamental problem is in the distinct difference in the ways you both approach your work. Your strengths lie in getting things done on time and under budget. Although Lora is aware of these constraints, her creativity and perfectionism sometimes make her prolong projects continually looking for the best approaches. On her most recent assignment, Lora seemed more intent than ever on doing things her way. Despite what you felt were clear guidelines, she was two weeks late in meeting an important customer deadline. And while her product quality was high, as always, the software design was far more elaborate than what was needed at this stage of development. Looking over her work in your office, you feel more than a little frustrated and certain that you need to address matters with Lora.

Reinforcement: Mentoring

The following suggestions are activities you can do to practice and reinforce the behaviors needed in mentoring.

1. If there are individuals on your campus who act as mentors (or advisors) to first-time students, make an appointment to talk to one of these mentors. These mentors may be upper-division students or they may be professors or college staff employees. Ask them about their role as a mentor and the skills they think it takes to be an effective mentor. How do the skills they mention relate to the behaviors described here?

2. Athletic coaches often act as mentors to their younger assistant coaches. Interview a coach about her or his role as a mentor. What types of things do coaches do to instruct, teach, advise, and encourage their assistant coaches? Could any of these activities be transferred to an organizational setting? Explain.

NEGOTIATING

Negotiating is another interpersonal skill that managers use. For instance, they may have to negotiate salaries for incoming employees, negotiate for resources from their managers, work out differences with associates, or resolve conflicts with subordinates. **Negotiation** is a process of bargaining in which two or more parties who have different preferences must make joint decisions and come to an agreement.

Learning About Negotiation

You can be more effective at negotiating if you use the following six recommended behaviors.

1. *Research the individual with whom you will be negotiating.* Acquire as much information as you can about the person with whom you'll be negotiating. What are this individual's interests and goals? Understanding this person's position will help you to better understand his or her behavior, predict his or her responses to your offers, and frame solutions in terms of his or her interests.

2. *Begin with a positive overture.* Research shows that concessions tend to be reciprocated and lead to agreements. Therefore, begin bargaining with a positive overture and then reciprocate the other party's concessions.

3. *Address problems, not personalities.* Concentrate on the negotiation issues, not on the personal characteristics of the individual with whom you're negotiating. When negotiations get tough, avoid the tendency to attack this person. Remember it's that person's ideas or position that you disagree with, not him or her personally.

4. *Pay little attention to initial offers.* Treat an initial offer as merely a point of departure. Everyone must have an initial position. Such positions tend to be extreme and idealistic. Treat them as such.

5. *Emphasize win-win solutions.* If conditions are supportive, look for an integrative solution. Frame options in terms of the other party's interests and look for solutions that can allow this person, as well as yourself, to declare a victory.

6. *Create an open and trusting climate.* Skilled negotiators are better listeners, ask more questions, focus their arguments more directly, are less defensive, and have learned to avoid words or phrases that can irritate the person with whom they're negotiating (such as "generous offer," "fair price," or "reasonable

arrangement"). In other words, they are better at creating the open and trusting climate that is necessary for reaching a win-win settlement.

Source: Based on M.H. Bazerman and M.A. Neale, *Negotiating Rationally* (New York: The Free Press, 1992); and J.A. Wall, Jr. and M.W. Blum, "Negotiations," *Journal of Management*, June 1991, pp. 278–82.

Practice: Negotiating

Read through the following scenario. Write down some notes about how you would handle the situation. Be sure to refer to the six behaviors described for negotiating. Your professor will then tell you what to do next.

SCENARIO

As marketing director for Done Right, a regional home repair chain, you've come up with a plan you believe has significant potential for future sales. Your plan involves a customer information service designed to help people make their homes more environmentally sensitive. Then based upon homeowners' assessments of their homes' environmental impact, your firm will be prepared to help them deal with problems or concerns they may uncover. You're really excited about the competitive potential of this new service. You envision pamphlets, in-store appearances by environmental experts, as well as contests for consumers and school kids. After several weeks of preparations, you make your pitch to your boss, Patrick Wong. You point out how the market for environmentally sensitive

products is growing and how this growing demand represents the perfect opportunity for Done Right. Patrick seems impressed by your presentation, but he's expressed one major concern. He thinks your workload is already too heavy. He doesn't see how you're going to have enough time to start this new service *and* still be able to look after all of your other assigned marketing duties.

Reinforcement: Negotiating

The following suggestions are activities you can do to practice and reinforce the negotiating behaviors.

1. Find three people who have recently purchased new or used cars. Interview each to learn which tactics, if any, they used to get a better deal (lower price, more car features, and so forth). Write a short paper comparing your findings and relating it to the negotiating behaviors presented in this section.

2. Research current business periodicals for two examples of negotiations. The negotiations might be labor-management negotiations or they might be negotiations over buying and selling real estate or a business. What did the article say about the negotiation process? Write down specific questions that each party to the negotiation might have had. Pretend that you were a consultant to one of the parties in the negotiation. What recommendations would you have made?

PROVIDING FEEDBACK

Ask a manager about the feedback he or she gives employees and you're likely to get an answer followed by a qualifier! If the feedback is positive, it's likely to be given promptly and enthusiastically. However, negative feedback is often treated very differently. Like most of us, managers don't particularly enjoy communicating bad news. They fear offending the other person or having to deal with the recipient's defensiveness. The result is that negative feedback is often avoided, delayed, or substantially distorted. However, it is important for managers to provide both positive and negative feedback.

Learning About Providing Feedback

You can be more effective at providing feedback if you use the following six specific suggestions.

1. *Focus on specific behaviors.* Feedback should be specific rather than general. Avoid such statements as "You have a bad attitude" or "I'm really impressed with the good job you did." They're vague and although they provide information, they don't tell the recipient

enough to correct the "bad attitude" or on what basis you concluded that a "good job" had been done so the person knows what behaviors to repeat or to avoid.

2. *Keep feedback impersonal.* Feedback, particularly the negative kind, should be descriptive rather than judgmental or evaluative. No matter how upset you are, keep the feedback focused on job-related behaviors and never criticize someone personally because of an inappropriate action.

3. *Keep feedback goal oriented.* Feedback should not be given primarily to "unload" on another person. If you have to say something negative, make sure it's directed toward the recipient's goals. Ask yourself whom the feedback is supposed to help. If the answer is *you*, bite your tongue and hold the comment. Such feedback undermines your credibility and lessens the meaning and influence of future feedback.

4. *Make feedback well timed.* Feedback is most meaningful to a recipient when there's a very short interval between his or her behavior and the receipt of feedback about that behavior. Moreover, if you're particu-

larly concerned with changing behavior, delays in providing feedback on the undesirable actions lessen the likelihood that the feedback will be effective in bringing about the desired change. Of course, making feedback prompt merely for the sake of promptness can backfire if you have insufficient information, if you're angry, or if you're otherwise emotionally upset. In such instances, "well timed" could mean "somewhat delayed."

5. *Ensure understanding.* Make sure your feedback is concise and complete so that the recipient clearly and fully understands your communication. It may help to have the recipient rephrase the content of your feedback to find out whether or not he or she fully captured the meaning you intended.

6. *Direct negative feedback toward behavior that the recipient can control.* There's little value in reminding a person of some shortcoming over which he or she has no control. Negative feedback should be directed at behavior that the recipient can do something about. In addition, when negative feedback is given concerning something that the recipient can control, it might be a good idea to indicate specifically what can be done to improve the situation.

Source: Based on P.L. Hunsaker, *Training in Management Skills* (Upper Saddle River, NJ: Prentice Hall, 2001), pp. 60–61.

Practice: Providing Feedback

Read through the following scenario. Write down some notes about how you would handle the situation. Be sure to refer to the six behaviors described for providing feedback. Your professor will tell you what to do next.

SCENARIO

Craig is an excellent employee whose expertise and productivity have always met or exceeded your expectations.

But recently he's been making work difficult for other members of your advertising team. Like his co-workers, Craig researches and computes the costs of media coverage for your advertising agency's clients. The work requires laboriously leafing through several large reference books to find the correct base price and add-on charges for each radio or television station and time slot, calculating each actual cost, and compiling the results in a computerized spreadsheet. To make things more efficient and convenient, you've always allowed your team members to bring the reference books they're using to their desks while they're using them. Lately, however, Craig has been piling books around him for days and sometimes weeks at a time. The books interfere with the flow of traffic past his desk and other people are having to go out of their way to retrieve the books from Craig's pile. It's time for you to have a talk with Craig.

Reinforcement: Providing Feedback

The following suggestions are activities you can do to practice and reinforce the behaviors in providing feedback.

1. Think of three things that a friend or family member did well recently. Did you praise the person at the time? If not, why? The next time someone close to you does something well, give him or her positive feedback.

2. You have a good friend who has a mannerism (for instance, speech, body movement, style of dress, or whatever) that you think is inappropriate and detracts from the overall impression that he or she makes. Come up with a plan for talking with this person. What will you say? When will you talk with your friend? How will you handle his or her reaction?

READING AN ORGANIZATION'S CULTURE

The ability to read an organization's culture can be a valuable skill. For instance, if you're looking for a job, you'll want to choose an employer whose culture is compatible with your values and in which you'll feel comfortable. If you can accurately assess a potential employer's culture before you make your job decision, you may be able to save yourself a lot of anxiety and reduce the likelihood of making a poor choice. Similarly, you'll undoubtedly have business transactions with numerous organizations during your professional career, such as selling a product or service, negotiating a contract, arranging a joint work project, or merely seeking out who controls certain decisions in an organization. The

ability to assess another organization's culture can be a definite plus in successfully performing those pursuits.

Learning About Reading an Organization's Culture

You can be more effective at reading an organization's culture if you use the following behaviors. For the sake of simplicity, we're going to look at this skill from the perspective of a job applicant. We'll assume that you're interviewing for a job, although these skills are generalizable to many situations. Here's a list of things you can do to help learn about an organization's culture.

1. *Observe the physical surroundings.* Pay attention to signs, posters, pictures, photos, style of dress, length

of hair, degree of openness between offices, and office furnishings and arrangements.

2. *Make note of those with whom you met.* Was it the person who would be your immediate supervisor? Or did you meet with potential colleagues, managers from other departments, or senior executives? Based on what they revealed, to what degree do people interact with others who may not be in their particular work area or at their particular organizational level?

3. *How would you characterize the style of the people you met?* Are they formal? Casual? Serious? Laid-back? Open? Not willing to provide information?

4. *Look at the organization's human resources manual.* Are formal rules and regulations printed there? If so, how detailed are these policies?

5. *Ask questions of the people with whom you meet.* The most valid and reliable information tends to come from asking the same questions of many people (to see how closely their responses align) and by talking with individuals whose jobs link them to the outside environment. Questions that will give you insights into organizational processes and practices might include the following: What is the background of the founders? What is the background of current senior managers? What are their functional specialties? Were they promoted from within or hired from outside? How does the organization integrate new employees? Is there a formal orientation program? Are there formal employee training programs? How does your boss define his or her job success? How would you define fairness in terms of reward allocations? Can you identify some people here who are on the "fast track"? What do you think has put them on the fast track? Can you identify someone in the organization who seems to be considered an oddball or deviate? How has the organization responded to this person? Can you describe a decision that someone made that was well received? Can you describe a decision that didn't work out well? What were the consequences for the decision maker? Could you describe a crisis or critical event that has occurred recently in the organization? How did top management respond? What was learned from this experience?

Source: Based on S.P. Robbins, *Organizational Behavior*, 9th ed. (Upper Saddle River, NJ: Prentice Hall, 2001), p. 513.

Practice: Reading an Organization's Culture

Read through the following scenario. Write down some notes about how you would handle the situation. Be sure to refer to the suggested behaviors for reading an organization's culture. Your professor will tell you what to do next.

SCENARIO

After spending your first three years after college graduation as a freelance graphic designer, you're looking at pursuing a job as an account executive at a graphic design firm. You feel that the scope of assignments and potential for technical training far exceed what you'd be able to do on your own and you're looking to expand your skills and meet a brand-new set of challenges. However, you want to make sure you "fit" into the organization where you're going to be spending more than eight hours every workday. What's the best way for you to find a place where you'll be happy and where your style and personality will be appreciated?

Reinforcement: Reading an Organization's Culture

The following suggestions are activities you can do to practice and reinforce the behaviors associated with reading an organization's culture.

1. If you're taking more than one course, assess the cultures of the various classes in which you're enrolled. How do the classroom cultures differ? Which culture(s) do you seem to prefer? Why?

2. Make some comparisons of the atmosphere or feeling you get from various organizations. Because of the number and wide variety that you'll find, it will probably be easiest for you to do this exercise using restaurants, retail stores, or banks. Based on the atmosphere that you observe, what type of organizational culture do you think these organizations might have? On what did you base your decision? Which type of culture do you prefer? Why? If you can, interview three employees at this organization for their descriptions of the organization's culture. Did their descriptions support your interpretation? Why or why not?

RUNNING PRODUCTIVE MEETINGS

As a manager, you'll spend a good deal of your workday in meetings. And, undoubtedly, there will be instances when you will be responsible for running meetings. Great meetings don't just happen—they're designed to be great. How can you make sure that your meetings are productive?

Learning About Running Productive Meetings

You can be more effective at running productive meetings if you follow these eight suggestions.

1. *Prepare and distribute an agenda well in advance of the meeting.* An **agenda** defines the meeting's purpose for participants and the boundaries between rel-

evant and irrelevant discussion topics. Also, the agenda can serve as an important vehicle for pre-meeting discussions with participants.

2. *Consult with participants before the meeting to ensure proper participation.* Let all participants know that their input is valuable and that you welcome their speaking up at the meeting when they have something to offer.

3. *Establish specific time parameters for the meeting; specify when it will start and end.* This step helps keep the meeting on time and focused on the important matters.

4. *Maintain focused discussion during the meeting.* Items not on the agenda should not be given substantial time during the meeting. If an issue is important, maybe another meeting, with its own agenda, should be held to address that issue.

5. *Encourage and support participation by all meeting attendees.* If you have done a good job in the second step, participants should come prepared to talk but still may need some encouragement at the meeting. Sometimes direct questions about what they think will get them to talk.

6. *Encourage the clash of ideas.* Remember that you want as much information about a topic to surface as possible. Disagreements are fine. They indicate that different voices are being heard. Better to work the differences out than to have them surface later.

7. *Discourage the clash of personalities.* Disagreements can enhance the process, but they should be substantive disputes. Differences caused by personal issues are a disaster in a meeting.

8. *Bring closure by summarizing accomplishments and allocating follow-up assignments.* This step lets participants understand what occurred in the meeting and what they may have to do before the next meeting. This is, in essence, planning.

Source: Based on S.P. Robbins and D.A. DeCenzo, *Fundamentals of Management*, 3rd ed. (Upper Saddle River, NJ: Prentice Hall, 2001), pp. 136–37; G. Imperato, "We Have to Start Meeting Like This!" *Fast Company*, April 1999, pp. 204–10; S. Armour, "Meetings Inspire High-Tech Survival Skills," *USA Today Online* [www.usatoday.com], January 22, 1999; J. Champy, "Wasteful Meetings," *Forbes*, November 2, 1998, p. 173; and J. Grossman, "We've Got to Start Meeting Like This," *Inc.*, April 1998, pp. 70–74.

Practice: Running Productive Meetings

Read through the following scenario. Write down some notes about how you would handle the situation described. Be sure to refer to the suggestions for running productive meetings. Your professor will then tell you what to do next.

SCENARIO

You manage a group of six skilled technicians in the radiology department of a large hospital. You need to meet with them to discuss the hospital's unpopular new vacation policy and to devise your department's vacation schedule for the coming year. In keeping with the new policy, only one person will be allowed to take vacation at any given time. Anna, the newest member of the department, is out sick but has agreed to participate in the meeting by telephone. Ravi and Helen, senior members of the department, both want to take the same week off. Draft your agenda for the meeting and allocate specific time intervals for each topic of discussion.

Reinforcement: Running Productive Meetings

The following suggestions are activities you can do to practice and reinforce the behaviors associated with running productive meetings.

1. You are probably involved in a student project team or maybe are part of a team at work. Practice running the meeting the next time this group meets. (If at work, make sure you check this with your manager first.) Be sure to follow the suggested behaviors for running productive meetings. After the meeting, analyze what happened. Was the team able to stick to its agenda? Why or why not? Was discussion focused on the important issues? Why or why not? Did all meeting attendees participate? Why or why not? Were ideas freely and openly exchanged? Were any personality clashes obvious? If so, what did you do to discourage them? How did you end the meeting? What did this experience teach you about running productive meetings?

2. Interview managers from three different organizations about how they conduct meetings. What specific tips have they discovered for running productive meetings? What problems have they encountered when conducting meetings? How did they deal with these problems?

SCANNING THE ENVIRONMENT

Anticipating and interpreting changes that are taking place in the environment is an important skill that managers need. Information that comes from scanning the environment can be used in making decisions and taking actions. And managers at all levels of an organization need to know how to scan the environment for important information and trends.

Learning About Scanning the Environment

You can be more effective at scanning the environment if you use the following suggestions:

1. *Decide which type of environmental information is important to your work.* Perhaps you need to know changes in customers' needs and desires or perhaps you need to know what your competitors are doing. Once you know the type of information that you'd like to have, you can look at the best ways to get that information.

2. *Regularly read and monitor pertinent information.* There is no scarcity of information to scan, but what you need to do is read those information sources that are pertinent. How do you know which information sources are pertinent? They're pertinent if they provide you with the information that you identified as important.

3. *Incorporate the information that you get from your environmental scanning into your decisions and actions.* Unless you use the information you're getting, you're wasting your time getting it. Also, the more that you find you're using information from your environmental scanning, the more likely it is that you'll want to continue to invest time and other resources into gathering it. You'll see that this information is important to your being able to manage effectively and efficiently.

4. *Regularly review your environmental scanning activities.* If you find that you're spending too much time getting nonuseful information or if you're not using the pertinent information that you've gathered, you need to make some adjustments.

5. *Encourage your subordinates to be alert to information that is important.* Your employees can be your "eyes and ears" as well. Emphasize to them the importance of gathering and sharing information that may affect your work unit's performance.

Source: Based on L.M. Fuld, *Monitoring the Competition* (New York: Wiley, 1988); E.H. Burack and N.J. Mathys, "Environmental Scanning Improves Strategic Planning," *Personnel Administrator*, 1989, pp. 82–87; and R. Subramanian, N. Fernandes, and E. Harper, "Environmental Scanning in U.S. Companies: Their Nature and Their Relationship to Performance," *Management International Review*, July 1993, pp. 271–86.

Practice: Scanning the Environment

Read through the following scenario. Write down some notes about how you would handle the situation described. Be sure to refer to the suggestions for scanning the environment. Your professor will then tell you what to do next.

SCENARIO

You're the assistant to the president at your college. You've been asked to prepare a report outlining the external information that you think is important for her to monitor. Think of the types of information that the president would need in order to do an effective job of managing the college right now and over the next three years. Be as specific as you can in describing this information. Also identify where this information could be found.

Reinforcement: Scanning the Environment

The following suggestions are activities you can do to practice and reinforce the behaviors associated with scanning the environment.

1. Select an organization with which you're familiar either as an employee or perhaps as a frequent customer. Assume that you're the top manager in this organization. What types of information from environmental scanning do you think would be important to you? Where would you find this information? Now assume that you're a first-level manager in this organization. Would the types of information you'd get from environmental scanning change? Explain.

2. Assume you're a regional manager for a large bookstore chain. Using the Internet, what types of environmental and competitive information were you able to identify? For each source, what information did you find that might help you do your job better?

SETTING GOALS

Employees should have a clear understanding of what they're attempting to accomplish. In addition, managers have the responsibility for seeing that this is done by helping employees set work goals. Setting goals is a skill every manager needs to develop.

Learning About Setting Goals

You can be more effective at setting goals if you use the following eight suggestions.

1. *Identify an employee's key job tasks.* Goal setting begins by defining what it is that you want your employees to accomplish. The best source for this information is each employee's job description.

2. *Establish specific and challenging goals for each key task.* Identify the level of performance expected of each employee. Specify the target toward which the employee is working.

3. *Specify the deadlines for each goal.* Putting deadlines on each goal reduces ambiguity. Deadlines, however,

should not be set arbitrarily. Rather, they need to be realistic given the tasks to be completed.

4. *Allow the employee to actively participate.* When employees participate in goal setting, they're more likely to accept the goals. However, it must be sincere participation. That is, employees must perceive that you are truly seeking their input, not just going through the motions.

5. *Prioritize goals.* When you give someone more than one goal, it's important for you to rank the goals in order of importance. The purpose of prioritizing is to encourage the employee to take action and expend effort on each goal in proportion to its importance.

6. *Rate goals for difficulty and importance.* Goal setting should not encourage people to choose easy goals. Instead, goals should be rated for their difficulty and importance. When goals are rated, individuals can be given credit for trying difficult goals, even if they don't fully achieve them.

7. *Build in feedback mechanisms to assess goal progress.* Feedback lets employees know whether their level of effort is sufficient to attain the goal. Feedback should be both self-generated and supervisor generated. In either case, feedback should be frequent and recurring.

8. *Link rewards to goal attainment.* It's natural for employees to ask, "What's in it for me?" Linking rewards to the achievement of goals will help answer that question.

Source: Based on S.P. Robbins and D.A. DeCenzo, *Fundamentals of Management*, 2nd ed. (Upper Saddle River, NJ: Prentice Hall, 1998), p. 80.

Practice: Setting Goals

Read through the following scenario. Write down some notes about how you would handle the situation described. Be sure to refer to the eight suggestions for setting goals. Your professor will then tell you what to do next.

SCENARIO

You worked your way through college while holding down a part-time job bagging groceries at Food Town supermarket chain. You like working in the food industry and when you graduated, you accepted a position with Food Town as a management trainee. Three years have passed and you've gained experience in the grocery store industry and in operating a large supermarket. About a year ago, you received a promotion to store manager at one of the chain's locations. One of the things you've liked about Food Town is that it gives store managers a great deal of autonomy in running their stores. The company provides very general guidelines to its managers. The concern is with the bottom line; for the most part, how you get there is up to you. Now that you're finally a store manager, you want to establish an MBO-type program in your store. You like the idea that everyone should have clear goals to work toward and then is evaluated against those goals.

Your store employs 90 people, although except for the managers, most work only 20 to 30 hours per week. You have six people reporting to you: an assistant manager; a weekend manager; and grocery, produce, meat, and bakery managers. The only highly skilled jobs belong to the butchers who have strict training and regulatory guidelines. Other less skilled jobs include cashier, shelf stocker, cleanup, and grocery bagger.

Specifically describe how you would go about setting goals in your new position. Include examples of goals for the jobs of butcher, cashier, and bakery manager.

Reinforcement: Setting Goals

The following suggestions are activities you can do to practice and reinforce the behaviors in setting goals.

1. Where do you want to be in five years? Do you have specific five-year goals? Establish three goals you want to achieve in five years. Make sure these goals are specific, challenging, and measurable.

2. Set personal and academic goals you want to achieve by the end of this college term. Prioritize and rate them for difficulty.

SOLVING PROBLEMS CREATIVELY

In a global business environment, where changes are fast and furious, organizations desperately need creative people. The uniqueness and variety of problems that managers face demand that they be able to solve problems creatively. Creativity is a frame of mind. You need to expand your mind's capabilities—that is, open up your mind to new ideas. Every individual has the ability to improve his or her creativity, but many people simply don't try to develop that ability.

Learning About Solving Problems Creatively

You can be more effective at solving problems creatively if you use the following 10 suggestions.

1. *Think of yourself as creative.* Although this may be a simple suggestion, research shows that if you think

you can't be creative, you won't be. Believing in your ability to be creative is the first step in becoming more creative.

2. *Pay attention to your intuition.* Every individual has a subconscious mind that works well. Sometimes answers will come to you when you least expect them. Listen to that "inner voice." In fact, most creative people will keep a notepad near their bed and write down ideas when the thoughts come to them. That way, they don't forget them.

3. *Move away from your comfort zone.* Every individual has a comfort zone in which certainty exists. But creativity and the known often do not mix. To be creative, you need to move away from the status quo and focus your mind on something new.

4. *Determine what you want to do.* This includes such things as taking time to understand a problem before beginning to try to resolve it, getting all the facts in mind, and trying to identify the most important facts.

5. *Look for ways to tackle the problem.* This can be accomplished by setting aside a block of time to focus on it; working out a plan for attacking it; establishing subgoals; imagining or actually using analogies wherever possible (for example, could you approach your problem like a fish out of water and look at what the fish does to cope? Or can you use the things you have to do to find your way when it's foggy to help you solve your problem?); using different problem-solving strategies such as verbal, visual, mathematical, theatrical (for instance, you might draw a diagram of the decision or problem to help you visualize it better or you might talk to yourself out loud about the problem telling it as you would tell a story to someone); trusting your intuition; and playing with possible ideas and approaches (for example, look at your problem from a different perspective or ask yourself what someone else, like your grandmother, might do if faced with the same situation).

6. *Look for ways to do things better.* This may involve trying consciously to be original, not worrying about looking foolish, eliminating cultural taboos (like gender stereotypes) that might influence your possible solutions, keeping an open mind, being alert to odd or puzzling facts, thinking of unconventional ways to use objects and the environment (for instance, thinking about how you could use newspaper or magazine headlines to help you be a better problem solver), discarding usual or habitual ways of doing things, and striving for objectivity by being as critical of your own ideas as you would those of someone else.

7. *Find several right answers.* Being creative means continuing to look for other solutions even when you think you have solved the problem. A better, more creative solution just might be found.

8. *Believe in finding a workable solution.* Like believing in yourself, you also need to believe in your ideas. If you don't think you can find a solution, you probably won't.

9. *Brainstorm with others.* Creativity is not an isolated activity. Bouncing ideas off of others creates a synergistic effect.

10. *Turn creative ideas into action.* Coming up with creative ideas is only part of the process. Once the ideas are generated, they must be implemented. Keeping great ideas in your mind, or on papers that no one will read, does little to expand your creative abilities.

Source: Based on J. Calano and J. Salzman, "Ten Ways to Fire Up Your Creativity," *Working Woman*, July 1989, p. 94; J.V. Anderson, "Mind Mapping: A Tool for Creative Thinking," *Business Horizons*, January–February 1993, pp. 42–46; M. Loeb, "Ten Commandments for Managing Creative People," *Fortune*, January 16, 1995, pp. 135–36; and M. Henricks, "Good Thinking," *Entrepreneur*, May 1996, pp. 70–73.

Practice: Solving Problems Creatively

Read through the following scenario. Write down some notes about how you would handle the situation. Be sure to refer to the 10 suggestions for solving problems creatively. Your professor will then tell you what to do next.

SCENARIO

Every time the phone rings, your stomach clenches and your palms start to sweat. And it's no wonder! As sales manager for Brinkers, a machine tool parts manufacturer, you're besieged by calls from customers who are upset about late deliveries. Your boss, Carter Hererra, acts as both production manager and scheduler. Every time your sales representatives negotiate a sale, it's up to Carter to determine whether or not production can actually meet the delivery date the customer specifies. And Carter invariably says, "No problem." The good thing about this is that you make a lot of initial sales. The bad news is that production hardly ever meets the shipment dates that Carter authorizes. And he doesn't seem to be all that concerned about the aftermath of late deliveries. He says, "Our customers know they're getting outstanding quality at a great price. Just let them try to match that anywhere. It can't be done. So even if they have to wait a couple of extra days or weeks, they're still getting the best deal they can." Somehow the customers don't see it that way, however. And they let you know about their unhappiness. Then it's up to you to try to soothe the relationship. You know this problem has to be taken care of, but what possible solutions are there? After all, how are you going to keep from making your manager mad or making the customers mad?

Reinforcement: Solving Problems Creatively

The following suggestions are activities you can do to practice and reinforce the behaviors associated with solving problems creatively.

1. Take out a couple of sheets of paper. You have 20 minutes to list as many medical or health care related jobs as you can that begin with the letter *r* (for instance, radiologist, registered nurse). If you run out of listings before time is up, it's OK to quit early. But try to be as creative as you can.

2. List on a piece of paper some common terms that apply to both *water* and *finance*. How many were you able to come up with?

Additional skills materials are available on PRISM (PRactical Interactive Skills Modules) which can be found on R.O.L.L.S. (Robbins OnLine Learning System) at www.prenhall.com/robbins. The 12 scenarios included in PRISM cover the following skills:

Scenario 1: Designing Motivating Jobs
Scenario 2: Choosing an Effective Leadership Style
Scenario 3: Environmental Scanning and Reading an Organization's Culture
Scenario 4: Developing Trust
Scenario 5: Acquiring Power and Managing Resistance to Change
Scenario 6: Assessing Cross-Cultural Differences
Scenario 7: Mentoring
Scenario 8: Disciplining and Providing Feedback
Scenario 9: Coaching and Creating Effective Teams
Scenario 10: Delegating
Scenario 11: Active Listening and Interviewing
Scenario 12: Setting Goals and Solving Problems Creatively

NOTES

CHAPTER 1

1. Information from company's Web page (www.thethinkers.com), June 12, 2000; and N.K. Austin, "Tear Down the Walls," *Inc.*, April 1999, pp. 66–76.

2. Information from Catalyst Web page (www.catalystwomen.org), June 15, 2000.

3. D. Drickhamer, "America's Best Plants," *IW*, October 18, 1999, pp. 40–41.

4. H. Fayol, *Industrial and General Administration* (Paris: Dunod, 1916).

5. For a comprehensive review of this question, see C.P. Hales, "What Do Managers Do? A Critical Review of the Evidence," *Journal of Management*, January 1986, pp. 88–115.

6. H. Mintzberg, *The Nature of Managerial Work* (New York: Harper & Row, 1973).

7. See, for example, L.D. Alexander, "The Effect Level in the Hierarchy and Functional Area Have on the Extent Mintzberg's Roles Are Required by Managerial Jobs," *Academy of Management Proceedings* (San Francisco, 1979), pp. 186–89; A.W. Lau and C.M. Pavett, "The Nature of Managerial Work: A Comparison of Public and Private Sector Managers," *Group and Organization Studies*, December 1980, pp. 453–66; M.W. McCall Jr. and C.A. Segrist, *In Pursuit of the Manager's Job: Building on Mintzberg, Technical Report No. 14* (Greensboro, NC: Center for Creative Leadership, 1980); C.M. Pavett and A.W. Lau, "Managerial Work: The Influence of Hierarchical Level and Functional Specialty," *Academy of Management Journal*, March 1983, pp. 170–77; Hales, "What Do Managers Do?"; A.I. Kraut, P.R. Pedigo, D.D. McKenna, and M.D. Dunnette, "The Role of the Manager: What's Really Important in Different Management Jobs," *Academy of Management Executive*, November 1989, pp. 286–93; and M.J. Martinko and W.L. Gardner, "Structured Observation of Managerial Work: A Replication and Synthesis," *Journal of Management Studies*, May 1990, pp. 330–57.

8. Pavett and Lau, "Managerial Work."

9. S.J. Carroll and D.A. Gillen, "Are the Classical Management Functions Useful in Describing Managerial Work?" *Academy of Management Review*, January 1987, p. 48.

10. H. Koontz, "Commentary on the Management Theory Jungle—Nearly Two Decades Later," in H. Koontz, C. O'Donnell, and H. Weihrich (eds.), *Management: A Book of Readings*, 6th ed. (New York: McGraw-Hill, 1984); Carroll and Gillen, "Are the Classical Management Functions Useful in Describing Managerial Work?"; and P. Allan, "Managers at Work: A Large-Scale Study of the Managerial Job in New York City Government," *Academy of Management Journal*, September 1981, pp. 613–19.

11. R.L. Katz, "Skills of an Effective Administrator," *Harvard Business Review*, September–October 1974, pp. 90–102.

12. K.B. DeGreene, *Sociotechnical Systems: Factors in Analysis, Design, and Management* (Upper Saddle River, NJ: Prentice Hall, 1973), p. 13.

13. T. Aeppel, "Power Generation," *Wall Street Journal*, April 7, 2000, pp. A1+; "Rethinking Work," *Fast Company*, April 2000, p. 253; "Workplace Trends Shifting Over Time," *Springfield News Leader*, January 2, 2000; p. 7B+; Expectations: The State of the New Economy," *Fast Company*, September 1999, pp. 251–64; T.A. Stewart, "Brain Power: Who Owns It . . . How They Profit from It," *Fortune*, March 17, 1997, pp. 105–10; G.P. Zachary, "The Right Mix," *Wall Street Journal*, March 13, 1997, pp. A1+; W.H. Miller, "Leadership at a Crossoads," *IW*, August 19, 1996, pp. 42–56; M. Scott, "Interview with Dee Hock," *Business Ethics*, May/June 1996, pp. 37–41; and J.O'C. Hamilton, S. Baker, and B. Vlasic, "The New Workplace," *Business Week*, April 29, 1996, pp. 106–17.

14. *Occupational Outlook Handbook, 2000–01 Edition*, U.S. Department of Labor, Bureau of Labor Statistics available online at www.bls.gov/ocohome. htm, July 1, 2000.

CHAPTER 2

1. E. Thornton, L. Armstrong, and K. Kerwin, "Toyota Unbound," *Business Week*, May 1, 2000, pp. 142–46; information from company Web site (www.toyota.com), May 25, 2000; S. Spear and H.K. Bowen, "Decoding the DNA of the Toyota Production System," *Harvard Business Review*, Septem-

ber–October, 1999, pp. 96–106; and R.L. Simison, "Toyota Finds Way to Make a Custom Car in 5 Days," *Wall Street Journal*, August 6, 1999, p. A4.

2. C.S. George Jr., *The History of Management Thought*, 2nd ed. (Upper Saddle River, NJ: Prentice Hall, 1972), p. 4.

3. Ibid., pp. 35–41.

4. F.W. Taylor, *Principles of Scientific Management* (New York: Harper, 1911), p. 44. For other information on F.W. Taylor, see M. Banta, *Taylored Lives: Narrative Productions in the Age of Taylor, Veblen, and Ford* (Chicago: University of Chicago Press, 1993); and R. Kanigel, *The One Best Way: Frederick Winslow Taylor and the Enigma of Efficiency* (New York: Viking, 1997).

5. See for example, F.B. Gilbreth, *Motion Study* (New York: Van Nostrand, 1911); and F.B. Gilbreth and L.M. Gilbreth, *Fatigue Study* (New York: Sturgis and Walton, 1916).

6. G. Colvin, "Managing in the Info Era," *Fortune*, March 6, 2000, pp. F6–F9; and A. Harrington, "The Big Ideas," *Fortune*, November 22, 1999, pp. 152–153.

7. H. Fayol, *Industrial and General Administration* (Paris: Dunod, 1916).

8. M. Weber, *The Theory of Social and Economic Organizations*, ed. T. Parsons, trans. A.M. Henderson and T. Parsons (New York: Free Press, 1947).

9. E. Mayo, *The Human Problems of an Industrial Civilization* (New York: Macmillan, 1933); and F.J. Roethlisberger and W.J. Dickson, *Management and the Worker* (Cambridge, MA: Harvard University Press, 1939).

10. See, for example, A. Carey, "The Hawthorne Studies: A Radical Criticism," *American Sociological Review*, June 1967, pp. 403–16; R.H. Franke and J. Kaul, "The Hawthorne Experiments: First Statistical Interpretations," *American Sociological Review*, October 1978, pp. 623–43; B. Rice, "The Hawthorne Defect: Persistence of a Flawed Theory," *Psychology Today*, February 1982, pp. 70–74; J.A. Sonnenfeld, "Shedding Light on the Hawthorne Studies," *Journal of Occupational Behavior*, April 1985, pp. 111–30; S.R.G. Jones, "Worker Interdependence and Output: The Hawthorne Studies Reevaluated," *American Socio-*

logical Review, April 1990, pp. 176–90; S.R. Jones, "Was There a Hawthorne Effect?" *American Sociological Review*, November 1992, pp. 451–68; and G.W. Yunker, "An Explanation of Positive and Negative Hawthorne Effects: Evidence from the Relay Assembly Test Room and Bank Wiring Observation Room Studies," paper presented, Academy of Management Annual Meeting, August 1993, Atlanta, Georgia.

11. W.C. Taylor, "Whatever Happened to Globalization?" *Fast Company*, September 1999, pp. 228–36; and S. Zahra, "The Changing Rules of Global Competitiveness in the 21st Century," *Academy of Management Executive*, February 1999, pp. 36–42.

12. R.W. Judy and Carol D'Amico, *Workforce 2020* (Indianapolis: Hudson Institute, August 1999).

13. G.W. Loveman and J.J. Gabarro, "The Managerial Implications of Changing Work Force Demographics: A Scoping Study," *Human Resource Management*, Spring 1991, pp. 7–29.

14. E. LeBlanc, L. Vanderkam, and K. Vella-Zarb, "America's 50 Best Companies for Minorities," *Fortune*, July 10, 2000, pp. 190–200.

15. *The Facts About Small Business 1999* (Washington, DC: U.S. Small Business Administration, Office of Advocacy), available from SBA Online Web site (www.sba.gov/advo), May 19, 2000, p. 1; and "On the Continent, On the Cusp," *New York Times*, May 14, 2000, pp. BU1+.

16. D.A. Menasce and V.A.F. Almeida, *Scaling for E-Business* (Upper Saddle River, NJ: Prentice Hall PTR, 2000).

17. Menasce and Almeida, *Scaling for E-Business*; M. Lewis, "Boom or Bust," *Business 2.0*, April 2000, pp. 192–205; J. Davis, "How It Works," *Business 2.0*, February 2000, pp. 112–115; and S. Alsop, "e or Be Eaten," *Fortune*, November 8, 1999, pp. 86–98.

18. Alsop, "e or Be Eaten."

19. D. Pottruck and T. Pearce, *Clicks and Mortar* (San Francisco: Jossey-Bass, 2000).

20. G. Hamel, "Reinvent Your Company," *Fortune*, June 12, 2000, pp. 98–118; A. Hargadon and R.I. Sutton, "Building an Innovation Factory," *Harvard Business Review*, May–June 2000, pp. 157–66;

and S. Caudron, "The Economics of Innovation," *Business Finance*, November 1999, pp. 23–27.

21. M.S. Malone, "Which Are the Most Valuable Companies in the New Economy?" *Forbes ASAP*, May 29, 2000, pp. 212–14.

22. See, for example, B. Krone, "Total Quality Management: An American Odyssey," *The Bureaucrat*, Fall 1990, pp. 35–38; A. Gabor, *The Man Who Discovered Quality* (New York: Random House, 1990); J. Clemmer, "How Total Is Your Quality Management?" *Canadian Business Review*, Spring 1991, pp. 38–41; M. Sashkin and K.J. Kiser, *Total Quality Management* (Seabrook, MD: Ducochon Press, 1991); J.W. Dean Jr. and D.E. Bowen, "Management Theory and Total Quality: Improving Research and Practice Through Theory Development," *Academy of Management Review*, July 1994, pp. 392–418; C.A. Reeves and D.A. Bednar, "Defining Quality: Alternatives and Implications," *Academy of Management Review*, July 1994, pp. 419–45; R.K. Reger, L.T. Gustafson, S.M. Demarie, and J.V. Mullane, "Reframing the Organization: Why Implementing Total Quality Is Easier Said Than Done," *Academy of Management Review*, July 1994, pp. 565–84; T.C. Powell, "Total Quality Management as Competitive Advantage: A Review and Empirical Study," *Strategic Management Journal*, January 1995, pp. 15–37; J.R. Hackman and R. Wageman, "Total Quality Management: Empirical, Conceptual, and Practical Issues," *Administrative Science Quarterly*, June 1995, pp. 309–42; T.A. Stewart, "A Conversation with Joseph Juran," *Fortune*, January 11, 1999, pp. 168–70; and J. Jusko, "Tried and True," *IW*, December 6, 1999, pp. 78–84.

23. J. S. Brown and P. Duguid, "Balancing Act: How to Capture Knowledge Without Killing It," *Harvard Business Review*, May–June 2000, pp. 73–80; J. Torsilieri and C. Lucier, "How to Change the World," *Strategy and Business*, 2nd Quarter 2000, pp. 17–20; E.C. Wenger and W.M. Snyder, "Communities of Practice: The Organizational Frontier," *Harvard Business Review*, January–February 2000, pp. 139–45; S.R. Fisher and M.A. White, "Downsizing in a Learning Organization: Are There Hidden Costs?" *Academy of Management*

Review, January 2000, pp. 244–51; R. Myers, "Who Knows?" *CFO*, December 1999, pp. 83–87; and M.T. Hansen, N. Nohria, and T. Tierney, "What's Your Strategy for Managing Knowledge?" *Harvard Business Review*, March–April 1999, pp. 106–16.

24. A.L. Delbecq, "Spirituality for Business Leadership," *Journal of Management Inquiry*, June 2000, pp. 117–28; D.P. Ashmos and D. Duchon, "Spirituality at Work: A Conceptualization and Measure," *Journal of Management Inquiry*, June 2000, pp. 134–45; R. Cacioppe, "Creating Spirit at Work: Re-visioning Organization Development and Leadership—Part 1," *The Leadership and Organization Development Journal*, vol. 21, no. 1 (2000), pp. 48–54; M. Conlin, "Religion in the Workplace," *Business Week*, November 1, 1999, pp. 150–58; M. McDonald, "Shush. The Guy in the Cubicle Is Meditating," *U.S. News & World Report*, May 3, 1999, p. 46; J. Braham, "The Spiritual Side," *IW*, February 1, 1999, pp. 48–55.

25. Ashmos and Duchon, "Spirituality at Work," p. 139.

26. Conlin, "Religion in the Workplace,"and I.I. Mitroff and E.A. Denton, *A Spiritual Audit of Corporate America* (San Francisco: Jossey-Bass, 1999).

CHAPTER 3

1. B. Paik Sunoo, "HR in Lotusland," *Workforce*, June 2000, pp. 74–79, available at Workforce Online (www.workforce.com), May 31, 2000.

2. For insights into the symbolic view, see J. Pfeffer, "Management as Symbolic Action: The Creation and Maintenance of Organizational Paradigms," in L.L. Cummings and B.M. Staw (eds.), *Research in Organizational Behavior*, vol. 3 (Greenwich, CT: JAI Press, 1981), pp. 1–52; D.C. Hambrick and S. Finkelstein, "Managerial Discretion: A Bridge between Polar Views of Organizational Outcomes," in L.L. Cummings and B.M. Staw (eds.), *Research in Organizational Behavior*, vol. 9 (Greenwich, CT: JAI Press, 1987), pp. 369–406; J.A. Byrne, "The Limits of Power," *Business Week*, October 23, 1987, pp. 33–35; J.R. Meindl and S.B. Ehrlich, "The Romance of Leadership and the Evaluation of Organizational Performance," *Academy of Management Journal*, March 1987,

pp. 91–109; C.R. Schwenk, "Illusions of Management Control? Effects of Self-Serving Attributions on Resource Commitments and Confidence in Management," *Human Relations*, April 1990, pp. 333–47; and S.M. Puffer and J.B. Weintrop, "Corporate Performance and CEO Turnover: The Role of Performance Expectations," *Administrative Science Quarterly*, March 1991, pp. 1–19.

3. T.M. Hout, "Are Managers Obsolete?" *Harvard Business Review*, March–April 1999, pp. 161–68; and Pfeffer, "Management as Symbolic Action."

4. L. Smircich, "Concepts of Culture and Organizational Analysis," *Administrative Science Quarterly*, September 1983, p. 339; D.R. Denison, "What Is the Difference between Organizational Culture and Organizational Climate? A Native's Point of View on a Decade of Paradigm Wars," paper presented at Academy of Management Annual Meeting, 1993, Atlanta, GA; and M.J. Hatch, "The Dynamics of Organizational Culture," *Academy of Management Review*, October 1993, pp. 657–93.

5. K. Shadur and M.A. Kienzle, "The Relationship Between Organizational Climate and Employee Perceptions of Involvement," *Group & Organization Management*, December 1999, pp. 479–503; and A.M. Sapienza, "Believing Is Seeing: How Culture Influences the Decisions Top Managers Make," in R.H. Kilmann et al. (eds.), *Gaining Control of the Corporate Culture* (San Francisco: Jossey-Bass, 1985), p. 68.

6. C.A. O'Reilly III, J. Chatman, and D.F. Caldwell, "People and Organizational Culture: A Profile Comparison Approach to Assessing Person-Organization Fit," *Academy of Management Journal*, September 1991, pp. 487–516; and J.A. Chatman and K.A. Jehn, "Assessing the Relationship between Industry Characteristics and Organizational Culture: How Different Can You Be?" *Academy of Management Journal*, June 1994, pp. 522–53.

7. A.E.M. Va Vianen, "Person-Organization Fit: The Match Between Newcomers' and Recruiters' Preferences for Organizational Cultures," *Personnel Psychology*, Spring 2000, pp. 113–49; K. Shadur and M.A. Kienzle, "The Relationship Between Organizational Climate and Employee Perceptions of Involvement"; P. Lok and J. Crawford, "The Relationship Between Commitment and Organizational Culture, Subculture, and Leadership Style," *Leadership & Organization Development Journal*, vol. 20, issue 6/7, 1999, pp. 365–74; C. Vanadenberghe, "Organizational Culture, Person-Culture Fit, and Turnover: A Replication in the Health Care Industry," *Journal of Organizational Behavior*, March 1999, pp. 175–84; and C. Orphen, "The Effect of Organizational Cultural Norms on the Relationships between Personnel Practices and Employee Commitment," *Journal of Psychology*, September 1993, pp. 577–79.

8. See, for example, D.R. Denison, *Corporate Culture and Organizational Effectiveness* (New York: Wiley, 1990); G.G. Gordon and N. DiTomaso, "Predicting Corporate Performance from Organizational Culture," *Journal of Management Studies*, November 1992, pp. 793–98; J.P. Kotter and J.L. Heskett, *Corporate Culture and Performance* (New York: Free Press, 1992), pp. 15–27; J.C. Collins and J.I. Porras, *Built to Last* (New York: HarperBusiness, 1994); Collins and Porras, "Building Your Company's Vision," *Harvard Business Review*, September–October 1996, pp. 65–77; and R. Goffee and G. Jones, "What Holds the Modern Company Together?" *Harvard Business Review*, November–December 1996, pp. 133–48.

9. E.H. Schien, *Organizational Culture and Leadership* (San Francisco: Jossey-Bass, 1985), pp. 314–15.

10. J. Forman, "When Stories Create an Organization's Future," *Strategy & Business*, Second Quarter 1999, pp. 6–9; D.M. Boje, "The Storytelling Organization: A Study of Story Performance in an Office-Supply Firm," *Administrative Science Quarterly*, March 1991, pp. 106–26; and C.H. Deutsch, "The Parables of Corporate Culture," *New York Times*, October 13, 1991, p. F25.

11. E. Ransdell, "The Nike Story? Just Tell It!" *Fast Company*, January–February 2000, pp. 44–46.

12. A.M. Pettigrew, "On Studying Organizational Cultures," *Administrative Science Quarterly*, December 1979, p. 576.

13. Ibid.

14. Cited in J.M. Beyer and H.M. Trice, "How an Organization's Rites Reveal Its Culture," *Organizational Dynamics*, Spring 1987, p. 15.

15. A. Bryant, "The New Power Breakfast," *Newsweek*, May 15, 2000, p. 52.

16. P. LaBarre, "Success: Here's the Inside Story," *Fast Company*, November 1999, pp. 128–32; and A. Law, *Creative Company: How St. Luke's Became "The Ad Agency to End All Ad Agencies"* (New York: Wiley, 1999).

17. This box is based on "Diversity Today," special advertising section in *Fortune*, June 12, 2000, pp. S1–S24; O.C. Richard, "Racial Diversity, Business Strategy, and Firm Performance: A Resource-Based View," *Academy of Management Journal*, April 2000, pp. 164–77; A. Markels, "How One Hotel Manages Staff's Diversity," *Wall Street Journal*, November 20, 1996, pp. B1+; C.A. Deutsch, "Corporate Diversity in Practice," *New York Times*, November 20, 1996, pp. C1+; D.A. Thomas and R.J. Ely, "Making Differences Matter: A New Paradigm for Managing Diversity," *Harvard Business Review*, September–October 1996, pp. 79–90; "The Challenge of Managing Diversity in the Workplace," *Black Enterprise*, July 1993, pp. 79–90; T.H. Cox Jr. and S. Blake, "Managing Cultural Diversity: Implications for Organizational Competitiveness," *Academy of Management Executive*, August 1991, pp. 45–46; and T.H. Cox Jr., "The Multicultural Organization," *Academy of Management Executive*, April 1991, pp. 34–47.

18. This box is based on S. Thurm, "The Ultimate Weapon," *Wall Street Journal*, April 17, 2000, pp. R18+; S. Jurvetson, "Turning Customers into a Sales Force," *Business 2.0*, March 2000, pp. 231–36; and S. Mott, "Winning One Customer at a Time," *Business 2.0*, March 2000, pp. 269–76.

19. T.S. Mescon and G.S. Vozikis, "Federal Regulation—What Are the Costs?" *Business*, January–March 1982, pp. 33–39.

20. See, for instance, A.S. Hayes, "Layoffs Take Careful Planning to Avoid Losing the Suits That Are Apt to Follow," *Wall Street Journal*, November 2, 1990, p. B1.

21. D. Tapscott, *Growing Up Digital: The Rise of the Net Generation* (New York: McGraw-Hill, 1998).

22. T. Donaldson and L.E. Preston, "The Stakeholder Theory of the Corporation: Concepts, Evidence, and Implications," *Academy of Management Review*, January 1995, pp. 65–91.

23. J.S. Harrison and C.H. St. John, "Managing and Partnering with External Stakeholders," *Academy of Management Executive*, May 1996, pp. 46–60.

24. J. Kotter and J. Heskett, *Corporate Culture and Performance* (New York: The Free Press, 1992).

25. Harrison and St. John, "Managing and Partnering with External Stakeholders."

CHAPTER 4

1. M. Wallengren, "Mixing Salsa with Islam," *Latin Trade*, June 2000, pp. 32–33; and information from company's Web site (www.cemex.com), June 12, 2000.

2. G. Koretz, "Things Go Better with Multinationals—Except Jobs," *Business Week*, May 2, 1994, p. 20.

3. The idea for this quiz is adapted from R.M. Hodgetts and F. Luthans, *International Management*, 2nd ed. (New York: McGraw-Hill, 1994).

4. N. Adler, *International Dimensions of Organizational Behavior*, 3rd ed. (Cincinnati: South-Western, 1996).

5. P.R. Harris and R.T. Moran, *Managing Cultural Differences*, 4th ed. (Houston: Gulf Publishing Co., 1996); R.T. Moran, P.R. Harris, and W.G. Stripp, *Developing the Global Organization: Strategies for Human Resource Professionals* (Houston: Gulf Publishing Co., 1993); Y. Wind, S.P. Douglas, and H.V. Perlmutter, "Guidelines for Developing International Marketing Strategies," *Journal of Marketing*, April 1973, pp. 14–23; and H.V. Perlmutter, "The Tortuous Evolution of the Multinational Corporation," *Columbia Journal of World Business*, January–February 1969, pp. 9–18.

6. E.L. Andrews, "European Union's Tough but Relentless Drive to Expand," *New York Times*, December 20, 1999, p. C22.

7. H. Cooper, "The Euro: What You Need to Know," *Wall Street Journal*, January 4, 1999, pp. A5+.

8. J.S. McClenahan, "NAFTA Works," *IW*, January 10, 2000, pp. 5–6.

9. "NAFTA: Five-Year Anniversary," *Latin Trade*, January 1999, pp. 44–45.

10. C. Sims, "Chile Will Enter a Big South American Free-Trade Bloc," *New York Times*, June 26, 1996, p. C2.

11. T. Purdum, "Africa Zone Created," *Industry Week*, November 20, 2000, p. 12.

12. D.A. Aaker, *Developing Business Strategies,* 5th ed. (New York: John Wiley & Sons, 1998); and J.A. Byrne et al., "Borderless Management," *Business Week*, May 23, 1994, pp. 24–26.

13. See, for example, G. Hofstede, *Culture's Consequences: International Differences in Work-Related Values* (Beverly Hills, CA: Sage Publications, 1980), pp. 25–26; G. Hofstede, *Culture and Organizations: Software of the Mind* (London: McGraw-Hill, 1991); G. Hofstede, "Cultural Constraints in Management Theories," *Academy of Management Executive*, February 1993, pp. 81–94; and C.C. Chen, X-P Chen, and J.R. Meindl, "How Can Cooperation Be Fostered? The Cultural Effects of Individualism-Collectivism," *Academy of Management Review*, April 1998, pp. 285–304.

14. G. Hofstede, *Culture's Consequences*; and G. Hofstede, "The Cultural Relativity of Organizational Practices and Theories," *Journal of International Business Studies*, Fall 1983, pp. 75–89.

15. Hofstede called this last dimension "masculinity versus femininity," but we have changed it because of the strong sexist connotation in his choice of terms.

16. C.M. Solomon, "The World Stops Shrinking," *Workforce*, January 2000, pp. 48–51; V. Frazee, "Selecting Global Assignees," *Global Workforce,* July 1998, pp. 28–30; and C.M. Solomon, "Staff Selection Impacts Global Success," *Personnel Journal*, January 1994, p. 42; and R.L. Tung, "Human Resources Planning in Japanese Multinationals: A Model for U.S. Firms?" *Journal of International Business Studies*, Fall 1984, p. 146.

17. J.T. Gullahorn and J.E. Gullahorn, "An Extension of the U-Curve Hypothesis," *Journal of Social Sciences*, January 1963, pp. 34–47.

CHAPTER 5

1. Information from company's Web site (www.digitalmafia.com), August 30, 2000; and T.K. Muhammad, "Talking Tech and the Stock Market," *Black Enterprise*, January 2000, pp. 45–46.

2. A.B. Carroll, "A Three-Dimensional Conceptual Model of Corporate Performance," *Academy of Management Review*, October 1979, p. 499.

3. M. Friedman, *Capitalism and Freedom* (Chicago: University of Chicago Press, 1962); and Friedman, "The Social Responsibility of Business Is to Increase Profits," *New York Times Magazine*, September 13, 1970, p. 33.

4. Information from Avon's Web site (www.avoncrusade.com), May 19, 2000.

5. E.P. Lima, "Seeding a World of Transformation," *IW*, September 6, 1999, pp. 30–31.

6. C. Caggiano, "Is Social Responsibility a Crock?" *Inc.*, May 1993, p. 15.

7. This section is based on R.J. Monsen Jr., "The Social Attitudes of Management," in J.M. McGuire (ed.), *Contemporary Management: Issues and Views* (Upper Saddle River, NJ: Prentice Hall, 1974), p. 616; and K. Davis and W.C. Frederick, *Business and Society: Management, Public Policy, Ethics*, 5th ed. (New York: McGraw-Hill, 1984), pp. 28–41.

8. See, for example, R.A. Buccholz, *Essentials of Public Policy for Management*, 2d ed. (Upper Saddle River, NJ: Prentice Hall, 1990).

9. See S.P. Sethi, "A Conceptual Framework for Environmental Analysis of Social Issues and Evaluation of Business Response Patterns," *Academy of Management Review*, January 1979, pp. 68–74.

10. See, for example, D.J. Wood, "Corporate Social Performance Revisited," *Academy of Management Review*, October 1991, pp. 703–08.

11. S.L. Wartick and P.L. Cochran, "The Evolution of the Corporate Social Performance Model," *Academy of Management Review*, October 1985, p. 763.

12. Ibid., p. 762.

13. See, for instance, P. Cochran and R.A. Wood, "Corporate Social Responsibility and Financial Performance," *Academy of Management Journal*, March 1984, pp. 42–56; K. Aupperle, A.B. Carroll, and J.D. Hatfield, "An Empirical Examination of the Relationship between Corporate Social Responsibility and Profitability," *Academy of Management Journal*, June 1985, pp. 446–63; J.B. McGuire, A. Sundgren, and T. Schneeweis, "Corporate Social Responsibility and Firm Financial Performance," *Academy of Management Journal*, December 1988, pp. 854–72; D.M. Georgoff and J. Ross, "Corporate Social Responsibility and Management Performance," paper presented at the National Academy of Management Conference, Miami, August 1991; S.A. Zahra, B.M. Oviatt, and K. Minyard, "Effects of Corporate Ownership and Board Structure on Corporate Social Responsibility and Financial Performance," paper presented at the National Academy of Management Conference, Atlanta, August 1993; "Social Responsibility and the Bottom Line," *Business Ethics*, July–August, 1994, p. 11; D.B. Turban and D.W. Greening, "Corporate Social Performance and Organizational Attractiveness to Prospective Employees," *Academy of Management Journal*, June 1996, pp. 658–72; S.A. Waddock and S.B. Graves, "The Corporate Social Performance–Financial Performance Link," *Strategic Management Journal*, April 1997, pp. 303–19; and S.L. Berman and others, "Does Stakeholder Orientation Matter? The Relationship Between Stakeholder Management Models and Firm Financial Performance" *Academy of Management Journal*, October 1999, pp. 488–506.

14. D.J. Wood and R.E. Jones, "Stakeholder Mismatching: A Theoretical Problem in Empirical Research on Corporate Social Performance," *International Journal of Organizational Analysis* (1995), pp. 229–67.

15. See A.A. Ullmann, "Data in Search of a Theory: A Critical Examination of the Relationships among Social Performance, Social Disclosure, and Economic Performance of U.S. Firms," *Academy of Management Review*, July 1985, pp. 540–57; R.E. Wokutch and B.A. Spencer, "Corporate Saints and Sinners: The Effects of Philanthropic and Illegal Activity on Organizational Performance," *California Management Review*, Winter 1987, pp. 62–77; K.E. Aupperle, "The Use of Forced Choice Survey Procedures in Assessing Corporate Social Orientation," pp. 269–80; R.P. Gephart Jr., "Multiple Methods for Tracking Corporate Social Performance:

Insights from a Study of Major Industrial Accidents," pp. 359–85; R. Wolfe and K. Aupperle, "Introduction to Corporate Social Performance: Methods for Evaluating an Elusive Construct," pp. 265–68, in J.E. Post (ed.), *Research in Corporate Social Performance and Policy*, vol. 12, 1991; Wood and Jones, "Stakeholder Mismatching: A Theoretical Problem in Empirical Research on Corporate Social Performance"; and A. McWilliams and D. Siegel, "Corporate Social Responsibility and Financial Performance: Correlation or Misspecification?" *Strategic Management Journal*, May 2000, pp. 603–09.

16. McGuire, Sundgren, and Schneeweis, "Corporate Social Responsibility and Firm Financial Performance."

17. A. McWilliams and D. Siegel, "Corporate Social Responsibility and Financial Performance: Correlation or Misspecification?" *Strategic Management Journal*, June 2000, pp. 603–09.

18. Information from Domini Social Investments Web site, (www.domini.com), August 1, 2000; R. Wherry, "The Cleans & The Greens," *Forbes*, June 12, 2000, p. 412; S. Scherreik, "A Conscience Doesn't Have to Make You Poor," *Business Week*, May 1, 2000, pp. 204–08; and P. Keating, "Know What You Own," *Money*, November 1999, pp. 79–81.

19. G.P. Alexander, "Establishing Shared Values through Management Training Programs," *Training and Development Journal*, February 1987, pp. 45–47.

20. Ibid.; J.L. Badaracco Jr. and R.R. Ellsworth, *Leadership and the Quest for Integrity* (Boston: Harvard Business School Press, 1989); and T. Chappell, *Managing Upside Down: The Seven Intentions of Values-Centered Leadership* (New York: William Morrow, 1999).

21. Information from Tom's of Maine Web site (www.tomsofmaine.com), August 1, 2000.

22. Information from Herman Miller Web site (www.hermanmiller.com), August 1, 2000.

23. R. Kamen, "Values: For Show or For Real?" *Working Woman*, August 1993, p. 10.

24. Badaracco and Ellsworth, *Leadership and the Quest for Integrity*.

25. J. Bamford, "Changing Business as Usual," *Working Woman*, November 1993, pp. 62+.

26. This section is based on P. Shrivastava, "Environmental Technologies and Competitive Advantage," *Strategic Management Journal*, Summer 1995, pp. 183–200; S.L. Hart, "A Natural-Resource-Based View of the Firm," *Academy of Management Review*, December 1995, pp. 986–1014; and S.L. Hart, "Beyond Greening: Strategies for a Sustainable World," *Harvard Business Review*, January–February 1997, pp. 66–76.

27. J.L. Seglin, "It's Not That Easy Going Green," *Inc.*, May 1999, pp. 28–32; W.H. Miller, "What's Ahead in Environmental Policy?" *IW*, April 19, 1999, pp. 19–24; and P. Shrivastava, "Environmental Technologies and Competitive Advantage," p. 183.

28. S.L. Hart, "Beyond Greening," p. 68.

29. Worldwatch Institute, "Earth Day 2000: What Humanity Can Do Now to Turn the Tide," Web site for Worldwatch Institute (www.worldwatch.org), August 2, 2000; and L. Brown and Staff of the Worldwatch Institute, *State of the World* (New York: Norton, 1987–1996).

30. C. Marsden, "The New Corporate Citizenship of Big Business: Part of the Solution to Sustainability?" *Business & Society Review*, Spring 2000, pp. 9–25; R.D. Klassen and D.C. Whybark, "The Impact of Environmental Technologies on Manufacturing Performance," *Academy of Management Journal*, December 1999, pp. 599–615; H. Bradbury and J.A. Clair, "Promoting Sustainable Organizations with Sweden's Natural Step," *Academy of Management Executive*, October 1999, pp. 63–73; F.L. Reinhardt, "Bringing the Environment Down to Earth," *Harvard Business Review*, July–August 1999, pp. 149–57; I. Henriques and P. Sadorsky, "The Relationship Between Environmental Commitment and Managerial Perceptions of Stakeholder Importance," *Academy of Management Journal*, February 1999, pp. 87–99; and M.A. Berry and D.A. Rondinelli, "Proactive Corporate Environmental Management: A New Industrial Revolution," *Academy of Management Executive*, May 1998, pp. 38–50.

31. The concept of shades of green can be found in R.E. Freeman, J. Pierce, and R. Dodd, *Shades of Green: Business Ethics and the Environment* (New York: Oxford University Press, 1995).

32. See, for example, A.B. Carroll, "The Pyramid of Corporate Social Responsibility: Toward the Moral Management of Organizational Stakeholders," *Business Horizons*, July–August 1991, pp. 39–48.

33. This section has been influenced by K.B. Boal and N. Peery, "The Cognitive Structure of Social Responsibility," *Journal of Management*, Fall–Winter 1985, pp. 71–82.

34. K. Davis and W.C. Frederick, *Business and Society*, p. 76.

35. F.D. Sturdivant, *Business and Society: A Managerial Approach*, 3rd ed. (Homewood, IL: Richard D. Irwin, 1985), p. 128.

36. G.F. Cavanagh, D.J. Moberg, and M. Valasquez, "The Ethics of Organizational Politics," *Academy of Management Journal*, June 1981, pp. 363–74. See F.N. Brady, "Rules for Making Exceptions to Rules," *Academy of Management Review*, July 1987, pp. 436–44 for an argument that the theory of justice is redundant with the prior two theories. See T. Donaldson and T.W. Dunfee, "Toward a Unified Conception of Business Ethics: Integrative Social Contracts Theory," *Academy of Management Review*, April 1994, pp. 252–84 and M. Douglas, "Integrative Social Contracts Theory: Hype Over Hypernorms," *Journal of Business Ethics*, July 2000, pp. 101–10 for discussions of integrative social contracts theory.

37. D.J. Fritzsche and H. Becker, "Linking Management Behavior to Ethical Philosophy—An Empirical Investigation," *Academy of Management Journal*, March 1984, pp. 166–75.

38. L. Kohlberg, *Essays in Moral Development: The Philosophy of Moral Development*, vol. 1 (New York: Harper & Row, 1981); L. Kohlberg, *Essays in Moral Development: The Psychology of Moral Development*, vol. 2 (New York: Harper & Row, 1984); J.W. Graham, "Leadership, Moral Development, and Citizenship Behavior," *Business Ethics Quarterly*, January 1995, pp. 43–54; and T. Kelley, "To Do Right or Just To Be Legal," *New York Times*, February 8, 1998, p. BU12.

39. See, for example, J. Weber, "Managers' Moral Reasoning: Assessing Their Responses to Three Moral Dilemmas," *Human Relations*, July 1990, pp. 687–702.

40. J.H. Barnett and M.J. Karson, "Personal Values and Business Decisions: An Exploratory Investigation," *Journal of Business Ethics*, July 1987, pp. 371–82; and W.C. Frederick and J. Weber, "The Value of Corporate Managers and Their Critics: An Empirical Description and Normative Implications," in W.C. Frederick and L.E. Preston (eds.) *Business Ethics: Research Issues and Empirical Studies* (Greenwich, CT: JAI Press, 1990), pp. 123–44.

41. L.K. Trevino and S.A. Youngblood, "Bad Apples in Bad Barrels: A Causal Analysis of Ethical Decision-Making Behavior," *Journal of Applied Psychology*, August 1990, pp. 378–85; and M.E. Baehr, J.W. Jones, and A.J. Nerad, "Psychological Correlates of Business Ethics Orientation in Executives," *Journal of Business and Psychology*, Spring 1993, pp. 291–308.

42. B.Z. Posner and W.H. Schmidt, "Values and the American Manager: An Update," *California Management Review*, Spring 1984, pp. 202–16; R.B. Morgan, "Self- and Co-Worker Perceptions of Ethics and Their Relationships to Leadership and Salary," *Academy of Management Journal*, February 1993, pp. 200–14; G.R. Weaver, L.K. Trevino, and P.L. Cochran, "Corporate Ethics Programs as Control Systems: Influences of Executive Commitment and Environmental Factors," *Academy of Management Journal*, February 1999, pp. 41–57; and G.R. Weaver, L.K. Trevino, and P.L. Cochran, "Integrated and Decoupled Corporate Social Performance: Management Commitments, External Pressures, and Corporate Ethics Practices," *Academy of Management Journal*, October 1999, pp. 539–52.

43. B. Victor and J.B. Cullen, "The Organizational Bases of Ethical Work Climates," *Administrative Science Quarterly*, March 1988, pp. 101–25; J.B. Cullen, B. Victor, and C. Stephens, "An Ethical Weather Report: Assessing the Organization's Ethical Climate," *Organizational Dynamics*, Autumn 1989, pp. 50–62; Victor and Cullen, "A Theory and Measure of Ethical Climate in Organizations," in Frederick and Pre-

ston (eds.) *Business Ethics*, pp. 77–97; R.R. Sims, "The Challenge of Ethical Behavior in Organizations," *Journal of Business Ethics*, July 1992, pp. 505–13; and V. Arnold and J.C. Lampe, "Understanding the Factors Underlying Ethical Organizations: Enabling Continuous Ethical Improvement," *Journal of Applied Business Research*, Summer 1999, pp. 1–19.

44. T.M. Jones, "Ethical Decision Making by Individuals in Organizations: An Issue-Contingent Model," *Academy of Management Review*, April 1991, pp. 366–95.

45. Ibid., pp. 374–78.

46. Information from the Global Compact Web site (www.unglobalcompact.org), August 14, 2000; J. Cohen, "Socially Responsible Business Goes Global," *In Business*, March/April 2000, p. 22; and C.M. Solomon, "Put Your Ethics to a Global Test," *Personnel Journal*, January 1996, pp. 66–74.

47. Series of posters called "Sears Ethics and Business Practices: A Century of Tradition," in *Business Ethics*, May/June 1999, pp. 12–13; and B.J. Feder, "The Harder Side of Sears," *New York Times*, July 20, 1997, pp. BU1+.

48. Trevino and Youngblood, "Bad Apples in Bad Barrels," p. 384.

49. "Global Ethics Codes Gain Importance as a Tool to Avoid Litigation and Fines," *Wall Street Journal*, August 19, 1999, p. A1; and J. Alexander, "On the Right Side," *World Business*, January/February 1997, pp. 38–41.

50. P. Richter, "Big Business Puts Ethics in Spotlight," *Los Angeles Times*, June 19, 1986, p. 29.

51. F.R. David, "An Empirical Study of Codes of Business Ethics: A Strategic Perspective," paper presented at the 48th Annual Academy of Management Conference, Anaheim, California, August 1988.

52. "Ethics Programs Aren't Stemming Employee Misconduct," *Wall Street Journal*, May 11, 2000, p. A1.

53. A.K. Reichert and M.S. Webb, "Corporate Support for Ethical and Environmental Policies: A Financial Management Perspective," *Journal of Business Ethics*, May 2000; G.R. Weaver, L.K. Trevino, and P.L. Cochran, "Corporate Ethics Programs as Control Systems:

Influences of Executive Commitment and Environmental Factors"; G.R. Weaver, L.K. Trevino, and P.L. Cochran, "Integrated and Decoupled Corporate Social Performance: Management Commitments, External Pressures, and Corporate Ethics Practices"; R.B. Morgan, "Self- and Co-Worker Perceptions of Ethics and Their Relationships to Leadership and Salary"; and B.Z. Posner and W.H. Schmidt, "Values and the American Manager: An Update."

54. L. Nash, "Ethics without the Sermon," *Harvard Business Review*, November–December 1981, p. 81.

55. Associated Press, "Cheating Rampant in Workplace, Study Says," *Springfield News Leader*, April 5, 1997, p. A5.

56. T.A. Gavin, "Ethics Education," *Internal Auditor*, April 1989, pp. 54–57.

57. W. Penn and B.D. Collier, "Current Research in Moral Development as a Decision Support System," *Journal of Business Ethics*, January 1985, pp. 131–36.

58. J. Weber, "Measuring the Impact of Teaching Ethics to Future Managers: A Review, Assessment, and Recommendations," *Journal of Business Ethics*, April 1990, pp. 182–90.

59. T. Kelley, "Charting a Course to Ethical Profits," *New York Times*, February 28, 1998, pp. BU1+.

60. See, for instance, P.F. Miller and W.T. Coady, "Teaching Work Ethics," *Education Digest*, February 1990, pp. 54–55.

61. See, for example, A. Stark, "What's the Matter with Business Ethics?" *Harvard Business Review*, May–June 1993, pp. 38–48; "More Big Businesses Set Up Ethics Offices," *Wall Street Journal*, May 10, 1993, p. B1; W.D. Hall, *Making the Right Decision: Ethics for Managers* (New York: John Wiley & Sons, 1993); S. Gaines, "Handing Out Halos," *Business Ethics*, March–April 1994, pp. 20–24; and L.S. Paine, "Managing for Organizational Integrity," *Harvard Business Review*, March–April 1994, pp. 106–17.

62. Associated Press, "Cheating Rampant in Workplace, Study Says"; and H. Fountain, "Of White Lies and Yellow Pads," *New York Times*, July 6, 1997, p. F7.

63. C. Kleiner and M. Lord, "The Cheating Game," *U.S. News & World Report*, November 22, 1999, p. 56; and C.R. Campbell, C.O. Swift, and L. Denton, "Cheating Goes Hi-Tech: Online Term Paper Mills," *Journal of Management Education*, December 2000, pp. 726–40.

64. Ibid, pp. 55–66.

PART 2

1. P. Strozniak, "25 Growing Companies," *Industry Week*, November 20, 2000, p. 76.

2. T.L. Hatten, *Small Business: Entrepreneurship and Beyond* (Upper Saddle River, NJ: Prentice Hall, 1997), p. 5; and J.W. Carland, F. Hoy, W.R. Boulton, and J.C. Carland, "Differentiating Entrepreneurs from Small Business Owners: A Conceptualization," *Academy of Management Review*, vol. 9, no. 2, 1984, pp. 354–59.

3. "The New American Evolution: The Role and Impact of Small Firms," a report prepared by the Office of Economic Research of the U.S. Small Business Administration's Office of Advocacy, *SBAOnline*, found at [www.sbaonline.gov/ADVO/stats/], December 21, 2000.

4. P. Almeida and B. Kogut, "The Exploration of Technological Diversity and Geographic Localization in Innovation: Start-Up Firms in the Semiconductor Industry," *Small Business Economics*, vol. 9, no. 1, 1997, pp. 21–31.

5. R.J. Arend, "Emergence of Entrepreneurs Following Exogenous Technological Change," *Strategic Management Journal*, vol. 20, no. 1, 1999, pp. 31–47.

6. "The Facts About Small Business," a report prepared by the Office of Advocacy of the U.S. Small Business Administration," *SBAOnline*, [www.sbaonline.sba.gov/advo/stats/], December 23, 2000.

7. "Economic Growth Linked to Levels of Business Start-Ups," *GEM2000 Report*, found online at [www.babson.edu/press/gemGrowth2000.html], December 22, 2000.

8. P.F. Drucker, *Innovation and Entrepreneurship: Practice and Principles* (New York: Harper & Row), 1985.

9. W. Royal, "Real Expectations," *Industry Week*, September 4, 2000, pp. 31–34.

10. M.A. Verespej, "25 Growing Companies," *Industry Week*, November 20, 2000, p. 70.

11. T. Purdum, "25 Growing Companies," *Industry Week*, November 20, 2000, p. 82.

12. G.S. Stodder, "Goodwill Hunting," *Entrepreneur*, July 1998, p. 119.

13. E. Updike, "The Straightest Arrows," *Business Week Enterprise*, October 12, 1998, p. ENT 2.

CHAPTER 6

1. Information from company Web site (www.cannondale.com), June 12, 2000; and The Associated Press, "Cannondale Dives into Dirt Bikes," *Springfield News Leader*, June 4, 2000, p. 12B.

2. W. Pounds, "The Process of Problem Finding," *Industrial Management Review*, Fall 1969, pp. 1–19.

3. R.J. Volkema, "Problem Formulation: Its Portrayal in the Texts," *Organizational Behavior Teaching Review*, 11, No. 3 (1986–87), pp. 113–26.

4. M.W. McCall Jr. and Robert E. Kaplan, *Whatever It Takes: Decision Makers at Work* (Upper Saddle River, NJ: Prentice Hall, 1985), pp. 36–38.

5. H.A. Simon, *The New Science of Management Decision* (New York: Harper & Row, 1960), p. 1.

6. See H.A. Simon, "Rationality in Psychology and Economics," *Journal of Business*, October 1986, pp. 209–24; and A. Langley, "In Search of Rationality: The Purposes Behind the Use of Formal Analysis in Organizations," *Administrative Science Quarterly*, December 1989, pp. 598–631.

7. F.A. Shull Jr., A.L. Delbecq, and L.L. Cummings, *Organizational Decision Making* (New York: McGraw-Hill, 1970), p. 151.

8. See, for example, J.G. March, *A Primer on Decision Making* (New York: Free Press, 1994), pp. 8–25; and A. Langley, H. Mintzberg, P. Pitcher, E. Posada, and J. Saint-Macary, "Opening Up Decision Making: The View from the Black Stool," *Organization Science*, May–June 1995, pp. 260–79.

9. J.G. March, "Decision-Making Perspective: Decisions in Organizations and Theories of Choice," in A.H. Van de Ven and W.F. Joyce (eds.), *Perspectives on Organization Design and Behavior* (New York: Wiley-Interscience, 1981), pp. 232–33.

10. See N.McK. Agnew and J.L. Brown, "Bounded Rationality: Fallible Decisions in Unbounded Decision Space," *Behavioral Science*, July 1986, pp. 148–61; B.E. Kaufman, "A New Theory of Satisficing," *Journal of Behavioral Economics*, Spring 1990, pp. 35–51; and D.R.A. Skidd, "Revisiting Bounded Rationality," *Journal of Management Inquiry*, December 1992, pp. 343–47.

11. See, for example, B.M. Staw, "The Escalation of Commitment to a Course of Action," *Academy of Management Review*, October 1981, pp. 577–87; D.R. Bobocel and J.P. Meyer, "Escalating Commitment to a Failing Course of Action: Separating the Roles of Choice and Justification," *Journal of Applied Psychology*, June 1994, pp. 360–63; C.F. Camerer and R.A. Weber, "The Econometrics and Behavioral Economics of Escalation of Commitment: A Re-examination of Staw's Theory," *Journal of Economic Behavior and Organization*, May 1999, pp. 59–82; V.S. Rao and A. Monk, "The Effects of Individual Differences and Anonymity on Commitment to Decisions," *Journal of Social Psychology*, August 1999, pp. 496–515; and M. Keil, "A Cross-Cultural Study of Escalation of Commitment Behavior in Software Projects," *MIS Quarterly*, June 2000, pp. 299–326.

12. See K.R. Hammond, R.M. Hamm, J. Grassia, and T. Pearson, "Direct Comparison of the Efficacy of Intuitive and Analytical Cognition in Expert Judgment," *IEEE Transactions on Systems, Man, and Cybernetics SMC-17* (1987), pp. 753–70; W.H. Agor (ed.), *Intuition in Organizations* (Newbury Park, CA: Sage Publications, 1989); O. Behling and N.L. Eckel, "Making Sense Out of Intuition," *The Executive*, February 1991, pp. 46–47; and L.A. Burke and M.K. Miller, "Taking the Mystery Out of Intuitive Decision Making," *Academy of Management Executive*, October 1999, pp. 91–99.

13. V. Pospisil, "Gut Feeling or Skilled Reasoning?" *IW*, March 3, 1997, p. 12.

14. Information for this box came from C. Kanchier, *Dare to Change Your Job and Your Life*, 2nd ed. (Indianapolis, IN: Jist Publishing, 2000); and S. Hagevik, "Responsible Risk Taking," *Journal of Environmental Health*, November 1999, pp. 29+.

15. A.J. Rowe, James D. Boulgarides, and Michael R. McGrath, *Managerial Decision Making, Modules in Management Series* (Chicago: SRA, 1984), pp. 18–22.

16. Information for this box came from B.C. McDonald and D. Hutcheson, "Dealing with Diversity Is Key to Tapping Talent," *Atlanta Business Chronicle*, December 18, 1998, pp. 45A+; P.M. Elsass and L.M. Graves, "Demographic Diversity in Decision-Making Groups: The Experience of Women and People of Color," *Academy of Management Review*, October 1997, pp. 946–73; and N.J. Adler (ed.), *International Dimensions of Organizational Behavior*, 3rd ed. (Cincinnati: South-Western College Publishing, 1997).

CHAPTER 7

1. Information from company's Web site (www.gazoontite.com), June 12, 2000; S. Furman and M.S. Foley, "Nothing to Sneeze At," *Success*, June 2000, p. 58; and J. Hodges, "Bricks for Branding," *Business 2.0*, February 2000, pp. 95–98.

2. See, for example, J.A. Pearce II, K.K. Robbins, and R.B. Robinson Jr., "The Impact of Grand Strategy and Planning Formality on Financial Performance," *Strategic Management Journal*, March–April 1987, pp. 125–34; L.C. Rhyne, "Contrasting Planning Systems in High, Medium, and Low Performance Companies," *Journal of Management Studies*, July 1987, pp. 363–85; J.A. Pearce II, E.B. Freeman, and R.B. Robinson Jr., "The Tenuous Link Between Formal Strategic Planning and Financial Performance," *Academy of Management Review*, October 1987, pp. 658–75; D.K. Sinha, "The Contribution of Formal Planning to Decisions," *Strategic Management Journal*, October 1990, pp. 479–92; N. Capon, J.U. Farley, and J.M. Hulbert, "Strategic Planning and Financial Performance: More Evidence," *Journal of Management Studies*, January 1994, pp. 22–38; C.C. Miller and L.B. Cardinal, "Strategic Planning and Firm Performance: A Synthesis of More Than Two Decades of Research," *Academy of Management Journal*, March 1994, pp. 1649–85; and P.J. Brews and M.R. Hunt, "Learning to Plan and Planning to Learn: Resolving the Planning School/Learning School Debate," *Strategic Management Journal*, December 1999, pp. 889–913.

3. R. Molz, "How Leaders Use Goals," *Long Range Planning*, October 1987, p. 91.

4. K. Naughton, "Ford Goes for the Green," *Newsweek*, August 7, 2000, p. 62; J. Ball, "Ford Contacts Environmentalists Behind Scenes," *Wall Street Journal*, May 15, 2000, p. B2; and B. Morris, "This Ford Is Different," *Fortune*, April 3, 2000, pp. 122–36.

5. Annual Reports from Lands End Inc. (2000), Colgate-Palmolive Company (1999), and SBC Communications Inc. (1999).

6. See, for instance, C.K. Warriner, "The Problem of Organizational Purpose," *Sociological Quarterly*, Spring 1965, pp. 139–46; and J. Pfeffer, *Organizational Design* (Arlington Heights, IL: AHM Publishing, 1978), pp. 5–12.

7. J.D. Hunger and T.L. Wheelen, *Strategic Management*, 7th ed. (Upper Saddle River, NJ: Prentice Hall, 2000).

8. P.N. Romani, "MBO By Any Other Name Is Still MBO," *Supervision*, December 1997, pp. 6–8; and A.W. Schrader and G.T. Seward, "MBO Makes Dollar Sense," *Personnel Journal*, July 1989, pp. 32–37.

9. R. Rodgers and J.E. Hunter, "Impact of Management by Objectives on Organizational Productivity," *Journal of Applied Psychology*, April 1991, pp. 322–36.

10. For additional information on goals, see, for instance, P. Drucker, *The Executive in Action* (New York: HarperCollins Books, 1996), pp. 207–14; and E.A. Locke and G.P. Latham, *A Theory of Goal Setting and Task Performance* (Upper Saddle River, NJ: Prentice Hall, 1990).

11. Several of these factors were suggested by J.S. Armstrong, "The Value of Formal Planning for Strategic Decisions: Review of Empirical Research," *Strategic Management Journal*, July–September 1982, pp. 197–211; and R.K. Bresser and R.C. Bishop, "Dysfunctional Effects of Formal Planning: Two Theoretical Explanations," *Academy of Management Review*, October 1983, pp. 588–99.

12. Brews and Hunt, "Learning to Plan and Planning to Learn: Resolving the Planning School/Learning School Debate."

13. Ibid.

14. A. Campbell, "Tailored, Not Benchmarked: A Fresh Look at Corporate Planning," *Harvard Business Review*, March–April 1999, pp. 41–50.

15. J.H. Sheridan, "Focused on Flow," *IW*, October 18, 1999, pp. 46–51.

16. H. Mintzberg, *The Rise and Fall of Strategic Planning* (New York: Free Press, 1994).

17. Ibid.

18. Ibid.

19. G. Hamel and C.K. Prahalad, *Competing for the Future* (Boston: Harvard Business School Press, 1994).

20. J. Moore, "The Death of Competition," *Fortune*, April 15, 1996, pp. 142–43.

21. D. Miller, "The Architecture of Simplicity," *Academy of Management Review*, January 1993, pp. 116–38.

22. This box is based on K. Girard and S. Donahue, "Crash and Learn: A Field Manual for Ebusiness Survival," *Business 2.0*, June 28, 2000, found on Web site (www.business2.com), September 19, 2000; and S. Hamm and A. Reinhardt, "How Fast Is Net Fast?" *Business Week E.Biz*, November 1, 1999, pp. EB52–EB54.

23. Brews and Hunt, "Learning to Plan and Planning to Learn: Resolving the Planning School/Learning School Debate."

CHAPTER 8

1. Information from WNBA Web site (www.wnba.com), August 17, 2000; L.A. Woellert, "For the WNBA, It's No Easy Layup," *Business Week*, May 1, 2000, pp. 102–06; and C. Hawn, "A Dud of Their Own," *Forbes*, November 29, 1999, p. 80.

2. J.W. Dean Jr. and M.P. Sharfman, "Does Decision Process Matter? A Study of Strategic Decision-Making Effectiveness," *Academy of Management Journal*, April 1996, pp. 368–96.

3. T.L. Wheelen and J.D. Hunger, *Strategic Management and Business Policy*, 7th ed. (Upper Saddle River, NJ: 2000), p. 3.

4. "A Solid Strategy Helps Companies' Growth," *Nation's Business*, October 1990, p. 10.

5. See, for example, H. Mintzberg, *The Rise and Fall of Strategic Planning* (New York: Free Press, 1994); S.J. Wall and S.R. Wall, "The Evolution (Not the Death) of Strategy," *Organizational Dynamics*, Autumn 1995, pp. 7–19; and J.A. Byrne, "Strategic Planning: It's Back!" *Business Week*, August 26, 1996, pp. 46–52.

6. N. Capon, J.U. Farley, and J.M. Hulbert, "Strategic Planning and Financial Performance: More Evidence," *Journal of Management Studies*, January 1994, pp. 22–38; C.C. Miller and L.B. Cardinal, "Strategic Planning and Firm Performance: A Synthesis of More Than Two Decades of Research," *Academy of Management Journal*, December 1994, pp. 1649–65; D.J. Ketchen, Jr., J.B. Thomas, and R.R. McDaniel Jr., "Process, Content and Context: Synergistic Effects on Performance," *Journal of Management*, Vol. 22, No. 2 (1996), pp. 231–57; and P.J. Brews and M.R. Hunt, "Learning to Plan and Planning to Learn: Resolving the Planning School/Learning School Debate," *Strategic Management Journal*, December 1999, pp. 889–913.

7. See, for example, M. Li and R.J. Litschert, "Linking Strategy-Making Process and Environment: A Theory," paper presented at the 1993 Academy of Management Meeting, Atlanta, Georgia; D. Marline, B.T. Lamont, and J.J. Hoffman, "Choice Situation, Strategy, and Performance: A Reexamination," *Strategic Management Journal*, March 1994, pp. 229–39; and D. Miller, T.K. Lanta, F.J. Milliken, and H.J. Korn, "The Evolution of Strategic Simplicity: Exploring Two Models of Organizational Adaption," *Journal of Management*, 22, No. 3 (1996), pp. 863–87.

8. "Sports Sales Get Extreme," *Springfield News Leader*, February 12, 2000, p. 7A.

9. C.K. Prahalad and G. Hamel, "The Core Competence of the Corporation," *Harvard Business Review*, May–June 1990, pp. 79–91.

10. Information from company's Web site (www.startec.com), January 17, 2000; and C. Ghosh, "Plugged In," *Forbes*, April 5, 1999, pp. 70–71.

11. See, for example, J.B. Barney, "Organizational Culture: Can It Be a Source of Sustained Competitive Advantage?" *Academy of Management Review*, July 1986, pp. 656–65; C. Scholz, "Corporate Culture and Strategy—The Problem of Strategic Fit," *Long Range Planning*, August 1987, pp. 78–87; S. Green, "Understanding Corporate Culture and Its Relation to Strategy," *International Studies of Management and Organization*, Summer 1988, pp. 6–28; T. Kono, "Corporate Culture and Long-Range Planning," *Long Range Planning*, August 1990, pp. 9–19; and C.M. Fiol, "Managing Culture as a Competitive Resource: An Identity-Based View of Sustainable Competitive Advantage," *Journal of Management*, March 1991, pp. 191–211.

12. J.P. Kotter and J. L. Heskett, *Corporate Culture and Performance* (New York: Free Press, 1992).

13. Box based on R.J. Lewicki, D.D. Bowen, D.T. Hall, and F.S. Hall, *Experiences in Management and Organizational Behavior*, 3rd ed. (New York: John Wiley & Sons, 1988), pp. 261–67; A. Williams, "Career Planning: Build on Strengths, Strengthen Weaknesses," *The Black Collegian*, September–October 1993, pp. 78–86; C.C. Campbell-Rock, "Career Planning Strategies That Really Work," *The Black Collegian*, September–October 1993, pp. 88–93; B. Kaye, "Career Development—Anytime, Anyplace," *Training and Development*, December 1993, pp. 46–49; W. Wooten, "Using Knowledge, Skill, and Ability (KSA) Data to Identify Career Pathing Oportunities," *Public Personnel Management*, Winter 1993, pp. 551–63; C. Mossop, "Values Assessment: Key to Managing Careers," *CMA—The Management Accounting Magazine*, March 1994, p. 33; and A.D. Pinkney, "Winning in the Workplace," *Essence*, March 1994, pp. 79–80.

14. See W.F. Glueck, *Business Policy: Strategy Formulation and Management Action*, 2nd ed. (New York: McGraw-Hill, 1976), pp. 120–47; J.A. Pearce II, "Selecting Among Alternative Grand Strategies," *California Management Review*, Spring 1982, pp. 23–31; and T.T. Herbert and H. Deresky, "Generic Strategies: An Empirical Investigation of Typology Validity and Strategy Content," *Strategic Management Journal*, March–April 1987, pp. 135–47.

15. P. Haspeslagh, "Portfolio Planning: Uses and Limits," *Harvard Business Review*, January–February 1982, pp. 58–73.

16. *Perspective on Experience* (Boston: Boston Consulting Group, 1970).

17. R. Rumelt, "Towards a Strategic Theory of the Firm," in R. Lamb (ed.), *Competitive Strategic Management* (Upper Saddle River, NJ: Prentice Hall, 1984), pp. 556–70; M.E. Porter, *Competitive Advantage: Creating and Sustaining Superior Performance* (New York: Free Press, 1985); J. Barney, "Firm Resources and Sustained Competitive Advantage," *Journal of Management* 17, No. 1 (1991), pp. 99–120; M.A. Peteraf, "The Cornerstones of Competitive Advantage: A Resource-Based View," *Strategic Management Journal*, March 1993, pp. 179–91; and J.B. Barney, "Looking Inside for Competitive Advantage," *Academy of Management Executive*, November 1995, pp. 49–61.

18. T.C. Powell, "Total Quality Management as Competitive Advantage: A Review and Empirical Study," *Strategic Management Journal*, January 1995, pp. 15–37.

19. See R.J. Schonenberger, "Is Strategy Strategic? Impact of Total Quality Management on Strategy," *Academy of Management Executive*, August 1992, pp. 80–87; C.A. Barclay, "Quality Strategy and TQM Policies: Empirical Evidence," *Management International Review*, Special Issue 1993, pp. 87–98; T.E. Benson, "A Business Strategy Comes of Age," *Industry Week*, May 3, 1993, pp. 40–44; R. Jacob, "TQM: More Than a Dying Fad?" *Fortune*, October 18, 1993, pp. 66–72; R. Krishnan, A.B. Shani, R.M. Grant, and R. Baer, "In Search of Quality Improvement Problems of Design and Implementation," *Academy of Management Executive*, November 1993, pp. 7–20; B. Voss, "Quality's Second Coming," *Journal of Business Strategy*, March–April 1994, pp. 42–46; M. Barrier, "Raising TQM Consciousness," *Nation's Business*, April 1994, pp. 62–64; and special issue of *Academy of Management Review* devoted to TQM, July 1994, pp. 390–584.

20. This box based on D. Tapscott, D. Ticoll, and A. Lowy, *Digital Capital* (Boston: Harvard Business School Press, 2000); L. Gomes, "Copycats," *Wall Street Journal*, April 17, 2000, p. R43; K. Mieszkowski, "Let Your Customers Lead," *Fast Company*, April 2000, pp. 210–26; and A. Slywotzky,

"How Digital Is Your Company?" *Fast Company*, February–March 1999, pp. 94–113.

21. Information on Ericsson from Hoover's Online (www.hoovers.com), September 20, 2000; and S. Reed, "Ericsson: Wireless Workhorse," *Business Week*, July 10, 2000, p. 110.

22. See, for example, M.E. Porter, *Competitive Strategy: Techniques for Analyzing Industries and Competitors* (New York: Free Press, 1980); Porter, *Competitive Advantage: Creating and Sustaining Superior Performance*; G.G. Dess and P.S. Davis, "Porter's (1980) Generic Strategies as Determinants of Strategic Group Membership and Organizational Performance," *Academy of Management Journal*, September 1984, pp. 467–88; Dess and Davis, "Porter's (1980) Generic Strategies and Performance: An Empirical Examination with American Data—Part I: Testing Porter," *Organization Studies*, No. 1 (1986), pp. 37–55; Dess and Davis, "Porter's (1980) Generic Strategies and Performance: An Empirical Examination with American Data—Part II: Performance Implications," *Organization Studies*, No. 3 (1986), pp. 255–61; M.E. Porter, "From Competitive Advantage to Corporate Strategy," *Harvard Business Review*, May–June 1987, pp. 43–59; A.I. Murray, "A Contingency View of Porter's 'Generic Strategies,'" *Academy of Management Review*, July 1988, pp. 390–400; C.W.L. Hill, "Differentiation versus Low Cost or Differentiation and Low Cost: A Contingency Framework," *Academy of Management Review*, July 1988, pp. 401–12; I. Bamberger, "Developing Competitive Advantage in Small and Medium-Sized Firms," *Long Range Planning*, October 1989, pp. 80–88; and D.F. Jennings and J.R. Lumpkin, "Insights between Environmental Scanning Activities and Porter's Generic Strategies: An Empirical Analysis," *Strategic Management Journal*, 18, No. 4 (1992), pp. 791–803.

23. D. Miller and J. Toulouse, "Strategy, Structure, CEO Personality, and Performance in Small Firms," *American Journal of Small Business*, Winter 1986, pp. 47–62.

24. Hill, "Differentiation versus Low Cost or Differentiation and Low Cost"; R.E. White, "Organizing to Make Business Unit Strategies Work," in H.E. Glass

(ed.), *Handbook of Business Strategy*, 2d ed. (Boston: Warren Gorham and Lamont, 1991), pp. 24.1–24.14; D. Miller, "The Generic Strategy Trap," *Journal of Business Strategy*, January–February 1991, pp. 37–41; and S. Cappel, P. Wright, M. Kroll, and D. Wyld, "Competitive Strategies and Business Performance: An Empirical Study of Select Service Businesses," *International Journal of Management*, March 1992, pp. 1–11.

CHAPTER 9

1. Information from Cnn.com Web site (www.cnn.com/ASIANOW/time/magazine), W. Mellow, "Blazing Refrigerators," *Asia Now*, May 8, 2000.

2. S.C. Jain, "Environmental Scanning in U.S. Corporations," *Long Range Planning*, April 1984, pp. 117–28; see also L.M. Fuld, *Monitoring the Competition* (New York: John Wiley & Sons, 1988); E.H. Burack and N.J. Mathys, "Environmental Scanning Improves Strategic Planning," *Personnel Administrator*, April 1989, pp. 82–87; J.B. Thomas, S.M. Clark, and D.A. Gioia, "Strategic Sensemaking and Organizational Performance: Linkages among Scanning, Interpretation, Action, and Outcomes," *Academy of Management Journal*, April 1993, pp. 239–70; R. Subramanian, N. Fernandes, and E. Harper, "Environmental Scanning in U.S. Companies: Their Nature and Their Relationship to Performance," *Management International Review*, July 1993, pp. 271–86; R. Subramanian and others, "An Empirical Examination of the Relationship Between Strategy and Scanning," *The Mid-Atlantic Journal of Business*, December 1993, pp. 315–30; S. Kotha and A. Nair, "Strategy and Environment as Determinants of Performance: Evidence From the Japanese Machine Tool Industry," *Strategic Management Journal*, vol. 16 (1995), pp. 497–518; B.K. Boyd and J. Fulk, "Executive Scanning and Perceived Uncertainty: A Multidimensional Model," *Journal of Management*, 22, No. 1 (1996) pp. 1–21; and D.S. Elkenov, "Strategic Uncertainty and Environmental Scanning: The Case for Institutional Influences on Scanning Behavior," *Strategic Management Journal*, vol. 18 (1997), pp. 287–302.

3. T.L. Wheelen and J.D. Hunger, *Strategic Management*, 7th ed. (Upper Saddle River, NJ: Prentice Hall, 2000), pp. 52–53.

4. B. Gilad, "The Role of Organized Competitive Intelligence in Corporate Strategy," *Columbia Journal of World Business*, Winter 1989, pp. 29–35; B.D. Gelb, M.J. Saxton, G.M. Zinkhan, and N.D. Albers, "Competitive Intelligence Insights from Executives," *Business Horizons*, January–February 1991, pp. 43–47; L. Fuld, "A Recipe for Business Intelligence," *Journal of Business Strategy*, January–February 1991, pp. 12–17; G.B. Roush, "A Program for Sharing Corporate Intelligence," *Journal of Business Strategy*, January–February 1991, pp. 4–7; J.P. Herring, "The Role of Intelligence in Formulating Strategy," *Journal of Business Strategy*, September–October 1992, pp. 54–60; R.S. Teitelbaum, "The New Role for Intelligence," *Fortune*, November 2, 1992, pp. 104–07; and K. Western, "Ethical Spying," *Business Ethics*, September–October 1995, pp. 22–23.

5. C. Davis, "Get Smart," *Executive Edge*, October/November 1999, pp. 46–50.

6. B. Ettore, "Managing Competitive Intelligence," *Management Review*, October 1995, pp. 15–19.

7. Western, "Ethical Spying."

8. W.H. Davidson, "The Role of Global Scanning in Business Planning," *Organizational Dynamics*, Winter 1991, pp. 5–16.

9. Wheelen and Hunger, *Strategic Management*, p. 67.

10. J.W. Verity, "Clearing the Cobwebs From the Stockroom," *Business Week*, October 21, 1996, p. 140.

11. See J.K. Glassman, "The Year of Gazing Dangerously," *Business Month*, March 1990, pp. 13–14; A.B. Fisher, "Is Long-Range Planning Worth It?" *Fortune*, April 23, 1990, pp. 281–84; J.A. Fraser, "On Target," *Inc.*, April 1991, pp. 113–14; P. Schwartz, *The Art of the Long View* (New York: Doubleday/Currency, 1991); S. Davis, "Twenty Tips for Developing 20/20 Vision for Business," *Journal of Management Development*, September 1993, pp. 15–20; G. Hamel and C.K. Prahalad, "Competing for the Future," *Harvard Business Review*, July-August 1994, pp. 122–28; F. Elikai and W. Hall, Jr., "Managing and Improving the Forecasting Process,"

Journal of Business Forecasting Methods & Systems, Spring 1999, pp. 15–19; L. Lapide, "New Developments in Business Forecasting," *Journal of Business Forecasting Methods & Systems*, Summer 1999, pp. 13–14; and T. Leahy, "Building Better Forecasts," *Business Finance*, December 1999, pp. 10–12.

12. P.N. Pant and W.H. Starbuck, "Innocents in the Forest: Forecasting and Research Methods," *Journal of Management*, June 1990, pp. 433–60; Elikai and Hall, "Managing and Improving the Forecasting Process;" and M.A. Giullian, M.D. Odom, and M.W. Totaro, "Developing Essential Skills for Success in the Business World: A Look at Forecasting," *Journal of Applied Business Research*, Summer 2000, pp. 51–65.

13. This section is based on Y.K. Shetty, "Benchmarking for Superior Performance," *Long Range Planning* 1, April 1993, pp. 39–44; G.H. Watson, "How Process Benchmarking Supports Corporate Strategy," *Planning Review*, January–February 1993, pp. 12–15; N. Banerjee, "Firms Analyze Rivals to Help Fix Themselves," *Wall Street Journal*, May 3, 1994, p. B1+; S. George and A. Weimerskirch, *Total Quality Management: Strategies and Techniques Proven at Today's Most Successful Companies* (New York: John Wiley & Sons, 1994), pp. 207–21; S. Greengard, "Discover Best Practices," *Personnel Journal*, November 1995, pp. 62–73; J. Martin, "Are You as Good as You Think You Are?" *Fortune*, September 30, 1996, pp. 142–52; J.I. Sanchez and J.I. Kraus, "Adopting High-Involvement Human Resource Practices: The Mediating Role of Benchmarking," *Group & Organization Management*, December 1999, pp. 461–78; R.L. Ackoff, "The Trouble with Benchmarking," *Across the Board*, January 2000, p. 13; V. Prabhu, D. Yarrow, and G. Gordon-Hart, "Best Practice and Performance Within Northeast Manufacturing," *Total Quality Management*, January 2000, pp. 113–21; "E-Benchmarking: The Latest E-Trend," *CFO*, March 2000, p. 7; and E. Krell, "Now Read This," *Business Finance*, May 2000, pp. 97–103.

14. Benchmarking examples were found in the following: "Benchmarkers Make Strange Bedfellows," *IW*, November 15, 1993, p. 8; G. Fuchsberg, "Here's Help

in Finding Corporate Role Models," *Wall Street Journal*, June 1, 1993, p. B1; and A. Tanzer, "Studying at the Feet of the Masters," *Forbes*, May 10, 1993, pp. 43–44.

15. This section is based on T. Gutner, "Better Your Business, Benchmark It," *Business Week*, April 27, 1998, pp. ENT4–6.

16. T. Leahy, "Necessary Evil," *Business Finance*, November 1999, pp. 41–45; J. Fanning, "Businesses Languishing in a Budget Comfort Zone?" *Management Accounting*, July/August 1999, p. 8; "Budgeting Processes Inefficiency or Inadequate," *Management Accounting*, February 1999, p. 5; A. Kennedy and D. Dugdale, "Getting the Most From Budgeting," *Management Accounting*, February 1999, pp. 22–24; G.J. Nolan, "The End of Traditional Budgeting," *Bank Accounting & Finance*, Summer 1998, pp. 29–36; J. Mariotti, "Surviving the Dreaded Budget Process," *IW*, August 17, 1998, p. 150.

17. See, for example, S. Stiansen, "Breaking Even," *Success*, November 1988, p. 16.

18. S.E. Barndt and D.W. Carvey, *Essentials of Operations Management* (Upper Saddle River, NJ: Prentice Hall, 1982), p. 134.

19. E.E. Adam Jr. and R.J. Ebert, *Production and Operations Management*, 5th ed. (Upper Saddle River, NJ: Prentice Hall, 1992), p. 333.

20. See, for instance, C.E. Gray and E.W. Larsen, *Project Management: The Managerial Process* (Columbus, OH: McGraw-Hill Higher Education, 2000); J.D. Frame, *Project Management Competence: Building Key Skills for Individuals, Teams, and Organizations* (San Francisco, CA: Jossey-Bass, 1999); D. Stamps, "Lights! Camera! Project Management!" *Training*, January 1997, p. 52; and J.W. Weiss and R.K. Wysocki, *5-Phase Project Management* (Reading, MA: Addison-Wesley, 1992), p. 3.

21. P. Gordon, "Track Projects on the Web," *Information Week*, May 22, 2000, pp. 88–89.

22. S. Caudron, "Frontview Mirror," *Business Finance*, December 1999, pp. 24–30; and J.R. Garber, "What if . . .?" *Forbes*, November 2, 1998, pp. 76–79.

23. S. Caudron, "Frontview Mirror," p. 30.

PART 3

1. G.B. Knight, "How Wall Street Whiz Found a Niche Selling Books on the internet," *Wall Street Journal*, May 15, 1996, pp. A1+.

2. N.F. Krueger, Jr., "The Cognitive Infrastructure of Opportunity Emergence," *Entrepreneurship Theory and Practice*, Spring 2000, p. 6.

3. P. Drucker, *Innovation and Entrepreneurship* (New York: Harper & Row, 1985).

4. B. McClean, "This Entrepreneur is Changing Underwear," *Fortune*, September 18, 2000, p. 60.

5. A. Cohen, "eBay's Bid to Conquer All," *Time*, February 5, 2001, pp. 48–51.

6. S. McFarland, "Cambodia's Internet Service is in Kids' Hands," *Wall Street Journal*, May 15, 2000, p. A9A.

7. Information on Whole Foods Market from Hoovers Online [www.hoovers.com], January 31, 2001.

8. A. Eisenberg, "What's Next: New Fabrics Can Keep Wearers Healthy and Smelling Good," *New York Times*, February 3, 2000, pp. D1+.

9. S. Greco, "The Start-Up Years," *Inc. 500*, October 21, 1997, p. 57.

10. T. Stevens, "Master of His Universe," *Industry Week*, January 15, 2001, pp. 76–80; and R. Grover, "Back From a Black Hole," *Business Week*, May 29, 2000, p. 186.

11. E. Neuborne, "Hey, Good-Looking," *Business Week*, May 29, 2000, p. 192.

CHAPTER 10

1. Information from J.S. McClenahen, "CEO of the Year," *Industry Week*, November 20, 2000, pp. 38–44; company's Web site (www.nokia.com), June 12, 2000; J. Fox, "Nokia's Secret Code," *Fortune*, May 1, 2000, pp. 160–74; and A. LaTour, "Finland's Nokia Posts 76% Jump in Pretax Profit for First Quarter," *Wall Street Journal*, April 28, 2000, p. A17.

2. See, for example, R.L. Daft, *Organization Theory and Design*, 6th ed. (St. Paul, MN: West Publishing, 1998).

3. This section based on J.A. Byrne, "The McKinsey Mystique," *Business Week*, September 20, 1993, p. 70; B. Dumaine, "Payoff from the New Management," *Fortune*, December 13,

1993, pp. 103–10; J.A. Byrne, "The Horizontal Corporation," *Business Week*, December 20, 1993, pp. 76–81; R. Semler, "Why My Former Employees Still Work for Me," *Harvard Business Review*, January–February 1994, pp. 64–74; R.A. Lutz, "Implementing Technological Change with Cross-Functional Teams," *Research-Technology Management*, March–April 1994, pp. 14–18; and G.M. Parker, *Cross-Functional Teams* (San Francisco: Jossey-Bass, 1994).

4. For a discussion of authority, see W.A. Kahn and K.E. Kram, "Authority at Work: Internal Models and Their Organizational Consequences," *Academy of Management Review*, January 1994, pp. 17–50.

5. D. Van Fleet, "Span of Management Research and Issues," *Academy of Management Journal*, September 1983, pp. 546–52.

6. R. Gibson, "Interstate Bakeries Is Able to Mine Profit from a Golden Cake," *Wall Street Journal*, January 31, 1997, pp. A1+.

7. C. Tohurst, "Companies March on the Morale of Their Workers," *Australian Financial Review*, November 13, 1998, p. SP2.

8. A. Ross, "BMO's Big Bang," *Canadian Business*, January 1994, pp. 58–63.

9. See, for example, H. Mintzberg, *Power In and Around Organizations* (Upper Saddle River, NJ: Prentice Hall, 1983); J. Child, *Organization: A Guide to Problems and Practices* (London: Kaiser & Row, 1984).

10. T. Burns and G.M. Stalker, *The Management of Innovation* (London: Tavistock, 1961); and D.A. Morand, "The Role of Behavioral Formality and Informality in the Enactment of Bureaucratic versus Organic Organizations," *Academy of Management Review*, October 1995, pp. 831–72.

11. A.D. Chandler, Jr., *Strategy and Structure: Chapters in the History of the Industrial Enterprise* (Cambridge, MA: MIT Press, 1962).

12. See, for instance, R.E. Miles and C.C. Snow, *Organizational Strategy, Structure, and Process* (New York: McGraw-Hill, 1978); D. Miller, "The Structural and Environmental Correlates of Business Strategy," *Strategic Management Jour-*

nal, January–February 1987, pp. 55–76; H.L. Boschken, "Strategy and Structure: Reconceiving the Relationship," *Journal of Management*, March 1990, pp. 135–50; H.A. Simon, "Strategy and Organizational Evolution," *Strategic Management Journal*, January 1993, pp. 131–42; R. Parthasarthy and S.P. Sethi, "Relating Strategy and Structure to Flexible Automation: A Test of Fit and Performance Implications," *Strategic Management Journal*, 14, no. 6 (1993), pp. 529–49; D.C. Galunic and K.M. Eisenhardt, "Renewing the Strategy-Structure-Performance Paradigm," in B.M. Staw and L.L. Cummings, (eds.) *Research in Organizational Behavior*, vol. 16 (Greenwich, CT: JAI Press, 1994), pp. 215–55; and D. Jennings and S. Seaman, "High and Low Levels of Organizational Adaptation: An Empirical Analysis of Strategy, Structure, and Performance," *Strategic Management Journal*, July 1994, pp. 459–75.

13. See, for instance, P.M. Blau and R.A. Schoenherr, *The Structure of Organizations* (New York: Basic Books, 1971); D.S. Pugh, "The Aston Program of Research: Retrospect and Prospect," in A.H. Van de Ven and W.F. Joyce (eds.), *Perspectives on Organization Design and Behavior* (New York: John Wiley, 1981), pp. 135–66; and R.Z. Gooding and J.A. Wagner III, "A Meta-Analytic Review of the Relationship between Size and Performance: The Productivity and Efficiency of Organizations and Their Subunits," *Administrative Science Quarterly*, December 1985, pp. 462–81.

14. J. Woodward, *Industrial Organization: Theory and Practice* (London: Oxford University Press, 1965).

15. See, for instance, C. Perrow, "A Framework for the Comparative Analysis of Organizations," *American Sociological Review*, April 1967, pp. 194–208; J.D. Thompson, *Organizations in Action* (New York: McGraw-Hill, 1967); J. Hage and M. Aiken, "Routine Technology, Social Structure, and Organizational Goals," *Administrative Science Quarterly*, September 1969, pp. 366–77; and Miller et al., "Understanding Technology-Structure Relationships."

16. D. Gerwin, "Relationships between Structure and Technology," in P.C. Nystrom and W.H. Starbuck (eds.), *Handbook of Organizational Design*, vol. 2

(New York: Oxford University Press, 1981), pp. 3–38; and D.M. Rousseau and R.A. Cooke, "Technology and Structure: The Concrete, Abstract, and Activity Systems of Organizations," *Journal of Management*, Fall–Winter 1984, pp. 345–61.

17. F.E. Emery and E. Trist, "The Causal Texture of Organizational Environments," *Human Relations*, February 1965, pp. 21–32; P. Lawrence and J.W. Lorsch, *Organization and Environment: Managing Differentiation and Integration* (Boston: Harvard Business School, Division of Research, 1967); and M. Yasai-Ardekani, "Structural Adaptations to Environments," *Academy of Management Review*, January 1986, pp. 9–21.

18. H. Mintzberg, *Structure in Fives: Designing Effective Organizations* (Upper Saddle River, NJ: Prentice Hall, 1983), p. 157.

19. R.J. Williams, J.J. Hoffman, and B.T. Lamont, "The Influence of Top Management Team Characteristics on M-Form Implementation Time," *Journal of Managerial Issues*, Winter 1995, pp. 466–80.

20. See, for example, R.E. Hoskisson, C.W.L. Hill, and H. Kim, "The Multidivisional Structure: Organizational Fossil or Source of Value?" *Journal of Management* 19, no. 2 (1993) pp. 269–98; I.I. Mitroff, R.O. Mason, and C.M. Pearson, "Radical Surgery: What Will Tomorrow's Organizations Look Like?" *Academy of Management Executive*, February 1994, pp. 11–21; T. Clancy, "Radical Surgery: A View from the Operating Theater," *Academy of Management Executive*, February 1994, pp. 73–78; E. Pinchot and G. Pinchot, *The End of Bureaucracy and the Rise of the Intelligent Organization* (San Francisco: Berrett-Koehler Publishers, 1994); T. Peters, "Crazy Times Call for Crazy Organizations," *Success*, July–August 1994, pp. 24A+; and T.H. Davenport and J.E.K. Delano, "On Tomorrow's Organizations: Moving Forward, or A Step Backwards?" *Academy of Management Executive*, August 1994, pp. 93–98.

21. See, for example, H. Rothman, "The Power of Empowerment," *Nation's Business*, June 1993, pp. 49–52; B. Dumaine, "Payoff from the New Management"; J.A. Byrne, "The Horizontal Corporation," and J.R. Katzenbach and

D.K. Smith, in *The Wisdom of Teams* (Boston: Harvard Business School Press, 1993); L. Grant, "New Jewel in the Crown," *U.S. News & World Report*, February 28, 1994, pp. 55–57; D. Ray and H. Bronstein, *Teaming Up: Making the Transition to a Self-Directed Team-Based Organization* (New York: McGraw Hill, 1995); and D.R. Denison, S.L. Hart, and J.A. Kahn, "From Chimneys to Cross-Functional Teams: Developing and Validating a Diagnostic Model," *Academy of Management Journal*, December 1996, pp. 1005–23.

22. C. Fishman, "Whole Foods Is All Teams," *Fast Company*, Greatest Hits, vol. 1 (1997), pp. 102–13.

23. P. LaBarre, "This Organization Is Dis-Organization," *Fast Company* Web page (www.fastcompany.com), April 16, 1997.

24. M.F.R. Kets deVries, "Making a Giant Dance," *Across the Board*, October 1994, pp. 27–32; and information on company from Hoover's Online (www.hoovers.com), October 3, 2000.

25. See, for example, G.G. Dess, A.M.A. Rasheed, K.J. McLaughlin, and R.L. Priem, "The New Corporate Architecture," *Academy of Management Executive*, August, 1995, pp. 7–20.

26. For additional readings on boundaryless organizations, see "The Boundaryless Organization: Break the Chains of Organizational Structures," *HR Focus*, April 1996, p. 21; R.M. Hodgetts, "A Conversation with Steve Kerr," *Organizational Dynamics*, Spring 1996, pp. 68–79; J. Gebhardt, "The Boundaryless Organization," *Sloan Management Review*, Winter 1996, pp. 117–19; and M. Hammer and S. Stanton, "How Process Enterprises Really Work," *Harvard Business Review*, November–December 1999, pp. 108–18. For another view of boundaryless organizations, see B. Victor, "The Dark Side of the New Organizational Forms: An Editorial Essay," *Organization Science*, November 1994, pp. 479–82.

27. This box is based on D. Tapscott, D. Ticoll, and A. Lowy, "Human Capital in the Business Web," *Workforce*, on Workforce.com Web site (www.workforce.com), June 6, 2000; R. Gulati and J. Garino, "Get the Right Mix of Bricks & Clicks," *Harvard Business Review*, May–June 2000, pp. 107–14; M. Sawhney and D. Parikh, "Break Your Bound-

aries," *Business 2.0*, May 2000, pp. 198–207; and T.A. Stewart, "Three Rules for Managing in the Real-Time Economy," *Fortune*, May 1, 2000, pp. 333–34.

28. P.M. Senge, *The Fifth Discipline: The Art and Practice of Learning Organizations* (New York: Doubleday, 1990).

29. J.M. Liedtka, "Collaborating across Lines of Business for Competitive Advantage," *Academy of Management Executive*, April 1996, pp. 20–37; and G. Szulanski, "Exploring Internal Stickiness: Impediments to the Transfer of Best Practice within the Firm," *Strategic Management Journal*, Winter Special Issue, 1996, pp. 27–43.

CHAPTER 11

1. M. Hofman, "Lost in the Translation," *Inc.*, May 2000, pp. 161–62.

2. T. Dixon, *Communication, Organization, and Performance* (Norwood, NJ: Ablex Publishing Corporation, 1996), p. 281; P.G. Clampitt, *Communicating for Managerial Effectiveness* (Newbury Park, CA: Sage Publications, 1991); and L.E. Penley, E.R. Alexander, I.E Jernigan, and C.I. Henwood, "Communication Abilities of Managers: The Relationship to Performance," *Journal of Management*, March 1991, pp. 57–76.

3. C.O. Kursh, "The Benefits of Poor Communication," *Psychoanalytic Review*, Summer–Fall 1971, pp. 189–208.

4. D.K. Berlo, *The Process of Communication* (New York: Holt, Rinehart & Winston, 1960), pp. 30–32.

5. Clampitt, *Communicating for Managerial Effectiveness*.

6. J. Manion, "He Said, She Said," *Materials Management in Health Care*, November 1998, pp. 52–62; G. Franzwa and C. Lockhart, "The Social Origins and Maintenance of Gender Communication Styles, Personality Types, and Grid-Group Theory," *Sociological Perspectives*, vol. 41, no. 1 (1998), pp. 185–208; and D. Tannen, *Talking From 9 to 5: Women and Men in the Workplace* (New York: Avon Books, 1995).

7. Berlo, *The Process of Communication*, p. 103.

8. A. Mehrabian, "Communication Without Words," *Psychology Today*, September 1968, pp. 53–55.

9. See, for instance, S.P. Robbins and P.L. Hunsaker, *Training in InterPersonal Skills*, 2nd ed. (Upper Saddle River, NJ: Prentice Hall, 1996); M. Young and J.E. Post, "Managing to Communicate, Communicating to Manage: How Leading Companies Communicate With Employees," *Organizational Dynamics*, Summer 1993, pp. 31–43; J.A. DeVito, *The Interpersonal Communication Book*, 6th ed. (New York: HarperCollins, 1992); and A.G. Athos and J.J. Gabarro, *Interpersonal Behavior* (Upper Saddle River, NJ: Prentice Hall, 1978).

10. Cited in "Heard It Through the Grapevine," *Forbes*, February 10, 1997, p. 22.

11. See, for instance, N.B. Kurland and L.H. Pelled, "Passing the Word: Toward a Model of Gossip and Power in the Workplace," *Academy of Management Review*, April 2000, pp. 428–38; N. DiFonzo, P. Bordia, and R.L. Rosnow, "Reining in Rumors," *Organizational Dynamics*, Summer 1994, pp. 47–62; M. Noon and R. Delbridge, "News from Behind My Hand: Gossip in Organizations," *Organization Studies*, vol. 14, no. 1 (1993), pp. 23–26; and J.G. March and G. Sevon, "Gossip, Information and Decision Making," in J.G. March (ed.), *Decisions and Organizations* (Oxford: Blackwell, 1988), pp. 429–42.

12. J. Rohwer, "Today, Tokyo. Tomorrow, the World," *Fortune*, September 18, 2000, pp. 140–52; J. McCullam and L. Torres, "Instant Enterprising," *Forbes*, September 11, 2000, p. 28; J. Guyon, "The World Is Your Office," *Fortune*, June 12, 2000, pp. 227–34; S. Baker and others, "The Wireless Internet," *Business Week*, May 29, 2000, pp. 136–44; and R. Lieber, "Information is Everything . . ." *Fast Company*, November 1999, pp. 246–54.

13. McCullam and Torres, "Instant Enterprising."

14. Based on P. Sloan, "New Ways to Goof Off at Work," *U.S. News & World Report*, September 4, 2000, p. 42; and M. Conlin, "Workers, Surf at Your Own Risk," *Business Week*, June 12, 2000, pp. 105–06.

15. K.C. Laudon and J.P. Laudon, *Essentials of Management Information Systems* (Upper Saddle River, NJ: Prentice Hall, 1995), p. 234.

16. J. Rohwer, "Today, Tokyo. Tomorrow, the World,"; and S. Rosenbush and B. Einhorn, "The Talking Internet," *Business Week*, May 1, 2000, pp. 174–88.

17. S. Baker and others, "The Wireless Internet"; A. Cohen, "Wireless Summer," *Time*, May 29, 2000, pp. 58–65; and K. Hafner, "For the Well Connected, All the World's an Office," *New York Times*, March 30, 2000, pp. D1+.

18. Hafner, "For the Well Connected, All the World's an Office."

CHAPTER 12

1. C. Murphy, "The Next French Revolution," *Fortune*, June 12, 2000, pp. 156–68; J. Tagliabue, "Sprechen Sie Technology?" *New York Times*, May 5, 2000, pp. C1+; and D. Woodruff, "In New Europe, Mobile Workers Find Jobs in Nations Offering Best Opportunities," *Wall Street Journal*, August 5, 1999, p. A14.

2. P.M. Wright and G.C. McMahan, "Theoretical Perspectives for Strategic Human Resource Management," *Journal of Management* 18, no. 1 (1992), pp. 295–320; A.A. Lado and M.C. Wilson, "Human Resource Systems and Sustained Competitive Advantage," *Academy of Management Review*, October 1994, pp. 699–727; and J. Pfeffer, *Competitive Advantage Through People* (Boston: Harvard Business School Press, 1994).

3. J.B. Arthur, "Effects of Human Resource Systems on Manufacturing Performance and Turnover," *Academy of Management Journal*, June 1994, pp. 670–87; M.A. Huselid, "The Impact of Human Resource Management Practices on Turnover, Productivity, and Corporate Financial Performance," *Academy of Management Journal*, June 1995, pp. 635–72; M.J. Koch and R.G. McGrath, "Improving Labor Productivity: Human Resource Management Policies Do Matter," *Strategic Management Journal*, May 1996, pp. 335–54; B. Becker and B. Gerhart, "The Impact of Human Resource Management on Organizational Performance: Progress and Prospects," *Academy of Management Journal*, August 1996, pp. 779–801; M.A. Youndt, S.A. Snell, J.W. Dean, Jr., and D.P. Lepak, "Human Resource Management, Manufacturing Strategy, and Firm Performance," *Academy of Management Journal*, August 1996, pp. 836–66; J.T. Delaney and M.A. Huselid, "The Impact of Human Resource Management Practices on Perceptions of Organizational Performance," *Academy of Management Journal*, August 1996, pp. 949–69; M.A. Huselid, S.E. Jackson, and R.S. Schuler, "Technical and Strategic Human Resource Management Effectiveness as Determinants of Firm Performance," *Academy of Management Journal*, January 1997, pp. 171–88; A.S. Tsui, J.L. Pearce, L.W. Porter, and A.M. Tripoli, "Alternative Approaches to the Employee-Organization Relationship: Does Investment in Employees Pay Off?" *Academy of Management Journal*, October 1997, pp. 1089–1121; and J. Kurtzman, "An Interview With Jeffrey Pfeffer," *Strategy & Business*, Third Quarter 1998, pp. 85–94.

4. "Human Capital a Key to Higher Market Value," *Business Finance*, December 1999, p. 15.

5. Y.J. Dreazen, "Labor Unions Turn to Mergers in Pursuit of Growth," *Wall Street Journal*, September 1, 2000, p. A2; "Foreign Labor Trends—Germany," U.S. Department of Labor, 1999; "Foreign Labor Trends—Japan," U.S. Department of Labor, 1994–1995; and "Foreign Labor Trends—Mexico," U.S. Department of Labor, 1999.

6. P. Digh, "Religion in the Workplace," *HRMagazine*, December 1998, p. 88.

7. T.J. Bergmann and M.S. Taylor, "College Recruitment: What Attracts Students to Organizations?" *Personnel*, May–June 1984, pp. 34–46; and A.S. Bargerstock and G. Swanson, "Four Ways to Build Cooperative Recruitment Alliances," *HRMagazine*, March 1991, p. 49.

8. J.R. Gordon, *Human Resource Management: A Practical Approach* (Boston: Allyn and Bacon, 1986), p. 170.

9. See, for example, J.P. Kirnan, J.E. Farley, and K.F. Geisinger, "The Relationship between Recruiting Source, Applicant Quality, and Hire Performance: An Analysis by Sex, Ethnicity, and Age," *Personnel Psychology*, Summer 1989, pp. 293–308; and R.W. Griffeth, P.W. Hom, L.S. Fink, and D.J. Cohen, "Comparative Tests of Multivariate Models of

Recruiting Sources Effects," *Journal of Management*, 23, no. 1 (1997), pp. 19–36.

10. J. Spiers, "Upper Middle Class Woes," *Fortune*, December 27, 1993, p. 80; and M. London, "Redeployment and Continuous Learning in the 21st Century: Hard Lessons and Positive Examples from the Downsizing Era," *Academy of Management Executive*, November 1996, pp. 67–79.

11. G.W. England, *Development and Use of Weighted Application Blanks*, rev. ed. (Minneapolis: Industrial Relations Center, University of Minnesota, 1971); J.J. Asher, "The Biographical Item: Can It Be Improved?" *Personnel Psychology*, Summer 1972, p. 266; G. Grimsley and H.F. Jarrett, "The Relation of Managerial Achievement to Test Measures Obtained in the Employment Situation: Methodology and Results," *Personnel Psychology*, Spring 1973, pp. 31–48; E.E. Ghiselli, "The Validity of Aptitude Tests in Personnel Selection," *Personnel Psychology*, Winter 1973, p. 475; I.T. Robertson and R.S. Kandola, "Work Sample Tests: Validity, Adverse Impact, and Applicant Reaction," *Journal of Occupational Psychology*, 55, no. 3 (1982), pp. 171–83; A.K. Korman, "The Prediction of Managerial Performance: A Review," *Personnel Psychology*, Summer 1986, pp. 295–322; G.C. Thornton, *Assessment Centers in Human Resource Management* (Reading, MA: Addison-Wesley, 1992); C. Fernandez-Araoz, "Hiring Without Firing," *Harvard Business Review*, July–August, 1999, pp. 108–20; and A.M. Ryan and R.E. Ployhart, "Applicants' Perceptions of Selection Procedures and Decisions: A Critical Review and Agenda for the Future," *Journal of Management*, 26, no. 3 (2000), pp. 565–606.

12. S. Randall, "An Overview of Personality Testing in the Workforce," Workforce Online (www.workforce.com), December 13, 2000; and S. Randall, "Legal Challenges to Personality Tests," Workforce Online (www.workforce.com), December 13, 2000.

13. C.A. Townsley, "Planning and Administration of Assessment Centers," Center for the Study of Workteams Reports, online at www.workteams.unt.edu/reports, November 3, 2000.

14. R.L. Dipboye, *Selection Interviews: Process Perspectives* (Cincinnati: South-Western Publishing, 1992), p. 6.

15. See, for instance, R.D. Arveny and J.E. Campion, "The Employment Interview: A Summary and Review of Recent Research," *Personnel Psychology*, Summer 1982, pp. 281–322; and M.M. Harris, "Reconsidering the Employment Interview: A Review of Recent Literature and Suggestions for Future Research," *Personnel Psychology*, Winter 1989, pp. 691–726.

16. See, for example, S.L. Premack and J.P. Wanous, "A Meta-Analysis of Realistic Job Preview Experiments," *Journal of Applied Psychology*, November 1985, pp. 706–20; and J.A. Breaugh and M. Starke, "Research on Employee Recruitment: So Many Studies, So Many Remaining Questions," *Journal of Management*, vol. 26, no. 3 (2000), pp. 405–34.

17. S.L. Robinson, M.S. Kraatz, and D.M. Rousseau, "Changing Obligations and the Psychological Contract: A Longitudinal Study," *Academy of Management Journal*, February 1994, pp. 137–52.

18. J. Jusko, "Never a Dull Moment," *IW*, March 20, 2000, pp. 14–16.

19. Information from Training Supersite Web site, www.trainingsupersite.com, December 13, 2000.

20. See, for example, J.C. Szabo, "Boosting Workers' Basic Skills," *Nation's Business*, January 1992, pp. 38–40; and R. Henkoff, "Companies That Train Best," *Fortune*, March 22, 1993, pp. 20–25.

21. R.D. Bretz, Jr., G.T. Milkovich, and W. Read, "The Current State of Performance Appraisal Research and Practice: Concerns, Directions, and Implications," *Journal of Mangement*, June 1992, p. 331.

22. This section based on R.I. Henderson, *Compensation Management*, 6th ed. (Upper Saddle River, NJ: Prentice Hall, 1994), pp. 3–24.

23. L.R. Gomez-Mejia, "Structure and Process of Diversification, Compensation Strategy, and Firm Performance," *Strategic Management Journal* 13 (1992), pp. 381–97; and E. Montemayor, "Congruence between Pay Policy and Competitive Strategy in High-Performing Firms," *Journal of*

Management, 22, no. 6 (1996), pp. 889–908.

24. E.E. Lawler III, G.E. Ledford Jr., and L. Chang, "Who Uses Skill-Based Pay and Why," *Compensation and Benefits Review*, March–April 1993, p. 22; and Ledford, "Paying for the Skills, Knowledge and Competencies of Knowledge Workers," *Compensation and Benefits Review*, July–August 1995, pp. 55–62.

25. M. Rowland, "For Each New Skill, More Money," *New York Times*, June 13, 1993, p. F16; and C. Lee, K.S. Law, and P. Bobko, "The Importance of Justice Perceptions on Pay Effectiveness: A Two-Year Study of a Skill-Based Pay Plan," *Journal of Management*, 26, no. 6 (1999), pp. 851–73.

26. M. Rowland, "It's What You Can Do That Counts," *New York Times*, June 6, 1993, p. F17.

27. D.E. Super and D.T. Hall, "Career Development: Exploration and Planning," in M.R. Rosenzweig and L.W. Porter (eds.), *Annual Review of Psychology*, vol. 29 (Palo Alto, CA: Annual Reviews, 1978), p. 334.

28. S.E. Sullivan, "The Changing Nature of Careers: A Review and Research Agenda," *Journal of Management*, 25, no. 3 (1999), pp. 457–84; D.T. Hall, "Protean Careers of the 21st Century," *Academy of Management Executive*, November 1996, pp. 8–16; M.B. Arthur and D.M. Rousseau, "A Career Lexicon for the 21st Century," *Academy of Management Executive*, November 1996, pp. 28–39; N. Nicholson, "Career Systems in Crisis: Change and Opportunity in the Information Age," *Academy of Management Executive*, November 1996, pp. 40–51; and K.R. Brousseau, M.J. Driver, K. Enertoh, and R. Larsson, "Career Pandemonium: Realigning Organizations and Individuals," *Academy of Management Executive*, November 1996, pp. 52–66.

29. Hall, "Protean Careers of the 21st Century."

30. M.B. Arthur and D.M. Rousseau, *The Boundaryless Career: A New Employment Principle for a New Organizational Era* (New York: Oxford University Press, 1996).

31. M. Cianni and D. Wnuck, "Individual Growth and Team Enhancement: Moving toward a New Model of Career

Development," *Academy of Management Executive*, February 1997, pp. 105–15.

32. D.E. Super, "A Life-Span Life Space Approach to Career Development," *Journal of Vocational Behavior*, Spring 1980, pp. 282–98; see also E.P. Cook and M. Arthur, *Career Theory Handbook* (Upper Saddle River, NJ: Prentice Hall, 1991), pp. 99–131; and L.S. Richman, "The New Worker Elite," *Fortune*, August 22, 1994, pp. 56–66.

33. R. Henkoff, "Winning the New Career Game," *Fortune*, July 12, 1993, pp. 46–49; "10 Tips for Managing Your Career," *Personnel Journal*, October 1995, p. 106; and A. Fisher, "Six Ways to Supercharge Your Career," *Fortune*, January 13, 1997, pp. 46–48.

34. Interview with Bill Gates, "Bill Gates on Rewiring the Power Structure," *Working Woman*, April 1994, p. 62; F. Moody, "Wonder Women in the Rude Boys' Paradise," *Fast Company* Web Page (www.fastcompany.com), April 17, 1997.

35. R. Leger, "Linked by Differences," *Springfield News-Leader*, December 31, 1993, pp. B6+.

36. P. Brimelow, "Is Sexual Harassment Getting Worse?" *Forbes*, April 19, 1999, p. 92.

37. A.B. Fisher, "Sexual Harassment, What to Do," *Fortune*, August 23, 1993, pp. 84–88.

38. P.M. Buhler, "The Manager's Role in Preventing Sexual Harassment," *Supervision*, April 1999, p. 18; and "Cost of Sexual Harassment in the U.S.," *The Webb Report: A Newsletter on Sexual Harassment* (Seattle, WA: Premier Publishing, Ltd.), January 1994, pp. 4–7 and April 1994, pp. 2–5.

39. "U.S. Leads Way in Sex Harassment Laws, Study Says," *Evening Sun*, November 30, 1992, pp. A1+; and W. Hardman and J. Heidelberg, "When Sexual Harassment Is a Foreign Affair," *Personnel Journal*, April 1996, pp. 91–97.

40. Although the male gender was referred to in this case, it is important to note that sexual harassment may involve persons of either sex sexually harassing others or a person of the same sex harassing another individual. (See, for instance, *Oncale v. Sundowner Offshore Service Inc.*, 118 S. Ct. 998.)

41. A. Fisher, "After All This Time, Why Don't People Know What Sexual Harassment Means?" *Fortune*, January 12, 1998, p. 68; and A. R. Karr, "Companies Crack Down on the Increasing Sexual Harassment by E-Mail," *Wall Street Journal*, September 21, 1999, p. A1.

42. See K.A. Hess and D.R.M. Ehrens, "Sexual Harassment—Affirmative Defense to Employer Liability," *Benefits Quarterly*, Second Quarter 1999, p. 57; J.A. Segal, "The Catch-22s of Remedying Sexual Harassment Complaints," *HRMagazine*, October 1997, pp. 111–17; S.C. Bahls and J.E. Bahls, "Hand-Off Policy," *Entrepreneur*, July 1997, pp. 74–76; J.A. Segal, "Where Are We Now?" *HRMagazine*, October 1996, pp. 69–73; B. McAfee and D.L. Deadrick, "Teach Employees to Just Say No," *HRMagazine*, February 1996, pp. 86–89; G.D. Block, "Avoiding Liability for Sexual Harassment," *HRMagazine*, April 1995, pp. 91–97; and J.A. Segal, "Stop Making Plaintiffs' Lawyers Rich," *HRMagazine*, April 1995, pp. 31–35. Also, it should be noted here that under the Title VII and the Civil Rights Act of 1991, the maximum award that can be given, under the federal act, is $300,000. However, many cases are tried under state laws that permit unlimited punitive damages, such as the $7.1 million that Rena Weeks received in her trial based on California statutes.

43. B.E. Ashforth, G.E. Kreiner, and M. Fugate, "All in a Day's Work: Boundaries and Micro Role Transitions," *Academy of Management Review*, July 2000, pp. 472–91; J.R. Edwards and N.P. Rothbard, "Mechanisms Linking Work and Family: Clarifying the Relationship Between Work and Family Constructs," *Academy of Management Review*, January 2000, pp. 178–99; J. Sammer, "Maintaining Employee Equilibrium," *Business Finance*, October 1999, pp. 81–84; M.A. Verespej, "Work vs. Life," *IW*, April 19, 1999, pp. 37–42; and F.J. Milliken, L.L. Martins, and H. Morgan, "Explaining Organizational Responsiveness to Work-Family Issues: The Role of Human Resource Executives as Issue Interpreters," *Academy of Management Journal*, October 1998, p. 585.

44. K.H. Hammond and A.T. Palmer, "The Daddy Trap," *Business Week*, September 21, 1998, pp. 56–64.

CHAPTER 13

1. Information from company's Web site (www.panamco.com), June 12, 2000; and S. Van Yoder, "Thirst for Success," *IW*, May 15, 2000, pp. 34–39.

2. S. McCartney, "Airlines' Reputations Hinge on the Basics, Study Shows," *Wall Street Journal*, April 27, 2000, p. B4; and B. O'Reilly, "The Mechanic Who Fixed Continental," *Fortune*, December 20, 1999, pp. 176–86.

3. The idea for these metaphors came from B.H. Kemelgor, S.D. Johnson, and S. Srinivasan, "Forces Driving Organizational Change: A Business School Perspective," *Journal of Education for Business*, January/February 2000, pp. 133–37; G. Colvin, "When It Comes to Turbulence, CEOs Could Learn a Lot From Sailors," *Fortune*, March 29, 1999, pp. 194–96; and P.B. Vaill, *Managing as a Performing Art: New Ideas for a World of Chaotic Change* (San Francisco: Jossey-Bass, 1989).

4. K. Lewin, *Field Theory in Social Science* (New York: Harper & Row, 1951).

5. See, for instance, T. Peters, *Thriving on Chaos* (New York: Alfred A. Knopf, 1987); and T. Peters, "Thriving in Chaos," *Working Woman*, September 1993, pp. 42+.

6. M. Davids, "Wanted: Strategic Planners," *Journal of Business Strategy*, May–June 1995, pp. 30–38.

7. L. Smith, "New Ideas from the Army (Really)," *Fortune*, September 19, 1994, pp. 203–12.

8. J. Jesitus, "Change Management: Energy to the People," *IW*, September 1, 1997, pp. 37, 40.

9. D. Lavin, "European Business Rushes to Automate," *Wall Street Journal*, July 23, 1997, p. A14.

10. See, for example, W.L. French and C.H. Bell Jr., *Organization Development: Behavioral Science Interventions for Organization Improvement*, 4th ed. (Upper Saddle River, NJ: Prentice Hall, 1990); C.L. Walck, "Organization Development in the USSR: An Overview and a Case Sample," *Journal of Managerial Psychology*, March 1993, pp. 10–17; T.C. Head and P.F. Sorensen, "Cultural Values and Organizational Development: A Seven-Country Study," *Leadership & Organization Development Journal*, March 1993, pp. 3–7; M.P.

O'Driscoll and J.L. Eubanks, "Behavioral Competencies, Goal Setting, and OD Practitioner Effectiveness," *Group & Organization Management*, September 1993, pp. 308–26; A.H. Church, W.W. Burke, and D.F. Van Eynde, "Values, Motives, and Interventions of Organization Development Practitioners," *Group & Organization Management*, March 1994, pp. 5–50; N.A. Worren, K. Ruddle, and K. Moore, "From Organizational Development to Change Management," *Journal of Applied Behavioral Science*, September 1999, pp. 273–86; G. Farias, "Organizational Development and Change Management," *Journal of Applied Behavioral Science*, September 2000, pp. 376–79; W. Nicolay, "Response to Farias and Johnson's Commentary," *Journal of Applied Behavioral Science*, September 2000, pp. 380–81; and S. Hicks, "What Is Organization Development?" *Training & Development*, August 2000, p. 65.

11. See, for example, B.M. Staw, "Counterforces to Change," in P.S. Goodman and Associates (eds.), *Change in Organizations* (San Francisco: Jossey-Bass, 1982), pp. 87–121; and A.A. Armenakis and A.G. Bedeian, "Organizational Change: A Review of Theory and Research in the 1990s," *Journal of Management*, 25, no. 3 (1999), pp. 293–315.

12. J.P. Kotter and L.A. Schlesinger, "Choosing Strategies for Change," *Harvard Business Review*, March–April 1979, pp. 107–09; P. Strebel, "Why Do Employees Resist Change?" *Harvard Business Review*, May–June 1996, pp. 86–92; J. Mariotti, "Troubled by Resistance to Change," *IW*, October 7, 1996, p. 30; and A. Reichers, J.P. Wanous, and J.T. Austin, "Understanding and Managing Cynicism about Organizational Change," *Academy of Management Executive*, February 1997, pp. 48–57.

13. Kotter and Schlesinger, "Choosing Strategies for Change," pp. 106–11; K. Matejka and R. Julian, "Resistance to Change Is Natural," *Supervisory Management*, October 1993, p. 10; C. O'Connor, "Resistance: The Repercussions of Change," *Leadership & Organization Development Journal*, October 1993, pp. 30–36; J. Landau, "Organizational Change and Barriers to Innova-

tion: A Case Study in the Italian Public Sector," *Human Relations*, December 1993, pp. 1411–29; A. Sagie and M. Koslowsky, "Organizational Attitudes and Behaviors as a Function of Participation in Strategic and Tactical Change Decisions: An Application of Path-Goal Theory," *Journal of Organizational Behavior*, January 1994, pp. 37–47; V.D. Miller, J.R. Johnson, and J. Grau, "Antecedents to Willingness to Participate in a Planned Organizational Change," *Journal of Applied Communication Research*, February 1994, pp. 59–80; P. Pritchett and R. Pound, *The Employee Handbook for Organizational Change* (Dallas: Pritchett Publishing, 1994); R. Maurer, *Beyond the Wall of Resistance: Unconventional Strategies That Build Support for Change* (Austin: Bard Books, 1996); D. Harrison, "Assess and Remove Barriers to Change," *HR Focus*, July 1999, pp. 9–10; L.K. Lewis, "Disseminating Information and Soliciting Input During Planned Organizational Change," *Management Communication Quarterly*, August 1999, pp. 43–75; J.P. Wanous, A.E. Reichers, and J.T. Austin, "Cynicism About Organizational Change," *Group & Organization Management*, June 2000, pp. 132–53; K.W. Mossholder, R.P. Settoon, A.A. Armenakis, and S.G. Harris, "Emotion During Organizational Transformations," *Group & Organization Management*, September 2000, pp. 220–43; and S.K. Piderit, "Rethinking Resistance and Recognizing Ambivalence: A Multidimensional View of Attitudes Toward an Organizational Change," *Academy of Management Review*, October 2000, pp. 783–94.

14. Based on N.G. Carr, "Being Virtual: Character and the New Economy," *Harvard Business Review*, May–June 1999, pp. 181–90; B. Kaye, "Career Development—Anytime, Anyplace," *Training & Development*, December 1993, pp. 46–49; A.D. Pinkney, "Winning in the Workplace," *Essence*, March 1994, pp. 79–80; C.B. Bardwell, "Career Planning & Job Search Guide 1994," *The Black Collegian*, March–April 1994, pp. 59–64; and W. Kiechel III, "A Manager's Career in the New Economy," *Fortune*, April 4, 1994, pp. 68–72.

15. See T.H. Fitzgerald, "Can Change in Organizational Culture Really Be Man-

aged?" *Organizational Dynamics*, Autumn 1988, pp. 5–15; B. Dumaine, "Creating a New Company Culture," *Fortune*, January 15, 1990, pp. 127–31; P.F. Drucker, "Don't Change Corporate Culture—Use It!" *Wall Street Journal*, March 28, 1991, p. A14; J. Martin, *Cultures in Organizations: Three Perspectives* (New York: Oxford University Press, 1992); D.C. Pheysey, *Organizational Cultures: Types and Transformations* (London: Routledge, 1993); C.G. Smith and R.P. Vecchio, "Organizational Culture and Strategic Management: Issues in the Strategic Management of Change," *Journal of Managerial Issues*, Spring 1993, pp. 53–70; P. Bate, *Strategies for Cultural Change* (Boston: Butterworth-Heinemann, 1994); and P. Anthony, *Managing Culture* (Philadelphia: Open University Press, 1994).

16. E. Nelson, "Rallying the Troops at P&G," *Wall Street Journal*, August 31, 2000, pp. B1+; and P. Galuzka, "Is P&G's Makeover Only Skin Deep?" *Business Week*, November 15, 1999, p. 52.

17. See, for example, R.H. Kilmann, M.J. Saxton, and R. Serpa (eds.), *Gaining Control of the Corporate Culture* (San Francisco: Jossey-Bass, 1985); and D.C. Hambrick and S. Finkelstein, "Managerial Discretion: A Bridge between Polar Views of Organizational Outcomes," in L.L. Cummings and B.M. Staw (eds.), *Research in Organizational Behavior*, vol. 9 (Greenwich, CT: JAI Press, 1987), p. 384.

18. Based on C. Lindsay, "Paradoxes of Organizational Diversity: Living within the Paradoxes," in L.R. Jauch and J.L. Wall (eds.), *Proceedings of the 50th Academy of Management Conference*, San Francisco, 1990, pp. 374–78.

19. This section is based on M. Hammer and J. Champy, *Reengineering the Corporation: A Manifesto for Business Revolution* (New York: HarperBusiness, 1993); H. Gleckman, J. Carey, R. Mitchell, T. Smart, and C. Rouch, "The Technology Payoff," *Business Week*, June 14, 1993, pp. 56–68; T.A. Stewart, "Reengineering: The Hot New Managing Tool," *Fortune*, August 23, 1993, pp. 40–48; G. Fuchsberg, "Small Firms Struggle with Latest Management Trends," Wall Street Journal, August 26, 1993, p. B2; M. Barrier, "Re-engineering Your Company," *Nation's Business*, February 1994, pp. 16–22; J.P. Womack and D.T. Jones, "From Lean Production to the Lean Enterprise," *Harvard Business Review*, March–April 1994, pp. 93–103; and Y.F. Jarrar and E.M. Aspinwall, "Integrating Total Quality Management and Business Process Re-Engineering: Is It Enough?" *Total Quality Management*, July 1999, pp. S584–S593.

20. "Workplace Stress Is Rampant, Especially with the Recession," *Wall Street Journal*, May 5, 1992, p. A1; V.M. Gibson, "Stress in the Workplace: A Hidden Cost Factor," *HR Focus*, January 1993, p. 15; J. Iacovini, "The Human Side of Organization Change," *Training and Development*, January 1993, pp. 65–68; R. Waxler and T. Higginson, "Discovering Methods to Reduce Workplace Stress," *Industrial Engineering*, June 1993, pp. 19–21; C.L. Cordes and T.W. Dougherty, "A Review and an Integration of Research on Job Burnout," *Academy of Management Review*, October 1993, pp. 621–56; M.A. Verespej, "Stressed Out," *IW*, February 21, 2000, pp. 30–34; and J. Laabs, "Time-Starved Workers Rebel," *Workforce*, October 2000, pp. 26–28.

21. Adapted from R.S. Schuler, "Definition and Conceptualization of Stress in Organizations," *Organizational Behavior and Human Performance*, April 1980, p. 189.

22. Ibid., p. 191.

23. S.E. Jackson, "Participation in Decision Making as a Strategy for Reducing Job-Related Strain," *Journal of Applied Psychology*, February 1983, pp. 3–19; C.D. Fisher, "Boredom at Work: A Neglected Concept," *Human Relations*, March 1993, pp. 395–417; C.A. Heaney, et al., "Industrial Relations, Worksite Stress Reduction and Employee Well-Being: A Participatory Action Research Investigation," *Journal of Organizational Behavior*, September 1993, pp. 495–510; P. Froiland, "What Cures Job Stress?" *Training*, December 1993, pp. 32–36; C.L. Cooper and S. Cartwright, "Healthy Mind, Healthy Organization—A Proactive Approach to Occupational Stress," *Human Relations*, April 1994, pp. 455–71; and A.A. Brott, "New Approaches to Job Stress," *Nation's Business*, May 1994, pp. 81–82.

24. See R.S. Schuler, "Time Management: A Stress Management Technique," *Personnel Journal*, December 1979, pp. 851–55; and M.E. Haynes, *Practical Time Management: How to Make the Most of Your Most Perishable Resource* (Tulsa: Penn Well Books, 1985).

25. M. Marriott, "The Workout Ethic Gets Taken to Work," *New York Times*, March 20, 1996, pp. B1+.

26. "Take Five," *Personnel Journal*, September 1996, p. 24.

27. R.M. Kanter, "From Spare Change to Real Change: The Social Sector as Beta Site for Business Innovation," *Harvard Business Review*, May–June 1999, pp. 122–32.

28. These definitions are based on T.M. Amabile, "A Model of Creativity and Innovation in Organizations," in B.M. Staw and L.L. Cummings (eds.), *Research in Organizational Behavior*, vol. 10 (Greenwich, CT: JAI Press, 1988), p. 126.

29. R.W. Woodman, J.E. Sawyer, and R.W. Griffin, "Toward a Theory of Organizational Creativity," *Academy of Management Review*, April 1993, pp. 293–321.

30. This box based on E. Abrahamson, "Change Without Pain," *Harvard Business Review*, July–August 2000, pp. 75–79; E. Cochran, "The E Gang," *Forbes*, July 24, 2000, pp. 145–72; A. Hargadon and R.I. Sutton, "Building an Innovation Factory," *Harvard Business Review*, May–June 2000, pp. 157–66; C.M. Christensen, "Coping with Change," *Executive Edge*, February/March 2000, pp. 28–32; S. Caudron, "The Economics of Innovation," *Business Finance*, November 1999, pp. 23–27; and C. Salter, "Fast Change at Tivoli Systems Inc.," *Fast Company*, April 1999, pp. 130–44.

31. F. Damanpour, "Organizational Innovation: A Meta-Analysis of Effects of Determinants and Moderators," *Academy of Management Journal*, September 1991, pp. 555–90; S.D. Saleh and C.K. Wang, "The Management of Innovation: Strategy, Structure, and Organizational Climate," *IEEE Transactions on Engineering Management*, February 1993, pp. 14–22; J.F. Coates and J. Jarratt, "Workplace Creativity," *Employment Relations Today*, Spring 1994, pp. 11–22; G.R. Oldham and A. Cummings, "Employee Creativity: Personal and Contextual Factors at Work," *Academy of Management Journal*, June 1996, pp. 607–34; and

J.B. Sorensen and T.E. Stuart, "Aging, Obsolescence, and Organizational Innovation," *Administrative Science Quarterly*, March 2000, pp. 81–112.

32. P.R. Monge, M.D. Cozzens, and N.S. Contractor, "Communication and Motivational Predictors of the Dynamics of Organizational Innovations," *Organization Science*, May 1992, pp. 250–74.

33. E. von Hippel, S. Thomke, and M. Sonnack, "Creating Breakthroughs at 3M," *Harvard Business Review*, September–October 1999, pp. 47–57.

34. See, for instance, Amabile, "A Model of Creativity and Innovation in Organizations," p. 147; M. Tushman and D. Nadler, "Organizing for Innovation," *California Management Review*, Spring 1986, pp. 74–92; R. Moss Kanter, "When a Thousand Flowers Bloom: Structural, Collective, and Social Conditions for Innovation in Organization," in Staw and Cummings, (eds.), *Research in Organizational Behavior*, vol. 10, pp. 169–211; G. Morgan, "Endangered Species: New Ideas," *Business Month*, April 1989, pp. 75–77; S.G. Scott and R.A. Bruce, "Determinants of Innovative People: A Path Model of Individual Innovation in the Workplace," *Academy of Management Journal*, June 1994, pp. 580–607; T.M. Amabile, R. Conti, H. Coon, J. Lazenby, and M. Herron, "Assessing the Work Environment for Creativity," *Academy of Management Journal*, October 1996, pp. 1154–84; A. deGues, "The Living Company," *Harvard Business Review*, March–April 1997, pp. 51–59; and G. Hamel, "Reinvent Your Company," *Fortune*, June 12, 2000, pp. 98–118.

35. J.M. Howell and C.A. Higgins, "Champions of Change," *Business Quarterly*, Spring 1990, pp. 31–32; P.A. Carrow-Moffett, "Change Agent Skills: Creating Leadership for School Renewal," *NASSP Bulletin*, April 1993, pp. 57–62; T. Stjernberg and A. Philips, "Organizational Innovations in a Long-Term Perspective: Legitimacy and Souls-of-Fire as Critical Factors of Change and Viability," *Human Relations*, October 1993, pp. 1193–2023; and J. Ramos, "Producing Change That Lasts," *Across the Board*, March 1994, pp. 29–33.

36. W.J. Broad, "A Tiny Rover, Built on the Cheap, Is Ready to Explore Distant Mars," *New York Times*, July 5, 1997, p. 9.

PART 4

1. J. Hovey, "25 Growing Companies," *Industry Week*, November 20, 2000, p. 66.

2. R.D. Schatz, "A Perfect Blendship," *Business Week Enterprise*, March 1, 1999, p. ENT 20.

3. I.O. Williamson, "Employer Legitimacy and Recruitment Success in Small Businesses," *Entrepreneurship Theory and Practice*, Fall 2000, pp. 27–42.

4. R.L. Heneman, J.W. Tansky, and S.M. Camp, "Human Resource Management Practices in Small and Medium-Sized Enterprises: Unanswered Questions and Future Research Perspectives," *Entrepreneurship Theory and Practice*, Fall, 2000, pp. 11–26.

5. Ibid.

6. "Best Employer," *Working Woman*, May 1999, p. 54.

7. Heneman, Tansky, and Camp, "Human Resource Management Practices in Small and Medium-Sized Enterprises: Unanswered Questions and Future Research Perspectives."

8. Based on G. Fuchsberg, "Small Firms Struggle with Latest Management Trends," *Wall Street Journal*, August 26, 1993, p. B2; M. Barrier, "Re-engineering Your Company," *Nation's Business*, February 1994, pp. 16–22; J. Weiss, "Reengineering the Small Business," *Small Business Reports*, May 1994, pp. 37–43; and K.D. Godsey, "Back on Track," *Success*, May 1997, pp. 52–54.

9. R. Kiener, "Hitting on All Cylinders," *Nation's Business*, June 1999, pp. 57–58.

10. G.N. Chandler, C. Keller, and D.W. Lyon, "Unraveling the Determinants and Consequences of an Innovation-Supportive Organizational Culture," *Entrepreneurship Theory and Practice*, Fall, 2000, pp. 59–76.

11. Ibid.

12. J. Jusko, "Turning Ideas Into Action," *Industry Week*, October 16, 2000, pp. 105–06.

CHAPTER 14

1. Information from company's Web site (www.plumtree.com), June 12, 2000; and L. Kroll, "The Plumtree Software Soap Opera," *Forbes*, May 29, 2000, pp. 96–100.

2. Based on G. Fuchsberg, "Small Firms Struggle with Latest Management Trends," *Wall Street Journal*, August 26, 1993, p. B2; M. Barrier, "Re-engineering Your Company," *Nation's Business*, February 1994, pp. 16–22; J. Weiss, "Reengineering the Small Business," *Small Business Reports*, May 1994, pp. 37–43; and K. Dunlap Godsey, "Back on Track," *Success*, May 1997, pp. 52–54.

3. The idea for these metaphors came from P.B. Vaill, *Managing as a Performing Art: New Ideas for a World of Chaotic Change* (San Francisco: Jossey-Bass, 1989).

4. D.W. Organ, *Organizational Citizenship Behavior: The Good Soldier Syndrome* (Lexington, MA: Lexington Books, 1988), p. 4.

5. In the area of job satisfaction, see, for example, A.O. Agho, C.W. Mueller, and J.L. Price, "Determinants of Employee Job Satisfaction: An Empirical Test of a Causal Model," *Human Relations*, August 1993, pp. 1007–27; J.E. Mathieu, D.A. Hofmann, and J.L. Farr, "Job Perception–Job Satisfaction Relations: An Empirical Comparison of Three Competing Theories," *Organizational Behavior and Human Decision Processes*, December 1993, pp. 370–87; L.H. Pelled and K.R. Xin, "Down and Out: An Investigation of the Relationship Between Mood and Employee Withdrawal Behavior," *Journal of Management*, 25, No. 6 (1999), pp. 875–95; and R.W. Griffeth, P.W. Hom, and S. Gaertner, "A Meta-Analysis of Antecedents and Correlates of Employee Turnover: Update, Moderator Tests, and Research Implications for the Next Millennium," *Journal of Management*, 26, No. 3 (2000), pp. 463–88. In the area of job involvement, see I.M. Paullay, G.M. Alliger, and E.F. Stone-Romero, "Construct Validation of Two Instruments Designed to Measure Job Involvement and Work Centrality," *Journal of Applied Psychology*, April 1994, pp. 224–28. In the area of organizational commitment, see D.M. Randall, "Cross-Cultural Research on Organizational Commitment: A Review and Application of Hofstede's Value Survey Module," *Journal of Business Research*, January 1993, pp. 91–110; R.J. Vandenberg and R.M. Self, "Assessing Newcomers' Changing

Commitments to the Organization During the First Six Months of Work," *Journal of Applied Psychology*, August 1993, pp. 557–68; A. Cohen, "Organizational Commitment and Turnover: A Meta-Analysis," *Academy of Management Journal*, October 1993, pp. 1140–57; and M. Clugston, J.P. Howell, and P.W. Dorfman, "Does Cultural Socialization Predict Multiple Bases and Foci of Commitment?" *Journal of Management*, vol. 26, no. 1 (2000), pp. 5–30. In the area of organizational citizenship behavior, see, for example, P.M. Podsakoff, S.C. Mackenzie, J.B. Paine, and D.G. Bachrach, "Organizational Citizenship Behaviors: A Critical Review of the Theoretical and Empirical Literature and Suggestions for Future Research," *Journal of Management*, 26, No. 3 (2000), pp. 513–63.

6. I. Ajzen and M. Fishbein, *Understanding Attitudes and Predicting Behavior* (Upper Saddle River, NJ: Prentice Hall, 1980); and A.J. Elliott and P.G. Devine, "On the Motivational Nature of Cognitive Dissonance: Dissonance as Psychological Discomfort," *Journal of Personality and Social Psychology*, September 1994, pp. 382–94.

7. L. Festinger, *A Theory of Cognitive Dissonance* (Stanford, CA: Stanford University Press, 1957).

8. "Trident's Employee Satisfaction Survey," *Workforce Online* (www.workforce.com), August 9, 2000.

9. V.H. Vroom, *Work and Motivation* (New York: John Wiley, 1964); M.T. Iaffaldano and P.M. Muchinsky, "Job Satisfaction and Job Performance: A Meta-Analysis," *Psychological Bulletin*, March 1985, pp. 251–73; and C. Ostroff, "The Relationship between Satisfaction, Attitudes, and Performance: An Organizational Level Analysis," *Journal of Applied Psychology*, December 1992, pp. 963–74.

10. See, for example, J.B. Herman, "Are Situational Contingencies Limiting the Job Attitude–Job Performance Relationship?" *Organizational Behavior and Human Performance*, October 1973, pp. 208–24; and M.M. Petty, G.W. McGee, and J.W. Cavender, "A Meta-Analysis of the Relationship between Individual Job Satisfaction and Individual Performance," *Academy of Management Review*, October 1984, pp. 712–21.

11. C.N. Greene, "The Satisfaction-Performance Controversy," *Business Horizons*, February 1972, pp. 31–41; E.E. Lawler III, *Motivation and Organizations* (Monterey, CA: Brooks/Cole, 1973); Petty, McGee, and Cavender, "A Meta-Analysis of the Relationship between Individual Job Satisfaction and Individual Performance"; B.M. Staw and S.G. Barsade, "Affect and Managerial Performance: A Test of the Sadder-but-Wiser vs. Happier-and-Smarter Hypotheses," *Administrative Science Quarterly*, June 1993, pp. 304–28; and S.P. Brown and R.A. Peterson, "The Effect of Effort on Sales Performance and Job Satisfaction," *Journal of Marketing*, April 1994, pp. 70–80.

12. See, for example, E.A. Locke, "The Nature and Causes of Job Satisfaction," in M.D. Dunnette (ed.), *Handbook of Industrial and Organizational Psychology* (Chicago: Rand McNally, 1976), pp. 1297–1350; P.W. Hom, R. Katerberg Jr., and C.L. Hulin, "Comparative Examination of Three Approaches to the Prediction of Turnover," *Journal of Applied Psychology*, June 1979, pp. 280–90; R.P. Tett and J.P. Meyer, "Job Satisfaction, Organizational Commitment, Turnover Intention, and Turnover: Path Analyses Based on Meta-Analytic Findings," *Personnel Psychology*, Summer 1993, pp. 259–93; T.A. Judge, "Does Affective Disposition Moderate the Relationship between Job Satisfaction and Voluntary Turnover?" *Journal of Applied Psychology*, June 1993, pp. 395–401; S.S. Kohler and J.E. Mathieu, "Individual Characteristics, Work Perceptions, and Affective Reactions Influences on Differentiated Absence Criteria," *Journal of Organizational Behavior*, November 1993, pp. 515–30; J.R. Rentsch, "Influence of Cumulation Strategies on the Long-Range Prediction of Absenteeism," *Academy of Management Journal*, December 1995, pp. 1616–34; T.A. Judge and J.J. Martocchio, "Dispositional Influences on Attributions Concerning Absenteeism," *Journal of Management*, 22, No. 6 (1996), pp. 837–61; Clugston, Howell, and Dorfman, "Does Cultural Socialization Predict Multiple Bases and Foci of Commitment?"; and Griffeth, Hom, and Gaertner, "A Meta-Analysis of Antecedents and Correlates of Employee Turnover: Update, Moderator Tests, and Research Implications for the Next Milliennium."

13. See, for example, A.P. Brief, *Attitudes in and Around Organizations* (Thousand Oaks, CA: Sage, 1998), pp. 44–45; P.E. Spector, *Job Satisfaction: Application, Assessment, Causes, and Consequences* (Thousand Oaks, CA: Sage, 1997), p. 3; M.A. Konovsky and D.W. Organ, "Dispositional and Contextual Determinants of Organizational Citizenship Behavior," *Journal of Organizational Behavior*, May 1996, pp. 253–66; D.W. Organ and K. Ryan, "A Meta-Analytic Review of Attitudinal and Dispositional Predictors of Organizational Citizenship Behaviors," *Personnel Psychology*, Winter 1995, p. 791; R.H. Moorman, "Relationship Between Organization Justice and Organizational Citizenship Behaviors: Do Fairness Perceptions Influence Employee Citizenship?" *Journal of Applied Psychology*, December 1991, pp. 845–55; J. Fahr, P.M. Podsakoff, and D.W. Organ, "Accounting for Organizational Citizenship Behavior: Leader Fairness and Task Scope Versus Satisfaction," *Journal of Management*, December 1990, pp. 705–22; T.S. Bateman and D.W. Organ, "Job Satisfaction and the Good Soldier: The Relationship Between Affect and Employee 'Citizenship,'" *Academy of Management Journal*, December 1983, pp. 587–95; and C.A. Smith, D.W. Organ, and J.P. Near, "Organizational Citizenship Behavior: Its Nature and Antecedents," *Journal of Applied Psychology*, October 1983, pp. 653–63.

14. I. Briggs-Myers, *Introduction to Type* (Palo Alto, CA: Consulting Psychologists Press, 1980); C.K. Coe, "The MBTI: Potential Uses and Misuses in Personnel Administration," *Public Personnel Management*, Winter 1992, pp. 511–22; J. Austin Davey, B.H. Schell, and K. Morrison, "The Myers-Briggs Personality Indicator and Its Usefulness for Problem Solving by Mining Industry Personnel," *Group & Organization Management*, March 1993, pp. 50–65; and W.L. Gardner and M.J. Martinko, "Using the Myers-Briggs Type Indicator to Study Managers: A Literature Review and Research Agenda," *Journal of Management*, 22, No. 1 (1996), pp. 45–83.

15. J.M. Digman, "Personality Structure: Emergence of the Five-Factor Model," in M.R. Rosenweig and L.W. Porter (eds.), *Annual Review of Psychology*, vol. 41 (Palo Alto, CA: Annual Review, 1990), pp. 417–40; O.P. John, "The Big Five Factor Taxonomy: Dimensions of Personality in the Natural Language and in Questionnaires," in L.A. Pervin (ed.), *Handbook of Personality Theory and Research* (New York: Guilford Press, 1990), pp. 66–100; M.K. Mount, M.R. Barrick, and J.P. Strauss, "Validity of Observer Ratings of the Big Five Personality Factors," *Journal of Applied Psychology*, April 1996, pp. 272–80; P.J. Howard and J.M. Howard, "Buddy, Can You Paradigm?" *Training and Development Journal*, September 1995, pp. 28–34; and S.E. Seibert and M.L. Kramer, "The Five-Factor Model of Personality and Its Relationship With Career Success," *Academy of Management Proceedings*, 1999, CD-ROM: CAR: A1.

16. M.R. Barrick and M.K. Mount, "Autonomy as a Moderator of the Relationship between the Big Five Personality Dimensions and Job Performance," *Journal of Applied Psychology*, February 1993, pp. 111–18; see also Barrick and Mount, "The Big Five Personality Dimensions and Job Performance: A Meta-Analysis," *Personnel Psychology*, 44 (1991), pp. 1–26.

17. This section is based on D. Goleman, *Emotional Intelligence* (New York: Bantam, 1995); J.D. Mayer and G. Geher, "Emotional Intelligence and the Identification of Emotion," *Intelligence*, March–April 1996, pp. 89–113; J. Stuller, "EQ: Edging Toward Respectability," *Training*, June 1997, pp. 43–48; R.K. Cooper, "Applying Emotional Intelligence in the Workplace," *Training & Development*, December 1997, pp. 31–38; "HR Pulse: Emotional Intelligence," *HRMagazine*, January 1998, p. 19; M. Davies, L. Stankov, and R.D. Roberts, "Emotional Intelligence: In Search of an Elusive Construct," *Journal of Personality and Social Psychology*, October 1998, pp. 989–1015; and D. Goleman, *Working With Emotional Intelligence* (New York: Bantam, 1999).

18. J.B. Rotter, "Generalized Expectancies for Internal versus External Control of Reinforcement," *Psychological Monographs* 80, No. 609 (1966).

19. See, for instance, D.W. Organ and C.N. Greene, "Role Ambiguity, Locus of Control, and Work Satisfaction," *Journal of Applied Psychology*, February 1974, pp. 101–02; and T.R. Mitchell, C.M.

Smyser, and S.E. Weed, "Locus of Control: Supervision and Work Satisfaction," *Academy of Management Journal*, September 1975, pp. 623–31.

20. R.G. Vleeming, "Machiavellianism: A Preliminary Review," *Psychological Reports*, February 1979, pp. 295–310.

21. Based on J. Brockner, *Self-Esteem at Work* (Lexington, MA: Lexington Books, 1988), chapters 1–4.

22. See M. Snyder, *Public Appearances/ Private Realities: The Psychology of Self-Monitoring* (New York: W.H. Freeman, 1987).

23. Snyder, *Public Appearances/Private Realities*; and J.M. Jenkins, "Self-Monitoring and Turnover: The Impact of Personality on Intent to Leave," *Journal of Organizational Behavior*, January 1993, pp. 83–90.

24. N. Kogan and M.A. Wallach, "Group Risk Taking as a Function of Members' Anxiety and Defensiveness," *Journal of Personality*, March 1967, pp. 50–63; and J.M. Howell and C.A. Higgins, "Champions of Technological Innovation," *Administrative Science Quarterly*, June 1990, pp. 317–41.

25. J.L. Holland, *Making Vocational Choices: A Theory of Vocational Personalities and Work Environments*, 2d ed. (Upper Saddle River, NJ: Prentice Hall, 1985).

26. See, for instance, M.J. Martinko (ed.), *Attribution Theory: An Organizational Perspective* (Delray Beach, FL: St. Lucie Press, 1995); and H.H. Kelley, "Attribution in Social Interaction," in E. Jones et al. (eds.), *Attribution: Perceiving the Causes of Behavior* (Morristown, NJ: General Learning Press, 1972).

27. See A.G. Miller and T. Lawson, "The Effect of an Informational Option on the Fundamental Attribution Error," *Personality and Social Psychology Bulletin*, June 1989, pp. 194–204.

28. See, for example, S.T. Fiske, "Social Cognition and Social Perception," *Annual Review of Psychology*, 1993, pp. 155–94; and G.N. Powell and Y. Kido, "Managerial Stereotypes in a Global Economy: A Comparative Study of Japanese and American Business Students' Perspectives," *Psychological Reports*, February 1994, pp. 219–26.

29. B.F. Skinner, *Contingencies of Reinforcement* (East Norwalk, CT: Appleton-Century-Crofts, 1971).

30. Based on R.M. Bramson, *Coping with Difficult People* (Garden City, NY: Anchor Press/Doubleday, 1981); J.D. O'Brian, "De-Clawing the Chronic Complainer," *Supervisory Management*, June 1993, pp. 1–2; R. Cooper, "Dealing Effectively with Difficult People," *Nursing*, September 1993, pp. 97–100; A. Urbaniak, "How to Supervise Problem Employees," *Supervision*, September 1993, pp. 10–13; and K. Mannering, *Managing Difficult People: Proven Strategies to Deal with Awkwardness in Business Situations* (Philadelphia, PA: Trans-Atlantic Publications, Inc., 2000).

CHAPTER 15

1. Company information from Web site [www.strawberryfrog.com], June 12, 2000; and S. Ellison, "Ad Firm Strawberry Frog in Amsterdam Thinks Big but Wants to Stay Small," *Wall Street Journal*, April 3, 2000, pp. A43D+.

2. B.W. Tuckman and M.A.C. Jensen, "Stages of Small-Group Development Revisited," *Group and Organizational Studies* 2, No. 3 (1977), pp. 419–27; and P. Buhler, "Group Membership," *Supervision*, May 1994, pp. 8–10.

3. L.N. Jewell and H.J. Reitz, *Group Effectiveness in Organizations* (Glenview, IL: Scott, Foresman, 1981); and M. Kaeter, "Repotting Mature Work Teams," *Training*, April 1994, pp. 54–56.

4. G. Prince, "Recognizing Genuine Teamwork," *Supervisory Management*, April 1989, pp. 25–36; R.F. Bales, *SYMLOG Case Study Kit* (New York: Free Press, 1980); and K.D. Benne and P. Sheats, "Functional Roles of Group Members," *Journal of Social Issues*, 4 (1948), pp. 41–49.

5. S.E. Asch, "Effects of Group Pressure upon the Modification and Distortion of Judgments," in H. Guetzkow (ed.), *Groups, Leadership and Men* (Pittsburgh: Carnegie Press, 1951), pp. 177–90.

6. See, for instance, E.J. Thomas and C.F. Fink, "Effects of Group Size," *Psychological Bulletin*, July 1963, pp. 371–84; and M.E. Shaw, *Group Dynamics: The Psychology of Small Group Behavior*, 3rd ed. (New York: McGraw-Hill, 1981).

7. See R. Albanese and D.D. Van Fleet, "Rational Behavior in Groups: The Free-Riding Tendency," *Academy of Management Review*, April 1985, pp. 244–55.

8. See, for example, L. Berkowitz, "Group Standards, Cohesiveness, and Productivity," *Human Relations*, November 1954, pp. 509–19; and B. Mullen and C. Copper, "The Relation between Group Cohesiveness and Performance: An Integration," *Psychological Bulletin*, March 1994, pp. 210–27.

9. S.E. Seashore, *Group Cohesiveness in the Industrial Work Group* (Ann Arbor: University of Michigan, Survey Research Center, 1954).

10. This section is adapted from S.P. Robbins, *Managing Organizational Conflict: A Nontraditional Approach* (Upper Saddle River, NJ: Prentice Hall, 1974), pp. 11–14. Also see D. Wagner-Johnson, "Managing Work Team Conflict: Assessment and Preventative Strategies," Center for the Study of Work Teams, University of North Texas (www.workteams.unt.edu/reports/), November 3, 2000; and M. Kennedy, "Managing Conflict in Work Teams," Center for the Study of Work Teams, University of North Texas (www.workteams.unt.edu/reports/), November 3, 2000.

11. See K.A. Jehn, "A Multimethod Examination of the Benefits and Detriments of Intragroup Conflict," *Administrative Science Quarterly*, June 1995, pp. 256–82; K.A. Jehn, "A Qualitative Analysis of Conflict Type and Dimensions in Organizational Groups," *Administrative Science Quarterly*, September 1997, pp. 530–57; and K.A. Jehn, "Affective and Cognitive Conflict in Work Groups: Increasing Performance Through Value-Based Intragroup Conflict," in C. DeDreu and E. Van deVliert (eds.), *Using Conflict in Organizations* (London: Sage Publications, 1997), pp. 87–100.

12. K.W. Thomas, "Conflict and Negotiation Processes in Organizations," in M.D. Dunnette and L.M. Hough (eds.), *Handbook of Industrial and Organizational Psychology*, 2nd ed., Vol. 3 (Palo Alto, CA: Consulting Psychologists Press, 1992), pp. 651–717.

13. J. Grossman, "We've Got to Stop Meeting Like This," *Inc.*, April 1998, pp. 70–74.

14. I.L. Janis, *Victims of Groupthink* (Boston: Houghton Mifflin, 1972); R.J. Aldag and S. Riggs Fuller, "Beyond Fiasco: A Reappraisal of the Groupthink Phenomenon and a New Model of Group Decision Processes," *Psychological Bulletin*, May 1993, pp. 533–52; and T. Kameda and S. Sugimori, "Psychological Entrapment in Group Decision Making: An Assigned Decision Rule and a Groupthink Phenomenon," *Journal of Personality and Social Psychology*, August 1993, pp. 282–92.

15. See, for example, A.L. Delbecq, A.H. Van de Ven, and D.H. Gustafson, *Group Techniques for Program Planning* (Glenview, IL: Scott, Foresman, 1975); L.K. Michaelson, W.E. Watson, and R.H. Black, "A Realistic Test of Individual vs. Group Consensus Decision Making," *Journal of Applied Psychology* 74, No. 5 (1989), pp. 834–39; R.A. Henry, "Group Judgment Accuracy: Reliability and Validity of Postdiscussion Confidence Judgments," *Organizational Behavior and Human Decision Processes*, October 1993, pp. 11–27; P.W. Paese, M. Bieser, and M.E. Tubbs, "Framing Effects and Choice Shifts in Group Decision Making," *Organizational Behavior and Human Decision Processes*, October 1993, pp. 149–65; N.J. Castellan Jr. (ed.), *Individual and Group Decision Making* (Hillsdale, NJ: Lawrence Erlbaum Associates, 1993); D. Gigone and R. Hastie, "The Common Knowledge Effect: Information Sharing and Group Judgment," *Journal of Personality and Social Psychology*, November 1993, pp. 959–74; and S.G. Straus and J.E. McGrath, "Does the Medium Matter? The Interaction of Task Type and Technology on Group Performance and Member Reactions," *Journal of Applied Psychology*, February 1994, pp. 87–97.

16. F.A. Shull, A.L. Delbecq, and L.L. Cummings, *Organizational Decision Making* (New York: McGraw-Hill, 1970), p. 151.

17. This model is substantially based on the work of P.S. Goodman, E. Ravlin, and M. Schminke, "Understanding Groups in Organizations," in L.L. Cummings and B.M. Staw (eds.), *Research in Organizational Behavior*, vol. 9 (Greenwich, CT: JAI Press, 1987), pp. 124–28; and J.R. Hackman, "The Design of Work Teams," in J.W. Lorsch (ed.), *Handbook of Organizational Behavior* (Upper Saddle River, NJ: Prentice Hall, 1987), pp. 315–42.

18. F. Friedlander, "The Ecology of Work Groups," in Lorsch (ed.), *Handbook of Organizational Behavior*, pp. 301–14.

19. V.U. Druskat and S.B. Wolff, "The Link Between Emotions and Team Effectiveness: How Teams Engage Members and Build Effective Task Processes," *Academy of Management Proceedings*, on CD-Rom, 1999; and M.E. Shaw, *Contemporary Topics in Social Psychology* (Morristown, NJ: General Learning Press, 1976), pp. 350–51.

20. C.G. Andrews, "Factors That Impact Multi-Cultural Team Performance," Center for the Study of Work Teams, University of North Texas (www.workteams.unt.edu/reports/), November 3, 2000; P.C. Earley and E. Mosakowski, "Creating Hybrid Team Cultures: An Empirical Test of Transnational Team Functioning," *Academy of Management Journal*, February 2000, pp. 26–49; J. Tata, "The Cultural Context of Teams: An Integrative Model of National Culture, Work Team Characteristics, and Team Effectiveness," *Academy of Management Proceedings*, on CD-ROM, 1999; D.I. Jung, K.B. Baik, and J.J. Sosik, "A Longitudinal Investigation of Group Characteristics and Work Group Performance: A Cross-Cultural Comparison," *Academy of Management Proceedings*, on CD-ROM, 1999; and C.B. Gibson, "They Do What They Believe They Can? Group-Efficacy Beliefs and Group Performance Across Tasks and Cultures," *Academy of Management Proceedings* on CD-ROM, 1996.

21. Based on L. Copeland, "Making the Most of Cultural Differences at the Workplace," *Personnel*, June 1988, pp. 52–60; C.R. Bantz, "Cultural Diversity and Group Cross-Cultural Team Research," *Journal of Applied Communication Research*, February 1993, pp. 1–19; L. Strach and L. Wicander, "Fitting In: Issues of Tokenism and Conformity for Minority Women," *SAM Advanced Management Journal*, Summer 1993, pp. 22–25; M.L. Maznevski, "Understanding Our Differences: Performance in Decision-Making Groups with Diverse Members," *Human Relations*, May 1994, pp. 531–52; and F. Rice, "How to Make Diversity Pay," *Fortune*, August 8, 1994, pp. 78–86.

22. See, for example, J.R. Hackman and C.G. Morris, "Group Tasks, Group Interaction Process, and Group Performance Effectiveness: A Review and Proposed Integration," in L. Berkowitz (ed.), *Advances in Experimental Social Psychology* (New York: Academic Press, 1975), pp. 45–99; and M.J. Waller, "Multiple-Task Performance in Groups," *Academy of Management Proceedings* on disk, 1996.

23. M. Beyerlein and C. Harris, "Introduction to Work Teams," presentation at 9th Annual International Conference on Work Teams, 1998.

24. B. Dumaine, "The Trouble with Teams," *Fortune*, September 5, 1994, p. 86.

25. Based on C.E. Larson and F.M.J. LaFasto, *TeamWork* (Newbury Park, CA: Sage Publications, 1989); and E. Sundstrom, K.P. DeMeuse, and D. Futrell, "Work Teams," *American Psychologist*, February 1990, p. 120.

26. C. Rance, "Doing the Team Thing," *The Age*, November 28, 1998, pp. E1–2.

27. See, for example, G.M. Parker, *Cross-Functional Teams* (San Francisco: Jossey-Bass, 1994), pp. 35–39; M.E. Warkentin, L. Sayeed, and R. Hightower, "Virtual Teams Versus Face-to-Face Teams: An Exploratory Study of a Web-Based Conference System," *Decision Sciences*, Fall 1997, pp. 975–93; A.M. Townsend, S.M. DeMarie, and A.R. Hendrickson, "Virtual Teams: Technology and the Workplace of the Future," *Academy of Management Executive*, August 1998, pp. 17–29; and D. Duarte and N.T. Snyder, *Mastering Virtual Teams: Strategies, Tools, and Techniques* (San Francisco: Jossey-Bass, 1999).

28. C. Joinson, "Teams at Work," *HRMagazine*, May 1999, pp. 30–36.

29. M. Cianni and D. Wanuck, "Individual Growth and Team Enhancement: Moving Toward a New Model of Career Development," *Academy of Management Executive*, February 1997, pp. 105–15.

30. G.M. Spreitzer, S.G. Cohen, and G.E. Ledford, Jr., "Developing Effective Self-Managing Work Teams in Service Organizations," *Group & Organization Management*, September 1999, pp. 340–66.

31. G. Imperato, "Real Tools for Virtual Teams" *Fast Company*, July 2000, pp. 378–87.

32. L. Grant, "New Jewel in the Crown," *U.S. News & World Report*, February 28, 1994, p. 56.

33. S. Sherman, "Secrets of HP's 'Muddled' Team," *Fortune*, March 18, 1996, pp. 116–20.

34. See Sundstrom, DeMeuse, and Futrell, "Work Teams"; Larson and LaFasto, *TeamWork*; J.R. Hackman (ed.), *Groups That Work (and Those That Don't)* (San Francisco: Jossey-Bass, 1990); D.W. Tjosvold and M.M. Tjosvold, *Leading the Team Organization* (New York: Lexington Books, 1991); G.R. Jones and G.M. George, "The Experience and Evolution of Trust: Implications for Cooperation and Teamwork," *Academy of Management Review*, July 1998, pp. 531–46; A.R. Jassawalla and H.C. Sashittal, "Building Collaborative Cross-Functional New Product Teams," *Academy of Management Executive*, August 1999, pp. 50–63; R. Forrester and A.B. Drexler, "A Model for Team-Based Organization Performance," *Academy of Management Executive*, August 1999, pp. 36–49; V.U. Druskat and S.B. Wolff, "The Link Between Emotions and Team Effectiveness: How Teams Engage Members and Build Effective Task Processes"; M. Mattson, T. Mumford, and G.S. Sintay, "Taking Teams to Task: A Normative Model for Designing or Recalibrating Work Teams," *Academy of Management Proceedings*, on CD-ROM, 1999; J.D. Shaw, M.K. Duffy, and E.M. Stark, "Interdependence and Preference for Group Work: Main and Congruence Effects on the Satisfaction and Performance of Group Members," *Journal of Management*, 26, No. 2 (2000), pp. 259–79; and G.L. Stewart and M.R. Barrick, "Team Structure and Performance: Assessing the Mediating Role of Intrateam Process and the Moderating Role of Task Type," *Academy of Management Journal*, April 2000, pp. 135–48.

35. Larson and LaFasto, *TeamWork*, p. 75.

36. S. Allred, "Team Reward Systems," Center for the Study of Work Teams, University of North Texas (www.workteams.unt.edu/reports/), November 3, 2000; T.R. Zenger and C.R. Marshall, "Determinants of Incentive Intensity in Group-Based Rewards," *Academy of Management Journal*, April 2000, pp. 149–63; B.L. Kirkman and B. Rosen, "Powering Up Teams," *Organizational Dynamics*, Winter 2000, pp. 48–65; and R. Cacioppe, "Using Team-Individual Reward and Recognition Strategies to Drive Organizational Success," *Leadership & Organization Development Journal*, 20, issue 6/7 (1999), pp. 322–31.

37. P.E. Brauchle and D.W. Wright, "Fourteen Team Building Tips," *Training &*

Development, January 1992, pp. 32–34; R.S. Wellins, "Building a Self-Directed Work Team," *Training & Development*, December 1992, pp. 24–28; S.T. Johnson, "Work Teams: What's Ahead in Work Design and Rewards Management," *Compensation and Benefits Review*, March–April 1993, pp. 35–41; V.A. Hoevemeyer, "How Effective Is Your Team?" *Training & Development*, September 1993, pp. 67–71; S.G. Cohen and G.E. Ledford Jr., "The Effectiveness of Self-Managing Teams: A Quasi-Experiment," *Human Relations*, January 1994, pp. 13–43; and J. Panepinto, "Maximize Teamwork," *Computerworld*, March 21, 1994, p. 119.

38. D.M. Enlen, "Team Goals: Aligning Groups and Management," *Canadian Manager*, Winter 1993, pp. 17–18; and A.M. O'Leary, J.J. Martocchio, and D.D. Frink, "A Review of the Influence of Group Goals on Group Performance," *Academy of Management Journal*, October 1994, pp. 1285–1301.

39. C. Meyer, "How the Right Measures Help Teams Excel," *Harvard Business Review*, May–June 1994, pp. 95–103; D.E. Yeatts and C. Hyten, *High-Performing Self-Managed Work Teams: A Comparison of Theory and Practice* (Thousand Oaks, CA: Sage, 1998); R. Cacioppe, "Using Team-Individual Reward and Recognition Strategies to Drive Organizational Success"; T.R. Zenger and C.R. Marshall, "Determinants of Incentive Intensity in Group-Based Rewards"; and S. Allred, "Team Reward Systems."

40. T.A. Stewart, "The Great Conundrum—You vs. the Team," *Fortune*, November 25, 1996, pp. 165–66.

41. B. Geber, "The Bugaboo of Team Pay," *Training*, August 1995, pp. 27 and 34.

42. P.K. Zingheim and J.R. Schuster, "The Team Pay Research Study," *Compensation & Benefits Review*, November–December 1995, pp. 6–10; G. Flynn, "Teams Won't Push for More Pay," *Personnel Journal*, January 1996, p. 26; J.H. Sheridan, "'Yes' to Team Incentives," *IW*, March 4, 1996, pp. 63–64; V. Frazee, "Recognize Team Success," *Personnel Journal*, September 1996, p. 27; and B. Nelson, "Does One Reward Fit All?" *Workforce*, February 1997, pp. 67–76.

CHAPTER 16

1. C. Dahle, "The New Fabric of Success," *Fast Company*, June 2000, pp. 252–70.

2. R. Katerberg and G.J. Blau, "An Examination of Level and Direction of Effort and Job Performance," *Academy of Management Journal*, June 1983, pp. 249–57.

3. A. Maslow, *Motivation and Personality* (New York: McGraw-Hill, 1954); A. Maslow, D.C. Stephens, and G. Heil, *Maslow on Management* (New York: John Wiley & Sons, 1998); M.L. Ambrose and C.T. Kulik, "Old Friends, New Faces: Motivation Research in the 1990s," *Journal of Management*, 25, No. 3 (1999), pp. 231–92; and "Dialogue," *Academy of Management Review*, October 2000, pp. 696–701.

4. See, for example, D.T. Hall and K.E. Nongaim, "An Examination of Maslow's Need Hierarchy in an Organizational Setting," *Organizational Behavior and Human Performance*, February 1968, pp. 12–35; E.E. Lawler III and J.L. Suttle, "A Causal Correlational Test of the Need Hierarchy Concept," *Organizational Behavior and Human Performance*, April 1972, pp. 265–87; R.M. Creech, "Employee Motivation," *Management Quarterly*, Summer 1995, pp. 33–39; J. Rowan, "Maslow Amended," *Journal of Humanistic Psychology*, Winter 1998, pp. 81–92; J. Rowan, "Ascent and Descent in Maslow's Theory," *Journal of Humanistic Psychology*, Summer 1999, pp. 125–33; and Ambrose and Kulik, "Old Friends, New Faces."

5. D. McGregor, *The Human Side of Enterprise* (New York: McGraw-Hill, 1960).

6. F. Herzberg, B. Mausner, and B. Snyderman, *The Motivation to Work* (New York: John Wiley, 1959); F. Herzberg, *The Managerial Choice: To Be Effective or to Be Human*, rev. ed. (Salt Lake City: Olympus, 1982); Creech, "Employee Motivation"; and Ambrose and Kulik, "Old Friends, New Faces."

7. Ambrose and Kulik, "Old Friends, New Faces."

8. D.C. McClelland, *The Achieving Society* (New York: Van Nostrand Reinhold, 1961); J.W. Atkinson and J.O. Raynor, *Motivation and Achievement* (Washington, DC: Winston, 1974); and D.C. McClelland, *Power: The Inner Experience* (New York: Irvington, 1975).

9. McClelland, *The Achieving Society*.

10. McClelland, *Power*; D.C. McClelland and D.H. Burnham, "Power Is the Great Motivator," *Harvard Business Review*, March–April 1976, pp. 100–10.

11. D. Miron and D.C. McClelland, "The Impact of Achievement Motivation Training on Small Businesses," *California Management Review*, Summer 1979, pp. 13–28.

12. "McClelland: An Advocate of Power," *International Management*, July 1975, pp. 27–29.

13. Ambrose and Kulik, "Old Friends, New Faces."

14. J.C. Naylor and D.R. Ilgen, "Goal Setting: A Theoretical Analysis of a Motivational Technique," in B.M. Staw and L.L. Cummings (eds.), *Research in Organizational Behavior*, vol. 6 (Greenwich, CT: JAI Press, 1984), pp. 95–140; A.R. Pell, "Energize Your People," *Managers Magazine*, December 1992, pp. 28–29; E.A. Locke, "Facts and Fallacies about Goal Theory: Reply to Deci," *Psychological Science*, January 1993, pp. 63–64; M.E. Tubbs, "Commitment as a Moderator of the Goal-Performance Relation: A Case for Clearer Construct Definition," *Journal of Applied Psychology*, February 1993, pp. 86–97; M.P. Collingwood, "Why Don't You Use the Research?" *Management Decision*, May 1993, pp. 48–54; M.E. Tubbs, D.M. Boehne, and J.S. Dahl, "Expectancy, Valence, and Motivational Force Functions in Goal-Setting Research: An Empirical Test," *Journal of Applied Psychology*, June 1993, pp. 361–73; and Ambrose and Kulik, "Old Friends, New Faces."

15. J.B. Miner, *Theories of Organizational Behavior* (Hinsdale, IL: Dryden Press, 1980), p. 65.

16. J.A. Wagner III, "Participation's Effects on Performance and Satisfaction: A Reconsideration of Research and Evidence," *Academy of Management Review*, April 1994, pp. 312–30; and J. George-Falvey, "Effects of Task Complexity and Learning Stage on the Relationship between Participation in Goal Setting and Task Performance," *Academy of Management Proceedings on Disk*, 1996.

17. J.M. Ivancevich and J.T. McMahon, "The Effects of Goal Setting, External Feedback, and Self-Generated Feedback on Outcome Variables: A Field Experiment," *Academy of Management Journal*, June 1982, pp. 359–72.

18. J.R. Hollenbeck, C.R. Williams, and H.J. Klein, "An Empirical Examination of the Antecedents of Commitment to Difficult Goals," *Journal of Applied Psychology*, February 1989, pp. 18–23; see also J.C. Wofford, V.L. Goodwin, and S. Premack, "Meta-Analysis of the Antecedents of Personal Goal Level and of the Antecedents and Consequences of Goal Commitment," *Journal of Management*, September 1992, pp. 595–615; and Tubbs, "Commitment as a Moderator of the Goal-Performance Relation."

19. A. Bandura, "Self-Efficacy: Toward a Unifying Theory of Behavioral Change," *Psychological Review*, May 1977, pp. 191–215; and M.E. Gist, "Self-Efficacy: Implications for Organizational Behavior and Human Resource Management," *Academy of Management Review*, July 1987, pp. 472–85.

20. E.A. Locke, E. Frederick, C. Lee, and P. Bobko, "Effect of Self-Efficacy, Goals, and Task Strategies on Task Performance," *Journal of Applied Psychology*, May 1984, pp. 241–51; and M.E. Gist and T.R. Mitchell, "Self-Efficacy: A Theoretical Analysis of Its Determinants and Malleability," *Academy of Management Review*, April 1992, pp. 183–211.

21. A. Bandura and D. Cervone, "Differential Engagement in Self-Reactive Influences in Cognitively-Based Motivation," *Organizational Behavior and Human Decision Processes*, August 1986, pp. 92–113.

22. See J.C. Anderson and C.A. O'Reilly, "Effects of an Organizational Control System on Managerial Satisfaction and Performance," *Human Relations*, June 1981, pp. 491–501; and J.P. Meyer, B. Schacht-Cole, and I.R. Gellatly, "An Examination of the Cognitive Mechanisms by Which Assigned Goals Affect Task Performance and Reactions to Performance," *Journal of Applied Social Psychology* 18, No. 5 (1988), pp. 390–408.

23. B.F. Skinner, *Science and Human Behavior* (New York: Free Press, 1953); and Skinner, *Beyond Freedom and Dignity* (New York: Knopf, 1972).

24. This box based on R. McNatt, "The Young and the Restless," *Business Week*, May 22, 2000, p. 12; "On the Job," *Wall Street Journal*, April 11, 2000, p. B18; P. Kruger, "Does Your Job Work?" *Fast Company*, November 1999, pp. 181–96; and M.A. Verespej, "What Each Generation Wants," *IW*, October 18, 1999, pp. 14–15.

25. The same data, for instance, can be interpreted in either goal-setting or reinforcement terms, as shown in E.A. Locke, "Latham vs. Komaki: A Tale of Two Paradigms," *Journal of Applied Psychology*, February 1980, pp. 16–23. Also see Ambrose and Kulik, "Old Friends, New Faces."

26. See, for example, R.W. Griffin, "Toward an Integrated Theory of Task Design," in L.L. Cummings and B.M. Staw (eds.), *Research in Organizational Behavior*, vol. 9 (Greenwich, CT: JAI Press, 1987), pp. 79–120; and M. Campion, "Interdisciplinary Approaches to Job Design: A Constructive Replication with Extensions," *Journal of Applied Psychology*, August 1988, pp. 467–81.

27. S. Caudron, "The De-Jobbing of America," *Industry Week*, September 5, 1994, pp. 31–36; W. Bridges, "The End of the Job," *Fortune*, September 19, 1994, pp. 62–74; and K.H. Hammonds, K. Kelly, and K. Thurston, "Rethinking Work," *Business Week*, October 12, 1994, pp. 75–87.

28. M.A. Campion and C.L. McClelland, "Follow-Up and Extension of the Interdisciplinary Costs and Benefits of Enlarged Jobs," *Journal of Applied Psychology*, June 1993, pp. 339–51; and Ambrose and Kulik, "Old Friends, New Faces."

29. See, for example, J.R. Hackman and G.R. Oldham, *Work Redesign* (Reading, MA: Addison-Wesley, 1980); and Miner, *Theories of Organizational Behavior*, pp. 231–66; and Ambrose and Kulik, "Old Friends, New Faces."

30. J.R. Hackman and G.R. Oldham, "Development of the Job Diagnostic Survey," *Journal of Applied Psychology*, April 1975, pp. 159–70.

31. J.R. Hackman, "Work Design," in J.R. Hackman and J.L. Suttle (eds.), *Improving Life at Work* (Glenview, IL: Scott, Foresman, 1977), p. 129; and Ambrose and Kulik, "Old Friends, New Faces."

32. "Involve Your Customers," *Success*, October 1995, p. 28.

33. Ibid.

34. J.S. Adams, "Inequity in Social Exchanges," in L. Berkowitz (ed.), *Advances in Experimental Social Psychology*, vol. 2 (New York: Academic Press, 1965), pp. 267–300; and Ambrose and Kulik, "Old Friends, New Faces."

35. P.S. Goodman and A. Friedman, "An Examination of Adams' Theory of Inequity," *Administrative Science Quarterly*, September 1971, pp. 271–88.

36. See, for example, M.R. Carrell, "A Longitudinal Field Assessment of Employee Perceptions of Equitable Treatment," *Organizational Behavior and Human Performance*, February 1978, pp. 108–18; R.G. Lord and J.A. Hohenfeld, "Longitudinal Field Assessment of Equity Effects on the Performance of Major League Baseball Players," *Journal of Applied Psychology*, February 1979, pp. 19–26; and J.E. Dittrich and M.R. Carrell, "Organizational Equity Perceptions, Employee Job Satisfaction, and Departmental Absence and Turnover Rates," *Organizational Behavior and Human Performance*, August 1979, pp. 29–40.

37. P.S. Goodman, "An Examination of Referents Used in the Evaluation of Pay," *Organizational Behavior and Human Performance*, October 1974, pp. 170–95; S. Ronen, "Equity Perception in Multiple Comparisons: A Field Study," *Human Relations*, April 1986, pp. 333–46; R.W. Scholl, E.A. Cooper, and J.F. McKenna, "Referent Selection in Determining Equity Perception: Differential Effects on Behavioral and Attitudinal Outcomes," *Personnel Psychology*, Spring 1987, pp. 113–27; and C.T. Kulik and M.L. Ambrose, "Personal and Situational Determinants of Referent Choice," *Academy of Management Review*, April 1992, pp. 212–37.

38. P.S. Goodman, "Social Comparison Process in Organizations," in B.M. Staw and G.R. Salancik (eds.), *New Directions in Organizational Behavior* (Chicago: St. Clair, 1977), pp. 97–132.

39. V.H. Vroom, *Work and Motivation* (New York: John Wiley, 1964).

40. See, for example, H.G. Heneman III and D.P. Schwab, "Evaluation of Research on Expectancy Theory Prediction of Employee Performance," *Psychological Bulletin*, July 1972, pp. 1–9;

and L. Reinharth and M. Wahba, "Expectancy Theory as a Predictor of Work Motivation, Effort Expenditure, and Job Performance," *Academy of Management Journal*, September 1975, pp. 502–37.

41. See, for example, V.H. Vroom, "Organizational Choice: A Study of Pre- and Postdecision Processes," *Organizational Behavior and Human Performance*, April 1966, pp. 212–25; L.W. Porter and E.E. Lawler III, *Managerial Attitudes and Performance* (Homewood, IL: Richard D. Irwin, 1968); and Ambrose and Kulik, "Old Friends, New Faces."

42. This four-step discussion was adapted from K.F. Taylor, "A Valence-Expectancy Approach to Work Motivation," *Personnel Practice Bulletin*, June 1974, pp. 142–48.

43. See, for instance, M. Siegall, "The Simplistic Five: An Integrative Framework for Teaching Motivation," *The Organizational Behavior Teaching Review* 12, No. 4 (1987–88), pp. 141–43.

44. J.R. Billings and D.L. Sharpe, "Factors Influencing Flextime Usage Among Employed Married Women," *Consumer Interests Annual* (1999), pp. 89–94; and I. Harpaz, "The Importance of Work Goals: An International Perspective," *Journal of International Business Studies*, First Quarter 1990, pp. 75–93.

45. L.B. Ward, "If It's Friday, This Might Be Your Flex-Time Day Off," *New York Times*, March 31, 1996, p. F11.

46. "Health Club Membership, Flextime Are Most Desired Perks," *Business West*, September 1999, p. 75.

47. Hewitt Associates, "Survey of Work/Life Benefits and Work/Life Scheduling," *Employee Benefit Plan Review*, July 2000, p. 5.

48. This box based on S.N. Mehta, "What Minority Employees Really Want," *Fortune*, July 10, 2000, pp. 180–86; K.H. Hammonds, "Difference Is Power," *Fast Company*, July 2000, pp. 258–66; "Building a Competitive Workforce: Diversity, the Bottom Line," *Forbes*, April 3, 2000, pp. 181–94; and "Diversity: Developing Tomorrow's Leadership Talent Today," *Business Week*, December 20, 1999, pp. 85–100.

49. G. Hofstede, "Motivation, Leadership, and Organizations: Do American Theo-

ries Apply Abroad?" *Organizational Dynamics*, Summer 1980, p. 55; and P.R. Harris and R.T. Moran, *Managing Cultural Differences*, 4th ed. (Houston: Gulf Publishing Company, 1996).

50. Ibid.

51. J.K. Giacobbe-Miller, D.J. Miller, and V.I. Victorov, "A Comparison of Russian and U.S. Pay Allocation Decisions, Distributive Justice Judgments, and Productivity Under Different Payment Conditions," *Personnel Psychology*, Spring 1998, pp. 137–63.

52. S.L. Mueller and L.D. Clarke, "Political-Economic Context and Sensitivity to Equity: Differences Between the United States and the Transition Economies of Central and Eastern Europe," *Academy of Management Journal*, June 1998, pp. 319–29.

53. I. Harpaz, "The Importance of Work Goals: An International Perspective," *Journal of International Business*, First Quarter 1990, pp. 75–93.

54. G.E. Popp, H.J. Davis, and T.T. Herbert, "An International Study of Intrinsic Motivation Composition," *Management International Review*, January 1986, pp. 28–35.

55. R.K. Abbott, "Performance-Based Flex: A Tool for Managing Total Compensation Costs," *Compensation and Benefits Review*, March–April 1993, pp. 18–21; J.R. Schuster and P.K. Zingheim, "The New Variable Pay: Key Design Issues," *Compensation and Benefits Review*, March–April 1993, pp. 27–34; C.R. Williams and L.P. Livingstone, "Another Look at the Relationship between Performance and Voluntary Turnover," *Academy of Management Journal*, April 1994, pp. 269–98; and A.M. Dickinson and K.L. Gillette, "A Comparison of the Effects of Two Individual Monetary Incentive Systems on Productivity: Piece Rate Pay versus Base Pay Plus Incentives," *Journal of Organizational Behavior Management*, Spring 1994, pp. 3–82.

56. "Performance-Based Incentives: Four Approaches," *Business Ethics*, January–February 1997, p. 10.

57. Cited in D.L. McClain, "Tricks for Varying the Pay to Motivate the Ranks," *New York Times*, November 15, 1998, p. BU-5.

58. "More Than 20 Percent of Japanese Firms Use Pay Systems Based on Performance," *Manpower Argus*, May 1998,

p. 7; and "Bonus Pay in Canada," *Manpower Argus*, September 1996, p. 5.

59. H. Rheem, "Performance Management Programs," *Harvard Business Review*, September–October 1996, pp. 8–9; G. Sprinkle, "The Effect of Incentive Contracts on Learning and Performance," *Accounting Review*, July 2000, pp. 299–326; and "Do Incentive Awards Work?" *HRFocus*, October 2000, pp. 1–3.

60. R.D. Banker, S.Y. Lee, G. Potter, and D. Srinivasan, "Contextual Analysis of Performance Impacts on Outcome-Based Incentive Compensation," *Academy of Management Journal*, August 1996, pp. 920–48.

61. J. Case, "The Open-Book Revolution," *Inc.*, June 1995, pp. 26–50; A. Kleiner, "The Open-Book Policy," *WorldBusiness*, September–October 1996, pp. 52–53; and J. Case, "Opening the Books," *Harvard Business Review*, March–April 1997, pp. 118–27.

62. R.C. Yafie, "Pass the 10Q, Partner," *Journal of Business Strategy*, January–February 1996, pp. 53–56; and J.P. Schuster, J. Carpenter, and J.P. Kane, *The Power of Open-Book Management* (New York: John Wiley, 1996).

63. J. Fierman, "Winning Ideas from Maverick Managers," *Fortune*, February 6, 1995, pp. 66–80; and J.A. Byrne, "Management Meccas," *Business Week*, September 18, 1995, pp. 126–28.

64. Ibid.

65. See, for instance, M. Alpert, "The Care and Feeding of Engineers," *Fortune*, September 21, 1992, pp. 86–95; and G. Poole, "How to Manage Your Nerds," *Forbes ASAP*, December 1994, pp. 132–36.

66. This box based on S. Wetlaufer, "Who Wants to Manage a Millionaire?," *Harvard Business Review*, July–August 2000, pp. 53–60; C. Taylor, "Is This the End.Com?" *Time*, July 3, 2000, pp. 43–45; T. Spencer, "Paycheck, Health Benefits, and a Mercedes," *Fortune*, June 26, 2000, p. 336; M. Conlin, "Workers, Surf at Your Own Risk," *Business Week*, June 12, 2000, p. 105; E. McDonald, "Breathing Underwater," *Forbes*, May 15, 2000, p. 188; C. Hymowitz, "Motivating Employees in Volatile Era Means Managing Expectations," *Wall Street Journal*, May 2, 2000, p. B1; E. Ackerman, "Optionaires,

Beware!" *U.S. News & World Report*, March 6, 2000, pp. 36–38; and R. Mitchell, "How to Manage Geeks," *Fast Company*, June 1999, pp. 174–80.

67. G. Fuchsberg, "Parallel Lines," *Wall Street Journal*, April 21, 1993, p. R4; and A. Penzias, "New Paths to Success," *Fortune*, June 12, 1995, pp. 90–94.

68. S.W. Kelley, "Discretion and the Service Employee," *Journal of Retailing*, Spring 1993, pp. 104–26; and S.S. Brooks, "Noncash Ways to Compensate Employees," *HRMagazine*, April 1994, pp. 38–43.

69. C. Yang, A.T. Palmer, S. Browder, and A. Cuneo, "Low-Wage Lessons," *Business Week*, November 11, 1996, pp. 108–16.

70. E.A. Locke, D.B. Feren, V.M. McCaleb, K.N. Shaw, and A.T. Denny, "The Relative Effectiveness of Four Methods of Motivating Employee Performance," in K.D. Duncan, M.M. Gruneberg, and D. Wallis, (eds.), *Changes in Working Life* (London: John Wiley, 1980), pp. 363–83.

CHAPTER 17

1. Information from company's Web site (www.bobrossauto.com), June 12, 2000; and G. Gallop-Goodman, "All in the Family," *Black Enterprise*, June 2000, pp. 159–66.

2. See S.A. Kirkpatrick and E.A. Locke, "Leadership: Do Traits Matter?" *Academy of Management Executive*, May 1991, pp. 48–60.

3. K. Lewin and R. Lippitt, "An Experimental Approach to the Study of Autocracy and Democracy: A Preliminary Note," *Sociometry* 1 (1938), pp. 292–300; Lewin, "Field Theory and Experiment in Social Psychology: Concepts and Methods," *American Journal of Sociology* 44 (1939), pp. 868–96; Lewin, Lippitt, and R.K. White, "Patterns of Aggressive Behavior in Experimentally Created Social Climates," *Journal of Social Psychology* 10 (1939), pp. 271–301; and Lippitt, "An Experimental Study of the Effect of Democratic and Authoritarian Group Atmospheres," *University of Iowa Studies in Child Welfare* 16 (1940), pp. 43–95.

4. B.M. Bass, *Stogdill's Handbook of Leadership* (New York: Free Press, 1981), pp. 289–99.

5. R.M. Stogdill and A.E. Coons (eds.), *Leader Behavior: Its Description and Measurement, Research Monograph No. 88* (Columbus: Ohio State University, Bureau of Business Research, 1951). For an updated literature review of Ohio State research, see S. Kerr, C.A. Schriesheim, C.J. Murphy, and R.M. Stogdill, "Toward a Contingency Theory of Leadership Based upon the Consideration and Initiating Structure Literature," *Organizational Behavior and Human Performance*, August 1974, pp. 62–82; and B.M. Fisher, "Consideration and Initiating Structure and Their Relationships with Leader Effectiveness: A Meta-Analysis," in F. Hoy (ed.), *Proceedings of the 48th Annual Academy of Management Conference*, Anaheim, California, 1988, pp. 201–05.

6. R. Kahn and D. Katz, "Leadership Practices in Relation to Productivity and Morale," in D. Cartwright and A. Zander (eds.), *Group Dynamics: Research and Theory*, 2nd ed. (Elmsford, NY: Row, Paterson, 1960).

7. R.R. Blake and J.S. Mouton, *The Managerial Grid III* (Houston: Gulf Publishing, 1984).

8. L.L. Larson, J.G. Hunt, and R.N. Osborn, "The Great Hi-Hi Leader Behavior Myth: A Lesson from Occam's Razor," *Academy of Management Journal*, December 1976, pp. 628–41; and P.C. Nystrom, "Managers and the Hi-Hi Leader Myth," *Academy of Management Journal*, June 1978, pp. 325–31.

9. F.E. Fiedler, *A Theory of Leadership Effectiveness* (New York: McGraw-Hill, 1967).

10. L.H. Peters, D.D. Hartke, and J.T. Pholmann, "Fiedler's Contingency Theory of Leadership: An Application of the Meta-Analysis Procedures of Schmidt and Hunter," *Psychological Bulletin*, March 1985, pp. 274–85.

11. See E.H. Schein, *Organizational Psychology*, 3rd ed. (Upper Saddle River, NJ: Prentice Hall, 1980), pp. 116–17; and B. Kabanoff, "A Critique of Leader Match and Its Implications for Leadership Research," *Personnel Psychology*, Winter 1981, pp. 749–64.

12. P. Hersey and K. Blanchard, "So You Want to Know Your Leadership Style?" *Training and Development Journal*, February 1974, pp. 1–15; and P. Hersey and K.H. Blanchard, *Management of*

Organizational Behavior: Utilizing Human Resources, 6th ed. (Upper Saddle River, NJ: Prentice Hall, 1993).

13. See, for instance, C.F. Fernandez and R.P. Vecchio, "Situational Leadership Theory Revisited: A Test of an Across-Jobs Perspective," *Leadership Quarterly*, vol. 8, no. 1 (1997), pp. 67–84; and C.L. Graeff, "Evolution of Situational Leadership Theory: A Critical Review," *Leadership Quarterly*, vol. 8, no. 2 (1997), pp. 153–70.

14. V.H. Vroom and P.W. Yetton, *Leadership and Decision-Making* (Pittsburgh: University of Pittsburgh Press, 1973).

15. V.H. Vroom and A.G. Jago, *The New Leadership: Managing Participation in Organizations* (Upper Saddle River, NJ: Prentice Hall, 1988). See especially chapter 8.

16. V.H. Vroom, "Leadership and the Decision-Making Process," *Organizational Dynamics*, vol. 28, no. 4 (2000), pp. 82–94.

17. R.J. House, "A Path-Goal Theory of Leader Effectiveness," *Administrative Science Quarterly*, September 1971, pp. 321–38; House and T.R. Mitchell, "Path-Goal Theory of Leadership," *Journal of Contemporary Business*, Autumn 1974, p. 86; and House, "Retrospective Comment," in L.E. Boone and D.D. Bowen (eds.), *The Great Writings in Management and Organizational Behavior*, 2nd ed. (New York: Random House, 1987), pp. 354–64.

18. J. Indrik, "Path-Goal Theory of Leadership: A Meta-Analysis," paper presented at the National Academy of Management Conference, Chicago, August 1986; R.T. Keller, "A Test of the Path-Goal Theory of Leadership with Need for Clarity as a Moderator in Research and Development Organizations," *Journal of Applied Psychology*, April 1989, pp. 208–12; J.C. Wofford and L.Z. Liska, "Path-Goal Theories of Leadership: A Meta-Analysis," *Journal of Management*, Winter 1993, pp. 857–76; and A. Sagie and M. Koslowsky, "Organizational Attitudes and Behaviors as a Function of Participation in Strategic and Tactical Change Decisions: An Application of Path-Goal Theory," *Journal of Organizational Behavior*, January 1994, pp. 37–47.

19. B.M. Bass, "Leadership: Good, Better, Best," *Organizational Dynamics*, Winter 1985, pp. 26–40; and J. Seltzer and

B.M. Bass, "Transformational Leadership: Beyond Initiation and Consideration," *Journal of Management*, December 1990, pp. 693–703.

20. B.J. Avolio and B.M. Bass, "Transformational Leadership, Charisma, and Beyond." Working paper, School of Management, State University of New York, Binghamton, 1985, p. 14.

21. Cited in B.M. Bass and B.J. Avolio, "Developing Transformational Leadership: 1992 and Beyond," *Journal of European Industrial Training*, January 1990, p. 23.

22. J.J. Hater and B.M. Bass, "Supervisors' Evaluations and Subordinates' Perceptions of Transformational and Transactional Leadership," *Journal of Applied Psychology*, November 1988, pp. 695–702.

23. Bass and Avolio, "Developing Transformational Leadership;" R.T. Keller, "Transformational Leadership and the Performance of Research and Development Project Groups," *Journal of Management*, September 1992, pp. 489–501; J.M. Howell and B.J. Avolio, "Transformational Leadership, Transactional Leadership, Locus of Control, and Support for Innovation: Key Predictors of Consolidated-Business-Unit Performance," *Journal of Applied Psychology*, December 1993, pp. 891–911; and J.P. Schuster, "Transforming Your Leadership Style," *Association Management*, January 1994, pp. 39–43.

24. J.R. Hagerty, "A Free Spirit Energizes Home Depot," *Wall Street Journal*, April 11, 2000, p. B1+.

25. See, for example, R.J. House, "A 1976 Theory of Charismatic Leadership," in J.G. Hunt and L.L. Larson (eds.), *Leadership: The Cutting Edge* (Carbondale: Southern Illinois University Press, 1977), pp. 189–207; W. Bennis, "The 4 Competencies of Leadership," *Training and Development Journal*, August 1984, pp. 15–19; J.A. Conger and R.N. Kanungo, "Behavioral Dimensions of Charismatic Leadership," in J.A. Conger, R.N. Kanungo and Associates, *Charismatic Leadership* (San Francisco: Jossey-Bass, 1988), pp. 78–97; G. Yukl and J.M. Howell, "Organizational and Contextual Influences on the Emergence and Effectiveness of Charismatic Leadership," *Leadership Quarterly*, Summer 1999, pp. 257–83; and J.M. Crant and T.S. Bateman,

"Charismatic Leadership Viewed From Above: The Impact of Proactive Personality," *Journal of Organizational Behavior*, February 2000, pp. 63–75.

26. J.A. Conger and R.N. Kanungo, *Charismatic Leadership in Organizations* (Thousand Oaks, CA: Sage, 1998).

27. R.J. House, J. Woycke, and E.M. Fodor, "Charismatic and Noncharismatic Leaders: Differences in Behavior and Effectiveness," in Conger and Kanungo, *Charismatic Leadership*, pp. 103–04; D.A. Waldman, B.M. Bass, and F.J. Yammarino, "Adding to Contingent-Reward Behavior: The Augmenting Effect of Charismatic Leadership," *Group & Organization Studies*, December 1990, pp. 381–94; S.A. Kirkpatrick and E.A. Locke, "Direct and Indirect Effects of Three Core Charismatic Leadership Components on Performance and Attitudes," *Journal of Applied Psychology*, February 1996, pp. 36–51; J.A. Conger, R.N. Kanungo, and S.T. Menon, "Charismatic Leadership and Follower Outcome Effects," paper presented at the 58th Annual Academy of Management Meetings, San Diego, CA, August 1998; "Charismatic Leaders Spur Results," *Workforce*, March 1999, p. 19; G.P. Shea and C.M. Howell, "Charismatic Leadership and Task Feedback: A Laboratory Study of Their Effects on Self-Efficacy," *Leadership Quarterly*, Fall 1999, pp. 375–96; and R.W. Rowden, "The Relationship Between Charismatic Leadership Behaviors and Organizational Commitment," *Leadership & Organization Development Journal*, January 2000, pp. 30–35.

28. J.A. Conger and R.N. Kanungo, "Training Charismatic Leadership: A Risky and Critical Task," in Conger and Kanungo, *Charismatic Leadership*, pp. 309–23; S. Caudron, "Growing Charisma," *Industry Week*, May 4, 1998, pp. 54–55; and R. Birchfield, "Creating Charismatic Leaders," *Management*, June 2000, pp. 30–31.

29. House, "A 1976 Theory of Charismatic Leadership;" R.J. House and R.N. Aditya, "The Social Scientific Study of Leadership: Quo Vadis?" *Journal of Management*, vol. 23, no. 3, 1997, pp. 316–23; and J.G. Hunt and others, "The Effects of Visionary and Crisis-Responsive Charisma on Followers: An Experimental Examination," *Leadership Quarterly*, Fall 1999, pp. 423–48.

30. This definition is based on M. Sashkin, "The Visionary Leader," in Conger and Kanungo, *Charismatic Leadership*, pp. 124–25; B. Nanus, Visionary Leadership (New York: Free Press, 1992), p. 8; and N.H. Snyder and M. Graves, "Leadership and Vision," *Business Horizons*, January–February 1994, p. 1.

31. Nanus, *Visionary Leadership*, p. 8.

32. Based on Sashkin, "The Visionary Leader," pp. 128–30.

33. S. Caminiti, "What Team Leaders Need to Know," *Fortune*, February 20, 1995, pp. 93–100.

34. Ibid., p. 93.

35. Ibid., p. 100.

36. N. Steckler and N. Fondas, "Building Team Leader Effectiveness: A Diagnostic Tool," *Organizational Dynamics*, Winter 1995, p. 20.

37. R.S. Wellins, W.C. Byham, and G.R. Dixon, *Inside Teams* (San Francisco: Jossey-Bass, 1994), p. 318.

38. Steckler and Fondas, "Building Team Leader Effectiveness," p. 21.

39. See J.R.P. French Jr. and B. Raven, "The Bases of Social Power," in D. Cartwright and A.F. Zander (eds.), *Group Dynamics: Research and Theory* (New York: Harper & Row, 1960), pp. 607–23; P.M. Podsakoff and C.A. Schriesheim, "Field Studies of French and Raven's Bases of Power: Critique, Reanalysis, and Suggestions for Future Research," *Psychological Bulletin*, May 1985, pp. 387–411; R.K. Shukla, "Influence of Power Bases in Organizational Decision Making: A Contingency Model," *Decision Sciences*, July 1982, pp. 450–70; D.E. Frost and A.J. Stahelski, "The Systematic Measurement of French and Raven's Bases of Social Power in Workgroups," *Journal of Applied Social Psychology*, April 1988, pp. 375–89; and T.R. Hinkin and C.A. Schriesheim, "Development and Application of New Scales to Measure the French and Raven (1959) Bases of Social Power," *Journal of Applied Psychology*, August 1989, pp. 561–67.

40. This box based on S.A. Culbert and J.J. McDonough, *The Invisible War: Pursuing Self-Interest at Work* (New York: John Wiley, 1980); J. Pfeffer, *Power in Organizations* (Marshfield, MA: Pitman, 1981); H. Mintzberg, *Power In and Around Organizations* (Upper Saddle River, NJ: Prentice Hall, 1983); and S.P. Robbins

and P.L. Hunsaker, *Training in InterPersonal Skills: TIPS for Managing People at Work*, 2nd ed. (Upper Saddle River, NJ: 1996).

41. M. Thompson, "Aye, Aye, Ma'am," *Time*, March 27, 2000, pp. 30–34.

42. J.M. Kouzes and B.Z. Posner, Credibility: *How Leaders Gain and Lose It, and Why People Demand It* (San Francisco: Jossey-Bass, 1993), p. 14.

43. Based on L.T. Hosmer, "Trust: The Connecting Link between Organizational Theory and Philosophical Ethics," *Academy of Management Review*, April 1995, p. 393; R.C. Mayer, J.H. Davis, and F.D. Schoorman, "An Integrative Model of Organizational Trust," *Academy of Management Review*, July 1995, p. 712; and G.M. Spreitzer and A.K. Mishra, "Giving Up Control Without Losing Control," *Group & Organization Management*, June 1999, pp. 155–87.

44. P.L. Schindler and C.C. Thomas, "The Structure of Interpersonal Trust in the Workplace," *Psychological Reports*, October 1993, pp. 563–73.

45. See Kouzes and Posner, *Credibility*, pp. 278–83.

46. This section is based on F. Bartolome, "Nobody Trusts the Boss Completely—Now What?" *Harvard Business Review*, March–April 1989, pp. 135–42; and J.K. Butler Jr., "Toward Understanding and Measuring Conditions of Trust: Evolution of a Conditions of Trust Inventory," *Journal of Management*, September 1991, pp. 643–63.

47. W.A. Randolph, "Navigating the Journey to Empowerment," *Organizational Dynamics*, Spring 1995, pp. 19–32; R. Hanson, R.I. Porterfield, and K. Ames, "Employee Empowerment at Risk: Effects of Recent NLRB Rulings," *Academy of Management Executive*, April 1995, pp. 45–56; R.C. Ford and M.D. Fottler, "Empowerment: A Matter of Degree," *Academy of Management Executive*, August 1995, pp. 21–31; J.S. McClenahen, "Empowerment's Downside," *IW*, September 18, 1995, pp. 57–58; D. Brady, "An Executive Whose Time Has Gone," *Business Week*, August 21, 2000, p. 125; and C. Robert and T.M. Probst, "Empowerment and Continuous Improvement in the United States, Mexico, Poland, and India," *Journal of Applied Psychology*, October 2000, pp. 643–58.

48. H. Stock, "Processor Pampers Employees to Keep Them Happy and in the Fold," *American Banker*, May 11, 2000, p. 12.

49. See, for instance, M. Billard, "Do Women Make Better Managers?" *Working Woman*, March 1992, pp. 68–71, 106–07; and S.H. Applebaum and B.T. Shapiro, "Why Can't Men Lead Like Women?" *Leadership & Organization Development Journal*, December 1993, pp. 28–34.

50. See J. Grant, "Women as Managers: What They Can Offer to Organizations," *Organizational Dynamics*, Winter 1988, pp. 56–63; S. Helgesen, *The Female Advantage: Women's Ways of Leadership* (New York: Doubleday, 1990); A.H. Eagly and B.T. Johnson, "Gender and Leadership Style: A Meta-Analysis," *Psychological Bulletin*, September 1990, pp. 233–56; J.B. Rosener, "Ways Women Lead," *Harvard Business Review*, November-December 1990, pp. 119–25; "Debate: Ways Men and Women Lead," *Harvard Business Review*, January–February 1991, pp. 150–60; A.H. Eagly, S.J. Karau, and B.T. Johnson, "Gender and Leadership Style among School Principals: A Meta-Analysis," *Educational Administration Quarterly*, February 1992, pp. 76–102; H. Collingwood, "Women as Managers: Not Just Different—Better," *Working Woman*, November 1995, p. 14; B.S. Moskal, "Women Make Better Managers," *IW*, February 3, 1997, pp. 17–19; F.J. Yammarino, A.J. Dubinsky, L.B. Comer, and M.A. Jolson, "Women and Transformational and Contingent Reward Leadership: A Multiple-Levels-of-Analysis Perspective," *Academy of Management Journal*, February 1997, pp. 205–22; and M. Gardiner and M. Tiggemann, "Gender Differences in Leadership Style, Job Stress and Mental Health in Male- and Female-Dominated Industries," *Journal of Occupational and Organizational Psychology*, September 1999, pp. 301–15.

51. Gardiner and Tiggemann, "Gender Differences in Leadership Style, Job Stress and Mental Health in Male- and Female-Dominated Industries."

52. H. Aguinis and S.K.R. Adams, "Social-Role Versus Structural Models of Gender and Influence Use in Organizations: A Strong Inference Approach," *Group & Organization Management*, December

1998, pp. 414–46; and A.H. Eagly, S.J. Karau, and M.G. Makhijani, "Gender and the Effectiveness of Leaders: A Meta-Analysis," *Psychological Bulletin*, vol. 117 (1995), pp. 125–45.

53. R. Sharpe, "As Leaders, Women Rule," *Business Week*, November 20, 2000, pp. 74–84.

54. S. Helgesen, *The Female Advantage*.

55. G.H. Dobbins, W.S. Long, E.J. Dedrick, and T.C. Clemons, "The Role of Self-Monitoring and Gender on Leader Emergence: A Laboratory and Field Study," *Journal of Management*, September 1990, pp. 609–18.

56. F.W. Swierczek, "Leadership and Culture: Comparing Asian Managers," *Leadership & Organization Development Journal*, December 1991, pp. 3–10.

57. Cited in House and Aditya, "The Social Scientific Study of Leadership," p. 463.

58. R.J. House, "Leadership in the Twenty-First Century," in A. Howard (ed.), *The Changing Nature of Work* (San Francisco: Jossey-Bass, 1995), p. 442.

59. This box based on E. Corcoran, "The E-Gang," *Forbes*, July 24, 2000, pp. 145–72; M. Stepanek, "How to Jump-Start Your E-Strategy," *Business Week E-Biz*, June 5, 2000, pp. EB97-EB100; P. Labarre, "Leaders.com," *Fast Company*, June 1999, pp. 95–112; and G. Colvin, "How to Be a Great E-CEO," *Fortune*, May 24, 1999, pp. 104–10.

60. Ibid.

61. House and Aditya, "The Social Scientific Study of Leadership," p. 463.

62. House, "Leadership in the Twenty-First Century," p. 443; M.F. Peterson and J.G. Hunt, "International Perspectives on International Leadership," *Leadership Quarterly*, Fall 1997, pp. 203–31; and J.R. Schermerhorn and M.H. Bond, "Cross-Cultural Leadership in Collectivism and High Power Distance Settings," *Leadership & Organization Development Journal*, vol. 18, issue 4/5 (1997), pp. 187–93.

63. S. Kerr and J.M. Jermier, "Substitutes for Leadership: Their Meaning and Measurement," *Organizational Behavior and Human Performance*, December 1978, pp. 375–403; J.P. Howell and P.W. Dorfman, "Substitutes for Leadership: A Statistical Refinement," paper presented at the 42nd Annual Academy of Management Conference, New York, August 1982; J.P. Howell, P.W. Dorfman, and S. Kerr, "Leadership and Substitutes for Leadership," *Journal of Applied Behavioral Science* 22, No. 1 (1986), pp. 29–46; J.P. Howell, D.E. Bowen, P.W. Dorfman, S. Kerr, and P.M. Podsakoff, "Substitutes for Leadership: Effective Alternatives to Ineffective Leadership," *Organizational Dynamics*, Summer 1990, pp. 21–38; and P.M. Podsakoff, B.P. Niehoff, S.B. MacKenzie, and M.L. Williams, "Do Substitutes for Leadership Really Substitute for Leadership? An Empirical Examination of Kerr and Jermier's Situational Leadership Model," *Organizational Behavior and Human Decision Processes*, February 1993, pp. 1–44.

PART 5

1. S. Greengard, "25 Growing Companies," *Industry Week*, November 20, 2000, p. 76.

2. P.B. Robinson, D.V. Simpson, J.C. Huefner, and H.K. Hunt, "An Attitude Approach to the Prediction of Entrepreneurship," *Entrepreneurship Theory and Practice*, summer 1991, pp. 13–31.

3. B.M. Davis, "Role of Venture Capital in the Economic Renaissance of an Area," in R.D. Hisrich (ed.), *Entrepreneurship, Intrapreneurship, and Venture Capital* (Lexington, MA: Lexington Books, 1986), pp. 107–18.

4. J.M. Crant, "The Proactive Personality Scale as Predictor of Entrepreneurial Intentions," *Journal of Small Business Management*, July 1996, pp. 42–49.

5. J. Chun, "Type E Personality," *Entrepreneur*, January 1997, p. 10.

6. Information from company's Web site [www.sapient.com], January 22, 2001; "America's Fastest-Growing Companies," *Fortune*, September 4, 2000, available online at [www.fortune.com]; and S. Herrera, "People Power," *Forbes*, November 2, 1998, p. 212.

7. "Saluting the Global Awards Recipients of Arthur Andersen's Best Practices Awards 2000," *Fortune Online* [www.fortune.com], January 16, 2001.

8. T. Purdum, "Winning with Empowerment," *Industry Week*, October 16, 2000, pp. 109–10.

9. P. Strozniak, "Rescue Operation," *Industry Week*, October 16, 2000, pp. 103–04.

10. M. DePree, *Leadership Jazz* (New York: Currency Doubleday, 1992), pp. 8–9.

11. J.C. Collins and J.I. Porras, *Built to Last: Successful Habits of Visionary Companies* (New York: HarperBusiness, 1994).

12. P. Strozniak, "Teams at Work," *Industry Week*, September 18, 2000, pp. 47–50.

13. Ibid.

CHAPTER 18

1. C. May Yee, "Singaporean Sari Store Is Undone by Fraud Online," *Interactive Wall Street Journal* (www.interactive.wsj.com), May 11, 2000.

2. K.A. Merchant, "The Control Function of Management," *Sloan Management Review*, Summer 1982, pp. 43–55.

3. E. Flamholtz, "Organizational Control Systems as a Managerial Tool," *California Management Review*, Winter 1979, p. 55.

4. W.G. Ouchi, "A Conceptual Framework for the Design of Organizational Control Mechanisms," *Management Science*, August 1979, pp. 833–38; and Ouchi, "Markets, Bureaucracies, and Clans," *Administrative Science Quarterly*, March 1980, pp. 129–41.

5. B. Nelson, "Long-Distance Recognition," *Workforce*, August 2000, pp. 50–52.

6. S. Kerr, "On the Folly of Rewarding A, While Hoping for B," *Academy of Management Journal*, December 1975, pp. 769–83.

7. H. Koontz and R.W. Bradspies, "Managing through Feedforward Control," *Business Horizons*, June 1972, pp. 25–36.

8. E. MacDonald, "More Accounting Firms Bar Risky Clients," *Wall Street Journal*, April 25, 1997, p. A2.

9. W.H. Newman, *Constructive Control: Design and Use of Control Systems* (Upper Saddle River, NJ: Prentice Hall, 1975), p. 33.

10. Information on Marriott International and Lightbridge from Hoover's Online, (www.hoovers.com), December 1, 2000; and A. Murr, "Final Answer: It Crashed," *Newsweek*, April 10, 2000, p. 46.

11. See, for instance, Newman, *Constructive Control*.

12. Information from Hoovers Online (www.hoovers.com), December 1, 2000; and

N. Shirouzu and J. Bigness, "7-Eleven Operators Resist System to Monitor Managers," *Wall Street Journal*, June 16, 1997, p. B1.

13. This box based on Nelson, "Long Distance Recognition;" L. Guernsey, "You've Got Inappropriate Mail," *New York Times*, April 5, 2000, pp. C1+; M.A. Verespej, "Inappropriate Internet Surfing," *Industry Week*, February 7, 2000, pp. 59–64; M.A. Verespej, "Everybody's Gone Surfing," *Industry Week*, January 10, 2000, p. 11; and R. Karaim, "Setting E-Privacy Rules," from *Cnnfn Online* (www.cnnfn.com), December 15, 1999.

14. E. Bott, "Are You Safe? Privacy Special Report," *PC Computing*, March 2000, pp. 87–88.

15. L. Guernsey, "The Web: New Ticket to a Pink Slip," *New York Times*, December 16, 1999, pp. D1+; and K. Naughton, "CyberSlacking," *Newsweek*, November 29, 1999, pp. 62–65.

16. R. Karaim, "Setting E-Privacy Rules;" and L. Guernsey, "You've Got Inappropriate Mail."

17. E. Bott, "Are You Safe? Privacy Special Report."

18. Ibid.

19. R. Karaim, "Setting E-Privacy Rules."

20. K. Naughton, "CyberSlacking."

21. A.M. Bell and D.M. Smith, "Theft and Fraud May Be an Inside Job," *Workforce Online* (www.workforce.com), December 3, 2000.

22. D. Buss, "Ways to Curtail Employee Theft," *Nation's Business*, September 1993, pp. 36–38.

23. J. Greenberg, "The STEAL Motive: Managing the Social Determinants of Employee Theft," in R. Giacalone and J. Greenberg (eds.), *Antisocial Behavior in Organizations* (Newbury Park, CA: Sage, 1997), pp. 85–108.

24. B.P. Niehoff and R.J. Paul, "Causes of Employee Theft and Strategies That HR Managers Can Use for Prevention," *Human Resource Management*, Spring 2000, pp. 51–64; and G. Winter, "Taking at the Office Reaches New Heights: Employee Larceny Is Bigger and Bolder," *New York Times*, July 12, 2000, pp. C1+.

25. This section is based on J. Greenberg, *Behavior in Organizations*, 7e (Upper Saddle River, NJ: Prentice Hall, 2000), pp. 396–97.

26. A.H. Bell and D.M. Smith, "Why Some Employees Bite the Hand That Feeds Them," *Workforce Online* (www.workforce.com), December 3, 2000.

27. A.H. Bell and D.M. Smith, "Protecting the Company Against Theft and Fraud," *Workforce Online* (www.workforce.com), December 3, 2000; J.D. Hansen, "To Catch a Thief," *Journal of Accountancy*, March 2000, pp. 43–46; and J. Greenberg, "The Cognitive Geometry of Employee Theft," in *Dysfunctional Behavior in Organizations: Nonviolent and Deviant Behavior* (Stamford, CT: JAI Press, 1998), pp. 147–93.

28. E.F. Sygnatur and G.A. Tuscano, "Work-related Homicides: The Facts," *Bureau of Labor Statistics Online Report* (www.bls.gov), December 4, 2000; and P. Temple, "Real Danger and 'Postal' Mythology," *Workforce*, October 2000, p. 8.

29. "Ten Tips on Recognizing and Minimizing Violence," *Workforce Online* (www.workforce.com), December 3, 2000.

30. R. McNatt, "Desk Rage," *Business Week*, November 27, 2000, p. 12.

31. M. Gorkin, "Key Components of a Dangerously Dysfunctional Work Environment," *Workforce Online* (www.workforce.com), December 3, 2000.

32. "Ten Tips on Recognizing and Minimizing Violence"; M. Gorkin, "Five Strategies and Structures for Reducing Workplace Violence"; "Investigating Workplace Violence: Where Do You Start?"; and "Points to Cover in a Workplace Violence Policy," all articles from *Workforce Online* (www.workforce.com), December 3, 2000.

CHAPTER 19

1. J. Millman, "The World's New Tiger on the Export Scene Isn't Asia; It's Mexico," *Wall Street Journal*, May 9, 2000, pp. A1+.

2. U.S. Census Bureau, *Statistical Abstract of the United States: The National Data Book* (Washington, DC, 1999), p. 555; and P. Brimelow, "Creation and Destruction," *Forbes*, March 8, 1999, p. 62.

3. *World Fact Book 2000*, available online (www.odci.gov/cia/publications/factbook/), December 14, 2000.

4. M. Magnet, "The Productivity Payoff Arrives," *Fortune*, June 27, 1994, p. 82.

5. "Price Discipline," *U.S. News & World Report*, April 25, 1994, p. 17.

6. J. Ordonez, "McDonald's to Cut the Cooking Time of Its French Fries," *Wall Street Journal*, May 19, 2000, p. B2.

7. C. Fredman, "The Devil in the Details," *Executive Edge*, April–May, 1999, pp. 36–39.

8. T. Mudd, "The Last Laugh," *Industry Week*, September 18, 2000, pp. 38–44.

9. T.P. Pare, "A New Tool for Managing Costs," *Fortune*, June 14, 1993, p. 129.

10. "Manufacturing Is in Flower," *Time*, March 26, 1984, pp. 50–52.

11. J.H. Sheridan, "Managing the Value Chain," *Industry Week*, September 6, 1999, available online (www.industryweek.com).

12. Ibid., p. 5.

13. Ibid., p. 1.

14. Ibid.

15. Ibid., p. 3.

16. S. Leibs, "Getting Ready: Your Suppliers," *Industry Week*, September 6, 1999, available online (www.industryweek.com).

17. D. Bartholomew, "The Infrastructure," *Industry Week*, September 6, 1999, p. 1, available online (www.industryweek.com).

18. G. Taninecz, "Forging the Chain," *Industry Week*, May 15, 2000, pp. 40–46.

19. R. Normann and R. Ramirez, "From Value Chain to Value Constellation," *Harvard Business Review on Managing the Value Chain* (Boston: Harvard Business School Press, 2000), pp. 185–219.

20. S. Leibs, "Getting Ready: Your Customers," *Industry Week*, September 6, 1999, p. 4, available online (www.industryweek.com).

21. Ibid., p. 3.

22. S. Leibs, "Getting Ready: Your Suppliers," p. 2.

23. J.H. Sheridan, "Managing the Value Chain;" S. Leibs, "Getting Ready: Your Company," *Industry Week*, September 6, 1999, available online (www.industryweek.com); S. Leibs, "Getting Ready: Your Customers;" and S. Leibs, "Getting Ready: Your Suppliers."

24. J.H. Sheridan, "Managing the Value Chain," p. 3.

25. Leibs, "Getting Ready: Your Customers," p. 4.

26. J.H. Sheridan, "Managing the Value Chain," pp. 2–3; S. Leibs, "Getting Ready: Your Company," pp. 3–4; S. Leibs, "Getting Ready: Your Customers," pp. 1 and 4; D. Bartholomew, "The Infrastructure," p. 6.

27. G. Taninecz, "Forging the Chain."

28. S. Leibs, "Getting Ready: Your Company," p. 4.

29. S. Leibs, "Getting Ready: Your Suppliers," p. 1.

30. S. Leibs, "Getting Ready: Your Customers," p. 1.

31. D. Drickhamer, "On Target," *Industry Week*, October 16, 2000, pp. 111–12.

32. S. Leibs, "Getting Ready: Your Suppliers," p. 2.

33. Ibid.

34. G. Taninecz, "Forging the Chain," p. 44.

35. J.H. Sheridan, "Managing the Value Chain," p. 3.

36. D. Bartholomew, "The Infrastructure," p. 3.

37. W. Royal, "Too Much Trust?" *Industry Week*, November 2, 1998, available online (www.industryweek.com).

38. J.H. Sheridan, "Managing the Value Chain," p. 4.

39. J. Teresko, "The Dawn of E-Manufacturing," *Industry Week*, October 2, 2000, pp. 55–60.

40. D. Bartholomew, "E-Business Commentary—Quality Is Still Job One," *Industry Week*, September 4, 2000, available online (www.industryweek.com).

41. J. Jusko, "Tried and True," *Industry Week*, December 6, 1999, pp. 78–85.

42. Ibid., p. 78.

43. G. Hasek, "Merger Marries Quality Efforts," *Industry Week*, August 21, 2000, pp. 89–92.

44. Ibid.

45. J.S. McClenahen, "Unstoppable Improvement," *Industry Week*, October 16, 2000, pp. 85–86.

46. G. Hasek, "Extraordinary Extrusions," *Industry Week*, October 16, 2000, pp. 79–80.

47. W. Royal, "Spotlight Shines on Maquiladora," *Industry Week*, October 16, 2000, pp. 91–92.

48. See B. Whitford and R. Andrew (eds.), *The Pursuit of Quality* (Perth: Beaumont Publishing, 1994).

49. D. Drickhamer, "Road to Excellence," *Industry Week*, October 16, 2000, pp. 117–18.

50. "U.S., Italy Lead in Rise of ISO 9000 Certificates," *Industry Week*, November 13, 1999, available online (www.industryweek.com).

51. G. Hasek, "Merger Marries Quality Efforts."

52. C.H. Deutsch, "Six Sigma Enlightenment," *New York Times*, December 7, 1998, pp. C1+.

53. G. Hasek, "Merger Marries Quality Efforts."

54. Ibid.

55. Ibid.

CHAPTER 20

1. S. Kirsner, "Are You Experienced?" *Wired*, July 2000, p. 190; "Seattle's $240M Question: Are You Experienced?" *USA Today*, June 26, 2000, p. 1; K. Swisher, "While Bill Gates Has His World Rocked, Paul Allen Is on a Roll," *Wall Street Journal*, June 12, 2000, pp. B1+, and R. Covington, "A Swoopy, Funky Fun House of Rock," *Smithsonian Magazine*, June 2000, pp. 68–78.

2. T.L. Wheelen and J.D. Hunger, *Strategic Management,* 7th ed. (Upper Saddle River, NJ: Prentice Hall, 2000), p. 231.

3. R.E.S. Boulton, B.D. Libert, and S.M. Samek, "Learning to Juggle," *Business 2.0*, June 27, 2000, pp. 250–63.

4. Ibid.

5. This box based on R. Balu, "Exit Strategies," *Fast Company*, April 2000, pp. 352–65.

6. J. Teresko, "Using R&D to Drive Growth," *Industry Week*, March 15, 1999, pp. 22–30.

7. "Strong Reputations Mean Business," *Marketing Management*, Fall 1999, p. 4.

8. "Investors Love the Top Ten and So Do Job Seekers," *Fortune*, February 21, 2000, available online (www.fortune.com); and A.B. Fisher, "Corporate Reputations," *Fortune*, March 4, 1996, pp. 90–96.

9. C. Gore and E. Gore, "Knowledge Management: The Way Forward," *Total Quality Management*, July 1999, pp. S554–60.

10. S.L. Mintz, "A Knowing Glance," *CFO*, February 2000, pp. 52–57.

11. Ibid.

12. R. Lieber, "Numbers Talk!" *Fast Company*, October 1999, pp. 362–73.

13. Ibid.

14. P.F. Drucker, *Management: Tasks, Responsibilities, Practices* (New York: Harper & Row, 1974), p. 456.

15. C. Fredman, "The Completely PC Workforce," *Executive Edge*, August/September 2000, pp. 44–48.

16. A.M. Ristow, T.L. Amos, and G.E. Staude, "Transformational Leadership and Organizational Effectiveness in the Administration of Cricket in South Africa," *South African Journal of Business Management*, March 1999, pp. 1–5.

17. This box based on S.M. Mehta, "What Minority Employees Really Want," *Fortune*, July 10, 2000, pp. 180–186; and E. LeBlanc, L. Vanderkam, and L. Vella-Zarb, "America's 50 Best Companies for Minorities," *Fortune*, July 10, 2000, pp. 190–200.

18. "Top Performing Companies," *Fortune*, found online (www.fortune.com), December 17, 2000.

19. R. Levering and M. Moskowitz, "How We Pick the 100 Best," *Fortune*, January 8, 2001, available online (www.fortune.com).

20. G. Hasek, "The World's 100 Best," *Industry Week Online* (www.industryweek.com), December 18, 2000.

21. "ACSI Methodology," American Customer Satisfaction Index, available online (www.bus.umich.edu/research/nqrc/acsi.html), December 17, 2000.

22. J. Rosenfeld, "Down-Home Food, Cutting-Edge Business," *Fast Company*, April 2000, pp. 56–58.

23. P. Landers, "Japan Tech Star Sticks to Manufacturing," *Wall Street Journal*, April 24, 2000, p. A22.

24. Wheelen and Hunger, *Strategic Management*, pp. 236–37.

25. T. Leahy, "Capitalizing on Economic Value Added," *Business Finance*, July 2000, pp. 83–86.

26. Wheelen and Hunger, *Strategic Management*, p. 237.

27. K. Lehn and A.K. Makhija, "EVA and MVA As Performance Measures and Signals for Strategic Change," *Strategy & Leadership*, May/June 1996, pp. 34–38; and A.B. Fisher, "Creating Stockholder Wealth: Market Value Added," *Fortune*, December 11, 1995, pp. 105–16.

28. Wheelen and Hunger, *Strategic Management*, p. 236.

29. T. Leahy, "Tailoring the Balanced Scorecard," *Business Finance*, August 2000, pp. 53–56.

30. Wheelen and Hunger, *Strategic Management*, p. 238.

31. Leahy, "Tailoring the Balanced Scorecard."

32. Ibid.

33. Ibid.

34. "Mercedes-Benz Benchmarking Saves DaimlerChrysler $100 Million," *Industry Week*, October 27, 2000, available online (www.industryweek.com).

35. M. Simpson and D. Kondouli, "A Practical Approach to Benchmarking in Three Service Industries," *Total Quality Management*, July 2000, pp. S623–S630.

36. K.N. Dervitsiotis, "Benchmarking and Business Paradigm Shifts," *Total Quality Management*, July 2000, pp. S641–S646.

37. T. Leahy, "Extracting Diamonds in the Rough," *Business Finance*, August 2000, pp. 33–37.

38. Ibid.

39. Hasek, "The World's Best 100."

40. Ibid.

41. J. Rosenfeld, "Want to Lead Better? It's Simple," *Fast Company*, March 2000, pp. 58–60.

42. J. Mariotti, "What Gets Measured Gets Done?" *Industry Week*, February 15, 1999, p. 94.

43. A.M. Weber, "Why Can't We Get Anything Done?" *Fast Company*, June 2000, pp. 168–80.

44. Mariotti, "What Gets Measured Gets Done."

45. T. Leahy, "10 Cures for Performance Reporting Anxiety," *Business Finance*, December 1999, pp. 63–65.

46. P. Roberts, "The Art of Getting Things Done," *Fast Company*, June 2000, pp. 162–64.

47. This box based on E. Gunn, "Shop From Us, Buy From Them," *Business 2.0*, December 26, 2000, pp. 116–18; K. Belson, "Yahoo Japan Wins Hoorays," *Business Week*, June 19, 2000, p. 104; R.O. Crockett, "A Digital Doughboy," *Business Week E-Biz*, April 3, 2000, pp. EB78-EB86; D. Rocks, "Reinventing Herman Miller," *Business Week E-Biz*, April 3, 2000, pp. EB89–EB96; C. Pickering, "Tight Fit," *Business 2.0*, April 1, 2000, available online (www.busines2.com); and "10 Companies That Get It," *Fortune*, November 8, 1999, pp. 115–17.

48. J. McClenahen, "What Is a Best Practice Anyway?" *Industry Week*, March 24, 1997, available online (www.industryweek.com).

PART 6

1. Information from company's Web site [www.gloryfoods.com], January 22, 2001; and C. Shook, "Making Haste Slowly," *Forbes*, September 22, 1997, pp. 220–22.

2. G.R. Merz, P.B. Weber, and V.B. Laetz, "Linking Small Business Management with Entrepreneurial Growth," *Journal of Small Business Management*, October 1994, pp. 48–60.

3. L. Beresford, "Growing Up," *Entrepreneur*, July 1995, pp. 124–28.

4. J. Summer, "More, Please!" *Business Finance*, July 2000, pp. 57–61.

5. T. Stevens, "Pedal Pushers," *Industry Week*, July 17, 2000, pp. 46–52.

6. P. Lorange and R.T. Nelson, "How to Recognize—and Avoid—Organizational Decline," *Sloan Management Review*, Spring 1987, pp. 41–48.

7. S. D. Chowdhury and J.R. Lange, "Crisis, Decline, and Turnaround: A Test of Competing Hypotheses for Short-Term Performance Improvement in Small Firms," *Journal of Small Business Management*, October 1993, pp. 8–17.

8. C. Farrell, "How to Survive a Downturn," *Business Week*, April 28, 1997, pp. ENT4–ENT6.

9. R.W. Pricer and A.C. Johnson, "The Accuracy of Valuation Methods in Predicting the Selling Price of Small Firms," *Journal of Small Business Management*, October 1997, pp. 24–35.

10. P. Hernan, "Finding the Exit," *Industry Week*, July 17, 2000, pp. 55–61; D. Rodkin, "For Sale by Owner," *Entrepreneur*, January 1998, pp. 148–53; A. Livingston, "Avoiding Pitfalls When Selling a Business," *Nation's Business*, July 1998, pp. 25–26; and G. Gibbs Marullo, "Selling Your Business: A Preview of the Process," *Nation's Business*, August 1998, pp. 25–26.

11. T. Stevens, "Striking a Balance," *Industry Week*, November 20, 2000, pp. 26–36; and S. Caudron, "Fit to Lead," *Industry Week*, July 17, 2000, pp. 63–68.

Chapter 1

page 3: Jeff Sciortino Photography; page 4: Rafael Fuchs Photography; page 9: Mike Malone/Malone & Co. Photography, Inc.; page 12: courtesy of Martha Barkman; page 14: used with permission of United Airlines, Worldwide Communications; page 17: © Reuters NewMedia Inc./CORBIS; page 19: Joe Raymond/South Bend Tribune; page 21: courtesy of Shannon McMurtrey; page 21: courtesy of James Amalfitano; page 24: David Fields Photography.

Chapter 2

page 27: Mamoru Tsukada/Aria Pictures; page 29: Frank La Bua/Pearson Education/PH College; page 30: Raeanne Rubenstein/Index Stock Imagery, Inc., page 32: Courtesy S. C. Williams Library, Stevens Institute of Technology, Hoboken, NJ; page 33: UPI/Corbis; page 37: Mark Peterson/Corbis/SABA Press Photos, Inc.; page 39: courtesy of Gordon Wadge; page 41: Mark Richards; page 43: ad concept: Terry Chan, Ryan Crowther, Elaine Sher, Becky Yiu; ad design: Marcel DaSilva, Mariana Prins; photography and photo editing: Daniel Morisette; page 47: Solectron Corporation; page 49: Seth Resnick Photography; page 50: courtesy of Marilyn Farrar-Wagner; page 50: courtesy of Adam Ferguson; page 53: Randall Scott Photographics.

Chapter 3

page 55: Robert Karpa Photography; page 57: Bob D'Amico/ABC/Liaison Agency, Inc.; page 58: Bob D'Amico/ABC/Liaison Agency, Inc.; page 61: courtesy of Trenham Ian Weatherhead; page 63: W. L. Gore & Associates, Inc.; page 64: © 2000 Hewitt Associates LLC; page 67: Jean-Marc Giboux/Liaison Agency, Inc.; page 69: Robert Visser/Corbis/Sygma; page 72: Jose L. Pelaez/Corbis/Stock Market; Page74: David Lassman/The Image Works; page 76: © AFP/CORBIS; page 79: courtesy of Ricardo Mendiola; page 79: courtesy of Lynee Pauk; page 82: MicroStrategy, Inc.

Chapter 4

page 83: Keith Dannemiller/Corbis/SABA Press Photos, Inc.; page 88: courtesy of Ford Motor Company; page 92: Lugio Blanco/Notimex, S.A. de C.V.; page 94: Horacio Paone/New York Times Pictures; page 99: Christopher Calais/Contact Press Images Inc.; page 101: Karen Kusmauski/Matrix International, Inc.; page 105: courtesy of Doug Heatherly; page 108: David Karp/AP/Wide World Photos.

Chapter 5

page 111: Hosea Johnson/Montgomery Group; page 113: William J. VanderDecker/Merck & Co., Inc.; page 117: Corbis/Sygma; page 121: DDB Dallas, Phillips Petroleum Company; page 123: Detroit News photograph by Morris Richardson;

page 125: Francis Li/Liaison Agency, Inc.; page 127: © Jason Furnari/CORBIS; page 129: courtesy of Boeing Aircraft Company; page 130: David Levenson; page 134: Fannie Mae; page 137: courtesy of Lois Boyle; page 137: courtesy of Amanda Quebbeman.

Chapter 6

page 149: Cannondale Corp.; page 153: Churchill & Klehr Photography; page 164: Jeff Sciortino Photography; page 165: William Neumann/William Neumann Photography; page 169: courtesy of Stacy Renee Unger; page 169: courtesy of Lynee Pauk; page 172: Bernard Boutrit/Woodfin Camp & Associates.

Chapter 7

page 175: Mark Richards; page 178: AP/Wide World Photos; page 180: Jill Connelly; page 164: Fred Mertz; page 185: courtesy of Gerrit Grunert; page 187: Alex Wong/Liaison Agency, Inc.; page 189: Sergio Dorantes; page 191: Carrie Lundy; page 191: Gyl Kovalik; page 194: Lend Lease Corporation.

Chapter 8

page 197: © 2000 NBA Entertainment. Photo by Frank Veronsky; page 202: Ray Ng Photography; page 203: Michael L. Abramson Photography; page 204: © 2000 Doug Knutson; page 206: Donna Terek Photography; page208: © Paulo Fridman/CORBIS SYGMA; page 209: Tom Salyer Photography, Inc.; page 211: Bob Berg Photography; page 214: Marco Hillen/Hillen Fotografie; page 217: courtesy of Ted V. Schaefer; page: 217; courtesy of Donald Weeks; page 220: Dave Buston/CP Picture Archive.

Chapter 9

page 223: © Dan Groshong/CORBIS SYGMA; page 226: Najlah Feanny/Stock Boston; page 229: courtesy of David Raphael; page 231: Mary Katz/NYT Pictures, published 2/16/99; page 237: Aaron Lee Fineman/NYT Pictures, published 9/10/99; page 240: Herman Miller, Inc.; page 241: KPMG; page 243: courtesy of Richard Unger; page 243: courtesy of Cindy Brewer; page 246: Viktor Korotayev/Archive Photos.

Chapter 10

page 253: Nokia; page 257: James Schnepf Photography, Inc.; page 260: TII Industries; page 261: Holland Productions; page 265: courtesy of Dan J. Shapiro; page 264: Scott Montgomery Photography; page 268: Bill Aron/PhotoEdit; page 269: New York Times Pictures; page 272: Mercedes-Benz; page 273: Chris Maynard/NYT Pictures; page 275: courtesy of Susan Colegrove; page 275: courtesy of Joe L. Jakubielski; page 278: R H Buckman and Associates.

Chapter 11

page 281: Kathrin Miller; page 285: James Keyser Photography; page 287 (montage of 6 photos): Paul Ekman, Ph.D./Paul Ekman, Ph.D., Professor of Psychology; page 290: Ozier Muhammad/NYT Pictures, published 12/15/99; page 294: Chris Usher Photography; page 297: Andre Pichette Photography; page 299: Boeing Commercial Airplane Group; page 300: courtesy of Michael J. Stabile; page 300: courtesy of Jeff Sneed; page 303: M. Granitsas/The Image Works.

Chapter 12

page 305: John Giannini/New York Times Pictures; page 306: Rich Frishman/Rich Frishman Photography and Videograph Inc.; page 308: Philippe Lopez/Philippe Lopez; page 310: John Schults/Archive Photos; page 317: Tracy Kroll; page 318: courtesy of Suzanne J. Cohen; page 320: John Riley; page 323: Daniel Lincoln Photography; page 325: John Giannini/New York Times Pictures; page 327: © Ray Ng; page 330: courtesy of Marvin Fisher; page 330: courtesy of Stacy Renee Unger; page 333: Jilly Wendell.

Chapter 13

page 337: Tom Salyer/Black Star; page 339: Rina Castelnuovo/New York Times Pictures; page 341: Catherine Ledner; page 344: Michael L. Abramson; page 346: Alan Levenson; page 350: Tom Wagner/Corbis/SABA Press Photos, Inc.; page 353: Gary Tramonita/New York Times Pictures; page 357: Greg Miller Photography; page 358: courtesy of Rick Allen Gladden; page 358: courtesy of Adam Ferguson; page 361: Porter Gifford/Liaison Agency, Inc.

Chapter 14

page 369: Eric Millette Photography; page 371: Robert Holmgren Photography; page 376: Barbara Gentile; page 379: Dan Krauss/New York Times Pictures; page 381: Tom Wagner/Corbis/SABA Press Photos, Inc.; page 385: David Levenson; page 388: Wendy Earl Productions; page 392: courtesy of Lee Lesser; page 392: courtesy of Karen Armstrong; page 395: © B. Daemmrich/CORBIS SYGMA.

Chapter 15

page 397: Karin Drakenberg; page 401: Mark Van S.; page 404: George Lange; page 413: David Barry/Julian Richards Agency; page 414: © 1997 Tres Watson/Hot Link; page 415: David Zadig; page 416: Chuck Eaton; page 418: courtesy of Jeff Wasson; page 418: courtesy of Peter Nalen.

Chapter 16

page 413: Mary Ellen Mark; page 424: Sam Jones Photography; page 426: Horacio Paone/New York Times Pictures; page 429: Robbie

McClaran/Corbis/SABA Press Photos, Inc.; page 431: Gail Albert Halaban/Corbis/SABA Press Photos, Inc.; page 433: EW Productions; page 438: Richard Termine Photography; page 439: Allan Barnes Photography; page 445: Gary Hershorn/Archive Photos; page 447: Darryl Estrine Photography; page 452: courtesy of Cindy Brewer; page 452: courtesy of Stacey Ficken; page 455: Blair Jensen Photography.

Chapter 17

page 457: Ross Communications Group; page 464: Tim Rue/Black Star; page 467: Laura Pedrick/Laura A. Pedrick; page 471: Nicole Bengiveno/New York Times Pictures; page 476: Louise Gubb/Corbis/SABA Press Photos, Inc.; page 477: T. Michael Keza Photography; page 479: page 480: © Axel Koestser/CORBIS SYGMA; © Dudley Reed/CORBIS; page 484: courtesy of Jason Downing; page 484: cour-

tesy of Pete G. Johnson; page 487: Atsushi Tsukada/AP/Wide World Photos.

Chapter 18

page 495: Ng Han Guan; page 497: Angela Prada de Almwis; page 503: courtesy of Vick Cavallaro; page 504: Shawn G. Henry; page 506: © 2000 Jamie Tanaka, All Rights Reserved; page 507: Evan Kafka; page 510: Graham Trott; page 511: Yoshikazu Tsuno/Agence France-Presse; page 513: Versus Technology, Inc.; page 519: courtesy of Wayne Price; page 519: courtesy of Diane Dudley; page 522: Mark Richards.

Chapter 19

page 425: Titus Lokananta; page 527: Rocky Thies Photography; page 528: Michael McLaughlin/Julian Richards Agency; page 530: Paula Lerner/Aurora & Quanta Produc-

tions; page 531: T. Simon Photography; page 533: T. Simon Photography; page 536: T. Simon Photography; page 541: Robert Houser/Robert Houser Photography; page 544: PAC International Ltd.; page 547: courtesy of Debra Barnhart; page 542: courtesy of Candice Mathers.

Chapter 20

page 553: Steve Gottlieb Photography; page 555: © 2000 Jamie Tanaka, All Rights Reserved; page 557: Jonathan Player/New York Times Pictures; page 560: Steven Senne/AP/Wide World Photos; page 564: Katherine Lambert; page 561: AP/Wide World Photos; page 567: John Mireles Photography; page 568: Craig Cunningham; page 571: courtesy of Catherine Holmes; page 571: courtesy of Adam Ferguson; page 574: © Willy Rizzo/CORBIS SYGMA.

NAME INDEX

H

Halo effect A general impression of an individual based on a single characteristic, 387

Harvesting Exiting a venture when an entrepreneur hopes to capitalize financially on the investment in the venture, 578

Hawthorne Studies A series of studies during the 1930s that provided new insights in individual and group behavior, 38–40

Hierarchy of needs theory Maslow's theory that there is a hierarchy of five human needs: physiological, safety, social, esteem, and self-actualization, 425–26

Higher-order needs, 426

High-high leader A leader high in both initiating structure and consideration behaviors, 461

High-performance work practices Work practices that lead to both high individual and high organizational performance, 306–7

Human relations view of conflict The view that conflict is a natural and inevitable outcome in any group, 405

Human resource management Activities necessary for staffing the organization and sustaining high employee performances, 307–9

current issues in, 326–29

decruitment in, 311, 312

employee training in, 319–20

issues in entrepreneurial ventures, 366

orientation in, 318–19

process of, 307–26

reasons for importance of, 306–7

recruitment in, 311–12

selection in, 312–17

Human resource planning The process by which managers ensure that they have the right number and kinds of people in the rights places, and at the right times, who are capable of effectively and efficiently performing assigned tasks, 309–10

Human resources

meeting future needs in, 310

variables in, 357

Human skills The ability to work well with other people individually and in a group, 11

Hygiene factors Factors that eliminate job dissatisfaction but don't motivate, 428

I

Idea champion Individuals who actively and enthusiastically support new ideas, build support, overcome resistance, and ensure that innovations are implemented, 357

Ideas

evaluating, 250

generating, 250

Immediate corrective action Corrective action that corrects problems at once to get performance back on track, 503

Immigration Reform and Control Act (1986), 309

Implementation Conveying a decision to those affected and getting their commitment to it, 155

Importing An approach to going global that involves selling products at home that are made overseas, 95

Independent social audits, 135

Individual behavior, 370

reason for looking at, 370–71

Individualism A cultural dimension that describes when people are supposed to look after their immediate family, 100

Individual ranking A multiperson comparison that requires the evaluator to list employees in order from lowest to highest, 322

Industrial Revolution The advent of machine power, mass production, and efficient transportation, 30–31

Industry rankings as measures of organizational performance, 559–60

Informal communication Communication that is not defined by the organization's structural hierarchy, 293

Informal groups, 398

Informational roles Managerial roles that involve receiving, collecting, and disseminating information, 9

Information controls, 563–65

Information overload The information we have to work with exceeds our processing capacity, 289

Information Processed and analyzed data, 564

Information systems as controls, 564–65

Information technology, 296–99

effect of, on organizations, 299

Initiating structure The extent to which a leader was likely to define and structure his or her role and the roles of group members in the search for goal attainment, 461

Innovation The process of taking a creative idea and turning it into a useful product, service, or work method, 144, 354. *See also* Learning organization; Knowledge management

continuing importance of, 366–67

creativity versus, 354

at e-business, 355

in entrepreneurship, 42–43, 143–45

managing, 338–57

stimulating, 354–57

Instant messaging Interactive real-time communication that takes place among computer users logged on the computer network at the same time, 297

Integration, 161

Integrative social contracts theory A view of ethics that proposes that ethical decisions should be based on empirical (what is) and normative (what should be) factors, 125

Intellectual property Proprietary company information that's critical to its efficient and effective functioning and competitiveness, 539

Intelligence, emotional, 379–80

Interactionist view of conflict The view that some conflict is necessary for a group to perform effectively, 405

Internal forces for change, 339

International context, ethics in, 130

Interpersonal communication Communication between two or more people, 283

barriers to effective, 288–91

methods of, 284–87

overcoming barriers to effective, 291–93

process of, 283–93

Interpersonal roles Managerial roles that involve people and other duties that are ceremonial and symbolic in nature, 9

Interview, 315–16; 594–95

Intranet An internal organizational communication system that uses Internet technology and is accessible only by organizational employees, 45, 298

Intuitive decision making A subconscious process of making decisions on the basis of experience and accumulated judgment, 158

Iowa, University of, studies, 460–61

ISO 9000 A series of international quality management standards that set uniform guidelines for processes to ensure that products conform to customer requirements, 544–45

Issue intensity, 128–29

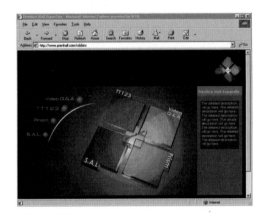 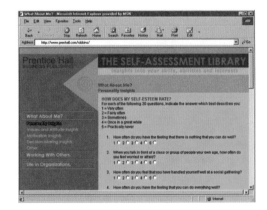

www.prenhall.com/robbins

> **R.O.L.L.S. ROBBINS ONLINE LEARNING SYSTEM WEB SITE**

This dynamic new Web site is where you'll find valuable resources, including:

- **Management FAQ's** (Frequently Asked Questions answered by the authors themselves!)

- **PRISM** (PRactical Interactive Skills Modules)—the PRISM Web site presents different "virtual" management situations in an organization called MediaPlex. The interactive decision-tree design of the management situations gives students the chance to try different management approaches and to learn why certain approaches are better than others. You'll find the pin code included in every new student text.

- **Self-Assessment Library Version 2.0** — more than 40 exercises will help students learn about themselves and how they relate to others! (also available on a convenient CD-ROM)

- **Testing, Testing . . . 1, 2, 3** — offers suggested responses to the text's questions.